Encyclopedia of American Business History and Biography

Banking and Finance to 1913

Edited by

Larry Schweikart
University of Dayton

A Bruccoli Clark Layman Book

 Facts On File ®

New York • Oxford • Sydney

Encyclopedia of American Business History
and Biography:
Banking and Finance to 1913
Copyright © 1990 by Bruccoli Clark Layman, Inc., and
Facts On File, Inc.

Library of Congress Cataloging-in-Publication Data

Banking and Finance to 1913/edited by Larry E. Schweikart.
    p. cm.–(Encyclopedia of American business history and biography)
  Includes bibliographical references.
  ISBN 0-8160-2193-7
  1. Banks and banking–United States–History. 2. Finance–United States–History. 3. Bankers–United States–Biography.
I. Schweikart, Larry. II. Series.
HG2461.B33 1990
332.1'0973–dc20
                                        89-29581
                                        CIP

British CIP information available on request

Designed by Quentin Fiore

Printed in the United States of America

10 9 8 7 6 5 4 3 2 1

For Adam

Encyclopedia of American Business History

Contents

Foreword

The Encyclopedia of American Business History and Biography chronicles America's material civilization through its business figures and businesses. It is a record of American aspirations—of success and of failure. It is a history of the impact of business on American life. The volumes have been planned to serve a cross section of users: students, teachers, scholars, researchers, and government and corporate officials. Individual volumes or groups of volumes cover a particular industry during a defined period; thus each *EABH&B* volume is freestanding, providing a history expressed through biographies and buttressed by a wide range of supporting entries. In many cases a single volume is sufficient to treat an industry, but certain industries require two or more volumes. When completed, the *EABH&B* will provide the fullest available history of American enterprise.

The editorial direction of *EABH&B* is provided by the general editor and the editorial board. The general editor appoints volume editors whose duties are to prepare, in consultation with the editorial board, the list of entries for each volume, to assign the entries to contributors, to vet the submitted entries, and to work in close cooperation with the Bruccoli Clark Layman editorial staff so as to maintain consistency of treatment. All entries are written by specialists in their fields, not by staff writers. Volume editors are experienced scholars.

The publishers and editors of *EABH&B* are convinced that timing is crucial to notable careers. Therefore, the biographical entries in each volume of the series place businesses and their leaders in the social, political, and economic contexts of their times. Supplementary background rubrics on companies, inventions, legal decisions, marketing innovations, and other topics are integrated with the biographical entries in alphabetical order.

The general editor and the volume editors determine the space to be allotted to biographies as major entries, standard entries, and short entries.

Major entries, reserved for giants of business and industry (e.g., Henry Ford, J. P. Morgan, Andrew Carnegie, James J. Hill), require approximately 10,000 words. Standard biographical entries are in the range of 3,500-5,000 words. Short entries are reserved for lesser figures who require inclusion and for significant figures about whom little information is available. When appropriate, the biographical entries stress their subjects' roles in shaping the national experience, showing how their activities influenced the way Americans lived. Unattractive or damaging aspects of character and conduct are not suppressed. All biographical entries conform to a basic format.

A significant part of each volume is devoted to concise background entries supporting and elucidating the biographies. These nonbiographical entries provide basic information about the industry or field covered in the volume. Histories of companies are necessarily brief and limited to key events. To establish a context for all entries, each volume includes an overview of the industry treated. These historical introductions are normally written by the volume editors.

We have set for ourselves large tasks and important goals. We aspire to provide a body of work that will help reduce the imbalance in the writing of American history, the study of which too often slights business. Our hope is also to stimulate interest in business leaders, enterprises, and industries that have not been given the scholarly attention they deserve. By setting high standards for accuracy, balanced treatment, original research, and clear writing, we have tried to ensure that these works will commend themselves to those who seek a full account of the development of America.

—William H. Becker
General Editor

Acknowledgments

This book was produced by Bruccoli Clark Layman, Inc. James W. Hipp is the series editor. Michael D. Senecal was the in-house editor.

Production coordinator is James W. Hipp. Systems manager is Charles D. Brower. Photography editor is Susan Todd. Layout and graphics supervisor is Penney L. Haughton. Copyediting supervisor is Bill Adams. Typesetting supervisor is Kathleen M. Flanagan. Typography coordinator is Sheri Beckett Neal. Charles Lee Egleston and Laura Ingram are editorial associates. The production staff includes Helen Baucum, Rowena Betts, Anne L. M. Bowman, Joseph M. Bruccoli, Teresa Chaney, Patricia Coate, Sarah A. Estes, Willie M. Gores, Cynthia Hallman, Susan C. Heath, David Marshall James, Kathy S. Merlette, Ellen McCracken, Laura Garren Moore, Laurrè Sinckler, and Betsy L. Weinberg. Jean W. Ross is permissions editor.

Walter W. Ross and Jennifer Toth did the library research with the assistance of the reference staff at the Thomas Cooper Library of the University of South Carolina: Lisa Antley, Daniel Boice, Faye Chadwell, Cathy Eckman, Gary Geer, Cathie Gottlieb, David L. Haggard, Jens Holley, Jackie Kinder, Marcia Martin, Jean Rhyne, Beverly Steele, Ellen Tillett, Carol Tobin, and Virginia Weathers.

Usually this section is read only by either the terminally bored or the dearly beloved of the author. Nevertheless, I take great pleasure in expressing my thanks to several individuals who made this volume possible. Lynne Pierson Doti, Charles Calomiris, Ed Perkins, and Ben Klebaner all read the introductory essay and offered comments. Whether or not I took their advice was a different story, and therefore any errors that remain in the introduction are mine and mine alone. Some contributors performed heroic duties, taking over where other authors could not finish, or accepting entries that we both knew would be particularly difficult. Among those who aided this volume with their special efforts, I would like to thank Lynne Pierson Doti, Michael Konig, Carol Martel, Jim Smallwood, and Richard Timberlake. At the University of Dayton, Linda McKinley singlehandedly organized and orchestrated the assignments, contracts, and typing, and Jenny Wharton provided timely typing assistance. My wife, Dee, patiently left me in front of the word processor from time to time, while my son, Adam, desperately wanted to help type despite the fact that at 16 months he can't quite read yet. His wonderful distractions account for the dedication in this volume.

–L. S.

Introduction

Few businesses in American history have suffered from the confusions and controversies that have surrounded banking. Modern Americans, for example, frequently associate Savings and Loan Associations, Mutual Savings Associations, stock and bond brokerage houses, investment banks, and even finance companies with the commercial banks and banking functions with which they come in daily contact. Indeed, in the 1980s climate of financial deregulation, the lines between many of those activities have grown increasingly fuzzy. In 1989 officials even permitted, for the first time since the passage of the Glass-Steagall Act during the Great Depression, some commercial banks to enter into limited investment banking activities. Of course, American financial enterprises have common roots, and the multiplicity of institutions that dot modern America (many of them experiencing severe difficulties) represent different paths to providing capital for a wide spectrum of commercial, industrial, governmental, and leisure activities.

Banks, in addition to operating in a certain shroud of mystery that has always surrounded money, probably have been the subject of more hostility and vituperation than any other businesses in American history, except, perhaps, the railroads. Even a cursory reading of the American past finds such phrases concerning banks: "money bags of the east," "Billions for bankers, debt for the People," and "money changers waxing richer and richer." John Davis, an important voice of the late-nineteenth-century farmers' groups in Kansas, referred to the banking system as "The Financial Devil Fish of America." One only has to look at the titles in the library to appreciate the characterizations. Authors refer to "the Money Changers," or claim to reveal, as William Grieder does, the "Secrets of the Temple."

Why have banks received such abuse and garnered such suspicion? Have they developed differently from other business institutions? If so, why did they develop differently, and how? What characteristics of banks have evoked such confusion and such negative perceptions from the public? European banks seem to have inspired more benign feelings from local populations. The Italians, then later the English and the Scots, developed impressive banking systems that not only stimulated commerce but, in the case of the Medicis in Italy, supported the arts as well. Several types of banks existed at the time the states established their banking systems: Americans looked to the Bank of England for a centralized organization, or to the Scottish free banks for a more laissez-faire approach. Ultimately, though, American financial institutions varied widely in their form and characteristics exactly because they were governed by the states. A textile mill was a textile mill in Lowell or in Charleston, but a Boston bank differed a great deal from a South Carolina bank.

American banking developed several distinctive features, the most important of which was the dual banking system of nationally chartered banks and state-chartered banks. That dual system sprang from the struggle for control over finance that mirrored the battle for states' rights over other issues. The practical effects of the struggle appeared in laws dealing with minimum capitalization, branching, deposit insurance, and other regulations spanning the period from independence to 1913. Toward the end of the nineteenth century, the debate also involved disagreements about the location of the nation's financial power.

Virtually all merchants dabbled in financial services in colonial times. The principal medium of exchange, gold and silver coins (specie), came mostly from Spanish colonies in the western hemisphere. But merchants disliked carrying coin, due to its weight and bulk. In frontier areas of the Old Northwest and, later, the Great Plains and Far West, traders and merchants exchanged otter, beaver, or deer pelts (which they loosely termed "fur" money) in lieu of coin. They would have much preferred specie but could not get it. They accepted paper as a second choice if they could locate paper money that retained its value.

Paper money arose from the issuance of bills of credit by colonial legislatures. The first bills were issued in 1690 to finance a Massachusetts military expedition against the French in Canada. Most of the colonies had the power to print money to meet government expenditures. By 1755 every colony issued paper money. Most also established land banks, wherein borrowers received bills of credit by offering land as collateral. But the British government realized the potential problems in granting such freedoms and attempted to rescind the privileges. In 1751 and 1764, as part of England's attempt to shore up its control over its overseas empire, the Crown prohibited certain colonies from issuing further bills of credit, and its continuing attempts to restrict note issue provided one of the sources of irritation that eventually sparked the American Revolution. The Continental Congress authorized the printing and expenditure of bills of credit even before the Declaration of Independence. During the French and Indian War, as Elmus Wicker, Charles W. Calomiris, and others have demonstrated, colonies maintained the value of their currencies by regularly collecting them in taxes, but the failure to apply vigorous taxation during the revolutionary period doomed the currency to depreciation.

Although by 1800 more than 30 banks existed in the United States, two stood out in the financial affairs of the country's first decades of independence: the Bank of North America and the First Bank of the United States (BUS). Toward the end of 1781 the Second Continental Congress, which had raised funds in 1780 by printing paper money, concluded that it needed a more stable and reliable revenue system. In 1780 a group of merchants had participated in organizing the so-called Pennsylvania Bank, which generated money for a single purpose–supplying the armed forces. Meanwhile, Robert Morris, a merchant who had contributed much time, effort, and fortune toward keeping George Washington's troops in the field, was chosen by the Continental Congress in February 1781 as superintendent of finance and took it upon himself to issue paper money, "Morris Notes," secured by his own reputation. However, he realized that such a tactic provided only a short-term solution and forcefully advocated the creation of a privately owned bank to supply a sound currency. Morris played a key role in organizing that Philadelphia bank, capitalized initially with the pro-

ceeds of a French loan, and, despite objections from members of the Congress who contended that the Articles of Confederation did not provide for such activity, Morris secured a charter for the bank from the state of Pennsylvania. The nation's first commercial bank, the Bank of North America, opened in early January 1782. Other states followed suit, chartering banks in Boston, New York, Providence, Baltimore, and, by the end of the century, many other cities. The Bank of North America prospered, but the man who brought it into existence could not manage his own fortune after the bank lost its charter. Morris died in a debtors' prison in 1806, a result of his own speculation in western lands.

The BUS owed its existence to a brilliant young foreign-born visionary, Alexander Hamilton. As the country's first secretary of the treasury, Hamilton well understood the necessity of forming an institution and an environment to deal with the financial affairs of the nation beyond his own tenure as secretary. Indeed, as Calomiris points out in his essay on Hamilton, the secretary established the precedent that the Treasury Department, rather than Congress, would set the agenda for financial policy, thus insulating it from yearly budgetary squabbles. Or, in Calomiris's words, Hamilton achieved his ends through "extra-Constitutional" means. Hamilton's genius emerged in developing a system of tariff-based revenues that generated sufficient funds to maintain interest payments on federal government bonds. He also sought to avoid making the finances of the nation dependent on annual appropriations from Congress, which could suddenly or unexpectedly revoke spending authority. To that end he favored a sinking fund, which, as Calomiris points out, contributed to a degree of government inertia by subordinating new debt to old debt, except, of course, in the case of war or other extreme emergencies. The sinking fund was more than rhetoric, and through it and his other measures Hamilton restored the faith of creditors who loaned funds to the United States. In another example of Hamilton's genius for ensuring stability, he (and Secretary of State Thomas Jefferson, who seldom agreed with Hamilton on anything) insisted on using the Spanish dollar as a currency standard, to prevent Congress from devaluing the nation's money. He and Jefferson also favored using the decimal system (even though Spanish dollars traditionally had been divided in eighths), which made the money convenient for use in commercial transactions.

Hamilton's proposal for a national bank–the BUS–also reflected his desire to create permanent institutions not subject to the whims of legislators. The BUS gave the country the advantages of sound paper currency consistently convertible to specie, without turning those powers over to Congress, and it provided a fiscal device for government to place loans and collect taxes. It had one obvious Hamiltonian feature in that its charter ran for 20 years–a long time–and had Hamilton been able to control politics he would have bestowed it with permanent life. But neither Congress nor Hamilton could endow it with central banking powers. The BUS had the advantage of interstate branches (something that only a few banks, under extremely special circumstances, have enjoyed since); it held the government's deposits, and its notes were receivable for all public dues. Its total capital of $10 million made it by far the largest business enterprise in the nation. The bank also was essentially a private bank, with the U.S. government a 20 percent shareholder. It had the power to force smaller state-chartered banks to maintain a level of reserves sufficient to exchange for their own notes when the BUS presented them for collection. If a given state bank did not have enough BUS notes on hand with which to redeem its own notes, then it had to pay out the difference in specie. But scholars still debate whether the BUS was effective at that game (if indeed it actually viewed the regulation function as part of its job or ever seriously undertook to perform it), with J. Van Fenstermaker and Peter Temin in the forefront of those contending that the effect of that power was minimal.

The BUS carried on its other tasks well, lending the federal government more than $13 million, establishing a sound circulating currency that seldom if ever fell below par, and providing loans to individuals and businesses, especially those engaged in trade. It was not openly afflicted by partisan bitterness. The same could not be said for the states. New York in the late 1790s, for example, witnessed a situation in which the two chartered banks, both dominated by the Federalists, refused to lend money or discount the paper of Republican businessmen. The revolt against the New York Federalist banks ultimately spawned the Manhattan Company, founded largely through the efforts of Aaron Burr. Originally a water company, it conducted its business through "the Bank of the Manhattan Company," which appropriated half of the company's total capital. With the barrier broken, other Republican banks gained entry into the market. In 1816 DeWitt Clinton pioneered the savings bank, an institution aimed at the ordinary public rather than the wealthy. Clinton envisioned attracting depositors who had only small amounts to save. The New York legislature delayed its charter, however, so that when the Bank for Savings received the legislature's approval in 1819, it no longer represented the first savings bank in the nation. Legislatures tended to sharply limit the types of loans savings banks could make, a practice that lingered until the deregulation movement of the 1980s.

During the first decades of the new century, banking expanded in several areas, with the authorized capital stock of chartered banks increasing from $3 million to $168 million between 1790 and 1830. As Benjamin J. Klebaner has noted, banks multiplied by a factor of twelve during the first two decades of the 1800s. Banking growth characterized most areas, but it boomed in New England particularly. The period from 1800 to 1825 saw New England banks grow at an astounding rate: statistics compiled by Van Fenstermaker and his colleagues suggest that New England banking expanded by more than 20 percent annually in those years. Bank assets, loans, and deposits kept pace with the number of banks, and by 1820 every town aspired to have its own bank.

Since merchants routinely conducted some banking activities, exactly what did those communities want? The term "bank" meant several things to the public. First, most true banks had a charter from the state, or, in the case of the BUS, the federal government. Those charters established the length of the corporation's life (usually 20 to 25 years), set capitalization requirements, defined special conditions such as required loans to the state or contributions to required funds (some states paid for their universities out of bank profits), and determined whether or not the bank had the right to branch if the state had no general law. Charters endowed banks with tremendous respectability, but, more important, they generally constituted an authorization from the state for the bank to issue notes. No bank maintained 100 percent convertibility of its notes to specie; that is, at no time could all the depositors of a bank present their notes for conversion into the gold and silver in the bank's vaults. Nevertheless, legislatures constantly threatened to penalize banks that "suspended" (refused to pay out their limited supply of specie during a run). Then, as today, the only ways to break a run were to obtain more money (reserves) or find a way to keep people from withdrawing their deposits (rebuild public confidence). Banks in the period before the Civil War kept their own reserves.

The New York Safety Fund and the somewhat more successful regional networks such as the Suffolk System and various clearinghouse associations were brief and unsuccessful, and no national banking reserve existed as a lender of last resort to bail out banks if they experienced difficulties. Even the BUS operated under no obligation to rescue failing banks, nor did it have the means to do so if runs occurred everywhere at once as in the Panic of 1837. With no lender of last resort, banks simply refused to give people specie for notes for "temporary" periods of time. (No banker ever admitted that a suspension was permanent!) Evidence unearthed by Temin in his study of the Jacksonian economy suggests, however, that banks also "discounted" for business customers or other banks during crisis periods. The discounting procedure consisted of a banker agreeing to pay only a portion of a note's value in specie, with the noteholder having the option to retain the note for full-value presentation at a later date. Legislators frowned on any interruption of what they considered "normal" disbursement of specie, and state laws often required the revocation of the charter of an offending bank. Unfortunately, crisis periods sometimes forced general suspensions during which all banks refused to convert their notes to specie. Lawmakers intent on punishing banks found that their actions promised to leave their states bankless. During the crises legislatures waxed vitriolic in the chambers of the statehouses, and when flush times returned the lawmakers quickly passed relief bills and released the banks from their charter forfeitures.

It is important to understand, however, that in the antebellum period dozens of institutions issued notes under various guises. Steamboat companies, insurance companies, railroads, cities and towns, and even private merchants printed and circulated their own money. Such currency often even came to bear the name of the founder: "Mills Money" in Texas and "George Smith's Money" in Illinois and Wisconsin both had widespread appeal. Legislatures desperately tried to rein in such rogue ac-

tivities, but with little success. Between 1830 and 1861 they eliminated the problem through the other extreme, general incorporation laws that in essence let any individual or group start a bank by meeting uniform conditions of incorporation.

Those laws did not see widespread adoption until mid century. Until they did, chartered banks had to compete with so-called "private" (unincorporated) banks in lending and exchange operations. State legislatures also created some banks, known as state banks, to act as agents of the states themselves. Otherwise, all state-chartered banks were privately owned. But not all private banks were incorporated with state charters. To make matters even more confusing to modern observers, all chartered banks were "state" banks in that they held state-granted charters, but contemporaries clearly understood which banks were operated for profit and which banks were political tools. Heaped upon those confusions, state banks created as agents of the states differed drastically in the level of participation or control by the state government. The Bank of the State of South Carolina, for example, had to compete with prosperous chartered banks such as the Bank of Charleston and the Bank of South Carolina. On the other hand, Alabama legislators intended the Bank of Alabama to serve as a source of loans for borrowers it deemed most worthy—the planters—and sought from the outset to make it a monopoly bank with several branches. It not only failed to attain monopoly status, since it never completely eliminated the Bank of Mobile, but it failed, and the state ultimately liquidated it at a great loss of cash and credibility. Many states, however, saw the need for a state bank that stood as one competitor in a large market, because such institutions handled the financial activities of the state.

State-dominated banks that achieved monopoly status were not long for this world. Some of the most spectacular bank collapses have involved state institutions. Even so, governments exhibited persistence and ingenuity in injecting themselves into financial affairs. While some states sought to consolidate all banking functions into the hands of the government, others favored using the credit of the state to back bond issues that chartered banks could use to make loans. Disastrous results accompanied both efforts. Mississippi, one notorious example, had in the 1830s used the "full faith and credit" of the state to back bonds that a number of banks sold to obtain capital. One bank had $15 million in capital (more than the First BUS). When the Panic of 1837 struck, the state repudiated its "full faith and credit" thanks largely to the oratory of state senator Jefferson Davis. During the Civil War the Confederacy, under Davis's leadership, approached many of the same lenders whose debts Mississippi had earlier repudiated, and they not surprisingly refused the Confederacy's credit requests.

Banks in operation by 1830 included state-chartered, privately owned banks, unchartered private banks, state-monopoly banks, state banks that had no monopoly status, and the BUS. Several other variations of financial institutions and structures supplemented those major forms. Mutual savings banks differed from commercial banks chiefly in that they were non-profit organizations. The depositors owned all the assets; any profits earned were credited to their accounts. The first mutual savings bank, the Philadelphia Savings Fund Society, opened in 1816, and by 1860 mutual savings banks numbered more than 270, most of them serving small depositors, workers, and tradesmen. Virtually all mutuals operated in the Northeast. Improvement banks, another variant, provided the vehicle for the formation of organizations such as the Manhattan Company. Proponents of improvement banks generally argued that they made possible low-return, long-term activities such as canal building, hotel construction, or the expansion of utilities through linkage to high-return banking activities. They also encouraged the public to support internal improvements. In addition to the Manhattan Company, which evolved into the modern Chase National Bank, New York's famous Chemical Bank had its origins as an improvement bank called the New York Chemical Manufacturing Company. Later in the century, another variation of financial institution arose, the building and loan association, which operated along lines similar to the mutual savings associations, except that building and loan associations focused on housing construction. Yet another financial intermediary appeared as a means to finance the revolutionary war debts. A group of New York merchants who agreed to standardize their bond-sales operations in 1817 formed the New York Stock Exchange. Although the Exchange in its formative years handled only 30 securities—mostly state and local government bonds—it grew to handle the bonds of railroads, mining companies, and banks.

Two other groups affected the nation's banking and financial systems, although measuring their impact remains an elusive goal. One group, Americans who acted as agents for foreign banks, usually developed reputations for their own banking skills and on occasion opened their own banks. Perhaps the most famous trio of agents-turned-bankers, Louisiana's Edmond Jean Forstall, Wall Street's August Belmont, and Boston's Thomas Wren Ward, enhanced their careers as representatives of the Lizardis of Paris and later the Rothschilds of Paris and the Baring Brothers, respectively. Not only did American agents of foreign banks channel capital into the United States, they established permanent networks that eventually benefited all American bankers. And they learned the ropes of banking and eventually opened domestic banks that helped the United States gradually pull away from reliance on outside capital. The second group, known as "private bankers," conducted banking businesses without state charters. They lacked the official authority to issue notes, although many of them did so anyway, and quite frequently in times of crisis, they provided a reliable source of exchange. No historian has expressed confidence in existing estimates of the number of private banks. Most agree that the existing estimates have almost certainly undercounted their numbers and underestimated their impact. Some of those known as private bankers also were called "factors." Factors, located almost completely in the South and generally called "cotton factors," conducted middleman operations in which they purchased cotton for cash and then sold the cotton at the ports for a profit. Because they advanced funds and traveled inland, factors diminished the demand for banks in inland planting areas until state laws made establishing a bank almost as cheap and easy as dealing with a factor. Finally, banks received assistance in their lending from the credit agents of Dun and Bradstreet, who performed detailed (and often extremely personal) credit checks on merchants who enjoyed widespread respect.

That myriad of financial institutions and operatives made up the American banking system in the antebellum period. From 1791 to 1836, with an interlude of five years, the United States also had a national bank. The First BUS had not been rechartered when it expired in 1811. It had aroused concerns about special privilege and earned the enmity of the Jeffersonians as a remnant of Federalist policies. However, during the War of 1812, the nation tripled its debt by issuing short-term, interest-bearing treasury notes that, as Jeffrey Hummel points out, "were little different from government-issued paper money." The number of state-chartered banks increased and prices rose to all-time-high levels. Circulation of bank notes expanded by 50 percent after the demise of the BUS, and by August 1814 most banks had suspended specie payment because of the runs inspired by the war atmosphere. President James Madison, who had supported renewal of the charter of the First BUS, initiated legislation for a new bank as a means to help finance the wartime debt through his secretary of the treasury, Alexander Dallas. Congress passed a bill creating the Second BUS in 1816. Stephen Girard, whose private bank had taken over the business of the Philadelphia office of the First BUS and whose personal influence in financial circles allowed him to form a syndicate that rescued the federal government from falling revenues in 1813, added his voice to those advocating a national bank. Consequently, the government appointed him one of the directors. The new bank, like its predecessor, had a 20-year charter. It had a larger capital base ($35 million), of which the government again owned 20 percent. The Second BUS received the right to issue $35 million in notes, but no notes under $5. It also obtained the government's deposits, for which it paid no interest, and it transferred federal funds between the states with no charge. Headquarters for the BUS remained in Philadelphia.

BUS assets surpassed $40 million after only one year of operation, but low reserves in 1818 caused the bank to curtail loans, and its president, a Pennsylvanian named William Jones, soon lost his job to a South Carolinian, Langdon Cheves. An ally of former Speaker of the House Henry Clay and a personal friend of prominent Baltimore banker Alexander Brown, Cheves immediately choked off credit issued by the BUS. Many blamed the BUS and Cheves for the Panic of 1819. In fact, the BUS did not cause the inflationary bulge, as some historians have charged, nor did Cheves cause the contraction. As Edwin J. Perkins has shown, Jones's policies had already tightened credit, and, at the most, Cheves's policies caused the BUS to act "as a drag on an economy already suffering from a liquidity shortage." The bank survived its first crisis, and Cheves, until the recent revisions by Perkins, won acclaim as a hard-nosed banker who saved the BUS. But the bank received harsh criticism, mostly from debtors who had suffered foreclosure, and

that criticism was rekindled during the Jackson years.

In 1819 many of the arguments Alexander Hamilton thought he had put to rest when he secured the charter for the First BUS resurfaced when several state governments attempted to tax the Second BUS. Maryland levied a tax of $15,000 against any bank not chartered by the state, and when it attempted to collect from the BUS, a landmark Supreme Court case, *McCulloch* v. *Maryland*, resulted. Chief Justice John Marshall reiterated Hamilton's reasoning that the "necessary and proper" clause of the Constitution permitted Congress to charter a national bank. Consequently, the Court unanimously ruled that no state could tax the operations of the BUS (or any other federal agency).

The BUS directors must have suspected that Cheves was not the manager that several generations of historians assumed him to be, and they replaced him in 1823 with Nicholas Biddle, a Philadelphian who immediately boosted the bank's income and, hence, its dividends. Traditionalist interpretations of the bank's operations during the Biddle years, especially Bray Hammond's *Banks and Politics in America from the Revolution to the Civil War* (1957), held that the BUS under Biddle restricted the activities of the state banks by acting as a quasicentral bank. The BUS indeed dwarfed other banks. It accounted for 20 percent of the nation's loans, and its notes made up perhaps 25 percent of the total, although again historians have tended to underestimate the money supply by a considerable margin. Even so, by any standards, the BUS wielded substantial influence. But could it control the state banks? More recent scholarship by Temin and Van Fenstermaker finds that assertion dubious. Public use of bank money increased under Biddle, and state banks widely supported the Second BUS.

Under Biddle the bank did make important changes, however. Biddle personally selected—or influenced the selection of—BUS branch cashiers, who remained loyal to him. Except for the president of the United States and the postmaster general, possibly no other civilian commanded such patronage. But Biddle's control over the branches extended well beyond politics. He instituted uniform reporting procedures, inspections, and note redemption policies that required the branches to transfer state bank notes back to the source of issue as soon as possible, expanding the BUS stock of specie. He instituted a policy of paying out loans in the bank's notes, which gave the BUS currency a national circulation. The bank embarked on a path of expansion under Biddle, not just in notes and loans, but also in the foreign-exchange market.

Biddle's bank profited from one advantage denied all other American banks at the time: its ability to establish interstate branches. No other bank could diversify the way the BUS could. It could lend to New England merchants, Louisiana sugar growers, Ohio farmers, Atlantic Coast shippers, and still protect itself in the Philadelphia foundries or the Chillicothe land markets. Many states, particularly those in the North, prohibited branching. southern states, with their credit demand in rural areas, looked more favorably upon branching. Branching proved superior to simply chartering more unit banks because it permitted a single bank to diversify its portfolio and take advantage of the lower capitalization costs of establishing branches over new unit banks. In that respect the South was actually quite innovative. Not only did southern banks make extensive use of branches, they often opened "agencies" that emitted notes but did not redeem them. Evidence suggests that agencies may have generated loans, but they did not accept deposits. While some banks extended their agencies across state lines, no banks dared attempt to establish full-fledged branches in another state; that remained the sole domain of the BUS.

Thus, the Second BUS had important political clout through its branch patronage and also enjoyed unparalleled portfolio diversification through its interstate branching. The bank's huge capital endowed it with yet another advantage. And Biddle conducted intense if not always successful foreign-exchange operations, in which he learned the limits of the bank. In 1828, for example, he attempted to stem the outflow of specie through BUS credit rationing. However, the Alexander Brown family, which had plenty of funds of its own, continued to ship specie abroad and earned generous returns. Few observers appreciated that check on the bank's powers, and it remained only one instance in which the expanding empire of the BUS had been restrained. Consequently, many voices warned about the dominance of the BUS. Few people gave much credence to those warnings in the flush times of the late 1820s. Nevertheless, the presence of antibank sentiments had not completely disappeared since the earliest days of the Republic. An entirely new battle, in

which banks symbolized the differences between Jacksonian Democrats and their opponents, who eventually coalesced into a party called the Whigs, dominated American politics from the early 1830s until the mid 1840s.

Andrew Jackson, elected president in 1828, did much to encourage the polarization of society over economic issues. Seen as the champion of the "common man," of the rising group of voters who no longer had to meet property qualifications to participate in the political process, Jackson exploited his rural roots and his fame as a war hero to rail against the "privileged classes." Cheated out of the presidency in 1824 by the "corrupt bargain"–so his supporters claimed–Jackson focused his campaign rhetoric on equality and emphasized the notion of rotation in office, which the party generously lubricated through its patronage appointments. Given those views, it is easy to see why the BUS posed a threat, even before the famed Bank War: it offered a tempting target for the charges of privilege (which it certainly had), and over the years it had aggregated a tremendous patronage power itself.

But modern historians, especially those subscribing to the interpretations of either Arthur Schlesinger, Jr., in his *Age of Jackson* (1945) or Bray Hammond, whom historians for years posited as opposites, accepted the dichotomy between antibank Jacksonians and probank Whigs. Although some correction of those views took place in the 1970s, the record still suggested that Jackson opposed any national bank, that he favored "states' rights," and that he believed in a decentralized government. Historians thus tended to view his war on the BUS as exhibiting all of those positions. Nothing could be further from the truth. Jackson, in fact, had instructed Amos Kendall in 1829 to prepare plans for a Democratic national bank, and as pointed out by this author, Edwin Perkins, and others, Jackson made extremely specific objections to the BUS recharter, to which Biddle could have complied if he wished. Indeed, more than a little evidence suggests that the Democrats disliked the BUS only because it was not their national bank, and that their antibank activities merely provided a smoke screen for their further centralization of national financial activities.

The Bank War itself probably represents the most controversial (and to students, the most interesting) aspect of banking and finance in American history. Biddle brought on the battle by attempting to recharter the bank in 1832, four years ahead of schedule. He had skirmished with Jackson over the nominations of various branch directors and knew that Jackson wished some unspecified revisions in the BUS charter. By bringing up the recharter issue in an election year wherein Jackson promised to win handily, Biddle asked for certain defeat. If Jackson vetoed a recharter, Biddle and his supporters hoped to use it against him during the campaign. Biddle self-assuredly pressed for the recharter legislation at a time when a few "courtesy calls" to the White House would have in all probability ensured Jackson's approval. Instead, Biddle not only alienated the president, he failed to satisfy Jackson's specific demands in the new charter. The singsong line taught to high-school students about the Bank War, "Biddle Blundered Badly," appropriately sums up the result. Unable to override the veto, Biddle had as his only recourse deposing Jackson in the 1832 general election. In Perkins's words, Biddle "made a gross miscalculation." He printed up and distributed thousands of copies of the veto message, hoping that the voters would turn on Jackson. Most Americans who read the message got an entirely different point, and they tended to respond to Jackson's charges of BUS partisanship and elitism. They found the specific charter provisions of the BUS confusing, and Jackson's adroit political managers painted the issue in stark colors. Biddle never could have won.

With Jackson reelected, Biddle's problems grew even more serious and more immediate. In 1833 Jackson withdrew the government deposits from the BUS and put them in state-chartered private banks loyal to the administration, known as the "pets." Biddle tried to use the powers of the BUS, through a sharp credit constriction, to force Jackson to change his mind. He justified the contraction on the grounds that the loss of deposits demanded it. In his personal correspondence, however, Biddle left little doubt that he sought to precipitate a recession. He succeeded only in turning many of his supporters against him while lending credibility to those who contended that the bank remained hostile to the needs of the average citizen. Finally resigned to the inevitable demise of the bank, Biddle sold off branches and arranged a state charter from Pennsylvania so that the Philadelphia office could continue. He shrewdly maintained many offices in the form of agencies throughout New England and New York, and he entertained visions of a powerful private bank with a vast expanse of international enterprises, including investment banking, commercial banking, foreign exchange, and cotton consignment. The state-chartered version of the bank, while important, never achieved the level of international influence Biddle sought for it. He remained active in the management of the bank's affairs until 1839, and even after that he returned periodically to assist. But the effects of the Panic of 1837 eventually took their toll, and in 1841, after the bank had suspended specie payments for the third time, the state of Pennsylvania cited charter violations and closed it. Biddle's exit from the financial scene ended the career of the most important nonpolitician to imprint American commercial banking.

Biddle had contributed to, if not caused, the contraction in 1833-1834, and certainly the government, and Jackson, did their part by keeping the American banking and financial system in a state of chaos for several years. First, Congress reduced the gold content of the dollar in 1834. Second, revenue from increased land sales doubled the ordinary revenue that such sales usually produced for the government, giving the government a budget surplus of $35 million. In 1836 Congress decided to distribute that surplus to the states, and the process of redistribution tied up the government deposits for several months, which may have disrupted the system. Third, Andrew Jackson issued his Specie Circular in 1836, wherein buyers had to pay gold or silver for public lands. That action also disrupted interbank balances of specie. None of those events or even the cumulative activities of the government caused the Panic of 1837, however. Rather, it occurred because of a complex set of international forces that began with Mexican silver inflows to the United States in the 1830s, which in turn allowed the United States to ship silver to China to pay for Chinese goods. The Chinese used the silver in part to pay the British for opium. And the British added the silver to their reserves, which they used to provide loans to canals, railroads, and other businesses in the United States. When the Mexican silver sources dried up, it set off a chain reaction that reduced the amount of silver reserves in British vaults, and the British responded by raising interest rates, which in turn set off the American depression. Peter Temin, whose quantitative analysis of the panic seems uncontested at present, thus thoroughly refuted the Schlesinger-Hammond interpretations that ascribed credit or blame to Jackson or the BUS.

But contemporaries did not hesitate to draw lessons from the events of the 1830s. Editorialists such as Amos Kendall, editor of the *Argus of Western America* and later an auditor in the Treasury Department, thought banks "disgusting" and advocated a constitutional amendment prohibiting the chartering of additional banks. Kendall admitted that the nation needed banks, and unlike other critics of the banking system he supported the true laissez-faire concept of competing bank notes. He dismissed the idea of a uniform national currency as "an absurdity"; along with other theorists of the day, such as William Gouge, he opposed the BUS as an artificial means of granting subsidies to one group at the expense of another. (It did not seem to bother Kendall that he supported Jackson's plan for a national bank, which merely changed the group receiving the subsidies.) Whereas Kendall concerned himself more with power and politics, Gouge represented one of the first (and certainly up to that time the most influential) thinkers on money and banking in the nation. Gouge, who borrowed from the earlier writings of George Tucker, edited the *Philadelphia Gazette* and later edited the *Journal of Banking*. He won fame for his *Short History of Paper Money and Banking in the United States*, which appeared in 1833. Gouge berated banks as the products of a "moneyed aristocracy" and denounced limited liability laws for stockholders. He advocated "hard money"–specie–and contended that paper money resulted in increased prices and economic disruption. Gouge allowed for credit, but he insisted on the separation of credit from money through a system of promissory notes. Nevertheless, unlike other hard-money fanatics, Gouge proposed a gradual reduction of paper money over a ten-year period. The first step in Gouge's planned reforms required the divorce of government from banking.

Other hard-money theorists, including Amasa Walker, echoed Gouge and Kendall in the 1850s. Walker, in his articles in *Hunt's Merchant and Commercial Review*, argued for 100 percent specie reserves in banks. And the most famous of the hard-money advocates was not an economic theorist in any sense of the word, but a politician. Thomas Hart "Old Bullion" Benton, one of only two prominent nineteenth-century politicians to be nicknamed in commemoration of his metallic cause (Richard P. "Silver Dick" Bland was the other), had forcefully argued for a requirement that banks hold 100 percent specie reserves. Benton had suffered losses from his investment in the Bank of Missouri when it failed, at which point he formulated his hard-money ideas. Ironically, Missouri had only recently emerged from a business climate in which trappers and traders exchanged "fur" money; paper money constituted a wonderful convenience. Unlike many other Jacksonians, however, Benton actually opposed all banks, Whig or Democrat. After working with Jackson to eliminate the BUS, he adamantly refused to play any part in "put[ting] up a wilderness of state banks."

Modern economists tended to dismiss hard-money theorists such as Kendall and Gouge because of the obvious limitations a purely metallic currency put on economic growth. But the relationship of gold and silver to paper currency, when combined with competitive notes issue, proved quite effective in maintaining the stability of the banking system in the antebellum economy. Arguably, the Panic of 1819 occurred when the BUS withdrew from maintaining convertibility of the state bank notes, and the Panic of 1837 stemmed from international forces over which American banks had virtually no control. In both cases the system had operated outside the control of the BUS. Gouge and other "metallists" often preached wildly contradictory messages, however, contending on the one hand that individuals should have greater freedom from government intrusion into their economic lives, and on the other hand clamoring for requirements to limit individuals' choices regarding the types of money they wanted. Gouge remained adamant: "Paper-money Banking is *essentially bad*." He ended up a bureaucrat, serving as an inspector in the Independent Treasury System.

A few notable probank intellectuals achieved some measure of influence, including Richard Hildreth, who published *The History of Banks* in 1837 and expanded and updated it in 1840 under the title *Banks, Banking, and Paper Currencies*. Hildreth championed competition, and he and economist Henry C. Carey, in his *Credit System in France, Great Britain, and the United States* (1838), argued for the necessity of banks and the criticality of their functions. Carey and Hildreth remained if not less popular than Gouge and Amasa Walker, at least less quotable.

Carey, along with many hard-money Jacksonians, later became a proponent of greenbacks and monetary inflation. The migration from the position of hard-money metallism to greenback inflationism on the surface seems surprising and is only understandable in the context of egalitarianism. At the time Gouge railed against paper money, the Jacksonians claimed it constituted a source of inequality. Yet in practice, the Democrats far exceeded the Whigs in abusing paper-note issue, chiefly through their state monopoly banks. In the South and the West, where Democrats had uncontested control of the state legislatures, they tended toward one of three excesses: either they supported state monopoly banks (as in Arkansas, Alabama, Missouri, and Indiana); or they used the credit of the state to back banks with bond issues (as in Florida and Mississippi); or they passed laws prohibiting banks altogether (in Wisconsin, Minnesota, Illinois, Texas, Arkansas, Iowa, and Nebraska at one time or another). None of those approaches benefited the state economies. Missouri's state bank failed, as did Arkansas'. The latter state joined Texas in prohibiting banks, and the two suffered for years without credit or exchange facilities beyond a few renegade merchants who operated on the fringe of the law. Alabama, after a disastrous brush with a state monopoly, righted itself and adopted standard competitive banking. Only Indiana's state bank experienced any degree of success, and that was due largely to the superlative administration of its president, Hugh McCulloch, who well understood the advantages of competition and even supported free-banking laws when they appeared. Elsewhere, government interference in banking, regardless of its slant, produced unhappy and unexpected results. Mississippi and Florida languished until after the Civil War. In Nebraska, after the state's legislators passed a free-banking law, they found that several institutions sprang up overnight along the Iowa border, capitalized and run by out-of-staters. More astounding to Nebraskans, the founders of those banks were Iowa Democrats who had prominent antibank, hard-money reputations in their home state.

Usually laws prohibiting banks failed to deter banking completely. Entrepreneurs constantly found ways around the restrictions, and the public proved eager to acquire banking services. In California, for example, the state prohibited note-issuing banks, but within two years 16 banks appeared in San Francisco alone. So many other banks popped up in the Golden State that the government, lacking any effective means to restrain them, simply gave up. William Ralston and D. O. Mills immediately founded the Bank of California with a whopping $2 million capitalization. Prohibition sparked other ingenious methods of evasion. To circumvent Wisconsin's prohibition, a Scotsman, George Smith, established the Wisconsin Marine and Fire Insurance Company and issued notes. His commitment to always redeem notes in specie, and his reputation for doing just that, made him the most powerful financier in the Midwest. Smith even loaned money to the state of Wisconsin, the very entity that ostensibly prohibited him from making the loan. Instead of the notes circulating at a discount, "George Smith's Money" was literally as good as gold and constituted much of the circulating medium in Wisconsin, northern Illinois, and parts of Iowa and Minnesota in the early 1840s. His notes brought a premium of 1 to 2 percent in Chicago, meaning that Chicagoans willingly paid $1.02 for a $1 Smith note. Smith later purchased a Georgia bank for the sole purpose of issuing notes in Chicago, and his money constituted three-fourths of the city's money supply.

Smith could no more redeem all his notes than other bankers could, but his operations illustrated the strengths and weaknesses of fractional reserve banking. Basically, the concept assumes that all of a bank's depositors (or note holders, in the antebellum period) would never demand their deposits (or present their notes for redemption) at the same time. Bankers determined profitable (but, to them, practical and safe) ratios of reserves to notes, or, later, reserves to deposits. Smith, like modern bankers, also knew that money was lost, stolen, or destroyed, and that a tremendous amount of lag time, known to bankers as "float," was inherent in the system. Certainly the float in the antebellum period vastly exceeded that of modern times, wherein computers can make transactions in seconds. Most of all, though, Smith relied on another fundamental element of banking: the psychological element of public confidence. Once the public determined it could redeem Smith money at any time, it no longer asked on a regular basis. (In essence, the public inverted the old joke about never being able to get a loan until you did not need one.)

Other bankers and writers had gradually moved past the hard-money theories of the Jacksonians and entered a new era of thinking about banks and money. For example, Alexander

B. Johnson, a New York banker, published one of the earliest management guides on banking in the United States. His *Treatise on Banking* appeared in 1850 and refreshingly proclaimed an end to the rigidities of hard money. Johnson offered instead a model of a competitive money economy in which the value of different bank notes fluctuated with demand. He also outlined principles that several generations of bankers later followed, urging them to rely on their own instincts, know their customers personally, and study their lenders and their situations. Personal banking of the type Johnson espoused remained predominant in all but the largest cities until well into the second decade of the twentieth century, even as banks gradually professionalized. According to research by Naomi Lamoreaux, New England banks started to change their management in the Jacksonian Era, making fewer "insider" loans to directors and officers, and hiring professionals to fill the position of cashier (the major managing officer in most nineteenth-century banks). The new professionalism gave little place to hard-money sentiments.

As the Jacksonian hard-money views faded, new solutions to the problems of "privilege" associated with banks arose, often from some of the same Jacksonians who had favored prohibition or stricter regulation of banks. The "Free Banking Era," as Hugh Rockoff has termed it, resulted from one of the new solutions, the passage of free banking laws. Michigan passed the first such law in 1837, and a year later New York did likewise out of desperation when the chartering process in the state "became so shameless and corrupt that it could be endured no longer," according to Millard Fillmore. Under free banking laws any group (or individual) that raised a stipulated amount of capital was automatically eligible to receive bank charter. The banks had the authority to issue notes, but only up to the value of government bonds that the banks purchased and placed on deposit with a state agency. Free entry seemed appealing at first. Entrepreneurs in Michigan must have thought so, for they opened 40 banks within a year after passage of the act. Enthusiasm soon waned however, as several free banks failed and as the bankers came to understand the disadvantages of the bond security system. The states stipulated the "acceptable" securities and thus seriously limited the banks' portfolio choices. Free banks found themselves holding large amounts of what in today's terminology are called non-performing assets. In that respect free banking did not mean laissez-faire banking. Bankers also seem to have attributed some degree of prestige to charters and may have preferred them over free entry.

On the other hand, if the states failed to write the laws with care, and therefore tended to allow the bonds deposited to be assessed according to their par value (the amount on the face of the bond) as opposed to their market value, free banking offered an opportunity for shenanigans. Specifically, a banker could post, say, $100,000 in bonds (par) that really only were worth $50,000. After issuing $100,000 in notes and receiving in return either specie or the good notes of other banks, the banker had a temptation to skip town with the bank's assets, forfeiting the $100,000 (par) bonds that were only worth $50,000. He stood to make as much as $50,000. Or he could use the notes to purchase more bonds, increase the capital of the bank, and continue to leverage to the point of instability. As Arthur Rolnick and Warren Weber have shown, the par/market problem particularly afflicted Minnesota and Michigan; in Minnesota, 11 of 16 free banks closed. Minnesota free banks had their fortunes tied to railroad bonds, and when the bonds plunged in 1859, the banks closed. Contrary to the views of previous generations of historians, however, the free bank failures correlated to capital losses on assets, not to fraud or "wildcatting." Overall, free banks exhibited a much higher degree of stability than historians previously had thought, and Rockoff and Rolnick and Weber have made much-needed revisions in the historical assessment of free banking.

Free banking was just one of the many innovations tried by the states before the Civil War. In the case of free banking, states wanted to ensure greater equality of opportunity. Most other experiments focused on improving bank stability and liquidity, as in the case of the Suffolk System, the New York Safety Fund, and the New York Clearing House Association. The Suffolk System attempted to solve the problem of "foreign notes" from other areas circulating at a discount in the local economy. In the mid 1820s Boston's Suffolk Bank found a method of achieving a par currency by purchasing all of the country bank notes held by other banks in Boston. Other banks in the city misjudged the profit in agreeing to the Suffolk's suggestion. Suffolk Bank, on the other hand, dominated the country note-exchange business. The Suffolk plan had a unique feature in that country banks had to keep a permanent $2,000 deposit in the Suffolk's vaults in addition to an amount sufficient to redeem notes that reached Boston. The balances did not pay interest, and understandably the country banks wanted out of the system. Many of them got out in 1858, when they formed the Bank of Mutual Redemption as a competitor. Shortly thereafter the Civil War disturbed the money markets, thus ending the Suffolk System's regulatory regime. As a result, evaluating the performance of the Suffolk System is difficult. The system did have one undeniable achievement: it forced a par-value currency throughout New England and ended the fluctutations in value between notes.

Another mechanism emerged for clearing checks and serving as a lender of last resort when Boston banks established the Boston Clearing House in 1852. New York followed suit a year later, with the New York Clearing House Association. Those associations provided central locations for check clearing on a regional basis, and the systems developed an efficient clearing mechanism that relied on certificates exchanged for deposits with the associations. Clearinghouse associations and the Suffolk System both arrived at currency-exchange mechanisms that reduced the discounts on notes. But the clearinghouses also provided an important service that the Suffolk System lacked, namely the ability to use deposits in the capacity of "lender of last resort" during a crisis. The New York Clearing House used its newfound powers for the first time during the Panic of 1857 and then routinely thereafter. Much earlier, in 1829, New York had developed yet one other device for ensuring stability, the Safety Fund. The Fund levied an assessment of .05 percent of bank capital on all banks in the city for the purpose of establishing an emergency reserve fund. A board of commissioners made routine inspections to ensure compliance. Those favorable to the Safety Fund point out that it paid off 100 cents on the dollar, but it was designed to prevent runs, not pay off depositors after the fact, and from that perspective it failed during the Panic of 1837. Despite the fund's poor performance, the idea of a deposit guaranty fund has bobbed up periodically throughout American financial history, especially after the Panic of 1907, when the state of Oklahoma instituted its famous Deposit Guaranty Law, ultimately with similarly disappointing results.

Nationally, the hope of a uniform or par currency that various regions accepted without a discount disappeared with the death of the BUS. In its place the Democrats under Martin Van Buren created the Independent Treasury System (also known as the Sub-Treasury or the "divorce" because it divorced the government from banking) in 1840. Repealed a year later, the Independent Treasury was reestablished in 1846 and technically remained open until 1920. Democrats developed the Independent Treasury along the lines suggested by William Gouge, with the government acting as its own banker, paying and receiving in gold and silver or treasury notes. Whigs continued to clamor for a national bank, and thought they had achieved that end when William Henry Harrison won the 1840 election. He disappointed them by dying only a few months later, and his successor, John Tyler, who gave no indication that he intended to do anything but approve the new bank, flabbergasted the Whigs by vetoing the bank bill.

Two sets of issues in the antebellum period actually represented different sides of the same problem. Both the constant agitation for a national bank and the smorgasbord of state measures such as the free-banking laws, the Suffolk System, the Safety Fund, and the clearinghouses, all attempted to solve certain anomalies in the banking system: they sought to attain regular convertibility, institute circulation at par among the thousands of bank notes, ensure bank solvency, and provide a lender of last resort (to one degree or another). One mechanism used only sparingly, mostly in the South and parts of the West, branch banking, solved most of those problems. Branching had accounted in some measure for the success of the Indiana State Bank. Several southern states, including Virginia, Louisiana, Tennessee, and South Carolina, permitted branches (and many others allowed agencies). Branches smoothed out fluctuations related to local economies. If the tobacco crop was bad one year, trade and shipping in the coastal areas nevertheless might have enjoyed a profitable season: all of the banks' assets were not tied to the fortunes of one sector of the economy. Canada's banking system, which allowed branching, never experienced the disasters that periodically swept down on its southern neighbors.

Because the state monopoly banks had collapsed and left states with either stable and generally healthy systems or with bank prohibition, the first period that allowed a true comparison of banking efficiency, the 1850s, yielded surprising results. J. Van Fenstermaker, in a paper all but hidden by his oft-cited book, *The Development of American Commercial Banking*, demonstrated that dividends in the period before 1830 in selected southern banks matched those paid in the North. Scholars have contended that the statistics do not compare apples to apples and have assured themselves that the presence of the Safety Fund, the clearinghouses, the Suffolk System, and other innovations meant that northern banks were far superior to their southern cousins. In the 1850s, however, southern banks spurted again. More important, when the Panic of 1857 struck, southern banks scarcely felt the effects, while the northern money centers experienced widespread chaos. The panic itself was brought on by the activities of the New York cashier of the Ohio Life and Insurance Company, a bank that invested much of its $2 million capital in railroads. Whether the cashier had speculated with the bank's money on his own account or had advanced loans to a particular railroad that went bad remains a matter of mystery. At any rate, the failure of Ohio Life triggered a panic, made worse by the arbitrary activities of speculators who took advantage of a New York law to pull specie out of the banks in that city.

Several banks in the South did not even suspend, and throughout the panic southern banks looked extremely healthy. By the end of the decade they had clearly established themselves as the equals of northern banks. The West, on the other hand, went almost totally without banks—or money—in good times as well as bad. One pioneer in Kansas in the 1850s lamented that there "is no money in Kansas." Even a decade later, merchants in Montana and other areas of the West experienced severe money shortages despite the abundance of gold dust and nuggets. Banks in the frontier areas sprang up as a consequence of the money and currency shortages, not the absence of credit. Expectedly, bankers came from the ranks of gold-dust brokers and merchants. Those individuals not only had business expertise, but they also had the necessary affluence to assure customers that they could trust their money with the merchants. In the West especially, bankers needed one other physical manifestation, an impressive-looking bank building with an equally impressive-looking vault holding a secure-looking safe. The key word was "looking." On the

frontier, with its open and democratic character, much more so than in the Northeast or South, symbols went a long way toward establishing a man's credentials as a banker. Female bankers in the nineteenth century simply did not exist (or if they did, no record of them remains). The most noted female involved in finance in the nineteenth century, Hetty Green, the "Witch of Wall Street," never owned or attempted to own a bank. At any rate, to succeed in the West, a good suit, a considerable girth, and an impregnable vault in a building that had impressive looks (by frontier standards, at least) constituted the basic ingredients for starting a bank.

Perhaps few would express surprise at those qualifications. However, the results they yielded in at least one area might surprise all but the most well read Western history buffs: there were virtually no bank robberies in most of the West before 1900. Given the tremendous lore that has developed around such activities, this requires some caveats: Minnesota and Missouri, along with parts of Texas, no longer constituted the West for many settlers. Minnesota, a solid part of the Midwest, endured the famous raid at Northfield, and the James brothers plied their trade throughout Missouri. But historians have turned up no bank robberies in Arizona prior to 1900, nor have histories of banking in Oklahoma, Wyoming, or Colorado mentioned any robberies, except a planned attempt by Butch Cassidy that never got off the ground. Other state histories are notable for their absence of stories of successful bank heists before 1900.

Several factors account for the difference between myth and reality. First, many of the images portrayed by Hollywood and western writers reflect the activities in Missouri, Minnesota, and Texas. Second, screenplay and novel writers seem to have underestimated the tremendous difficulty associated with robbing a bank. The bank usually stood smack dab in the middle of town; small towns quickly noticed a pack of strangers in long coats (and mobilized accordingly), while larger towns had more than enough firepower to protect local citizens' savings. Even more detrimental to successful thievery, however, were the buildings themselves. Penetrating a vault constituted a major undertaking and, once accomplished, merely allowed access to the safe. Traditional safes followed the ball design, in which a bottom box area held papers and the like while a cast-iron ball with a combination door in the middle protected the cash. Rounded edges made blowing the door almost impossible, and separating the top ball from the bottom box left the crook with an incredibly heavy iron ball. The heist either had to be carried out at night–when explosions tended to wake the residents–or during the day, when a posse proved willing and able to trail the culprits. Nor could bandits count on passive resistance from bankers, tellers, or even nearby stores. As late as the 1920s, Nevada banker George Wingfield (whose biography appears in the subsequent banking volume in this series) continued to issue shotguns to all his banks, and he wrote the merchants in adjoining stores to remind them to keep their guns ready in case of irregularities. Since many bandits commonly carried a bounty on their heads, local custom was to shoot first and count your cash later.

The absence of bank robberies certainly did not mean that banks never lost money through embezzlement, creative bookkeeping, or defaulted loans. But banks proved too formidable a target once the teller had taken money on deposit. Trains and stagecoaches offered much more tempting targets and involved much less risk. That still did not let banks completely off the hook: in many cases bankers either conducted freighting operations or had originated from them. The most famous freighting/banking operation, still in existence as of this writing, Wells, Fargo & Company, is synonymous with money on the move. Henry Wells not only pioneered express and communications on the frontier, he also founded American Express, a modern credit card and traveler's check operation. The stage line that he founded with William Fargo stretched to California by the early 1850s. Soon thereafter numerous financiers branched out from freighting, steamboating, mercantile businesses, and gold-dust exchange to start banks. Ambitious entrepreneurs who created or fostered the development of powerful banking institutions in the late nineteenth century–William Chapman Ralston and Isais W. Hellman in California, Henry Corbett, William Ladd, and Henry Failing in Oregon, "Major" Rufus Palen in New Mexico, the Kountze brothers in Nebraska and Colorado, David H. Moffat, Jr., in Colorado, and, of course, Wells and Fargo–played important roles in contributing to the business (and usually social) climates of their states. In addition, several easterners had encouraged western growth through their investments, beginning in the Old Northwest–Ohio, Michigan, Illinois, Indiana,

and Wisconsin–with investors such as John Murray Forbes, George Smith, and Alfred Kelly. Others, such as John Jacob Astor, financed much of the Pacific Northwest fur trade early in the century. Others, such as J. & W. Seligman & Company, stretched banking interests into mining areas such as Montana.

The West benefited from the clash between the other two sections when the Civil War broke out in 1861. Railroads wove their way toward the Great Plains and the Rockies, and, after the war, disaffected Confederates found haven. But four years later the financial effects of the war were not so favorable, and, indeed, other sections found that the Northwest had drastically increased its control over both the banking and monetary systems of the country through the changes instituted during the war by the administration of Abraham Lincoln and his capable secretary of the treasury, Salmon P. Chase.

As Richard H. Timberlake explains, the National Bank and Currency Acts of 1863 and 1864, envisioned as a way to "create an institutional demand for the burgeoning volume of government securities" that the Union needed to finance the war, took on a life of their own. With no southerners in Congress to restrain the Republicans, the government established a national bank system in which all banks in the national system had to obtain charters from the federal government. The system featured central reserve cities, and country banks in outlying communities. Banks in reserve cities had to hold greenbacks or specie equal to 25 percent of national bank notes issued, while the country banks only had to hold 15 percent in reserves. The system achieved many of the goals of the numerous mechanisms that states had earlier tried, such as the clearinghouses, uniform note appearance, and a steady market for notes to trade at par value. National banks had to hold government bonds as collateral for the notes, thus ensuring brisk bond sales. Congress found that state banks had little interest in joining the system and as a result decided to prohibit note issue by state chartered banks. It accomplished that by placing a 10 percent tax on non-national bank note issues, driving them out of existence. Many Jacksonians, such as Secretary Chase, had moved into the Republican administration, and those who had always had a centralizing bent found in the Lincoln administration the opportunity to put into action their plans for centralizing control of the banking system, at least to the degree that they could accomplish it. The era of competitive money in the United States came to an end, much to the disadvantage of the South and West, areas that had supported the Jacksonians and, later, voted Democratic.

Whether the greenbacks issued during the war indeed carried legal-tender status remained a matter of controversy for several years, until the Supreme Court heard the *Hepburn* v. *Griswold* case in 1870. Ironically, Chase, the former hard-money advocate who had served as secretary of the treasury when Congress passed the Legal Tender Act in 1862, had since attained the position of chief justice of the United States. He had a chance to disavow his earlier actions and took advantage of the opportunity. Congress was incensed at the Court's ruling (on questions of legislative authority more than financial issues). It had already increased the size of the court and the new appointees of Ulysses S. Grant voted with the earlier minority to reverse the *Hepburn* decision in 1872. Greenbacks thus became legal tender for all debts public and private.

Giving money legal-tender status did little to endow it with the qualities of stability or value. Congress in fact had done that, perhaps by accident, when it authorized that the government accept the money for taxes. That proved a crucial difference between the financing efforts of the Union and the Confederacy. Christopher G. Memminger, the Confederate secretary of the treasury, resisted giving legal-tender status to Confederate notes and relied on bond sales to support the Confederacy. The Confederate Congress, which rarely adhered to Memminger's proposals, rejected his advice, and the value of Confederate money fell accordingly. Whether Confederate financial policies ever would have succeeded even in the event of Southern military victory still evokes controversy. At any rate, the Union victory sealed the doom of the Confederate financial system. The Southern banking system all but disappeared, as well, after the banks had diverted their specie into war loans. Southern banks also lost huge amounts following the sudden change in the status of the former slaves, who had served as collateral on many loans. Finally, Southern banks that managed to survive the war found themselves at a severe disadvantage when it came to acquiring national bank charters.

Certainly the Republican Congress did not intend to grant any charters to loyal Confederates, nor did Congress leap to confer charters on the freed-

men. Moreover, the original National Banking Act limited total note allocation to $300 million, with Secretary Chase authorized to make half the allocation on the basis of population (therefore mostly in the North) and half on the basis of "existing banking capital, resources, and business" (again the North). As Timberlake points out, national banks in the South comprised 4 percent of all national banks and received only 3 percent of the national bank notes in 1870. However, because the banks had to trade off profits in note issue against other profitable activities, such as lending, southern banks did not issue more money because their lending activity constituted a more powerful incentive. The inelasticity of note issue, caused by penalties associated with issuing national bank notes, prevented the national bank system from dominating the nation as many had predicted.

At first, the number of national banks surged as the Republicans hoped (see the table, "Banks in the United States, 1834-1910"). State banks, which comprised all of the country's 1,562 banks in 1860, fell to 325 in 1870, while national banks totaled 1,612. The trend still seemed in the national system's favor a decade later, with national banks exceeding 2,000 in number. But during that same time, the number of state banks almost quadrupled; by 1890 they almost quadrupled again, and by 1910 they doubled yet again. The growth in the number of national banks, meanwhile, slowed considerably. They fell behind state banks in 1890, and by 1910 trailed by nearly 11,000. The dramatic shift occurred primarily because states passed laws making it easier to obtain a charter and requiring less capitalization than national chartering laws; thus, the states undercut one of Congress's main objectives in setting up the national system.

If the National Banking and Currency Acts failed to make national banks the dominant form of banking in the nation, they succeeded in providing the market for government securities for which their authors hoped. Chase realized that the North would not accept burdensome taxes, and finding a means of financing the war constituted his top priority as treasury secretary. Congress initially authorized him to borrow $250 million (later increasing that by $500 million) through the sale of bonds. Chase also negotiated for three specie loans of $50 million, which brought gold into the government's vaults. Unfortunately, that action drained the gold from the banks, which suspended. Congress frantically passed the Legal Tender Act, which permitted Chase to issue $100 million worth of interest-free treasury notes. Chase, earlier in his career a hard-money man, retreated to take the position that the war made the new paper money issues "a political necessity." He also decided to hire Jay Cooke, a close friend and salesman extraordinaire, to unload the slow-selling bonds. Cooke sold $400 million worth of bonds in less than two years, earning a tidy commission in the process.

Cooke represented a new breed of financiers not commonly seen before the 1850s–investment bankers. Investment banking differed from commercial banking in that investment bankers did not make short-term loans or deal in note issues, but provided the large capital backing for projects such as railroads, and later utilities and steel, through their underwriting of bond sales. Quite frequently that entailed forming a syndicate of several banking concerns, so large were the demands of the railroads in particular. Cooke, neither the first nor the most famous of the new breed, certainly gained notoriety as a result of his activities. He mastered the sale of bonds through newspaper advertisements and pioneered the use of pamphleteering as a sales device for banks. Many criticized him for the profits (at least $1 million) he made on the government bond sales, forgetting that he constantly had to wait or nag the government for his rightful recompense. Still others blamed him for causing the 1873 financial panic when the failure of his Jay Cooke & Company, after valiantly bracing the sagging sales of the Northern Pacific Railroad, caused financial turmoil. (Richard H. Timberlake, elsewhere in this volume, attributes the panic to a sharp reduction in the volume of bank reserves, a reduction brought on by the government.)

Other bankers, including Levi P. Morton, the Speyers, and John S. Kennedy, played an important role in extending the railroads westward and in developing the American capital market. No one, however, influenced banking in the nineteenth century as much as J. P. Morgan. Under the political traditions of earlier ages, Morgan probably would have earned the title, "the Great," for his contributions. Separating Morgan from other financiers was the fact that above even raising great sums of capital and operating a highly profitable banking house, Morgan had a managerial genius that enabled him to reorganize the recipients of that capital, usually railroads, on a permanently profitable basis. Using

the contacts of his father, Junius Morgan, and his alliance with Drexel & Company, Morgan underwrote and distributed railroad bonds in America, England, and Europe. He and his partners earned a great reputation for turning some of the most troubled roads into solid lines.

Morgan's preeminence as an investment banker in the postbellum period grew after he guided his company and many of the railroads through the depression of 1873. His importance also grew because of the stability of his firm during the so-called Populist Era. The deflation in prices that lasted from the end of the Civil War almost until the end of the century caused many critics to complain that the national banking and monetary system still contained flaws (even though on that count the banking system was blameless). Two significant flaws still afflicted the system: the absence of national branch banking and the strength of the unit banks' lobbies in most states, which reduced the abilities of banks to diversify their portfolios. Where the economy relied on a single industry–mining in parts of Colorado, for example–banks found themselves at the mercy of international metals prices. The absence of branching also contributed to another concern, the inelasticity of money. Overlaying those troubles, the deflation that, before 1879, was brought about by the expectations of a return to the gold standard and after 1879 by a long-term worldwide deflation, led to new agitation by farmers and miners for an increase in the money stock through government purchase and coinage of silver.

The silver issue emerged due to a scarcity of the metal that led Congress in 1873 to abandon the coinage of silver dollars, an action critics called the "crime of '73." Suddenly, however, the quantity of silver rose with new discoveries and increased production from silver mines. Silverites pressed Congress to purchase and coin as much silver as the mines could turn out at the previous ratio of 16 ounces of silver to 1 ounce of gold. Since the new increases in silver meant that silver came out of the ground at a ratio of 17 to 1, the silverites anticipated a resulting inflation. With the help of Sen. Richard P. "Silver Dick" Bland, the silver lobby pushed the Bland-Allison Act through Congress in 1878, wherein the government remonetized silver by authorizing the Treasury to purchase between $2 million and $4 million worth of the metal each month to coin silver dollars. In 1890 Congress passed the Sherman Silver Purchase Act, which required the Treasury to buy 4.5 million ounces of silver at market prices and, rather than coin silver dollars, issue legal-tender treasury notes redeemable in gold. The Sherman Act marked an important change: the government bought not a dollar value of silver but a specified quantity. Coinciding with the silverite agitation, the rising Populist movement (officially founded in 1890) provided a natural pool of allies. The Populists favored any means of inflating the currency, including either silver coinage at a 16 to 1 ratio or new greenback issues. Even without their efforts, the quantity of silver had already increased, and along with it the total amount of all currency in circulation.

Populist pressures for inflation and uncertainty over the nation's commitment to the gold standard touched off a gold drain. Historians have called the resulting disequilibrium the Panic of 1893. More than any previous panic, it represented a crisis of confidence, not in the banking system itself, but in the nation's ability to master its finances. Indeed, it revived Hamilton's concerns about politicians controlling the money supply, for Congress had the power to restrict the sale of bonds necessary to protect the gold standard. Into the breach stepped J. P. Morgan. Despite shabby treatment from President Grover Cleveland—the president forced Morgan to wait in an outer room while he and his advisors determined the least embarrassing way to ask the banker for his support—Morgan formed a syndicate with August Belmont & Company and the Rothschilds to deliver 3.5 million ounces of gold to the U.S. Treasury. Essentially, Morgan prevented the nation from defaulting on its promise to pay gold for its dollars. Yet the man who bore much of the responsibility for turning the country's railroad system into an efficient engine of progress, and whose personal efforts and influence alone saved the United States from humiliation in international financial circles, nevertheless topped the list when writers issued their polemics against the "robber barons."

Indeed, bankers suffered some embarrassment as a result of Morgan's rescue, if only because they realized the inability of the commercial banking system to deal with such troubles. A new generation of writers had cleared the way for such reform, many of them arguing for a final commitment to the gold standard (William Graham Sumner and Horace White), increased incorporation of modern statistical and economics methods in banking and finance (Davis Rich Dewey), and improved bank chartering laws that fostered more accurate examinations (John Jay Knox). Others expressed concern about the inelasticity of the currency. Francis Amasa Walker, Amasa Walker's son, departed from the strict 100 percent reserve concepts of his father to argue for an international bimetallic standard. Walker favored a money supply that made use of silver, greenbacks, and anything serving as a medium of exchange. As Walker illustrated, the numerous reformers hardly agreed on the specific ingredients of reform and often fought over the merits of the gold standard, bimetallism, and the "real bills" doctrine. They left to the national and state regulators the chore of coping with the booming numbers of banks, which exploded as the national and state authorities in the dual system competed to grant charters. The office of the comptroller of the currency had expanded its staff in the latter part of the century, although it by no means kept up with the increasing number of national banks. And both national and state governments remained reactive agencies in the late 1800s, although banks engaged in more self-regulation than is generally believed.

Increasingly, thanks to Morgan's efforts, banking had developed its own divisions and managerial hierarchies. The "one-man bank" started to disappear in favor of more professional organizations, except in parts of the West. Directors played less of a role in the management of banks, and increasingly the position of cashier required professionally trained individuals rather than friends, relatives, or part owners. As bank management changed, so too did attitudes about making loans based on such personal characteristics as reputation, looks, or a man's word; instead, banks increasingly demanded collateral. Many states passed new banking laws, often establishing agencies for regulating or at least examining banks. States demanded publication of balance sheets. Faced with certain regulation of one kind or another, bankers formed statewide bankers' associations in the late-nineteenth and early-twentieth centuries. Those associations spoke for banking interests and provided lobbying services. The founding of the American Bankers Association in 1876 represented a major step for bankers. Within less than half a decade the association took positions on the uniformity of state laws and bank crime, and then established a clearinghouse section in 1906. *A Journal of the American Bankers Association* entered into publication two years later.

The professionalization of banking allowed bankers for the first time to address on a national level the important weaknesses that remained in the system, which crisis situations exposed all too clearly. Expedients developed in earlier times proved unsatisfactory. Clearinghouses provided only temporary remedies for sharp fluctuations in the system. The treasury secretaries had attempted to use government deposits in large national banks to "manage" interest rates with equally poor results. Consequently, voices for reform emerged. John Jay Knox, who was comptroller from 1872 to 1884, had forcefully advocated a more flexible currency, but it took the Panic of 1893 to spark the bankers into action. Following that panic, A. Barton Hepburn, president of the Third National Bank of New York (and later chairman of Chase National Bank) called the currency system "ill-conceived, unresponsive to the various interests of our great nation, and prejudicial to renewed and stable prosperity." At the American Bankers Association convention in Baltimore in 1894, he and Charles Christopher Homer, a Baltimore banker, put into motion a plan that ultimately served as the basis for the Federal Reserve Act.

Labeled the "Baltimore Plan," it advocated a guaranty fund supplied by the federal government and provided an emergency elastic note issue capacity based on a bank's capital, with the emergency money taxed at a stiff rate to ensure that banks did not permanently abuse their "emergencies." Supported by Hepburn and Horace White, the Baltimore Plan served as a basis for continued discussion of reform at the Indianapolis Monetary Convention in 1897 and in a study by the Currency Commission of the American Bankers Association, which Hepburn chaired. Hepburn also published a *History of Coinage and Currency* in 1903, which turned up the reform temperature further.

By the early 1900s most observers expected some kind of banking and monetary reform to occur. Most citizens, especially bankers, detested the idea of running to Morgan and his partners in each new crisis. Indeed, the power of Morgan and other New York banks narrowed the range of choices available to reformers. Any attempt to centralize the system raised questions not only about whether private hands or the government should run it, but where the focus of power would be

(New York, Washington, or scattered in several reserve cities). The debate revived the Populists' fears of a "money power" based in New York and spurred opposition in the American Bankers Association by powerful unit bankers, who envisioned any kind of national branch-banking law as sounding their death knell. Unit bank laws revived the old Jacksonian suspicions about banks, but in fact became self-fulfilling prophecies: banks were to be feared because they could grow so big they abused power, so they must be kept small. But small banks without branching tended to fail, and when they did, "common man" was most hurt because he lost his savings. So small banks were to be feared. And so on. Thus, two separate battles developed within the broader context of banking reform, either of which had the potential to derail the reform efforts completely: branch versus unit banking and "country" versus "city" banking, understood to mean banks in every part of the country versus banks in New York City. To complicate matters, under those tensions yet another, more theoretical, debate had developed over the nature of credit. Many bankers accepted the "real bills" doctrine of money, meaning that money should represent self-liquidating, short-term loans backed by "real," tangible goods. Others had only started to suspect that the nation's money supply had long since ceased to represent such goods, and that the credit needs of the country far exceeded those allowed by the "real bills" doctrine.

The different contingents played against each other in many ways. New York bankers such as Frank Arthur Vanderlip, who favored branching, also supported a centralized system with the central bank located in New York City. And clearly the unit bankers never appreciated the gravity of the threat posed to them by the central government. The notion that by centralizing control over banking and money in the hands of the federal government the units banks would emerge with less power never seemed to have occurred to many of the antibranch, anti-New York leaders.

At any rate, armed with previous investigations into national banking reform, the movement coalesced sometime before the Panic of 1907, perhaps as early as 1906, when Jacob Henry Schiff, a senior partner in Kuhn, Loeb & Company, delivered an attack on the national banking system at the New York Chamber of Commerce. As a result of Schiff's prodding, the chamber named a five-man committee, including Vanderlip of National City Bank, Isador Straus, Charles Conant, and John Claflin, all of whom specifically were recommended by former secretary of the treasury Lyman J. Gage or A. Barton Hepburn. The committee sent Conant to Europe to study banking systems there, and the committee's report recommended a central bank such as existed in Britain, France, and other countries. The 1907 depression added weight to the reformers' arguments. Morgan again used his enormous wealth and influence to try to quell the money markets, lending $25 million at 10 percent interest to the New York banks (as opposed to the U.S. Treasury, which only deposited $19 million in those banks during the crisis). The Panic of 1907 led to passage of the Aldrich-Vreeland Act of 1908, which authorized the secretary of the treasury to issue emergency currency during future panics. More important, however, it created the National Monetary Commission to make recommendations to prevent future crises. That committee, too, went to Europe, and upon its return chairman Nelson W. Aldrich completely accepted the need for a national bank.

As Aldrich's committee studied the banking problem, the members met privately with many important bankers, including Vanderlip, Paul Warburg (whose entry will appear in the post-1913 volume), Morgan, and others. They sought to separate politics from banking, but in fact many of the assumptions seemed foregone conclusions. For example, the government was not going to tolerate New York as the center of the new system. And most observers suspected that the national branch concept was doomed. Aldrich and his committee hoped to deliver their report to Congress in 1911, but even by late 1910 they had not worked out any of the details. Thus, in November 1910, in a setting that some could well have labeled "conspiratorial," Vanderlip, Warburg, Aldrich, Henry Davison (a Morgan partner), and A. Piatt Andrew, a Harvard professor, met in secrecy on Jekyll Island, Georgia, where they outlined the scope, functions, management, and organization of the new system. But the plan floated listlessly in Congress before it finally met defeat, largely because it promised increased centralization of power in government hands.

During and after the Aldrich committee's efforts to reform the system, new concerns arose over the power of the large New York banks. In 1912, Louisiana congressman Arsène P. Pujo, through the House Committee on Banking and Currency, conducted an investigation into the "Money Trust." The committee called witnesses, including Morgan (who made a memorable appearance), and requested information from more than 30,000 banks. The committee's report, issued in February 1913, contributed to the passage of the Federal Reserve Act. It revealed great concentration of financial assets among the nation's largest banks, and showed, through their directorships, holding companies, and stock ownership, that their control over the wealth of the country was deeper than most Americans thought. For example, George F. Baker, the chairman of First National Bank of New York, held 58 directorships in 1912, in companies worth billions of dollars, and Morgan's power dwarfed even Baker's.

A few months after the Pujo Committee issued its report, Rep. Carter Glass of Virginia, chairman of the House Committee on Banking and Currency, introduced a bill to create the Federal Reserve System. Both houses of Congress quickly passed the bill, and President Woodrow Wilson signed it before the end of the year. Those wishing to deflate the power of the New York banks thought they had won a major victory, because the new system had 12 reserve banks scattered throughout the country (Missouri had two), and cities such as Minneapolis and Atlanta had reserve banks. Each Federal Reserve bank was a corporation, which the member banks in its district "owned" through each bank's required investment of 6 percent of its paid-up capital and surplus. The member banks chose most of their directors, but although those directors chose the officers, the member banks themselves did not directly vote for anyone on the governing committee, the Board of Governors. Instead, the president of the United States appointed five members of the board, and both the comptroller of the currency and the secretary of the treasury served as ex officio members.

The Federal Reserve System sought to contain runs through the rapid transfer or availability of funds from the Reserve banks. It had no system of deposit insurance, although several states, patterning themselves on the basis of the Oklahoma Deposit Guaranty Law, either had already enacted or would soon pass similar laws. The new system also had another flaw. Its supporters intended it to act as an apolitical body, but with the comptroller and the treasurer, as well as five appointees of the president, on the board, that hope faded. On the other hand, by placing the board's headquarters in the Treasury building and by creating 12 district banks, supporters thought they had diluted the power of the New York banking community, an equally erroneous assumption. As Eugene White has shown, the New York Federal Reserve bank quickly took the lead and dominated the policies, if not the affairs, of the system. Not only had the hope to have an apolitical system been thwarted, but the notion that the Federal Reserve would reduce the dominance of New York by giving all banks access to loans previously available (or so critics assumed) to the "Money Trust" also went astray. Rather than witnessing a mass movement to obtain national bank charters to gain access to the system's loans, banks retained their state charters and became correspondents with national banks. Thus, in some ways, the Federal Reserve reinforced the Money Trust.

Reserve banks "regulated" the money supply, to the extent that was possible, through their discounting to member banks (that is, the short-term borrowing of Reserve funds). To expand bank credit the Reserve banks lowered the discount rate; to contract credit, they increased it. In theory, reserve banks discounted according to the "real bills" doctrine; in practice, lending officers at the Reserve banks determined the "eligibility" of bills offered for discount, thus effectively separating money from any rigid standard. That marked the system's solution to the third dilemma posed to the reformers, the problem of elasticity. As Richard H. Timberlake explains, the authors of the Federal Reserve Act so thoroughly expected the gold standard

to continue to operate that they built into the act few links between the Reserve system and gold. Consequently, discretionary discounting, increasingly based on government intervention, soon, as Timberlake puts it, "divorced the results of decision-making from those who had a self-interest in maintaining the integrity of the system." Certainly the act had sought to insulate the Federal Reserve through several layers of checks and compromises. But in many ways, the advantages that Hamilton so deftly crafted for the Treasury had escaped the framers of the Federal Reserve Act.

To analyze the subsequent developments of the banking and monetary system is beyond the scope of this volume, however, and another volume, covering the period from 1913 to the present, will soon appear. Consequently, the subjects in this work have been limited to those making their *primary* impact in the pre-1913 period. Banks or individuals alive during the years covered here but whose main banking activities came later (such as A. P. Giannini) will appear in the subsequent book. Nevertheless, by 1913 the fundamental elements of the banking system in American had jelled. The Great Depression brought considerable trauma and fundamental reforms, but even then banking reflected the concepts of the nineteenth century. Not until the deregulation of the 1980s did critics challenge assumptions that had, up to that point, guided the development of the nation's banking and financial system.

Banks in the United States 1834-1910

Year	National Banks	Non-National Banks	Total
1834	----	506	506
1840	----	901	901
1850	----	824	824
1860	----	1,562	1,562
1870	1,612	325	1,937
1880	2,076	1,279	3,355
1890	3,484	4,717	8,201
1900	3,731	9,322	13,053
1910	7,138	18,013	25,151

Sources: U.S. Bureau of the Census, *Historical Statistics of the United States: Colonial Times to 1970*, 2 volumes (White Plains, New York: Kraus International Publications, 1989), II: 1019-1021, 1024-1035; Larry Schweikart, "Southern Banks and Economic Growth in the Antebellum Period: A Reassessment," *Journal of Southern History*, 53 (February 1987): 26-27.

Encyclopedia of American Business History and Biography

Banking and Finance to 1913

Albany Regency

by David T. Beito

University of Nevada at Las Vegas

In the first 50 years of American independence, political parties–in the sense of formalized, permanent organizations–barely existed. The Albany Regency of New York, a highly organized system of alliances designed to perpetuate political power as much as to promote a political program, represented a watershed in that it helped make the two-party system an accepted, and even praised, feature of politics. The Regency also helped demonstrate some of the strengths and weaknesses of the Jacksonian alliance of government and business through Martin Van Buren's attempt to regulate New York banks by means of a Safety Fund.

The Regency grew out of the rough and tumble of New York state politics. By the second decade of the eighteenth century the Jeffersonian Republicans enjoyed almost unchallenged domination of the local and state political scene. The once-powerful Federalists had fallen to rump status and no longer posed a serious threat. Left without significant opposition, the Republicans slowly fell prey to factionalism. By 1817 party divisions had coalesced into two groups (both claiming the title Republican), the Clintonians and the Bucktails. The Clintonians were followers of former presidential candidate DeWitt Clinton, who became governor in 1817. The Bucktails, so named for the bucktail each wore on his hat at party meetings, gradually fell under the sway of Albany senator Martin Van Buren. While the division owed much to personalities and geography, it also reflected shifting ideological concerns. The Clintonians favored interventionist government policies, including state funding of internal improvements such as the Erie Canal. They also had a rather loose view of party discipline, based on Clinton's "patrician" style of leadership. The Bucktails, on the other hand, initially favored a more negative and limited conception of government. They accused the Clintonians of aban-

Martin Van Buren, leader of the Albany Regency and president of the United States from 1837 to 1841 (portrait by Eliphalet Fraser Andrews; courtesy of the U.S. Department of State)

doning the small-government ideals of Jefferson in favor of Hamiltonian policies.

Between 1817 and 1821 the Bucktails embarked on an all-out campaign to wrest control of the legislature and governorship from Clinton's faction. They set up a statewide governing council, in effect a political machine, including such Van Buren allies as William L. Marcy, Roger Skinner, Silas Wright, Jr., Edwin Crosell, and Benjamin F. Butler. In the election of 1821 Van Buren was elected U.S. senator. In 1822 Van Buren and his allies, having won control of the legislature and the governor's office from the Clintonians, began to turn their attention to national politics. Van Buren had become disillusioned with the policies of the Monroe administration. He accused Monroe of forsaking Republican ideals to promote "fusion" with the remnants of the Federalist party.

The political success of the Van Buren faction in New York was fostered in large part by the adoption of efficient organizational techniques. The newspaper the *Albany Argus* became an important promotional vehicle for the party program. The Van Burenites also set up subordinate organizations in each county of the state and made skillful use of committees of correspondence to coordinate campaigns. They put a high premium on party loyalty, allowing, even encouraging, dissent in party councils but expecting all members to fall into line when a final decision had been made. But they were not immune to unfavorable political fallout. The legislature's expulsion of Clinton as president of the commission overseeing the construction of the Erie Canal was widely criticized. Opposition journalists dubbed the Van Buren faction the "Albany Regency" in attacks that brought Clinton back to the governorship in 1824.

The Clinton debacle reflected the increasing self-consciousness of Regency leaders on the national level as well. As the 1824 presidential election approached Van Buren and other Regency leaders launched a national campaign "to commence the work of a *general resuscitation* of the *old democratic party.*" The Regency rallied behind presidential candidate William H. Crawford and helped to engineer his nomination by the Republican caucus in the U.S. Senate, the traditional method of choosing the party candidate. The caucus system broke down when Crawford's opponents rejected the process. This made all but official a split in the national party. Soon after the election of John Quincy Adams, Van Buren began to build a separate national (now called Democratic) party organization to oppose the new administration's policies, especially its promotion of internal improvements. The presidential campaign of Andrew Jackson, who had been defeated along with Crawford in 1824, served as the vehicle for this movement. Through an extensive network of committees of correspondence and pro-Jackson journals, Van Buren and his allies linked their efforts with strong party organizations in Virginia, Tennessee, Kentucky, and other

states. On election day 1828 the Regency was instrumental not only in carrying New York for Jackson (thus winning him the presidency) but electing Van Buren governor of New York. The 1828 campaign witnessed the pinnacle of party organization in New York and included such innovations as partisan songs, buttons, and parades.

In his short tenure as governor Van Buren worked to curtail internal improvements and lower licensing requirements for state auctioneers. His most controversial proposal, however, the bank Safety Fund, proved to be at odds with the Regency's stated dedication to limited government. The Safety Fund required banks in the state to pay into a general fund that would be used to redeem the notes of those banks threatened with failure. Essentially, it constituted one of the first efforts to guarantee deposits, although depositors specifically had no more claim than any other note holders. The law establishing the Fund imposed unprecedented inspection requirements on the banks, leaving the Regency open to accusations from its opponents, mostly in the newly formed Whig party, of creating "licensed monopolies." In retrospect, other more limited regulatory systems of the day provided greater safety than the Fund. Although Van Buren resigned as governor in 1829 to become Jackson's secretary of state, he continued to direct New York party affairs from Washington, cooperating closely with Jackson's attorney general, Butler.

In 1832 Jackson chose Van Buren as his vice-presidential candidate. In large part the nomination was a reward for the Regency's support for Jackson's program of state's rights, including his veto of the Maysville Road Bill in 1830. When Jackson vetoed recharter of the Bank of the United States in 1832, the Regency embraced the war against the "monster bank" with full vigor. It made effective use of slogans such as "The Democracy, Against the Aristocracy and the Bank."

By the late 1830s the Regency had come under increasing electoral pressure. Although Democratic presidential nominee Van Buren carried New York in 1836 and won the election, the Whig party, employing campaign tactics pioneered by the Regency and the national Democrats, captured both houses of the New York legislature. The state party suffered further damage from internal factionalism. In 1835 Democratic dissidents, dubbed "locofocos" by their opponents at Tammany Hall, formed the Equal Rights party. Locofoco leaders such as journalist William Leggett considered Van Buren and the Regency insufficiently dedicated to the ideals of laissez-faire.

The Locofocos rejoined the party in 1837 out of enthusiasm for Van Buren's plan to divorce banking from the federal government through an independent treasury. That may have healed one party split, but it helped to create another when Democratic governor Marcy criticized Van Buren for his support of the Locofoco program. Even the Regency's mouthpiece, the *Albany Argus*, questioned Van Buren's financial policies. The 1838 election proved to be a disaster for Regency Democrats. The Whigs defeated Marcy and elected William H. Seward as governor. In the 1840 presidential election Van Buren proved unable to carry his home state. After his defeat for reelection he continued to play an important role in New York politics. Nevertheless, his opponents in the New York party, led by Marcy, remained in control of the state organization. By the early 1840s the Albany Regency had effectively ceased to exist.

References:

Lee Benson, *The Concept of Jacksonian Democracy: New York as a Test Case* (Princeton: Princeton University Press, 1961);

James C. Curtis, *The Fox at Bay: Martin Van Buren and the Presidency, 1837-1841* (Lexington: University Press of Kentucky, 1970);

Frank Otto Gattell, "Sober Second Thoughts on Van Buren, the Albany Regency, and the Wall Street Conspiracy," *Journal of American History*, 53 (June 1966): 19-40;

John Niven, *Martin Van Buren: The Romantic Age of American Politics* (New York: Oxford University Press, 1983);

Robert V. Remini, *Martin Van Buren and the Making of the Democratic Party* (New York: Columbia University Press, 1959);

Ivor Debenham Spencer, *The Victor and the Spoils: A Life of William L. Marcy* (Providence, R.I.: Brown University Press, 1959);

Major L. Wilson, *The Presidency of Martin Van Buren* (Lawrence: University Press of Kansas, 1984).

Nelson W. Aldrich

(November 6, 1841-April 16, 1915)

by Benjamin J. Klebaner

City College, CUNY

CAREER: Junior partner, Waldron & Wightman (1865- ?); councilman (1869-1871), president, Providence Common Council (1871-1873); state representative, Rhode Island (1874-1878); U. S. representative, state of Rhode Island (1878-1881), U.S. senator, state of Rhode Island (1881-1911); president, United Traction & Electric Company (1892-1902); chairman, National Monetary Commission (1908-1912).

Nelson Wilmarth Aldrich, key Republican senator for three decades, influenced tariff, railroad, and currency legislation in a direction favorable to business interests. Some called him the "general manager of the United States."

Born on November 6, 1841, on a farm in Foster, Rhode Island, Aldrich was the oldest of three children of Anan E. and Abby Ann Burgess Aldrich. He was a descendant of George and Katherine Aldrich, who migrated from Derbyshire, England, to Dorchester, Massachusetts, in 1631, and (on his mother's side) of Roger Williams. He received a common-school education in East Killingly, Connecticut, and attended the East Greenwich (Rhode Island) academy for a year, as the family had limited means. At seventeen he was a grocer's boy, then a helper in a fish market. In the spring of 1862 he left a job with Waldron & Wightman, a leading Providence wholesale grocery firm, to enlist in the 10th Rhode Island Volunteers. After serving several months in the defense of the nation's capital, an attack of typhoid fever led to his discharge in September. He returned to Waldron & Wightman and in 1865 was made a junior partner, at the age of twenty-four.

Elected to the Providence Common Council in 1869, he served as president from 1871 to 1873. For the next five years he served in the Rhode Island House of Representatives. In 1878 he won election to the U.S. House of Representatives and

Nelson W. Aldrich

reelected in 1880. In October 1881 he was chosen to fill the Senate seat vacated by the death of Gen. Ambrose E. Burnside. Aldrich won reelection from the Rhode Island legislature in 1886, 1892, 1898, and 1904. Assigned to the Finance Committee, he served as chairman from 1899 to 1911. For many years he chaired the Committee on Rules. Theodore Roosevelt referred to Aldrich as "the leader of the Senate"; others called him "boss of the Senate."

Aldrich had contemplated retiring from the Senate when his term ended in 1892, as he was anxious to increase his wealth. Friends worked out an arrangement that enabled him to prosper while continuing in office. United Traction & Electric Company (UTE) was formed to modernize Rhode Island's street railways. John E. Searles, secretary and treasurer of the Sugar Trust, led a group of businessmen who agreed to finance up to $7 million to acquire for UTE four Providence-area horse-drawn traction companies. With Aldrich as president until 1902, UTE expanded and electrified the lines. The properties were sold to United Gas Improvement Company, a Philadelphia holding company, in 1902. In 1906 Aldrich helped negotiate a sale of the traction companies to the New Haven Railroad, then intent on acquiring a monopoly on transportation in New England. In addition to his highly profitable traction investments, Aldrich also invested in sugar, rubber, tobacco, banking, and utilities. His estate was appraised at $7 million, all of which he bequeathed to his widow, Abby P. Chapman (whom he married in 1866), and children.

In managing tariff bills throughout his Senate career Aldrich aimed to take care of the interests of all sections and states with "a policy of nationalism." Legislation, as he put it in 1890, should "fairly represent the average judgment of the majority of Congress upon the interests of the whole people as well as upon the claims of sections and interests." He declared on the Senate floor in 1892 that the purpose of the protective duties was "to maintain the existing high level of . . . earnings of American workmen." For those goods where the United States had "equal natural advantages" with other nations, duties should equal the difference between the normal cost of making the product in the United States and in the foreign country where the cost was lowest. Aldrich would admit free "articles in the production of which their countries have permanent natural advantages." Proclaiming "the industrial ascendancy of the United States" in 1900, he described protective policy as "expansion through a better diversification of national industries and a more thorough organization and development of national forces."

In tariff debates Aldrich demonstrated impressive knowledge of industry details and generally supported high rates. He first made his mark with respect to wool, cotton, and sugar provisions in the 1883 tariff bill, which increased rates in those areas. By 1888 he had more influence than such senior senators as John Sherman and William B. Allison. The McKinley Act of 1890, which raised

rates on a variety of imports still higher, was largely his handiwork. He voted against the Wilson-Gorman tariff reduction bill of 1894. Significantly, the 1894 bill abandoned the "reciprocity" provisions of the 1890 bill, which had given the president the capacity to respond flexibly to tariff rate changes in other countries. In 1897, however, when Congress considered the Dingley bill, Aldrich opposed certain extreme rates voted by the House, helping to amend the House version until it satisfied the Senate. The final version of the Dingley bill revised many Wilson-Gorman rates upward and reestablished reciprocity.

Public antagonism to extreme protection led the Republican party to include tariff revision in its 1908 platform. President William H. Taft, who won election with a promise to lower rates, praised the Payne-Aldrich Act of 1909, claiming that of 874 changes made in the Dingley bill, 654 represented decreases. Sen. Robert La Follette of Wisconsin, however, denounced the bill as "the most outrageous assault of private interests upon the people recorded in tariff history." Nevertheless, the 1909 act did reduce the average ad valorem duty to about 42 percent, from Dingley's 52 percent.

Regarding railroad regulation, Aldrich expressed displeasure with parts of the Interstate Commerce Commission Act of 1887. The act set up a commission to ensure fair rate practices by railroad companies. He feared that the long- and short-haul clause, which was intended to end the railroad practice of favoring the long hauler, might harm his region: the new commission might exercise its power either "to build up or destroy communities." When President Roosevelt proposed what became the Hepburn Act of 1906 (which increased the commission's jurisdiction and its powers of enforcement and allowed it to set maximum rates), Aldrich fought successfully for broad judicial review of commission decisions.

Aldrich also made important contributions to the nation's financial history. The Gold Standard Act of March 1900 was passed during Aldrich's first session as chairman of the Senate Finance Committee. The act placed the United States on a monometallic gold standard, defining a dollar as 25.8 grains of gold, nine-tenths fine. Aldrich explained that "we intend under all circumstances to keep all forms of our currency equal in value with gold." He did not consider this "reaffirmation of the gold standard" to be inconsistent with the Republican

Drawing by Robert Carter of Aldrich during his tenure as chairman of the National Monetary Commission (New York World, *June 13, 1909)*

commitment to international bimetallism in the 1896 platform. Already, on January 13, 1891, he had proclaimed his strong advocacy of "the restoration of silver," conditioned on international agreement. The last proved impossible to attain.

The bank panic of 1907 forced banks to suspend convertability of deposits and to resort to makeshift substitutes for cash for a time. The panic brought home to Aldrich the urgency of providing emergency currency in periods of panic. Aldrich called not only for a currency based on bank assets (including both federal bonds and commercial paper) but also for utilization of the bonds of railroads and state and local governments as collateral in times of necessity. The Aldrich-Vreeland Act of 1908 authorized the secretary of the treasury to approve the use of "any securities, including commercial paper, held by a banking association" as collateral for notes issued by "national currency associations" composed of groups of national banks. The outbreak of World War I in 1914 led to a brief

panic. This time the banking system could satisfy the scramble for cash. Issues of emergency currency under the act reached $380 million by the end of November.

The Aldrich-Vreeland Act also established a National Monetary Commission to seek means of mitigating the severity of future financial crises. Aldrich's original purpose in supporting the commission provision was to sidetrack further currency reform, but he changed his mind as the investigation moved forward. The commission, chaired by Aldrich, was composed of nine senators, nine representatives, and several business-community and academic advisers, was empowered to summon witnesses and examine papers to obtain helpful information. Many commissioners also went abroad to study European banking practices. Soon after returning from the European investigations in 1908, Aldrich wrote to Paul M. Warburg, a Wall Street investment banker who led the movement for reform: "I am going to have a central bank in this country." Aldrich declined nomination for reelection to the Senate in 1910 so that he could devote his entire time to the work of the commission. He aspired to cap his long career in public life with nonpolitical legislation vital to the material well-being of all Americans, to "make the United States the financial center of the world."

The commission finally issued its report to Congress on January 8, 1912. It recommended that a National Reserve Association, capitalized at some $300 million from voluntary state and national bank stock subscriptions, be organized with 15 districts. The association would have the power to set a uniform discount rate on loans made to member banks. Aldrich described the proposed association as "a cooperative union of all the banks . . . with very limited and clearly defined functions . . . an evolution of the clearinghouse plan modified to meet the needs of an entire people."

President Taft, who claimed the commission's work was vitally important in his annual message to Congress in 1911, failed to push the plan vigorously in the face of the election battle in 1912. Supporters of Theodore Roosevelt's Bull Moose campaign opposed placing U.S. currency and credit "in private hands, not subject to effective public control." The Democrats, led by Woodrow Wilson, opposed Aldrich in their rhetoric but planned to use aspects of the commission plan in financial legislation of their own. There was also opposition to some of the details of the proposal, particularly to the idea of a centralized organization, which aroused fear of Wall Street dominance of the Reserve Association.

The 1913 Federal Reserve Act did not carry Aldrich's name, but many considered Aldrich "the real author of the reform which has given us the Federal Reserve," as his obituary in the *New York Times* stated. A. Barton Hepburn, a leading student of American currency history as well as a banker, thought the act was the Aldrich bill "in all essential features." Warburg (who had worked closely with Aldrich) thought the senator had rendered "invaluable service . . . by boldly cutting loose" from antiquated principles, so that the legislation that did pass necessarily embodied many "principles and essential features" of the Aldrich bill.

H. Parker Willis, the banking expert relied on by Carter Glass in drafting the Federal Reserve bill, grudgingly acknowledged that in matters of machinery and techniques the act resembled the Aldrich plan closely but insisted that in theory and purpose the two differed widely. The chief difference, however, was the abandonment of the Aldrich idea of a central noncommercial institution for a group of nominally independent reserve banks.

Aldrich retired after his tenure on the National Monetary Commission. After retirement he enjoyed sailing his yacht *Omera* and fishing, and he expanded his collections of art and books. He died on April 16, 1915, and was buried in Providence.

Publications:

Suggested Plan for Monetary Legislation (Washington, D.C.: Government Printing Office, 1911; revised, 1911);

"Banking Reform in the United States," *Proceedings of the Academy of Political Science*, 4 (1913): 31-91.

Reference:

Nathaniel W. Stephenson, *Nelson W. Aldrich: A Leader in American Politics* (New York: Scribners, 1930).

Archives:

The papers of Nelson W. Aldrich are in the Manuscript Division of the Library of Congress.

American Bankers Association

by Benjamin J. Klebaner

City College, CUNY

A convention held in Saratoga Springs, New York, from July 20 to 22, 1875, "to bring bank officers and bankers into closer relations, with a view to the advancement and protection of mutual interests" attracted 332 bankers from 32 states and territories. James T. Howenstein, cashier of the Valley National Bank, a St. Louis correspondent of country banks, initiated the drive for an association. Never before had so many bankers assembled. Their interests were "of a social as well as of a business nature," Howenstein reminisced at the 1895 convention. A national organization would help in the battle to eliminate Civil War taxes on banks and burdensome state usury laws. The following year the American Bankers Association (ABA) took permanent form at a convention held on the grounds of the Philadelphia Centennial Exhibition from October 3 to 5. The ABA is one of the oldest surviving trade associations.

The 1876 constitution set forth its purposes: "to promote the general welfare and usefulness of banks and banking institutions, and to secure uniformity of action, together with the practical benefits to be derived from personal acquaintance and from the discussion of subjects of importance to the banking and commercial interests of the country, and especially in order to secure the proper consideration of questions regarding the financial and commercial usages, customs and laws which affect the banking interests of the entire country." In 1881 a new concluding clause was added: "and for protection against loss by crime."

In addition to national and state banks, savings banks and trust companies were eligible to join. Membership numbered around 1,600 in the first decade, and 1,713 in 1883; it more than doubled by 1899 and doubled again from 1899 to 1905. More than 14,300 banks were on the rolls of the ABA in 1913. Headquarters resided in rented quarters in the Wall Street area until May 1923.

Lyman J. Gage, president of the American Bankers Association from 1883 to 1886 and U.S. secretary of the treasury from 1897 to 1901.

Within a decade of the formation of the ABA, bankers began to organize statewide associations, beginning with Texas in 1885. Thirty years later Rhode Island completed the roster of the 48 states and the District of Columbia. There were 34 state associations by November 1902, when the Organization of Secretaries of State Bankers' Associations was formed to further cooperation of the state associations with the ABA. In 1910 this became the State Association Section.

In 1882 the ABA endorsed uniformity of state laws governing business to facilitate interstate commerce. In 1897 the Committee on Uniform Laws appointed the previous year sought uniformity in negotiable instruments, appearing before various legislatures for the purpose. The Law Committee subsequently expanded its recommendations; by 1913 it advocated approved drafts of state legislation for uniform warehouse receipts and uniform bills of lading. In addition, the association sought state action on false statements to obtain credit, derogatory statements affecting banks, checks or drafts without funds, burglary with explosives, liability for forged or raised checks, payment of deposits in two names, payment of deposits in trust, and competency of bank notaries.

To deal with bank crime, in 1894 a Standing Protective Committee was appointed that retained Pinkerton's National Detective Agency in December. Over the next decade nonmembers suffered more than six times the number of burglaries and ten times the amount of losses that ABA members incurred. The association's success in apprehending and prosecuting criminals encouraged many banks to join.

The association set up a Protective Department at its headquarters in August 1909. In 1913 its rogues' gallery had 3,000 photographs on file. The manager kept in close touch with state associations on protection matters. Dissatisfaction with Pinkerton's led to the naming of William J. Burns International Detective Agency as the official ABA protective agency in 1910. Burns conducted investigations on behalf of the ABA.

To accommodate the divergent and specialized interests of the growing membership, the ABA formed special sections (called divisions since 1920). Five sections were organized before 1914, encompassing trust companies (1896), savings banks (1902), clearinghouses (1906), the American Institute of Banking (1908), and state bankers association secretaries (1910). The trust company section boasted 1,363 members in 1913.

A "Conference of Clearing Houses" was organized at the 1899 ABA convention. It declared the practice of charging exchange fees for out-of-town check collection to be proper and advocated that clearinghouses set the clearing fee in each locality. In 1906 the conference became the Clearinghouse Section; it promoted formation of new clearinghouses and expansion of their functions. By fall

1911–five years after the Chicago clearinghouse introduced the practice–36 clearinghouses examined members on a regular basis. In 1911 the section devised a universal numerical system for check routing: each U.S. bank was assigned a designated transit number. By 1913 more than half of all checks carried that number, which saved time and labor in the check-sorting process.

The ABA began what developed into an extensive program of employee education with the sponsorship of the Institute of Bank Clerks at the 1900 convention. Lyman J. Gage, ABA president from 1883 to 1886, initiated the drive that resulted in sponsorship of the institute in a speech given at the 1884 convention. The institute was made a section of the ABA in 1908 and renamed the American Institute of Banking (AIB). Graduates of its program received a certificate after passing final examinations. The AIB had 64 chapters with 13,587 members in 1913, including 713 who belonged to the Correspondence Chapter, but the great majority were in various city chapters.

In July 1908 the ABA began to publish a monthly *Journal of the American Bankers Association*. At first it emphasized ABA activities, serving as "the mouthpiece of the officers and the committees of the Association." It also carried articles on the principles and practice of banking and finance.

The ABA has always been concerned with a variety of policy issues affecting banking. The first convention had the issue of bank taxes on the agenda. Year after year conventions called for reduction or abolition of Civil War levies on bank capital, deposits, and national bank notes, which bankers considered harmful to business and banking. The 2-cent stamp tax on checks was singled out as a nuisance. In March 1883 Congress repealed all but the tax on national bank notes.

From the beginning the ABA endorsed resumption of specie payments. Banks cooperated with the Treasury when resumption took effect on January 1, 1879. Bankers viewed silver as a threat to prosperity, and steadfastly rejected bimetallism. The ABA opposed the 1878 Bland-Allison Act and the 1890 Sherman Silver Purchase Act, repealed in 1893. Bankers identified sound money with gold and the Gold Standard Act of 1900 offered cause for rejoicing.

With the Panic of 1873 still fresh in the minds of the audience, the first convention (and many later ones) discussed causes and means of preventing money panics. In 1894 the "Baltimore Plan" for an elastic currency secured by bank assets gained favor. A distinguished currency commission, formed in 1906, led the discussion in the ABA. The commission welcomed the Aldrich-Vreeland Act of 1908, which provided for emergency currency issues by banks as "legislative sanction" for the asset-currency idea. The 1911 convention endorsed the Aldrich National Monetary Commission plan "for the establishment of a cooperative agency of all the banks to be known as the National Reserve Association of the United States" (in the words of the ABA resolution). That association would hold reserves of all the banks, rediscount their commercial paper, and expand note issues based on gold and commercial paper.

Several features of the Federal Reserve Act passed by Congress in 1913 aroused strong ABA opposition. Bankers feared that lack of banker representation on the Federal Reserve Board might lead to control of finance by politicians and incompetent management of the Federal Reserve banks. Compulsory national bank membership was held to be a socialist taking of bank capital. Acting president Arthur M. Reynolds described the proposed bill in his address to the 1913 convention as "an invasion of the liberty of the citizen in the control of his own property by putting under government management enormous individual investments and a branch of the country's business which should be left to individual effort."

Government in banking proved a source of concern expressed since 1908 in ABA resolutions opposing the acceptance of small-deposit accounts by federal post offices and state laws providing for guaranty of deposits. After the postal savings system was enacted in 1910, the ABA worked to confine its activities. Eight states sponsored deposit guaranty schemes from 1908 to 1917; all succumbed by March 1930.

In its first 39 years the ABA had 28 presidents, as the practice of one-year terms began only in 1892. Seven came from New York City banks, and three each from Chicago and St. Louis. Perhaps the best-known presidents were George S. Coe (1881-1883), Lyman J. Gage (1883-1886), Myron T. Herrick (1901), and George N. Reynolds (1908). By 1913 the ABA had a staff of 29 at a headquarters that, together with the elected officers, was "working continuously for the best interests of its membership," as proclaimed in the official history printed with the 1913 convention proceedings.

References:
American Bankers Association, *Proceedings of the . . . Annual Convention* (New York: American Bankers Association, 1875-1913);

Richard Hill, *Fifty Years of Banker Education* (New York: American Institute of Banking, 1950);

Wilbert M. Schneider, *The American Bankers Association: Its Past and Present* (Washington, D.C.: Public Affairs Press, 1956).

John Jacob Astor

(July 17, 1763-March 29, 1848)

by Michael F. Konig

Westfield State College

CAREER: Fur trader, shipowner, and general merchant (1786-1808); owner and president, Pacific Fur Company (1808-1813); owner and president, Southwest Fur Company (1808-1817); owner and president, American Fur Company (1808-1834); director, Globe Insurance Company (1814-1834); director, Bank of the United States (1816-1819); president, New York branch, Bank of the United States (1816-1819); co-owner and president, John Jacob Astor and Son (1816-1834); director, Mohawk & Hudson Railroad (1828-1831).

John Jacob Astor, one of the preeminent businessmen of his day, was a financier, fur trader, and land speculator. Born in the German village of Waldorf in the Duchy of Baden in 1763, the fifth child of Jacob Astor, a butcher, and Maria Magdelena Vorfelder, Astor never enjoyed affluence as a child but received a better-than-average education. He worked as his father's assistant in butchering, delivering meat, and tending shop but exhibited little enthusiasm for this occupation. Upon the death of his mother, Astor decided to shift for himself and left his German village home for London. Local accounts state that upon his departure in 1779 he pledged "to be honest, to be industrious, and never to gamble." In London, Astor found work with his brother George, who had previously migrated to the city.

By 1783 Astor determined to leave London and embark for America. He departed in November aboard the *North Carolina*, and according to various sources he established the foundation for his later fabulous personal fortune during the voyage. Officers of the Hudson's Bay Company, a prominent British fur trading enterprise, were among the vessel's cabin passengers. These men fascinated the young Astor with stories of their trade enterprises and relations with the American Indians. The *North Carolina* entered Chesapeake Bay early in Jan-

John Jacob Astor circa 1824, in a portrait said to have been made in Switzerland

uary 1784 and became icebound for more than two months. The additional time allowed Astor to question the Hudson's Bay Company officers as to almost every detail pertaining to the fur trade. By the time the vessel broke free of its ice entrapment he had settled upon fur trading as his future occupation.

Journeying north from Baltimore, Astor arrived in New York City in April 1784. There he found his brother Henry Astor and Henry's wife, Dorothea Pessenger. Accounts of Astor's early life in New York are somewhat sketchy and even conflicting. It appears that he may have worked for a period as an apprentice to a local baker, George Dietrich. Astor later secured employment at various times with several furriers, including a Quaker merchant named Robert Bowne. While working for Bowne, Astor purchased and sold furs on a small scale and made his first voyage to England with that commodity. He also made various trips to the outlying parts of New York State as a fur peddler. By 1786 he established his own place of business on Water Street in New York. There he augmented his fledgling fur trading business by selling musical instruments.

During these early years of his business activity, Astor married Sarah Todd. Connected to the Brevorts, a well-respected and socially elite New York family, Todd brought Astor a dowry of $300 in cash and a business associate who possessed "great piety and . . . considerable business ability."

Astor and his wife continued to work hard, plan new enterprises, and consistently demonstrate a talent for simply "giving the least and getting the most" in their business transactions. Often Astor made trips related to his fur trading into the nearby frontier and even as far as Montreal. To facilitate this business Astor set up a web of agents through the upper Hudson Valley. He also formed a business connection with Peter Smith, a former clerk and import merchant from New York. Contemporaries described Smith as being "fully as precocious in his financial ability" as Astor. Their relationship lasted until Smith's death in 1837.

By 1790 Astor had also established a connection with the London firm of Thomas Backhouse and Company. That relationship brought him into contact with a relative of the London Backhouse, William Backhouse, a prominent New York merchant. With the support of Backhouse, Astor's fur trading business continued to grow, but at only a moderate pace because the British had retained military posts in the northwestern United States. As a result, furs that Astor purchased in Canada could not be shipped directly to the United States but had to go first to London. That situation changed in 1794, when John Jay negotiated his famous and unpopular treaty with the British, a major provision of which required the British to abandon their western military posts. After the completion of this evacuation in 1796, furs could be shipped directly from the Old Northwest and Canada to New York. Abandoned British forts served as storage facilities for the furs. This and the fact that Astor arranged with the Northwest Company, a Canadian fur trading concern, to add to his stock by direct importation

from Montreal, contributed to the rapid expansion of his business. By 1800 he had amassed a personal fortune of $250,000 and was acknowledged as the leading trader in the fur business.

According to Kenneth W. Porter, Astor's entrance into the China trade grew naturally out of his success as a fur trader and general merchant. On one of his visits to London an official at the East India House provided Astor with a license to trade freely in any foreign market monopolized by the East India Company. After the Revolution, American ships required permits from the East India Company to trade in China. Whatever the case, Astor initiated his China trade enterprises with the vessel *Severn*. This ship had been built in New York City in 1792 and had arrived back in that city in 1801 after an extended commercial tour of Canton. Astor, together with business associates John Titus and William Laight, retained this vessel to return with a diverse cargo that included silk and satin goods, souchong teas, India lutestrings and taffetas, colored sinchews, Canton and Waukin furs, spices, sugar, and chinaware. Astor tied his dealings with China to Europe by shipping more than 18,000 pounds of souchong tea to the prominent British tea merchants Strobel, Martin and Bordeaux. He also shipped another 4,500 pounds of souchong to a merchant, Joseph Pitcairn, in Hamburg, Germany. These trading enterprises involved the transporting of beaver and otter skins and gold bullion to the Orient in exchange for silks, spices, and teas.

By 1803 Astor had become the sole owner of the *Severn* and had made the China trade one of his chief interests. His shipments of furs to the Orient became more frequent and the profits exceedingly handsome. A typical cargo bound for Canton might be valued as high as $166,000 and would be comprised of choice furs from Montreal, numerous kegs of ginseng, bales of cotton, and a considerable sum of specie. These goods would be exchanged for a sizable cargo of "Hyson, Young Hyson, Hyson-skin, Souchong, Congo, and Singlo Teas of superior quality," plus usually some Chinese porcelain for ballast in the ships to offset the buoyant tea.

Astor sold the *Severn* in 1805 but continued his China trade with the "flat bottomed" ship, the *Beaver*. Much larger than the *Severn*, the *Beaver*'s capacity for 1,100 tons of cargo increased Astor's profits. A single voyage often yielded the entrepreneur more than a $50,000 profit. By 1806 Astor had increased his China trade operations with the pur-

Portrait of Astor by Gilbert Stuart

chase of an additional vessel, the *Magdelena*. An examination of the shipping log of the *Magdelena*'s first voyage that same year reveals the variety of furs sent by Astor to Canton. These included otter, fox, and beaver skins as well as substantial amounts of ginseng and blackwood. The vessel returned to New York in 1807 with a full cargo of "teas, nankeens, silks and china wares." Yet all had not proceeded smoothly in the China trade. British squadrons repeatedly harassed Astor's two vessels. This problem foreshadowed difficulties and danger ahead. Astor became so concerned by these problems that he determined to lessen his responsibility and chance for loss by involving others with him in the ownership of the *Beaver* and the *Magdelena*. He continued his orient trade, although in a reduced manner, when in 1807 he sent the *Magdelena* to Calcutta. The ship returned as quickly as possible with a cargo of cotton, indigo, and sugar.

By the time of the *Magdelena*'s return the international situation had deteriorated even further. In order to protect American interests on the high seas, President Jefferson had instituted an embargo on all foreign shipping. Faced with these difficult prospects, Astor demonstrated tremendous inventiveness and ingenuity in his business dealings. He sold his remaining interest in the *Magdelena* and searched for loopholes in the Embargo Act. In effect Astor succeeded in causing the president to suspend the embargo in his favor. Producing a Chinese businessman, Punqua Winchong, who wished to return to his homeland, Astor presented his case for a voyage to the Orient. Convincing such close presidential advisers as James Madison and Albert Gallatin that the return of Winchong would improve relations between China and the United States, Astor presented a strong case to Jefferson. The president saw this as an opportunity to raise his own standing in the international community and acceded to Astor's request. Astor used the opportunity to trade for a sizable cargo of teas, silks, and nankeens. But the whole scenario was a ruse. Winchong was neither a prominent merchant nor was he even from Hong Kong. Little embarrassment from this episode tainted either the president or Astor, however, since by the time of the *Beaver*'s return from the Orient the embargo had been relaxed, at least as far as the China trade was concerned.

Astor continued to increase his activities and profits associated with the China trade. At the same time, the Louisiana Purchase presented him with unlimited opportunities for the extension of his fur trading business. By 1807 he began to contest the hold of the Mackinac Company, another Canadian fur trading enterprise in the upper Mississippi Valley. Yet Astor ambitiously envisioned more. He confided to DeWitt Clinton, mayor of New York City and later governor of New York State, a prominent promoter of the Erie Canal project, that he intended to bring the whole of the United States fur trading territory under his personal control. Astor foresaw that New York would serve as the headquarters of this activity and that two arteries of transportation would link that city to the frontier—one overland, the other from New Orleans up the Mississippi River. Such a far-flung enterprise required a line of trading posts along the exploration route taken by Lewis and Clark. This route ran from St. Louis to the Pacific Ocean and would provide his operations with a distinct advantage over the Canadians. Communications and shipments of supplies would be more direct, and the furs could be sent easily from New York to far-reaching markets. The Canadians, on the other hand, found their markets restricted to only London or the United States.

In 1808 Astor incorporated, through a charter granted by the New York legislature, all of these widespread designs in his enterprise, the American Fur Company. Astor constituted this company's sole owner and received President Jefferson's enthusiastic support. Jefferson had determined that the fur trade of the West should be monopolized by American citizens.

Astor's plans materialized slowly. The hostility of traders already established in St. Louis made his entrance there difficult, even hazardous. Thus Astor planted a central establishment for his fur trading enterprise at the mouth of the Columbia River on the Pacific Coast. He planned to locate subordinate posts at various locations toward the interior. Through this enterprise, the famous but ill-fated Pacific Fur Company, Astor could gather furs where they were most abundant, the Pacific Northwest, and ship them from a location nearest their richest market, China. He founded the central post, Astoria, in 1811, but the enterprise, which he had begun with high hopes, never succeeded.

Astor had outfitted a vessel, the *Tonquin*, to assist with the building of the new post. The *Tonquin* had been designated to bring needed supplies and building materials. It first sailed to Canton, then to the Hawaiian Islands, and finally reached the mouth of the Columbia River in the spring of 1811. There the crew helped to lay the foundation for Astoria. While details of what ultimately befell the *Tonquin* are sketchy, it appears that after the vessel was anchored at Astoria, Indians boarded, massacred the crew, and destroyed the ship. Most of the blame for this tragedy has fallen to the *Tonquin* captain, Jonathan Thorn, who had on several occasions angered some of the Indian groups of the Pacific Northwest involved in the fur trade. Thorn considered the Indians contemptible and aroused them to such a degree that they suggested the trading of furs for knives on a basis highly favorable to the Astoria group. Astor had previously warned Thorn never to allow a large number of Indians aboard the *Tonquin* at one time. Thorn failed to follow this advice and conducted the exchange of furs for knives while on board. After making their deals the Indians turned upon the crew and "proceeded to hack the Astorians to shreds."

By 1812 the Northwest Company had sent two expeditions from Lake Superior to the Pacific Northwest to contest Astor's Pacific Fur Company operations. Hostile Indians blocked the first of these, and Astor fully anticipated that his men at Astoria could thwart the other. During the next several months, however, the situation changed dramatically. The *Tonquin*'s loss threatened the permanence of Astoria, and Astor determined to reinforce the post by sending it another ship, the *Forester*, loaded with guns, ammunition, and other equipment. This action refutes the claim of some biographers that after 1812 Astor cared little for the fate of Astoria. Following considerable delay, the *Forester*, sailing from England under British colors and convoy, set out for the Pacific Northwest. Yet because of the War of 1812 the vessel never reached Astoria, and Astor could not gain positive assurance that he could send another vessel from New York without it being molested.

From that point the fortunes of the Pacific Fur Company quickly deteriorated. By January 1813 word reached the post of the declaration of war. The Northwest Company successfully landed a new fur trading expedition in the region with the express mission of wresting the Columbia River area from the Americans. Since the British navy had blockaded New York City, Astor could not send another vessel to reinforce the Astoria traders. Realizing that the situation had become untenable, he gave permission to his agent in charge of Astoria, Duncan McDougall, to sell the post to the British. Thus the Northwest Company came to possess Astoria for $58,000, a fraction of its value, and rechristened the post Fort George.

Though Astor suffered reverses during the war, he enjoyed more than compensating gains. His Manhattan real estate continued to increase in value. The rise of New York as the nation's commercial and financial nexus during the first decades of the nineteenth century contributed dramatically to heightened Manhattan real estate prices, and Astor had invested much of the profits of his China trade in Manhattan real estate. That seems to have been a common Astor investment pattern. He put profits accrued from commercial enterprises into land. Evidence suggests that his fur trading activities had not undergone an expansion sufficient enough to finance all of his real estate ventures, but in 1804 and 1805 Astor invested about $80,000 each year in Manhattan holdings. The War of 1812 curtailed his commercial activities and profits; thus his real estate investments somewhat declined. In 1813 Astor purchased $30,000 worth of Manhattan holdings, and in 1814 those holdings were valued at

The Montreal warehouse used by Astor from about 1800 to store furs obtained from the Northwest Company (drawing by Henry Scott; courtesy of the Public Archives of Canada)

$42,000. By 1819 his investment totals had surpassed $715,000.

A common misconception has arisen that portrays Astor as having never disposed of any of his Manhattan real estate during the period from 1800 to 1820. That misconception distorts the fact that on several occasions Astor sought to sell some of his holdings as soon as possible after he purchased them. In fact, by 1820 he had received more than $180,000 for property he had sold outright, while during the same period he received only $10,000 in income from long-term leases.

Of course, the sale of Manhattan real estate always accrued for Astor a substantial profit. In 1805 he paid to a George Clinton $75,000 for a tract of land called Greenwich Village. At the time of Astor's purchase the land had been divided into 243 lots. During the next few years Astor sold those lots for an average price of nearly $1,000 apiece, thus making a profit of $168,000, or more than 200 percent. In some cases Astor took a mortgage on the lots sold for the full value of the purchasing price, to be paid in two or three years with interest and providing that if the grantee should de-

fault in either principal or interest, Astor could have the property sold at auction and recompense himself out of the proceeds for principal, interest, and expenses. Astor instituted other schemes on several occasions. They indicate that Astor garnered considerable profits in a short time by buying and selling Manhattan lots, or by purchasing larger tracts to be divided and sold. In short, Astor was a marvelous short-term speculator and real estate financier.

The war presented Astor with other opportunities to add to his wealth. By 1814 the federal government, desperately short of funds to prosecute the fighting, turned to Astor for financial support. Working in conjunction with a powerful financial group from Philadelphia, Girard and Parish, Astor purchased a large block of government bonds at from 80 to 82 cents on the dollar. He and his financial collaborators paid for those bonds with bank notes worth approximately one-half their face value.

Although the war ended the Pacific Fur Company branch of Astor's incorporated American Fur Company, the Southwest Fur Company branch of that enterprise remained operative if only on a limited basis. The determination of Astor eventually to monopolize the fur trade, both within the boundaries of the United States and over as much unclaimed North American territory as possible, also remained. By 1815 Astor, then fifty-two years of age and in the prime of his life, stood ready to fulfill this ambition. He planned a new offensive to drive beyond the Great Lakes and up the Missouri River, a campaign which would gain him control of the rich St. Louis trade.

In 1816 Congress struck a mortal blow at the interests of Astor's competitors, chiefly Canadian traders who conducted their business within the territory of the United States. The federal government established severe penalties by confiscating the goods of unlicensed foreign traders. All of the forces of the federal government stood in support of Astor's scheme to eliminate his competitors. Yet this situation did not fully satisfy him because swift application of the new regulations could interfere with his own plans to force out his few American rivals.

Astor turned to the secretary of state, James Monroe, for assistance and requested that some Canadian fur traders and their Indian coworkers be allowed to continue their activities. In that manner the Indians could be kept involved in the fur trade, and Astor could solidify his dealings with them before other American competitors entered the field. Incredibly, Monroe forwarded this brazen request to President James Madison. The president rightfully ignored it, but this episode demonstrates the lengths to which Astor would go to dominate the American fur trading business. Those as well as other actions earned for Astor a deserved reputation for high-handedness and even ruthlessness.

On another occasion he demanded that the federal government send troops to the western frontier to protect his trading operations from competitors and from Indians. Again the government ignored such a request, but it had become apparent that, in his own thinking, Astor had linked his own success on the frontier with that of the growing new nation's.

By 1817 the American Fur Company incorporated the operations of the Southwest Fur Company. During the preceding decade the American Fur Company had been little more than a paper entity, but after the war it became a dynamic enterprise. Astor owned nearly all of the company's stock and supplied all of its capital. He sold all of

the furs received by the company and gave all of the orders.

The American Fur Company reflected Astor's commitment to extensive organization, in many ways predating the managerial hierarchies that have become the vogue in studies of business history. His operation encompassed both fur and China traders spread over a vast geographic region and involved far-flung world markets. While Astor occupied the position of ultimate authority, his son, William Astor, played an increasingly important role in the operation of the trading concern after 1816. From that date the Astors tied their fur trade business to their China trade operations through a second company, John Jacob Astor and Son.

The American Fur Company's managerial hierarchy required three separate business locations, each directed by a nearly autonomous manager, in order to adequately oversee its operations. John and William Astor oversaw the collection, packaging, and shipment of furs in New York. A subordinate manager, William Matthews, outfitted traders and directed their trips into the interior from Montreal. Ramsay Crooks and Robert Stuart managed trading operations in the Mackinac region. The Mackinac post, which served as the northwestern focal point of the business, grew into a rather sophisticated community. Office buildings, storerooms, sleeping quarters, a retail store, and facilities for a blacksmith, carpenter, and silversmith comprised the physical layout of this trading center.

Boatmen, voyageurs, and interpreters, directed by clerks and outfit traders, comprised the next level of the American Fur Company worker hierarchy. Those outfits annually journeyed into the interior from the Montreal and Mackinac centers and traveled to a series of small forward posts near Detroit and Chicago or in the area of Prairie du Chien. Out on the trading frontier, wages and responsibilities varied greatly. The company paid the interpreters, boatmen, and voyageurs niggardly wages while the clerks and outfit traders drew pay as well as profits from the local fur operations.

At the bottom level, on the frontier, traders profited from using the furs themselves as money, although usually a warehouse stood to receive the interest. Little paper money circulated, and specie currency was equally scarce. Thus the trappers, traders, and merchants occasionally used furs, pelts, and hides as a medium of exchange. (Early visitors to California, for example, noted the widespread

Astoria, the central post for Astor's Pacific fur trading enterprise from 1811 to 1813 (drawing by Henry James Warre; courtesy of Yale University Library)

practice of using otter furs for money.) While this practice undoubtedly went on without Astor's knowledge—indeed, it is unlikely that he cared as long as no substantial profits existed—his trading operations nevertheless acted in this way as primitive banks of issue, even as they displayed an embryonic managerial hierarchy.

Expansion of trading territories and the elimination of competition constituted the major organization of strategy of the American Fur Company. In line with that objective, Astor mounted his offensive in the Old Northwest in 1818. Despite the outcome of the war and the strength of his own company, he continued to face significant competition from independent traders. Canadian traders continued to trap in certain parts of the region in violation of the law. At Detroit, David Stone and Company, an enterprising and well-financed trading concern, constituted a threat. Yet because the American Fur Company controlled the Mackinac outpost this meant that it essentially dominated the Old Northwest trading region. From that center Astor directed his traders, many of whom were Canadian, into the Minnesota wilderness and on to the Sandy Lake source of the Mississippi River. There they came into contact with Sioux Indians. Proceeding

further, with easy portages, they reached the Red River of the North. This route allowed Astor's men to gain access to Fort Snelling and Traverse des Sioux, both prominent outposts of the fur trade.

Another route of Astor's brigades ran up Green Bay from Lake Michigan, utilizing the Fox River. A portage put them on the Wisconsin River, which ran into the Mississippi, which brought the Astor men into contact with the Winnebago Indians, important participants in the trade. Astor's bateaux and canoes also traveled down Lake Michigan to Milwaukee, the Chicago River, and other points, into the land of the Chippewa Indians, and from there moved down the Des Plains and Illinois rivers through the lands of the Fox, Peoria, and Potowatomie Indians, all good hunters.

Furs poured into Mackinac from these sources. Astor's agents then loaded these on cargo canoes and transported them down Lake Huron, then across Lake Erie to Buffalo. There other Astor men loaded the furs on wagons and shipped them to Albany. There they were finally shipped by boat down the Hudson River to New York City.

The activity of Astor's fur trading agents also resulted in the establishment of Detroit as a major trading center. Into this settlement came furs from Ohio, Indiana, and southern Michigan. This area became one of the most productive in the Old Northwest. Astor's traders took thousands of mink, muskrat, raccoon, opossum, skunk, otter, beaver, wildcat, wolf, deer, and fox. Pelts also came into Detroit from the Canadian territory east of Lake Huron, but this trade ended in 1821, when Americans were barred from operating on Canadian soil.

Other events in Canada affected Astor's operations. The Hudson's Bay Company waged a desperate war for control of the country west of the Great Lakes. Every effort of the Northwest Company to break up the monopoly of the Hudson's Bay Company had failed. Agents of the Northwest Company tried in vain to gain security by establishing undisputed areas of trade. Both companies employed the most violent traders, who often murdered their rivals. This rivalry finally ended with a merger of the two enterprises. The combined organization operated under the Hudson's Bay Company name. Astor thus had a single Canadian opponent with whom to battle for control of the Old Northwest and upper Missouri River trading areas.

The owners of all the fur trading enterprises treated their lowest employees, the humble *engagés,* with incredible disdain. Contemporary accounts stated that the *engagés* performed all of the menial tasks, working "more like beasts than like men." Annual wages for these employees usually totaled no more than $100 per year, in addition to a few perquisites such as articles of clothing, tobacco, salt, or soap. As Astor became more dominant in the field he dispensed with the perquisites except for providing his employees a small ration of "blé d'Indi," a type of Indian corn. He also reduced the *engagés'* wages to $250 for three years, but, as if that did not satisfy his desire for profit, Astor condoned the practice of cheating them out of the money due them. If a company or outfit trader whom Astor employed to supervise directly the *engagés'* activities could by any means avoid paying them their full wages, Astor looked upon this favorably. Goods that the *engagés* might require to survive, or some article that might break up the hardship and monotony of their lives, such as tobacco, or liquor, Astor sold them at a scandalously high markup. Often the *engagés* ended three years of back-breaking work heavily indebted to the company, thereby being forced to reengage for another term. Quite nat-

urally, these employees of the American Fur Company came to hate their employer.

As one prominent historian recounts, Astor's growing dominance of the fur trading business after the War of 1812 created an "evil pyramided system." Again, Astor predated such practices as the mining company towns, establishing a fur trade version of debt peonage. The company furnished goods to its own traders at enormous profits, which made it impossible for it to lose money. To break even, the outfit traders had to resort to all types of deceit, trickery, and misconduct in their relationships with the *engagés* under their supervision. Because of the inescapable financial burden placed upon them by Astor, certain company traders would even kill an *engagé* to prevent paying out a few hundred dollars.

Astor's tightfisted wage policy reflected his mania for cost control. He tracked every conceivable expense. He kept ledgers on each trading outfit, listing the value of each item provided to the group by the company and the value of all furs collected. In addition, Astor kept a second set of books for John Jacob Astor and Son. Those accounts reflected the cost and sale of items imported from China and the volume of furs sold there. Another account ledger depicted the profits and losses on all voyages to China. On some occasions those accounts reflected transactions that took many years to complete. Because of their detail and accuracy Astor could easily scan these separate accounts and determine his financial condition.

Astor used the information he obtained from his detailed accounting records to increase profits and reduce costs. In that sense he operated at a level of sophistication unmatched by other businessmen of his era. His ability to monitor costs and to assess the potential of markets led to his withdrawal from the China trade in 1824. Among all of the major fur traders, Astor first recognized the declining European markets for silks and tea and the dwindling demand for furs in China.

Some accounts record that Astor made a fight to keep liquor out of the Indian trade and that he insisted that they receive high-quality merchandise for their furs. But these small acts of altruism scarcely allayed the negatives that Astor brought to the fur trading business. He treated the Indians involved in the trade decently only because of the competition for their services by the British or Canadians.

Later, when supplying the Indian traders liquor became essential to dominance of the upper Missouri fur business, any reticence on the part of Astor to engage in such a practice vanished. Canadian traders, desperate to stave off Astor's advance, flooded the region with liquor in hopes of depriving him of Indian labor. By 1822 Astor ordered his posts and outfitters to use liquor as freely as they deemed necessary. Very quickly Astor became the largest supplier of liquor to the Indian population on the American frontier. A federal territorial law passed by Congress in 1822 prohibited such liquor trafficking, but government Indian-affairs agents experienced great difficulty in enforcing that dictate. From 5,000 to 8,000 gallons of Astor liquor flowed through to the Mackinac trading post alone during each season. One of Astor's biographers states that in view of such substantial illegal shipments, government officials responsible for restricting the trade "appear to have been afflicted with spasmodic blindness." Actually, Astor's liquor shipments moved effortlessly through the frontier because he had bribed key Indian-affairs agents and territorial officials, including Michigan's territorial governor, Lewis Cass. Of course, the general effect of liquor on the frontier was disastrous. Stated Col. Josiah Snelling, the famed frontier commander, "the neighborhood of the trading houses where whiskey is sold presents a disgusting sense of drunkenness, debauchery, and of nearly all the murders committed in the Indian country."

Despite those actions Astor still experienced determined opposition in the form of independent traders. Some of these independents invaded "company territory" and offered higher prices for pelts from Indians and *engagés* than Astor would pay. A few succeeded for a short time, but usually Astor's agents quickly put them out of business. They accomplished this by luring intruders into the American Fur Company field with annual stipends or share contracts.

Even Astor found that he could not buy off all competitors. When one independent arrived in Wisconsin in the early 1820s and dealt directly with the Indians, Astor's agents warned him that he risked both life and property. Astor's agents paid a local Indian chief to kill the trader, but that attempt failed, and the trader survived and remained a competitor for years.

In 1832 Congress considered a new bill intended to completely eradicate the flood of liquor into the upper Missouri trading region. As a prominent Astor biographer explained, "The law of 1822 had provided that liquor should be excluded; the law of 1832 was to state that liquor should really be excluded."

Astor, who had begun his American Fur Company operations by forbidding his agents from engaging in frontier liquor trafficking, exerted his great personal influence against the 1832 congressional bill. But in that effort Astor lost the support of Lewis Cass. The former Michigan territorial governor had been elevated to the position of secretary of war and in his new position demonstrated a new responsibility for the welfare of the Indians. The bill passed and, in contrast to the 1822 law, significantly decreased the amount of liquor brought into the upper Missouri River area.

Other determined independent traders working out of St. Louis resisted Astor's growing dominance. Astor, in turn, met this resistance with greater determination. In the winter of 1821-1822 he succeeded in persuading Congress to abolish the government trading posts that it had started constructing as early as 1796. In the spring of 1822 he established in St. Louis the western department of the American Fur Company.

Astor employed all of his standard operational techniques—price-cutting, the supply of large quantities of liquor, and the use of political influence—to overwhelm his opponents. Astor absorbed his chief competitor in the region, the Columbia Fur Company, in 1827 and utilized its field operations to push even farther west and south. These expanded operations placed the American Fur Company in direct competition with the Rocky Mountain Fur Company of Thomas Fitzpatrick, James Sublette, and Jim Bridger.

While Astor's fur trading business expanded, however, his profits did not often rise accordingly. Accounts by those involved in the western fur trade out of St. Louis testified as to the disappointing profits. Astor referred to these low yields when he requested, unsuccessfully, that the federal government impose a duty on foreign furs. Yet other contemporary accounts speak of traders reaping substantial profits on the frontier between the years 1815 and 1830.

Whatever the profit margins, the American Fur Company and the Rocky Mountain Fur Company competed intensely for control of the fur producing regions west of St. Louis. In order to enhance his position Astor merged with another major St. Louis fur trading competitor, Bernard Pratte and Company. This merger, coupled with his previous purchase of the Columbia Fur Company, situated the American Fur Company to penetrate effectively not only the upper Missouri region but also other areas west of the Mississippi River.

Despite these takeovers and his continued operational policies of price and wage reduction, Astor found it difficult to compete with the Rocky Mountain Fur Company. The leading partners and trade outfitters of that company made spectacular gains in opening up the trans-Mississippi West. Unlike Astor, who virtually never visited the fur trading regions (let alone operated from bases in the wilderness), Sublette, Fitzpatrick, and Bridger had bravely ventured to and through the Rocky Mountains and had tapped new and rich fur-bearing regions and established strong and profitable ties with Indian groups such as the Blackfeet, the Flathead, and the Pend d'Oreille. Rocky Mountain's knowledge of the geography of the region far exceeded that of the outfits sent west by the American Fur Company. Some of Astor's far-western expeditions, which ventured up the Missouri, met with disaster at the hands of some of these same Indian groups.

The opportunities for profit continued to dwindle substantially for all parties participating in the far-western fur trade. The trade perpetuated itself as long as it did because it developed an inertia of its own. But by June of 1834 Astor determined to sell all of his fur interests. He did so, and for the remainder of his days never again engaged in commerce.

Astor did, however, remain associated with a major real estate enterprise in the west. That involved his attempt to establish a thriving community at Green Bay. The Panic of 1837 ruined what could have been a very successful investment. At the same time Astor initiated an unwise policy of nonresident land ownership within the community. These owners did not conscientiously attend to the welfare of their holdings.

Astor, at seventy years of age when he began this enterprise, failed to keep himself informed as to proper methods of western land development. He could not avoid thinking of Green Bay lands in terms of New York City. He charged far too much for Green Bay lots and thus never secured an adequate number of purchasers before the financial crash of 1837 occurred.

Although Astor concluded his fur trading enterprises by 1834, he still remained active in various Manhattan real estate ventures. Between 1820 and 1848 he invested more than $1.25 million in this area. This money came from varied sources. The amount of money Astor received from the rentals of his land-holdings surpassed the total amount he invested. Therefore the rising value of his Manhattan property, coupled with its increased rental returns, created a profitable inertia for further real estate investment.

Astor had exhibited noteworthy ruthlessness in the fur trade, and it would be natural to assume that he displayed the same characteristic when he acquired his Manhattan real estate. Such a trait would have translated into a large percentage of his property being obtained through the foreclosing of mortgages. But extant records do not demonstrate such an occurrence. During Astor's entire career he became the mortgager in nearly 500 separate real estate transactions but came to acquire less than 70 pieces of property by foreclosure. Nearly all of Astor's foreclosures occurred after the Panic of 1837. That severe economic downturn placed tremendous pressure on New York real estate owners. Since Astor had divested himself of his fur trading enterprise, he possessed sufficient capital to purchase large quantities of Manhattan real estate that had temporarily dropped in value.

Prior to 1820 Astor usually disposed of his real estate holdings in a quick and profitable manner. After 1820 he disposed of his land in fee simple, or on a long-term-lease basis for lump sums. His returns from these types of transactions totaled nearly $995,000. After 1820 Astor accrued significant profits from short-term leases on his New York property as well. The rapid growth of New York City after 1820 led Astor on several occasions to lease rather than sell. He rightly surmised that many newcomers to the city could not afford to buy a lot and build, but could lease and build. Astor also realized that, in view of the rise in Manhattan real estate values, retaining ownership of his property would be more profitable in the long term. Between 1820 and 1848 New York residents desperately required housing. That factor relieved Astor of the need to improve his lots to attract tenants. Thus his profit margin from these leased lots was even greater. Astor's methods of property management in Manhattan yielded for him during the last decade of his life more than $1.25 million. Irrespective of his methods in the fur trade, Astor exhibited considerable courage and foresight in his Manhattan real estate purchases.

He battled powerful rivals in both his China trade and fur trading enterprises. But none possessed his vision of the future of New York City as the center of the nation's commercial activity. That vision, realized through his shrewd real estate enterprises in Manhattan, made Astor the richest man in the United States and one of the richest in the world.

Because he owned ships and buildings in New York City, Astor became cognizant of the financial possibilities of the insurance industry. Between 1814 and 1834 he served as director of the Globe Insurance Company. He also held the same position for New York Fireman's Insurance and the Hope Insurance companies. By the 1830s he directed the New York Life Insurance and Trust Company. Despite the fact that Astor held these rather impressive positions, his insurance dealings constituted only a small fraction of his overall business activities.

The same can be said for Astor's banking activities. He supported the chartering of the Second Bank of the United States (BUS) in 1816. In fact, he played a major role in this episode because of his large subscriptions to war loans during the War of 1812. During the war he purchased large amounts of U.S. government securities, support the bank desperately needed. As a result of those efforts, the Board of Directors of the New York branch of the BUS elected Astor as its president.

Astor served for only a short period in this position and focused most of his efforts toward procuring suitable directors for the institution. At the same time he served as a director of the parent BUS. But by 1819 Astor had left both of these positions. Again, although his contributions to national banking enterprises were not monumental, Astor played a substantial role in strengthening the banking community. Overall, however, he expanded the scope of finance into new areas.

The quality of mind that Astor brought to his various commercial, real estate, and moneylending enterprises naturally led him into other businesses and even cultural enterprises. Astor always exhibited a recreational interest in the theater. Contemporaries claimed that he refused to break a theater engagement on the day he learned of the *Tonquin* disaster. Not surprisingly, in 1806 he purchased for $50,000 the Park Theater in New York. In typical Astor fashion he rented this facility at a rather high quarterly rate. The rate proved so high, in fact, that the theater tenant, Thomas Cooper, unsuccessfully complained that Astor should reduce the sum. The Park Theater burned down in 1820, but Astor remodeled it in 1834.

Astor also invested in Manhattan hotels. In 1828 he purchased the City Hotel, the foremost institution of its kind in New York. Fire also damaged this facility, but it proved a profitable investment, as Astor derived $15,000 annually from the City Hotel at the time of his death. More important, Astor erected the Park Hotel in 1834. Some deft real estate maneuvering preceded the construction of this hotel, because a certain John G. Coster, who owned a home on a lot which Astor desired for the hotel location, refused to sell. Apparently Coster held out for a considerable time and ultimately sold his property to Astor for an extremely high price. After Astor came into possession of Coster's home, he learned that the original owner still occupied the building, at which time Astor ordered the house torn down around Coster.

Designed by the famous Boston architect Isaiah Rogers, the Park Hotel was a large and magnificent structure. But Astor never considered having the hotel managed for his own account. In 1835 he conveyed the facility to his son, William, who in turn leased it on a long-term basis. Astor valued the Park Hotel at more than $750,000, and it constituted one of his more profitable investments. The annual rent of the facility actually brought him only $120,000, a rather small amount when all the money, time, and effort he had expended during the facility's planning and construction is considered.

Astor not only demonstrated an interest in the financial prospects offered by transoceanic trade, he also sought to reap rewards through railroad investment. He became a major shareholder in the Mohawk & Hudson Railroad, the forerunner of the New York Central. Elected director of that line in 1828, 1829, 1830, and 1831, Astor served as one of its most important promoters. By 1834 he had sold most of his stock in the company and after that date rarely showed much interest in other railroad enterprises.

The investment in government securities dominated much of Astor's attention during his later years. He also purchased large quantities of municipal and state bonds, as well as those of the federal government. Astor spent much of the 1830s in Great Britain and purchased U.S. government securities through his London agents. His commitment to this enterprise increased during the next decade. Astor made these purchases in an attempt to establish trust funds for his children and grandchildren. During the last year of his life he transferred more than $250,000 worth of these securities to some of these descendants.

Astor also invested heavily in New York State and Ohio securities. His New York securities totaled at least $500,000. Astor's purchase of more than $1 million worth of Ohio bonds stemmed from his interest in that state's profitable canal-building program. He also bought Indiana, Pennsylvania, and Missouri securities, but at a more modest level. The combined total of his state security holdings surpassed $2 million. By contrast, his investments in municipal bonds were small. His will indicated that he possessed $100,000 in New York City bonds and $50,000 in New Haven municipal bonds. Astor's commitment to the large-scale purchase of these types of securities grew during the later years of his life because they constituted safe investments requiring little hands-on management.

Accounts vary as to Astor's commitment to philanthropic endeavors. Upon his death his eulogist, Washington Irving, described him as "highly and deservedly esteemed for his extraordinary philanthropy." Though he did demonstrate a modest commitment to benevolent and philanthropic enterprises, he did not deserve such a tribute. Near his death Astor himself commented that "the disposition to do good does not always increase with the means." Between 1836 and 1838 his personal records reveal only one instance of unsolicited philanthropic support, when he donated a check for $100 to assist a group in New Jersey that had suffered damage by a tornado. Those same records, however, do not reveal refusals of requests for contributions to charitable or philanthropic agencies.

Whatever the extent of Astor's philanthropies during his lifetime, there is ample evidence that his will left to public purposes a much larger amount. This document stipulated a $30,000 bequest to the German Society of New York City and a $25,000 donation to Columbia College for the purpose of establishing a professorship of the German language and literature. An additional bequest of $25,000 went to the Association for the Relief of Respectable Aged Indigent Families. Various codicils to Astor's

will increased the amounts of some of these bequests and provided significant sums for other benevolent agencies. One such codicil provided for the bequest of the remarkable sum of $400,000 for the establishment of a public library in his name, and another left $50,000 to the poor of Waldorf, Astor's German home. Nevertheless, other codicils to Astor's will reduced certain philanthropic bequests.

Astor's greatest benefaction, the Astor Library, represented his greatest interest outside of business. It also reflected Astor's association with prominent literary figures of New York City during the 1830s and 1840s. The bequest that established the library may have affected his unwillingness to part with more of his fortune for other such enterprises. When knowledge of Astor's large bequest for the library became public, various agencies and societies besieged him for donations. All told, Astor's contributions to philanthropic interests totaled $507,000, a sizable amount; but when compared to the monetary commitment for such purposes by later American men of wealth such as Andrew Carnegie and John D. Rockefeller, Astor's appears rather tightfisted and miserly.

While Astor's career was a part of American history, he remained European in many facets of his personality. He always spoke with a distinct German accent and spent more than one-third of his eighty-four-year lifespan in Europe. Except for the trips to Europe he never traveled extensively. He never visited the exotic ports his ships frequented during the years of his China trade. Nor did he travel a great deal within the United States. He journeyed from New York north to his Montreal enterprises but no farther. Once he considered visiting St. Louis, but he abandoned the idea. While Astor played a dominant role in far-western affairs, he never saw the Mississippi River or the Rocky Mountains. New York City constituted the sphere of his American existence. Because he never experienced the Far West firsthand and largely perceived the region as simply a valuable resource for the augmentation of his personal fortune, Astor does not stand as an attractive figure in the historical saga of the American frontier. That, coupled with the factor of his parsimonious character, render him a rather easy target for criticism.

Upon Astor's death on March 29, 1848, several prominent contemporaries offered mixed appraisals of his character. In his eulogy Irving ascribed to Astor both a sense of public spirit and benevolence. Yet many thought that Irving had been paid handsomely for such praise. The *New York Herald* stated of Astor, "He has exhibited at best but the ingenious powers of a self-invented money-making machine." An earlier biographer described him as selfish, grasping, and ruthless, evidenced by the fact that he left his faithful employee of many years, Fitz-Greene Halleck, the poet, a paltry annuity of $200.

Though often exaggerated, accounts of his extreme parsimony and exacting acquisitiveness abound. Historical documentation attests to his merciless aggression in prosecuting the fur trade. The high-handed tactics of his employees on the frontier reflected his influence over and contempt of Washington officials. Astor's men interfered with government agents and acted with arrogance and even lawlessness until he left the business. Stated one agent, "They entertain, as I know to be a fact, no respect for our citizens, agents, officers or the Government or its laws or general policy." In a variety of enterprises, ranging from the fur trade to real estate, insurance, banking, and investment, the amassing of wealth constituted Astor's passion.

Yet the author of the most comprehensive Astor biography, Kenneth W. Porter, qualifies this assessment. According to Porter, Astor worked within the values and mores established by the business community of his time, and he had striven specifically to become the greatest single force within that community. In addition, Porter contends that Astor did not fail to recognize his social responsibilities, but that his "extraordinary far-seeing qualities on the economic horizon" appeared to limit this social vision. Essentially Astor was a businessman, the pre-eminent one of his era, whose understanding of management structure far surpassed that of his contemporaries. And gauging his character, by his business abilities alone, Astor stands unsurpassed in the art of buying and selling and in wielding economic power.

References:

Hiram M. Chittenden, *The American Fur Trade of the Far West* (3 volumes, New York: Francis P. Harper, 1902; 2 volumes, Stanford, Cal.: Academic Reprints, 1954);

John D. Haegar, "Business Strategy and Practice in the Early Republic: John Jacob Astor and the American Fur Trade," *Western Historical Quarterly*, 19 (May 1988): 183-202;

Washington Irving, *Astoria, or Anecdotes of an Enterprise Beyond the Rocky Mountains*, edited by Edgeley W. Todd (Norman: University of Oklahoma Press, 1964);

Dale L. Morgan, ed., *The West of William Ashley; the International Struggle for the Fur Trade of the Missouri, the Rocky Mountains, and the Columbia, with Explorations beyond the Continental Divide, recorded in the Diaries and Letters of William H. Ashley and his Contemporaries, 1822-1838* (Denver: Old West, 1964);

Paul C. Phillips and J. W. Smurr, *The Fur Trade*, 2 volumes (Norman: University of Oklahoma Press, 1961);

Kenneth W. Porter, *John Jacob Astor, Business Man*, 2 volumes (Cambridge, Mass.: Harvard University Press, 1931);

David J. Wishart, *The Fur Trade of the American West, 1807-1840, A Geographical Synthesis* (Lincoln: University of Nebraska Press, 1979).

George F. Baker

(March 27, 1840-May 2, 1931)

by Michael F. Konig

Westfield State College

CAREER: Clerk, New York state banking department (1856-1863); pay teller (1863-1865), cashier (1865-1877), president (1877-1909), chairman, First National Bank of New York (1909-1926).

George Fisher Baker, son of George Ellis and Eveline Stevens Baker, was born in Troy, New York, on March 27, 1840. The family moved to Williamsburg (later Brooklyn), New York, a few years later. His father pursued a varied career, working as a shoe merchant, serving as a member of the New York state legislature, and holding the position of private secretary to Secretary of State William H. Seward. Baker received his education at the Williamsburg School in Dedham, Massachusetts, and at Seward University in Florida, New York.

Baker's banking career began at the age of sixteen, when he took a position as clerk in the New York state banking department in Albany. In 1863, with John Thompson and Thompson's sons, he established the First National Bank of New York. Thompson, a financier who had managed to recover from losses incurred during the Panic of 1857, foresaw that the recently passed National Banking Act of 1863 provided opportunity for new banking ventures. Thompson had invited Baker, who through his father was connected to many of the leaders of the Republican party, to invest in the new undertaking. Baker bought 30 shares of the new bank's stock for $3,000, an investment of all of his personal savings. The First National Bank opened on Wall Street on July 22, 1863, and was an immediate success, in some measure due to the fact that Baker's father opened an account as Disbursing Agent of the U.S. State Department. The bank also developed profits from the sale of government bonds, and its capital stock of $200,000 increased to $500,000 by April 1864. By 1865 Baker, who began work as the bank's teller, had become the cashier. The financial success of the First Na-

George F. Baker

tional Bank during the Civil War years, which was similar to that of Jay Cooke & Company, depended to a large extent upon federal-government bond financing. The termination of the Civil War reduced this source of earnings. By 1869 Baker had become the active head of the First National Bank, and he had started to search for new avenues of financial opportunity for the institution. He had also married Florence Tucker of Louisville, Kentucky.

The Panic of 1873 dramatically affected the development of the First National Bank and Baker's position within the institution. Thompson, president of the bank, suffered severe setbacks to his personal credit and eventually sold his interest in First National to Baker. During the panic Baker had made a favorable impression on the financial community through his dealings with Jay Cooke & Company. This prominent Philadelphia financial institution suspended its American operations in 1873 because of overextended railroad speculation. Baker worked closely with Cooke's New York office in an attempt to explore new avenues for profitable investment for First National. According to Sheridan Logan the members of the Cooke firm in New York "had proved their ability, had conducted their business profitably, and had only been dragged down by the Philadelphia associations." If Cooke wanted a profitable New York and federal-government connection, Baker could provide that opportunity. Although the members of this firm were in bankruptcy, they still possessed sufficient capital to help Baker purchase Thompson's controlling interest in 1877. After that transaction and perhaps as part of the agreement, Baker appointed several of the Cooke men as officers of the First National Bank. A new phase in the history of the institution had begun. Baker, the bank's new president, charted this direction.

During the first six years after the Panic of 1873 the bank made considerable strides in the recovery of its assets. Much of the recovery was achieved through the bank's involvement with the federal government's plans to refund the Civil War debt. Between 1871 and 1879 the Treasury Department refunded more than half of the accumulated government debt by selling new bonds bearing interest rates ranging between 4 and 5 percent. A powerful European financial syndicate headed by N. M. Rothschild and Sons, of London, with which the First National Bank was associated, purchased many of these new issues. Since First National constituted one of the few American banks within this syndicate it came to acquire very large Treasury deposits. By 1879 its financial statement showed deposits of businesses and individuals at $11.9 million and more than $128 million in federal funds.

Other powerful American banks resented what they termed the "treasury pet" position of First National. But the bank worked hard for the profits it accrued from the sale of bonds, and Baker proved his capabilities, thereby achieving "a position of leadership in the financial world which was never impaired." In any case the bond enterprise had brought about two other important develop-

ments for Baker and First National. Baker was elected a trustee of the powerful Mutual Life Insurance Company, and, more important, First National was able to establish a close working relationship with the House of Morgan, as J. P. Morgan had also been a member of the Rothschild syndicate.

By 1881 Baker had moved the First National Bank to a new eight-story location, the United Bank Building, at 2 Wall Street in New York City. The institution remained at this location, jointly owned and occupied by First National and the Bank of the Republic until the firms merged in 1901, throughout Baker's life. It operated no branches, virtually ignored small depositors and borrowers, and developed business relationships with only a handful of out-of-town associates. That manner of operation may have appeared somewhat outdated in later years. But Baker's management techniques were remarkably shrewd and efficient and were copied by others in the field well into the twentieth century. At the same time, Baker's continued occupancy of his Wall Street building (a building surrounded by structures of considerably more height by 1900) made a clear, even arrogant, statement. At a time when prime Manhattan real estate had become exorbitantly expensive, forcing owners to construct high-rise structures that brought them greater rental returns, the eight stories of the First National Bank building clearly demonstrated that Baker did not require rental returns. In that respect Baker imitated Morgan, whose Manhattan headquarters also stood in strikingly low contrast to the surrounding skyline.

Throughout his career Baker invested mainly in "home industries," an undertaking relatively unaffected by foreign markets, tariffs, or international affairs. One of the more secure of the home industries was railroads, and First National was involved in several railroad reorganizations in the 1880s and 1890s. One of the more noteworthy of these reorganizations involved the Richmond & Danville Railroad, which later became part of the Southern Railway. Baker teamed with Morgan (on the latter's first railroad enterprise) to purchase the bankrupt Richmond Terminal and use it as a major facet of a restructuring that involved the establishment of an entirely new company. The Richmond Terminal encompassed a sizable railroad operation, including not only the Richmond & Danville but also the East Tennessee, Virginia & Georgia Railroad. The

The United Bank Building, Wall Street headquarters of the First National Bank and the Bank of the Republic, shortly after completion in 1881

Central Railroad and Banking Company comprised the remainder of the terminal's operations, which had been run into receivership by owners and officers described as "more concerned with their own speculative profits than with the company's stability." The owners finally appealed to Baker and Morgan, who took control of the reorganization process. By liquidating less profitable lines and by establishing a voting trust that controlled the terminal's property for a period of five years, Baker and Morgan accomplished what many thought impossible–the re-creation of a profitable rail operation during the depression of 1893.

Such a successful venture required a close relationship between Baker and Morgan. The two men shared similar outlooks and opinions and enjoyed a

healthy friendship based on mutual respect and trust. In his study of the Morgan financial empire, Vincent P. Carosso quotes Morgan's son, who summed up their relationship when he stated that "Mr. Baker was closer to my father than any other man of affairs. . . . They understood each other perfectly, worked in harmony, and there was never any need of written contracts between them." The two great bankers confided in each other so often that one of their contemporaries referred to Baker as "Mr. Morgan's Secretary of the Treasury." As a result of this relationship the First National Bank became a valuable source of funds for investment by J. P. Morgan & Company.

In 1897 Baker became a member of a group of powerful financiers that included J. Rogers Maxwell and J. Kenney Todd. This group acquired control of the Central Railroad of New Jersey, which was then in receivership, and resurrected it upon a profitable basis. Baker accomplished the same feat with the Delaware, Lackawanna & Western Railroad.

By that time Baker's reputation in financial matters had risen to such a point that others increasingly sought his services. Stockholders of railways, banks, and insurance companies turned to the First National president for financial guidance. As a result, at the time Baker restructured the Central Railroad of New Jersey and the Delaware, Lackawanna & Western, he served as director of 31 companies.

This diversification of Baker's business activities resulted in his appointment to the finance committee of the United States Steel Corporation when it was formed in 1901. Often referred to as the nation's first "Billion Dollar Trust," U.S. Steel was built by Morgan through his purchase of Federal Steel, certain properties of John D. Rockefeller, and, most important, Carnegie Steel. This new combination represented 60 percent of the steel-making capacity of the nation, and Baker served as one of its original directors.

Also in 1901, in conjunction with Morgan and the great rail magnate James J. Hill, Baker purchased the Chicago, Burlington & Quincy Railroad to provide an entrance into Chicago for Hill's Northern Pacific Railroad. That scheme intentionally left out E. H. Harriman, the owner of the revitalized Union Pacific Railroad. As a result Harriman attempted to purchase control of the Northern Pacific by enlisting the aid of the powerful financial concern of Kuhn, Loeb & Company. In response, brokers for the Baker, Morgan, and Hill group competed in a bidding war for Northern Pacific stock. This had a debilitating effect on the price of other stocks held by the competitors and caused a panic on Wall Street. The conflict finally ended with the creation of a new company, Northern Securities, headed by the Baker-Morgan-Hill faction, which allowed the participation of the Harriman group in the consolidation of the Northern Pacific and the Chicago, Burlington & Quincy. A year later the attorney general of the United States, at the behest of President Theodore Roosevelt, initiated a lawsuit aimed at breaking up of Northern Securities on grounds that it stood "in restraint of trade and violated antitrust laws."

By that time the capitalization of the First National Bank had increased to $10 million with the merger of First National with the Bank of the Republic. In addition to his aforementioned activities, Baker held directorates in 43 banks and corporations, including American Telephone and Telegraph, United Electric Light and Power, and Guaranty Trust. First National did not issue a statement of its combined earnings until 1926, when the bank and its subsidiary, First Security, showed net earnings of $16,779,569 and an annual dividend rate of 100 percent for 1925. These figures demonstrate how Baker's financial expertise kept First National strong and liquid. On one occasion Baker remarked to his son, "It is cheap insurance to keep strong." That strategy served the bank in good stead during the financial panic of 1907.

Through Baker's direction in 1908 the First National Bank created the First Security Company, which bought and sold stocks and bonds for the patrons of First National. Dealings in real estate, securities, stock, and other holdings comprised a majority of First Security's activities. Drawing upon assets provided by First National, First Security began operations with a capitalization of $10 million.

The economic dislocation caused by the Panic of 1907 led to an investigation of monetary conditions in the United States by a subcommittee of the Banking and Currency Committee of the House of Representatives. Congressman Arsène P. Pujo of Louisiana served as the chairman of this subcommittee. When this investigatory body convened, Baker had become known throughout financial circles as a member of Wall Street's "Big Three," a powerful banking triumvirate composed of himself, Morgan, and James Stillman, president of National City

Bank. The Panic of 1907 had led to a considerable consolidation in finance, similar to the consolidation that had brought stability and order to the railroad industry during the 1890s. Baker, Morgan, and Stillman had been the most active bankers involved in railroad revitalization, and the Big Three also led the combination movement within the nation's financial community after 1907.

The Pujo investigation covered a broad range of subjects, among them the methods bankers used to finance industrial development and the influence that firms such as the First National Bank and J. P. Morgan and Company exercised over their corporate clients. Prior to appearing before the subcommittee, Baker and Morgan (but not Stillman, who had retired) were required to provide a substantial amount of information pertaining to the number and size of their institutions' deposit accounts, the corporate securities they had acquired or underwritten, the directorships they held, and the investments they had made in other financial institutions. While the committee found no evidence of illegal activity by Baker, Morgan, or anyone else, the exposure of so much power held by so few (Baker alone held 58 directorships involving billions of dollars of assets in 1912) added to already mounting pressure for congressional action in finance.

The Pujo investigation contributed to the passage by Congress of the Federal Reserve Act of 1913, as the federal government attempted to wrest control of the nation's monetary affairs from powerful financiers such as Baker and Morgan by placing the reserve banks in cities across the country, thus diluting New York's power. The system of Federal Reserve banks established by the act included a branch in New York, which opened for business in 1914. The First National Bank, as required by law, invested 6 percent of its paid-in capital and surplus in the new institution, thereby joining the system. An era of change had dawned in the American financial world. Morgan died shortly after his 1913 appearance before the Pujo subcommittee, and a federal income tax law that took effect in 1914 further illustrated the intention of the progressive reformers to protect the American people from the abuses of what was called the "Money Trust."

While such occurrences as President Roosevelt's breakup of Northern Securities reduced Baker's directorships outside of the banking community, First National continued to be a powerful financial institution throughout the 1920s. The bank's shares, which had never sold for less than $500 after 1900, sold for as much as $8,500 during the height of the bull market of 1929.

Baker died in New York on May 2, 1931. By that time his list of financial achievements and personal philanthropies had become truly impressive. The Baker Trust bequeathed gifts of $2 million to the American Red Cross, $2 million to Cornell University, $1 million to Dartmouth College, $1 million to the Metropolitan Museum of Art, $750,000 to the New York Hospital, $700,000 to Harvard University, and $500,000 to the American Museum of Natural History.

References:
Vincent P. Carosso, *The Morgans: Private International Bankers, 1854-1913* (Cambridge, Mass.: Harvard University Press, 1987);

Sheridan Logan, *George F. Baker and His Bank, 1840-1855: A Double Biography* (N.p.: Privately published, 1981);

Albert Bigelow Paine, *George Fisher Baker: A Biography* (New York: Knickerbocker, 1920).

Bank of California

by Lynne Pierson Doti

Chapman College

The Bank of California has a past as colorful as the gold rush. The certificate of incorporation was filed in San Francisco on June 13, 1864, for the state's first joint-stock corporation empowered to engage in commercial banking. The bank opened on July 5 with D. O. Mills as president and William C. Ralston as cashier. Both men were respected San Francisco citizens, borne to the state with the tide of the 1849 migration.

D. O. Mills arrived in Sacramento in the fall of 1849 with a small schooner of goods for delivery to his two merchant brothers, who had preceded him. Mills, although only twenty-five years old, had achieved the position of cashier at a Buffalo, New York, bank before leaving for California. After working briefly with his brothers he opened a new bank in Sacramento. Mills established a conservative reputation in the management of the Sacramento bank and in other financial ventures; Ralston selected him as president partly to solidify the new bank's image.

Ralston worked on Mississippi riverboats before leaving for California, but he stopped in Panama on the way and took a job on the Pacific side of the Isthmus. He distinguished himself, becoming a partner when his company reorganized in 1853. Ralston moved to San Francisco that year, and the company entered the banking business in 1856. As individuals changed their interests, they reorganized the firm several times, but Ralston was listed as partner in each of the successive businesses. As manager of Donohue, Ralston & Company, Ralston quarreled with a partner because Ralston wanted to loan money to a firm in Oregon. "If you are to lend money outside California that way we had better dissolve the partnership," the partner reportedly said. Ralston envisioned a bank serving the Pacific Coast, and he began to gather capital to fulfill his dream.

The Bank of California began operating with $2 million of paid-up capital stock, and San Franciscans welcomed it as the first commercial bank in the far west. The new bank opened with 506 deposit accounts and more than $1.6 million in credit. Mills and Ralston tried to hire only the best people available and insured the continued prestige of the bank by building attractive and impressive quarters in 1867. The site (400 California Street) is still occupied by the bank's main office; the present building was constructed in 1907.

Bank panics and runs occurred regularly in the late nineteenth century. San Francisco's premier bank was not totally immune, but Ralston's unusual character and connections gave support through many crises. Once, during an 1868 earthquake, a crack appeared in the wall of his office. A piece of the building's cornice fell into the street. Ralston interrupted his work only to reprimand his employees for their fear: "Whoever does not stand up to business with strictness and cheerfulness

The Bank of California, San Francisco, 1868

today can never put foot in here again." On that same day he bought land on which he planned to build the world's largest, most elaborate hotel, the Palace. At another point, in 1869, the city experienced a liquidity crisis. An unusual amount of gold had been shipped out of state, and the U.S. Mint in San Francisco temporarily closed. Although the Sub-Treasury in San Francisco held $14 million in gold coin, the government refused to allow its release. Bankers were in a panic, and knowing a run would develop quickly put a stop to business. Ralston asked two friends to meet him at the bank late in the evening. They walked together to the Sub-Treasury, where Ralston entered unchallenged. He returned with several sacks of gold coin and directed his friends to carry them to the bank. A bank official there sent them back with gold bars equal in value to the coin. The operation continued until nearly $1 million was exchanged. The next morning a line formed at the bank's doors, but the display of gold piled along the tellers' counters averted a run.

The Bank of California did close on August 26, 1875, when rumors of a run threatened the supply of coin. The next morning the directors asked Ralston to resign from the bank. He died that afternoon, aged only forty-nine, as he swam in San Francisco Bay. He had tied the bank's future irretrievably to the fortunes of Nevada silver mines, and the bonanza failed him that summer. He had committed a vast fortune to the building of the Palace Hotel and had bid unsuccessfully for control of a new water system for the city. He had financed furniture factories, woolen mills, a silk industry, vineyards, clockworks, and a tobacco industry, all of which suffered from the competition imposed by the transcontinental railroad, which Ralston also helped fund. For these efforts, many of them failures, he died with debts of $9 million.

By 1873 D. O. Mills had retired from the bank, sold his stock, and embarked on a world tour. Ralston succeeded him to the presidency. The bank reopened on October 2, 1875, with Mills again as president, and $2.5 million in gold coin on hand. Deposits rose by more than $700,000 on the first day of business. Ralston's dream hotel opened the same day.

Mills retired as president again in 1878. A leading citizen and former San Francisco mayor, William Alvord, assumed the position. He retained the post until 1905, overseeing growth in the assets from about $11 million in 1879 to nearly $36 million in 1905. In that year the bank acquired the London and San Francisco Bank, which had branches in Portland, Tacoma, and Seattle. That acquisition gave the bank the unique advantage of being the only national bank with out-of-state branches, a distinction assured when changes in the law prohibited other banks from making similar acquisitions. Homer S. King was president of the bank from 1904 to 1909. He was succeeded by Frank B. Anderson, who was president until 1925 and chairman of the board until 1935.

References:

Ira B. Cross, *Financing An Empire: History of Banking in California* (Chicago, San Francisco & Los Angeles: Clarke, 1927);

Neill Wilson, *400 California Street: The Story of the Bank of California* (San Francisco: Bank of California, 1964);

Wilson, *400 California Street: A Century Plus Five* (San Francisco: Bank of California, 1969).

Bank of Italy

by Michael F. Konig

Westfield State College

Shortly after World War II the Bank of Italy, which had been renamed the Bank of America National Trust and Savings Association in 1930, became the largest bank in the world. With 538 branches in 317 California cities and towns in 1954, the bank possessed well over $8 billion in resources. Despite that enormous financial power the Bank of America functioned in many respects similar to the original Bank of Italy founded by A. P. Giannini in 1904 in San Francisco. The bank always served persons of moderate means or people who had never used a bank. As Giannini put it, the Bank of Italy began and remained a financial institution for "the little fellow."

Giannini also organized the Bank of Italy because San Francisco banks tended to ignore the North Beach Italian colony of that city. Many of the Bank of Italy's early patrons were immigrants, unsophisticated in the ways of financial affairs. Giannini served that clientele so ably that he spread branches of the bank throughout San Francisco and eventually Los Angeles, at a time when branch banking constituted a controversial issue. State and federal regulatory agencies only gradually modified their positions in favor of branch banks, in effect following the lead of Giannini and the Bank of Italy.

The earthquake and fire of 1906 devastated San Francisco and left the city's financial district in ruins. Among all the San Francisco banks the Bank of Italy resumed operations most quickly after the disaster. Giannini's fortitude in dealing with that crisis and then the Panic of 1907 contributed to the rise of the Bank of Italy's reputation. The bank not

A. P. Giannini, founder of the Bank of Italy, with his son, Mario (courtesy of BankAmerica Archives)

only made its branch functions available to California's urban residents but also to the state's agricultural entrepreneurs. Giannini established a policy of accepting farm mortgages at interest rates well below the norm, reflecting the desire of the bank's founder to protect the small borrower as well as his desire to expand his operation. As Marquis James and Bessie R. James put it, "it was the first bank to move on a large scale into lending fields that had once been bonanzas for loan sharks." Giannini also initiated the practice of advertising in order to attract the legions of small borrowers he sought to serve.

Giannini died in 1949, but by 1936 he had already relinquished control of the Bank of America

to his son Lawrence Mario Giannini. The younger Giannini initiated broad developments in installment banking after he became president. Under Mario Giannini the institution grew faster than ever.

References:

Julian Dana, *A. P. Giannini: Giant in the West* (New York: Prentice-Hall, 1947);

Marquis James and Bessie R. James, *Biography of a Bank: The Story of the Bank of America* (New York: Harper, 1954).

Bank of North America

by B. R. Burg

Arizona State University

Throughout the course of the American Revolution the United States was beset by severe military, political, and foreign policy problems. The nation's continuous shortage of funds compounded those difficulties. Even in the closing months of 1781, when it appeared the long struggle for independence was about to end in victory, prevailing uncertainties kept the government from dealing effectively with its financial predicament. Chief among those were that the terms of a binding peace treaty were far from agreed upon, and the unofficial truce instituted by Parliament after George Washington defeated Lord Cornwallis at Yorktown could have been abrogated by the English at any time.

The Second Continental Congress—the de facto national government through most of the conflict—had initially raised funds by printing unsecured paper money and by borrowing in the United States and abroad. By 1781 those methods of finance proved no longer suitable. The paper currency issued by Congress was virtually worthless within a few years after its issue, and even though the war moved toward a successful conclusion, few private citizens willingly hazarded additional loans. Foreign sources of revenue also dried up. Neither France nor Spain demonstrated any enthusiasm for

lending more money to the new nation after their own objectives (the defeat of Britain and the partial dismemberment of her empire) seemed at hand. Although several banks existed in the fledgling nation, they lacked the resources to finance the war effort. Those small banks, in fact, were scarcely more than associations organized to provide merchants short-term credit for their overseas business.

A measure of relief from the most pressing fiscal difficulties came with the organization of the Pennsylvania Bank in 1780. That institution was formed when some ninety merchants and wealthy residents of Philadelphia banded together and pledged to supply the American forces. As a boost to its credibility the Second Continental Congress placed its full faith and credit behind the effort in order to protect the lenders. The Pennsylvania Bank supplied more than £300,000 on the government's assurance of repayment. The funds arrived at a time when they were desperately needed, and the country's difficulties were mitigated, at least temporarily. Still, the Pennsylvania Bank constituted merely an association of men willing to provide a subscription for the army rather than a true bank in the modern sense of the term. It generated money for one type

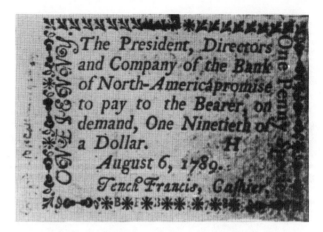

One-penny note issued by the Bank of North America (courtesy of the Library of Congress)

of government expenditure but engaged in no other banking functions.

Many men knowledgeable in fiscal matters saw the need for a genuine bank that would lend money to the nation as well as to private citizens, provide an adequate circulating medium, and carry on other financial operations. Inspired by the example of the Bank of England, Alexander Hamilton, then a twenty-four-year-old aide to George Washington, formulated a plan for such an institution in the late 1770s. Robert Morris, one of the country's most successful businessmen, also occupied himself with the task. Hamilton's efforts had little effect during the war years, but Morris enlisted other men of property and political influence to join him in securing legal permission to found a bank. His plan, submitted to the Congress in May 1781, culminated in the granting of a charter dated December 31 of that year. The Bank of North America, the continent's first true commercial banking institution, opened its doors on Chestnut Street in Philadelphia a week later.

Backers of the project, confident of its approval long before the authorization of the charter, had begun preparing to conduct business in autumn 1781. According to their plan, 1,000 shares of bank stock were to be offered to the public at a price of $400 per share, payable in cash. Buyers investing $2,000 or more were offered credit and only had to prepay 50 percent, with the balance due in three months. A meeting of investors at the City Tavern on November 1 selected a board of directors and named Thomas Willing, a leading Philadelphia businessman, as president.

Only $70,000 was initially subscribed for the bank, but the arrival of a loan of more than $400,000 in specie from France to the U.S. govern-

ment eased worries over capitalization. However, once it appeared that a national bank would be established, another difficulty surfaced. Questions arose as to the legality of the United States government chartering a bank. Robert Morris and his supporters argued in the affirmative, stressing the country's dire need, and their arguments prevailed over those more concerned with theoretical nuance than with impending national bankruptcy. Complaints about the illegality of the bank continued even after it began operation and were not finally laid to rest until spring of 1782 when the state of Pennsylvania granted a second charter.

Like others who championed the bank, Morris contended it would facilitate the war effort and promote prosperity after the nation secured independence. "I am . . . determined," he wrote to John Jay, "that the bank shall be well supported, until it can support itself, and then it will support us." Morris's advocacy involved more than rhetoric. He was one of the bank's heaviest subscribers, and his confidence was handsomely rewarded. From the time it commenced operations, the bank proved exceedingly profitable. Its success enabled the government to offer the shares it owned for sale to the public in 1782. The availability of those shares produced a scramble to purchase them, with buyers fully aware of the 12 percent to 16 percent returns posted by the bank during its first year.

Morris and other wealthy Americans profited from their interest in the bank, and the entire nation benefited from the institution. Its bills—the first in America convertible to specie—eased the problems created by the lack of a stable medium of exchange. The bank also loaned much-needed funds to the government, generated confidence in the national economy after years of wartime uncertainty, and in part contributed to the revival of the country's credit. Dutch lenders, for example, provided the newly emerging nation with $1.25 million shortly after the bank received its charter.

The success of the Bank of North America naturally encouraged imitators. Commercial banks soon received charters from the state legislatures of Maryland, Massachusetts, and New York. In Philadelphia, too, widespread admiration for the bank developed. As the bank's successes and profits accumulated, other groups, encouraged by its example, attempted to organize commercial banks of their own. The Bank of North America greeted such proposals for competition less than enthusiastically, however, and its directors used their considerable political strength to prevent another group from founding a similar institution in 1784.

Frustrated at every turn, opponents of the bank attacked it furiously, and their efforts achieved some degree of success. They secured the repeal of its Pennsylvania charter in 1785 after allegations of the institution's "evil effects," but their victory profited them little. The bank continued to operate on the basis of its national charter until two years later when the state rechartered it.

After the end of the revolutionary war, and following the difficult transition to peacetime, the American economy expanded. Throughout the 1790s and into the first decade of the next century, continuous warfare in Europe produced ample markets for the nation's products, and all sections of the country benefited. The Bank of North America shared in the general prosperity, but profits naturally fell from the high levels of earlier years. A second bank was chartered in Philadelphia by 1794, and other new banks appeared elsewhere in Pennsylvania and in several other states. The increased competition, combined with ineffective leadership and obvious favoritism in making business decisions, restrained growth and limited the rate of return for investors in the Bank of North America.

The nation's banking industry grew steadily during most of the nineteenth century. State authorities rechartered banks, chartered new banks, enacted free banking laws, and expanded the capital of existing banks. As a result, an adequate circulat-

ing medium existed for most regions, and westward expansion was expedited. Banks prospered when the economy expanded, but they also suspended specie payment during difficult times such as those during the latter years of the War of 1812, the Panic of 1837, and the Panic of 1857. The fortunes of the Bank of North America closely paralleled those of the industry. When the Civil War divided the nation, it subscribed to its pro rata share of treasury notes and made large loans to the government even though, like other banks, it was forced to suspend specie payments.

The directors of the Bank of North America reorganized it under the National Currency Act of 1864 as a national bank, but the government allowed it to deviate from provisions of the legislation in at least one particular. The comptroller of the currency bowed to the pressures of history. After reviewing petitions from stockholders and directors, he permitted the bank to conduct business under the original name. It did not add the word "national" to its title.

There was nothing noteworthy about the Bank of North America after its first few years of existence. By the 1790s it was the oldest bank in the nation and certainly one of the best capitalized, but its operations were no different from those of any other banking institution. It continued in business throughout the nineteenth century and on until 1929 when it was absorbed by a competitor, the Pennsylvania Company for Insurance on Lives and Granting Annuities.

References:

J. Van Fenstermaker, *The Development of American Commercial Banking, 1782-1837* (Kent, Ohio: Kent State University Press, 1965);

James W. Gilbart, *The History of Banking in America* (London: Longman, Rees, Orme, Brown, Green & Longman, 1837; reprinted, New York: Kelley, 1967);

Benjamin Klebaner, *Commercial Banking in the United States: A History* (Hinsdale, Ill.: Dryden Press, 1974);

Lawrence Lewis, Jr., *A History of the Bank of North America* (Philadelphia, 1882).

The Bank War and the Specie Circular

Two events in President Andrew Jackson's second administration, long thought by historians to have had significant effects on the nation's economy, have undergone substantial historical revision in the past 20 years. The Bank War involved Jackson's successful attempt to end the affairs of the Second Bank of the United States (BUS). The Second BUS, chartered in 1816 for 20 years, had generated no great hostility on the president's part during his first administration. For several reasons, some of which still remain unclear or controversial, Nicholas Biddle, the president of the BUS, attempted to force a recharter of the bank in 1832 ahead of schedule. According to most authorities on Biddle, he saw an opportunity to enhance his own power and political capital at the expense of Jackson, who, he reasoned, would not dare veto the recharter of an institution as popular as the BUS in an election year. But Jackson, not altogether fond of banks, had certain specific objections to the BUS charter, and he found Biddle totally unresponsive to any changes he suggested. Convinced he could not deal with Biddle or the BUS, Jackson vowed to destroy the bank and shrewdly painted it in his speeches as an institution for "elites" without the interests of the "common man" at heart. Biddle won the first battle when Congress rechartered the bank, but Jackson vetoed the bill in 1832, and the BUS forces failed to override the veto. Worse, Biddle had angered Jackson even more, and the president promptly ordered the removal of the government deposits–the government constituted the largest single depositor in the BUS– and put them in pro-Democratic state banks called "pet banks." Although the BUS hung on for three more years, it was dead as a national bank. Biddle managed to obtain a state charter from Pennsylvania, but his dream of a powerful national institution capable of influencing international finance vanished.

Traditional historians such as Bray Hammond portrayed the bank as an important restraint on the excesses of the state banks and depicted the war as one of Wall Street, with its rising entrepreneurial class, against Chestnut Street, where the bank's Philadelphia headquarters was located. Liberal revisionists such as Arthur Schlesinger, Jr., saw the Bank War as an episode in the rise of democracy over aristocracy. Despite their differences, however, both accepted the ability of the bank to effect major changes in the American economy. Peter Temin presented a powerful critique of those assumptions and convincingly showed that the BUS lacked the ability to influence the economy as much as the traditionalists thought.

Until the revisions by Temin, Richard H. Timberlake, and others, however, historians assumed that the BUS indirectly controlled the money supply and that its demise loosed the forces of the state banks to generate a burst of inflation. They further assumed that Jackson, whom they blamed for starting the inflation by killing the bank, then caused the Panic of 1837 in part through the issue of his Specie Circular of 1836. The traditionalists had argued that as a result of the inflation generated by the state banks, speculators had used the new note issues to purchase western lands. As a way of curtailing the notes flowing into the Treasury, Jackson ordered that only gold and silver (specie) be accepted for payment of land purchased from the federal government. According to the traditionalists, the effects of that order–combined with the disruptions caused by pulling the deposits out of the state banks and putting them in the pet banks and by the concurrent distribution of the U.S. government surplus to the states that Jackson had also ordered–caused so much chaos in the nation's financial market that a panic ensued. Specifically, the critics claimed, the Specie Circular abruptly halted western land sales and caused falling land prices, initiating the depression.

That view only held as long as the BUS could be shown to have the influence in the American economy ascribed to it by the traditionalists. Again, Peter Temin showed that inflows of Mexican silver had undergirded the inflation–if specie-backed note growth was really inflation in the nineteenth-century understanding of the concept–and a sudden rise in British interest rates had induced the panic. In short, the Bank War and the Specie Circular had minimal effects on the nation's economy.

The Bank War had effects in areas other than the economy, though. Historian Robert Remini has argued that the war was political, not economic, in the first place, and that Jackson repelled a powerful political threat from Biddle. Moreover, Jackson greatly expanded the domain of the executive branch during the events from 1832 to 1836 and

added to the federal government's increasing power at the expense of the states and private institutions such as the BUS.

See also:

Thomas Hart Benton, Nicholas Biddle, Isaac Bronson, Henry Clay, Thomas Ellicott, Financial Panics during the Nineteenth Century, First Bank of the United States, William M. Gouge, Amos Kendall, Second Bank of the United States, Hugh Lawson White.

–Editor

August Belmont

(December 8, 1813-November 24, 1890)

by Gregory S. Hunter

ITT Corporation

CAREER: Associate, House of Rothschild (1828-1890); owner, August Belmont & Company (1837-1890); Austrian consul general to the United States (1844-1850); U.S. chargé d'affaires at The Hague (1853-1857); chairman, Democratic National Committee (1860-1872).

August Belmont was a prominent Wall Street figure and a leader of the Democratic party in the Civil War and Reconstruction Eras. His international expertise also enabled him to serve as a diplomat during the administration of President Franklin Pierce.

Belmont was born on December 8, 1813, in the village of Alzey in the Rhenish Palatinate region of Germany. His father, Simon Belmont, was a community leader who served as president of the local synagogue for many years. Belmont's mother was Frederika Elsass Belmont. He had one sister, Elizabeth, and a brother, Joseph.

Tragedy came early to young Belmont's life. His mother died when he was seven, followed one month later by the death of his brother. Less than a year later Belmont went to Frankfurt, forty miles to the north, to live with his grandmother, Gertrude, and her husband, Hajun Hanau, who had connections to the Rothschilds.

In Frankfurt Belmont attended a Jewish school called the *Philanthropin*. The proprietor, Dr. Michael Hess, was quite progressive and even

August Belmont (daguerreotype by Mathew Brady; courtesy of the Library of Congress)

opened the school to Christian children. While Belmont thrived in the school his father had chronic difficulty meeting the tuition payments. In 1828 his father had to remove him because the tuition payments had fallen so far in arrears.

After he left school Belmont's relatives convinced their Frankfurt friends, the Rothschilds, to train the boy for a business career. His association with the Rothschilds thus began in 1828, when he was fifteen. In October of that same year Belmont's grandmother died, leaving him virtually on his own. The Rothschilds first made Belmont an apprentice at their Frankfurt branch. Clearly learning the business from the bottom up, he began by sweeping floors, polishing furniture, and running errands. Young Belmont was neat and punctual; he worked industriously at whatever tasks the Rothschilds gave him. He also showed drive and initiative, rising daily at five o'clock to have a private tutor instruct him in French, English, composition, and arithmetic.

The Rothschilds recognized Belmont's talents and hard work and, after a few years, advanced him through the ranks. In 1832 they gave Belmont a confidential clerkship and in 1834 made him secretary and traveling companion to one of the partners. The latter responsibility significantly broadened his horizons, as he traveled to Paris, Naples, and the Vatican. While in Italy Belmont learned to speak Italian and spent much of his leisure time in art galleries. That led to a lifelong interest in and support of the arts.

The turning point in Belmont's life and career came in 1837. Because of the instability of the Spanish Empire the Rothschilds decided that they needed a reliable agent in Havana to watch over their interests. Belmont accepted the assignment and sailed for Havana via New York City. He reached New York on May 14 and walked into the midst of a financial crisis: the Panic of 1837 had begun just one week before; all New York City banks had suspended specie payments.

The New York commercial community was hard hit by the financial downturn and resulting panic, with many businesses failing. Among the businesses affected was the Rothschilds' American agent, J. L. and S. I. Joseph & Company, which failed on March 17, leaving liabilities of $7 million.

Belmont therefore faced a dilemma. While he had instructions from the Rothschilds to go to Cuba, it was obvious that the Rothschild interests in the United States were at great risk. Because of the slow communications with Europe it would

take several months to receive new instructions from the partners. Belmont concluded that the situation required immediate action, and he decided to delay his Cuban departure: he stayed in New York to look after the Rothschilds' concerns.

Belmont established a firm, August Belmont & Company, and rented a room at 78 Wall Street. When the Rothschilds learned of his actions they approved and appointed Belmont's company their new American agent. The Rothschilds gave him a $10,000 annual salary, a princely sum in the then-depressed city.

Because of its powerful international connection Belmont's firm quickly became a success. Within three years Belmont amassed a personal fortune of more than $100,000, making him one of the richest men in New York City. From 1837 to 1842 he sorted out the complicated Rothschild interests in the United States. He served as their disbursing agent and dividend collector, even after the immediate crisis passed, and his affiliation with the Rothschilds extended to the close of the century.

August Belmont & Company also became a power in its own right. Belmont was involved in foreign exchange, commercial and private loans, acceptance of deposits, and the handling of commercial paper. By the time of the Mexican War Belmont's firm had sufficient resources to underwrite a large portion of the loans made to the U.S. Treasury.

As Belmont's financial success grew, he became more involved in New York society. He wintered in New York City and summered upstate in Saratoga Springs. In 1841 he experienced another aspect of gentlemanly society, as a party in a duel to defend a lady's honor. A man by the name of Edward Heyward had asserted in public that Belmont was sleeping with a married woman he frequently visited in Saratoga Springs. Belmont demanded satisfaction from Heyward, and the two traveled to Elkton, Maryland, to fight the duel, prohibited by New York laws. Heyward fired first, shattering Belmont's hip. Though incapacitated for quite a while, he recovered and returned to the city. For the rest of his life, however, Belmont walked with a pronounced limp.

From 1844 to 1850 Belmont assumed the added responsibility of serving as consul general for the government of Austria. This consulship gave Belmont further independence from the Rothschilds. While the appointment of a prominent American businessman as an agent of a foreign government may seem strange today, it was quite common in nineteenth-century America. The appointment, however, came to haunt Belmont in later years, when his political involvements made his European connections an easy target for partisan attacks.

During that time Belmont grew increasingly "American" in the personal as well as business aspects of his life. In 1844 he became a naturalized citizen of his adopted country. Five years later, on November 7, he married Caroline Slidell Perry, the fourth daughter of Matthew C. Perry and the niece of former congressman John Slidell of Louisiana. Caroline, nicknamed "Tiny," was Perry's eighth child and a renowned beauty of nineteen when she and Belmont met. He offered his bride an entire New York city block as a wedding present. By this marriage Belmont joined an old and prominent American family. The couple eventually had six children, all of whom they reared as Episcopalians. Though Belmont attended church regularly, he never was baptized. Nevertheless he became an outcast in the American Jewish community because of his involvement with Christians and the perceived renunciation of his faith.

Belmont and his wife originally lived at 72 Fifth Avenue. In the 1850s Belmont purchased and renovated a mansion at 109 Fifth Avenue, on the corner of 18th Street. According to all accounts the house was magnificent. The picture gallery Belmont had built was the first in New York City to include skylights. The house also had the first private ballroom in the city. The Belmonts frequently hosted and entertained guests in their mansion. Belmont won acclaim as one of the first gourmets in America, and the fine food and drink at his house constituted a source of much conversation in social circles.

As a change of pace Belmont bought a 1,200-acre farm on Long Island a few years later. Called the Nursery Farm, it was located in Babylon and was virtually a self-contained community. The farm had a 24-room mansion; a 30-acre lake; fields and silos for corn, hay, wheat, and rye; pastures for cows and horses; and even a bowling alley. The pride of the farm, however, was its stables, where Belmont hoped to raise the best racehorses in America. So that Belmont could watch his equine investments, the farm had a private one-mile-long racetrack complete with grandstands. Belmont emerged as one of the most influential figures in American horse racing during the second half of the nine-

teenth century. He served as president of the American Jockey Club and helped transform racing from a casual pastime into a professional sport.

Belmont's family connections led to his involvement with politics. In 1851 John Slidell, Belmont's wife's uncle, tried to secure the upcoming Democratic presidential nomination for his friend, Secretary of State James Buchanan of Pennsylvania. In order to win the nomination, it became clear that Buchanan needed to win New York State. At Slidell's urging Belmont agreed to head Buchanan's New York campaign. Despite Belmont's hard work, Buchanan lost the 1852 nomination to Franklin Pierce.

In a show of party unity, Belmont worked for Pierce's election and even made a generous financial contribution to the Democratic National Committee. Belmont's involvement, however, developed into a campaign issue with anti-Semitic overtones. The Whigs charged that Belmont had tried to buy votes for Pierce, and they also questioned Belmont's loyalty on the basis of his ties to the emperor of Austria and the Rothschilds. Despite those charges Pierce beat the Whig candidate, Winfield Scott, in the general election. The accusations, however, recurred regularly in Belmont's subsequent political campaigns.

With the victory in hand Belmont began his own campaign to secure a diplomatic appointment. He reminded the Pierce administration about his active role in the election and stressed his experience in international finance. Belmont hoped to secure the position in Naples, a city he had come to love while working for the Rothschilds. Because of the various political demands on Pierce, Belmont did not receive the Naples post. Rather, the president appointed Belmont chargé d'affaires at The Hague in the Netherlands.

Belmont sailed for Europe on August 20, 1853. His primary mission was to negotiate a commercial treaty opening the Dutch East Indies to American consuls. After much negotiation Belmont signed a consular convention on January 22, 1855. The agreement, however, went beyond Belmont's original instructions: it permitted the United States to establish consulates in all Dutch colonial ports open to foreign commerce, not just the Dutch East Indies. The Senate ratified the convention in March of the same year. Belmont achieved a second major diplomatic success in 1857 when he concluded the

Belmont's mansion at 109 Fifth Avenue, New York City

first-ever extradition treaty between the United States and the Netherlands.

Although in Europe, Belmont closely followed American politics. As the 1856 presidential election approached, he promoted Buchanan for the Democratic nomination. Buchanan eventually defeated Pierce, marking the first time in American history that an elected president desirous of another term failed to secure renomination.

When Buchanan won the general election, Belmont angled for an appointment to a more prestigious diplomatic post. In particular Belmont wanted to serve in Madrid, for that would give him the opportunity to pursue a long-standing plan of his for the United States' acquisition of Cuba. Despite Belmont's long association with Buchanan the new administration ultimately offered him nothing more than a reappointment to his current position at The Hague. When Belmont learned of this, he resigned and returned to the United States. Belmont's furniture, artwork, wine cellar, and personal belongings required 250 crates to ship home.

Belmont returned to a city in the midst of another panic. Many businesses had failed; unemployment and crime had risen. During that crisis

Belmont contributed generously to several charities. He also did something to try to raise the spirit of the city: he arranged a public exhibition of his art collection. This was a first in New York City and was well received in the press. Ever the art patron, Belmont eventually installed a large art gallery in his Fifth Avenue mansion.

Upon his return Belmont reclaimed his place at the head of the New York social scene. He brought his chef back with him from Europe, raising dinner parties to a new pinnacle. Belmont typically seated up to 200 people at gold place settings. Each guest had a personal footman to serve and remove plates. He also used his private ballroom for lavish parties that lasted until dawn. The cost of all this socializing was high: Belmont's monthly wine bill alone exceeded $20,000.

On the political side, Belmont's falling-out with Buchanan had consequences for the Democrats. Belmont immediately switched his loyalty to Stephen A. Douglas, the senator from Illinois and presidential aspirant. Throughout that period of mounting tension over the slavery issue, Belmont was most concerned with the practical aspects of disunion. He opposed both the Southern secessionist oratory and the "irrepressible conflict" ideas of New

York's Republican senator William H. Seward. He constantly looked for a middle ground.

Belmont believed with Douglas that each state should decide whether or not to permit slavery within its borders. One region should not impose its will on another, just as one person should not tell another how to run his household. Belmont personally opposed slavery. Since coming to the United States he had refused to recognize slaves as negotiable property. He never accepted title to slaves in payment nor recognized them as security for loans. But despite his personal beliefs he refused to impose them on anyone else. To the last he hoped by reason and compromise to prevent secession.

Belmont manifested his pro-Union sympathies in organizing the Democratic Vigilant Association in October 1859. That group of prominent New York merchants who did a great deal of business with the South tried to find a common ground that would avoid sectional conflict.

But as the election of 1860 approached, the conflict could not be dodged. During the campaign Belmont worked diligently for Douglas, especially in the Northeast. After Douglas's nomination by the Northern wing of the split Democratic party, the convention chose Belmont to head the National Committee, not just for his financial position but because of the energy and organizational ability he had shown when working for Douglas.

The 1860 campaign was a factious one, with four candidates competing for the office of president. Belmont found it extremely difficult to raise money because of that split. In a desperate measure to stop Abraham Lincoln's election, he organized fusion tickets in several states, composed of electors for Douglas, John Bell, and John C. Breckinridge. Belmont hoped to deny Lincoln the required number of electoral votes, thereby throwing the election into the House of Representatives. Despite those efforts Lincoln won the election, and Southern secessionist rhetoric rose to an even higher pitch.

Even after the election Belmont tried to promote unity and prevent secession. All of that came to a sudden halt, however, with the attack on Fort Sumter in South Carolina. Once the war was under way Belmont turned from conciliator to proponent of a vigorous military effort. He raised and supplied the first German-American regiment of the Union Army. Officially called the First New York Regiment of Rifles, the group was unofficially known as the "Blenker Regiment" after its com-

mander, Col. Louis Blenker. Belmont himself was precluded from military service by the leg injury he had sustained in the 1841 duel.

Troubles continued for the Democratic party. Belmont and the Democrats were stunned on June 3, 1861, by the sudden death of Stephen A. Douglas. For the second time in his political life Belmont had no leader to serve. In addition, a great void existed in the party: it remained badly divided in the North, and many of its stalwarts had seceded with the South. Driven by circumstances, Belmont became the de facto party leader. He also assumed real power for the first time in his political career. That power was limited, however, by the war in progress, for even as leader of the "loyal opposition" he had to tread lightly. Nevertheless, Belmont continued to work both for the Union and the Democrats.

Although Belmont could not join the military, two areas in his personal skills and contacts helped the Union cause: preventing European recognition of the Confederacy and marketing Union bonds at home and abroad. Belmont plunged into both efforts with his usual energy. On the diplomatic side Belmont used his financial contacts, primarily with the Rothschilds, to reach the ears of British and French government officials. In war financing, the North competed against the South for European capital. Belmont particularly feared Rothschild financing of the South, for this would jeopardize his personal political situation as well as the Northern war effort. Belmont's entreaties successfully prevented the Rothschilds from lending money to the Confederate government.

In June 1861 Belmont sailed for Europe, ostensibly for a family vacation. But he also had the blessing of the Lincoln administration to confer informally with various European governments and to assess their support, financial and otherwise, for the Union war effort. Belmont issued several reports to Lincoln on the foreign situation during his year in Europe. He continued to communicate with the Lincoln administration until after the Battle of Gettysburg in July 1863. By that time Union victories had made foreign intervention unlikely. Furthermore, the approaching 1864 election made contact between the two parties of dubious propriety.

In the postwar period the Democrats opposed the Radical Republicans at every turn and hoped for the rapid return of the South to the Democratic fold. Belmont remained chairman of the Demo-

Belmont in later life (courtesy of the Museum of the City of New York)

cratic National Committee until 1872. In that capacity he presided over the electoral defeats suffered by George B. McClellan and Horatio Seymour. Throughout that time he tried to restore the unity of the Democratic party and heal the wounds of the Civil War.

After twelve years of service Belmont resigned the chairmanship of the committee at the end of the 1872 convention. He had hoped to resign years sooner but did not wish to leave on a losing note. Despite Belmont's best efforts, however, the Democrats never won the presidency under his leadership. But he did change the nature of the chairmanship of the national committee from a part-time campaign-oriented position into an ongoing assignment crucial to the success of the political organization. That, perhaps, constituted Belmont's most enduring contribution to the Democratic party he

loved so dearly. After his resignation Belmont abandoned politics, Fifth Avenue, and Wall Street, spending ten months on a European vacation with his family.

Belmont returned to the United States in the fall of 1873. For the third time in his life he stepped off a boat to find the country in a financial panic. The stock market had crashed, causing numerous business failures. Before the crisis ended, Wall Street was transformed, and many of the old regulars disappeared. Among the casualties was Jay Cooke and Company, one of the most powerful firms in the nation.

Since Belmont was more conservative than many of his business associates, he avoided immediate ruin. Fortunately he also had tied up many loose ends and questionable loans before departing for Europe. Nevertheless, to remain solvent Belmont had to withdraw from all outside activities and focus exclusively on his finances. "I have to curtail my business to a point which renders all profits impossible," he wrote, "hold onto what property I have left, and retrench my expenditure."

Also contributing to Belmont's withdrawal from politics was the illness of his daughter Jeannie. While she had been an invalid for some time, her condition worsened after 1873. On numerous occasions her brothers and sisters left for balls and social events while Jeannie remained confined to her bed. During that period Jeannie's care so consumed the Belmonts that they seldom hosted dinners or other gatherings. That led the opposition *New York Times* to ask: " What has become of the great Mr. Belmont? . . . Is he dead, socially and politically, or is he only sleeping, as they say on the tombstones? . . . Surely Mr. Belmont should make himself seen among his party at the moment. . . . Mr. Belmont may not be a Jefferson, but he is pretty near all the Democrats have left."

Jeannie died on October 15, 1875. Belmont wrote, "It was the first deathbed at which I have ever stood and it was that of my beloved child!" He remained withdrawn for quite some time. "My father is still very much depressed," Perry Belmont wrote to Thomas F. Bayard. "If he could only interest himself in politics, it would be a great thing."

Despite Belmont's mourning, the great prospects for Democratic success in the 1876 election ultimately induced him to return to politics. Though a lukewarm supporter of Democratic candidate Samuel J. Tilden, Belmont worked hard for the ticket.

He also contributed $10,000 to the Tilden campaigns in Indiana and Ohio. When the results of the electoral college became a subject of dispute, Belmont played a behind-the-scenes role in trying to resolve the conflict between Tilden and Republican Rutherford B. Hayes. At the conclusion of the affair Belmont made clear his belief that Tilden's failure to push his cause aggressively enough had cost the Democrats their best opportunity for the presidency in two decades.

After the election Belmont again turned his attention to his family and the social scene. In 1878 he became actively involved with the New York Academy of Music. The academy had lost money for a quarter of a century and had never assembled a permanent opera company. One music critic called its efforts "spasm opera." In 1878 the stockholders refused to pay a new assessment, ousted the current directors, and elected a new board. As a longtime supporter of actors, singers, and dancers, Belmont proved a natural choice to lead the academy and was elected its president.

With customary energy Belmont set out to transform the academy into a quality opera company. He hired a European director with an international reputation, James Henry Mapleson. He also brought in a "star," Hungarian soprano Etelka Gerster. The academy gained popularity as the quality of its offerings increased. Having a subscription to the academy series symbolized one's arrival in New York society. Even in that regard Belmont maintained control over the social scene: as president of the academy he determined who could purchase boxes at the opera.

As 1880 approached, Belmont returned to politics, supporting Thomas F. Bayard for the Democratic presidential nomination. When Bayard failed to receive the nod, Belmont decided to sit out the election. While he still contributed financially to the Democrats he observed more than participated in subsequent years. However, a new Belmont, son Perry, emerged as a political leader, winning election to the House of Representatives in 1880.

The election of 1884 brought the elder Belmont out of retirement one last time. Again he supported Bayard, who ultimately lost the Democratic nomination to Grover Cleveland, governor of New York since 1882 and perhaps the strongest Democratic presidential candidate since the Civil War. As the campaign moved into high gear, Belmont felt slighted by the Democratic National Committee,

which asked him for neither advice nor money until October. The slight eventually was redressed, and Belmont worked for the ticket in the remaining weeks before election day. Cleveland won the election, and Belmont wrote that he was "delighted to have lived long enough to see Democracy once more triumphant."

Since Belmont was an elder statesman of the party one would have expected him to have great influence in the new administration. That, however, was not the case. Although he wrote letters of recommendation for people seeking federal appointments, he had only limited effect. On most political matters Cleveland consulted with Perry Belmont rather than with the father. The press also left Belmont alone after 1884–he no longer constituted an important enough Democrat to attack.

Belmont's health deteriorated rapidly after 1884. His eyesight continued to fail, relegating him to a world of shadows. He suffered increasingly from dyspepsia and rheumatism. His leg injury from the 1841 duel became more painful as time progressed. Making matters worse, an August 1886 fall down the stairs at his home left Belmont bedridden for weeks.

In his last few years Belmont seldom left his home. He turned over most business affairs to his son and namesake, August, Jr., whom he had groomed for the role for many years. The death of another son, Raymond, on January 30, 1887, further depressed and disoriented Belmont. Raymond shot himself with a pistol; authorities never determined if the death was an accident or a suicide.

Perhaps realizing that his remaining years were numbered, Belmont tried to heal some of the political wounds caused by his active campaigning over the years. He even became friends with former opponent Roscoe Conkling. He also remained in touch with the dwindling pool of his old friends. Much of Belmont's correspondence during that period shows his dismay at the changes sweeping the nation and a longing for the America of his youth.

But even to the end Belmont could not turn his back on his adopted city and nation. In 1890 the mayor of New York appointed Belmont to the city's rapid transit commission. Belmont accepted the position, stating that he would resign if the duties became too burdensome. He also came to the aid of George Westinghouse, the inventor and manufacturer. Westinghouse had suffered great losses in the stock market and came to Belmont only after everyone else had refused his requests for financial assistance.

In November 1890 organizers of a horse show at Madison Square Garden asked Belmont to serve as a last-minute replacement for a judge who was forced to withdraw. Belmont threw himself into his duties, perspiring greatly while in the Garden. He then stepped outside into the cold air to summon his carriage. After a restless night's sleep he complained of a fever and cough. A doctor diagnosed Belmont's condition as pneumonia, he soon lapsed into a coma, and he never regained consciousness. He died at three o'clock on the morning of November 24, 1890.

Belmont's funeral was held at the Church of the Ascension, where he and Caroline had been married forty-one years earlier. Among the twelve pallbearers were J. P. Morgan, former president Grover Cleveland, governor of New York David B. Hall, and newspaper editor Manton Marble. Politicians of both parties attended the funeral. That provided a fitting symbol of the unity Belmont had tried to build in the tumultuous war years and a tribute to the degree to which the immigrant banker had become part of the American political scene.

After the funeral a special train carried Belmont's casket to Newport, Rhode Island, where he was buried next to his two children. In keeping with Belmont's wishes all of his horses were sold after his death. The rest of his property and fortune, estimated to be worth between $10 and $50 million, was left to his wife, Caroline, and their remaining children. In assessing Belmont's life one obituary aptly summarized his various contributions:

"He will be remembered as a man who, combining solid business qualities with a noteworthy aptitude for the less serious affairs of life, contributed, certainly in as large a measure as any other of its citizens, to make the city of New York an agreeable place of residence."

Publications:

A Few Letters and Speeches of the Late Civil War (New York: Privately printed, 1870);

Letters, Speeches and Addresses (New York: Privately printed, 1890).

References:

David Black, *The King of Fifth Avenue: The Fortunes of August Belmont* (New York: Dial, 1981);

Richard J. Gottheil, *The Belmont Family: A Record of Four Hundred Years* (Norwood, Mass.: Plimpton, 1917);

Irving Katz, *August Belmont: A Political Biography* (New York: Columbia University Press, 1968);

Louis M. Sears, "August Belmont: Banker in Politics," *Historical Outlook*, 24 (April 1924): 151-154.

Archives:

The records of August Belmont & Company, along with much of Belmont's political correspondence, were destroyed in a 1912 fire at the Equitable Building. There are collections of Belmont's papers at the Houghton Library of Harvard University, the Library of Congress, the Massachusetts Historical Society, the New York Public Library, and the New-York Historical Society. Belmont correspondence can also be found in the manuscript collections of such contemporaries as Thomas F. Bayard and Stephen A. Douglas. Hundreds of Belmont's letters remain in the custody of his descendants.

Thomas Hart Benton

(March 14, 1782-April 10, 1858)

by Janet L. Coryell

Auburn University

CAREER: State senator, Tennessee (1809); U.S. senator, state of Missouri (1820-1850); U.S. representative, state of Missouri (1852-1854).

Thomas Hart Benton, Missouri senator from 1820 to 1850, spoke eloquently for conservative western interests on land, banking, and tariff issues. Often overshadowed by the nineteenth-century political triumvirate of John C. Calhoun, Henry Clay, and Daniel Webster, Benton maintained a Jeffersonian-Jacksonian vision of America as a land of equal opportunity. During his congressional career he promoted the beliefs that land should be easily obtainable for settlement west of the Appalachians, that the tariff should benefit all parts of the national economy, and that banking should be controlled to prevent overextension of note issues. Known as "Old Bullion," the Missouri senator emerged as one of the most visible proponents of a currency composed predominantly of specie.

Benton was born near Hillsborough, North Carolina, on March 14, 1782. His father, Jesse Benton, a lawyer, mill owner, and land speculator, died of tuberculosis in 1791, leaving a widow, Ann Gooch Benton, eight children, and a heavily indebted estate. Benton's mother spent four years after her husband's death clearing the debts, all the while impressing her children with the necessity of paying back debts as a matter of honor. In 1798 Benton left to study at the University of North Carolina at Chapel Hill. His matriculation was inauspicious; he seemed possessed of an ungovernable temper. In a brawl shortly after his arrival he drew a pistol on a fellow student and was stopped from shooting the boy only by the timely arrival of one of the professors. His atrocious behavior continued; three months into the term the school expelled him for stealing money from his companions. He returned home in disgrace, his education temporarily postponed.

Thomas Hart Benton (engraving by John Rogers)

About 1801 Benton's family moved to Tennessee to homestead on the West Harpeth River, 25 miles south of Nashville, on land Benton's father had obtained prior to Tennessee's statehood. Benton taught school from 1804 to 1805 while reading law. He was admitted to the Tennessee bar in 1806 and elected to the state senate in 1809. A Jeffersonian, Benton pushed for reform of the court system, sponsoring a bill to combine law and equity courts and to expand the number of court seats to ensure speedier service. He also campaigned for preemptive land laws, which offered first right of purchase to homesteaders who settled on land to which they did not have legal title. Benton's interest in promoting such a policy reflected his interest in the lands on which his father had speculated. Jesse Benton had claimed more than 30,000 acres in Tennessee and other western lands, but his son never managed to homestead more than the Harpeth River property. Debts from his father's speculative ventures, which his mother had to struggle to pay, ultimately turned Benton against land speculation. That opposition later led him to a belief in the necessity of government promotion of hard-money and tight-credit policies to prevent speculation and the debt that often accompanied it.

As a lawyer in Tennessee, Benton became acquainted with Andrew Jackson, whom he first met when Jackson served as judge for the Superior Court of Law and Equity, Mero District. Jackson had known relatives of Benton's in North Carolina and soon became friends with the Tennessee Bentons. Growing success as a lawyer took Benton away from the state senate, and his growing friendship with Jackson led him into service in the War of 1812. Commissioned as a captain of a volunteer infantry company in April 1812, Benton made colonel in less than a year. He served as an aide to Jackson until a quarrel between them over Jackson's support of a challenger who dueled with Benton's younger brother, Jesse, led to a hotel shoot-out with Jackson and some of his friends. Benton shot Jackson in the shoulder; Jackson's friends stabbed Benton five times. Jackson recovered and did without Benton's aid for the rest of the war, sending him to Nashville as a recruiter instead of into battle. By war's end Benton realized he could scarcely succeed in a city where he had tried to kill its leading son and war hero, so he moved to St. Louis, Missouri.

In St. Louis Benton worked as a lawyer specializing in land claims and titles. In 1817 another duel ended with the death of Benton's opponent, Charles Lucas. It also ended Benton's need to prove himself with firearms. He never dueled again and regretted to his own dying day the death of Lucas. Another misadventure in 1817 also had a lifelong impact. He invested in the Bank of St. Louis, where improvident loans and a fear that the bank's cashier had absconded with funds led Benton and a minority bloc of the bank's stockholders to seize the bank's assets and padlock the building. Benton was arrested but not convicted; the bank eventually reopened but failed within a year. The Panic of 1819 further reinforced Benton's fear of speculation in

banking. Although the panic did not reach Missouri until 1821, when it came the Bank of Missouri, of which he was a stockholder and director, failed. Benton was saddled with a $7,000 debt to the U.S. government for his share of the government's deposits and interest in the bank. In response to this crisis his own fiscal ideology evolved into a belief that paper money should be fully backed by specie. Benton had purchased the *St. Louis Enquirer* in 1819 and used the newspaper to promote his hard-money ideas. But hard-money advocacy ran contrary to the trend in Missouri, where speculators and entrepreneurs wanted easy credit so they could do more business. Missouri had long suffered from an inadequate circulating medium, with such items as animal skins and pelts often serving as money. Paper money promised to be a more portable and popular alternative, especially among new settlers. Benton represented instead the interests of established businesses and conservative farmers, who wanted tighter credit to offset the perilously cyclical economy.

In 1820, as the dust settled from the federal controversy over slavery that led to the Missouri Compromise, Benton was elected U.S. senator from the new state. As he had during his tenure in the Tennessee senate, he sought to encourage western settlement by making it easier to own land. In April 1824 he proposed a "graduation-donation" land policy, suggesting that the government gradually lower the price of public lands if they had not sold within five years of their first offering and "donate" unsold lands to homesteaders upon three-year occupancy. He argued that the policy would engender money enough that the protective tariff could be eliminated. A Graduation Act along those lines became law in 1854, after Benton had left the senate, but its passage owed much to his persistence and vision.

While Benton's ideology encompassed the Jeffersonian ideal of equality of opportunity, he did not embrace the Jeffersonian notion of limited government. In addition to his land policy, Benton, in concert with westerners such as Henry Clay, promoted internal improvements, roads, and canals to link West with East and to promote trade. He advocated using river routes up the Missouri and Columbia to establish trade with the West Coast and thus with the Orient, and called for both a transcontinental road and a railroad to the Pacific. Benton also led the fight to repeal the salt tax in Missouri, be-

Benton, circa 1825 (portrait by Matthew Harris Jouett; courtesy of the Cleveland Museum of Art)

cause salt, the sole food preservative available, was an essential commodity. He also spoke in favor of postroads to ensure effective postal service beyond the Mississippi.

An assignment to the Committee on Military Affairs brought about a reconciliation between Benton and Andrew Jackson, who was elected senator from Tennessee in 1823. By 1828 Benton had rejected Henry Clay to support Jackson's bid for the presidency. He did not follow Jackson wholeheartedly, however, and maintained support for much of Clay's "American System." He supported the tariff of 1828, for instance, because it provided protection for lead, fur, and indigo, Missouri products all. But in 1830, in the midst of the heated debates over South Carolina's nullification of the tariff, he proposed a reduction in rates, hoping to promote an alliance between the South and West. Neither southerners nor antinullifiers supported Benton's fence-straddling bill, and he withdrew it. By the time the crisis came to a head in 1832, Benton stood apart from both Jackson and Clay, opposing Jackson's threat to use troops to force South Carolina into compliance with federal authority and call-

ing Clay's compromise tariff bill an unfair tax on the South.

On fiscal policy Benton showed most clearly his allegiance to Jackson. Jackson's 1832 veto of the bill to recharter the Bank of the United States (BUS) had repercussions throughout the president's second term, and with his vocal support of Jackson's veto Benton emerged as a national hard-money advocate. Like Jackson, Benton opposed the BUS on several grounds. Both men thought the bank was too independent of federal control. They also saw it as corrupt. In his veto message Jackson argued that, since only a tiny minority of Americans owned stock in the bank, the basis of its existence was exclusionary. In addition, foreigners owned much of the stock, and some stockholders worked for the federal government. Conflicts of interest inevitably led to undue influence exercised by the bank over political matters. Jackson and Benton also opposed the power of the BUS to present state-bank notes to the issuers for redemption because the drafts tended to drain specie from the western banks to the East, exacerbating the West's chronic short supply of silver and gold.

Jackson's veto message articulated many of Benton's concerns about the bank, but it did set up conditions for a compromise with BUS forces. BUS president Nicholas Biddle was, however, determined to turn the contest into a political referendum on the BUS rather than meet Jackson's criticisms. He lost. Benton supported Jackson's veto as well as the president's decision to remove federal deposits from the BUS and deposit them in state "pet" banks. But Benton did not trust state banks to issue sound paper currency any more than the BUS; in fact, he more and more thought paper money unsound even when fully backed by specie.

After Jackson's veto, a financial panic in 1834 led Benton to charge that Biddle had created the panic to ensure recharter of the BUS. His accusation had a certain amount of truth, and his view was reinforced when the bank expanded credit in September 1834 after Biddle lost the support of business leaders in major cities for his tightened credit policies.

After the short-term panic had subsided Benton outlined on the Senate floor his idea for a financial system based strictly on hard money. He argued that the Constitution provided only for specie currency, but he offered to bow to the increasing complexity of the financial system by allowing for specie-backed large bank notes and large bills of exchange. He declared his opposition to the issue of notes of less than $20 and proposed the revaluation of gold to suppress such issues. In the existing system, he argued, "if a bank stops payment [of specie], the holders of the small notes, who are usually the working part of the community, are the last to find out, and the first to suffer."

Benton's logical and erudite two-day speech in favor of specie earned him the nickname "Old Bullion," and he won in his effort to revalue gold. The old silver-to-gold ratio, defining the weight of a silver dollar in relation to a gold dollar, was upped from 15 to 1 to 16 to 1. The revaluation bill passed with bipartisan approval, and the economy improved, partly spurred by the more rational valuation of specie. Benton's popularity soared. A Democratic convention meeting in Mississippi unofficially nominated him to run as vice-president in 1836 (he declined consideration), and some saw Benton as next in line for the presidency after Jackson's hand-picked successor, Martin Van Buren, served the anticipated eight years. The close ties between Benton and Jackson were further strengthened when Benton used the last days of Jackson's second term to work on the expunction from the *Congressional Record* of Henry Clay's 1834 Senate resolution censuring Jackson for his veto of the BUS recharter bill. He succeeded in January 1837 and sent the pen used to delete the censure to Jackson as a gift. In appreciation Jackson bequeathed the pen to Benton in his will.

In 1836, continuing to press for the adoption of a hard-money policy, Benton proposed a "Specie Resolution" that would require payment for public lands to be made only in gold and silver. The resolution never passed, but Jackson adopted Benton's ideas in an executive order, the Specie Circular of July 1836. Unintended consequences resulted from the order. The circular strove to prevent the speculation rampant under paper money, but because specie was so scarce in the West, many who wanted to buy land found themselves shut out. The order exacerbated an increasingly difficult economic situation. The increased demand for specie strained the resources of western banks; a decline in cotton prices added to their difficulties. Most important, the effects of higher British interest rates, mandated by a fall in Mexican silver output, finally reached the United States. In May 1837 New York City's banks suspended payment of their bank notes and the

Contemporary drawing of Benton addressing the U.S. Senate during his successful fight in 1837 to expunge from the Congressional Record *a resolution censuring Andrew Jackson for his veto of a bill to recharter the Bank of the United States*

Panic of 1837 began. In 1839 a bumper crop of cotton brought still lower prices for that important export commodity, and the national depression deepened.

Benton saw the Panic of 1837 as another artificial creation, part of a plot to force the recharter of the BUS, despite the fact that southern cotton farmers and New England industrialists alike cited the higher British rates as the source of their troubles. But Nicholas Biddle made a more obvious and easy target on whom to blame the financial distress.

In his home state for a reelection campaign in 1838 Benton saw that Missouri's hard-money policy meant the state suffered little in the early years of the panic. The state's economy also benefited from trade along the Santa Fe Trail, which ran from Independence, Missouri, west to the silver mines of Santa Fe in Mexico. Since Missouri had plenty of specie, Benton reasoned, other states that followed his hard-money course would also have it in abundance. But he never acknowledged the hardships under which frontier regions that lacked specie labored. Nor did he acknowledge the weaknesses in his own state's economy caused by the state banking monopoly. He never explained where the United States could obtain enough specie for a currency such as he envisioned, nor did he pause to note that many of the coins circulating in the United States were Spanish. Benton's ideas were popular among many conservative Missourians. However, it was not state banks but a central bank that would be able, through its note-issue functions, to keep the money supply close to 100 percent specie equivalence more easily than could a myriad of state banks. Thus, Benton's opposition to the central bank system exemplified in the BUS took him away from, not closer to, his goal of hard money.

Reelected by a large margin, Benton returned to Washington to meet in a special session of Congress called by President Van Buren to announce plans for dealing with the panic. Van Buren refused to recharter the BUS or revoke the Specie Circular. Instead he proposed an "Independent Treasury" system in which the government would keep its own funds separate from the banking system of the United States. The Independent Treasury Bill was introduced in special session in 1837, and Benton led the fight for the president's program. He made clear his opposition to new state bank charters as well, saying, "I did not join in putting down the Bank of the United States to put up a wilderness of state banks." Passed by the Senate but tabled by the House, the Independent Treasury plan stalled in 1838, and the administration met the continuing financial crisis by issuing treasury notes to raise funds. Benton was aghast at what he considered Van Buren's connivance regarding the paper issue and refused to vote for the notes, even though failure of the bill would have meant the government could not meet its payroll. The bill passed, however, and the special session ended with the government in the black.

Van Buren's Independent Treasury Bill finally passed in 1840, with Benton's wholehearted support. In addition to providing a Sub-Treasury system for the deposit of federal funds, in lieu of the state banks, specie was made the only acceptable currency for payment to the government, which meant that specie would decline as a percentage of the circu-

lating medium, not increase as Benton had hoped. Benton thought he was seeing the triumph of his hard-money program. In fact, he was spared from seeing the disappearance of specie as a part of the currency (and the subsequent collapse of trade) when, in 1841, Clay and the Whigs attempted to reestablish a national bank and forced the repeal of the Sub-Treasury system. The Clay forces failed to recharter the bank, however, and federal money was again transferred to state banks until the Independent Treasury was restored in 1846.

Benton did not oppose the Whig program of looser credit without an alternate plan to increase revenue. In 1838 he led a fight for a new graduation bill to lower prices on unsold public lands. Benton's support for such a policy was ironic. Support of the graduation bill showed he wanted to encourage frontier land purchases, but his hard-money ideology, his support of the restriction of federal payments in specie, tended to tighten credit because it stressed state banks. The graduation bill did pass the Senate, despite opposition from the Whigs, led by Clay, and leading Democrats James Buchanan and John C. Calhoun. It foundered in the House, however, and Benton put the issue on the back burner.

Benton continued to advocate hard-money policies in the Senate and in his home state. In the wake of the panic-induced collapse of banks in the South and Old Northwest he stood well outside the party's mainstream that advocated free incorporation of banks. Benton's reelection campaign in 1844 focused less on fiscal policy than on the Texas question raised by Calhoun's proposal that Texas be annexed and divided into five separate slave states. Benton opposed Texas annexation first on the grounds that it would be an unjust act of war against Mexico. In addition he protested against the extension of slavery into the new territories, declaring to his fellow southerners in the Senate that while he was a slaveowner and would preserve the rights of slaveholders in existing slave regions, he would vote his convictions on the issue of extension even if it meant political suicide. Most Missourians, anxious to expand the plantation system, favored Calhoun's position. In a Missouri growing increasingly hostile not only to Benton's hard-money ideology but also to his seeming antislavery stance, he won by only a slim margin.

Back in Washington for what would be his last Senate term, Benton, with his Senate colleagues, was increasingly consumed by the issue of the extension of slavery into U.S. territories. Texas joined the Union as a slave state on December 29, 1849. When Representative David Wilmot of Pennsylvania attached to an appropriations bill a proviso prohibiting the extension of slavery into territories acquired from Mexico as a result of the Mexican War, Benton opposed it, citing the danger to the Union rather than the constitutionality of congressional legislation against territorial slavery. But in 1849 Benton used the provisions of the Northwest Ordinance of 1787 as a precedent to argue that Congress could legislate against slavery. (One of the provisions of the ordinance creating the Northwest Territories defined all persons born in the region as freemen.) In debates over an omnibus bill proposed by Henry Clay to resolve the problem of the admission of California, the organization of new territories, and other issues, Benton opposed compromise, arguing that Clay's proposal to extend the Missouri Compromise line dividing the nation into free and slave sections would lead to war. If Congress gave in to secessionists' demands for opening the West to popular sovereignty, they would continue to blackmail Congress until they had complete control of the government. For Benton, disunion posed a far greater threat than attacks on slavery, and he voted accordingly. But his negative stance on the bills that turned out to be the Compromise of 1850 guaranteed his political demise in the senatorial election of that year.

Benton continued to serve his nation and state after his defeat. He was elected to the House of Representatives for one term beginning in 1852 and ran for governor of Missouri in 1856. Though he lost the governorship, Benton did not lose interest in politics. He began an insider's account of Congress called *Thirty Years' View* in 1854, finishing the two-volume work in 1856, even after losing most of his manuscript in a house fire in 1855. He then began to edit an *Abridgement of the Debates*

of Congress from 1789 to 1856, a 16-volume work that occupied his last days, along with a book refuting the Dred Scott decision, published in 1857. On April 9, 1858, he dictated the last words of the 16th volume of the *Debates;* on April 10 he died of intestinal cancer. Two days later his grandson, McDowell Benton Jones, the son of his eldest daughter, also died. Grandfather and grandson were buried together in St. Louis. Benton was preceded in death by his wife, Elizabeth McDowell Benton, in 1854, and by his three sons, James McDowell Benton, Benton McDowell Benton, and John Randolph Benton. His daughters, Eliza Benton Jones, Susan Benton de Boileau, Jessie Benton Fremont, and Sarah Benton Jacobs, survived him.

Publications:

Thirty Years' View; or, A History of the Workings of the American Government for Thirty Years, from 1820 to 1850, 2 volumes (New York: Appleton, 1854-1856);

Historical and Legal EXAMINATION of that Part of the Decision of the Supreme Court of the United States in the DRED SCOTT CASE, Which Declares the Unconstitutionality of the Missouri Compromise Act, and the Self-Extension of the Constitution to Territories, Carrying Slavery Along With It (New York: Appleton, 1857);

Abridgement of the Debates of Congress from 1789 to 1856, 16 volumes, edited by Benton (New York: Appleton, 1857-1863).

References:

William N. Chambers, *Old Bullion Benton: Senator from the West* (Boston: Little, Brown, 1956);

Elbert B. Smith, *Magnificent Missourian: The Life of Thomas Hart Benton* (Philadelphia: Lippincott, 1958).

Archives:

Most of Thomas Hart Benton's papers were destroyed when his house burned in 1855. Those remaining are at the Missouri Historical Society, St. Louis, and the Missouri State Historical Society, Columbia.

Nicholas Biddle

(January 8, 1786-February 27, 1844)

by Edwin J. Perkins

University of Southern California

CAREER: Personal secretary to John Armstrong, U.S. ambassador to France (1804-1807); lawyer, Philadelphia, Pennsylvania (1807-1811); state assemblyman, Pennsylvania (1810-1811); state senator, Pennsylvania (1814-1816); director (1819-1821), president, Bank of the United States (1823-1839).

Nicholas Biddle was the nation's foremost commercial banker during the first half of the nineteenth century, and he ranks high among the most important financial leaders in American history. He was president of the Second Bank of the United States (BUS) from 1823 until 1839. During his tenure in office, the BUS exerted a powerful impact on the American economy, in part because it performed at least some of the functions typically associated with modern central banking. The confrontation between Biddle and President Andrew Jackson over rechartering the bank in 1832 ranks among the nation's most publicized political controversies. When the national charter expired in 1836, Biddle obtained a substitute from the state of Pennsylvania. In the late 1830s the bank engaged heavily in speculative activity linked to the cotton market and never fully recovered. Biddle resigned the presidency in March 1839, and two years later the bank went into liquidation.

Nicholas Biddle was born on January 8, 1786, the fourth son of Charles and Hannah Shepherd Biddle. His father was a successful Philadelphia merchant; his mother had been reared in North Carolina. Biddle was an intellectually precocious child. His parents enrolled him at the University of Pennsylvania at age ten. Three years later he transferred to the College of New Jersey, at Princeton, where he entered the sophomore class. The college had a modern curriculum for its era: in addition to the classics the faculty offered courses in mathematics, science, composition, public speaking, history, and philosophy. In his political views

Nicholas Biddle, 1837 (engraving by John Sartain from a portrait by Thomas Sully)

young Biddle leaned toward the Federalist party and expressed dislike for the ideas of Democrats such as Thomas Jefferson and Thomas Paine. He graduated in September 1801 at age fifteen, the youngest person to receive a degree from the college up to that date.

For the next two years Biddle lived at home in Philadelphia and continued his education, including a sampling of books on the law, on his own. In 1804 he was offered the opportunity to serve as personal secretary to John Armstrong, who had just been named U.S. ambassador to France. For most of the following three years, from October 1804 to July 1807, young Biddle lived in Paris and traveled throughout much of Europe. He was present in the American embassy when Napoleon's continental system was in effect and thus witnessed important events during a period of high activity in Franco-American diplomacy. During his stay in Paris he became well acquainted with James Monroe, who was also stationed at the embassy. Monroe, as president, later named him to serve as one of five government directors of the Second BUS.

Upon returning to Philadelphia in 1807, Biddle joined his brother William's law office. He handled mostly civil cases, especially debt collections. As a young man he had a wide range of interests that extended far beyond the world of business and law. For example, he contributed regularly to a local magazine, *Port Folio*, which published articles on culture, art, and history. Indeed, his literary reputation earned him an invitation in 1810 to edit for publication the lengthy journals compiled by the famous explorers Lewis and Clark on their expedition across the continent to the Pacific Coast from 1804 to 1806. Later that same year the Republican party (Federalists had virtually disappeared) nominated him to run for Pennsylvania's lower house; he was elected, and so too was his father, but to the state's upper chamber.

On January 8, 1811, his twenty-fifth birthday, Biddle made his first major legislative speech. He spoke to oppose a motion urging Pennsylvania's two U.S. senators to vote against the recharter application of the First Bank of the United States. (At that early date U.S. senators were elected by the state legislature, not directly by popular vote, and they frequently received pointed advice from the state capital.) The First BUS had been a controversial institution since its creation in 1792, with much of the criticism focused on its alleged unconstitutionality. The power and depth of his three-hour address came as somewhat of a surprise to members of the legislature, since Biddle was a political unknown and an assemblyman who had revealed no public association with the bank issue.

Biddle defended the national bank in practice and in principle. He rebutted every argument against its continuation. He asserted that the institution was not unduly influenced by foreign stockholders nor did it tend to widen the division between the rich and poor, as critics contended. On the contrary, he argued, the First BUS, despite a large number of foreign stockholders, had contributed greatly to the stability of the American financial system and generally promoted economic development. Biddle claimed that banks, on balance, constituted democratic institutions because they expanded the range of credit opportunities, thus lessening the financial power of wealthy households over their neighbors. The final vote in the Pennsylvania legislature went against his position, but Biddle had forcefully identified himself as an articulate spokesman for the concept of a large national bank.

In an extremely close vote in Congress a few months later, the charter of the First BUS failed to gain renewal. The bank liquidated its assets and paid off all its creditors and investors in full. The timing of its demise proved most unfortunate because the nation soon entered into the War of 1812, and the national bank's assistance in raising funds to fight the war was sorely missed.

In the fall of 1811 Biddle married Jane Craig, and the union made a substantial impact on his career plans. Jane was the daughter of a moderately wealthy Philadelphia widow who owned several valuable properties in the local area. After their October wedding the couple traveled to Washington, D.C., visited Secretary of State James Monroe, and paid their respects to President James Madison. Returning to Philadelphia, Biddle retired from the practice of law and assumed management of the Craig family estate called "Andalusia," located about 15 miles outside the city. He intended to concentrate henceforth on agriculture, politics, and civic affairs. He finished the editorial work on the Lewis and Clark collection around this time, and it appeared in print a few years later.

Biddle was no mere gentleman farmer, but someone who, although completely inexperienced, pursued the challenge of farm management quite seriously. He had a keen interest in scientific experimentation regarding both crops and livestock, and he relayed his discoveries to other interested agriculturalists in speeches and articles. In his address to the Philadelphia Society for the Promotion of Agriculture in January 1822, for example, Biddle talked about the modern equipment and innovative techniques that he had successfully employed on his estate.

Biddle had declined to stand for reelection to the Pennsylvania lower house after his initial term, but he won election to the state's upper chamber in 1814. Public debate about reviving a national bank filled the air, and Biddle avidly supported the idea. He went on record declaring that any new bank should have dual goals: generating profits for stockholders and providing vital aid to the government in crisis. During that period he maintained a steady correspondence with government officials in Washington, including a monthly exchange of letters with President Monroe. Biddle had ambitions for high political office, but not much materialized over the next few years. He ran unsuccessfully for the U.S. House of Representatives in 1818, and again in 1820. Meanwhile, President Monroe in January 1819 named him as one of the five directors representing the federal government on the board of the directors of the headquarters office of the Second BUS in Philadelphia.

The Second BUS had received congressional approval in 1816 and opened its doors under the leadership of William Jones, a Philadelphian who had questionable business credentials but strong political connections. During the first year of operations the bank originated a large volume of loans in its branches located near the nation's southern and western frontiers. Specie reserves dropped dramatically, and by the summer of 1818 the bank flirted with suspension and possible failure. A sharp curtailment of loan obligations in the second half of 1818 turned the situation around, but criticism of Jones's management persisted. A congressional investigating committee was appointed late in the year, and it issued a report in January 1819 highly critical of Jones—who immediately resigned.

Biddle was a newly appointed member of the board of directors that recruited South Carolina's Langdon Cheves to assume the bank's presidency in March 1819. Biddle supported Cheves's candidacy and continued to offer his support throughout the difficult months surrounding the Panic of 1819. The former president had been too permissive in his lending policies, Biddle believed, and the stark contrast of Cheves's cautious conservatism attracted him.

Yet, as the months passed, Biddle entertained doubts about the new president's overly restrictive program. After the panic atmosphere had subsided Cheves continued to hold tight on the credit reins and to accumulate larger specie reserves. By the end of 1820 the bank's ratio of reserves to bank-note and deposit liabilities had climbed to more than 60 percent. If a reserve ratio of 30 percent represents a reasonable level of safety for a large bank with a

chain of branch offices throughout the states, then Cheves's hoard of specie was double the amount necessary for prudent operations. Moreover, by stressing excessive safety over the legitimate credit requirements of farmers and merchants, the bank acted as a drag on the economy rather than as an aid to a quick rebound.

Biddle was upset too because Cheves's limitations on lending reduced the volume of earning assets and prevented the bank from generating sufficient interest revenues to resume the payment of dividends to long-suffering stockholders. Still, he voted to reelect Cheves at the board meeting in January 1821. He took the occasion to criticize rather vocally the policy of permitting borrowers who offered bank stock as collateral to negotiate loans that ran as high as the stock's nominal par value. Since dividends had been suspended, the market value of bank stock had fallen below par, and Biddle felt strongly about the impropriety of making loans that were not, in actuality, fully secured by adequate collateral. As a consequence he wrote President Monroe a spirited letter of resignation in December 1821 and left the board.

In the fall of 1822 Cheves announced his impending retirement. The outgoing president wanted Thomas Ellicott of Baltimore, another staunch conservative, to succeed him, but too many people remained unconvinced about his qualifications. The names of Albert Gallatin, the former treasury secretary, and Thomas Willing, former president of the First BUS, surfaced, but they expressed an unwillingness to serve. Through a process of elimination Biddle's name moved to the forefront of the list. His main support came from an influential group of Philadelphia stockholders. His old friend President Monroe added an endorsement. At the first board meeting in 1823 Biddle was elected the bank's third president, and he promptly assumed office on January 7, one day shy of his thirty-seventh birthday.

The institution over which he presided was by far the largest business enterprise in the nation. Its capital of $35 million was gigantic by contemporary standards. By law the bank was the only institution granted permission to establish a multibranch system throughout the United States. It had branches located in 16 commercial cities throughout the nation, including an outlet in most states. Under Jones's administration the branches had operated in autonomous fashion. From 1819 to 1822

Biddle in his early years (portrait by Henry Inman)

Cheves had placed strict limitations on the loans of certain offices in the southern and western states, but he had never shown much interest in coordinating the operations of all the branches.

Biddle planned to make sweeping changes in the bank's financial strategies and its administrative practices. He wanted to improve the bank's profitability, which had weakened because of the losses sustained during the panic and because of Cheves's ultraconservative asset management in the early 1820s. The bank resumed semiannual dividend payments in the second half of 1821, but the annual payout in 1822 only reached 3.5 percent of the original issue price. Under Biddle, profits rose steadily if not spectacularly. By 1827 the dividend rate rose to 6 percent and two years later to 7 percent, a figure that Biddle thought reasonable. He did not return additional profits to stockholders in cash dividends but used the funds to build up retained earnings (called a surplus account in the nineteenth century); by 1836 he had added about $6.5 million to capital through the retention of earnings.

Biddle exercised vastly more administrative control over the Second BUS than his two predecessors. He paid strict attention to the management of

the branch offices and particularly to the selection of the personnel in charge of decision making. The two key officials in each branch location were the president and cashier. The branch's board of directors elected a president from among its ranks, which meant that the successful candidate was a local businessman who had the solid support of peers in the mercantile community.

Biddle made his influence felt in the branches by offering recommendations regarding the composition of the various local boards. He suggested names for new directors whenever vacancies arose. Biddle favored men with outstanding mercantile credentials, with little consideration given to their political leanings. He preferred men with substantial liquid wealth who relied only occasionally on commercial bank financing. He tried to rule out individuals proposed as board members on the basis of political patronage alone. Over time the president hoped to depoliticize the 17 separate boards of directors and to make the Second BUS a highly professional institution, and he succeeded on that score admirably in most people's estimation—but not, unfortunately, in the estimation of President Andrew Jackson and a few of his closest advisers. When a vote to elect the president of a local branch was scheduled, Biddle likewise offered a list of rank-ordered names. Local boards almost always agreed with his first selection for the presidency, since careful negotiations between powerful community leaders and the headquarters office in Philadelphia had invariably preceded the actual vote.

To keep him apprised of local developments in the branch cities, Biddle had a group of confidential correspondents with whom he regularly exchanged facts, rumors, and opinions. Often his confidants served as members of the local board, but others included prominent business leaders unconnected with the bank. Biddle valued his network of confidants because his sources provided vital information on local developments and kept him current about economic trends in every section of the country.

The main vehicle for realizing centralized administrative control under the direction of the bank's Philadelphia headquarters was through the office of cashier. Depending on how managerial responsibilities were divided in the various branches, the cashier was either the first or the second most important official in terms of fundamental decision making. The directors in Philadelphia appointed all the branch cashiers, which meant that Biddle had an instrumental role in their selection, and that cashiers considered themselves accountable primarily to him rather than to local boards. Over the years Biddle replaced the existing branch cashiers, selected originally from pools of local candidates, with loyal bank employees who were first properly trained in the Philadelphia office and then rewarded with appointments in the branches. By promoting largely from within the organization Biddle hoped to attract outstanding employees and to strengthen the institution both geographically and internally.

Besides exerting control over the selection of managerial personnel in the branches, Biddle instituted various formal and informal mechanisms to keep posted on branch operations. He demanded a steady flow of critical information from the local offices. Financial statements and accounts came into Philadelphia, and, after careful review, Biddle frequently returned them with requests for further clarification. Instructions on the management of loan portfolios and operational details flowed out to local presidents and cashiers. To check on the accuracy of accounting records and to discourage fraud, Biddle scheduled regular inspections by teams of cashiers from the main office or assembled from personnel posted to other branches. His chief assistant, Thomas Cadwalader, headed some of the review panels.

Biddle was in many ways the forerunner of the modern business executive. He sought the best means of effectively managing a large, geographically dispersed enterprise. He employed innovative techniques, which explains why contemporaries often depicted his methods as dictatorial and uncompromising. Although he centralized policy-making, he still placed a great deal of emphasis on the sound judgment and responsibility of local boards and local bank officers. The financial historian Fritz Redlich drafted a succinct personality profile: "He was forceful and strong-willed, but at the same time urbane, even-tempered, and considerate of the well-being and interests of his collaborators and subordinates. Biddle considered a certain harshness of disposition, which he undoubtedly possessed, as indispensable for dealing with debtors and employees." Redlich added: "He was able equally to grasp a total situation and to master detail, and being a man of both thought and action, he was an unusual specimen of the genus business administrator."

In addition to administrative reform Biddle launched several new policy initiatives to improve the performance of the Second BUS. Both Jones and Cheves had been tentative about how to handle the routine inflow of bank notes issued by hundreds of independent state banks into the Second BUS's branch network. At one point Cheves had ordered the offices in the southern and western states to pay out the accumulated notes of the various state banks when making new loans to credit customers. Biddle altered the policy. He planned instead to transfer the state bank notes to the branch nearest the issuing bank as soon as possible and to present them to the issuers for redemption immediately upon receipt.

The advantages of that policy were several-fold. The inflow of gold and silver bolstered the branches' own reserves. Equally important, the constant pressure on the specie reserves of the state banks made their managers think twice about expanding the volume of outstanding bank notes beyond prudent levels. Through its vigorous specie-redemption policy the Second BUS acted as a de facto commercial banking regulator; it acted as a watchdog over the entire American banking system, preventing the overexpansion of loans and bank notes by individual state banks. In negotiating customer loans Biddle ordered his cashiers to pay out the currency of the Second BUS in every circumstance. As a result its currency became truly national in scope. By 1830 the notes issued by the various branches were interchangeable at par, or at most up to a 1 percent discount, in the Philadelphia and New York money markets. In 1827 Biddle introduced branch drafts as a supplement to bank notes, and their use facilitated the transfer of funds within the organization.

Biddle changed the general character of loans in the bank's portfolio. Cheves had favored so-called accommodation loans of indeterminate length secured by other financial assets such as stocks and bonds—including the bank's own outstanding stock. Biddle wanted to concentrate more on discounting mercantile paper maturing within 30 to 90 days. His emphasis on short-term paper and a high degree of liquidity coincided more closely with the prevailing theories of respected economists about the primary purposes of commercial banks. Indeed, Biddle's elevated reputation, granted him by the nation's leading financial historians in the late-nineteenth and early-twentieth centuries, rests in large part on the president's decision to allow his lending policies to be guided by the "real-bills doctrine" of commercial banking. While Biddle was drawn to the logic of the real-bills approach, he was not single-minded in its pursuit, and when altered circumstances–different seasons and different locales–suggested the wisdom of negotiating loans with longer maturities based on other collateral, he showed enough flexibility to make sensible adjustments. The bank was not strictly a private enterprise but a partially public institution accountable to the national electorate, and, as a consequence, Biddle had to make some effort to meet the varied credit needs of customers in every branch city.

Biddle used the bank's geographical spread to become heavily involved in exchange operations: the purchase and sale of drafts with varying maturity dates drawn in one locale on a designated payee in a distant city. By the mid 1820s the Second BUS actively engaged in markets for both domestic and foreign exchange. Exchange profits generated less than 10 percent of net earnings in 1824, but their contribution rose to as much as two-fifths of net earnings by the early 1830s. Domestic exchange generated the largest volume of business, since the bank was ideally situated to serve citizens with intersectional debts in the transfer of moneys between trading and financial centers. Domestic bills typically matured in three to four months. The expanding transportation network, including canals and railroads, fostered interregional trade, which in turn created opportunities for profitable operations in domestic exchange. Evidence suggests that Biddle encountered little competition in the market for domestic exchange. The Second BUS had the structural organization to handle those operations expeditiously, and its transactions fees, usually in the range of 0.5 to 2 percent of a bill's face value, were generally much lower than other firms asked to perform identical services.

In the field of foreign exchange the Second BUS operated its account in conjunction with the House of Baring. The agency arrangement was already apparently in place when Biddle assumed the presidency, but the volume of transactions expanded under his administration. By the mid 1820s the bank had emerged as the market leader in the purchase and sale of sterling bills, and it remained in the lead until the federal charter expired in 1836. Again, the bank's geographical network created the conditions conducive to profitable foreign exchange operations. The main competition in the foreign exchange market came from the Anglo-American merchant banking firm headed by Baltimore's Alexander Brown, which also possessed a network of branch offices and agencies in major port cities. The Browns generally deferred to the Second BUS in establishing rates for the sale of first-class sterling bills. The bank's bills sold for the very highest prices because customers willingly paid a premium to acquire sterling obligations backed by an enormous capital and the unparalleled reputation of the Barings.

Biddle used the bank's domineering presence in the exchange markets, domestic and foreign, as an effective tool for exerting influence over American financial markets. Whether he deserves classification as a full-fledged central banker is questionable, but few can doubt that Biddle intervened in financial markets with the goal of smoothing out geographical and seasonal fluctuations and creating greater economic stability. He shifted the bank's resources from section to section to provide seasonal funding for the foreign trade sector, thereby leading to a dampening in the amplitude of exchange-rate movements. He had the capital and the organizational network that allowed a quick response to price signals and money rates emanating from various markets throughout the nation.

In the late fall and winter months Biddle ordered the purchase of large amounts of sterling bills of exchange from cotton shippers through the southern branches. In spring and summer he reversed the process and sold heavily to meet the requirements of importers based along the Atlantic coast. Through his vast correspondence he carefully monitored reports of prevailing exchange rates in the major ports, north and south, in an effort to determine exactly when to start and halt seasonal operations. The sale of huge quantities of sterling bills, without offsetting purchases until months later, was made possible by drawing upon the credit lines made available by Baring Brothers in London. Prior to 1829 the credit line was £100,000; thereafter it rose to £250,000 (roughly $1.25 million). By 1830 the bank earned between $75,000 to $100,000 annually from foreign exchange operations.

In addition to seasonal smoothing of the financial markets, Biddle demonstrated in 1825 that he was prepared to serve the public interest in a crisis. The late fall always proved a period of vulnerability for the U.S. banking system during the nineteenth century. Beginning in September and October, deposits in the eastern money centers were systematically diverted to farm regions to finance the shipment of recently harvested crops. In early November 1825, with reserves low, a panic atmosphere brewed in Philadelphia and New York. In the sudden scramble for liquidity, commercial banks refused to renew maturing loans of many mercantile customers, which threatened some with bankruptcy.

After a few weeks of turmoil Biddle took decisive action to stabilize the situation. He ordered branch managers in the money centers to expand their volume of loans. "The object," he told one correspondent, "should be to ease the community." He hoped to send a clear signal to participants in the financial markets that the Second BUS was not going to pull in its horns as Cheves had done in 1819 and 1820. He planned to use the bank's vast resources to provide leadership—by rekindling the flagging confidence of state bankers and mercantile borrowers alike.

As it happened the downturn was short-lived, and the economy was robust again by the summer of 1826. Monetary historians have invariably given Biddle high marks for the boldness and good judgment he displayed in 1825, and they have awarded him most of the credit for preventing a sharp correction from degenerating into prolonged depression. He demonstrated, for the first time in U.S. history, the effectiveness of responsible and timely action by the nation's largest and most influential banking institution.

On another occasion, in 1828, Biddle used the bank's position in an effort to achieve a very different result. Because of heavy demand the rates for sterling bills had started inching up steadily. In November rates finally moved beyond the specie export point, the threshold price at which American firms found it less costly to ship specie across the Atlantic than to acquire foreign bills of exchange from brokers and dealers. Biddle feared that the continued loss of specie reserves would drive up interest rates, restrict credit facilities, and possibly trigger a panic. Therefore he decided upon a policy of credit rationing; in early January 1828 the president instructed branch managers to freeze the loans of all merchants and dealers suspected of drawing down specie from banks for export.

Biddle's effort to exert influence over international specie flows proved largely ineffective, how-

ever, because other leading dealers in the foreign exchange market operated well beyond his reach. The Browns, for example, had substantial capital resources of their own and were thus free of any reliance on loans from commercial banks. While exchange rates remained high, the Browns sold bills at market prices and continued to ship specie to England at a handsome profit, thwarting Biddle's retention program.

These circumstances led to some acrimony between Biddle and Alexander Brown, the Brown family patriarch. Biddle was upset to learn that the Browns were, in his judgment, placing the pursuit of private greed above their responsibility for the public welfare. Brown disputed the contention and expressed anger over Biddle's allegedly unwarranted attempt to forcefully intervene in the foreign-exchange market. Brown thought the normal price-stabilization mechanism associated with the maintenance of a specie standard should be allowed to run its course and that specie exports were necessary to achieve that end. One lesson emerging from that episode was that there were clear limits on Biddle's power over markets and other independent firms; although the Second BUS remained the dominant force in the foreign-exchange field, it had neither a dictatorial nor a monopolistic position.

The most famous political confrontation over the institutional structure of the American banking system revolved around Biddle and President Jackson. Both men were self-assured, stubborn, and, ultimately, uncompromising. Jackson envisioned himself as a champion of the masses in the battle against privilege and monopoly. He dealt mainly in the realm of rhetoric, emphasizing democratic ideology. In contrast Biddle focused on the practicalities, namely that the Second BUS had benefited the nation as a whole, irrespective of class, and contributed to steady economic growth. As generally happens in such classic confrontations, elements of truth existed on all sides. The issue came to a head in the debate over a congressional bill to recharter the bank in 1832. In the showdown Jackson won and Biddle lost. This disastrous defeat for the proud banker dealt him a setback from which he never fully recovered—although he remained at the helm of the bank for seven additional turbulent years.

The operation of the large nationally chartered bank had been controversial since the inception of the First BUS in 1791. Many critics had challenged its constitutionality, among them Thomas Jefferson and James Madison. Some saw the bank as a vehicle for expanding the power of the urban rich at the expense of yeoman farmers. In their presidential terms, however, Jefferson and Madison and some of their followers modified their opposition to the bank in light of its seemingly positive influence on the economy. But reservations persisted. In a very close congressional vote in 1811, the First BUS was denied recharter. In 1816, after the War of 1812, Congress created the Second BUS, modeled after its predecessor but with a capital more than three times larger, and another 20-year charter life.

Not long after the national bank's reestablishment came the Panic of 1819, and the Second BUS received much criticism for alleged mismanagement. Former opponents revived old doubts about its propriety. After Biddle took over the presidency in 1823 the bank made new enemies within the ranks of state bankers, who resented Biddle's policy of regularly presenting their bank notes for redemption in specie. By the mid 1820s the Second BUS was not a highly popular institution for one reason or another. Over the next few years, however, the owners and managers of state banks in most regions grew more accustomed to conducting operations under the bank's controlling mechanisms. State bankers discovered that in the stable environment they were still able to earn a satisfactory, and now much more predictable, return on equity. By the end of the decade Biddle had won over the majority of his critics within the banking field—and along with them most of the politicians who represented the interests of state bankers in Congress.

Indeed, Biddle succeeded with every major group except diehard constitutionalists, hard-money advocates, and those who remained suspicious of banks in general and of large banks in particular. Unfortunately, the most prominent person fitting into all three opposition categories was President Jackson. Ironically, Biddle had voted for Jackson in 1824, when John Quincy Adams had won, and again in 1828 when the "Hero of New Orleans" proved victorious. No one had raised the future of the bank as a serious issue in the 1828 campaign, which pleased Biddle greatly and gave him a false sense of security.

Biddle knew that Jackson harbored no friendship for the banking community, but he had no idea of the depth of the president's animosity to the continuance of the Second BUS under the existing charter provisions. Historians have speculated for years about the underlying reason for Jackson's attitudes toward banks. Some claim his views stemmed from an incident early in his career, when he pursued wealth and fame in Tennessee. In a routine business transaction Jackson had endorsed a debt instrument that went sour when the signer defaulted, and bankers allegedly pursued him for years to make it good, adding penalty fees along the way. Other experts believe that Jackson opposed only certain types of banks and that he might have supported a national bank organized under a revised charter, which would have exercised even greater central control over the money stock and the various state systems. Numerous hypotheses seem plausible under the circumstances.

In his inaugural address in 1829 Jackson mentioned the bank only in passing. He suggested that continuance of the bank might require alterations in some charter provisions, but he failed to specify its shortcomings. In private correspondence and conversations with White House visitors, however, Jackson openly criticized the bank. Biddle, aware of the hostility, tried to play the political game—within limits. While his first criterion was always competence, the bank president nonetheless took pains to recommend the election of new directors to the boards of local branches who were reportedly friendly to Jackson. But the appeasement strategy failed because Jackson still took offense at a few of the names put forward, and he accused Biddle of trying to pack some local boards with enemies of his administration. Whether Jackson believed the composition of local boards represented a genuine threat to his reelection campaign or whether he simply looked for any excuse to attack the Second BUS will remain forever the subject of conjecture.

Trying to size up Jackson always proved difficult, but it was a task that Biddle could not ignore because the bank's charter was due to expire in 1836. The question in Biddle's mind was whether to press for recharter in the presidential election year of 1832 or to wait until 1835 or 1836. Most political observers expected Jackson to win reelection handily in 1832 in the absence of unforeseen developments, which meant that he would likely hold the power to wield the presidential veto under either the earlier or later option. Biddle mulled over the situation, consulted with his allies in Washington, and finally made the fateful decision to go ahead in

Lithograph of the Bank of the United States made in 1839, the year Biddle resigned as the bank's president

1832. He reasoned that a solid majority in Congress, but probably not two-thirds, favored continuation of the bank as currently organized, and that Jackson would hesitate to veto any bank bill for fear of the possible loss of the upcoming election.

Biddle received encouragement to seek recharter from Henry Clay and other political opponents of Jackson. They hoped to use the bank issue to defeat him. If recharter became law despite Jackson's opposition it would undermine presidential prestige; if, on the other hand, he made a veto stick, the issue could be used against him in the campaign. Some bank supporters placed political opportunism above all other considerations. Many hoped for a presidential veto, followed by Jackson's certain defeat in the fall election, and the subsequent enactment of recharter legislation under a new administration. Henry Clay, the Whig candidate for the presidency in 1832, was foremost in this category.

After deciding in late 1831 to allow congressional allies to introduce legislation in the upcoming session, Biddle asked friends within the administration to raise the issue with Jackson in private and test his reaction. The initial reports offered surprising encouragement. Secretary of State Edward Livingston met with Jackson in January 1832 and reported that the president seemed firmly committed to only four modifications in the charter terms. According to Livingston, Jackson desired no

further government investment in bank stock, but he wanted to retain the right to appoint five directors to the board of the head office in Philadelphia, plus one government director to each local board. The president wanted a time limit established on how long the bank could hold real estate acquired as a result of loan defaults, and he proposed that the Second BUS pay taxes on its branch offices at the same rates paid by state banks. In correspondence with Charles Ingersoll, the bank's Washington lobbyist, in late February, Biddle readily acceded to Jackson's alleged requests: "In truth I believe there is no change desired by the President which would not be immediately assented to by the Bank." The banker felt confident—overly confident in view of the consequences.

Despite foreknowledge of Jackson's views, the bank's congressional supporters did not seek to open a dialogue with the White House aimed at negotiating minor modifications in charter terms. The recharter bill differed in no significant way from the original legislation of 1816. Biddle foolishly deferred to the political judgment of his supposed friends and allies. The failure to alter the charter terms in line with Jackson's expressed preferences was the first in a long chain of tactical blunders. Believing in the wisdom of maintaining the bank as a nonpolitical institution, a befuddled Biddle allowed himself to become the tool of a powerful political faction headed by Whig aspirants for the presidency.

In the debate on the bill on the Senate floor that May, Thomas Hart Benton, Democratic senator from Missouri, and other friends of the administration offered a series of amendments. All but one were voted down. The approved amendment gave Congress authority to prohibit the issuance of banknotes in sums below $20. Jackson later cited four of the rejected amendments in the presidential veto message as important deficiencies in the recharter terms. In retrospect none of the proposed alterations threatened the viability of the bank. But the anti-Jackson faction was in no mood for compromise, and another opportunity to save the bank in only slightly modified form drifted by.

After passing both houses of Congress with comfortable margins, the recharter bill moved forward to the White House. Jackson returned it on July 10 accompanied by a thundering veto message. Written in concert with some of his closest advisers, the message contained both exaggerated rhetoric and substantive arguments. Most historical accounts have concentrated on the flamboyant language in the beginning and closing paragraphs. Jackson dubbed the bank a monopolistic monster and accused it of favoring the rich over the poor. By vetoing the bank bill he claimed to be protecting the typical voter from the greed of monied aristocrats—in other words, people such as Biddle.

The presidential veto message was more than hyperbole, however. In addition to the perennial argument about the unconstitutionality of all national banking legislation, Jackson raised six other specific objections to the charter terms. Most of the complaints were raised in the earlier correspondence between Biddle and his Washington agents in January or later in May during the congressional debate. Jackson's objections fell into the following categories: the bank's alleged monopoly status; the number of foreign shareholders; varying rules for accepting bank notes from private parties versus financial institutions; the Supreme Court's mandated exemption of the bank from local and state taxation; and the allegedly excessive size of its capitalization.

Rather than analyzing the potential impact on the Second BUS by altering the bill to satisfy most, or at least some, of Jackson's complaints, Biddle and his congressional allies tried to line up sufficient votes to override the veto. The effort was futile from the outset because the initial divisions in both houses had not attracted the necessary margin of two-thirds. When the vote to override failed, Biddle next targeted the defeat of Jackson in the fall election. Political observers expected the bank issue to play a huge role in the campaign. In one of the most foolish electoral strategies in American political history, Biddle and his friends printed up thousands of copies of Jackson's veto message and distributed them throughout the nation. They planned to demonstrate conclusively the weakness and shallowness of the president's arguments against the bank. But the tactic backfired, and Jackson won the election handily in November 1832.

Biddle had made a gross miscalculation. He had neither sufficient votes in Congress nor in the general electorate to guarantee the continuation of the bank beyond 1836 under the existing charter terms. He claimed throughout the controversy that he was interested primarily in promoting the public welfare, which meant in that context perpetuating the charter of the bank. Unfortunately, he was too stubborn and rigid to consider the possibility of opening a genuine dialogue with Jackson or Jackson's allies about a possible compromise bill.

Biddle rejected every one of the opposition's proposals for altering the charter terms, because, in his view, none promised to improve the bank's operations. Wholly engrossed in refuting every one of Jackson's arguments, he failed to give proper consideration to the possibility of acceding to most, if not all, of the president's expressed demands. Especially after the publication of the veto message, a more contemplative bank president might have measured the magnitude of the damage likely to flow from catering to the whims of an angered chief executive. If Biddle had been more flexible and politically astute, he would have realized that, irrespective of its merits, a revised bank bill incorporating most of the new proposals would not have undermined the viability and stability of the institution. The following alterations would have met most of Jackson's stated objections: voiding the exclusive, monopolistic charter privileges; terminating the eligibility of foreigners to remain as stockholders; equalizing policies for private parties and state banks regarding the acceptance of bank notes; subjecting the branch offices to state taxation on their real estate holdings; and reducing the size of the capitalization to perhaps $25 million. Those changes would have created a less imposing enterprise, but they would not have destroyed nor severely crippled the institution. Biddle and his supporters aimed for all or nothing and got the latter. Their uncompromising attitude was irresponsible given the circumstances, since they had the most to lose in the event the Jacksonians triumphed.

Biddle also gave the continuance of his career as bank president the highest priority. Biddle and Jackson were clear rivals for political and economic power, and the president had determined that the bank and Biddle, its proud president, had accumulated too much independent authority. From Jackson's perspective, perpetuating the existing national charter was incompatible with the maintenance of a free and democratic society. Any compromise solution would have probably required a pledge from Biddle to step down from the presidency before the next scheduled election in January 1833. Biddle's retirement would have given Jackson the opportunity to participate in the selection of a successor. But no such offer was forthcoming, and Biddle remained at the helm throughout Jackson's second term.

The president's reelection hardly ended the bank war. The Second BUS still had more than three years under its national charter, and Biddle had no intention of leaving his post. The conflict heated up again in 1833 when Jackson decided to withhold the U.S. government's sizable deposits from the bank and place all incoming money in various state banks around the country—the so-called "pet" banks owned and managed by friends of the administration. In response to the loss of sizable deposits, Biddle ordered a sharp reduction in loans outstanding. The curtailment inconvenienced many borrowers with long-standing relationships with the bank, and it triggered a mild business contraction in some localities. The pet banks receiving government deposits eventually expanded the volume of their discounts, and the net effect of that transfer on the overall economy was fairly minimal.

Meanwhile, Biddle received sharp criticism for restricting credit facilities so drastically. He explained publicly that he had merely behaved prudently in response to Jackson's denial of government deposits, but many doubters remained unconvinced about his real motives. Their suspicions were well-grounded, for in private correspondence Biddle held out the possibility of precipitating a recession, which might lead, in turn, to Jackson's political reversal on the recharter issue. Government deposits declined by $10 million from 1832 to

1834, but Biddle managed to reduce outstanding credit by roughly $17 million during the same period. If the Second BUS could mete out enough economic punishment, he hoped to maneuver Jackson into agreeing to a three-year extension of the charter, up to 1839. By that date a new occupant would likely sit in the White House, and the whole issue could be reassessed in a less inflammatory atmosphere.

Once again Biddle's stratagems produced negative results. His curtailment of credit facilities in 1833 and 1834 angered many former allies. Congressional friends introduced resolutions in both houses to censure Jackson for removing the deposits in violation of law. The Pennsylvania state legislature debated a complimentary motion in support of the Second BUS, but the governor came out against the motion, and the state legislature decided to drop the matter. Biddle lost ground even in his home state. Under the leadership of Henry Clay, the Senate voted 26 to 20 to censure Jackson, but the House failed to act. His victory in the Senate was merely symbolic—and hollow.

By 1835 Biddle had reconciled himself to the loss of the national charter, and he shifted his attention to the possibility of substituting a state banking charter issued by the Pennsylvania legislature. Meanwhile he arranged the sale of the majority of the existing branch offices, including their assets and liabilities, to investors who planned conversions into state banks. Nine branches were sold in 1835 and nine more in the winter of 1836, while three offices were closed and their accounts transferred elsewhere. The sales totaled more than $15 million, with the bank accepting payment in notes maturing over three to five years.

In late February 1836 the board of directors accepted in principle the charter plan offered by the Pennsylvania legislature. It called for the annual payment of a $100,000 bonus (license fee) over the 20-year charter period. Biddle settled with the federal government by agreeing to repurchase its 70,000 shares of common stock at $115.50 per share—$100 par value plus $15.50 of retained earnings—in four equal annual installments starting in 1837. The remaining stockholders received one share in the new corporation for every share currently held. Over the next three or four years, however, ownership concentrated in the hands of foreigners and residents of Pennsylvania in about equal proportions.

In addition to the Philadelphia headquarters, Biddle decided to maintain a scaled-down network of branch offices and agencies. In New England he retained the New York and Boston offices because they were major mercantile centers; he added Pittsburgh, Erie, and New Brighton in Pennsylvania to please the state legislature; and he placed outlets in New Orleans, Mobile, Natchez, and Columbus, Georgia, to handle financial transactions associated with the shipment of cotton. The bank found itself less strategically positioned than in the past, and its powers were slightly curtailed, but it remained the largest private business enterprise in the nation. It had suffered damage to its prestige but its vast capital remained intact.

Under the state charter, which took effect in March 1836, Biddle turned his attention increasingly to the cotton market and to developing an investment banking connection in London. First, however, he had to deal with the Panic of 1837, which struck U.S. financial markets with a fury in the spring. In May the bank suspended specie payment along with other institutions in the American commercial banking system. Biddle resumed payment in August 1838; by then he had accumulated specie reserves of $7 million. After operating for more than two years as a state bank, the balance sheet showed exceptional strength.

Biddle made major changes in his ties to the English market. The joint account arrangement with Baring Brothers ended in late 1837 by mutual agreement. He sent a trusted associate, Samuel Jaudon, overseas to handle the bank's affairs in London. Biddle had visions of a grand international enterprise—a financial institution that would deal in a whole range of services ranging from commercial to investment banking plus foreign-exchange operations and other related activities. He had plans for opening a Paris office as well. To initiate the entry in Anglo-American investment banking, the bank sponsored the sale of a $12 million bond issue by the state of Illinois.

He had equally ambitious plans for involvement in the cotton market. In Liverpool his son Edward became one of the principals in Humphreys & Biddle, a firm organized to handle the sale of cotton consignments and to accept bills of exchange drawn against American shipments. Biddle, convinced that the nation's economic problems in the fall of 1837 stemmed mainly from an oversold cotton market, vowed to use the bank's resources to reverse the tide. Moreover, he hoped to profit personally from the turnaround. In 1837 and 1838 the bank financed about $9 million of cotton consignments through its southern network and Humphreys & Biddle. Biddle's profits on those transactions totaled somewhere in the neighborhood of $1.4 million.

Accused months later of speculating in cotton contrary to the mission of a prudent banker, Biddle stated emphatically that the institution had never purchased a bale of cotton in its own name. Instead it had merely provided the financing for individuals and mercantile firms. Biddle was technically correct, but he himself was one of the principal borrowers, and, since he participated handsomely in the profits of Humphreys & Biddle, it could be argued that he advanced substantial funds to an enterprise in which he held a large stake.

Indeed, financial historians have remained perplexed over Biddle's changed behavior after the bank's conversion to a state charter in March 1836. Prudent and cautious as a banker from 1823 to 1835, he followed a much more speculative course during the next three years. In previous years he had criticized directors and officers who borrowed heavily from the bank to finance their own business ventures. Yet in late 1837 he borrowed funds on a massive scale in his own name. Biddle used the loans to purchase cotton in the southern states on the calculated gamble that prices that had fallen sharply in the winter and spring of 1837 would recover the next year. On that occasion the gamble paid off, but he exposed the bank to a huge risk in embarking on that venture. He also set a bad precedent because efforts by his successors to intervene in the cotton market in later years produced heavy losses.

Biddle defended himself by explaining that his actions were motivated by a deep sense of responsibility for the health of the American economy in the aftermath of the Panic of 1837. Every commercial bank had suspended payment, and thousands of mercantile firms faced the prospect of bankruptcy. He saw a strong cotton market as the one essential ingredient for recovery, and he put the bulk of the corporate and personal resources at his disposal into supporting the market. While his expressed motivations sounded pure and patriotic, as a state banker Biddle no longer had such wide-ranging responsibilities to the commercial community. Perhaps he subconsciously tried to prove to former president Jackson and successor Martin Van Buren that he and the bank still had the will and the power to help in the prevention of a financial catastrophe. If Biddle tried to cast himself in the role of a national "hero," his plan ultimately failed. He did contribute to a rebound in 1838, but cotton prices dropped again in the early 1840s, and the whole economy remained sluggish until 1843. The broader problems were larger in scope than Biddle and his bank had the power to correct.

Biddle stepped down from the presidency in March 1839 at age fifty-three, after 16 years in office. He was succeeded by Thomas Dunlop, a prominent Philadelphia merchant. Over the next several years the bank faced a series of crises, relating largely to maintaining liquidity at home and abroad. Its foreign-exchange account was badly mismanaged. Directors made an effort to reestablish an agency agreement with the Barings in May 1839, but the proposal fell through in August. As a result of a domestic specie drain that continued into the fall months, the bank suspended payment in October.

After the second suspension of specie payments, Biddle returned to assist bank management in an unofficial capacity during much of the next year and a half. He was instrumental in inaugurating another massive intervention in the cotton market through the southern outlets in November 1839, although he did not actually oversee operations as in 1837. Problems persisted in England and the United States. Biddle engineered the removal of Dunlop from the presidency and his replacement with Jaudon, who returned from overseas. Conflicts between Biddle and the board of directors over strategies for strengthening the bank's position arose in the spring of 1840. Meanwhile, nothing went right for the bank. It suspended payment for a third time in February 1841, and Pennsylvania regulators, citing charter violations regarding the maintenance of specie payments, ordered the bank liquidated. The bank's ignoble end damaged all those associated with its management as a state-chartered institution—including Biddle. Although no longer officially in charge when the doors closed for the last time, he had been identified with the bank for so long that critics, as well as historians, blamed him, at least partially, for the unfortunate outcome.

In the presidential campaign of 1840 William Henry Harrison, the Whig candidate, was elected, and there was talk about appointing Biddle to the post of secretary of the treasury. But Biddle declined consideration. Harrison also thought about calling for recharter of a national bank, but Biddle advised against it. Proposing a third national bank, he told Harrison, would raise an issue "that might be turned to mischief against the new administration before it had time to strengthen itself." Biddle and his wife aimed for the post of ambassador to Austria, since he had promised her a stay in Europe someday, but the administration denied the request.

For the next few years Biddle lived in retirement at his estate outside Philadelphia. He suffered through a series of illnesses and died on February 27, 1844, at age fifty-eight. Huge successes marked his career as president of the Second Bank of the United States from his election by stockholders in 1823 until the ill-fated showdown with Andrew Jackson over the recharter issue in 1832. On the basis of his performance during the first nine years in office, financial historians have cited him as one of the most innovative and effective bankers in the nation's history.

Publications:

Meriwether Lewis and William Clark, *Travels to the Source of the Missouri River and Across the American Continent to the Pacific Ocean*, edited by Biddle (London: Longman, 1814);

Commercial Regulations of the Foreign Countries with which the United States have Commercial Intercourse, edited by Biddle (Washington, D.C.: Gales & Seaton, 1819);

The Correspondence of Nicholas Biddle Dealing with National Affairs, 1807-1844, edited by Reginald C. McCrane (Boston & New York: Houghton Mifflin, 1919).

References:

Ralph Catterall, *The Second Bank of the United States* (Chicago: University of Chicago Press, 1903);

Thomas Govan, *Nicholas Biddle: Nationalist and Public Banker, 1786-1844* (Chicago: University of Chicago Press, 1959);

Robert Remini, *Andrew Jackson and the Bank War* (New York: Norton, 1967);

Walter B. Smith, *Economic Aspects of the Second Bank of the United States* (Cambridge, Mass.: Harvard University Press, 1953).

Archives:

Collections of Biddle's incoming and outgoing letters are located at the family estate "Andalusia," near Philadelphia; the Historical Society of Pennsylvania, in Philadelphia; Princeton University; and the Library of Congress.

Bills of Exchange, Sight Drafts, and Bills of Credit

Bills of exchange were eighteenth-century financial instruments that facilitated trade by making conversion to a foreign currency. Such bills represented a sum payable at a future date, usually after the goods in transit arrived. By the nineteenth century domestic bills of exchange also circulated, for the purpose of drawing funds on a bank or business in another section of the country. Someone in New Orleans, for example, might need to draw on an account in New York.

Sight drafts were special bills of exchange payable when they arrived at the account on which they were drawn (that is, when the payer saw it). "Time drafts" usually had a specified date marked on the bill, and the holder could not exchange that bill before the designated time. Sometimes the two instruments were combined, so that a bill would not fall due until 30 to 60 days after sight. As nineteenth-century communication and transportation improved, the time period between "sight" and "time" narrowed to three days.

Bills of credit were possibly early IOUs or advances against goods, but by late colonial times they were exchanged as money—paper monetary instruments payable on demand. As with many definitions, the terms "bill of credit" or "bill of exchange" depend entirely on the time and place of usage.

–Editor

Richard P. Bland

(August 19, 1835-June 15, 1899)

by Hans Eicholz

University of California, Los Angeles

CAREER: Teacher, Ohio County, Kentucky (1854-1855); teacher, Wayne County, Missouri (1855); miner and prospector, California (1855-1859); lawyer, Utah Territory-Nevada (1859-1865); treasurer, Carson County, Utah Territory (1860-1864); lawyer, Rolla, Missouri (1866-1869), Lebanon, Missouri (1869-1872); U.S. representative, state of Missouri (1872-1895, 1897-1899).

Congressman Richard P. "Silver Dick" Bland was the principal leader of the free-silver movement during the last quarter of the nineteenth century. Long before William Jennings Bryan made silver the core issue of the 1896 presidential campaign, Bland took the floor of the House of Representatives to protest the "Crime of 1873," the coinage act whereby the government discontinued the minting of silver. Responding to the periodic inability of the gold-based currency system to meet the demand for cash, inflationists argued that the demonetization of silver constituted a plot on the part of eastern bankers to squeeze the earnings of western and southern agrarians by shrinking the money supply. In the 1870s Bland led the fight to inflate the currency through government purchase and coinage of silver, and he continued to promote the silver interest to the end of his congressional career.

Richard Parks Bland was born on August 19, 1835, near Hartford, Kentucky, to Edward and Margaret Parks Bland. His father was educated as a Presbyterian minister but chose to become a farmer instead. He died in 1842, and his wife died seven years later. Bland was forced to care for the family from an early age, plowing the farm and assisting neighbors for six or seven dollars a month. By winter he usually had saved enough to afford a modicum of schooling. When he reached the age of eighteen, he was accepted into the Hartford Academy and took a yearlong course in teacher training. He taught in Ohio County, Kentucky, for two

Richard P. Bland

terms, and in 1855 he taught one term in Wayne County, Missouri, after moving there in the spring of that year. That same year he moved to California, where he worked as a miner and prospector. He moved to Virginia City in the Utah Territory (now part of Nevada) in 1859. By that time he had completed his law studies, and he began a practice in Virginia City. In 1860 Bland was admitted to the U.S. District Court in the Utah Territory. He also served as treasurer of Carson County, from 1860 to 1864. He moved back to Missouri in 1866 to practice law in Rolla and then moved again in 1869 to the town of Lebanon. In 1873 he married Virginia

Elizabeth Mitchell; the couple had nine children.

In 1872, as Ulysses S. Grant and Horace Greeley dueled for the presidency, Bland was nominated for Congress by the Democratic party and was elected by a margin of 800 votes over his Republican opponent. Except for one term (1895-1897), he served continuously in the House of Representatives until his death. An exemplar of the rugged individualist, Bland appealed to his constituency's Jeffersonian sense of liberty and equality. Holding to the old-liberal tradition of free trade and anti-imperialism, he delivered a barrage of forceful critiques against the National Bank Act of 1863, the national-bank monopoly over the money supply, American military expansion, and tariff policy. During his first term, in 1873, a coinage act making gold the sole basis of U.S. currency passed Congress. Also in 1873 the discovery of Nevada silver deposits more extensive than any uncovered since 1859 inaugurated a new "silver rush" and greatly increased the supply of the metal. In 1875 Bland was appointed chairman of the Committee on Mines and Mining. Shortly thereafter a bill providing for the issue of certificates on the gold and silver bullion deposited with government assay offices was referred to the committee. The certificates were to be redeemable in specie but were not to be considered legal tender. The committee tacked on a free-coinage provision to compel the government to mint silver and gold at the established 16 to 1 ratio without limitation, as the precious metals were presented by the then-oversupplied Nevada miners for purchase.

The 16 to 1 silver-gold ratio, established in 1834, had led to the gradual disappearance of silver dollars from circulation because the new ratio overvalued gold in reference to international markets and made it profitable to sell silver for gold overseas. Because the silver in a silver dollar had come to be worth more in gold than the face value of the coin, the government found it expedient to stop coining silver dollars. But the Nevada discoveries, combined with the adoption of the gold standard in several European countries (which decreased European demand for silver), pushed silver prices down to a point where it became profitable again (from the point of view of silver interests) to coin silver at 16 to 1. Gold-standard supporters, who feared the inflation silver coinage would bring and preferred the stability of monometallic international exchange, filibustered the bill for three months after its introduc-

tion in the Senate, and it expired when Congress adjourned in August 1876. Thus began Bland's crusade for a bimetallic standard, which earned him the sobriquet "Silver Dick." In 1876 Bland received an appointment to a congressional "Silver Commission" to study the issue, and in 1879 he joined the House Committee on Coinage, Weights, and Measures. He became chairman of the committee in 1883.

Bland and the silver forces finally pushed a silver purchase act through Congress in 1878, but not without compromise. Bland's original free-coinage proposal was amended by Iowa congressman William B. Allison to require the federal government to purchase not the total amount of silver presented, but only between $2 million and $4 million worth per month at the market price. Under this Bland-Allison Act, however, the Treasury tended to purchase only the minimum amount, which had little inflationary effect. The legislation did provide silver miners with a secure, if limited, market for their product. The overvalued silver dollars coined under the act tended to remain in domestic circulation.

Over the next decade Bland continued to fight for a true bimetallic standard, for the restoration of silver to its pre-1873 status. In 1886 monometallists threatened even Bland-Allison, but the silver forces prevented a repeal. Then, in 1890, the Sherman Silver Purchase Act was passed. By that time some $380 million in silver had been coined under Bland-Allison. Although the Sherman Act required the Treasury to purchase almost twice as much silver as before, nearly the entire output of the Nevada mines, Bland opposed the legislation, claiming it still failed to provide an adequate solution to the currency problem. By 1893, however, gold forces had gathered the support not only of most Republicans but also of many eastern Democrats, and Bland found reason to support the Sherman Act in lieu of a bill authorizing free silver coinage. On August 11 he warned fellow Democrats in his famous "Parting of the Ways" speech that the western wing of the party would rather bolt than surrender the cause of free silver. But it came too late. On November 1 Congress repealed the Sherman Silver Purchase Act and returned the country to a gold standard. Silver prices, which had been supported almost solely by the government's purchases, collapsed, and many Nevada mines failed. In 1896 Bland emerged in the eyes of many as the logical Democratic party candidate for president and even led in the first three rounds of balloting at the convention. Lacking the charismatic style and wide popularity of William Jennings Bryan, however, his hopes faded, and Bryan pulled ahead, convincing Bland to withdraw from the race. Refusing nominations for vice-president and Missouri governor, Bland decided to run again for his House seat and was triumphantly reelected. Bryan lost the presidency to William McKinley, and the silver issue never again assumed the importance it had when Bland led the way.

The money issue had plagued the country since its founding, originating in conflicts between Jeffersonians and Hamiltons over the First Bank of the United States. The Jeffersonians sought to limit the power of government over economic matters, while the Hamiltonians supported a strong governmental role in finance. Bland and the silverites represented the last-ditch effort of the Jeffersonian tradition, but by that time the central government was more powerful, and the nation was more closely connected to the outside world. For Bland intimately tied the cause of free silver to other issues, especially banking and the tariff. The same interests that promoted tight credit tended also to support high tariffs, which kept the cost of living high. Bland saw it as an us-against-them contest. The national bankers, he believed, wanted to maintain the demand for their notes by driving out silver. By fighting for a bimetallic standard, Bland also fought against other centralizing forces.

In place of the national banks, Bland favored putting control of the money supply directly into the hands of Congress through the issue of treasury notes. While that seemingly represented an increased governmental financial role, to Bland it represented the only practical means to eradicate what he considered a banker's monopoly. Reliance on treasury-note issues would tie the currency to the government's most democratic body. Moreover, because the circulation of national-bank notes was related to the national debt (national banks were required to back their issues with government bonds), Bland reasoned that the national banking system would become a means by which politicians justified a perpetual debt and thereby created an internal financial incentive in favor of government expansion and militarism. What he stood for in a speech given on May 13, 1882, he continued to support for the remainder of his career: "Centralization may protect wealth, but it destroys liberty. Following Jefferson and the teachings of the democratic party, I am opposed to building up corporations in this country upon theories of centralized government."

Though never a brilliant speaker, Bland always received credit for thorough preparation and clear reasoning. His sincerity gained him the respect of both friend and foe. In 1898 he devoted his remaining days in the House fighting U.S. involvement in Cuba. He died on June 15, 1899.

Reference:

William Vincent Byars, ed., *"An American Commoner": The Life and Times of Richard Parks Bland* (Columbia, Mo.: E. W. Stephens, 1900).

Branch Banks and Agencies

When a bank received a charter, on occasion the provisions would allow for the bank to open branch offices at other locations. Branches had all the powers of the parent bank. They could accept deposits, emit notes by exchanging them for gold and silver (specie) or through loans, and initiate their own loans. The branches' independence and autonomy depended on their charter provisions. In some cases branches acted as offices of the parent bank, and thus they could draw on the reserves of that bank in times of crisis or to generate new loans. Money, therefore, transferred freely and easily, and the parent bank assumed all the responsibilities for the branch, counting its assets and liabilities as those of the bank. In other cases the branches actually functioned as independent units, even to the point of having their own boards of directors, and reported to a central board that only supervised general charter compliance, not bank policy. That type of organization did not lend itself to easy transfer of funds or centralized bookkeeping.

Branching had tremendous advantages over "unit banking" (that is, banking wherein branching did not occur, usually because laws prohibited it). First, branches carried the name identity of the parent bank, leading to greater customer confidence. Second, many states had no capital requirements for the branches themselves, only the parent bank. Thus, the stockholders could establish as many branches as they chose without investing additional funds. Third, branches established in different regions of a state greatly diversified the bank's loan risk. While one branch might deal primarily in agricultural loans, a branch in another sector of the state might lend primarily to businesses. Thus illiquid rural loans were pooled with more liquid commercial loans. Finally, the reserves of the parent bank always stood behind the notes and loans of the branches.

The first branch bank in the United States was the First Bank of the United States (BUS), which had eight branches. Both it and the Second BUS, which ultimately had 25 branches, possessed an important advantage over all state-chartered branch banks in that they could establish branches across state lines (as true interstate branch banks). An example of a cohesive branch system in which one branch was liable for the debts of the others was the State Bank of Indiana (called "a bank of branches"), while the State Bank of Alabama represented an autonomous branch system.

Some banks sought to avoid interstate branching prohibitions by establishing "agencies." Although little is known about agencies, they apparently lacked the authority to issue new notes but could extend loans and receive deposits as well as conduct basic exchange functions. The powers of interstate branches and agencies decreased sharply after the Alabama Supreme Court ruled in *Bank of Augusta* v. *Earl* (1837) against "foreign corporations" doing business in Alabama. Agencies kept a low profile after that, although they continued to conduct operations in several states.

See also:

First Bank of the United States, National Bank and Currency Acts, National Banks and State Banks, Second Bank of the United States.

—Editor

Isaac Bronson

(1760-May 1838)

by Carol Noland

Arizona State University

CAREER: Surgeon, revolutionary war; merchant and trader (1780s-1792); stockbroker, Philadelphia (1792), New York (1793-1807); director and president, Bridgeport Bank (1807-1832); cofounder, New York Life Insurance and Trust Company (1830); cofounder, Ohio Life Insurance and Trust Company (1834).

Isaac Bronson was director and president of the Bridgeport Bank, in Bridgeport, Connecticut, cofounder of the New York Life Insurance and Trust Company and the Ohio Life Insurance and Trust Company, and a major supporter of the national bank movement in the Jacksonian era. Born in 1760 in Middlebury, Connecticut, he was the son of a Connecticut farmer who was also a member of the Connecticut state legislature. He studied medicine without the benefit of college and became a junior surgeon during the American Revolution. After the war he abandoned medicine and traveled to India and Europe to take advantage of the expanded trade routes of American merchants.

In 1792 Bronson returned to the United States and settled in Philadelphia. There he speculated in national and state securities. In 1793 he moved to New York City and continued in the trading of stocks. An indication of Bronson's success in stock speculation was his purchase of a summer home near Fairfield, Connecticut, in 1796. He married Anna Olcott, and the couple had ten children.

While in New York Bronson cofounded the Merchants Bank of New York, but after a few years he dissolved that partnership and returned to Connecticut. In 1807 he joined the Bridgeport Bank of Bridgeport, Connecticut, founded in 1806. Bronson acquired the controlling interest of that bank and from 1807 to 1832 served as a member of the board of directors and as its president. In his capacity as president Bronson oversaw general operations and instituted policies of the bank. During his ten-

Isaac Bronson (Historical Collections, Bridgeport Public Library)

ure Bronson insisted that the bank maintain high reserves and redeem its notes on short notice. As a means to that end he supported the "real bills" doctrine, which was a policy of lending money for commercial transactions for 60 days only, with no renewals. The actual goods in transit acted as security. The borrower returned the bank's notes after delivery of the trade goods and completion of the transaction. Bronson believed that if the bank had its paper returned every 60 days, it could never overextend itself. Most considered that a very conservative policy because it furnished credit to merchants for trade but provided little help to those producing the goods.

Opponents of the policy thought that banks should also supply credit for businessmen to undertake new enterprises. Bronson, however, believed that investing in speculative enterprises was inflationary and an unnecessary risk of the bank's resources. He thought that individual financiers should invest their own capital in manufacturing and agricultural ventures because they could sustain losses on risk-taking ventures without affecting other areas of the economy. Bronson himself purchased lands throughout New York State and lent money to farmers and town residents. He even speculated on some manufacturing enterprises, including a gold mine in North Carolina.

After 1815, however, the national economy developed rapidly and generated a tremendous demand for capital. Individual financiers no longer could supply surplus capital or deal with all the nation's investment needs. Bronson, therefore, reluctantly admitted the necessity of commercial banks to expand their functions by investing their capital in secure farm mortgages and government securities. He remained a financial conservative, nevertheless, refusing to speculate, or invest in manufacturing.

Bronson's conservatism eventually caused him to lose control of the Bridgeport Bank and the support of the Bridgeport directors. Even though in 25 years, from 1807 to 1832, the Bridgeport Bank had redeemed all of its notes and had lost only $50, on a trade exchange, the directors felt that Bronson's conservative policies were no longer practical and took it upon themselves to provide more credit to merchants and capitalists. When the directors ignored Bronson's objections, he sold all of his shares in the bank and vowed never again to hold stock in a commercial bank. Bronson may have taken some consolation in the fact that the Bridgeport Bank became so overextended that within four years it suspended specie payments.

In 1829, when the North Carolina legislature debated the banking question, the *Raleigh Register,* on February 3, published Bronson's views on sound banking. On July 11 of that same year Condy Raguet, editor of the *Free Trade Advocate and Journal of Political Economy,* published a statement by Bronson of "General Propositions Explanatory of the Elementary Principles of Banking." Raguet held Bronson's opinion on finance in the highest regard and used many of Bronson's ideas in his own book on banking.

Bronson won respect in the political arena as well. New York congressman Churchill C. Cambreleng, chairman of the House Ways and Means Committee, often consulted Bronson regarding the banking system and strongly supported Bronson's principles. Aware that Bronson believed that a national bank was necessary to check the state banks' operations, Cambreleng urged Bronson to draft a proposal and lobby for a new national bank to replace the previous bank, which President Andrew Jackson had refused to recharter in 1832. On February 20, 1833, a committee of New York merchants presented a pamphlet entitled "Outline of a Plan for a National Bank with Incidental Remarks on the Bank of the United States" to Congress. While the pamphlet appeared in the form of a committee report, the influence of Bronson's views stood out.

Like Bronson, most conservative bankers believed that commercial banks could not both support the movement of trade goods and provide investment capital for the agricultural sector without resorting to unnecessary speculation. They believed that the investment function should be isolated in an independent institution. In 1830 Bronson and his son Arthur worked with other financial conservatives, mostly New York City bankers, to establish the New York Life Insurance and Trust Company (NYLTC). Bronson cowrote the institution's charter and proved instrumental in securing the state legislature's approval. He worded the charter and the bylaws to prevent speculative investments and negligent administration. The charter specified that the company's capital stock had to be invested in real estate mortgages within the state. Bronson also included clauses that gave the state the power to amend or repeal the charter and required the company to submit an annual report to the state chancellor, who could order further investigation if necessary. The company's bylaws gave the trustees, through several standing committees, the power to determine the utilization of company funds. The trustees, then, had created an institution to stand as a defense against the loose banking practices of the time.

The purpose of the trust company was to invest the finances of New York citizens in farm mortgages, personal notes of respected financiers, and occasional manufacturing enterprises. Essentially a savings institution based on conservative financial principles for those of moderate or substantial wealth, the trust company did contribute to economic expansion, although its directors selected its investments carefully. The company concentrated its activities in three areas: loans on personal security, loans on real estate mortgages, and loans on the stock of corporations. The NYLTC, however, did not want the power to circulate notes, since the trustees assumed that the responsibility for the periodic redemption of notes would jeopardize the company's primary investment function. Bronson believed that trust companies would eliminate the need for commercial banks to invest their capital in speculative enterprises, thus allowing them to specialize in the short-term financing of trade and circulation of notes.

The NYLTC had a very successful beginning. Deposits into the trust climbed from $232,123 in 1831 to $662,111 in 1834, and foreign deposits totaled $1,204,508 in 1834. By 1835 the NYLTC held a total of $5 million in deposits in addition to its $1 million capital stock. Due to the initial success of the NYLTC, the New York financiers considered the possibility of establishing similar firms in western and southern states. The Bronsons participated in the establishment of the Southern Life Insurance and Trust Company, the Alabama Life Insurance and Trust Company, and the Ohio Life Insurance and Trust Company (OLTC). The records of the OLTC show that the Bronsons, led by Isaac, wrote the OLTC's charter, acquired legislative approval from the state, and selected the officers and stockholders.

The Bronsons established a trust company in Ohio for three reasons. First, Ohio desperately needed capital and required more financial institutions. Second, the Bronsons saw the OLTC as a good stock investment and as a means of investing in western lands without having to relocate and assume personal supervision. They envisioned the trust as an important part of an overall plan for western development. Finally, conservative financiers intended that the Ohio firm would be an example of sound banking principles for the entire nation. Thus they established the OLTC not only as an agency for moving eastern capital into the western economy but also as a prototype for a national bank.

In 1834 the Ohio state legislature chartered several new banks with a combined capital of $4.4 million, of which it authorized $2 million for the OLTC. The legislature also granted the OLTC the

power to issue notes. The Bronsons had combined the functions of a trust company and a commercial bank (in addition to insurance activities) in the Ohio firm in order to demonstrate that a large financial institution could both finance trade and mobilize capital for the agricultural sector without encouraging speculation. They invested the capital in real estate mortgages and used it as security for the company's banking operations. In the first two years of the firm's existence, deposits increased the company's investment capital by nearly $1.5 million. The OLTC soon emerged as Ohio's most important financial institution both because it was the largest and because a substantial majority of its capital stock and deposits came from the East.

Despite its promising beginning the OLTC ultimately disappointed the Bronsons. The antibank faction in Ohio expressed concern over the company's broad powers and near-monopoly status and tried unsuccessfully to repeal the company's charter in the legislatures of 1835 and 1836. Opponents were also disturbed by the fact that New Yorkers were the primary stockholders in the company. They did not like the idea of "foreigners" controlling their money.

The Bronsons also had internal problems. Ohio at the time experienced an economic boom, which encouraged the trustees to liberalize their banking policies. The Bronsons interpreted that as a violation of the trust's charter and bylaws. In 1835 the trustees altered a bylaw that had called for immediate foreclosure when a borrower missed a payment. Under the new policy the trustees allowed a two-year grace period before foreclosure.

The most serious violation of conservative practices occurred when the company issued loans on the borrower's credit or reputation. The institution also granted renewals on notes beyond 100 days and at times did not call in its notes or outstanding balances for fear of alienating its customers. The Bronsons, however, believed that such practices were inflationary and threatened the bank's credit and its investments in real estate mortgages. Isaac Bronson once commented that the Ohio firm's practices "may be politically good policy; but it is what I should call practically bad banking."

Although eastern financiers held three-quarters of the stock and five of the twenty seats on the board of trustees, they had little control over the company's direction. It took only six board members to make a quorum, and eastern financiers often could not attend regular meetings due to time and distance. Local businessmen who responded to the needs of the local community determined the company's policies.

Despite the apparent prosperity of the OLTC the company suspended specie payments in May 1837. The Bronsons saw the suspension as a "moral failure of the trust company to operate according to its contract with the public." Suspension, therefore, represented the final violation of the conservative banking principles supported by Isaac Bronson. Thoroughly disappointed with the OLTC, the Bronsons sold their stock, and Arthur Bronson resigned from the board of trustees in September 1837.

After the OLTC experience Isaac Bronson was, once again, convinced of the need for a national bank to control state financial institutions. With the election of Martin Van Buren as president, Bronson believed that the political environment had grown more favorable toward a national bank. While his son went to Washington to lobby for a fiscal agency, Bronson proposed his plan to the secretary of the treasury. In a letter to the secretary Bronson argued that the deposit banks, in failing to regulate currency issues, had jeopardized the government's financial resources. Bronson believed in a simple solution: "All reflecting men ... now admit that without some controlling power over the issues of state banks there can be no security for our currency."

Bronson's proposed agency, a "U.S. Bank of Deposit and Exchange," would secure public funds and regulate the currency, although it would not have the power to issue notes. That would allow the agency to control the issue of all other banks impartially. It would function somewhat like the Bank of the United States, collecting and periodically redeeming the notes of state banks. Despite the rationality of Bronson's proposal, it failed to win approval from Congress. When Bronson died in May 1838, the movement for a national bank lost its most ardent supporter.

Even though Isaac Bronson did not see the development of a national bank based on his principles, contemporaries considered him a very successful and influential financial theorist. His contributions to banking theory and practice earned him a place of honor among nineteenth-century bankers.

References:

John Denis Haeger, *The Investment Frontier* (Albany, N.Y.: State University Press, 1981);

Fritz Redlich, *The Molding of American Banking: Men and Ideas*, 2 volumes (New York: Johnson Reprint Co., 1968);

Abraham Venit, "Isaac Bronson: His Banking Theory and the Financial Controversies of the Jacksonian Period," *Journal of Economic History*, 5 (November 1945): 201-214.

Alexander Brown

(1764-March 4, 1834)

by Edwin J. Perkins

University of Southern California

CAREER: Owner, Alexander Brown & Company (1800-1808); senior partner, Alexander Brown & Sons (1808-1834).

Alexander Brown, founding partner of the powerful and influential Anglo-American merchant banking house that bore his name, was born in Ireland in 1764 and died in Baltimore, Maryland, on March 4, 1834. He had four talented sons, who joined the family enterprise and were instrumental in the firm's growth and rise to prominence. The second son, George, remained in Baltimore and became his father's chief assistant, but each of the other three sons established offices linked to the family enterprise in separate cities: William in Liverpool in 1810; John in Philadelphia in 1818; and James in New York in 1825. The firm eventually became involved not only in mercantile activities but also in the provision of a wide range of financial services for the American foreign trade sector.

By the time of Alexander Brown's death the family firm had become one of the nation's foremost Anglo-American merchant banking houses. Best known as Brown Brothers & Company in the United States (with offices in New York and Philadelphia) and as Brown, Shipley & Company in England (with offices in Liverpool and London), it remained among the leaders in the foreign exchange and letter-of-credit markets throughout most of the nineteenth century. In the twentieth century three prominent financial services firms proudly traced their origins back to the founder: Brown Brothers Harriman & Company, a private commercial bank in New York City; Alex. Brown & Sons, a major investment banking firm headquartered in Baltimore; and Brown, Shipley & Company, a London merchant banking firm that was absorbed by Merrill Lynch & Company in the 1970s.

Alexander Brown

Unfortunately little is known about Alexander Brown's life in Ireland before he decided to immigrate to the United States. At some point in his early life he lived and worked in Ballymena, a village at the tip of northeastern Ireland about 20 miles from the Irish Sea. Just prior to his departure for the United States at the end of the eighteenth century, he was heavily involved in the linen trade. Irish linens, woven from the carefully processed fibers of flax plants, were exported to overseas markets around the globe. In the 1790s Brown reportedly worked as an auctioneer at the White Linen Hall, located in Belfast, the major commercial city in northern Ireland and the center of the island's linen trade. Alexander had befriended the successful linen merchant William Gihon; members of the Gihon family operated a small shop on Castle Street in Belfast and also maintained connections with linen suppliers in the village of Ballymena.

When Brown arrived in Baltimore in 1800, at age thirty-six, the port had undergone unprecedented growth. In the last decade before the break with Great Britain, Baltimore had grown to become a port city of about 7,000 residents. The revolutionary war and its immediate aftermath severely disrupted the trading patterns of most Atlantic port cities, but the volume of business in the Baltimore area continued to expand. By the turn of the century the city had a population of more than 25,000, and it rivaled the older and more established ports of Philadelphia, New York, and Boston.

Alexander Brown selected Baltimore as his final destination because his brother Stewart had preceded him to the Maryland port and had opened a general mercantile store in 1797. Alexander set sail across the Atlantic Ocean with his wife and eldest son, William, while the younger children went to boarding schools in England. An advertisement announcing the opening of his "Irish linen warehouse" appeared in a Baltimore newspaper in December 1800. Much of his inventory came from William Gihon and other former business associates in northeastern Ireland. Alexander Brown & Company prospered from the outset, and the owner broadened the scope of his operations to include a wide range of mercantile activities. His second son, George, joined the firm in 1808, and the title changed to Alexander Brown & Sons. By that date, the capital account had climbed to $120,000.

Brown typified the all-purpose merchant of the early-national period, dabbling in various types of transactions in both goods and services. Within half a decade he had moved beyond the confines of the Baltimore market to conduct business in cities farther south. In 1803 Brown arranged through an agent in Savannah, Georgia, to purchase cotton for direct shipment to the English market. This operation was apparently among the first in a long series of transactions that kept the Brown firm heavily involved in the Anglo-American cotton market, in one capacity or another, for the next three decades. Over the years the Browns invested their own funds in cotton cargoes, authorized advances to other American shippers consigning cotton to the firm's overseas office for sale to English textile mills, and purchased the foreign bills of exchange drawn by hundreds of American cotton exporters and cotton factors.

Alexander Brown became involved in the foreign exchange market within a few years of commencing operations in Baltimore. The sterling bill of exchange, a draft drawn by an American payee against an account maintained in Great Britain, was already a familiar device for making international payments and settling transatlantic debts. Local and regional markets for foreign bills had functioned sporadically wherever importers and exporters had intermingled since the seventeenth century, but no specialized dealers existed who bought or sold sterling bills throughout the year. By the first decade of the nineteenth century foreign exchange markets in the major port cities had become more active in response to the expanded volume of trade, but they remained institutionally immature. Exchange rates–the prices associated with buying or selling foreign moneys, mainly British sterling in the American market–experienced sharp and unpredictable fluctuations that depended on several factors, among them the state of the economy and how closely the demand for making monetary transfers across the oceans matched the supply of funds available during any given week or month. When exchange rates climbed too high, Americans with overseas debts due for settlement had the option of shipping specie–gold or silver–if adequate supplies of hard money were available.

In the early years Brown entered the foreign exchange market primarily in the capacity of a broker, an intermediary between exporters with sterling bills of exchange to sell and importers seeking to buy bills for transmittal to England. He bought sterling bills from responsible drawers, endorsed them himself, and then sold them, presumably at a profitable margin, to third parties in a fairly short period of time. One major risk involved the possibility that a draft might be dishonored ("bounced" is a modern synonym) and Brown, as a legal endorser, might be called upon to make good the draft if the drawer went bankrupt.

One of the most momentous events in the firm's history occurred when the firm founded its Liverpool office in 1810. William Brown had initially tried to open a branch office in Philadelphia in 1808, but that venture failed because President Thomas Jefferson's embargo temporarily restricted

American overseas trade. William returned to Ireland and married Sara Gihon, the daughter of Alexander's former associate, in 1809; the next year he opened the Liverpool office. That port city along England's western coast stood less than 50 miles downriver from Manchester, the center of the nation's booming cotton textile manufacturing. Liverpool linked its rise to the American cotton trade, which expanded continuously from 1790 until the Civil War.

The Brown family's decision to open a direct link with England was unique in several respects. First, none of the other major Anglo-American merchant banking houses possessed such a tight multinational organizational structure. The Baring and Peabody firms, two of the Browns' greatest rivals, conducted business in American ports through agency agreements with a series of independent firms headed by persons generally unrelated by blood or marriage. Second, rival merchant banking houses normally maintained their English headquarters in London, not in provincial Liverpool. Nevertheless Liverpool emerged as the main port of entry for American produce during the nineteenth century. Unlike its major competitors, the Brown family enterprise was not an English merchant banking house with subordinate outlets in the United States; it was instead a truly Anglo-American firm, with partners on both sides of the Atlantic exercising a substantial degree of managerial authority. By placing his branch office in Liverpool, a port city more than 150 miles northwest of London, William put himself in a superior position to oversee the firm's growing business in handling cotton consignments on commission.

The establishment of an English branch marked only the first step in Alexander Brown's plan for geographical expansion. In 1818 the third son, John, made a successful venture into the Philadelphia market, exactly one decade after William had failed. The youngest son, James, who spent several years learning the business in Liverpool under William's tutelage, opened the firm's New York office in 1825. New York had far outdistanced its rivals along the Atlantic Coast and emerged as the nation's foremost commercial center; the opening of the Erie Canal consolidated its leading position and spurred the city forward to realize even greater development.

No other merchant banking firm possessed multiple branch offices inside the United States.

The offices in Liverpool, Philadelphia, and New York complemented the activities of the original office in Baltimore. In later years the firm opened branches in Boston, New Orleans, and Mobile, and it maintained enduring agency agreements with cooperating mercantile houses in Charleston and Savannah. Steady profits accompanied organizational expansion. In 1821 the capital account passed the $1 million mark, and by the time of Alexander's death in 1834 it topped $4.5 million.

Although the Browns eventually made the decision to specialize in financial services markets, the American offices never abandoned their commitment to mercantile transactions during the lifetime of the founder. After the severe business recession from 1819 to 1821 the volume of imports handled by the Baltimore and Philadelphia branches stagnated. James's opening of the New York branch in 1825 breathed new life into this sphere of the business. The inauguration of packet boat lines between New York and Liverpool in the early 1820s encouraged a flood of imports, and many of the arriving shipments were sold at auction. The Browns imported European goods on their own account and solicited consignments from others. In an effort to give a further boost to their commission business in 1831, the Browns hired William Bowen to act as their permanent representative in Manchester with instructions to solicit consignments for the American branches from the region's numerous textile manufacturers.

Once the Liverpool branch opened, the American branches and agencies positioned themselves to solicit consignments of American raw materials, primarily cotton, for sale in the English market. The handling of consignments evolved into a lucrative business, with the normal commission at 2.5 percent of the sales proceeds. The Browns built their reputation by emphasizing the avoidance of speculation—meaning in this context that they generally sold arriving consignments immediately, refusing to withhold them in the hope of benefiting from a future advance in market prices that might never occur. Moreover, the Browns invited consignors interested in trying to maximize sales receipts through speculative marketing strategies to take their business elsewhere. On the basis of their conservative policies, the Liverpool office had risen by 1820 to become the second largest recipient of cotton consignments in port–12,700 bales, or about 3 percent of total cotton imports. That same year, in

The Baltimore office of Alexander Brown & Sons, circa 1909

addition to cotton, the firm also handled consignments of flour and tobacco. Functional specialization on finance had not yet developed, and the Browns allowed the scope of their operations to expand in all directions in the 1820s.

The risks associated with cotton shipments arose from two sources. In some cases the Browns entered into agreements with agents and customers to buy cotton in the United States and ship it overseas on joint account. In those instances the Browns accepted the risk of profit or loss routinely associated with mercantile transactions. Their second exposure to risk arose from the practice of authorizing advances to consignors directing cotton to the Liverpool office. Offering advances constituted a standard financial device used by consignees to attract and hold customers. Advances were based on the latest reliable reports of market prices in the English market. The Browns generally held the size of a customer's advances to a fairly conservative range, typically two-thirds to three-fourths of the estimated sales proceeds of a given consignment. If prices dropped sharply during the intervening weeks during which the cargo transited between an American port and Liverpool, it was possible for the sales proceeds to produce less than the earlier advance. In those cases the Browns had to apply to their American customer for sufficient funds to cover the shortage. Serious problems arose when a general crisis drove down prices in the English market in a matter of weeks and threatened a large number of firms on both sides of the Atlantic with possible bankruptcy. The Browns' cautious policies served them well, however, and shielded them from overwhelming losses during major economic crises, including the financial panics in 1819, 1837, and 1857.

The Browns had an edge on almost every other competitor after 1810 because by combining elements of their mercantile and financial functions they could handle more expeditiously the granting of advances against consignments. Other British consignees, without complementary financial services, were only able to authorize the granting of an advance; drawers still had to locate local buyers prepared to pay cash for their bills of exchange. The Browns not only authorized advances, but because of their simultaneous involvement in the foreign exchange market, they negotiated—or bought outright—the bills as soon as they were drawn, and of course at generally favorable exchange rates. Yet the Browns never put consignors under any obligation to sell the authorized bills of exchange drawn on the Browns' Liverpool office to the firm's American representatives. If third parties, seeking absolutely safe overseas remittances, willingly paid high rates for sterling bills drawn on William's Liverpool office, the Brown partners assumed an indifferent stance. Indeed, the willingness of third parties to pay premium prices for the Browns' bills only enhanced the prestige and reputation of the family enterprise.

The opening of the Liverpool branch in 1810 had a profound effect on the character of the firm's foreign exchange business as well. The Baltimore office and later other links in the Browns' network could take advantage of the opportunity to draw bills of exchange directly on the Liverpool office. Alexander Brown graduated from the status of broker to foreign exchange dealer. The Liverpool connection gave the firm the ability to draw a sterling bill on any business day throughout the year and, equally important, in the exact sum tailored to meet the needs of the customer. Bills drawn instantaneously in precise amounts commanded higher prices, which translated into greater profits. Until the market became much more competitive in the 1850s, the Browns tried to maintain a margin of 1.5 percent between their quoted buying and selling rates, and they rarely bargained with potential customers over prices, irrespective of the size of the potential transaction.

By conducting business with the Browns an American importer with large sums due overseas could avoid the problem of seeking out and eventually purchasing a whole series of sterling bills drawn by a number of exporters, in uneven amounts, on different English drawees with varying credit reputations. Instead that importer could deal directly with the Browns, who offered convenience and safety at only slightly higher exchange rates. Meanwhile, in the reverse operation, the American outlets could wait for opportune times, hoping for a drop in exchange rates, before buying covering sterling bills on sound English drawees to remit to the Liverpool office for collection.

The ability to coordinate activities on both sides of the Atlantic permitted the Browns to conduct foreign exchange operations on either a "covered" or "uncovered" basis. Covered operations involved the purchase of sterling bills on third party drawees prior to selling drafts drawn on the Liverpool office. Those operations were safer because the firm already possessed the offsetting remittances and knew at what rates it had acquired them. Uncov-

ered operations reversed the process: the American outlets sold sterling bills on the Liverpool office and then acquired the remittances to balance sales at some later date—weeks or even months later.

The uncovered account involved greater risk. It was predicated on two assumptions: that exchange rates in the months ahead would decline sufficiently to enhance profit margins and that a sufficient volume of offsetting remittances on sound drawees would be available for purchase in the market. But even the most carefully laid plans were vulnerable to the unpredictable twists and turns of economic and political events. If exchange rates suddenly rose rather than fell, or if American exporters stopped generating sufficient quantities of bills of exchange, a substantial potential for heavy losses arose. Viewed from another angle, the maintenance of an uncovered foreign exchange account resembled short selling in the stock market. Of course, the Browns never completely subjected themselves to the mercy of trends in the foreign exchange markets; if conditions deteriorated too much, the American outlets provided the Liverpool office with current funds through other means—the transfer of specie or the shipment of salable commodities such as cotton.

The Browns initially hesitated to operate an uncovered account even for short periods. As Alexander and his sons gained experience, however, they became much bolder. In the early 1820s they occasionally delayed coverage for up to three months. In later years the Browns operated uncovered exchange accounts for up to six months, taking advantage of profit opportunities arising from the seasonal character of American foreign trade.

As a general rule American importers received a disproportionate volume of their shipments during the spring and summer months. The heavy demand for sterling bills to pay the importers' overseas debts drove exchange rates up from May to September. In the fall, however, when American cotton and grains were harvested and shipped overseas, the huge supply of bills generated by American exporters drove rates downward. The Browns' strategy called for the American branches to act as net sellers of foreign exchange in the spring and summer; meanwhile, William's Liverpool office borrowed funds in the English money market where interest rates were typically lower than in the United States. In fall and winter the American outlets became net buyers, and they gradually covered their deficit balances with Liverpool. By April or May the American and Liverpool accounts reached equilibrium, and again a new seasonal cycle started.

In their efforts to take profitable advantage of normal seasonal fluctuations in trading patterns, the Browns acted unintentionally, and probably unwittingly, to reduce the amplitude of rate movements above and below the par figure of $4.86 to the English pound. The firm's year-round involvement helped to smooth out the foreign exchange market and therefore made it easier for all participants in the American nineteenth-century foreign trade sector to finance their various activities. By providing this specialized service in most of the major American ports, the Browns contributed greatly to the institutional maturation of American financial markets.

Once the firm had become established in the foreign exchange field, the partners discovered that a passive stance usually produced higher margins on exchange transactions. By 1820 the Baltimore branch reported that its sterling bills typically sold for up to 1 percent more than the prevailing rates on "ordinary bills." Until the emergence of the Second Bank of the United States (BUS) as the primary dealer in foreign exchange after 1823, the Browns apparently deferred to no other drawers in regard to the prices commanded for their sterling bills.

An important surviving letter from the Baltimore partners, Alexander and son George, to William in Liverpool, written in March 1821, reveals much about the nature of U.S. foreign exchange markets and the firm's place within them. The Baltimore office warned its counterpart overseas to make preparations to meet the burden of financing a large volume of sterling sales over the next few months without immediate reimbursement, because the American branches planned to sell steadily while exchange rates remained high. Alexander and George anticipated that imports would drop off soon given the prevailing sterling rates, and they hoped to cover their position sometime later when the rates had fallen. In the event William had any fears about his ability to sustain the financing of this temporary deficit based on his existing resources, the Baltimore partners volunteered to transfer to Liverpool some of the corporate stocks held in the firm's investment portfolio for use as collateral for a loan in the London money market. In planning their strategies the Browns possessed the flexibility to transfer assets from branch to branch and country to country. As a rule they held second-

The sons of Alexander Brown: George, John, William, and James. A portrait of their father hangs in the background.

ary reserves, mostly investments in the stocks and bonds of sound issuers in the United States where returns were higher, but they did not hesitate to shift resources overseas if it appeared that the Liverpool branch might be subject to undue pressure in financing anticipated deficits.

In the correspondence of 1821 the Baltimore partners also discussed the pattern of exchange rates in the major port cities in the mid-Atlantic region. "When Exchange is stationary we have generally found Phila. and this place full as good as New York." But when sterling rates fluctuated New York led the way: "It's the greatest market and always rises or falls there first." The partners cited the close relationship between the arrival and departure of transatlantic packet ships in the New York port and the corresponding movements in exchange rates. Taken in their entirety, the partners' remarks suggest just how much the foreign exchange markets in those three critical ports had become integrated by the early 1820s. Improvements in transportation and communications plus greater specialization by firms such as the Browns' in response to the growing size of urban economies had, in combination, led to much progress in creating a fairly uniform regional market for foreign exchange several years in advance of the initiatives launched by the Second BUS under Nicholas Biddle after his ascension to the presidency in 1823.

In truth, the rise of Biddle's BUS to a position of preeminence in the foreign exchange market in the mid 1820s was not detrimental to the Browns' operations. The national bank had opened a chain of branch offices in all the major American port cities, and it offered vigorous competition in the purchase and sale of sterling bills throughout the year in every geographical region. The bank conducted its foreign exchange business in cooperation with the House of Baring, and Biddle used the bank's enormous capital—$35 million—to dominate virtually every significant financial market in the nation. The Browns quickly moved into a second tier of exchange dealers ranking immediately behind the market leader. The bank's domineering position aided the Browns in planning their seasonal strategies because Biddle maintained a continuous market for sterling bills. As a result the Browns' American outlets sold heavily in the summer and early fall with little anxiety about covering their accounts in upcoming months. If purchasing bills from exporters proceeded slowly over the winter, the Browns always had the option of covering their Liverpool account with absolute certainty, if less profit, by transferring sterling bills bought from the national bank.

The Browns also discovered that they could regulate more carefully the volume of their sales and purchases by adjusting their rates vis-à-vis the bank. By moving their rates slightly up or down compared to the bank's buy-and-sell quotations, the Browns encouraged or discouraged transactions through the functioning of the impersonal pricing mechanism. The Baltimore branch remarked in 1828: "We could sell largely by taking .25 percent less, but shall probably sell as much as we like at the bank's price." Three years later, in 1831, the same office assessed the situation as follows: "We have now got to that standing that we get the same price for Exchange as the Bank U. States; . . . we believe we are the only private bill drawers that are able to obtain Bank U.S. price." When the Second BUS failed in its recharter efforts in 1832 and then liquidated its assets on schedule in 1836, the Brown firm moved at once into the leadership position in the American foreign exchange market, and it retained that high ranking for the next half century.

The opening of the Liverpool office presented the Browns with the opportunity to enter another financial market—the issue of letters of credit to American importers. This field was one of the last that the Browns entered in full force because a merchant banking house had to devote a good many years to building up its international reputation for financial integrity. Indeed, the letter-of-credit market was oligopolistic from the outset. A letter of credit was a device by which third parties, in this case the Browns, guaranteed the final payment of bills of exchange drawn by American importers purchasing goods from overseas suppliers. The Browns in essence allowed other merchants to conduct business in places far and wide on the basis of their own outstanding credit reputation. For that service they charged a commission, initially 2.5 percent of the amount of money guaranteed under each letter of credit.

The business was potentially very lucrative because under normal circumstances the Browns were not required to tie up any of their own funds in those transactions; they remained only contingently liable for their customers' debts. Many merchants gladly paid the fee required to obtain a document guaranteeing their overseas debts because it gave them the opportunity to buy goods in foreign markets where their own credit standing was slight or even nil. Meanwhile, foreign suppliers willingly sold to Americans about whom they knew little, since the Browns, or other well-known merchant bankers, stood behind the transaction.

The major risk in issuing letters of credit involved judging the reliability and credit worthiness of the American importer. The U.S. branches took the applications for credits, gathered the appropriate information about financial standing and character, and made the final decision about issuance, specifying the terms and amounts involved. The typical letter authorized the customer to draw sterling drafts, subject to certain limitations, which became payable 60 to 90 days after the seller had transmitted them to the Browns' Liverpool office. Upon determining the authenticity of the transaction the Liverpool office accepted the sterling bills and promised payment to the holder on the assigned due date. The resulting instrument, called a bankers' acceptance, remains the same term used today in reference to roughly similar transactions.

Before the acceptance matured, the American office assumed the responsibility of making certain that its local customer had remitted sufficient funds to Liverpool to cover the debt obligation. If an American importer failed to make the proper remittance, the Browns had to come up with the moneys from their own capital resources. When customers defaulted, the Browns sometimes recovered all or part of the deficiency, but on other occasions the losses proved unrecoverable. Potential losses in letter-of-credit operations, even when few in number, typically involved large amounts, and only one or two bad accounts could easily overwhelm the commissions earned from hundreds of reliable customers.

The first reference to the issuance of a letter of credit in the Browns' surviving records, dated 1820, to a Baltimore merchant, George Peabody, authorized him to draw bills of exchange totaling approximately $7,000. (Ironically, Peabody, after moving to London, later became one of the Browns' main competitors in this field.) The volume of business picked up dramatically with the opening of James's New York office in the mid 1820s. In the boom times of the early 1830s the Browns expanded their letter-of-credit volume substantially, as did many of the other Anglo-American merchant banking houses. Like other major issuers the firm was surprised by the sudden impact of the Panic of 1837. Only timely aid to William's Liverpool branch by the Bank of England saved the house from probable failure. Most of its illiquid debts stemmed from the letter-of-credit sphere of their business activities. When the firm finally settled all accounts, the partnership wrote off debts of about $300,000, a figure less than 5 percent of capital. Many competitors failed to weather the storm, however. In the aftermath of the panic the Browns moved into the leadership position in the American letter-of-credit market and retained that ranking for most of the next half century.

By the 1830s Alexander Brown could look back upon a long, varied, and enormously successful business career. He started out as a general merchant emphasizing the importation of linens from his Irish homeland. From that modest base in Baltimore he and his four sons built an Anglo-American merchant banking firm of the first rank, with branch offices in Liverpool, Philadelphia, and New York. The capital account of Alexander Brown & Sons grew from about $100,000 in 1810 to more than $4.5 million at his death–a steady increase of just over 15 percent per annum. During his lifetime Brown conducted a myriad of business activities: importing and exporting goods on his own account, financing the exports and imports of other U.S. merchants, dealing in foreign exchange, plus limited involvement with ship ownership, insurance underwriting, and investment banking. He was one of the last and most prosperous of the traditional, all-purpose merchants–those urban entrepreneurs who had dominated the major port cities in the colonial era and throughout the early national period.

After the founding partner's death the firm altered its strategies. James in New York and William in Liverpool assumed leadership, and over the next several decades they narrowed the range of business functions primarily to foreign exchange and letter-of-credit operations. The performance of those two financial services for the U.S. foreign trade sector carried the House of Brown to the pinnacle of Anglo-American merchant banking during the middle decades of the nineteenth century.

References:

Aytoun Ellis, *Heir of Adventure: The Story of Brown, Shipley & Co., Merchant Bankers* (London: Privately printed, 1960);

Ralph W. Hidy, *The House of Baring in American Trade and Finance: English Merchant Bankers at Work, 1763-1861* (Cambridge, Mass.: Harvard University Press, 1949);

John A. Kouwenhoven, *Partners in Banking: An Historical Portrait of a Great Private Bank, Brown Brothers Harriman & Co., 1818-1968* (New York: Doubleday, 1968);

Edwin J. Perkins, *Financing Anglo-American Trade: The House of Brown, 1800-1880* (Cambridge, Mass.: Harvard University Press, 1975).

Archives:

The letterbooks and financial records of the Brown family partnerships are found in two locations. The Library of Congress holds material generated by the Baltimore branch office, titled Alexander Brown & Sons. The New-York Historical Society and the New York Public Library hold information on the New York and Liverpool offices under the name Brown Brothers & Co.

Henry Charles Carey

(December 15, 1793-October 13, 1879)

by John W. Malsberger

Muhlenberg College

CAREER: Publisher (1814-1835); political economist (1835-1879).

The most influential American political economist of the nineteenth century, Henry Charles Carey broadly challenged the doctrines of the British neoclassical economists. Carey posited an optimistic set of theories that saw a harmony of interests between sections of the economy, leading to boundless growth and the betterment of all individuals. He trumpeted the virtues of high protective tariffs, banks, and limited liability laws, which he believed promoted economic harmony. His ideas not only reflected the spirit of the buoyant capitalism of nineteenth-century America, but also helped shape the industrial character of that capitalism.

Born in Philadelphia on December 15, 1793, Carey was the eldest son of Matthew Carey, an Irishman banished from his country in 1782 because of his protests against British rule. In his adopted land the elder Carey became a noted publisher, bookseller, economist, and philanthropist. The young Carey received little formal education, but was apparently taught much by his father. In addition to learning the publishing trade, he also absorbed his father's economic ideas, based largely on Alexander Hamilton's economic nationalism, and his intense Anglophobia.

In 1814 Carey became a partner in his father's publishing company and, following his father's retirement five years later, assumed control of what was then the largest publishing house in America. Included among the authors it published were Washington Irving, Thomas Carlyle, and Sir Walter Scott. By reading the wide array of manuscripts submitted to the firm, Carey broadened his education and whetted his appetite for intellectual pursuits. In 1835 he retired from active management of the publishing house (he officially removed himself from the partnership in October 1838) and devoted the re-

Henry Charles Carey (engraving by John Sartain)

mainder of his life to the study of political economy.

When Carey began his work on political economy, the eighteenth-century classical theories of Adam Smith and his nineteenth-century neoclassical followers, including David Ricardo, Thomas Malthus, and, later, John Stuart Mill, dominated the discipline. (Smith's work, which developed in opposition to British mercantilism, held great promise for the economic well-being of individuals.) Smith contended that economies operated according to immutable laws, and that an economy in which individuals could pursue their interests free of all government interference would automatically yield the most equitable distribution of goods and services. In the hands of the neoclassicists, however, Smith's theories took on a decidedly more pessimistic tone. Thomas Malthus predicted (in his earlier writings only, however) that the geometric rate of population growth would inevitably outstrip the sustaining ability of the land and lead to famine and social dislocation. David Ricardo's theory of rent came to similarly dire conclusions. He argued that the most fertile lands were settled first, and that an expanding population, by bringing increasing amounts of marginal land into cultivation, would at some point be unable to feed its inhabitants. Because the supply of land was inelastic, an expanding society invariably produced concentrations of wealth in the hands of landlords, who charged higher rents as productive land became more scarce. Foreseeing a future dominated by an increasingly inequitable distribution of wealth, inevitably leading to warfare between labor and capital, the neoclassicists, in contrast to Smith, held out only bleak prospects for individual welfare.

Carey's first economic work, *Essay on the Rate of Wages*, published in 1835, began his assault on these neoclassical theories. He accepted the classical contention that natural laws governed economies but insisted that the neoclassicists had drawn incorrect inferences about this economic truth from British history. Instead, Carey drew his version of immutable economic law from the situation in America. He asserted that the rapid economic and population expansion America had achieved in the Era of Good Feelings refuted Ricardo's and Malthus's arguments that natural limits to a nation's growth existed. Furthermore, America's practically unlimited potential for expansion arose not from neoclassical resource-based factors, but from the freedom established by republican government and a classless society. He resurrected Smith's optimistic appraisal of the economic future, but through a linkage of economic theory to political and social factors particular to America.

In this work Carey also expanded the neoclassical definition of capital in a way that strongly endorsed the American social system. Capital could not be regarded simply as material wealth used to produce more wealth, but, rather, should be defined broadly to include knowledge and talent. Anyone capable of using his ability to manipulate the natural world was, in Carey's view, a capitalist. Con-

sequently, the sharp division between labor and capital posited by the neoclassicists did not exist. Carey used that expanded definition of capital to undermine further the neoclassical position that inherent limits to economic growth existed. Workers' wages need not be restrained by rapid population growth and growing scarcity of land, Carey implied. Again drawing on the American experience (which Ricardo had explained, in the words of Paul K. Conkin, as the result of "distinctive and temporary natural advantages"), Carey maintained that wages would rise as long as ability, education, and industriousness expanded.

Carey continued his challenge to neoclassical theory in a three-volume work, *Principles of Political Economy*, published between 1837 and 1840. He continued to dispute Malthus's gloomy predictions, contending that as industrialization enhanced the technical capacity of society, the output of goods and services would expand more rapidly than population. He also predicted (correctly, as it turned out) that the birthrate would decline as industrialization progressed, something Malthus and Ricardo doubted. Carey believed that the desire for individual betterment would restrain population expansion in industrial society.

Ricardo's theory of rent was also taken to task in *Principles of Political Economy*. Carey made a survey of patterns of settlement and cultivation in the United States, Mexico, Great Britain, France, Italy, Greece, South America, and the Pacific Islands that indicated to him that productive land would remain freely available in spite of population expansion. He found, contrary to Ricardo, that the people often first settled the poorest, not the most fertile, land. Populations progressed to more fertile lands only when increases in wealth and labor enabled them to do so. Thus, an expanding population would not inevitably drive land prices beyond the reach of most renters or automatically increase the wealth of landlords. Rather, the world contained potential enough in land to sustain healthy growth far into the future.

The arguments Carey developed about population, rent, and land in *Principles of Political Economy* led him, in turn, to his most important conclusion, expressed with greater force than in *Essay on the Rate of Wages:* that societies were not composed of competing economic interests but were united in a harmony of complementary interests. Because land yielded little without the application of labor and capital, Carey asserted that the return to landowners (rent) was no different than the return on capital (interest) or the return to labor (wages). Since no commodity commanded more than the value of the labor required to reproduce it, technological gains would steadily reduce the relative value of labor in those commodities, thereby expanding workers' purchasing power. Capital's share of society's wealth, which the neoclassicists had argued would create sharp divisions between competing economic interests as it expanded, would in Carey's view remain relatively constant. The future did not promise war, pestilence, and famine. Rather, the harmony of interests promised peace, prosperity, and happiness.

Banks played a central role in Carey's theory of the harmony of economic interests. Beginning with his 1838 work, *The Credit System in France, Great Britain, and the United States*, Carey became a strong proponent of banking activities such as credit extension, note issue, and the investment of deposits, which he considered essential to economic expansion. To promote the chartering of banks, Carey also championed limited-liability laws that made individual investors responsible for the failure of a business only to the extent of their investment in it. The abolition of unlimited liability would benefit everyone by spurring economic growth.

The economic collapse following the Panic of 1837, which called into question Carey's belief that the American potential for growth was practically unlimited, forced him to rethink some of his earlier positions and produced some important changes in his views. Foremost among those changes was his attitude toward international trade. Until the early 1840s Carey had followed the free-trade principles of Adam Smith and eighteenth-century French economist Jean Baptiste Say. But the economy began its rebound only after the 1842 passage of a highly protective tariff bill, which convinced him that throughout its history America had prospered under protection and had been threatened by free trade. From that point on Carey became an uncompromising advocate of high protective tariffs. The Anglophobia inherited from his father also apparently influenced Carey's conversion to economic nationalism, since his writings consistently stressed the danger Britain posed to America's economic independence. He also may have been frightened away from free trade by several failed business ventures. In the late 1830s Carey invested heavily in a New Jer-

sey paper mill and in a Pennsylvania iron mill, but both enterprises went bankrupt, and he attributed their failure to the intense foreign competition allowed by low tariffs prior to 1842.

Carey fully and loudly proclaimed his devotion to economic nationalism in his works on political economy published in the late 1840s. In *The Past, the Present, and the Future* (1848) and *The Harmony of Interests, Agricultural, Manufacturing, and Commercial* (1849-1850) he not only expanded his attack on classical theory but also took direct aim at Britain's policy of free trade. British policy, he contended, was not designed to promote the interests of all commercial nations, but rather was a subtle effort to expand England's hegemony over the international economy. To guard against that outcome Carey insisted that the United States pursue a strict course of economic nationalism, using high tariffs both to protect its infant industries and to stimulate internal improvements. Such a course would not penalize any section or interest group. Since America was composed of complementary economic interests, high tariffs would benefit manufacturing, agriculture, and commerce by increasing the wealth and efficiency of the whole society.

Carey's economic nationalism reached a wide audience between 1849 and 1857, when he regularly contributed editorials to Horace Greeley's *New York Tribune*, then a strong advocate of American protectionism. Although his arguments left him vulnerable to criticism as an apologist for big business, his theories had a broad appeal to most Americans, partly because of their implicitly chauvinistic tone but also because they seemed to provide a scientific basis for protective tariffs. Carey's advocacy of economic nationalism helped provide an intellectual rationale for protection just as the United States entered its great period of industrial expansion.

Although Carey focused most of his attention on protective tariffs and on refuting the ideas of neoclassical economics, he was also associated with other causes. His belief that a harmony of interests united society, for example, led him to stress the importance of conserving the natural environment, which he saw as a vital component of that harmony. Anticipating the argument of later environmentalists, Carey reminded his readers that those who plundered the nation's resources undermined its productive capacity. He saved much of his most damaging criticism for the cash-crop system of southern planters, which exhausted the region's soil.

Carey during the time of his publishing career

Carey expanded his attack on the South's plantation economy in 1853 with the publication of an antislavery tract, *The Slave Trade, Domestic and Foreign: Why It Exists, and How It May Be Extinguished.* Influenced by the publication of Harriet Beecher Stowe's *Uncle Tom's Cabin* (1852), Carey's work on the slave trade was undoubtedly written to add support to the abolitionist cause, but it also provided another opportunity for him to condemn Britain. He compared southern slavery to British rule in Ireland and argued that since both had produced pauperism and social degradation, Britain could claim no moral superiority over the United States.

Following the Civil War, Carey also became a proponent of monetary inflation, eventually joining the Greenback party to promote the cause. His support, however, in no way marked a departure from his earlier ideas. He viewed monetary inflation as a logical extension of his philosophy of growth. Monetary inflation, by devaluing the U.S. dollar, also increased the price of imported goods and thus served the same purpose as protective tariffs.

Throughout his career Carey's ideas on political economy reflected his desire to promote the development of the American economy. But he continued to reflect many of the classical principles of Adam Smith. He did not so much reject classical economic theory as adapt it to the conditions of nineteenth-century America. Though contemporary economists often ridiculed his work, it was perfectly attuned to the buoyant capitalism of the period. Carey's ideas also captured the hearts and minds of American businessmen, politicians, and newspaper editors because they separated the United States from the depravity of the Old World. By providing a set of hopeful assumptions with which to view the future, Carey's ideas played a major role in expanding the climate of confidence essential for American industrialization.

Selected Publications:

The Geography, History and Statistics, of America, and the West Indies (London: Sherwood, Jones, 1823);

Essay on the Rate of Wages (Philadelphia: Carey, Lea & Blanchard, 1835);

The Harmony of Nature (Philadelphia: Carey, Lea & Blanchard, 1836);

Principles of Political Economy, 3 volumes (Philadelphia: Carey, Lea & Blanchard, 1837-1840);

The Credit System in France, Great Britain, and the United States (London: J. Miller / Philadelphia: Carey, Lea & Blanchard, 1838);

Answers to the Questions: What Constitutes Currency? What are the Causes of Unsteadiness of the Currency? and What is the Remedy? (Philadelphia: Lea & Blanchard, 1840);

Beauties of the Monopoly System of New Jersey (Philadelphia: C. Sherman, 1848);

The Frauds, Falsifications, and Impostures of Railroad Monopolists (N.p., 1848);

Letters to the People of New Jersey, on the Frauds, Extortions, and Oppressions of the Railroad Monopoly (Philadelphia: Carey & Hart, 1848);

The Past, the Present, and the Future (Philadelphia: Carey & Hart, 1848; London: Longman, Brown, Green & Longmans, 1848);

The Harmony of Interests, Agricultural, Manufacturing, and Commercial, 2 volumes (Philadelphia: Skinner, 1849,1850);

The Railroad Monopoly (Philadelphia: L. R. Bailey, 1849);

Proceedings of the Late Railroad Commission (Philadelphia: L. R. Bailey, 1850);

The Prospect: Agricultural, Manufacturing, Commercial, and Financial (Philadelphia: Skinner, 1851);

How To Increase Competition for the Purchase of Labor, and How to Raise the Wages of the Laborour (New York: Finch, 1852);

How to Have Cheap Iron (New York, 1852);

Letter Addressed to a Cotton Planter of Tennessee (New York: Finch, 1852);

The Working of British Free Trade (New York: Finch, 1852);

Letters on International Copyright (Philadelphia: A. Hart, 1853);

The Slave Trade, Domestic and Foreign: Why It Exists, and How It May Be Extinguished (Philadelphia: A. Hart, 1853; London: Low, 1853);

The North and the South (New York: Office of the Tribune, 1854);

Letters to the President, on the Foreign and Domestic Policy of the Union (Philadelphia: Lippincott / London: Trübner, 1858);

Principles of Social Science, 3 volumes (Philadelphia: Lippincott / London: Trübner, 1858-1859);

The French and American Tariffs Compared (Detroit: J. Warren, 1861; Philadelphia: Collins, 1861);

Financial Crises: Their Causes and Effects (Philadelphia: H. C. Baird, 1863);

The Paper Question (Philadelphia: Collins, 1864);

The Currency Question (Philadelphia: Collins, 1865);

The Farmer's Question (Philadelphia: Collins, 1865);

The Iron Question (Philadelphia: Collins, 1865);

Letters to the Hon. Schuyler Colfax (Philadelphia: Collins, 1865);

The Railroad Question (Philadelphia: Collins, 1865);

The Way to Outdo England Without Fighting Her (Philadelphia: H. C. Baird, 1865);

British Free Trade, How It Affects the Agriculture and the Foreign Commerce of the Union (New York: Iron Age, 1866; Chicago: J. A. Norton, 1866);

Contraction or Expansion? Repudiation or Resumption? (Philadelphia: H. C. Baird, 1866);

The Public Debt, Local and National: How to Provide For Its Discharge While Lessening the Burden of Taxation (Philadelphia: H. C. Baird, 1866);

The Resources of the Union (Philadelphia: H. C. Baird, 1866);

Reconstruction: Industrial, Financial and Political (Philadelphia: Collins, 1867);

Review of the Decade 1857-67 (Philadelphia: Collins, 1867);

The Finance Minister, the Currency, and the Public Debt (Philadelphia: Collins, 1868);

How Protection, Increase of Private and Public Revenues, and National Independence March Hand in Hand Together (Philadelphia: Collins, 1869);

Resumption: How It May Profitably Be Brought About (Philadelphia: Collins, 1869);

Shall We Have Peace? Peace Financial, and Peace Political? (Philadelphia: Collins, 1869);

Currency Inflation: How It Has Been Produced, and How It May Profitably Be Reduced (Philadelphia: Collins, 1870);

Wealth: Of What Does It Consist? (Philadelphia: H. C. Baird, 1870);

A Memoir of Stephen Colwell (Philadelphia: H. C. Baird, 1871);

The International Copyright Question Considered (Philadelphia: H. C. Baird, 1872);

Miscellaneous Works of Henry C. Carey (Philadelphia: H. C. Baird, 1872);

The Unity of Law (Philadelphia: H. C. Baird, 1872);

Capital and Labor (Philadelphia: Collins, 1873);

Of the Rate of Interest; and of its Influence on the Relations of Capital and Labor (Philadelphia: Collins, 1873);

The British Treaties of 1871 & 1874 (Philadelphia: Collins, 1874);

Miscellaneous Papers on the National Finances, the Currency, and Other Economic Subjects (Philadelphia: H. C. Baird, 1875);

Appreciation in the Price of Gold (Philadelphia: Collins, 1876);

Commerce, Christianity, and Civilization, versus British Free Trade (Philadelphia: Collins, 1876);

Resumption: When, and How, Will It End? (Philadelphia: Collins, 1877);

How to Perpetuate the Union (N.p., n.d.);

Ireland's Miseries, Their Cause (New York: Tribune, n.d.).

References:

Paul K. Conkin, *Prophets of Prosperity: America's First Political Economists* (Bloomington: Indiana University Press, 1980);

William Elder, *A Memoir of Henry C. Carey* (Philadelphia: H. C. Baird, 1880);

A. D. H. Kaplan, *Henry Charles Carey: A Study in American Economic Thought* (Baltimore: Johns Hopkins University Press, 1931);

Charles Levermore, "Henry C. Carey and His Social System," *Political Science Quarterly*, 5 (December 1890): 553-582;

James Moore Swank, *History of the Manufacture of Iron in All Ages*, second edition (Philadelphia: American Iron & Steel Institute, 1892).

Central Banks

Modern Americans associate the term "central bank" with an institution that engages in deliberate, planned, and discretionary management of the money supply. A central bank is usually a relatively large, nationally created and chartered institution empowered to create money (that is, issue bank notes). It not only holds the reserves of other domestic banks but also holds international monetary reserves, and thus it serves as a focal point for international financial exchanges. As one of its primary responsibilities, a central bank handles government financial transactions and usually holds government deposits. Part of its obligation to government involves making loans to the government, presumably on a basis no other bank could or would.

American concepts of central banks derive in great measure from the colonists' experiences with the Bank of England (created in 1694), although the Swedish Riksbank predated it by almost 30 years. To Americans in the early Republic, discussions of a central bank concentrated on the control of the country's gold reserves and on the questions of loans and note issue. The control over large gold and silver (specie) reserves allowed the central bank to operate as a "lender of last resort"—essentially to make loans to commercial banks in distress when no other bank could. That position, however, eventually entailed some regulatory functions, for, faced with limited resources, in a crisis the central bank had to determine who was deserving of its assistance. In normal times the bank had to pursue policies that would, if at all possible, prevent distress in the commercial banking sector. Ultimately such policies took on the aura of "political" decisions, and therefore the banks, especially in the United States, fell victim to considerable criticism, for policy decisions always favored some groups or sectors of the economy over others. For that reason central banks have always been the source of much hostility in the United States.

Central banking in the United States originated with the First Bank of the United States (BUS). Historians and economists still dispute whether either the First or Second BUS had true central banking powers or if either used what powers they had. Scholarly opinion seems to have arrived at the consensus that neither bank, despite the relatively large size of each at the time of creation (1791 and 1816, respectively), attempted to wield central banking powers to any great extent. Although both had a large number of notes in circulation compared to any other bank, historians doubt that either controlled the money supply. Nevertheless, the public frequently believed that both banks could influence the economy in a significant way. Both banks, for example, issued notes acceptable for payment to the government, but BUS notes never carried "legal tender" status, meaning that no one was obliged to accept them in payment for goods or services. The First BUS failed to receive a recharter in 1811, and people blamed the financial disruptions that occurred over the subsequent five years in part on the absence of a national bank. Congress saw a new BUS as a means to bolster the sale of government bonds and thus help finance the debt from the War of 1812. Therefore Congress chartered the Second BUS, modeled along the same lines as the first, in 1816. It had a 20-year charter and like the first was authorized to do something no other bank could: establish branches in the states. Nevertheless, both were commercial banks first and foremost and conducted their operations as such.

The details of the "Bank War," which ended the life of the Second BUS, appear elsewhere in this volume. With the expiration of the national charter for the Second BUS in 1836 (or its virtual emasculation in 1833 when President Andrew Jackson ordered the deposits withdrawn), the United States no longer had a central bank of any type. The Treasury Department conducted some central banking activities, but no mechanism of centralized control of the money supply existed again until the creation of the Federal Reserve System in 1913. Unlike the First or Second BUS, the Federal Reserve banks did not engage in commercial banking but instead acted as "bankers' banks." They held the reserve deposits of the member banks and made loans to them from the pool of deposits (called "discounting" commercial paper). As envisioned, the Federal Reserve System proposed to provide central banking functions and an elastic money supply and was empowered to regulate banks in a limited sense through the management of the member banks' reserves or by the interest rate it charged on its loans to member banks (called the "discount rate"). In addition, the Federal Reserve banks examined member banks.

Unlike other central banks, the Federal Reserve featured 12 district Reserve banks located in cities across the country, which at first remained highly independent of each other. Despite the forces that had succeeded in establishing the central bank, enough opposition remained against concentrating the power of money in the United States (especially in New York City) that Congress sought to distribute the representation and benefits of the bank throughout the country, with the South and West

heavily represented among Reserve cities. Each Reserve bank had jurisdiction over all commercial banks in its district, and although only national banks were required to become members, the founders envisioned state banks joining. That did not become a reality in the early years of the system. Federal Reserve banks issued a new form of paper money, supplanting the national bank notes, called Federal Reserve notes.

With the creation of the Federal Reserve System the forces that had lobbied for a central bank saw their vision come to fruition. How it behaved over the ensuing decades is a matter for a subsequent volume in this series.

See also:

Nelson W. Aldrich, George F. Baker, The Bank War and the Specie Circular, Salmon P. Chase, Federal Reserve Act, First Bank of the United States, Legal Tender Cases, National Bank and Currency Acts, Second Bank of the United States, Frank Arthur Vanderlip.

—Editor

Salmon P. Chase

(January 13, 1808-May 7, 1873)

by Roberta Sue Alexander

University of Dayton

CAREER: Teacher, Washington, D.C. (1827-1829); lawyer, Cincinnati, Ohio (1830-1849); city councilman, Cincinnati (1840-1841); U.S. senator, state of Ohio (1849-1855); governor of Ohio (1856-1860); U.S. secretary of the treasury (1861-1864); chief justice of the United States (1864-1873).

Salmon Portland Chase, leading mid-nineteenth-century Republican politician, secretary of the treasury during the Civil War, and chief justice of the United States during the Reconstruction Era, influenced Americans' views of freedom and liberty, banking and finance, and federal versus state power during the most important transitional period in American history. Born on January 13, 1808, in Cornish, New Hampshire, to Ithamar and Janet Ralston Chase, Chase grew up in a family struggling to achieve middle-class economic stability. Despite those tough circumstances, he began a classical education in the nearby town of Windsor, Vermont, as a youngster. Chase's father, a farmer and prominent member of his community, served regularly in the New Hampshire state legislature as a Federalist. In addition to farming and politics, Ithamar Chase tried his hand in the operation of a glass factory and a tavern. Both enterprises failed, and when he died in 1817, the family faced severe economic hardship. To help ease the financial crisis, at age twelve Chase went to Ohio to live with his uncle, Philander Chase, a minister in the Episcopal church who was just embarking for Worthington to take up new duties as bishop of Ohio.

Under his uncle's care, first in Worthington and then in Cincinnati (after Philander Chase became president of Cincinnati College), Chase continued his classical studies. But he was unhappy under the care of the rigid and stern man and gladly returned east when Philander Chase left for England to raise money to establish Kenyon College. Back in

Salmon P. Chase (courtesy of the National Archives, Brady Collection)

New England, Chase worked as a teacher, attended Royalton Academy in Vermont, and in 1826 graduated Phi Beta Kappa from Dartmouth College.

In December 1826 Chase moved to Washington, D.C., where he hoped to establish a school to earn money to pursue his goal of a career in law and politics. Only one student enrolled. Chase eventually joined A. R. Plumley's classical school, where he taught the sons of some of Washington's most prominent leaders, including those of Kentucky senator Henry Clay and Attorney General William Wirt. Wirt became Chase's mentor, friend, and role model. After more than two years of reading law under Wirt's careless guidance, Chase sought admission to the bar in 1829. The examining committee, although not impressed by Chase's mediocre performance, agreed to waive the three-year minimum study requirement after Chase explained his intention to leave Washington immediately to begin practice in the West.

At the age of twenty-two Chase arrived in Cincinnati and was quickly admitted to the Ohio bar. After struggling for several years as a fledgling attorney he formed several advantageous partnerships, and business increased. Through his association with Daniel Caswell he became solicitor of the Cincinnati branch of the Bank of the United States and then the Lafayette Bank. Also beginning in 1833, he published a three-volume collection, *Statutes of Ohio and the Northwestern Territory* (1833-1835), which brought him recognition if not much money. It became a standard legal reference work in the state. By 1835 Chase had achieved a measure of financial stability with his own law firm and his own junior partner. By 1845 the firm earned close to $10,000 annually, allowing Chase to invest his discretionary funds in real estate. He became recognized as an expert in banking, commercial, and land law.

Chase was an attractive man, standing higher than six feet tall, "with a broad and majestic form." Once established in the community he quickly found a suitable mate, Catherine Jane "Kitty" Garniss, whom he married on March 4, 1834. In November 1835 they celebrated the birth of a daughter, Catherine Amelia. But Chase's happiness was short-lived. Within a month, Kitty died from complications of childbirth. Chase, in Philadelphia at the time, after receiving assurance that Kitty's health had improved, was stricken with guilt and grief. Tragedy continued to plague his personal life. In 1839 Catherine Amelia died of scarlet fever. The pain of this loss was eased somewhat by the companionship of Eliza Ann Smith, whom Chase had married earlier that year. Their first daughter, Catherine Jane (Kate), lived to adulthood, but two other daughters died within their first years. Then, after a long illness, Eliza died in 1845. Chase's third wife, Sarah Belle Dunlop Ludlow, whom he married in 1846, died in 1852, leaving Chase with one other daughter, Janet (Nettie) Ralston. A second child, Josephine Ludlow, died before her first birthday.

Historians have speculated that because of those tragedies Chase determined to avoid close rela-

tionships and subordinate his private life to his professional duty. Contemporaries characterized him as "aloof," with a "forbidding" personality. Some depicted him as a pompous elitist, smug and inflexible. Many found him humorless, puritanical, ponderous, and without charm. Still, despite his aloofness, Chase remained devoted to his family. He provided money and loans to his brothers and sisters, even when such aid put him into debt. He was also a loving, overindulgent father.

From his first years in Cincinnati, Chase actively engaged in philanthropic activities. He was instrumental in establishing a lyceum for the city and also worked in the temperance movement, in St. Paul's Episcopal Church, and for an organization that distributed Bibles to the public. Only slowly and with some reluctance, however, did he become associated with the antislavery movement—an association that became the hallmark of his concerns and his career. Originally a Whig, he aligned himself with conservatives such as Nicholas Longworth and Josiah Lawrence, president of the Lafayette Bank, who favored colonization of slaves and worked to rid Cincinnati and the nation of African-Americans. In July 1836, however, an antiabolitionist incident in the city caused a transformation in Chase's thinking when a mob attacked local abolitionist newspaperman James G. Birney and destroyed his press. The mob then spent an evening looting the city's black neighborhoods. Cincinnati abolitionists, including Chase's sister and brother-in-law, Abigail and Isaac Colby, feared for their lives. Abigail sought refuge in Chase's home. Chase, appalled at the mob's disregard for personal liberty and freedom of the press, defied the mob, blocking their way into a hotel where they thought Birney was hiding. Later he acted as Birney's attorney in damage suits. He took those actions despite the potential political and economic risk entailed by alienating Longworth, Lawrence, and other leaders of the Cincinnati business community.

After the riots in Cincinnati Chase became more actively involved in the antislavery cause. While he never considered himself an abolitionist because of his belief that the federal government could not interfere legally with slavery in the states that chose to protect it, he struggled to limit slavery to the southern states and to undermine the enforcement of federal fugitive slave laws in Ohio. He developed a legal defense against the return of runaway slaves and against the prosecution of those who helped them escape, which earned him the title "Attorney General for Runaway Negroes."

No court ever accepted Chase's primary argument against fugitive slave laws. He maintained that the statutes were violations of the basic principle of the Declaration of Independence that all had a "natural right to human liberty." Neither the federal government nor the free states, therefore, had any obligation to aid in the capture of runaways. On the contrary Chase insisted that the federal government had an obligation to divorce itself from the defense or protection of slavery. The Supreme Court rejected that argument in *Prigg* v. *Pennsylvania* as it upheld the constitutionality of federal fugitive slave laws, but Chase's position formed the basis for one of the major arguments of the Republican party against slavery in the territories. It also inspired part of Justice John McLean's dissent in the Dred Scott decision of 1857.

Chase developed other arguments in his work for runaways that proved more successful in the courts. He maintained that the fugitive slave law was inoperable in Ohio and other northern states because the Northwest Ordinance made slavery illegal north of the Ohio River. Any runaway entering Ohio became free by virtue of this ordinance and by Ohio law. Chase also contended that Ohio personal liberty laws took precedence over slaveowners' rights of comity. Any slave voluntarily brought to Ohio, even as a temporary sojourner, was technically not a fugitive and therefore not subject to the fugitive slave law. While most courts rejected Chase's arguments in cases dealing with southern runaways, Chase had some success when the slave fled his or her master while sojourning in Ohio. He argued that the fugitive slave law did not apply in those cases because the slave had not run from a slave state to a free state. The former slave had merely left the master once the master had voluntarily taken the slave to a free state. With that defense Chase was able to gain acquittals in a few cases where his defendants were charged with violating the fugitive slave law.

In addition to defending runaway slaves and abolitionists who aided their escapes, Chase attacked racial discrimination against free blacks in the areas of education, legal rights, and suffrage. He also helped establish and continued throughout his life to support the Cincinnati Orphan Asylum for Colored Children. Later he helped establish Wilberforce University, an institution dedicated to the higher education of Ohio blacks.

By 1840 Chase was recognized as a leading opponent of slavery and an eloquent spokesman for equal rights. The antislavery mission transformed his entire political ideology. Originally a pro-national-bank Whig who disdained Andrew Jackson and the common man Jackson symbolized, Chase reassessed these views as he increased his involvement in antislavery work. He had become active in politics soon after arriving in Cincinnati, serving as a delegate at the 1831 National Republican convention that nominated Henry Clay for president. He became a Whig when that party coalesced in 1834 and supported William Henry Harrison for president in 1836. In the late 1830s he resisted the temptation to join the antislavery Liberty party movement, preferring to move the Whigs to a more active role in the battle. In 1840 Chase was elected to the Cincinnati city council as a "Log Cabin" Whig in support of Harrison. But after newly elected president Harrison died in 1841 and John Tyler, a Virginia slaveholder, became president and titular head of the Whig party, Chase renounced his Whig ties and joined the third-party Liberty movement. He had come to support the Jacksonian abolition of the Bank of the United States and the idea of an independent treasury system, believing that national banks constituted a system of unfair privilege. The Whig party's failure to embrace antislavery left him nothing to support. He campaigned for the Liberty candidate for the Ohio governorship in 1842 and supported Birney (though not his abolitionist stance) for the presidency in 1844. In 1846, as the Liberty party was losing steam, he wrote, "I do not at all concur in Whig views of public policy. . . . I do not believe in a high tariff, in a Bank of the United States, or a system of corporate banking." It is difficult to determine the cause of Chase's dramatic shift in fiscal ideology. Perhaps he came to oppose the national bank because it supported cotton planters. But personal associations and antagonisms could also be contributing factors. Increasingly, Chase's personal and political enemies, like Cincinnati's conservative bankers, were those who both opposed his slavery work and supported Whig economic views.

By the mid 1840s, despite his leadership in the Liberty party, in terms of major-party allegiance Chase considered himself a Democrat, or, more specifically, a Free Democrat, a Free-Soil Democrat, or

The Chase family home in Columbus, Ohio

an Independent Democrat. That is, he came to acknowledge "the great principles of the old party . . . , such as the sub-treasury and free trade," while rejecting its proslavery stance. He was unwilling to align himself formally with the national party as long as it refused to adopt a firm stand against the extension of slavery into the territories. He attended the Ohio Democratic party convention in January 1848, but the convention failed to endorse the Wilmot Proviso prohibiting territorial extension of slavery. Chase began to search seriously for a way to bring Liberty party moderates together with antislavery Democrats and Whigs to form a national coalition based on the proviso. During the summer of 1848 he helped organize the Free Soil party. He wrote much of its platform and persuaded his old Liberty party friends to support Martin Van Buren for president. The new party did so well in Ohio that when the new state legislature convened in Columbus, Free Soilers held the balance of power. Chase campaigned vigorously for the open Senate seat, and after months of deadlock he persuaded state Democrats to throw their support to him. The Democrats still held much of his affections, as he explained upon entering the Senate in

1849: "I am a Democrat, and I feel earnestly solicitous for the success of the Democratic organization and the triumph of its principles. The doctrines of the Democracy on the subjects of trade, currency, and special privileges commend the entire assent of my judgment."

While campaigning for the Senate, Chase also lobbied state legislators to modify Ohio's black code. During the campaign Free Soilers promised to work for equal rights, and Chase continued to remind them of the need to fulfill that pledge. Although the Free Soilers did not get everything they wanted, the legislature did amend the codes. Blacks gained the rights to enter Ohio without posting a bond, to testify in court without restriction, and to attend segregated public schools, but they still could not serve on juries, receive relief in poorhouses, or vote.

When Chase arrived in Washington to take his seat in the Senate, Democratic party leaders rejected him, denying him both committee assignments and the opportunity to participate in the Democratic caucus. As a third-party senator, he found himself relegated to a peripheral role. Still, he emerged as an able antislavery advocate, opposing the Compromise of 1850 and the Kansas-Nebraska Act of 1854. He also gained public works projects for his constituents—a custom-house and a marine hospital in Cincinnati and a canal around Portland Falls on the Ohio River. On economic issues he espoused the traditional Democratic belief in a minimal role for the federal government, opposing federal funding for internal improvements and railroad land grants. But the Democratic party was changing. When Stephen Douglas, one of the party's major leaders, pushed for subsidies for the Illinois Central Railroad, Chase "could do no more than try to reduce the acreage granted and the privileges given to the railroad companies."

Chase also worked to expand the base of the Free Soil party. His "Appeal of the Independent Democrats in Congress to the People of the United States," published in a January 1854 issue of the Washington newspaper *National Era*, was one of the more effective ways he sought to woo northern Democrats to Free Soilism. He appealed to whites to oppose the Kansas-Nebraska proposal on the basis of free soil and free labor rather than the principle of black justice and portrayed the act as "an atrocious plot" to spread slavery to the North. He believed that the clear threat to liberty posed by the bill would stimulate a major party realignment.

After the passage of the Kansas-Nebraska Act, Chase concentrated on organizing antislavery elements under a new party banner. In addition to seeking allies among disillusioned Democrats, he actively recruited former Whigs. By 1855 two major elements fought for control of the newly developing Ohio Republican party. Members of the Whig, Know-Nothing, conservative faction maintained a mild antislavery extension position. They expressed a willingness to accept the restoration of the Missouri Compromise line in the hope of ending agitation over slavery on a basis acceptable to both Northerners and Southerners. Many also held nativist, anti-Catholic ideas. While they took conflicting stands on economic issues, they tended to advocate the activist positions on banking and taxation favored by the business community. The Democratic-Free Soil element was composed of radical antislavery men who refused to compromise on the issue of the extension of slavery into the territories. They also opposed the nativist, anti-Catholic views of the Know-Nothings. Because of their focus on slavery issues they tended to be indifferent to eco-

nomic issues, although many held extreme laissez-faire viewpoints.

Chase successfully worked to unite those two factions on his own terms, so he could head a winning ticket in the upcoming Ohio gubernatorial election. The July 13, 1855, fusion convention in Columbus wrote the platform Chase advocated and nominated him for governor. While the Whig faction comprised the majority at the convention, the Free Soilers refused to compromise on the key issues of antislavery and nativism. They insisted that Chase head the party's ticket as a symbol of good faith on the part of the former Whigs. The platform denounced the Kansas-Nebraska Act and remained silent on Know-Nothingism. On economic issues it merely pledged, in vague language, a frugal administration and "a just and equal basis of taxation." Some Know-Nothing men, unwilling to accept the platform and Chase's nomination, held their own convention and nominated another candidate for governor.

The campaign centered on slavery issues; economic considerations played only a limited role. The newspaper the *Ohio State Journal* compared this new political era with the past. During the nation's early history, it wrote, foreign policy questions dominated politics. Then, in the first decades of the nineteenth century, "our internal industrial affairs commanded our attention. This was the era of banks, tariffs, and internal improvements." Now, it continued, economic issues were settled; "the great and absorbing questions" of the 1850s were "territorial extension and slavery propagandism." Still, many bankers and conservative businessmen worried about Chase's economic positions. Whig Republicans worked hard to persuade them that only a united party would enable them to reverse the antibusiness, antibanking policies of the previous Democratic administrations. But, in southern Ohio, with its strong economic ties to the South and more nativist and antiblack attitudes, Chase ran well behind the rest of the Republican ticket. Cincinnati businessmen feared that the election of an "abolitionist" would destroy their trade with the South.

In the three-man race for governor, Chase won a plurality of 48.5 percent of the vote while the Republican party gained a comfortable margin in both houses of the legislature. As governor Chase proposed many of the reform measures he had advocated for the past 25 years, such as improving the penal system, establishing facilities to care for the mentally ill and the disabled, and expanding women's rights. He also asked the legislature to establish a state-supported agricultural college and a railroad commission. While the legislature enacted a married woman's property law in response to Chase's urgings, it failed to act on his other proposals.

Chase and the Whig-dominated Republican party worked together more effectively on banking and tax reform. While Chase was known for his pro-Democratic economic views, which included support for hard money and a suspicion of banks and bankers, as governor he proposed both banking and tax reforms that the Republican majority quickly enacted. New laws exempted many banks from taxation and permitted taxpayers to deduct debts from credits. Chase also supported Whig-Republican legislation that would have expanded free banking in Ohio, but Ohio voters rejected the proposal in a state constitution-mandated referendum. He worked to get around that result. While the 1851 Ohio constitution required popular ratification of all new banking laws (hence the referendum), the state supreme court ruled that the free-banking law enacted in 1851 was unimpaired by the provisions of the constitution. On that basis Chase advocated the expansion of free banking via amendments to the 1851 banking act. Amendments, he claimed, did not need popular approval for they were not new laws. While that idea proved useful in the future, Chase never had the opportunity to implement the idea; the Democratic-controlled legislature elected in 1857 blocked all of his efforts in that direction.

Chase's 1857 reelection campaign, like the campaign of 1855, focused mainly on slavery issues, especially on the recent Supreme Court decision in *Dred Scott* v. *Sanford*. Banking and other economic issues rarely surfaced. But two major scandals, one involving favoritism on the part of the Democrats on the issue of contracts for the repair of the state's canal system and the other involving embezzlement by both the current Republican and former Democratic state treasurers, enlivened and complicated the campaign. Both scandals tended to damage Republicans more than Democrats. In addition, the financial panic of 1857 resulted in the collapse of many banks—including the large Ohio Life Insurance and Trust Company, whose collapse may have started the panic—and caused increased opposition to the Republican free-banking position. Demo-

crats, taking advantage of these events, captured control of the legislature, but Chase won reelection as governor, albeit by the narrowest margin in Ohio's history.

Chase's most important accomplishment in his second term was his successful reform of the state's militia system. He also worked with some success to settle the issue of the disposition of the increasingly unprofitable state-controlled canal system. In his first term Chase's Democratic philosophy of minimal involvement in economic activity led him to propose the sale of the canals. While both parties tended to support the plan, it failed because businessmen opposed it. In 1859 the Democrats enacted a measure to lease the canals. Chase and the Republicans supported the leasing principle but opposed the particular provisions of the statute. History proved the Republicans right; the law's stringent requirements discouraged bids. Not until a Republican legislature enacted a new statute in 1861 did Ohio successfully lease its canals to private business interests.

Chase worked hard as governor to increase his popularity and solidify his position within the Republican party. Despite his support of Whig-sponsored economic policies and his willingness to modify his antitariff views, however, he never could attract those former-Whig Republicans, who resented his Democratic party connections and his strong antislavery position. Because of that opposition, along with his inability to create a well-functioning political machine, in 1860 Chase failed to achieve his dream—nomination and election as president of the United States.

Despite Chase's failure to unite his home state's delegation behind him for the presidential nomination, he campaigned diligently for the Republican ticket. After the election Ohio Republicans rewarded him with a U.S. Senate seat after they again won the governorship and control of the state legislature. But Chase never took the seat. Abraham Lincoln, recognizing Chase's loyalty to the party as well as his ability to add antislavery weight to the cabinet, offered him the position of secretary of the treasury. With some reluctance, Chase accepted the position. He wondered whether serving the Senate might be better for the nation and for his political career. He would have preferred the job of secretary of war. He had never seemed particularly enlivened by economic and financial issues.

Once he accepted the position of secretary of the treasury, Chase devoted all his energies to his diverse tasks. Most historians conclude that he did a capable job. He found lenders for the millions of dollars in loans the government sought, controlled trade in the war zone, administered the greenback program, and supervised confiscated property and abandoned slaves. He also called for such bold new policies as a national banking system and a graduated income tax. Finally, Chase pushed for a firm policy of emancipation and a vigorous prosecution of the war.

Making the large and rapidly expanding Treasury bureaucracy function efficiently and honestly and solving the problems of war financing initially constituted Chase's chief tasks. He was only partially successful, but many have wondered if anyone could have achieved as much in the same situation. Chase had to create an effective means for a horse-and-buggy nation to finance a modern war. In the 1850s the federal budget averaged less than 2 percent of the gross national product. During the Civil War budgets increased to more than 15 percent of output.

Chase expanded the Treasury Department dramatically. From 383 clerks in 1861, the Treasury grew by 1864 to include 2,000 clerks along with new assistant treasurers, custom-house officials, and internal revenue agents spread throughout the country. One of Chase's most difficult jobs consisted of filling those positions with competent, honest people. His record in that regard was spotty. Many accused Chase of primarily concerning himself with building a loyal political machine that would pave the way for his nomination as president in 1864. Chase certainly appointed those loyal to him to many Treasury positions, but other cabinet officers also did so. Moreover, historians have recognized the competence of Chase's leading appointees. Finally, Chase and George Harrington, his assistant secretary, initiated an examination system to expand the number of qualified, nonpolitical appointees and to promote those most qualified. Chase also was the first treasury secretary to employ women in government, initially hiring them as currency counters and later as assistants and clerks. Still, he remained conscious of his opportunity to create a powerful machine. Many unqualified and corrupt people served in his department, and Chase arrogantly protected his right to appoint whom he pleased. On several occasions he threatened to re-

Chase as secretary of the treasury, 1861 (courtesy of the Chase Manhattan Archives)

sign over patronage disputes. Finally, in 1864 (after the presidential election), much to Chase's surprise and chagrin, Lincoln accepted his resignation when he tried again to use the bluff to get his way on a patronage matter.

While Chase continued to play politics during his tenure at the Treasury, he worked long hours attempting to deal with the enormous financial problems besetting the nation. The Panic of 1857, coupled with the incompetence of the Buchanan administration, had created a $75 million federal debt—the highest the country had ever amassed. With the government's bonds selling below par and a national tradition of low federal taxation, the only federal revenue sources, besides a few negligible taxes, were the low tariff of 1857 and land sales. Clearly, new taxes would be needed. But that required time not only for congressional action but also for collection. Chase assumed, however, as did nearly everyone at the time, that the war would be short. He saw borrowing as a logical short-term solution to the nation's money needs. But borrowing proved a problem, too. No national banking system existed. The government had to find a market for its debt from the myriad state banks. About 1,600 state banks operated, issuing more than 7,000 varieties of bank notes, but much of that currency was unsound. To compound the problem, the Independent Treasury Act of 1846, which Chase had supported, prohibited the government from depositing its bonds in interest-bearing banks. Even more exasperating, the statute required the government to pay its bills in specie.

When Congress convened on July 4, 1861, Chase presented a plan that proved inadequate in meeting the nation's needs. Assuming the war would only last a few months and reluctant to request politically unpopular taxation, Chase proposed to raise $80 million largely via tariffs and land sales. New internal or direct taxes, including a tax of 3 percent on incomes of more than $800, amounted only to $20 million of that total. He also called for confiscation of Confederate property. While Congress quickly enacted Chase's recommendations, the necessary funds failed to materialize. Only $2 million in direct taxes arrived at the Treasury Department by the end of the year, and the income tax was not to be collected until 1863.

To supplement this $80 million, Congress authorized Chase to raise $250 million through the sale of 20-year bonds at 7 percent interest along with short-term treasury notes, one issue maturing in three years and paying 7.3 percent interest and another bearing no interest but redeemable upon demand in specie. Chase hoped that those "demand notes" would become the basis for a national currency. He found it very difficult, however, to peddle the debt proposal to cautious bankers in the insecure war atmosphere. After long negotiations, he finally convinced major bankers to subscribe to a series of three $50 million loans spread out in 60-day intervals. The bankers sold the treasury notes to the public to replace the specie they had loaned the government. Problems soon arose because Chase, against the bankers' wishes, insisted that the banks turn over gold to the Treasury in return for government notes.

The loan program soon ran into problems. Long a hard-money advocate, Chase feared that if he did not insist on gold payments from the beginning, he would soon have to accept bank notes in exchange for treasury notes, which he believed would undermine the economy. He rejected the bankers' plan, which would have allowed them to treat the treasury-note transactions in the same manner they handled loans to businesses—crediting their payments to the government while the government

paid its creditors by check, thereby maintaining their gold reserves. Congress had indirectly approved the plan when it amended the Independent Treasury Act to allow Chase to deposit the proceeds from loans in "solvent specie-paying banks" instead of in subtreasuries.

At first Chase's system worked. But tariffs and taxation revenues did not materialize at the rate expected, and government expenditures greatly exceeded Chase's estimates, running to $2 million per day before the end of 1861. For a variety of reasons, including Europe's desire for neutrality in the Civil War, the North's failure to win on the battlefield, and European antipathy toward the newly enacted high Morrill tariff, Chase's attempt to borrow money abroad also failed. Then, on December 30, American bankers, having depleted their gold reserves with their first two $50 million subscriptions, suspended specie payments. The economy faced a serious crisis, and soldiers and government contractors went unpaid.

In that tense atmosphere Congress debated a variety of paper-money schemes. The proposed legal-tender bill would authorize the secretary of the treasury to issue $100 million worth of no-interest treasury notes in small denominations, which would circulate as "lawful money, and a legal tender in payment of all debts, public and private." Fifty million dollars of the previously authorized demand notes would also circulate as legal tender. Chase initially opposed the measure as inflationary and harmful to the nation's credit. He clung to the belief that traditional borrowing, along with taxes and confiscation of rebel property, could provide sufficient funds. But under pressure from leading bankers and Republican politicians, probably including President Lincoln, he reluctantly came to support the legislation as "a political necessity . . . [and] a war necessity." With Treasury support and after sometimes acrimonious debate, Congress enacted the Legal Tender Act in February 1862. By 1863 it had authorized the issuance of $450 million in no-interest legal-tender notes, which came to be called "greenbacks."

The Legal Tender Act stabilized war finance. Not only did it provide the government with sufficient funds to pay its ever-increasing expenses, it also gave the nation a circulating currency. Although the greenbacks depreciated, inflation in the North during the Civil War was mild compared to conditions in the South at the same time or for the nation during the American Revolution. The relative stability was due to such conservative provisions in the Legal Tender Act as the requirement that bond interest and import duties be paid in gold. The provision that made greenbacks acceptable currency for payment of taxes further secured the notes in the minds of the people.

In addition to passing the Legal Tender Act, Congress enacted most of the proposals Chase recommended in his 1861 report. Most important, it authorized Chase to borrow an additional $500 million by issuing new "five-twenty bonds," bearing an interest of 6 percent, redeemable after five years, and maturing in twenty years. Legal-tender notes, the "five-twenty bonds," and the earlier demand notes served as the prime means of government finance for the rest of the war.

In July 1862 Congress enacted a comprehensive revenue bill that taxed almost every aspect of the economy. The income provision levied a tax of 3 percent on incomes between $600 and $10,000 and 5 percent on incomes exceeding $10,000 (increased in 1864 to 5 percent on incomes of more than $600 and 10 percent on those of more than $10,000). Luxuries, including tobacco, liquor, and yachts, faced excise taxes. Congress also approved license taxes, stamp taxes, inheritance taxes, and value-added taxes. By fiscal 1864-1865, the tax system produced $209 million—five times the total receipts for 1860. Congress also enacted new tariff duties. Finally, it created the Internal Revenue Bureau in the Treasury Department. For the first time the national government had the ability to collect its income taxes independent of the states.

Not until February 1863 did Congress, by narrow margins, pass the National Banking Act for which Chase had lobbied so hard. The plan, proposed in his December 1861 report to Congress and modeled after New York State's 1838 Free Banking Law, provided the government with an efficient means of selling its bonds and enabled the treasury secretary to curb unreliable state-bank currency. The act created an association of banks authorized to issue up to $300 million in uniform national notes. Banks gaining federal charters had to deposit with the government U.S. bonds amounting to at least half their capital. They would then be authorized to issue notes in the amount of 90 percent of the bonds they purchased. The federal government retained the bonds as security. Member banks also had to comply with a minimum specie reserve re-

quirement. Because the initial act also permitted state banks to issue government notes up to the amount of 80 percent of the U.S. bonds they held, few bankers elected to apply for a national charter. They preferred the less regulated and potentially more profitable state-bank form. By December 1863 only 134 national banks operated. Not until March 1865, nine months after Chase stepped down at the Treasury, did Congress complete the system as he had initially requested it. By placing a 10 percent tax on all state-bank notes, Congress drove many of the banks out of business and ended the use of their notes. By the end of 1865, 1,650 national banks circulated more than $400 million in notes.

While the National Banking Act benefited the government and the nation in many ways, after the war many in the South and West began to complain about regional discrimination. Because national banks in the North could issue more notes and because there were more northern banks to issue such notes, by the 1880s westerners and southerners came to believe that a "monied conspiracy" existed, restraining economic growth in their areas. Chase, a "westerner" himself, never envisioned such results.

As secretary of the treasury, Chase greatly modified his essentially Jacksonian economic stance. He supported higher tariffs and lobbied for the national banking system embodied in the 1863 act. Reluctantly, he even went along with Congress's legal-tender scheme. He demonstrated more courage than most politicians in 1863 by calling for increases in federal taxation, urging Congress to "provide for at least one-half of our whole expenses" through income and other taxes. While Congress agreed to increase the income tax in 1864, taxation never produced enough to achieve Chase's goal.

In other ways, however, Chase clung to his Jacksonian orientation. He maintained his hard-money position as long as possible, opposing legal tender and, in 1861, insisting that bankers deliver specie in return for government bonds. When bankers urged Chase to sell government securities on the open market in Europe and the United States, Chase refused, arguing that "it did not comport with the dignity of the Federal government to trade and dicker in Wall Street and State Street and Chestnut Street." He thought selling government bonds much below par would lower the morale of the na-

Francis B. Carpenter's painting of Abraham Lincoln's cabinet on the occasion of the first reading of the Emancipation Proclamation (left to right): Edwin Stanton, Chase, Lincoln, Gideon Welles, Caleb Smith, William Seward, Francis P. Blair, and Edward Bates (courtesy of the U.S. Capitol Historical Society)

tion. Furthermore, Chase consistently supported short-term debt in such forms as the five-twenty bonds rather than the long-term bonds most bankers favored. Finally, he sought a public subscription to government bonds rather than rely on sales to bankers. The government launched an advertising campaign to appeal to the public's sense of patriotism as well as profit. The firm of Jay Cooke & Company sold bonds to small investors in towns and villages throughout the North, fulfilling Chase's desire to "democratize" government borrowing. One historian estimated that "nearly a million northerners—one out of every four families—bought war bonds."

Chase's record as secretary of the treasury is much disputed. The Union financed the war effort mainly through borrowing. Chase failed to insist on a comprehensive taxation policy at the outset. While almost every politician in 1861 agreed with Chase that the war would be brief, Chase can be criticized for clinging to his view longer than most. Not until 1863 did he call for a comprehensive fiscal program. Still, funds for taxation paid for 21 percent of war expenses while paper money financed an additional 13 percent. The Confederacy, in comparison, raised less than 1 percent of its war needs by taxation and never made its notes legal tender for private transactions. The cost of living rose approximately 80 percent in the North as compared to about 9,000 percent in the Confederacy. After

much caution and fumbling during the first year, Chase and Congress implemented a plan to finance a modern war while maintaining a prosperous economy. That most of the fighting and destruction occurred in the South contributed greatly to this relative prosperity, but Chase's policies certainly helped. Chase must also receive credit for creating a national banking system that, when finally completed in a series of statutes passed by Congress from 1863 to 1865, served as the national financial system until Congress established the Federal Reserve in 1913.

On the other hand, Chase's behavior often fell short of modern ethical standards. Most questionable was his relationship with the powerful Philadelphia banker Jay Cooke. Unable to sell the five-twenty bonds to banks as fast as he thought necessary, and anxious to democratize government borrowing, Chase hired Cooke, his close personal friend, as a special agent. He gave Cooke an exclusive right to sell the bonds, for which the banker received a commission of .25 percent. Cooke paid all expenses, including advertising costs and local agents' salaries. Still, he profited handsomely from the monopoly privilege. By the end of 1863 he had sold $400 million worth of bonds, bringing him a $1 million commission. In two years, after expenses, Cooke earned an estimated $220,000. While politicians and bankers howled at this sweetheart deal, Chase defended it as a necessary war measure.

Chase was cognizant of the need to avoid the appearance of cronyism, but just as Cooke profited as special agent, Chase benefited from private dealings with Cooke. Because the two kept those dealings separate from Cooke's work as special agent, nothing strictly illegal ever occurred. But many questioned the propriety of such a private relationship. Not only did Cooke serve as Chase's investment banker, he also frequently loaned Chase money and provided him and his family with gifts and hospitality.

Chase also administered a department filled with corrupt agents. While he had competent, honest, and hardworking bureau chiefs, many collection agents and other officials succumbed to the temptations of bribery and favoritism. Smuggling, biased trade licensing, and uneven tax collection plagued the department.

Finally, most of the Treasury agents were patronage appointees, selected for political advantage rather than for competence. Chase might have been no worse than the other department chiefs in that regard, but the activities of many of those men in his 1864 presidential campaign exposed the secretary to renewed charges of excess ambition and party disloyalty.

In addition to his job as head of the Treasury Department, Chase believed that, as a member of the president's cabinet, he had a duty to help formulate military and public policies, especially as they related to his main interest—race relations—and Lincoln initially encouraged that role. In May 1861 Lincoln authorized Chase to frame orders for the organization of regular and volunteer troops in Kentucky, Tennessee, and Missouri. Because Lincoln saw Secretary of War Simon Cameron as incompetent, he not only welcomed Chase's advice on military matters but also responded to his eventual call to replace Cameron with Edwin M. Stanton. Ironically, however, once Lincoln appointed Stanton, he no longer heeded Chase's advice. Lincoln and Stanton worked well together and closed their ears to the criticism of Union generals by Chase and others. Chase urged Lincoln and Stanton to wage a more aggressive war and to appoint bold generals such as John Pope, Joseph Hooker, and James A. Garfield, who favored, at least in theory, a policy of advance and a strategy of emancipation—and, perhaps not incidentally, Chase's political ambitions.

Chase undertook congressionally-assigned duties as administrator of confiscated and abandoned lands until Congress placed that function in the War Department in 1862. Acting in that capacity, he initiated the famed Port Royal experiment. He selected Boston abolitionist Edward L. Pierce to supervise a group of freed people on the lower South Carolina coast, and the former slaves turned the confiscated land they had been granted into cotton farms. However, as often happened with Chase, he also succumbed to pressures from friends. Following the recommendation of his son-in-law, Rhode Island governor William Sprague, Chase appointed William H. Reynolds to oversee the production and sale of cotton on Port Royal. Reynolds, more concerned with efficient cotton production and distribution than with the interests of the former slaves, continually interfered with Pierce's efforts. Chase had a second opportunity to develop his egalitarian policies when Congress again put the Treasury Department in charge of abandoned lands in 1863. He insisted that former slaves working such lands receive "sufficiently liberal wages" to support their families. He also proposed a land reform that would have divided plantations and encouraged landowners to sell small plots to the freed people.

For Chase, these efforts provided just a beginning. To enable blacks to protect themselves, Chase advocated unconditional emancipation, the enlistment of freedmen in the army, and the idea that slaveowners should not be compensated for the loss of slave property. He urged Lincoln to alter his Emancipation Proclamation to incorporate the unconditional emancipation idea and to extend the policy even to conquered areas of the South. While Chase failed to convince Lincoln on those points, the president did accept Chase's suggestion that the proclamation declare emancipation "an act of justice." Chase also campaigned for the proposed Freedmen's Bureau Bill, which would set up an agency to distribute land to freedmen, and for limited black suffrage. He hoped for a comprehensive Reconstruction policy that would ensure blacks equal rights and an equal opportunity to participate in government.

By 1864 Radical Republicans, not pleased with Lincoln from the outset, perceived him to be politically vulnerable as the war continued to drag on and Lincoln hesitated to commit to unconditional emancipation. They hoped to replace him with someone more likely to defeat the Democratic nominee, to prosecute the war vigorously, and pursue policies of racial fairness. Chase's liberal position on the freedmen question and his criticism of Lincoln's record made him a logical choice.

While never admitting that he sought the presidency, Chase worked to make himself available. For example, he put his own picture on the $1 greenback. Moreover, newspapers supporting his candidacy received an abundance of Treasury Department advertisements. He made no attempt to stop his friends from organizing a campaign for his nomination. Known as the Pomeroy Committee, it included, in addition to Senator Samuel C. Pomeroy of Kansas, Ohio senator John Sherman and Massachusetts senator Henry Wilson; Ohio congressmen James A. Garfield, James Ashley, Robert C. Schenck, and Rufus P. Spalding; and *Cincinnati Gazette* correspondent Whitelaw Reid. Jay Cooke and Chase's son-in-law William Sprague provided important financial support.

The Pomeroy Committee's earnest efforts, however, proved so embarrassing that Chase renounced them. In early February 1864 the committee circulated throughout the Midwest, through the franking privileges of several congressmen, an inflammatory, anti-Lincoln pamphlet that found its way into many Northern newspapers. Entitled "The Next Presidential Election," the article attacked Lincoln's abilities as commander in chief. While never mentioning Chase specifically, the pamphlet asserted "that because people had 'lost all confidence' in Lincoln's ability to suppress the rebellion, the party needed in his place 'a statesman profoundly versed in political and economic science, one who fully comprehends the spirit of the age in which we live.'" The infamous "Pomeroy Circular," in which the committee called upon Republicans to nominate Chase, followed later in the month. The circular argued that Chase had demonstrated the ability as secretary of the treasury to lead the nation to a successful military conclusion and an honorable and lasting peace.

The publications backfired. Instead of stirring up anti-Lincoln feelings, they brought Chase new charges of excessive ambition and disloyalty. Leading politicians and the Republican rank and file rallied to Lincoln and his more moderate policies on war, race, and Reconstruction. The endorsement by the Ohio Republican legislative caucus of Lincoln's renomination proved most embarrassing.

Chase reacted meekly, contending that he knew nothing of the Pomeroy Committee and that he had no desire to challenge Lincoln for the nomination. Few believed Chase's denials, but the renunciation stopped whatever Chase boom may have been developing. As a final gesture, Chase offered to resign his cabinet post. If Lincoln had accepted the resignation, Chase would have been free to challenge him. Lincoln preferred to keep Chase restrained in the Treasury Department. There his effective work added to the growing reputation of the administration while his deficiencies worked to his personal disadvantage.

After Lincoln received the nomination in early June, Chase became expendable. During Lincoln's first term Chase often threatened to resign, most commonly over patronage disputes but occasionally over differences in policy. Lincoln conceded the point and refused the resignation every time. Once Lincoln no longer needed Chase politically, however, he refused to put up with his demands. When Chase sent Lincoln yet another resignation letter over a new patronage matter, Lincoln accepted the letter. Much to his dismay, Chase found himself out of a job. He wrote in his diary, "So my official life closes."

Chase's problems in his relations with Lincoln typified the troubles he had throughout his career. He speculated in a letter to Whitelaw Reid that "the root" of the problems he had with Lincoln was "a difficulty of temperament. The truth is that I have never been able to make a joke out of this war." One Republican senator, however, summarized the attitudes of many when he said, "Chase is a good man, but his theology is unsound. He thinks there is a fourth person in the Trinity." Chase refused to recognize his faults, however. He believed Lincoln had treated him unfairly. Clearly bitter, he wrote in his diary that his only crime was his "unwillingness to have offices distributed as spoils." Lincoln, he wrote, "had never given me the active and earnest support I was entitled to and even now Congress was about to adjourn without passing sufficient tax bills." He was proud of his accomplishments and thought he had "laid broad foundations" for a solid economy.

Chase began to hope for a return to a place of prominence when Chief Justice Roger B. Taney died in October 1864. On the day Chase found out that Lincoln had accepted his resignation as secretary of the treasury, Massachusetts congressman

Samuel Hooper informed him that despite their differences, the president had indicated his intention to appoint Chase to the position if a vacancy developed. Three years earlier Chase had told Lincoln that he "preferred judicial to administrative office and would rather . . . be Chief Justice of the United States than hold any other position that could be given to me." By informing Hooper of his interest in Chase as chief justice, Lincoln may have been trying to let Chase down gently. But it also proved an effective device for keeping Chase in the president's camp. Some speculate that it was Lincoln's hint to Hooper, coupled with Taney's failing health, that led Chase to stump for Lincoln during the fall campaign.

Lincoln considered Chase an appealing choice as chief justice for several reasons. Chase would help solidify radical support for the administration, which had waned because of Lincoln's moderate war and Reconstruction policies and his acceptance of Chase's resignation as treasury secretary. Perhaps more important, Lincoln assumed Chase would be correct on the key issues the Court would have to face, especially the legal-tender question, the problem of military arrests and trials, and emancipation policies. Lincoln explained that because "we cannot ask a man what he will do," he wanted someone "whose opinions are known." Chase had supported emancipation, vigorous prosecution of the war, and the issue of legal-tender notes (the last albeit with great reluctance). The chief criticism of a Chase nomination and Lincoln's greatest fear was that Chase would politicize the Court and continue his efforts to gain the presidency. But the advantages outweighed the disadvantages, and on December 6 Lincoln sent his name to the Senate, which quickly confirmed him. The new chief justice assumed office immediately.

During his first years as chief justice Chase indeed politicized the Court. He found himself bored with the tedium of the job and considered resigning because he missed the excitement of politics. He believed his experience made him more valuable as an advisor to policymakers. Moreover, he had not practiced law for many years and had no judicial experience. Those considerations made it easy for him to conclude that no conflict existed between his position on the bench and his desire to help the new president, Andrew Johnson, formulate effective policies on Reconstruction and black rights. Chase visited both the White House and Congress often. In 1865

Chase as chief justice of the United States, about 1870 (courtesy of the National Archives)

he also undertook, perhaps with Johnson's encouragement, a tour of the South to provide the president with a report on conditions so he could shape an appropriate plan for Reconstruction. After interviewing Unionists as well as former Confederates, Chase concluded that while Southern whites were generally docile, a continued military presence coupled with black suffrage was necessary to protect the freed people and to ensure that only loyal Southerners would rule. Most whites, Chase wrote, were "disarmed" but "not reconciled" and "hardly acquiescent." He had no qualms about publicly pronouncing those views. In an address to Charleston freedmen during his tour, he declared that the vote would become "the freedmen's weapon in peace." Chase argued that blacks were entitled to the vote because as free people they were citizens.

Unable to convince Johnson that his positions on suffrage and land redistribution were constitutional, Chase supported Congress's break with the president. While he did not actively campaign during the 1866 congressional elections, he became increasingly frustrated because he could not "throw off the judicial robes" and help to uphold "the right." Still, he did so quietly by a letter campaign aimed at achieving ratification of the Fourteenth Amendment and black suffrage.

In more direct ways, Chase's job as chief justice involved him with Reconstruction politics and policies. While he was an early supporter of military occupation of the South until a secure Reconstruction policy could be put into effect, Chase remained cautious about the problems that could arise between the military and the judiciary. Insisting on the maintenance of judicial independence, he refused to allow Supreme Court justices to attend court in the South until "the complete restoration of the southern states" allowed the courts to function without military interference. Not until June 1867, believing then that military interference in civil procedures had ended, did Chase open court in the South. That policy alienated many of the more radical Republicans.

Chase also became involved in Jefferson Davis's treason trial. The public clamored for a quick trial, but the courts had an obligation to ensure fairness. The president and his cabinet decided to hold the trial in Virginia district court, arguing that it constituted the proper tribunal because it encompassed the former Confederate capital, Richmond. As one of the courts in Chase's circuit, the chief justice could allow the district judge to preside, or he could take charge of the trial himself. He moved cautiously, urging delay to avoid the dangers the trial posed for both the nation and his political ambitions. Many feared that a Richmond jury might fail to convict Davis, thereby embarrassing the presiding judge and northern Reconstruction efforts. As the northern desire for revenge against Davis abated, Chase continued to delay, to promote his policy of universal amnesty coupled with universal suffrage. In 1867 he put off the trial, weakly claiming that Supreme Court business took too much of his time. In 1868 he again postponed the trial because of the Johnson impeachment hearings. In addition, he offered a new argument against any trial, maintaining that the Fourteenth Amendment, because it barred Davis and other Confederate leaders from holding office, "precluded any other punishment." Finally, in December 1868, Johnson issued a universal amnesty proclamation. In February 1869 Chase got what he had worked for when the government dismissed the case against Davis.

Chase also entered into political conflicts over control of Reconstruction policies when he undertook his constitutionally-mandated function as the presiding officer of the Senate during the spring 1868 impeachment trial of Andrew Johnson. Chase by that time openly questioned what he perceived as the harshness of Congressional Reconstruction, and especially the efficacy and legality of the use of military courts in the South, thereby displeasing many leading Republican congressmen. His insistence that the impeachment trial follow strict legal procedures further angered those who viewed the trial in purely political terms. Besides the obvious political implications, Chase grappled with the very nature of impeachment. Many have contended that the impeachment process is intended to ensure that the president faithfully execute the law; there is no need for the president to have committed an indictable offense. Based on that assumption, evidence need not specifically pertain to violations of federal crimes. Chase advocated a more narrow, conservative view of impeachment. He believed that such trials should constitute legal proceedings to judge charges of indictable offenses. In that view the Senate had to follow strict rules of evidence.

After hard negotiation with Senate leaders, Chase agreed to a compromise. He would have the power to rule on all points of law, but the Senate, by a majority vote, could override his decisions. Throughout the trial Chase and the senators differed over the introduction of evidence, and the Senate overruled Chase on several occasions, especially over the issue of allowing Johnson's attorney the opportunity to present evidence concerning the president's motives for violating the Tenure of Office Act. Johnson wanted to show that he violated an unconstitutional law to protect executive prerogatives and to test the act's legality. The Senate, over Chase's objections, refused to allow evidence supporting that defense. It did grant Chase the full powers of president of the Senate. Chase had contended that as chief justice during an impeachment trial, he acted as the constitutionally sanctioned presiding officer. As such, he had all the prerogatives of the president of the Senate, including the right to break ties. The Senate upheld Chase on that point over the objections of Massachusetts senator Charles Sumner, who argued that because Chase was not a member of the Senate, he was not entitled to a vote. While Chase clearly favored Johnson's acquittal, his leadership at the trial remained important to ensure proper decorum and an air of impartiality.

Despite Chase's proclivity to politicize the Court during the Reconstruction period, he helped steer a divided court through difficult cases dealing with issues of Reconstruction and finance. He wrote a majority of the opinions himself, at least until 1870, when a stroke impaired his abilities. During his eight years on the bench he was in the minority only 33 times.

The Chase Court was the most activist in the Court's history to date. In the eight years of his service the Court overturned ten federal statutes, compared with only two during the Court's previous 75-year history. It also invalidated numerous state statutes. In a case involving a military trial conducted during the Civil War, the Court criticized the executive's use of military commissions in areas far from the military theater, although Chase and three others argued that Congress legally could have authorized such commissions. The Court also invalidated state and federal test oaths. In several early cases the Court indirectly challenged Congress's Reconstruction policies, but it avoided a direct confrontation with Congress on Reconstruction, refusing to prevent the president or other executive officials from performing their duties under Reconstruction legislation and, in *Texas* v. *White*, upholding the congressional right to make the final determination of when a state was ready to be restored to the Union.

In other disputes, the Court asserted its power and limited the scope of congressional authority. In *U.S.* v. *Dewitt*, for example, Chase and the other Democrats on the Court struck a blow for states' rights by prohibiting Congress from using its commerce powers to interfere with intrastate trade. In *Collector* v. *Day* the Court placed limits on the federal taxation power by declaring salaries of state government officials exempt from federal income tax.

In other cases, the Court supported expanded federal economic control. Even in *Collector* v. *Day* the Court gave no hint that it viewed federal income tax legislation, in general, as unconstitutional. In the License Tax Cases the Court upheld the provisions of the Internal Revenue Act of 1864 that outlawed the sale of lottery tickets and liquor without a license, arguing that the licenses constituted "mere receipts for taxes" and did not interfere with the state's ability to regulate economic activities within its borders. State laws against the sale of such items superseded the federal license. In *Veazie Bank* v. *Fenno* the Court sustained the most impor-

tant provision of the National Bank Act—the 10 percent tax on state-bank notes. Chase, in a classic statement of judicial restraint, wrote for the majority: "The judicial cannot prescribe to the legislative departments of the government limitations upon the exercise of its acknowledged powers, and that as a means to provide a currency for the whole country, Congress might restrain the issue of their [the states'] notes." He granted that "the power to tax may be exercised oppressively," but if that occurred recourse lay in the political arena, not with the courts. That landmark decision established an important precedent, allowing the federal government to exercise its tax powers for a wide range of regulatory purposes.

In several bank tax cases the Court upheld federal law if the statutes explicitly exempted certain bank assets from taxation. But when Congress remained silent, the Court allowed states to exercise their tax powers. The Court applied similar principles in cases concerning state taxation of railroads, refusing to view such taxation as an impermissible interference with the federal regulation of interstate commerce. Similarly, the Court allowed state regulation of insurance companies doing business in more than one state. In sum, the Chase Court seemed almost as willing as the earlier Taney Court to allow full range to state police powers.

In cases dealing with the issue of legal-tender notes the Court vacillated. In *Lane County* v. *Oregon* it ruled that states did not have to accept legal-tender notes for payment of state taxes. *Bronson* v. *Rhodes* limited the legal-tender quality of those securities by enforcing a contract that specified the payment of specie. *Hepburn* v. *Griswold* invalidated the Legal Tender Act, at least as it applied to debts contracted before its passage. In the words of leading constitutional scholar Stanley I. Kutler, the Court by that decision offered "one of its historically most extreme and involved justifications for judicial intervention" and "one of the most dubious examples of judicial review" in its history. Chase, writing for the majority, argued that Congress had no expressed or implied power to make treasury notes a legal tender. He presented an elaborate economic analysis to demonstrate that making paper money legal tender was unnecessary, thereby injecting policy judgments into constitutional law. Finally, he concluded that the act, as it applied at least to debts contracted before its passage, "arbitrarily" altered contracts, thereby violating both the spirit and the letter of the Constitution "contrary to justice and equity." The act had impaired the obligation of contract and deprived creditors of property without due process in violation of the Fifth Amendment. Chase granted that the Constitution prohibited only the states from impairing the obligation of contract but expanded the provision in a loose interpretation: "Those who framed and those who adopted the Constitution, intended that the spirit of this prohibition should pervade the entire body of legislation." The minority took a more expansive view of congressional power and a more restrained view of the Court's proper role, arguing that Congress, not the courts, should determine if legislation was "necessary." The minority also maintained that "this whole argument of the injustice of the law . . . is too abstract and intangible for application to courts of justice."

The Hepburn ruling lasted only a short time. In April 1869 Congress increased the size of the Court from seven to nine justices. By the end of March 1870 President Ulysses S. Grant's two new appointees took their seats and immediately voted with the Hepburn minority to hear two new cases concerning the constitutionality of the Legal Tender Act. On January 15, 1872, by a five-to-four vote, the Court reversed Hepburn and upheld the congressional power to issue treasury notes and make them legal tender for all debts, public and private, contracted either before or after the statute's passage.

On the issue of racial equality Chase consistently upheld the egalitarian position, often in dissent. Early in his career as chief justice, in an important symbolic act, he admitted John S. Rock as the first black lawyer to practice before the Supreme Court. Later, Chase had the opportunity to translate his egalitarian beliefs into constitutional law. In civil rights matters Chase was a strong nationalist with a broad view of federal power. He maintained that the Civil Rights Act of 1866, which guaranteed blacks legal equality, was constitutional under the authority granted Congress by the Thirteenth Amendment. In the circuit court case *In re Turner* he declared that a Maryland apprenticeship statute regulating blacks violated the Civil Rights Act and therefore the Thirteenth Amendment. Elsewhere, he contended that the Thirteenth Amendment prevented the enforcement of all contracts dealing with slavery even if they were made before the amendment's adoption. Finally, Chase opposed the narrow decision in the Slaughterhouse Cases,

which greatly restricted those rights protected by the federal government under the Fourteenth Amendment.

In addition to dealing with cases related to issues raised by the Civil War and Reconstruction, the Chase Court, in enforcing the Taney Court decision in *Gelpcke* v. *Dubuque*, anticipated the ways the courts would alter common law to protect business from a regulation-minded society. Before the Civil War, by using an instrumental view of the law, judges adapted the common law to the needs of the rapidly expanding economy. Viewing law as an instrument to stimulate individual initiative and risk taking, judges and legislators eased the requirements for incorporation and bankruptcy, approved subsidies for railroads and other enterprises, granted broad eminent-domain powers to private corporations, and developed new doctrines in the areas of torts and contracts to favor the entrepreneur over the established money interests. The law adapted to promote change and growth with little appreciation for stability and no talk of applying principles of natural law. After the Civil War the public's outrage over the abuses of many of those privileges, especially by the railroads, led to calls for regulation and more equitable law. In response business and sympathetic judges moved from an instrumental approach to the law, which emphasized results, to a formal approach, which concentrated on procedures and principles—especially the principles established in the previous decades favoring business interests. Legal formalism, with its antilegislative bias, mandated that judges exercise an activist judicial review to prevent state lawmakers from enacting statutes violating individual interests in the name of the public good. In trying to depoliticize the law, legal formalists praised judge-man common law as rational and called upon judges to examine the substance of statutes to ensure that they did not violate individual liberties.

While legal formalism had not yet come to dominate judicial thinking in the early postwar years, *Gelpcke* v. *Dubuque* cheered the hearts of investment and banking leaders, who opposed the increasing tendency of government to repudiate public debt. In the antebellum years state and local governments irresponsibly increased their debts to attract railroads and other industries. Like other states, Iowa competed for railroads by issuing state bonds to subsidize private rail corporations. But Iowa's constitution limited the state's debt to

$100,000 and forbade state investment in private corporations. However, the Iowa legislature gave in to pressure from the city of Dubuque and enacted legislation authorizing cities to issue those bonds, bypassing the constitutional limits. Dubuque issued more than $100,000 in bonds to subsidize railroad construction not only in the city but throughout the state. When the projected economic boom failed to materialize and construction lagged behind expectations, Dubuque and other cities had to increase taxes to avoid default on the bond interest. Initially the Iowa courts upheld the legislative action. But as taxes increased, the public elected new judges more responsive to public interests, who reversed earlier decisions. In response, bondholders sued in federal court to protect their investment. The federal judge, faced with conflicting state court decisions, upheld the most recent precedent. Bondholders then appealed to the Supreme Court, which promoted a more stable investment climate by ruling that Iowa had to honor the bonds. By overturning a state court's interpretation of state statutes and the state constitution, the Supreme Court expanded its power, ignoring a long-standing precedent recognizing the finality of state courts in interpreting their own laws and constitutions. Iowa refused to recognize the Supreme Court's decision. Chase, as Taney's successor, issued writs of mandamus against state officials to compel them to raise taxes to pay off the bonds. Federal officers imprisoned those who refused. Iowa finally buckled under Chase's firm policy and recognized the validity of all the bonds it had issued or authorized.

Despite his success as chief justice, Chase never abandoned his desire for the presidency. In 1868 he again quietly sought the nomination–this time as a Democrat. The switch in political affiliation was not merely due to expediency. Throughout 1867 he grew increasingly critical of the militarism of the Republican Reconstruction program. Besides, Chase had left the Democratic party primarily because of his position on slavery. He had worked hard to bring northern Democrats into the Liberty and later the Free Soil and then the Republican parties. As late as the 1850s he referred to himself as an Independent Free Democrat. In the 1851 Ohio elections he supported Democratic over third-party candidates. Most important, he had long supported Democratic economic principles.

The chief difference between Chase and the Democrats in 1868 came over black suffrage. Since

the war, Chase had advocated federal enfranchisement of blacks. Democrats were generally opposed to black suffrage on any grounds but by 1867 had softened their position by arguing that the decision on suffrage properly belonged to the states. To win the 1868 presidential nomination, Chase had to be willing to compromise. He conceded the "wisdom and expediency" of allowing the states to decide who should vote and agreed to run on a platform calling for universal suffrage "to be applied in the states by the states." Chase also waffled on the other major political issue of the day. Long a hard-money man, he opposed Congressman George Pendleton's scheme to redeem the war-issued five-twenty government bonds in greenbacks. But because his true position would alienate most Ohio and other midwestern and western Democrats, he presented the party with a vague statement calling for "the honest payment of the public debt" but opposing any "special favor" to creditors.

Despite his willingness to modify his positions, Chase never had a chance for the nomination. He still held views much in advance of the Democrats on race, reconstruction, and suffrage. He would have had a very difficult time defending the platform the party approved, which endorsed the use of greenbacks, condemned Reconstruction for promoting "negro supremacy," and omitted any support for universal or black suffrage. More important, Chase had been too closely identified as a Radical Republican for too long; he had too many enemies among the Democrats.

After his failure to receive the nomination Chase withdrew to the security of the Supreme Court. He took no part in the 1868 campaign, not even taking the time to return to Ohio to vote. After that election he involved himself in politics only once more. He launched a letter-writing campaign after Congress sent the Fifteenth Amendment, prohibiting racial discrimination in voting, to the states for ratification. He worked hard behind the scenes to secure the ratification of the amendment in Ohio.

Once Chase partially recovered from his 1870 stroke he resumed an active role on the Supreme Court. But his health quickly deteriorated again. On May 6, 1873, while visiting his youngest daughter and her husband, he suffered a stroke and died the next day. Thousands attended the May 9 funeral at St. George's Episcopal Church in New York. After lying in state at the Supreme Court,

Chase was buried at Oak Hill Cemetery in George-town, Washington, D.C.

Chase led a rewarding life, dedicated to the eradication of injustice and the promotion of equality and fair play. As a prominent antislavery advocate and Radical Republican he helped raise the consciousness of much of the nation. He was an adequate secretary of the treasury at an enormously difficult time. Besides finding the resources to fund the war, his policies furthered the consolidation of federal power and the development of national economic institutions. His national banking system, while somewhat limiting in the West and the South, stimulated new growth throughout the rest of the country. As chief justice of the Supreme Court, he helped move that institution toward an activist role that would eventually promote laissez-faire economics over state and federal regulations. But Chase was also a cautious justice who clung to outmoded ideas. By opposing the Legal Tender Act he showed how his Jacksonianism limited his vision in the area of finance. Still, he won respect for his many achievements. An arrogant, aloof man, he never truly gained the affection of the people. But, as Abraham Lincoln once observed, Chase was "about one and a half times bigger than any other man I ever knew."

Publications:

"The Life and Character of Henry Brougham," *North American Review*, 33 (July 1831): 227-261;

"The Effects of Machinery," *North American Review*, 34 (January 1832): 220-246;

Statutes of Ohio and the Northwestern Territory Adopted or Enacted from 1788 to 1833 Inclusive, Including a Preliminary Sketch of the History of Ohio, edited by Chase, 3 volumes (Cincinnati, 1833-1835);

Reclamation of Fugitives from Service (Cincinnati: R. P. Donogh, 1847);

"Diary and Correspondence of Salmon P. Chase," *Annual Report of the American Historical Association of 1902*, edited by Edward G. Bourne and others, volume 2 (Washington, D.C.: American Historical Association, 1903);

Inside Lincoln's Cabinet: The Civil War Diaries of Salmon P. Chase, edited by David Herbert Donald (New York: Longmans, Green, 1954);

Advice After Appomattox: Letters to Andrew Johnson, 1865-1866, edited by Brooks D. Simpson, LeRoy P. Graf, and John Muldowny (Knoxville: University of Tennessee Press, 1987).

References:

Frederick J. Blue, *Salmon P. Chase: A Life in Politics* (Kent, Ohio: Kent State University Press, 1987);

Eric Foner, *Free Soil, Free Labor, Free Men: The Ideology of the Republican Party Before the Civil War* (New York: Oxford University Press, 1970);

Bray Hammond, *Sovereignty and an Empty Purse: Banks and Politics in the Civil War* (Princeton: Princeton University Press, 1970);

Albert B. Hart, *Salmon P. Chase* (Boston: Houghton, Mifflin, 1899);

Stanley I. Kutler, *Judicial Power and Reconstruction Politics* (Chicago: University of Chicago Press, 1968);

Eugene H. Roseboom, *The Civil War Era, 1850-1873*, volume 4 (Columbus: Ohio State Archaeological & Historical Society, 1944);

Jacob W. Schuckers, *The Life and Public Services of Salmon Portland Chase* (New York: Appleton, 1874);

Robert P. Sharkey, *Money, Class and Party: An Economic Study of the Civil War and Reconstruction* (Baltimore: Johns Hopkins University Press, 1959).

Archives:

The major collections of Chase's papers are found at the Library of Congress, the National Archives, the Ohio Historical Society, and the Historical Society of Pennsylvania. The Cincinnati Historical Society and the New Hampshire Historical Society house smaller collections. University Publications of America has assembled a microfilm edition of Chase's papers under the editorship of John Niven.

Chase/Manhattan Companies

by Gregory S. Hunter

ITT Corporation

Chase Manhattan Bank was formed by the 1955 merger of two major New York City institutions: the Bank of the Manhattan Company and the Chase National Bank. Not only did the banks merge, but two nineteenth-century banking traditions merged as well.

The Manhattan Company was chartered in 1799 to supply New York City with water. A particularly virulent yellow fever epidemic the year before spurred public-minded citizens to address the ongoing problem of the city's water supply. The New York City common council initially favored the establishment of a municipal waterworks and so petitioned the state legislature. The council changed its mind, however, upon appeal by a bipartisan group including both Alexander Hamilton and Aaron Burr. Particularly compelling were Hamilton's arguments about the debt burden such a large-scale municipal project would generate. That set the stage for the chartering of a private water company.

At this point the traditional telling of the Manhattan Company story becomes a saga of deceit. Beyond dispute is the fact that Aaron Burr inserted a clause into the proposed charter permitting the company to use "surplus" capital in any legal way. Burr probably intended to use that clause as a way of increasing the profits of a public-works enterprise that otherwise faced a bleak financial future. The major point of dispute was the cooperation of the Federalists in this endeavor, which ultimately broke the Federalist monopoly over banking in New York City. Were the Federalists duped? Or did they understand Burr's intentions and hope to profit also from the enterprise? Amid the after-the-fact incriminations it is impossible to determine the truth, though most historians hold to the belief that Burr tricked the Federalists into supporting the company.

The issue of surplus capital was not an idle one, for the Manhattan Company's charter permit-

John Thompson, founder of the Chase National Bank in 1877

ted a capitalization of $2 million, quite large for the time. Another uncommon feature of the charter involved a grant of perpetual life to the corporation. During the first half of the nineteenth century state legislatures used periodic charter expiration to retain control over corporations, especially those in the financial area. In the case of the Manhattan Company that control was noticeably lacking. For example, the state failed to force the Manhattan Company to join the Safety Fund system after 1829.

Banking quickly emerged as the primary use of the Manhattan Company's surplus capital, though for a short period the company also involved itself in insurance and annuities. In addition to its New York City banking operations, the company operated two branches from 1809 to 1819 in the upstate villages of Utica and Poughkeepsie. The Manhattan Company became a leader in politics as well as finance. The company's president, Henry Remsen, was a personal friend and frequent correspondent of DeWitt Clinton. They worked closely together on matters affecting the well-being of the Manhattan Company and their own political faction.

Because of the company's primary focus on banking, the waterworks tended to receive minimum managerial attention and financial resources. That changed only when public criticism of the Manhattan Company's water-supply efforts grew so pronounced that it threatened the continued existence of the company. The Manhattan Company supplied New York City with water until the mid 1840s, when the municipal Croton system entered full operations. In order not to jeopardize its charter, however, the Manhattan Company continued to pump water even after the construction of the Croton system. In fact, the company pumped water daily from a well in the Wall Street area until the 1920s.

The Chase National Bank was founded in 1877 by John Thompson, a well-known banking figure of the day. Thompson previously had been associated with the First National Bank of New York. He also published *Thompson's Bank Note Reporter*, a newsletter tracing changes in the price of bank notes. Thompson named the bank after his friend Salmon P. Chase, Lincoln's secretary of the treasury and the father of the national banking system. Chase's association with the bank, however, extended no further than the honorific attachment of his name to the institution.

Throughout the nineteenth century the Chase National Bank was blessed with outstanding leaders. Henry White Cannon succeeded Thompson in 1887 and guided the bank into the next century. Previous to joining Chase, Cannon was comptroller of the currency under President Chester A. Arthur. Cannon's familiarity with banks throughout the nation enabled him to develop Chase's role as a correspondent bank for other banks. By the end of the nineteenth century the Manhattan Company and Chase National Bank had emerged as leaders of the New York financial community.

References:

Nelson M. Blake, *Water for the Cities: A History of the Urban Water Supply Problem in the United States* (Syracuse: Syracuse University Press, 1956);

Gregory S. Hunter, "The Manhattan Company: Managing a Multi-Unit Corporation in New York, 1799-1842," Ph.D. dissertation, New York University, 1989;

Beatrice G. Reubens, "Burr, Hamilton, and the Manhattan Company," *Political Science Quarterly*, 72 (December 1957): 578-607; 73 (March 1958): 100-125;

John Donald Wilson, *The Chase: The Chase Manhattan Bank, N.A., 1945-1985* (Boston: Harvard Business School Press, 1986).

Archives:

The records of both the Manhattan Company and the Chase National Bank can be found in the Chase Manhattan Archives in New York City.

Langdon Cheves

(September 17, 1776-June 26, 1857)

by Edwin J. Perkins

University of Southern California

CAREER: State representative, South Carolina (1802-1806); attorney general, South Carolina (1806-1808); U.S. representative, state of South Carolina (1811-1815); speaker, U.S. House of Representatives (1814-1815); associate justice, South Carolina Supreme Court (1818-1819); chairman, Charleston branch, Bank of the United States (1818-1819); president, Bank of the United States (1819-1823).

Langdon Cheves (pronounced Chiv-is) served as president of the Second Bank of the United States (BUS) from 1819 to 1823. During his tenure in office, the American economy suffered through the Panic of 1819 and an ensuing depression that persisted into the early 1820s. Financial historians in the early twentieth century generally credited Cheves with saving the Second BUS from possible failure in the crisis atmosphere of 1819 and putting it on a sound footing for the future, but subsequent research has indicated that his reputation as the bank's savior was grossly exaggerated and, moreover, that his lending policies in 1820 and 1821 exacerbated the economic contraction and hampered recovery. After serving four years, Cheves retired in 1823 and was succeeded in the presidency by Nicholas Biddle.

Cheves's father, Alexander Cheves, was a Scotsman who immigrated to South Carolina in 1761. Working at first as an itinerant peddler, by 1772 Alexander Cheves had accumulated the financial resources to buy a 200-acre farm on the banks of the Little River in western South Carolina near the towns of Greenwood and Abbeville. Langdon Cheves was born in this backcountry region on September 17, 1776, and he seems, at least on the surface, to have experienced a difficult childhood. His mother, Mary, died when he was only three, and thereafter he lived at various times with relatives.

Langdon Cheves

After the British occupied Charleston during the Revolution, Alexander Cheves cast his lot with the Loyalists. When the British army abandoned the city for Nova Scotia in 1782, Alexander sailed with the fleet, leaving Langdon in the care of brother Thomas's household. Three years later, in 1785, Thomas died, and under an amnesty program Alexander returned to the state and took Langdon, then aged ten, with him to Charleston, where the father opened a small shop. After two more years of schooling Langdon went to work for local merchant James Joffray, a native of Glasgow, and he soon rose to the position of chief clerk. When Joffray died, young Cheves decided to pursue a career in the law.

Cheves began a legal apprenticeship with Judge William Marshall in 1796. A year later, at age twenty-one, he was admitted to the South Carolina bar after passing a brief oral examination. For the next several years he periodically traveled the backcountry in the entourage of a circuit judge, soliciting clients as he went along. By the turn of the century Cheves had established his legal reputation, and he often argued cases before judges sitting on the U.S. District Court based in Charleston. His earnings were reportedly in the neighborhood of $20,000 annually, a very handsome income for that era.

Cheves launched his political career in 1802, when he was elected to South Carolina's lower legislative chamber. Although he apparently sympathized with the Federalist party in the early years of his service, he soon became a staunch supporter of President Thomas Jefferson's program of economic coercion to force the British to respect American rights on the open seas, and he converted to the Republican cause. Within a few years Cheves became chair of the lower chamber's Ways and Means Committee, and in that capacity he got an early taste of high finance. In 1806, at age thirty, he was named attorney general of the state of South Carolina.

In December 1810 Cheves won election to the U.S. House of Representatives from the Charleston district. Another new member of the House representing South Carolina was John C. Calhoun. Cheves and Calhoun emerged as prominent members of the younger generation of "War Hawks" who arrived in Washington in 1811 intent on pushing for a political and military showdown with Great Britain. Cheves gained appointment to the Ways and Means Committee, and shortly thereafter he became its second ranking member. Sometime before Congress declared war in 1812, with Cheves voting in the affirmative, he moved up to chair of Ways and Means. In that position he was involved in negotiations with Secretary of the Treasury Albert Gallatin about raising sufficient funds, mainly through bond sales, to support the war effort. The expiration of the charter of the First BUS, after Congress had refused renewal, made funding the war vastly more difficult.

When Henry Clay of Kentucky was named a member of President James Madison's peace commission in January 1814, Cheves succeeded as Speaker of the House, elected on the first ballot by a vote of 94 to 59. Possibly anticipating Clay's reassumption of the speakership after the peace, Cheves announced in May 1814 that he would not stand for re-

election to the House in the upcoming congressional elections. But Cheves's legislative service lasted a little longer than he had anticipated because Madison called Congress back into session in the fall of 1814, which meant performing the duties of speaker for several additional months.

During the session convened in late 1814 and lasting into 1815, Secretary of the Treasury Alexander J. Dallas proposed the creation of a second national bank with a capital of $50 million, a fivefold increase in capital over the expired national bank. In a crucial test on January 2, 1815, Cheves, as House Speaker, cast the last negative vote to tie the total at 81, preventing the bill's passage. The next day a vote to reconsider received a large majority, and the members sent the bill to a select committee for more tinkering. With capitalization reduced to $30 million, the altered bank bill passed both the House and Senate, but President Madison vetoed the legislation because he claimed that it did not promise sufficient support for financing the ongoing war with Great Britain. Soon thereafter, news about the successful negotiation of the treaty ending the war reached the United States by ship from Europe. The old Congress adjourned in early March 1815–just before the newly elected Congress was scheduled to be sworn in for the next session. At age thirty-nine, Cheves's legislative career had ended by his own volition.

Cheves went home to resume his law practice in Charleston on a full-time basis after having spent much of the last five years in Washington. About 18 months later, in December 1818, the state's General Assembly elected him to serve as an associate justice on South Carolina's highest court. Meanwhile, the directors of the headquarters office of the Second BUS in Philadelphia had nominated him to serve as a member of the subsidiary board of directors for the Charleston branch office. At a meeting of the Charleston board the members selected Cheves to serve as chairman. Over the next two years he was closely involved with the operations of the bank's office in Charleston.

During the initial 18 months under the administration of bank president William Jones, the Second BUS had made a large volume of loans at branch offices closest to the western frontier. As a result of the absence of central coordination and the lack of internal control over lending policies at the various branches, the bank found itself overextended in the spring of 1818, and its specie reserves had dwindled to a very low level. Six months later Congress appointed a special committee to investigate the bank's status, and its report released in January 1819 contained sharp criticism of the president's performance. Jones almost immediately resigned, and an interim president was installed.

In the search for a new permanent president Cheves's name headed the list of possible candidates from the outset. The former Speaker of the House was widely known and much respected. Alexander Brown, the prominent Baltimore merchant banker, extended strong and influential support. The fact that Cheves had served merely as a director of the Charleston branch and had never actually been engaged in the management of a banking institution, large or small, was not viewed by the directors voting in Philadelphia as a serious handicap. Meanwhile, they considered his reputation for conservatism one of his most important attributes.

Cheves took over the reins of the bank in March 1819. The most comprehensive historical account of what occurred during his tenure in office can be traced back to a lengthy document that Cheves penned in the late summer of 1822. He described his actions over the last three and a half years and provided the underlying rationale. Cheves presented the summary essay to the bank's directors and stockholders, which the *Niles Weekly Register*, a leading business publication with a wide circulation, published in its October 1822 issue.

Not surprisingly, Cheves gave himself exceedingly high marks when it came to measuring his performance as bank president. For decades the majority of financial historians, including scholars Ralph Catterall and Bray Hammond, accepted Cheves's version of events at face value and congratulated him for his valiant efforts. When Cheves arrived in Philadelphia in March 1819, he claimed that he had found the bank absolutely "prostrate" and in imminent danger of suspending payment; the prospect of complete failure loomed on the horizon. To meet the crisis Cheves took steps to tighten credit and build reserves. He forbade the western branches to issue any new notes. Before the end of 1819 the ratio of specie reserves to bank-note and deposit liabilities had reached 33 percent, and during the following year the reserve ratio climbed to more than 60 percent. Cheves claimed in the 1822 document that he played an instrumental role in rescuing the bank from almost certain collapse.

During his tenure in office a few contemporary critics blamed his tight credit policies for causing the so-called Panic of 1819 and for prolonging the subsequent depressed level of business activity. Writing a decade later, William Gouge, an ally of President Andrew Jackson, asserted in his *Short History of Paper Money and Banking in the United States*, published in 1833, that under Cheves "the bank was saved and the people were ruined." In his 1822 essay Cheves absolved himself of any blame for causing the panic, claiming that he had merely adhered to policies instituted earlier. He denied having ordered an accelerated curtailment of loans in his first few months in office. He likewise defended his conservative lending policies in 1820 and 1821. Until recently most financial historians have agreed with Cheves's own assessment; Catterall, the first professional scholar to study the bank in depth, concluded: "Cheves's management of the bank, on the whole, was excellent."

In the 1980s, however, historians subjected those glowing assessments of Cheves's performance as BUS president to substantial revision. A review of the bank's financial statements in the period from 1818 to 1823 suggests a rather different scenario. Cheves did not actually "save" the bank during his first few months in office because, as a result of the policies Jones had implemented in the summer of 1818, including a sharp curtailment of loans, the bank had passed the crisis point six months earlier. The reserve ratio at the end of 1817 had dropped as low as 12 percent, a genuinely precarious number, but by December 1818 that same ratio was up to 21 percent and was climbing. Cheves may have believed he faced a liquidity crisis in March 1819, but he based his judgment on his banking naiveté and his exceedingly conservative outlook.

The Panic of 1819 struck soon after Cheves arrived in Philadelphia. In his defense, no financial historian to date has disputed Cheves's claim that the bank's actions after he assumed the presidency were not directly linked to the onset of the financial crisis. Nor have historians held him responsible for the financial dislocations that occurred over the remainder of the year. On the other hand the policies that Cheves pursued in 1820 were questionable since he did nothing to promote economic recovery. Rather than easing monetary conditions, he continued to call in loans and build specie reserves. By the end of 1820 the reserve ratio had climbed to 61 percent. By that date, the bank held one-third of the total specie reserves in the U.S. banking system. Cheves tried to protect a bank that required no further safety measures. His argument that the policy of contracting loans and building reserves had been initiated by his predecessor and was, therefore, not a policy for which he could be held accountable is specious. Cheves exerted full control after March 1819, and he operated under no obligation to persist in policies of the Jones administration.

If we assume that a holding of 30 percent reserves represents a prudent figure for a quasi-central institution like the Second BUS or any domineering commercial bank in a given financial system, then Cheves held nearly $4 million in excess reserves for no legitimate reason. The bank in truth acted as a drag on an economy already suffering from a liquidity shortage. He could have used the excess reserves to expand the money supply by up to 17 percent. If Cheves had acted in a less conservative manner he could have alleviated much hardship, prevented thousands of bankruptcies, and possibly pulled the nation out of the recession months earlier. Gouge exaggerated when he blamed Cheves for "ruining the people," but it can be accurately stated that the bank president had done nothing to relieve widespread distress at a time when he clearly had the power to act in a more positive manner. Excessive conservatism was the root cause of his failure to meet fully his overall responsibilities to the general public and to the bank's numerous stockholders.

In sum, Cheves's reputation as a banker merits a reassessment comparable to his policy of 1820: sharp deflation. His skills as an administrator of the nation's largest financial institution were minimal at best, and the praise that he received from contemporary supporters, and repeated by subsequent historians, was based on his tendency to rank absolute safety above every other economic consideration. Cheves was too conservative, even for a banker.

After retiring from the bank Cheves lived in Pennsylvania for the remainder of the decade. He served on the government commission that arbitrated American claims against the British stemming from the War of 1812. In 1830 he purchased a rice plantation along the Savannah River in South Carolina, and a few years later he inherited a cotton plantation near Columbia. By 1840 Cheves held title to more than 180 slaves and strongly defended the slave system.

When the Second BUS closed its doors in 1836, after President Andrew Jackson's veto of the application for recharter, Cheves applauded the outcome. In a public debate regarding the wisdom of chartering a third national bank Cheves expressed stern disapproval. The former BUS president had become one of the institution's staunchest opponents, arguing that a national bank with an extensive branch system posed a threat to states' rights. Echoing the sentiments of Jackson, Cheves called the proposals for a successor bank "inexpedient, unnecessary, and dangerous." Later, a bill to establish a third national bank passed through Congress in the early 1840s, but President John Tyler vetoed it. The idea was not revived until the creation of the Federal Reserve System in the early twentieth century.

Cheves died in his eightieth year in Columbia, South Carolina, on June 26, 1857. Seven years earlier he had appeared before a convention of southern politicians in Nashville to urge secession from the union by joint action of all the slaveholding states. In old age, this former House Speaker and previous president of the nation's largest and most powerful financial institution for a term of nearly four years, vigorously renounced the very concept of a national bank and, indeed, called for the breakup of the nation itself.

Publication:

"Exposition of the President of the Bank to Stockholders," *Niles Weekly Register*, 23 (October 12, 1822): 89-96.

References:

Ralph Catterall, *The Second Bank of the United States* (Chicago: University of Chicago Press, 1903);

William Gouge, *A Short History of Paper Money and Banking in the United States* (Philadelphia: Printed by T. W. Ustick, 1833);

Archie Vernon Huff, Jr., *Langdon Cheves of South Carolina* (Columbia: University of South Carolina Press, 1977);

Edwin J. Perkins, "Langdon Cheves and the Panic of 1819: A Reassessment," *Journal of Economic History* (1983): 455-461.

Archives:

Langdon Cheves's papers are located in the archives of Duke University and at the South Carolina Historical Society, Charleston.

Henry Clay

(April 12, 1777-June 29, 1852)

by Larry Schweikart

University of Dayton

CAREER: Lawyer (1797-1803); state legislator, Kentucky (1803-1806, 1807-1810); U.S. senator, state of Kentucky (1806, 1810-1811, 1831-1842, 1849-1851); U.S. representative, state of Kentucky (1812-1814, 1816-1820); member, U.S. peace commission to Ghent (1814); U.S. secretary of state (1825-1828).

The "Sage of Ashland," or "Harry of the West," as he was sometimes called, Henry Clay was a statesman, diplomat, politician, and, above all, the symbol for the short-lived and ill-fated Whig party. Born on April 12, 1777, in Hanover County, Virginia, Clay grew up in his mother's home after his Baptist preacher father died when Clay was four years old. His father, the Reverend John Clay, left the family with virtually no money. Clay had eight brothers and sisters, and when his mother, Elizabeth Hudson, remarried, seven more children by her new husband, Henry Watkins, joined the family. Clay had only the most basic education–much of it under "a drunken remittance man"–and when his parents moved to Kentucky to open a tavern, Clay (then fifteen years of age) remained in Richmond to work as a store clerk. After a year of work in the store Clay's stepfather persuaded the clerk of the high court of chancery of Virginia to give young Clay a job. There he gained more than temporary employment. He met George Wythe, the first law professor in the state and a man who had signed the Declaration of Independence, and whom Thomas Jefferson has tutored. Wythe took young Clay under his wing and led him through a study of the classics and law in return for Clay's services as a private secretary. Clay furthered his education under former Virginia governor Robert Brooke and opened a legal practice in Lexington, Kentucky, in 1797.

At twenty years of age the attorney quickly emerged as Lexington's foremost criminal lawyer.

Henry Clay (engraving by W. J. Edwards from a daguerreotype by Mathew Brady)

Although he once served as a state prosecutor, he apparently resigned in disgust over the conviction of a slave for murder, and he turned his special temperament and legal talents to defense. Accordingly, "no person . . . ever invoked the aid of [Clay] without being saved." And the law rewarded Clay as well: he not only prospered from his practice but engaged in profitable land speculation in the booming frontier areas of Kentucky. In 1799 he married Lucretia Hart, whose family had considerable local connections and no small amount of wealth. Clay made political contacts that served him in good stead for the rest of his life. He became involved in the 1798 campaign to expand the franchise in Kentucky and to emancipate slaves. Although a new constitution containing broadened voting privileges passed, emancipation failed, and Clay let the matter ride for the time. Whatever support he lost over that issue he regained with his attacks on the federal Alien and Sedition Acts passed during the administration of President John Adams. His passionate and eloquent speeches on behalf of Thomas Jefferson during the presidential campaign of 1800 paved the way for his election to the Kentucky state legislature in 1803. He argued on behalf of the Kentucky Insurance Company, a corporation that faced the repeal of its charter on the grounds that it had illegally gained banking powers. Clay showed that the state had a contract with the company, and the contract could not be broken. Clay won a well-publicized acquittal for Aaron Burr at a Kentucky grand-jury investigation involving Burr's conspiracy to seize lands in the Southwest, although he later said that Burr had "hoodwinked" him, and he never forgave the vice-president.

The Burr defense propelled Clay into an appointment in 1806 to fill the unexpired term of John Adair in the U.S. Senate. Only twenty-nine years of age, he had already formulated the essentials of his "American System," and it hardly looked like anything his old hero Jefferson would have favored. In the Senate Clay forcefully argued for federal funding of roads, canals, and internal improvements—items all clearly favorable to western interests but items all guaranteed to expand the role and scope of the national government. Clay returned to the Kentucky legislature in 1807 and won election as speaker of the house. He repeatedly attacked the Federalists, whose programs in many ways more resembled his own than the Republicans, and even engaged in a duel with Humphrey Marshall, a leading Kentucky Federalist. (In addition to dueling, Clay had distinguished himself in Washington as a gambler.)

All of those "frontier" traits tended to increase Clay's local popularity, and after he returned to the U.S. Senate in 1810, his colorful manner and brilliant eloquence warmed the coldest of Washington hearts. His speeches on behalf of his western constituents won him the admiration of even his opponents, and his leadership abilities ensured that he only needed an opportunity to shine. But it did not come in the Senate, where, despite his impassioned support for high tariffs to protect

Lexington's hemp interests and his calls for the annexation of Spanish territory, he remained a young man in a club of senior statesmen. He participated in the 1811 defeat of the bill to recharter the Bank of the United States (BUS)—again, an ironic touch given that his later career frequently hinged on his support of the Second BUS. He maintained that the bank had gone beyond the bounds of its original charter and that it was "worse than usurpation to establish it [the bank] for a lawful object, and then extend to it other objects which are not lawful." Clay perceived what few others had, namely that the BUS could have a significant role in monetary policy. He also had close ties to Kentucky's frontier speculators, and they, along with many state bankers, opposed the national bank. In foreign affairs, his fevered attacks on Great Britain stoked the fires of war against the English, whom he claimed had incited the Indians into hostilities against frontier settlers. Although his Senate term expired in 1811, Clay's constituency immediately returned him to Washington as a congressman, where he joined a similar group of young, aggressive legislators, many of them from the West. Like Clay, those "War Hawks" had made much of their political careers on calls for the United States to declare war on Britain and in the process end impressment of seamen and, they hoped, take Canada. Clay's defiant speeches spurred the Congress to elect him speaker of the House of Representatives—the youngest man ever to hold the position.

Once in office as speaker, Clay immediately established and wielded remarkable control. He knew parliamentary rules intimately, and he carefully stacked all the major committees with friends such as Felix Grundy of Tennessee, Langdon Cheves of South Carolina, Joseph Desha of Kentucky, and Peter B. Porter of New York, all of whom served as chairmen. Soon Clay had radically changed the focus of power in Washington, making the speakership one of the most important positions in government. Whenever possible he increased the power and visibility of the western-states delegations. In so doing he virtually ensured the success of almost every major measure he championed before he ever took the floor to deliver the coup de grace, his own masterful speech. The first test of his power came over the issue of war, and Clay's young committee chairmen ran roughshod over older, less energetic party loyalists. They passed bills for new shipyards, appropriated money for ship timber, and author-

Lithograph of Clay's Virginia birthplace

ized the president to call out 100,000 militia. Clay and Congress then pressured President James Madison into hostilities. The resulting short conflict damaged the national pride both of the Americans, who lost several lopsided early battles and saw Washington, D.C. burned (if only by accident), as well as the British, who enjoyed success over the ragtag militias only to lose head-to-head conflicts with regulars at Lundy's Lane and suffer a humiliating defeat in New Orleans after the war had officially ended.

Clay, of course, had as much a role in the peace as he had in precipitating the war. Named as one of five commissioners to Ghent in 1814, he and the other delegates obtained few material concessions from the British. But in reality, the war had left the country with several advantages that required no bargaining: the Indians in the northwest areas had been subdued and the British presence removed, and European powers came to recognize the United States as a force, at least in the Western Hemisphere. The war also made a hero of "Old Hickory," Andrew Jackson, who emerged as a politi-

cal star, one destined to collide with "Harry of the West."

Clay did not perceive as much immediately, however, for his career continued to blossom. Upon his return from Ghent in 1815 he returned to the House and was reelected to the position of speaker. He developed the position of speaker into a different office than it had been. He used procedural changes to refer bills to a committee rather than have each measure taken up by the Committee of the Whole. Not only was that practice becoming unwieldy, but Clay perceived the committee system as a means to direct legislation to the exact source of his strength, the chairmen he had appointed. Moreover, the speaker appointed all committees, hence Clay controlled the placement of legislation and the appointment of those who considered it in addition to chairing the proceedings, a power he wielded ruthlessly. During his years as speaker Clay was involved in nine major issues, including the bank recharter and the tariff. He had roughly a two-to-one ratio of victories to defeats on those issues, and he won on all the crucial votes, such as those on the War of 1812 and the Missouri Compromise. Not until the twentieth century did speakers again display the talent or the willingness to use the powers of the office in such a manner as Clay. He gained a reputation as a dictator at times and always needed adulation and public acceptance. Characterized as "over-sanguine when skies were fair," yet capable of sinking into the depths of despondency, and a "prima donna," Clay vented unrestricted jealousy on some political opponents, such as Zachary Taylor. Late in life he delivered a speech in the midst of some of his most bitter opponents, so moving them, "strong and cold men as they were, are said to have wept like children."

Without the war issue, Clay focused his energies on internal developments beneficial to the West. A series of measures, known as the American System, consisted of protective tariffs, road and harbor improvements, and a national bank. Clay saw the system as encouraging New England's industries through the tariffs; generating demand for western farm goods and raw materials used in the factories; facilitating their easy transportation and shipping through road, river, and harbor improvements; and stabilizing the national money supply through a uniform currency. The bank, he contended, also would provide increased credit to the growing West and South. Finally, Clay called for recognition of the newly independent Latin American republics, partly because they adopted democratic systems and partly because they offered large, untapped markets for American goods. Moreover, solidarity with the Latin republics would encourage the removal of Mexico from the control of Spain and further open the Mississippi River to trade.

In 1816 Congress approved one of the major programs in the American System by chartering the Second Bank of the United States. Clay had set up the passage by naming his friend John C. Calhoun to a special committee examining the necessity of a uniform national currency. Calhoun eventually succeeded in pushing the bill through. Like its predecessor, the Second BUS had predominantly private ownership, with only one-fifth of its capital held by the U.S. government. It had branches scattered across the country, especially in the South and West—Ohio had two branches, in Chillicothe and Cincinnati—and offered some stability of note exchange on a national basis. Historians for some time thought that both the national banks acted as quasi-regulators of the state-chartered banks in that

the BUS, if its management thought that a particular local bank had inflated its notes, could stockpile that bank's notes and make a "raid" in which it presented the notes to the bank and demanded immediate redemption in BUS notes or specie. That, in turn, was supposed to have made the BUS quite unpopular with the state banks.

This theory failed to explain the first serious test of the BUS in 1819, a panic year, when the BUS scarcely prevented the state banks from inflating. Langdon Cheves of South Carolina, one of Clay's War Hawk allies in 1812, was appointed president of the BUS in 1819. As shown by Richard H. Timberlake, the Treasury actually used the BUS to cloak its austere fiscal-monetary policy through which it retired the federal government's treasury notes issued between 1812 and 1814. Those high-denomination bills did not circulate for ordinary transactions but instead found their way into banks' reserves, where they became the base for further note issues. The resulting inflation, then, clearly had its origins in the federal war financing effort, not the "speculative tendencies" of private bankers. Similarly, the contraction that took place was a natural response to the purge of these treasury notes from the system. The BUS merely acted in accordance with this process, with Cheves contracting the loans. It appeared to the farmers and merchants that the BUS had caused the contraction, when, in reality, the contractions were symptoms, not causes. Throughout the panic Clay supported the BUS, understanding that while it lacked the power to control the rest of the economy, it did have to manage its own affairs on a paying basis. As is usually the case, borrowers howled when required to repay, and in many cases the hard-nosed South Carolinian Cheves simply ordered the BUS to foreclose on mortgages. Clay had fought his first battle over the bank: whether he won or not is questionable. He had alienated some of his frontier farm- and small-merchant support. But the view that the state banks uniformly despised the BUS is groundless, and Clay maintained his base among state bankers and the Lexington merchant community.

A much larger battle, involving slavery, also took shape in 1819. Missouri sought admission to the Union as a slave state, an act Thomas Jefferson described as "a firebell in the night." The crisis manifested both Clay's great strength—his ability to fashion a compromise out of almost any conflict—and his fatal weakness—believing that all issues were sub-

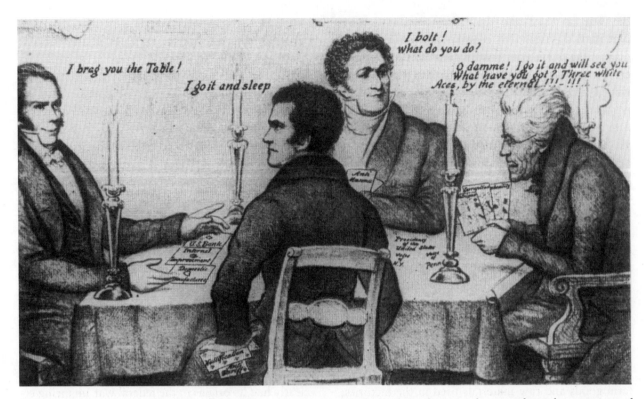

Contemporary cartoon by Edward W. Clay representing ideological rivalries in the presidential campaign of 1832. From the left, Clay presents his hand, the program of the American System; John C. Calhoun discreetly holds his anti-tariff and nullification cards from play; anti-Masonic candidate William Wirt declares his intention to remain in the race; and President Jackson frets over Clay's threat. Jackson won the election and dealt the American System a serious blow (courtesy of the New-York Historical Society).

ject to compromise. That capacity for compromise has indicated the line of separation between those politicians Americans have traditionally revered, such as Abraham Lincoln, and Clay. His inability to portray himself as firmly antislavery cost him more than mere elections. Clay sought a solution that even Lincoln endorsed, namely setting up an African colony for the slaves. Unlike Lincoln, he failed to see the necessity for keeping slavery out of the western territories. He toiled to develop a compromise. His efforts culminated with the Missouri Compromise, in which Missouri entered the Union as a slave state and Maine as a free state, and an imaginary line was drawn across the country at the 36° 30" parallel above which no new state could admit slavery and below which no new state could prohibit it. For that he won acclaim as the "great pacificator," but even as the compromise went into effect, Martin Van Buren and William Crawford met to form the structure of a new political party, the Democratic Republicans, Clay's nemesis for the rest of his life.

The remainder of Clay's program also ran into trouble. In theory internal improvements should have benefited the South and West, making the roads and waterways into effective links for southern and western goods heading for northern markets. He intended the tariff to protect northern industries, whose finished goods would flow back to the West and South. Always linked economically, the regions would find, he argued, that they had more common interests than differences. Bound together, even slavery could not drive them apart. Moreover, the commercialism of the North would influence the South and eventually make slavery extinct. He failed to notice the high costs of the tariff on the South, and he soon found that many of his southern friends, such as John C. Calhoun, placed allegiance to their states and region ahead of allegiance to the nation. He also failed to see that his programs gave the federal government sweeping new powers, and that it was only a matter of time before the North, with its growing population, used those powers against slavery. Ironically, the Democratic Republicans relied on economic inducements—patronage, or "spoils"—in the manner of Clay's American System but on a more individualistic level. Both the Whigs and the Democrats fundamentally believed that the voters could be "bought" and that they would subordinate important moral issues such as slavery to economic issues. Like Clay, the Democrats also failed to notice that the corollary of their program was a rapidly growing federal government that could turn its powers against slavery.

Clay continued his personal political rise, although he suffered a temporary and surprising setback in 1816 when President James Monroe named John Quincy Adams, not Clay, as his secretary of state. That position in the early years of the Republic had proved to be the jumping off point for the presidency. Monroe had offered him several positions, but the Kentuckian remained in the House until 1820 and marshaled his support for a presidential try in 1824. But he ran last, well behind both Adams and Andrew Jackson, who had stolen his western base. No candidate had a majority, meaning that the House of Representatives decided the election. Clay's poor showing eliminated him during the very time that he could have used his position as speaker to swing the House to his cause. He drifted into the greatest blunder of his political life. Finding Jackson personally unacceptable (he claimed Jackson's only qualification for the presidency was "killing two thousand five hundred Englishmen at New Orleans"), Clay threw his support to John Quincy Adams, and with Clay's votes the New Englander won the election. Not only had Clay disobeyed the Kentucky legislature's instructions to vote for Jackson, but he then accepted Adams's invitation to serve as secretary of state in the new administration. Historians have searched in vain for evidence of a "corrupt bargain." Clay simply failed to appreciate the appearance of his action. As for the two men's policies, they had similar goals of uniting the nation through roads and canals, and both approved of a high tariff. Under other circumstances, no one would have found it suspicious that Clay and Adams joined forces.

By the mid 1820s Clay entered a period in his political life when his most cherished programs seemed to yield results exactly opposite their intent. The most important of those setbacks, the tariff of 1828, in many ways provided a prelude to the Civil War. The extremely high tariff, passed when the South sought to embarrass the North by giving the northerners what they wanted, backfired and stuck the South with increases in many areas of up to 33 percent. South Carolina threatened secession over

the "tariff of abominations." In turn, Andrew Jackson, elected president in 1828, threatened to hang the ringleader of the movement, Clay's one-time War Hawk partner, John C. Calhoun. Clay quickly attempted to repair the damage by fashioning a lowered tariff in 1832 that proved acceptable to the West and South. But one of the major planks in his American System had sustained a direct hit, and soon another of his pillars, the BUS, was in the line of fire.

Clay had lost his chance for the 1828 election by accepting the position of secretary of state. He became identified with the New England faction of John Quincy Adams, the last vestige of the Federalist image in American politics. Against a candidate who spouted slogans of democracy at every turn and who promised to populate the government with the "common man," Clay had no chance. His American System had atrophied under Adams, and the laudable calls for aiding the Latin American republics stirred few American voters. The 1828 tariff had alienated sections of the South, while Jackson had beaten the Kentuckian to the punch with the backwoods and frontier vote.

Clay may have run those drawbacks through his mind before he threw his support in 1832 behind Nicholas Biddle and his attempt to recharter the Second BUS four years before its charter was due to expire. Certainly neither he nor Biddle ever thought Jackson capable of successfully opposing the recharter bill. Clay thought he had a no-lose situation on his hands. To an extent he was correct: recent historical scholarship had revised the view that entrepreneurs and state bankers disliked the BUS or that the BUS ever really acted as a "central" bank. Yet Jackson colored the bank question in such terms. What Clay did not realize was that while Jackson lacked the support to stop the recharter in Congress, he had enough votes to sustain a veto, and, already in his second term, he was a lame duck with nothing to lose politically by vetoing the bill.

Indeed, in each of the Jackson presidential elections, in 1824, 1828, and 1832, Clay played to Jackson's strength, allowing himself to appear as the candidate of "big government" and Jackson as the candidate of the common man. He never pointed out that Jackson had developed plans for his own national bank, or that the Democrats universally supported either state monopoly banks or state bond support of private banks when they had legislative majorities, or that the Jacksonians' fetish

*Clay in middle life (courtesy of the
Boston Athenaeum)*

about driving small notes out of existence would have ground all exchange among small businessmen and merchants to a halt. Nor did Clay ever point out the degree to which Jackson himself had greatly expanded the federal government. And, for his part, the Kentuckian harbored some concerns about the extent of federal power. When a measure was put forward in 1837 to authorize an issue of treasury notes, which were used as bank reserves, Clay warned the act would turn the government into a huge bank, with Secretary of the Treasury Levi Woodbury as "the great cashier." His own conception of the secretary's office was that it was "altogether financial and administrative." The secretary had no legislative powers, nor could Congress delegate any to him. At any rate, Clay's vision of a voter uprising against Jackson on the bank issue never materialized.

So Clay returned to the Senate, where his role in developing a compromise over the tariff problem enhanced his status as a negotiator. As the central spokesman of the Whig party, Clay remained a firm critic of the Jackson administration. When the panic of 1837 set in and the new Van Buren administration was pinned with the blame, Clay saw another chance for national election fade. Thurlow

Weed of New York pushed the Whigs to nominate Gen. William Henry Harrison of Ohio for president in 1840. A candidate who epitomized frontier values but had none of Clay's big-government baggage, Harrison won the election, then promptly died. His successor, John Tyler of Virginia, opposed Clay's grandiose plans for aggressive federal action. Clay forced his program through the Congress but met a stone wall in Tyler, who vetoed another BUS recharter bill. Frustrated, Clay left the Senate in 1842, despite a string of impressive victories.

He thought he had one more chance at the presidency. From his home in Kentucky he prepared for his final campaign. The Whigs had been split by Tyler's actions, yet Clay remained popular and by far had the clearest Whig vision of the future. Tyler had pressed for the annexation of Texas as a slave state, an act that almost certainly guaranteed war with Mexico. Clay's own frontier followers favored taking Texas. He waffled over the most important issue of his political career. At first he opposed annexation; then he tried to win southern and western support by promising to annex Texas after he was elected if it could be achieved "without war." The South rejected his appeal, and in the 1844 election he lost all but two southern states. James K. Polk, a Tennessean committed to annexation, won, and soon the nation had its war. Clay's son was a casualty of the war Clay sought to avoid.

In 1848 the party passed him over in favor of Gen. Zachary Taylor, ending Clay's last chance to attain the presidency. The Whigs, in nominating Taylor, alienated Clay and a sizable faction of Whigs, initiating the final decline of the party. Even John J. Crittenden, Clay's longtime lieutenant, who had often sought to develop Clay's views on the Kentucky farmers and mechanics, in that campaign had to abandon his friend Clay for the sure winner, Taylor.

The cessation of hostilities with Mexico in 1848 brought Clay new troubles. New settlers poised themselves to enter the vast western conquests. Although Clay had attempted to move his party to outright opposition of slavery in the territories, clearly southerners, who had fought to acquire the lands, demanded their share of the spoils. In his last great contribution to the Union cause, Clay fashioned yet another compromise, a series of five bills together called the Compromise of 1850. Clay had returned to the Senate in 1849 and, along with Illinois senator Stephen A. Douglas, promoted the settlement that admitted California as a free state, allowed the organization of other territories in the Mexican cession according to "popular sovereignty" (Douglas's phrase for the policy of allowing each new state to vote on whether to admit slavery), and established a much stronger fugitive slave law. The compromise suffered from severe weaknesses: northerners perceived the fugitive slave law as an attempt to force them into support of a system they hated; the concept of popular sovereignty led to bloody struggles to settle western territories by rival groups intent on achieving victories for free soil or slavery at the polls; and the entire basis of Clay's earlier masterpiece, the Missouri Compromise, was eroded by admitting California and the Mexican cession territories on new terms.

On an even deeper level, Clay's repeated failures to attain the nation's highest office showed that his vision of a unified nation with an active national government was simply at odds with the desires of most Americans of the day. Jackson had succeeded by carefully shrouding some of the same goals in more states' rights rhetoric. Indeed, Clay was probably too honest to aspire to the nation's highest office. Yet he also badly misjudged the divisions brought about by slavery. He always assumed that proper economic incentives–a national bank, protective tariffs, internal improvements–could overcome moral objections to continued union (which he shared). In 1849 he proposed a program for gradual emancipation, although he never pressed it with the zeal he gave to other causes.

In another respect, also, Clay had confidence in the Union. He thought that improved communication and trade would tie the nation evermore tightly together. He only wanted to buy time, and indeed, the Compromise of 1850 did just that. But Clay was out of time. After a period of failing health he died on June 29, 1852. He left debts of more than $50,000, and only four of his eleven children survived him. Of those–all sons–one became insane from an accident; Thomas H. Clay became Abraham Lincoln's minister to Guatemala and died

in 1871; James B. Clay served as chargé d'affaires in Portugal during the Taylor administration and died in 1863; and John M. Clay, the last surviving member of the family, died in 1887.

Henry Clay's American System was the natural successor to Alexander Hamilton's Federalist programs, which sought to centralize aspects of the economy. As the leader of the Whig party for much of its existence, he championed the ideas of national economic unity, symbolized more than anything else by the Bank of the United States. But he attempted to straddle the slavery issue, which alienated him from much of his natural northern and northwestern constituency. It was fitting that Abraham Lincoln admired the Kentuckian, even delivering a eulogy for Clay. But Lincoln refused to budge on slavery. Despite the fact that the Republicans adopted much of the Whig program–Clay's program–Harry of the West got little of the credit because he had not championed abolition.

Publications:

Calvin Colton, ed., *The Papers of Henry Clay*, 10 volumes (New York: Putnam's, 1904);

James F. Hopkins and others, eds., *The Papers of Henry Clay*, 4 volumes to date (Lexington: University of Kentucky Press, 1959-   ).

References:

Clement Eaton, *Henry Clay and the Art of American Politics* (Boston: Little, Brown, 1957);

George R. Poage, *Henry Clay and the Whig Party* (Gloucester, Mass.: Peter Smith, 1965);

Larry Schweikart, "Focus of Power: A Reappraisal of Speaker Henry Clay," *Alabama Historian* (Spring 1981): 18-24;

Richard Timberlake, *The Origins of Central Banking in the United States* (Cambridge, Mass.: Harvard University Press, 1978);

Glyndon G. Van Deusen, *The Life of Henry Clay* (Boston: Little, Brown, 1937).

Archives:

The papers of Henry Clay are located at the Library of Congress.

Henry Clews

(August 14, 1834-January 31, 1923)

by Kurt Schuler

George Mason University

CAREER: Clerk, Wilson G. Hunt & Company (1849-1857); partner, Stout, Clews & Mason (later Livermore, Clews & Company) (1857-1873); president, Henry Clews & Company (1878-1923).

Henry Clews, financier and writer, was born in Hilderstone, Staffordshire, England, on August 14, 1834. His parents were James C. Clews, a china manufacturer, and Elizabeth Kendrick Clews. Clews had three older brothers and three sisters. His family intended him to become a minister in the Church of England. He was to have begun his career as a curate under his cousin, the vicar of Wolstanton. Clews's cousin supervised his education, an excellent one for the time.

When Henry Clews was fourteen, his father invited him on a business trip to the United States. The purpose of the trip was to determine whether the china firm should establish a factory to serve the American market. "The hustle and the bustle that contrasted so vividly with the slow and easy style which prevailed in my native country" so thrilled Clews that he persuaded his father to let him stay. He landed a job as a clerk with Wilson G. Hunt & Company, one of the largest importers of wool goods in New York City. He found the financial aspect of the business more to his taste than its merchandising aspect. In eight years with the firm he acquired a thorough knowledge of commercial credit.

For several years Clews tried to gain membership in the New York Stock Exchange, but the older members frustrated his efforts, as they did the efforts of many like-minded young men. Quick on the heels of the Panic of 1857, Clews hit upon a tactic to force his way in. He placed newspaper advertisements offering to buy and sell stock for a commission of one-sixteenth of a dollar on each trade, half the going rate. Customers flocked to him, and the exchange admitted him to prevent an in-

Henry Clews (engraving by H. B. Hall & Sons)

formal market from developing outside its control. Clews was then only twenty-three years old. The firm he helped found, Stout, Clews & Mason (later Livermore, Clews & Company), worked in note brokerage and investment banking. Mainly through Clews's keen speculations and forceful personality, it became one of the best-known on Wall Street.

The threat of civil war troubled the bond market in early 1861. Clews's firm was the only large investment banker to purchase an issue of 5 percent, 20-year treasury bonds shortly before the Lincoln administration entered office. Though the firm lost money reselling the bonds to its clients, it gained a good reputation with the Treasury. On the eve of the war Clews visited Washington to offer to buy another block of treasury bonds. However, conversations with southern politicians convinced him that, contrary to general expectation, a long conflict lay ahead. He hurried back to sell all the securities he held. When war broke out, he had a great pile of cash, which he used to advantage in the bond market. Clews's firm bought a one-year, 12 percent issue that financed the Union government's initial war spending. After unsuccessful attempts to sell longer-term notes directly to investors, the Treasury chose Livermore, Clews & Company as one of three firms to sell a $250 million issue of 7.3 percent, three-year bonds. Clews's firm became second only to Jay Cooke & Company as a war bond underwriter, selling large amounts through its European agents. For investors with the fortitude to hold the bonds, they ultimately saw great profits. Secretary of the Treasury Salmon P. Chase once remarked that "if it had not been for Henry Clews and Jay Cooke, I should never have been able to sell enough of the 7-30 notes and 5-20 bonds to carry on the war."

Henry Clews was not yet an American citizen when war broke out. Upon his naturalization he became an ardent Republican. His sincerely held political beliefs fit perfectly with his financial interests. He helped found the Union League, the foremost Republican club in New York City. He despised President Andrew Johnson's lukewarm support of the rights of freed slaves and, with at least equal passion, Johnson's tirades against war bond speculators. Johnson went so far as to suggest that the Union should repudiate its war debts, because according to him war bond speculators had already received a fair return on their investment, and the excess they would get until the bonds matured constituted usury.

Clews became a close friend of Ulysses S. Grant, working behind the scenes for Grant's victories in the presidential elections of 1868 and 1872. Grant twice offered Clews the job of secretary of the treasury, but Clews preferred to remain a businessman. He also refused the important post of collector of customs for New York harbor, recommending instead Chester A. Arthur, who received the appointment. Clews called upon his friendship with Grant on two great occasions. The first was during Jay Gould and James Fisk's attempt to corner the gold market in September 1869. Trade in New York was paralyzed because customs duties had to be paid in gold, and foreigners who could afford to sit tight kept their goods aboard ship until the price of gold fell. Gould and Fisk had corrupted Grant's brother-in-law and the assistant treasury secretary in New York to keep the government's gold supplies off the market. On "Black Friday" (September 24), when the stringency reached new proportions, Clews sent telegrams to Grant and to the secretary of the treasury urging them to sell gold to relieve the market, which they did, ending the corner but plunging many Wall Street firms into bankruptcy. The second occasion on which Clews called upon his friendship with Grant was when Grant was dying. Clews gently persuaded him to be buried in New York City rather than in several other locales vying for the honor.

Two honors that the Grant administration successfully urged on Clews included appointment as the U.S. government's financial agent abroad, replacing Baring Brothers, and a recommendation to the Japanese government that it ask Clews to serve as an expert adviser on financial reform. In the early 1870s Japan introduced Western forms of organization and legal practices into its banking system. Clews and several other financiers explained the workings of the American system to a visiting Japanese delegation. He also arranged for the first modern-style Japanese bank notes to be engraved and printed in the United States. For his assistance the Japanese government awarded him a decoration, just one of many honors he received during his lifetime.

Locally, business and political interests drew Clews into the fight against "Boss" William Marcy Tweed's ring of political cronies. Tweed's Tammany Hall Democrats regained control of New York City's government in 1866 after being out of office during the Civil War. The Democrats initiated a large public-works program, financed by bond issues. Some of the proceeds went into the pockets of the Tweed ring. In July 1871 a disgruntled auditor opened secret city account books to the press. Bankers refused to lend to the city government when they learned the true extent of its borrowing. Clews argued that every banking house in the city would suffer if the city's credit collapsed. He helped organize a bipartisan reform group, the Committee of Seventy, to run candidates against Tammany Hall in the approaching November elections. As the date approached, the scandal widened and many Tammany officials resigned or went to jail. The reform ticket won handily. Clews later turned down the Republican party's offer to be its mayoral candidate.

The remarkable sixth sense Clews had for anticipating panics failed him in 1873. His firm had eagerly reentered the market for underwriting Southern state bonds after the Civil War. In the aftermath of the Panic of 1873, Georgia defaulted. The $2 million of Georgia bonds that Clews's firm held became worthless, bankrupting him. He had to sell his seat on the New York Stock Exchange. At thirty-nine he saw 15 years' painstaking effort to accumulate wealth wiped out in an instant. But his financial genius propelled him to the top again: in 1876 he rejoined the stock exchange and two years later opened a new firm, Henry Clews & Company, which engaged in commission business only and made no speculations.

Clews married in 1874. His wife, Lucy Madison Worthing, of Kentucky, was the grandniece of President James Madison. They had two children: Henry Jr., an artist, and Elsie, a writer.

Clews won fame as a popular speaker and a prolific writer on financial and civic topics. He was particularly concerned with upholding the reputation of Wall Street against charges that it was a den of thieves or a gambling casino. His memoir *Twenty-Eight Years in Wall Street* (1887) took pains to stress the high degree of trust necessary in financial dealings. Yet much of the book's interest lay in Clews's inside account of the barely legal stock manipulations of such characters as Jay Gould, Cornelius Vanderbilt, and Daniel Drew. The book's forthright, businesslike style and mildly sensational tales made it a success, so much so that toward the end of his career Clews expanded it as *Fifty Years in Wall Street* (1908).

In old age Clews relinquished day-to-day management of Henry Clews & Company to a nephew, James B. Clews. Another nephew, John H. Clews, who was also a partner in the firm, died in 1907. Clews's son, Henry Jr., displayed no business aptitude. Clews kept an eye on the firm's operations and frequented its offices when he was not enjoying his fine vacation house in Newport, Rhode Island. Civic causes, which had always claimed a large share of his time, grew still more important. He served as the treasurer of several organizations, including the Society for the Prevention of Cruelty to Animals, the American Geographical Society, and, during World War I, the Dollar Christmas Fund for Destitute Belgian Children. Of all the civic causes Clews supported, the American Peace and Arbitration League was particularly dear to his heart. He at one time served as its president and proved a tireless publicist for its advocacy of peaceful settlement of international disputes. (The League and its foreign counterparts were instrumental in establishing the World Court in The Hague, Netherlands.)

In his eighty-ninth year Clews suffered a long illness. He died on January 31, 1923, at home in New York of chronic bronchitis and was buried in Woodlawn Cemetery in the Bronx.

Clews saw his role in financing the Union government's Civil War debt as his proudest accomplishment, and it stands today as his chief claim to a place in history. As the *Commercial and Financial Chronicle* remarked at his death, "He represented the better part of Wall Street, a place which renders indispensable services and maintains the highest standards of rectitude in dealings."

Publications:

Twenty-Eight Years in Wall Street (New York: Irving, 1887); enlarged as *Fifty Years in Wall Street* (New York: Irving, 1908);

Financial, Economic, and Miscellaneous Speeches and Essays (New York: Irving, 1900);

The Wall Street Point of View (New York & Boston: Silver, Burdett, 1900).

DeWitt Clinton

(March 2, 1769-February 11, 1828)

by B. R. Burg

Arizona State University

CAREER: State assemblyman and senator, New York (1797-1802); U.S. senator, state of New York (1802-1803); mayor, city of New York (1803-1807, 1809-1810, 1812-1815); Erie Canal commissioner (1810-1824); governor of New York (1817-1822, 1824-1828).

DeWitt Clinton was a New York political leader, land speculator, city planner, canal promoter, and banker during the early decades of the nineteenth century. His public career spanned a period of extraordinarily rapid growth for the new nation. Not only had America moved boldly westward in those years but the center of economic and political power had shifted. The nation transferred its capital southward to the banks of the Potomac, farmers by the thousands migrated to the Ohio Valley, New York City overtook Philadelphia as the commercial center of the nation, and the state of New York expanded its role as one of the chief agricultural areas in North America. During those unsettling years of social, political, and economic change, Clinton held major political offices, led in formulating a plan for the development of Manhattan Island, was a guiding spirit in almost every stage of the planning and construction of the Erie Canal, championed various civic improvement projects, and was an advocate of legal reform long before many of his fellow New Yorkers accepted it. He was the first governmental leader to favor a statewide system of free public education, and, as a true visionary in the field, he led a movement for the professionalization of teachers, supported the establishment of school libraries, and strove to provide education for women and for the speech and hearing impaired. Clinton also advocated programs to aid the poor and directed at least some of his involvement in banking toward this end.

DeWitt Clinton was born on March 2, 1769, in Orange County, New York, to James and Mary

DeWitt Clinton (portrait by Samuel F. B. Morse)

DeWitt Clinton. His father rose to the rank of major-general during the American Revolution, and his father's brother George became the first governor of the state of New York. Young Clinton was educated at Kingston Academy, then one of the best grammar schools in the state. After completing his course of study he set out for New Jersey to enroll at Princeton College. While passing through New York City he had a change of heart. He decided to attend Columbia, where he became the first student to matriculate after the Revolution. Clinton graduated at the head of his class in 1786 and then studied law for three years. Admitted to the bar in 1790, he made little use of his legal training except to further the land speculations he engaged in with John Jacob Astor and others. He took a job as private secretary to his uncle, George Clinton, and served as secretary to both the State Board of Regents and the State Board of Fortification.

Clinton's various public employments and family background made him a force to be reckoned with in New York politics throughout the 1790s, and by the beginning of the next century he had assumed leadership of the New York Republican party. His rise to power when scarcely thirty years old, as his enemies conceded, resulted from more than family connections. A man of consummate ability, Clinton possessed an uncanny talent for attracting supporters through the blend of a forceful personality and an unfailing skill at dispensing political favors. Although widespread distribution of patronage characterized the previous Federalist administrations, the ambitious young New Yorker made far more effective use of it when the Republicans gained power. He was assiduous, even compulsive, in his efforts to replace Federalist officials with loyal members of his own party.

When he received an appointment to the U.S. Senate in 1802, after the resignation of John Armstrong, it appeared he would become a leading member of that body. Clinton gained considerable favor with the Republican national leadership by providing unswerving support for their programs. On the critical question of selecting a proper response when the Spanish governor of New Orleans closed the port to American shipping, Clinton strongly opposed the Federalist demands for the use of force to reopen it. He also introduced the Twelfth Amendment to the Constitution, providing for the present method of electing the president and vice-president.

Clinton's reasons for resigning from the Senate in 1803 to become mayor of New York are not entirely clear. He may have decided he could help his family by returning home, or perhaps he thought that the power and dignity of the mayoral office—far greater than they are today—would give him broader latitude in the exercise of his talent and ambitions. The annual salary of $15,000 surely had appeal. In 1796 he married Maria Franklin, daughter of wealthy Quaker merchant Walter Franklin, and they wasted little time beginning a family that ultimately numbered ten children.

By the time Clinton graduated from college and became involved with the Republican party in the late 1780s, the nation's banking system had grown rapidly. No one assumed any longer that each major city would have only one commercial bank and that legislatures would prohibit the chartering of competitors. The Bank of North America in Philadelphia struggled against newer banking houses, and in New York a similar situation had developed. Clinton observed banking closely and the political struggles it engendered in his state, but his interest and early involvement left relatively little historical record. It is much easier to trace his public life and his work as organizer and chief promoter of the Erie Canal than to chronicle his early career in banking.

Banking in New York was divided along the same party lines as state politics during the last years of the eighteenth and first years of the nineteenth centuries. The legislature granted charters, and the party ascendant at any specific time determined which of the numerous applicants would receive permission to incorporate. Political pressure and the competitive atmosphere created complex alliances among those seeking charters, and the same names appeared repeatedly as directors or officers of banks seeking and receiving permission to conduct business.

The earliest political conflict over banking came in the late 1790s, when partisan bitterness was amplified by accusations that the two chartered banks in New York City, both dominated by Federalists, refused to lend money to or discount the commercial paper of Republican merchants. By 1799 frustrated Republicans decided to found their own financial institution. They hoped to aid those of similar ideological disposition and to benefit financially from breaking the banking monopoly held by the Federalist-dominated Bank of New York and the local branch of the Bank of the United States.

The Republicans labored long to organize their own bank and secure a charter, but even with party leader Clinton as their ally they found it a daunting task. The established banks were not anxious for competition from any quarter, and the proposed bank's leader, Aaron Burr, was a personal and political enemy of Alexander Hamilton, the moving spirit behind the Federalists' Bank of New York. Despite the political power wielded by Burr, Clinton, Brockholst Livingston, and the apostate Federalist Samuel Osgood, the opposition then denied the Republicans' petition. The Republicans tried a new strategy. Burr put together a bill incorporating a company to supply New York City with pure water. The capital available for the company totaled $2 million, but in the event the company could not use all of it immediately, the articles of agreement empowered the directors to lend or otherwise invest the temporary surplus of funds. The Federalists strove mightily to stop the legislation, but Burr's manipulative skill and the fear that contaminated water would bring another epidemic of yellow fever enabled the Republicans to secure a permanent charter for their "water works" in 1799. The Republicans' strategy of engaging in banking through another business front proved so successful that by the mid 1800s it remained the most popular method of entering banking in the face of legislative opposition.

Operating under the name of the Manhattan Company, workers began laying pipe, and by the close of 1801 the company supplied water to more than 1,400 homes. Notwithstanding the company's success as a public utility, the association conducted its main business through what was styled "The Bank of the Manhattan Company," which used approximately half of the original capitalization for its business. Later, relying heavily on political influence of the Clintons and Livingstons, other Republican banks received charters in New York.

During Thomas Jefferson's first presidential administration, when Clinton served as Republican senator and mayor of New York, Republican banks in the state flourished. Their coffers were filled by the federal funds the president provided in a bid to debilitate or even destroy the financial underpinning of the opposition. Federalists tried to maintain their influence over state financial activities by organizing a Merchants' Bank of New York in 1803, but the legislature, which was by then hostile to their purposes, rejected their charter application.

The highly politicized climate in the state's financial establishments hardly diminished when Jefferson left office. Republicans remained in power and thwarted the Federalists at every turn. As late as 1812 Republican governor Daniel D. Tompkins worked assiduously to prevent chartering of the Bank of America, which he considered too strongly influenced by the opposition.

While political struggles dominated New York politics, the international situation for the United States became more precarious with each passing year. British impressment of American seamen, the seizure of American ships, the confiscation of car-

goes, and attempts by England and France to blockade American ports made it increasingly likely the United States would be drawn into the Anglo-French conflict. Jefferson and his Republican majority in Congress labored doggedly to preserve U.S. neutrality. They responded to the threat from across the Atlantic with the Embargo Act of 1807, which in effect prohibited almost all American ships from putting to sea. The president hoped that by suspending the nation's maritime commerce British and French provocations would be avoided and the United States would not be forced into a war to salvage national honor. Jefferson also presumed that by denying the warring powers access to American shipping and American products they would be coerced into halting their depredations against American ships and sailors.

New York's merchants and bankers regarded the embargo as an outrage certain to drive them into bankruptcy. The pressure made Clinton's political position excruciatingly difficult. He first sided with his city's business interests and opposed the embargo, but as a loyal Republican he found it difficult to maintain that position for long. The party's political machine supported the national leadership on the issue, and Clinton had to accommodate them without alienating local bankers and merchants. It proved an impossible task. Fortunately, Congress repealed the embargo early in 1809, and the confrontation ended without serious damage to Clinton's career. The only lasting result was that Clinton emerged from the fracas with a reputation for equivocation.

Although a Republican, Clinton's handling of the political storm generated by the embargo earned him considerable admiration from the Federalist party. Rumors also circulated that despite Republican opposition, he strongly advocated one of their favorite projects, the establishment of the Merchants' Bank in New York. As a result the Federalists nominated him to be their presidential candidate in 1812. He seemed particularly attractive to Federalist leaders not only because of shared ideological perspectives but because they assumed he would move quickly to halt the war begun only a few months earlier by Republican president James Madison. The war was anathema to the large shippers and traders who dominated the commercial life of Pennsylvania, New York, and New England. They knew America could not stand against the might of the Royal Navy, and they predicted accurately that when hostilities commenced the nation's merchant fleet would be driven from the seas. To preserve their wartime prosperity, they reasoned, they needed to elect a man who would return the country to a neutral stance and allow them to trade again with all belligerents.

The Federalist party had already started its decline by 1812. Their last successful presidential candidate, John Adams, was elected in 1796, and their strength in Congress diminished gradually over the years. By the time they chose Clinton to lead them in a presidential election, their narrow advocacy of the economic interests of northern seaboard commercial leaders had destroyed their support elsewhere in the nation and reduced them to the status of a regional party. Not only did the Federalists have an inadequate political base, but they pursued a badly flawed election-year strategy. They planned to defeat the Republicans on the war issue, but in the autumn of 1812 the struggle against England remained popular in the southern and western areas of the country. The disenchantment with Madison that followed the multiple defeats sustained by American military forces had not set in by election time, and the incumbent overwhelmed Clinton by an electoral margin of 128 to 89. Clinton's loss revealed the sectional nature of the Federalist party. He carried New York and most of New England, but nothing else.

Serving as the Federalist presidential candidate temporarily destroyed Clinton's influence with Republicans, even those in his own state. The Bank of America received a charter against his wishes, the decline of the Federalists continued, and he lost his post as mayor of New York in 1815. Still, the succession of rebuffs did not persuade him to retire from public life. Instead he turned his efforts toward combining his own philanthropic interests with his knowledge of banking and the pursuit of personal gain. He set out to organize a bank where the working classes could deposit their funds safely, earn interest, and make withdrawals as needed. A group of New Yorkers who shared Clinton's motives in founding such a savings bank joined him in the project. Those were level-headed businessmen who sought pecuniary reward and not social reform, but like the English social commentators whose works influenced them, they saw that it was to their advantage to help the poor help themselves. By allowing the lower classes a stake in preserving economic and social stability they secured their own position and in the process reduced the cost of programs designed to ameliorate conditions for the poor and the destitute.

The concept of a savings bank was new in America when Clinton and his associates proposed it in 1816. Previously, banks had engaged solely in business lending, note issue, the processing of commercial paper, and in the financing of local or national government. A limited number of wealthy investors rather than a large corps of small depositors provided deposits. The administrative structure for the proposed savings bank essentially resembled those of the nation's commercial banks, with a board of directors, a president, vice-presidents, and a cashier. In dealing with the investors—depositors in this case—the organizers adopted English models. Five percent was to be paid on all accounts of $5 to $49. Larger amounts earned 6 percent. Only whole dollars were to be taken in deposit (i.e., no small-change bills), and the bank recorded transactions in passbooks furnished to the customers. Officers balanced accounts and entered interest once per year. Accounts derived interest from investments made in the United States, the state of New York, New York City, or wherever the directors saw fit.

All went well in the initial stages of the bank's organization. Serious difficulties did not develop until the group applied to the state legislature for a charter. In selecting the term "savings bank" they aroused the antagonism of the growing number of elected officials who opposed banks on principle. Legislators did not understand the distinction between the entirely new concept of a savings bank and the commercial banks with which they were familiar. The lack of comprehension combined with the tactical error made by using the word "bank" in the title of the bill doomed the application. Even the ploy of changing the name of the legislation from "An Act to Incorporate an Association by the Name of the Saving-Bank of the City of New York" to "An Act to Incorporate an Association by the Name of the Saving Corporation of the City of New York" failed.

Clinton's political advice aided the organizers the following year when they again attempted to obtain a charter. To head the enterprise they chose Matthew Clarkson, a widely respected citizen whose name had long been associated with undertakings designed for the general improvement of the city. His selection, Clinton explained, would be "a passbook

The locks of the Erie Canal at Lockport, New York. Clinton served as canal commissioner from 1810 to 1824 (courtesy of the New York Public Library Picture Collection).

to public approbation." This time, instead of organizing a bank, the moving spirits of the project constituted themselves as a "Society to Prevent Pauperism." In doing so they followed both American and English models. Clinton had seen subterfuge work in gaining a charter for the Manhattan Company 20 years earlier, as had another of the savings bank organizers, Brockholst Livingston, who was also a founder of the Manhattan Company. Across the Atlantic philanthropic groups that had influenced American organizations like Clinton's "Society to Prevent Pauperism" often operated banks. The Liverpool Mechanics', Servants', and Labourers' Fund was established in 1813 by the Society for Bettering the Condition and Increasing the Comforts of the Poor in the Town and Neighborhood of Liverpool. In a similar manner, the Edinburgh Society for the Suppression of Mendacity in Scotland was the parent organization of the Edinburgh Savings Bank.

The new name and an altered political situation in 1817 made it more likely the charter would be granted. In that year Daniel D. Tompkins resigned as New York governor to become the nation's vice-president, and a Republican caucus selected Clinton to replace him. In his message of January 27, 1818, he expounded on the evils of pauperism, and he suggested among other remedies founding a savings bank. He explained that the bank would aid the poor to become self-sufficient; they would then no longer be supported by the government. Taxes could then be reduced. By the time Clinton gave his address, savings banks already existed in Boston, Baltimore, Philadelphia, and Salem, and New York legislators drew on the experience of those other cities. After discovering that the savings banks had achieved success elsewhere, and with the prospect of lowered expenditures before them, they approved the scheme. On January 5, 1819, the charter and bylaws of the New York Bank for Savings were passed.

The following year the directors petitioned the legislature, asking for permission to expand the types of loans the bank could make. They wanted to provide credit to the government of New York City and to underwrite real estate transactions. Governor Clinton gave his approval to the request, but by that time his hold over the Republican party had weakened. The legislature refused to follow his lead, and they denied the Bank's petition.

The refusal to allow the savings bank to expand the type of loans it provided was symptomatic of the disenchantment with banks that appeared in New York during the Panic of 1819. In Clinton's annual message to the state legislature that year he raged against a system that had expanded out of control and demanded legislative action to curb the industry. "I . . . submit it to your serious consideration," he told the legislators, "whether the incorporation of banks in places where they are not required by the exigencies of commerce, trade or manufactures, ought to be countenanced." Such institutions, he added, having but few deposits of money, must rely for their profits principally upon the circulation of their notes, and they are therefore tempted to extend themselves beyond their faculties.

The legislators responded to the governor's address, using the opportunity to flog a few of their own whipping boys. They blamed the disordered state of the economy on South American revolutions, the siphoning off of specie by the China trade, the importation of luxuries by Americans, and, in line with Clinton's complaint, they named "the improvident increase of banking institutions" as one of the problems.

At the same time Clinton dealt with the banking problems of 1819 and organized the savings bank, he also took an interest in promoting construction of a canal from the Great Lakes to the Hudson River. He had been involved in canal projects since the turn of the century, but not until 1816 did he seriously devote himself to the task of solidifying public opinion behind the idea that a canal could actually be constructed. He organized meetings everywhere in New York and went to Albany to persuade lawmakers of the need for the project. As head of the committee to promote the idea, he wrote an appeal for support that became the most widely publicized of the 30 or so memorials on the subject presented to the New York legislature. Clinton was well prepared to argue his case. He understood the economic benefits that would accrue, was conversant with engineering and construction technology, and thoroughly appreciated the complexities of financing a project of the magnitude he proposed. He explained that canals combined economy, safety, and certainty in transportation. The cost of shipping a ton of goods 100 miles by canal was approximately $1, he claimed, while the same single-ton cargo sent overland by wagon cost $32.

Clinton's efforts succeeded despite complaints about the cost and squabbles that pitted various factions of the Republican party against one another. On April 17, 1816, the assembly approved the plan and created a new canal commission, with Clinton as president. The commission set to work examining routes and exploring suggestions on ways to connect Lakes Erie and Champlain with the Hudson River. It also applied to Congress for financial aid.

In the midst of the bustle of organizing the effort to build a canal, Clinton lived through one of the most hectic periods of his life. His wife of more than 20 years died, and a short time later he began courting. Catherine Jones, the object of his suit, was the daughter of a prominent physician. He married her in 1819.

Clinton's efforts on the canal project were partially deflected by political difficulties during his term as governor. The problems, as before, stemmed from his close ties with the opposition party. The obvious commercial benefits promised by the canal gained him enthusiastic approbation from leading Federalists. This angered Martin Van Buren, who superintended the Tammany wing of the New York Republicans and was closely allied with the party's Virginia leadership. Little doubt existed in Clinton's mind of the potential his enemies possessed for disrupting or even halting construction of the canal before it reached completion. He forestalled attempts to terminate the canal's route at any one of several points short of Lake Erie by beginning construction on the middle sections and extending it eastward and westward simultaneously so that no segment along the route would derive any benefit until after completion of the entire length. That stratagem proved effective, but it was more than such exercises in political trickery that swept away opposition to the canal by the time of the final vote to authorize completion in 1819. Economic hard times had spread throughout America by then, and lowered wages and prices made it possible for construction to proceed at a reduced cost. Excavation expenses dropped 30 to 40 percent. Overexpanded credit, the collapse of markets at home and abroad, foreclosures, and the failure of many banks all had their effects. Farmers west of the Seneca River sank deeply in debt, and they had to accept employment as construction laborers as the only way to keep their land from the hands of creditors. Their self-serving enthusiasm for the canal, coupled with their willingness to work at depressed wage levels, gave Clinton the tools he needed to manipulate the legislature. The canal obviously reduced the effects of economic decline, but its usefulness in alleviating widespread financial distress along the route was not part of the rhetoric offered to gain the last necessary appropriations. The deliberate use of public-works projects to provide employment only came much later. Instead, the belief that completion of the canal would herald the return of prosperity proved to be the driving consideration in its approval.

Clinton succeeded far less in protecting his own political base than at accruing support for the canal. His personal power eroded rapidly during his term of office, and in 1822 he retired from political life without making another attempt to secure the governorship. His retirement did not placate his political enemies. In 1824 he lost his position as canal commissioner, a job he had held since 1810. That final act of revenge went too far. Clinton and the canal were linked closely in the popular mind, and fierce opposition emerged from this move. Huge meetings were held in Albany and in New York City to protest the action, and resolutions of praise were drafted everywhere to support the ejected commissioner. Even more outrage appeared in western villages, where the canal remained especially popular. Thurlow Weed's *Rochester Telegraph* called Clinton's firing a "deed which will ever blacken the annals of the State." The editor wrote that "Every contemptible effort to rob Mr. Clinton of his well-earned fame, serves only to identify him still more indissolubly with these great national works. Clinton does 'swim' triumphantly upon his 'big ditch,' where he will continue to 'swim' long after the memory and offenses of his enemies are forgotten and forgiven."

The partisan vindictiveness directed against Clinton caused a reaction among New York voters, and in the autumn of 1824, only eight months after he was forced off the canal commission, the citizens again elected him governor. The following year the project on which he had labored so long at last began operation. Workers finished construction on the 362 miles from Buffalo to Albany and on the 71-mile Champlain Canal. The triumphant emergence of New York over New Orleans as the shipping and transfer point for the agricultural products of the Old Northwest had begun.

Clinton's political fortunes remained precarious after the opening of the canal system. He re-

fused an appointment as U.S. minister to England offered him by President John Quincy Adams, preferring instead to remain in the United States and nurture his presidential ambitions. Unfortunately for his candidacy, Clinton lacked the broad-based political support necessary for serious consideration. His flirtations with the Federalists over the years had hurt him within the ranks of his own party, and his states-rights views were unpopular in the North. He not only supported Andrew Jackson in an area of the country that favored Adams but was a leading Mason at a time when anti-Masonic fervor had grown to an important element in American politics.

DeWitt Clinton's contributions to New York and to the nation went far beyond his political achievement and his commercial activities. His enthusiasm for the expansion of agriculture fueled his interest in natural science. He discovered a native American wheat, a new fish, and published papers on pigeons, swallows, and rice. He held membership in many scientific societies in America and abroad. His *An Introductory Discourse Delivered Before the Literary and Philosophical Society of New York*, published in 1815, was one of the most comprehensive statements of technical information available in America up to that time.

Clinton was also deeply involved in the arts. He inaugurated the translation of New York's Dutch archives, was a guiding spirit in the founding of the New-York Historical Society, and was actively involved in many other civic and cultural organizations. Clinton's deep concern with the promotion of religion led him to serve as vice-president of both the American Bible Society and the educational society of the Presbyterian Church. Unlike so many enthusiastic American Protestants in the early nineteenth century, he harbored no hostility to the Roman Catholic Church. He succeeded in having the political disabilities of New York's Catholics removed in 1806, and he defended the secrecy of the confessional in a case where a priest was called as a witness.

Even though he was a leader of manifold accomplishments, Clinton is best known for the Erie Canal. His labor, dedication, and political skill brought the dream of a nation connected by economical and rapid transportation a step closer to reality. His vision inspired others who organized and invested in canal systems throughout Pennsylvania, into the Ohio Valley, and westward to the banks of the Wabash. In personal terms, the canal probably remains the last instance of a mighty public-works project being so closely associated with the name of one man.

Clinton's unexpected death in 1828 simplified New York politics by removing a leader all factions regarded with suspicion. His philosophy usually aligned him with the Republicans, but he was at heart an aristocrat and was more comfortable in the company of New York's Federalists. Similarly, he advocated states' rights in the tradition of Thomas Jefferson, yet he espoused Alexander Hamilton's active support for internal improvements and the growth of manufacturing. His wide-ranging and at times ambiguous political positions prevented him from gaining national prominence and damaged his career in the state of New York. Though personally unpopular with many, most generally regarded Clinton as a man of liberal principles and vast administrative ability. In the end, however, his abilities, his commitment to progress and prosperity, and the divisions among his political enemies all contributed to give him the opportunity to build a distinguished record as a champion of westward expansion and commercial growth.

Publications:

"Letters opposing the ratification of the United States Constitution," as A Countryman, *New York Journal*, November 1787;

A Vindication of Thomas Jefferson (New York: D. Denniston, 1800);

An Introductory Discourse Delivered Before the Literary and Philosophical Society of New York (New York: D. Longworth, 1815);

Memoir on the Antiquities of the Western Parts of the State of New York (Albany, N.Y.: I. W. Clark, 1818);

The Canal Policy of the State of New York; Delineated in a Letter to Robert Troup, Esquire, as Tacitus (Albany, N.Y.: E. & E. Hosford, 1821).

References:

John Bigelow, "DeWitt Clinton as a Politician," *Harper's New Monthly Magazine*, 50 (February 1875): 409-417; (March 1875): 563-571;

Dorothy Bobbé, *DeWitt Clinton* (New York: Minton, Balch, 1933);

James Renwick, *Life of DeWitt Clinton* (New York: Harper, 1840);

Ronald E. Shaw, *Erie Water West, A History of the Erie Canal, 1792-1854* (Lexington: University of Kentucky Press, 1966).

Archives:

Clinton's papers are located at the Columbia University Library, the New York Public Library, and the New-York Historical Society.

Commercial Banks and Investment Banks

All early American banks owed their existence to the daily operations they conducted on behalf of merchants, including lending, exchanging drafts for specie (gold or silver coin) or other drafts on local merchants' accounts, and issuing notes against a specie reserve. Thus they were viewed as "commercial banks," meaning they facilitated commerce. Most of their operations involved short-term loans (usually outstanding for no more than six months) that were secured by the goods themselves as collateral. Those loans came to be referred to as "short-term, self-liquidating paper." Few banks prior to the Civil War had the resources to back large-scale projects, and none had the resources to finance more than minor business development. Even when a bank undertook a large-scale project it acted as an adjunct of a business, such as a railroad company, which sold its own bonds to finance its construction. The bank merely facilitated the bond sales and usually did not underwrite the railroad's construction. Since traditionally commercial banks concentrated on providing banking services for businesses rather than individuals, their assets consisted of the short-term, self-liquidating loans to businesses. Even when they made loans on real estate, they tended to use the real estate as collateral on a business loan. On the liabilities side, banks focused on short-term liabilities, such as checking accounts (known as demand deposits) for businesses.

For those projects too large for individual commercial banks to finance, such as railroad construction, a new institution emerged called the investment bank. Investment banks provided capital by helping businesses create and sell securities, although investment banks also advanced some funds to the businesses during the sales period, a procedure called "underwriting." While commercial banks also engaged in underwriting before 1933, investment banks existed specifically for that purpose. The securities created and sold by the investment banks could take the form of stocks or bonds. Bonds represented a loan made to the company with a guaranteed interest payable at a specified time. Stock represented a share of ownership in the company, and thus stockholders had a lower priority on the claims of the company's assets than bondholders if the company went into liquidation. On the other hand, as part-owners, stockholders could control the company through their voting rights.

Jay Cooke gave investment banking a great deal of respectability when he managed the sales of U.S. government bonds to finance the Union victory in the Civil War. But the most famous of the investment bankers, J. P. Morgan, made his fortune by financing railroad reorganizations. Eventually his firm's wealth made it, for all practical purposes, the "lender of last resort" for most commercial banks during panics. Most of the investment bankers at one time or another had specialized in railroads, with Daniel Drew being among the earliest and most infamous, although as they grew more comfortable in investment banking activities they involved themselves in other businesses. Frequently the size of a railroad reorganization dwarfed the resources of a single investment bank, even Morgan's or Kuhn, Loeb & Company. At those times, the financiers formed syndicates in which they shared the risk—and the profits—with other houses. Often, syndicates involved firms overseas, and foreign bankers proved reliable outlets for bond sales.

By 1900, although no laws prohibited commercial banks from engaging in investment banking, or vice versa, each type of bank remained relatively confined to its own specialty, except for some of the largest New York and Chicago commercial banks.

See also:

Jay Cooke, Daniel Drew, Otto Kahn, J. P. Morgan, Junius S. Morgan, Jacob Schiff, Joseph Seligman, James Speyer.

—Editor

Confederate Finance

by Jeffrey Rogers Hummel

Independent Institute

Delegates representing six Southern state governments assembled at Montgomery, Alabama, in February 1861. Having just seceded from the United States, those states now established a rival central government. Within two months the newly formed Confederate States of America, joined by five additional slave states, was at war with the Union. Waging the Civil War dominated Confederate finance until the rebellion's collapse four years later.

The Confederacy's conventional military strategy ensured that its wartime expenditures, like the Union's, would be staggering. President Jefferson Davis appointed Christopher G. Memminger, a South Carolina lawyer, as the first Confederate secretary of the treasury. Although a hard-money man, Memminger, like his Union counterpart, Salmon P. Chase, ended up turning to a mixture of heavy taxation, borrowing, and fiat money. The South, however, could not call upon wealth as abundant as that available to the North. Its financial system, although arguably as sophisticated, had previously financed agriculture, not industry.

Consequently, taxation covered perhaps as little as 5 percent of the South's total war costs compared with 20 percent for the North. That was not for want of trying, even though the Confederacy, like the Union, at first expected a brief conflict, which in both cases resulted in some delay before the combatants resorted to truly confiscatory taxes. No sooner was the Confederate government established than it imposed import duties modeled upon the U.S. tariff. It also imposed export duties, something the United States Constitution prohibited. Yet the Federal blockade and the Confederate cotton embargo severely circumscribed revenue from those sources.

The Confederate Congress made a first stab at internal taxation on August 19, 1861, with a direct levy upon real estate, slaves, and all other property except Confederate bonds and money. Because the central government still lacked the necessary bureaucratic machinery, however, this tax was to be collected through the state governments, which received a discount for rapid payment. Most Southern states therefore converted the direct tax into a war loan by issuing state bonds to finance their shares. That not only undercut the tax's impact but also competed against the borrowing of the Confederate central government.

So on April 24, 1863, the Confederacy imposed a comprehensive revenue measure that included a 10 percent excess profits tax, license taxes ranging as high as $500, ad valorem excise taxes of 8 percent, sales taxes varying between 2.5 and 10 percent, a graduated income tax, and a 10 percent tax in kind. The marginal rates of the income tax varied from 1 to 2 percent for salaries and 5 to 15 percent for other income. Farmers paid the tax in kind by directly surrendering their agricultural products. The Southern economy's comparative lack of monetary development necessitated that expedient, but the high-handed behavior of the "TIK men" who enforced it engendered widespread resistance, particularly in North Carolina.

The Confederate Congress passed further tax measures in February and June 1864 and March 1865 to extend and strengthen the act of April 1863. These bills also added a 10 percent tax on gold and silver plate, a new 5 percent direct tax on land, and a 25 percent tax on holdings of coin, bullion, and foreign exchange. But they came too late to generate significant revenue.

Secretary of the Treasury Memminger secured more than one-third of his government's income through borrowing (compared with nearly two-thirds in the North). At the behest of the state governments most Southern banks outside of New Orleans had suspended specie payments to the general public during the secession crisis. As a result they had enough gold and silver in their vaults to

Confederate treasury note, 1864. The Confederacy issued more than $1 billion in currency during the course of the Civil War, most of it, like this note, redeemable in specie two years after the ratification of a peace treaty with the Union (courtesy of the Chase Manhattan Bank Money Museum).

cover much of the first Confederate loan, amounting to $15 million at 8 percent annual interest.

A second loan for $100 million, authorized by the Confederate Congress on August 19, 1861, fared less well. Planters partly paid for the bonds with cotton and other commodities rather than money. Produce loans of that sort became the most conspicuous feature of the Confederacy's later domestic borrowing and were fiscally analogous to the tax in kind.

The produce loans also linked Confederate finance and diplomacy. Hoping that the need for cotton would bring foreign intervention, Southerners decided at the outset of the war to embargo the crop until European nations granted recognition. The government did not directly enforce the policy, but only because President Davis did not wish to antagonize Britain and France needlessly. Local committees of public safety and state governments policed the cotton embargo instead, while the produce loans helped siphon off accumulating stockpiles.

Southern cotton reaching Europe in the first year of the war dropped to about 1 percent of its peacetime level. The tax in kind further contributed to the central government's holdings. Although the staple could not directly feed or equip Southern soldiers, it brought in supplies through an illicit but flourishing trade with the enemy. Despite a formal ban, the Davis Administration allowed military commanders to monopolize the exchange of cotton across the lines. When the cotton embargo finally

proved a diplomatic fiasco, the Confederate government became the market's largest exporter as well.

The government's cotton eventually served as collateral for a major foreign loan. Negotiated in 1863 through the French financier Emile Erlanger, the loan's nominal value was $14.5 million in specie. The bonds for this loan, convertible into cotton at below its market price, sold well at first. But as Rebel forces suffered military reverses, the sale of the bonds lagged in Europe, and Confederate agents threw away some of the proceeds trying to hold up the price. The South eventually realized only $8.5 million from the loan, with commissions to Erlanger and Company accounting for much of the difference.

During the course of the war, the Confederacy received more than $2 million in donations—from churches, ladies' societies, and patriotic citizens. A sequestration law, passed in response to the Union confiscation acts, expropriated all Northern private property within Confederate jurisdiction. The law, along with the seizure of such U.S. government assets as the New Orleans mint, provided some additional resources.

But overall the South was far less successful with taxation and borrowing than the North and therefore relied far more extensively upon paper money. The Confederate Congress started on March 9, 1861, with an issue of $1 million of one-year treasury notes bearing 3.65 percent interest. The government soon replaced those with $20 million of non-interest-bearing two-year notes, authorized in May 1861. By August Congress had provided for $100 million more. The Confederate government accepted the notes for most tax payments (except export duties) at par. Still more helpful in making them circulate was the willingness of the seceding state governments and the state banks to receive the notes. Indeed, Secretary Memminger had compelled the conservative New Orleans banks to suspend specie payments so that treasury notes would fully replace gold and silver as the Confederacy's circulating medium.

The Confederate Treasury ultimately issued well over $1 billion in currency, more than twice the amount in greenbacks issued by the Union. Most of it consisted of non-interest-bearing treasury notes supposedly redeemable in specie two years after the end of the war. There were also a few interest-bearing issues in denominations of $100 or more. Moreover, the individual states injected $45 million in paper currency of their own. Local governments and private companies often issued "shinplasters," paper that filled the need for money of small denomination. Widespread counterfeiting, some done by the North, added to the flood.

Only Southern state banks exercised restraint in the matter of money creation. Having no central bank or national banking system to encourage their expansion, the banks raised reserve ratios throughout the war and partially neutralized the increase in high-powered money. Despite the suspension of specie payments and use of Confederate treasury notes as reserves, bank notes circulated at a premium as the war dragged on.

The South's monetary expansion nonetheless spurred ruinous hyperinflation. The blockade, the fall in real output, and mounting territorial losses, of course, fueled the monetary depreciation. A Confederate dollar was worth 82.7 cents in specie in 1862, 29 cents in 1863, and 1.7 cents in 1865. Between 1860 and 1864 prices less than doubled in the North but rose 2,676 percent in the South. The price increases worked great hardship on the Southern people. As this hidden tax on cash balances diverted resources, prices climbed faster than incomes. Real wages fell by almost two thirds. Food riots swept through Richmond and other Southern cities in the war's third year, with wives and mothers in the forefront of the rioters.

The Confederate Congress attempted a complicated currency "reform" in February 1864, but it amounted to nothing more than a phased devalua-

tion and repudiation. After April 1, 1864 (or July 1 west of the Mississippi), the Treasury accepted the bulk of its outstanding currency either for taxes, as payment for bonds, or in exchange for new currency at a devalued rate of $3 for $2. After January of the following year, the government ceased to accept its old currency except for small bills, although it continued to issue new currency.

The so-called currency reform did little to arrest the accelerating breakdown in the monetary system, and Secretary Memminger, who had recommended a far more drastic repudiation, resigned four months after its enactment. President Davis replaced him with another South Carolinian, George A. Trenholm. Trenholm was a wealthy businessman. His import-export firm, Fraser and Company, was heavily involved in blockade running and already had close connections with the Confederate Treasury. Trenholm, however, assumed his post too far into the war to have much independent influence on policy.

The Rebel government never made its paper money legal tender for private transactions as did the Federal government. It did, however, force much of the money into circulation through the impressment of supplies. Commanders in the field initiated the practice, and the Confederate Congress formally systematized impressments in 1863. The Commissary and Quartermaster bureaus seized food and other items, including slave labor, in exchange for Confederate currency at officially fixed prices. Because the fixed prices were invariably lower than the inflationary market prices, shortages became rampant.

After Union forces split the Confederacy along the Mississippi River in the summer of 1863, the Trans-Mississippi Department became partially autonomous from the Confederate capital in Richmond. Confederate officials in the Trans-Mississippi, however, were not granted authority to issue paper money. Because the quantities of Confederate currency smuggled across the Mississippi proved insufficient, commanders in that region had to rely increasingly upon impressed supplies, though they had no Confederate currency to offer in exchange.

Impressments made Southerners suffer almost as much from the proximity of their own armies as from Union invasions. Nearly every Southern-state governor protested vigorously against the practice. That grievance, along with others such as the arbitrary tax in kind and the skyrocketing inflation, led to growing disaffection throughout the Confederacy and a general erosion in Southern morale. Thus, the accumulating excesses of Confederate finance actually contributed to the Confederacy's final defeat in the spring of 1865.

References:

E. Merton Coulter, *The Confederate States of America, 1861-1865* (Baton Rouge: Louisiana State University Press, 1950);

Judith Fenner Gentry, "A Confederate Success in Europe: The Erlanger Loan," *Journal of Southern History,* 36 (1970): 157-188;

John Munro Godfrey, *Monetary Expansion in the Confederacy* (New York: Arno, 1978);

Eugene Lerner, "The Monetary and Fiscal Programs of the Confederate Government, 1861-1865," *Journal of Political Economy,* 62 (December 1954): 506-522;

Lerner, "Money, Prices, and Wages in the Confederacy, 1861-65," *Journal of Political Economy,* 63 (February 1955): 70-98;

Gary M. Pecquet, "Money in the Trans-Mississippi Confederacy and the Confederate Currency Reform Act of 1864," *Explorations in Economic History,* 24 (April 1987): 218-243;

John Christopher Schwab, *The Confederate States of America, 1861-1865: A Financial and Industrial History of the South During the Civil War* (New York: Scribners, 1901);

Larry Schweikart, *Banking in the American South: From the Age of Jackson to Reconstruction* (Baton Rouge: Louisiana State University Press, 1987);

Emory M. Thomas, *The Confederate Nation: 1861-1865* (New York: Harper & Row, 1979);

Richard Cecil Todd, *Confederate Finance* (Athens: University of Georgia Press, 1954).

Jay Cooke

(August 10, 1821-February 16, 1905)

by Joseph F. Rishel

Duquesne University

CAREER: Partner, E. W. Clark & Company (1843-1857); partner, Jay Cooke & Company (1861-1873).

Jay Cooke, named in honor of Supreme Court Chief Justice John Jay, was born August 10, 1821, the third of four surviving children of Eleutheros and Martha Carswell Cooke. His mother's ancestors came from Northern Ireland; his father descended from English Puritans who settled in Salem in the 1630s. From colonial times the Cooke family were truly pioneers, and for succeeding generations they kept ever on the move westward to Connecticut and New York. In 1816, only four years after his marriage, Eleutheros Cooke moved his family west from the Lake George region of New York. They floated down the Ohio River on a flatboat before finally settling near what is now Sandusky, Ohio, the year of Jay Cooke's birth.

Historians have seen the Cookes' continuing frontier experience as having a profound influence on Jay Cooke's character. Eleutheros Cooke's ancestors never rose above the status of yeoman farmers or small tradesmen, but he did. He read law before leaving New York and practiced in Sandusky. He served several terms in the Ohio legislature and one term (1831-1833) as a Whig in the U.S. House of Representatives. In public life he gained a reputation as an advocate of internal improvements: roads, canals, and, later, railroads.

In Sandusky young Cooke grew up under the combined influence of a prosperous home filled with books and periodicals, a father who instilled leadership qualities, and a devoutly Methodist mother. Unlike his college-educated brothers, Cooke preferred to end his education at the village school at age fourteen, although he did attend Adams Academy in Sandusky in the winter of 1838. After clerking in local stores and learning bookkeeping, Cooke joined a mercantile house in St. Louis, but he was ruined in the Panic of 1837. He returned home for a year before going to Philadelphia to work for the Washington Packet & Transportation Company, whose president, William G. Moorhead, had married his sister. Cooke acted as a general clerk. The company hauled passengers and freight via the Pennsylvania Canal to Pittsburgh. It was begun in part by money borrowed from the Bank

Jay Cooke

of the United States of Pennsylvania. The possibilities of using the government for private gain were not lost on Cooke. As always, he made the most of his situation. One of his duties consisted of placing newspaper advertisements. Unlike the stodgy announcements of other carriers, those of the Washington Company were true advertisements, extolling the comfort and speed of its service as well as giving usable information such as freight rates. Cooke's early realization of the value of publicity in part may have accounted for his later success as an investment banker.

Cooke had worked with the company less than a year when it collapsed, but the eighteen-year-old frontier boy had learned a great deal about business and the world. And the world started to notice the talented and ambitious Cooke. While moonlighting at Philadelphia's Congress Hall Hotel in the financial district—he did bookkeeping to pay his room rent—Cooke came to the attention of Enoch W. Clark, a stock and exchange broker. Although the jobless Cooke already had returned home to Ohio, Clark nonetheless offered him a position as a clerk. He quickly abandoned his plans to start farming and returned to Philadelphia to begin a banking career in April 1839. E. W. Clark & Company was one of the leading stock and exchange houses in the city, and Cooke could scarcely contain his enthusiasm. Writing to his brother only a month after beginning his new job, he related, "This business is always good and those who follow it always in time become rich." Only a minor distinction between private bankers and brokers existed. Merchants and others borrowed mostly from brokers instead of banks. Thus, brokers acted as a kind of intermediary between borrowers and lenders and in doing so assumed the risks inherent in lending. But they also discounted business paper as much as 18 percent and dealt in out-of-town drafts and bank notes. By knowing which state banks were solvent and how much to discount their notes, speculators could make a lot of money. But they could also lose money. Thanks to Jacksonian policies, which cared more for creditors than for the safety of deposits, banking remained a largely unregulated, even chaotic, business. Cooke quickly developed a facility for it and as a result gained the increased confidence of Clark. Thirteen-hour days, six days a week were not unusual for Cooke, and in the course of a normal day Clark entrusted Cooke to reconcile overdrafts of as much as $100,000 with the banks. Such practices were common and were extremely important to the continued existence of the firm.

Using his experience and knowledge, Cooke wrote a column on money and brokerage banking for Philadelphia's *Daily Chronicle* in the spring of 1840. His column, hardly the very first of its genre—one had appeared five years earlier—nevertheless proved clearer and more comprehensive than others. In the absence of financial periodicals, Cooke put himself on the cutting edge of a new type of journalism. His column continued for about a year. Writing it had consumed too much of his leisure time, which he otherwise spent playing the flute or attending the Methodist Episcopal church.

In 1841 Cooke met and fell in love with Dorothea Elizabeth Allen, whose deceased father had been a Maryland planter of some prominence. The Allen family had migrated there from Ireland. "Libby," as Cooke called Dorothea, was only fifteen when they met, so the couple waited three years before marrying. A year later, in 1845, Jay, Jr., was born. By 1857 the Cookes had eight children, three of whom died in infancy. At the behest of his wife, Cooke became an Episcopalian. Since much of the Philadelphia elite preferred the Episcopal church, membership in it profoundly affected Cooke's career. He established contacts that greatly helped him in business, and within that church he met his closest friends and supporters.

However, well before his religious conversion, Cooke was made a one-eighth partner in E. W. Clark & Company. He remained a partner from 1843 to 1857. Those years witnessed enormous growth and expansion for the United States and equally great opportunity for Clark & Company. In partnership with others, Clark branch houses were opened in St. Louis; New Orleans; New York; Burlington, Iowa; and Springfield, Illinois. By the middle of the 1840s Clark & Company referred to itself as a banking house instead of a brokerage house, though the distinction between the two was still not clear. In so doing, it widened or perhaps changed its field of business. Clark & Company bought and sold state and city bonds on commission. The Mexican War gave Clark & Company and Cooke the first opportunity to sell federal government securities, and that experience proved invaluable to Cooke later, when he marketed Civil War bonds. Since the firm incurred virtually no risk, it emerged from the war stronger and richer and took advantage of the boom times of the 1850s. In addition to state and municipal bonds, the firm sold railroad securities and western lands. Cooke's older brother, Pitt, a real estate agent in Sandusky, was hired in 1855 to obtain land mostly in Iowa and Minnesota, some of which Jay Cooke owned. He had become a senior member of the firm by the time the Panic of 1857 struck. Money was tight, and some branches of Clark & Company were caught short. The Philadelphia partners dissolved their business. Some of the other branches of the firm reorganized, but not the Philadelphia house. Cooke did not rejoin the remaining Clark houses.

For three years Cooke formed no new business relationships but remained on what he called a "free foot." In the aftermath of the Clark liquidation, he settled his obligations so conscientiously that his father and his brother Pitt reprimanded him for extreme generosity. Still, Cooke retained what he called a "fair fortune." He also busied himself with the Sunday school movement and with settling the estate of Clark, who had died in 1856. From 1858 to 1860 he reorganized transportation concerns that the panic had devastated. Reorganizations ensued, involving such firms as the Sunbury & Erie Railroad, the Pennsylvania Canal, and the Franklin Railroad. In those ventures Cooke reacquainted himself with his brother-in-law, William Moorhead, and Harris C. Fahnestock. Moorhead was then the president of the Philadelphia & Erie Railroad, and Fahnestock was a young teller in the Bank of Harrisburg and treasurer for the Franklin Railroad. Although Cooke profited from the transactions, the experience and contacts he made proved even more valuable. For instance, his work on the affairs of the Vermont Central brought him into contact with a group of railroad men who later interested him in the Northern Pacific. Despite their effect on his later life, such endeavors only temporarily diverted Cooke's financial career.

After the death of Clark, Cooke had considered establishing his own banking house, but the 1857 panic put a temporary hold on his plans. When Cooke and William Moorhead founded Jay Cooke & Company on January 1, 1861, less than two months after Abraham Lincoln's election to the presidency, business had recovered from the panic, but the political situation rapidly deteriorated. The Union was falling apart, throwing the business picture into uncertain focus. When Cooke and Moorhead established the partnership–Cooke had two-thirds interest–Moorhead furnished the capital and prestige, and Cooke took over the management. At thirty-nine he had considerable funds of his own, perhaps $150,000. The firm was a true partnership, not a corporation, and as such had no charter (31 such firms existed in Philadelphia at the time). Jay Cooke & Company dealt in bank notes, bills of exchange, and stock. It also discounted paper and received deposits.

As the Cooke firm got started, both the political and financial conditions of the country worsened. The fall in imports reduced customs revenues, forcing the U.S. Treasury to resort to borrowing. In the first half of 1861 federal debt increased by nearly 50 percent. Bonds were marketed through competitive bidding, with the government acting as its own broker. Secretary of the Treasury Salmon P. Chase marketed the bonds at a set amount rather than according to what the market would bear. As a result, many bankers refused to accept them. With so much bad feeling between the bankers and the Treasury, Jay Cooke saw an opportunity. His brother Henry D. Cooke owned a newspaper in Ohio that had vigorously supported Chase as governor of the state and later as senator. Eleutheros Cooke wrote to both of his sons urging, "Now is

Letter from Secretary of the Treasury Salmon P. Chase to Cooke asking for a loan (Ellis Paxson Oberholtzer, Jay Cooke: Financier of the Civil War, *1907)*

the time for making money, by honest contracts out of the government."

Jay Cooke & Company obtained a $200,000 share of the $2.5 million bond issue and part of another in April 1861, the same month the Confederates bombarded Fort Sumter. By that time Secretary Chase was forced to accept bids lower than what he had earlier accepted. Then Cooke envisioned a different scheme for selling the government debt. He conceived of the idea of marketing war bonds to the general public, based on patriotic appeal, rather than to bankers, who had only a mercenary motive for their purchases.

An opportunity to implement the idea occurred when the Pennsylvania legislature voted $3 million for the defense of the state. But it had had poor credit ever since it defaulted on canal bonds in the 1840s. Selling bonds to Pennsylvania citizens of-

fered an ideal solution. Cooke had little trouble convincing the state of his scheme despite the skepticism of other Philadelphia bankers. Along with the old and respectable Drexel & Company, Jay Cooke & Company was appointed general agent for the sale of the Pennsylvania loan, and Cooke went about his task like the salesman he was. He placed advertisements in the newspapers. Handbills exhorting the public to come to the aid of the Commonwealth "in this hour of trial" blanketed the state. He also publicized that the state would reward investors' patriotism with 6 percent interest.

To the astonishment of nearly everyone except Cooke, the loan was oversubscribed. The state treasurer wrote to Secretary Chase telling him of Pennsylvania's success and suggesting that the federal government do the same. Meanwhile, the war was getting underway in earnest, and Henry Cooke was in Washington urging Chase not to market bonds in Europe until domestic capital had been exhausted. Henry also enlisted the aid of another Ohioan he had supported, Sen. John Sherman, a member of the Senate Finance Committee. Things fell into place for the Cookes, but not entirely. Cooke would have preferred to have been sole agent for the marketing of the treasury bonds, but that was not politically possible, for the war demanded not two or three million, but hundreds of millions of dollars in sales. Many bankers had to share in the federal bonanza. Jay Cooke & Company, however, received the appointment as bond agent for greater Philadelphia and all of New Jersey.

Selling the bonds was not easy. The war had shaken public confidence in the nation's monetary system. Rampant hoarding of gold, silver, and even copper coins occurred. Banks suspended specie (gold) payments in December 1861. Financing the war through the banks proved impossible. In February 1862 Jay Cooke & Company opened its Washington house. It was not really a branch, but a partnership organized separately from the Philadelphia firm. Cooke and Moorhead were partners in the new house, as were Henry Cooke and Fahnestock. Henry lacked business experience, but he had unquestioned credentials as a lobbyist. Jay Cooke did not normally approach public officials directly; he depended upon Henry, who eventually grew acquainted with everyone in Washington worth knowing, including newspapermen.

The establishment of the Washington house brought Cooke much closer to Secretary Chase. Not only did Cooke & Company receive more business but Cooke assumed the role of an unofficial adviser to the secretary. Due to his concern with skill and honesty and his wish not to give Chase "cause to regret his confidence," Cooke faced a problem that he had for the rest of the war: getting adequate compensation for his work. When, for instance, the firm purchased gold for the U.S. Treasury, no clear understanding existed concerning how the government intended to pay the firm.

Because the Lincoln administration expressed caution about raising taxes to the degree the emergency demanded, by 1862 the government had issued huge quantities of paper money commonly called greenbacks. Even that failed to supply enough cash, and that same year the government sought to sell $500 million in bonds paying 6 per-

cent interest. The government could retire them in five years; otherwise they matured in twenty (thus they were known as five-twenties). The Treasury had difficulty marketing them at par (full price) because bankers wanted to discount them (pay less than full price and in effect get more than 6 percent interest). When in October 1862 Chase appointed Jay Cooke & Company as special agent for marketing the five-twenties, he set the stage for a revolution in the American system of securities distribution. He had not named Cooke the exclusive agent, but older banking houses tended to back away from the sale. As a consequence Cooke vastly enlarged his operation and engaged some 2,500 agents to sell the five-twenties in every state and territory still loyal to the Union. Hundreds of thousands of posters and handbills as well as newspaper advertising greatly aided those agents. Newspapers that received Cooke advertising were expected to carry favorable stories of the loan on their own free of charge. Aside from their patriotic appeal to the small investor, the advertisements frequently took the form of question and answer, to educate the public to that form of investing. The ads answered everyday questions clearly and simply. Speculation in gold, draining away potential investment capital, and Union losses on the battlefield compounded Cooke's difficulties in selling the bonds. He even asked President Lincoln to remove General McClellan from his command. The continued issuance of greenbacks did not help sales either, for they caused inflation.

At the center of the chaotic monetary arrangement lay the system of state banks, many of which emitted their own currency. Secretary Chase wanted a national banking system, but Congress opposed such a step. Chase convinced Cooke to assist him, so Cooke put his advertising system to work. He persuaded the newspapers in which he advertised to support a national banking system and gave the clippings to congressmen from their home-district newspapers. Congress passed the National Banking Act in 1863. Following that, Cooke wrote a pamphlet titled "How to Organize a National Bank under Secretary Chase's Bill" (1863). Under the new law the first bank to be chartered was the First National Bank of Philadelphia, of which Cooke was the second largest of the 73 incorporators, and he appointed two of the bank's directors.

Thereafter Cooke did all he could to encourage the spread of national banks throughout the

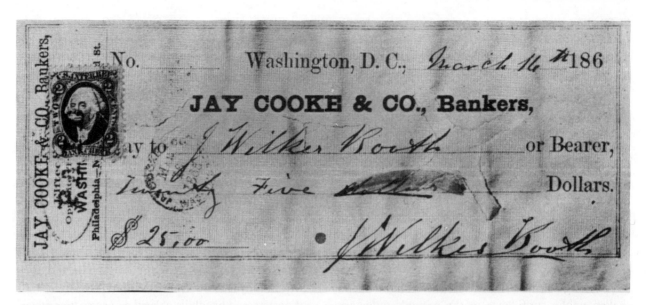

A check on Jay Cooke & Company written by John Wilkes Booth (Ellis Paxson Oberholtzer, Jay Cooke: Financier of the Civil War, *1907)*

country. One of those was the First National Bank of Washington, D.C., in which he also had an interest.

The establishment of a national banking system greatly aided the sales of the five-twenty bonds. By May 1863 sales reached as high as $5 million per day, and the Treasury was unable to supply bonds fast enough. After the Battle of Gettysburg sales grew even stronger. Before the loan was subscribed, perhaps a million citizens had purchased bonds. Despite the huge volume of business, Cooke's profit actually comprised much less than the 0.125 percent commission. Cooke & Company, not the government, absorbed the costs of drafts, counterfeits, subagent irregularities, and the like. Although the firm actually received about one-sixteenth of 1 percent profit ($220,054.49), a widespread notion among politicians and many newspapers held that Cooke had profited excessively at the time of the loans completion on January 21, 1864. The profit was not excessive, but the war generated other business for the firm. For the years 1862 to 1864 the Philadelphia and Washington houses combined realized $1,264,813.87 in profits, of which Cooke received $300,000.

For a year after the closing of the 6 percent loan (the five-twenties), Cooke sold no government securities, although he did work closely with the Treasury. He and Chase attempted to stop the wild speculation in gold by selling treasury reserves, but to little effect. Then, to Cooke's chagrin, Chase resigned in June 1864. The new secretary of the trea-

sury was William P. Fessenden, with whom Cooke was not acquainted. Cooke wrote to Chase, "those New Yorkers have told Fessenden that they don't consider me a financier, but only a good advertiser of patent medicines." But the Treasury needed an advertiser, for sales on later bond issues lagged badly, and even Fessenden had to turn to Cooke in 1864 and again in 1865. Jay Cooke & Company was appointed as general subscription agent for 7.3 percent interest-bearing bonds maturing in three years (known as seven-thirties). Cooke threw himself into the sale of the seven-thirties as he had with the five-twenties: employing newspaper advertisements, circulars, posters, and the like. It had taken Fessenden seven months to sell $133 million of the seven-thirties; Cooke sold $600 million of them in less than six months, most of that after Gen. Robert E. Lee's surrender.

At the end of the war Cooke was internationally known, but his reputation exceeded his assets. At the end of 1865 the Philadelphia house had made a total of $1,137,302 (with one-tenth going to charity and two-thirds of the remainder to Cooke), and the Washington house had made $720,000 divided among four partners. That fell far short of what critics claimed Cooke had made.

He planned on making more money, however, by greatly enlarging and refurnishing the Philadelphia office. The new office was an extravagant marble palace (Cooke never could save money), but it was in the wrong city. The war had put Philadelphia out of the running for the position of financial center of the United States. Since New York had emerged as the uncontested leader of American finance, Cooke opened a house there on Wall and Nassau streets in 1866. Cooke no longer found it possible to manage the firm's affairs as closely as he once had. His brother Henry was a liability, but Jay was too devoted to him to discharge him. Thus Henry headed the Washington office, Fahnestock managed the New York office, and Jay ran the Philadelphia office. Each office was run on a departmentalized basis, imparting a degree of modern bureaucratization to the business. One man could no longer effectively control operations.

With the strain of the war effort behind him, Cooke devoted more time to his family. He built a mansion on Gibraltar Island in Lake Erie near Sandusky. The family summered there, and Cooke indulged his love of fishing. In 1866 he built a 50-room mansion, called Ogontz, one of the most costly homes of its time. Since the home stood in a location north of Philadelphia and far from an Episcopal church, Cooke built one, nicknamed the five-twenty church. In the manner of Victorian millionaires, he also turned to collecting art.

The Appomattox surrender did not mean the end of government monetary problems. The debt had to be funded, greenbacks stabilized, and the continuing gold problem solved. Cooke & Company continued to deal in government securities and also dealt in new areas, including life insurance. Cooke conceived of the idea whereby the company's profits should go to the stockholders. He also succeeded in getting a federal charter, the first ever for an insurance company. He was a major stockholder of the National Life Insurance Company of the United States of America. Although the company prospered, it did not make as much money as Cooke would have liked. He also entered other investment fields. After several unprofitable ventures in coal and iron, Cooke took an interest in transportation once again. By 1869 there was less money to be made in government securities and more to be made in railroads. Cooke also engaged in real estate purchases to develop transportation links. The upper Mississippi basin had long held Cooke's interest, and in 1866-1867 he and Moorhead each purchased 19,000 acres near Duluth, Minnesota, then a seven-house village. Cooke visited it in 1868 and wrote, "I felt sure that vast cities would grow up at Duluth & Superior [Wisconsin]." He attempted to promote the Lake Superior & Mississippi Railroad

Cooke at eighty

(which was to connect the two bodies of water), but its bonds did not sell well.

Despite the unfavorable reception for the bonds, Cooke became interested in another more grandiose plan for a railroad, the Northern Pacific. It was to cross the entire tier of northern states and territories, connecting Lake Superior to the Pacific. A group of New Englanders had founded the road in 1864, but the enterprise failed when they could not raise enough funds. It was then purchased by the so-called Vermont Clique, who in 1869 tried to involve Cooke in selling the bonds of the Northern Pacific. Even though he had earlier refused a role in a railroad that was to cross 2,000 miles of unoccupied territory, his interest in Duluth overruled his otherwise clear head. Cooke hesitated before associating himself with the largest business enterprise ever undertaken in the United States, but when his agents, having traversed the proposed route, returned with glowing reports of its geography and climate, Cooke joined the enterprise on January 1, 1870.

In agreeing to become agent for the Northern Pacific, Cooke undertook the task of raising more than $100 million. Although the Northern Pacific received considerable support in the form of land grants, the federal government refused to guarantee its bonds as it had those of the Union Pacific and Central Pacific roads. A London office was opened in 1870 to promote the sale of bonds (the Rothschilds were approached as potential partners, but they refused), but European sales remained sluggish. Crews undertook to build the road out from Duluth, but Tacoma (the proposed terminus) was still 1,800 miles away, and his partners grew increasingly anxious. In June 1872 Fahnestock wrote to him, "no enterprise of such magnitude has ever before been so entirely dependent upon one house or rather one man." Further remonstrating Cooke, Fahnestock told him what he probably already knew: "You are the Northern Pacific Railroad, and you have the additional delicate responsibility of the trusteeship, making you morally liable to every man and woman holding the bonds." He went on to say that "a large proportion of the lands are practically valueless," although Cooke did not believe that. Yet many small investors, prompted by Cooke's promotion, purchased bonds based on little more than the judgment and integrity of Jay Cooke & Company.

The Northern Pacific needed more than integrity to help meet its obligations to bondholders. Any unforeseen contingency could bring ruin to the railroad and to Cooke & Company as well. And contingencies indeed arose. The Franco-Prussian War broke out in 1870, virtually drying up available capital in Germany and France and tightening it in other nervous European countries. Other troubles also surfaced. It was an open secret that the St. Paul & Pacific Railroad, a subsidiary of the Northern Pacific, was in trouble and had received no help from the parent company. Continued speculation in gold disturbed the money market just when Cooke tried to raise funds through a syndicate (a word he is credited with Anglicizing from the French word *syndicat*). Congress again refused to support the project with an appropriation or a guarantee of its bonds. Since the railroad went from Duluth to virtually nowhere, it generated little revenue. The Cooke houses either had to make continual cash advances to the line or watch it collapse. Yet Cooke refused to abandon it. Fahnestock wrote to him, "We are in a perfectly helpless situation."

By September 1873 Wall Street was jittery after the collapse of the New York Warehouse & Security Company, which had assumed too heavy a burden in financing a railroad. Then, on September 13, Kenyon, Cox & Company, of which Daniel Drew was a partner, collapsed. Finally on September 18, 1873, the New York house of Jay Cooke & Company failed, followed almost immediately by the Philadelphia and Washington houses and the First National Bank of Washington, D.C. Cooke had precipitated the Panic of 1873. Pandemonium enveloped the stock exchange. Outside the Cooke offices pitiful crowds gathered and stared at the closed doors while across the street, at the exchange, stocks tumbled.

The failure of Jay Cooke & Company touched off the panic, but the underlying causes were far greater. For some time an overexpanded economy had awaited a correction. Moreover, unscrupulous promoters had fraudulently sold worthless bonds and watered-down stock. While Cooke was more of a victim of the panic than a perpetrator, there were still accounts to be settled in the aftermath of the tragedy, with Cooke hoping to satisfy the creditors without declaring bankruptcy. His brother Henry supported him (Henry had transferred more than $100,000 of his estate to his wife), but Fahnestock and Moorhead refused to help. Events soon acquired a force of their own, however, as a creditor prevailed upon the court to declare Jay Cooke & Company bankrupt on November 26, 1873. The firm had liabilities of $11,134,878; assets amounted to $3,440,332, most of which were in the form of bills receivable. The homes of the partners and other miscellaneous personal and real estate were valued at just under $4 million. The settlement of the affairs of the First National Bank of Washington, D.C., was complicated by the fact that Jay Cooke & Company owed the bank $827,000. In addition, the Cookes owned almost three-quarters of its stock. The bank went into receivership and met its obligations in full by 1876.

The bondholders of the Northern Pacific were not as fortunate. Creditors finally agreed to a complicated formula devised by the courts in 1890, giving them cash, asset scrip, and shares in three companies. It is not known what percentage of their initial investments the creditors finally received, but Cooke later insisted that they more than recovered their losses if they retained the stock. (According to

Ellis Paxson Oberholtzer, Cooke's foremost biographer, "At the prices of 1882 for the shares of Northern Pacific and its old allies it was computed that the estate had already paid its creditors $1.56 for each dollar of its indebtedness.")

For a while Cooke lived at his daughter's home and occupied a desk at her husband's firm, Chas. D. Barney & Company. Cooke's son-in-law had worked for Jay Cooke & Company, and the new firm acted as its successor but on a much-reduced scale. In 1878 an old business associate called on Cooke to interest him in a Utah silver mine. It had good prospects, but it was located 150 miles from a railroad. Cooke went to Utah to see the mine for himself and assess the situation. Although he had no capital, at age fifty-seven Cooke still possessed business capabilities, powers of persuasion, and prestige. He incorporated the Horn Silver Mining Company in 1879 and immediately promoted the needed funds for the construction of a railroad–all within a year. Having learned his lesson from his involvement in the Northern Pacific, Cooke refused to have any part in the ownership of the company or to take any responsibility for investors. For his efforts, he received commissions and 40,001 shares of stock in the company. Incredibly, the mine struck it rich. One mining journal of the time described it as "unquestionably the richest silver mine in the world now being worked." In 1880 Cooke sold his stock for $800,000. That, along with his commission and dividends, netted him nearly a million dollars. In less than seven years Cooke had lost one fortune and gained another. He was soon flooded with offers from other mining companies. The sale of the Great Republic Mine in Montana and the St. Eulalie in Mexico further increased his estate.

His wealth restored, Cooke turned to a journey of the heart: he repurchased Ogontz. The home was too large, so he leased it free of charge to a private school for girls. He repurchased Gibraltar and spent much of his time fishing there. But Cooke's business career had ended. He did not even care to manage his own estate, preferring to leave the task to his sons-in-law.

Cooke had one more adventure in him. In 1891 he took the promised journey on the Northern Pacific Railroad. The last remaining link had been completed in 1888, and the company gave him a private car. He was feted at Duluth, Tacoma, and many points in between, his vision for the Northwest vindicated at last.

Cooke spent the remainder of his life at Gibraltar and in Philadelphia. He devoted himself to church work and activities at Philadelphia's Union League, of which he was a founding member. Having a fear of the ocean, he never went to Europe. His health failed only slowly. Several days after giving his annual reception at Ogontz School, he died, February 16, 1905, aged eighty-three. In tribute to his greatness, the city of Philadelphia lowered its flags to half-staff.

References:

Henrietta M. Larson, *Jay Cooke: Private Banker* (Cambridge, Mass.: Harvard University Press, 1936; New York: Greenwood, 1968);

Ellis Paxson Oberholtzer, *Jay Cooke: Financier of the Civil War*, 2 volumes (Philadelphia: Jacobs, 1907; New York: Kelley, 1968).

Archives:

The papers of Jay Cooke are at the Historical Society of Pennsylvania and the Baker Library, Harvard University. Baker also holds the manuscript for his unpublished memoirs.

Henry Winslow Corbett

(February 18, 1827-March 31, 1903)

by Larry Schweikart

University of Dayton

CAREER: Dry goods clerk, Bradford & Birdsell (1843-1846), Williams, Bradford and Company (1846-1851); owner, H. W. Corbett Company (1851-1871); vice-president (1869-1898), president, First National Bank of Portland (1898-1903); U.S. senator, state of Oregon (1867-1873); partner, Corbett, Failing and Company (1871-1893), Corbett, Failing & Robertson (1893-1898); owner, *Oregonian* (1872-1877); president, Security Savings & Trust Company (1890-1903).

Born in Westshore, Massachusetts, on February 18, 1827, Henry Winslow Corbett lived in New York for most of his first sixteen years. After graduating from Cambridge Academy in New York at the age of thirteen he worked in a local store for three years before departing for New York City with his life's savings–$22. He worked as a clerk in the dry goods firm of Bradford & Birdsell for three years, then took a better position with Williams, Bradford and Company, also a dry goods firm. There also he met future Oregon banking colleague C. H. Lewis. By October 1850 Corbett had enough contacts among New York wholesale merchants to acquire more than $24,000 worth of cargo (for which he paid $13,000 in cash and obtained the rest on acceptance from Williams, Bradford), which he planned to sell in Portland, Oregon. On January 20, 1851, he booked passage for Panama, crossed the isthmus, and sailed north to San Francisco. He arrived in Portland to sell the New Yorkers' merchandise on consignment. For that purpose Corbett launched H. W. Corbett Company in April 1851. He made further trips back to New York, via the Panama route before the completion of the Union Pacific Railroad, to supplement the speculative but prosperous enterprise, which profited from the boom in the Willamette Valley that had gone on since the beginning of the gold rush of 1848. Gold stimulated other sectors of the economy, including agriculture and lum-

Henry Winslow Corbett (Oregon Historical Society CN1528)

ber. At the end of his first month he had accumulated sales of more than $14,000. Most potential rivals did not reach Oregon until later in 1851, by which time Corbett had firmly established himself. During the first two years of the business Corbett sold goods at 50 to 300 percent above their cost in New York.

Although Corbett introduced many progressive business practices (such as closing on Sunday), by and large the trade remained conservative, for his New York partners cautiously watched costs.

When they raised questions about the rising costs of the trade in 1852, Corbett returned to New York to assuage their worries. He remained in New York as a buyer for a year, leaving the business in the hands of two Oregon associates, but decided to stake his claim in Oregon once and for all in 1853.

He arrived in the midst of a new Oregon immigration, although the growing San Francisco market had started to compete more than ever before. A depression struck Oregon in 1854, the result of the gold outflow to San Francisco. Corbett personally directed the business during these years, reinvesting the profits on a regular basis. Maintaining steady lines of supply to New York, Corbett devised a system of purchasing and paying, remitting to major New York firms and later to the Wells Fargo Nevada National Bank in San Francisco. On occasion Corbett found the need to purchase Portland produce and sell it in San Francisco through Abernethy, Clark & Company, sponsors of the Oregon and California Packet Line. By 1857 Corbett was worth more than $50,000. He kept a high quality of goods and avoided a reputation for shoddiness.

Despite Corbett's comment that he "was afraid of bankers," he soon appreciated the profits available in offering banking services in addition to dry goods. In the 1860s he made loans, received deposits, and traded in the gold dust that streamed in from Corbett's Idaho business connections. He had interests in railroads, steamship companies, and telegraph companies; and his business contacts in Idaho, established in the 1850s principally from his dry goods business, allowed him to extend credit throughout the region. His chief Oregon competitor, Henry Failing, noted that while "Corbett . . . has never made money as fast as we have . . . [he] has now a large capital in his business and a great deal outside which he can call in at any moment." Corbett and Failing became friends when Corbett's sister, Emily, married Failing. The two men shared a general sense of business conservatism and in 1869 joined their resources to gain control of the First National Bank of Portland (established in 1865 by A. M. and L. M. Starr). Failing became president and Corbett vice-president, and Corbett served as chief executive officer after Failing's death in 1898. First National was the first of Oregon's national banks and the first formed on the coast. During Corbett's lifetime capital stock increased from $100,000 to $700,000 and deposits reached $7 mil-

lion. It became the largest bank in the Pacific Northwest.

Shortly after forming the bank, in 1871, the brothers-in-law combined their merchandise businesses to create Corbett, Failing and Company. This company, in turn, was replaced by Corbett, Failing & Robertson in 1893, at which time the line of general merchandise was discontinued and the firm centered its trade on wholesale hardware. Sales exceeded those of all other hardware firms in the region. Meanwhile, in the 1870s Corbett and Failing turned management of the banking arm of the firm over to other members, while they involved themselves in other businesses. From 1867 to 1873 Corbett served as U.S. senator from Oregon. As senator Corbett restored oceangoing mail service between San Francisco and Portland and specialized in harbor and navigation legislation directed at Oregon.

Corbett also came to hold extensive interests in stagecoach, telegraph, hotel, iron, insurance, railroad, and other businesses, and he had extensive real estate holdings. In 1890 he organized the Security Savings & Trust Company of Portland and served as its president until his death. He also participated in the Title Guarantee & Trust Company of Portland. His iron interests included the Willamette Steel & Iron Works, and he joined in 1865 with William S. Ladd and Failing to form the Oregon Iron Works at Oswego. His connection with these men led him to invest in the Portland Hotel Company, and he served as president of that enterprise beginning in 1888. As early as 1865 he won a contract for transporting the mails to San Francisco. He promoted city and suburban railways and was a member of the board of directors of the Street Railway Companies. From 1872 to 1877 he took over ownership of the *Oregonian* newspaper while its previous owner, Henry Pittock, worked his way out of financial difficulties. He also presided over the Portland Board of Trade and chaired the Lewis and Clark Exposition Association in 1905.

Corbett was married twice, in 1853 to Caroline E. Jagger (she died in 1866), then to Emma L. Ruggles in 1867. Corbett had two sons by Caroline, Henry Jagger and Hamilton, both of whom died relatively young. Henry Jagger Corbett's death came just at the time he had prepared to take over his father's businesses. Corbett died in Portland on March 31, 1903. He left a reputation for shrewd, even ruthless business dealings, but he also had a kind and generous side. At the time of his death his estate was valued at $5 million. His grandson, Henry Ladd Corbett, returned to Oregon from Harvard University to take over the family businesses.

In the hands of the Corbett descendants, First National Bank continued to prosper. The president from 1903 to 1927, Abbot Mills, saw the bank through a period of particularly good growth, marked by the traumatic difficulties of one of Portland's other pioneer institutions, Ladd & Tilton. First National survived and entered into an association with A. P. Giannini's Transamerica Corporation in 1938. Before and during World War II the bank began a program of rapid branch expansion, under which it acquired 39 banks with deposits of more than $73 million through a subsidiary of Transamerica called O. N. Hood.

Henry Corbett made it possible. A man of public vision and personal vigor, he contributed more than his share to Portland's development. His great-est contribution was the bank, which survived more than 100 years.

References:

Orrin K. Burrell, *Gold in the Woodpile—An Informal History of Banking in Oregon* (Eugene: University of Oregon Press, 1967);

Joseph Gaston, *Portland, Oregon: Its History and Builders* (Chicago: Clarke, 1911);

Albert R. Gutowsky, "History of Commercial Banking in Oregon," *Oregon Business Review*, 24 (August 1965);

E. Kimbark MacColl, *Growth of a City: Power and Politics in Portland, Oregon, 1915-1950* (Portland: Georgian Press, 1979);

MacColl, *The Shaping of a City: Business and Politics in Portland, Oregon, 1885-1915* (Portland: Georgian Press, 1976).

Archives:

The papers of Henry Corbett and Corbett, Failing and Company are at the Oregon Historical Society in Portland.

W. W. Corcoran

(December 27, 1798-February 24, 1888)

by Janet L. Coryell

Auburn University

CAREER: Partner, W. W. Corcoran & Company (1817-1823); clerk, Bank of Columbia (1823-1828); real estate and suspended debts manager, Washington, D.C., branch, Bank of the United States (1828-1836); note broker (1837-1840); partner (1840-1848) senior partner, Exchange Bank of Corcoran & Riggs (1848-1854).

William Wilson Corcoran, banker and philanthropist, was born on December 27, 1798, in Georgetown, D.C. His father, Thomas Corcoran, had emigrated from Ireland in 1783 and married Hannah Lemmon of Baltimore County, Maryland. The couple had twelve children, six of whom survived into adulthood. Thomas Corcoran was a merchant and real estate salesman and was politically active as a Democrat, serving as magistrate and as mayor of Georgetown and as a member of the Levy Court. Appointed by President Thomas Jefferson as a justice of the peace, Thomas Corcoran continued his affiliation with the Democratic party as a member of Andrew Jackson's Georgetown presidential campaign committee in 1828, and he also served as Georgetown postmaster before his death in 1830.

The link between the Democrats and the Corcorans was maintained by W. W. Corcoran, Thomas's youngest son. Corcoran was educated in a traditional classical curriculum in Georgetown schools and spent one year at Georgetown College (now Georgetown University), but in 1815, at age seventeen, he quit his studies to go into business with two older brothers, James and Thomas, Jr. Their dry goods store met with success, and in 1817 Corcoran opened a branch store called W. W. Corcoran & Company. All three men prospered and eventually expanded their business into an auction and commission house. In 1823, however, the company went bankrupt with debts of $28,000; the brothers paid their commercial debts completely and paid the rest at 50 cents on the dollar. Eventually, in 1847, Corcoran paid all creditors in full with interest, to the tune of almost $46,000, an hon-

W. W. Corcoran

orable gesture that did much to enhance his reputation.

After his business failed, Corcoran took over his father's real estate investments and invested in the real estate market himself. In 1828 a clerkship with the Bank of Columbia ended when the bank failed. Its assets were assigned to the Washington, D.C., branch of the Bank of the United States (BUS), where Corcoran took over as real estate and suspended debts manager.

On December 23, 1835, Corcoran eloped with fifteen-year-old Louise Amory Morris, daughter of Navy commander Charles Morris. The more-than-twenty-year age difference grieved Louise's parents, who refused to speak to either husband or wife until the birth of their first child in September 1836. The couple had two more children, but childbirth sapped the health and morale of Louise Corcoran. Only one child, daughter Louise, survived past infancy. Mrs. Corcoran died in 1841 at

only twenty-one years of age; Corcoran never remarried.

Corcoran's association with the BUS ended in 1836, when the Washington branch of the bank closed after the bank's federal charter expired. The demise of the primary fiscal agent of the government provided an opportunity for Washington financiers to take over BUS services. Corcoran first moved into the vacated territory with a brokerage firm in 1837. He then helped form a banking firm, the Exchange Bank of Corcoran & Riggs, in 1840.

Corcoran's partner was George Washington Riggs, son of New York banker Elisha Riggs, with whom Corcoran had speculated in real estate prior to opening his brokerage firm. In addition, Corcoran had bought U.S. treasury notes for Elisha Riggs during the Panic of 1837, to Riggs's considerable benefit. As a private banker, Riggs had strong connections with the New York, Philadelphia, and Baltimore banks, connections that proved valuable to his son George and to Corcoran.

The Exchange Bank of Corcoran & Riggs opened in Washington on April 15, 1840. The bank issued no notes, focusing instead on buying U.S. treasury notes to resell to New York banks for investment. Corcoran & Riggs benefited from a close link with George Newbold, president of the New York-based Bank of America, for whom Corcoran had briefly worked as the Washington correspondent. Newbold's alliance with treasury secretary Levi Woodbury to fight the BUS's attempt to drain specie from New York banks in 1839 also provided Corcoran & Riggs with an ally in the Washington financial world. Woodbury commonly kept Corcoran informed of bids on treasury notes so Corcoran & Riggs could undercut the competition. The government's business helped Corcoran & Riggs get on its feet rapidly, and the firm turned a profit of almost $5,000 in its first year of operation.

Corcoran & Riggs continued to concentrate on building its business in Washington while maintaining substantial interests in New York City and some secondary business in Baltimore. In 1841, however, the incoming Whig administration promised erosion of the firm's inside track with the Treasury Department. The death of President William Henry Harrison after one month in office and the accession of John Tyler proved fortuitous for the firm. Tyler, a former Democrat, vetoed many of the Whig party's financial measures, including the national bank proposed to replace the old BUS. The resulting split in the party led Tyler to seek support where he could find it, and his new treasury secretary, Walter Forward, had no qualms about using public financiers linked to former Democratic administrations, including Newbold's Bank of America. When the government borrowed $7 million to cover a deficit resulting from the 1841-1842 depression, Newbold took $2 million and Corcoran & Riggs 20 percent of that. The link between Newbold, Corcoran & Riggs, and the Washington administration was secure. Corcoran & Riggs was still a small firm but was well on the way to becoming the primary depository of the government's funds.

Using Corcoran & Riggs as primary depository presented the government with both ideological and political advantages. As a private and unincorporated firm, the bank escaped accusations of enjoying special privilege or of corruption. Since Corcoran & Riggs did not issue notes, it avoided attack by hard-money advocates. The firm's discretion and its conservative approach to moneylending, especially to politicians, further enhanced its prestige in Washington. And Corcoran's growing circle of political friends practically guaranteed the firm's survival; the Democrats' success in the off-year elections of 1842 provided a politically favorable climate. In June 1845 Robert Walker, treasury secretary under President James K. Polk, made Corcoran & Riggs the sole federal depository.

Corcoran did not immediately move to capitalize on the firm's good fortune. He had worked long and hard to achieve his monopoly; he maintained the firm's conservative style in order to solidify its position. He continued to wine and dine the leading Democratic and Whig politicians, many of whom borrowed money from his bank.

Corcoran's friendship with Walker proved particularly lucrative. After the Independent Treasury Act of August 1846 was signed Corcoran worked with Walker to prevent a financial panic by the New York banks contracting credit. Seeing the change from "pet" banks to a subtreasury system as inevitable, Corcoran lobbied the government to ensure the gradual withdrawal of its specie from Corcoran & Riggs and corresponded with Wall Street leaders to ensure cooperation. As a result Corcoran & Riggs held on to the accounts of many government agencies and, in the end, enjoyed a federal patronage almost as lucrative as its earlier monopoly.

As successful as Corcoran & Riggs was with federal patronage, it was the firm's financing of the Mexican War that made Corcoran's fortune. In February 1847 the Treasury Department floated an $18 million loan. Corcoran & Riggs offered to pay a .125 percent premium on the treasury bonds and wound up holding $14.7 million. They sold the bonds at 104 to 107 percent of par value, primarily to American investors, until January 1848, when the price slipped below par. Even with the drop in prices the firm made $250,000 profit on the loan by February 1848. Later that spring Congress authorized another bond issue, this time for $16 million. But Corcoran had to deal with growing market conservation and a partner, who was far less daring than Corcoran and disinclined to mirror his optimistic approach to investment. George Riggs finally quit, and his son, Elisha Riggs, Jr., replaced him as junior partner to Corcoran.

With the less cautionary and less powerful junior partner, Corcoran moved to capitalize on his political friendships. Using market information from Secretary Walker, Corcoran submitted a bid of 103.02 percent of par and won more than $14 million of the $16 million loan. But after a strong start, a combination of factors, including the saturation of the American bond market, increasing competition from commercial investment opportunities, and slight demand for the bonds in Europe pulled the price down to a low of 101 percent. Corcoran decided to travel to England to try to revive interest in the American bonds. Authorized as an American agent for the Treasury Department to sell $5 million, Corcoran managed, in a tight and conservative market, to sell $3 million and receive options for $1 million more. Though they sold at 93.75 percent of par, English investors held onto the bonds long enough to allow the market in the states to rebound, and by the end of 1848 the price rose to 107; by the spring of 1849, to 115; by December 1849, to 120. By the completion of the loan's liquidation in 1851 Corcoran had netted approximately $755,000 profit from his personal account with the Treasury Department as well as his (far greater) share of the firm's profit.

Corcoran's friendships across the political spectrum, particularly among Southerners, stood him in good stead as incoming Whigs attempted to reduce his firm's link to the Treasury Department in 1849. Rep. Robert Toombs of Georgia, for instance, emphasized Corcoran's Southern background in urging

Corcoran in an 1871 portrait (courtesy of the Corcoran Gallery of Art)

the administration of President Zachary Taylor to maintain its tie with Corcoran & Riggs; when Millard Fillmore became president after Taylor's death in 1850 the support continued. When Franklin Pierce's term began in 1853 the government severed the link as the new treasury secretary, James Guthrie, withdrew all government deposits from private agencies and at last completed the move to the subtreasury system.

The deaths in 1853 of Elisha Riggs and his son Joseph, the men who served as Corcoran & Riggs' New York City connections, and Corcoran's long-held ambition to play the part of a wealthy gentleman of leisure convinced him to retire in 1854 at the age of fifty-five. Thereafter, he continued to enlarge his personal fortune. He took a share in the Maynard Arms Company in 1856 and held a one-third interest in the patent on the Maynard carbine as well. He continued his real estate investments, pur-

chasing lots in Georgetown, St. Louis, Manhattan and, by the 1860s, became the largest landowner in the District of Columbia. He also made considerable sums as a claims agent for individuals with claims against the federal government, using his political contacts and occasionally bribery to bring 5 to 10 percent commissions. Corcoran's share of claims he won from the Mexican Claims Commission as both agent and claimant, for example, amounted to over $15,000; in 1885 he amused himself by lobbying Congress for payment of small claims half a century old. Such lobbying added little to his fortune but did keep Corcoran's foot in the door of the political world he so enjoyed. Finally, the long-term nature of his investments in government bonds, railroads, and land grants meant Corcoran stayed active in the business world long after his claimed "retirement." He also embarked upon a philanthropic career with donations to temperance and mental health reform movements (Dorothea Dix, the mental health reformer, had carte blanche) and church organizations.

Corcoran continued to dabble in politics, strongly supporting James Buchanan's presidential bid in 1856. He served as a major source for Democratic Party funding for both candidates and newspapers. Corcoran long had been Buchanan's financial adviser, and after the election the president visited Corcoran frequently at his Lafayette Square mansion across from the White House. But their close friendship dissolved in anger over Buchanan's failure to support Southern demands during the secession crisis and the two never spoke again.

During the early years of the Civil War Corcoran's pro-Southern sympathies led to his harassment by Unionist forces. He was briefly arrested; Federal troops occupied his Washington properties; union forces seized his son-in-law, George Eustis, Jr., private secretary to Confederate diplomat John Slidell, in the infamous *Trent* affair. From December 1861 through October 1862 Corcoran, determined to be comfortable as he joined his daughter and her family in Paris, expatriated $470,000 in cash and securities from the United States to avoid the wartime income tax, and Secretary of War Edwin Stanton seized property and confiscated rents to punish him. His old firm, renamed Riggs & Company in 1854, continued to prosper during the war, holding all of the Army of the Potomac's deposit and exchange draft business while continuing to trade with Southerners. After the war Riggs &

The original Corcoran Gallery of Art, Washington, D.C., opened in 1872. The gallery moved to a new Washington location in 1897.

Company remained the major chartered bank in the Washington-Richmond area, with only the private Thomas Branch & Sons as competition.

Corcoran's expatriation ended in 1867, after his daughter, Louise, died of tuberculosis. Her father brought her body home to Washington from Cannes where they had settled, then resumed his philanthropic endeavors. The Corcoran Gallery of Art, which he had begun in 1859, opened in 1872, with the nucleus of the collection coming from Corcoran's own. He founded the "Louise Home" in 1869 for destitute gentlewomen and aided churches and colleges, making generous gifts to the University of Virginia, the College of William and Mary, the Virginia Military Institute, and Washington and Lee University. His later years were marked by physical and family troubles; he suffered a fall in 1870 and failing eyesight required surgery in 1871. In 1872 his son-in-law died in France, leaving him with three grandchildren for which to care.

In spite of his age and his physical difficulties Corcoran continued his active participation in public life. He served as vice-president of the Washington Monument Society and provided loans to speed completion of the work. His autobiography, *A Grandfather's Legacy*, was published in 1879. The continued exclusion of the Democrats from the seat of political power after the Civil War convinced Corcoran to contribute to their revival by funding

Democratic candidates and the leading Democratic newspaper, the *Washington Union*. In 1884 the Democrats at long last recaptured the White House and the eighty-six-year-old philanthropist found himself enjoying White House receptions once again. After a stroke in 1887, Corcoran died on February 24, 1888.

Publication:

A Grandfather's Legacy (Washington, D.C.: Privately published, 1879).

References:

Henry Cohen, *Business and Politics in America from the Age of Jackson to the Civil War: The Career Biography of W. W. Corcoran* (Westport, Conn.: Greenwood, 1971);

Irving Katz, "Confidant at the Capital: William W. Corcoran's Role in Nineteenth-Century American Politics," *Historian*, 29 (1967): 546-564;

Robert T. Sweet, "Selected Correspondence of the Banking Firm of Corcoran & Riggs, 1844-1858, Showing the Emergence of Washington as a Financial Center," Ph.D. dissertation, Catholic University, 1982.

Archives:

The papers of W. W. Corcoran are at the library of Congress. The Riggs National Bank, Washington, holds material relating to Corcoran & Riggs and Corcoran & Company.

Currency *(see* Notes, Currency, and Legal Tender*)*

Deposits, Reserves, and Fractional Reserve Banking

Deposits made up those funds brought by individuals or businesses to a bank or financial intermediary for safekeeping. To induce the customer to part with his money for a period of time, banks often paid interest–a fee–to the depositor.

Once deposits came into a bank, they added to the institution's reserves; that is, the pool of money it held back (refrained from lending) in order to meet the daily demands of depositors wishing to withdraw their money or convert their notes into gold or silver (specie). No bank ever maintained $100 on reserve for every $100 worth of deposits–it would go out of business. Instead, banks operated on the principle of "fractional reserve banking," in which they loaned out all but a portion of their deposits and kept only a small reserve. The money they loaned out might itself be put on deposit at another bank, with the process repeating itself. Economists have termed that process the "money multiplier" and have discovered that $1 in deposits generates $2.70 after the money multiplier has taken effect.

The ratio of reserves to outstanding notes or deposits constituted the "reserve ratio." It varied according to the financial tenor of the times. Usually in antebellum times a ratio of 8 to 15 percent proved sufficient, and generally the healthier the bank, the lower a reserve ratio it could carry, because customers knew their money was safe. In panic times bankers had to bolster their reserves, but even then, sometimes, they could not meet the demand by customers for their money or to convert the banks' notes into specie. At those times the banks "suspended" and essentially refused to pay in specie or allow depositors to withdraw money (although they still welcomed new deposits).

See also:

Financial Panics during the Nineteenth Century; Notes, Currency, and Legal Tender; Specie, Hard Money, and "Suspension."

–Editor

Davis Rich Dewey

(April 7, 1858-December 13, 1942)

by James Smallwood

University of Texas at Tyler

CAREER: Teacher, Chicago, Illinois (1879-1881); principal, Hyde Park High School, Chicago (1881-1883); instructor (1886-1888), assistant professor (1888-1889), associate professor (1889-1892), professor, Massachusetts Institute of Technology (1892-1942); managing editor, *American Economic Review* (1911-1940).

Born in Burlington, Vermont, on April 7, 1858, Davis Rich Dewey was the son of Archibald Sprague Dewey and Lucina Rich Dewey. The older brother of John Dewey, famed philosopher of pragmatism in American education, Davis Dewey was educated in the public schools of Burlington and later attended the University of Vermont, from which he graduated in 1879.

Dewey's family circumstances were modest. Descended from generations of hardy Vermont farmers, Dewey's father originally tilled the soil but broke with family tradition when he entered the grocery business in Burlington. Davis Dewey was perhaps fortunate that his brother was born when Davis was but eighteen months old. The boys grew up together and ultimately proved to be good influences on each other. Their mother instilled a love of learning in both boys. Although they often played together, more important than that, they studied together and drew inspiration from each other. Both tended to be "bookish."

At the University of Vermont, Dewey found yet more intellectual stimulation. He was exposed to the major fundamental issues of the day—philosophical, religious, political, and economic. His interests broadened as he heard more and more professors and read more and more books. As he matured as a student, he discovered that he preferred history, political science, and economics. As he had at home as a youngster, at the university Davis enjoyed the company of his brother. Although they studied in different academic fields, each provided in-

Davis Rich Dewey (courtesy of the MIT Museum)

tellectual support for the other. They graduated together in 1879, both receiving A.B. degrees. In 1910 the university awarded Davis an honorary LL.D. in recognition of his lifetime achievements.

After graduating the brothers embarked on long and successful careers in secondary and higher education as teachers, administrators, and researchers. Although he would not be as well known as his younger brother, Davis Dewey's contributions to education, particularly as a research scholar, eventually won him national recognition; even the federal government utilized his expertise by naming him as a consultant for various projects.

First, however, Dewey had to pay his educational dues. He taught in secondary school at Hyde Park, a neighborhood in Chicago, Illinois, from 1879 to 1881. In his high-school teaching career he gave instruction primarily in history and political science. From 1881 to 1883 he served as principal of Hyde Park High School. In the fall of 1883 he followed his brother to the graduate school of Johns Hopkins University in Baltimore, Maryland.

For approximately 15 months the brothers again gave emotional and intellectual support to each other, although the pair split when John Dewey graduated and accepted an invitation to join the faculty at the University of Michigan. Johns Hopkins awarded Davis Dewey a Ph.D. in history and economics in 1886. Immediately he found employment at the Massachusetts Institute of Technology (MIT) as an instructor in history and political science. That same year he married Mary Caroline Hopkins, the daughter of Judge and Mrs. James C. Hopkins of Madison, Wisconsin. The Deweys had two children, Bradley and Dorothy. Bradley Dewey served in the armed forces, rising to the rank of colonel. He later became the founding president of the Dewey & Almy Chemical Company. Dorothy Dewey married A. Barr Comstock.

After Dewey had performed satisfactory work at MIT for two years, he accepted an assistant professorship of economics and statistics. The next year, 1889, MIT promoted him to associate professor and in 1892 to full professor.

An intrepid researcher, Dewey quickly became a widely published scholar. A year after he joined MIT, his *Elementary Notes on Graphic Statistics* appeared. The next year, 1888, Schofield Press of Boston released a work Dewey had originally not intended to publish. Soon after joining MIT he had produced a manual on political history. Dewey had intended the manual for the use of MIT freshmen, but Schofield convinced him to allow its publication and regional distribution. In 1892 Dewey produced an article entitled "Statistics of Suicides in New England," which appeared in the June/September 1892 issue of *Publications of the American Statistical Association*. In 1899 he edited a volume by Francis Amasa Walker entitled *Discussions in Economics and Statistics*.

Dewey also participated in several professional associations and presented many academic papers to scholarly audiences. With each appearance he enhanced his growing professional reputation. In 1888 he attended the third annual meeting of the fledgling American Economics Association (AEA) in Philadelphia and read a paper on "The Study of Statistics," published the next year in the association's *Proceedings*. In 1894 he appeared before the AEA annual meeting and read "Irregularity of Employment." That paper, too, was published in the *Proceedings*.

By the 1890s Dewey had developed into a prominent figure in Massachusetts, widely known not just for his teaching and research but also for his public service. In 1895 the state's governor appointed him chairman of the Massachusetts board that investigated and reported on the problems of unemployment. Two years later he assisted state commissions that investigated public charities and reformatories in Massachusetts. During 1900 he served as a consultant for the U.S. Bureau of the Census. He advised the bureau as an expert on business payrolls and wrote the section of the census report entitled "Employees and Wages." In 1903 he was a member of another state commission, which examined job relations between workers and employers.

Meanwhile, Dewey continued his research and writing. In 1903 the Carnegie Institute released a volume entitled *The Economic History of the United States;* Dewey contributed the chapter on "Money and Banking." More important, the publishing house of Longmans, Green published his *Financial History of the United States* in 1903. A volume containing 600 pages, the book was comprehensive in scope. It examined the country's financial history from colonial times to 1903. Dewey periodically released revised editions to update the story, until 1939. The professor, who had grown to maturity in the era of Social Darwinism and laissez-faire capitalism, tended toward conservatism in his interpretation of economic history. He treated his subjects somewhat coldly in his chapters on President Andrew Jackson's war on the Bank of the United States and, in a revised edition, on the beginning of Franklin D. Roosevelt's New Deal. True to his academic training, which urged objectivity, Dewey scrupulously attempted to present opposing views.

Dewey's *Financial History* remains a classic. Writing in a tight, logical framework suggestive of the idea that history approximated science, he produced a solid, factual work still consulted by teachers and students. Johns Hopkins University recognized his achievement in 1904, when univer-

*Dewey's parents, Archibald S. and Lucina R. Dewey (Dewey Papers, Special Collections,
Morris Library, Southern Illinois University, Carbondale)*

sity officials gave Dewey the John Marshall Prize for his effort.

Another of Dewey's important scholarly works was *National Problems, 1885-1897* (1907), a volume in Harper & Brothers American Nation Series, edited by historian Albert Bushnell Hart, the same editor with whom he had worked to produce the *Financial History*. With the publication of the new book, reading audiences learned more about Dewey's conservative political and economic orientation. In 343 pages he generally supported the conservative establishment of the era. In chapter 1 Dewey upheld his era's racism against the American Indian. When referring to the Indians' laments about whites stealing their lands, he concluded: "The immediate problem was the adjustment of Indian barbarism to Anglo-Saxon civilization." To Dewey, the Anglo theft of millions of acres of land became an Indian problem–their inability to adjust. As for the labor strife of the industrial era, Dewey dismissed it by claiming that labor engaged in "an established policy of terrorism."

Dewey also subscribed to the "Dunning School" interpretation of the Civil War and Reconstruction Era. Blacks were "ignorant" and "inferior." In economics he supported monopoly capitalism, citing the advantages of trusts and noting that the industrialists were "statesmen."

Dewey also justified American imperialism in the book: "As the government of Hawaii was unstable, there was a growing disposition on the part of some of the American commercial interests . . . to bring about a protectorate, if not annexation, by the United States." Dewey neglected to mention that the invasion of American capitalism was the destabilizing element.

Yet Dewey had his progressive side, as was befitting an intellectual living at the turn of the century. He noted that in the presidential election of 1896, wherein the reformer William Jennings Bryan went down in defeat, Republican industrialists in the East intimidated many of their workers into voting for William McKinley, the conservative standard-bearer. He also sincerely noted that much of the country's labor strife stemmed from the cyclical nature of the economy.

At the time of its publication, *National Problems* helped solidify Dewey's academic reputation, which he furthered in 1910 when he coauthored with John Thom Holdsworth a monograph on economic history, published by the federal government– *The First and Second Banks of the United States.*

Dewey's birthplace in Burlington, Vermont (courtesy of L. L. McAllister)

That new publication reaffirmed Dewey's conservative views. Consistently he supported the captains of finance, defending them from all hostile critics.

Dewey's other contributions to national life continued to enlarge his academic reputation. From 1886 to 1906 he served as secretary of the American Statistics Association. He edited the association's quarterly journal and also led membership drives that, in time, greatly increased the number of member-scholars. Dewey also presided as president of the AEA in 1909. He became a trustee of the Massachusetts Agricultural College (later Massachusetts State College) in 1900, a position he held until 1939.

In 1911 Dewey became the managing editor of the *American Economic Review* (*AER*), a post he held until 1940. That appointment represented a pinnacle; still young in terms of career and scholarly development, Dewey had captured the attention of his seniors in academe. Under his editorial and managerial guidance the *AER* eventually became one of the ranking international journals of the twentieth century, noted for solid articles that tried to analyze scientifically the economic issues of the era.

The same year he took over the *AER*, Dewey also became chairman of the faculty at MIT, a post he held until 1913. In 1912 Dewey assumed the du-

ties of coordinator of MIT's courses in engineering administration, an assignment he held until 1930. Furthermore, in 1919-1920 he directed the economic section of the Office of Information and Educational Services, a part of the relatively new Department of Labor. As is true in so many academic case studies, Dewey's administrative chores coupled with the responsibilities of editing a major academic journal took much of his time. He sacrificed much of his personal research and writing.

Years later, in 1930, MIT recognized Dewey's career accomplishments by offering him a new administrative assignment. He accepted appointment as head of the Department of Economics and Statistics, an appointment he held until the year of his death. Dewey's tenure as head of his department was characterized by objectivity, attention to detail, and cordiality with colleagues. His administrative posts did not entirely stop his research. In 1922, with Martin Joseph Shugrue, he coauthored a study on *Banking and Credit*.

In his later years Dewey continued to emphasize public service. He became a fellow of the American Academy of Arts and Sciences and tried to further the careers of younger scholars. Likewise, he joined the International Statistics Institute. In 1928 President Calvin Coolidge appointed Dewey a member of a board to investigate and analyze ques-

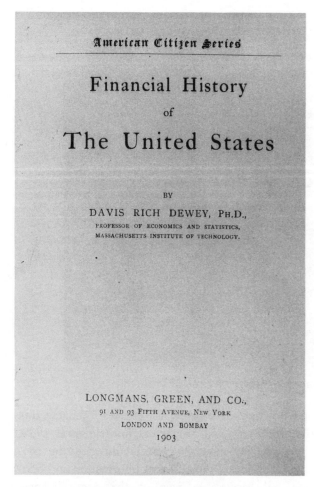

*Title page for Dewey's textbook
of economic history*

tions of working conditions and wages for the railroad industry in the American West. That investigation involved thousands of railway workers on approximately 50 trunk lines and subsidiaries.

In the early 1930s, under President Herbert Hoover, Dewey served as a member of yet other national labor commissions, which usually convened whenever railroad strikes or strikes by urban laborers appeared imminent. In the same areas of government concern, between 1931 and 1933 Dewey was named to three more boards of labor-management arbitration.

After a lifetime of achievement, Dewey died on December 13, 1942, at his home in Cambridge, Massachusetts, at eighty-four years of age. A conservative spokesman for his times, he had produced a mountain of research and a shelfful of books and articles. As the longtime editor of the *American Economic Review* he supervised and aided a host of younger scholars whose papers his journal published. His long tenure at MIT helped maintain the college's national reputation. It is fair to say that MIT grew with every honor that Dewey won, with every publication, and with every action in the arena of public service.

Publications:

Elementary Notes on Graphic Statistics (Boston: Schofield, 1887);

Political History since 1815: History Notes for the Use of First-Year Students (Boston: Schofield, 1888);

Financial History of the United States (New York & London: Longmans, Green, 1903; final revision, 1939);

National Problems, 1885-1897 (New York & London: Harper, 1907);

The First and Second Banks of the United States, by Dewey and John Thom Holdsworth (Washington, D.C.: Government Printing Office, 1910);

State Banking before the Civil War, with *The Safety Fund Banking System in New York, 1829-1866*, by Robert E. Chaddock (Washington, D.C.: Government Printing Office, 1910);

Banking and Credit: A Textbook for Colleges and Schools of Business Administration, by Dewey and Martin Joseph Shugrue (New York: Ronald Press, 1922).

References:

Harry M. Campbell, *John Dewey* (New York: Twayne, 1971);

Paul K. Crosser, *The Nihilism of John Dewey* (New York: Philosophical Library, 1955).

Archives:

Davis Rich Dewey's papers are at the library of the Massachusetts Institute of Technology, Boston, Massachusetts.

Discounting

The term "discounting" referred to a process by which banks received their interest "up front" by giving someone less than par (face) value of the bills or IOUs brought to the bank for exchange. For example, a merchant might bring $1,000 worth of IOUs to a bank, but the bank would only pay $900, taking the balance in interest as it collected the IOUs. Another use of the term discounting involved note discounting. In the antebellum period, when hundreds of different bank notes circulated, the notes of banks in one part of the country might be presented for redemption in gold or silver (specie) at a bank in another. Because of either the uncertainty of the notes' value—due to lack of sufficient informa-

tion about faraway markets—or due to the costs of transporting the notes back to the bank of origin, the bank at which the notes were presented might discount the note by taking a fee for exchanging it. A final use of the term involved special circumstances during panics when banks suspended (refused to pay gold or silver for notes). However, evidence suggests that for other banks or large business customers, banks might pay notes at a discount, say 5 to 10 percent. Thus, if another bank were desperate for specie, it could obtain specie by receiving only 90 to 95 percent on the notes it presented.

—Editor

Daniel Drew

(July 29, 1797-September 18, 1879)

by Carol M. Martel

Arizona State University

CAREER: Drover, circus worker (1815-1834); steamboat company operator (1834-1856); partner, Drew, Robinson and Company (1839-1852); independent speculator and financier (1852-1875); director, Erie Railroad (1854-1868).

Daniel Drew, a colorful Wall Street figure often called "Uncle Daniel" or "the Great Bear of Wall Street," speculated and manipulated the stock market and especially starred in the Erie War, which pitted Drew, Jim Fisk, Jr., and Jay Gould against Cornelius Vanderbilt for control of the Erie Railroad. He figured prominently in the unregulated expansion of post-Civil War Wall Street and claimed to be the first great Wall Street "speckilator." Born on July 29, 1797, in Carmel, New York, a small town in upstate Putnam County, he grew up on his father's 100-acre stock farm. His father, Gilbert Drew, was an elderly man raising a second family with his second wife. His mother, Catherine Muckleworth Drew, of whom he always spoke affectionately, taught him to fear damnation and observe the outward forms of Christianity. During the winter months Drew obtained a meager education at the neighborhood country school. Throughout his life his speech reflected his lack of education. He cultivated his country clothes, manners, and accent even after he moved to the city. Even when he was at his wealthiest he spent little on his personal appearance. He wore old, often slovenly clothes and for a cane often used a broken umbrella shaft.

Drew's father died when the boy was fifteen, and he went to New York to look for employment, but he found none because of the War of 1812. He therefore enlisted in the army to earn the $100 bonus paid for substitutes. He saw no fighting, spending three months at Fort Gansevoort, opposite New York. He returned to his mother and the farm but in 1815 decided to take his bonus and the

Daniel Drew, 1850s

little money his father had bequeathed to buy cattle to drive to New York City butchers. Over the next 50 years Drew turned that $100 into a fortune that at one time may have amounted to $16 million.

Drew interrupted cattle droving at one point to work for circuses that quartered for the winter in nearby towns. He probably toured with them also, learning early the arts of huckster and barker that he used to good advantage on Wall Street. He was offered part ownership of one show but then underwent the first of his several religious conversions. He left the circus to return to being a drover. A wave of prosperity swept the nation as it recovered from war, and New York City called for more meat for its rapidly growing population.

In 1820 Drew married Roxanna Mead, a Putnam County girl and the sister of his brother Thomas's wife. She was even less educated than her husband and apparently could not sign her name. The couple had three children, a son and two daughters, one of whom died in infancy.

Drew soon started to deal in livestock, buying cattle from farmers and driving them to New York City. He acquired a reputation as a sharp trader who frequently used unscrupulous tactics. Bouck White, the source of many intriguing though undocumented stories about Drew, claimed that Drew bought cattle on credit and often did not pay the farmers all they had coming from the sale. Instead he moved on to a new group of farms. In 1820 he established his base of operations at the famous Bull's Head Tavern in the Bowery. The tavern was the principal headquarters and exchange point for New York City drovers, with yards for 1,500 cattle. Drew leased the tavern in 1829 and became an innkeeper. He often functioned as a banker for the drovers, cashing their certificates and saving them a long trip downtown to Wall Street.

Drew went into partnership with two other drovers and traded in cattle and horses with such success that they extended operations into Pennsylvania and Ohio, where prices were cheaper and quality higher. He was the first drover to bring a herd to New York from west of the Ohio River. The trek across the Allegheny Mountains with 2,000 head took two months and gained Drew a profit of $12 per head. He later brought herds from as far away as Illinois. On one of his cattle drives a lightning bolt killed Drew's horse and intensified his already intense interest in fire-and-brimstone religion.

A popular story is that the phrase "watered stock" originated with Drew. Once he bought a large herd of starved cattle at a cheap price and arranged to sell them to fur trader John Jacob Astor's brother, Henry Astor, who owned a leading New York City butcher business. Drew brought the cattle to the Bull's Head, turned them loose in a pasture with bags of salt, and would not let the thirst-maddened animals drink until just before the buyer's arrival. The cattle then gorged themselves full of water and gained about 50 pounds per head, which made them look fat and heavy. Henry Astor paid a good price for them. While Astor never

bought cattle from Drew again, he possessed enough guile to recommend Drew to his competitors, and so the practice took hold. Stock watering took on another definition when companies issued more shares of stock than 100 percent of their assets could cover.

Drew left the cattle business in 1834 to enter the highly competitive steamboating business on New York's inland waterways. He bought an interest in a steamboat line from Peekskill to New York City on the Hudson River, investing $1,000 in the steamboat the *Water Witch*. At that time Cornelius Vanderbilt enjoyed a near monopoly of the Hudson River business. Victimized by Vanderbilt's price-cutting techniques, Drew lost about $10,000 in his first season. Back the next year with the aid of financing provided by others anxious to defeat Vanderbilt, Drew cut prices until everyone running steamboats on the Hudson lost money. Much to the chagrin of Drew's supporters, when Vanderbilt offered to buy him out, Drew accepted. Drew then began to challenge the Hudson River Association (HRA), which ran boats from Albany to New York City, with similar price-cutting techniques. He formed a pool with the HRA but then entered into a partnership in a competing service. He encouraged the HRA directors to buy out the service, thus making a tidy profit for himself.

In 1839 Drew broke with the HRA to establish the People's Line, which constructed spectacular boats such as the *Isaac Newton,* the *New World,* the *St. John,* the *Dean Richmond,* and the *Drew,* outfitting them more and more luxuriously to attract customers. The 300-foot-long *Isaac Newton* had berths for 500 passengers. The HRA could not compete for long against the well-financed People's Line, which employed with great success the price-cutting strategy Drew had perfected in earlier ventures. Drew acquired the Stonington Line on Long Island Sound in 1847 in a partnership with George Law. In 1849 Drew and some associates purchased the Champlain Transportation Company, running a line of five steamers from Whitehall to the Canadian end of Lake Champlain. After seven years he sold out at a profit.

In 1839 Drew founded the brokerage and banking firm of Drew, Robinson and Company with some of his steamboat profits. He knew his partner, Nelson Robinson, from their days in the droving business. The firm became known as one of the most successful houses in New York City. Drew

Engraving of Drew from a daguerreotype by Mathew Brady

soon found he could make more money speculating in stock than by running steamboats, and he disengaged himself from his steamboat concerns. In 1852 Drew and Robinson decided amicably to dissolve the firm, and from that time Drew operated independently.

Drew especially prospered in the trading of railroad stocks. In 1850 he and Vanderbilt, who understood just as well as Drew that railroads promised greater future profit than steamboats, bought a controlling interest in the Boston & Stonington Railroad, which connected to the Stonington steamboat line. In 1853 Drew made heavy investments in the New York & Erie Railroad. He decided that a position as director of the road would increase his opportunity for profits, and he bought controlling interests in two small connecting railroads and a line of steamboats connecting the Erie road with the West. When he announced he planned to give Vanderbilt's New York Central Railroad a better deal on the use of those connecting lines, the Erie board made him a director and the road's treasurer.

Drew took advantage of the board's decision to move the terminus of the Erie Railroad from Piermont, New York, to Jersey City, New Jersey, by spreading rumors that a tunnel project necessary to the completion of the move was in danger of being left uncompleted. Erie stock dropped in price as a result, and Drew loaned the road nearly $2 million, taking chattel mortgages–mortgages on the company's rolling stock–as security.

Drew and Vanderbilt then clashed over plans for the Harlem Railroad, in which they both had invested in 1857. When the advantage of extending the Harlem line became evident, Drew purchased more shares of the road's stock and prevailed upon the New York City Common Council to allow the expansion. Then he sold shares short–that is, he sold borrowed shares and promised to repay those who lent their stock with purchases made later, at what he hoped would be a lower market price. Then he got an injunction prohibiting the planned expansion. Vanderbilt stopped a potential plunge in Harlem stock by convincing another court to reverse Drew's injunction. Luckily for Drew, he was barely able to cover his short sales from his own holdings. Drew again tried to profit on the Harlem Railroad through short sales in a plot with members of the New York legislature, which defeated another plan for expansion, again in the hope that Harlem stock would decrease. Instead, large purchases by Vanderbilt and John Tobin drove the stock price from 90 to 284 in five months. Drew had sold short on more shares than were available and had to ask Vanderbilt to cover for him to the tune of $500,000. That left him thirsting for revenge.

Drew tried to obtain his revenge in the Erie War of 1868. After Drew released 58,000 shares of Erie Stock and the price per share declined from 95 to 47, he profitably covered another round of short sales. But Vanderbilt bought the low-priced stock and worked with other large Erie stockholders to have Drew ousted from the board in October 1867. Drew succeeded in being reinstated by agreeing to act in Vanderbilt's behalf as director, and Drew's colleagues James Fisk, Jr., and Jay Gould also became directors. In February 1868 Drew went back on his promise to Vanderbilt by compelling the Erie board to authorize a $10 million bond issue, convertible under the road's charter to 100,000 shares of new stock. Without revealing that he had the power to create the new shares, Drew sold short. Vanderbilt attempted to prevent a stock issue through a court in-

1873 cartoon satirizing the effect of Drew's financial hardship on the seminary he endowed. When he declared bankruptcy in 1876, creditors claimed the capital he used to generate interest for the endowment (courtesy of Drew University Library).

junction, but Drew had his own injunction issued and printed the new shares. Drew, Fisk, and Gould had the new stock "stolen" to prevent Vanderbilt's injunction from being enforced, then placed it on the market. They covered the short sales at the reduced price, in effect taking $7 million Vanderbilt had invested in the Erie. Vanderbilt swore warrants for the arrest of the trio, but before the warrants could be served they moved the railroad's headquarters out of jurisdiction, into New Jersey.

Drew, Fisk, and Gould then got the New Jersey legislature to charter the Erie in that state and embarked upon a rate war with Vanderbilt's New York Central. Then they bought legislation in Albany legalizing the $10 million bond conversion. As the price of New York Central stock fell, Drew agreed to authorize an Erie purchase of Vanderbilt's remaining Erie stock in October 1868. Fisk and Gould agreed to the deal, in which Drew took personal profits, only when Drew agreed to leave the Erie board.

Drew tried another short sale at Fisk and Gould's expense in 1869, but the two successfully kept the price of the Erie stock high, and Drew covered only at great loss. He took another loss in 1870, when he sold short on the stock of the Chicago & North Western Railroad at the same time Gould was pushing up the price. Other reverses, then the Panic of 1873, forced Drew to retire in March 1875 and declare bankruptcy in March 1876. He died on September 18, 1879.

An essay on the Erie War by Charles Francis Adams, Jr., and Henry Adams, in their *Chapters of Erie* (1871), called Drew "shrewd, unscrupulous, and very illiterate–a strange combination of superstition and faithlessness, of daring and timidity–often good-natured and sometimes generous." He regarded his position as railroad director as a means of manipulating stock for his own advantage. For years Drew had been the leading bear of Wall Street. While treasurer of Erie he advanced the railroad large sums that it could not have obtained elsewhere. He was at once "a good friend of the road and the worst enemy it had as yet known."

During his heyday Drew contributed generously to the Methodist church. He was much a part of the religious spirit of the age, of revivals and prayer meetings and wrestling with the devil. On Sundays his soul belonged to God, but on weekdays he rationalized that religious spirit with the buccaneering tactics of Wall Street. Drew was also a significant benefactor of the Drew Theological Seminary in Madison, New Jersey, but because he had maintained possession of the capital for the endownment and paid the interest to the seminary, that source of funding dried up when he went bankrupt. The seminary opened in November 1867. He also contributed heavily to the Drew Seminary for Young Ladies in Carmel, New York, donating land, buildings, and $25,000 for a library in addition to a substantial endowment.

Drew's career was inseparable from the story of Wall Street, of the city in which he lived, and of his nation. As biographer Clifford I. Browder described him in all his roles, Drew was "an astute money manager, suffering repentant sinner, cheat, philanthropist, and bankrupt." He was "so human it hurts, so American it agonizes."

References:

Charles Francis Adams, Jr., and Henry Adams, *Chapters of Erie* (Boston: Osgood, 1871);

Clifford I. Browder, *The Money Game in Old New York: Daniel Drew and His Times* (Lexington: University Press of Kentucky, 1986);

John Steele Gordon, *The Scarlet Woman of Wall Street* (New York: Weidenfeld & Nicolson, 1988);

Edward Hungerford, *Men of Erie* (New York: Random House, 1946);

Bouck White, *The Book of Daniel Drew* (New York: Doubleday, Page, 1910).

Anthony Joseph Drexel

(September 13, 1826-June 30, 1893)

by James M. Smallwood

University of Texas at Tyler

CAREER: Clerk (1839-1847), partner, Drexel & Company (1847-1893); real estate investor and developer (1855-1893); partner, Drexel, Morgan & Company (1871-1893).

Born on September 13, 1826, in Philadelphia, Pennsylvania, Anthony Joseph Drexel was the son of Francis Martin Drexel, an immigrant who had been born in the Austrian Tyrol, and Catherine Hookey Drexel. The boy (known as Tony to his family and friends) had one older brother, Francis, Jr. For a time Drexel's father pursued the life of a wandering artist and then became an art collector, but to secure a more stable income he founded a brokerage firm, Drexel & Company, in 1837 and established its headquarters in Philadelphia. Early in the company's history it engaged primarily in currency brokerage; its major activity was "money shaving"– trading the paper money issued by state-chartered banks.

Drexel's early education rested in the hands of private tutors, but in 1839, when he reached the age of thirteen, his father took control of the youth's continuing quest for knowledge. The senior Drexel took his son to his firm's office and trained the youth first as a clerk and later as a broker and banker. Drexel's older brother also worked for the firm. At home at night and under their father's guidance, the sons also studied music and languages. A rigorous disciplinarian, the senior Drexel insisted that his sons work hard but rewarded their diligence with promotions and with ever-increasing responsibilities. While still only a teenager, Drexel was sent by his father to New Orleans to accept a large shipment of gold and to escort it safely to Philadelphia.

As a reward for his job performance, Drexel became a partner in Drexel & Company in 1847, at

Anthony Joseph Drexel (engraving by Samuel Sartain)

the age of twenty-one. That same year he met, courted, and married Ellen Rozet, daughter of a local Philadelphia merchant of French antecedents. The union appeared to be a happy one, and in time a son, Anthony Joseph Drexel, Jr., was born. In the coming years Ellen Drexel dedicated herself to her son and to her husband and his business career.

As Drexel & Company amassed more capital and the family acquired more financial experience, the company moved beyond trading in bank notes.

The firm bought and sold domestic and foreign bills of exchange; accepted deposits; and made loans, at first short-term notes to local merchants and later long-term loans to corporations. By the time Drexel became a partner in his father's business, the firm had evolved into a full-fledged private bank. A demonstration of its new status and growing reputation came during the Mexican War of 1848. Drexel & Company aided the U.S. Treasury Department by selling, at par or above, approximately $49.2 million worth of 20-year bonds.

After the war ended, the firm expanded its business in securities and financed international trade. In 1854 it gained its first direct representation on Wall Street by acquiring an interest in a respected house. By 1863 the Drexels had become senior partners in the Wall Street firm that at the time was styled Drexel, Winthrop & Company.

Francis Martin Drexel died in 1863, and Drexel and his older brother assumed full management of Drexel & Company. Francis, Jr., took over as the nominal head of the house, but Anthony remained the management leader, making the key decisions affecting the firm.

The senior Drexel's death coincided with the opening of a new era in the financial history of the United States. Some of the trends of the new era included the organization of a national banking system, a large increase of public debts, a tremendous increase in the issue of industrial securities, and the expansion of the national rail network.

In the later nineteenth century Drexel & Company evolved into a house of international investment brokers. The firm established working relationships with banking houses in such locations as London, Paris, New York, and San Francisco. The company processed a veritable flood of investment securities related to national and public debts, the improvement of urban real estate, industrialization, the building of railways, and the development of mining.

Drexel received credit as the directing "genius" and organizational "mastermind" of Drexel & Company. By 1863 he had maintained daily contact with the firm for nearly a quarter of a century. Drexel possessed excellent financial judgment, which led him to emphasize conservatism and financial stability; a spontaneous, decisive intellect; and a penetrating mind capable of discerning the feasibility of complex financial undertakings. He also worked hard and was totally dedicated to his business. His peers considered him well-informed, decisive, dedicated, thrifty, diligent, and resourceful.

In addition to devoting a great amount of time to the firm, Drexel also actively participated in Republican party politics. He supported the victorious candidacy of Abraham Lincoln for the presidency. Drexel had joined the newly created Republican party in the late 1850s, largely because the party endorsed the Wilmot Proviso (which would have limited the territorial expansion of slavery) and because the Republicans had adopted a strong national economic program. Drexel continued in his support of the Republicans after the war as an influential member of the Union League. In 1872 he endorsed and worked for the election of Ulysses S. Grant. After Grant took office, Drexel led a small group of northern businessmen who exercised great influence on the new president.

Although he demonstrated an interest in politics, Drexel's first and greatest love remained his business. In the early 1870s he made a momentous decision. His dissatisfaction with the New York house led him to form an alliance with the House of Morgan. After counseling with Junius S. Morgan, Drexel brought Junius and his son, John Pierpont, into his inner circle, and Drexel, Morgan & Company was created. The alliance strengthened both houses.

The new firm, with capital of $1 million, opened for business on July 1, 1871. The elder Morgan immediately proved his importance: he was well-informed about American and European business and finance in general, and as one of the heads of a leading merchant bank he had access to reliable information about current business affairs on both continents. Finally, Junius Morgan had an excellent reputation for sound judgment. Those qualities were much appreciated by Drexel.

Drexel benefited greatly from the new alliance. With J. P. Morgan in charge of Drexel's New York office, that office gained a young, energetic, self-assured, and ambitious leader who already had a national reputation in finance. Moreover, J. P. Morgan also helped Drexel's house in Paris, by implementing management reforms that improved operations there.

In the 1870s and 1880s the Drexel-Morgan partnership established itself as the preeminent private domestic and foreign bank in the United States. It expanded greatly in the late nineteenth century by adding new members. Both senior partners proved adept at choosing talented junior partners. As Drexel once said, the selection of partners "must be done with the greatest of caution." After the elder Morgan died in 1890, the first new partner, recruited after an exhausting search, was S. Endicott Peabody, a Bostonian who had developed his own banking firm (Cuyler, Peabody & Company). Peabody brought Drexel and J. P. Morgan much general mercantile and banking experience at a time when the senior partners had already decided to get help in monitoring commercial credits so they could concentrate more attention on developing government loans.

In selecting Peabody as a partner, Drexel and J. P. Morgan established a pattern that lasted well into the future. They recruited new partners for one of two purposes: to supervise some aspect of the firm's internal operations, such as commercial credits and foreign exchange; or to engage in public relations, interacting with clients in the private sector or with government officials.

Yet, in the period prior to Junius Morgan's death, Drexel and the two Morgans remained undisputed leaders of their firm. They agreed that they must protect the firm's credit by maintaining liquidity at all times. All three knew that even in the best of economic times rumors could undermine the best houses. In 1877 Drexel, Morgan faced the widespread rumor that the house was overextended. The rumor dissipated, in part because J. P. Morgan could report to his father that the firm "had in Bank and Call-Loans money enough to pay in two hours every dollar we owed to every one, assuming that every depositor we had should draw every cent of money out instantly without notice—consequently our whole business was being conducted with our own means in our business without any regard to what any of the partners might have outside. How many firms do you suppose, doing such a business as we are, could make that statement?" Drexel, Morgan and Company easily became the most successful financial house of the late nineteenth century. Increasingly the firm contributed to the overall process of industrialization in the United States and in Europe.

The Drexel family's far-flung business interests always demanded much of Anthony Drexel's time; his time became even more precious when his older brother died in 1885. Thereafter Drexel assumed sole responsibility for Drexel & Company, which entered into another era of expansion as

American trade assumed an increasingly international character. In his later years Drexel coordinated the erection of a new bank and office building in Philadelphia.

Yet Drexel & Company and the Drexel partnerships were not Drexel's only concerns. He had numerous real estate holdings both within and outside Philadelphia. Over the years the increase in value of his holdings added greatly to his private fortune. Further, as one of the landlords of working-class homes and apartments in the central city, Drexel proved reform-minded. In overseeing repairs and in planning remodeling schemes he had great success in improving the housing conditions of his tenants.

Drexel also took an interest in the publishing business. He became part owner of the *Philadelphia Public Ledger,* one of the city's best-managed papers. The editor and principal owner of the *Ledger,* George W. Childs, one of Drexel's lifelong friends, enjoyed a national reputation as a journalist and publisher.

Shortly before his death Drexel gave attention to the promotion of industrial education. His interest in industrial training befitted the times. In the course of his life Drexel had witnessed the steady industrial development of the United States. His firm had helped finance a part of that development, from railroads to bridge companies to foundries. In the early 1890s Drexel donated $3 million for the founding of a new school—Drexel Institute—in Philadelphia.

Drexel Institute, opened to students in 1892, stressed technological education. The school was also noted for its flexible scheduling, featuring night classes for working young people and older adults. Drexel Institute also refused to discriminate with respect to class, sex, race, or religion. It offered free scholarships and low tuition for paying students. The institute sponsored concerts, lecture series, and other cultural programs—free for students and the general public. Drexel Institute continued in later years to expand its offerings, eventually attaining university status.

As Drexel's fortune continued to grow, he donated much of it to philanthropic causes. He made sizable donations to local hospitals, churches, and charitable institutions. With Childs he cofounded the Childs-Drexel Home for Aged Printers in Colorado Springs, Colorado.

In the autumn of 1892 Drexel's health declined. In the early summer of 1893 he traveled to Europe for the healthier climate. He sought the advice of Europe's finest doctors. June of 1893 found Drexel trying to recover at a famous spa in western Bohemia. But he continued to decline; on June 30, 1893, he died at the famous watering place near Carlsbad, Germany. He left an estate estimated to be worth $25 to $30 million.

References:

Vincent P. Carosso, *The Morgans: Private International Bankers, 1854-1913* (Cambridge, Mass.: Harvard University Press, 1987);

George W. Childs, "Anthony Drexel," in *Public Ledger Almanac* (Philadelphia: Public Ledger, 1894);

Edward Hopkinson, Jr., *"Drexel & Co.": Over a Century of History* (New York: Newcomen Society, 1952);

A New Home for an Old House (Philadelphia: Drexel & Company, 1927);

E. P. Oberholtzer, *Philadelphia: A History of the City and its People,* 4 volumes (Philadelphia & Chicago: Clarke, 1912).

Archives:

The papers of Anthony Joseph Drexel are at Drexel University.

Thomas Ellicott

(November 10, 1777-October 6, 1859)

by John Landry

Brown University

CAREER: President, Union Bank of Maryland (1819-1834); director, Baltimore & Ohio Railroad (1827); trustee for the bankruptcy of the Bank of Maryland (1834-1839).

Thomas Ellicott, friend and adviser to Secretary of the Treasury Roger B. Taney in the early 1830s, influenced the decision to replace the Second Bank of the United States (BUS) with a system of depository state banks. While president of one of those "pet" banks he engaged in private speculations that threatened to discredit the entire system of depository banks.

Little is known of Ellicott's personal life. Born on November 10, 1777, in Bucks County, Pennsylvania, he was the son of Andrew Ellicott by a second marriage. Andrew Ellicott's sons by his first marriage were the enterprising brothers who set up a complex of grist mills near Baltimore. While Thomas Ellicott and his brother, Andrew, Jr., eventually moved to Maryland in 1797 and shared the ownership of a grist mill there, they never achieved the scale of operations of their half brothers.

Along with owning the mill, Thomas Ellicott joined in the promotion of the Baltimore & Ohio Railroad, and he served on the board of that railroad in its first year of operation, 1827. In 1833 he served as the president pro tem of the permanent committee of the New York Convention of the

Friends of Domestic Industry, a protariff group. A Quaker, he was by several accounts a vigorous and domineering man. He married Martha Miller; the couple had eight daughters and one son.

Ellicott achieved prominence as the president of the Union Bank of Maryland, in Baltimore. The directors of that institution first elected him in 1819, at the age of forty-two, after a scandal in which the previous president had lost one-fourth of the bank's capital. In a few years the bank restored its standing, but not all observers credited Ellicott with the improvement. Langdon Cheves, the outgoing president of the Second BUS, was sufficiently impressed with Ellicott in 1822 to propose him as his successor. Ellicott's fellow Baltimore bankers, however, had a low opinion of his abilities, and they successfully opposed the appointment.

Ellicott also may have damaged his chances for Cheves's post by antagonizing officials of the Washington branch of the BUS. Willing to cooperate with the national bank when he first took over the Union Bank, he joined with smaller Baltimore banks in early 1822 in an attempt to reduce the circulation of notes from banks of the District of Columbia. In May the cashier of the Washington BUS branch complained of Ellicott's intervention. Ellicott's attempts to take on for his own bank some of the regulatory activities of the BUS contin-

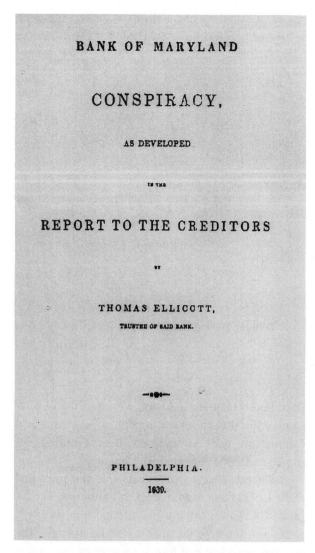

BANK OF MARYLAND

CONSPIRACY,

AS DEVELOPED

IN THE

REPORT TO THE CREDITORS

BY

THOMAS ELLICOTT,

TRUSTEE OF SAID BANK.

PHILADELPHIA.

1839.

Title page for Ellicott's version of events surrounding an 1833 sale of Tennessee bonds and the subsequent failure of the bank that financed the sale (courtesy of the Enoch Pratt Free Library)

ued after 1822, leading to complaints from the latter's branches in Baltimore and elsewhere.

In waging those petty battles with the branches Ellicott came to oppose the monopoly granted to the BUS. That opposition, combined with his aggressive personality, isolated him from most other bankers in Baltimore. He managed to gain the friendship and confidence of Taney, then a lawyer from rural Maryland. After arriving in Baltimore in 1823 Taney served as director and as counsel for the Union Bank. Ellicott's skirmishes with the national bank confirmed Taney's preexisting distrust of that powerful institution. Taney reported that despite the contrary opinion of many Baltimoreans, Ellicott impressed him as an honest, conscientious, and knowledgeable man. Taney was instrumental in blocking an attempt by several stockholders to remove Ellicott from the Union Bank presidency in the late 1820s.

As Andrew Jackson's attorney general in 1833 Taney found himself the lone cabinet member to favor the president's aim of letting the BUS charter expire. Jackson therefore made him secretary of the treasury. Once in those unfamiliar waters, Taney relied heavily on Ellicott, whom he then considered his closest adviser. Jackson as early as 1829 had considered replacing the BUS with a national bank of a more democratic character, one that indeed would have many of the central-bank powers ascribed to the BUS. Ellicott, both directly and through Taney, lobbied instead for the system of depository state banks that the administration adopted in October 1833. While the original pet system lasted only three years, it was replaced, under the Deposit-Distribution Act of 1836, by a system granting federal deposits to many more state banks. Jackson's reversal of his earlier position favoring a national bank helped to delay the advent of organized central banking for many decades.

Ellicott's intimacy with Taney made his bank a natural choice for depository status. The Union Bank was initially the only pet bank in Baltimore and one of only seven in the country. Fearing that the national bank would try to destroy the new system by manipulating its accounts with those banks, Taney gave Ellicott and the other pet bankers transfer drafts against the Treasury's account at the national bank. Rather than save the drafts as protection against any sudden demands from the national bank, Ellicott used them immediately to shore up a faltering bank in Baltimore, the Bank of Maryland. That bank neared collapse as a result of the speculative activities of its president, Evan Poultney, in association with Ellicott.

In early 1833 Poultney, having already managed to buy up almost all of his bank's stock, underwrote bonds for the state of Tennessee to the value of $500,000. Joining Poultney in that speculation, apparently, were his brother, Samuel, and Ellicott's son, William, who had married a Poultney. All had combined with Poultney in the private banking partnership of Poultney, Ellicott & Company. The directors of the Bank of Maryland may have played a part as well.

Unable to sell the bonds quickly at a high profit, Poultney and his associates used them for security in the purchase of a large amount of stock in

Ellicott's Union Bank. As those and other of their ventures went poorly, the speculators found their bank, the Bank of Maryland, which in effect had financed their ventures, short of cash. With the help of Ellicott they convinced the Union Bank to purchase the Tennessee bonds, of questionable value, at 108 percent of par. Ellicott, who apparently dominated his board, had his bank pay for the bonds with the transfer drafts. Poultney thereupon paid Ellicott $25,000 as a commission.

Taney soon found out about Ellicott's improper use of the drafts, but he did not demand repayment. At a time when the new depository system was fragile and under great scrutiny by the opponents of the federal administration, he feared causing a series of failures in Baltimore, beginning with the Bank of Maryland and possibly including his depository bank. Although shaken by his friend's behavior, Taney kept Ellicott in his confidence. When the BUS's policy of contraction in late 1833 and early 1834 caught the Union Bank in an overextended position, Taney also helped to strengthen that bank.

In response to the contraction, Ellicott called for cooperation between the depository banks. He suggested a confederation of the banks under the central direction of Reuben Whitney, a former director of the BUS who had become an opponent of that bank. Taney, who had tried to prevent other pets from making surprise demands on the weakened Union Bank, nevertheless rejected the plan. Ellicott also proposed a system of pet banks strengthened by special privileges and monopolies granted by state governments. That proposal suggests that Ellicott fought the BUS not because he opposed the granting of monopolies to banks, but because the existence of the BUS diminished his powers as a state banker.

In March 1834 the Bank of Maryland failed, along with two other banks in Baltimore. Only limited help from the BUS and Taney's diversion of federal funds from the pet bank in Philadelphia prevented a panic in Baltimore and allowed Ellicott to survive a run on his bank.

In May 1834, with the situation still precarious, Ellicott demanded extensive new aid from the Treasury. He threatened to surrender the federal deposits and to support a move to recharter the BUS if not satisfied. Tired of putting good money in an unreliable institution, and feeling betrayed by someone who he had thought genuinely opposed a na-

tional bank on principle, Taney called Ellicott's bluff.

By then thoroughly disillusioned with Ellicott, Taney, who still owned shares in the Union Bank, threw his support behind a new attempt by several stockholders to remove Ellicott from the presidency. Despite the intervention of Poultney, Ellicott & Company, which by then controlled a large block of shares of the Union Bank, Ellicott was replaced as president by Hugh Evans in July 1834. The exasperated Democratic administration in Washington accepted Evans, a Whig, because of the great respect other bankers had for him.

When the Bank of Maryland failed in March 1834, its officers offered the trusteeship to Ellicott, still president of the Union Bank. Ellicott accepted after managing to obtain the unanimous approval of his fellow bank presidents in the city. A public meeting of the bank's creditors, however, demanded two additional trustees, to which Ellicott reluctantly consented.

Over Ellicott's opposition the other trustees launched successful suits against Poultney, Ellicott & Company for losses sustained by the bank, and against Ellicott himself for the commission he had received on the sale of the Tennessee bonds. Ellicott, for his part, claimed that the two trustees had conspired with the directors of the Bank of Maryland to put the blame for their failed speculations on Poultney, Ellicott & Company.

Ellicott continued as trustee despite losing the suit, but after 1834 he left the state and abandoned most of the work to the other trustees. His wife had inherited an estate in Avondale, Pennsylvania, in 1834, and he seems to have spent the rest of his life there. In his later years he worked on a genealogy of the Ellicott family. He died in 1859 and was buried in Chester County, Pennsylvania.

In an administration intent on changing the nation's banking system, but with little firsthand knowledge of financial matters, Thomas Ellicott occupied an influential position. He himself opposed the BUS mainly because it curbed his own ambitions as the president of an important state bank. His lobbying helped to bring about the short-lived system of depository banks, while his abuse of his status as a pet banker weakened the new system in its early months.

Publication:

Bank of Maryland Conspiracy as Developed in the Report to the Creditors (Philadelphia, 1839).

References:

Stuart Bruchey, ed., "Roger Brooke Taney's Account of His Relations with Thomas Ellicott in the Bank War," *Maryland Historical Magazine*, 53 (1958): 58-74, 131-152;

Frank Otto Gatell, "Secretary Taney and the Baltimore Pets: A Study in Banking and Politics," *Business History Review*, 39 (1965): 205-227.

Henry Failing

(January 13, 1834-November 8, 1898)

by Larry Schweikart

University of Dayton

CAREER: Various positions, L. F. de Figanere & Company (1846-?); bookkeeper, broker, Eno, Mahoney & Company (?-1851); partner, J. Failing & Company (1851-1871); mayor, city of Portland (1864-1875); president, First National Bank of Portland (1869-1898).

Henry Failing, Portland pioneer and founder of one of Oregon's most important banks, was born in New York City on January 13, 1834, to Josiah and Henrietta Ellison Failing. Failing's parents came from upper New York State in the Mohawk Valley. Josiah Failing held a position as a city government official. After Failing attended New York public schools until he reached the age of twelve, he went to work in the New York City countinghouse of L. F. de Figanere & Company. This firm, partly owned by a French minister from Bordeaux, gave Failing contact with French dealers in the city. As a result he learned to speak French fluently. He rose to the rank of accountant in the company, then took a position as bookkeeper at the dry goods store of Eno, Mahoney & Company, under the tutelage of Amos R. Eno, a New York millionaire who was the senior partner. Eno later expressed regret that he had not retained Failing. At Eno's company Failing learned business methods and brokerage, and at age seventeen he left with his father and younger brother, John W. Failing, for Oregon.

The three reached Portland on June 9, 1851, after a three-month trek that included crossing the Panama isthmus and a voyage up the coast to San Francisco. They founded a business on Front Street in Portland, called J. Failing & Company, that sold

Henry Failing

dry goods and other mercantile commodities. Josiah Failing immediately entered into politics, serving on the city council in 1852. The following year he won election as mayor of Portland (preceding another banker, William Ladd). After several years in the merchandise business and politics, Josiah Failing retired to work for the Baptist church, leaving the business to his eldest son. The young entrepreneur promptly increased the size of the stock and began to branch out in his business connections.

Failing married Emily Phelps Corbett, banker Henry Corbett's sister, in 1858 (the couple had four daughters) and joined in Portland civic affairs. At various times he served as president of the Portland Art Museum, on the Public Library Association, and on the University of Oregon's Board of Regents (eventually as chairman). He contributed $10,000 to the construction of the Portland Library. An active member of the First Baptist Church, he served as president of the Baptist Society. As treasurer of the city's Children's Home he aided needy infants. Along with William S. Ladd and Corbett, Failing purchased the land for and planned the Riverside cemetery. He read widely in literature and science and emphasized the value of a classical education in public speeches. He was a trustee and treasurer of Pacific University and a trustee of a school for the deaf in Salem.

Failing became politically connected with the Union party, the Civil War combination of Republicans and War Democrats, and in 1864 he was elected mayor of Portland. During his tenure the city obtained a new charter and embarked on a system of street improvements. Toward the end of his third term Portland experienced a fire that destroyed more than 20 downtown blocks and caused $670,000 in damages. Failing's insistence that Portland not accept outside financial help during the crisis led to his defeat in 1875.

Failing gained his banking experience when he and brother-in-law Corbett purchased control of the First National Bank of Portland from A. M. and L. M. Starr in 1869. In 1871 they created Corbett, Failing and Company, merging their separate dry goods businesses. Corbett, except for the years 1867 to 1873, when he served as U.S. senator from Oregon, presided over the mercantile business, while Failing was president of the bank until his death in 1898.

Failing's success largely rested on his "uncanny powers of exact calculation." As president of Portland's Water Committee beginning in 1885, for example, his estimates of revenues and expenses always proved remarkably exact: one year an estimate of $100,000 in expenses was only off by $211, while in another year a revenue estimate of $232,000 was off by less than $190. Failing also built a reputation for honesty, industry, and good judgment.

First National Bank funded and helped to reorganize the rail transportation and street railway companies of Portland. In 1891 the bank participated in the organization of the Union Power Company, an electrical rail line company created by Charles R. Swigert. Failing also served as vice-president of the City and Suburban Railway Company from 1891 to 1898 and was a director of the Oregon Railway & Navigation Company. He was also president of Northern Pacific Terminal Company, incorporated in 1882, and he served on the board of commissioners of the Port of Portland from 1891 to 1897. First National also extended large loans for the Portland Gas Company, in which Failing held stock.

Still, banking, not transportation, remained Failing's central enterprise. The bank grew steadily but experienced some difficulty during the Panic of 1893, when it had to bail out much of the banking community in the Northwest with money obtained from the well-capitalized Meier and Frank general store. First National survived, and by 1895 it and the other pioneer Portland bank, Ladd & Tilton, had combined total assets that exceeded by four times those of the other seven Portland banks combined.

Failing, along with Corbett and fellow Portland banker C. H. Lewis, also participated in the creation of Security Savings and Trust Company in 1890. Although the headquarters of Security Savings and First National were in the same building, they remained separate until 1914. Founded by First National's cashier, Abbot Low Mills, and C. F. Adams, Security Savings had secured $5 million in outside money, but Failing and Corbett convinced the young bankers that a smaller bank, controlled by the two men and other local owners, would better serve Portland. They agreed, and Failing obtained just under a 20 percent interest in the new venture.

Prior to his death Failing suffered from physical problems and chronic insomnia. Every night one of his daughters read him to sleep. He apparently took his business worries home, and contemporaries expressed concern that the financial panics of 1893 and 1896 had placed too much strain on him. He died on November 8, 1898.

Failing's business success made him a power in Portland society until his death. He amassed significant wealth, with his prime downtown properties worth $1.5 million in 1898, but he never acquired truly huge holdings. Even a severe critic of Portland's business community concluded of Failing and colleagues Corbett and William Ladd (of Ladd & Tilton) that they "contributed more than their fair share." Failing did more than donate to charity. He founded or directed a dozen or more important and profitable businesses, not the least of which was the First National Bank. In the long run, those businesses contributed more to Portland than his charity.

References:

Orrin K. Burrell, *Gold in the Woodpile—An Informal History of Banking in Oregon* (Eugene: University of Oregon Press, 1967);

Joseph Gaston, *Portland, Oregon: Its History and Builders* (Chicago: Clarke, 1911);

E. Kimbark MacColl, *The Growth of a City: Power and Politics in Portland, Oregon, 1915-1950* (Portland: Georgian Press, 1979);

MacColl, *The Shaping of a City: Business and Politics in Portland, Oregon, 1855-1915* (Portland: Georgian Press, 1976).

William George Fargo

(May 20, 1818-August 3, 1881)

by Robert J. Chandler

Wells Fargo Bank

CAREER: First freight agent, Auburn & Syracuse Railroad (1841-1842); messenger, Pomeroy & Company (1842-1843); post agent, Livingston, Wells & Pomeroy (1843-1845); partner, Wells & Company (1845-1846); partner, Livingston & Fargo (1846-1850); secretary (1850-1868), president, American Express Company (1868-1881); mayor, Buffalo, New York (1861-1865); president, Wells, Fargo & Company (1870-1872).

William George Fargo was a builder of the express business in the United States. He helped found two important financial institutions, the American Express Company and Wells, Fargo & Company. He devoted his managerial talents to American Express, assuring its survival and growth.

Born on May 20, 1818, in Pompey, New York, Fargo was the eldest of 12 children born between 1818 and 1843 to William C. Fargo and Tracy Strong Fargo. As a boy he worked on his father's farm in summer and in winter attended school. When Fargo was thirteen, mail contractor Daniel Butts hired him to carry the mail on a 43-mile circuit around Pompey. Carrying the mail acquainted young Fargo with the rapid delivery of news. He later dabbled at innkeeping and the grocery business, and in 1840 he opened a short-lived store with a brother. That same year he married Anna H. Williams of Pompey. Of their eight chil-

William George Fargo (engraving by E. G. Williams & Brothers)

dren, only William, Helen, and Georgiana lived to adulthood.

In 1841 Fargo entered the transportation business when he became the first freight agent at Auburn, New York, for the Auburn & Syracuse Railroad. There he attracted the attention of Henry Wells, a proprietor for the express service of Pomeroy & Company. In 1842 Fargo became a messenger for Pomeroy & Company, carrying valuables on the 24-hour rail journey between Albany and Buffalo. The next year he was promoted to post agent and settled in Buffalo. Also in 1843 the company became Livingston, Wells & Pomeroy, with the addition of William A. Livingston as partner.

Fargo's tact and courage impressed Wells, and on April 1, 1845, Fargo became a partner in a new concern, Wells & Company, which offered express services from Buffalo to Detroit and Chicago. In 1846, when Wells moved to New York City to concentrate on the business to Buffalo, Fargo and Livingston formed Livingston & Fargo. They became the western connection of Wells's operation. Livingston remained at Buffalo, while Fargo, at Detroit, was eight days distant during the winter months. Two brothers, James and Charles Fargo, and brother-in-law Samuel P. Wormley also joined Livingston & Fargo.

On March 18, 1850, Fargo's business horizons expanded with the formation of the American Express Company, a joint-stock association with two virtually autonomous divisions. Livingston & Fargo became Livingston, Fargo & Company and controlled the western business. In the East, Wells & Company and Butterfield, Wasson & Company combined to form Wells, Butterfield & Company under the direction of John Butterfield, the largest stockholder in American Express. Henry Wells, as president, acted as peacemaker between line superintendent Butterfield and company secretary Fargo. The two rivals made directors' meetings battlegrounds, as each worked to increase his power at the expense of the other. Due to the hostility American Express was not venturesome. The directors usually united only to fend off competitors and to form affiliates to enter new territories. American Express fathered Wells, Fargo & Company in 1852 (for which Fargo served as director), the United States Express Company in 1854, and the National Express Company in 1855. By 1855 banker Danford N. Barney was president of all three. Until 1915, besides founder Fargo, six Fargo brothers, a brother-in-law, and six nephews served American Express.

Conflict on the American Express board of directors spilled over into other endeavors, including the Overland Mail Company. In September 1857 John Butterfield used his friendship with President James Buchanan to gain a government contract to provide faster mail service to California. To please the South, the proposed 2,700-mile route would connect St. Louis, Missouri, to San Francisco, California, via El Paso, Texas, and Los Angeles. Its scheduled transit time of 21 days cut a week off steamer mail service. Though the Overland Mail Company was primarily an American Express enterprise, the route traversed territory served by Adams and Wells Fargo, and their support was essential. The Overland Mail Company had eleven directors. Eight were expressmen, drawn from the owners of the four major expresses serving the south and west, and three were line superintendents. As the latter could be removed at pleasure, and their duties were along the stagecoach route, power rested with the expressmen in New York City.

On October 23, 1857, the express proprietors signed circulars addressed to their respective stockholders urging investment in the Overland Mail Company, and revealing interlocking directorates. The signers for American Express included John Butterfield, president of the Overland Mail Company; William Fargo; American Express treasurer Alexander Holland, Butterfield's son-in-law; and Hamilton Spencer, a director friendly to Butterfield. The Adams representatives were its president, William B. Dinsmore, vice-president of the Overland Mail; and Johnston Livingston, who was also a director of American Express and Wells Fargo. Danford N. Barney and Elijah P. Williams, Fargo's brother-in-law, signed for Wells Fargo and the United States Express Company; Barney headed both. Counting those who served on both boards, American had five Overland Mail directors, and Wells Fargo had four.

Wells Fargo and Adams loaned money for construction of the Overland line, which began running in September 1858, and for operations in 1859 when government appropriations failed to materialize. Butterfield covered Adams from loss, but beginning in August 1859 Barney and Williams protested Wells Fargo's vulnerability and Butterfield's extravagance. Spencer left the board in November, depriving Butterfield of an ally. Tensions increased, and Butterfield's feelings may have been imagined, considering his actions in January 1860 at an American Express board meeting. Henry Wells wrote, "All of the profanity that one head could hold, or one tongue utter, was used to express his friendship toward me and Fargo." A showdown between Fargo and Butterfield came two months later. On March 19 Fargo moved that Wells Fargo seize all Overland Mail Company property to secure its $160,000 loan, and Benjamin P. Cheney, a Wells Fargo director, joined the Overland Mail board. The next day brought compromise. Fargo withdrew his motion, but Butterfield was out as president and Dinsmore was in.

Butterfield's defeat lessened his interest in American Express operations and increased Fargo's ambitions. Fargo secured Butterfield's support to elect brother James C. Fargo to the American Express board. If successful, Henry Wells discovered, "Barney and the Fargos would have entire control of the three Companys," American Express, United States Express, and Wells Fargo. "It did not take me a great while to put a stopper on this move," Wells wrote on January 19, 1861.

The Civil War brought peace to the American Express boardroom, great prosperity for the express companies, and political advancement to Fargo. He owned the *Buffalo Courier,* and in 1861 and 1863 Democrats elected him mayor of Buffalo. Fargo supported the war, raised men, and backed his Pompey neighbor, New York governor Horatio Seymour. As Fargo prospered, he built a great mansion, supported the Episcopal church, and gave much of his wealth to charity.

In the 1860s Fargo also directed Wells, Fargo & Company. It expanded eastward from California as miners struck gold and silver in Nevada, Idaho, and Montana. By 1861 the Overland Mail route went through Salt Lake City, and a railroad soon followed. On April 15, 1863, Wells Fargo sent directors Barney, Cheney, and Fargo overland to California "for the purpose of looking after the interests of this Company." On May 18 the three, also representing the Overland Mail Company, met stagecoach king Ben Holladay in Denver. Holladay controlled the overland route east of Salt Lake City. In June they arrived in California and stayed for six weeks. They discussed overland matters with Wells Fargo's general agent, Louis McLane, who also owned the Pioneer Stage line running to Virginia City, Nevada, via Placerville, and his brother Charles, who shortly became president of the Placerville & Sacramento Valley Railroad.

The McLanes and other San Francisco Democrats supported the Sacramento Valley Railroad and its affiliates. Since 1856 Wells Fargo had used the Sacramento Valley Railroad running from Sacramento to Folsom. At first Wells Fargo supported an affiliate building from Folsom over the Sierra mountains by way of Auburn, but then switched to the Placerville route, which had the best wagon road to the Comstock silver mines. Louis McLane and Wells Fargo president Barney signed the Placerville & Sacramento Valley Railroad bonds, while Wells Fargo advanced $250,000. Wells Fargo bought 2,000 tons of rails and fixtures, which in 1865 brought the tracks to Shingle Springs. Not surprisingly, in December 1864 Wells Fargo quietly purchased the Pioneer Stage Company. Sacramento Republicans opposed Wells Fargo, and they, with the encouragement of the Lincoln administration, formed the Central Pacific Railroad to cross the mountains by way of Auburn. In August 1865 the Central Pacific stopped Wells Fargo's bid for a trans-Sierra line by buying the Sacramento Valley Railroad.

Fargo's 1863 trip laid the foundation for the "grand consolidation" of November 1, 1866, which combined the Pioneer, Overland Mail, and Holladay stage lines under the Wells Fargo name and made Louis McLane president. Wells Fargo, through its express and stagecoaching network and its banking house in Salt Lake City, gained control of the gold coming out of Idaho and Montana, removed Holladay's competing express, banking, and stagecoaching company, and blocked the westward expansion of Adams, American Express, and the United States Express companies.

In 1866 American Express claimed Fargo's energies. Merchants Union Express entered American Express territory in upstate New York, gained rail contracts, cut rates, and captured business. Both companies suspended dividends and suffered losses but would not surrender. An express agreement in December 1867 apportioning territory hurt American Express the most. Wells wished to endure further losses to crush the foe, while Fargo wanted to compromise through merger. The fifty-year-old Fargo became president of American Express Company, and on November 27, 1868, the two expresses merged.

After serving 18 years on a wrangling board of directors, Fargo welcomed a change. In 1867 Butterfield had suffered a stroke, and in 1868 Wells lost his power. An executive committee rather than the directors set policy, and three made a quorum: president Fargo, line superintendent James C. Fargo (Fargo's brother), and treasurer Holland. Another brother, Charles Fargo, ran affairs at Chicago.

No sooner had Fargo settled the difficulty with Merchants Union Express than a similar crisis arose with Wells Fargo. Operating a large-scale stagecoach empire in the midst of Indian wars taxed Wells Fargo's resources, and in 1867 it suspended its dividend. On July 1, 1868, the Pacific Union Express Company began to challenge Wells Fargo in California and Nevada, cutting rates and capturing a large portion of Wells Fargo's bullion- and letter-carrying business. Partners included D. O. Mills, president of the Bank of California; Henry Bacon, previously the junior partner of the banking house of Page, Bacon & Company, which failed in 1855; and Josiah Stanford, a pioneer petroleum distributor and Leland Stanford's brother.

Lloyd Tevis made an exclusive express contract for the Pacific Express with Central Pacific Railroad president Leland Stanford, who ordered Wells Fargo off the railroad by October 1. At Omaha, Nebraska, on October 4 Tevis, Mills, and Bacon met William and Charles Fargo and A. H. Barney, Wells Fargo's new president. In return for one-third of Wells Fargo's stock, Wells Fargo gained the exclusive contract, and that agreement soon brought the collapse of the Pacific Union Express. Fargo became president of Wells Fargo in 1870, restored the dividend in 1871, and in 1872 turned the office over to Tevis, who served for 20 years.

Fargo's other interests included railroads. For many years he was a vice-president of the New York Central Railroad, that prime American Express carrier, and he worked to push the Northern Pacific Railroad across the Great Plains. On September 22, 1871, the town of Fargo, North Dakota, was named for Fargo. That same year he lost an election for the New York state senate. The collapse of Jay Cooke & Company, the Northern Pacific's bond seller, ended Fargo's dream of completing a transcontinental railroad line and precipitated the Panic of 1873.

William George Fargo's executive ability enabled him to size up men, organize business, make decisions, and get results. He overcame competitors and prospered in the post-Civil War era. He died on August 3, 1881.

References:

American Express Company, *Promises to Pay* (New York: American Express, 1977);

John J. Giblin, *Record of the Fargo Family* (New York: American Bank Note Company, 1907);

Peter Z. Grossman, *American Express: An Unauthorized History* (New York: Crown, 1987);

W. Turrentine Jackson, "A New Look at Wells Fargo, Stagecoaches, and the Pony Express," *California Historical Society Quarterly*, 45 (December 1966): 291-324;

Robert D. Livingston, "Pacific Expresses: Many with Short Lives," *Western Express*, 36 (October 1986): 9-16;

Livingston, "Wells and Fargo: Western Travelers," *Western Express*, 33 (January 1933): 17-20;

Noel Loomis, *Wells Fargo* (New York: Crown, 1968);

A. L. Stimson, *History of the Express Business* (New York: Baker & Godwin, 1881).

Archives:

Material on William George Fargo can be found at the corporate archives of the American Express Company in New York City, and Wells Fargo bank in San Francisco.

Federal Reserve Act

by Richard H. Timberlake

University of Georgia

The bill to create the Federal Reserve System was introduced in the House of Representatives in the late summer of 1913 by Carter Glass of Virginia, who was chairman of the House Committee on Banking and Currency. A similar bill was initiated in the Senate by Robert Owen of Oklahoma. A third bill was initiated by Senator Gilbert Hitchcock of Nebraska as a substitute measure for the Glass-Owen bill. Hitchcock's measure emerged as the focal point for populist and conservative opposition to what many regarded as the establishment's institution. After extended debate and much compromise, which absorbed more than 1,200 pages in the *Congressional Record,* the House passed the bill 298 to 60; the Senate passed it 43 to 25; and President Woodrow Wilson signed it into law on December 23, 1913.

The institution that emerged from the legislation was not a central bank, or so its proponents claimed. They thought of it as a federal system of autonomous, regional, reserve-holding, supercommercial banks. The label "central bank" was politically unacceptable to the leaders of the Democratic party. It had monopolistic connotations left over from the Jacksonian "war" against the Second Bank of the United States 80 years earlier. Since Democrats had won not only the presidency but also a majority in both houses of Congress in 1912, any reform institution they created had to avoid the central bank label.

The new act, when made operational, resulted in a system of 12 Federal Reserve banks located in the different regions of the United States. Every Reserve bank was a corporation owned by member banks in its district. Each member bank received an annual statutory dividend of 6 percent of the amount it had invested in the Reserve bank. The member bank's required investment was 6 percent of its paid-up capital and surplus. Member banks also chose most of the directors of the Reserve banks, who in turn chose the officers. The president of a Federal Reserve bank was a corporate executive and was paid accordingly. Annual salaries originally ranged from $9,000 for the presidents of the less prestigious Reserve banks to $30,000 for the president of the New York bank. (To get an equivalent in 1989 dollars, these salaries would have to be multiplied by a factor of at least ten.)

The Federal Reserve System's Board of Governors was a separate organization housed in the U.S. Treasury building in Washington. Supporters of the new system thought of it as a governmental oversight committee that would verify the legitimacy of the 12 reserve banks' operations. It was a body meant to "coordinate the operations of the Reserve Banks as a whole." The president of the United States appointed five members of the board, who the Senate had to confirm. Each member received an annual salary of $12,000. The secretary of the treasury served both as an ex officio member of the board, as did the comptroller of the currency, and as chairman. His annual salary of $12,000, already determined by his role as secretary, set the salary scale for the five appointed members. After the passage of the Banking Act of 1935, most of the Fed's key decisions emanated from the Federal Open Market Committee (FOMC), a group that consisted of the seven members of the Board of Governors and five of the twelve Reserve bank presidents. The president of the New York Fed had a permanent seat on the FOMC. The other eleven Fed bank presidents took turns filling the four remaining seats. The FOMC as of 1989 has complete technical control over the supply of common money in the economy.

The Federal Reserve System had many institutional roots. It took several of its provisions, such as reserve requirements and the classifications of reserve city banks and central reserve city banks, from the national banking system. Many of its sponsors saw it as a public utility, with the Federal Reserve Board somewhat like the Interstate Commerce

THE WHITE HOUSE
WASHINGTON

December 23, 1913

My dear Senator:

Now that the fight has come to a successful issue, may I not extend to you my most sincere and heartfelt congratulations and also tell you how sincerely I admire the way in which you have conducted a very difficult and trying piece of business? The whole country owes you a debt of gratitude and admiration. It has been a pleasure to be associated with you in so great a piece of constructive legislation.

Cordially and sincerely yours,

Woodrow Wilson

Hon. Robert L. Owen,
United States Senate.

Letter from President Woodrow Wilson congratulating Oklahoma senator Robert Owen on the passage of the Federal Reserve Act (Noble Foster Huggson, Epochs in American Banking, *1929)*

Commission. Others saw the board as a "Supreme Court of Finance" because its members had ten-year tenures (fourteen years after 1935), and because their decisions and actions were supposed to be beyond the reach of political influence. Critics of pre-Fed policy attributed most of the monetary mischief that had occurred to the actions of the Treasury Department. The Fed's supporters contended that the new system would take the Treasury out of monetary policy. How that view squared with the inclusion of the secretary of the treasury as chairman of the board and the housing of the Board in the treasury building no one ever explained.

The Federal Reserve System's most important effect was to displace the unofficial system of clearinghouse associations that had emerged over the previous 60 years. Not only had the clearinghouses greatly enhanced the efficiency of the payments system, they had also served capably as lenders of last resort in times of bank crisis and monetary panic. Their operations in that role, while unexceptionable in stopping panics, had manifested an aura of funny-money illegality. Supporters of the Federal Reserve Act saw it as a means for legitimizing those clearinghouse functions.

No one expected or even imagined that the Federal Reserve banks would usurp the functions of the gold standard. The Fed banks had as their principal monetary function the promotion of form-seasonal elasticity of the money supply; that is, the maintenance of a reasonable degree of constancy in the existing stock of money by enabling commercial banks to convert one form of money–demand deposits–into another form–currency–without undue costs or significant changes in the total stock of money. The Fed banks would thereby prevent the fi-

Cartoon by Césare depicting the Federal Reserve telling financial panic to "Move On" (New York Sun, November 17, 1914)

nancial trauma associated with fractional reserve bank credit crises.

Because the gold standard still remained inviolate, and in fact explicitly reaffirmed in the Federal Reserve Act itself, legislators wrote few safeguards in the way of effective checks and balances into the act. The Reserve banks, with the approval of the Board of Governors, set their discount rates at levels relative to existing market rates depending on their assessment of the state of business activity at the time. To encourage the extension of bank credit they lowered discount rates, and to dampen banking exuberance they raised rates. The discount rate supposedly constituted their primary, and almost exclusive, means of monetary control. The act explicitly fixed member bank reserve requirements and sought to limit severely all open-market operations, particularly in government securities.

Reserve bank discounting, besides being regulated by Reserve bank discount rates, was supposed to be confined to "eligible" paper; that is, to short-term, self-liquidating commercial paper that emerged from the financing of the actual production and marketing of goods and services in the real economy. That concept, known as the "real-bills doctrine," played a prominent role in the congressional debates. It reflected an idea that seemed sensible to everyone: the creation of money should occur in conjunction with the production of real goods and services. It also seemed compatible with the goal of an elastic currency and a relatively stable price level. It was (and is), however, a fundamentally flawed doctrine because the prices assigned to the "real" commercial paper by the bank or central bank making the loan were not fixed by statute but were subject to the discretion of the banks' loan officers. Thus, the optimism or pessimism of the hour often determined the "eligibility" of the bills offered for discount.

The Federal Reserve Act in the final analysis resulted in more, not less, government influence in the monetary and banking system. By taking the basic production of money via the gold standard out of the private sector and subjecting it to governmental intervention, it divorced the results of decision-making from those who had a self-interest in maintaining the integrity of the system.

References:

Board of Governors of the Federal Reserve System, *The Federal Reserve Act* (Washington, D.C., 1983);

William Greider, *Secrets of the Temple: How the Federal Reserve Runs the Country* (New York: Simon & Schuster, 1987);

A. Barton Hepburn, *A History of Currency in the United States,* revised edition (New York: Macmillan, 1924);

J. Lawrence Laughlin, *The Federal Reserve Act, Its Origins and Problems* (New York: Macmillan, 1933);

Lloyd W. Mints, *A History of Banking Theory* (Chicago: University of Chicago Press, 1945);

Harold L. Reed, *The Development of Federal Reserve Policy* (Boston: Houghton Mifflin, 1922);

Richard H. Timberlake, Jr., *Origins of Central Banking in the United States* (Cambridge, Mass.: Harvard University Press, 1978);

Robert Craig West, *Banking Reform and the Federal Reserve* (Ithaca: Cornell University Press, 1977);

Eugene Nelson White, *The Regulation and Reform of the American Banking System, 1900-1929* (Princeton: Princeton University Press, 1983);

H. Parker Willis, *Federal Reserve System* (New York: Ronald Press, 1923).

Financial Panics during the Nineteenth Century

by Richard H. Timberlake

University of Georgia

Financial panics are disruptions in those markets in which securities of all kinds are bought and sold. Of necessity the institutions affected include the commercial banking system and central banks or government treasuries that may supply money to the economy.

Industrial recessions and depressions, by way of contrast, reflect disrupted conditions in markets for factors of production and for finished goods and services. Such episodes may include financial panics and may be triggered by them, but the two types of disequilibrium may also be largely independent. Usually a financial panic is short-term and often centered in the banking sector, while general economic maladjustment may affect many sectors of the economy and linger for years.

The financial panics identified during the nineteenth century were associated with several different kinds of banking and monetary developments. All of them followed circumstantially either from banking legislation or from special monetary activities of the federal government.

Through most of the nineteenth century the gold standard ruled the monetary system of the United States. Congress, in compliance with the Constitution, specified the legal-tender relationship between a weight of gold and a weight of silver in two sums of dollars. The first specification of a bimetallic standard occurred in 1792. The gold content of the dollar was then reduced by about 6 percent in 1834 and 1837 so that the mint value between the two metals became 15.988 to 1 and stayed that way for almost 100 years.

Economic historians have generally identified four major panics in the nineteenth century, the first of which was the Panic of 1818-1819. That disturbance had its source in the federal government's issues of treasury notes between 1812 and 1814. Those notes were interest-bearing currency that Congress authorized to cover part of the fiscal deficits in-

Wall Street during the Panic of 1857 (courtesy of the Museum of the City of New York)

curred during the War of 1812. The interest on them–5.4 percent per year–was payable only for one year. The notes were not reissuable once they came back into the Treasury, and, most important, they were a tender in all payments due to and from the federal government. While they avoided the Constitution's proscription against full legal-tender paper money, their necessary acceptance by the federal government ensured that virtually all households, business firms and banks would also accept them when tendered.

Their denominational levels (at first, none was issued for a sum less than $100) precluded their use in ordinary transactions. But for banks they proved highly desirable because they bore a good rate of interest and could be considered viable reserves for most purposes. The commercial banks, therefore, acquired them as the Treasury sold them to finance the war. Once they became bank reserves the notes served as the base for further issues of bank notes and deposits, which were then used for most ordinary payments by both the government and the private sector.

The treasury notes triggered the classic operation of a "cheaper" money replacing a "dearer" money. The new money started prices rising. Imbedded in the general price structure were the fixed mint prices of the precious metals. These prices could only be changed by a legislative act that was not politically acceptable. Thereupon, the precious metals went out of circulation as their commodity values exceeded their fixed monetary values. Banks and government suspended specie (gold and silver) payments, and the price level rose until 1815, when the issues of treasury notes ceased.

The readjustment necessary to restore specie payments for common money was complicated by the formation of the Second Bank of the United States (BUS) in 1816. The Treasury Department used the bank as a convenient buffer for carrying out the austere fiscal-monetary policy by which it retired the treasury notes. The last of the notes went out of existence by late 1817, and the banking system made its ragged adjustment during 1818-1819. Much of that adjustment included the systematic contraction of bank loans and discounts, and of notes and deposits, due to the reduced reserve base that no longer included government currency.

Prices fell unmistakably—first from 1814 to what seemed to be a plateau in 1816, then again until 1820. The total decline reached 30 percent from the peak in 1814 to genuine resumption in 1819. At that time prices had fallen to where they had been in 1811.

As with all financial and monetary contractions, the symptoms appeared to the layman as causes. Banks that failed had "speculated and overtraded." Critics found the Second BUS especially culpable. The monetary fasting and cleansing that the Treasury initiated was evident to no one, except perhaps the secretary of the treasury, and he best served his own interests by denying all complicity.

Even after specie payments resumed in 1819, prices continued to fall both in the United States and in the rest of the world due to a growth rate in real product that exceeded the corresponding growth rate in the monetary metals. From 1820 until 1834 U.S. prices fell by about 17 percent.

Another panic, perhaps the worst in the nineteenth century, occurred in 1837. After Congress devalued the dollar in 1834, land sales began to burgeon. Andrew Jackson's "war" against the Second BUS also reached its zenith at this time. For about two years (1834-1836) land sales generated double the ordinary revenue the federal government usually received. The outstanding federal debt was paid off entirely, and an estimated $35 million balance accrued in the depository ("pet") banks to the credit of the U.S. Treasury.

Congress passed a law in June 1836 that called for the Treasury to distribute this money to the credit of the several states. The distribution, which began in January 1837, required that a small part of the money actually transferred be withdrawn from a few of the depository banks in some states in order to pay the distributional shares due other states. That money, which also included bank reserves in the form of specie, was not immediately redeposited in other banks until the recipient state governments disposed of it. Redistribution of government deposits took several months and, by its effect on bank reserves, triggered the Panic of 1837. One year later, when the specie was back in the banks and specie payments were resumed, the financial sector again assumed a healthy look that continued until the middle of 1839.

The long business decline from 1839 to 1843 represented a real economic adjustment to the world's continually declining rate of increase in monetary gold stocks. It was not marked by any particular financial crisis in the U.S. economy at any stage, although certainly several banks failed during that period. Those failures generally represented serious mismanagement that the panic only exposed. For example, the State Bank in Alabama, heavily leveraged in real estate and slaves, collapsed along with the price of land.

The 1850s witnessed a significant increase in the world's gold stocks due to increased supplies from California and Australia. Enhanced gold production made the U.S. economy a net exporter of gold and a net importer of other goods and services. Greatly increased imports generated significant increases in tariff revenues for the Treasury. At the same time the banking system financed extensive railway construction. When the rate of increase in monetary gold waned around 1856, the New

SAVED FROM WILD PANIC.

STOCK EXCHANGE TREMBLES.

INDUSTRIALS RESCUED JUST IN TIME BY OUTSIDE MILLIONS.

S. V. WHITE GOES DOWN WITH A CRASH.

GENERAL ELECTRIC DARTS DOWN LIKE A KITE AND THEN UP AGAIN—OTHER INDUSTRIALS HAVE AMAZING FLUCTUATIONS—DREXEL MORGAN AND VANDERBILT INTERESTS LEAP INTO THE BREACH—MORE FAILURES THAT SEEMED TRIVIAL IN THE GENERAL DANGER—A BREATHING-SPELL AT LAST.

"The worst is probably over." That was the general expression of opinion in Wall Street circles yesterday at the close of a day of terrible strain, such as has not been felt in the Stock Exchange community in many years. Not that the failures announced were of sensational import, nor that the general declines in prices have not been exceeded on numerous previous occasions. The significance of the situation lay in its threatening

Headlines in the New York Times, *May 6, 1893*

York City banks found themselves unable to sustain credit demands of importers. Short-term interest rates increased in the summer of 1857 as banks scrambled for reserves. The Treasury, recognizing the banks' difficulties, carried out open-market operations in government securities until its specie balances were almost exhausted, but it could not prevent suspension of payments in October. The actual suspension lasted only six weeks, general resumption occurred in mid December 1857, and the nation suffered minimal economic hardship.

The Civil War Era witnessed a major change in the U.S. monetary system, when the federal government printed and spent into circulation almost $500 million of non-interest-bearing, fully legal-tender paper currency. The three Legal Tender Acts that authorized the U.S. notes, or "greenbacks," provided the banks with a base with which they more than tripled the stock of common money (notes and deposits). The price level rose, by 1865, to more than double its 1860 value, and all metallic currency disappeared from the monetary system. Since all ultimate payments could be made in greenbacks, the monetary system was on a greenback standard from 1862 to 1879.

The federal government tried different means between 1866 and 1878 to reduce the quantity of greenbacks and thereby the price level so that resumption could occur. Various acts of Congress in the post-Civil War period effected a permissive constancy in the stock of bank-issued money but also reduced somewhat the total volume of bank reserves. By September 1873 New York City banks had insufficient specie and greenbacks to meet both the demands for foreign exchange and the demands of interior banks to finance the marketing costs of harvest crops. During September and October reserves of New York City national banks declined from more than $50 million to $17 million, and the banks suspended greenback redemptions of their own notes.

Fiscal receipts of the federal government also declined significantly. The secretary of the treasury felt obliged by December to reissue some of the greenbacks that the government had previously retired. That circumstance relieved the crisis, so that banks could again redeem their own (national bank) notes and deposits with greenbacks.

Thereafter, laws passed in 1874 and 1875 abolished the legal limit on national bank note issues and provided as well for a further reduction in greenbacks. By May 1878 Treasury policy had reduced the stock of greenbacks to $346.7 million, which Congress fixed by law as a permanent government issue. Together with increased real output over the period, that reduction generated a decline in prices sufficient to bring about resumption of specie payments on January 1, 1879.

Back on an operational gold standard with silver serving practically as a subsidiary currency, the U.S. economy experienced a three-year boom (1879-1882) during which time prices rose by 20 percent. A short, sharp readjustment to that boom occurred in 1884, but it lasted only a few weeks and had no profound repercussions.

Silver politics and silver money of various kinds occupied an important place in the monetary system during the 15-year period from 1878 to 1893. The Bland-Allison Act of 1878 required the U.S. Treasury to buy $2 million to $4 million worth of silver every month and coin the silver into standard silver dollars. Only a minor fraction of the coined silver would circulate; so in 1886 Congress provided for the issue of silver certificates backed dollar-for-dollar by silver bullion in the Treasury. Once the silver money took the form of paper currency, it circulated as readily as greenbacks or national bank notes.

The price of silver continued to fall. The coined silver was clearly subsidiary in that its material value was significantly less than its monetary value. The prosilver bloc in Congress, which consisted of western silver-state Republicans and southern and western populists, engineered new legislation in 1890–the Sherman Silver Purchase Act. This act called for annual government purchases of a quantity of silver–4.5 million ounces per month–rather than a dollar value as specified by Bland-Allison.

This new silver policy at first increased the quantity of silver currency as well as the total amount of all currency in circulation. It also induced international expectations that the U.S. monetary system would not be able to sustain a viable gold standard. Gold, therefore, ebbed from the banking system and the Treasury. In 1890 the ratio of Treasury gold to total outstanding government-backed currencies (U.S. notes, national bank notes, and treasury notes of 1890) was 32 percent. By 1893 the ratio had fallen to 18 percent, and it finally bottomed at 13 percent in 1895.

The national election of 1892 brought Grover Cleveland back into the presidency. Cleveland, even though a Democrat, had strong antisilver views. Shortly after his inauguration in March 1893 he called for a special session of Congress to repeal the silver purchase provision of the Sherman Act.

The bitter controversy that marked the session was not between Democrats and Republicans, but between prosilver and antisilver forces in both parties. Since the repeal bill came from the administration, the Democrats generated most of the acrimony. The repeal act finally passed and the president signed it on November 1, 1893.

The U.S. Treasury immediately retired the notes of 1890 as they came in as fiscal revenues, and total currency in circulation declined 12 percent from late 1893 to mid 1896. Prices, likewise, showed a modest peak in 1892 and a general decline of about 10 percent to the trough of late 1896.

The monetary uncertainty resulting from silver agitation generated both foreign and domestic demands for the U.S. Treasury's stock of monetary gold. The resulting disequilibrium, which was not quite a panic, manifested itself in the summer of 1893. Internal and external demands drained gold from New York City banks and from the U.S. Treasury. Foreign-owned U.S. securities came home for redemption. Short-term interest rates rose. The result was a currency "famine," by which was meant an extraordinary demand for fully legal-tender Treasury currency that was itself legally redeemable in gold.

In the face of that pressure the New York Clearing House Association and other similar associations around the country issued supplemental short-term currency. That action relieved the crisis by effectively blocking the drains of bank reserves. The clearinghouse currency provided a fresh supply of high-powered money in the presence of a manifest demand for the same.

Once the crisis had passed, the cessation of silver purchases, an enhanced world production of gold, and the abatement of uncertainty over the status of the currency eased the monetary tightness. After the elections of 1896 the U.S. economy enjoyed an era of business euphoria that can only be described as "golden."

References:

Rendigs Fels, *American Business Cycles* (Chapel Hill: University of North Carolina Press, 1959);

Milton Friedman and Anna J. Schwartz, *A Monetary History of the United States, 1867-1960* (Princeton: Princeton University Press, 1963);

A. Barton Hepburn, *A History of Currency in the United States*, revised edition (New York: Macmillan, 1924);

Murray Rothbard, *The Panic of 1819* (New York: Columbia University Press, 1951);

Larry Schweikart, *Banking in the American South from the Age of Jackson to Reconstruction* (Baton Rouge: Louisiana State University Press, 1987);

O. M. W. Sprague, *History of Crises Under the National Banking System* (National Monetary Commission, 61st Congress, 2nd Session; Senate Document No. 538: Washington, D.C., 1910);

Peter Temin, *The Jacksonian Economy* (New York: Norton, 1969);

Richard H. Timberlake, *Origins of Central Banking in the United States* (Cambridge, Mass.: Harvard University Press, 1978).

First Bank of the United States

by Jeffrey Rogers Hummel

Independent Institute

The First Bank of the United States (BUS, 1791-1811) was America's earliest nationally chartered bank under the Constitution. A prior attempt to establish such a bank under the Articles of Confederation had occurred at the end of the revolutionary war. Robert Morris, a wealthy Philadelphia merchant who led the nationalist faction in the Continental Congress, became superintendent of the newly created Department of Finance in 1781. From this post he embarked upon various measures designed to make the central government more powerful. Among them was securing a legally dubious congressional charter for the Bank of North America. The nationalists, however, lost control of Congress in late 1783, and Morris resigned his post, while the Bank of North America, having already obtained a charter from the state of Pennsylvania, continued operation as the country's first commercial bank.

Morris's failure helped inspire the Philadelphia convention that replaced the Articles of Confederation. Less than two years after the new Constitution went into effect, on December 13, 1790, Secretary of the Treasury Alexander Hamilton proposed another nationally chartered bank to Congress. Patterned after the Bank of England, the BUS plan comprised a crucial feature of Hamilton's ambitious fiscal program, which involved full funding of the $55 million revolutionary war debt, national assumption of $20 million worth of state war debts, and collection of a tariff, a whiskey excise, and other internal taxes. Hamilton hoped those measures would tie the allegiance of private monied interests to the central government. A national bank, in his words, was "a political machine of the greatest importance to the state."

The proposal for a Bank of the United States aroused passionate opposition from the emerging Republican party, under the leadership of Congressman James Madison and Secretary of State Thomas

Jefferson. They feared the consolidation of central power that Hamilton's program entailed. Nevertheless, the proadministration Federalist party secured congressional approval for the bank bill. President George Washington then solicited written opinions from his cabinet. Jefferson, upholding a strict construction of the Constitution, argued against the charter. Hamilton, in contrast, justified a national bank with a loose interpretation of the Constitution's "necessary and proper" clause. Bowing to Hamilton's arguments, Washington signed the charter bill on January 25, 1791.

The BUS charter ran for 20 years and included a pledge that Congress would not establish any other banks during that period. The bank's authorized capital stock was $10 million, one-fifth of which the national government subscribed. Only $2 million of the total capital had to be paid in gold and silver coin (specie), the country's prevailing money both de facto and de jure. To help the Treasury float the growing national debt, the remaining stock could be purchased with government securities.

The bank received the legal authority to make loans and discount bills so long as it charged no more than 6 percent annual interest. It was also empowered to accept deposits and issue notes. The latter, mostly redeemable upon demand for specie, circulated as paper currency. The bank could issue up to $10 million in notes, and the federal government promised to receive the notes for all payments. In addition, the bank became the primary depository for the funds of the national government, although the Treasury continued to deposit some money with state-chartered banks throughout the existence of the First BUS.

BUS stock did not go on sale until July 4, 1791. Within a few hours it was fully subscribed. One-third of the members of Congress and many other public officials ended up owning shares. The

The First Bank of the United States, Philadelphia, 1791-1811

stockholders elected a board of directors on October 21, and Thomas Willing, partner of Robert Morris and head of the Bank of North America since its founding, was chosen president. The bank's main office opened in Philadelphia, and by the spring of 1792 it had branches in Boston, New York, Baltimore, and Charleston, South Carolina.

The BUS did not wield the control over the money stock associated with modern central banks. When the bank started business, the United States contained only four other commercial banks, each with a state charter. Yet the bank was the country's largest corporation, and its privileged connection with the national government, along with its monopoly on interstate branch banking, gave it a commanding position within the economy. As the number of state banks grew to 22 within the national bank's first five years, its dependable notes helped encourage the general circulation of paper over specie. The bank's directors could either make loans to state banks, which encouraged currency expansion, or restrain the issues of state banks through the adverse clearing of bank notes.

Upon the election of Jefferson as president in 1800, the Republicans swept into control of both houses of Congress. They did not, however, repeal the BUS charter, due to the reservations of Albert Gallatin, Jefferson's secretary of the treasury. Gallatin found the national bank convenient for the collection, safekeeping, transfer, and paying out of government funds. The bank, moreover, made direct short-term loans to the Treasury and marketed government securities. Jefferson's administration merely sold off the government's remaining shares in the bank. The Republican fiscal policy of drastic debt retirement meanwhile whittled down the bank's combined holdings of government securities and direct government loans from its peak of about $10 million in 1795.

The BUS appears to have been conservatively managed and earned respectable 8 to 10 percent annual returns for its stockholders, including the government. Additional branches set up in Norfolk (May 1800), Washington (January 1802), Savannah (August 1802), and New Orleans (October 1805) gave it a total of eight. One of the bank's few surviving balance sheets, for February 1809, reveals the following assets: $5 million in specie reserves; $2.2 million in government securities; $800,000 due from state banks; $15 million in loans to private individuals, chiefly payable in 60 days; and $500,000 in real estate. Its liabilities included $4.5 million of notes in circulation and $8.5 million of deposits. The bank thus had a reserve ratio of 38 percent for notes and deposits.

The secretary of the treasury was authorized to call for financial reports from the bank as often as once a week. But the Treasury never offered those reports for congressional or public scrutiny. The resulting secrecy surrounding the bank's operations aroused popular suspicions. The growing amount of its stock owned outside the country, mainly by British investors, further contributed to those suspicions despite the fact that foreigners could neither legally serve as directors nor even vote by proxy for directors.

The bank's charter came up for renewal in 1811. Gallatin, still secretary of the treasury, persuaded President Madison to press for renewal. The fact that the state banks almost universally supported rechartering attests to their friendly relations with the national bank. The Republican rank and file in Congress, however, balked. Even with the combined support of the Madison administration and the Federalists, the recharter bill met defeat in both houses by a single vote. Secretary Gallatin thereupon oversaw an orderly liquidation of the BUS, and its branches were sold to various state banks. Within five years, however, a second national bank took the place of the first.

References:

E. James Ferguson, *The Power of the Purse: A History of American Public Finance, 1776-1790* (Chapel Hill: University of North Carolina Press, 1961);

Bray Hammond, *Banks and Politics in America: From the Revolution to the Civil War* (Princeton: Princeton University Press, 1957);

John Thom Holdsworth, *The First Bank of the United States* (Washington, D.C.: National Monetary Commission, 1910);

Benjamin J. Klebaner, *Commercial Banking in the United States: A History* (Hinsdale, Ill.: Dryden, 1974);

John Jay Knox, *A History of Banking in the United States* (New York: Bradford Rhodes, 1900);

Burton Alva Konkle, *Thomas Willing and the First American Financial System* (Philadelphia: University of Pennsylvania Press, 1937);

Lawrence Lewis, *A History of the Bank of North America* (Philadelphia: Lippincott, 1882);

John R. Nelson, Jr., *Liberty and Property: Political Economy and Policy Making in the New Nation, 1789-1812* (Baltimore: Johns Hopkins University Press, 1987);

Curtis P. Nettels, *The Emergence of a National Economy, 1775-1815* (New York: Holt, Rinehart & Winston, 1962);

Fritz Redlich, *The Molding of American Banking: Men and Ideas* (New York: Johnson Reprint Co., 1968);

William Graham Sumner, *The Financier and Finances of the American Revolution* (New York: Dodd, Mead, 1891);

Richard H. Timberlake, Jr., *The Origins of Central Banking in the United States* (Cambridge, Mass.: Harvard University Press, 1978);

James O. Wettereau, "New Light on the First Bank of the United States," *Pennsylvania Magazine of History and Biography,* 61 (July 1937): 236-285.

John Murray Forbes

(February 23, 1813-October 12, 1898)

by James E. Fell, Jr.

United Banks of Colorado

CAREER: Clerk, J. & T. H. Perkins & Company, Boston (1828-1829); clerk, partner, Russell & Company, China (1830-1838); merchant, Boston (1838-1846); director and president, Michigan Central (1846-1855); director (1857-1898), president (1878-1881), chairman, Chicago, Burlington & Quincy Rail Road Company (1881-1898); chairman and treasurer, Chicago, Burlington & Northern (1885-1892).

John Murray Forbes was a merchant, financier, and general entrepreneur. He made his original fortune as a merchant in China. After returning to the United States he gradually engaged in mobilizing capital in Boston, New York, and London to finance the construction of western railroads, most notably the Michigan Central and the Chicago, Burlington & Quincy, through what was known as "the Forbes group."

Forbes came from a family of wealthy Boston merchants. He was born on February 23, 1813, the third son and one of the eight children of Ralph Bennet Forbes and Margaret Perkins Forbes. Despite the family's wealth and stature, his father was something of a ne'er-do-well; he was plagued by gout (some said he drank too much) and did not provide well for his family. He was largely an invalid during John's early years and died when John was eleven years old.

Forbes's elder brothers went to work in the merchant trade very early, which allowed John to remain in school longer than the others. But he eagerly pursued a career in business. In 1828, at fifteen years of age, he left school to work for the firm of J. & T. H. Perkins & Company, one of Boston's great merchant houses, which his uncles owned. Forbes also eagerly followed the example of his older brother Thomas and sailed for Canton, China. But he embarked for the Far East in July

John Murray Forbes (courtesy of the Chicago, Burlington & Quincy Railroad)

1830 with a heavy heart, for he had just learned that his brother had been lost at sea.

When Forbes arrived in Canton, he worked as a clerk for Russell & Company, a Boston merchant house owned by other uncles. He rapidly mastered operations and advanced quickly. His balding forehead made him look older than he actually was, which may have helped him. He returned to Boston in 1833 and married Sarah Hathaway of New Bedford, Massachusetts, in early 1834, then returned to Canton, where he learned he had been made a secret partner in Russell & Company during his first tour of service. He left China again in December 1836.

The Panic of 1837 created a crisis for Forbes and Russell & Company. Both survived, but only to face internal problems a year later. As a result, Forbes emerged as the controlling principal in the partnership. Nevertheless, he moved away from his mercantile interests. Although he might have remained a merchant, during the 1840s he invested in enterprises spawned by the industrial revolution. By the late 1840s his interests had clearly shifted to western railroad construction.

The panic had also left several publicly funded western roads unfinished and in desperate straits. One of those, the Michigan Central, ran from Detroit to Kalamazoo. It came to Forbes's attention through the efforts of John W. Brooks, a skilled engineer from New Hampshire, and James F. Joy, an energetic lawyer from Massachusetts. They wanted to buy the line from the state of Michigan and complete the track to Chicago, but they lacked the money. Brooks went to Boston, where he convinced Forbes that the project had merit. Forbes agreed to raise the money to save the road, which he did primarily through his mercantile connections in Boston and New York. The project brought together for the first time the talents of Forbes, Brooks, and Joy, who worked closely together in western railroad construction for the next 30 years.

In September 1846 Forbes was made president of the newly organized Michigan Central Railroad Company. Forbes and his colleagues successfully raised the capital they needed and completed the line to Lake Michigan in 1849 and around the southern tip of the lake to Chicago in 1852. With the Michigan Central's construction came the development of a so-called "Forbes group," a coterie of investors and managers who had intangible ties but who worked together on a series of railroad ventures that formed a "family" of roads.

In 1851, as the Michigan Central neared Chicago, the Forbes group thought of obtaining traffic from areas west of Chicago. Partly through the efforts of Joy and Brooks, the group acquired three railroad lines in Illinois and in 1855 organized the Chicago, Burlington & Quincy Rail Road Company. As it financed that line, the Forbes group also built lines farther west—the Hannibal & St. Joseph in Missouri, the Burlington & Missouri in Iowa,

and the Burlington & Missouri in Nebraska. Ultimately those lines were consolidated into the Chicago, Burlington & Quincy and the road extended to Denver, Colorado, by 1882.

By that time, however, the Forbes group had fallen apart, to some degree, because of the growing conflicts of interest of Joy and Brooks, who had investments in other roads, particularly those building along north-south axes as opposed to the east-west orientation of those controlled by the Forbes group. The matter came to a head in the "revolution of 1875," when a group headed by Forbes ousted Joy and his supporters from the Chicago, Burlington & Quincy board. This ended the Forbes-Brooks-Joy association. In the aftermath of the struggle, Forbes served three years as president of the line, until he stepped up to chairman and his nephew Charles E. Perkins became president. Forbes remained a member of the board until he died in 1898.

Forbes's view of railroad construction was conservative—he wanted his lines to be built in a sequential, developmental manner. In this rational, logical approach construction moved ahead in connection with the expansion of settlement. The Forbes group generally followed this strategy in building the Michigan Central from Kalamazoo to Chicago and in constructing the Chicago, Burlington & Quincy across Illinois, Iowa, and Nebraska to Denver.

Forbes himself remained something of a contradiction. He had an eighteenth-century style of business—one that emphasized close family connections, a personal sense of integrity and responsibility, and the conservative philosophy of his mercantile family. Yet in business he committed himself to innovation that truly changed the American transportation system.

Publications:

Letters and Recollections of John Murray Forbes, 2 volumes, edited by Sarah Forbes Hughes (Boston: Houghton, Mifflin, 1899);

Reminiscences of John Murray Forbes, 3 volumes, edited by Hughes (Boston: Ellis, 1902);

Letters of John Murray Forbes, 3 volumes, edited by Hughes (Boston: Ellis, 1905).

References:

Thomas C. Cochran, *Railroad Leaders, 1845-1890: The Business Mind in Action* (Cambridge, Mass.: Harvard University Press, 1953);

Arthur M. Johnson and Barry E. Supple, *Boston Capitalists and Western Railroads* (Cambridge, Mass.: Harvard University Press, 1967);

John Lauritz Larson, *The Bonds of Enterprise: John Murray Forbes and Western Development in America's Railway Age* (Cambridge, Mass.: Harvard University Press, 1984);

Richard C. Overton, *Burlington Route: A History of the Burlington Lines* (New York: Knopf, 1965);

Henry Greenleaf Pearson, *An American Railroad Builder: John Murray Forbes* (Boston: Houghton Mifflin, 1911);

Duncan Yaggy, "John Forbes: Entrepreneur," Ph.D. dissertation, Brandeis University, 1974.

Archives:

Materials pertaining to John Murray Forbes are located in the John Murray Forbes Papers of the Baker Library, Harvard Graduate School of Business Administration, Boston, Massachusetts; in the Forbes Family Papers (microfilm) of the Massachusetts Historical Society, Boston; in the James F. Joy Papers of the Michigan Historical Collections, Ann Arbor; in the Erastus Corning Papers of the Albany Institute of History and Art, Albany, New York; in the Burlington Railroad Archives of the Newberry Library, Chicago; and in the Michigan Central Railroad Archives of the New York Central System, Detroit.

Edmond J. Forstall

(November 7, 1794-November 16, 1873)

by Irene D. Neu

Indiana University

CAREER: Partner, Gordon & Forstall (1823-1825); partner, Gordon, Forstall & Company (1825-1835); comptroller, Consolidated Association of the Planters of Louisiana (1829); partner, M. de Lizardi & Company (1835-1838); president, Citizens' Bank of Louisiana (1836-1838); state representative, Louisiana (1836-?); partner, E. J. Forstall & Company (1838-1865); agent, Hope & Company, Amsterdam (c.1843-1873); sugar planter (1845-1873); agent, Baring Brothers & Company, London (1849-1873); partner, Edmond J. Forstall & Sons (1865-1873).

Edmond Jean Forstall, merchant, banker, and sugar planter, was a promoter of antebellum Louisiana's property banks and was strongly influential in the passage of the state's controversial Bank Act of 1842. Born in New Orleans on November 7, 1794, he was the eldest of the six children of Edouard Pierre Forstall and Celeste de la Villebeauve. Through his mother and his father's mother he descended from some of the earliest French settlers in Louisiana, but his paternal grandfather, Nicolas Michel Forstall, was born in Martinique, the son of an Irish father and an Irish or English mother. Nicolas Forstall arrived in New Orleans prior to 1762, and by Edmond's day the Forstalls were thoroughly French Creole in outlook and manners.

Edouard Forstall is a shadowy figure. Born in 1768, he died in New Orleans in 1822. As early as 1797 reports circulated that he owed "great sums of money," but in Edmond's youth his father headed a household of 24 persons, including 14 or 15 slaves.

Doubtless Edmond Forstall received an education of sorts, but no record of it remains. In 1806, at the age of twelve, he went to work for a merchant. In later years he said that when he began his career he was "pennyless and without commercial friends," but this must be discounted as the hyperbole of a successful man looking back over the distance he had come. In the close-knit Forstall family of the early nineteenth century there were several merchants, and it seems likely that Forstall began his career in the countinghouse of one of them.

In the years before the building and integration of America's East-West transportation lines, most of the surplus produce of the Ohio and Mississippi valleys came downriver to New Orleans. There the commodities of the interior of the country—the corn and pork, the tobacco, the cotton and sugar—found their way into the local market or were transferred to coastwise or oceangoing vessels for shipment to East Coast and European ports. Through New Orleans, also, passed manufactured goods from Europe for distribution over a wide area of the lower South and Mexico. From Latin

Portraits painted in 1836 by Vaudechamp of Edmond Forstall with a daughter, Désirée, and Clara Forstall, Forstall's wife, with a son, Eugene (collection of Olga and Yvonne Tremoulet)

America came coffee and cocoa, to be carried upriver to the shelves of storekeepers throughout America's great central valley. So important was the entrepôt at New Orleans that it had been the primary factor in the Louisiana Purchase just three years before Forstall entered his apprenticeship.

The War of 1812 interrupted trade and paralyzed commercial New Orleans, but shortly after news of the Treaty of Ghent reached the city in February 1815, new mercantile houses appeared. One of those was Gordon, Grant & Company, on St. Louis Street. By 1819, if not earlier, Forstall had associated with Alexander Gordon, the resident partner. In 1823 the firm reorganized as Gordon & Forstall, and with the addition of a third partner in 1825 it became Gordon, Forstall & Company. Forstall was the managing partner, Gordon having taken up residence in Liverpool, where he became the managing partner of Alexander Gordon & Company.

On July 19, 1823, at the age of twenty-eight and on the strength of his new partnership, Forstall married Clara Durel, a member of a New Orleans mercantile family. The couple had eleven children: five sons and six daughters. Forstall greatly enjoyed the role of paterfamilias, and supporting his growing family constituted a responsibility that he never shirked.

The firm of Gordon, Forstall & Company, located on Royal Street near the Louisiana State Bank, sold imported goods on consignment, advanced money on cotton shipments to Liverpool, bought cotton on account, and, as factors, managed the affairs of sugar planters. The firm's local customers included planters, dealers in the Mexican trade, and country storekeepers. New Orleans merchants especially prized the Mexican trade, for Mexico had little produce to export and paid for the bulk of its imports in specie and silver bullion. In 1824 Gordon & Forstall had set up Gordon, Tuyes & Company, a branch house in Tampico. The Tampico firm sold goods of all kinds on consignment from European houses, thus bypassing New Orleans, but Gordon, Tuyes & Company remitted the specie it received to England through Gordon, Forstall & Company whenever the premium on exchange, or operations in the New Orleans produce market, promised a profit. Use of such remittances, plus that portion of what Forstall described as "their own active capital" that the firm devoted to cotton operations, permitted Gordon, Forstall &

Company to consign nearly 8,000 bales of cotton to Liverpool during the 1827-1828 buying season, an amount that represented commitments of no less than $250,000.

In the 1830s both Forstall and Gordon associated themselves with the Lizardi brothers, merchant bankers of Paris, London, and Liverpool. After October 1835 the New Orleans house was known as M. de Lizardi & Company, the partners being Manuel de Lizardi, Edmond Forstall, and his brother, Placide Forstall. Edmond Forstall remained the managing partner. In London, Gordon became a partner of F. de Lizardi & Company. The Lizardis' Paris house was known as Lizardi Hermanos. As the years advanced (or, as Forstall would have said, "as time rolled"), both sugar factoring and the selling of European goods on consignment became less important to the New Orleans firm, while produce and exchange operations grew more important. Forstall remained active in the produce market and retained his reputation as a first-rate judge of cotton and tobacco, but the seasonal nature of produce operations allowed him months at a time to concentrate on other matters.

Like many young merchants of his day, Forstall early showed an interest in banking. In 1818, at the age of twenty-four, he became a director of the newly chartered Louisiana State Bank and with characteristic energy set out to learn all that he could about banking. Ever an avid reader and tireless investigator, he became an authority on the history and practice of banking in the western world. On the local level he found the Louisiana State Bank an admirable school. As a director he was often present on discount days when the businessmen of the city applied for loans and renewals. Thus he expanded his knowledge of the commercial affairs of New Orleans and the financial position of individual merchants and firms. When on June 6, 1829, Governor Peter Derbigny appointed him comptroller of the first property bank, the Consolidated Association of the Planters of Louisiana, Thomas Baring, then in the United States, assured his partners in London that Forstall had been "a long time in the routine of the banks."

In connection with the property banks of Louisiana, Forstall, who always described himself as a merchant and planter, earned his reputation as a banker. Property banks, often inaccurately called plantation or land banks, enjoyed a considerable popularity in the South, particularly in Louisiana,

in the decade before the Panic of 1837. "An act to incorporate the subscribers to the Consolidated Association of the Planters of Louisiana" became law on March 16, 1827. The charters of the Union Bank of Louisiana and the Citizens' Bank, both property banks, dated from 1832 and 1833, respectively. Forstall was associated with all three institutions.

Property banks resembled other commercial banks in that they issued bank notes, accepted deposits, and discounted commercial paper. They differed from other banks primarily in their method of raising capital. Incorporated banks ordinarily sold stock for cash; property banks sold bonds secured by a pool of stockholders' mortgages. An investor in a property bank obtained his stock by mortgaging his real estate, and sometimes his slaves, to the bank. The bank then sold bonds, based on its mortgage pool (and, as it developed, the faith and credit of the state), to raise its capital. In its inception, the Consolidated Association of the Planters of Louisiana was what its name implied: an association through which rural property owners had access to the long-term credit that the New Orleans commercial banks often denied them. Later, one-third of its mortgages were given on city property. Both the Union and Citizens' banks had an urban orientation from the beginning.

Property banks provided an ingenious vehicle for expanding capital and credit in an area chronically short of both. The Louisiana property banks alone disposed of some $17 million worth of bonds, mostly in Europe. Thus, in the 1830s those banks constituted an important instrument for channeling the foreign capital into the United States. Previous to the introduction of foreign capital by the property banks, Forstall claimed in 1843, cotton received at New Orleans did not exceed 200,000 bales a year. By 1843 it exceeded 400,000 bales. Sugar, which hardly reached 75,000 hogsheads annually in the 1820s, reached 125,000 to 140,000 in the 1840s.

Although Forstall was closely identified with the early history of the Louisiana property banks, no evidence suggests that he had anything to do with the inception of the first of them, the Consolidated Association of the Planters of Louisiana. Jean Baptiste Moussier, a New Orleans merchant of unknown background, conceived and suggested the plan. His inspiration may have come from the Prussian *Landschaften,* agricultural credit institutions that one authority suggests could have served as models for the property banks, or Moussier may have had knowledge of the colonial land banks, or perhaps his thinking was nudged by a provision in the charter of the Bank of Louisiana (1824) that required the bank to lend $2 million in the form of mortgages to planters. Whatever the source of his ideas, he was indisputably the "father" of the first property bank.

Forstall's appointment as comptroller of the Consolidated Association brought to the bank "what the planters had not–knowledge of the place–exchanges & commercial affairs," but perhaps his appointment stemmed less from his commercial acumen than from the directors' exaggerated idea of his influence with Baring Brothers & Company, the leading firm of London merchant bankers engaged in American trade and finance. As a matter of record, Forstall's relationship with the Barings was limited to a scant acquaintance with Thomas Baring, one of the partners, and that was an indirect result of the Consolidated Association's earlier efforts to market bonds in Europe.

The association had entrusted placing the bonds to Hughes Lavergne, Forstall's predecessor in the office of comptroller. Lavergne, a planter and former secretary of state of Louisiana, was related to Forstall, having married one of his many cousins. The two men were of an age and seem to have been confidants. When Lavergne arrived in England in the summer of 1828 to offer the Consolidated Association's bonds to London capitalists, he first called on Alexander Gordon, Forstall's former partner in Liverpool. Together Lavergne and Gordon went to London to see the Barings and discovered that they had been expected. A letter from Stephen Girard, the Philadelphia banker, who had interests in Louisiana heralded their arrival.

Barings contracted to buy 750 bonds of $1,000 each at 95 percent of par. The bonds came in three series, reimbursable in London in five, ten, and fifteen years, at the fixed rate of 4s. 3d. to the dollar. Five percent annual interest on the bonds was also payable in London, at the fixed rate of 4s. 6d. to the dollar. Those comprised the first American bonds sold in Europe at a fixed rate of return in sterling, a stipulation that Gordon and Lavergne, after some debate, had become convinced was "the condition *sine qua non* of the negotiation." Barings also agreed to accept on consignment for the account of the Consolidated Association the remaining 1,750 bonds of its permissible $2.5 million

issue, principal and interest payable in London at the same fixed rates as had been agreed to for the 750 bonds sold to the Barings.

Less than a month after the signing of the contract, Thomas Baring set out for the United States to look into "the Louisiana concern," that is, the Consolidated Association. He arrived in New Orleans on Christmas Eve, and Forstall for the first time met a member of the Baring firm. Making the most of the opportunity, he had several long conversations with Baring and subsequently wrote him a nine-page letter, setting forth in minute detail the business carried on by himself and his associates in New Orleans, Tampico, and Liverpool. From that time Forstall kept Baring informed of the affairs of the Consolidated Association, with Lavergne as one of his sources. Soon he had something significant to report, for the directors of the association refused to sanction that part of the contract with Barings that concerned the bonds that the London firm had agreed to sell on account of the association. The directors demanded renegotiation of the contract.

Forstall learned that the directors were insisting upon two basic changes: Barings must be held to a minimum limit at which they might sell bonds on account of the association, and those bonds must be reimbursable in New Orleans rather than in London. In early April 1829 Louis Allard, one of the Consolidated Association's directors, went north to meet with Thomas Baring, who had left New Orleans but was still in the United States, and propose to him the desired changes in the contract. Unable to wring concessions from Baring, Allard attempted to sell a bloc of bonds in northern financial centers, but met with no success. The directors of the association, hard-pressed by stockholders who felt themselves entitled to loans, and desperately in need of funds, turned to Forstall, who, as a merchant, understood international finance. Appointed comptroller of the Consolidated Association, Forstall was directed to renew negotiations with Thomas Baring.

Baring refused to change the terms of the original contract but offered in the name of his house to buy outright 500 more bonds of $1,000 each on substantially the same terms that Barings had purchased the first 750, a proposal that the board accepted. By the end of 1829 Barings was reporting sales of the association's consigned bonds and remitting the proceeds to New Orleans. Nonetheless, in the middle of December Forstall was forced to re-

Citizens' Bank, New Orleans, circa 1890. Forstall served as president of the bank from 1836 to 1839 (photograph by George François Mugnier, courtesy of the Louisiana State Museum).

sign from the comptrollership, having come to be regarded in some quarters as an agent of foreign capitalists.

The inescapable conclusion is that Forstall had only himself to blame. Always a loquacious person who greatly enjoyed the position of man of substantial affairs, he could hardly have resisted the temptation to boast of his acquaintanceship with Thomas Baring, and he doubtless gave the impression that he had more than a little influence with Baring Brothers & Company. Like almost any other man, Forstall enjoyed making money, but he enjoyed even more being in the center of things.

"Forstall is very zealous in whatever he undertakes," Joshua Bates, a partner in Baring Brothers & Company once remarked to Bostonian Thomas Wren Ward, "but," continued Bates, "I never saw a man that carried so much vanity. . . . He unfortunately for him sincerely believes that no one can do business as well as he can." To which Ward replied, "Mr. Forstall has all the faults you say, but is still quite an uncommon person." Shortly after Thomas Baring came to know Forstall he described him as

"a hard worker and clever[,] perhaps a little too sanguine & might be speculative."

In a career marked by more than one setback, Forstall's high opinion of his own abilities and his incurable optimism stood him in good stead. Philosophically accepting the necessity of leaving the comptrollership of the Consolidated Association, he continued to exercise such influence as he could in the bank through Lavergne "and a few other friends." The knowledge he had gained by his short-lived official relationship with the association he used to advantage in his future banking career. During a sojourn in Europe in the summer of 1830 he sounded out Barings on the possibility of their interest in the bonds of a second property bank in New Orleans. It appeared that they indeed had such an interest.

Back in New Orleans, Forstall prepared the charter for the Union Bank of Louisiana, following closely that of the Consolidated Association. Only residents of Louisiana who owned revenue-producing property might hold stock, with the amount of their subscriptions limited to the appraised value of their property minus double the amount of any prior encumbrances. When the pool of mortgages reached $8 million, the bank was privileged to sell $7 million worth of state-guaranteed bonds to raise its working capital. The bonds had a par value of $1,000 each, were divided into four equal series maturing in 12, 15, 18, and 20 years, and carried interest of 5 percent per annum, payable semiannually. The state received one-sixth of the bank's profit; the remainder accumulated in a fund for the redemption of the bonds.

The bill to charter the Union Bank of Louisiana became law on April 2, 1832. Forstall was among the managers appointed by Governor Andre Bienvenu Román to receive subscriptions to the stock of the bank. His fellow managers included Martin Duralde, recorder of mortgages in New Orleans and a son-in-law of Henry Clay; Dominique Bouligny, a former U.S. senator; Matthew Morgan, who became the bank's first president; and S. W. Oakey, a prominent Jacksonian. With the stock heavily oversubscribed, the founders soon organized the bank and chose commissioners. Forstall was one of the commissioners; the other was Samuel Jaudon, cashier of the New Orleans branch of the Bank of the United States.

In New York City on August 14, 1832, Forstall and Jaudon signed a contract with Baring

Brothers & Company and Prime, Ward, King & Company, the Barings' New York correspondents, for sale of the Union Bank's bonds. The Barings' principal American agent, Thomas Wren Ward, signed for the London bankers, and at this time Forstall came to know Ward, with whom he formed a lifelong friendship. The contract covered the entire $7 million Union Bank loan. Baring Brothers and Prime, Ward, King & Company contracted to buy 5,500 of the 7,000 bonds, while Barings undertook to market the remaining 1,500 bonds "on account and risk" of the Union Bank, with an option to buy those securities as well.

Of the 5,500 bonds, Baring Brothers took 3,700 and Prime, Ward, King & Company 1,800, at a premium of 6 1/14 percent, or 106 1/14 percent of par in New Orleans. The difference between that figure and the 95 percent of par that Baring Brothers paid for Consolidated Association bonds in 1828 testified to the improved demand for American securities abroad. The Union Bank bonds, like the Consolidated Association bonds, were reimbursable in London, and the interest on them was payable there, on the same terms as those given to the Consolidated Association four years earlier, that is, the principal at the rate of 4s. 3d. to the dollar, the interest at the rate of 4s. 6d.

At least one provision of the contract indicated that the New Orleans financial community, including Forstall, had learned a lesson from the experience of the Consolidated Association. The first property bank had to manage the transfer of funds from the sale of its bonds in London by selling 90-day sight drafts on Baring Brothers & Company in the American market. More often than not the bank failed to command the 8 percent premium necessary to spare it a loss on the exchange. With that example before it, the Union Bank insisted upon payment in America–in New York, Philadelphia, or New Orleans–making it the business of Baring Brothers and their agents to manage the exchange and absorb any loss.

The lack of Union Bank minutes makes it impossible to assess Forstall's continuing role, if any, in the Union Bank. In October 1834, in a letter to Thomas Baring, he remarked that the bank was doing a large and safe business and that it would probably develop into the most powerful bank in the United States in less than five years. The stock, he added, was scarce at 15 percent premium. In the same letter Forstall showed his interest in yet a

third property bank, the recently chartered Citizens' Bank of Louisiana, with a permitted capital of $12 million. Commissioners prepared to leave for England to attempt a sale of the new institution's bonds, and he had taken the liberty of giving a few lines of introduction to Baring to one of the commissioners, Charles Lesseps. Destined for the presidency of the Citizens' Bank, Forstall at that point had no official connection with it.

The charter of the Citizens' Bank dated from April 1, 1833, but not until March 23, 1835, did the directors choose Forstall to fill a vacancy on the board. Then they promptly appointed him chairman of the committee on exchange and a member of the committee to revise the rules. He was also charged with acquiring land for a banking house. Disappointed in the ability of Lesseps and his fellow commissioner, Dusuau Delacroix, to place the bank's bonds in Europe, the directors at the beginning of May revoked the commissioners' powers and appointed a committee of three, including Forstall, to suggest a new plan for the sale of the bonds. As in the case of the Consolidated Association, Forstall brought to the Citizens' Bank a knowledge of banking and the international money market that few, if any, other members of the board shared.

The committee delegated to place the bank's bonds prepared its report in three days. Members thought the failure of the commissioners' negotiations abroad could in no way affect a future sale of the bonds, for "a more favorable moment than the present has perhaps never presented itself for the disposal of American Stocks in Europe." The committee recommended the appointment of four new commissioners, any two of whom be empowered to act, to proceed immediately to Philadelphia and New York to offer the bonds to the leading houses in those places. Failing a sale in the United States, two commissioners should proceed to Europe to open negotiations with the capitalists of London, Paris, and Amsterdam. Having unanimously adopted the report, the board appointed the suggested commissioners, Forstall among them. Subsequently, the board voted them a commission of 2 percent on the first $3 million worth of bonds sold, 1 percent on $3 million to $6 million worth, and one-half on those more than $6 million. Thus, for the first time Forstall stood to gain financially from placing property bank bonds, for he had accepted no commission from either the Consolidated Association or the Union Bank.

The new commissioners placed no bonds in the North, and when they approached the London capital market they had no better luck than the earlier commissioners had had, despite Forstall's personal appeal to Thomas Baring. Forstall then went on to Amsterdam, where he was more successful. On September 1, 1835, acting for the commissioners, he signed a contract with Hope & Company, international bankers, for the sale of $3 million worth of Citizens' Bank bonds at par in London. Alexander Gordon, one of Forstall's fellow commissioners, later signed. On November 24 the bank's board of directors approved the contract unanimously. With exchange on London quoted in New Orleans at 9 percent premium, Forstall had made a good bargain, but the contract was a conditional one, dependent upon the Louisiana legislature's pledging the faith of the state for the payment of the bonds.

An earlier attempt on the part of the Citizens' Bank to obtain the state's pledge, as both the Consolidated Association and the Union Bank had succeeded in doing, had come to nothing. Now the directors appointed a committee that included Forstall to present the matter anew to the legislature.

Largely the work of Forstall, the bank's petition to the legislature pointed to the "happy precedents" that the legislature had set in pledging the state's faith to earlier issues of bank bonds. It suggested that the desired pledge in the present instance would subject the state to little or no risk, while giving life to "an institution calculated to promote the best and most important interest of our Country." It maintained that the experience of several years had demonstrated "the decided Superiority of Banks resting on the principles of the Citizens' Bank over . . . monied institutions differently organized," for in addition to the ample security that the property banks afforded, they introduced into the country the large amounts of foreign capital "so necessary to the full and rapid development of the great internal resources of our State." Finally, the petition urged the expediency of bringing the Citizens' Bank into immediate operation to ease "the almost unavoidable embarrassment which will follow the winding [up] of that Colossal institution," the Bank of the United States.

Despite opposition from enemies of the Citizens' Bank in the legislature, a bill pledging the state's backing of its bonds became law on January 30, 1836. On the same day the bank's directors met and, on the motion of Forstall, accepted the act. At the time John A. Merle was president of the bank, but Forstall had taken over the leadership of the board of directors. In March, when Merle refused to accept another term as president, Forstall was unanimously elected in his place. The bank then prepared to open for business.

Forstall was very conscientious as president of the bank, conceiving it as his duty to keep the terms of the bank's charter and bylaws, to hold sacred the bank's obligation to its bondholders, to insure that "the Bank abstain using her deposits, unless fully prepared to meet them under all circumstances," and always to subordinate the other business of the bank to its function as issuer of currency. Believing that bank-note currency had no value in itself, but merely represented gold or silver, he insisted that the Citizens' Bank should so conduct its business as to be always specie-paying. "I deemed it my first duty in putting the Citizens' Bank in movement," he later wrote, "to lay down as a fundamental rule,–That the Bank should hold at all times an amount of gold and silver equal to one third of its whole cash responsibilities, *id est: Deposits and Bank-money in circulation* and also short commercial paper, maturing in rapid succession so as to create a daily income, to the full extent of such responsibilities."

The Citizens' Bank, according to Forstall, divided its loans into two classes: first, loans "on short commercial paper, for the purpose of meeting the 2/3rds of deposits and bank-money unrepresented by gold and silver"; and second, long-term loans on the stock of the bank (as required by the charter), and on "accommodations for the furtherance of agriculture and industry. . . . The Loans of the first class were considered the movement of the Bank. The Loans of the second class, the dead weight."

A month before Forstall assumed the presidency of the bank F. de Lizardi & Company, the bank's London agents, notified the directors that Hope & Company had bought 3,375 more of the bank's bonds at face value ($1.5 million), and that the Amsterdam firm would remit one-third of the purchase price at the end of February, one-third at the end of April, and one-third at the end of May,

Etching of the Mississippi riverfront at New Orleans, 1850. Early in his career Forstall often went to the river to purchase cotton (courtesy of The Historic New Orleans Collection, 533 Royal Street, 1978.34).

or earlier. Secure in the knowledge of funds in Europe, the Citizens' Bank initiated exchange operations in New Orleans, drawing on both F. de Lizardi & Company and Lizardi Hermanos, the bank's agents in Paris.

Given the close ties between the Lizardi firms in Europe and Forstall's mercantile firm in New Orleans, it was probably unwise of Forstall to accept the presidency of the Citizens' Bank. That he saw no conflict, but rather a merging, of interest could not be doubted, but he provided his critics, of whom a man of his ebullient personality had many, with arguments to use against him when opportunity offered. Opportunity was not long in coming.

The financial crisis of 1837 hit New Orleans in March, bringing down a number of commercial houses. In May, 14 New Orleans banks suspended specie payments. The Citizens' Bank was not among them, but nonetheless rumors began to circulate in the city that the bank had lent Lizardis of London the $1.5 million that Hope & Company had paid for the bonds that the Dutch firm had taken earlier in the year. The amount, critics alleged, had secretly been placed in the account of F. de Lizardi & Company to cover its debts to the Amsterdam bankers. At Forstall's insistence the Citizens' Bank directors ordered an investigation of the affairs of the bank, including the negotiating of the bonds in ques-

tion and the state of the accounts with "Messrs Lizardis of this place, of London, and of Paris and the nature of the transactions of said Houses with this Bank." The committee reported no irregularity in either the sale of the bonds or the accounts of the Lizardi firms with the bank, but this hardly meant the end of Forstall's problems.

On June 29, according to the Citizens' Bank minutes, he begged the permission of the directors "to express disapprobation of the extraordinary and unaccountable conduct" of the bank's agents in London and Paris. News had just arrived that Lizardi Hermanos had refused to honor the bank's bills of exchange, claiming that the bank had no credit in its account with the firm. Subsequently F. de Lizardi & Company confessed that it had failed to keep the Paris house in funds as it promised to do by the terms of its agreement with the bank. Rather, the London firm had used the credits from Hope to honor the drafts of American correspondents during the London financial crisis of April and early May, counting on remittances from America to restore the bank's account. The remittances failed to arrive. An embarrassed Forstall offered to resign from the presidency of the bank, but the directors, doubtless fearing that his withdrawal at that time would further damage the bank's reputation both at home and abroad, refused his resignation.

In the early summer information arrived in New Orleans that Lizardi Hermanos again had funds from London and since the end of May had been honoring the bank's bills. It was also learned that the Lizardis were about to dissolve their Paris partnership. Not waiting upon that event, the Citizens' Bank changed its Paris agency to Andre & Cottier, and instructed F. de Lizardi & Company to keep the new agency in funds to cover the bank's drafts on it.

Meanwhile, local criticism of the Citizens' Bank continued. The bank, it was alleged, was refusing to expand its loans for the relief of hard-pressed debtors and to cooperate with the city's other banks in alleviating the community's financial distress. Given Forstall's conservative stance, there was doubtless truth in the first allegation, but the second lacked firm foundation. Forstall expressed a willingness to cooperate, but not to compromise his principles. According to the *New Orleans Bee* the ill will directed at the bank arose from its being "a Creole institution"—a reflection of the persisting split between the "Americans" in Louisiana and the persons of French and Spanish background whose families had resided there before the Louisiana Purchase.

Evidence exists that not all the community's ire in 1837 and 1838 was directed against the bank alone, but some of it against Forstall personally. At least he complained that of all the commercial houses in New Orleans, the city's banks forced only his to take up its paper in full (more than $800,000 worth from March to October 1837), while the banks renewed the paper of other houses every 60 days, minus only 10 percent. Moreover, rumors circulated that Forstall drew an exorbitant salary as president of the bank. (It was, in fact, $3,000 a year.)

While Citizens' Bank bonds continued to sell in Europe during the summer of 1837 and into 1838, the events of March and April 1837 continued to reverberate in the affairs of the bank and of the Lizardi firms in New Orleans and London. To honor the drafts of their American correspondents, F. de Lizardi & Company, in addition to using the funds of the Citizens' Bank that it had in hand, had sold 1,175 of the bank's bonds below the limits set by the bank and had borrowed £43,000 from the Bank of England on protested bills that were the property of the Citizens' Bank. At the same time, to meet anticipated demands on the bank incident

upon the protest of the bank's bills in Paris, the bank held in New Orleans specie it intended to reimburse to F. de Lizardi & Company for a portion of the bank's drafts on the London firm. Still, F. de Lizardi & Company owed a large sum to the bank and, to settle the account, in October 1837 contracted to buy 1,500 of the bank's bonds, paying for them at 6, 9, and 12 months. M. de Lizardi & Company guaranteed payment. The company met the first installment but not the second, even though the bank had granted an extension of time. In September 1838 the bank withdrew its London agency from Lizardis, transferring it to Reid, Irving & Company.

Forstall, meanwhile, was losing the confidence of a majority of the bank's directors. By the end of August his position had become untenable, and on the 31st he resigned as director and president. His differences with the directors seemed to arise from his dual position as president of the bank and New Orleans agent of F. de Lizardi & Company, but Emile Philippe Grenier, whose Ph.D. dissertation of 1942 is the starting point for anyone who seeks to understand property banks, maintained that in reality the board's animosity arose from Forstall's insistence upon strict and regular operation of the bank following the Panic of 1837, when the business community demanded an expansion of credit. During his tenure as president Forstall had regularly lectured the board on good, that is, conservative, banking practices, and his lengthy letter of resignation was a final instruction on the way to run the bank. Less than a month after his resignation, according to Forstall, he refused an appeal from "a large and respectable majority" of the stockholders to resume the presidency of the bank.

Early in 1839 a committee of stockholders, appointed by the directors to investigate the general situation of the bank and more particularly the change of agencies in London and Paris, published its report, along with pertinent documents. Only then were the full details of the Forstall-Lizardi operations revealed. The gist of the report suggested that while the general affairs of the bank were in good order, the directors had acted wisely in changing the London agent. The report ignored the change of agent in Paris, probably because Lizardi Hermanos had passed into liquidation.

Reelected to the bank's board in February 1839, Forstall served actively for at least a year. At the end of 1840 and for six months into 1841 he traveled in Europe as the bank's confidential agent, charged with selling its remaining bonds. In that he was only minimally successful, for the demand for American bonds in Europe remained low, but he increased his knowledge of European capital markets.

In the early 1840s the Citizens' Bank was poorly managed. In May 1842 rumors of its insolvency, in part the result of unwise loans to cotton speculators, caused a run on the bank. After having resumed specie payments following the general suspension of 1839 the bank again suspended on May 30, 1842. At the beginning of August the state's attorney general brought suit for forfeiture of the bank's charter. He charged that the bank failed to keep on hand the required specie to back its circulation, that it had exceeded the permissible limits on its long-term loans, and that it had not settled its balances with other banks as prescribed by law. On October 25 a decree of the district court declared the bank's charter forfeit. Governor Román appointed Forstall president of the bank's Board of Managers, whose duty it was, in accordance with state law, to oversee the bank's liquidation. Working 18 hours a day, Forstall thoroughly investigated the bank's condition, only to be removed from office in March 1843 by "a locofoco [that is, a Democratic] administration." Later the state restored the Citizens' Bank charter, and the bank survived into the twentieth century.

In December 1838 Forstall and his partners had agreed to dissolve their New Orleans commercial concern, with the terminal illness of Miguel de Lizardi perhaps the deciding factor. Liquidation of the firm proved complicated, for in addition to the intermixture of its affairs with those of the Citizens' Bank, the individual partners, or the firm, or both had interests in the Red River Rail Road Company, the Louisiana Sugar Refining Company, the North Levee Steam Cotton Press, and the Tobacco Warehouse Company—all of which had to be disentangled. The Forstalls, for reasons unknown, were deeply indebted to the Lizardis. New Orleans notarial records and the Citizens' Bank minutes for the 1840s include many entries concerned with the settlements between the former M. de Lizardi & Company and its debtors and creditors, and between the Forstalls and the Lizardis. As late as 1843 Edmond Forstall made what he hoped was a final offer to the heirs of Miguel de Lizardi, confessing to a correspondent that until he received the Lizardis' response he would be in "a complete Purgatory." His

A Forstall home in New Orleans (Louisiana Collection, Tulane University Library, New Orleans.

entire fortune went into the settlement. During those trying years the Forstall brothers continued their commission business under the rubric of E. J. Forstall & Company.

In 1843 the property banks and the state moved to repudiate the bank bonds that Forstall had been so highly instrumental in selling in Europe a decade earlier. Feeling that his honor was involved, he bent his efforts to reversing the repudiation. He lobbied in the state legislature and in Washington, wrote countless letters and pamphlets, went to Europe to negotiate terms with the foreign bondholders, and bore the calumny heaped upon him by Louisiana debtors. His campaign was successful, for by the end of the decade most of the bonds had been paid off or renegotiated, and Forstall had earned the respect of European bankers. As a direct result he became the New Orleans agent of both Baring Brothers & Company of London and Hope & Company of Amsterdam, buying cotton on their account, managing their exchange business, and overseeing their other interests in the city. That entailed keeping an eye on the property banks, but Forstall promised that in the future he would remain free of mercantile and financial commitments on his own account, confining himself entirely to the commission business. That ended his banking career, for his agreements with the Barings and Hopes continued until his death in 1873.

A second and perhaps more significant dimension of Forstall's association with banking paralleled his active service in the banks. That was his contribution to banking legislation. Elected to the Louisiana House of Representatives in the summer of 1836, while president of the Citizens' Bank, Forstall was appointed a member of the joint committee of the House and Senate charged with investigating the financial institutions of the state. Such a joint committee was appointed at each session but had been a mere form prior to Forstall's service on that of 1836-1837, when, as the *New Orleans Bee* (December 15, 1837) put it, "the examination of the banks was conducted in a systematic and rigorous manner that admitted of no concealment or evasion." Forstall wrote the committee's report, which, the *Bee* averred, "was drawn up with a clearness and amplitude of elucidation that would have done honour to any financial officer of any country." That report constituted the genesis of the Louisiana Bank Act of 1842.

The report of 1837 advocated what Forstall regarded as the "fundamental rules" of good banking. First, it called for fractional specie reserves against a bank's total cash liabilities (that is, bank note circulation and deposits), not circulation alone, as was the policy of many, if not most, banks at that time. Second, the report urged that banks restrict loans that sustained their liabilities to advances on short-term commercial paper, "payable on a fixed day, and moving in a rapid circle," for even the most secure long-term paper was of no use to a bank in meeting its debts that were payable on demand. With that report Forstall began his crusade to hold all the banks of Louisiana to the principles that he practiced as president of the

Citizens' Bank, principles that he thought embodied the essence of sound banking.

The financial crisis of 1837 and the resultant call for reform banking legislation provided Forstall with a further opportunity to lobby his point of view. "In 1838," he wrote to Ward a decade later (February 11, 1847), "I presented a law, as member of the H[ouse] of R[epresentatives], which I believed would have saved our Banking Institutions." Incorporating the principle of set specie reserves against both currency and deposits, and providing for a three-man Board of Currency to supervise the execution of its provisions, the bill, according to Forstall, "was opposed by the whole commerce of New Orleans. . . . [S]till I succeeded after a battle of 60 days in passing it through both Houses of the Legislature." The merchants of New Orleans opposed the bill for the same reason that Forstall was squeezed out of the presidency of the Citizens' Bank later that year. The community needed easier, not more restricted, credit. Doubting the constitutionality of one or more of the bill's provisions, Governor Edward D. White vetoed it. Not until 1842, when Forstall no longer served in the legislature, did a bill based upon the principles of his report of 1837 become law.

Bipartisan political support greeted the bank bills of 1838 and 1842. The legislative and public debates of 1838 would seem to mark the Democrats as the party favoring the restrictive banking legislation advocated by Forstall. By implication, at least, the Whigs emerged as advocates of freer banking. A predominantly Democratic House of Representatives voted overwhelmingly in favor of the bank bill, though not strictly along party lines, and a Whig governor vetoed it. But the Senate passed it unanimously, and seven of the thirteen senators who voted to override the governor's veto were members of his own party. Forstall himself changed his affiliation from the Democratic to the Whig party in 1837 or early 1838 but did not regard his party allegiance as a reason for changing his opinion concerning the way to run banks.

The vote on the Bank Act of 1842 was even less clearly a party matter than that on the bank bill of 1838. The Senate in 1842 had a Democratic majority of one, while the House was made up of twenty-eight Whigs and twenty-two Democrats. The ten senators (five Democrats, three Whigs, and two men of unknown party) who voted on the final version of the bill unanimously favored it. In the

House, where the bill carried by a vote of 29 to 13, more Whigs than Democrats opposed it, but almost as many Whigs as Democrats favored it, and without the Whig votes the bill could not have passed. Moreover, Albert Hoa, a Whig, introduced the bill into the Senate, and Governor Román, also a Whig, approved it. Sometime later a eulogist claimed for Solomon W. Downs, the Democratic chairman of the Senate Finance Committee in 1842, the credit for the bank act of that year, but added that the law was "the old project of 1838," that is, Forstall's bill.

Forstall's role in the legislative struggle that preceded the passage of the Bank Act of 1842 is not precisely known, but surely it was an important one. He was a passionate man with a firm belief that there was a right way–his way–to conduct a bank and to insure the stability of a banking system. He willingly worked hard for the adoption of his ideas, and he was not without political influence. In January 1842 he served as secretary of a public meeting in New Orleans held in support of the pending bank measure. An old friend of Senator Hoa, he enjoyed ties of kinship with Governor Román. To assume that both men listened to him is not to assume too much. An observer once remarked (in connection with another matter and at another time) that Forstall's exertions to impress "the truth" upon "the officers of government, and upon the members of both Houses" had "amazing" effectiveness. The hard times of the early 1840s caused men of both parties to be receptive to a change in banking laws. In those circumstances they accepted Forstall's fundamental rules.

The rules that the Bank Act of 1842 prescribed for Louisiana's chartered banks were the rules that Forstall had laid down for the Citizens' Bank in 1836: the division of loans into two classes, "the movement of the bank" and "the dead weight"; and the requirement that a bank hold specie reserves to the amount of one-third of its deposits and note issue, as well as short-term commercial paper to the full extent of its cash liabilities.

Linked with Forstall's faith in his fundamental rules was his insistence upon accountability of the banks to the people of the state. In commenting upon the refusal of two New Orleans banks to reply to a legislative inquiry of 1837, he wrote: "The readiness on the part of the monied institutions to meet such inquiry, is in itself . . . the surest pledge and guarantee of the soundness of the princi-

ples on which these establishments are conducted, and of the fidelity with which the duties confided to the directors are performed." Doubtless his unsuccessful efforts as president of the Citizens' Bank to persuade the Louisiana banks to cooperate with and to control each other buttressed his conviction that the state should exercise control. The bank bill of 1838 provided for a Board of Currency, appointed by the governor, to oversee the administration of the bill's provisions. That idea carried over into the Bank Act of 1842, in which the powers given to the Board of Currency were both supervisory and investigative. The act's insistence upon the strict accountability of the banks to the state, no less than the provisions governing bank liabilities, showed Forstall's influence on the legislation.

Not even Forstall's staunchest admirers could claim for him originality of thought. His ideas about banking grew out of his wide study of earlier and contemporary financial institutions and out of his experience in the banking community of New Orleans. He was proud of his accumulated knowledge and often cited his sources–the writings of Albert Gallatin, the histories of the Bank of England, the Bank of France, and the "ancient Bank of Amsterdam." Long before 1842, and even before 1837, the essentially conservative New Orleans bankers advocated the practice of holding fixed specie reserves against cash liabilities.

In 1847 Forstall described for a friend the financial chaos in which the Bank Act of 1842 had taken shape: "The Banks were prostrated, public and private credit was ruined–repudiation tacit or open was making rapid progress in the public mind. . . . I threw myself to the rescue," he added, "and succeeded in obtaining the Bank laws of 1842." Thus he claimed entire credit not only for the act of February 5 but for a cluster of subsequent laws as well.

Anyone who knows that a piece of major legislation is of necessity the result of many political deals and compromises may be amused at Forstall's pretensions, but his neighbors and acquaintances appeared to agree with him. At least he was a very unpopular man in New Orleans in the mid 1840s. How much of that unpopularity stemmed from the businessmen's belief in his responsibility for the restrictive banking legislation (which had as its immediate effects the tightening of credit and the liquidation of banks unable to conform to the fundamental rules); how much from his strenuous efforts

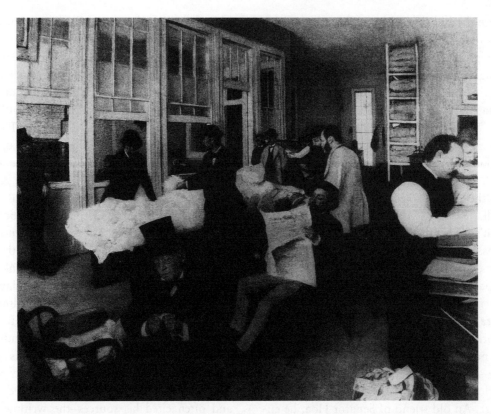

Edgar Degas's 1873 painting, The Cotton Market, New Orleans, *showing the character of the cotton-buying operations in which Forstall engaged toward the end of his career (courtesy of the Museum of Pau, France)*

to thwart repudiation of the property bank bonds (in which he was seen as an agent of foreign capitalists); and how much from the doubtless annoying officiousness with which he carried out his duties as president of the Board of Managers of the Citizens' Bank, is now impossible to say. When the Board of Managers removed him, an action that he saw as politically motivated, the new administration willingly continued in office four other managers of the Citizens' Bank and those of the Consolidated Association, all of whom had been named by the preceding administration. Apprised of this, Samuel Labouchere, a Hope & Company partner, wrote sadly from Amsterdam, "It is evident that the hostility is chiefly directed against said friend [that is, Forstall]."

In 1847 Forstall claimed that the laws of 1842 had lifted the banks of Louisiana "from a state of complete prostration to their former efficiency, and are now the strongest Banks in the Union." He added that his own work in bringing about this happy situation "remained thankless." But in 1853, when the Louisiana legislature was considering a free banking bill, he was called to testify as an authority on the earlier bank law. In 1877,

four years after his death, *Bankers' Magazine* learned from "old bank officers in New Orleans" that Forstall had been "the gentleman most influential in framing the act of 1842."

Historians, for the most part, have accepted the opinion of the old bank officers and long agreed with *Bankers' Magazine* as to the outstanding merits of "Forstall's" bank act. William Graham Sumner, in his *History of Banking in the United States,* published in 1896, wrote of the Louisiana act that "it may justly be regarded as one of the most ingenious and intelligent acts in the history of legislation about banking." Bray Hammond, writing in 1957, echoed that opinion. Fritz Redlich devoted an entire chapter of his *Molding of American Banking* (1951) to the Louisiana act, pointing out that it was the first law in America that aimed at both a specie basis for currency and at liquidity and elasticity, "the prerequisites of what came to be considered sound banking in modern times."

But a younger generation of historians has taken a new look at the famous Louisiana bank act and has come to different conclusions. Robert Roeder, who has studied the commercial community of antebellum New Orleans, regards the act of 1842 as a mixed blessing. He suggests that while it provided for greater stability in the banking system, the price was high in the form of a contracted volume of credit and a consequent retardation of commerce and manufacturing.

George D. Green, in his *Finance and Economic Development in the Old South: Louisiana Banking, 1804-1861* (1972), analyzes the entire act and is sharply critical of it, including Forstall's fundamental rules. While loans on commercial paper were safe in times of prosperity, Green argues, they proved disastrous when whole communities were unable to meet their obligations. A currency based in part on such loans expanded in good times and contracted in bad, thus reinforcing the swings of the business cycle. Two other reforms written into the act Green sees as "a popular alternative" to the fundamental rules and the Board of Currency: "frequent publicizing of the financial condition of the banks, and weekly settlements in specie of any balances accumulated between banks as they received each other's notes during the routine course of business." Rather than viewing those measures as alternatives to his fundamental rules, Forstall doubtless saw them as reinforcements of his rules. They were embedded in the bill of 1838, and he had long advocated interbank specie settlements. While more popular than the fundamental rules, according to Green, "the settlement rule was no more a foolproof regulator of the money supply than was Forstall's commercial paper rule," for "if all banks expanded their issues together at about the same rate . . . settlement of specie balances would do little to prevent inflationary money issues."

Larry Schweikart in his *Banking in the American South from the Age of Jackson to Reconstruction* (1987) shows how the act of 1842 played into the hands of Louisiana's antibank Democrats. After its passage restrictive bank sentiment grew in the state. The Constitution of 1845 entirely prohibited the chartering or rechartering of banks, thus limiting the state's incorporated banks to those already established, but by 1853 tight credit prompted the Louisiana legislature to pass a free banking act.

While the legislature debated the free banking bill, Forstall did all that he could to urge the incorporation into it of his fundamental rules. But following the lead of New York, Louisiana's Free Bank Act required that currency issues be backed by government bonds—in the case of Louisiana by state

and municipal bonds. Deposits remained under the reserve requirements of the Bank Act of 1842: specie equal to at least one-third of the bank's liabilities, and short-term commercial paper equal to the remainder. Forstall was initially pleased with the act but later criticized the use of government bonds to back bank notes, since it tied circulation to the availability of such bonds and therefore failed to respond to the needs of business.

The comparative stability of the New Orleans banks during the Panic of 1857 was widely, if wrongly, credited to the strict reserve requirements under Louisiana law. Debates in both the New York and Massachusetts legislatures took note of the Louisiana experience. Partly through the influence of Samuel Hooper, a Boston merchant, banker, legislator, and admirer of the Louisiana banking system, legislators wrote reserve requirements similar to those of that state into the Massachusetts Bank Law of 1858. The *New Orleans Times* noted the influence of Forstall's ideas in the national banking legislation of 1863, and it was no coincidence that Hooper was then a member of the federal House Banking Committee.

Forstall's personal fortunes changed abruptly for the better upon the death of his aunt, Lise Forstall Poeyfarré, in 1845. At that time he acquired his sugar plantation in St. James Parish, on the Mississippi, 64 miles north of New Orleans, and from that time until his death he seems to have had no severe financial problems. Besides his income from his estate, which he estimated at $35,000 to $40,000 annually, he received $2,000 a year from Hope & Company, and beginning in 1849, £1000 sterling a year from Baring Brothers, plus commissions on any business that he transacted for the two houses. In addition, Baring Brothers put him in the way of other business, which, with their own, according to a Baring partner, brought him $20,000 to $30,000 annually.

When in the early 1850s Baring Brothers took an interest in transacting payment of the indemnity that the United States owed Mexico for the annexation of territory following the Mexican War, Forstall went to Mexico three times as the London firm's agent, spending a month there in 1850 and six months each in 1851 and 1852. The first time he arrived in Mexico City to find that an agent of Rothschild's had preceded him, but in the latter two years he arranged the transfer of millions of dollars, working under great difficulties. When leaving

Mexico in 1852 he accompanied a *conducta* (a military caravan) that transported silver for the payment of British holders of Mexican bonds from Mexico City to Vera Cruz and saw the silver safely aboard ship for transport to England.

Although nothing pleased Forstall more than immersion in business affairs, he was a person of wide interests. When in Paris in 1841 as agent of the Citizens' Bank, and while negotiating on his own account with the Lizardis, he spent many hours in the French archives searching out records of early Louisiana. He helped to revive the Louisiana Historical Society in the 1840s and also supported local educational institutions. In 1842, before he was himself a sugar planter, he spent six months in Washington lobbying for a sugar tariff. During the busiest years of his life he frequently wrote articles on banking, sugar planting, and the tariff for the *New Orleans Bee, DeBow's Review,* and the *National Intelligencer.*

After the mid 1840s Forstall divided his time between New Orleans and his plantation. Steamboats were numerous on the Mississippi, and the trip between the two places took only five to nine hours, depending upon the season of the year, the number of stops, and the direction of travel. Just prior to receiving the Baring agency, Forstall moved his family from New Orleans to the St. James estate. When the family returned to the city in 1849 they settled in a house on Carondelet Street, which Forstall subsequently purchased from the Barings. In 1857 the Forstalls established themselves in a newly built residence on St. Louis Street. Designed by James Gallier, a well-known New Orleans architect, the house still stands.

During the Civil War, Forstall continued to manage the affairs of Baring Brothers and of Hope & Company in New Orleans, and in so doing ran afoul of Gen. Benjamin F. Butler, who, after New Orleans fell to the Union on May 1, 1862, took command of the city. In February of that year the Citizens' Bank had entrusted $800,000 in Mexican silver dollars to Forstall, as agent for Hope & Company. The money was destined for payment of interest on Citizens' Bank bonds held in Europe. Forstall placed the funds under the protection of the Dutch consul, but Butler sequestered the silver, together with other contents of the vault that had been deposited in it for safekeeping, on the ground that some of the vault's holdings belonged to citizens in rebellion. Subsequently Butler released the

$800,000, but not before the episode had become a cause célèbre in the foreign community of New Orleans and had found its way into the annals of New Orleans under occupation.

Because of his sugar estate, Forstall suffered heavy losses in the war, including his equity in more than 130 slaves, but he was not prostrated financially as he had been after the Panic of 1837. In 1865, for the purpose of levying the direct tax that Congress had decreed for "insurrectionary districts," Forstall's city property was valued at $61,000 and his St. James estate at $85,000. Those surely represented low appraisals, for earlier the plantation was said to be worth in excess of $300,000. In 1864 one of Forstall's sons wrote to another son, "Papa sings poverty more than ever—I pray God never to make me poorer than he is."

In 1865, when he was seventy-one, Forstall wrote to the Barings that in view of the large interests passing through his hands he thought it wise to associate with himself in his agency and commission business his sons Oscar and Ernest and his son-in-law, Adolph Schreiber. The new firm was known as Edmond J. Forstall & Sons. Gradually after that he released responsibility for his commercial affairs to his younger partners.

As he freed himself from his urban concerns, Forstall spent more and more time on his plantation. In 1867 he formally claimed it as his domicile. His new sugar mill was described as one of the best in Louisiana. To keep a close eye on the processing of the cane, he had a room built for himself adjacent to the mill, and there he died of what the *New Orleans Bee* described as an inflammation of the lungs, early on Sunday morning, November 16, 1873, in his eightieth year. The Archbishop of New Orleans conducted the funeral rites, and the body was entombed in St. Louis Cemetery No. 2 in New Orleans.

Although Forstall in his last years was more planter than man of business, he never lost interest in banking. As late as 1871, in a letter to the Barings, he wrote almost ten pages on the affairs of the Citizens' Bank, of which he clearly had intimate knowledge. By that time the antebellum banking system of Louisiana was widely admired and Forstall's role in forming it generally recognized. Italian senator Guilio Adamoli, who visited New Orleans in 1867, described Forstall as "a prominent banker," a clue perhaps to his reputation among his peers.

As banker and lawmaker Forstall had earned a place in nineteenth-century banking history.

Publications:

An Analytical Index of the Whole of the Public Documents Relative to Louisiana Deposited in the Archives of the Department "De la Marine et des Colonies" at Paris (New Orleans, 1841);

Agricultural Productions of Louisiana, Embracing Valuable Information Relative to the Cotton, Sugar and Molasses Interests, and the Effects upon the Same of the Tariff of 1842 (New Orleans, 1845).

References:

George D. Green, *Finance and Economic Development in the Old South: Louisiana Banking, 1804-1861* (Stanford: Stanford University Press, 1972);

Emile Philippe Grenier, "Property Banks in Louisiana," Ph.D. dissertation, Louisiana State University, 1942;

Bray Hammond, *Banks and Politics in America from the Revolution to the Civil War* (Princeton: Princeton University Press, 1957);

Leonard C. Helderman, *National and State Banks: A Study of Their Origins* (Boston: Houghton Mifflin, 1931);

Ralph W. Hidy, *The House of Baring in American Trade and Finance: English Merchant Bankers at Work, 1763-1861* (Cambridge, Mass.: Harvard University Press, 1949);

Irene D. Neu, "Edmond Jean Forstall and Louisiana Banking," *Explorations in Economic History*, 7 (Summer 1970): 383-398;

Fritz Redlich, *The Molding of American Banking: Men and Ideas*, volume 2 (New York: Hafner, 1951);

Larry Schweikart, *Banking in the American South from the Age of Jackson to Reconstruction* (Baton Rouge: Louisiana State University Press, 1987).

Archives:

Material on Edmond J. Forstall can be found in the Baring Brothers & Company Papers in the Public Record Office, Ottawa (microfilm copies are in the National Archives, Washington, D.C.); the archives of Baring Brothers & Company, London; the Canal Bank Collection (including the minute books of the Citizens' Bank of Louisiana), Tulane University, New Orleans; the Consolidated Association of the Planters of Louisiana Collection, Department of Archives and Manuscripts, Louisiana State University, Baton Rouge; the Hope & Company Records in the archives of Hope & Mees, Amsterdam; and the Thomas Wren Ward Papers, Massachusetts Historical Society, Boston.

Fractional Reserve Banking *(see* Deposits, Reserves, and Fractional Reserve Banking*)*

Free Banking and Wildcat Banking

by Hugh Rockoff

Rutgers University

For more than two decades, from the expiration of the charter of the Second Bank of the United States (BUS) in 1836 to the passage of the National Banking Act in 1863, the regulation of banking in the United States was left to the states. The federal government tried (without complete success) to divorce itself completely from the banking system through the Independent Treasury System, under which the federal government was supposed to transact its business only in gold or silver, leaving the private sector to deal with banks. That period was unique. Under the First and Second Banks of the United States, under the National Banking Act, and of course under the modern system inaugurated by the establishment of the Federal Reserve in 1913, the federal government has had a major role in banking.

The period is known to financial historians as the Free Banking Era. While the term has suggested complete laissez-faire to laymen and even to a few historians, in fact free banking had a very specific and limited meaning. It referred to the free banking laws, which, with minor although significant variations, were adopted by many states in those years. The standard free banking law contained two provisions that distinguished it from other contemporary forms of bank regulation. First, the law provided that any group able to raise a certain amount of capital would automatically receive a bank charter. That contrasted sharply with the older system of chartered banking, in which a special legislative act was required to start a bank. Thus, free banking assured free entry. The charter system was characterized by a tendency to grant charters to established interests and on occasion by corruption of the legislature. It is not surprising, therefore, that free banking was especially popular in the rapidly developing frontier areas of the West.

Second, the free banking law provided that banks could issue notes to circulate as hand-to-hand currency, but such currency had to be backed by specified government bonds (or in a few cases other securities), generally of equal or greater value than the notes issued. The banks deposited those bonds with a state authority. In the event the bank failed to redeem its notes on demand, the authority would sell the bonds and redeem the notes. Since bank notes constituted a substantial portion of the money supply, that was far from a trivial requirement. Under most traditional bank charters banks were somewhat freer in the assets they could choose to back their notes. They could, for example, hold the short-term unsecured business loans typical of the period. So in that respect the free banking law proved more restrictive than traditional charters. The law, in other words, was based on a conscious decision to balance the reduced safety of the banks against the increased safety for note holders (but not shareholders or depositors) provided by the bond security system.

The law gave note holders more protection than other investors in a bank because note holders had limited control over the character of the notes they held. In the course of a transaction someone might accept, perhaps without noticing, a note from a distant and unfamiliar bank. It might be mixed with other, more familiar, notes. Should the unfamiliar bank fail, the note holder would normally have no recourse against the person who had given him the note. A mechanism existed for handling that problem. In magazinelike publications called bank note reporters, merchants and others involved in trade could find the prices (percentage discounts) prevailing for various notes. By checking in such a reporter one could determine what allowance to make for the fact that the note had strayed far from home or that the bank that issued it was in financial difficulty. Nevertheless, the protection provided by that mechanism was imperfect. Since the character of a bank could change quickly with little outward sign, even the bank note reporters

Antebellum cartoon expressing public antipathy toward wildcat banking

could supply only approximate information. Depositors and shareholders, on the other hand, were assumed to be making an informed decision. Moreover, it was thought that notes were more likely to be held by the poor or middle classes, while deposits and common stocks were considered investments of the wealthy.

It did not go unnoticed by the states passing free banking laws that by forcing banks to back their notes with government bonds they would strengthen the market for those bonds. Many states therefore made their own bonds one of the eligible securities, if not the only one, creating a conflict of interest for the legislature. On the one hand, reducing the amount of notes a bank could issue for a given amount of collateral made the bank notes safer; on the other hand, increasing the number of notes, within certain limits, might strengthen the market for a state's bonds. Limiting the range of assets in which a bank could invest with the funds generated by note issue increased certain risks. State bonds hardly constituted perfectly safe assets in this period. States could and did default on their bonds. A

random event, large deficits in the state budget for example, perhaps caused by an unexpected decline in tax revenues, had the potential to damage the credit of the state and with it the integrity of the state's banking system.

It is important to emphasize that banking was free only in contrast with the system of state chartering then the norm, and only with respect to entry. Restrictions in addition to the bond security provision applied to free banks as well as other banks. Banks had to redeem deposits and bank notes on demand in specie. Indeed, under free banking the law called upon state authorities to sell immediately all the bonds deposited and redeem all the notes, if even one note came to the state authority because a bank failed to redeem it. Banks could not protect themselves against runs by issuing notes that contained a clause permitting the bank to delay payment in the event of an emergency. Immediate redemption on demand tended to make the system as a whole unstable. In addition bank loan rates were subject to the state usury laws. Finally, banks could not invest directly in real estate.

The adoption of free banking was not a uniform process. New York, Michigan, and Georgia adopted free banking laws shortly after Andrew Jackson sealed the fate of the Second BUS. The movement then lost momentum until the 1850s, when several states adopted the law, notably Ohio in 1851 and Louisiana (in a modified form) in 1853. The free banking movement comprised part of a general economic and banking expansion. Legislatures were overwhelmed with applications to start new banks, and free banking laws were one answer. Another was simply to grant charters in the old way, but more freely. A more liberal chartering policy, moreover, was one way the legislature could defuse the pressure for a free banking law. In short the free banking movement was part of a great expansion in the banking system, but there were several causes for this expansion (including the discovery of gold in California and Australia), and the role of free banking itself was complex.

The movement toward free banking remained strong and perhaps gathered speed as the Civil War approached. The National Banking Act was in some ways simply a free banking law for the nation as a whole, although the conditions of entry do not seem to have been as free in practice as they were intended to be. In calling for a national system, President Abraham Lincoln and his secretary of the

Treasury, Salmon P. Chase, argued that bond-secured notes issued by private banks would provide the type of currency most congenial to America's economic and political system. The national system provided even greater safety and uniformity than the state systems that had gone before. The national system also strengthened the market for federal bonds and provided a currency for certain western states whose systems had suffered because they were based on bonds issued in the South. The adoption of the national banking system, far from a rejection of free banking, affirmed it.

In some cases, however, free banking produced wildcat banking, one of the most romantic and least understood manifestations in American banking history. Wildcat banking was a rare phenomenon. It appears to have happened for brief periods after the introduction of free banking in Michigan, Indiana, and Minnesota, and on a few other occasions, although authorities disagree on whether all of those cases can legitimately be called wildcat banking. Some authors contend that independent events that undermined the value of the stocks being deposited as backing for the bonds explain the high rates of bank failure in some of these states.

Consider how wildcat banking might happen. Suppose that the securities required as collateral for bank notes could be had for less or only slightly more than the value of the notes to be issued on them. Then the possibility for some profitable but highly unstable banking existed. To take the simplest case, if bonds sold for, say, $95 and notes could be issued on them to the tune of $100, then it would be simple enough to take $95, purchase some bonds, issue $100 in notes, invest $95 in more bonds, issue $100 in notes, and so on. On each round our wildcat banker would make a profit of $5. Even if the bonds sold for more than $100, our wildcat banker could still use the note issue to leverage the purchase of a large mass of bonds. Once the bank failed, and the note holder had been paid from the deposited bonds, he could presumably still sue the bank for the remainder, but in practice such a suit probably proved futile.

Finding people to buy such notes was a problem, and many attempts at wildcat banking proved unsuccessful simply because no one could be found to take the notes at par. Of course such a game was likely to meet with more success in a relatively unsophisticated community, and then only the first

time around. That may be part of the reason why wildcat banking was more frequent in the West than in the eastern financial centers. And the requirement that the notes be redeemable in specie on demand was also a problem for the potential wildcatter. The more specie held in reserve, the longer the bank could expect to survive, but the lower its profits were. Wildcat banks typically held very little specie. Instead, they relied on the practice of operating in out-of-the-way places to forestall redemption as long as possible. One story, probably apocryphal, is that wildcat bankers got their name from their tendency to locate in unsettled land where wildcats still roamed. The wildcat bankers were not necessarily engaged in legal fraud, although many broke various laws. But they did mislead the public.

Free banking, it should be emphasized, typically did not produce such disasters. If the legislature made the collateral requirements strict enough, it would not pay to try to turn a quick profit through wildcatting. Indeed, if the collateral requirements (or other restrictions) were made too tight, it might not pay to set up free banks at all, as happened in some states. Frequently an experience with wildcat banking led to a tightening of the collateral requirements. Even in the rare cases of wildcat banking themselves it must be noted that losses were seldom as high as some historical accounts have presumed. Remember that the wildcat banker hoped to profit from the opportunity to leverage the purchase of a large mass of securities, or in the extreme case to profit from small gaps between the value of notes and the value of bonds held as collateral. In the end, the holder of a note might lose nothing (except for the inconvenience of having to redeem the note) or at most a few cents on the dollar. Many of the losses under free banking occurred not because of wildcat banking but rather a decline in the value of the underlying securities.

Most of the time the advantages of free banking outweighed the problems of wildcatting. Free banking meant equality of opportunity. No longer were political connections required to enter banking. That constituted no small issue in an era characterized by rapid immigration, massive internal migration, and the breakdown of old party structures and the emergence of new ones. For another, free banking may have led to an improved allocation of bank capital, although the evidence on this point is still far from clear. It was true in the West, where rapid economic growth made it difficult to forecast the areas that would need banking facilities. But it was also true in the East. During the free banking era New York City shouldered its way past Boston and Philadelphia to become the nation's and one of the world's leading financial centers. Determining the exact role of free banking in that process is difficult. Presumably New York's role in the dispersal of midwestern agricultural products would have assured it a major position in any case. But it also seems likely that free banking influenced the pace at which the city emerged.

References:
Hugh Rockoff, *The Free Banking Era: A Re-examination* (New York: Arno, 1975);

Arthur Rolnick and Warren Weber, "Free Banking, Wildcat Banking, and Shinplasters," *Federal Reserve Bank of Minneapolis Quarterly Review*, 6 (Fall 1982): 10-19.

Albert Gallatin

(January 29, 1761-August 12, 1849)

by B. R. Burg

Arizona State University

Albert Gallatin (courtesy of the National Archives, Brady Collection)

CAREER: Merchant, Boston, Massachusetts (1780-1783); tutor, Harvard College (1781); merchant, farmer, manufacturer, land speculator, Ohio Valley (1783-?); Pennsylvania assemblyman (1790-1792); U.S. senator, state of Pennsylvania (1793-1794); U.S. representative, state of Pennsylvania (1795-1801); U.S. secretary of the treasury (1801-1814); various diplomatic posts (1813-1827); president, National Bank of New York (1831-1839).

Albert Gallatin, land speculator, politician, secretary of the treasury, diplomat, and economic theorist, descended from an old and distinguished European family. Orphaned at the age of nine, a distant relative cared for him and provided him with an excellent education. He was raised in the sophisticated society of late-eighteenth-century Geneva and graduated from the local academy in 1779. As a student he found the political atmosphere of his native city stifling. He rejected the aristocratic notions of his family, preferring instead to associate with the more radical student elements. The young man became an ardent admirer of Jean Jacques Rousseau and readily espoused his calls for the rejection of conventional society and a return to nature. After declining an appointment as a lieutenant colonel in a Hessian regiment hired by George III for service in the American colonies, he embarked for America a few weeks before his nineteenth birthday.

Gallatin did not journey to America in response to romantic notions about warring against tyranny or aiding humanity to shed the fetters of past oppression. Unlike many others who came from Europe to fight against the British, Gallatin made the pilgrimage across the Atlantic to secure his own freedom. When he arrived in Massachusetts in the summer of 1780, there was no indication of the eventual outcome of the war, but the unsettled nature of the conflict did not trouble him. The newly arrived immigrant first entered the tea business, then traded his stock for an inventory of West Indian products that he took to Maine to sell. Back in Boston by October 1781, he taught an extracurricular French course at Harvard, attended only by students whose parents gave them special permission to enroll.

While in Boston Gallatin met Jean Savary de Valcoulon, a young Frenchman with wondrous dreams of America's future. In his native Lyons, Savary had already failed in business, but, determined to recoup his fortunes and visit the land whose founding principles he supported, he crossed the Atlantic as the representative of René Rapicault, a businessman who had claims against the state of Virginia. Gallatin became Savary's interpreter in 1783, and the two journeyed to Philadelphia. There they heard talk of the fortunes to be made from speculation in western land, and they learned that George Washington had already acquired vast tracts on the frontier, as had Robert Morris, the great Revolutionary War financier. Gallatin made inquiries about available lands and with Savary decided where to make the best purchases. The two bought 120,000 acres in the Ohio Valley, land along the Great Kanawha and Ohio Rivers, and scattered blocks near the confluence of the Ohio and Mississippi. Gallatin obtained much of his share of the land by promising payment from funds he stood to inherit when he reached the age of twenty-five.

The speculation failed to develop as successfully as the partners had hoped. Indian depredations along the frontier made settlement impossible, and their lands remained vacant. Still, the two men determined to make their fortunes. By late 1785 they leased a house and five acres on George's Creek not far from the Monongahela, where they established a store. Gallatin later purchased a 400-acre farm in the area. He named it Friendship Hill.

In the three years that followed, Gallatin, by then a jack-of-all-trades, tended the store, engaged in farming, read widely, and traveled from Maine to Virginia with the intention of investing more heavily in land. On one of his visits to Richmond he was smitten with the daughter of a boardinghouse keeper and courted her. Sophia Allègre became his wife on May 14, 1789. With his new bride Gallatin returned to Friendship Hill in the summer, but his marriage met with tragedy. Sophia died in October and was buried in an unmarked grave near the Monongahela.

Gallatin expanded his western land holdings during those years and sought ways to increase their value. One of his schemes to bring settlers westward involved friends in Switzerland. The turmoil of the French Revolution reached Geneva by 1794, and many in that city had given thought to migrating to America. With a combination of the spirit that brought him across the ocean and the acquisitiveness that became part of his character after arriving, Gallatin evolved a plan that would help his friends, appeal to his own sensibilities, and produce profit. He proposed to found a settlement of Genevans in the New World, a settlement where Swiss artisans and men of letters could live, prosper, and hold fast to their native ways.

He envisioned a stock company held jointly by Americans and Genevans, and he received encouragement from members of the small Swiss community in Philadelphia, who assured him they would purchase shares. The next step, to find a suitable location for the settlement, led Gallatin to travel to New York in 1785 to explore the area west of the Hudson. In the end he decided to plant the community nearer to home. He wrote disparagingly of the high prices and infertility of land in New York and of the strong aristocratic influences in the state. "In Pennsylvania not only we have neither Livingstones [sic] nor Rensselaers, but from the suburbs of Philadelphia to the banks of the Ohio I do not know of a single family that has any extensive influence. An equal distribution of property has rendered every individual independent, and there is amongst us true and real equality."

After his return to Pennsylvania Gallatin discovered the political situation had improved in Geneva, and there would be no mass migration to the settlement he organized. Still, the bad news did not cause him to abandon the scheme. He remained enthusiastic about the project, as did the Swiss in Philadelphia. Gallatin and four other investors formalized an arrangement in July 1795 that provided funds for a retail store to serve as the nucleus of the undertaking.

The partners set out in August for the property Gallatin purchased at Wilson's Port in western Pennsylvania. It comprised 650 acres and contained three mill sites. "With a good store," he wrote, "we will, in a great degree, command the trade of this part of the country." He also made purchases on his own account directly across the Monongahela from the company's land. Every unsold lot in the tiny town of Greensburg was bought by him, as were 22 acres of bottomland nearby.

The partners discovered that their dreams far exceeded what they could sustain by their initial investment of $10,000, and by September they had to double their contributions. They entered into a new partnership, known as Albert Gallatin and Company. As the name of the venture implied, Gallatin was the largest subscriber, having invested some $6,000. The group planned to construct a store and millhouses, then build several houses and offer them for sale in their town, which they named New Geneva.

The venture continually met with problems, but none as unsettling as those that occurred in late 1796 with the collapse of the western land-speculation boom. Robert Morris, by that time one of America's wealthiest men and most active speculators, saw his fortune ruined. He was carted off to the Prune Street debtors' prison, and Gallatin, like so many of Morris's creditors, held thousands of dollars of his worthless notes. If the collapse of Morris's paper fortune was not bad enough for Gallatin, his situation grew even more difficult that winter when the results of the general economic downturn then plaguing the nation affected his own enterprise. Business at the store came to a virtual halt, and the company's goods remained unsold on the store's shelves.

At one point Gallatin became so disaffected with his American experiment that he toyed with the idea of returning to Geneva, but he could not retrieve the money he had invested in land and gave up the idea. Fortunately he salvaged the situation when the undeclared war between France and the United States brought him a new business opportunity in 1798. The Pennsylvania legislature ordered 12,000 stands of arms for the militia to repel the French invasion that the Adams administration claimed was inevitable. Gallatin thought the invasion fears exaggerated and the expenditure unnecessary, but he managed to obtain a profitable government contract to supply some of the weapons. He delivered the first two shipments to the state by 1800, long after it was clear that the French had no interest in launching a military adventure on American soil.

At the same time he engaged in supplying Pennsylvania with arms, Gallatin also benefited from another business enterprise. A glassworks he established several years earlier operated at a profit by then, despite problems with cold weather and a strike by the workers. During the winter of 1798-1799 it sold almost £600 worth of merchandise to customers in Pittsburgh and Kentucky.

Gallatin attained those two commercial successes only after a complete reorganization of the company in 1799. He took over the entire enterprise that year, and under his sole direction the company reversed its decline.

If the returns from the investment of his inheritance failed to produce all Gallatin hoped to achieve socially and financially, his reputation as one of the few gentlemen settled on the banks of the Monongahela at least had political advantages. His relative prosperity and many talents launched him on a political career that spanned four decades. He had his first taste of American-style democracy as a member of a conference held in Harrisburg, Pennsylvania, in 1788. The meeting was called to examine ways to modify the constitution drafted for the United States in Philadelphia the previous year and awaiting approval by the requisite nine state conventions. Gallatin's presence at the meeting placed him in the camp of those who feared that if the nation adopted the newly written constitution it might well destroy the independence of the states. The resolutions he composed indicated a distinct preference for the Articles of Confederation, the document under which the United States was governed at the time. The modifications Gallatin and his fellow delegates suggested would have made the proposed constitution little different from the Articles. They called for retaining a single-house legislature, an executive with severely restricted powers, brief terms for government officials, and a Supreme Court with a narrowly defined jurisdiction.

The United States adopted the Constitution without the changes proposed by the Pennsylvania meeting in 1788, but Gallatin was not disheartened after his first foray into politics failed to affect the course of national events. The following year he again tried his hand at politics, but that time on a smaller scale. As a member of the conference that revised the Pennsylvania state constitution during the winter of 1789-1790, he participated in discussions on suffrage, representation, taxation, and the court system. His service at the conference showed him to be a man of ability, and in the fall of 1790 he was elected to represent Fayette County in the state legislature. There he proved an efficient worker and a popular representative. He won reelection the following year and in 1792 as well.

Although most often in the minority, Gallatin arrived at his positions only after careful consideration. During one term, according to his own testimony, he was a member of 35 separate committees, and he drafted all of their reports and drew up all of their bills. He had a particular concern with social issues such as the creation of a statewide system of public education and the abolition of slavery.

Although his interests covered a broad range of subjects, Gallatin's greatest contribution came in the realm of public finance. The measures he advocated while a member of the Pennsylvania legislature were remarkably similar to those then being enacted at the behest of Alexander Hamilton, President Washington's secretary of the treasury. Gallatin called for paying the state debt in specie, the elimination of state paper money, better management of funds derived from the sale of public lands, the establishment of a continuous source of revenue, and the creation of a Bank of Pennsylvania. If the state followed his program, he estimated the people of Pennsylvania could go for as long as 40 years without a direct tax.

As a representative from the frontier Gallatin cleaved close to the Republican party line. Testimony to the respect he earned came when the Federalist-dominated state legislature elected him to the U.S. Senate in 1793. Unfortunately for his political career, the Federalists in the national government were less enamored of his abilities than had been the case in Pennsylvania. The upstart Republican called for a detailed statement of the nation's finances from the secretary of the treasury, which piqued Federalist stalwarts. Hamilton objected to what he characterized as "hectoring," and Gallatin's audacity in discommoding a leader of the opposition cost him dearly. By a vote of 14 to 12 the Senate expelled him on the grounds that he had not held U.S. citizenship for the required nine years.

Gallatin was not unduly distressed by ejection from the Senate, and, in any case, there was much beyond national politics to claim his attention. In November 1793 he married again. His second wife differed greatly from Sophia, the Richmond landlady's daughter with whom he had run off four

years before. Hannah Nicholson of New York was a woman from a distinguished and influential family. Her father was Commodore John Nicholson, her uncles and brothers were naval officers, and her sisters had all married members of Congress.

When Gallatin returned to Friendship Hill with his bride, he found an extremely volatile political situation along the frontier. The entire western part of the state, enraged over an excise tax on whiskey levied in Hamilton's revenue bill of 1791, verged on rebellion. Gallatin well appreciated the antagonism the whiskey tax created. A general feeling predominated that the tax discriminated against the poor, and hostility to the measure had increased since it had gone into effect two years earlier. Petitions against the tax circulated initially, but they had no effect. Frustration at the failure to gain repeal led to increasing radicalism, and by early 1792 violence was widespread. The lives of revenue officers were endangered, property was destroyed, and the authority of the U.S. government collapsed in the western counties. A protest meeting held in Pittsburgh during late August resulted in a series of resolutions demanding social and commercial ostracism for those who cooperated with government enforcement efforts.

Gallatin supported the measure as did other members of the frontier aristocracy, but it is impossible to tell if he and others of his class actually favored the measures or if they endorsed them for political expediency. Wealthier residents of the area found themselves caught between the government, their own desire for stability, concern over their property, and the threat posed by the antitax mobs that grew increasingly violent and destructive toward those who did not openly support their cause. Gallatin, clearly a moderate in the crusade against the levy on whiskey by 1794, spoke out against violent opposition to the government. He opposed regional secession, a measure advocated by some, and he denied the radicals' claim that their revolt was analogous to the American Revolution. He also endeavored to explain that Shays' Rebellion, a 1786 farmers' revolt in Massachusetts, produced disastrous results for the participants. Any illegal opposition would not only be crushed, he maintained, but the result would make "the people abject and the government tyrannic."

Years later, when he reflected upon his stand during the Whiskey Rebellion—and when the danger of mob violence directed against his person or prop-

Friendship Hill, Gallatin's Pennsylvania country home from about 1785

erty no longer existed–he regretted the tone of the resolutions he supported in 1792. He called the endorsement "my only political sin."

During the height of the crisis over the excise tax Federalist supporters of strong measures to put down the rebellion blamed those they labeled foreign agitators for the problem. They claimed that men such as Irish-born William Findley, Scotsman Hugh Henry Brackenridge, and Gallatin had incited the mobs to armed resistance. When Hamilton accompanied the troops sent to Pittsburgh to subdue the rebels, some said his purpose was to demonstrate that Gallatin was somehow disloyal to the country. Whatever the validity of the rumor about Hamilton's motives, the assertions that foreign-born radicals led the uprising lacked truth. Gallatin and Findley were moderates, as were many of those wrongly accused of advocating either war or secession.

When the rebellion evaporated, after President Washington made clear his intention to use the army to overwhelm any challenge to the authority of the United States, Gallatin emerged triumphant.

He had taken a moderate stand, at least within the context of frontier politics, and at the same time persuaded his neighbors he was neither a traitor nor had he abandoned their cause. In 1794 they elected him to the first of three consecutive terms in the U.S. House of Representatives.

The six years Gallatin served as a representative in Congress, 1795-1801, were critical times in the history of the new republic. George Washington retired, the political-party system that had come into existence was used in the first truly contested presidential election, and war in Europe created tremendous foreign policy pressures as well as expansive commercial opportunities for America. In his time as a representative from western Pennsylvania, Gallatin participated in the various tumults over Jay's Treaty, the XYZ Affair, the Alien and Sedition Acts, and the undeclared naval war with France. Throughout his terms he suffered repeated attacks from the opposition Federalists, who denounced him as a foreigner, ridiculed his accent, and portrayed him as a chief fomenter of the Whiskey Rebellion. He endured it all with equanimity and at the same time demonstrated his grasp of the issues before the House and his considerable abilities in debate. By 1797 he was recognized as the leader of the minority Republican party in the House of Representatives.

In the disputed election of 1800, when Republicans Thomas Jefferson and Aaron Burr each received 73 electoral votes, Gallatin led the fight in the House to assure that Jefferson was not robbed of the presidency by his running mate. The Federalist majority determined to make the best of their unanticipated opportunity to deprive the Virginian of the nation's highest office, but Gallatin's skill and firmness carried the day. On the 36th ballot Jefferson secured the requisite number of votes, and Burr went down to defeat.

Gallatin gained recognition as an expert on public finance by 1800, and he insisted that the Department of the Treasury be held accountable to Congress. He played an instrumental part in founding the House Committee on Ways and Means and urged that the government spend no money except for the specific purpose for which it was appropriated. As a minority member he never saw his financial program enacted in its entirety, but during those years he evolved the ideas on fiscal policy that guided him throughout his service under Presidents Jefferson and James Madison.

Few observers doubted that Jefferson would name Gallatin secretary of the treasury after the election of 1800. When Gallatin took office he brought his usual driving enthusiasm to the job. As he once explained to the president, he did not choose to be a payer of bills, a collector of revenues, and a keeper of records. He undertook his work with a clear social and political program and insisted on shaping policy to produce his vision of the nation's future. He wanted a place free from the oppressive burdens of military preparedness, untrammeled by the diplomatic fetters of the Old World, free from party factionalism, undisturbed by class antagonism, and without the weight of opprobrious taxation. He thought that the nation's geographical isolation would keep it out of war, and thus the government, without the need of expenditures for engorged military and diplomatic establishments, could remain small and economical. Hence, the nation would prosper. He envisioned surplus revenues devoted to productive ends, with money spent on education and internal improvements designed to stimulate commerce. The abundant raw materials, the fertile land, and an educated population would ensure prosperity.

Gallatin soon discovered that stating principles was far easier than applying them to a functioning economy. Even though he used the efficient organization Hamilton built at the Treasury Department, difficulties abounded for the new secretary. After assuming office he quickly encountered the sinking fund, a device the Federalists adapted from England for setting aside money specifically to retire the public debt. While a member of the House of Representatives he had exhibited contempt for the fund, arguing that the device complicated finances and facilitated the accrual of additional obligations. He did not alter his opinion when he became secretary of the treasury. He maintained that the fund, although not intrinsically evil, provided a tempting opportunity for abuse. Still, he could not eliminate it no matter what he believed. A large segment of the population saw it as an effective check on the powers of the treasury secretary, and the public would have interpreted any move to abolish it as an attempt by Gallatin to manipulate public funds for his own dubious ends.

When Gallatin took over the Treasury Department, the public debt exceeded $82 million. It could be retired within 16 years, he calculated, if the government set aside $7.3 million per annum for interest and principal payments. Such a schedule presented no difficulty. The customs duties would provide almost $10 million per year. Sale of public lands, the postal service, and a tax on whiskey stills would provide more than $1 million more. In all, the United States would have revenue enough to pay the debt, according to his estimate, with more than $3 million to spare each year.

Gallatin's first battle as secretary was to preserve the whiskey tax. He and his neighbors in the West had long opposed it, but upon his appointment to the Treasury Gallatin abandoned his earlier position. As the man most responsible for the nation's fiscal well-being he argued for retaining the levy. Its abolition, he declared, made collection of other excise taxes uneconomical. Despite his pleas Congress had different views. They followed the lead of the eccentric but brilliant John Randolph of Roanoke and repealed the tax.

Foreign-policy problems created additional obstacles to the implementation of Gallatin's plans. The unanticipated war with the Barbary pirates in Jefferson's first term required naval expenditures far beyond the demands of peacetime. Trade was also constricted to some extent by the maritime restrictions and depredations the warring nations of France and England inflicted on American merchant shipping. Complicating Gallatin's task, the two leading Republicans, Jefferson and Madison, demonstrated a total lack of interest and enthusiasm for fiscal matters.

Despite the many economic difficulties the country faced in the first decade of the nineteenth century, America became prosperous more rapidly than even Gallatin anticipated. Even though Congress had repealed by 1802 most internal duties, such as those that precipitated the Whiskey Rebellion, the government experienced no shortage of revenue. The nation profited immensely from the war in Europe, and by 1806 the Treasury Department showed a surplus of $4 million.

Unfortunately, the sound financial position of the United States dramatically reversed. As the Napoleonic Wars continued, the increasing loss of blood and treasure grew more and more burdensome for both England and France. Each nation became less tolerant of the other's use of American merchant ships to supply its military effort. Desperate to gain any advantage in the conflict, the English set out to restrict American commerce with their enemy, and the French attempted to do the same. The vessels of both countries captured American ships, confiscated the cargoes, and declared paper blockades to destroy the nation's commerce. Jefferson found his latitude for maneuver restricted in the situation: war or submission offered the two most conspicuous alternatives, but instead he marked out another path. He sought to use economic pressure as a weapon for persuading the belligerents to end their violations of American neutrality.

Through a series of measures beginning with the Nicholson Nonimportation Act of 1806, Jefferson and his successor, James Madison, employed a series of boycotts, embargoes, and subtle threats to coerce the European powers. Gallatin, although unenthusiastic about the measures, doggedly supported both presidents. The Embargo Act of 1807, which he viewed as a poorly drafted measure that provided no penalties for violations and failed to deal with vessels in the coasting trade, especially distressed him.

Gallatin complained that the embargo hurt the economy of the United States far more than it damaged the British. The French alone gained from the American measure. Napoleon's coastal patrols confiscated American ships arriving in French harbors, he explained, on the premise that they all must be British, since the embargo prohibited international trade to and from American ports. Meanwhile, in ports from New England to the deep South trade languished, vessels rotted at their berths, and sailors idled away their unproductive and uncompensated days.

The relationship between England and the United States steadily deteriorated after Madison's inauguration in 1809, and in June 1812, riding a crest of cries for hostilities by the "War Hawks," Congress declared war. Open conflict compounded Gallatin's already serious problems at the Treasury Department. When he reported to Congress in December, he explained that revenues were down, the nation faced a $20 million shortfall, and there seemed to be little chance of making it up through borrowing. Lenders in Philadelphia furnished almost $6 million for the war effort and New York only slightly less, but the amounts remained inadequate. In New England, where "Mr. Madison's War" was exceedingly unpopular, Boston bankers provided a mere $75,000. Congress refused to recharter the Bank of the United States (BUS) despite Gallatin's pleas, further disrupting the nation's finances.

When only $4 million was subscribed of an $11 million loan offered to banks by the government early in 1813 the secretary sought new ways for increasing revenue. He decided to turn to the general public for financing.

Even before his plan for instituting a popular subscription to finance the war could be put into operation, however, Gallatin received news that caused him to alter the scheme. Millionaire David Parrish, a native of Hamburg, Germany, living in America, attempted to organize a syndicate of wealthy men to underwrite a large loan. He was joined by the French-born Stephen Girard, one of Philadelphia's merchant princes, and by Gallatin's friend, the redoubtable John Jacob Astor. The government's offer of a .25 percent interest premium to any person or group accumulating subscriptions of $100,000 or more persuaded Parrish that the syndicate would make a fortune. The three men pledged almost $10 million, and an assortment of investors another $6 million. The lenders completed the transaction in time to prevent the United States accounts from being overdrawn, and Gallatin, in his greatest financial operation of the war, successfully kept the nation's credit secure.

Even though he had succeeded in obtaining funds to support America's military effort, the secretary of the treasury was discouraged by the destruction of his scheme to pay the country's debts and by the necessary abandonment of the plan he and Jefferson developed to build a system of canals from Maine to Georgia. He found the most demoralizing feature of wartime politics to be the bitterness and intensity of Federalist opposition to the war and to his policies. As the country plunged $123 million into debt, the Federalists not only rejected his plea to recharter the BUS (the creation of their own Alexander Hamilton) and failed to subscribe to the loans needed to prosecute the war, but they also opposed the secretary on virtually every other measure.

The continuing opposition persuaded him by 1813 that he could no longer serve effectively as secretary of the treasury. When the Russian czar offered to mediate the conflict between Britain and the United States, Gallatin asked President Madison to send him as a negotiator, and Madison granted the request. Along with James A. Bayard and John Quincy Adams, he journeyed to St. Petersburg. Unfortunately, the six months the delegation spent in the Russian capital were wasted. The British refused to accept the czar's mediation, and the mission ended in failure. Gallatin assumed he would return to the cabinet post he continued to hold at least nominally, but the assumption was incorrect. When the British offered to negotiate directly with the United States, the president again added Gallatin to a newly appointed delegation, composed of Bayard, Adams, Henry Clay, and Jonathan Russell. At the same time President Madison relieved him of his duties as secretary of the treasury since he could not have been effective in both positions simultaneously.

Although continual squabbling ensued among the American diplomats over who among them should actually lead the negotiating team, Gallatin more than the others labored diligently on the work at hand. He did most of the drafting and exhibited considerable patience in dealing with British demands. In the negotiations Adams was committed to maintaining the right of Massachusetts mariners to fish off the Newfoundland coast while Clay remained equally intent on preserving the interests of westerners, namely American access to the Missis-

sippi River. Beyond their conflicts on matters of substance, the two proved temperamental opposites. The ambitious Clay already envisioned a career well beyond Congress and frequently sought to bolster his reputation at home. Gallatin had the additional task of compromising their policy disagreements without damaging their monumental egos.

The treaty ending the war between the United States and Britain was signed at Ghent on December 24, 1814. On the way back to the United States Gallatin visited Geneva after an absence of 35 years. He then went on to London, where, with Adams and Clay, he concluded a commercial treaty between the United States and Britain. He returned home in September 1815.

Gallatin faced several difficult choices when he arrived in America. Friends urged him to run for Congress, John Jacob Astor offered him one-fifth of a highly profitable business, Secretary of State James Monroe asked him to return to Europe as minister to France, and, when Alexander J. Dallas resigned as secretary of the treasury, President Madison offered to restore Gallatin to the post. Gallatin had little difficulty making his decision. Residence at Friendship Hill in western Pennsylvania or in Washington, D.C., had little to recommend it compared to life in Paris. He declined to resume his old position as secretary of the treasury, saying the job required a younger man. Then, the fifty-five-year-old Gallatin set off with his family in 1816 for a seven-year sojourn in the French capital.

The most serious diplomatic problems between the United States and France after the War of 1812 involved the claims for compensation lodged against the French. In the years before the War of 1812 many American merchants and shippers suffered from the various measures proclaimed by Napoleon in his efforts to hinder British trade. After the Duke of Wellington's victory at Waterloo and the return of the Bourbon monarchy, many on the western side of the Atlantic saw what they thought was an opportunity to obtain redress from the newly restored French king. Their hopes proved illfounded. The royal government was as unresponsive to American claims as the unpredictable Bonaparte had been, and Gallatin made no progress extracting payments. He managed to clear up several disagreements relating to the Louisiana Purchase, but these minor matters skirted the real troubles. The only substantive contribution he made

Washington Square offices of the New-York Historical Society, 1845. Gallatin was president of the society from 1843 to the time of his death in 1849 (Gleason's Pictorial, September 4, 1852).

during those years involved the aid he gave Richard Rush, U.S. minister to the Court of St. James. In 1818 he assisted Rush in negotiating the establishment of a boundary between the United States and British North America that ran from the Lake of the Woods to the Rocky Mountains. As part of the boundary settlement the two nations agreed to joint occupation of the Oregon Country for a period of ten years.

Although he won few diplomatic successes, Gallatin and his family enjoyed their stay in Paris. The diary kept by son James reveals their joyous participation in the continuous festivals and entertainments around which diplomatic life in the French capital revolved.

When Gallatin returned to America in 1823, the political situation drifted in a state of flux. The Federalists no longer existed as an organized political party, and without an effective opposition to unite them, the Republicans were riven by factionalism. Each segment of the party claimed to be the bearer of the true Jeffersonian tradition and sought with determination to elect its favorite as president. Gallatin, deterred by what he perceived as a decline in the nation's political standards, only reluctantly involved himself in those struggles. And when one

wing of the party nominated him as a vice-presidential candidate but later asked him to withdraw his name, he made the decision to abandon public service for the life of a gentleman farmer. With his $2,000 per year income he retired to the new mansion he built at Friendship Hill.

Gallatin spent only a year at his home in western Pennsylvania. After living in Paris his family yearned for the more sophisticated cities of Europe in preference to the American wilderness. When declining health forced the resignation of Rufus King, American minister to England, President John Quincy Adams asked Gallatin to replace him. He accepted the offer without hesitation. Gallatin's negotiations in London were far more successful than his earlier diplomatic efforts in Paris. During his tenure as U.S. minister to the Court of St. James, the United States renewed several commercial treaties with England; the joint occupation of Oregon was continued indefinitely; and the two nations made progress on compromising other minor differences between them.

Gallatin's public career ended when he returned from England in 1827, but that time he did not return to Friendship Hill. He settled in New York and four years later became the president of

213

John Jacob Astor's National Bank of New York. He served as chief executive of the bank until 1839. Even though he avoided active participation in politics, Gallatin wrote extensively on political and economic topics. During his years in Europe he had refined his notions of international economics and had poised himself to act on his newly acquired principles after resettlement in America. He and his old acquaintance, banker Alexander Baring of the House of Baring, had been deeply impressed by the resilience of the French economy to the shocks administered by the Napoleonic Wars, the invasion of the Allied powers, and the reparations extracted from the restored Bourbon monarch. Gallatin believed that the free circulation of gold and silver in France had enabled the nation to exhibit so much fiscal durability.

Many improvements could be made in the American economy, Gallatin thought. The country theoretically adopted a bimetallic currency years earlier, during the tenure of Alexander Hamilton as secretary of the treasury, and the nation's mints coined both silver and gold at a ratio of fifteen to one. The value of gold soon exceeded that fixed rate, and by the 1820s most of the gold in American coffers had drifted to Europe, leaving the United States with a silver-dollar currency. Gallatin urged Andrew Jackson's secretary of the treasury, Samuel D. Ingraham, to institute a true bimetallic system for the United States. This could be done, he explained, by setting the ratio of silver to gold at between 15.58 and 15.69 to 1.

The French experience also persuaded the returned diplomat that France had gained strength from allowing only one bank to issue paper money, and then only in notes of $100 or more. He conceded that his ideas made him an "ultra-bullionist," but he was sophisticated enough to understand that a "French solution" to America's economic problems faced a political uphill climb, given the power of the many banks throughout the country and their insistence on issuing small-denomination notes. Indeed, the Jacksonians' war on the "small change notes" absorbed much of the party's attention and may have ultimately wrecked its more grandiose financial schemes.

Word of his views reached Robert J. Walsh, Jr., editor of the influential *American Quarterly Review*. Walsh labored under the influence of Nicholas Biddle, the president of the Second Bank of the United States, which had received a charter in 1816 after Gallatin left the post of secretary of the treasury. Walsh frequently published articles supporting the BUS position on fiscal policy, and he saw that Gallatin's ideas could give him another opportunity to be helpful to Biddle. In the early 1830s the BUS president foresaw the possibility that Congress would decline to renew the charter when it expired in 1836, and he suspected that Jackson had several proposals for his own national bank. Hence, Biddle had worked assiduously to obtain support of influential Americans in securing renewal long before the critical date, and Walsh reasoned that a work by a respected former secretary of the treasury and an avowed Jeffersonian would carry considerable weight with Congress.

In the spring of 1830 Walsh asked Gallatin to write an article for the *Review*, and he accepted. Biddle obligingly provided more than a dozen bundles of information and the services of his own nephew as an assistant. Throughout the months he labored on the project Gallatin constantly communicated with Biddle. The former secretary of the treasury told Biddle that it was far from certain the charter could be renewed under any circumstances. When the First BUS failed to gain recharter by Congress in 1811, he explained, it had resulted in opposition to himself and to President Madison. The situation had altered dramatically since then. Although in retrospect Gallatin was wrong, he believed that the private banking system that had spread across the nation by the time Jackson took his inaugural oath constituted a powerful political force determined to eliminate the Second BUS as a competitor. (Many of the private bankers, in fact, supported the BUS.) Gallatin advised Biddle to counter the opposition in two ways. Initially, the BUS would have to accept modifications in its charter to give the government a greater share of its profits. It would also have to encourage private banks to make loans to farmers on the security of their acreage. Biddle failed to respond to Gallatin's suggestions, although he reviewed the manuscript before Walsh received it for publication in the December 1830 issue of the *American Quarterly Review*.

Biddle, anxious to show his appreciation for the support, offered $1,000 in payment for the piece. Gallatin declined despite his need for money. Accepting remuneration, he thought, would make it appear he supported a renewal of the charter for payment rather than principle. There must be no challenge to his motives, he told Biddle. He declined a fee of $500 from the *Review* for the same reason.

Nicholas Biddle was delighted not only with the article but with the author's willingness to provide a longer version to be published as a pamphlet for distribution to congressmen and to other men of power and influence. The BUS underwrote the cost of publication.

The final version of Gallatin's pamphlet, entitled *Considerations on the Currency and Banking System of the United States*, appeared in February 1831 (and was republished in *The Writings of Albert Gallatin*, 1879). Gallatin drew most of his arguments from the fiscal ideas he acquired while in France. Gold and silver constituted the only true forms of money, he insisted. Paper currency had nothing to recommend it except availability. The supply could not be controlled, thus it produced instability, depreciation, and ultimately disaster. The free circulation of gold and silver in the United States must be encouraged, he wrote, and he again urged the establishment of a 15.7-to-1 ratio between the two metals. In the pamphlet he argued that no institution had been as crucial in promoting financial stability as the BUS. Neither did any question about the constitutionality of the institution remain: the Constitution authorized Congress to enact "necessary and proper" legislation for the welfare of the nation. The BUS had also proved exceedingly useful for the U.S. government and the country at large in facilitating commercial transactions. If the Treasury Department or some other governmental body assumed its functions, only ineptitude and incompetence in the management of financial affairs would result, he claimed.

When Gallatin's pamphlet saw publication, the BUS charter had several years left before expiration. Nicholas Biddle thought it dangerous to wait until the expiration date, and Henry Clay, Whig presidential candidate in 1832, shared Biddle's fears. They reasoned that in an election year the odds of obtaining favorable treatment from Congress favored their cause, and Clay would improve his chances of defeating Jackson in the fall if he could list rechartering the bank among his achievements.

Biddle and Clay correctly assumed Congress would accede to their wishes. The bill to continue the BUS passed the Senate and the House of Representatives. Unfortunately for their plans, Andrew Jackson vetoed it. The intensity of the president's opposition was made clear by the raging denunciation

of the bank contained in the message to Congress that accompanied his veto, although Jackson offered the bank's supporters several points on which to compromise and save the bank. The president's action disturbed Gallatin, but events following the veto distressed him much more. Jackson ordered federal funds withdrawn from the BUS and deposited in state banks (known as the "pets"), a measure Gallatin regarded as entirely unnecessary. The BUS then retaliated by sharply reducing loans and presenting notes to state banks, demanding payment in specie. Interest rates rose rapidly, business failures followed, runs on banks ensued, and numerous banks closed as a result. Biddle explained the policy, saying he had simply tried to prepare the bank for its impending liquidation. Gallatin thought the reasoning specious. He and others claimed Biddle tried to create financial panic in the nation and thereby force Jackson and the Democrats to call a truce in their war against the bank. All the while, the bank's supporters ignored the loopholes in Jackson's veto message.

New York was particularly hard hit by the bank's policy of contraction. A "Union Committee of Merchants" organized to put pressure on Biddle and on state and national governments. The committee chose Gallatin to chair the effort. After several conferences with Biddle failed to alter the policy, the committee adopted the only tactic available. It produced a report critical of the bank's actions and hoped to gain popular support by circulating it widely. Not surprisingly, the committee chose Gallatin to draft it. When his report was made public in the spring of 1834, carrying the signatures of two dozen powerful merchants, it was clear he blamed more than BUS policy for the difficulties. Biddle's removal of the deposits represented unnecessary interference with the bank's operations and unconscionable meddling with the affairs of the secretary of the treasury, Gallatin admitted, but added that Jackson also shared the blame. The president exceeded his constitutional authority, interfered with Congress, and used the veto indiscriminately. In a comment certain to elevate the spirit of the Whigs, Gallatin charged Jackson with thinking he could do no wrong and forgetting that the people, not the chief executive, were sovereign in America.

Gallatin included an addendum to Congress with the report. It suggested changes in the nation's currency and banking systems. The recommendations included a prohibition against circulation of notes with a value of less than $5, a regulation allowing banks to lend no more than two-thirds of their resources, and an upper limit of 6 percent profit on their capital.

The report and the addendum, although unanimously endorsed by the New York merchants, had little effect. Relaxation of charter requirements by the states and the anticipation of vast profits to be made after the demise of the BUS resulted in more bank incorporations in the 1830s. In Jackson's mind, the new banks fueled speculation, and he sought to control the frenzy by requiring all payment for public lands to be made in specie rather than bank notes. Neither Jackson nor Gallatin suspected that the influx of Mexican silver flows, which had permitted the prosperity of the early 1830s, had dried up and had the effect of forcing British interest rates higher. Thus, Jackson, thinking the problem lay within his control, made matters worse by distorting the specie flow within the United States. A rash of bank failures followed as specie moved westward in large quantities. By spring the Panic of 1837 swept the nation, and the country's economy fell into a serious depression, although one characterized by the bankruptcies of railroads and banks rather than by long lines of unemployed people.

Again, Gallatin was selected to chair a committee to deal with the difficulty. Fellow bankers and merchants appointed him to lead a group to obtain emergency aid from the governor of New York. The state legislature had authorized the sale of stock for the construction of several canals. Gallatin and his committee wanted $3.5 million of the stock for loans to local banks that would then sell it to satisfy the English demand for specie. The state ignored the suggestion, and the drain on New York City's banks continued. In the midst of the panic Gallatin warned bankers against suspending specie payment. His own bank faced no danger, at least in the short term, but his reasons for opposing suspension went far beyond the interests of his own institution. He predicted that if the city's banks suspended specie payment, every bank in America would follow. His words again went unheeded. New York banks suspended specie payment, and Gallatin's own bank soon followed suit.

Once the New York banks made the decision, Gallatin moved with dispatch to try to discourage banks elsewhere in America from adopting the same policy. He also worked to persuade banks in

New York to resume specie payment as soon as possible. He remembered that after the War of 1812 bankers in many cases delayed resumption so they could benefit from the chaotic financial circumstances then prevailing. He suggested several measures to the governor for ensuring it did not happen again. Banks should be forbidden to loan more than twice their capital, he advised, and it would be prudent to limit the dividends of all banks unwilling or unable to resume specie payment. Again, Gallatin's suggestions for stringent fiscal policies were ignored. The legislature moved in a direction opposite from that he recommended and liberalized rather than constricted regulations dealing with banking operations. He was aghast to learn of the passage of a new law allowing banks unable to make specie payment to continue doing business while at the same time New York City banks were forced by statute to honor the notes of banks located in the countryside at a fixed discount. (Indeed, that very feature of the New York law turned a temporary money crisis in 1857 into a full-fledged panic as speculators—arbitragers, really—took advantage of the fixed discount rates in the city to make their fortunes. In the process, they started runs on the major banks.) Within weeks every bank in the land abandoned specie payment, and the number of business failures multiplied.

Late in the summer of 1837, while America still languished in the grip of what to that time constituted its most serious economic downturn, Gallatin met with a group of New York bankers to work out a plan for recovery. After three days of deliberation the group sent a letter to every bank in the nation. It announced a convention at year's end and urged the resumption of specie payment on a fixed date. Much of the letter bore Gallatin's imprint, and, as in the case with his earlier memorials and reports, there appeared little positive response to the initiative. Banks in the major cities reacted coldly or with outright hostility to the proposal. In nine states no banks even bothered to respond. Those that replied said weakly that they would resume payments when the foreign-exchange situation improved and the metropolitan banks made it possible.

The obvious lack of enthusiasm for the convention portended its subsequent failure. Almost 100 delegates attended the meeting in late December, but they represented only 17 of the 26 states. They proffered various views of the origins of the eco-

Portrait of Gallatin by William H. Powell (courtesy of the New-York Historical Society)

nomic woes, but were far from unanimous about what course to follow. Representatives from the Northwest as well as from the South suggested a resumption of specie payment as soon as possible, but elsewhere few supported the plan. Bankers from Baltimore, Boston, and Philadelphia favored adjournment until the following April, when they could predict better the situation in regard to crops, foreign exchange, and other factors. Gallatin, with the backing of the New York delegation, proposed to resume specie payments nationally on July 1, 1838, but the members rejected his suggestion.

Although discouraged by the lack of cooperative spirit, Gallatin continued to work for a solution. He sought support from bankers and government officials for organizing another national conference. He authored two reports issued under the name of the New York committee, and, as might be expected, both argued for resumption.

The next in the series of bankers' conventions called to deal with the panic assembled on April 11, 1838, but again only seventeen states were represented. The New York banks by that time were prepared to resume specie payment, but, as had been the case previously, there was no unanimity. A report reached the meeting that President Martin Van

Buren was considering placing federal funds in subtreasury depositories, and the news effectively destroyed any possibility the convention would have even partial success. Gallatin spoke passionately of the evils perpetrated on the nation's economy by the Jackson and Van Buren administrations, but his words had limited effect. New York banks agreed to resume specie payment on May 10, 1838, but they took the action as a result of a state law requiring them to do so. They were not persuaded by Gallatin's arguments. Before dissolving, the convention took the obligatory step of voting to work toward resuming specie payments everywhere in the nation.

A part of the failure to deal decisively with financial difficulties, Gallatin believed, could be traced to the machinations of Nicholas Biddle. He had operated the BUS under a charter from the state of Pennsylvania since the expiration of its federal mandate in 1836, but he hoped to regain the national charter. If Biddle's forces convinced President Van Buren that to solve the nation's economic woes the government needed to recharter the bank, Biddle and the shareholders would not only profit tremendously, but the steady progress of New York toward replacing Philadelphia as the country's financial capital would be halted. As late as 1838 it seemed possible to Gallatin that Van Buren might agree to support recharter of a national bank, but Samuel Ward, a leading New York banker, negotiated a loan of $5 million in gold bars from the Bank of England and frustrated the scheme. Specie payment was then resumed in New York. Boston banks followed the example of New York banks, and in a short time the remainder of the nation's banks did the same.

The Panic of 1837 abated by the time Ward made his dramatic move, and the economic situation continued to improve over the next several years. Prosperity would have returned to the United States, and the banking industry would have stabilized late in 1838 or early 1839 without Gallatin's unremitting labor. Yet to argue that his efforts were entirely without effect would be inaccurate. His continuous proselytizing not only aided in passing the New York law requiring the resumption of specie payment, but his persuasive arguments and passionate declamations helped prepare the mood of bankers everywhere to accept it sooner than would have been the case without his efforts.

Gallatin resigned as president of the National Bank of New York in June 1839, a year after resumption became general throughout America. His son James was chosen to replace him. Despite his retirement he remained a trenchant observer of the economy and was quick to comment when he judged anything amiss. He expressed his outrage late in 1839 when the BUS again suspended specie payment and other banks in the South and West followed its example. As he had done so many times before, the presiding elder of the industry took pen in hand. His pamphlet, *Suggestions on the Banks and Currency of the Several United States*, published in June 1841 (republished in *The Writings of Albert Gallatin*), contained 36,000 words and was supplemented by detailed appendices. Gallatin distributed the blame widely for the most recent difficulties. He again charged the policies of Jackson and Van Buren with responsibility for much of the problem and denounced Nicholas Biddle's fiscal chicanery for encouraging speculation and wasting much of the BUS capital. *Suggestions on the Banks and Currency* differed from his earlier writings in that he placed a portion of the blame on the people, who had bought too many foreign products, borrowed too much foreign capital, and, like the bankers, thrived on wild speculation.

The election of William Henry Harrison as the first Whig president in 1840 revived the question of the need for a national bank. Throughout the campaign Whig orators had thundered against the Jacksonians who allowed Biddle's bank to expire, and they blamed the Panic of 1837 on its absence. The need to found another national bank comprised a central plank in their platform, and once the Whigs attained office the political struggle over recharter resumed. Although Harrison's death within weeks after his inauguration made John Tyler president, it was widely assumed that despite his Democratic antecedents the second Whig to attain the presidency would support one of the Whig party's most important measures.

Gallatin favored a national bank if it would guarantee a sound currency, but by 1841 he doubted it could. Referring to the divisive nature of the political situation, he thought that recharter was not a cause "worth dying for.... I would at least wait until the wishes of the people were better ascertained." Gallatin need not have worried. For reasons not entirely understood by either Whigs or

Democrats, Tyler vetoed two recharter bills, making it certain there would be no third BUS.

While embroiled in the controversies over currency and banking, Gallatin also deeply engaged in the raging debate over tariff policy. He had long championed free trade. As an early admirer of Adam Smith, he had written against protection in 1796 and again in 1810. When hostilities with England neared in 1812, he temporarily supported a higher tariff to encourage manufacturing in the event of war, but he wished to safeguard the nation rather than tax ordinary Americans or hamper competition.

Gallatin was disturbed by the sectional division on tariff questions that became a central feature of American political life in the late 1820s. He hoped to serve as a conciliator when he attended an 1831 free-trade convention at Philadelphia. Like the other New Yorkers in the delegation he regarded himself as a moderate on the subject. His hopes were dashed shortly after the meeting convened. Adamant free traders from the southern states dominated the meeting, with 44 of the 205 delegates from South Carolina and only 72 from north of Virginia. He was particularly disturbed by the attacks on the constitutionality of the tariff. He saw in them an implication of unconstitutionality for all federal law.

Even with the convention's incendiary rhetoric few members had the inclination to follow it with corresponding action. The members chose Gallatin to draft the convention's memorial to Congress. The act of selecting him, a known moderate, indicated a spirit of compromise ruled among the delegates not otherwise reflected in their speeches. His *Memorial of the Committee Appointed by the "Free Trade" Convention held in Philadelphia* (1832) argued against the Whig's advocacy of high import duties to protect and encourage manufacturing.

As Gallatin worked on the memorial every segment of the free-trade movement besieged him with advice. He patiently gathered facts, figures, and a myriad of economic details. When he presented his draft for consideration, a general enthusiasm settled in among the free-trade leadership. He maintained, as opponents of the tariff had always done, that the most productive industries were the most profitable. Any manufacturing enterprise requiring perpetual protection posed a liability to the taxpayers and to the nation. High tariffs not only encouraged smuggling, he explained, but the insidious practice of extending protection to an ever-expanding number of industries in order to obtain broad-based political support ensured their continuation. Not only did tariff protection discriminate against the South, he claimed, but it discriminated against some northern industries to the benefit of others. Gallatin proposed a downward adjustment of tariffs over a period of years to a point where they secured adequate revenue for the government and aided only deserving industries. He suggested that a rate of between 20 and 25 percent would adequately provide for the nation's needs.

Henry Clay launched a bitter attack on the memorial Gallatin wrote at the behest of the free-trade convention. Clay knew it presented a serious challenge to his "American System," as he styled his own protectionist economic ideology. To counter Gallatin's influence he not only attacked his arguments but in desperation besmirched his character. Clay proclaimed that even after 40 years serving his adopted country, the Geneva-born Gallatin remained an alien at heart. "Go home to your native Europe," he exclaimed, "and there inculcate upon her sovereigns your utopian doctrines of free trade, and when you have prevailed upon them to unseal their ports and freely admit the produce of Pennsylvania, and other States, come back and we shall be prepared to become converts, and to adopt your faith."

The congressional struggle over tariff policy in 1832 and 1833 climaxed in one of the most vituperative political confrontations in the country's history. Clay's supporters at first seemed to carry the day with the Tariff of 1832, which scarcely lowered rates. South Carolinians were enraged, and at a state convention they declared the new tariff bill null and void. Secession seemed a possibility at that juncture, but a willingness to compromise emerged from several quarters, as long as compromise could be had without the apparent abandonment of principle. Jackson threatened to use force to collect federal revenues in South Carolina but quietly negotiated for tariff reduction. The South Carolinians at the same time made clear their willingness to accept lower rates rather than an abandonment of the tariff, but even as they accepted compromise they "nullified" legislation allowing the president to use force to collect tariffs in their state.

Gallatin took no direct part in the uproarious politics of the tariff, and his unpopularity with both Whigs and Jacksonian Democrats makes it impossible to estimate how much influence his writings had on the combatants. When the confrontation was settled in 1833, the solution resembled in most respects the one he had favored. Schedules were to be reduced gradually over a ten-year period until they reached 20 percent ad valorem rates.

Gallatin gained an important position as an American economic theoretician during the decade from 1830 to 1841 when he published numerous pamphlets, letters, and papers on banking, currency, and the tariff. He derived many of his ideas from European models, but Americans found them new and refreshing. The primary significance of his shrewd observations was that he brought them together in a coherent financial program, one of the first ever proffered in the United States. In an era when Americans discovered the principles enunciated by Adam Smith in his *The Wealth of Nations* (1776) Gallatin was one of the first to cull ideas from the work and place them in a context designed to alleviate specific economic difficulties facing the nation.

Gallatin had a long, but not particularly distinguished, diplomatic career. Although he met with successes and failures during his service in foreign capitals, the successes were not out of the ordinary nor were the failures disastrous. His most conspicuous involvement was as a delegate in the negotiations that ended the War of 1812. He willingly submerged himself in the details of drafting an agreement that won him the respect and gratitude of his fellows, and his suavity and manners undoubtedly proved an asset to the American representatives. As one of a five-member delegation, none of whom wished to submit to the will of the others, and each of whom claimed to be the man most responsible for the Treaty of Ghent, Gallatin's role remains difficult to evaluate.

With the exception of Alexander Hamilton no one had more influence on the fiscal policies of the United States during its formative years than Albert Gallatin. His keen intellect and voracious appetite for detail in an area that many officeholders avoided gave him an overwhelming advantage over opponents of every political persuasion. His positions on financial matters were not always consistent with his sentiments or philosophy. Early in his career he supported states' rights and limited powers for the central government. Like Jefferson, his perceptions altered radically when he assumed power. As secretary of the treasury he came to support measures usually associated with Hamilton and the Federalist opposition. He endorsed a strong banking system superintended by a national bank, accepted the need for internal taxes during wartime even though he once opposed them, and supported Jefferson and Madison in their attempts to coerce the British with economic pressure even though he would have railed against John Adams or any other Federalist chief executive had the same measures been enacted under their administrations.

His moral victory on the tariff question did not persuade Gallatin to retire from public life. He continued his often controversial comments on every phase of American politics and fiscal policy. Over the years he chaired meetings, wrote reports, and attended conferences. At the age of eighty-four he was still speaking out, denouncing the annexation of Texas in 1845 as the prelude to a war of aggression by the United States against Mexico.

In addition to his leadership in the area of public finance, his political career, and the diplomatic posts he held, Gallatin actively participated in cultural and intellectual enterprises. He was a founder of the University of the City of New York in 1831 and in 1843 was made president of the New-York Historical Society. His most absorbing intellectual inquiry was a study of American Indian tribes. A founder of the American Ethnological Society in 1842, he defrayed publication costs of the first two volumes of its *Transactions*. He regarded his books on Indians as his most significant writings.

Gallatin suffered ill health during the winter of 1848-1849, and his condition worsened in the spring when Hannah, his wife of 56 years, died. While sick, he was taken to the home of a daughter at Astoria, Long Island. There, at eighty-eight years of age, he died, on August 12, 1849.

Publications:

Memorial of the Committee Appointed by the "Free Trade" Convention held in Philadelphia (New York, 1832);
The Writings of Albert Gallatin, 3 volumes, edited by Henry Adams (Philadelphia: Lippincott, 1879).

References:

Henry Adams, *The Life of Albert Gallatin* (Philadelphia: Lippincott, 1879);
Raymond Walters, Jr., *Albert Gallatin, Jeffersonian Financier and Diplomat* (New York: Macmillan, 1957).

Archives:

The major collection of Albert Gallatin's papers is located at the New-York Historical Society in New York City.

Stephen Girard

(May 20, 1750-December 26, 1831)

by Gregory S. Hunter

ITT Corporation

CAREER: Sea merchant, financier (1774-1812); owner, Stephen Girard's Bank (1812-1831); director, Bank of the United States (1816-1817).

Stephen Girard was a prominent merchant and financier as well as one of the leading figures in early-nineteenth-century Philadelphia society. He exemplified a vanishing breed of "private" bankers at a time when states moved toward the standard of incorporated banks.

Girard was born on May 20, 1750, in Bordeaux, France, the second oldest of ten children. His father, Pierre, was a naval officer, burgess of the city, and captain of the port. His mother, Odette Lafargue, died when he was twelve, leaving Girard much on his own. As a child Girard received little education, with some biographers attributing this to the fact that he probably was born blind in one eye.

Despite his educational deficiencies Girard soon made a name for himself in the seafaring trade. At the age of fourteen he first went to sea, serving as a cabin boy on a half-dozen voyages to the Caribbean. He was licensed as a captain, master, and pilot before he reached the age of twenty-four, an unusual event for the time.

Girard struck out on his own in 1774, making his first independent voyage on a ship to Haiti. The voyage did not work out as planned, and Girard found himself heavily in debt. To help with his financial obligations he agreed to transport a shipment of coffee and sugar from the Caribbean to New York. While he eventually satisfied his debt, the experience so affected him that for the remainder of his life he avoided doing business on credit.

The bustling port of New York offered numerous possibilities for the young sea captain. He made several voyages for the firm of Thomas Randall and Company and accumulated both nautical experience and business acumen. Girard soon

Stephen Girard (Gale International Portrait Gallery)

used his savings to purchase a half-interest in a ship, thereafter becoming master of his own fate.

As the situation between England and the colonies came to a head, Girard continued his voyages to the Caribbean. During the summer of 1776 the risk of capture by the British, combined with a rough return voyage, forced Girard to dock in Philadelphia rather than New York City. Though Girard was in Philadelphia at the time of the writing of the Declaration of Independence, he did not become involved in the political situation. Nevertheless, the war affected him: the treacherous nature of wartime sea travel led Girard to suspend trading activities. He therefore turned his energies to merchandising.

His presence in Philadelphia also led to a change in Girard's personal situation. In 1777 he married Mary Lum, a shipbuilder's daughter. Their happy times together did not last long, however. Mary Girard suffered from a mental illness that grew worse over time. Girard eventually had to commit her to the Pennsylvania Hospital, where she died in 1815. The situation with his wife caused Girard to become more and more reclusive as he grew older.

After the Revolution Girard returned to commerce. He initially focused on the West Indies, though he later also traded with Europe and Asia. Girard owned up to six ships at any one time and a total of eighteen over the course of his life. He named the flagships of his fleet after philosophers of his native France: *Montesquieu*, *Rousseau*, and *Voltaire*. In Girard's mind commerce was a noble enterprise that also advanced the development of nations.

The Napoleonic Wars in Europe jeopardized that commerce, however. Girard had much of his wealth located not in Philadelphia but in ships and cargoes spread across Europe. In 1807 Girard acted to shore up his foreign financial position. In October he dispatched a trusted assistant, Mahlon Hutchinson, Jr., to Europe to represent his interests. Correspondence with Girard's London agents at that time, Baring Brothers, shows no indication of a desire to remove funds from Europe.

The situation soon changed dramatically. In an effort to avoid conflict with both France and Great Britain, President Thomas Jefferson in late December embargoed all foreign trade. Over the next few months Girard centralized his European assets in London, using favorable exchange rates to transfer his funds from pounds sterling to dollars.

Beginning in 1808 Girard also explored options for repatriating his assets to the United States. With each shift of the political climate Girard changed his instructions to Hutchinson and Baring Brothers. Those maneuvers indicate the uncertainty of commercial relations between the United States and Europe. In general, Girard's options for transferring assets from Europe involved buying goods in Europe and shipping them to America, purchasing U. S. government stock, or purchasing shares in the Bank of the United States (BUS). While the shipment of goods across the Atlantic was risky, the purchase of stock also involved financial dangers. Exchange rates on U.S. government stock fluctuated

widely as the threat of war ebbed and flowed. Similarly, the uncertainty over the rechartering of the BUS affected its stock price. At that time Girard also dispatched three more assistants to Europe to help settle affairs.

At first Girard spread the financial risk by using all three options for repatriation of funds. Gradually he moved away from the maritime option and focused on the purchase of stock, especially BUS stock. That seemed like a good investment for Girard: if the bank received a new charter, its stock price would rise; even if the bank was not rechartered the liquidation value of the stock would be considerable.

By 1812 Girard had repatriated more than $1 million in assets. He had to decide how to employ those funds domestically in the face of disrupted foreign trade and an impending war. After due consideration of all his options, Girard opened in May a nonchartered "private" bank to replace the defunct Philadelphia office of the BUS. Girard's bank differed from other private banks, however, because it was not an unincorporated association; rather, the bank remained under Girard's sole ownership. Few individuals in early-nineteenth-century America could have undertaken a similar venture alone. Girard's personal contributions led to a bank capital of $1.5 million by January 1814; the bank's capital reached its highest level, $3 million, in January 1827. The bank quickly became a success, due in part to Girard's willingness to defer profits. Since there were no shareholders, he did not have to pay dividends. In the bank's early years Girard reinvested profits in the business, rejecting current income in favor of greater size and economic power. The combination of long-term objectives, personal wealth, and the residual reputation of the BUS made Girard's bank a major player on the local and national scenes.

Girard's importance in financial circles was apparent during the War of 1812. When the United States declared war on Britain in June 1812, the nation found itself in a precarious financial condition: tariff revenues had declined because of the hostilities, the government did not wish to institute new taxes to finance the war, and the opposition of the New England states to the war made the prospects of their economic assistance bleak.

The federal government therefore requested a loan of $11 million, primarily drawn from the Mid-Atlantic region. The subscriptions, however, totaled

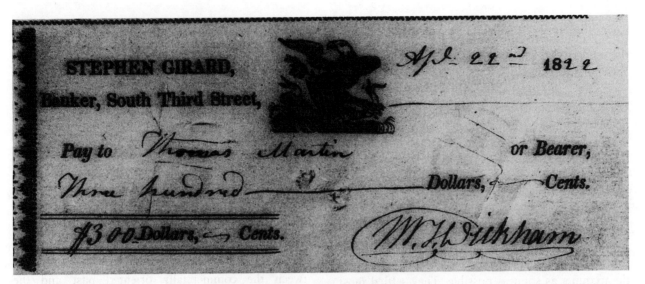

Check written on Stephen Girard's Bank

a disappointing $6 million. In 1813 Congress authorized another loan of up to $16 million, with prospects for success appearing just as limited. Public subscriptions eventually reached just $5.8 million, placing the financing of the war in jeopardy. Coming to the aid of the Treasury, Girard, David Parish, and John Jacob Astor formed a syndicate to raise the additional $10 million through the sale of government stock. Girard's stated as a condition for participating that his bank be recognized on an equal footing with Philadelphia's chartered institutions. He also hoped to benefit from the deposit of federal funds in his bank. Whatever his motives, Girard's actions, along with those of Parish and Astor, proved crucial in restoring public confidence in the U.S. Treasury.

As the war came to an end additional fiscal challenges awaited the country and Girard. A heavy drain on specie forced the banks of the nation to suspend specie payments in August 1814. Girard retrenched, drastically curtailing loans made by his bank. In the midst of this depression plans for a second national bank crystallized, with Girard acting as one of the leading players in the drama. Secretary of the Treasury A. J. Dallas consulted with Girard on the structure of the new bank. Both men viewed a national bank as key to returning federal finances to stability. Girard eventually was appointed one of the five commissioners to receive up to $28 million in bank stock subscriptions from the public. When subscriptions fell $3 million short of this total, Girard stepped forward as head of the syndicate and purchased all of the remaining shares. He therefore assured prompt opening of the bank.

When the Second Bank of the United States was officially organized on October 28, 1816, Girard served as one of five directors appointed by the government. As a further indication of Girard's importance, the directors held the organizational meeting in Girard's banking house in Philadelphia.

Girard's association with the Second BUS, however, lasted only a short time. He soon found himself at odds with the president of the bank, William Jones. Girard advocated that the bank's main office in Philadelphia issue all notes and distribute them to the various branches. In Girard's opinion that approach would promote uniform currency and centralized control of the bank. Ignoring Girard's advice, Jones instituted a system in which each branch issued its own notes; those notes in turn were redeemable at any other branch. In other matters as well Girard disagreed with Jones and the majority of directors. Realizing the futility of his opposition, Girard resigned as a director in December 1817.

After that time Girard's dealings with the Second BUS consisted of little more than pro forma settlements of accounts. Girard's close association with the Treasury also ended by 1820. During its last decade Girard's bank focused on its dealings with the other Philadelphia banks. The bank had reached the point where its chartered counterparts fully accepted it. In some ways, in fact, the institution was indistinguishable from its chartered competitors. The major difference between Girard's bank and the chartered banks was Girard's more conservative policies: he focused on short-term notes backed by commercial transactions, full specie reserves, and limited use of post notes. Girard also refused to pay interest to attract depositors, believing that the security of his institution should be enough to encourage business.

One additional difference existed. Unlike the other Philadelphia banks, Girard's bank was as mortal as its founder. When Stephen Girard died of pneumonia the day after Christmas in 1831, his bank died with him. Before his death Girard had made provisions for the settlement of the bank's affairs. At the end of 1831 the bank had assets of more than $6 million, loans outstanding of more than $3.2 million, and individual accounts in excess of $500,000. Out-of-town correspondent banks, informed of Girard's death, received instructions to settle accounts as soon as possible. They settled most outstanding loans by the middle of 1832, though collection efforts continued for five more years. As the trustees settled accounts they transferred funds to Girard's already sizable estate.

Girard's 1826 will reflected a lifelong interest in philanthropy and public service. As early as 1793 Girard gave liberally of his time and money during a severe yellow fever epidemic. He went so far as to volunteer for 60 days as superintendent of the "fever hospital" at Bush Hill, working closely with the patients on a daily basis. In keeping with that spirit Girard's will included the following bequests: $140,000 to relatives and several charities; $300,000 to the Commonwealth of Pennsylvania for internal improvements; $500,000 to the city of Philadelphia; and the remainder of more than $6 million in trust to the city for educating poor white orphan boys. No previous American had ever made such a large bequest for charitable and civic purposes. Disgruntled relatives challenged Girard's will, which the Supreme Court eventually upheld. Girard College stands today as a monument to its benefactor's ideals.

Over the course of his eighty-one years Stephen Girard had a profound impact on his city and the nation. Donald R. Adams, Jr., has summarized his importance and contribution: "Girard was at the same time a link with the past and a precursor of things to come in the financial world. As a product of the eighteenth century, he exhibited many characteristics of his mercantilist past. However, as a financier of great influence, wealth, and flexibility, he foreshadowed the great investment bankers who were to dominate the latter half of the nineteenth century. Perhaps it is in this role as a bridge between the commercially oriented past and the dynamic era of domestic growth that Girard should be remembered."

References:

Donald R. Adams, Jr., *Finance and Enterprise in Early America: A Study of Stephen Girard's Bank, 1812-1831* (Philadelphia: University of Pennsylvania Press, 1978);

Henry Atlee Ingram, *The Life and Character of Stephen Girard* (Philadelphia: Hart, 1884);

John Bach McMaster, *The Life and Times of Stephen Girard, Mariner and Merchant*, 2 volumes (Philadelphia & London: Lippincott, 1918);

Stephen Simpson, *Biography of Stephen Girard* (Philadelphia: Bonsal, 1832);

Harry Emerson Wildes, *Lonely Midas: The Story of Stephen Girard* (New York: Farrar & Rinehart, 1943).

Archives:

Stephen Girard's manuscripts are held by Girard College in Philadelphia. A microfilm version totaling 663 reels is available for research at the American Philosophical Society Library in Philadelphia.

William M. Gouge

(November 10, 1796-July 14, 1863)

by Kurt Schuler

George Mason University

CAREER: Publisher and editor, *Philadelphia Gazette and City Advertiser* (1823-1831); clerk, U.S. Department of the Treasury (1834-1841, 1843-1851, 1853-1856, 1859-1862); editor, *Journal of Banking* (1841-1842); accountant, State Bank of Arkansas (1857-1858).

William M. Gouge, financial journalist and government official, was born in Philadelphia on November 10, 1796. His father was a druggist. The family, which included a sister, was apparently well off, for Gouge once wrote that he enjoyed a higher station in life as a young man than he did in middle age.

The details of Gouge's early life remain obscure. He developed strong interests in banking and finance. In May 1823, when he was twenty-six years old, he and Stevenson Smith acquired the *Philadelphia Gazette and City Advertiser* upon the owner's death. The *Gazette*, a well-established daily paper, had been founded in 1788 as the *Federal Gazette*. Under Gouge it achieved less success than it might have because of its unpopular editorial policies, which he later estimated cost the paper one subscriber per day. Gouge used the *Gazette* to espouse monetary reform. He advocated abolishing small-denomination bank notes (those under $5), a position he adopted from Adam Smith and one that later established itself in American monetary orthodoxy. Though strongly Democratic, the paper avoided attacking the Bank of the United States (BUS) for fear of losing the bulk of its readers.

Gouge's friends included Condy Raguet, editor of the *Philadelphia Free Trade Advocate*, and Roberts Vaux, a Quaker philanthropist. In March 1829 all signed a petition to the state legislature "opposed to the chartering of any new banks." The petition, the product of "a large meeting of workingmen and others," was probably written by Raguet and Gouge. Philadelphia intellectuals, not workingmen, dominated the meeting. Among them were Wil-

liam J. Duane, a prominent lawyer who later became Andrew Jackson's secretary of the treasury, and Reuben M. Whitney, a businessman and former BUS director.

In February 1831 Gouge gave up his editorship of the *Gazette*. In November a Delaware newspaper employed him to report the debates of the state constitutional convention. He spent most of the two years after leaving the *Gazette* preparing *A Short History of Paper Money and Banking in the United States*, first published in February 1833. The book found a wide audience as debate over rechartering the BUS grew heated. It went through five American editions by 1842, one of which sold for only 25 cents, and many newspapers serialized it. At the time it was probably the best-read work on economics in America. Certainly the prominent Jacksonian radicals William Legget, Orestes Brownson, and William Cullen Bryant praised it lavishly. It delighted many within the Jackson administration, including Frank Blair, editor of the *Washington Globe* and a member of Jackson's Kitchen Cabinet. The book also enjoyed success abroad. The *Revue Universelle* of Brussels published an abridged French translation. The radical English writer and member of Parliament William Cobbett issued an abridged version entitled *The Curse of Paper Money and Banking*. He used Gouge's historical evidence to argue against making Bank of England notes legal tender and against repealing usury laws.

Gouge's *Short History of Paper Money and Banking in the United States* displays wide knowledge of banking theory and especially of American banking history. Gouge read extensively at the excellent libraries in Philadelphia and corresponded with knowledgeable persons throughout the country to gather information for the book. It consisted of a theoretical "Inquiry into the Principles of the American Banking System" and the "Short History"

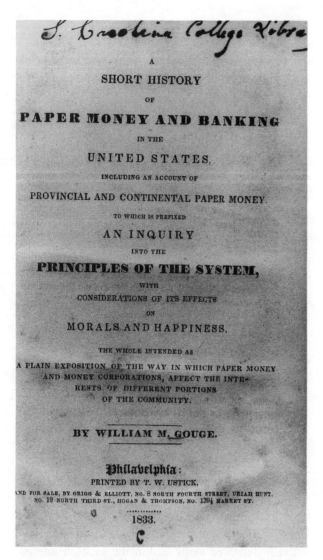

A

SHORT HISTORY

OF

PAPER MONEY AND BANKING

IN THE

UNITED STATES,

INCLUDING AN ACCOUNT OF

PROVINCIAL AND CONTINENTAL PAPER MONEY.

TO WHICH IS PREFIXED

AN INQUIRY

INTO THE

PRINCIPLES OF THE SYSTEM,

WITH

CONSIDERATIONS OF ITS EFFECTS

ON

MORALS AND HAPPINESS,

THE WHOLE INTENDED AS

A PLAIN EXPOSITION OF THE WAY IN WHICH PAPER MONEY
AND MONEY CORPORATIONS, AFFECT THE INTE-
RESTS OF DIFFERENT PORTIONS
OF THE COMMUNITY.

BY WILLIAM M. GOUGE.

Philadelphia:

PRINTED BY T. W. USTICK,

AND FOR SALE, BY GRIGG & ELLIOTT, NO. 8 NORTH FOURTH STREET, URIAH HUNT,
NO. 19 NORTH THIRD ST., HOGAN & THOMPSON, NO. 139½ MARKET ST.

1833.

Title page for Gouge's book arguing against a paper-money banking system

proper. According to the "Inquiry" banks were dangerous because they were, to use Thomas Jefferson's term, "a moneyed aristocracy." The powers granted to corporations reduced those of individuals and governments. Limited stockholder liability for corporate debts diminished the incentive to conduct business prudently. The result was "that want of moral feeling and responsibility which characterizes corporations." The defects of corporate organization were so great, Gouge contended, that corporations could only survive if governments protected them from competition. As evidence, he cited the prohibitions that existed in most states against banking without a government charter.

For Gouge, as for many of his contemporaries, limited liability constituted a mark of special privilege. General incorporation laws did not come

into existence in the United States until the 1860s. Until then only banks, insurance companies, canals, turnpikes, and railroads usually received corporate charters. State governments often helped finance such enterprises, sometimes in return for bribes or political favors. However, Gouge ignored the fact that practices varied widely among states. New England states granted bank charters liberally; consequently, their charter requirements offered few obstacles to competition. Elsewhere, especially in New York, securing a charter often required extensive bribery and legislative battling.

Gouge maintained that government favors such as charters and acceptance of bank notes for taxes implicitly placed government credit behind the banks, enabling them to "coin money out of paper." Unlike some writers of the era, Gouge recognized the equivalence of bank deposits and bank notes. He stated clearly the difference between 100 percent reserve banking and fractional reserve banking. As a sort of shorthand, though, he restricted consideration to notes—"paper money"—in most of his arguments. He thought paper money had no real benefits. It merely raised prices and deranged economic activity. In a hard-money system money and credit remained distinct. Creditors granted credit directly to borrowers through bills of exchange, ledger entries, and promissory notes. Underlying economic realities kept the supply and demand for credit in harmony. In a paper-money system, on the other hand, bank credit and money were the same as far as people within that country were concerned. Banks separated borrowers from ultimate creditors, which encouraged imprudent lending. Banks could expand credit for long periods even though underlying economic realities failed to justify it. Thus, prices rose. Eventually, though, higher domestic prices made a country's export goods more expensive than those of other countries. Foreigners who held notes of the country's banks, instead of buying the country's export goods, demanded specie (gold or silver), draining bank reserves and forcing banks to contract credit. A depression followed.

The frequent suspensions of specie payments that Americans had experienced, under both government note issue and bank-note issue, comprised an unavoidable part of the American banking system, Gouge contended. He argued that, contrary to the opinion of many eminent economists, obliging banks to redeem their notes in specie on demand did not confine bank credit expansion within narrow limits. Convertibility was, rather, only a very loose check on banks, a "contrivance" designed to dupe the public into accepting bank notes.

Again in this case Gouge ignored differences among state practices. New England states strictly enforced banks' obligation to redeem notes in specie. Redemption demands from within that region proved far more important in checking bank credit expansion than redemption demands from abroad. At the time Gouge wrote, there had never been a general suspension of specie payments among New England banks, and note quality was higher there than anywhere else in the country. Other states, especially in the South, often helped banks evade the obligation to redeem notes in specie. Convertibility there was in some cases a dead letter. Suspension of payments could last for years, and bank notes in such states traded at steep and irregular discounts to specie.

Gouge argued that banks had harmful social effects as well as harmful economic effects; indeed, he called banks "the principal cause of our social evils." He claimed that paper-money issue redistributed wealth from the laboring poor to the rich, undermining morals and decreasing the standard of communal honesty by encouraging reckless speculation. "Wages," he wrote, "appear to be among the last things that are raised by an increase of Bank medium. The working man finds all the articles he uses in his family raising in price, while the money rate of his own wages remains unchanged." Ironically, many years later the Populists and other paper-money advocates drew their strongest support from workingmen.

Despite Gouge's hostility to paper money, he did not advocate revolutionary measures to abolish it. He realized that a sudden contraction of bank-note issues would depress prices and upset the basis on which economic activity then rested. Therefore, he proposed gradually reducing bank-note issues to zero by prohibiting first the lower and then the higher denominations, over a ten-year period. He took encouragement from recent measures by some states to prohibit notes under $5. He probably was unaware that the supply of small notes and tokens grew rapidly during his life. Gouge produced statistics to show that suppressing small notes would still leave ample specie available to pay for other imports. Even if abolishing bank notes should take 20 or 30 years, he concluded, it "is but a short period in the lifetime of a nation."

An essential step in getting rid of the paper-money system was to separate government finance from banking, Gouge thought. That would remove the temptation to grant government favors to banks in exchange for bribes. He proposed that the federal government (and, by implication, state governments) establish a system of subtreasury offices to keep its funds and hold nothing but specie. The federal government already collected taxes at many points; setting up subtreasury offices at the chief ones would require few additional personnel. Its practice of depositing its funds at the BUS was unnecessary and dangerous, Gouge contended. It enlisted government support for the bank's purely private ends. It encouraged on a national scale the paper-money system Gouge thought he had shown to be so destructive at the state level. And although the government had not lost any money through the bank so far, no guarantee existed that such would be the case in the future, especially during wartime. A war lasting two years or more (such as the War of 1812 had) would certainly compel the bank to suspend specie payments or curtail credit, either of which would produce a calamity. However, "Let Bank notes be withdrawn, and such an accumulation of gold and silver coin will be made by individuals, that in no possible exigency will there be a real scarcity of money."

The second, historical part of the *Short History of Paper Money and Banking* attempted to demonstrate that experience bore out Gouge's theories. It comprised the first thorough research into the history of the American banking system considered as a whole. Its facts were quite reliable, though its interpretations often were not.

Before the first issue of paper money, Gouge claimed, the supply of specie had proved adequate for the demands of trade, though not plentiful enough to satisfy all those who desired overly cheap credit. Attempts to prevent the export of coins by raising their legal-tender value had raised nominal prices without accomplishing the desired end. The Massachusetts colonial government made the first issue of paper money in the United States, in 1690, initially to pay soldiers, later to fund government expenses and to try to help trade. In later decades other colonies followed the Massachusetts example. All saw their currency depreciate against specie. Gouge stressed the harmful political and moral effects of the colonial issues. Making them legal tender was "an act of tyranny." However, in contrast to bank paper money, colonial issues had had the peculiar merit of being so ill-managed that they destroyed confidence and prevented credit from spreading to the "pernicious" extent possible under a system of bank credit. The Continental currency continued the colonial tradition of depreciating paper-money issues. Gouge saw the currency as "a tax, the expenses of collecting which were many times as great as the sum brought into the treasury. The benefit the government derived from it was in no way commensurate with the burden it imposed on the people," which fell disproportionately on the patriotic and the poor.

Gouge deprecated the banks that the federal government had used as its fiscal agents. He felt the Bank of North America got far more benefit from its involvement with the government than the government ever got from the bank. The First BUS was inessential–the expiration of its charter in 1812 did not interrupt the progress of industry–and undemocratic. The Second BUS did not restore specie payments in the South and West after it started operations; it merely brought inconvertible state-chartered banks' notes to par with one another, but not with specie. Furthermore, it caused the Panic of 1819, and by its policy of reducing exchange rates among the regions of the nation removed "the only effective check on overtrading." (That remained consistent with Gouge's emphasis on external demand for specie rather than local demand as the brake on credit expansion.)

The history of state banking systems, according to Gouge, followed a similarly dreary path of inflation, depression, suspension of payments, and moneyed monopoly. He compared the actions of banks to "that of so many drunken men passing along the street together, occasionally supporting one another, and occasionally knocking one another down. Their motion is vacillating, tottering. It is rarely in a straight line." The "vibrations of Bank medium" had been frequent and severe.

Gouge's peroration stressed that "Paper-money Banking is *essentially bad*." He rejected the idea that more liberal granting of charters would allay the banking system's bad effects, claiming, "It would be as rational to attempt to abolish a political aristocracy by multiplying the number of nobles." To institute a good system required exertion, but not so much as many imagined. "Nine Americans in ten, if not ninety-nine in a hundred, have an interest in the downfall of the paper-money and money corporation system, and it is impossible for them not to see, sooner or later, where their true interest lies."

The success of the *Short History* prompted Secretary of the Treasury Levi Woodbury to offer Gouge a clerkship in the secretary's office. Roberts Vaux encouraged Gouge to accept the post, which Gouge assumed in June 1834 at a salary of $1,000 per year. That month the anti-Jackson Democratic Congressman William F. Gordon of Virginia introduced a bill proposing to remove the federal government's deposits from the state-chartered "pet banks," where they had resided since the government ran down its deposits in the BUS beginning October 1833. Condy Raguet persuaded Gordon to introduce the bill. It died, but in January 1835 Congressman Roger Gamble of Georgia introduced a similar bill. Gamble, like many congressional Democrats, opposed the BUS, but he was also angry that the Jackson administration had not sought Congress's approval to shift deposits to the state banks. His bill ordered the secretary of the treasury to study the separation of government finances from banking. In anticipation that it might pass, Woodbury ordered Gouge to gather materials on the question.

Gouge proceeded cautiously, treating the matter abstractly in a report entitled "A Memoir on the Expediency of Establishing Subtreasury Offices" that he gave to Woodbury in April 1835. Reuben M. Whitney, who had signed Gouge's 1829 workingmen's petition, held a position above Gouge in the Treasury Department. Whitney had changed his views in the intervening years and now supported the pet-bank system. Gouge carefully avoided arousing Whitney's opposition. The House of Representatives tabled Gamble's bill by a narrow vote and passed instead the administration's bill regulating the pet banks, so Gouge's report never became public. Gouge applied for a job as one of the clerks to supervise accounts in the state banks under the new law but was passed over for a man with less experience. Though not promoted, he did get a $400 raise in salary, to $1,400 per year. To his chagrin, he was passed over for another promotion in favor of the ex-husband of one of Woodbury's relatives.

In August 1836, shortly before the last session of Congress of the Jackson administration, Gouge wrote the president a long memorandum, based on the research he had done earlier for Woodbury, about the practicability of separating government funds from the banking system. Two of Jackson's friends, Amos Kendall and the late Roberts Vaux, had encouraged Gouge to do so. Jackson's own actions also gave Gouge hope of a hearing for antibank views. In his 1830 address to Congress, Jackson touched on the possibility of divorcing the state from banking, switching from his position of the previous year, which had favored a new national bank. And one of the few times that Gouge met Jackson, Jackson remarked to him that "The American Banking system has done more moral evil than the temple of Juggernaut."

Gouge contended that the American banking system rested on four legs: bank cupidity, public ignorance about paper-money banking, state government support, and federal government support. If the federal government removed its deposits from the state banks, the public would become aware of the dangers of the banking system and require state governments to withdraw state deposits also, leaving the banks politically and economically isolated. By that means Jackson could achieve the monetary system that Thomas Jefferson had desired, but that Alexander Hamilton had thwarted with what Gouge characterized as a system of aristocratic commercial privilege (that is, special charters).

The federal government could easily dispense with state banks and paper money, Gouge said. The extra expense of keeping government gold in separate subtreasuries would be small, and even that would be offset by the safety of the subtreasury system, for the government would never have to worry that a bank failure would wipe out some of its funds. Gouge tried to dispose of the objection that such a policy might cause a depression. Appealing to economic principle, he said that, since the supply of specie always answered to its effective demand, no shortage of specie could exist. Furthermore, it would be in neither the public's interest nor the government's to demand a sudden massive withdrawal of specie from circulation into government vaults. Finally, believing as he did that the amount of precious metals in circulation provided a barometer of a monetary system's health, Gouge claimed that no other policy would so effectively replace bank notes with gold in everyday use.

Jackson apparently read Gouge's memorandum carefully, but he took no action on it. Shortly after American banks suspended specie payments in the financial panic of May 1837, Gouge published

a revised version of the memorandum as *An Inquiry into the Expediency of Dispensing with Bank Agency and Bank Paper in the Fiscal Concerns of the United States*. He did so without informing the administration because, as he disingenuously explained to Woodbury, he did not want to give the impression that his views had official standing. The banks' suspension of payments threatened to paralyze government finances, and the new president, Martin Van Buren, called a special session of Congress for September to resolve the issue. In June Gouge sent Van Buren a delicately worded report listing the important issues and proposing policies to handle them. On the question of whether to accept credit for customs and excise taxes, Gouge suggested allowing delays of payment as long as six months. He recommended postponing the October payment of surplus federal government revenue to the states until the next year or even indefinitely. On the question of whether to issue treasury notes temporarily, Gouge strongly opposed non-interest-bearing notes payable for federal taxes and proposed that if notes must be issued, they should be interest-bearing and not payable for taxes. He also advocated the establishment of a subtreasury system to handle the government's funds, and he recommended that the government accept payment only in specie. He proposed a combination of incentives and threats to get the government's frozen deposits out of state banks and recommended that the government tolerate suspension of gold and silver payments in the District of Columbia, where it could pass a law to end the suspension, for 60 to 90 days at the most.

At the special session Van Buren proposed the subtreasury (or independent treasury) system Gouge had advocated in the *Short History of Paper Money and Banking* and in the memorandum to Woodbury. After heated debate the Senate passed the subtreasury bill, but the House defeated it in March 1838. Congress did approve interest-bearing treasury notes receivable for taxes and postponed dispensing the budget surplus, as Gouge had recommended. The subtreasury bill died again in the next Congress, but a wave of bank suspensions of specie payments in 1839 gave it new appeal, and it narrowly passed both houses of Congress, as the Independent Treasury Act, in June 1840. Gouge hoped for some reward as the idea's originator, but got none, prompting him to complain to Van Buren. For some time Gouge had worked as a traveling inspector of the pet banks, a job that worsened his rather delicate health. He asked Van Buren for a raise to $1,600 or, if not, requested that his unemployed brother-in-law be given a job as his assistant. Otherwise, Gouge said, the responsibility of supporting his brother-in-law's family devolved on him. Since he did not mention having a family of his own to support, it seems he was a bachelor.

Whether Van Buren granted Gouge's request is not known. Gouge still worked in the Treasury in 1841, when the Whig administration of William Henry Harrison and John Tyler came into office. Thomas Ewing, the new secretary of the treasury, fired Gouge in April "on account of my Democracy," as Gouge put it. Forty-four years old, he returned to Philadelphia and started the fortnightly *Journal of Banking* in June. Intended to provide running commentary on current events to supplement the *Short History of Paper Money and Banking*, it reached for a broad audience. Gouge took particular pleasure in noting the defects of the American banking system, such as discounts on circulating notes, embezzlements, and bank failures. News of the failure of the BUS and the subsequent trial of its president, Nicholas Biddle, occupied considerable space in the *Journal*. In addition to news, the *Journal* contained articles on banking theory (it reprinted the *Short History of Paper Money and Banking*), accounts of foreign banking systems, parables, and even poetry, such as this "Epigram-Impromptu":

Of modern books, the best I know—
  The author all the world is thanking—
One written more for use than show,
  Is quaintly titled, "*Gouge* on Banking."

But still improvements might be made,
  Whilst books on books the world is scrouging,
Let *Biddle* try to help the trade,
  And write one titled, "Banks on *Gouging*."

The Whigs' repeal of the Independent Treasury and their attempt (which President Tyler unexpectedly vetoed) to establish a new national bank angered Gouge, who thundered against them in the *Journal*. He contended that any plan to keep government deposits in banks was "UNCONSTITUTIONAL" because "The object of the framers of the constitution, was that ours should be a *hard money* government." Paper-money banking owed its origin and its continued existence to the demands of government finance, especially govern-

ment debt. Therefore, government deposits in banks posed extreme danger, he claimed.

Gouge reiterated his proposal of the *Short History* for gradually introducing a purely metallic currency by prohibiting first lower and then higher denominations of all bank notes not backed 100 percent by gold and silver. He contended that the existing currency system relied so heavily on bank notes because "a medium of less value will always displace a medium of greater value." That incorrect formulation of Gresham's Law failed to add that such a displacement only happens when the two media have the same legal-tender sanction; otherwise the medium of less value trades at a discount to the medium of greater value. Gouge took pains to show that, should paper money be prohibited, adequate gold and silver existed to replace it. He estimated that in the United States the amount of the precious metals then in circulation already totaled "about half the sum required to enable us to dispense entirely with the use of paper *as money*." The country could easily obtain the balance in the normal course of trade over the next ten or twelve years.

In a series on "The True Principles of Commercial Banking" published in the journal, Gouge distinguished the granting of credit from "coining" paper money. He adhered to the so-called real-bills doctrine of Adam Smith and other writers, which held that bank credits could not be inflationary if issued to finance short-term movements of goods from production to sale. However, in the banking practice of his own day, Gouge believed that this healthy form of banking, which could be carried on entirely by bills of exchange and without paper money, had mixed with unhealthy paper-money banking, which fostered speculation and business cycles. Like other proponents of the real-bills doctrine, he particularly condemned mortgage lending as an inappropriate activity for banks. He rejected the idea, which Smith and others had inconsistently held alongside the real-bills doctrine, that a paper currency always convertible into gold and silver regulates itself. "Paper money is merely the representative of a *debt* due by the issuer to the holder. Gold and silver may be said to represent the *labor* and the *capital* which have been employed in producing them." Hence convertible bank paper cannot really be said to be founded on gold and silver, or to have "that *stability* of value which every currency ought to possess." To remedy the suspension of convertibility that banks outside of New England and New York had made in 1839 and again in 1841, Gouge proposed at a minimum that governments forbid banks to pay dividends until they had resumed payments for at least three months.

The *Journal of Banking* never achieved success; it had only 1,600 subscribers. Gouge was disappointed that bankers, especially, seemed reluctant to subscribe. It ceased publication in July 1842, one year after its first issue.

Sometime in that period Gouge's mother died. An acquaintance, the Philadelphia Democratic Congressman Charles Brown, remarked that the circumstances were "particularly affecting." Gouge's father had probably been dead for some time. Brown wrote the Whig secretary of the treasury, Walter Forward, imploring him to give Gouge a job as a special agent. Brown noted Gouge's poverty and pointed out that his knowledge of banking theory was useless for business but could benefit the government. Forward, a Pennsylvanian, appointed Gouge a customs agent in New York. Gouge wrote occasional free-lance essays on banking, as he had done since the 1830s. Over the years his work appeared in the *United States Magazine and Democratic Review*, the *Washington Globe, Hunt's Merchants' Magazine*, and the *Bankers' Magazine and Statistical Register*. In October 1843 the next treasury secretary, John C. Spencer, offered Gouge a post in Washington. Gouge accepted, even though he preferred the diversions of a large city to the quiet of the small town that Washington then was, partly because they kept him from dwelling on his mother's death.

The Democratic administration of James K. Polk reestablished the Independent Treasury System in August 1846. In August 1848 Secretary Robert J. Walker appointed Gouge a traveling inspector of the system. Gouge traveled through most of the country east of the Mississippi, at a salary of $6 per day plus 10 cents per mile in expenses. He continued his hobby of collecting banking statistics and historical material.

In April 1851 a Whig administration again fired Gouge. He journeyed to Texas. Stranded in Austin by floods in the surrounding region, he passed the time by doing research. The result was *The Fiscal History of Texas*, which appeared in 1852. The book expounded his belief that "The paper-money disease is hereditary with us Americans. If it is subdued in one form, it breaks out in another." He condemned the treasury notes the Texas government issued before Texas joined the United States. Gouge viewed the partial repudiation of public debt as an "infamy." Though "A public debt is a public evil," once undertaken for however foolish a purpose, it is a lawful obligation and ought to be paid, he argued. Gouge found a correspondence between periods of paper money issue and periods of economic hardship in Texas. He observed with pleasure that as a republic and a state, Texas prohibited banking. (Such prohibitions were common in western states during the 1840s, but did not stop banking from appearing under other guises. Insurance companies and other allegedly nonbanking concerns issued notes and accepted deposits.)

Gouge was by that time fifty-six years old. Experience had shown him that he could not make an adequate living by writing. Accordingly, he went from Philadelphia down to Washington to ask the new Democratic secretary of the treasury, James Guthrie, for a job. He stressed his "thorough acquaintance with the duties of what may be called the Statistical and political-Economical work of your bureau." Guthrie appointed him a clerk in the secretary's office.

Gouge traveled widely as an inspector of the Independent Treasury System, of steamboats, and of naval hospitals. His report on the Independent Treasury claimed that the system, though imperfect in some of its details because it was not adequately funded, had done much good and promised to do more. He particularly stressed that it had avoided the losses that failures had caused under the pet-bank system, and that it held the banking system somewhat in check by preventing the even greater inflation that would occur if all the country's gold and silver resided in banks. To reduce shipments of the precious metals among subtreasury branches, Gouge proposed that they issue drafts on one another. That would allow settlers to avoid carrying gold and silver over long distances, since they could get a draft in the East and use it to pay for lands in the West, where payments had to be made at the subtreasury branch nearest the land. However, to discourage the drafts from circulating as currency, Gouge suggested that each draft be made payable only at one branch. The Treasury adopted the proposal.

As an inspector of steamboats Gouge traveled the Mississippi and its tributaries. At least once he experienced the boiler room fires that frequently endangered wooden vessels of the era. In a parallel to his views on bank regulation, he held that steamboat regulation, though incompatible with perfect freedom of contract, was justified by the public's inability to judge adequately the safety of the boats. Once the government put safety regulations in place, though, Gouge believed that competition should determine the service offered.

At the end of his 1855 report on naval hospitals Gouge wrote, "I pen these remarks with the expectation of being separated, for a time, from the Treasury Department." Eventually, if not immediately, he went to Arkansas, which he had occasionally visited as a Treasury agent. In 1857 and 1858 he and A. H. Rutherford served as accountants for the State Bank of Arkansas, which languished in the midst of a long drawn-out liquidation. It and a twin, the Real Estate Bank of Arkansas, had operated as monopolies, and both had failed from graft, corruption, and mismanagement. What Gouge saw further confirmed his antibank views.

Following his Arkansas assignment Gouge returned to the Treasury Department. By that time his salary was $1,600 per year, and he held the post of third-class clerk. In March 1862, two months after it had suspended specie payments and effectively disbanded important features of the Independent Treasury System, the Lincoln administration dismissed him. Gouge died on July 14, 1863, in Trenton, New Jersey, at the age of sixty-six.

Gouge unquestionably was the most influential American banking theorist of his day. He also influenced later hard-money economists, especially Amasa Walker, whose popular textbooks reproduced Gouge's views in modified form. Despite the cost to his financial security, Gouge consistently and outspokenly defended hard money throughout his adult life. His chief practical accomplishment was the Independent Treasury System, which enjoyed wide political popularity, especially after it enabled the government to avoid in the Panic of 1857 the fiscal crisis it suffered in the Panic of 1837.

Publications:

A Short History of Paper Money and Banking in the United States, Including an Account of the Provincial and Continental Paper Money. To Which is Prefixed an Inquiry into the Principles of the System (Philadelphia: T. W. Ustick, 1833);

An Inquiry into the Expediency of Dispensing with Bank Agency and Bank Paper in the Fiscal Concerns of the United States (Philadelphia: William Stavely, 1837);

The Fiscal History of Texas. Embracing an Account of Its Revenues, Debts, and Currency, from the Commencement of the Revolution in 1834 to 1851-2. With Remarks on American Debts (Philadelphia: Lippincott, Grambo, 1852);

Report of the Accountants of the State Bank of Arkansas, Made to the Governor, in Pursuance of Law, by Gouge and A. H. Rutherford (Little Rock: Johnson & Yerkes, 1858).

References:

Joseph Dorfman, "William M. Gouge and the Formation of Orthodox American Monetary Policy," introduction to Gouge's *A Short History of Paper Money and Banking* (New York: Kelley, 1968);

Lloyd W. Mints, *A History of Banking Theory in Great Britain and in the United States* (Chicago: University of Chicago Press, 1945);

Benjamin G. Rader, "William Gouge: Jacksonian Economic Theorist," *Pennsylvania History*, 30 (October 1963): 443-453.

Archives:

Gouge's official letters are at the National Archives: in the Andrew Jackson Papers, the Martin Van Buren Papers, the Levi Woodbury Papers, and the Treasury file relating to Gouge. Some personal letters are in the Henry Lee Papers at the Massachusetts Historical Society and the Blair Papers at Princeton University Library.

Hetty Green

(November 21, 1834-July 3, 1916)

by Janet L. Coryell

Auburn University

CAREER: Private banker and moneylender (1870-1910).

Hetty Green, the so-called "Witch of Wall Street," was the most recognized "ready-money" lender on Wall Street at the turn of the century and the richest woman in America at the time of her death in 1916. Tales of her miserliness and eccentricities were legion. She posed as a poor woman to obtain free medical care at charity hospitals, ate at soup kitchens, lived in a succession of cold-water flats and two-room walkups to avoid paying taxes, and once pulled a pistol on railroad magnate Collis P. Huntington during the course of a business discussion. Her black bonnet, moth-eaten seal cape, and cheap black dress so long worn it had turned green painted a portrait that provided her with her nickname, an appellation made still more appropriate by her shrewd gray eyes and sharp tongue. She was obsessed with making and hoarding money, and the key to her success involved no great secret, as she once remarked: "I believe in getting in at the bottom and out at the top. All you have to do is buy cheap and sell dear, act with thrift and shrewdness and be persistent." Green's instinct and talent parlayed her considerable inheritance into a fortune estimated at perhaps $200 million at her death. Her son, Edward, interviewed by the *New York Times* shortly afterward, called his mother a "one-man bank." "There [was] no better judge of commercial paper in the United States," he boasted, than this woman who always kept $20 million to $30 million in cash on hand for short-term loans.

Henrietta Howland Robinson was born on November 21, 1834, in New Bedford, Massachusetts, the firstborn and only daughter of Edward Mott Robinson and Abby Slocum Howland Robinson. The Howland and Robinson families were two of the oldest and wealthiest in New England. Hetty Robinson's great-grandfather Isaac Howland, Jr.,

Hetty Green

founded a whaling company that owned 30 ships and parts of more. Her grandfather, Gideon Howland, had a partial interest in the company, and his two daughters, her mother, Abby, and her maiden aunt, Sylvia Ann, had shares, as did her father, Edward "Black Hawk" Robinson. He came from a prominent Quaker family of Providence, Rhode Island, and entered the Howland firm about 1833, shortly after marrying Abby. "Black Hawk" Robinson was so called less for his hawklike features than for his ruthless business manner, which was said to parallel the ruthlessness of the Illinois Indian chief of the same name. He was not amused by the denomination: he fired anyone he heard call him "Black Hawk" just as he fired any worker he thought to be shirking his duties. A demanding and determined man dedicated to making money, Black Hawk possessed a ferocious temper. Nevertheless, he conducted himself honorably, according to Quaker principles. He believed in simplicity and thrift and taught his daughter to value those virtues above all others.

When Hetty Robinson was eighteen months old her parents celebrated the birth of their only other child, a son. Both births had taxed Abby Robinson's strength to the breaking point, so the family sent the daughter to live with her widowed grandfather, Gideon Howland, his stepmother-in-law, Ruth, and her aunt, Sylvia, who raised her even after her baby brother died. Gideon Howland ran his home with frugality, and all three adults continually impressed upon young Hetty the importance of simplicity in life. They taught her to ride, to drive a carriage, and to read, and, as her grandfather's sight failed, she read the financial news to him every morning. By the time she reached fifteen she knew the difference between bulls and bears and how stocks and bonds could be manipulated to make money.

Robinson had a limited formal education. At age ten she went to a Quaker boarding school run by Eliza Wing in Sandwich, Massachusetts. After three years of rigorous religious education and a memorably bad diet she returned to New Bedford for her grandfather's funeral and the reading of the will. Much to her chagrin, her grandfather left her nothing, dividing his $800,000 estate instead among his brothers, nieces, nephews, and daughters. She was disproportionately disappointed by what she viewed as a betrayal of her right to an inheritance, thus giving the first indications of a lifelong obsession with not only money but with her "rights," real or imagined. This obsession manifested itself first in thrift, then in complaints when any member of her family bought anything. She knew she would be the sole heir to both the Howland and Robinson fortunes and was determined to preserve them.

When Robinson's mother died intestate in February 1860, father and daughter agreed to abide by an attorney's decision regarding the division of the estate. Disregarding nineteenth-century traditions regarding property, the lawyer allotted Edward Robinson the personal property of his wife, worth some

$120,000, while Hetty Robinson inherited the $8,000 in real estate. Most of Edward Robinson's inheritance was in the form of a trust fund Abby had inherited from her grandfather. Sylvia Ann Howland claimed Abby Robinson had always intended the money to go to her daughter, Hetty, but Edward Robinson held fast to the cash. Sylvia had never liked her brother-in-law, and that imposition of his will led to their final break. A year later Edward Robinson dissolved the Howland whaling firm and moved to New York, where he became partner with William T. Coleman of Coleman & Company, shippers.

Hetty Robinson, then twenty-five, did not accompany her father to New York but instead lived with her aunt. Fully aware of how much she stood to inherit (by then about $2 million), she drove her invalid aunt to distraction with her petty economies. She cancelled food orders, dismissed servants, and badgered her aunt to change her will to eliminate all charitable bequests. She threw temper tantrums and sulked and swore until her aunt finally banished her from the house. She moved to New York and continued to plague her aunt with letters, protesting her affection, her resentment at her aunt's treatment of her, and her horror at gossip that her aunt continued to spend money on an addition to her house. She also kept an eye on her father and his lawyer, hoping to control the formulation of his will so the money would be hers outright. The usual nineteenth-century trust arrangement limited inheritances of women, who at that time were thought to be incapable of managing any more than the smallest sums of money.

On June 14, 1865, Edward Robinson died. On July 2 Sylvia Ann Howland died. Within two weeks Hetty Robinson's worth had gone from about $31,000 to, she estimated, about $7 million. But her father had given her only $1 million outright in his will; the rest remained in trust. Sylvia Howland's will proved an even bigger disappointment. She had left her niece only the income from just over $1 million, and that in trust. The rest of her $2 million went to friends and charities.

Enraged by the will, Robinson challenged the document on two counts. She held that her aunt was not of sound mind when she executed it, and that there was another will anyway—a cooperative will made between Robinson and her aunt that gave everything to the one who survived the other.

Only $100,000 of Sylvia Howland's fortune went to others besides Robinson under the second will.

The will was no doubt a forgery, but the case lasted almost six years, cost more than $150,000 in attorneys' fees, and produced 1,000 pages of testimony. Naturalist Louis Agassiz and Dr. Oliver Wendell Holmes testified for Robinson that the signatures of Sylvia Howland under suspicion were genuine. Innumerable others testified against the claim, declaring that someone had almost certainly traced the disputed signatures. The three signatures on the document looked so identical that noted mathematician Benjamin Pierce put the chances of them being coincidentally identical at one in 2.666 sextillion.

The court dismissed the lawsuit over the will in 1868 on a technicality and left Hetty Green with a lifetime hatred of both lawyers and judges. In the meantime she had married Edward Henry Green, a native of Bellows Falls, Vermont, and a highly successful trader with Russell & Sturgis of Manila, the Philippines. Her father had met Green in New York and introduced the two before his death. Edward Green had a net worth of about $1 million at the time of their marriage in New York City on July 11, 1867. Hetty, nevertheless, made him sign a prenuptial agreement making him responsible for all household expenses and absolving her from any responsibilities for his debts, this despite New York State's married woman property laws that protected her fortune from coming under his control. The Greens left for England soon after the wedding, in part to escape the possibility that Hetty might be charged with forging her late aunt's will. They lived in London until 1874, and there their two children, Edward Howland Robinson and Hetty Sylvia Ann Howland, were born.

In London Hetty Green moved into the financial market for the first time, primarily through purchasing U.S. gold bonds. Some she had inherited as a final settlement of Sylvia Howland's estate, others she bought outright. In one year of her London stay she made more than $1.25 million. U.S. bonds sold cheaply in London just after the Civil War, when rumors abounded that the federal government would pay interest in paper instead of gold, but their value crept upward in the early 1870s. Green held $600,000 worth of bonds in 1871 that by 1874 were worth $732,000. She bought thousands more on the London market, some for as low as 40 cents on the dollar. In addition, she invested heavily in railroads as offerings of those bonds exploded

in the 1870s. But marriage and more money did not appreciably change Green's approach to living. Her husband, paying the household bills, preferred to live in luxury. She lived with him, but continued to wear shabby clothes and pinch pennies. In one incident during their years in London, Green provided first aid to an injured passerby. A marchioness saw her, ragged and obviously destitute, and sent for her to offer her a job as a superintendent of a charity hospital with living quarters included. Green declined the offer without revealing her identity and later remarked how honored she was to be offered such a position. She prided herself on her ability to aid others as long as it did not involve spending any money. Her husband, on the other hand, enjoyed the good life. Their disparate views of the purpose and function of money eventually led to their separation.

The Panic of 1873 brought the Greens home in 1874. Hetty Green's heavy investments in railroads, particularly the Louisville & Nashville and the Rock Island, were hard hit: Rock Island stock dropped from 108 7/8 to 86 in just 16 days. Her husband had given her fundamentally sound advice on speculation, but he had not foreseen the panic, and from that point on Green grew more cautious, continually warning her bankers in New York, John J. Cisco & Son, not to confuse their two accounts.

From 1874 to 1885 the Greens resided in Edward's hometown of Bellows Falls. They spent winters in New York and Chicago, where Edward continued to speculate and Hetty continued to invest conservatively, primarily in real estate, and to raise the children. Her son, nicknamed Ned, was her pride and joy, but her strange obsession with saving money cost him a great deal. Not only did he and his sister suffer the taunts of other children because of their shabby appearances, but when Ned injured his knee in a sledding accident, his mother refused to take him to a doctor. She tried to treat the injury herself, but eventually, having applied hot sand as a poultice that burned the knee badly, she had to resort to a physician. She dressed herself and Ned in rags and got treatment for her son at Bellevue Hospital as a charity case. Incensed at her masquerade when he learned her identity, the doctor demanded his fee in advance; Green refused to pay and never returned. The worse Ned's knee got the more doctors she consulted, but she always tried to present herself as a charity case to avoid paying a fee. Finally, about 1888, the leg developed gangrene and had to be amputated. Edward Green, anxious to have the problem solved and eager to avoid a scene he knew would occur if Hetty found out the operation cost $5,000, paid the bill. Ned, a gregarious man, did not appear permanently traumatized by his mother's failure to secure medical aid. He knew she hated and distrusted doctors as much as lawyers and knew also of her frequent promises to make him the richest man in the world.

By the time of Ned's amputation the Greens no longer lived together. In 1885 Edward Green had gone bankrupt. His stock market adventures always had involved more risk than Hetty liked, but Edward loved the danger and could always get credit on the strength of her fortune, even after he had run through his own. In 1884 John J. Cisco, founder of John J. Cisco & Son, died. His son and namesake, a far more adventuresome financier, took over the bank and brokerage business. He extended credit to Edward Green not only because Hetty had $550,000 on deposit but also because she stored much of her treasure in bonds, mortgages, and securities, some $25 million worth, in one of the bank's vaults, free of charge. Edward's investments in late 1884 and early 1885 suffered from the nationwide business depression, and his Louisville & Nashville Railroad stock, which served as collateral for his loan account, had declined in worth far below the amount he owned. He also participated in an opium pool in which he lost a small fortune. Hetty, who had bailed Edward out of the market several times previously, expressed increasing concern over the management of the Cisco bank. In January 1885 she demanded that the bank transfer her money to the Chemical National Bank. Cisco refused unless Hetty paid Edward's debts, by that time more than $700,000. For two solid weeks Hetty besieged the bank's managers and lawyers with threats, tears, and pleas. They stood firm, managing to convince her that her prenuptial agreement with Edward was not enforceable, and she paid the debt, receiving Edward's Louisville & Nashville Railroad stock in exchange for cash.

The episode had several repercussions. Edward went to live at the Union League Club, where he continued to reside until just before his death in 1902. The marriage effectively ended, and from that point on it was Mrs. Hetty Green, not Mrs. Edward Green, who practiced her financial wizardry on Wall Street. When Hetty asked for her

The "Witch of Wall Street" in her trademark seal cape and black dress

money, she had nearly precipitated a financial panic. Her demand led the Cisco bank to make assignment for the benefit of its creditors, and only Jay Gould's reassurance that he considered the failure an isolated case and that he would buy any stock adversely affected kept the market from panicking.

Hetty Green gained immediate public notoriety as a result of her actions. When she withdrew her money from Cisco, she did so literally, loading securities worth more than $25 million into a hansom cab to transfer them to Chemical National. There she used any convenient desk to conduct business and refused all attempts by the bank to give her a private office. She stored her fortune in the bank's vault, but it soon outgrew the room and overflowed into second-floor offices. She stashed securities in trunks, portmanteaus, packing cases, and even a wagon and a buggy, though in a rare concession to the bank she did allow the wheels from the vehicles to be removed for easier storage. She kept much of her clothing in the bank so she could change in town and thought nothing of adding up her accounts while sitting cross-legged on the floor surrounded by her treasure. She kept her personal belongings at the bank whenever she left town and generally treated it as an extension of her home.

Green began to participate much more actively in the public markets. The next major business turndown, the Panic of 1890, involved a revolution, wheat failure, and assorted disasters in Argentina, which depressed Argentinian securities and threatened the existence of the Baring Brothers firm in London, which held millions of pounds worth of Argentine bonds. The market declined precipitously, but Green, convinced that the Bank of England would support Baring Brothers, bought heavily as the market hit bottom. She also had enough cash on hand to provide loans to individuals. While she always said that she never loaned at more than 6 percent, the rate provided for by New York State's usury law, loan rates on call during the panic went as high as 186 percent. Given her avarice, it would be illogical to assume she did not take advantage of the market demand.

In addition to raiding as a bear on the stock market Green continued to invest heavily in real estate. Between 1885 and 1890 she bought more than $17 million in properties in California, Texas, New York, Denver, St. Louis, Cincinnati, and Chicago, where she sent Ned to work as her agent. He relayed income of $40,000 per month to her; his salary was $3.00 per day. Ned's responsibility over his mother's properties gradually increased, and she eventually sent him to Terrell, Texas, to foreclose a $750,000 mortgage on the Texas & Midland Railroad. Green gave Ned the railroad to see what he could do, and he proved an administrative genius. His success was limited, however, by competition from Collis P. Huntington, who owned the Southern Pacific and was determined to control all the rails in Texas. In 1892 Huntington acquired stock in the Houston & Texas Railroad. The only stock he could not get was the $1 million in bonds and first and second mortgages on the road owned by Hetty Green. She refused all offers to settle and forced the road into receivership. Green's fight with Huntington made her popular with those he had trampled on in his rise to power in California; a group of San Franciscan admirers sent her a .44-caliber revolver. Huntington responded to her challenges by making Ned's life as uncomfortable as possible as they came into competition over another railroad, questioning Ned's land grants and titles in

the Texas courts for years. When Huntington finally went to New York to settle the argument with Green over the Texas railroads, he threatened to have her son put in jail. Hetty Green the mother proved far more forceful in her defense of Ned Green than Hetty Green the businesswoman: she pulled out the revolver and threatened to put a bullet through Huntington's heart. The railroad magnate fled, leaving his silk top hat behind.

The Greens eventually lost in Texas, but Hetty did at last exact some revenge on Huntington. In 1899, learning he was borrowing from a certain New York bank, she began to make deposits until her balance reached $1.6 million. After making sure Huntington was still borrowing and was weeks away from being able to repay his loans and still make a profit, Green went to the bank and demanded her money in cash. The bank resisted but finally called Huntington's loans to raise the necessary cash. Huntington survived the onslaught, but barely, and Green gleefully attributed his death the following year to the worry she had caused him.

After short-lived panics in 1901 and 1903 the stock market heated up again until a major crash came in 1907. Green sensed it coming as early as 1904, after the New York Central Railroad approached her for a loan. She called in her money quietly, converting all she had to cash or first mortgages. When the crash hit she was one of the few private bankers on Wall Street with money to lend, which she did, providing a loan of $6 million to the state of Texas alone. Despite accusations in the press she still maintained that she never loaned at rates greater than 6 percent. More likely, she also loaned money by having clients execute mortgages at rates considerably higher.

After her success in the Panic of 1907 Green exhibited more frequent instances of bizarre behavior. She became convinced that not only had her father and her Aunt Sylvia been murdered but that her husband had been murdered too. After her husband's death in Bellows Falls in 1902 she carried a pistol with her, which she also rigged up with string at the foot of her bed at night so it would go off if any intruders opened her door at whatever cheap boardinghouse she lived. The boardinghouses became cheaper and cheaper—two-room cold-water walkups in Hoboken, New Jersey, with aliases on the mailboxes. By moving frequently Green hoped to avoid establishing legal residence anywhere outside of Bellows Falls. An agreement with the town fathers there enabled her to pay taxes on property assessed at only $30,000. She never paid taxes in either New York City or New Jersey. Accompanying her as she moved all over Hoboken were her daughter and her pet dog, C. Dewey, whom she taught to waltz on his hind legs. Her eccentricities and paranoia increased yearly. She pleaded with Ned to come from Texas and care for her, a poor, lone woman surrounded by assassins. She granted newspaper reporters impromptu interviews in which she held forth in great detail on her accomplishments, abilities, and her reasons for living as she did. "I am in earnest," she once said, "therefore they picture me heartless. I go my own way, take no partners, risk nobody else's fortune, therefore I am Madame Ishmael, set against every man." She explained away her decrepit clothing: as a Quaker she merely tried to live up to the tenets of simplicity so much a part of her faith. Or perhaps it was foreordained: her mother had been frightened by a ragged tramp when pregnant with Hetty. The experience had "marked" the child, so she said: "I suffer, really, when I'm dressed up."

In 1909 Green supervised the wedding of her thirty-eight-year-old daughter to Matthew Astor Wilks, a fifty-seven-year-old millionaire. For a brief period Green lived like the multimillionaire she was. She bought new clothes for the wedding, visited a chic beauty parlor, and furnished a fine wedding breakfast by a French chef. Wilks was not the first suitor for Sylvia's hand, but all the others had fallen before Green's conviction that they only sought her fortune. Wilks had enough money to alleviate part of the suspicion; Green ensured the point by having Wilks sign a prenuptial agreement to relinquish any claim to Sylvia's property. The couple married on February 13, 1909; Sylvia was a widow by 1926, one month after she came into her full inheritance from her mother's estate.

Ned did not marry until age forty-eight, more than keeping a college graduation promise to his mother that he would not marry for 20 years. He married his longtime companion, a former prostitute and stripper, Mabel Harlow. Green knew of their alliance since Ned had brought Mabel with him when he returned to New York in 1910 to take over his mother's affairs. After Sylvia's marriage Green had lived alone in New Jersey and lavished all the affection of which she was capable on her dog; his death in March 1910 broke her heart

and her health. Ned rescued her from her Hoboken flat and installed her in a brownstone in the city. She alternated between that apartment and the home of the Countess Annie Leary, a close friend, still trying to move often enough to avoid establishing a New York residence. In April 1916, following a vociferous exchange with the countess's cook over the cost of a meal, Green suffered a paralytic stroke. Between then and July she suffered five or six additional small strokes and finally died on July 3, 1916. She succeeded in her lifelong goal of avoiding taxes; after years of contest over the will, Vermont was declared her residence. The state netted about $55,000 in taxes on her estate, estimated to be worth somewhere between $100 million and $200 million. Green left her money to her children, evenly divided, in trust for ten years.

Hetty Green exerted a powerful influence over Wall Street between 1890 and 1915. Mere rumors that she or her agents had started buying blocks of stock proved sufficient to send the market scrambling. But because she concentrated on buying in a bear market few could match her cash resources. Few could match her eccentricities either. After her death friends tried to explain her behavior. One suggested that most people would be a bit odd if they were as free as Green had been to follow their own inclinations. Another argued that Green "had her own theories of what was right and wrong, and lived up to them with all the tenacity of her strict New England conscience; and it didn't matter to her one bit what the world thought about it."

Her legacies were her millions and two children. The free-spending Ned indulged his every whim and died in 1936; Sylvia, a shy woman as eccentric as her mother, had three estates, all run-down; she never connected the pipes or used central heating so she could save money. Neither had children. At Sylvia's death from cancer in 1951, Hetty Green's fortune was at last spent, distributed to innumerable churches, charities, friends, relatives, and universities. Some $150 million went out into the world in a way that probably made the "Witch of Wall Street" turn in her grave.

References:
John T. Flynn, *Men of Wealth* (Freeport, N.Y.: Books for Libraries, 1941), pp. 215-249;

Arthur H. Lewis, *The Day They Shook the Plum Tree* (New York: Harcourt, Brace & World, 1963);

Ishbel Ross, *Charmers and Cranks* (New York: Harper & Row, 1965), pp. 26-60;

Boyden Sparkes and Samuel Taylor Moore, *The Witch of Wall Street: Hetty Green* (Garden City, N.Y.: Doubleday, 1948);

Peter Wyckoff, "Queen Midas: Hetty Robinson Green," *New England Quarterly*, 23 (June 1950): 147-171.

Alexander Hamilton

(January 11, 1755-July 12, 1804)

by Charles W. Calomiris

Northwestern University

CAREER: Captain, New York Militia (1776-1777); lieutenant colonel, Continental Army (1777-1781); receiver of continental taxes, state of New York (1782); delegate, Continental Congress, state of New York (1782-1783); lawyer, New York City (1783-1791, 1795-1804); director, Bank of New York (1784-?); delegate, Annapolis Convention (1786); delegate, Constitutional Convention (1787); U.S. secretary of the treasury (1791-1795).

Alexander Hamilton, recognized by contemporaries as the preeminent financier of his era, is best known to students of American history as one of the founding fathers–a distinction that embraces a wide range of accomplishments. As the first secretary of the treasury, or a close aide to General and President George Washington, or an influential supporter of the Constitution, Hamilton would have been assured a prominent place in American history. That he was all of these and more has made him an icon of American politics.

From the time American independence was assured, Hamilton's work focused on the goal of promoting a strong and stable government for the new country. He served briefly in the Continental Congress, from 1782 to 1783, but was frustrated by its inability to exert authority. He was selected to represent New York at the Annapolis Convention of 1786, which called for a constitutional convention the following year. While he attended the Constitutional Convention and eventually signed the Constitution, Hamilton's own views were more conservative than those of most other delegates, so he took little part in composing it. Once it was written, however, he was instrumental in gaining its ratification in New York. He is even better known, however, for his authorship (together with James Madison and John Jay) of *The Federalist*, a series of

Portrait of Hamilton by John Trumbull, 1792 (courtesy of the Yale University Art Gallery)

essays arguing for the adoption of the Constitution that has become a classic of political thought.

Hamilton's contribution to American history did not end with the ratification of the new form of government. He thought it his duty to ensure its inauguration on a sound basis, so he accepted Washington's appointment as the first secretary of the treasury. He used his position in the cabinet to influence the full scope of the administration's activities, engaging in a bitter battle with Secretary of State Thomas Jefferson in the process. Even after leaving the government in 1795, Hamilton continued to advise Washington and his cabinet, and Washington asked him to draft parts of the outgoing president's farewell address, a work that gained lasting fame and influence.

Hamilton's most enduring contribution to American government came through his work in the Treasury Department. His influential reports to the Congress provided detailed arguments for a variety of programs. The recommendations that were enacted established a stable currency, a national bank, a program for the orderly retirement of revolutionary war debts, and a revenue system based on the collection of tariffs. His *Report on Manufactures*, while largely ignored, offered a farseeing plan for American industrial development, demonstrating Hamilton's vision for a prosperous nation.

Hamilton understood that his actions as secretary of the treasury established precedents for the operation of the new government. He used the office to implement his own views on the proper role of the central government in the new federal system—views that earlier he had muted to strengthen the government and facilitate agreement during and immediately after the Constitutional Convention. He acted to strengthen the Treasury Department and the position of treasury secretary so that the department and his successors would be able to resist congressional pressures and implement the consistent financial policies he felt were essential. His efforts to repay the revolutionary war debts manifested his belief in the sanctity of contracts and were an important step in establishing that principle as the foundation of American commercial society. In the fight for the Bank of the United States, he established the principle of implied constitutional powers, on which much of the subsequent activity of the federal government has been based. Hamilton also established the principle of equal treatment for all nations in his tariff policies, further helping to ensure a predictable environment for American business.

Alexander Hamilton was born on the island of Nevis, in the British West Indies, on January 11, 1755, the second son of Rachel Faucette Lavien and James Hamilton, a merchant and the son of a landed family with ancient roots in Scotland. Hamilton and Lavien lived together from 1752 to 1765. Lavien's divorce from John Michael Lavien, a failed Danish or German planter from whom she had separated in 1750, was not granted until 1759. Danish

law (which prevailed in St. Croix, where they then lived) prohibited her remarriage. That Hamilton was an illegitimate child from a noble line may have contributed to his concern with reputation, evident throughout his life.

In 1765 James Hamilton left Lavien and the children. Three years later Lavien died. Hamilton, then thirteen, and his brother received some minor assistance from the family of his mother's half-sister, Ann Lytton; otherwise, they were penniless—the entirety of their mother's small estate went to her legitimate son by John Lavien. Little is known about Hamilton's early education, but he had apparently received an education at home and was literate in French as well as English.

About the time of his mother's death in 1768 Hamilton went to work for Nicholas Kruger, a local merchant. He remained in Kruger's employ for four years. Toward the end of that time Kruger left St. Croix for several months and put Hamilton in charge of the business. By that time Hamilton was writing more than business correspondence. He contributed a piece to the island newspaper entitled "Rules for Statesmen," which admired the British form of government—a view that he repeated to the Constitutional Convention in 1787. (Hamilton's publications can be found in the definitive collection of his published and unpublished work, *Papers of Alexander Hamilton*, 1961-1979).

In the summer of 1772 a severe hurricane hit St. Croix. Hamilton's account of the hurricane much impressed his friend and teacher, Rev. Hugh Knox, who had come to the island from Princeton, New Jersey, not long before. Knox had Hamilton's report published in the local paper and used the account in discussions with friends to raise money to send him to New York for formal education. Knox found several contributors and arranged that Hamilton attend preparatory school and college. In October 1772 Hamilton arrived in America. It had been almost five years since Hamilton wrote the first of his letters that has been preserved, in which he admitted, "my ambition is prevalent, so that I condemn the grovelling condition of a clerk or the like, to which my fortune, etc., condemns me, and would willingly risk my life, though not my character, to exalt my station."

After a year in the academy at Elizabethtown, New Jersey, studying Latin, Greek, and mathematics with great diligence, Hamilton enrolled at King's College in New York (later Columbia College). After a short time he changed his course of study from medicine to political economy and law. During his two years at King's Hamilton began his political career. In July 1774 he attracted attention with a fiery speech at a rally organized by New York patriots following the Boston Tea Party. The following winter he published several widely read tracts in favor of independence–*A Full Vindication of the Measures of the Congress, from the Calumnies of their Enemies; Remarks on the Quebec Bill;* and *The Farmer Refuted*–and contributed articles to the *New York Journal.*

Hamilton's political activity won him influential friends, and when in the spring of 1776 the New York legislature decided to raise an artillery company, he obtained a captain's commission. He was efficient, effective, and disciplined in his command and received praise for the actions in which he participated. He came to the attention of General Nathanael Greene, who befriended him. That connection brought him to the attention of General Washington, and within a year of his commission, Hamilton had transferred to an appointment as Washington's aide-de-camp with the rank of lieutenant colonel.

As Washington's aide Hamilton's duties included managing the general's correspondence and serving as his personal representative in conferences and missions. His knowledge of French made him an important liaison with the allied army in the later stages of the war. Most important, Hamilton found himself in a position to see firsthand all of the problems facing the Continental Army: finance, supply, organization, and the degree to which these problems were compounded by jealousies and dissension–in Congress, among local field commanders, and from state legislatures and governors. The experience impressed Hamilton with the benefits of centralized decision-making to achieve national goals, a common theme in his thinking in the years following the war.

Washington, speaking of his aides-de-camp, said, "I give in to no kind of amusement myself, and consequently those about me can have none, but are confined from morning till eve, hearing and answering the applications and letters." Hamilton was noted for his diligence and his ability to work without respite, but during winter lulls he also read widely, broadening his knowledge of political economy in particular.

While serving with Washington, Hamilton met and courted Elizabeth Schuyler, daughter of General Philip Schuyler, one of the wealthiest and most influential men in New York. While Hamilton's correspondence contains convincing evidence that this was a love match, Schuyler also became an important political ally, and the match greatly improved Hamilton's position in New York society.

Immediately following the war Hamilton was admitted to the New York bar. During the same period he wrote a series of essays arguing the merits of a strong central government entitled "The Continentalist" for the *New York Packet.* In July 1782 he was appointed receiver of continental taxes for the state of New York by Robert Morris, the superintendent of finance for the Continental government, with whom he had corresponded for some time over means to improve the country's finances. As receiver Hamilton directed his efforts toward reforming the tax system in New York and lobbying the New York legislature to provide funds for the army and for payment of the war debt. He found this an arduous and frustrating task. In his efforts to raise national funds from New York he met with the telling argument that there was no point in putting up money so long as other states did not. This form of jockeying, repeated in virtually all the states, proved one of the greatest defects of the Confederation.

While he failed to extract revenue, Hamilton impressed the legislature sufficiently to obtain a seat in New York's delegation to the Continental Congress, which he held from November 1782 until July 1783. That position also proved frustrating. Congress occupied itself with trying to raise money to pay the still-active army and the war debt, an endeavor in which it met with little success. Peace had removed the wartime sense of urgency and made it difficult to convince the states to contribute funds or levy common taxes for the support of the central government. Congress itself often failed to achieve a quorum.

Frustrated with the inability of Congress to raise funds to pay the army, Hamilton proposed to Washington that the general lead his army against Congress to apply pressure for settlement of military pay claims. Washington refused. Shortly thereafter an uprising motivated by the pay shortage arose within Washington's army, and only the general's personal efforts quashed it. Ironically, Hamilton acted as the congressional intermediary when a band of unpaid soldiers invaded Philadelphia, threatened the state government, and demanded their pay. Congress took flight to New Jersey until disciplined troops brought from West Point quelled the disturbance.

In November 1783 Hamilton left government service to open a law office on Wall Street. He often represented defendants being prosecuted under the antiloyalist statutes of the Continental government, arguing that the laws violated due process and that individuals could not be prosecuted ex post facto for complying with British laws while New York was under British rule. While engaged in his legal practice Hamilton continued to be active in civic affairs. He published his opinions in the newspapers, maintained an active correspondence with political leaders throughout the country, became a founding member of the New York Society for Promoting the Manumission of Slaves, and helped to found the Bank of New York in 1784.

The proposal for the Bank of New York emerged in part from a desire on the part of certain New York merchants for banking services like those provided by the Bank of North America, founded in Philadelphia three years before. It was also a way of circumventing a proposal by Robert R. Livingston for a land bank in New York. Hamilton and others feared that a bank capitalized predominantly on the basis of pledges on land would have dangerous weaknesses. The Bank of New York opened in June 1784 under a constitution drafted by Hamilton and with Hamilton as one of the directors. The bank took deposits, issued notes, and discounted notes and bills at 6 percent, repayable in bank notes or specie. The bank failed to secure a charter until 1791, however, due to public suspicion of banking. The public blamed the bank for a shortage of specie during the late 1780s that was actually the result of an unfavorable balance of payments with Britain. The bank's charter generally followed Hamilton's recommendations but limited the bank's capital-asset ratio to 25 percent and barred the bank from buying or selling stock– limitations that set precedents for future American banking regulation.

In 1786 Hamilton was appointed to represent New York at a meeting in Annapolis, Maryland, that had been called by Virginia "for the purpose of framing such regulations of trade as may be judged necessary to promote the general interest." The representatives of only five states appeared.

Lacking a quorum, the delegates decided to call for a broader conference in Philadelphia the following spring. The convention report, drafted by Hamilton, called attention to the inability of the central government to raise revenue without the consent of the individual states, the jealousy with which each state guarded its rights and defended its own view of the "fair" allocation of the fiscal burden of the national government, and the many impediments to national commerce both between states and with foreign nations. Also, competitive tariff policies of state governments weakened the national economy and worsened political quarrels among the states. It was in this environment that the delegates in Annapolis recommended that the Philadelphia assemblage "devise such further provisions as shall appear to [the delegates] necessary to render the constitution of the Federal Government adequate to the exigencies of the Union." Hamilton appeared before the New York legislature the following year and worked to persuade his colleagues that the state should send a delegation to the convention. He succeeded and with his father-in-law's assistance was appointed to that delegation.

Most of Hamilton's contributions to the Constitution devised in Philadelphia occurred before and after the convention. Serving on a delegation with two men who opposed the strengthening of the federal government and who eventually withdrew from the convention, Hamilton was often unable to influence decisions. Moreover, his distrust of congressional politics led him to advocate an essentially monarchical model of government. He outlined that extreme position in a five-hour speech early in the debates. His extremism may have helped pave the way for discussion of the milder but still radical proposals the convention adopted. Hamilton was absent from the convention for much of the summer, when the basic framework of the document was forged. He did serve on the Committee on Style, which prepared the final text, but the committee had little influence over content. In the end Hamilton signed the Constitution, viewing it as the best solution available to the country's problems.

Following the signing of the Constitution, Hamilton returned to New York and worked, with the collaboration of James Madison and John Jay, on the series of eighty-five essays for which he is best known today. *The Federalist*, as these essays became known, explained the mechanisms and ratio-

THE WALTON HOUSE.

The Walton House, first headquarters of the Bank of New York. Hamilton served as a director of the bank from the time it was chartered in 1784.

nales for the various provisions of the new Constitution and had a great influence on contemporaries. The work has since become a standard reference for Constitutional interpretation. Among the more than 50 essays written by Hamilton were numbers 6 through 9, on the costs of disunity and the political benefits of a stronger union; numbers 11 through 13, on the economic benefits of union; numbers 21 through 36, on the need for greater powers for the central government, with six of these on the common defense and seven on federal taxation; and numbers 62 and 63 and 65 through 82, advocating the importance of the powers of the Senate, the president, and the federal courts.

The first 46 essays of *The Federalist* are devoted to establishing the need for a stronger central government. Hamilton's contributions are concentrated among those essays. In view of his later role as the first secretary of the treasury, his essays on taxation are of particular interest. In number 11 he suggests that the federal form of government would increase commerce considerably, and that a government relying on indirect taxation would derive great fiscal benefits. In numbers 30 through 36 he discusses taxation at length, introducing his discussion with the remark that "money is . . . considered

as the vital principle of the body politic," a view that accords well with his later efforts to influence the role of government from the Treasury Department.

Madison had participated actively in the convention and had taken detailed notes on the proceedings. He was thus in a somewhat better position than Hamilton to comment on the political mechanisms of the Constitution. Nevertheless, Hamilton reserved for himself the essays on the Senate, president, and courts. Those essays reflect the core of Hamilton's political philosophy, a central feature of which is a pessimistic view of human nature. In number 6 he writes, "Men are ambitious, vindictive, and rapacious." He goes on to ask, "Are not popular assemblies frequently subject to the impulses of rage, resentment, jealousy, avarice, and of other irregular and violent propensities?" But Hamilton is optimistic that proper governmental institutions can counter such impulses: the Senate, the president, and the independent courts can check the passions of the people and the excesses of legislators. In number 62 he writes, "The necessity of a senate is . . . indicated by the propensity of all single and numerous assemblies to yield to the impulse of sudden and violent passions. . . . A body which is to correct this infirmity ought itself to be free from it, and consequently ought . . . to possess great firmness, and consequently ought to hold its authority by a tenure of considerable duration." In number 70 he explains the role of the president in restraining the mob influence of which he is so distrustful: "When occasions present themselves, in which the interests of the people are at variance with their inclinations, it is the duty of the persons whom they have appointed to be the guardians of those interests, to withstand the temporary delusion, in order to give them time and opportunity for more cool and sedate reflection." As for the courts, number 78 is unambiguous in assigning them a crucial role in protecting the right of the minority—and the Constitution itself—against the democratic majority: "The courts of justice are to be considered as the bulwarks of a limited Constitution against legislative encroachments."

Hamilton, among others, coaxed George Washington out of retirement to assume the presidency in the new government. Searching for the best possible assistance, Washington asked the former superintendent of finance, Robert Morris, for advice on how to deal with the country's heavy debt. Morris's reported reply was, "There is but one man who can tell you; that is, Alexander Hamilton." On September 11, 1791, Hamilton was appointed the first U.S. secretary of the treasury; the Senate confirmed his appointment the same day.

For five years, until early 1795, Hamilton worked to establish the Department of the Treasury as an institution fully capable of meeting the financial needs of the federal government. The new Constitution was most systematically put to the test in the formulation of Treasury policy. In the area of taxation, enforcement had previously been lax, and federal taxation had raised the greatest concern in the ratification fight. The competitive resistance to providing funds for the central government that characterized the behavior of the states under the Articles of Confederation came to an end, and with it, the inability to repay government obligations. Hamilton had to set up the new system of taxation, commission and build coastal cutters to enforce the customs, and respond to the requests of Congress for information and proposals. Furthermore, he had to devise a means for consolidating the outstanding war debts of the government, which involved determining the proper disposition of state war debts and a credible schedule for debt retirement.

Hamilton's reports to Congress highlighted his tenure as secretary of the treasury. The *Report on Public Credit* (1790) is the best known of the reports and was one of the most controversial among contemporaries. There Hamilton laid out his arguments in favor of the funding of the revolutionary war debts and the assumption by the federal government of the war debts of the states. In part Hamilton based his argument for funding and assumption on the idea that the federal government was morally obligated to honor the debt, noting that "the debt of the United States . . . was the price of liberty." He argued at length, however, for the practical benefits arising from securing the revenue to service the debt.

The first of those benefits was the reduced fiscal cost of borrowing as the result of the government's improved creditworthiness. A second advantage was the potential liquidity of government paper. Hamilton argued that bonds, the instruments of public debt, given a stable and credible value, would be useful for transacting business, and might mitigate the problem of deflation that had plagued the 1780s and thereby reduce the market interest rate. He also argued that a public debt of uncertain value stood as a handicap to the country's financial system. Third, making the wealthy classes of the country (who were government creditors) reliant on the federal government for redemption of the debts they held would generate greater future support for federal taxation and centralization of financial policy. Fourth, Hamilton believed in the sanctity of the contract. This belief is often couched in terms of the government's obligation to uphold the public credit, but there is a broader consideration as well. Hamilton believed that agreements between private parties, made freely and lawfully, should not be altered by political action. The uncertainty in commercial relations generated by the abandonment of that principle would be injurious to the nation's commerce. The Constitution itself comprised a form of voluntary contract—a significant innovation in the practice of government—and the legitimacy and stability of the union rested on the principle of its enforceability. A final consideration was that, absent federal assumption, the state taxes necessary to service the debts of the states would unfairly disadvantage the producers of the taxed articles. He wrote, "A state must always be checked in the imposition of taxes on articles of consumption, from the want of power to extend the same regulation to the other states, and from the tendency of partial duties to injure its industry and commerce."

While Hamilton's preference was to promise the holders of state debts the full amount due plus back interest at the agreed rate, he was conscious of the limited revenues that could be raised in that manner. Once more his sense of pragmatism came into play: "Every breach of the public engagements, whether from choice or necessity, is in different degrees hurtful to public credit. When such a necessity does truly exist, the evils of it are only to be palliated by a scrupulous attention, on the part of the government, to carry the violation no farther than the necessity absolutely requires, and to manifest, if the nature of the case admits of it, a sincere disposition to make reparation, whenever circumstances shall permit.... Those who are most commonly creditors of a nation ... will understand their true interest too well to refuse their concurrence in such modifications of their claims, as any real necessity may demand." Hamilton's plan was to offer creditors a menu of choices. They could retain their debt and hope for the best, or trade it in for debt funded through a sinking fund at a lower rate of return. The original debt was placed at 6 percent, while the funded-debt options of the various plans offered roughly a 4 percent yield. He justified the reduction on the grounds that, if Congress adopted his plan, government default risk would decline, and the market interest rate on government debt would fall to 4 percent. The credibility of the Federal commitment would derive from the employment of the sinking fund as well as the taxes to back it, and the establishment of a definite repayment schedule.

The main effect of the sinking fund provision in practice was to subordinate old debt (assumed state debt) to funded debt rather than raise the credibility of the federal debt commitment. There would have been no incentive for creditors to accept the lower-yield funded debt voluntarily had the estimated default rates been the same. Thus, while Hamilton cast it in the best possible light, the sinking fund was his way of reducing the real value of creditors' claims, putting less pressure on government coffers. To ensure fairness the loss would be spread among all creditors, and the creditors could choose from several financing options to best accommodate their needs.

The final plan adopted by Congress closely resembled Hamilton's proposal, shorn of the array of options Hamilton wanted to offer creditors. Arrears were funded at 3 percent while principal was funded at an average initial rate of 4 percent, rising after ten years, with a call provision allowing the government to redeem principal in limited amounts each year.

The second of Hamilton's congressional reports, the *Report on a National Bank*, was issued toward the end of 1790. It revealed another important element of Hamilton's strategy for managing the nation's finances. The bank proposed in the report was to act as the agent of the Treasury in the marketplace and as a source of low-interest credit to the government. It also would contribute to the expansion of liquidity, through the issue of notes.

The bank proposal attracted a great deal of opposition, partly because banks were largely unknown in the country and people were suspicious of them. A more important source of opposition was that the Constitution nowhere explicitly gave Congress the power to charter corporations. Hamilton's reply to the conservative legal opinions of Secretary of State Jefferson and Attorney General Edmund Randolph invoked his novel conception of constitutional "implied powers." Hamilton held that the "necessary and proper" clause of the Constitution justified the assumption of implied powers to carry out the expressed powers. He declared it was unrealistic to expect that the Constitution could enumerate all the powers necessary to run the government ("the power to lay a duty on a gallon of *rum* is only a particular *implied* in the general power to lay and collect taxes"). Hamilton's defense of the constitutionality of a national bank, which Congress accepted in authorizing the charter for the Bank of the United States (BUS) in 1791, had far-reaching consequences. In prohibiting the states from imposing taxes on the BUS in the case of *McCulloch* v. *Maryland* (1819), Chief Justice John Marshall defined the chartering of the bank as a power implied from the expressed federal power over national fiscal policy.

The *Report on the Establishment of a Mint* was issued shortly after the bank report, in early 1791. Congress adopted it with few changes and little controversy. Hamilton embraced Jefferson's proposal for a decimal currency but suggested establishing the new American currency at parity with the Spanish milled dollar, which was then the most widely used form of specie in circulation. Hamilton proposed a bimetallic standard in order to provide a flexible means to increase the money supply, but by settling on a coinage ratio of 15 to 1 he undervalued gold, and very little of that metal came to the mint until the 1834 rise in the mint ratio to 16 to 1 changed the de facto standard from silver to gold.

The *Report on Manufactures* (1791) took two years to produce, as Hamilton carefully gathered information from across the country. In it he set out his views on the course the country's economic development should take. Hamilton's central goal was to encourage the growth of domestic industry as the route to future prosperity. He drew on contemporary writers in political economy, among them Adam Smith. While he accepted the benefits of the division of labor and certain others of Smith's ideas, he rejected the invisible hand of laissez-faire economics. He preferred a more activist policy of protection and subsidy to promote domestic industry. This advocacy was politically premature in an overwhelmingly agricultural country, and Congress failed to act on the recommendations of the report.

Hamilton issued another report on the public credit in 1795, shortly before his resignation as treasury secretary. The report consisted of a series of recommendations to enable the government to retire the last of its debts without raising additional taxes. More significantly, it included procedural measures designed to maintain the public credit following Hamilton's departure. Chief among those was a recommendation that no loan be raised without a simultaneous provision for its retirement. Additions to the government sinking funds were also recommended, so that the government's debts would be retired in the order they were due. Congress passed the recommendations with only a few amendments.

Hamilton's reports to Congress reveal a unified conception of the role of the federal government and the means to carry out that role. His position as secretary of the treasury, and his definition of the duties that position entailed, allowed him to achieve most of his aims. By playing a critical role in the process of institution building in the nascent government, he strengthened the Treasury Department and extended its influence in economic planning. He broadly strengthened the executive branch by establishing the precedent that it, rather than Congress, should set the agenda for financial policy, and by championing policies that limited the potential for congressional discretion in the future.

Strengthening the executive at the expense of the legislature clearly was Hamilton's intent. He con-

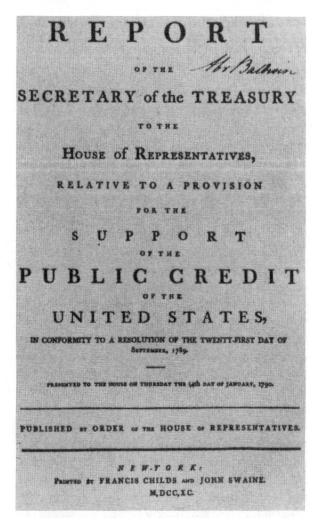

Title page for the first published version of Hamilton's Report on Public Credit *(Rare Book Division, Library of Congress)*

sidered Congress the greatest threat to the country's political stability and prosperity. Thus, he schemed to bypass Congress to the greatest extent possible, and, where not, to place Congress in a reactive role to proposals from the executive branch. If he could control the agenda and create mechanisms that were unlikely to be undermined by the acts of a diffuse opposition, he could insulate the country's financial engagements from congressional marauding.

It is instructive to examine Hamilton's reports in this light. The *Report on Public Credit* relies on a sinking fund, rather than annual appropriations, to ensure the servicing of the public debt. The establishment of a national bank allowed the country to gain the advantages of paper currency issue, without giving those powers to Congress, which had used them to excess in the financing of the Confederation government. His advocacy of the Bank of the

United States gave him the opportunity to promote the doctrine of implied powers (which Madison had propounded in *The Federalist* but later backed away from, preferring the strict constructionist position with Jefferson). The minting proposals relied on the Spanish milled dollar as the currency standard, thus depriving Congress of the power to debase specie money. Finally, the use of call provisions attached to debt encouraged timely taxation policy by allowing the government to benefit from tax-induced reductions in the market's valuation of default risk.

In setting the congressional agenda and acting as the initiator of financial proposals, Hamilton set an important precedent other treasury secretaries emulated. Until the founding of the Federal Reserve System, the treasury secretary played a unique role as formulator and coordinator of financial policy. Indeed, one could argue that a disadvantage of the current system is the division of powers among the various federal financial authorities (the Federal Reserve, Treasury, FDIC, FSLIC, FHLBB), and the intrusion of Congress as the overseer of Federal Reserve policy. This decentralization of power prevents any one entity from assuming a role of unchallenged leadership. Congressional paralysis in the 1980s, in reducing the federal deficit, or in reforming the deposit insurance systems, may be among the most convincing evidences for the wisdom of the Hamiltonian principle of centralizing financial leadership and placing it outside of Congressional control.

While at the Treasury, Hamilton had an influential voice within the cabinet. He stood against Secretary of State Jefferson's commitment to the alliance with France in favor of establishing friendly relations with Britain. He even advised British diplomats to bypass Jefferson and deal directly with the president. He opposed giving France preferential tariff treatment, arguing for the equal treatment of all foreign nations. As often occurred, Washington agreed with Hamilton, and Hamilton obtained nondiscriminatory tariffs along with regulations discriminating in favor of American vessels in international and coastal trade.

Hamilton usually convinced Washington to adopt what became the Federalist position. Animosity between Hamilton and Jefferson grew intense, with each trying to drive the other out of the cabinet. At the end of 1793 Jefferson resigned. In early 1795 Hamilton also left the cabinet to return to his law practice in New York, but he maintained his influence on the government, continuing to advise Washington and the new treasury secretary, Oliver Wolcott.

Hamilton's most important task as an outside advisor was composing Washington's *Farewell Address*. He received material Madison had prepared for a farewell speech at the end of Washington's first term and built around this an address that presented a clear statement of the foreign policy he had engineered with Washington.

Washington's departure meant John Adams's inauguration. While Adams and Hamilton had similar views, they disliked each other personally. So long as Adams retained Washington's cabinet, Hamilton continued to have influence in the government, but the feud between the two men eventually led Adams to purge the officials associated with Hamilton.

Hamilton continued to write for the New York newspapers as well as to practice law. In 1800 he published a vitriolic attack on Adams, the repercussions of which contributed to a split within the Federalists that allowed Jefferson to become president the next year. In 1804 remarks made by Hamilton about Aaron Burr, candidate for governor of New York, led Burr to challenge Hamilton to a duel. Hamilton accepted the challenge reluctantly, impelled by a concern over the consequences of refusing, and lost his life in the duel at Weehawken, New Jersey, on July 12, 1804.

Alexander Hamilton's great achievements as the first secretary of the treasury involved much more than the arrangement of the country's finances. They marked the continuation of his broader efforts to strengthen and redefine the federal union. In the process of advocating and creating a strong central government he laid the foundations for the emergence of the modern American economy. Appropriately, Hamilton is buried in the graveyard of Trinity Church, at the foot of Wall Street.

Selected Publications:

A Full Vindication of the Measures of the Congress, from the Calumnies of their Enemies, as A Friend to America (New York: J. Rivington, 1774);

The Farmer Refuted: or, A More Impartial and Comprehensive View of the Dispute between Great-Britain and the Colonies, as A Sincere Friend to America (New York: James Rivington, 1775);

The Federalist: a collection of essays, written in favour of the new Constitution, as agreed upon by the Federal convention, September 17, 1787, by Hamilton, James Madison, and John Jay (New York: J. & A. M'Lean, 1787);

[*Report on Public Credit.*] *Report of the Secretary of the Treasury to the House of Representatives, Relative to a Provision for the Support of the Public Credit of the United States* (New York: Francis Childs & John Swaine, 1790);

[*Report on a National Bank.*] *Report of the secretary of the Treasury, December 13, 1790. In obedience to the order of the House of Representatives, on the ninth day of April last, requiring the secretary to prepare and report, on this day, such further provisions as may in his opinion be necessary for establishing the public credit* (New York: F. Childs & J. Swaine, 1790);

[*Report on the Establishment of a Mint.*] *The secretary of the Treasury, having attentively considered the subject referred to him by the order of the House of representatives on the fifteenth day of April last, relatively to the establishment of a mint, most respectfully submits the result of his inquiries and reflections* (Philadelphia: Francis Childs & John Swaine, 1791);

Report of the Secretary of the Treasury of the United States, on the Subject of Manufactures (Philadelphia: Childs & Swaine, 1791);

Report of the secretary of the Treasury, for the improvement and better management of the revenues of the United States (Philadelphia: Francis Childs, 1795);

Papers of Alexander Hamilton, 27 volumes, edited by Harold C. Syrett and others (New York: Columbia University Press, 1961-1979).

References:

Claude G. Bowers, *Jefferson and Hamilton: The Struggle for Democracy in America* (Boston: Houghton Mifflin, 1953);

Jacob E. Cooke, *Alexander Hamilton* (New York: Scribners, 1982);

Louis Hacker, *Alexander Hamilton in the American Tradition* (New York: McGraw-Hill, 1957);

Forrest McDonald, *Alexander Hamilton: A Biography* (New York: Norton, 1979);

Broadus Mitchell, *Alexander Hamilton: A Concise Biography* (New York: Oxford University Press, 1976);

Mitchell, *Alexander Hamilton: The National Adventure, 1788-1804* (New York: Macmillan, 1962);

Mitchell, *Alexander Hamilton: Youth to Maturity, 1755-1788* (New York: Macmillan, 1957);

Richard B. Morris, *Witnesses at the Creation: Hamilton, Madison, Jay, and the Constitution* (New York: Holt, Rinehart & Winston, 1985);

Allan Nevins, *History of the Bank of New York and Trust Company, 1784 to 1934* (New York: Privately published, 1934);

Gerald Stourzh, *Alexander Hamilton and the Idea of Republican Government* (Stanford: Stanford University Press, 1970);

George Washington, *Washington's Farewell Address, in Facsimile, with Transliterations of all the Drafts of Washington, Madison & Hamilton,* edited by Victor Hugo Paltsits (New York: New York Public Library, 1935).

Archives:

The papers of Alexander Hamilton are at the Library of Congress.

Hard Money *(see* Specie, Hard Money, and "Suspension")

Isaias W. Hellman

(October 3, 1842-April 9, 1920)

by Michael F. Konig

Westfield State College

CAREER: Merchant and real estate speculator, Los Angeles, California (1865-1868); partner, Hellman, Temple and Company (1868-1871); cashier (1871-1876), president, Farmers and Merchants Bank of Los Angeles (1876-1903); regent, University of California (1881-1919); president, Los Angeles Clearing House Association (1887); president, Wells Fargo Nevada National Bank of San Francisco (1891-1920); president, Union Trust Company (1893-1916); president, Farmers and Merchants National Bank of Los Angeles (1903-1920); president, United States National Bank (1905-1914); president, Southern Trust Company (1908).

Isaias W. Hellman's distinguished career in banking not only reflected the evolution of California's financial industry during the late nineteenth and early twentieth centuries but also mirrored the growth and development of that state's major urban areas, Los Angeles and San Francisco. As founder of the Farmers and Merchants Bank of Los Angeles and director of the Wells Fargo Nevada National Bank and the Union Trust Company of San Francisco, Hellman played a vital role in the remarkable economic and demographic growth of southern California as well as in the rebuilding of San Francisco after the earthquake of 1906.

Hellman was born on October 3, 1842, in Beckendorf, Bavaria. With his brother, Herman Wolf Hellman, he migrated to Los Angeles in 1854. Isaias worked for his cousins, Samuel and Isaiah M. Hellman, who operated Hellman and Brothers, a dry goods, stationery, and clothing store, entering employment as a clerk. In return he received $25 per month as well as board and lodging. At first the lodging meant sleeping under the store counter. In 1861 and 1862 a series of floods caused extensive damage to the fledgling Los Angeles business district. The losses incurred by the Hellman brothers forced them to dissolve their partnership, and Isaias

Isaias W. Hellman

joined with Isaiah in a new version of the same business. In 1865 Isaias opened his own dry goods, clothing, and shoe store near the corner of Main and Commercial streets in Los Angeles. In addition to this prosperous enterprise Hellman became a speculator in Los Angeles real estate. Many of his purchases encompassed what would become entire blocks of the developing downtown area. Hellman also bought outlying properties, which he held for future subdivision. Those parcels, which were located just to the east of the city and in the vicinity of what are now the Los Angeles Memorial Coliseum and the University of Southern California, brought Hellman substantial profit. He also purchased a good deal of ranch land, some of which included

249

the 6,800-acre Los Alamitos Rancho, which had previously been owned by the early Los Angeles pioneer Abel Stearns.

Through his dry goods business and his real estate speculation, Hellman developed an interest in banking. He had become familiar with banking practices during business trips to San Francisco. In a corner of his store was a safe and a sign: "I. W. Hellman, Banker." During the 1860s Los Angeles merchants informally allowed their friends and customers to use their store safes as depositories for their valuables, including gold dust. Hellman was one of the first local figures to systematize the practice. He began to purchase gold dust, and miners deposited the money from the transactions with him. Los Angeles merchants and businessmen also made deposits at Hellman's store. He honored checks written on those deposits. Some of the miners later turned to farming and prospered. They remembered Hellman's initial courtesies and became important depositors in his later banking enterprises. By the late 1860s Hellman recognized the profits to be made through banking and disposed of his dry goods operation.

Joining in 1868 with William Workman, a well-known settler who had arrived in Los Angeles in 1841, and Workman's son-in-law, Francis P. F. Temple, Hellman formed his first large-scale banking enterprise, known as Hellman, Temple and Company. The building for their new institution, constructed by Pio Pico, the last Mexican governor of California, was situated on Main Street between Arcadia and Commercial streets. Workman and Temple each invested $50,000 in the new banking house, and Hellman contributed $25,000. Some of the bank's initial depositors included well-known figures of nineteenth-century Los Angeles such as Diego Sepulveda, for whom a prominent boulevard and outlying community would be named; William Wolfskill, the trapper and rancher; and Wolfskill's son-in-law, Henry Dwight Barrows. Barrows served as U.S. marshal during the Civil War and headed the Los Angeles County Republican party for many years.

Hellman's banking career began in a Los Angeles that was undergoing significant change. The predominance of Californios, residents of the region who had been Mexican citizens, was fading. Yet some of the more well-known of those Mexican-Americans continued to play a role in community affairs, as evidenced by Pio Pico's construction of the Hellman and Temple building. The city had also weathered some difficult times during the Civil War. A strong secessionist movement threatened the loss of southern California to the Confederacy. Individuals such as Wolfskill and Barrows, who had led the community through those difficulties, recognized in Hellman and his new bank a stable individual and institution upon which their personal financial futures, as well as that of southern California, could be built. Hellman's own life had also changed in 1870 with his marriage to Esther Neugass, of New York.

The appearance of banking institutions such as Hellman, Temple and Company was of enormous importance to southern California borrowers. Although these banks operated in technical violation of the state's constitutional prohibition against banking, California authorities never attempted to enforce the prohibition, and banks such as William Ralston's Bank of California advertised flagrantly, as did Hellman, Temple and Company. The banks offered loans at significantly lower rates than did private lenders. Such loans, usually available at a rate of 1.5 or 2 percent interest per month, proved essential to the building and commercial activity in the newly developing Los Angeles area.

Hellman, Temple and Company operated for only a short period. Differences in lending strategies led to the eventual dissolution of the partnership. In 1871 Hellman bought out Workman and Temple and established the more fiscally secure I. W. Hellman and Company as the original bank's successor. That company merged with the banking house of John G. Downey, and with the addition of new capital from 21 of the city's best-known and most affluent residents, the Farmers and Merchants Bank of Los Angeles was established. Because of the prominent stature of the bank's original investors, the Farmers and Merchants Bank received immediate respect throughout the Los Angeles area. The founders selected John Downey as the bank's first president and Hellman as its first cashier. The bank, capitalized at $500,000, had 23 trustees and shareholders (including Downey and Hellman); it was incorporated on February 22, 1871. Described as "safe" and "guaranteed," a local newspaper touted the new bank as a much needed alternative to sending Los Angeles-area savings to San Francisco banks. By October of 1871 the Farmers and Merchants Bank handled the accounts of more than 600 depositors, all of whom conducted their transactions in gold and silver, since the state in effect prohibited the issuance of bank notes. An 1865 amendment to the National Banking Act of 1863 had taxed such notes out of existence.

Hellman also played a key role in securing a line of the Southern Pacific Railroad to Los Angeles. During those years rail service, especially if it connected to a transcontinental line, could spell the difference between success or failure for fledgling frontier communities. Often railroads selected communities through which to run their lines on the basis of financial inducements, including tax advantages, rebates, kickbacks, and other quasi-bribes. Communities with stable financial institutions could make more attractive offers to the railroads. Such was the case with Los Angeles. Linkage to the Southern Pacific helped to ensure a period of growth and prosperity for Los Angeles and southern California.

Hellman and the Farmers and Merchants Bank experienced steady success until 1875. During that year the entire California economy underwent a series of shocks. The Nevada mining boom, to which the California economy was closely tied through Ralston's Bank of California, collapsed. At the same time the negative effects of the failure of Jay Cooke and Company in New York and Philadelphia reached the West Coast. Those and other factors, including a poor crop year, took their toll on the Los Angeles banks. Farmers and Merchants experienced a run by depositors but possessed ample funds to meet that emergency. It did, however, temporarily suspend operations.

When the panic struck, Hellman had been vacationing in Europe. Hearing reports of the deteriorating economic conditions in California, he quickly returned to the United States. From New York he ordered that checks drawn on the Farmers and Merchants Bank be honored at the offices of Hellman, Haas and Company, a wholesale grocery enterprise he had helped to found in Los Angeles in 1871. Thus, while the bank itself suspended operations for 30 days, its customers still conducted their financial transactions. That action endeared Hellman and the Farmers and Merchants Bank to the citizenry of Los Angeles, and the institution's seemingly impregnable solvency through the Panic of 1875 placed it in a much stronger position within the community.

Other Los Angeles banks failed to demonstrate the steadfastness exhibited by Hellman and

the Farmers and Merchants Bank during these difficulties. Hellman's former partners, Workman and Temple, had made several unwise loans prior to the panic. In 1876 the two turned to a ruthless Comstock Lode speculator, E. J. Baldwin, for temporary financial support. But when the Workman and Temple Bank finally closed its doors in 1876, Baldwin foreclosed on its property holdings. Workman, distraught by those financial reverses, took his own life.

Also in 1876 the Farmers and Merchants shareholders elected Hellman the institution's new president. Downey's temporary suspension of the bank's operation during the 1875 panic had brought him criticism. Downey continued his association with the bank as one of several elected directors, yet even that association was tarnished by internal management differences and even by litigation. In spite of those problems (and with support from Downey), Hellman pushed ahead with a program that eventually culminated in the founding of the University of Southern California. During the late 1870s southern California lacked the facilities for educational services beyond the high-school level. In July 1879 Hellman, Downey, and Ozro W. Childs, one of the original investors in the Farmers and Merchants Bank, gave 308 lots of land to a university foundation headed by a local judge, Robert M. Widney. Those lots formed the nucleus of the original campus site. The banking triumvirate of Hellman, Young, and Childs also helped to organize and fund such projects as the Main Street and Agricultural Park Railroad, one of Los Angeles's first streetcar lines.

Such successful endeavors enabled Hellman to exert more fully his authority over the bank's operations and policies as its president. His abilities in banking management and financial affairs came to be recognized as among the most capable in the industry. The historians of the Farmers and Merchants Bank, Robert G. Cleland and Frank B. Putnam, attribute this recognition of Hellman to the fact that his policies and decisions were "built upon the solid foundation of moral courage, simple integrity, and uncompromising conviction that the interests of the depositors were a bank's first responsibility."

As a corollary, Farmers and Merchants suffered from excess conservatism, which limited its growth. But Hellman steadfastly held out against overly speculative investment affairs, a trait that

The first Farmers and Merchants Bank building, Los Angeles, early 1870s. Hellman worked as cashier of the bank from 1871 to 1876, when he was made bank president.

would prove to be an important element in his success. Other California, and even foreign, bankers held a high regard for his conservative disposition. Later in life Hellman advised a young San Francisco woman, Wilhelmina Chapman, how to properly handle her newly inherited fortune. He informed the young heiress that many would approach her with speculative investment schemes and that she should carefully record all of these proposals in a little black book. But Hellman advised her not to invest in any of them. At the end of that year, she could total up how much money she had saved. Despite Hellman's reputation, his conservatism seemed extreme only when measured by the other, most wildly speculative bankers of the day in California. In addition, with rare exceptions, it was difficult not to make money in California during that period.

Under Hellman's direction the Farmers and Merchants Bank maintained sufficient cash reserves to deal with fiscal emergencies and offered loans only after a proposed project and borrower had been carefully scrutinized. Yet Hellman exhibited a compassionate nature toward those who did secure loans. One contemporary stated that Hellman never foreclosed on a mortgage unless there was no alternative. Part of this compassion stemmed from Hellman's Jewish faith and from his desire to avoid the criticism that many Jews received at that time, ostensibly for being ruthless in financial dealings.

Although a prominent member of the Los Angeles Jewish community, Hellman also advised the Roman Catholic Diocese of Monterey-Los Angeles on financial matters. His relationship with the Catholic Church had evolved from his friendship with Bishop Francis Mora. The two had met shortly after Hellman's arrival in Los Angeles, and they always remained close. Hellman also became president of Congregation B'nai B'rith of Los Angeles and, with Mora's encouragement, built a permanent synagogue for the community. That synagogue was dedicated for construction in 1872, and Hellman, at the time still less than thirty years of age, gave the major address at the ceremony. The speech not only illustrated his deeply held religious convictions but also provided an interesting historical portrait of the area's Jewish community. Hellman stated that the community had desired the construction of its own synagogue for many years. The congregation had been organized in 1862, but it had struggled to remain financially solvent. Hellman had faithfully served in the organization since its inception and by 1872 described it as in "a flourishing condition." He noted that the completed synagogue would not only serve as the gathering place for Sabbath services but also would provide a schoolroom for the instruction of the area's young Jewish population. During the 1880s the Diocese of Monterey-Los Angeles experienced financial difficulties, and it, too, turned to Hellman for advice and assistance. He recommended that the Diocese sell a valuable tract of land upon which an older church stood. Hellman predicted that the site would prove valuable for commercial development. Mora favored the sale, but others within the church hierarchy opposed the transaction, and it never took place.

Hellman also joined and participated in local booster organizations such as the Masonic Order, and the Olympic and Union Leagues. He also became involved in educational and other community affairs. In 1881 he was appointed regent of the University of California, a position he held until 1919. A newspaper reporting that event described Hellman as possessing "many notable qualities," including "a vigorous intellect," which would ensure that the institution would have "energetic" and "capable" leadership. Eventually Hellman established an endowment of $50,000, providing four scholarships at the university.

In March 1878 the California State Legislature passed a regulatory banking bill that provided for the appointment of three bank commissioners and required banks with state charters to submit to regular examinations and to file reports on their financial condition. That bill, in addition to other state impositions, caused most of the larger California banks, including the Farmers and Merchants, to reduce their capital. Such impositions, however, did not prevent the Farmers and Merchants, as well as other large Los Angeles banks, from participating in the population, real estate, and building boom which occurred in southern California during the 1880s.

Many factors contributed to that remarkable upswing in land speculation, building, and general business activity. These included the completion of the Southern Pacific Railroad's transcontinental line through Los Angeles and rising profits from navel or-

ange and grape production. Thousands flocked to southern California, especially from the Midwest, aided by low fares offered by railroad companies and real estate speculators. These speculators plotted out new towns surrounding Los Angeles, often with unrealistic optimism. Hellman and the other directors of the Farmers and Merchants Bank realized that they had to exercise a degree of restraint over their real estate lending policies. In 1887 Hellman suspended the use of the bank's funds for further real estate development. Other banks followed that example, and the boom almost immediately collapsed.

While the boom of the 1880s lasted only briefly, it led to the establishment of several new banks in the Los Angeles area. Hellman served on the boards of directors of some of those institutions, such as the Security Savings Bank and Trust Company and the Los Angeles Savings Bank. The unstable conditions created by the boom and bust events convinced prominent financial figures such as Hellman that cooperation within the local banking community was essential. As a result, the community created the Los Angeles Clearing House Association. This organization acted first and foremost as a means of clearing checks against member banks during times of crisis–especially panics and suspensions. But the Los Angeles Clearing House also functioned to gather and disseminate monetary information, consider questions of financial importance, and help the Los Angeles banks present a united front when matters of state legislation affected their affairs. Member institutions included the Farmers and Merchants Bank, the Los Angeles County Bank, the Southern California National Bank, the University Bank, and the Children's Safe Deposit Bank. Hellman was elected the association's first president.

By the 1890s both Los Angeles and the Farmers and Merchants Bank had grown considerably. The population of the city had increased almost 500 percent since 1880, and deposits at the Farmers and Merchants Bank had increased nearly as much. By 1890 deposits totaled $2,203,000, and loans and discounts had grown to $2,153,000. Hellman's reputation as a banker had risen even further. His expertise was common knowledge within the San Francisco banking community. His abilities had become so well-known that Collis P. Huntington, the most noteworthy economic and political figure in the state, recommended that Hellman assume control of the foundering Nevada Bank of San Francisco. Established by the "Irish Four" of John Mackay, James Flood, James Fair, and William O'Brien, the Nevada Bank had built its asset base upon much of the wealth drawn from the famous Comstock Lode, but suffered from chronic financial mismanagement. Hellman accepted the task and immediately worked to bring in new capital. He obtained funds from sources ranging from San Francisco to Los Angeles and from New York to London. He also transferred his residence to San Francisco and relinquished management responsibilities of the Farmers and Merchants Bank to his brother, Herman. Hellman retained the presidency of the Farmers and Merchants, but the main focus of his activities for the next several years centered on the merging of the Wells Fargo and Company Bank with the Nevada Bank of San Francisco to form the Wells Fargo Nevada National Bank. Hellman served as that institution's president from 1891, and from 1893 as president of the San Francisco-based Union Trust Company.

Hellman's entry into the San Francisco banking scene created quite a stir. A reporter from Los Angeles recounted that much of the commotion was caused by what San Franciscans believed to be Hellman's net worth, reportedly near $40 million. While that figure was exaggerated, it did not lessen the willingness of prominent San Francisco investors to support Hellman's banking activities. The 1891 reorganization of the Nevada Bank created the spectacle of numerous millionaires–many of them reportedly quite old and feeble–standing in line for hours waiting for a chance to purchase stock. The chance to be associated with a Hellman enterprise was too attractive to miss.

Hellman's association with Wells Fargo Nevada National and Union Trust demonstrated his stature as a leading California and national banking figure. He stamped that institution with his own character of conservatism. Local residents often referred to it as "the Hellman Bank." He correctly realized that the institution stood as a natural product of the American West and early California, and that residents of the state held complete confidence in its past achievements. The original Wells Fargo and Company had been established in 1852 as an outgrowth of American Express, a company formed by Henry Wells and William G. Fargo. The bank originally served the miners and other residents of San Francisco and by the 1860s had dozens of branches throughout California, Nevada, and Oregon. During the 1850s the directors of America's leading express companies formed the Overland Mail Company, better known as the Butterfield Stage Line. By the 1860s Wells Fargo controlled and expanded the line's operation into a 2,500-mile stagecoach empire. That operation ran throughout the West and, in a time before railroads crisscrossed the region, served as the most effective means of transportation there. At the same time the company initiated the famed Pony Express mail service. The short-lived Pony Express, replaced by transcontinental telegraph service in the 1860s, combined with the Wells Fargo stage operations to form a powerful symbol of efficient banking and express service that helped to tame and settle the West. Equally important, by the late 1800s the hundreds of Wells Fargo offices and agents (so many in Nevada that even the San Francisco Wells Fargo headquarters lost track of them) took on a number of "branch" banking functions, thus expanding the scope of Wells Fargo's operations, extending its territory, and diversifying its portfolio. Armed with this powerful interstate branch system and heralded by the stagecoach symbol and the deft reorganization of the company by the former California railroad magnate Edward H. Harriman, the foundations were laid upon which Hellman rebuilt the Wells Fargo Nevada National Bank's fortunes.

Although the Wells Fargo Nevada National was the second largest commercial bank in San Francisco after the Bank of California, Hellman's guiding philosophy was not simply oriented toward increased size. Upon his assumption of the bank presidency, Hellman remarked that "our ambition is not to be the largest bank in San Francisco, but to be the soundest and the best." Only a year after this statement the bank faced possible disaster. In April 1906 a tremendous earthquake and fire devastated San Francisco. Like most of the other business establishments, the Wells Fargo building was destroyed. Hellman reported to his board and to his depositors that the bank's vaults stood intact and that credit remained unaffected. Until the hot vaults could be safely opened, Hellman required ready cash to continue operating, and his close relationship with the Farmers and Merchants Bank allowed him the luxury of immediate access to it. By Wells Fargo Express he wired $5,000 from Farmers and Merchants and encouraged the officers of that institution to "keep strong in cash" and to make mod-

Third site of the Farmers and Merchants Bank, 1890s

erate loans available only to regular customers. Similar to his reaction to the financial panics of the 1870s and 1880s, Hellman's conservative maintenance of adequate cash reserves at Wells Fargo enabled the institution to remain strong throughout the earthquake crisis.

After the 1906 fire the bank jointly occupied a building with the Union Trust Company. By 1908 the company had a capital surplus of $2.6 million and deposits totaling $14 million. During the next five years the building was remodeled in order to facilitate more adequately the activities of the Wells Fargo Nevada National Bank. Located on the corner of Montgomery and Post streets, the building stood 12 stories high and possessed a total floor space of more than 20,000 feet. The bank's remodeled interior was designed by Weary and Alford Company of Chicago, prominent architects of the day, and constituted their largest undertaking on the Pacific Coast. The interior reflected the grandness of Gilded Age architecture, with its Greek and Byzantine themes. While not particularly human in scale, this design sought to create a positive environment and to uplift the general citizenry into a "more productive and community-oriented" state of mind.

The design of the Wells Fargo building and others like it constituted an important element in the resurgence of a sense of community pride in post-earthquake San Francisco.

As the director of the bank's reorganization program, Hellman required a highly qualified staff. The selection of these subordinate officers again demonstrated his sound banking judgment. Hellman chose his son, Isaias W. Hellman, Jr., as vice-president and manager. Contemporaries described the younger Hellman as a businessman of "keen intellect." He brought to his position a good deal of solid professional experience, including his past management of the Farmers and Merchants Bank and his experience as cashier of the Union Trust Company. Isaias, Jr., also held the position of vice-president and manager of the Union Trust Company until 1916, when he succeeded his father as president. Hellman also selected other highly qualified officers for the Wells Fargo Nevada National. J. K. Wilson, past president of the San Francisco National Bank, was brought in as an additional vice-president, and Frank B. King, a longtime Wells Fargo officer and a descendant of one of California's oldest Anglo families, was made cashier. Governed by such capable bankers, the institution continued to grow, so that by 1911 assets of the institution totaled more than $43 million.

Hellman's banking and business activities branched out in other directions as well. By 1908 he served as president of the newly formed Southern Trust Company in Los Angeles. Back in 1906 Hellman had reorganized this company out of the Mercantile Trust and Savings Bank. He also held the position of director of the United States National Bank of Portland, Oregon. Contemporaries described Hellman as southern California's largest landowner, as well as the holder of extensive San Francisco real estate. He and some of his financial associates had obtained control of the California Wine Association, and with this control came a virtual lock on the state's profitable grape and wine industry.

Control of this enterprise caused some controversy. Hellman and his partners had come to control the association through the purchase of more than $1 million worth of stock. Many who sold their stock feared that Hellman would raise the price of wine. But Hellman countered that charge, stating that the partners had not "formed a combination to raise the price of wine. That must be regulated by supply and demand." He realized that most California wine was produced for export, and therefore its price could not be significantly increased for fear of competition from producers outside of the state. Hellman wished to assist grape growers in keeping the existing price sufficiently high, thus encouraging the production of high-quality grapes. "We deal only in California wines," he stated, "and our ambition is to put the industry on a solid basis. . . . I believe in California enterprises, for I am a Californian. I have no interests in the East. This is my home and I expect to live and die here."

In 1910 the Union Trust Company moved into a handsome new building at the corner of Market Street and Grand Avenue in San Francisco. The structure had been designed by the famous architect Clinton Day and contained the finest vaults available. A fireproof floor protected the vaults and the safe-deposit boxes. The bankers and their builders had not forgotten the catastrophic events of April 1906. The rebuilt economy of the city purred along, aided by the growing bank. Total available cash at the Union Trust Company exceeded $16.6 million. Like the directors of the Wells Fargo Ne-

vada National Bank, those of Union Trust constituted some of the most prominent San Francisco and California businessmen, bankers, and financiers. They included John D. Spreckels, president of J. D. Spreckels and Brothers, specializing in sugar importation; Charles Holbrook, president of Holbrook, Merrill, and Stetson, Inc.; and Jacob Stern, president of Levi Strauss and Company.

Through all of his banking and business activities in San Francisco, Hellman still retained a keen interest in the Farmers and Merchants Bank. Although he had given up direct management of that institution, he once stated that he felt more pride in the Farmers and Merchants Bank than in any of the other institutions with which he had associated. He still assisted in making the bank's major policy decisions. For example, during the Panic of 1893 thousands of homeless flocked to the warm weather of southern California, thereby exacerbating the region's unemployment and relief problems. In Los Angeles bread lines were opened to the public, and state and local governments, totally strapped, called upon private citizens to feed large numbers of hungry and desperate men and women. Southern California banks were hard hit. The *Los Angeles Times* reported long lines of panicked depositors withdrawing their funds from the local institutions. The First National Bank of Los Angeles temporarily closed its doors, as did the Southern California National and University Banks. But Farmers and Merchants Bank weathered the storm, largely due to the action of Hellman. At the height of the calamity he shipped $250,000 in gold coin from his San Francisco firms. Bank officials stacked the money in plain sight in the bank building for the many anxious depositors to see. Hellman's preference for liquidity over profits looked wise. Still, the bank needed additional funds to meet customer demand. Hellman therefore traveled south to Los Angeles with an additional $500,000 in gold coin, which came directly from his personal resources and not from the Wells Fargo Nevada National Bank or the Union Trust Company. The new infusion of money, along with Hellman's mere presence, allayed the fears of the worried Farmers and Merchants depositors and prevented a full-scale bank run. The 1893 downturn, however, did significantly reduce total deposits at Farmers and Merchants, but only temporarily. Deposits shrank from $2,504,000 to $1,867,000, then quickly rebounded, so that by

Interior of the Farmers and Merchants National Bank in 1905, shortly after the bank moved to a choice site at Fourth and Main streets in Los Angeles. Farmers and Merchants received its national charter in 1903.

1908 they surpassed $5 million. At no time was the bank's stability threatened.

In 1894 Isaias W. Hellman, Jr., replaced Herman Hellman as the Farmers and Merchants Bank manager, and in 1901 the bank retained Jackson A. Graves, one of the city's leading attorneys, to assist in the management process. New directors such as Isaac N. Van Nuys, a longtime southern California resident and prominent real estate magnate, also came on board.

In 1902 Hellman proposed to the Farmers and Merchants board that the bank reorganize on the basis of a national charter, arguing that "much of our business is transacted with people who are used to the methods of the East, where national banks are the usual form, and it is our wish to conform with eastern customs and methods." He also noted that national banks had regular government inspections. A national charter promised Farmers and Merchants other benefits as well. National banks qualified as depositories for federal funds. In addition, the federal comptroller of the currency authorized the printing of national bank notes that bore the names of nationally chartered institutions, providing the institutions with favorable publicity.

The transition from a state to a national charter in effect involved the organization of a new bank. Articles of association had to be adopted and an organization certificate executed. Bylaws submitted by Graves were adopted, and Hellman issued to the old bank the formal proposal for national charter reorganization. That involved the capitalization of the new national bank at a paid-up total of $1 million divided into 10,000 shares. Five thousand of those shares were issued to the stockholders of the old state bank in exchange for safe deposit business, assets, and negotiable paper, the bank's articles of physical property, and the sum of $500,000 in gold coin. In addition to the stock, the shareholders of the old state bank, who became shareholders of the new national bank, received protection from all of the debts and liabilities associated with the state-chartered institution. They also were given the opportunity to purchase 2,500 additional shares of the national bank's capital stock at a cost of $200 per share.

The Farmers and Merchants National Bank of Los Angeles received national charter number 6,617, dated February 7, 1903, and opened for business on February 9 of that year. Its officers included Hellman as president and Herman Hellman and Graves as vice-presidents. Although 32 years had passed since the inception of the Farmers and Merchants Bank, several of its founders served as directors of the new national bank. Some of those founders' sons, including Isaias Hellman, Jr., and Ozro Childs, Jr., also served on the board. That continuity of leadership over three decades constituted a major factor in the sustained growth and success of the institution. The depositors' faith, bolstered by the bank's performance in the Panic of 1893, rose. By 1905 deposits at the new national bank totaled nearly $7 million.

An unfortunate event soon disrupted the harmony at the bank and ultimately led to a break between Hellman and his brother. The bank's cashier, Henry T. Fleishman, embezzled more than $100,000 of the bank's funds and disappeared. Fleishman was never arrested or brought to trial, but the bank attached his personal assets. He held a standard bond of $30,000, but the bank settled for less than that sum, and Hellman made up the difference from his own funds. Charles Seyles, an agent for the Southern Pacific Railroad, took over as the bank's new cashier.

Herman Hellman, who detested Fleishman, believed that his brother had mishandled the whole affair, and he left the Farmers and Merchants in 1903 to become president of Merchants National Bank of Los Angeles. He also initiated construction of the eight-story H. W. Hellman Building at the corner of Fourth and Spring streets. At the time of his death in 1906 he was president, vice-president, or director of twelve banks in Los Angeles and southern California in addition to Merchants National.

In 1905 Farmers and Merchants National moved to one of the most desirable locations in Los Angeles, the corner of Fourth and Main streets, immediately opposite the fashionable Van Nuys and Westminster hotels with their wealthy eastern clientele. At the same time Hellman helped form the United States National Bank, which occupied the building at North Main Street previously vacated by the Farmers and Merchants National. He served as president of this new institution until 1914.

The conversion of the Farmers and Merchants Bank to a national charter along with the erection of its new building reflected the growth and development of Los Angeles during the early twentieth century. Its population increased and industries such as citrus production, petroleum, and tourism boomed, and Los Angeles took on the character of a sophisticated urban center. With the destruction of San Francisco in the 1906 earthquake, Los Angeles emerged as an even more important commercial and financial center in the transformation of the American West, particularly the Pacific Coast. But the economy of Los Angeles remained vulnerable in several respects. The disaster of the San Francisco earthquake had placed a burden upon the financial resources of the southern California city. The Panic of 1907 produced a money shortage among the Los Angeles-area banks, many of which had earlier formed the Los Angeles Clearing House Association. In order to prevent a drastic reduction of their gold reserves, these associated banks issued certificates in denominational scrip with which depositors could conduct their daily transactions. In order to encourage the public's use of this clearinghouse scrip, the certificates were made to bear interest at a rate of 7 percent per annum.

In spite of those measures the panic exacted a toll on the Los Angeles banking community. Several area banks closed or merged. But the Farmers and Merchants National, again due to Hellman's conservative policies, survived intact. In some respects the institution prospered. Since Hellman insisted that the bank always carry in its vault large cash reserves, frequently totaling 45 percent of its deposits, Farmers and Merchants National always had ample funds to deal with emergencies. At the same time, it secured a great many of the clearinghouse association certificates. When the certificates were finally retired, the bank received the 7 percent return. By 1910 deposits amounted to more than $11.5 million, and total resources expanded to more than $16.6 million.

In 1911 Hellman sent the assistant cashier of Wells Fargo Nevada National, Victor H. Rossetti, to Farmers and Merchants National to investigate an embezzlement and to modernize some of the bank's operational procedures. Rossetti took over as cashier shortly afterward and worked closely with Hellman. The embezzlement involved a receiving teller, Wilson B. Evans, whom the bank had employed to handle some of its railroad accounts. Evans left on vacation, taking in his suitcase $60,000 of the bank's railroad remittances. His disappearance involved bizarre events. Using an alias, Evans engaged a schooner, the *Kate*, to pick him up near San Francisco. The schooner was believed to have provided a means of escape for individuals involved in dynamiting the *Los Angeles Times* building in October 1910. Later that month the *Kate* turned up in Acapulco, Mexico, where Mexican police held three of the men on board in connection with the *Times* explosion. Evans was also arrested. His extradition met with delay, and reports surfaced that he had died in Mexico. Ultimately the bank recovered less than $20,000 of the embezzled funds.

Farmers and Merchants National, like many major financial institutions, faced a period of uncertainty and confusion at the outbreak of World War I. Foreign trade dwindled and deposits shrank. General business activity in Los Angeles and California declined during the first months of the conflict. The city faced a shortage of currency, but the Los Angeles Clearing House Association, acting through the National Currency Association, made sufficient capital available to various area banks on a short-term-loan basis. After the initial shock the region's economy rebounded. Agricultural, manufacturing, and petroleum enterprises all prospered in the seller's market created by the war. The growth also reflected a continuing increase in the population of California's urban areas. By 1920 both San Francisco and Los Angeles had populations in excess of 500,000. At the same time the assessed valuation of San Francisco reached $820 million, while that of Los Angeles totaled nearly $1.3 billion. Activities at the Farmers and Merchants National expanded in kind. In 1915 the Traders Bank of Los Angeles vacated its quarters in the Hellman building on West Fourth Street. That building adjoined the Farmers and Merchants National building, and the bank expanded into the vacant space.

Still active after 50 years in business, Hellman died on April 9, 1920. California stood on the verge of a decade of remarkable growth. Farmers and Merchants National played an important role in the process. But because of Hellman's long-established policies, the bank refused to join in the speculative mania that historians have often associated with 1920s business and real estate activities. Farmers and Merchants National therefore substantially expanded its assets, deposits, and activities during the decade of the Great Depression. The bank continued to adhere to the fundamental principle

that the safety of the depositors' funds should be its chief concern throughout its existence as a separate institutional entity.

In 1956 Farmers and Merchants National merged with the Security-First National Bank of Los Angeles. The merger allowed its customers to benefit from the availability and convenience of Security-First's 147 branches, and the bank extended its service area into many new communities. The aggregate resources of the combined institution totaled $2,545,824,000. In addition, the bank still had access to Wells Fargo's funds and other monies, although it had no branch offices.

Hellman had founded the Farmers and Merchants Bank in 1871 and had served as its president for almost fifty years. He had witnessed and played a major role in the rise of two of the nation's great urban centers. He amassed a considerable fortune, including substantial amounts of valuable California real estate. He had also been thoroughly immersed in humanitarian and educational enterprises. Hellman's will provided for the distribution of $100,000 to Jewish charitable and benevolent institutions and $25,000 to the Catholic Orphans Asylum of Los Angeles. He left $50,000 to each of his seven grandchildren and $25,000 each to his brother, James Hellman, and his daughter-in-law, Frances J. Hellman. His will further stipulated the creation of a $2,000 trust fund for the poor of his native city, Beckendorf, Bavaria.

Hellman had also taken the time to enjoy and support cultural activities. He became fluent in four languages and was described as possessing a keen interest in national and international affairs. He was genuinely concerned for others, and his concern went beyond merely enhancing of his personal ends or fortune.

Through his business activities and personal character, Hellman had established a banking tradition of competence, honesty, and stability. Biographers state that during his early years in Los Angeles he befriended numerous merchants, farmers, and ranchers. Historian Ira B. Cross contends that the Farmers and Merchants Bank "undoubtedly" did more "toward fostering the development of southern California than any other bank in the state."

References:

Robert G. Cleland and Frank B. Putnam, *Isaias W. Hellman and the Farmers and Merchants Bank of Los Angeles* (San Marino, Cal.: Huntington Library, 1965);

Ira B. Cross, *Financing an Empire: History of Banking in California*, 4 volumes (Chicago: Clarke , 1927);

John M. Gwinn, *Historical and Bibliographical Record of Los Angeles and Vicinity* (Chicago: Chapman, 1902);

Leroy R. Hafen, *The Mountain Men and the Fur Trade of the Far West* (Glendale, Cal.: Clark, 1965);

"I. W. Hellman's Useful Career Ends," *Coast Banker* (November 1908): 17;

Michael F. Konig, "Henry Dwight Barrows: California Renaissance Man," in *Brand Book VI* (San Diego: Westerners Historical Association, 1979);

John Henry Nash, *In Memorium: Isaias W. Hellman* (San Francisco: Privately published, 1921);

Norton B. Stern, "Towards a Biography of Isaias W. Hellman: Pioneer Builder of California," *Western*

States Jewish Historical Quarterly, 2 (October 1969): 27-28;

Francis J. Weber, "Precedent for Ecumenism," *Western States Jewish Historical Quarterly*, 19 (January 1987): 158-160;

Wells Fargo Bank, *Wells Fargo Since 1852* (San Francisco: Wells Fargo Bank History Department, n.d.);

"Wells Fargo Nevada National Bank," *Coast Banker* (August 1911): 88-92;

Iris H. Wilson, *William Wolfskill: Frontier Trapper to California* (Glendale, Cal.: Clark, 1965).

Archives:

Some of Isaias W. Hellman's personal correspondence is at the Wells Fargo Archives, San Francisco, California.

A. Barton Hepburn

(July 24, 1846-January 25, 1922)

by Benjamin J. Klebaner

City College, CUNY

CAREER: Teacher, principal, St. Lawrence County, New York (1869-1871); lawyer, Colton, New York (1871-1872); school commissioner, second assembly district, New York (1872-1875); state assemblyman, New York (1875-1880); superintendent, New York Banking Department (1880-1883); receiver, Continental Life Insurance Company (1883-1886); lumber business (1883-1889); U.S. bank examiner, New York City, Brooklyn, Jersey City (1889-1892); U.S. comptroller of the currency (1892-1893); president, Third National Bank (1893-1897); vice-president, National City Bank (1897-1899); vice-president (1899-1904), president (1904-1911), chairman (1911-1917), chairman of the advisory board, Chase National Bank (1917-1922).

Alonzo Barton Hepburn, a leading banker and currency reformer in the late nineteenth and early twentieth centuries, was born in Colton (St. Lawrence County), New York, on July 24, 1846. He was the seventh of eight children of Zina Earl and Beulah Gray Hepburn. His paternal great-great-grandfather emigrated around 1700 from Abbey Mill (which he owned)–near Edinburgh, Scotland–to Stratford, Connecticut. Hepburn's first American ancestor on his mother's side came from London-

A. Barton Hepburn

derry, Ireland, in 1718 and settled in a Scotch-Irish colony in Worcester, Massachusetts. His parents were born in Vermont.

Hepburn described his childhood as one of "grim rigor and sad severity." After attending the village school, he entered St. Lawrence Academy in Potsdam (nine miles from his home) in 1861, graduating in the spring of 1867. A classmate later described him as a model student. Enrolled in Middlebury College in 1867, he left early in his sophomore year for lack of funds but continued to study on his own. In 1902 the college awarded him the A.B. He repaid his educational debts by working as a mathematics instructor at St. Lawrence Academy for one term, then as principal of the Ogdensburg Educational Institute for a year. While working in the schools he read law in the Ogdensburg office of Stillman, Foote, and James. He was admitted to the bar in November 1871. He enjoyed a busy practice in his hometown until its fortunes declined when the New York Central Railroad bypassed Colton.

In the fall of 1872 Hepburn entered public life with an appointment as school commissioner for New York's second assembly district, filling an unexpired term. He then won election for a full term. In 1874 he was elected to the New York state assembly as a Republican, taking his seat in January 1875. He won reelection four times with increasing majorities. He served on the Committee on Cities and on the Ways and Means Committee and chaired the committees on judiciary and apportionment and on insurance. Known for talking to the point, he had great influence on his colleagues.

In February 1879 Hepburn became chairman of a special committee of the legislature formed to investigate abuses in railroad management. The investigation grew out of agitation by business and farm groups over unfair railroad practices, including rate discrimination against particular shippers or localities. An 1882 act recommended by the committee established a bipartisan railroad commission empowered to investigate and make recommendations. The federal Interstate Commerce Commission Act of 1887 incorporated the commission's recommendation to ban the practice of charging more for a short haul, rejecting the railroads' argument that railroads based such discrimination on real costs and not on the existence, or the lack, of competition.

Hepburn's fine reputation led New York governor Alonzo R. Cornell to appoint him superinten-

dent of New York State's Banking Department in 1880. He served three years during a period of general prosperity. He advocated regular examinations of state-chartered institutions in order to prevent mismanagement. He believed that the public held national banks in highter esteem because they were "annually examined and vouched for." He argued that the 1882 failure of the Merchants Bank in Watertown pointed to the need for such preventative examinations. Regular examination of state banks became New York law in May 1884.

To increase the availability of services from incorporated banks, Hepburn recommended that minimum capital requirements for banks be reduced from $50,000 to $25,000 in places with fewer than 15,000 inhabitants. A July 1882 revision of the state's banking laws reduced the minimum for communities of fewer than 6,000.

When Democrat Grover Cleveland became New York governor in 1883, Hepburn declined reappointment to the commission. In February 1883 he was named receiver for the Continental Life Insurance Company of New York. He conducted the receivership with great skill, in the view of knowledgeable observers, until his discharge on August 9, 1886.

Hepburn also entered the lumber business in 1883. He had earlier acquired 30,000 acres of timberland in his native county for $15,000, and the superintendent's salary had proved inadequate to cover taxes and interest on the investment. He busied himself with making a market for his timber, the basis of his fortune, until 1889.

In June 1889 U.S. comptroller of the currency Edward S. Lacey named Hepburn bank examiner for New York City, Brooklyn, and Jersey City, the most important assignment in the system. In that position he urged banks to analyze the profitability of their accounts. For example, some banks gave immediate credit to customers depositing out-of-town checks, despite the lag in actual collection.

On July 27, 1892, at the age of forty-six, Hepburn became U.S. comptroller of the currency, filling Lacey's unexpired term. Leading New York City bankers and merchants had petitioned President Benjamin Harrison, urging Hepburn's appointment. He served less than nine months, deferring his resignation until April 25, 1893, so that Grover Cleveland, then president, could secure confirmation of his successor, James H. Eckels. Hepburn's tenure was the briefest of any comptroller in the agency's history. Thomas P. Kane, associated with the office for more than a generation, described Hepburn as "a man of exceptional attainments and executive force."

Hepburn left Washington for New York City to become president of Third National Bank. The bank was not a money-maker. It went into voluntary liquidation on May 20, 1897, and National City Bank, the leading bank in New York, acquired it. National City Bank had two objectives: to secure Third National's business–particularly its out-of-town depositors–and to gain Hepburn as a vice-president. "His ability, experience and reputation will strengthen our staff," bank president James Stillman stated. But Hepburn resigned after two years, preferring to be associated with a smaller bank.

Another former comptroller of the currency, Henry W. Cannon, had been at the head of Chase National Bank since 1886. Eager because of failing health for a competent banker to take his place, he personally solicited Hepburn. The fifty-two-year-old Hepburn was brought in as vice-president of Chase on January 24, 1899. He became president on February 9, 1904, upon Cannon's resignation from the post. When Cannon retired from management altogether in 1911, Hepburn was elected chairman of the board, "authorized to bind the Bank by his acts and signature with the same effect as if he were President," as the board of directors' resolution stated. On the occasion of his promotion to chairman, the board recorded its pleasure that under Hepburn, Chase had "grown steadily in importance, in strength, in public confidence, and in reputation for stability and conservative progress." He won praise for his "untiring application, capacity for searching analyses, foresight, breadth of view, rare judgment, and the wise courage which has made him a leader of men."

The seventy-one-year-old Hepburn resigned the chairmanship of Chase National on September 12, 1917. Named chairman of the bank's advisory board (a post created for him), he continued to enjoy the same legal powers as before. That innovation reflected the directors' unwillingness to lose Hepburn's counsel. After his death the position disappeared.

Hepburn succeeded "simply by hard, systematic work directed by every ounce of intelligence in me." He kept a proper record of facts and figures to which he could turn whenever the occasion arose. The bank launched a house organ, *The Chase*, in April 1918. Hepburn wrote in the opening article that "the bank that has a reputation of studying the wants and meeting the needs of its customers and giving them courteous, warm-blooded treatment . . . will find the volume of its business constantly increasing."

Chase, with its very substantial correspondent banking activity, had the reputation of a "bank of banks." In 1897 it had more accounts from out-of-town banks–some 2,000 from all over the country–than any other in New York; the correspondent accounts represented about 75 percent of Chase's deposit volume. Chase had almost 3,200 correspondent accounts in 1912, but by then National Park Bank had 4,200. Albert Wiggin, upon joining the bank as vice-president in 1904, cultivated nonfinancial firms, yet as late as September 1915 more than 60 percent of total deposits were from other banks. Chase held $41 million in total deposits in 1899, compared to National City's $105 million. A decade later Chase's deposits had increased to $80 million and National City's to $190 million.

Financier George F. Baker came to own a majority of Chase shares in the early 1900s, in contemplation of merging Chase into his First National Bank of New York. He later decided Chase's prospects were "too valuable to sacrifice."

Hepburn had an interest in sound money and published frequently on the subject. An 1893 paper for the Academy of Political and Social Science opposed attempts to restore state bank note issue, which he thought would bring "disaster to that class of our citizens who most need and have most right to ask protection from the Government." In March 1893 Hepburn wrote in the *North American Review* that "every currency should be sound, safe, elastic and good as gold." To qualify as sound money, a coin's value should equal commercial value of the bullion, while paper money and token money should be redeemable in sound coin. To the end of his life he viewed paper money as "a promise to pay real money–gold–on demand." Hepburn also played a public role in support of sound money. He served as treasurer and general secretary of the National Sound Money League, organized at the time of the 1896 presidential campaign to combat efforts to restore bimetallism.

Hepburn also concerned himself with the issue of monetary reform, and he generally advocated a currency expansion based on the backing of

Broadway offices of Chase National Bank from 1914 to 1928. Hepburn served in the bank's administration from 1899 to 1922.

bank assets as a solution to the problem of cyclical tight money. In 1894, as chairman of a subcommittee of the American Bankers Association's executive council, Hepburn urged the clearinghouse banks of Baltimore (the site of the annual convention) to draft a plan of currency reform. Years later Charles Hamlin, first governor of the Federal Reserve Board, hailed the Baltimore Plan, as the product of Hepburn's solicitation became known, as "the cornerstone of the Federal Reserve Act."

When the American Bankers Association established a Currency Commission in 1906, Hepburn became chairman, a position he held until his death. Hepburn's Currency Commission unanimously recommended a credit currency in November 1906. Such a currency would satisfy local demand; more currency could be issued, subject to a steep tax, "in cases of extreme need," as his article published by Hepburn in the *North American Review* of December 1906 pointed out. Until passage of the Federal Reserve Act in 1913, the Currency Commission devoted earnest and continued attention to banking issues.

According to Hepburn's article published in *Moody's Magazine* in October 1907, "a government-controlled central bank of issue, where the banks . . . can . . . discount their receivables, receiving the proceeds in bank-notes, [would] afford the best solution of the currency question, the interest rate and bank reserves." The identical conclusion appeared two years later in an essay published in *Century Magazine*.

As a long-standing advocate of a central bank, Hepburn was consulted on the Federal Reserve Bill by various congressmen and H. Parker Willis, expert adviser to the bill's author, Rep. Carter Glass of Virginia. Separate Federal Reserve banks would violate the principle of consolidation of reserves, Hepburn argued. He succeeded in persuading President Wilson that the banks should have the right and obligation to rediscount for one another; that made the system a central bank.

In Hepburn's view, one of the chief benefits of the Federal Reserve Act was that it did away with the bad effects of the Independent Treasury System. The antiquated system had significantly interfered with "the even tenor of general business," his Currency Commission informed Congress in 1913. The Subtreasury arrangement represented "an absurd governmental interference with the currency supply, affecting values, promoting speculation, retarding business, and disturbing the welfare of the people."

In January 1918 Hepburn became concerned that the United States would "lose the proud preeminence of being squarely on a gold basis, with the prestige that it will give us after the war." He later expressed pride that only the United States had "preserved the gold standard in its full integrity." But the nation could not afford complacency: "the time will never come when the sound banker and economist will not need to combat the idea that governmental fiat can create something out of nothing."

In 1919 the directors of the Federal Reserve Bank of New York elected Hepburn to succeed J. P. Morgan, Jr., on the Federal Advisory Council of the Federal Reserve Board. During his two years on the council he gave his duties priority over other matters. Benjamin Anderson credits Hepburn with defending sound policies while fighting dangerous ones.

Early in 1920 Hepburn stated that the country could have avoided panics in the past "under a proper currency system, such as we have now under the Federal Reserve Banks." A few months later a sharp economic downturn began. Hepburn told the *New York Globe* that the Federal Reserve had prevented the failure of sound businesses. Previous panics had swept those away together with unsound firms. In the 1924 edition of his *History of Currency in the United States* (originally published in 1903), he expressed the "hope that we have a credit and currency system which will assure stability as to metallic money, security and flexibility as to paper currency, to the end that prices may not be subject to ruthless disturbances and interest rates be reasonably uniform and equitable throughout the land."

Growing up in the Adirondack foothills, with the Raquette River at his door, Hepburn became an adept hunter and fisherman. As a seven-year-old he proudly possessed a three-and-a-half-pound shotgun. In a region where good marksmanship ensured good standing, Hepburn developed into one of the best shots. He went big-game hunting in British East Africa in his sixty-seventh year. He recounted his adventures in *The Story of an Outing* upon his return in 1913. He continued to hunt game in various lands for the rest of his life. He enjoyed salmon

fishing in Canada, an activity he described as "the King of Sports," for more than a dozen years. "The outdoor life sweetens all existence," he told B. C. Forbes. Hepburn went salmon fishing in the last summer of his life in Gaspé, Quebec. On his return he suffered a second stroke (he suffered his first during a trip to Tokyo in 1921), from which he never fully recovered.

Knocked down by a bus on New York City's Madison Square, Hepburn suffered a third stroke and died five days later, on January 25, 1922. He was buried in Canton next to the grave of Frederic Remington, a native son who became the great artist of the American West. Hepburn's estate was appraised at $7.5 million at the time of his death.

Hepburn's numerous benefactions came to $5 million. He gave Ogdensburg Hospital and Middlebury College $1.1 million each. A total of $535,000 went to the building of libraries in seven St. Lawrence County towns. The distinctively designed buildings became centers of social life, as Hepburn intended, by incorporating large halls on the ground floors. Williams College was given $301,250 and St. Lawrence University $276,500. Lesser amounts were donated to Princeton University, Wellesley College, and New York University. In 1917 Hepburn gave $60,000 for a professorship in American constitutional history at Tokyo University, to be taught by a Japanese.

Convinced of the importance of commercial education for the prosperity of New York City, Hepburn worked to set up a School of Commerce there. He played an instrumental role in the establishment of Columbia University's School of Business and gave $500,000 toward that end in February 1919. He later gave an additional $350,000.

Hepburn's leadership qualities were widely recognized. In New York it was said that he was "president of everything worthwhile but the United States." He was made an officer of the French Legion of Honor in 1912, commander of the Royal Order of George the First of Greece in 1919, and the Emperor of Japan honored him with the Second Class of the Order of the Sacred Treasure in 1921. He served as director of many corporations. He received honorary doctorates from Columbia University, Williams College, Middlebury College, St. Lawrence University, and New York University.

Hepburn married Hattie A. Fisher of St. Albans, Vermont, on December 10, 1873. The couple had two sons: Harold Barton and Charles

Fisher. The latter was a major during World War I and later a Cleveland businessman. Hepburn's first wife died in December 1881. On July 14, 1884, he married Emily Lovisia Easton, also a Vermont native, who had graduated from St. Lawrence Academy the previous year. They had two daughters: Beulah Easton, who married Robert Emmet, and Cordelia Susan, who married Paul Cushman.

A self-made man of wide-ranging interests, A. Barton Hepburn had a distinguished career in both the public and private sectors. Widely respected for his integrity and judgment, recognized as a leading spokesman for the financial community, he was a shining example of the American businessman at his best.

Selected Publications:

"National Banking and the Clearing-House," *North American Review*, 156 (1893): 365-376;

"State and National Bank Circulation," *Annals of the American Academy of Political and Social Science*, 3, no. 5 (1893): 573-580;

History of Coinage and Currency in the United States and the Perennial Contest for Sound Money (New York: Macmillan, 1903; London: Macmillan, 1903); revised and enlarged as *A History of Currency in the United States, with a Brief Description of the Currency Systems of All Commercial Nations* (New York: Macmillan, 1915); revised and enlarged again as *A History of Currency in the United States, with New Chapters on the Monetary and Financial Developments in the United States from 1914 to 1922* (New York: Macmillan, 1924);

"Credit Currency," *North American Review*, 183 (1906): 1171-1178;

"Currency Commission Plan," *Moody's* (October 1907): 479-487;

Artificial Waterways and Commercial Development (New York: Macmillan, 1909); revised and enlarged as *Artificial Waterways of the World* (New York: Macmillan, 1914);

"Is a Central Bank Desirable?," *Century*, 78 (1909): 950-957;

The Story of an Outing (New York & London: Harper, 1913).

References:

Joseph Bucklin Bishop, *A. Barton Hepburn: His Life and Service to His Time* (New York: Scribners, 1923);

B. C. Forbes, *Men Who Are Making America* (New York: Forbes, 1917);

Thomas P. Kane, *The Romance and Tragedy of Banking: Problems and Incidents of Governmental Supervision of National Banks*, 2 volumes (New York: Bankers Publishing Co., 1922).

Archives:

A. Barton Hepburn's papers are held at Columbia University and Chase Manhattan Bank.

Richard Hildreth

(June 28, 1807-July 11, 1865)

by James M. Smallwood

University of Texas at Tyler

CAREER: Lawyer (1830-1865); historian and author (1832-1865); co-owner and editor (1832-1834), editor, *Boston Daily Atlas* (1837-1839); editor, abolitionist newspapers, British Guiana (1840-1843); columnist, *New York Tribune* (1855-1861); U.S. consul to Trieste, Italy (1860-1864).

Richard Hildreth, destined to become best known as an editor and writer of political and economic history, was born in Deerfield, Massachusetts, on June 28, 1807, the son of the Reverend Hosea and Sarah McLeod Hildreth. He was descended from namesake Richard Hildreth, a freeman who came to Massachusetts in 1643.

Hosea Hildreth, who had graduated from Harvard College, became professor of mathematics at Phillips Exeter Academy four years after Hildreth was born; Hildreth entered the academy in 1816, at nine years of age. After graduating in 1822 he continued his education, first studying with a private tutor and then attending Harvard.

After graduating from Harvard in 1826, Hildreth studied law and was admitted to the bar in Suffolk County, Massachusetts, in 1830; he established his practice in Boston and Newburyport. In 1832 he became a co-founder of a newspaper, the *Boston Daily Atlas*. He took a small salary for himself and became an editorial writer for the *Atlas*. He also contributed articles to such popular journals as *American Monthly Magazine*, *Ladies' Magazine*, and *New-England Magazine*.

In 1834 Hildreth developed serious health problems, which forced him to sell his interest in the *Atlas* and move to Florida, where he lived for two years. He used his time in Florida to write an antislavery novel, *The Slave: or Memoirs of Archy Moore*, which saw publication in 1836 and was reissued in 1852 as *The White Slave: or, Memoirs of a Fugitive*.

*Richard Hildreth (*Second Publication of the Hildreth Family Association, *1922)*

Upon returning to Massachusetts Hildreth reestablished his connection—but not as an owner—to the *Atlas*, again becoming its primary editorial writer in 1837. His editorials often dealt with issues of national political importance. He opposed the temperance movement, which he believed threatened civil rights. He also thundered against the annexation of Texas, which he regarded as a conspiracy by the "slave power" to add another slave state to the Union (or perhaps even to divide Texas into several slaveholding states). Such opposition helps explain why President Andrew Jackson could not guide the annexation through Congress. In the 1820s Hildreth had joined the Jacksonian Democrats, but the Texas question drove him to embrace the Whig party.

Hildreth retired from the *Atlas* in 1839, when he and a new owner disagreed on matters of local politics. By the time he left the *Atlas* he had established himself as the preeminent business historian of Massachusetts. In 1837 he published a volume entitled *The History of Banks*. In 1840 he brought out an expansion of the 1837 study entitled *Banks, Banking, and Paper Currencies*. Those studies argued for free, open competition as the basis for the U.S. economy.

In 1839 Hildreth began to work actively for the Whig party, supporting William Henry Harrison for president in the election of 1840. Hildreth wrote Harrison's campaign biography, *The People's Presidential Candidate* (1839). The next year he wrote a tract entitled *The Contrast: or William Henry Harrison versus Martin Van Buren*. In the election year he also published *Despotism in America*, a discussion and criticism of the consequences of American slavery.

In 1840 Hildreth was also drawn into a theological controversy when he criticized some of the views of the noted Reverend Andrews Norton, who had questioned the idea of biblical literality. Hildreth's argument, published in 1840 as *A Letter to Andrews Norton on Miracles as a Foundation of Religious Faith*, first reviewed Protestant history, beginning with an overview of Martin Luther's beliefs, then recounted the miracles as told in the Gospels.

After the 1840 presidential campaign Hildreth spent three years in British Guiana, where he edited two abolitionist newspapers. He also compiled and edited a volume on Guiana's colonial laws and gathered enough material to publish a *Local Guide of British Guiana* (1843). Upon returning to the United States in 1843 he courted Caroline Neagus, of Deerfield, and the two were married on June 7, 1844. Although they had a happy, stable union, the couple never had children.

From the 1840s until his death in 1865 Hildreth achieved wide recognition as a writer whose treatment of diverse subjects was always "preeminently respectable" and objective. His later books and booklets include several works that attacked the institution of slavery and others that developed his mature thoughts on such topics as politics, morals, education, and temperance. In addition, from 1849 to 1852 he worked laboriously on a six-volume history of the United States, published as two separate three-volume works, which carried the story of the nation from its beginnings to 1821. He also contributed scholarly articles to the *Massachusetts Quarterly Review*, then edited and published by Unitarian clergyman Theodore Parker.

After the opening of Japan in 1854, Hildreth compiled all available data on the country and in 1855 published *Japan as It Was and Is*. Further, after the new Republican party was organized in 1854, Hildreth emerged as an ardent supporter, especially endorsing the new party's antislavery position. Yet he still had ample time to continue his writing. He published a revised six-volume U.S. history from 1856 to 1860. From 1855 to 1861 he contributed a regular column to the *New York Tribune*. He discontinued his *Tribune* column when—after Abraham Lincoln assumed the presidency—he was named consul to Trieste, Italy. Ill health forced Hildreth to resign his consulship in 1864. He retired to Florence, where he hoped he could recuperate, but he died there on July 11, 1865, and was buried near Theodore Parker in the Protestant graveyard.

Hildreth's fame came primarily from his historical works—particularly his books on banking and business and his multivolume general study on U.S. history. Contemporaries and later scholars have credited him with objectivity and with a solid and readable, if somewhat pedestrian, style. Throughout his career as an author he remained an advocate of laissez-faire economic doctrine.

Publications:

An Abridged History of the United States of America. For the Use of Schools. Intended as a Sequel to Hildreth's View of the United States, as Hosea Hildreth (Boston: Carter, Hendee & Babcock, 1831);

The Slave: or Memoirs of Archy Moore, 2 volumes, anonymous (Boston: J. H. Eastburn, 1836); expanded as *The White Slave; or, Memoirs of a Fugitive* (Boston: Tappan & Whittemore/Milwaukee: Rood & Whittemore, 1852; London: Routledge, 1852);

The History of Banks: To Which Is Added, A Demonstration of the Advantages and Necessity of Free Competition in the Business of Banking (Boston: Hilliard, Gray, 1837; London: J. S. Hodson, 1837); revised and enlarged as *Banks, Banking, and Paper Currencies* (Boston: Whipple & Damrell, 1840);

The People's Presidential Candidate; or The Life of William Henry Harrison, of Ohio (Boston: Weeks, Jordan, 1839);

The Contrast: or William Henry Harrison versus Martin Van Buren (Boston: Weeks, Jordan, 1840);

A Letter to Andrews Norton on Miracles as a Foundation of Religious Faith (Boston: Weeks, Jordan, 1840);

Despotism in America; or an Inquiry into the Nature and Results of the Slave-Holding System in the United States . . ., anonymous (Boston: Whipple & Damrell, 1840); revised and enlarged as *Despotism in America: An Inquiry into the Nature, Results, and Legal Basis of the Slave-Holding System in the United States* (Boston: John P. Jewett/Cleveland: Jewett, Proctor & Worthington, 1854; Boston: J. P. Jewett/New York: Sheldon, Lamport & Blakeman, 1854; London: Low, 1854);

Local Guide of British Guiana (Boston: Weeks, Jordan, 1843);

Theory of Morals: An Inquiry Concerning the Law of Moral Distinctions and the Variations and Contradictions of Ethical Codes (Boston: Charles C. Little & James Brown, 1844);

Native-Americanism Detected and Exposed. By a Native American (Boston: Printed for the author, 1845);

A Joint Letter to Orestes A. Brownson and the Editor of the North American Review: In Which the Editor of the North American Review is Proved to Be No Christian, and Little Better than an Atheist (Boston, 1845);

The Truth Revealed. Statement and Review of the Whole Case of the Reverend Joy H. Fairchild, from its Commencement to its Termination, Compiled from Original Documents by a Member of the Suffolk Bar, anonymous (Boston: Wright's Steam Press, 1845);

"Our First Men:" A Calendar of Wealth, Fashion and Gentility, Containing a List of Those Persons Taxed in the City of Boston, Credibly Reported to Be Worth One Hundred Thousand Dollars, with Biographical Notices of the Principal Persons, anonymous (Boston: Published by all the Booksellers, 1846);

The History of the United States of America, from the Discovery of the Continent of the Organization of Government under the Federal Constitution, 3 volumes (New York: Harper, 1849); revised as volumes 1-3 of *The History of the United States of America*;

The History of the United States of America, from the Adoption of the Federal Constitution to the End of the Sixteenth Congress, 1788-1821, 3 volumes (New York: Harper, 1851-1852); revised as volumes 4-6 of *The History of the United States of America*;

Theory of Politics: An Inquiry into the Foundations of Governments, and the Causes and Progress of Political Revolutions (New York: Harper, 1853);

Japan as It Was and Is (Boston: Phillips, Sampson/New York: J. C. Derby, 1855); revised as *Japan and the Japanese* (Boston: Bradley, Dayton, 1860);

The History of the United States of America, 6 volumes (New York: Harper, 1856-1860).

References:

William T. Davis, *Bench and Bar of the Commonwealth of Massachusetts* (Boston: Little, Brown, 1895);

F. L. Mott, *A History of American Magazines, 1741-1850* (New York: Doubleday, 1930);

Martha Pingal, *An American Utilitarian: Richard Hildreth* (New York: Columbia University Press, 1948).

Archives:

The best collection of material on Richard Hildreth is located at the Massachusetts Historical Society.

Charles Christopher Homer

(November 1, 1847-September 13, 1914)

by Carol M. Martel

Arizona State University

CAREER: Vice-president (1886-1889), president, Second National Bank of Baltimore (1889-1914); chairman, Baltimore Clearing House Association (1897-1911).

Charles Christopher Homer, a Baltimore banker, introduced a currency reform plan in 1894 that kicked off a reform movement culminating in the Federal Reserve Act of 1913. Homer was born on November 1, 1847, in Baltimore, the son of Christopher Homer, a prosperous businessman who had emigrated from Germany. Little is known of his childhood education. He graduated from Georgetown University in the District of Columbia in 1877, later earning a master's degree there. Homer began his business career as a glass and paint salesman. He established and directed his own provision business, Foss and Homer, until 1880. After that he went into banking, and in 1886 he became vice-president of the Second National Bank of Baltimore. Three years later he was promoted to president, a position he held until his death. The prominent Baltimore banker served many years as chairman of the Baltimore Clearing House Association. He also served as vice-president of the Savings Bank of Baltimore and the Safe Deposit and Trust Company.

In his leisure time Homer managed a large peach farm at Poole's Island, at the mouth of the Patapsco River in Maryland. He had a reputation of being well informed about banking and economics in general. His community interests included trusteeships of the Sheppard and Enoch Pratt Hospital and the Maryland Historical Society. On March 4, 1869, he married Frances M. Holthaus, daughter of Francis T. Holthaus of Baltimore. The couple had five children: Charles Christopher (who was president of the Baltimore Clearing House from 1915 to 1919), Francis Theodore, Henry Louis, Robert Baldwin, and a daughter who died in infancy. Homer died in Bremen, Germany, on September 13, 1914, just after the beginning of World War I.

The discussion of currency reform became serious after the financial crisis of 1893, which taught both the banks and the public a lesson. During panics the whole American banking system became paralyzed, as depositors quickly withdrew money in the large city banks. Several proposals for reform emerged, and they generally fell into three groups: currency reform, the creation of a central bank, and deposit insurance. Those bankers who championed reform mainly promoted currency reform. They warmed up only slowly to the idea of central banking, and even then they split over a central bank dominated by government or one run by private bankers. They especially disliked the idea of deposit insurance.

As a result of the 1893 panic the emphasis in reform proposals shifted from banking practices to the inelasticity of the national currency, which could not readily be decreased in slack seasons or increased in busy seasons and periods of emergency. Homer reasoned that the panic's roots lay in the fear that the government would not be able to maintain specie redemption of all its obligations. Alonzo Barton Hepburn, president of the Third National Bank of New York, described the currency system of the time as "ill-conceived, unresponsive to the various interests of our great nation, and prejudicial to renewed and stable prosperity." The two essential elements of a perfect currency were security and elasticity. After 1893 the business and financial community preferred to abolish bond-secured currency and issue a new national bank note that the assets of the issuing bank secured. One of the first proposals for this type of assets-based reform, the "Baltimore Plan," emanated from bankers themselves.

Homer and Hepburn figured among a group of men in the 1890s and 1900s who expounded the advantages of central banking. The reform movement centered in Chicago, an area of rapid bank growth. Midwestern city bankers devoted much time to organizing and running the American Bankers' Association (ABA). Most New York and other northeastern bankers directed their attention to state rather than national issues and so stayed fairly aloof from the early reform movement.

The Baltimore Plan for a safe and elastic currency, written by Homer with the help of Hepburn and Horace White, editor of the *New York Evening Post*, was presented by Homer to the 1894 ABA convention. As chairman of the ABA's subcommittee in charge of planning the convention, Hepburn had suggested to the Baltimore Clearing House banks that they draft a currency reform plan. Homer, described by Hepburn as "one of the most competent bankers of the country," told the convention that the plan represented the thought and practical experience of the observant businessmen of conservative Baltimore as expressed through the members of the Baltimore Clearing House. Hepburn and White commented on the proposal as if a group of Baltimore bankers had conceived it. This procedure, according to Robert Craig West, indicated the approach of some New York bankers, who preferred to remain in the background because of the prevalent fear of Wall Street.

Homer proposed revising the National Banking Act of 1863 by repealing the provision requiring the deposit of federal-government bonds to secure a bank's circulation. An expanded circulation would be established based on bank assets, amounting to three-fourths of the banks' unimpaired capital. Banks would be able to issue circulating notes to the amount of 50 percent of their paid-up, unimpaired capital, which could be increased by 25 percent in an emergency. A heavy tax would be placed on that emergency part of the circulation so that every bank would withdraw it as promptly as possible once it had served its purpose. That tax marked firmly the line of departure between ordinary and emergency circulation so that business might return to its normal state as quickly as possible.

The other primary change from the National Banking Act, a "guarantee fund" or safety fund for the circulation, proposed to ensure the soundness of the assets-based notes. The guarantee fund consisted of contributions from each bank of 2 percent of its circulation the first year, and after that one-half of 1 percent until the guarantee fund reached 5

percent of outstanding circulation. Security would be unconditionally guaranteed by the federal government, which would be required to redeem immediately notes of failed banks. Moreover, the government exposed itself to little financial risk because banks provided and maintained the fund from which to make such redemptions. Any surplus would be used for the benefit of the United States absolutely and without question and no longer constituted a part of an asset of any bank. Homer insisted that no association or individual could claim money from the guarantee fund except for redemption of insolvent banks. The government would have a prior lien on the assets of each failed bank and on the shareholders, to the extent of their liability, in order to replenish the guarantee fund.

Some of Homer's proposals reproduced provisions of the National Banking Act. A tax of one-half of 1 percent would be levied on the average amount of each bank's outstanding circulation. This tax would be paid to the U.S. treasurer to defray the expenses of the office of comptroller of the currency and for the printing and circulating of notes. Any surplus from that tax would go into the guarantee fund. Also, banks would still contribute 5 percent of their assets to a redemption fund to be maintained by the treasurer to redeem national bank notes. A bank's circulation could be retired at any time by depositing with the secretary of the treasury lawful money equal to the sum desired to be withdrawn.

The last section of Homer's proposal, taken from Canadian law, dealt with bank closings. It gave the treasurer authority to wind up the business of any insolvent bank and pay over to directors, liquidators, or other lawful parties the amount to the credit of the bank in the redemption fund.

When he introduced the plan, Homer argued that American banks historically had maintained a circulation equal to 40 to 50 percent of capital, so the plan would not create inflation or deflation. In his comments on the proposal Hepburn showed that the guarantee fund provided more than adequate backing for the proposed note issue. Both men argued that the plan provided a solution to the problem of an inelastic currency. The emergency currency ensured elasticity because banks could satisfy depositors' demands even if an unusual amount of currency was needed. The plan's premise was that Congress had the sole power to coin money and regulate its value, but government's money functions

Certificate of the Baltimore Clearing House. Homer served as president of the Clearing House Association from 1897 to 1911.

should end with the coining of gold and silver. The issue of auxiliary currency—paper money—that did not possess legal-tender quality ought to be left to the banks, relieving note issue from unreasonable restrictions and providing elasticity in the safety-fund principle.

As part of the reform agenda of the ABA, the Baltimore Plan constituted not a final solution but a means of focusing discussions of experts on banking and currency problems. Free-silver advocates hardly supported the reform plan willingly, but they would have criticized any plan that did not utilize silver. Hepburn castigated their control of monetary legislation as a "suicidal silver policy" that contributed to the 1893 economic crisis. Other bankers objected to the idea that note holders would hold a prior lien on the assets of a failed bank, but in fact they already did so under the National Banking Act and the banking laws of most states. The proposal also met with opposition from some New York bankers, and that opposition alone made the adoption of the plan unlikely. On the other hand, leaders of midwestern city banks, such as James Echels of Chicago and Frank Bigelow of Milwaukee, threw their support behind the reform plan. They hoped to improve their position relative to the New York bankers, but distrust of midwestern city bankers increased the politically powerful New York banking community's opposition to ABA reform plans. Country bankers, with their distrust of

city bankers, would have been more interested in a reform measure that recognized rural assets.

In December 1894 Homer, White, and Hepburn testified before the House Committee on Banking and Currency concerning the Baltimore Plan. White emphasized that the proposal dealt with only one part of the banking business, that of note issues. Homer outlined and defended the nine sections of the proposal, providing statistics to show that the proposed guarantee fund would be sufficient to cover all insolvent banks. He estimated current national bank capital as $700 million and bank-note circulation as $350 million. A guarantee fund of 5 percent would thus total $17.5 million. Investing that sum at 3 percent would yield an annual income to the fund of $525,000. According to the records of the comptroller's office, under the National Banking Act insolvent bank losses had amounted to $953,000, or about $30,000 annually. If the fund ever proved insufficient, additional money could come from the Treasury's own funds, which would be reimbursed upon replenishment of the guarantee fund. Homer insisted that no association or individual could claim money from the guarantee fund except for redemption of insolvent banks, and only the government would have title to surplus funds.

Homer then went on to criticize the rival plan of Secretary of the Treasury John Carlisle. The required deposit of 30 percent in Carlisle's guarantee fund seemed excessive and unwarranted by past ex-

271

perience. It proposed to relieve the government from the responsibility of redeeming a large portion of its own notes, which Homer considered a rather unmanly position. Contrary to Treasury policy, Homer recommended the issue of bank notes of less than $10, because maintaining such a minimum required people to carry too many coins. Homer also criticized the treasurer's proposal to allow each national bank to redeem national bank notes, since the system of central redemption through subtreasuries already worked efficiently. Money had already been deposited in a redemption fund, which Homer's proposal would retain, for the purpose of maintaining that centralized system. Homer also urged rigid supervision of banks by the comptroller of the currency. The comptroller could exercise a sharper and more effective supervision if the government stood ultimately liable than if the banks themselves were liable.

The committee doggedly attacked Homer, his proposals, and bankers in general. One congressman described the ABA convention as "bankers who considered nothing except their own immediate banking business and what would benefit that business." Homer replied that the "interest of the banks is the interest of the country" and that banks and depositors worked together as "staunch friends and allies." Another congressman derided the Baltimore Plan as "a careful and conservative action by a bankers' convention, the members of which know more about finances than all of us know, and as one of your men said . . . that we were entirely incompetent to deal with the question, or in fact, to deal with much of anything else. So long as you take that position, I do not know that I care to interrogate you further about it."

Although not a single supporter of the Baltimore Plan served on the House committee, the proposal marked the beginning of serious agitation for banking reform along asset currency lines. It laid the groundwork for acceptance of the "real bills" doctrine, the belief that credit should be based on commercial bills. If deposit bills were allowed to be counted as reserves in addition to gold, gold certificates, silver, and silver certificates, it would mean a great expansion of deposits.

Although the Baltimore Plan failed to lead to any immediate reform of the system, the business community continued to discuss the problem. The plan resulted in greater consideration of bank reform along assets-based lines. Within the ABA, pro-

posals of that type were introduced in subsequent conventions. Homer and other bankers also attended the Indianapolis Monetary Convention of 1897, although it primarily represented business interests. At the Indianapolis meeting a plan was introduced by J. Laurence Laughlin, a University of Chicago economist, that incorporated many aspects of the Baltimore Plan, such as the establishment of a redemption fund and a guarantee fund. The basic difference was that the Indianapolis proposal allowed banks to issue notes in an amount equal to their paid-up and unimpaired capital minus the amount invested in real estate. In 1906 the Currency Commission of the ABA presented a proposal well in line with the Baltimore and Indianapolis suggestions. None of those proposals became law, but their basic premise persisted: the concept of a currency supported by the assets of banking institutions.

Leading bankers never agreed among themselves on a reform measure during the 1890s and early 1900s. Historians have often suggested that the self-interest of bankers impeded reform. There were many conflicts of interest within the banking community, between national and state banks, city and country banks, large and small banks, and between sections of the country. There were also conflicts between supporters of a high-taxed emergency currency and a low-taxed credit currency, and between opponents of branch banking and central banking. Opposition to the Baltimore Plan arose from such men as Jacob Schiff, New York investment banker, George William, president of the Chemical National Bank of New York, and John Walsh, president of the Chicago National Bank. Schiff suggested that banks be entitled to encroach on their reserves in emergencies.

Banking and currency issues played an important role in nineteenth-century politics because the Constitution gave Congress control of monetary affairs. Only when the Federal Reserve System was activated in 1913 did those issues become removed from congressional jurisdiction and thus from normal political discourse, although they still remained somewhat politicized. Charles Homer played an important role in pushing reform in the direction of the Federal Reserve.

References:

Charles A. Hales, *The Baltimore Clearing House* (Baltimore: Johns Hopkins University Press, 1940);

Alonzo Barton Hepburn, "The Baltimore Plan of Currency Reform," *Forum*, 18 (1894): 385-395;

J. Laurence Laughlin, "The Baltimore Plan of Bank Issues," *Journal of Political Economy*, 3 (1894): 101-105;

Proceedings of the Annual Convention of the American Bankers' Association (1894);

Fritz Redlich, *The Molding of American Banking: Men and Ideas*, 2 volumes (New York: Johnson Reprint Co., 1968);

Robert Craig West, *Banking Reform and the Federal Reserve, 1863-1923* (Ithaca, N.Y.: Cornell University Press, 1974).

Improvement Banks

by Gregory S. Hunter

ITT Corporation

In addition to commercial and savings banks, which still exist, nineteenth-century America had a third major type of banking institution: the improvement bank. That entity combined the traditional banking functions of the century—note issue, discounting, and loans—with an internal-improvement firm such as a canal, railroad, or water company.

The reason for this combination of activities reflects the unique situation found in early America. State governments either could not or would not fund all of the required improvements to the economic infrastructure. States found it desirable, therefore, to have some improvements undertaken by private corporations chartered for those purposes. The problem, however, was that capital-intensive, internal-improvement companies traditionally paid small returns to their investors. That tended to discourage investment and diminish the capital available for the project.

One solution was to combine the low-return internal-improvement activity with a high-return activity such as banking. Investors in early banks received a very favorable return. For example, the Bank of Pennsylvania paid a dividend of 8.75 percent in 1782 and 14.5 percent in 1783.

The combination of banking with other activities is not as strange as it may appear. In the early part of the century, banks, like other corporations, were considered to be franchises: legislators bestowed incorporation upon activities considered to advance the public good. Banks advanced the public good by issuing and circulating notes that served as the de facto currency for a particular area. This link between public service and business corporations did not end until general incorporation statutes commonly appeared during the 1850s.

One example of an improvement bank, the New York Chemical Manufacturing Company, received its charter in 1823. In order to attract investment to the manufacture of chemicals, the legislature permitted the company to use for banking up to four-fifths of its total capital of $500,000. The company was involved in both activities during the 21-year term of its original charter. In 1844 the company divorced itself from manufacturing and became known as the Chemical Bank.

Examples illustrating the range of improvement banks included the Morris Bank and Canal Company (New Jersey); the Connecticut River Banking Company (Connecticut); the Susquehanna Bank and Bridge Company (Maryland); the Sanders Manufacturing Company (Kentucky); the Gas Light and Banking Company (Louisiana); the Grand Gulf Railroad and Banking Company (Mississippi); and the Texas Railroad, Navigation, and Banking Company. Still others backed canals and other fairly exotic businesses, including in one case a hotel.

Not all improvement banks, however, were specifically chartered. One of the most famous—or infamous—the Manhattan Company, chartered in 1799 to supply New York City with water, soon devoted most of its energies to banking. In that and similar cases the improvement objective of the corporate charter provided a shield to deflect public criticism from the nascent banking effort. In several instances public opposition to the establishment of a bank proved so intense that only the subterfuge of an improvement company led to the founding of a bank. For example, the Miami Exporting Company of Cincinnati, chartered in 1803 ostensibly to transport farm products to New Orleans, soon established a profitable banking business.

Despite these and similar cases of hidden banking activities, improvement banks performed a needed service in the first half of the nineteenth century. They helped raise capital for projects that otherwise might never have been undertaken, financing canals, railroads, water projects, gas lights, and roads. They are an often forgotten part of the American banking tradition.

References:

Joseph Stancliffe Davis, *Essays in the Earlier History of American Corporations* (Cambridge, Mass.: Harvard University Press, 1917; New York: Russell & Russell, 1965);

Bray Hammond, *Banks and Politics in America from the Revolution to the Civil War* (Princeton: Princeton University Press, 1957);

Fritz Redlich, *The Molding of American Banking: Men and Ideas*, 2 volumes (New York: Hafner, 1947; New York: Johnson Reprint Co., 1968);

Ronald Seavoy, *The Origins of the American Business Corporation, 1784-1855: Broadening the Concept of Public Service During Industrialization* (Westport, Conn.: Greenwood 1982).

Independent Treasury System *(see* Second Bank of the United States*)*

Investment Banks *(see* Commercial Banks and Investment Banks*)*

Alexander Bryan Johnson

(May 29, 1786-September 10, 1867)

by Jennifer Davis

University of Dayton

CAREER: Glass-factory owner, Utica, New York (1810-1811); financier, New York City (1811-1812); financier, Utica, New York (1812-1815); state director, Bank of Utica (1815-1816); owner, Utica Insurance Company (1816-1818); director and president, Ontario Branch Bank of Utica (1819-1855).

Alexander Bryan Johnson, banker and economic theorist, was born on May 29, 1786, in Gosport, England, the son of Bryan and Leah Simpson Johnson. Difficult times brought the senior Johnson to New York in 1797. Over the next four years Johnson's father moved north through New York in search of stable employment. Finally, in 1801, Johnson and his mother joined the elder Johnson in Utica, New York.

The family established a Mohawk River trading post in Utica. Alexander, who revealed a keen monetary sense at an early age, acted as the bookkeeper and financial adviser. That position provided a breeding ground for his banking ideas and also allowed for time to read. Philosophy, grammar, and etymology were Johnson's favorite topics. By 1810 Johnson grew restless and went seeking new business ventures.

Unfortunately, Johnson's first venture proved his least successful. Along with seventeen-year-old Henry Robert Schoolcraft, he opened a glass factory. Due to a large amount of pirating by rival glassblowers, the company had to close. Johnson took no loss on the venture, but he felt the "trouble and exertions" and the "anxiety and labor" that came from lack of profit. Although not a financial loss, the glass factory nonetheless constituted a personal failure.

In 1811 Johnson left Utica for New York City, where he invested what money he and his father had accumulated. After careful observation he chose bank notes for his investments. Apparently

Daguerreotype of Alexander Bryan Johnson (courtesy of Bryan Johnson Lynch, Reading, Vermont)

that was a good choice—the first-year profits were 22.7 percent. By 1812 war with Britain loomed on the horizon, and several investors questioned the future of their investments. Johnson's first reaction was to "accept the first loss and immediately sell," despite the fact that when war broke out he was counseled to wait it out. He refused the advice and quickly converted his notes into specie, fearing a financial loss. In doing so he formed the first of many personal philosophies: "to place too little respect for opinions that differed from my own." He then returned to Utica and reinvested his capital in local enterprises.

While in New York City, Johnson had spent a great deal of time studying banking methods and economics. He was fascinated by the financial workings of the large city. That fascination led to the publication of his first book, *An Inquiry into the Nature of Value and Capital*, in 1813. The privately published book did not achieve a high level of success, but it launched a prolific career in writings on economics, banking, and semantics.

By that time Johnson had reached the age of twenty-seven and still had no wife. His father urged him to marry. Soon after, he met and courted Abigail Adams, the granddaughter of President John Adams and niece of John Quincy Adams. They married in 1814 in the Episcopal Church of Utica. The marriage began Johnson's long relationship with the highly political Adams family.

In 1815 Johnson received an appointment as state director of the Bank of Utica. The appointment gave him a prestigious but not lucrative position. Johnson soon grew restless to start a new venture. He formed the Utica Insurance Company in 1816 and entered banking through the "back door." A restriction on the number of banks existed in New York at the time; however, the fine print on the company's charter escaped the notice of state attorney general Martin Van Buren, and thus the state inadvertently empowered the business to conduct banking operations. Business went well, but in August 1818 the state saw its mistake and forced Johnson to suspend operations. The legislature passed a law forbidding banking operations in any business not explicitly chartered as a bank.

Johnson then turned to the study of law. He ultimately gained admission to the bar but never practiced. Still, his thoughts once again turned to banking, and in June 1819 he became a director of the Ontario Branch Bank of Utica. After some poor decisions by the bank's cashier, a Mr. Lothrop, which caused credit problems, the directors asked Johnson to take over as cashier. Rather than damage relations with Lothrop, Johnson assumed the role of president, a position he held along with his directorship until 1855. To correct the credit problems, the bank, instead of borrowing, issued new notes and redeemed old ones. By November 1820 it had returned to sound condition.

Johnson had become very popular in New York, so much so that he considered running for the governorship. To facilitate his campaign, in 1821 he proposed a law to change the statute prohibiting naturalized citizens from running for the office of governor. The proposal was defeated, ending Johnson's political career before it ever really started, and for the rest of his life Johnson devoted himself to banking and finance.

During the 1830s Johnson also involved himself in several social movements as well. As the country sought faster and better means of transportation, Johnson invested his time and money in furthering the cause. He pushed for building and enlarging the canal system and expanding the railroad networks. He also worked on behalf of the Utica Lyceum and Temperance Society because he contended that education and sobriety were good business practices that ultimately furthered one's financial position.

One of the most interesting causes espoused by Johnson was the push for Sunday postal service. Johnson argued that business operations suffered unduly because of the lack of postal service on Sunday. His support for Sunday mail outraged church elders in Utica, who felt his beliefs "dishonored religion and truth." Tensions mounted and led to the excommunication of Johnson from the Presbyterian Church of Utica in 1834. He later joined the elite Grace Episcopal Church.

In 1838, after bearing nine children, Abigail Johnson died. Three years later Johnson remarried. His second wife, Eliza Masters, bore four children and died in 1852 when the family house burned. With thirteen children, Johnson married Mary Livingston six months later.

Over the next ten years Johnson paid close attention to the federal financial situation. While opposing a national bank, he had a deep interest in the production and maintenance of the nation's wealth. He advocated increasing production through the public use of money. To add incentive, the government should implement only minimal taxes for its functions to maintain the nation's monetary needs. Johnson's biggest break from mainstream thought came in the notion that government debts and bank reserves provided useful tools in increasing that wealth, an early version of the Federal Reserve Board's "monetary tools" approach.

The publication of *A Treatise on Banking* in 1850 marked the culmination of Johnson's banking theory. He advocated banking at its "utmost simplicity." He divided the book into three parts. The first dealt with banking as it existed in 1849. Johnson proclaimed that "the object of banking is making pecuniary gains for stockholders by legal operations." He denounced the rigidities of a hard-money standard that forced banks to redeem notes in specie on demand. He supported inconvertible notes that fluctuated according to the nation's needs. He warned that if the natural supply and demand processes broke down, the banks would cause disastrous inflation due to excessive quantities of paper money in the market. He sought a freer market where capital consisted of any "article that bears value in the market." That theory emphasized scarcity and paid little attention to demand.

The primary focus of the second section was on bank prosperity. Johnson recommended that bankers know the circumstances of their debtors. They should also know the signatures of their depositors to help eliminate forgeries. Johnson also advocated a "no frills" style of bank architecture. The third section of the book was closely linked to the second. In it Johnson recommended that bankers listen to financial advice but always be governed by their own judgment. The *Treatise* was widely read and earned Johnson the title "Philosophical Banker of Utica."

On September 10, 1867, Johnson quietly passed away. His funeral was the largest in Utica's history. He was buried at Forest Hills cemetery. His gravestone, befittingly, reads: "The Author of Many Books; A Lawyer by Education, A Banker during Active Life, a Student of Philosophy Always."

Publications:

An Inquiry into the Nature of Value and Capital (New York: Privately published, 1813);

The Philosophy of Human Knowledge, or A Treatise on Language (New York: G. & C. Carvil, 1828); republished as *A Treatise on Language: or, The Relation which Words Bear to Things* (New York: Harper, 1836);

A Treatise on Banking: The Duties of a Banker and His Personal Requests Therefore (Utica, N.Y.: Sewards & Thurber, 1850);

The Meaning of Words Analysed into Words and Unverbal Things, and Unverbal Things Classified into Intellections, Sensations, and Emotions (New York: Appleton, 1854);

A Guide to the Right Understanding of Our American Union; or, Political, Economical and Literary Miscellanies (New York: Derby & Jackson/Cincinnati: Derby, 1857);

Deep Sea Soundings and Explorations of the Bottom; or, The Ultimate Analysis of Human Knowledge (Boston: Privately published, 1861);

The Advanced Value of Gold, Suspended Specie Payments, Legal-Tender Notes, Taxation and National Debt, Investigated Impartially (Utica, N.Y.: Curtiss & White, 1862).

References:

Russell Blackwood and Charles Todd, eds., *Language and Value* (New York: Greenwood, 1968);

Mary P. Ryan, *Cradle of the Middle Class* (New York: Cambridge University Press, 1981).

Otto H. Kahn

(February 21, 1867-March 29, 1934)

by Hans Eicholz

University of California, Los Angeles

CAREER: Banker, Speyer and Company (1893-1895); partner, Kuhn, Loeb and Company (1897-1934).

Otto H. Kahn masterminded many of the most significant financial reorganizations of American railroads around the turn of the twentieth century. For that alone he has earned a notable place in the history of business, but that by itself does not do justice to a man of such wide-ranging interests and abilities. Possessing a deep appreciation for the arts, Kahn also became one of America's most successful benefactors of theater, painting, sculpture, music, and opera. To Kahn, art and business were both creative activities, and throughout his life he endeavored to combine the elements of both spheres. He once commented that the methods of railroad reorganization embodied "a certain element of romance; they call for constructive imagination. . . . It yields the joy of creation."

Born into an upper-middle-class family in the German city of Mannheim, Kahn was exposed to the lively cultural environment that characterized the late-nineteenth-century duchy of Baden. His father, Bernhard Kahn, had participated in the revolution of 1848 and had fled to America for a short time until amnesty was proclaimed. Returning to Germany, Bernhard Kahn entered the field of banking and married Emma Eberstadt.

Bernhard enjoyed intellectual pursuits, and the arts especially intrigued him. The Kahn family played host to numerous European artists, writers, and intellectuals. Bernhard Kahn's eight children carried on that passion for art. Otto Kahn's earliest desire was to study music. By the time he graduated from high school he had mastered seven musical instruments and had written two five-act tragedies in blank verse (never performed). The family decided, however, that he would follow his father's vocation. One brother had already been allowed to

Otto H. Kahn

enter the Royal Academy of Music in Berlin, and that the family deemed sufficient. But the Kahns always stressed the importance of artistic appreciation and learning, and in his leisure time Kahn attended university lectures on artistic and academic subjects.

When he turned twenty, Kahn decided to fulfill the required year of military service by joining one of the regiments of hussars, acquiring the soldierly bearing that remained with him throughout his life. At twenty-one he embarked upon his career as a banker, taking a position with the Deutsche Bank in Berlin. Shortly thereafter he was transferred to the London branch. Reveling in what he saw as the openness and intellectual liberality of English society, he became a British citizen. After a short time he attracted the attention of the Speyers in London, members of the prominent German banking family, who offered him a position in their New York firm of Speyer and Company. Intending to stay for only a short time, Kahn accepted the appointment and arrived in the United States in 1893. The challenges and opportunities in America soon convinced him to stay longer.

Possessing a passion for work and a creative financial imagination, Kahn attracted the attention of New York's banking community. During his first three years in America he made the acquaintance of Addie Wolff, daughter of Abraham Wolff, a senior member of Kuhn, Loeb and Company, and in 1896 Wolff and Kahn married. In 1897 Kahn joined the firm. Almost immediately the firm threw him into contact with the powerful Edward H. Harriman. The two became close friends and worked together on such projects as the reorganization of the Union Pacific Railroad, placing it on a solid financial foundation. The able Jacob H. Schiff, former head of the firm, had originally undertaken the task, but only the joint effort of Harriman and Kahn, his right-hand man, deserved credit for its completion. The men complemented each other nicely. Harriman, as Kahn described him, had "the genius of Bismarck, of a Roman Caesar. His dominion was based on rugged strength, iron will and tenacity." Kahn, on the other hand, was refined and polite and knew how to appeal to the kinder side of human nature. Together they made a formidable business team.

Over the course of his career Kahn added to his reputation as a financial genius by successfully reorganizing one troubled railroad after another. Those benefiting from his financial acumen included the Baltimore & Ohio, the Missouri Pacific, the Wabash, the Chicago & Eastern Illinois, and the Texas & Pacific. He also staved off the almost certain financial panic that would have ensued had the Pearson-Farquhar railroad syndicate failed in 1906. Having overextended itself in its attempt to unite a number of smaller roads into one transcontinental line, the firm required the organizing expertise of Kahn to rescue it from insolvency. Kahn also had a leading role in introducing American securities into France. In 1906 he brought $50 million worth of Pennsylvania bonds into the Paris market.

But for all of his success in finance, Kahn would probably wish to be remembered for his support of the arts. In 1903 he started the arduous task of restoring the Metropolitan Opera Company to its former position as America's premier opera company. Purchasing a large share of the company's stock, he quickly made his influence felt. The company had steadily lost ground to Oscar Hammerstein's rival Manhattan Opera House, and its grounds had fallen into disrepair. With the help of William K. Vanderbilt, Kahn bought out Heinrich Conried, the former director of the Metropolitan, in 1907. Shortly thereafter he took over Vanderbilt's share. He paid out approximately $350,000 of his own money just to cover the company's losses between 1908 and 1910. During the same period he paid Hammerstein $1.2 million to discontinue his rival opera house. After extensive reorganization and an infusion of new blood from Europe the enterprise achieved success.

Kahn also participated in other philanthropic activities, including trusteeships in the Carnegie Institute of Technology, the Massachusetts Institute of Technology, and Rutgers College. He vigorously promoted the Boston Opera Company, served as director of the Chicago Opera Company, helped found the New Theater in New York City, and was a member of the National Arts Club. In 1930 evidence surfaced that he had been a liberal benefactor of black artists, providing cash prizes for struggling individuals. He routinely provided assistance outside of the public eye, more concerned with the outcome than with the publicity.

In 1913 Kahn purchased the estate St. Dunstan's from the Earl of Londesborough, hoping to retire in England. He quickly abandoned the plan because, as he stated, "my roots had gone too deeply into American soil ever to be transplanted." During World War I he condemned German military strategy but never repudiated his German ties, and after the war he denounced the injustice of the Versailles treaty. He later became a naturalized American citizen.

The Great Depression hit Kahn hard. In the years 1930, 1931, and 1932 he paid no income tax. They were also years of declining health. Suffering from a heart condition and high blood pressure, he retired from all but his most essential activities. Maintaining his soldierly bearing, he concealed the severity of his condition up to the moment of his death. On March 29, 1934, while taking lunch with his business associates in the offices of Kuhn,

Loeb and Company, Kahn died of a heart attack. His wife, son, and three daughters survived him.

Reference:
B. C. Forbes, *Men Who Are Making America* (New York: Forbes Publishing Co., 1917).

Alfred Kelley

(November 7, 1789-December 2, 1859)

by Kirby Turner

Montgomery County Historical Society

CAREER: Prosecutor, Cuyahoga County, Ohio (1810-1822); president, Village of Cleveland (1814-1816); state representative and senator, Ohio (1814-1857); president, Commercial Bank of Lake Erie (1816-?); canal commissioner, state of Ohio (1822-1834); president, Columbus & Xenia Railroad (1847-1854); president, Cleveland, Columbus & Cincinnati Railroad (1847-1854); president, Cleveland, Painesville & Ashtabula Railroad (1851-1854).

Alfred Kelley is best remembered for his role in the passage of the Kelley Banking Act of 1845, which became the basis of the Ohio banking system until the Civil War. Not as widely known is Kelley's pivotal role in the development of the state's transportation and revenue systems.

Born on November 7, 1789, Kelley was the second son of Daniel and Jemima Stow Kelley of Middlefield, Connecticut. When he was ten years old his family moved to Lowville, New York, where his father soon established himself as a wealthy landowner and judge of the common pleas court. Kelley's education consisted of attending the common schools of Lowville and the academy in Fairfield, New York. He read law from 1807 to 1810 in a law office in Whitesboro, New York. In May 1810 he accompanied his uncle to Cleveland, where his parents and five brothers soon joined him. Kelley was admitted to the Ohio bar in the fall of 1810, becoming Cleveland's first attorney, and was then appointed Cuyahoga County prosecuting attorney. He held that post until 1822. When Cleveland became an organized village in 1814, Kelley was elected its first president. In 1816 he became president of the Commercial Bank of Lake Erie, and he and his family were prominent incorporators of the Cleveland Pier Company. Kelley first won election

Alfred Kelley

to the Ohio House of Representatives in 1814 and served in the house and senate until 1857.

Kelley first gained statewide prominence for his outspoken advocacy of a canal system for Ohio. The overwhelming success of the Erie Canal had led to a canal boom not only in Ohio but throughout the nation. Kelley and others promoted the canal as a means to tie the Ohio River, the Great Lakes, and New York City together and end the economic isolation of the state's interior. In 1822 Kelley accepted an appointment as a canal commissioner responsible for surveying canal routes. In

1825 he received an appointment as acting canal commissioner responsible for the funding and actual construction of the canal system. Kelley and his fellow commissioners oversaw the construction of the Ohio and Miami canals. In 1834 Kelley resigned from the post of acting canal commissioner.

The national economic panic beginning in 1837 severely strained Ohio's financial system. During the preceding boom years the state had overextended its credit to stimulate the building of canals and roads. The state borrowed to meet debt and interest payments and several times faced default. In 1841, as state fund commissioner, Kelley traveled to New York City to arrange a loan for the state. He raised $250,000 but had to pledge his personal security before the bankers would approve the loan. Many Ohio banks failed during the panic, and Ohio residents vociferously joined the national debate over monetary policy precipitated by President Andrew Jackson's veto of the bill to recharter the Bank of the United States. Since the 1830s Kelley, a Whig, had been a leader in that party's attempt to develop a centralized banking system in Ohio. Democrats known as Locofocos had strenuously opposed those efforts. In the elections of 1844 the Whig party gained control of the state legislature, which enabled them to implement centralizing financial policies. In 1845 the legislature passed the Kelley Banking Act. The law established a State Bank of Ohio with the ability to charter branches throughout the state. It was not a central bank, as the branches each conducted independent banking operations. The law required minimum capital of $50,000 and $100,000 for independent and insured banks, respectively. (A few older banks whose charters had not lapsed continued to operate independently of those systems.) Each branch's note circulation was limited to a percentage of its capitalization, and each had to deposit 10 percent of its circulation in Ohio stock or U.S. bonds to the Board of Control for a "safety fund" in case of failures. The Board of Control, with representatives from each of the branches, generally supervised the system. Existing banks could become branches by meeting the requirements or could remain independent. Each independent bank, whether new or existing, had to deposit with the state treasurer Ohio stock or U.S. bonds equal to the amount of its capital stock. Its notes would be issued under the supervision of the state

treasurer. The Kelley Banking Act produced a safe, reliable circulating medium that survived monetary panics in 1847, 1857, and 1861. The Ohio system's success in surviving the Panic of 1857 stood in sharp contrast to the history of neighboring Indiana, where more than one-third of the banks failed in 1857. Only one of Ohio's 54 banks failed.

Kelley had a major impact on the state's financial system in yet another area. Until 1846 Ohio's system of property taxation was erratic and inequitable at best, and, worse, it did not produce sufficient revenue for the state. The 1846 law sponsored by Kelley required that "all property in the state whether real or personal therein, unless excepted, shall be subject to taxation." The Kelley Revenue Act has continued to provide the basis for property taxation in Ohio up to the present time.

As canals faded in importance, Kelley turned his attention to the next revolution in transportation, railroads. From 1847 to 1854 he served as president of the Columbus & Xenia Railroad and the Cleveland, Columbus & Cincinnati Railroad. In 1851 he also became president of the Cleveland, Painesville & Ashtabula Railroad. He retired from those positions in 1854 and from political life in 1857. Kelley died on December 2, 1859, in Columbus, Ohio.

Though Henry Clay was reputed to have said that Kelley "had too much cast iron in his composition to be popular," he was held in high regard by his peers and the general public. Kelley was eulogized as the founder of the state's canal system, the preserver of its public credit, and the author of its system of banking and taxation.

References:

"A History of Banking in Ohio," *Ohio State Archaeological and Historical Society Publications*, 23 (1914): 316-317;

Walter Ramsey Marvin, "Alfred Kelley," *Museum Echoes* (Ohio Historical Society), 23 (February 1960): 11-14;

William E. Smith and Ophia D. Smith, *A Buckeye Titan* (Cincinnati: Historical and Philosophical Society of Ohio, 1953), pp. 261-317;

Francis P. Weisenburger, *The History of the State of Ohio*, volume 3: *The Passing of the Frontier* (Columbus: Ohio State Archaeological and Historical Society, 1941).

Amos Kendall

(August 16, 1789-November 12, 1869)

by David T. Beito

University of Nevada at Las Vegas

CAREER: Editor, *Argus of Western America* (1816-1829); fourth auditor, Department of the Treasury (1829-1834); U.S. postmaster general (1835-1840); journalist and newspaper publisher (1840-1845); business agent for Samuel F. B. Morse (1845-1859); president, Board of Trustees of the Columbia Institution for the Deaf and Dumb (1857-1869).

Political hack, devious wire puller, and shameless sycophant have been among the characterizations heaped on Amos Kendall, perhaps the most controversial member of Andrew Jackson's "kitchen cabinet." Epithets of this variety originated not only from Kendall's political opponents during the Jacksonian Era but also from later historians. Lynn J. Marshall, one of his biographers, portrayed Kendall as a "man on the make" ever ready to trim principle in the cause of personal advancement. In recent years, however, historians such as Richard B. Latner and Robert V. Remini have considerably improved Kendall's reputation. Latner writes, "To characterize Kendall or [newspaper editor and fellow Jackson confidant Francis P.] Blair as ambitious men-on-the-make endeavoring to replace one established elite with another ignores their Jeffersonian antipathy towards banking, their partiality for hard money, and their commitment to the concept of republican virtue."

Kendall was born in Dunstable, Massachusetts, on August 16, 1789, the son of strict Congregational parents. He grew up in modest circumstances and, despite poor health, worked hard on his father's farm. Through his own efforts and the help of his family he attended Dartmouth College in New Hampshire, where he graduated as class valedictorian in 1811. After graduation he read law at the firm of William Merchant Richardson in Groten, Massachusetts. He left Groten for Washington, D.C., in 1814, where he arranged employment

Amos Kendall

as a tutor to the family of Kentucky senator Jesse Bledsoe in Lexington. Circumstances changed, and he ended up taking a similar position in the family of Henry Clay. In October 1814 Kendall was admitted to the Kentucky bar. Shortly thereafter he took a position as postmaster in Georgetown, Kentucky.

In 1816 Kendall moved to Frankfort, the capital of Kentucky, to become editor for the newspaper *Argus of Western America*. Although the *Argus* had been in existence for several years, Kendall, through his cogent editorials, quickly widened the readership and prestige of the paper. By that time his political outlook, which changed little during his life, had taken shape. His editorials for the *Argus* centered on one issue in particular: the Second Bank of the United States (BUS). The Second

BUS remained Kendall's nemesis for the next 20 years and is crucial to an understanding of his career.

The First BUS had been dissolved in 1811. The federal government would not have a central bank until the creation of the Second BUS in 1816. The Second BUS had been created after a period of acute financial instability in the United States. The economy still had not completely recovered from the dislocation caused by the War of 1812. Local and state banks had overexpanded during the war, in part to help finance the federal government's war effort. The British invasion of Washington in August 1814 exacerbated an already shaky situation, inducing runs on many state banks. In the wake of the invasion the banks, with the support of the federal government, suspended specie payments. The crisis continued to worsen.

Despite the problems with the state banks and the fact that several prominent national politicians (including Henry Clay of Kentucky and John C. Calhoun of South Carolina) who had supported dissolution of the First BUS in 1811 now supported the creation of a second national bank, Kendall remained opposed to such a move. But, like many other misnamed "antibank" Jacksonians, he never supported abolition of banking per se. He was never comfortable with the practice of banking, however. Jacksonians such as William Leggett viewed banks, if shorn of certain government-granted privileges, as good and necessary. Kendall, on the other hand, found "the very thought of these [banking] institutions" to be "disgusting." Ideally, he supported a constitutional amendment to prohibit chartering of any additional banks, which he thought would lead to the disappearance of the "whole paper system." Nevertheless, he conceded that the "interest of banks is too deeply rooted, prejudice in their favor has taken too deadly a hold to be unhandled even by the tremendous convulsions into which they have thrown the whole community. All declare the system a public curse, but few can think of destroying it."

His critique went to the heart of the chief justification of a national bank, the provision of a uniform national currency. Kendall rejected the proposition that the achievement of a currency of uniform value was even a desirable goal. In his view, because the volume and character of trade varied in different parts of the country, so too should the value of bank notes. It was entirely proper that

bank notes be subject to the same laws of supply and demand as other commodities. Any attempt to impose uniform values without regard to local economic conditions would produce dangerous distortions in the flow of currency and specie. "The scheme," he wrote, "of sustaining a paper currency of uniform value throughout a country so commercial and extensive as the United States, is an absurdity," because if "bank-notes be issued in the interior which are everywhere equal to specie ... they will at once disappear from circulation, because, being available as exchange, they are in that locality worth more than the local bank-notes for specie itself, and are hoarded for sale or remittance. The result would be the same if there were no local bank-notes in existence."

Interestingly, in contrast to the then-standard labor theory of value of classical economics, Kendall argued that the value of economic goods, including money, originated from consumer demand. Writing in language that anticipated the subjective-value theorists of the Austrian School of Economics in the late nineteenth century, Kendall compared the fixed measurements of weights and measures to the more variable values produced by the marketplace. "The former you can divide and mark by lines and bounds," he declared, "but the latter is invisible, intangible, and not subject to human control. Until the operations of the mind and the various causes which put them in action are reduced to fixed rules, value can never be measured or reduced to a standard."

After the creation of the Second BUS in 1816, Kendall strongly supported Kentucky legislation, similar to anti-BUS legislation promulgated in other states, to levy a $50,000 tax on banks chartered outside the state. In 1819 opponents of the BUS suffered a stinging defeat when the Supreme Court rendered its decision in the case of *McCulloch* v. *Maryland*. The court upheld the constitutionality of the BUS and ruled that the states could not tax it. Chief Justice John Marshall declared in his opinion that the "power to tax involves the power to destroy."

In a series of editorials for the *Argus* Kendall rejected the court's opinion that the "necessary and proper" clause of the Constitution authorized the establishment of a national bank. Kendall thought the bank was neither a necessary nor a proper function of the government but "a business carried on by individuals for individual gain—a means for the accomplishment of private ends, and not for the execution of national powers." Kendall also criticized *McCulloch* v. *Maryland* as a violation of ideals of local self-government and popular sovereignty. The Constitution, he asserted, had been ratified by "independent and sovereign" states, who reserved all powers not expressly delegated to the federal government in the Constitution. The states had not authorized the creation of a national bank, therefore they had the right to tax or prohibit BUS branches. Kendall refused, however, to support strategies of nullification or secession to overturn the court's ruling, preferring instead to support the enactment of a constitutional amendment to prohibit federal bank charters.

Kendall's critique of the BUS complemented his general commitment to small government. "The United States," he argued during the tax legislation battle, "is governed too much. The destruction of the Bank will be an important check to overmuch government." In his view government's "true strength consists in leaving individuals and states as much as possible to themselves." He emphasized that the "only use of government is to keep off evil" and warned that governmental power if left unchecked would lead to the division of society into a producing class of taxpayers and a privileged class who "by an alliance with government ... extract from the people a goodly portion of their earnings." The only way for government to prevent this class division was to allow people to pursue their private interests without subsidizing one group at the expense of another. For Kendall the BUS represented an artificial subsidy to a privileged class.

Unlike some of his allies in Kentucky, however, Kendall always defended the inviolability of private contracts. He rejected compromises on private debt, such as stay laws, and remained skeptical of bankruptcy laws, which he condemned as being "for the benefit of knaves and swindlers."

In October 1818 Kendall married Mary Morefolk, who died in October 1823. The couple had four children. In January 1826 he married again, to Jane Kyle, and fathered an additional ten children.

After the election of John Quincy Adams in 1824 Kendall originally supported Henry Clay for president but switched to Andrew Jackson in 1826. The change in allegiance led to accusations of betrayal but when viewed in retrospect seems to have made perfect sense. Kendall's hard-money and small-government views fit much better with Jackson than Clay and his interventionist "American system." In the coming years Jackson became his personal hero. A mutual friend once concluded that "Andrew Jackson was Amos Kendall's idol. Hamilton did not support Washington, the young Whigs did not idolize Henry Clay, with a deeper devotion." In the 1828 presidential election Kendall and the *Argus* proved instrumental in carrying Kentucky for Jackson.

In 1829 the new administration rewarded him with an appointment as fourth auditor for the Department of the Treasury, a position he held for six years. A year later Kendall brought Francis P. Blair, his friend and associate at the *Argus,* to Washington, D.C., to edit the *Globe,* a new pro-administration newspaper. The *Globe* had been established with Jackson's blessing as a publicity outlet against the BUS. Kendall wrote many of the anti-BUS editorials in the paper. Both he and Blair gradually gained entry into Jackson's inner circle of advisers, the so-called "kitchen cabinet."

In his counsel to Jackson, Kendall's concern remained fixed, as it always had been, against the BUS. He played a major role in persuading Jackson to take a strong stand against the national bank, even though in 1829 he edited and commented on Andrew Jackson's own "Plan for a National Bank," in which Old Hickory revealed his intention merely to substitute a Democratic national bank for the BUS. Over the ensuing years Jackson dropped this plan, finding it difficult to reconcile his opposition to the BUS and his own proposal for a bank. At first Kendall made slow progress in swaying the "old hero." Jackson refused to include attacks on the BUS written by Kendall in his first and third annual messages to Congress. Eventually Kendall's persistent lobbying of the president paid off. Jackson assigned him a role in preparing the presidential message vetoing the recharter of the bank in 1832. The message rejected *McCulloch* v. *Maryland* on the grounds that the Supreme Court had overstepped its power: "The authority of the Supreme Court must not, therefore, be permitted to control the Congress, or the Executive when acting in their legislative capacities, but to have only such influence as the force of their reasoning may deserve." For Kendall and Jackson, the power of the BUS had to be nipped in the bud before it became a tangible threat to economic liberty. According to Terry L. Shoptaugh, Kendall "was condemning the B.U.S.

The last Washington, D.C., residence of the Kendall family. Kendall lived in Washington from 1829 to the time of his death in 1869.

for the power it *might* use as much as for what it had done." Jackson concluded the veto message with a ringing attack on government-granted privileges for the rich and powerful that he could have easily culled from one of Kendall's editorials for the *Argus* and the *Globe*.

The veto message represented a major departure in presidential-congressional relations. Previous presidents had rarely used vetoes, and then they dealt almost exclusively with constitutional issues. As historian Robert V. Remini put it, Jackson's veto message "for the first time invoked political, social and economic, as well as strictly legal arguments. . . . Hereafter the threat of a possible veto for any reason forced the Congress to carefully consider the President's wishes on *all* bills before legislating them."

The veto sparked a firestorm of criticism by Jackson's opponents. Nicholas Biddle, president of the BUS, called the veto message a "manifesto of anarchy." Another critic at the BUS excoriated it as "a most wretched production going so far to weaken every principle of the government." Biddle mistakenly believed that the veto would backfire and made plans to distribute 30,000 copies of the

message in the upcoming election campaign. Indeed Jackson made the conditions of the veto such that, had Biddle wanted to compromise, ample room existed. A few changes in the charter of the BUS—none of them critical to its operations or to Biddle's role—would have sufficed to allow Jackson to withdraw his opposition. Biddle, determined to force a battle, brushed aside the last opportunities for compromise.

Kendall worked tirelessly for Jackson's reelection in 1832. Along with Blair he created a special election journal called the *Extra-Globe*. To coordinate the national presidential campaign Kendall organized the Central Hickory Club. Through the club, which served as steering committee for Jackson's campaign, Kendall kept tabs on local party organizations throughout the country and urged party leaders on to greater efforts. To a Connecticut politician he inquired, "Have you an organization in your state? Whether you have or not . . . send me a list of names of Jackson men good and true in every township in the state . . . to whom our friends may send political information. I beg you to do this *instantly*."

285

In 1833 Kendall proposed a controversial plan to Jackson to transfer federal funds from the BUS into state-chartered banks, dubbed by critics "pet banks." At first he encountered determined opposition from Vice-President Martin Van Buren, a powerful influence on the president. According to Kendall's autobiography the two remained at loggerheads until they had a meeting to discuss the question. Kendall used the occasion to warn Van Buren that the BUS, if its power remained intact, would throw its weight behind the Whig party in coming elections. Several weeks later, again according to Kendall, Van Buren told him that "I had never thought seriously upon the deposit question until after my conversation with you; I am now satisfied that you were right and I was wrong."

In June 1833 Jackson took the first steps toward implementing removal of federal funds from the BUS. He appointed Kendall to tour the eastern seaboard to line up state banks willing to act as federal depositories. During these highly publicized travels Kendall met with bankers in Philadelphia, Baltimore, New York, and Boston, candidly admitting that the administration would give "politically friendly" (pro-Jackson) banks preference in the selection. When Kendall returned to Washington he reported to Jackson that seven banks in these cities had pledged to serve as depositories. In September Jackson gave his formal approval to removal. He assigned Kendall, along with Levi Woodbury, the task of preparing a presidential order to enact the withdrawal. By December 1833 the government had transferred virtually all its funds from the BUS to state banks.

In 1835 Jackson promoted Kendall from his position as fourth auditor of the Department of the Treasury to postmaster general. During his five years at the post office under Jackson and Martin Van Buren, Kendall retired the department's extensive debt, reformed its contracting procedures, and steered it clear of partisan politics. Kendall scrupulously cracked down on employees who used their positions for partisan campaigning. The most controversial decision of his tenure came in 1835, when (with Jackson's support) he permitted local postmasters to refuse delivery of "incendiary" abolitionist literature. A wide coalition, ranging from antislavery elements to stalwart Jacksonians such as Thomas Hart Benton, criticized the ban as a violation of first amendment rights. A resolution in the Senate

to overturn Kendall's decision failed passage by one vote.

Kendall left office in 1840 to write editorials in the *Globe* in favor of the reelection of Van Buren. He particularly promoted Van Buren's proposal to replace the pet banks as depositories for government funds with an "independent treasury." Kendall's defense of the independent treasury underscored his longtime dedication to the divorce of the national government from banking. He explained the plan as a method by which public money would "go into the Treasury and there remain untouched and inviolate, until drawn out to pay the expenditures of the government in pursuance of appropriations." Kendall later applauded the creation of the independent treasury as a second declaration of independence. "The former delivered the American people from the power of the British throne," he concluded, "the latter delivered them from the power of the British banks."

After Van Buren's defeat Kendall returned to his journalistic pursuits. He launched several periodicals, but none had lasting success. His life was further complicated by personal debt, poor health, and several unsettled suits brought by contractors during his tenure at the postal service. At one point a court imprisoned him for indebtedness and restricted his movements to the District of Columbia. It took a decision of the Supreme Court to overturn this conviction. A year later Congress passed a special appropriation to pay all of Kendall's legal fees arising from the postal litigation.

In 1845 telegraph inventor Samuel F. B. Morse hired him as his business agent. The position gave Kendall, who had made his career as a journalist and government official, the opportunity to prove his business and legal acumen. He tenaciously defended Morse's patents against a string of lawsuits and then resold the patent rights along particular telegraph routes. Kendall's experience as postmaster had given him useful knowledge about where such routes could be most profitably located. He directed the operations of several telegraph companies and linked them together through a parent company, the Magnetic Telegraph Company. Eventually he presided over the consolidation of most of the smaller firms into the American Telegraph Company.

As a telegraph entrepreneur Kendall earned a reputation for fairness and always proved willing to negotiate and compromise rather than confront.

One observer found it hard to believe that "this gentle, quiet, and soft-spoken man was the same whose nervous editorials aroused the resentment of the Whigs and the enthusiasm of the Democrats." When Kendall retired from management of the business in 1859, both he and Morse had become millionaires several times over. Kendall's estate was so large that after his death it took two years for his heirs (from his second marriage, to Jane Coyle in January 1826) to settle it in probate.

In 1857 Kendall founded the Columbia Institution for the Deaf and Dumb (later Gallaudet College). He served as president of the Board of Trustees of the college and endowed it heavily with his own funds. He also lobbied Congress for additional appropriations.

On the eve of the Civil War Kendall authored a "Letter on Secession" in which he attacked the constitutionality of the Southern position. Although he strongly supported the Union, he criticized the Lincoln administration for moving too quickly on emancipation and for failure to prosecute the war vigorously. In 1864 he played an active role in the presidential campaign of former Union general George B. McClellan. His last political effort came in 1868, when he authored a "Letter to Rutherford," a critique of the federal government's Reconstruction policies.

In the last few years of his life Kendall became an active member of the Baptist church and spent increasing time on charitable efforts. His second wife died in June 1864, and he survived all but four of his fourteen children. Kendall died on November 12, 1869, in Washington, D.C.

Publications:

Letters to John Quincy Adams (Lexington, Ky.: Printed by W. Tanner, 1823);

Secession. Letters of Amos Kendall; also, His Letters to Colonel Orr and President Buchanan (Washington, D.C.: Printed by H. Polkinhorn, 1861);

Letters Exposing the Mismanagement of Public Affairs by Abraham Lincoln, and the Political Combinations to Secure His Re-election (Washington, D.C.: Constitutional Union Office, 1864);

Letters on Our Country's Crisis (Washington, D.C.: Constitutional Union Office, 1864);

Autobiography of Amos Kendall, edited by William Stickney (Boston: Lee & Shepard, 1872; reprinted, New York: Peter Smith, 1949).

References:

Richard B. Latner, *The Presidency of Andrew Jackson: White House Politics* (Athens: University of Georgia Press, 1979);

Lynn J. Marshall, "The Authorship of Jackson's Veto Message," *Mississippi Valley Historical Review*, 50 (December 1963): 476;

Robert V. Remini, *Andrew Jackson and the Bank War: A Study in the Growth of Presidential Power* (New York: Norton, 1967), pp. 30-31, 82-83, 96-97, 112, 117, 124-125;

Edward M. Shepard, *Martin Van Buren* (Boston: Houghton, Mifflin, 1899), pp. 261, 275-276;

Terry L. Shoptaugh, "Amos Kendall: A Political Biography," Ph.D. dissertation, University of New Hampshire, 1984;

Major L. Wilson, *The Presidency of Martin Van Buren* (Lawrence: University Press of Kansas, 1984).

John Stewart Kennedy

(January 4, 1830-October 31, 1909)

by Saul Engelbourg

Boston University

CAREER: Partner, M. K. Jesup & Company (1857-1867); senior partner, J. S. Kennedy & Company (1868-1883); president pro tem (1883-1884, 1893), vice-president, Bank of the Manhattan Company (1884-1888).

John Stewart Kennedy supplied and financed American railroads during the great age of railroad building, becoming James J. Hill's financial intermediary when Hill obtained control of the St. Paul, Minneapolis & Manitoba Railway in 1878. From the early 1880s until his death Kennedy was a director of the Bank of the Manhattan Company and other financial institutions.

Born on January 4, 1830, Kennedy was the fifth son of John Kennedy and Isabella Stewart Kennedy of Blantyre, Lanarkshire, Scotland (in the vicinity of Glasgow). His family moved to Glasgow during his infancy. Leaving school at the age of thirteen, Kennedy worked as a clerk in a Glasgow shipping office. He remained there for four years while also attending classes both morning and afternoon. In 1847 he became a salesman for the Mossend Iron and Coal Company, a position he held for the next three years. Kennedy first visited the United States in June 1850 as a representative for William Baird & Company, an iron firm that sold railroad-related products, and on that trip he met his future partner, Morris Ketchum Jesup, a railroad commission merchant and private banker. In July 1852 Kennedy returned to the United Kingdom to head the Baird company's Glasgow office, a post he held until December 1856. (Jesup later served as supporter of noted polar expeditions, so much so that explorer Robert E. Peary named a site for him.)

Kennedy first became a significant actor in American economic and business history as a partner of Jesup from 1857 to 1867. During those years Kennedy not only absorbed the craft of negotiating as a mercantile skill but also formed the basis

John Stewart Kennedy

of the network of friends and acquaintances necessary to begin his own firm. During the decade Kennedy partnered with Jesup, the firm dealt with several developmental railroads.

In 1868 Kennedy opened his own railroad commission merchant and private banking firm, J. S. Kennedy & Company. It combined credit with trade and specialized in the discounting and creation of commercial paper; growth allowed specialization in the banking function. J. S. Kennedy & Company bought and sold railway bonds and stocks and negotiated loans, drew bills on London, and was a fiscal agent and banker for railroads. Engaging in the process of financing Anglo-American trade and financial intermediation, Kennedy mobilized and funneled the capital of a multitude of American and European investors in order to promote the economic development of America. He emerged as an independent entrepreneur just as changes in both the railroads, the manufacturers of specific railroad products, and the capital market combined to make the railroad commission merchant obsolescent. Consequently, he and his competitors gradually shifted from an emphasis on acting as a commission merchant to financing as a private banker.

Marrying Emma Baker on October 14, 1858, brought Kennedy a connection with an affluent and influential New York mercantile family of long standing. His brother-in-law, Henry M. Baker, entered J. S. Kennedy & Company as a partner in 1868. Kennedy soon added John Sanford Barnes, to whom Kennedy was distantly related in that Barnes's sister was married to Baker.

Following the induced withdrawal of both his initial partners, Baker in 1877 and Barnes in 1880, Kennedy reconstituted J. S. Kennedy & Company, this time with men junior in age. John Kennedy Tod, his nephew, was elevated to the rank of partner in 1880 coincident with the departure of Barnes. Oliver Hugh Northcote (sometimes he reversed his first and middle names) and Alexander Baring (a younger member of the famous British banking family), each of whom also had associated with the firm for several years, became partners in 1883.

Kennedy had business relations in his own name with railroads including the Texas & New Orleans; the Houston & Texas Central; the International & Great Northern; the Cedar Falls & Minnesota; the Indianapolis, Cincinnati & Layfayette; the St. Paul & Pacific; the St. Paul, Minneapolis & Manitoba; and other railroads. Also, he represented the Bowling Steel Company of England and the Cambria Iron Works of Pennsylvania.

In 1878 Kennedy completed financing the reorganization of the two bankrupt St. Paul & Pacific railroads, having wrestled as the agent for the Dutch bondholders with innumerable complexities since bankruptcy in 1872. Ultimately that constituted Kennedy's most profitable and enduring investment. His other railroad reorganizations conformed to the norm: in-and-out plus the transferal of operating control to new owners. That particular railroad transaction, as permanent as the others were

temporary, transformed Kennedy from merely rich to one of the most wealthy Americans of his time.

Like other private international banking houses, J. S. Kennedy & Company mobilized and transferred the savings of numerous European investors to the United States. In one such notable instance, Kennedy participated in 1873, along with William John Menzies of Edinburgh, Scotland, in the launching of the Scottish American Investment Company. Kennedy acted as its New York agent from 1873 to 1883 and for 15 years remained as a member of the Advisory Board. Confining its investing solely to the United States, the company quickly became one of the largest and most successful of Scottish investment companies.

Much of the credit for this extraordinary achievement, especially during the first decade and to a lesser extent later, belongs to Kennedy. As a result of his prescient skill as a money manager and investment adviser and of his ability to furnish timely investment intelligence, investors in the Scottish American Investment Company benefited from a return on investment higher than available elsewhere. The capital market allocated long-term funds throughout the international economy; with the help of Kennedy, the Scottish American Investment Company put most of its investment pool, acquired at a much lower cost than the cost of capital in the United States, into railroads, the most capital-intensive sector of the nineteenth-century American economy.

Kennedy had a net worth of about $500,000 in 1878 when the liquidators of the City of Glasgow Bank called on him to demonstrate his first-rate talents on behalf of the shareholders. The principal asset of the City of Glasgow Bank being certain American securities with a par value of more than $5 million, the liquidators of the City of Glasgow Bank asked Kennedy's company to represent them.

The liquidators received much more than anticipated on the American assets of the City of Glasgow Bank under their control. They capitalized on the recovery of security prices, and Kennedy's adroit tactics utilized a judicious combination of litigation and negotiation. Kennedy could take considerable satisfaction from his able representation of the liquidators of the bank. While his own monetary reward of $50,000 proved comparatively modest, he enriched himself in other ways. By resisting the opportunity to take advantage of the liquidators, Kennedy enhanced his standing.

During its 15 years as a railroad commission merchant and private international banker, J. S. Kennedy & Company took large, and Kennedy amassed a large personal fortune. The advertisements exemplify the transformation of a successful railroad commission merchant into a private banker. By the time Kennedy liquidated his firm in 1883, owing to nervous and physical exhaustion, the advertisements of J. S. Kennedy & Company no longer mentioned railroads and, instead, enumerated those financial activities appropriate to a private banker. The mature company reorganized and supplied railroads. It acted as an agent for banks, bankers, and railroads, issuing commercial credits and letters of credit and collecting dividends, coupons, and foreign and inland drafts. Its European correspondents included Melville, Evans & Company, London; C. J. Hambro & Son, London; H. Oyens & Sons, Amsterdam; and Hottinguer & Company, Paris.

Kennedy's 1883 "retirement" broadened his role as a financier with diverse interests in leading New York financial intermediaries. Following the president's resignation under pressure, Kennedy held the post of president pro tem of the Bank of the Manhattan Company from December 1883 until February 1884, when he became vice-president until he resigned for reasons of health in 1888.

The president of the bank resigned in May 1893 because of ill health, leaving Stephen Baker, Kennedy's nephew on his wife's side, the highest ranking officer. Since Baker had been a director since 1890 and vice-president only since 1891 and was therefore relatively inexperienced, Kennedy again took the helm, becoming president pro tem in August and retaining that post until mid December. Then he helped Baker navigate the Bank of the Manhattan Company through the shoals of the financial stress of the last two months of 1893. In 1890 and again in 1907 Kennedy advanced Bank of the Manhattan Company securities for use as collateral so that the bank could obtain clearinghouse loan certificates during the panics, when everyone sought liquidity above all. Although two other directors acted similarly, the amount of Kennedy's aid exceeded theirs.

Kennedy also served as a trustee of the Central Trust Company from 1882 until he died. Benefit-

ing from Kennedy's experience, the Central Trust was heavily involved in railroad securities as well as reorganizations. On several occasions it acted as the trustee for the St. Paul, Minneapolis & Manitoba (renamed the Great Northern). Kennedy's profitable investment in the Central Trust hardly compared to the leverage he commanded or the responsibility he exercised. Kennedy held similar positions with the National Bank of Commerce (1887-1909), the New York Life Insurance Company (1903-1906), the Title Guarantee and Trust Company (1895-1909), and the United States Trust Company of New York (1896-1909). As a result of his varied banking activities, Kennedy became a seminal figure in the history of American banking and in the New York business community. The trust companies lent to the emerging large industrial enterprises and assumed the function of trustees that corporation lawyers and private bankers had performed. In addition, they had perpetual life charters, an important advantage as the maturities of the bond issues lengthened.

The scale of Kennedy's bequests dwarfs that of many of his contemporaries with comparable financial resources perhaps because he had no children. Although the magnitude of his gifts certainly warranted it, by his own choice nothing was ever named after Kennedy to perpetuate his name. Equally important, unlike many contemporary philanthropists, he did much more than merely dole out his millions with an open hand. Instead, he took an active part in the management of those institutions to which he entrusted his funds, becoming a member of the boards of trustees or an officer. His contributions to New York City and to national cultural, social, and civic institutions were consequential. He enriched libraries and universities, hospitals and charities with his money, his presence, and his administrative skill.

Kennedy died on October 31, 1909, as one of America's richest men. Kennedy also died relatively unknown despite his wealth and civic accomplishments. The *New York Tribune* included Kennedy in its 1892 list of millionaires, but in spite of his achievements the newspaper knew so little about Kennedy that upon his death it identified the source of his wealth as "inherited." Kennedy had successfully shunned the limelight. Obituaries commended him as a philanthropist and generally allotted the most space to his will. But the obituaries avoided the question of how he had accumulated his fortune of $60 million and concentrated instead on the fact that he gave away roughly half this sum in his will to institutions in which he had participated.

Kennedy was a seminal figure in early railroad development. He played a vital part in the history of American banking. He is also an important figure in the evolution of the joint charity movement in New York and the United States. No wonder both Andrew Carnegie and J. P. Morgan chose to attend Kennedy's funeral.

References:

Saul Engelbourg, "John Stewart Kennedy and the City of Glasgow Bank," *Business and Economic History,* 15 (1986): 69-84;

Engelbourg, "John Stewart Kennedy and the Scottish American Investment Company," *Essays in Economic and Business History,* 6 (1988): 37-54;

Engelbourg, "John Stewart Kennedy: Railroad Commission Merchant, Private Banker, and Philanthropist," *Essays in Economic and Business History,* 4 (1986): 98-108;

Heather Gilbert, *The Life of Lord Mount Stephen* (Aberdeen, Scotland: Aberdeen University Press, 1976);

Gilbert, "The Unaccountable Fifth: Solution of a Great Northern Enigma," *Minnesota History,* 42 (Spring 1971): 175-177;

Ralph W. Hidy, Muriel E. Hidy, Roy V. Scott, and Don L. Hofsommer, *The Great Northern Railway: A History* (Boston: Harvard Business School Press, 1988);

"In Memory of John S. Kennedy," *Survey,* 23 (November 27, 1909): 276-278;

Albro Martin, *James J. Hill and the Opening of the Northwest* (New York: Oxford University Press, 1976);

Joseph Gilpin Pyle, *The Life of James J. Hill* (Garden City, N.Y.: Doubleday, Page, 1917);

R. E. Tyson, "Scottish Investment in American Railways: The Case of the City of Glasgow Bank, 1856-1881," in *Studies in Scottish Business History,* edited by Peter L. Payne (New York: Kelley, 1967), pp. 387-416;

Ronald B. Weir, *A History of the Scottish American Investment Company 1873-1973* (Edinburgh, Scotland: Scottish American Investment Company, 1973).

John Jay Knox

(March 19, 1828-February 9, 1892)

by Benjamin J. Klebaner

City College, CUNY

CAREER: Teller, Bank of Vernon (1849-1852); teller, Burnet Bank (1852-1856); cashier, Susquehanna Valley Bank (1856); partner, J. J. Knox & Company (1856-1862); clerk (1862), disbursing clerk, U.S. Department of the Treasury (1862-1865); cashier, Exchange National Bank of Norfolk (1865); clerk (1865-1867), deputy comptroller of the currency (1867-1872), comptroller of the currency, U.S. Department of the Treasury (1872-1884); president, National Bank of the Republic (1884-1892).

John Jay Knox, notable banking and currency figure of the post-Civil War era, was born in Augusta, New York, on March 19, 1828. He was the seventh of ten children and the third son born to John J. and Sarah Ann Curtiss Knox. Knox's Scotch-Irish great-grandfather came from Strabane in 1760. Knox's father opened a store in Augusta, in Oneida County, in 1811. Until 1863 he was president of the Bank of Vernon, which he established in

1839 with a capital of $81,700. He served on the board of trustees of Hamilton College for 47 years. On the occasion of his golden wedding celebration in October 1863, Augusta was renamed Knoxboro in his honor.

John Jay Knox's childhood included "sliding down the Brewery hill, fishing and bathing in the brook," picking apples, berries, and nuts, and eating sap from local maples, he reminisced in 1863. He attended Augusta Academy and Watertown Classical Institute. He graduated from Hamilton College in 1849 and became a teller at the Bank of Vernon at a salary of $300 a year.

In 1852 Knox left for Syracuse, where he took a job as a teller in the Burnet Bank. Four years later he joined the Susquehanna Valley Bank in Binghamton as cashier. Shortly thereafter he moved with a younger brother, Henry Martyn Knox, to St. Paul, Minnesota, where they conducted a private banking business, J. J. Knox & Company, for six years.

John Jay Knox

Secretary of the Treasury Salmon P. Chase, attracted by Knox's article in *Hunt's Merchant's Magazine* for February 1862 in support of Chase's proposal for a national banking system, hired him as a clerk in 1862 at a salary of $1,200 a year. Chase soon moved him to his own office and made him disbursing clerk. Knox prepared a salary table of the Treasury Department for every month and quarter of the year, which the Government Printing Office published in 1865.

Early in April 1865, offered the cashiership of the newly opened National Exchange Bank of Richmond and the same position at the Exchange National Bank of Norfolk at a salary of $2,500, Knox decided to accept the latter. Unable to find a way to reduce Exchange National's expenses, he informed the bank's president that he saw "no hope . . . to try to make the Bank prosperous." After a few months he resigned. Secretary of the Treasury Hugh McCulloch forthwith offered him his old clerkship. Returning to Norfolk on official business a year later, he congratulated himself heartily "in having escaped so promptly from the disagreeable, filthy & unhealthy Norfolk."

Knox had charge of the Treasury's mint and coinage correspondence from 1866 to 1873. He inspected the branch mints at San Francisco and Carson City, Nevada, in 1866. In 1867 his examination of the New Orleans Subtreasury revealed a $1.2 million defalcation, the largest federal government loss up to that time. Thanks to his collection efforts, the shortage was reduced to $681,000.

In an 1866 report to the secretary of the treasury, Knox urged a revision of the laws relating to the Mint System: since the last revision in 1837, coinage volume had increased thirteenfold. He recommended that a commission be appointed to find ways to increase Mint efficiency and receipts. The secretary thought so highly of the report that he included it in his *Report on the Finances* for 1866.

Secretary McCulloch promoted Knox to deputy comptroller of the currency on March 12, 1867. In December 1869 the new secretary of the treasury, George Boutwell, placed Knox in charge of the work of revising the laws governing the Mint. The Treasury transmitted a bill containing Knox's recommendations to Congress in April 1870. Knox proposed that the Mint discontinue coinage of the silver dollar. He pointed out that the silver dollar's bullion content was worth $1.03 in gold, and that, consequently, the silver dollar had not circulated since about 1837. Silver could be more profitably sold in the market rather than to the Mint. For trade with the Far East, Knox proposed coining a new silver dollar, 1.8 percent heavier than the one to be discontinued. Nearly three years elapsed between the introduction of the bill and the passage of the Coinage Act on February 12, 1873. The act substantially embodied Knox's recommendations. Probably no prior act of Congress had "received more care in its preparation, or was ever submitted to the criticism of so great a number of . . . experts," Knox asserted in his first talk at an American Bankers Association (ABA) convention, in August 1879. Among advocates of silver, however, Knox's name was forever anathema.

Ulysses S. Grant appointed Knox comptroller of the currency on April 25, 1872. Reappointed by Rutherford B. Hayes and Chester Arthur, Knox served as comptroller until April 30, 1884.

As comptroller Knox opposed repeal of statutory reserve requirements: depositors needed safeguards, though only "the experience of years" could determine the correct proportion "to protect the demand-liabilities of the bank." Private banks could remain relatively unregulated, but if corporations desired to organize "under the authority and seal of a great nation, care should be exercised that the authority obtained shall not be abused." Since inexperienced persons might organize a national bank, a place existed for statutory "judicious limitations ... known to characterize good banking." Such restrictions, however, did not make government the guardian of the bank or in any way responsible for the management of its funds. That remained the task of its officers and directors, who swore to exercise continuous vigilance. If the public called on the Office of the Comptroller of the Currency to detect defalcations or other violations, more frequent and more thorough examinations would be necessary. Modestly compensated bank examiners could not be expected to audit a bank. They usually examined a small bank in a single day, and larger ones, with the aid of an assistant, in two or three days. Unpopular in the beginning, bank examinations yielded excellent results. Supervisory examinations and mandatory reports of condition had contributed to the low rate of failure of the national banking system. Seventy-three banks failed during the dozen years Knox served as comptroller of the currency; 40 of those had capital of less than $100,000. Losses to depositors since 1863 averaged about one-twentieth of 1 percent of total national bank deposits.

By far the largest nineteenth-century national bank failure (measured by capital, not assets) was the National Bank of the State of Missouri. The state had sold its stock interest in mid 1866, a few months after the bank, capitalized at $2.5 million, received a national charter. Bank policy shifted from conservatism to speculation. Fraudulent management, excessive loans to officers and directors, and depreciation of its securities portfolio contributed to the bank's collapse in June 1877. Upon its liquidation all claims were paid in full with interest. Another troublesome failure involved Pacific National Bank of Boston, ordered closed on May 22, 1882. Disgruntled shareholders made serious charges against Knox, which he attributed to malice. On April 22, 1884, the House Banking Committee found nothing to indicate that Knox "was activated by an improper motive or was guilty of any intentional violation of the law."

Knox became commissioner of the Freedman's Savings and Trust Company by an act of February 21, 1881. For that additional responsibility the comptroller's salary was increased by $1,000. Though chartered by Congress in March 1865 to receive deposits of ex-slaves, the institution did not fall under federal supervision. The charter was amended in May 1870 to permit real estate loans. That led to its failure in mid 1874. Before Knox took over, some 40 cents on every dollar of deposits had been paid out. Knox was able to declare additional dividends of 22 percent to more than 61,000 deposit claims totaling just under $3 million. He pleaded, "It would be little more than just for Congress to make an appropriation for the payment in full of all the creditors of the Freedman's Bank, instead of allowing them to lose 40 percent of the scanty means which they had deposited in an institution organized, as they believed, for their benefit, and some of whose branches were controlled by officers of the government." Knox argued that "the government has assumed a quasi-moral responsibility to the beneficiaries of this trust, in the first place by the incorporation of the company without proper safeguards, and subsequently by permitting its own agents, the officers of the late Bureau for Refugees, Freedmen, and Abandoned Lands, to act as the agents of the company, thus leading the inexperienced and ignorant freedman to regard it in the light of a government institution, and as such to commit their earnings to its keeping." Congress refused to heed his plea, which he renewed over the next two years.

In contrast to the supervision of bank failures, the day-to-day activities of the office, invisible to the general public, lacked drama. Each year the office notified hundreds of banks of violations and brought the banks "under the discipline of the law." At the 1883 convention of the American Bankers Association, Knox confessed that "it has sometimes seemed as though the title of 'the scolding Comptroller' would be appropriate." But as a result of his wisdom and firmness many troubled banks were restored to a sound condition.

In 1869 Congress banned the certification of checks in amounts not warranted by deposit balances. Violations of the law led to the appointment of receivers for the National Bank of the Commonwealth in New York City in September 1873 and the New Orleans National Banking Association in October 1873. That November, Knox's *Annual Report* warned that he intended to "rigidly enforce" the law. In October 1879 he ordered a series of special examinations and again halted the practice. He admonished national banks to obey the law or leave the system.

Knox had been an ardent advocate of a national banking system even before the adoption of the national banking system. At his suggestion, an act of March 3, 1873, forbade the use of the term "national" in the title of a bank not organized under federal auspices. He reminded the nation that the system had been "established, not for the benefit of the stockholders of the banks, but for the benefit of all the people. Its ample basis of unimpaired capital, its large surplus, its large cash reserves, its secured circulation, its protection to depositors, and its general management, must commend it to every student of political economy."

Even so, the system had many enemies. President Hayes found it necessary to veto a funding act on March 3, 1881, because he feared it was "a step in the direction of the destruction of the National Banking system." One section would have prohibited new banks from organizing and prevented existing banks from increasing their capital.

That December, Knox urged Congress to extend the corporate status of national banks for another 20 years. Charters started to expire at the start of 1882, but only "after a long contest" did the president sign the legislation on July 12.

Hostility toward national banks was in part related to a mistaken impression that the banks gathered enormous profits on their note issues. In 1872 Knox estimated profits at not more than 3 percent. In 1883 he reported that profits on circulation were "nominal." Banks paying exceptionally large dividends often had a smaller circulation than others earning moderate dividends. Moreover, thousands of state and private banks denied note issue chose not to join the national banking system. In 1879 outstanding notes had totaled less than five-sixths of the maximum allowable. Organizers were attracted less by profits on circulation than by the reputation national banks enjoyed, "which is of great value to them in the accumulation of deposits."

Beginning in June 1874 national banks could retire their note issues and reclaim federal government bond collateral in excess of $50,000. Beginning in 1872 Knox had urged that the minimum compulsory bond purchase be reduced. A decade later Congress eased the minimum for banks with capital under $150,000, but Knox considered that unsatisfactory. U.S. bonds were then quoted at a premium; many national banks found the return on note issues unattractive. Congress finally eliminated the requirement in 1913.

Profits of national banks, Knox argued in 1872, were "not more than a fair remuneration upon capital." During his 12 years as comptroller, net earnings from all sources never came to as much as 5.5 percent on total capital and surplus, and sank to a low of 2.31 percent in the half-year ending September 1, 1878. Profits averaged 3.7 percent from 1872 to 1884. National bank shares probably had a wider distribution among people of "moderate means" than any other corporate stock.

National banks held more than one-fifth of the interest-bearing debt of the federal government during the 1870s. Knox made various proposals for refunding older issues over the years. In 1884 he recommended that the entire issue of 4 percent bonds be refunded into 2.5 percent bonds.

Knox left the comptroller's office on April 30, 1884, after completing only two years of his five-year appointment by Arthur. On at least two occasions prior to 1884 he had turned down offers of employment in the private sector. In the fall of 1869 he declined a cashiership in the Union Square National Bank in New York City, unwilling "to take hold of a bank that is not right in all important particulars," as he wrote to family. The bank (with a capital of $200,000) closed on December 15, 1871. A second offer, at double his Washington salary, came from another New York City bank in the spring of 1882, but he chose to remain for a third term as comptroller. In 1884 friends finally prevailed upon Knox to assume the lucrative position of president of the National Bank of the Republic. The New York City institution, organized in 1851, had converted to a national charter in 1865. The capital of $1,500,000 was owned by 450 shareholders. Only two had as much as $30,000 par value; one-third were New Englanders "of moderate means" who had been shareholders for 30 years.

As president of the National Bank of the Republic Knox attracted correspondent business, much of it unsolicited. He regularly sent out his bank's statement of condition to other banks but never directly solicited business already in another bank's hands. While making "every possible effort" to obtain the business of newly organized banks, he never tried to take business from his Wall Street neighbors. In seeking correspondent bank business, he never promised what he could not deliver.

Knox discontinued the practice of check overcertification at the bank, something he had fought as comptroller of the currency. The bank thereby lost some $600,000 in "remunerative bal-

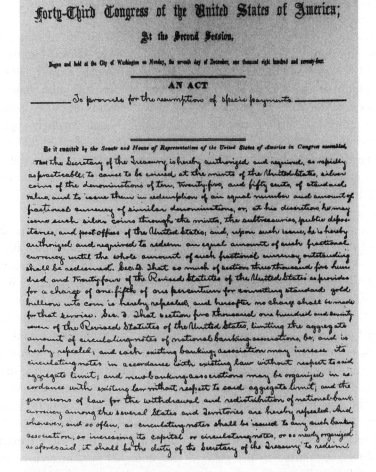

First page of the original copy of the Resumption Act of 1875, by which the U.S. Treasury resumed specie payment on January 1, 1879. Knox was comptroller of the currency at the Treasury from 1872 to 1884 (U.S. Department of State).

ances" but gained an increase in public confidence and a substantial increase in the price of its stock.

Knox looked upon his staff as associates and friends. He encouraged and instructed beginners to train for higher positions. He rewarded good service liberally. As comptroller he had commended his staff for their devoted service during the Panic of 1873. In November 1873 and again the following year he urged Congress to appropriate funds for those in his office who rendered "the most efficient and responsible service."

In mid 1887 Knox wrote his family that the National Bank of the Republic had earned almost 7 percent during the prior half-year. "The bank's progress has been more than equal to my expectations," he added. The bank's share of the total assets of the 48 national banks in New York City had been a modest 1.82 percent in the fall of 1883. It soared to 3.41 percent in 1889 only to retreat to 2.85 percent in October 1891. A year later (some

eight months after Knox's death) its share reached 3.59 percent. First National Bank of New York absorbed the bank in August 1901.

Knox spoke out for "real money," also known as "honest money," both as a government official and as a banker. The years preceding the Treasury's resumption of specie payments on New Year's Day 1879 had been marked by "the popular agitation of financial heresies," Knox believed. Resumption meant "that the . . . billions of business transactions of a single year shall each be measured by a fixed and true . . . standard of value," not the false standard of the paper dollar. All notes, including national bank notes, were promises to pay real money, "substitutes for real money."

Knox played an active role behind the scenes in the battle for resumption. He worked on arrangements that made the assistant treasurer of the United States a member of the New York Clearing House Association in October 1878. Under the direction of Secretary of the Treasury John Sherman, Knox was also significantly involved in negotiations for the sale of $50 million in government bonds preceding and following resumption.

Knox's September 1879 speech to the ABA convention revealed his elation at the success of the Treasury's return to specie payments: "the financial marvels of the first four months succeeding resumption day . . . are beyond all precedent. . . . No nation ever before resumed specie payments with $670 million of paper money in circulation." He wrote his family in 1880, "The past two years have been the most memorable in the history of the country in financial matters, and I am glad that I have fortunately been associated with the Government in its good work."

Knox also hoped the government would see fit to withdraw greenbacks from circulation. An April 1884 Supreme Court decision (*Julliard* v. *Greenman*) empowering Congress to issue such legal-tender notes at all times, not only during war emergencies, disappointed him. Knox feared that "every commercial crisis or sudden panic, or cry of hard times, may be succeeded by legislation which shall increase the issue of the greenback and reduce its value even below the level of the silver certificate."

Knox remained firmly committed to the gold standard. But he was "willing to agree to as free a use of silver as possible while still maintaining that standard," provided that the silver dollar be at par with the gold dollar. A switch to a silver standard would represent "the greatest financial evil that could befall the United States," he warned the House Committee on Coinage in February 1891. That November, in his last appearance before the ABA convention, he applauded Secretary of the Treasury Charles Foster for his "purpose to maintain gold payments," to redeem treasury notes based on silver and greenbacks "at all times in gold coin."

Greenbacks had "strangled national bank notes," Knox contended. The election of 14 Greenback party candidates to Congress in 1878 alarmed him. He warned against the substitution of treasury notes for national bank notes: that would mean "the volume of the currency will be controlled, not by the demands of business and the wants of the country, but by the views and action of political parties and of Congress." He thought national bank notes had many advantages: they were a homogeneous currency, fully secured, redeemable at a common point, and exempt from the discount

occasioned by an irregularity of value in different localities.

Knox also feared that Congress might restore state-chartered banks' circulation privileges, which had been "much abused' before the Civil War. Unwary holders of state bank notes had suffered losses averaging about 5 percent per year, he estimated. Though strongly opposed to state bank notes, Knox recognized that national banks wanted the state systems preserved. Federally chartered banks liked the option of taking out state charters as insurance against the threat of adverse federal legislation.

"The best currency is that which will most readily adapt itself to the needs of business," Knox maintained in 1879. The national bank note, he acknowledged, "was defective in the principle of elasticity." He warned, however, that it would be an irreparable error to obtain elasticity at the risk of safety. Antebellum state bank notes had proved "as elastic in value as in volume," he reminded the House Banking Committee in 1890. Knox had insisted on a bond-secured bank currency in 1882, opposing proposals for notes backed by general assets of national banks. By January 1890, however, he endorsed before the House Banking Committee a plan for notes 70 percent secured by U.S. bonds and 30 percent by general assets, supported by a safety fund accumulated by a semiannual tax of .5 percent on circulation.

Knox published only one book in his lifetime, *United States Notes: A History of the Various Issues of Paper Money by the Government of the United States* (1884). The preface described it as "a small volume containing a history of all the various issues of paper money by the Government." Knox's preface revealed his plan to publish "at some future day a volume worthy of the title of "History of Banking in the United States." A posthumous volume with that title appeared in 1900. Bradford Rhodes, editor of *Bankers Magazine*, and Elmer Youngman (associate editor) were also mentioned on the title page. The manuscript had been "carefully revised and brought up to date" by the two, who enlisted a corps of writers for the chapters dealing with individual states not covered by Knox. The 880-page work has remained the most ambitious treatment of the subject to the present.

Knox's *Annual Reports* as comptroller of the currency represent the bulk of his published writings. The *Annual Reports* discussed major currency and banking problems of the day and influenced congressional legislation. The volume for 1876 contains useful and comprehensive historical information. Colleges used the reports in courses on political economy. The 12 annual reports became "standard authorities on financial questions" and circulated more widely than almost any other government documents.

In 1884 Knox was elected to the Executive Council of the American Bankers Association, and he was reelected year after year. As first vice-president in November 1891, he would have become president at the 1892 convention had he lived. Knox was also a member of the elite Chamber of Commerce of the state of New York. He belonged to the Union League and to the University and Century Clubs in New York City. His alma mater's Phi Beta Kappa chapter (chartered in 1870) elected him a member in 1887. Hamilton College awarded him an honorary LL.D. degree.

On February 7, 1871, Knox married Caroline E. Todd, daughter of the much respected William B. Todd, the largest property holder in the District of Columbia at the time of his death in March 1872. Four sons and three daughters were born of this marriage: Caroline Todd (1871-1948), Elizabeth Irving (1873-1940), John Jay, Jr. (1874-1875), John Jay, Jr. (1876-1913), Irving Gillis (1877-1921), Herman Warren (1881-1931), and Adelaide Strong (1884-1941). Mrs. Knox was an accomplished pianist and was president of Babies' Hospital in New York City at the time of her death on August 15, 1922, in her seventy-sixth year.

Knox appreciated art, music, and poetry and had a genial and gentle disposition. His colleague Henry Cannon described him as "a man of the strictest and most unvarying integrity . . . dignified . . . cordial . . . thoughtful and courteous."

On January 21, 1892, Knox brought greetings from the thousand-member Chamber of Commerce of the state of New York at the opening of the headquarters of the Boston Chamber of Commerce. His talk featured reminiscences of pioneer days in St. Paul. He worked at his bank desk for the last time on February 4, 1892. He became sick on the evening of February 5 and died of pleuropneumonia at his home four days later. On February 12 a funeral service was held at St. Bartholomew's, the church to which he had belonged. Many prominent New Yorkers attended. The next day an Episcopal service was held in the Church of the Epiphany in Washington before a distinguished gathering. Knox was buried in Oak Hill Cemetery in Georgetown, D.C. He left his entire estate to his wife.

During Knox's long and distinguished career in Washington he was "the mainstay and pillar of the Treasury Department," Abram S. Hewitt, former Congressman and outstanding New Yorker, stated at the New York Chamber of Commerce's memorial meeting. In his eight years in New York City he presided over the growth of the National Bank of the Republic "to the full stature of the great banks of the city," wrote *Bankers Magazine*. Knox's death represented "a great loss, not merely to the financial circle of this city, but to the whole country," a *New York Times* editorial stated on February 10. London's *Bankers Magazine* remembered him as "one of the soundest authorities on currency and banking in America."

Publications:

Reports and Addresses of Comptroller Knox, 24 volumes (Washington, D.C. & New York, 1873-1883);

United States Notes: A History of the Various Issues of Paper Money by the Government of the United States (New York: Scribners, 1884; revised edition, New York: Scribners, 1885; London: Unwin, 1885; revised again, New York: Scribners, 1892);

A History of Banking in the United States, edited by Bradford Rhodes and Elmer Youngman (New York: B. Rhodes, 1900).

References:

Charles A. Conant, *A History of Modern Banks of Issue* (New York: Putnam's, 1896);

Edwin Leland Harper, "The Policy-Making Role of Federal Political Executives: The Case of the Comptroller of the Currency," Ph.D. dissertation, University of Virginia, 1968;

Thomas P. Kane, *The Romance and Tragedy of Banking: Problems and Incidents of Governmental Supervision of National Banks*, 2 volumes (New York: Bankers Publishing Co., 1922).

Archives:

The papers of the Knox family are at the New-York Historical Society.

Augustus Kountze

(November 19, 1826-April 30, 1892)

Herman Kountze

(August 21, 1833-November 20, 1906)

Luther Kountze

(October 29, 1841-April 17, 1918)

Charles B. Kountze

(March 4, 1845-November 18, 1911)

by James E. Fell, Jr.

United Banks of Colorado

The Kountze brothers—Augustus, Herman, Luther, and Charles B.—were the founders and developers of a group of loosely associated banks located primarily in the West. Except for the branch in New York, they founded the banks during times of early settlement and prospered as the population grew and the economy expanded. In that sense the Kountze brothers grew up with the country.

The four brothers were the sons of Christian Kountze and Margaret Zerbe Kountze. Christian Kountze was a linen peddler who emigrated from Saxony about 1820. Once in the United States he anglicized his name from Kunze to Kountze, then worked his way from New York to Pittsburgh and from there to Osnaburg (now Canton), Ohio, where he opened a store, became Osnaburg's first postmaster, and married Margaret Zerbe in 1826. The union produced twelve children, not all of whom survived to adulthood.

As the sons grew they went to work in their father's store in Osnaburg. He made each one a partner at the age of sixteen and gave each the sum of $100 at the age of twenty-one. That early experience produced deeply ingrained work habits along with a commitment to shared responsibility among the brothers. But despite their father's success, they did not intend to remain in Osnaburg. They looked farther west, where they saw opportunity in newly settled country.

Luther Kountze, founder of the Denver bank that became the Colorado National Bank in 1866

Augustus and Herman, the oldest brothers, took the lead. In the 1850s they went to Omaha, Nebraska Territory, where in 1857 they founded their first bank, known as Kountze Brothers. Despite the ravages of the Panic of 1857 the house survived, and the Kountzes became leading figures in the community. With the passage of the National Banking Act in 1863 the bank was reorganized, and its name was changed to First National Bank of Omaha. Edward Creighton, with whom the Kountzes would have a long association, became president, although the Kountzes held the controlling interest.

No sooner had the Kountzes opened their bank in Omaha than a party of prospectors discovered gold in the Rocky Mountains, some 500 miles to the west. That touched off the Pike's Peak gold rush of 1859, which prompted the founding of the city of Denver and led to the formation of Colorado Territory two years later. The Kountzes used Denver's first newspapers to advertise that their Omaha bank would receive gold shipments and dispose of the proceeds. This apparently produced little business, however, and, with Colorado booming, the brothers made the decision to launch a new bank in Denver, the transportation and distribution center for the mines. In 1862 Luther Kountze moved there to open another Kountze Brothers bank, which made loans and bought gold dust.

Not content with the bank in Denver, Luther Kountze looked farther afield to Central City, which lay in the heart of the gold region, about 50 miles to the northwest. He opened an office for Kountze Brothers there in 1863. It became the Rocky Mountain National Bank in 1866, the state's third national bank and the third the brothers controlled.

Despite the location of the Central City office, the key to the brothers' operations in Colorado was the bank in Denver, the territory's leading city. In 1866 the bank was reorganized as the Colorado National Bank of Denver. Its first five directors included Luther and Charles B. Kountze as well as the wealthy Creighton. Luther Kountze became the first president of Colorado National, followed by Augustus in 1869 and Charles in 1874. Charles would preside over the bank for the next 37 years.

By the early 1870s Colorado National had emerged as the second largest bank in the state. It was quite profitable and was known for its conservative management, which contrasted with the more daring First National Bank of Denver, Colorado's largest bank, headed by Jerome B. Chaffee and David H. Moffat, Jr.

Meanwhile, in 1868 Augustus Kountze had taken a special interest in Cheyenne, Wyoming, an important link in the Union Pacific Railroad's transcontinental route between Omaha and Salt Lake City. He persuaded his brothers to found a bank there, once again in partnership with Creighton, among others. To help run the new enterprise, Augustus brought in brother-in-law William Lewis Bart Berger, who had married Margaret Kountze. Although Berger and his associates might have made the Cheyenne bank a success, in 1870 the Kountzes sold out. Berger then moved to Denver, where he became cashier of the Colorado National Bank. By the mid 1870s he and Charles B. Kountze dominated the bank, as would their descendants for most of the next century.

Also in 1868 Luther Kountze left Denver for New York City, where he opened a private bank on Wall Street. That enterprise also prospered, and Luther and his family became prominent in New York social circles. By the early 1870s the Kountzes had made a decision to focus their energies on the banks in Denver, Omaha, and New York. That decision was reflected in the sale of the smaller Cheyenne and Central City banks.

The Kountzes knew that Colorado's mines comprised the bedrock of the territorial economy but that railroads made the mines profitable. Colorado National Bank became a principal financier of the Denver Pacific Railroad, which gave the city its first link with the Union Pacific track at Cheyenne. The Kountzes were also instrumental in founding and supporting the Denver South Park & Pacific Railway, which built west in the 1870s to tap many mining communities.

The 1880s were a prosperous time for both Colorado and the Colorado National Bank. The new state's economy boomed in response to the Leadville rush and the railroad construction emanating from Denver. But the Panic of 1893 brought the boom to a sudden halt. It destroyed many Colorado banks. Colorado National survived, although the financial crisis prompted the bank to diversify its loan portfolio.

By the early twentieth century the unity that had characterized the Kountze brothers' banking empire began to die with them. Augustus passed away in 1892, and his three brothers died in the early twentieth century—Herman in 1906, Charles B. in 1911, and Luther in 1918. A new generation—cousins—succeeded to what their fathers had founded, and while the younger generation worked together, the banks in Denver, Omaha, and New York evolved into more independent institutions than before.

What drove those enterprises even farther apart was the Great Depression. In 1930 the Colorado National Bank recorded the first loss in its history, and its loan portfolio deteriorated. In October the New York firm was declared insolvent, largely because of the collapse in the price of bonds, the firm's bread and butter for the previous 52 years. At the end of the year the New York house filed for bankruptcy. The collapse of the New York branch stunned the banks in Omaha and Denver. Depositors streamed in to withdraw their money. That hurt the Omaha bank the most. Trying to help their New York cousins, the Omaha Kountzes had become more heavily involved than their Denver cousins. As a result they were forced from the bank's board and management.

The Denver Kountzes did not escape unscathed, however. To help save Colorado National, in 1932 the Reconstruction Finance Corporation (RFC) bought $1.5 million in the bank's preferred stock, thus adding to its strength and liquidity. But there was a price. The RFC forced out George

Berger, Sr., who had been president of the bank for 23 years, and replaced him with Harold Kountze, Jr. The First National Bank of Omaha was soon after the subject of an RFC stock purchase. It also survived.

The Depression gradually ran its course, and World War II restored prosperity to Colorado and Nebraska. The Bergers and the Kountzes continued to run Colorado National until 1962, when Melvin J. Roberts became the first outsider in a century to be president. That trend continued, but not until 1985 did the last member of the Kountze family leave the ranks of senior management. In Nebraska the Kountzes' bank continued as one of the leading banks in the state.

Reference:

Thomas Jacob Noel, *Growing through History with Colorado: The Colorado National Banks, The First 125 Years, 1862-1987* (Denver: Colorado National Banks and Colorado Studies Center, University of Colorado at Denver, 1987).

Archives:

The Kountze Family Collection is in the Western History Department of the Denver Public Library.

William S. Ladd

(October 10, 1826-January 6, 1893)

by Larry Schweikart

University of Dayton

CAREER: Schoolteacher (1845-1848); merchant, W. S. Ladd & Company (1849-1851); partner, Ladd & Reed & Company (1852-1859); mayor, city of Portland (1854-1858); partner, Ladd & Tilton Bank (1859-1893); partner, Ladd & Reed Farm Company (?); partner, Oregon Iron & Steel Works (1862 [reorganized as Oregon Iron & Steel Company, 1882]); founder, Oregon Steam and Navigation Company (1862-1871); partner, Auburn Canal Company (1863); organizer, Ladd & Bush (1868); founder, Oregon Furniture Company (1874); founder, Portland Flouring Mills (1883); founder, Oregon Paving Contracting Company (1884); founder, Artificial Stone Company (1885); founder, Oregon Pottery Company (1885); founder, Portland Cordage Company (1888).

Early Oregon banker William Sargeant Ladd, born on October 10, 1826, in Holland, Vermont, was the son of Nathaniel Gould and Abigail Kelly Ladd. The Ladds were a middle-class family who saw to young Ladd's education at home before he attended public schools, where he had a reputation as a serious student. Nathaniel Ladd, a physician, headed the local abolitionist movement and wielded some influence in town. He put his son to work on a farm he purchased in 1841. At the age of nineteen Ladd began to teach in the local country schools. When news of the California gold rush reached New England, he held a position as a freight agent in a local shipping firm. He eventually won a promotion as manager of the freight department. While he worked in that capacity still other news–the tales of a former schoolmate, Charles Elliott Tilton–reached his ears. Tilton had moved to San Francisco, where he started a booming mercantile business. His sales network extended north up the coast to Portland, and he reported considerable opportunities for riches. Ladd decided to seek his own fortune in the West, and on February 27,

William S. Ladd (Oregon Historical Society 5162)

1849, he sailed for San Francisco. There he acquired a small stock of goods and traveled to Portland, where he sold wine, liquor, eggs, chickens, produce and other goods under the name W. S. Ladd & Company. Within a few months he had grossed over $2,000. In 1852 he entered into a partnership with Tilton, who advanced him more than $60,000 in gold to buy merchandise for his next sales expedition. Tilton lived in San Francisco and had accumulated a great deal of wealth in the China trade. A third New Englander, Simeon Reed, who had recently arrived in Portland, joined the firm and served as clerk and salesman. Ladd handled wholesale, and Reed, as one account noted, "was the best dressed bartender in early day Portland."

In 1853 Ladd moved the business into a new location on Front Street, and during this time he erected the first brick building in Portland. He also broadened the business to sell groceries and general merchandise. Like many other merchants, Ladd started to lend money at a monthly interest of 1 percent. Gradually he focused on banking, and he and Tilton opened a private bank, Ladd & Tilton, in 1859 with $50,000 in capital. The two had dissolved their mercantile business with Reed two years earlier. (The Oregon Constitution prohibited state-chartered banks.) The partners quickly increased their capital, and after only a year and a half the bank had deposits of more than $130,000. Ladd's uncle, Stephen Mead of New London, Connecticut, also provided capital, with each major partner investing $200,000 to refund the bank in 1869. (Ladd, in 1875, served as trustee of Mead's estate, and he invested more than $164,000 of the proceeds in Portland enterprises, as well as a large sum in the bank.)

Ladd & Tilton often held nonliquid investments, but it also held a high ratio of capital to deposits. In 1869 the bank, buoyed by Mead's investment, moved into new quarters, reflecting its growth. Shares in the bank proved extremely profitable, with each share worth more than $1 million after only six years. Ladd & Tilton did a vigorous gold dust exchange business, and also provided assay reports on gold. In 1880 Ladd and his son William Mead Ladd bought out Tilton, making the bank a completely Oregonian institution. Also that year the Oregon Supreme Court reviewed the state's constitutional prohibition against chartered banking, interpreting the law to mean only the prohibition of the issue of private bank notes (which by then had been effectively driven out of circulation across the nation anyway, due to the rise of the national banking system), and ruled that state-chartered banks were indeed constitutional. Consequently, Ladd & Tilton incorporated under the new interpretation of the law.

Ladd & Tilton also expanded its banking services by investing in other banks. In 1868 Ladd and Tilton obtained a half-interest in the Ladd & Bush Bank of Salem. Ladd permitted Asahel Bush a considerable degree of autonomy in running the bank in Salem. Ladd also purchased an interest in

the Dextor Horton National Bank in Seattle (later Seafirst).

Among his numerous nonbanking interests, Ladd actively participated in Oregon agriculture. He owned several valuable farms and stimulated agricultural development throughout the region by importing hogs, sheep, and thoroughbred horses and by breeding shorthorn and Guernsey cattle. His Broad Mead farm had the reputation of having the finest herd of shorthorn cattle on the Pacific Coast. In recognition of his efforts the regents of the Agricultural College at Corvallis (now Oregon State University) named him to the Board of Regents. Eventually his interest in farming broadened to include founding the Portland Flouring Mills in 1883, the largest milling operation in the Pacific Northwest.

Ladd also embarked on numerous other ventures, incorporating the Oregon Artificial Stone Company (1885), the Oregon Pottery Company (1885), and the Oregon Paving Contracting Company (1884). Those companies participated in a massive program of laying water pipes and paving the streets of Portland. Ladd proved an early sparkplug to the Portland Water Committee and advanced $20,000 from the bank to underwrite its activities. His interest and capital had given him an early edge, with the city in 1862 offering him a 30-year exclusive franchise to lay pipes for the city's water system; nothing materialized from that franchise, and Ladd sold his interest that same year. Still, when the Water Committee was authorized in 1886 to sell $700,000 in bonds, Ladd purchased more than one-fourth of them before the end of the next year.

The Portland banker also served as a director of the Portland & Willamette Valley Railroad and had interests in other railroads. He participated in founding the Oregon Steam and Navigation Company in 1862 with another Portland banker, John C. Ainsworth. That company turned in remarkable profits. After receiving an offer from Jay Cooke's Northern Pacific in 1871, Ladd sold his shares in that venture. When Cooke went bankrupt in 1873, Ladd again acquired shares in the company, then called the Oregon Railroad and Navigation Company, and sold that interest in 1879 to Henry Villard. Ladd also occasionally engaged in speculative ventures, including the Oregon Branch Pacific Railroad Company, a line that was intended to run from a point south of Eugene to the Pacific Railroad at Winnemucca, Nevada.

Portland offices of Ladd & Tilton Bank at the time of the 1894 flood

In the 1870s Ladd suffered a reoccurrence of a spinal injury he incurred as a young man, and he was paralyzed from the waist down for the rest of his life. By mid decade he found that he required considerable time to rest at Hot Springs, Arkansas.

The Ladd & Tilton Bank continued under the leadership of Ladd's son William Mead Ladd, who became president after his father's death on January 6, 1893. He retained most of the controlling interest in the bank. In 1907 the bank encountered difficulties when the Title Guarantee & Trust Company, of which Ladd was also president, collapsed, owing Ladd & Tilton more than $600,000. The Title Company's manager, J. Thornburn Ross, had participated in looting the bank. William S. Ladd had intended to use the Title Company to handle many of his (and later, his estate's) real estate interests. William Mead Ladd sold the family's interests to his brother-in-law Frederick B. Pratt of New York, to raise the $2.5 million to reimburse the company's depositors. Ladd retained the title of president until 1919. The bank survived the ordeal, but it revealed that the younger Ladd did not have his father's banking skills. The Oregon legislature also revised the state's banking laws in 1907, passing the Oregon Banking Act that forced all private Oregon banks to incorporate and thus open their books to public scrutiny. Ladd & Tilton incorporated in compliance with the law in 1909, on its fiftieth anniver-

sary. At that time the bank had $14.7 million in assets. It had been remarkably profitable and had contributed greatly to Portland's development.

William Mead Ladd, however, had come under the influence of Theodore B. Wilcox, director and president of the Portland Flouring Mills (another Ladd enterprise). Wilcox, according to one source, engineered the major investment decisions of the bank after William S. Ladd's death in 1893. Although Frederick Pratt, heir to an oil refining fortune and the husband of Caroline Ladd, owned a controlling interest, he found it difficult to keep tabs on the business from New York. The bank invested heavily in farming and forest products industries, including King's Food Products Company and the Bankers Discount Corporation, both financial fiascoes. In their early stages, however, they looked like winners. Thus, when offered a good price by the Wilcox Investment Company in 1919, Pratt sold. The new owner, Wilcox Investment, was run by Theodore B. Wilcox's son, Raymond.

By 1923 Ladd & Tilton had sunk $2.5 million into loans to King's Food Products, which operated fruit and vegetable packing plants in Salem and the Dalles, and a year later an Oregon governor's report on security frauds showed that the bank had nearly $1 million in uncollectable loans. A self-appointed vigilante group called the Financial Investigation Corporation exposed the loans to the public at every opportunity. It even backed the suit of a stockholder, Agnes B. Wigle, against the bank. In 1924 the directors of Wilcox Investment Company sought to escape and convinced Frederick Pratt to take back the bank. William Mead Ladd remained chairman of the board, but two Wilcox-related vice-presidents made lending decisions. After Pratt hired a troubleshooter to determine the condition of the bank's loans, he realized he had to sell, with losses of up to $15 million staring at him. Pratt found a buyer in the U.S. National Bank in 1925, closing the chapter on the Ladd family's banking interest. The assets given Ladd & Tilton in return for the deposits, however, did not always prove valuable. After transferring the assets, Ladd & Tilton filed new articles of incorporation for an investment company without banking functions called the Nassau Company. That company slowly liquidated the doubtful assets of the bank.

William S. Ladd had a reputation for thrift to the point of eccentricity, so much so that he replied to letters written to him by scribbling between the lines and was known to slice open envelopes and use the inner side for letter paper. He had a keen eye for property and accumulated vast real estate holdings in part out of forfeited mortgages and defaulted loans. By 1891 Ladd's holdings increased at a rate of 20 percent per month. For example, he had acquired 400 acres in one tract for $20 an acre in 1874; in 1909 the land sold for $5,000 an acre. At the time of his death in 1893 his estate exceeded $10 million. In addition to his wife, Caroline, Ladd's surviving family members including three sons, William Mead, Charles E., and John Wesley Ladd.

Ladd also had political, religious, and educational interests. In 1854 he was elected mayor of Portland, but he never held other major public offices. Although he had been raised a Methodist, he joined the Presbyterian church and actively participated in its affairs. He endowed a chair of practical theology for Presbyterians at the church seminary in San Francisco in 1886 for $50,000, on the condition that the synod of California endow another chair for a similar sum. Along with colleagues Henry Corbett and Henry Failing, Ladd selected and furnished the grounds for the Riverview cemetery. He championed the Portland Library Fund and donated a scholarship to the University at Salem. He also endowed a chair in the medical department of Portland State University.

A paradoxical man, Ladd had a reputation for generosity and penury, for caution and recklessness. Known to pinch pennies occasionally in business, he set aside 10 percent of his income for charitable purposes and established a trust fund of more than $500,000 for posthumous benefactions. Although he sold liquor early in his career, he personally abstained. He had great ambition and imagination, and the paralysis of his legs apparently did not slow him down. He carried considerable influence in all the civic affairs of Portland; the fact that his family risked great sums to keep Ladd & Tilton from collapsing in the 1920s testified to the character of the bank's founder.

References:

Orrin K. Burrell, *Gold in the Woodpile—An Informal History of Banking in Oregon* (Eugene: University of Oregon Press, 1967);

Joseph Gaston, *Portland, Oregon: Its History and Builders* (Chicago: Clarke, 1911);

E. Kimbark MacColl, *The Growth of a City: Power and Politics in Portland, Oregon, 1915 to 1950* (Portland: Georgian Press, 1979);

MacColl, *The Shaping of a City: Business and Politics in Portland, Oregon, 1885-1915* (Portland: Georgian Press, 1976).

Archives:

The William S. Ladd Papers and corporate records of Ladd & Tilton Bank are at the Oregon Historical Society, Portland.

Legal Tender (*see* Notes, Currency, and Legal Tender)

Legal Tender Cases

by Roberta Sue Alexander

University of Dayton

To help finance the increasingly costly Civil War, on February 25, 1862, the U.S. Congress passed the Legal Tender Act. The act authorized the secretary of the treasury to issue non-interest-bearing treasury notes in small denominations, which were to be "lawful money, and a legal tender in payment of all debts, public and private." Eventually the government issued $450 million of these "greenbacks." Eight years later, in *Hepburn* v. *Griswold*, the Supreme Court for the first time directly confronted the issue of whether that method of financing the Civil War was constitutional.

The *Hepburn* case involved a note, signed by a Mrs. Hepburn, in which she promised to pay Henry Griswold $11,250. The note, executed in 1860, fell due five days before Congress enacted the Legal Tender Act. But Hepburn did not fulfill her obligation as promised. Therefore, in March 1864 Griswold sued to recover principal and interest. The Court ruled that Hepburn must pay $12,720. Complying with the order, she remitted that amount in greenbacks. Griswold refused payment, insisting she pay in gold. After the Court of Errors of Kentucky agreed with Griswold, Hepburn appealed to the Supreme Court. The Court decided the case in conference on November 27, 1869, while Justice Robert Grier was still a member of an eight-person court, but when the opinion was read in February 1870, Grier had retired. By a four-to-three margin the Court declared the Legal Tender Act invalid as it applied to contracts made before the passage of the statute.

Chief Justice Salmon P. Chase, writing for the majority (including Justices Stephen J. Field, Nathan Clifford, and Samuel Nelson), argued that the Constitution gave Congress no expressed power to make treasury notes a legal tender. Moreover, the power could not be implied as a necessary and proper means to carry out constitutionally enumerated ends. Chase concluded that the act, as it ap-

Justice Samuel F. Miller, who wrote for the minority in the 1870 case Hepburn v. Griswold, *in which the Supreme Court ruled the Civil War issuance of legal-tender greenbacks unconstitutional. The Court, bolstered by two additional justices, reversed itself in the 1872* Legal Tender Cases *(courtesy of the Library of Congress, Brady-Handy Collection).*

plied at least to debts contracted before its passage, "arbitrarily" altered contracts, thereby violating both the spirit and the letter of the Constitution. The act was "contrary to justice and equity," impaired the obligation of contracts, and deprived a creditor of his property without due process of law in violation of the Fifth Amendment. Justice Samuel F. Miller, writing for himself and Justices Noah Swayne and David Davis, vigorously disagreed with the majority. The minority took a more expansive view of congressional powers and a more restrained view of the Court's proper role. They argued that it was up to Congress, not the courts, to determine if legislation was necessary and proper. As long as the means and the end were related, the minority argued, Congress could pick from among various means. They also maintained that "this whole argument of the injustice of the law . . . is too abstract and intangible for application to courts of justice."

The Republican party reacted angrily to the decision. Abraham Lincoln had appointed Chase chief justice on the assumption that he "was right" on the emancipation and legal-tender issues. Chase was the secretary of the treasury who requested and then administered the Legal Tender Act in the first place. But by 1869 Chase had become a Democrat, and the vote on the Court followed strict party lines, the Democratic justices opposing the statute and the Republicans supporting it.

The reaction by President Ulysses S. Grant and the Republican majority in Congress was not based on support for the continued use of greenbacks. That economic question, highly controversial at the time, divided members of both political parties. Rather, the Republicans expressed outrage at the Court's challenge to legislative authority and Republican wartime policies.

Moreover, the Court's arguments were constitutionally questionable. To nineteenth-century Americans, the overturning of a congressional statute constituted a profound judicial act. The Court to that time had declared only two other congressional laws unconstitutional. And its last such decision, *Dred Scott* v. *Sanford* (1857), proved disastrous to the Court's prestige. The reasoning in *Hepburn* v. *Griswold*, some believed, was not much better than that found in *Dred Scott*. As constitutional historian Stanley I. Kutler has concluded, *Hepburn* was "one of the most dubious examples of judicial review in the Court's history."

At any rate, the *Hepburn* ruling stood only a short time. In April 1869 Congress increased the size of the court to nine justices. Coupled with Justice Grier's resignation, that move gave Grant the opportunity to make two Court appointments. He announced his choices the day the Court issued the *Hepburn* decision. By the end of March the new justices—William Strong and Joseph P. Bradley, Jr.—had installed themselves, and they immediately voted with the Hepburn minority to hear two new

cases concerning the constitutionality of the Legal Tender Act. *Knox* v. *Lee* involved a flock of sheep brought to Texas by their owner, a Mrs. Lee from Pennsylvania. In March of 1863 the Confederate government confiscated the sheep as alien enemy property and sold them to a Mr. Knox. After the war Lee sued Knox for damages. The jury awarded her $7,368. But in his charge to the jury the judge reminded the jurors that payment would be made in greenbacks. Knox appealed to the Supreme Court, arguing that the judgment amount was higher than it should have been, because the jury had taken into account the value of greenbacks as against gold. The second case, *Parker* v. *Davis*, originated as a suit in equity. Davis sought to force Parker to comply with a contract, entered into before the enactment of the Legal Tender Act, to convey some land to him in return for a payment of a specified sum of money. When the Supreme Court of Massachusetts, in February 1867, ordered Parker to convey the land, he refused, for Davis planned to pay for it in greenbacks. The Massachusetts court ordered Parker to turn over the property; Parker appealed to the Supreme Court.

Due to several delays the Court did not read its opinion concerning what became known as the Second Legal Tender Cases until January 15, 1872, when by a five-to-four vote the Court reversed *Hepburn* and upheld Congress's power to issue treasury notes and make them legal tender for debts contracted either before or after the passage of the Legal Tender Act. Many charged Grant with packing the court, but the change was unwarranted. First, Grant nominated Strong and Bradley the day the court announced the Hepburn decision, and no evidence suggests that he knew the result of the decision before its reading. Grant merely exercised the same power every president has exercised; he chose to appoint judges to the Court based on his assumption that they would support his positions on the leading judicial issues of the day. Further, there is no evidence that Grant acted improperly by asking either nominee what his position would be on the legal-tender issue or by asking for any guarantees on any position.

The arguments developed by both sides in the Second Legal Tender Cases present interesting constitutional, economic, and monetary theories. The minority (the *Hepburn* majority), relying heavily on their view of the intent of the framers and ratifiers of the Constitution, contended that Congress had neither expressed nor implied power to define anything but coin as legal tender. Economic assumptions clearly influenced that conclusion. The minority believed that making treasury notes legal tender had not been necessary for the successful prosecution of the Civil War. Based on their reading of the history of treasury notes issued since the ratification of the Constitution, they concluded that notes circulated just as well without having the status of legal tender. Or, as they put it, "the real support of note circulation not convertible on demand into coin is receivability for debts due the government." Finally, the minority based their arguments on a narrow definition of money as gold or silver only. Legal-tender notes represented nothing more than "promises to pay money." Money had to have "a standard of value." Quoting former Supreme Court justice Joseph Story and the well-known English commentator on the common law, William Blackstone, the minority maintained that "money is a universal medium or common standard, by a comparison with which the value of all merchandise may be ascertained, or it is a sign which represents the respective values of all commodities." Therefore, only precious metals or paper redeemable upon demand in gold or silver can be money. The fact that the paper can be used to pay government taxes is irrelevant. To be money, the medium must have an "intrinsic," "universally acknowledged" value. That position, well accepted at the time, led bankers to adopt the "real bills" doctrine, by which bankers made loans based on self-liquidating, short-term, high-quality paper.

The majority disagreed with every point of the minority's analysis. They maintained that making treasury notes legal tender contributed to their stability. More important, they contended that the question was not up to the Court to decide. The Constitution assigned to Congress the role of determining fiscal policy. Congress believed that making these treasury notes legal tender was a necessary means to finance the Civil War; the Court should accept that judgment. The majority also defined "money" more broadly, as any medium that could be used to pay government debts. Since greenbacks were "receivable for all dues to the government, and payable for all dues from the government," they qualified. To support that argument the majority turned to the words of the Constitution. In Article I the Constitution grants Congress the power "to raise and support Armies" but stipulates that

"no Appropriation of *Money* to that Use shall be for a longer Term than two Years." Later it stipulates that "No *Money* shall be drawn from the Treasury, but in Consequence of Appropriations" by Congress. Greenbacks were certainly money in those senses.

The majority defended its position through an expansive view of congressional and federal power. Loosely interpreting the Constitution, they contended that the federal government had all the attributes of sovereignty. All governments, including that of the United States, they explained, must have the power of self-preservation. Unless the Constitution specifically denied a power to the national government, that government could exercise any power recognized as an attribute of sovereignty. The power to make its issue legal tender was, they concluded, "a power confessedly possessed by every independent sovereignty."

The minority feared that upholding the Legal Tender Act would open the door to the issue of more greenbacks, creating inflation and undermining economic stability and the creditor class. The majority maintained that overturning a statute that had been in effect for ten years and under which thousands of contracts had been negotiated would prove too disruptive. "Indeed," they concluded, "treasury notes have become the universal measure of values." If the Court now required the debts, contracted under the assumption that payment was to be made in greenbacks, to be paid in gold, it would create the "grossest injustice": "A large percentage is added to every debt, and such must become the demand for gold to satisfy contracts, that ruinous sacrifices, general distress, and bankruptcy may be expected."

The minority's fears were not realized. The decision had a negligible economic impact. The price of gold barely fluctuated, and the country quietly returned to the use of metal coins until the 1930s. In the 1930s the Supreme Court used the second set of cases as precedent to defend the government's right to define the country's money and thereby to abrogate private contracts if they prevented the government from exercising its rightful power. The cases still serve today as the constitutional basis for the issuance of paper money, although for the first time in a century economists have raised the question of whether the government should permit competitive paper money, issued by private sources, to circulate.

References:

Kenneth W. Dam, "The Legal Tender Cases," *Supreme Court Review*, 12 (1981): 367-412;

Charles Fairman, "Mr. Justice Bradley's Appointment to the Supreme Court and the Legal Tender Cases," *Har-*vard Law Review*, 54 (1941): 971-1034, 1128-1155;

Fairman, *Mr. Justice Miller and the Supreme Court* (Cambridge, Mass.: Harvard University Press, 1939);

Stanley I. Kutler, *Judicial Power and Reconstruction Politics* (Chicago: University of Chicago Press, 1968).

Hugh McCulloch

(December 7, 1808-May 24, 1895)

by Carol Noland

Arizona State University

CAREER: Lawyer, Fort Wayne, Indiana (1833-1835); cashier and manager, State Bank of Indiana, Fort Wayne branch (1835-1855); president, Bank of the State of Indiana (1856-1863); U.S. comptroller of the currency (1863-1865); U.S. secretary of the treasury (1865-1869; 1884-1885); partner, Jay Cooke, McCulloch & Company (1870-1873); partner, McCulloch & Company (1873-1877).

Hugh McCulloch was manager and later president of the Bank of the State of Indiana in the 1850s and early 1860s, comptroller of the currency under President Abraham Lincoln, and secretary of the treasury under Presidents Andrew Johnson and Chester Arthur.

Born on December 7, 1808, in Kennebunk, Maine, McCulloch was the son of Abigail Perkins and Hugh McCulloch. His father was a shipbuilder and West India merchant. Even though Hugh McCulloch, Sr., sustained serious financial losses during the War of 1812, he sent his son to Bowdoin College. McCulloch left school during his sophomore year and at the age of seventeen began teaching in Boston. In 1829 he gave up teaching and devoted himself to studying law. He was admitted to the bar in 1832 and moved to Fort Wayne, Indiana, in 1833 to start a law practice. In 1838 he met and married Susan Mann. They had four children, two sons and two daughters.

McCulloch continued his practice until 1835, when he received an appointment as cashier and manager of the Fort Wayne branch of the State Bank of Indiana. The first State Bank of Indiana was organized in 1817 with $1 million in capital and an 18-year charter. As that charter neared expiration in 1834, a second State Bank of Indiana was

Hugh McCulloch (courtesy of the National Archives, Brady Collection)

formed and was given a 25-year charter for ten branches. It had a total of $1.6 million in capital, one-half of which the state furnished. While its charter was in existence no other bank or corporate banking institution was permitted in the state. Only after the State Bank's charter expired did the state legislature pass a Free Bank Act, allowing anyone who deposited designated bonds with state officials as security for currency issued to start a bank.

McCulloch accepted the State Bank position with some hesitation because he had no practical knowledge of banking. Despite his reservations he quickly gained a reputation as an excellent financier, and in 1856 he accepted the presidency of the newly formed Bank of the State of Indiana. That bank was established in 1855 with 20 branches and $6 million in capital. McCulloch held the position until 1863. Under his leadership the bank continued to grow and thrive, so much so that it was one of the only state banks in the country, along with the Chemical Bank in New York and several Kentucky banks, to weather the Panic of 1857 without suspending specie payments (although numerous private banks easily sailed through the depression with few difficulties).

McCulloch's career in government came about rather unexpectedly. He traveled to Washington, D.C., in 1862 as a representative of state bankers to oppose projected national banking legislation. Under the proposed legislation all state banks would be required to give up their charters and adopt federal charters. Proponents viewed the proposal as a means of curtailing the so-called "wildcat" banking that had spread throughout the West. Wildcat banks were free banks that issued more notes than they could continuously redeem, and they had come into being as a result of the liberal entry provisions of state free banking laws. Wildcat banks received their name because of their reputation for establishing branches in remote areas, "where a wildcat wouldn't go," which made it difficult to redeem their notes. Wildcat banking in Indiana occurred because the state made bonds eligible at par when they actually sold at 80 percent of par (or less) in New York. Indiana successfully ended that problem in 1855 when the state's free banking law was amended to set the legal price of bonds below the market price. The federal government, however, sought to eliminate all wildcatting by eliminating free banking. Many states resented the proposed restriction on free banking and chose McCulloch, a strong advocate of state banking, to represent their interests.

The Republicans who supported the free banking restrictions also had several other priorities, some of them more important than ending wildcatting. They were concerned with centralizing control of the money supply and financing the Civil War through bond purchases by banks. After discussing the legislation with the secretary of the treasury,

Salmon P. Chase, McCulloch became convinced of the necessity of a national currency. He realized that the notes of the state banks fluctuated, and that in turn hindered the collection of public revenues. After a careful examination of the legislation McCulloch satisfied himself that it would provide a secure circulation. Chase in turn was so impressed with McCulloch that he offered him the position of comptroller of the currency, a position entrusted with overseeing the solvency of all participating banks and with giving final approval to petitions for national-bank charters. The legislation passed. McCulloch accepted and in 1863 began to administer the new National Banking Act.

In one of McCulloch's first acts as comptroller he recommended an amendment to the National Banking Act to bring all banks under federal supervision by making it easier for banks to join the system. McCulloch's plan did not work as well as he had hoped. While most banks initially took out national charters, some held on to their state charters. Even 1865 legislation that placed a prohibitive tax on notes issued by state banks could not persuade those banks to change their charter allegiance. State capitalization requirements fell far below the prohibitively high national-bank capitalization levels, and many states had loose examination procedures. Many bankers, on principle, resented the federal government "snooping" into their affairs, and certainly they had little confidence in the recommendations of federal examiners who had no sense of the territory or the borrowers. Thus the number of state banks eventually increased rather than decreased, giving rise to the dual banking system of state and nationally chartered banks characteristic of the post-Civil War period.

McCulloch remained comptroller until March 1865. Chase had resigned as secretary of the treasury in 1864 to become chief justice of the United States, and his successor, William P. Fessenden, withdrew at the beginning of Lincoln's second term. On the recommendation of both Chase and Fessenden, Lincoln appointed McCulloch to the secretaryship. When Andrew Johnson succeeded Lincoln as president, Johnson kept McCulloch on as secretary, and he held that office until the end of Johnson's administration in 1869.

McCulloch, assuming the office of secretary of the treasury at the end of the Civil War, immediately faced the problem of the greenbacks (specially issued national paper currency not backed by specie) that the government had emitted during the war. Those notes lacked legal-tender status because there was not enough gold to meet the great demand of the war. At the end of the war more than $450 million in greenbacks circulated. Secretary McCulloch favored retirement of the notes and a return to the gold standard as soon as possible. He maintained that since the issue of greenbacks constituted only a war measure, they should not remain in force in peacetime. He recommended that the government authorize him to sell U.S. bonds, with the proceeds to be used to retire the greenbacks from circulation. Congress concurred with McCulloch, as put forth in a House resolution, and favored an early resumption of specie payments, pledging active cooperation to that end. Despite the resolution, however, Congress authorized the retirement of only $10 million in greenbacks in the first six months and $4 million per month thereafter. The government achieved the final retirement of greenbacks 12 years later.

After McCulloch retired from the treasury in 1869, he joined the banking house of Jay Cooke & Company as a partner. He established the London branch of the firm under the name of Jay Cooke, McCulloch & Company. When the American branch of Jay Cooke & Company failed in 1873, McCulloch reorganized the London branch under the name of McCulloch & Company and experienced continued success for some time.

In 1884 the current secretary of the treasury,

Walter Q. Gresham, resigned, and President Arthur asked McCulloch to resume the secretaryship. McCulloch held the position until the end of Arthur's term in March 1885. He held office too briefly to make significant contributions to the Arthur administration, although he presided over continued national deflation, which began during his earlier tenure. He also oversaw a period of steady and impressive national growth, caused in no small part by adequate—if not altogether ingenious—banking and monetary policies.

Hugh McCulloch spent his retirement years in Washington, D.C., writing *Men and Measures of Half a Century*, which was published in 1888. The book is a reflection of his career, his political experiences, and his personal opinions concerning the issues of the time. McCulloch died at his home, "Holly Hill," Prince George's County, Maryland, on May 24, 1895.

Publication:

Men and Measures of Half a Century (New York: Scribners, 1888).

References:

Deane Carson, ed., *Banking and Monetary Studies* (Homewood, Ill.: Irwin, 1963);

Davis R. Dewey, *State Banking Before the Civil War* (New York: Johnson Reprint Co., 1972);

Walter Nugent, *Money and American Society, 1865-1880* (New York: Free Press, 1968);

Fritz Redlich, *The Molding of American Banking: Men and Ideas* (New York: Johnson Reprint Co., 1968);

William Gerald Shade, *Banks or No Banks* (Detroit: Wayne State University Press, 1972).

Christopher G. Memminger

(January 9, 1803-March 7, 1888)

by Gary M. Pecquet

Southwest Texas State University

CAREER: Lawyer, alderman, city of Charleston (1824-1836); state representative, South Carolina (1836-1852, 1856-1858, 1877); school commissioner, city of Charleston (1855-1885); senator, Provisional Congress of the Confederacy (1861-1862); Confederate secretary of the treasury (1861-1864).

Christopher Gustavus Memminger, antebellum South Carolina politician and secretary of the treasury for the Confederate States of America, was born on January 9, 1803, in the Dukedom of Wurtenberg, Germany, and died March 7, 1888. Memminger was the only son of Christopher Godfrey Memminger and Eberhardina Elisabeth Memminger. His father served as quartermaster of the Prince-Elector's Battalion of Jaegers (riflemen) and died in battle shortly after the birth of his son. During the ensuing political turmoil of the Napoleonic Wars, Memminger's mother brought him to Charleston, South Carolina, along with his maternal grandfather, John Michael Kohler. Mrs. Memminger, exhausted from the trip, succumbed to disease, leaving her son an orphan. At the age of four, young Memminger was formally entered into the "Orphan House" of Charleston.

C. G. Memminger was adopted at age eleven by Thomas Bennett, a prominent South Carolina gentleman who served as governor. His foster father recognized young Memminger's intellectual potential and provided the boy with excellent tutors. In 1815, at age twelve, Memminger enrolled in South Carolina College. He excelled in college and began studying for the bar of Charleston in 1820. Four years later Memminger became a naturalized citizen of the United States and was promptly admitted into the legal profession.

During the early days of his legal career Memminger married Mary Wilkinson of Georgetown, South Carolina. He also served as alderman of the city of Charleston and sought to reform the

Christopher G. Memminger (courtesy of the New-York Historical Society)

system of public schools. He won election to the state House of Representatives in 1836 and became chairman of the Ways and Means Committee in 1838. During his legislative career Memminger expressed strong views concerning banking and financial matters.

According to Memminger, banks existed for the convenience of the public. They should not be regarded as mere money-making institutions. They were not to take advantage of special circumstances in order to advance the interest of stockholders at the expense of the general community. (That view did not prevent him from serving as the legal representative of the Planters and Mechanics Bank in Charleston.) As chairman of the Ways and Means Committee, Memminger sought to guard the funds of depositors and keep the banks solvent by regulating their activities. In 1840 he introduced "An act to provide against the suspension of specie by the banks of South Carolina," which the legislature passed into law.

In 1837 Memminger sided with President Andrew Jackson in opposing the Second Bank of the United States. But Memminger at that time held no such opposition to the principle of a similar state-run bank. (The state of South Carolina did own and operate its own bank–the Bank of the State of South Carolina–in competition with several privately chartered banks.) The state bank directors thought Memminger should promote "legitimate commercial interests" and refrain from conferring a special privilege upon a few people or establishing an artificial standard of value. During the 1840s Memminger's opposition to the state bank hardened. It had extended several loans that the legislature found questionable, and it grew increasingly controversial. Memminger opposed the recharter of the state bank in 1848. He argued for a separation of the state and banking, declaring, "One of the greatest curses in our state is the vile concubinage of bank and state." The bank had corrupted politics, politicians were meddling in the banking business, and "foul disease and corruption ensue ... Bank First, State Second, Bank Master, State Slave, Bank head, State tail." Despite such magnificent oratory, the Bank of the State of South Carolina remained in operation.

Memminger supported the concept of slavery, but he often opposed the radical secessionists early in his career. In 1830 he published a satirical essay entitled *The Book of Nullification*. During the 1850s Memminger acknowledged the right of secession but considered it to be a grave course leading to war. As the events of the late 1850s increased tensions between North and South, Memminger finally sided with the secessionist forces in South Carolina. In 1860 Governor Christopher Gist appointed Memminger to a special ambassadorial post to the state of Virginia. Memminger was elected to the South Carolina Secession Convention and reputedly helped draft the secession ordinance. The convention also selected Memminger to become one of South Carolina's senators in the new Provisional Congress of the Confederacy.

The Provisional Congress of the Confederacy met in February 1861. It consisted of delegates from the seven states that had already seceded. The congress adopted a provisional constitution and selected Jefferson Davis as the president of the Confederacy and Alexander Stephens as vice-president. The president quickly appointed his cabinet. R. B. Barnwell was reported to be Davis's first choice for the secretary of the treasury, but Davis sought to please the South Carolina delegation by choosing Memminger instead. (Memminger continued to serve as senator through 1862.) Financial historian John C. Schwab remarked on Memminger's Treasury appointment, "He had displayed no peculiar fitness for the position of organizer and head of Confederate finances; and it must be said, while holding that position, his leadership evoked much criticism and little commendation." But Schwab also remarked, more charitably, "It is doubtful whether any other secretary would have handled the Confederate finances in a very different or more successful way."

Secretary Memminger patterned the Confederate Treasury along the same lines as the United States Treasury. By June 30, 1861, most of his appointments were made. The most critical function Secretary Memminger had to perform was to secure the necessary funds required to operate the new government and prosecute the war. The Provisional Congress reenacted the customs duties in effect under U.S. law before secession, but the receipts from those taxes fell to a trickle after the Union naval blockade went into effect. Memminger recommended internal taxation as early as May 1, 1861, but the Confederate Congress expressed considerable reluctance to adopt such new taxes because many believed that the war would last only a short time, and the central government did not yet have the administrative machinery to lay and collect the taxes.

The Congress did enact a war tax on August 19, 1861, which imposed taxes to be collected by the state governments. Legislators intended to utilize the existing tax-collecting machinery of the state governments without establishing a new administrative bureaucracy. The purpose of the act was completely defeated by the states, however. Only three of them actually laid and collected the taxes. The remainder borrowed the funds used to pay their share of the war tax.

Memminger had no recourse but to raise funds through the printing of Confederate treasury notes and the sale of Confederate bonds. He secured the support of Confederate currency by the Southern states. He persuaded Governor Thomas O. Moore to pressure Louisiana banks to suspend specie payments in November 1861. By then, all banks throughout the South had to accept Confederate treasury notes on deposit. All the state legislatures accepted Confederate currency in payment of taxes and public dues by January 1862. Those moves paved the way for the massive issue of Confederate treasury notes and their widespread acceptance by the public.

Memminger opposed proposals making Confederate treasury notes the official legal tender of the land because by March 1862 the notes circulated on par with bank notes. The law was unnecessary and would only arouse suspicion, he argued. Moreover, a legal-tender law might adversely affect creditors in the aftermath of the war.

The Confederacy also relied heavily on loans. The Provisional Congress approved its first loan act on February 28, 1861. The act authorized the Treasury to issue bonds valued at up to $15 million, bearing 8 percent interest payable semiannually in specie. A special export duty on cotton was earmarked to repay the loan, and Memminger was able to float successfully the amount of the loan by selling it at par value to Southern banks and the public. The bond sale remained the major debt of the Confederacy. Should the Confederacy have won the war, the export tax would have been collected and the loan repaid. On August 19, 1861, the Confederate Congress authorized a $100 million loan. That loan also paid 8 percent interest, but no special revenue source secured it, and consequently the bonds sold at market values below the $15 million loan. During 1862 and 1863 the Confederacy experimented with loans backed by Confederate cotton. In January 1863 Memminger indicated that most of the Southern states had better credit than the Confederate government itself and recommended that each state pledge to honor its quota of Confederate bonds. The states refused to approve the funding scheme, however.

Despite Memminger's urging, the Confederate Congress refused to enact any major taxes during 1862. That meant more treasury-note issues and bond sales, and that meant rampant inflation. The price of one U.S. gold dollar in Richmond increased from $1.10 in Confederate currency during the summer of 1861 to $1.50 by the following summer and to $3.00 by November 1862. During December 1863 the price of gold hit $20.00 Confederate. Only about 10 percent of Confederate government expenses were financed via taxation, and most of those taxes were enacted during the latter stages of the war.

The Confederate Treasury managed to maintain the values of Confederate bonds close to Confederate currency until the final months of the war. One-hundred-dollar bonds of the $100 million variety sold for $98 to $120 in Confederate treasury notes for most of the war. Traditional economic theory would predict that nominal interest would reflect expectations of rampant inflation and adverse war news (the Fisher effect). The Confederacy anchored the nominal interest rates by the use of call certificates. They originally earned 6 percent and could be converted into cash at their face value upon the pleasure of the holder. By the use of those certificates, war news and adverse inflation induced bondholders to alter their cash positions rather than bid up nominal interest rates. (The impact of adverse war news and inflationary expectations were fully evident in the gold prices of both Confederate currency and bonds.)

In the absence of substantial revenues, Memminger proposed to relieve the inflationary pressures by inducing the public to buy more bonds. Under the Funding Act of March 23, 1863, the holders of Confederate currency were given deadlines to convert their cash into bonds before interest rates fell to 7 percent. Call certificates were reduced to 5 percent interest. That approach proved inadequate to stem the tide of inflation in the face of massive currency issues to finance the war.

At the persistent urging of Memminger, the Confederate Congress enacted tax legislation during 1863 and 1864. The Tax Act of April 24, 1863, imposed an 8 percent ad valorem tax on those who held numerous commodities or any kind of money on July 1, 1863. It also imposed a 10 percent tax on the profits from the sale of various commodities. It imposed a license tax and an in-kind tax on agricultural produce. The law also provided for a graduated income tax to become effective on January 1, 1864. The marginal tax rates increased from 5 to 15 percent on all income other than salaries (which only carried a 1 to 2 percent tax rate). An even more comprehensive tax was enacted on February

Five-dollar Confederate note carrying a portrait of Memminger (Bureau of Engraving and Printing, U.S. Department of the Treasury)

17, 1864. The revenue from both of those acts, however, collected less than $180 million (less than 10 percent of Confederate war expenditures).

By July 9, 1863, federal troops occupied the entire Mississippi River Valley and severed the Trans-Mississippi states from the rest of the Confederacy. It became very difficult to communicate with the western region. The Confederate Congress, upon Memminger's recommendation, established an almost autonomous Treasury Department for the region. Peter W. Gray became the treasury agent of the Trans-Mississippi Department and attended many of the duties performed by Memminger in the East. The western Confederacy never received the authority to print money, however.

On December 7, 1863, Memminger recommended a sweeping monetary reform to the Confederate Congress. He hoped that by forcing the conversion of outstanding treasury notes into bonds, the value of future treasury-note issues would be enhanced and the Confederacy could be financed for another year. The Confederate Congress debated Memminger's proposals, and arguments from various special interests emerged. The congressmen from states that had been occupied by federal troops favored a drastic repudiation of the currency, while those from Confederate-held states favored more modest reform measures. In the end the Congress passed the Currency Reform Act of February 17, 1864. That act pleased no one and eventually led to Secretary Memminger's resignation.

The Currency Reform Act divided Confederate treasury notes into four classes by denomina-

tion. Most of the currency could be subject to a 33 percent tax beginning in April. Those funds could then be exchanged for a new issue of Confederate currency at the rate of three old dollars for two new ones. Outstanding treasury notes of the $100 denomination could be used to purchase 4 percent bonds before April and would lose two-thirds of their value on that date. Thereafter, those notes would cease to be tax receivable but would only be accepted in payment for 4 percent Confederate bonds. Moreover, the $100 bills were subject to a 10 percent tax on their face value every month after April. The $5 notes were subject to the 33 percent tax beginning in July instead of April, and the Confederate one-half-, one-, and two-dollar bills would retain their full face value without depreciation. All currency except the small bills was subject to a 100 percent tax beginning on January 1, 1865. That is, they would become worthless. Before that time, those holding the old currency could convert it into new currency at a three-for-two rate or exchange it for 4 percent bonds or certificates.

The plan significantly differed from Memminger's recommendations. He had favored an immediate repudiation, not a gradual one. He wanted the old notes repudiated in April, not the following January, and he did not recommend the three-for-two currency exchange. He had asked for $1 billion in new bonds. The Congress only authorized half that amount. Most important, Memminger did not want the bonds and certificates to remain tax receivable during 1864. The entire point of his proposal was to maintain the value of future issues by the 1864 taxes. The Congress defeated that purpose by allowing the old currency to be convertible into tax receivable assets.

The Currency Reform Act of 1864 provided another source of trouble for a region already destined for military defeat. Ordinary people had trouble calculating the proper prices for retail purchases while the various denominations of currency depreciated at different rates. The Confederate Treasury had to use a considerable portion of its new currency to refund the old notes rather than make necessary war purchases. Although the reform act seems to have kept inflation in check for the summer of 1864, by fall the price of gold soared once again. Memminger did not wait that long. He resigned his position in the government on June 15, 1864, because the Congress repeatedly refused to accept his recommendations on taxation and currency matters.

George A. Trenholm succeeded Memminger as treasury secretary and held the office until the fall of the Confederacy. His appointment by Davis did not represent a repudiation of Memminger's policies because Memminger frequently had conferred with Trenholm during his term in office. Trenholm was a leading Southern businessman who had been active in blockade-running expeditions. While Trenholm had a more conciliatory style than Memminger, the Congress generally ignored most of his suggestions nevertheless. As did his predecessor, Secretary Trenholm proposed a plan for reducing the currency in circulation. A bill embodying that recommendation passed the House but met opposition in the Senate and failed in a conference in February 1865.

Following the war Memminger was granted a full presidential pardon in 1867 by Andrew Jackson for his activities in support of the insurrection. He resumed his law practice and remained active for the duration of his life. In 1868 he became president of a newly formed company engaged in the manufacture of sulfuric acid and the superphosphates. In 1873 he became president of a railroad company. Following Reconstruction in 1877, Memminger won election to a term in the South Carolina legislature from his former district. Again he chartered the Ways and Means Committee, seeking to im-

prove the educational system of the state. Education had been a lifelong concern to Memminger. He had served as commissioner of the Charleston schools for more than 30 years beginning in 1855 and had served another 32 years on the executive board for South Carolina College.

After Memminger's first wife died in 1878, he promptly married her sister, Sarah Wilkinson. He died of natural causes on March 7, 1888, survived by his second wife and eight children.

Publications:

The Book of Nullification. By a Spectator of the Past (Charleston, S.C., 1830);

Address of the Hon. C. G. Memminger, special commissioner from the state of South Carolina, before the assembled authorities of the state of Virginia, January 19, 1860 (Richmond, 1860).

References:

Jefferson D. Bragg, *Louisiana in the Confederacy* (Baton Rouge: Louisiana State University Press, 1942);

Henry D. Capers, *The Life and Times of C. G. Memminger* (Washington, D.C., 1893);

George K. Davis and Gary M. Pecquet, "Interest Rates in the Civil War South," *Journal of Economic History* (forthcoming, 1990);

John M. Godfrey, *Monetary Expansion in the Confederacy* (New York, 1978);

Gary M. Pecquet, "Money in the Trans-Mississippi Confederacy and the Confederate Currency Reform Act of 1864," *Explorations in Economic History*, 24 (April 1987): 218-243;

John C. Schwab, *The Confederate States of America, 1861-1865: A Financial and Industrial History of the Civil War* (New York & London: Scribners, 1901);

Larry Schweikart, *Banking in the American South: From the Age of Jackson to Reconstruction* (Baton Rouge: Louisiana State University Press, 1987);

Schweikart, "Secession and Southern Banks," *Civil War History*, 31 (June 1985): 111-125;

Richard C. Todd, *Confederate Finance* (Athens: University of Georgia Press, 1954);

Wilfred B. Yearns, *The Confederate Congress* (Athens: University of Georgia Press, 1960).

Archives:

Secretary Memminger's official reports and correspondence have been compiled into several volumes that are available at Duke University and on microfilm at the National Archives.

D. O. Mills

(September 5, 1825-January 3, 1910)

by Lynne Pierson Doti

Chapman College

CAREER: Cashier, Merchants' Bank of Erie County (1847-1848); general merchant, Sacramento, California (1849-1850); president, Bank of D. O. Mills (1850-1862); president, Bank of California (1864-1872, 1875-1878); regent and treasurer, University of California (1868-1880).

D. O. Mills was one of many who came to California during the gold rush, but he found more wealth could be gained by supplying the everyday needs of the miners than by working with pick and pan. Before his immigration to California he was cashier of a bank in Buffalo, New York. Although he had that experience in banking, his reputation for honesty needed local verification before he could be trusted with the miners' and saloon keepers' funds, so, like many pioneer bankers in California, Mills first became a merchant.

With his eastern banking experience, and probably one of the most staid demeanors in the state of California, the word "respectable" quickly and permanently attached to his name. His reputation led to his enticement by William C. Ralston into the founding board of the Bank of California, capitalized at $2 million when it opened in 1864. Although he carried the title of president, Mills spent little time at the bank and retired in 1872 to spend more time in New York. He remained a director, however, and when the bank verged on failure in 1875, Mills came to the rescue. He later liquidated all of his California businesses, donated large sums to the University of California and to the state, and transferred his main residence to New York.

The fourth son of James and Hannah Ogden Mills, Darius Ogden Mills was born on September 5, 1825, in Westchester County, New York. His father was a prominent businessman in the town of North Salem, the center of the surrounding agricultural and grazing district. He served the town as postmaster and justice of the peace, and owned several

D. O. Mills (engraving by Alexander H. Ritchie from a photograph by Napoleon Sarony)

businesses. He had enough wealth to furnish even his fourth son with a good early education at North Salem Academy. The family moved to Sing Sing (later Ossining, New York) when James Mills bought a hotel and dock there, and Mills attended Mt. Pleasant Academy. At that excellent school he displayed talent in mathematics and evidence of his father's business acumen. The hotel did not do well, however, and the family's financial state declined when James Mills died in 1841. D. O. Mills finished his schooling the next year and, at seventeen, secured a clerkship in New York.

As a clerk Mills continued to develop his business skills and also a reputation for integrity. In 1847 a cousin on his mother's side invited him to

Buffalo to join in a banking venture. The cousin, E. J. Townsend, allowed him a one-third interest in the bank, the Merchants' Bank of Erie County, which operated under a special charter, accepting deposits and issuing notes. Mills was made cashier, a prestigious position equivalent to vice-president, with responsibility for investing the bank's funds. He made many friends and established a reputation among other bankers that served him well for many years.

He may not have been as contented as he appeared to be. News of the California gold rush stirred the longings of even the most settled young men of the day. Mills's two brothers, James and Edgar, were among the first to succumb to gold fever and embark on the long journey around Cape Horn. One evening Mills joined two of his friends, William R. Rochester and Joseph Stringham, to share leisure hours. Stringham, an older man working in the exchange business, knew of the gold already arriving from the mines. His stories inspired the young men, and suddenly Rochester proposed that the three of them go to California to take advantage of the opportunity. At once they all agreed and spent the night excitedly making plans to leave within a fortnight. The gray dawn and objections from families and business partners cooled Rochester's and Stringham's ardor. While most of Mills's relatives were no less strident in their objections, Mills's cousin Townsend supported the idea. Townsend offered to tend the bank alone and furnish Mills with credit in return for a share of any of the profits of the venture. In December 1848 Mills, without his friends, boarded a ship with a travel plan in hand that proposed to carry him to the Isthmus of Panama and overland to the Pacific shore, where he planned to travel to San Francisco on the first trip of the steamboat *California*.

In Panama, Mills encountered a chaotic situation. Gold seekers arrived there daily. Overland transportation was arduous; jungle heat, bandits, and malaria abounded. Even if a party crossed the isthmus, northbound steamers rarely arrived as planned because any ship that docked in San Francisco stood little chance of departing again. Sailors deserted their ships for the California mines, and merchants who found little other shelter for their wares eagerly occupied the empty hulls. Each month wharves stretched farther into San Francisco Bay to reach arriving ships, and dirt and debris replaced the bay's shoreline. Realizing the unlikeli-

hood of completing the voyage and frustrated by the circumstances–stranded with roughly 3,000 others on the isthmus–Mills and many others boarded a British ship southbound for Peru in search of an alternate means of transportation to California. At Callao, Peru, the sailing ship *Massachusetts* was engaged to take 100 of the forty-niners to San Francisco at a cost of $10,000. While the crew prepared the ship for the voyage, Mills visited Lima.

The trip north proved no more pleasant than preceding events. Mills was evicted from his private cabin by other passengers and spent most of the voyage dangling above the ship's decks in a lifeboat. On June 8, 1849, the ship arrived at the headlands of San Francisco, but the captain was reluctant to enter the bay. Mills and several others left the ship and secured a small boat. They stored their possessions on board and rowed through the Golden Gate.

Once in the city, Mills used his remaining funds to secure a stock of goods. He and a fellow passenger took the stock inland to Stockton. They sold the goods, but not at a profit. Several lessons resulted from that experience. Mills gained the trust of a ship captain, learned which goods sold most easily, and determined that Sacramento would be a more profitable center of operations than Stockton. With two old friends, with whom he became reacquainted in San Francisco, Mills determined to try merchandising again.

The trio purchased a variety of goods to fill a small schooner headed toward Sacramento. The venture represented a terrific gamble, since the freight bill alone totaled $5,000, the partners still owed for some of the goods, and their cash on hand stood at $40. As they unloaded the products, Mills quickly arranged their sale, collecting enough cash to pay the freight bill. With the remaining merchandise he established a store and gold exchange business. His brothers soon joined him in the operation.

Despite the success of his business and the unpleasantness of his earlier travel experience, Mills promptly embarked on a trip to the East. He took $40,000 in profits back to his partner in New York. Instead of closing their joint venture, however, Townsend added to Mills's funds, and together they purchased new goods for the California market. In the winter of 1849-1850 Mills returned to Sacramento. Among the goods shipped from New York was a large safe, which became the foundation for "The Bank of D. O. Mills," jointly owned by Mills, his brothers, and Townsend. Mills served as president of one of Sacramento's first banks.

Townsend and James and Edgar Mills continued as partners in this business until 1852, when Townsend withdrew. Edgar took over a branch of the bank in Columbia, which it had established in 1850. Columbia was the commercial center for one of California's most productive goldfields, and more than $55 million worth of gold dust passed over the counter of this branch.

D. O. Mills retained ownership of the Sacramento bank until 1862. By then he had established himself as California's most prominent banker. "The Luck of D. O. Mills" became the California phrase for good fortune. Beyond his luck, Californians considered Mills to possess foresight, integrity, and decisiveness. Never did he venture into town without wearing a high-collared white shirt and black suit and tie, which became his trademark. His bank accepted deposits of gold nuggets and dust, and the depositor received bank notes or credit at one of Mills's correspondent banks in the East, where the depositor's relatives or creditors could withdraw the funds. Loans were made with the notes, which formed the backbone of Sacramento commerce. Examples of those notes, the bank's large gold-scales, and other bits of bank memorabilia provide the decor for a current Sacramento restaurant called "The Bank of D. O. Mills."

By 1857 Mills decided he needed a vacation. He had married Jane Templeton Cunningham in 1854 and wanted his New York wife to see the vast wilderness of the West. To travel in comfort he outfitted an entire wagon train and traveled over the Rocky Mountains and Utah desert to Salt Lake City. He found the Mormon residents restless and suspicious. That year the "Utah War" had engulfed them, and among Mills's party was a representative of the federal government, which had sought to restrict the Mormons' freedom. Although Mills found the Indians friendly, he fled after some westbound travelers murdered Indians and caused an uprising.

To allow time for travel and leisure, Mills sold one-third of his bank to his brother Edgar and another to Henry Miller and retired from active management. Edgar became president of the bank, creating from it the National Gold Bank of D. O. Mills in 1872, then the National Bank of D. O. Mills & Company in 1883. Edgar Mills died in 1893, and the presidency passed to Henry Miller's

son Frank. The bank survived until it was purchased by California National Bank in 1925.

Shortly after giving up the management of the Sacramento bank Mills was approached with the idea of lending his name to another venture. William C. Ralston, a San Francisco banker and businessman, wanted to start a new bank that would be the state's largest from its inception. Ralston wanted the bank large enough to support a wide variety of industries, the fantastic production of the silver mines, and the blossoming trade with Mexico and the Orient. Naturally, Ralston contended, the state's foremost banker should be among the founders. Mills subscribed for 2,000 of the first 20,000 shares and was elected president. The founders soon added $3 million in additional funds, all paid up in gold. The Bank of California opened in July 1864 as the first bank in California to incorporate under an 1862 law permitting commercial banking.

Although Mills was president, he clearly planned to let Ralston run the bank from his position as cashier. Mills made his home in New York with his wife and two children and traveled extensively. He returned to California occasionally to reside at his estate at Millbrae and to consult on the operations of his Sacramento and San Francisco businesses. He built an impressive office building in San Francisco that still stands, served as regent and treasurer of the University of California, and was a charter trustee of the Lick Observatory.

Ralston made the Bank of California pay well. He gained control of most of the silver mines of the Comstock Lode in Nevada and made extensive investments in furniture factories, woolen mills, a cigar company, the railroads, and more. Predicted connections with the Orient also materialized; Ralston even provided Japan with financial assistance to purchase a locomotive and the Comstock silver used in their coinage. Ralston emerged as a public figure, and his personal habits became increasingly flamboyant. The public linked expensive horses, houses, diamonds, and actresses with his name. The conservative Mills could not have been comfortable with the situation.

The Bank of California encountered difficulties in 1869 and again in 1872. Silver prices had fallen, and lack of progress in the Sutro tunnel that was planned to link the mines to the eastern side of the Washoe Range, lessening dependence on the Bank of California's mills and rail lines, threatened the bank's grip on Comstock business. Furthermore, the completion of the transcontinental railroad brought competition to the many San Francisco industries Ralston had supported, and those industries started to falter. The manager of the Virginia City branch of the Bank of California, William Sharon, was indicted for conspiracy while running for a U.S. Senate seat. Mills, who had objected to hiring Sharon when Ralston first proposed it, wanted his resignation. When the bank's board of directors met on February 19, 1873, the state the bank had reached appalled Mills. The bank had loaned $3.5 million of the bank's capital to Sharon and the overextended Ralston. They were unable to pay interest on these loans, much less reduce the principal. Mills demanded the pair assume full personal responsibility for the debts. An agreement to that effect was drawn up and signed by Mills, Ralston, Sharon, and J. D. Fry, a business associate of Ralston's.

Ralston's debts did little to moderate his habit of conspicuous consumption, and Mills asked to be disassociated from the bank. His fellow directors realized that the departure of this paragon of sound banking would damage the reputation of the bank, particularly among the New York and foreign correspondent bankers Mills knew from his travels. To avoid a negative public reaction Mills remained on the board of directors, while Ralston was named president in June 1873. Mills issued a statement that the bank had never been in better shape, that "all the investments were sound," and departed for a world tour, leaving directions that his stock should be sold and his name be omitted from the list of directors for the following board meeting.

Mills returned from his trip dismayed to find himself still on the board and his 5,000 shares of stock still unsold. Not the sort of person to cause a fuss, he merely sold all of his shares, knowing that precluded his reelection to the board. Mills left town again, thinking his connection with the Bank of California had ended.

The situation at the bank continued to deteriorate. Ralston was involved in a new project, the construction of the largest and most elaborate hotel west of Chicago. Millions of dollars went for Angel Island bluestone, fine woodworking, tapestries, silk hangings, custom rugs, china, and a multitude of luxurious and innovative features, until even Sharon expressed alarm. The bank lost its dominance of the Comstock. Banking competitors entered the scene. The Nevada Bank of San Francisco was capitalized

at $5 million, and many of Ralston's depositors took their funds to the new bank. In December 1874 Ralston made a last attempt to gain control of a silver bonanza through the Ophir mine. He hired a broker who bought one-third of the mine's stock before the price soared. "Lucky Jim" Baldwin made enough money selling his share to Ralston to build a hotel and theater of his own. Sharon also sold his stock in Ophir, to pay the costs of his second, successful campaign for the Senate. But the stock's price dropped as quickly as it had flown. In a series of panics and recoveries, the market established a volatile but continuous decline.

On August 26, 1875, the market experienced a sharp drop, one that proved fatal to Ralston's fortune and that nearly destroyed the Bank of California. Bank of California cashier Thomas Brown anxiously noted the lack of coin in his vaults. Drained by financing the shipment of a very large wheat crop, and difficult to replenish due to the recent East Coast bank panic and recession, the coin in the city had dropped by nearly one-third since January. At the bank the morning hours saw steady activity. Mills worked at his desk. He had recently returned to town and discovered his name still listed among the directors. (Ralston had purchased 250 shares in Mills's name to keep the connection.) Sharon was also present. At the stock market, volume surged as prices on Comstock shares dropped. Sharon's broker, on the floor at the time, heard a rumor that Sharon was selling to pay his bank debts. Depositors descended on the Bank of California. Ralston had pulled his bank through numerous panics in the city, but his efforts proved fruitless. He ordered payments to cease only twenty minutes before the bank's normal closing time. The largest bank on the West Coast had failed.

The directors met the following morning. Mills revealed that he had loaned Ralston $750,000 in the few days since he had returned. It was discovered that this money had been used to retire an oversubscription of stock, that it had been insufficient to retire all of it, and the stock outstanding exceeded the capital of the bank. Ralston himself owed a large portion of the bank's debts. The situation seemed hopeless. The directors' first action was to ask Mills to request the resignation of the president. Mills proceeded to the adjoining room.

When he returned, the directors decided they had no option save bankruptcy. The newly retired

Ralston sought relief from the heat and stress with a swim in the bay, where he apparently suffered a heart attack. He died on the beach after rescue attempts failed.

While the state mourned Ralston's death, the bank directors sought a solution to the banks' problems, which quickly contaminated the other institutions on the West Coast. They reinstated Mills as president, and William Alvord, San Francisco's former mayor, was named vice-president. Examination of the bank records revealed $19.5 million in liabilities, $4.5 million of which Ralston owed. Ralston's paper was sold for $1.5 million. Mills, Sharon, and Thomas Bell worked to raise additional funds, including personal moneys, to reopen the bank. Also, the Oriental Bank Corporation of London granted $1.25 million to guarantee the redemption of the Bank of California notes. In total nearly $8 million was raised to support the bank, allowing the board of trustees, on September 30, to vote to reopen.

On October 2 the iron doors of the Bank of California building were thrown open to the cheers of the gathered crowd. Braced for a run with $2.5 million in gold coin on hand, by one o'clock Mills announced that deposits unexpectedly exceeded withdrawals. The stock exchange opened again, Ralston's Palace Hotel opened, and California entered a new era.

Mills was the man for that new era. Collar still high, the fifty-year-old was the type to lead the bank and the state from mining speculation to new investments: the telegraph; wheat, rice, and beef exports; timber; and the Southern Pacific Railroad to link the coast. Bankers organized a clearinghouse, which applicants could not join without the approval of their peers. The state required banks to publish statements of their condition, and in 1878 a state bank commission was set up. At that time Mills considered his job finished and again proclaimed his retirement.

He resigned the presidency of the bank in favor of Alvord, sold his office building in San Fran-

cisco, his interest in the Sacramento bank, his Tahoe timberland, and his other California investments. By 1880 he had no further business to attend to in California. He resigned his trusteeship with the university, leaving a $75,000 endowment for a chair in moral and intellectual philosophy. To the state where he had fared so well, he presented a statue, "Columbus before Queen Isabella," which was placed in the rotunda of the state capital.

In New York, Mills continued his business and philanthropic interests. He gradually invested his large wealth in many businesses. He became a director of Erie Railroad, the Lake Shore & Michigan Southern Railway, the New York Central & Hudson River Railroad, North Atlantic Steamship Company, Metropolitan Trust, International Paper, and others. He built a commercial building on Wall and Broad streets and Exchange Place that was the city's largest. In the public interest he presented to the city a $100,000 building on the Bellevue hospital grounds for the purpose of training male nurses, and he became a trustee of the Metropolitan Museum, the Museum of Natural History, the American Geographical Society, the Fordham Home for Incurables, and the Carnegie Foundation. He started a hotel in New York that provided room and board to young workingmen at reasonable prices. In his later years he continued to travel, collected art, and enjoyed the company of his children and grandchildren. He often spent winters at his California home at Millbrae, where he died on January 3, 1910.

References:

Ira Cross, *Financing an Empire: History of Banking in California* (San Francisco: Clarke, 1927);

George Lyman, *Ralston's Ring: California Plunders the Comstock Lode* (New York: Scribners, 1937);

Neill Wilson, *400 California Street: The Story of The Bank of California, National Association and its First 100 Years in the Financial Development of the Pacific Coast* (San Francisco: Bank of California, 1964).

David Halliday Moffat, Jr.

(July 22, 1839-March 18, 1911)

by James E. Fell, Jr.

United Banks of Colorado

CAREER: Messenger, assistant teller, New York Exchange Bank (1851-1855); teller, A. J. Stevens & Company (1855-1857); cashier, Bank of Nebraska (1857-1859); book dealer, Denver, Colorado Territory (1860-1866); adjutant general, Colorado Territory (1865-1867); cashier, First National Bank of Denver (1867-1880); treasurer, Denver Pacific Railroad (1867-1880); treasurer, Denver South Park & Pacific Railroad (1873-1880); owner, Colorado mining operations (1870s-1911); president, First National Bank of Denver (1880-1911); director, treasurer, Denver, Utah & Pacific Railroad (1880-1883); director, Denver Tramway Company (1885-1911); president, Denver & Rio Grande Railway (1887-1891); director, Denver Union Power Company (1890-1911); director, Denver, Northwestern & Pacific Railroad (1902-1911).

David Halliday Moffat, Jr., was arguably the leading businessman in nineteenth-century Colorado. For more than 30 years he served as president of the First National Bank of Denver, then the leading bank in the Rocky Mountains. Through the bank and his numerous investments in mines, railroads, and other ventures, he played a leading role in Colorado's development from 1860 to 1911.

Moffat was born on July 22, 1839, in Washingtonville, New York, the youngest of the eight children of David H. Moffat, Sr., and Eleanor Cutter Moffat. The family was moderately prosperous but hardly wealthy. The elder Moffat operated a store that apparently offered some banking services on the side. The younger Moffat went to work there at an early age.

Moffat left home at the age of twelve and moved to New York City, where, legend has it, he spent his first night in a packing crate. He soon found a job as a messenger at the New York Exchange Bank—a humble position, but one that helped launch his career in banking. By 1855 he

David Halliday Moffat, Jr. (courtesy of the Colorado Historical Society)

had advanced to the position of assistant teller. After four years in New York he joined an elder brother in Des Moines, Iowa, where he became a teller with A. J. Stevens & Company. In 1857 another group of entrepreneurs offered Moffat the position of cashier if he would move farther west to help start a bank in Omaha, Nebraska. Moffat accepted the challenge, but that bank failed in the recession that followed the Panic of 1857.

A short time after Moffat relocated in Omaha, an exploring party found gold in the Rocky Mountains, some 500 miles west. The discovery touched off the Pike's Peak gold rush of 1859. A year later Moffat succumbed to gold fever and departed for the new settlement of Denver City. He was then twenty-one years old—tall, lean, and ambitious, a young man with a receding hairline and a penchant for good wine and fresh oysters.

When Moffat arrived in Denver in March 1860, he did not initially go into the banking business. Instead, he formed a partnership with C. C. Woolworth and opened a stationery, book, and tobacco store; he also served as assistant postmaster and as the Western Union agent, working in the back office of the stationery store. The business prospered, and Moffat soon branched out, joining another New Yorker, Jerome B. Chaffee, in some real estate and mining ventures. Moffat also quickly made friends with Denver's leading figures, such as territorial governor John Evans.

Despite his mercantile success, Moffat eagerly wished to get back into banking. As early as 1863 he and others petitioned the U.S. comptroller of the currency to charter a national bank, but that initial effort failed because the group did not have enough capital. Moffat and his associates had to wait until they enlisted the aid of Evans, Chaffee and Eben Smith, a prosperous mine owner. Evans had political muscle in Washington, and Chaffee and Smith had the money necessary to capitalize a bank. In 1865 the comptroller finally granted a charter establishing the First National Bank of Denver; it quickly bought out the firm of Clark, Gruber & Company (founded in 1859 to purchase gold dust, mint coin, and provide commercial banking services) and opened for business, the first national bank in the Rocky Mountains. In 1867 Moffat was elected cashier.

As the 1860s and 1870s passed, both Moffat and the bank invested heavily in all phases of Colorado's economy. Moffat himself demonstrated a particular interest in railroads, notably the local lines that connected to the larger transcontinentals as well as the lines building west into the mountains. Those enterprises included the Denver Pacific, which brought the first railroad to Denver; the Denver South Park & Pacific, which built westward into the Rockies; and the Kansas Pacific, which came west across the plains. Few individuals contributed more to Colorado's railroad development than Moffat. Even after he sold his interest in those roads, he and the bank continued to invest in others.

In 1880 Moffat succeeded Chaffee as president of First National. Except for the sharp downturn that followed the Panic of 1893, the late

1800s were generally prosperous times in Colorado, and the bank enjoyed a period of vigorous growth. Moffat put his imprimatur on virtually every phase of the bank's activities—at one point, he owned nearly 75 percent of the stock—and his personal investments came to be nearly indistinguishable from those of the bank.

Over the years Moffat continued to invest in mines, particularly at the boom camps of Leadville in the late 1870s and 1880s and Cripple Creek and Creede in the 1890s. Those mining ventures had close ties to Moffat's railroad investments because Moffat and his associates quickly built spurs wherever possible to bring out the ore.

By 1902 Moffat was sixty-three years of age. He had built a fortune of $8 million and enjoyed the respect as the leading businessman in Colorado. He might have retired and enjoyed the fruits of his labor. Instead, he launched his most ambitious business venture, the Denver, Northwestern & Pacific Railroad, the so-called "Moffat Road." Moffat wanted to cross the front range of the Rockies northwest of Denver, tap various coal and agricultural areas, and build on to Salt Lake City and San Francisco.

When launched in 1902, the road was capitalized at $20 million. Denver's business elite invested heavily, although the board consisted principally of the officers of the First National Bank. Construction began immediately, but the difficult terrain slowed construction and drove up costs. The key was surmounting the continental divide at 11,700-foot Rollins Pass. Moffat's engineers recognized the need for a 6-mile tunnel under the divide, but that proved impossible in the short run. Instead, they laid rail over the pass. Costs mounted dramatically; heavy winter snows disrupted service, and an entire town seemed to live under the railroad's snow sheds during the winter.

Once across the pass, other problems befell the road. One was the growing opposition of Edward H. Harriman and the Union Pacific Railroad, whose line from Cheyenne to Salt Lake City ran only a few miles north. It was said that Harriman and his associates blocked Moffat's increasingly desperate efforts to raise capital. The Panic of 1907 further frustrated Moffat's efforts to attract money, and his mines began to play out.

By then, Moffat and First National Bank faced serious trouble. He had sunk almost his entire fortune into the railroad, and the bank had committed such an enormous sum to the project that it was in precarious shape–so much so that in 1908, the bank examiner wrote that because of the bank's investment in so many of Moffat's interests, many of them weak, he could not testify positively to its solvency.

Concern over the financial condition of the line absorbed much of Moffat's last years. He made numerous trips to New York to obtain more capital. Finally, in 1909, he managed to obtain a $4 million loan from Hallgarten and Company, but that constituted little more than a stopgap measure.

By 1911 Moffat was in failing health, but the financial demands of the railroad kept him traveling constantly in search of capital, particularly because the Hallgarten loans came due in May. But the sands of his life were fast running out, and he would not see the road to completion. While on another fund-raising trip to New York, he died suddenly at the Hotel Belmont on March 18, 1911.

In the months that followed came the public denouement. The "Moffat Road" was forced into receivership and the First National Bank to the brink of collapse, although it survived through the stewardship of the Leadville banker A. V. Hunter and the support of the Denver business elite. Creditors closed in on the Moffat estate, however, and

Moffat's wife, Frances, daughter Marcia, and nephew Frederick G. Moffat were left with very little. And rumors surfaced–never completely resolved–that Moffat had committed suicide because of his hopeless financial position.

Ultimately, the Denver, Northwestern & Pacific emerged from bankruptcy as the Denver & Salt Lake Railway and was completed to Salt Lake City. Later it merged with the Denver & Rio Grande Western Railway. In the 1920s public funds built the Moffat Tunnel under the continental divide and eliminated the costly route over Rollins Pass. The tunnel is the most direct railroad route between Denver and Salt Lake City.

References:

Eugene H. Adams, Lyle W. Dorsett, and Robert S. Pulcipher, *The Pioneer Western Bank–First of Denver: 1860-1980* (Denver: First Interstate Bank of Denver and State Historical Society of Colorado, 1984);

Harold A. Boner, *The Giants' Ladder: David H. Moffat and His Railroad* (Milwaukee: Kalmbach, 1962);

Steven F. Mehls, "David H. Moffat, Jr.: Early Colorado Business Leader," Ph.D. dissertation, University of Colorado, 1982.

Archives:

The papers of David Halliday Moffat, Jr., are at the Denver Public Library.

Monetary Expansion/Contraction and Elasticity

Banks created money in the nineteenth century by issuing notes against reserves (gold and silver held in their vaults). In the antebellum period, banks issued their own notes, and after the National Banking Act of 1863 national banks issued national bank notes. But the principle remained the same–banks emitted far more notes than they had reserves to redeem them. Such activity constituted "fractional reserve banking," whereby banks kept only a fraction of their total deposits on hand in their vaults and loaned out the rest.

In theory antebellum banks could increase the money supply by issuing more notes, and they could either issue the notes with or without additional specie. If the bank had no additional specie reserves, the additional note issue would threaten to place a strain on the convertibility of the notes to specie. Conversely, banks could contract the money supply by refraining from issuing notes even though their deposit base expanded. Sudden shifts in the economy could cause depositors to rush to banks to withdraw their funds, which banks often had tied up in long-term loans. Such occurrences could cause banks to fail. As banks failed, the loans normally created by the deposits they held were liquidated. Bank failures therefore accelerated contraction.

Contemporaries termed the ability of the banking system to expand and contract without disruption of the economy "elasticity." Achieving elasticity proved difficult in the nineteenth century because every fall farmers sold their crops, contracting the system as buyers drew upon their deposits before the farmers paid back loans. Each spring farmers needed new loans for planting, although no new deposits may have come in to back such expansion. Bank reformers in the late 1800s sought to solve the problem of elasticity more than any other. The Federal Reserve System, created in 1913, resulted from their efforts.

See also:

Nelson W. Aldrich, George F. Baker, Federal Reserve Act, Charles Christopher Homer, John Jay Knox, Jacob Schiff, Frank Arthur Vanderlip, Amasa Walker.

–Editor

John Pierpont Morgan

(April 17, 1837-March 31, 1913)

by Albro Martin

Bradley University, Emeritus

CAREER: Clerk, Duncan, Sherman & Company (1857-1860); manager, J. Pierpont Morgan & Company [New York agent for George Peabody & Company] (1860-1864); partner, Dabney, Morgan & Company (1864-1871); partner, Drexel, Morgan & Company (1871-1895); partner, J. P. Morgan & Company (1895-1913).

J. P. Morgan, as he is most frequently referred to, is one of the leading figures in the history of American banking and was the foremost practitioner of investment banking during its evolution into modern form. At his death in 1913 he ranked as one of the half-dozen most famous men in America, the acknowledged leader of such fundamental trends in American economic development as the reorganization of the railroad system and rationalization of much of heavy industry. He also rescued the commercial banking system as it existed before the creation of the Federal Reserve System. The power that he and his staff of able lieutenants wielded was highly controversial in American public affairs during his lifetime, and the changes they wrought have not yet fully become a part of the American consensus.

Few fathers ever laid a firmer foundation upon which their sons and heirs could follow in their footsteps than did Junius Spencer Morgan. Even fewer sons have made so much of the advantages thus received or fulfilled their fathers' faith in them so completely as "Pierpont," as Morgan was known by family and close friends. The Morgans had been firmly planted since the earliest days of the colony in the thin but rewarding soil of Massachusetts. The founder of the line, Miles Morgan, the son of a Welsh merchant of Bristol, England, came to America in 1636 and soon joined Col. William Pynchon's party of settlers headed for the Connecticut River Valley, where they founded Agawam, later Springfield. Whatever thoughts Miles Morgan may have had of himself as a scion of the merchant

John Pierpont Morgan (Gale International Portrait Gallery)

class, in America he and the next three generations of Morgans did what most immigrants to New England did: they farmed their original acres, enriched the community and the land with the cattle they raised, saved their money, and bought more land.

Using the Morgan family as a case, historians can trace the revolution that marked the rise of American commercial civilization during its first 200 years. The pioneers put their faith in "real" property, that is, land and its improvements. Even Morgan's grandfather Joseph Morgan, the first to be transformed from country squire to city dweller, stuck with real property. Morgan's father, Junius Morgan, came of age as the mercantile era was in full swing. By the time Morgan reached the age of seventeen, his father had established himself as an international merchant banker, in the business of buying and selling the kinds of vital goods and commodities that characteristically moved in international trade in the mid nineteenth century. The main goods were cotton, America's prime earner of foreign exchange before the Civil War, and, increasingly after 1830, English wrought-iron railroad rails, paid for by both the cotton exchange and the bonds of the railroad enterprises and several new midwestern states. That typified the era of trade in tangibles.

A banker, as the old style "sedentary merchants" had come to be thought of, had always made money by buying and selling the goods shipped between Europe, Africa, Asia, and the Americas. Increasingly, bankers dealt in foreign exchange and in making short-term, fully secured loans to highly reputable businessmen. Over the years men such as Junius Morgan learned the customs of international banking. They learned them well because they had helped create them, and they knew the consequences of failing to observe them. That environment prepared the way for the third and highest development of the banker's art: the conception, marketing, and monitoring of financial intangibles, that is, stocks and bonds, which J. P. Morgan and others perfected as a mechanism of economic development.

Junius Morgan had worked in his father's office during his free time as a boy, and at age fifteen he became a clerk for Alfred Welles, a merchant and banker in Boston. Five years later he moved to New York and entered into a partnership with Morris Ketchum, an important early figure in the railroad rails and supply industry. By 1836 Junius Morgan returned to Hartford, a partner in a wholesale dry goods firm renamed Mather, Morgan & Company. That year he married Juliet Pierpont, daughter of the Reverend John Pierpont, who possessed two features of a Boston Unitarian minister: a minor talent for poetry and an all-but-empty purse. John Pierpont Morgan was born on April 17 of the next year, on the eve of the first major American depression, and after him came four sisters but

no brothers, a fact that in due time ensured that his father's capital would pass almost intact to him.

Despite his family's attachment to Hartford, to which both father and son later gave generously for cultural institutions, greater opportunities beckoned from Boston. There, Junius spent the years from 1851 to 1854 as partner in J. M. Beebe, Morgan & Company, an important dry goods wholesaler. In 1854 Junius Morgan received a great opportunity to conduct business in England. While years would pass before American merchant banks operating in London would begin to share in the marshaling of capital within Europe, or even to tap the growing investible surpluses of English rentiers on a large scale, there was much business to be attended to for the accounts of American business concerns engaged in importing and exporting. One particularly successful American who had succeeded in London, then the financial capital of the world, was an aging bachelor named George Peabody. In 1854 Peabody actively sought a younger man to become his partner and continue the business after his retirement. Junius Morgan was by then one of the most prominent younger men in merchant banking in the small financial worlds of Boston and New York. In short order he received, and accepted, an offer from Peabody that eventually matured into J. S. Morgan & Company, the most prestigious American international banking house on the European Continent.

J. P. Morgan was only seventeen when the family left the United States to make a home in England. His parents returned only on frequent visits, but all the Morgans remained U.S. citizens throughout their lives. J. P. Morgan had inherited his father's tall, muscular build and his countenance, which was more intense than handsome. His health was uncertain, however, and he had to leave school more than once as both digestive and skin problems came and went. No such thing as organized athletics then existed in American schools, and Morgan does not seem to have spent much time in exercise. Neither in Europe nor in America did bourgeois fathers waste much time on activities outside the countinghouse, and Morgan, who took to the environment of the mid-Victorian office as enthusiastically as his father, had almost the same kind of apprenticeship. But he had the priceless advantage of a European education, if a rather disorganized one, during which he became fluent in French and German and acquired a cosmopolitan air that befitted a young man with great expectations in the booming field of international merchant banking. A good student in all his subjects, except when poor health sapped his enthusiasm, he demonstrated an especially strong aptitude for mathematics.

The Junius Morgans established themselves in modest middle-class comfort in London and sent their son to a Swiss boarding school in Vevey, where he remained from November 1854 to April 1856. Only nineteen and wanting to "starch up my German," he enrolled in the University of Göttingen, which had produced a number of Ph.D.'s for America's budding universities. He starched up his mathematics even more than his German, thus refining analytical powers that proved invaluable in an era when the human brain was the only computer available. From August, when the term ended, to spring of the following year, Morgan toured the Continent as far east as St. Petersburg and then enjoyed five very social weeks during "the season" in England. But he spent his days mostly in his father's countinghouse, tirelessly copying letters and documents for which neither typewriter, carbon paper, nor copying machine yet existed. But then it was time, he felt, to strike out on his own, and in August 1857 he took up a clerkship in Duncan, Sherman & Company, New York. He never forgot what he found going on around him, as the nation sank rapidly into the bitter depression of 1857-1859.

The flexibility and adaptability of American banking in that early period is revealed in the skill with which many, but by no means all, managed to readjust their credit policies to reflect new realities. In less than a year Morgan had received a liberal education in such pitfalls as the collapse of commodity prices and the inadequacy of the American banking system, still based on state-chartered, poorly regulated banks, and the money stringencies that made a joke of such firms as Duncan, Sherman's mere balance-sheet solvency. He saw the firm with which his father had so recently cast his lot, still called Peabody & Company, all but driven to the wall because it could not collect the credits it had extended in America, and for which it had more than $2 million in trade acceptances on its books. The value of friends was brought home to Morgan when the Bank of England agreed to lend Peabody's firm the huge sum of £800,000 upon its securing the written guarantees of 13 London banking establishments. Back in New York, Morgan watched as his own firm, Duncan, Sherman, strug-

gled successfully to raise a fraction of that amount to bail itself out. But there was far from enough gold to bail out everybody, and the process of survival of the fittest proceeded to its end, in a financial world where "fittest" meant the best past record and the best connections. By the end of 1858 many could see civil war coming in America, and normal trade would probably suffer accordingly, but the bankers had prepared themselves for the unknown. In London, Peabody had turned the leadership of the firm over to Junius Morgan, and J. P. Morgan, in New York, prepared to go into business for himself.

Morgan's years of experience with Duncan, Sherman, added to what he had already learned about international banking, made the serious, mature young man eager to go into business for himself. At Duncan, Sherman he had traveled extensively as far south as New Orleans, learning the cotton trade and doing an occasional commodity deal on his own. When the fortuitous conditions of international trade presented an opportunity, he seized it on the spot. His first independent transaction consisted of the purchase of a cargo of coffee, a commodity in which he lacked experience but about which he educated himself quickly, and he made a good profit. Antibusiness historians have sneered at the fact that Morgan hired a substitute to take his place in the Civil War draft, while he engaged in buying and selling gold. But the existence of a functioning market for gold, at a time when it had gone out of circulation but was still required, for example, to pay import duties, was a boon to the wartime economy. Substitutes were available for about $300. Vincent Carosso, leading historian of the House of Morgan, notes that 73,500 other American males did likewise, among them John D. Rockefeller. Future Americans would find equally legal and no more honorable means of avoiding an unpopular draft.

Morgan's wide acquaintances, both financial and social, in New York and the influence and help of J. S. Morgan in London guaranteed that no one at Duncan, Sherman should think of him as an ordinary junior clerk. He apparently set his own work schedule and late in 1859 was in London, discussing his future plans with his father. He was also seeing in London a great deal of a young American friend, Amelia Sturges, the daughter of old family friends, who had visited the Junius Morgans in England. His father counseled a delay in his son's big move, but by 1860 he was ready.

From Duncan, Sherman's offices at 11 Pine Street, in the heart of New York's financial district, Morgan moved in 1862 to a one-room office at 53 Exchange Place, which he shared with James Tinker, who imported iron rails, and one clerk who sufficed for both. Morgan's first firm seldom conducted anything but the most elementary transactions in foreign exchange, mostly selling bills of exchange for Peabody & Company. Years later he described a typical day in his routine to his son. "He once told me," J. P., Jr., recalled, "that he used to sell bills all the morning, post his books in the afternoon, and spend the evenings writing letters to George Peabody & Co., or to his father." A businessman's correspondence in those days comprised virtually the heart of his business (as any business historian lucky enough to find and be admitted to his subject's papers knows), for in it he exchanged the items of commercial intelligence on which he based successful deals; he cemented existing business relations and solicited new ones; and above all, he maintained the all-important confidential nature of business. A fair hand and a confident command of English grammar were vital, and many an ambitious young man, lacking them, found the way to even a modest clerical situation blocked. Morgan possessed the basics, but in addition he had a powerful, influential father to whom he remained devoted and with whom he shared long narratives of their activities though separated by an ocean.

By his late twenties Morgan was a striking young man, six feet tall and powerfully built, with piercing blue eyes and a bushy mustache. He shared rooms with George Peabody's nephew, Joe, at 45 West 17th Street, New York, then a fashionable part of the city. He was not drawn to the more casual social world outside the family circles of his many friends in the city, to whose homes he was constantly invited for Sunday dinner, followed by hymn singing. These occasions seem to have furnished all the gaiety he required. His company opened its offices six very full days a week except in summer, when some gave a Saturday half-holiday, and he spent most of his evening reading and attending to his ever-bulging correspondence portfolio.

This tranquil existence was interrupted in 1861 by the Hall Carbine affair. Reform-era American historians never hesitated to paint Morgan as a war profiteer in their narrative of his role in financing this weapons deal, but modern writers have revealed their accounts to be pure claptrap, no better than the sensational newspaper stories that appeared at the time and on which authors such as Gustavus Meyers based their diatribes. The U.S. House of Representatives investigated the matter and adduced no evidence against Morgan, but he learned a good lesson in the importance of public opinion to a banker, and the great care to be taken in the selection of clients.

On September 2, 1861, James Goodwin, J. P.'s cousin, joined Morgan's little firm as a partner, the immediate reason being J. P.'s imminent departure for Europe following his marriage to Amelia Sturges. The couple sailed for Liverpool and proceeded to Algiers, where they hoped that the climate would hasten her recovery from a supposed cold that had settled in her lungs. But the cold proved to be tuberculosis, and she died in Algiers in February 1862, after only four months and ten days of marriage.

Morgan remained a widower for more than three years, but he was also well aware of the old adjuration "one must marry." He had been confirmed in March 1861 as a member of St. George's Episcopal Church, of which he would always remain a loyal supporter and valuable layman. There he met Frances Tracy, whom Carosso describes as "slim, attractive, and charming" and "widely admired for her quiet beauty and vivacious personality." They married in May 1865, and once more Morgan left the office to Goodwin while he and his bride went off to London, Paris, and Switzerland for the honeymoon. Those long absences on the Atlantic and in Europe may seem to moderns as no more than pleasure junkets, but they were anything but vacations for J. P., who spent most of his days in talks with his father and in studying his firm's dealings. By that time the firm had attained a volume and a character that betokened big things to come for J. S. Morgan & Company and the Morgans' fledgling New York office as well.

On October 1, 1864, the partnership and firm of George Peabody & Company was terminated and succeeded by J. S. Morgan & Company upon the retirement of George Peabody. Morgan's only partner was Charles C. Gooch, who had been with the old firm and had a 17.5 percent interest in the new firm, of which the capital totaled £350,000. The partners had the use of the greater part of Peabody's capital, however, which the old bachelor obligingly left on interest with the firm until his death in 1869. The new firm remained in the same offices, at 22 Broad Street, for more than half a century. To all outward appearances, relates Carosso, it might have been a typical New York brownstone residence, for clients and customers entered not a bustling banking hall but a dignified "front parlor" where a partner greeted them. Once negotiations with clients reached the contract stage, of course, all legal niceties would be scrupulously covered, but the deal itself would conclude with a handshake by men who lived by the assertion that "my word is my bond."

In the same year Morgan strengthened his firm's standing by taking as a senior partner Charles H. Dabney, who as partner in charge of the accounts at Duncan, Sherman had taught young J. P. how to keep and interpret accounts by the still primitive system of that day. Dabney contributed only $25,000 of the new firm's total capital of $350,000, but he received 40 percent of the profits. Morgan contributed $200,000, most of which his father furnished, and also took 40 percent of the profits. Junior partner James Goodwin, who with the help of his father put in $125,000, received the remaining 20 percent. Dabney's presence put Dabney, Morgan & Company, as the new firm was called, on an equal footing with other international merchant banking firms in New York, but its basic strength remained the general realization on both sides of the Atlantic that Dabney, Morgan was the American representative of J. S. Morgan & Company. The two firms, often acting as one, competed for what was still the bulk of the business: financing international trade and dealing in commodities that ranged from coffee to guano and, above all, British wrought-iron railroad rails for the 36,000 miles of new railroad routes that America built in the boom years between the end of the Civil War and the onset of the 1873–1879 depression. The new railroads needed much more than rails, however. Their demands for fixed capital on long term proved all but insatiable for the next forty years. Looking at the heritage and the prospects of both Morgan firms, it is obvious that the rags-to-riches myth had little application to international banking. The real story lies in the brilliance with which they capitalized upon what they received from the past.

Before the coming of the railroad, the imperative for civilized societies to marshal large aggregations of capital and commit it, more or less irrevocably, to a single purpose was very small. Until the nineteenth century, such needs came almost exclusively from the sovereign, as the modern states of Europe made war after war upon each other in their struggle to assert national independence. The genie that ultimately escaped from the bottle and multiplied the needs for capital at a dizzying pace was technology. In the first quarter of the nineteenth century that genie had not been fairly uncorked, for the yearnings of society for better transport of humans and their produce had yielded nothing more demanding than the canal systems that were, nevertheless, the first large, impersonal, capital-intensive business enterprises. As the 1820s waned, however, men had learned not only how to harness steam, but to use it so efficiently that a boiler small and compact enough to travel at 20 miles an hour, while producing steam for an engine hauling several times its weight, made possible the first practical "locomotive" (literally, that which is capable of moving from one place to another). And once men had given up the notion that it required a paved vehicular roadway upon which to run and grasped the potential of the flanged wheel rolling on the iron rail, the steam railroad emerged as the key to man's mobility for the next 100 years.

New eras grow out of old eras, and it is the job of the historian to explain the continuity. The huge amounts of capital that such firms as the Morgans' marshaled to bring the world railroad system into being represented the wealth created by previous "great ideas," which the owners thereof desired to reinvest more profitably than ever. England, and to a lesser extent western Europe, offered the first such pools of surplus capital that entrepreneurs could tap, and the securities of one generation of railroad ventures after another found their way into the strongboxes of already successful entrepreneurs on that side of the Atlantic. The rails of Welsh ironmongers would be paid for with such securities, the profits of Lancashire textile magnates followed, and (in America as in Europe) ocean-shipping profits also financed the revolution in inland transportation. The process did not always produce happy results. Gradually the century that had brought so much that was new became the old century. The premier sources of wise investment counsel and the banking firms capable of effective monitoring of investments after they had made them led to the new field of investment banking. In

Europe the names of Rothschild and Baring stood out; in America the name of Morgan would eventually carry the most weight.

J. P. Morgan knew what the swift-moving changes in material civilization meant, and how deeply they ran. He had watched as his father, at the risk of giving his firm a "speculative" cast in the minds of ultraconservative Englishmen, helped Cyrus W. Field finance his Atlantic cable. Beginning in the 1850s Junius had stubbornly held on to his shares of the Atlantic Telegraph Company, and when the cable finally became a dependable means of instantaneous communication after ten heartbreaking years of repeated attempts, the value of the shares exceeded many times the £10,000 of Peabody & Company's money Junius had invested in them. Toward the end of the century, a few years after Alexander Graham Bell had beaten Elisha Gray to the patent office with a workable idea for a telephone, J. P.'s firm laid the financial foundations for the modern telephone system. The younger Morgan had also followed his father's handling of the tangled financial affairs of the Ohio & Mississippi Railroad in the 1850s and had seen how much more than peddling securities was involved in successful investment banking. Eventually this rickety railroad realized its true promise and comprised the Baltimore & Ohio's (B&O) extension west of Wheeling, West Virginia, to St. Louis. Whenever the B&O's impulsive president, John W. Garrett, got in financial hot water, which occurred frequently, he found that he could not do without the Morgans.

Morgan hastened to prepare himself to follow his father's lead in marshaling capital for the booming railroad industry. Only two months after crews had made the first tenuous rail connection between the east and west coasts at Promontory, Utah, he and his family set out on a trip to San Francisco. Even in the private Pullman sleeping car that the party had at its disposal, it was a strenuous venture, but the grandeur of a land that few Americans knew except from the paintings of such men as Albert Bierstadt awed everyone, and J. P. saw firsthand how much work remained before modern transportation could win the West. He also saw how great the capital requirements would be. Before leaving on the trip, he had conferred with Dabney and Goodwin (who seems to have done most of the spadework) on the firm's "first loan of any considerable size," as Goodwin put it: a $6.5 million issue of 7 percent first mortgage bonds of the Kansas Pacific Railway, whose huge land grant formed part of the collateral. The deal was concluded just a few days before J. P. returned to find the American railroad cauldron bubbling more vigorously than ever.

The railroad age called for much more than the passive ministrations of the old-style merchant banker. In 1869 the first struggle for control of a strategically important railroad property that J. P. was involved in came to be known as the "Susquehanna War." The 142-mile Albany & Susquehanna Railroad connected Albany and Binghamton, New York, forming a potentially valuable link between the anthracite coalfields of eastern Pennsylvania and New England. The road's promoter and president, Joseph H. Ramsey, found himelf beset by the powerful forces of Jay Gould and James Fisk, whose Erie Railroad connected with the Susquehanna at Binghamton. Fisk longed to form a through line to the New England market by connections with either the Boston & Maine or the Boston & Albany railroads at Albany. Real warfare ensued, with both forces at loggerheads inside a tunnel located midway on the route up the Susquehanna River. The governor had to call out the state militia to restore order and run the line under the command of a general until the legal and money men could straighten things out.

J. P., a vigorous thiry-two-year-old, consented to preside over a meeting of stockholders called to settle the issue. After much confusion, including at one point a split of the stockholders into separate meetings, Morgan succeeded in counting the proxies and declaring the Ramsey forces the winner. His most important service began at that point. A close friend of J. P. was Samuel Sloan, pioneer developer of the anthracite fields and president of the powerful Delaware, Lackawanna & Western Railroad, and bitter foe of Gould. Sloan used his influence to help J. P. merge the Susquehanna into the Delaware & Hudson Railroad and thereby frustrate Gould and the Erie in their efforts to break into the New England coal market.

By 1870 it was apparent to bankers on both sides of the Atlantic that providing America with the railroad facilities it required presented undreamed-of challenges. Indeed, although things drifted into abeyance during the middle years of the decade, no depression could restrain for long the inexorable advance of the iron horse, and the 1880s broke all records for new construction. There followed a decade of consolidation and rationalization of the fruits of this period of sometimes over-exuberant growth; after that came a period in which intensive development of the railroad system made even greater capital demands than the hectic years of extensive development. J. P. Morgan, strongly supported by his father and the family's invaluable connections, once more recast his firm, this time by a striking alliance with one of the oldest and most prominent families in American merchant banking.

On the eve of the American Revolution the second largest city in the British empire was Philadelphia. In the formative years of the nation the bustling city on the Delaware River estuary served as the financial capital of the new nation, in large measure because the first Bank of the United States (BUS) had been located there, and the much busier second BUS had established its main office there from its inception in 1819. Even before the statutory demise of the second BUS in the mid 1830s, however, Philadelphia had started to give way to New York in population, foreign trade, and financial importance. Most people attributed this development to New York's coup in obtaining easy access to the interior via the Erie Canal. Others said it was the unparalleled superiority of New York Port over those at any other place on the Atlantic seaboard. Either way, the low-gradient route of the chief trunk-line railroad between the seaboard and the Mississippi–the New York Central–soon sealed New York's preeminence for nearly a century.

The Drexel family had become a leader in Philadelphia banking circles under Francis M. Drexel, an Austrian immigrant, who died in 1863. His second son, Anthony J., took over management of the bank and in 1868 opened an office in Paris under John W. Harjes. The Drexel bank also had a New York office, but its poor performance demanded that it be provided with a more energetic manager forthwith. In 1871 Drexel called on Junius Morgan in London to seek the older man's advice. Their relations were very close, as J. S. Morgan & Company had been Drexel's correspondent bank in London and was almost as knowledgeable about Drexel's operations as they were. Morgan suggested J. P. as a partner for Drexel's New York firm, and the merging of two of the strongest American merchant banking families was soon arranged.

Drexel, Morgan & Company opened for business at J. P.'s old address, 53 Exchange Place, on July 1, 1871, with a capital of $1 million. Nearly all of the capital invested at that time was furnished by the Drexels, only $15,000 coming from J. P., whose contribution would be the management of the new firm. While Junius had a net worth of some $5 million at the time, his son's worth only totaled about $350,000. At that time half of the banks in the United States were still private partnerships and not subject to even the perfunctory regulation to which banks chartered under state laws or the National Banking Act were subject. Consequently, the leading private banks operated with great caution and sought as customers only individuals and firms of the highest character. The underwriting and distribution of American railroad bonds, in America and England, and only tentatively on the Continent, kept the partners busy from morning to night. The principals frequently found themselves passengers on the Cunard Line's *Etruria* or *Umbria*, or the White Star Line's *Oceanic*, which offered nine-day crossings to Liverpool (when their single screw propeller did not break its shaft or fall off in mid ocean). During the 1870s and 1880s the firm added junior partners, some of whom would become familiar figures in American finance as members of the firm, for example, Egisto Fabbri, Edward T. Stotesbury, and Charles H. Coster, who was one of the most knowledgeable American railroad experts in both finance and operation. In 1873 the firm moved into a new building put up by the Drexels at 23 Wall Street, an address ever afterward synonymous with American banking on the highest plane. By 1880 the firm employed 80 persons, all men.

An early undertaking by Drexel, Morgan, which it shared with other prominent firms, notably Seligman Brothers, Levi P. Morton, and August Belmont, involved refunding of the debt incurred by the United States during the Civil War. It was a frustrating business, as government officials were notoriously unpredictable until their signature was on a contract. Interest rates permitted by Congress were low, and the investing public refused to take the bonds except at unacceptable discounts as long as times were good and railroads' first mortgage gold bonds, bearing higher coupon interest rates and often discounted, were available. Interest rates, like prices in general, trended downward consistently to the end of the century, however, while first liens on railroad properties turned out to be less than an iron-clad guarantee of the soundness of many issues. By the end of the century government bonds sold at steep premiums, especially as Congress voted tiny budgets, the Treasury ran embarrassing surpluses, and no new bond issues were forthcoming.

Meanwhile a dilatory and politically conscious Congress sometimes had to be saved from itself, as when J. P. financed the army payroll without any prior guarantee of repayment from the government, to the extent of $2.5 million when Congress adjourned in 1871 without passing the appropriation bill. Such thankless tasks were made easier to bear when William H. Vanderbilt, son of the Commodore, who had died in 1877, sold some $10 million in government bonds through Drexel, Morgan at a steep premium. In the same year Drexel, Morgan participated in a $235 million gold refunding of U.S. debt bearing 4 percent and 4.5 percent interest, of which Morgan's firm took £55,000 for sale in England. During these years the chartered commercial banks grew in importance in investment banking, and Drexel, Morgan developed strong ties with the leading bankers, notably the First National's George F. Baker.

Drexel, Morgan, following the lead of J. S. Morgan & Company, found little opportunity in the bonds of foreign nations or enterprises in these years. Junius Morgan's successful flotation of the French loan that paid the heavy reparations demanded by Bismarck following the Franco-Prussian War had greatly added to his firm's prestige, but it was not representative of the general situation. American investors had no interest in foreign investments in these years, and Drexel, Morgan, while it joined underwriting syndicates along with Junius's firm, did not attempt to sell its allotment but sent them to London for disposal. Junius had some dealings in Argentina, a booming new nation upon which so many vain hopes would be pinned, but Drexel, Morgan steered clear of involvement except for such solid propositions as that of the Central & South American Telephone Company.

It was in the creation, underwriting, and sale of securities—mostly bonds—for the construction and equipping of railroad lines that American and European capital sources were most heavily and continuously tapped, and in railroading America reigned supreme. Clearly the expanding prestige and underlying financial strength of Drexel, Morgan and its London and Paris allies stemmed mainly from this fact.

In the 1870s Drexel, Morgan demonstrated both the will and the know-how to whip a leading railroad such as the B&O, which seemed to be constantly overextended, into shape and shepherd it through the first great depression (1873-1879) of the industrial age. In another decade or so the B&O, historically America's "first" railroad, had become an "attenuated nova," but the Morgans were riding higher than ever. The wealthiest man in America was William H. Vanderbilt, whose ruddy complexion, magnificent "Piccadilly weeper" sideburns, leadership in breeding and racing harness horses, and epochal public relations gaffe ("the public be damned") made him a symbol for the age of the "robber baron." His net worth, most of it represented by a 40 percent controlling block of the stock of the New York Central Railroad, hovered in the neighborhood of $100 million after he inherited it from his father in 1877, and when he died of apoplexy in 1885 it had doubled to $200 million. Vanderbilt was worried that his fortune was too concentrated in one area. The outrageous accusations that came out of the recently convened hearings by the lower house of the New York legislature under Alonzo Barton Hepburn concerned him even more and showed unmistakably that the politicians had looked upon the railroads as a means of making a political reputation.

In that context Morgan's network of contacts proved invaluable. Returning in 1879 from one of his frequent trips to Europe (he went at least once a year for the rest of his life), J. P. made the best of the opportunity to treat his shipmate, Billy Vanderbilt, as a captive audience on the subject of the management of large portfolios. Vanderbilt listened carefully, and the outcome was one of the biggest coups in investment banking to that day. Vanderbilt signed a contract to sell 150,000 shares of New York Central common at 120 through a syndicate headed by Drexel, Morgan & Company, which received an option to take another 100,000 shares. To this astonishing and unprecedented secondary offering of a security, yet another 100,000 shares were added.

English investors, weary of the boring 3 percent they received on domestic securities, nibbled at what seemed a once-in-a-lifetime opportunity, and a few conversations with London's most astute bankers and investors in genteel banking parlors and clubs soon produced for J. P. and his father the big breakthrough into British strongboxes that they had long sought. The Central was indeed a "good thing." It had confirmed control of the Lake Shore, which extended it from Buffalo to Chicago, and dominated entrance by rail to the western hemisphere's most important port. It was, if not the first, certainly the greatest and most efficient of the trunk-line railroads that operated over what was becoming the most heavily traveled trade route in history.

"Put all your eggs in one basket, and then watch that basket," said Andrew Carnegie when asked how he had established his fortune. J. P. Morgan knew that the people who bought New York Central common stock from his firm would expect him to watch *that* basket, and thus the firm's reputation for caring what happened to its issues after they had been sold was made. Morgan became a member of the Central's board of directors, and the firm opened an office in London for the sole convenience of English holders of Central stock. Drexel, Morgan's syndicate had established a price of $131 a share, and eventually the syndicate was a great success. But initially sales were slow, and most went to a few very rich men such as Jay Gould. The Morgans held on to theirs, banking the generous dividends, exuding confidence in the stock, and nervously watching the storm clouds of vicious rate competition that gathered in the railroad industry. American banking and American railroading henceforth were more closely allied than ever, a fact that produced at one and the same time the world's most efficient transportation system and a public relations problem that dogged both bankers and railroad men for the next century.

Nation-building and railroad-system-building were important contributions of such firms as Drexel, Morgan and their London counterpart, and they involved financing with more than a little risk. When Frederick Billings took over the shaky Northern Pacific Railroad project in 1880, for example, he proposed to Drexel, Morgan a $10 million financing in support of construction from eastern Montana on to the West Coast. He shortly increased this request to $40 million, an astounding sum for those days, but which nonetheless was oversubscribed. Drexel, Morgan had the vital cooperation of Winslow, Lanier & Company, August Belmont & Company, and J. S. Morgan & Company in comanaging the syndicate. The acceptance of such a large financing for a transcontinental railroad reflected the enhanced prestige of its new management under Billings, but also the remarkable enthusiasm for railroad building that made the decade of the 1880s the railroad decade par excellence.

Meanwhile, Drexel, Morgan was being called on more and more frequently to help nurse sick old railroads such as the Reading back to health. This valuable property, the leading factor in the anthracite coal business in eastern Pennsylvania, nevertheless had been badly managed by its former head, Franklin B. Gowen, who had killed himself. The reorganization went slowly as the late 1880s unfolded, and it all had to be done over again when the depression of the 1890s put the company in receivership. But out of the first round came the famous Morgan voting trust, which, as ultimately refined, gave the bankers absolute control of the company, its policies, and its management until the company attained prescribed performance goals. Drexel, Morgan was well paid for its work, but the $100,000 fee for supervising the trust was less important than the priceless contacts it made in America and Europe, the 5 percent fee ($1 million) for underwriting the $20 million bond issue, and the 6 percent interest it received on temporary cash advances during the reorganization. In the long run Drexel, Morgan benefited most from the continuing relationship thus established with the client, which made it, in effect, its banker. New business rises out of old business, and in a field of such rapidly increasing technical complexity, it does so regularly.

No banking firm in America, publicly chartered or private, had a bigger stake in the smooth operation of the American railroad system than Drexel, Morgan & Company. The bankers had placed many millions of dollars in American railroad securities with investors in the United States and abroad who depended upon the dividends and interest they paid. But the American railroad system was anything but tranquil as the new mileage built in the epochal decade of the 1880s was put in operation and went looking for traffic to carry. Formal passenger and freight tariffs, often ignored in the past, were now routinely replaced by negotiations that broke all of the common law definitions of what constituted "reasonable and proper" rates. Rebating, discrimination, even drawbacks (paying a valued shipper part of the tariff charged their competitors) constituted common practices, and the mighty trunk-line railroads did not escape. Adventurous parties attempted to "blackmail" the New York Central by duplicating its highly profitable main line from New York to Buffalo with the New York, West Shore & Buffalo Railroad. W. H. Vanderbilt had caved in a few years earlier when a syndicate headed by George I. Seney, president of New York's Metropolitan Bank, did the same thing with the "Nickel Plate" (New York, Chicago & St. Louis Railroad) between Cleveland and Chicago, but this time he decided to fight. He was convinced that the Pennsylvania Railroad was the power behind the West Shore. No tangible basis for believing this has been found, but Vanderbilt proceeded conspicuously to finance the South Pennsylvania Railroad, an abortive venture intended to parallel the Pennsylvania's main line on the south from Harrisburg to Pittsburgh. The situation was extremely delicate. Notwithstanding Andrew Carnegie's support, the new rail capacity was not needed, and if it had been completed and placed in operation the ability of even the trunk lines to earn their bond interest and dividends would have been jeopardized. J. P. Morgan threw all his prestige behind a settlement. Inviting Chauncey Depew, president of the Central, and George Roberts, his stubborn counterpart on the mighty Pennsylvania, on board his steam yacht, the *Corsair*, on a muggy July day in 1885, Morgan wined and dined the two men and then cruised up and down the Hudson past the city as he negotiated a compromise. The Central bought the West Shore, and the Pennsylvania bought what there was of the South Pennsylvania, which was only a few unfinished tunnels and the footings for a bridge at Harrisburg.

The newspapers the next day reveled in the exciting story of three men making such earthshaking decisions and noted that "rates are to be put back on a paying basis." But stability of rate schedules remained impossible under the primitive organizational structure of the railroads of that day, which gave great power to individual freight agents, and before the nation grew into its new railroad mileage. Congress intended the Act to Regulate Interstate Commerce (1887) to end the question of the role of the states in bringing order to the railroad industry, but in prohibiting pooling, the only form of concerted action with which the railroads had had any success at all, it foreclosed any constructive role for government regulation at that time. Morgan, believing that the act nevertheless did imply that rate pacts, as long as they did not provide for apportionment of tonnage or revenues, would be allowed–or, at least being determined to put this reasonable con-

clusion to the test–brought a number of leading railroad executives together in his Madison Avenue residence to organize what he called the Interstate Commerce Railway Association. Not all of those invited came, and of those who did few seemed to share Morgan's optimism. The Trans-Missouri (western) and Joint Traffic (eastern) rate bureaus took over the not inconsiderable accomplishments of the pool organizations, but the onset of depression in 1893, coupled with vigorous antitrust prosecution ending in Supreme Court decisions against the carriers, reduced the bureaus to a statistical function by 1898. Before the end of the century, however, the railroads revolutionized traffic management practices, and a volume of traffic descended upon the railroads that no one had foreseen. The situation changed overnight, it seemed, and America's railroads became the strongest element in its industrial picture. Drexel, Morgan & Company could take much of the credit.

From 1890 onward all occasions seemed to conspire to propel J. P. Morgan to first rank and finally absolute leadership in American investment banking. From then on the company went from one landmark financing to another, and its signal accomplishments, in the last stages of large-scale investment banking as it existed down to the Great Depression, are so numerous as to preclude more than a discussion of the most notable. Two events before the 1890s ended placed J. P. firmly in the driver's seat of the four firms–New York, Philadelphia, London, and Paris–that comprised what people freely called J. P. Morgan & Company. On April 8, 1890, Junius Spencer Morgan, who had retired from active participation in the Old Broad Street firm to a villa on the Italian Riviera, was killed in a carriage accident. He was nearly seventy-seven years old. His entire estate, amounting to some $12 million exclusive of art objects, went to his son after the usual bequests. Three years later the elder Tony Drexel died, and his son chose not to continue with the firm. In 1895 the name of the New York office was changed to J. P. Morgan & Company, and the Philadelphia office, while continuing to be called Drexel & Company, was made subordinate to New York under the supervision of Edward T. Stotesbury. The Paris firm became Morgan, Harjes & Company. J. P. was senior partner in each of the four.

What had traditionally operated as a private business–the underwriting of securities flotations by private interests—became painfully public when Morgan, now de facto leader of the American financial community, consented to help a desperate Grover Cleveland—a Democrat, but a conservative—over a major crisis in his second term. It had come rapidly. With the onset of the brutal 1890s depression, the jerry-built American monetary system, already creaking under the stresses of a modernizing world, threatened to grind to a halt. London remained firmly in control of international finance, and a nation's gold supply was vital, for gold was still considered the only "true" form of money in an age when fiat money ("greenbacks") with no gold reserve behind it was anathema, and the function of checking account money based on demand deposits in commercial banks was still poorly understood. The government required gold not merely to redress temporary imbalances in imports and exports, but to pay out over the counters of the U.S. Treasury and thousands of banks across the country to holders of paper money who wanted gold for whatever reason. The nation had argued and struggled for a decade and a half following the Civil War about the "money question" before the Treasury quietly resumed paying out gold in return for the nation's paper money, whether National Bank Notes secured by U.S. government bonds in the vaults of the issuing federally chartered commercial banks or U.S. Notes backed by nothing but the vague promises of Congress. Several years before, in the "Crime of '73," knowledgeable bureaucrats in the Department had—not just quietly, but silently—recommended dropping the silver dollar from the list of coins to be minted by the U.S. Mint, silver having been for some time too valuable in relation to gold to be used as a monetary metal at the statutory ratio. But by the late 1880s the world supply of silver had greatly increased with the opening of mines in the Rocky Mountain West. A rising tide of sentiment to remonetize silver was unmistakable. Moreover, inflationists demanded that Congress do so at a ratio so favorable (16 to 1) that, as sophisticated bankers knew, silver would be exchanged for gold as fast as the "cartwheels" (silver dollars) could be banged out by the Mint, and the nation would quickly find itself on a de facto silver standard, alongside such second-class nations as China, Mexico, and India. Indeed, gold already flowed out of the Treasury at alarming rates into hoards large and small as confidence waned, and the Treasury realized it would have to replenish stocks by selling bonds for gold.

But to whom? Americans would simply draw it out again in a meaningless short circuit. The gold would have to represent a net addition to U.S. stocks: that is, the bonds would have to be sold abroad, insofar as they could. Thus the Treasury could not market its bonds at auction, eschewing the services of bankers and brokers as it usually did. It would have to have the services of someone such as J. P. Morgan, who had the contacts, the influence, and the reputation for carrying out the obligations that huge sums demanded. There ensued an exhausting series of negotiations, carried on personally by Morgan and his senior associates by means of heavy use of the Atlantic cable to London and the Pennsylvania Railroad to Washington. In the end the syndicate that J. P. Morgan & Company formed along with August Belmont & Company and the Rothschilds as coleaders delivered to the Treasury 3.5 million ounces of pure gold, at $17.80441 per ounce, at least one-half from Europe, and undertook, moreover, to keep their eagle eyes peeled for a renewed threat to treasury stocks and to scrape up more gold if and when needed.

The affair of the gold purchases opened the floodgates to new excesses of American political demagogy, fanned by the opportunistic Joseph Pulitzer and his *New York World* newspaper. William Jennings Bryan grabbed the standard of "free coinage of silver at a ratio of 16 to 1" and ran it, almost literally, into the side of a stone wall: the American workingman's contempt for anything but "good, hard 'mun,' " meaning gold. Few Americans have ever understood the real issue or appreciated the profoundly valuable service that Morgan and his fellow bankers rendered the nation in this instance. Still, demagogy had its day, as it would for the rest of Morgan's life. Men such as Morgan knew that they would be vindicated, if at all, long after their deaths. Meanwhile, Jacob Schiff, head of Kuhn, Loeb & Company, remarked that Cleveland's action to save the gold standard showed "statesmanship, patriotism, and courage," and in our day a young John Fitzgerald Kennedy included Cleveland's highly unpopular policy in the crisis in his book *Profiles in Courage*. But there have been few to speak for the bankers, from whom, it seems, no good cometh.

At the same time that Morgan and his firms poured out their energies toward a solution of the gold crisis, which yielded them little compensation and much excoriation, they were heavily engaged in salvaging a large segment of the American railroad system. The depression of the 1890s sounded the death knell for the Victorian railroad corporation, often representing thousands of miles of railway built in anticipation of traffic that had yet to materialize, carried at rates for which no industry-wide stabilizing influence had been found, and paid for by funds raised by the sale of bonds at high "real" rates of interest. (Ten percent, twelve percent, or even higher rates of interest were more typical.) Many a western road had eagerly accepted a bonding company's offer that would net it barely 70 cents on the dollar when all discounts and commissions were deducted, to be paid back in perhaps 20 years in a period of constantly declining prices for the goods the shippers had to sell. By the late 1880s men such as John Murray Forbes, dean of Boston railroad investors, and his good friend James J. Hill, premier western railroad leader, anticipated stormy times. By 1893 railroads in many parts of the country struggled to pay such high rates of interest under such unfavorable economic conditions at a time when fresh capital could be raised at 3 percent on good risks and government bonds sold at nearly twice par, paying barely 2 percent.

Onerous interest charges were just one problem. The entire American railroad system needed rethinking and reorganizing. Many lines were strategically weak although their potential was substantial. Men such as Hill and Henry Lee Higginson, Boston investment banker, spoke freely of the need for massive consolidations into a few systems under sensible, cooperative system builders, and if J. P. Morgan said little, as was his lifelong policy, he surely thought so. As he told a Congressional investigating committee years later, "I like a little competition," but "without you have control, you cannot do anything."

By the end of 1893 some of the most respected names in American railroading were casting about for a way out of their difficulties. Without a bankruptcy law on the federal statute books in those years (the Constitution reserves this power to the federal government), railroad lawyers had learned to fall back on traditional receivership procedures well established in the equity branch of the common law. No bankruptcy courts, no bankruptcy judges: it was up to the railroads, their creditors, and their legal and financial counsels to work

Morgan at sixteen (courtesy of the Pierpont Morgan Library)

out the carriers' salvation. J. P. Morgan & Company and a few other prestigious and well-seasoned private banking firms found themselves in a position to furnish "one-stop" reorganization services in what was invariably beneath the surface of unpaid bond coupons, a highly complex set of problems requiring specialized experience of the highest order.

The oldest railroad in the nation–the B&O–and some of the newest, such as the Northern Pacific, defaulted on their bonds. So did all of the other transcontinentals except for Hill's Great Northern and C. P. Huntington's Southern Pacific. In the South, especially the Southeast, the jumble of poorly built, badly managed, and often looted railroads no more neared effective cooperation with each other than had the states of the Confederacy during the Civil War, and the results turned out just as badly. Many household names such as the Boston & Maine and the Erie were in extremis. The former road had been taken over by the Reading, which was about to join it on the receivers' bench. Morgan and his men put them all back on the track one way or another: the Erie, refinanced; the Boston & Maine merged with the New York, New Haven & Hartford, a constructive move until reformist Louis D. Brandeis got in position to place a well-aimed dagger in its back; and the Reading, which had once more fallen afoul of a megalomaniac leader, went through the Morganization process one more time. The leader, one Angus McLeod, refusing Morgan's directives, found himself out on the street and all but reduced to pushing the peanut wagon, which he had sworn he would rather do than take orders from J. P. Morgan. This was the age of anthracite, the fine, long-burning Pennsylvania hard coal that the Reading and the Erie were in a position to supply to the cold Northeast, and they would flourish in the coming 30 years of prosperity.

In the southeastern region, and in the far Northwest, the Morgan men left their deepest mark on the American railroad system. By 1890 the railroads of the South had been struggling from the ashes of the war to make themselves into efficient, rational transportation systems, with fair progress in the former and almost none in the latter goal. The one-crop system, carried on primarily by illiterate, malnourished, and sickly poor whites and blacks under a form of feudalism, caused a powerful drag on economic growth. Even those southern railroads in good shape were poor, while the worst were all but inoperable. They all chronically lacked long-term capital, and without it they could make no real improvement.

One important effort at consolidation of a number of railroads offering through service (with connections) from Washington, D.C., in the East via Richmond, Atlanta, Birmingham, and Chattanooga to St. Louis and Memphis in the West had been achieved under a holding company named the Richmond Terminal, dominated by the Richmond & Danville Railroad. It had steamed along gingerly as long as prosperity endured but sank promptly under the first blows of hard times. J. P. Morgan & Company's reorganization of the Richmond Terminal into a new railroad, the Southern—the best documented of the firm's reorganizations—reveals the vital importance of the small but vigorous group of lieutenants with whom Morgan had surrounded himself. The demanding work that he delegated to them called for nothing less than absolute devotion as day after long working day passed. Charles H. Coster, a Morgan partner, and Samuel Spencer,

hired as a consultant after he had told off the directors of the B&O Railroad (he had been president of the line), very largely created the new Southern Railway that emerged from the wreckage of the Richmond Terminal.

The Southern reorganization offered a classic example of the science of rebuilding a railroad in a financial sense. Morgan's firm had to evaluate all of the many issues of securities, from the first mortgage bonds of the most viable and strategically valuable line to the common stock of the most wretched (a few of which were excluded from the final system plan), and the managers had to find a place for them in the structure. Senior securities generally went unscathed; other issues of mortgage bonds had their interest rates reduced and in some cases were lowered to second mortgage status; the least valuable debt issues generally became preferred stock. The common was offered a place at the very end of the parade, namely, the shareholders were assessed a cash amount per share to raise funds for badly needed improvements, and if they refused to pay, their shares were canceled. Of course the Morgan "trademark" graced the reorganization: the voting trust, which endured until the preferred paid a dividend for a stated number of years. The Southern performed beautifully in good times thereafter, and sturdily in bad, and paid its obligations. Management steadily improved it when there were profits to be plowed back. In the 1970s recasting of the American railroad system, it merged with the Norfolk & Western, a highly successful coal carrier, and is one of the most profitable in the business. Coster and Spencer, whose services would have been invaluable to the railroad industry in the years ahead, did not fare so well. Coster, overworked when struck by pneumonia, died in 1900, and Spencer was killed a few years later by one of his own trains that rammed his business car while it stood at a wayside station.

The railroad reorganization in which Morgan took the greatest pride was the Northern Pacific (NP), to which he devoted more of his own time than most. Inefficiently and even corruptly built and operated, this transcontinental represented the first single enterprise all the way from the Mississippi to the Pacific and captivated the imagination of millions of Americans. Its leadership sadly lacked competence, however, and in the years just before it resorted to receivership in 1893, it had shown unmistakable signs of being operated primarily for the benefit of top management. Cynicism at the top inevitably produces cynicism in the ranks, and the true promise of the NP as a moneymaker was increasingly subordinated by operating employees who shirked their duties in a manner that outraged observers such as James J. Hill. Henry Villard, the line's now-and-then president, remained back East and gave only hit-and-miss attention to the railroad as he concentrated on other interests, notably the organization of the General Electric Company. Particularly infuriating to Hill, the NP had a practice of building parallel lines to his Great Northern (GN), the northernmost transcontinental, thus inciting rate wars, rate discriminations, and similar abuses that stem from lack of cooperation.

Hill himself had decided to go after the NP and run it in sensible tandem with the GN, and he would have except that the state of Minnesota challenged him in the courts. What he could not achieve by formal consolidation, he could attain by a "syndicate" of rich men acting in concert. The bondholders' committee of the NP, whose counsel had carried on endless negotiations and profited mightily thereby, welcomed the unbeatable team of Morgan and Hill, who reorganized the NP in one of the few examples of a "team" effort that reappeared in Morgan's career. But Morgan, ostensibly fearing cries of "monopoly," was in no hurry to turn control over to Hill and kept the voting trust alive. He insisted on naming two incompetents in turn as president of the reorganized and by then increasingly profitable line. The overworked Charles Coster bore the brunt of Hill's discontent, but when Coster died in March 1900, that was enough for Morgan, whose other lieutenants were more than fully occupied with great new projects that kept crowding in. That November Morgan wired Hill in St. Paul–Hill, in fact, was actually ensconced at the Netherlands Hotel a few blocks away, awaiting the outcome–as follows: "The voting trustees at their meeting two o'clock dissolved the voting trust. Many congratulations."

Three generations of historians and less objective observers have struggled to understand these events that repeatedly shook the financial world at the end of the old century. They have concentrated on them primarily as financial undertakings, designed above all to produce rich profits for the stockholders of the reorganized enterprises and fat commissions for the bankers who, as people once said about philosophers, "baketh no bread." Such bi-

ases, which are still a long way from having been outgrown, have gained strength from the fact that the bankers usually received large amounts of a new issue of stock in addition to management fees and commissions on new security issues underwritten. Few have bothered to note that stock–that is, evidence of equity in such profits as remain after all other claims, including bond interest and preferred stock dividends, have been satisfied–placed no necessary financial burden on the reborn enterprises. The par value, moreover (which many states still required of common stock shares) meant absolutely nothing. A large block of the new, untested common stock of a reorganized company that operated under a voting trust and was forbidden to pay any dividends until it reached a certain level of profitability nevertheless gave the bankers a share in the future growth of the company, if any, on the grounds that they would be largely responsible for it.

Few of the men in Morgan's firm, or even Morgan himself, could have articulated all they knew about the revolution that took place in corporate finance, and none of them devoted the time or talent to explanations, thinking, no doubt correctly, that no one would have believed them if they had. "College tack-head philosophers," as James J. Hill dubbed the unsophisticated faculties of the raw new state universities, routinely denounced all of this high-flown finance as mere thievery. But what should historians make of the obtuseness of the dignified, celebrated, and no doubt learned Harvard economics professor William Z. Ripley, who ranted against no-par-value stock (almost universal in modern times) and bemoaned the fact that in many cases the stock of certain companies, which may have sold in the hundreds of dollars, had been reduced to a few dollars by the money men–thus giving ample evidence that the company had been "looted"? None of the bankers' adversaries in public or intellectual life could propose rational alternatives to a system based on direction of troubled enterprises by a few powerful leaders of proven integrity.

At least this much was clear, however, to Morgan and a few other leaders in the field of investment banking: they bore a far greater responsibility than merely keeping their clients financially robust and busy making money and floating new securities. Preservation of committed capital, for which these men were more responsible than anyone else in the last analysis, was at the heart of the matter.

Morgan stood at the head of a group of remarkable men who nearly half a century before had taken upon their shoulders the job of coaxing the western world's flow of investible capital into enterprises of great social significance, bearing mainly upon the economic development of the United States, and for realizing the expectations held out by their prospectuses. Above all, they had to protect the capital in place from the many dangers, from within and without, to which the tentative character of human affairs subjected it, for if they failed in that, such capital would cease to reproduce itself and to yield the profits whereby it might grow ever greater in the future.

Envious Wall Streeters could hardly have believed, as the old century died, that the Morgan men would be handed yet more business of such proportions as the reorganization of the American railroad system. Railroads, however, were not the only industry that would feel the cathartic effects of the 1890s depression. They were America's first "big business," and for a long time, except for petroleum, the only really big business, that is, an enterprise of large, primarily fixed capital, widely owned by investors, and managed, at least day to day, by professional managers who seldom owned a commanding share of the company and often were not even rich men. Large-scale industrial (that is, manufacturing) enterprises blossomed rapidly, however, as the 1890s came to an end. If manufacturing, for example, with its thousands of production-line workers performing highly repetitive functions to turn out masses of goods, represented the mark of industrial America, it is only because of the notable events of the turn of the century that brought the virtues and the vices of consolidation and integration to American manufacturing.

Until the invention and perfection of the Bessemer and later the open hearth processes (both obsolete today) for making large tonnages of steel at low cost in the latter half of the nineteenth century, only one industry—petroleum and its products—had attained giant size and integrated structure. As late as the 1890s steel meant a few large, highly efficient producers of raw ingot steel and the prime staple finished product, railroad rails, around which were a highly undisciplined and largely uncoordinated mass of producers of finished goods, such as wire (thousands of tons of it, for enclosing the grazing lands of the West, for example); nails (the nation's biggest building boom so far was about to

begin); sheet, for a growing list of applications, most notably the tinplated cans in which an emerging food industry was packing more and more of the bounty of American farms; plate (much of it for what became Teddy Roosevelt's Great White Fleet as the American navy was rebuilt; tubes, required in great quantity for a nation that still looked to steam boilers for its prime energy source; structural shapes (columns, beams, and girders for the dawning skyscraper age); and so on.

The mightiest of the basic steel producers was Andrew Carnegie, for whom business, even when it was bad, was pretty good. Carnegie did not like a trend that he saw rising in the American steel business: uncoordinated integration, backward into blast furnaces, Bessemer converters, and even into ore properties and fleets of lake steamers, and forward into finished goods, by basic steel producers. If everybody did this, resulting excess capacity of the steel industry would destroy any hope of profitable operation. Meanwhile many a plant, especially those from which all the profits were regularly siphoned by family members who lived on their dividends, became ever more worn-out and obsolete. Their operating costs were high, but they had to keep turning out goods, for they had other fixed costs as well. Withal, the tariff kept prices up so that the industry circumvented a necessary death rate, which a free market would provide. Indeed, the statement still repeated in the 1980s, that the United States had excess steel-making capacity in the 1890s, is only a half-truth: the nation did not have too much low-cost capacity. The problem was how to concentrate production in the efficient mills that existed, maintain output at a profitable level—steel men knew, if statesmen affected not to, that future growth depended upon present profits—while still providing for the inefficient producers. A trust offered a logical solution, but the most successful of the trusts had fared badly under increasingly tighter application of the Sherman Antitrust Act of 1890. "The tariff is the mother of the trusts," opponents of booming capitalism shrieked, taking a potshot at their two most important perennial issues, even if most of them did not quite understand the shibboleth.

The sequence of events that produced the world's first billion-dollar manufacturing corporation, the United States Steel Company, in 1901, began in earnest in the early 1890s, with such figures as John W. "Bet-a-Million" Gates, who success-

*Morgan in 1889 (courtesy of the Pierpont
Morgan Library)*

fully consolidated small barbed-wire manufacturers
into larger ones and ended up with American Steel
& Wire Company in 1898. Another such consolidator was William H. Moore, who, in association
with Daniel G. Reid and William B. Leeds, did the
same thing with one small tinplate operator after
another until they ended up with such firms as
National Steel Company, American Steel Hoop,
American Sheet Steel, and American Can. Morgan
and his men had kept their eyes on them, and they
were delighted to work with Elbert Gary and Robert Bacon to arrange a merger of Gates's Illinois
Steel Company and the leading industrial beltline
railroad in the Chicago area, the Elgin, Joliet & Eastern, into the Federal Steel Company. A consolidation followed that included 14 of the nation's
largest steel tube manufacturers into National Tube,
which made 85.5 percent of the millions of miles of
steel tubing consumed by the nation each year.
These moves produced what Andrew Carnegie had
never faced before: a major, integrated, low-cost producer of finished goods that also made its own raw
steel. A customer had become a competitor, for
most of the tube companies had long rolled their
tubes from Carnegie ingots.

These aggressive men had pushed the American steel industry off dead center, and if J. P. Morgan had intended to get things moving, he got his
wish. Carnegie was not napping–he was "watching
that basket" of his. Some years before he had acquired lakefront property then used only for iron-ore docks, on the shores of Lake Erie at Conneaut.
He also acquired several railroad lines running between Pittsburgh and Conneaut, ultimately consolidated as the Bessemer & Lake Erie Railroad, hauling iron ore and other materials south to his steel
mills and finished steel north to connections at various points with all of the trunk-line railroads, all of
which eagerly wanted to carry his goods at competitive rates to all the world. It was a virtually impregnable position that no other factor in the steel
industry could match, or would want to, as long as
Carnegie remained a producer of raw steel. But
when he heard about the National Tube deal, he
charged back across the Atlantic from an extended
visit to Scotland and announced his intention to proceed immediately to build the largest and most efficient, fully integrated tube mill in the world at
Conneaut.

Gary, Bacon, and Carnegie's leading man,
Charles Schwab, realized that either there would be
a little cooperation or a lot of the worst kind of competition. Schwab talked up a merger of the Morgan
and Carnegie steel interests, while both principals remained in the background. Schwab, main speaker
at the annual dinner of steel men at New York's University Club in December 1900, launched his trial
balloon to an enthusiastic reception. Soon he had
Carnegie's approval. By all standards, his price was
steep: $480 million for all the properties, with
Carnegie's share to be paid for in gold bonds bearing 5 percent interest. Carnegie wrote the price on
a slip of paper and gave it to Schwab, who carried
it to Morgan. "I accept this price," said Morgan,
for he knew that neither the par value of the Carnegie securities nor the value of the company's physical assets bore any resemblance to the actual
earning power of the company, much less to what
it could be made to earn with fully coordinated, well-planned direction from the top. (When Morgan and
Carnegie consummated the deal in person, Morgan
congratulated the Scotsman on being "the richest
man in the world." Carnegie, in fact, gave away
more than $300 million of his return.)

Organization, subsequent financial management of U.S. Steel in its early years, and tending its banking needs constituted the most demanding as- signments of J. P. Morgan & Company up to that time. "Judge" Elbert H. Gary, Morgan's longtime legal counsel, became chief executive officer of the new corporation, while Robert Bacon and, after Bacon left to join the U.S. State Department, George W. Perkins led Morgan's participation in its affairs. Making the consolidation work like an effi- cient, rational business was not accomplished over- night; indeed, not until the threat of antitrust prosecution had been finally removed in the 1920s, and Myron C. Taylor had overhauled the com- pany's management structure, did it begin to realize the profitability that Morgan, Schwab, and Gary had foreseen in 1900.

Critics charged that the capitalization of the company was mostly water. They also alleged that the syndicate, in charging U.S. Steel a fee of $50 mil- lion for its services, of which J. P. Morgan & Company's share was $12.5 million, was vastly over- paid. In fact they seldom noted that the *entire* fee was paid in preferred and common stock, the latter with very little market value for several years there- after. Nor did they mention the fact that the Mor- gan companies had incurred expenses of more than $1 million cash to earn a fee largely payable in the fu- ture. Least understood of all by the general public and their self-serving mentors was the unacceptable waste that would inevitably have beset the Ameri- can industrial economy if the problems it faced at the dawn of the new century had not been met and solved.

If a recasting of the existing American indus- trial structure at the turn of the century was the main task that flowed from the remarkable series of technological innovations of the previous century, this did not preclude the growing importance of mar- shaling capital for new industries that science cre- ated out of the whole cloth. No better example exists than electricity and its most striking applica- tions, illumination and communication. By 1892 the two leading electrical goods manufacturers, Edison General Electric and Thompson-Houston Electric, had developed so many interfirm relations that merger seemed logical. Morgan had taken an early interest in Thomas A. Edison's experiments with electric light and arranged financing for the in- ventor's first move to exploit his accomplishments. Henry Villard, the promotional genius of the North- ern Pacific Railroad whose powers seemed to lapse when he had to face the difficult task of making a

new enterprise work, pressed his plan upon Mor- gan and the two Bostonians, Henry L. Higginson and Thomas Jefferson Coolidge, with whom Mor- gan worked. Villard wanted to have the Edison company take over Thompson-Houston, with an im- portant role for himself, but when the dust settled, it was the plan worked out by Morgan and Coster, in which Thompson-Houston took over the Edison Company, that prevailed, and they persuaded Vil- lard to resign. Charles A. Coffin of Thompson- Houston became G.E.'s first president at Morgan's suggestion, and the company started an almost un- broken record of growth to mammoth size and world influence.

Meanwhile the American telephone industry was ready to assume intelligent structure and coordi- nated leadership. Upon the expiration of Alexander Graham Bell's original patents in the mid 1890s, there had followed a period during which indepen- dent telephone companies attempted to compete side- by-side against the Bell system. At the turn of the century many business and professional men found it necessary to have two telephones so that their cus- tomers would be sure to reach them from the phone *they* had. As a consequence, American Tele- phone & Telegraph Company (AT&T) stood on the edge of rampant growth. Use of the telephone had rapidly become routine and universal, and this called for huge amounts of capital that the Boston capital market could not meet. Kidder, Peabody & Company, AT&T's longtime banker in Boston, had relations of long standing with J. P. Morgan & Com- pany, and the two firms, each of which was guaran- teed 25 percent of all telephone financing until the early 1920s, headed syndicates underwriting hun- dreds of millions of dollars in bonds. The first issue, for $150 million, required hard work on the part of the managers to get it off the ground, but after that the telephone company regularly per- formed as one of J. P. Morgan & Company's most profitable clients.

Today's banker, beset by a thousand obstacles from government red tape and the law's delay, can only marvel at the volume of work that Morgan and a half dozen senior lieutenants initiated, devel- oped, nurtured, and brought to fruition. As an exam- ple, while the U.S. Steel consolidation was creating the world's largest industrial corporation, the com- pany was also arranging the merger of the Mc- Cormick and the Deering agricultural machinery interests. These two large, closely owned, and fa-

*Wall Street offices of J. P. Morgan & Company,
circa 1900*

mous factors in the mechanization of American farming had long competed with each other vigorously and sometimes rancorously. Harmonizing them was a feat that depended upon the diplomatic talents of the firm's newest member, George W. Perkins. The International Harvester Company resulted, and it led its industry for some 80 years until men of less wisdom and no diplomatic talents destroyed it.

Less successful experiences included the firm's participation in the fledgling automobile industry, at least at the beginning. In 1896 the London house of Morgan had sought New York's participation in a $2 million issue of first mortgage bonds for the Studebaker Brothers Manufacturing Company, the world's largest manufacturer of farm wagons and carriages. Coster seems to have taken a fancy to the enterprise and, after his usual intensive examination of the fine old firm's creditworthiness revealed no problem, recommended acceptance of $1 million of the issue. The automobile had not graduated from rich man's toy to a utilitarian transportation medium, however, and the bonds did not sell. Morgan's loss on its share wiped out all the profits on subsequent issues of new stock in the company. Twelve years later Morgan firmly rejected a request for financing from William C. Durant, who ac-

quired automotive parts suppliers right and left in no detectable pattern, to round out General Motors, his big merger of automobile manufacturing firms. Nevertheless, when Durant, like all compulsive gamblers, ran short of cash, J. P. Morgan & Company did take, at thirdhand, a small participation in an underwriting of General Motors' notes. Meanwhile, Morgan's firm had participated in an attempt to shore up the moribund United States Motor Company, whose only asset apparently was its highly popular Maxwell car, with the resulting loss of an undisclosed amount. Not even the Maxwell stockholders would subscribe to its bonds.

J. P. Morgan & Company's orientation toward the conservative investor who invested for the long run and judged his banker primarily by the performance of the securities he sold him, is emphasized by the fact that the company did only a small fraction of its business in the securities of new and untried enterprises, however well recommended. Until the end of Morgan's life, railroad financings remained the heart of the business, although in his later years he could see the approaching end of the long, exacting, yet romantic job of providing the means of linking the nation's thousands of communities by rail.

The informed judgment by himself and his senior associates as to the financial strength of an enterprise, and the character of the men who came to him to finance their undertakings, provided the only bases J. P. Morgan claimed for deciding to participate in an underwriting. He would have been the last to suggest that any sure-fire system existed, and indeed, he and his firm made their share of mistakes, with the size of the mistakes growing as the volume of business transacted grew. The financial penalties were not always as important as the publicity and attendant embarrassment that ensued.

It was not the countless hours of conferences, negotiations, and working out of details, not nearly all of which could be left to the partners, that were the real cost of organizing and then taking apart the Northern Securities Company in the period 1901-1904. The glaring publicity, the likes of which Morgan had never endured, and resulting criticism, became the new national issue. It ensured the nomination and election of Theodore Roosevelt to a full term as president in his own right—the first vice-president who acceded to the presidency upon the death of his principal to be so honored—and stoked the furnace of the Progressive movement that gathered steam for the fight against the undisputed power of American big business and big finance. This power made many a small businessman uncomfortable, especially the inefficient ones or those who had not kept up with the times.

The Northern Securities Company was a holding company organized for the sole purpose of holding the capital stock of the Northern Pacific and Great Northern Railroads, each of which held in turn about one-half of the capital stock of the Burlington Railroad, which James J. Hill had acquired right under the nose of Edward H. Harriman. In a few years beginning at the depth of the 1890s depression, Harriman had gained control of the Union Pacific, which had a line running to the Pacific Northwest from its main line in Wyoming to a line that it controlled down the Columbia River. The Burlington also had such a line from its main line in Nebraska to a connection with the NP at Billings, Montana. Obviously, absolute control of the Pacific Northwest transportation lay with anyone who could control both northwestern lines, and effective control of the traffic policies of the Burlington could be attained by wresting control of the NP from the syndicate of rich men headed by Hill and Morgan. Harriman almost did it, but Hill fought him to a standstill, for, as he told his wife, if Harriman had won the NP, "we would not have held it [his and his associates' NP and GN stock] a day longer than we could have sold it," and the plans he had for the Northwest would have gone by the board. But the fight kicked over the applecart in New York when the infamous "Northern Pacific corner" developed, creating panic and nearly ruining dozens of brokers and bankers.

Morgan emerged as the arbiter of the affair and pried enough stock loose from the combatants to save the day for the shorts on Wall Street. He got them to agree to formation of the holding company to prevent any further warfare. Morgan had come to believe almost that the holding-company device offered the answer to all their antitrust problems. In this case it merely confirmed and made legally binding the spirit of cooperation that had existed in the "syndicate" of investors that held the Hill roads together. A holding company, moreover, took no part in the formulation or execution of business policy by its constituent corporations but only collected and distributed their dividends to the owners of the combine. Adequate competition, ensuring against "monopoly" rates (whatever that meant),

was assured by the presence of the Union Pacific, while it was common knowledge that the Chicago, Milwaukee & St. Paul Railway was about to build its own transcontinental line to Puget Sound. If anything, Hill remarked, "We have too many railroads in Washington State already."

In politics, however, appearances, not substance, are what count, and western politicians had long since learned the power of the "railroad problem" to excite the electorate, who had no more interest in "free silver" and were bored with the tariff as well. Although the state of Minnesota had bungled its chance at this juicy issue, a master politician occupied the White House, and he was determined to stay there until March 4, 1909. The suit brought by the Department of Justice went to the Supreme Court, which voted 5 to 4 to require the Northern Securities Company to divest itself of its GN and NP stock. The decision turned entirely upon the apparent possession of potential power to do great harm, although in just what way no one clearly stated. Among the dissenting justices, Oliver Wendell Holmes barely concealed his disgust with the decision. "Great cases, like hard cases, make bad law," he wrote, because cases are usually great for reasons having nothing to do with the merits of a case. The decision prompted the court to enunciate in 1911 the "rule of reason," which declared that the Sherman Act's condemnation of acts in restraint of trade was not absolute. Hill always considered the decision a repudiation of all he and others tried to do to stabilize western railroading, but Morgan, who had expressed reluctance to appeal beyond the Circuit Court level, was more concerned with what the publicity might do to another financing of his that was soon to sink, of its own weight, beneath the waves.

As the new century dawned, its promise for English and American transatlantic shipping was clouded. Steamship companies registered under several other flags, whose nations worked for lower wages and endured poorer living conditions than even the English sailors, much less the Americans, were taking away the business, and merger seemed to be a solution. Even the White Star Line, a prominent factor in the luxury passenger business, had lost out to the better-managed Cunard Line, which stiff-armed suggestions that it join the merger. The English government did not think much of it either, especially when officials announced the inclusion of Germany's Hamburg-America line. Parliament reacted by granting Cunard a big subsidy for the *Mauretania* and the *Lusitania* that it was building, two ships that achieved fame in very different ways.

Details of the wheel-spinning at J. P. Morgan & Company to make a go of International Mercantile Marine (IMM), as the combine was called, provide less instruction than the reasons for the failure. Morgan, in judging proposed mergers, thought primarily in terms of market control rather than functional considerations such as forward and backward integration or economies of scale. In the case of the IMM debacle, which cost J. P. Morgan & Company in its New York and London offices a total of nearly $2 million, no functional merits seem readily apparent, while market control was out of the question. With the entry of more and more foreign flag vessels into the business and the flourishing of tramp steamers, which called at ports and offered to take away whatever freight waited on the docks at whatever the shipper would pay, proud rulers of the sea such as the United States and Great Britain shared a less and less profitable total business with a growing horde of competitors, including the aggressive vessels of Japan.

J. P. Morgan had been in his grave some eight months as the year 1913 ended, and so he was spared the shock of learning that the New York, New Haven & Hartford Railroad had passed its quarterly dividend, thus ending an unbroken 40-year record of payments. But Morgan had watched the steady decline of the New Haven for 10 years, and his own man, Charles S. Mellen, was nominally responsible. Aggressive, abrasive, and tactless, Mellen was the wrong man in the wrong place at the wrong time. Apparently Morgan misconstrued these faults as evidence of strength, and he had put Mellen at the helm of the Northern Pacific when the voting trust still operated. In doing so he risked James J. Hill's good will, for Hill could not stand the man. Mellen had not lasted any longer than it took Hill to fire him once Hill acquired full command of the NP. But Morgan seems to have felt he owed Mellen another chance, and the good, gray New Haven, which ran along so eventlessly, seemed just the place.

It proved a fatal mistake, for the New Haven faced serious technological, operating, and financial problems. Traffic grew apace after 1897, and the capacity of the road had to be increased. Moreover, the New York Central's fabulous New York district rebuilding program, which produced Grand Central Station and electrification into the northern suburbs, propelled modernization. Operating in some of the most heavily urbanized and densely populated country, the New Haven faced growing competition from all manner of transportation agencies: "traction" (streetcar) and especially interurban lines took away much of its lucrative short-haul passenger traffic, while a renaissance of coastal shipping between New England ports and New York cut into freight traffic and kept rates low. Moreover, prices of everything it took to run a railroad had risen steadily, especially labor; yet the Interstate Commerce Commission firmly resisted any efforts to raise rates across the board until the U.S. Railway Administration granted relief during World War I.

The typical Morgan solution seemed to be consolidation. By 1913 the company's debt had been increased to pay for a long list of competing enterprises, none of which had any future, at prices so inflated as to suggest collusion between buyer and seller. Included was the Boston & Maine Railroad, which would have made a good match if Louis D. Brandeis had not made it a cause célèbre. With the onset of the sharp business recession of that year, the bubble burst.

Under the supervision of Morgan's son, J. P., Jr. ("Jack"), the Morgan men worked long and hard to get the New Haven out of trouble. Howard Elliott, an excellent example of the new breed of professional railroad executives, took over, avoided receivership, and finally regained financial soundness. If that had been all that was involved, J. P. Morgan & Company would have suffered no aftereffects. The notoriety, however, especially at a time when reformers such as Brandeis used an approach to judging business policies that was new and fresh, if badly flawed, promised to be an enduring incubus.

Another major disappointment in these years, although far from being the fault of Morgan and his lieutenants, was the failure to develop a substantial business in underwriting the bond issues of foreign governments or the securities of foreign enterprises. Morgan and his most sophisticated partners, notably Robert Bacon and George W. Perkins, spent untold hours in trying to develop the areas of the globe that seemed ready for development. Morgan never believed that the oriental nations could float a bond issue at an acceptable rate; he refused to close with both Chinese and Japanese representatives who pressed him, and his judgment was borne out. Russia, likewise, seemed far from promising de-

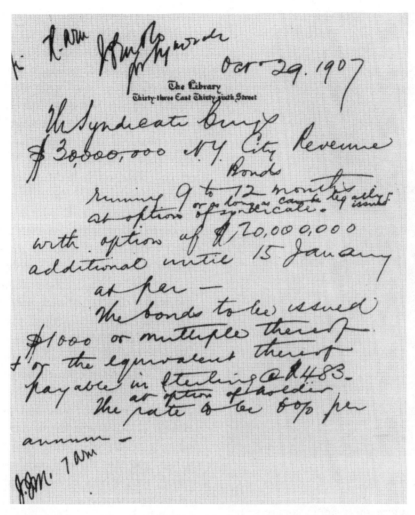

Morgan's authorization of a bond purchase to support the credit of New York banks during the Panic of 1907

spite Count Witte's attempts at industrialization. The czar's penchant for wars he could not possibly win and the incompetence and corruption of his regime gave sound businessmen pause. Morgan steadfastly turned down Russian loans (although the London office found it awkward to do so and took some), and the dramatic events of 1917 proved Morgan right again. The coldness of American bankers toward foreign investment, in the event if not in principle, has subsequently defeated the best efforts of Leninists to fit history into his model of capitalist imperialism.

South America kept knocking at the door of American capital sources, but few if any of the enterprises into which J. P. Morgan & Company ventured returned profits worthy of the time and attention they demanded. Even more of a disappointment, especially to the expansionist administrations of Theodore Roosevelt and William Howard Taft,

was the matter of financing railroads for China. These ancient peoples have subsequently spent more time almost emerging from oriental medievalism than one could ever have anticipated when the revolution of 1911 deposed the last emperor. Several years before, American investment bankers, notably J. P. Morgan & Company, had become involved in lengthy negotiations to raise money with which Edward H. Harriman could further his dreams of bringing rail transportation to the Chinese masses. The great powers of Europe were far from ready to work together on such a project, however, much less to grant the policy of the "open door," which the United States and Great Britain favored. The negotiations for the larger loans got nowhere.

These overseas experiences took a backseat to developments at home, however, with the "Money Trust" controversy the most memorable. Whatever

Morgan at the Pujo hearings, 1912

from the smallest farmers' bank in Arkansas to the most dignified New York trust company, was safe. In fact the New York trust companies comprised a new wrinkle in the banking business, and their ability to survive a crisis with much smaller reserves against deposits had gone entirely untested. As several, most notably the Knickerbocker Trust Company, prepared to close their doors against the mob when their cash ran out, New York's leading bankers converged on J. P. Morgan to head their concerted effort to stem the tide and save what was worthy of saving. J. P. Morgan & Company was no central bank with sovereign powers, to be sure, but it could channel funds, in the shape of loans, to worthy institutions (which simply meant those with loans made on good collateral—mostly real estate—and whose difficulties were not of their own making). Most accounts suggest that Morgan, sitting like an oriental potentate in the elegant library beside his Madison Avenue mansion, passed Solomonic judgment on which banks should live and which should die, as underlings spread mortgages and other securities before him, and in between visits he passed the time by playing solitaire or studying new artworks. Saving the American banking system, and thus the monetary system of the entire nation, took weeks of work and exacted a heavy toll on the seventy-year-old man who received grudging credit for the success, and mindless condemnation for the trouble in the first place.

One lesson that Washington had learned from the Panic of 1907 was that the electorate's mind-set against any kind of central banking system, which went back to the Age of Jackson and the ascendance of the Democratic party, had been greatly modified by the panic, and that, literally, this kind of thing could not be allowed to continue. Republican leaders such as Sen. Nelson Aldrich showed a fatal lack of imagination in moving toward creation of a more or less conventional central bank along the lines of the Bank of England. The Republican party had come apart at the seams, and once the heavily Democratic Congress elected in 1910 convened in 1911, the Democrats took charge of remodeling the system. A long and wearying struggle ensued before the Federal Reserve System, a bundle of compromises with the past consisting of not one but 12 central banks, emerged in 1913. The high point, at least to the newspapers, was the hearings before the Pujo Committee on the "money trust," and

value there has been over the years in congressional investigations of highly controversial and politically charged issues, they have seldom educated either the politicians who conduct them or the masses who have come to look upon them as entertainment. This was especially true of such complex technical matters as the monetary system in a capitalist society. J. P. Morgan's career ended in a blaze of headlines and recriminations that was the last thing he would have wanted but was the inevitable result of nearly a century of a vigorous young country's attempt to get along without a bossy central "bank of last resort." The depression of 1893-1897 had been set off by a collapse of the half-baked National Bank system, and each fall thereafter, when demands for currency expanded as crops went to market, bankers all across the country had nervously waited for disaster to strike. And strike it did in 1907. By that time deposit banking had grown enormously, giving a new lease on life to state-chartered banks whose numbers grew prodigiously. When the depositors lined up before the paying tellers' windows to demand their money, no bank, particularly the appearance of the leading witness on December 18 and 19, 1912: J. P. Morgan.

The Pujo Committee's exotic-sounding name was that of Arsène P. Pujo of Louisiana, chairman of the House Banking and Currency Committee, but its real leader was its counsel, Samuel Untermeyer, a wealthy New York corporate lawyer who had become increasingly anti-big-business. Untermeyer's bias stemmed perhaps not quite as much from his experience in defending such enterprises as from his surging ambition for a political career. Although the popular appeal of the word "trust" was not lost on men in public life, the term "money trust" did not mean, in the minds of the more sophisticated, that a formal consolidation of big banks, centered on New York City, held most of the nation's money in a viselike grip and absolutely controlled its availability. Instead they interpreted it as meaning a few men, such as J. P. Morgan, George F. Baker of the First National Bank, James Stillman of the National City Bank, to name the most well-known, collusively exercised effective power to a similar end.

Untermeyer got hardly anywhere with Morgan, for the banker steadfastly refused to disclose any details of the transactions his firm or he, personally, had engaged in, while refusing to rise to the bait of any of the counsel's leading questions. The verbatim testimony suggests that Untermeyer seriously underestimated his adversary, and many of Morgan's answers were the last that counsel seems to have expected. For example:

> UNTERMEYER: You are an advocate of combination and cooperation as against competition, are you not?
> MORGAN: Yes. Cooperation I should favor.
> UNTERMEYER: Combination as against competition?
> MORGAN: I do not object to competition, either. I like a little competition. . . . Without you have control, you cannot do anything.
> UNTERMEYER: . . . Is that the reason you want to control everything?
> MORGAN: I want to control nothing. . . .
> UNTERMEYER: Is not commercial credit based primarily upon money or property?
> MORGAN: No, sir, the first thing is character . . . Before money or anything else. Money cannot buy it . . . because a man I do not trust could not get money from me on all the bonds in Christendom.

Four months after his appearance before the Pujo Committee, J. P. Morgan lay dying in a suite at the Grand Hotel in Rome. Many of his close friends and associates attributed his rapid decline to the hearings and the attendant criticism, but as many others disagreed. He had often been sick during his lifetime, for his constitution was never as good as his commanding presence suggested, and a lifetime devoted to hard, demanding work in stuffy offices, sometimes around the clock, with all the stresses that undenied leadership of American merchant banking brought, had taken its toll. He had habitually worked hard for however long it took to get affairs in shape for his growing roster of bright young men to look after, and then taken increasingly long vacations from New York and from America. Never a single-minded accumulator of wealth, he left an estate of $68 million, not including artworks valued at $50 million and now priceless. The really rich in those days included the industrial magnates, such as John D. Rockefeller, or Andrew Carnegie, who had given several times as much to libraries. "And to think," said Carnegie when the terms of the will were announced, "he was not a rich man."

Morgan cared nothing for games, took little if any exercise beyond walking around the gentleman farm that he had delighted in, and seems to have had no interest in music or drama. His church, St. George's, was his chief interest along with his art collection, for which he made handsome accommodation in a beautiful museum next to the Madison Avenue mansion. His oceangoing steam yachts, each named in turn *Corsair,* were the scene of many of his most relaxing moments. He enjoyed the company of beautiful, intelligent, talented, and accomplished women. Among his favorites were singer Lillian Russell and actress Maxine Elliott. If he felt the need for extramarital sexual gratification, he did it with such discretion that no evidence of it remains. On the record, and probably off as well, he was a model husband to his second wife, Frances Louise Tracey, and kind father to three daughters and one son, "Jack," who followed him as head of the Morgan firms after his father's death.

Even for a man whose firm had so much to offer, Morgan was remarkably fortunate in hiring well-bred, if not always well-born, young men to work themselves to death for him, but he asked no more of them than he had given at the same age. Coster's loss in 1900 was a blow, but new partners were not wanting, most notably George W. Perkins, a brilliant self-made man who had already made an outstanding career at the New York Life Insurance Company; Robert Bacon, Harvard's "Greek God of the Class of '79," without whom the steel consolidation would have had a much rougher time, and who went from Morgans & Company to Washington as assistant secretary of state, and at the tag end of Roosevelt's administration, as secretary; and Charles Steele, whose years as a leading railroad lawyer made him an expert on that industry and just about everything else.

Morgan's spirits had been on the downgrade for some time when he died. He knew that the traditions of the private merchant bank as the principal instrument for marshaling the investable capital of the civilized nations were passing. Behind the meaningless term "finance capitalism," so beloved of Progressive historians, lurked a wrongheaded, physiocratic view of the money man as a sterile growth upon society that could do no constructive good and constantly threatened to do real harm. The very concept of trust—of giving a man just one chance to betray one's confidence in him—and the policy of absolute secrecy where a client's financial affairs were concerned, which had been the basis of our commercial civilization from earliest times, were passing. "The time is coming when all business will have to be done in glass pockets," Morgan declared after the Northern Securities decision condemned the possession of great economic power in the abstract.

If he had such fears, he did not live to see them borne out. By the mid 1920s nearly all the great economic leaders of his era had died. Commercial banks grew increasingly important in the underwriting of industrial securities, but what had worked so well in Germany, whose economic development in the Morgan era otherwise so closely par-

alleled America's, worked poorly for American commercial banks in the 1920s, and no leader remotely approaching the stature of a Morgan, a Schiff, a Belmont, or a Baker emerged. The increased competition for investable funds led to ill-advised efforts by many to broaden the market and embrace unsophisticated small savers. With the arrival of the Great Depression American investment banking had fallen into disarray and disgrace. A new underwriting industry had virtually to be created, under the leadership of the brilliant James M. Landis and his Securities & Exchange Commission. In the long run, however, institutions have proved no substitute for men and women of character who exercise personal responsibility. J. P. Morgan would not have been surprised, for his philosophy belongs not merely to his era, but to the ages.

References:

Vincent P. Carosso, *The Morgans: Private International Bankers, 1854-1913* (Cambridge, Mass.: Harvard University Press, 1987);

Louis Corey, *The House of Morgan: A Social Biography of the Masters of Money* (New York: Grosset & Dunlap, 1930);

Albro Martin, *James J. Hill and the Opening of the Northwest* (New York: Oxford University Press, 1976);

Joseph Wall, *Andrew Carnegie* (New York: Oxford University Press, 1970).

Archives:

This essay is based heavily upon Vincent P. Carosso's *The Morgans: Private International Bankers, 1854-1913*; indeed, it could not have been written before the appearance of this superb work of scholarship, in the preparation of which Professor Carosso had the assistance of his wife, the late Rose C. Carosso. The book includes a highly detailed bibliographical note and hundreds of notes on the text. It will stand for many years as the definitive study of the firm that Junius and J. P. Morgan headed. Carosso also details the existence and availability of the Morgan Archives.

Junius S. Morgan

(April 13, 1813-April 8, 1890)

by Steven Wheeler

New York Stock Exchange Archives

CAREER: Clerk and partner, Alfred Welles, Boston (1833-1834); partner, Morgan, Ketchum & Company (1834-1836); partner, Howe, Mather & Company (1836-1850), Mather, Morgan & Company (1850-1851); director of several railroad and insurance companies (1836-1854); partner, J. M. Beebe, Morgan & Company (1851-1854); partner, George Peabody & Company (1854-1864); partner, J. S. Morgan & Company (1864-1890).

Junius Spencer Morgan was a prominent, late nineteenth-century private banker whose London-based firm financed a great deal of American commerce and railroad expansion. He was patriarch of the Morgan banking dynasty.

One of three children and an only son, Junius Morgan was born to Sarah Spencer and Joseph Morgan, a farmer and entrepreneur, in West Springfield, Massachusetts, on April 13, 1813. Four years later the family moved to Hartford, Connecticut.

Junius Morgan received his education at several private academies and helped out on the family farm during his youth. In 1829, at the age of sixteen, he began his business career when his father apprenticed him to Boston merchant and banker Alfred Welles. He worked as a clerk in the store, made occasional sales trips, performed limited banking operations, and became a partner of the firm in 1833. The next year Morgan's father arranged a partnership for him with Morris Ketchum, a prominent Wall Street private banker who conducted a general banking and brokerage business. The firm was renamed Morgan, Ketchum & Company. Two years later Morgan returned to Hartford and became the junior partner in the wholesale dry goods firm Howe, Mather & Company. He supervised the firm's clerks and traveled throughout New England, New York, and southern states buying cotton, paying bills, and collecting accounts. His

Junius S. Morgan (courtesy of the Pierpont Morgan Library)

shrewd judgment helped keep the firm solvent during the Panic of 1837.

During his years as Howe & Mather's junior partner Morgan proved himself a capable businessman, winning recognition from Hartford's business and civic community. He was invited to serve as a director of several local companies, including the Hartford Fire Insurance Company and the New Haven & Hartford Railroad. In 1836 Morgan married Juliet Pierpont of Boston, who gave birth to their only son, John Pierpont, a year later.

Early in 1850 Morgan became senior partner and the firm changed its name to Mather, Morgan & Company. But Morgan had wider ambitions and made a trip to Europe to investigate opportunities to expand his business into international trade and meet some leading merchant bankers and transatlantic traders. Upon his return to the United States he formed a partnership with James M. Beebe & Company of Boston, a prominent wholesale dry goods merchant with a strong import trade. To Beebe's international ties Morgan brought additional capital, years of mercantile experience, and many domestic business connections. The firm was renamed J. M. Beebe, Morgan & Company, and over the next few years its annual sales tripled to $7 million.

In 1854, at the age of forty-one, Junius Morgan joined in a partnership with George Peabody & Company, a leading American merchant banker in London. Morgan agreed to a ten-year partnership and moved his family to London. The firm actively engaged in three major areas of merchant banking: financing import/export trade by providing commercial credits to traders shipping a wide variety of goods between Europe and America; commodities trading (particularly exports of British iron rails to the United States); and securities operations–selling the stocks and bonds that channeled foreign capital into American railroads and other business enterprises.

The firm's strong ties to the New York financial community caused it major problems during the Panic of 1857. Although fundamentally sound, the near failure of Duncan, Sherman & Company and several of its other important correspondents threatened Peabody & Company with collapse. A loan from the Bank of England saved the firm from failure, and, as the panic subsided, George Peabody & Company fully recovered. The panic emphasized to Morgan the danger of accepting too many credits from any single house and the need to supervise the firm's agents and correspondents better.

Morgan's business philosophy always followed a conservative track. He held his integrity and reputation as his firm's most important asset: he took few risks, and any that were taken were carefully weighed. Any proposed business venture was thoroughly scrutinized and had to earn his complete confidence.

After 1859, as Peabody's failing health prompted him to turn more and more responsibility over to his partner, Morgan became the effective head of George Peabody & Company. Finally, Peabody retired in 1864, and the firm's name was changed to J. S. Morgan & Company. The new firm continued in the same premises, with the same staff, the same business connections, and many of the same clients. Senior partner at the age of fifty-one, Morgan made all policy at the firm, deciding how the firm's resources were to be applied and what new propositions to accept and developing new business. In 1867 the firm entered an entirely new arena, the government loan business, when it successfully sold the entire foreign distribution of a loan for the government of Chile.

The business deal that brought the Morgan firm to the forefront of London's international bankers was the French Loan of 1870. In the midst of fighting the Franco-Prussian War, the French government found itself unable to obtain financing from any other major banking house in London. Napoleon III turned to Morgan to raise £10 million to continue the war. The 6 percent loan sold strongly at first but slowed months later when Paris fell to Bismarck's armies. Morgan held the unsold bonds, and the entire issue was redeemed at par in 1873. The loan brought great profits to the Morgan house and firmly placed it among the elite of London's merchant banks.

In the 1870s and 1880s J. S. Morgan & Company participated in some of the most important syndicates that underwrote loans for the United States, European, and Latin American countries. The most prestigious was the European/American syndicate that sold a series of loans refunding the U.S. Civil War debt (1871-1879). Its $1.4 billion in federal bonds was the largest and most significant issue of its time.

J. S. Morgan & Company strengthened its position in international finance by its connection with the New York banking house of Junius Morgan's son, John Pierpont Morgan. That alliance grew even stronger when the Drexel, Morgan & Company partnership was formed in 1871, linking prominent houses in New York, Philadelphia, and Paris to the London firm.

Cooperating with his son's New York firm, Junius Morgan attained a leadership position in financing the American railroad construction boom of the 1870s-1890s. The firm preferred to fund only established, well-managed railroads, as they were more profitable, safer, and more respectable, bringing additional prestige to the firm. In addition to selling a line's securities the firm also held deposits and acted as transfer agent and registrar of the company's stocks and bonds. Important accounts included the Baltimore & Ohio, the New York Central (the firm sold a large portion of William H. Vanderbilt's shares in 1879), and the Union Pacific. The firm financed extensions and improvements to lines, consolidated short lines into larger, regional networks, and, when necessary, reorganized and rehabilitated financially troubled railroads. Moreover, the company broke important ground by restructuring many of these roads under a new hierarchy of professional managers.

Junius Morgan headed J. S. Morgan & Company until his death in 1890, and the firm continued to be an important force in international and corporate finance, but in the 1880s his son and the New York firm of Drexel, Morgan & Company assumed an even greater leadership role in world finance.

On April 3, 1890, Junius Morgan suffered head injuries in a carriage accident near his villa at Monte Carlo. He died five days later on April 8, just a week shy of his seventy-seventh birthday. His body was interred in the family plot in Hartford, Connecticut. His estate is estimated to have been worth $10 million. Most of it passed to his son, who also succeeded his father as senior partner of J. S. Morgan & Company.

Reference:

Vincent P. Carosso, *The Morgans: Private International Bankers, 1854-1913* (Cambridge, Mass.: Harvard University Press, 1987).

Archives:

Some of Junius S. Morgan's papers, particularly relating to his early business career, are at the Pierpont Morgan Library in New York City. Additional personal papers and business records of J. S. Morgan & Company are at Guildhall Library, London.

Robert Morris

(January 31, 1734-May 8, 1806)

by B. R. Burg

Arizona State University

CAREER: Partner, Willing and Morris (1754-1777); state assemblyman, Pennsylvania (1775-1779, 1780-1781, 1785-1788); delegate, Second Continental Congress (1775-1778); U.S. superintendent of finance (1781-1784); delegate, Annapolis Convention (1786); delegate, U.S. Constitutional Convention (1787); U.S. senator, state of Pennsylvania (1787-1795).

Robert Morris, financier of the American Revolution, was born in England near the city of Liverpool. By the age of thirteen he had migrated to America to live in Maryland with his father, an agent for a Liverpool merchant engaged in the tobacco trade on Chesapeake Bay. He attended school in Philadelphia for a short time, and then, following the practice common in both England and the American colonies during the eighteenth century, he became an apprentice. He was sent to learn the intricacies of trade and commerce at

Willings, a leading Philadelphia mercantile house. The firm sent flour and wheat to Ireland and Britain; lumber and provisions to the West Indies; imported English dry goods; dealt in salt, lemons, and wine from the Iberian Peninsula; and purchased molasses from Jamaica, Barbados, and other sugar islands. Willings also handled bills of exchange and warehouse receipts, using an efficient network of correspondents on both sides of the Atlantic and throughout the Caribbean. In addition to trading, currency transactions, and note exchanges, the company transported cargoes on the ships of its own small fleet.

Morris received training in all aspects of the firm's business. He served not only in Philadelphia but also sailed as a supercargo on voyages to the West Indies, where French privateers once captured him. He became a trusted employee, and by 1754 the twenty-year-old Morris joined Thomas Willing, son of the founder, as a partner in the renamed firm of Willing and Morris.

Portrait of Robert Morris by Gilbert Stuart

The Seven Years' War created serious problems for the firm, but despite uncertain markets, enemies at sea, embargoes, and the vicissitudes of conducting trade in time of war, the partners prospered. During those early years Willing rather than Morris took charge of the firm's activities, but that changed. A gap exists in the surviving historical materials for the period from 1761 to 1775, but it appears that by 1775 Morris had assumed management of most of the company's affairs. How or why the change in leadership occurred is uncertain, but under Morris's direction the partnership continued to prosper and expanded beyond shipping, banking, and mercantile pursuits. It acquired land in several of the colonies, including the Orange Grove Estate, a southern plantation large enough to employ more than 100 slaves. By the time of the American Revolution, Willing and Morris was one of the largest and most powerful companies in British North America. Morris had acquired a palatial home outside Philadelphia, and, as he explained to a correspondent, "It is known that besides our capital in trade we possess valuable landed estates, [and] that we are totally free from encumbrances."

After the Seven Years' War concluded in 1763, both partners actively opposed British policies designed to tax and control the colonies. They joined other merchants from Philadelphia and coastal towns in denouncing various Parliamentary enactments. Morris took a conspicuous part in opposing the 1765 Stamp Act. In that year he signed a nonimportation agreement with the hope that economic pressure from the colonies in North America would force Parliament to accede to American demands for repeal. In October he served on a citizens' committee charged with prohibiting the Philadelphia stamp-tax collector from performing his duties.

The intensity of feeling dividing Britain from her colonies subsided to a degree after the repeal of the Stamp Act in 1766 and the repeal of the Townshend Duties in 1770, but the respite proved temporary. Several coercive acts passed in 1774 by Parliment in reaction to the Boston Tea Party again inflamed the passions of the colonists. The purpose of the acts, which closed the port of Boston until such time as the British felt normal commerce would be resumed, was to punish both the town of Boston for the destruction of the East India Company's tea the year before and to chastise the entire colony of Massachusetts Bay for various expressions of hostility to Royal government manifested over the previous decade.

When the First Continental Congress assembled at Philadelphia in the autumn of 1774 to decide how to respond to the coercive legislation, Morris had not yet committed himself to any specific course of action. By the following spring, however, he concluded that the colonists had to counter by force arbitrary Parliamentary enactments. According to family legend, the news of the battles of Lexington and Concord turned him into a champion of colonial rebellion. As a member of the Pennsylvania Assembly beginning in 1775, he regularly favored strengthening the colony's defenses, but in his ardor for the cause he still guarded his interests as a merchant. He voted against legal-tender laws whenever they were proposed. He accepted appointments to several positions of responsibility in the assembly, most notably the committee to secure munitions. In that position he oversaw the acquisition of military materiel, but the assembly discovered his considerable commercial experience was especially useful in negotiating arrangements to pay for what they purchased.

Morris became a delegate to the Second Continental Congress in 1775 and throughout his early service opposed suggestions that the colonies separate from England. Not until a month after the Continental Congress adopted the Declaration of Independence did he affix his signature.

The most important assignment he received in Congress was to the Secret Committee on Commerce, where he replaced his business partner, Thomas Willing. The work of the committee, although never clearly delineated, included purchasing and paying for most of the equipment and supplies needed for the war effort. As chief purchasing agent for the United States, Morris displayed the enthusiasm with which he pursued all of his commercial and political activities, and he soon gained control of the entire procurement process.

After the Congress fled from Philadelphia in December 1776, Morris remained in the city making heroic efforts to supply a revolution that, to many, appeared doomed. The only powers allotted him for conducting his frustrating and difficult tasks stemmed from those he held simply as a member of important congressional committees. The scope and complexity of his obligations caused him to go far beyond those delegated powers to satisfy the army's needs. Only by exceeding his authority was Morris able to circumvent monumental difficulties and acquire materiel and financing. Due mainly to Morris's efforts, George Washington's troops remained in the field against the British through the winter of 1776-1777.

When he first became involved in revolutionary politics, Morris stated he would probably devote little time to business affairs until the conflict ended. But within two months after commencement of the war he found himself deeply involved in commercial ventures, and the pace of his business activities hardly slackened until 1781, when he undertook especially heavy public responsibilities in the last years of the struggle for independence.

The appointment to the Secret Committee suited Morris's desire to serve the cause of the colonies and his own purse as well. Like other officials and envoys of the Second Continental Congress he often combined his own trading activities with those of the government. He conducted transactions through his Philadelphia mercantile firm during the time he controlled military purchasing, and he regularly mixed public and private cargoes and public and private funds. The confusion of goods and accounts makes difficult attempts to reconstruct his commercial transactions and to evaluate his public service. Other factors, such as primitive bookkeeping methods, shipments unaccompanied by bills of lading, and the fact that years often elapsed before the delivery of orders, render it impossible to trace Morris's business dealings during the war years.

As the war continued Morris grew increasingly wealthy. The quantum growth of his personal fortune, linked as it was to the military supply system, caused concern in the Congress about the nature and propriety of his activities. John Adams, in his notes for September 24, 1775, wrote that there was "An uneasiness, among some of the Members concerning a Contract with Willing and Morris, for Powder, by which the House, without any Risque at all will make a clear Profit of 12,000£ at least. . . . All think it is exorbitant." Adams correctly estimated the representatives' judgment, but Morris did little to alleviate their suspicions of impropriety. He lost no chance to make a profit or to collect his commissions when acting as a broker. "The present oppert'y [opportunity] of improving our Fortunes ought not to be lost," he proclaimed, "especially as the very means of doing it will contribute to the Service of our Country at the same time."

In an attempt to expand his profits Morris enlisted the services of his half brother, Thomas, in the company's affairs. Thomas Morris was traveling in Europe on unlimited funds when war broke out. His knowledge of European mercantile firms and his natural abilities made him an inestimable asset, the older brother thought, particularly since Congress appointed him as a purchasing agent. The young man was snatched from a profligate life and placed under the tutelage of Silas Deane, also an agent of Congress, who was serving in France. Deane, like the elder Morris, had an extraordinary ability to analyze economic trends and blend public business with the pursuit of wealth.

By selecting his brother to handle complicated financial dealings, Morris made one of his few misjudgments during the war years. Thomas Morris, it appears, had a deeper commitment to pleasure than to revolution. He neglected the oftentimes tedious work involved in mercantile operations and was exceedingly irresponsible. Word trickled across the Atlantic that he selected dubious merchants as partners and irritated friends and business associates. In due time the trickle turned into a cataract of complaints from almost everyone with whom he dealt. When tales of his younger brother's ineptitude reached Congress, Morris first defended him, but reports of his negligence and imcompetence grew to such intensity that Robert could not justify or ignore them. In December 1777 he reviewed his brother's actions before the Congress, offered apologies to those the young man offended, and asked that he be removed from public office.

Despite concern over Morris's obvious pursuit of personal profit, members of Congress recognized his considerable abilities. They made him a member of the committee that drafted instructions for American envoys in France and appointed him to a committee on fortifying seaports. By October 1777 he had emerged as one of the leaders of the Congress, sharing power with Richard Henry Lee of Virginia and the Adamses of Massachusetts.

Under the Pennsylvania Constitution, Morris was ineligible to be elected to the Continental Congress a second time, but he did not retire from public life after his term expired in 1778. He remained a member of the Pennsylvania Assembly and continued his exertions for the American cause.

When Morris left the Continental Congress, his departure marked not only a break in his political career but in his business arrangements as well. In that year the earlier dissolution of his partnership with Thomas Willing was made public. Morris then embarked on his own, and, for the first time since the beginning of the Revolution, he devoted himself solely to commerce. Between 1778 and 1781 he expanded his commercial interests to the point where he was acknowledged to be the most prominent merchant in the nation. Within that short span of years he joined or formed nine major partnerships and several arrangements with somewhat less than full-scale partnership status. At the same time, he superintended the development of mercantile connections that expanded the number of products he traded, facilitated complicated banking functions necessary for his mercantile operations, and poured more wealth into his already well-filled coffers.

Morris expended much of the gain from his trading activities in his baronial style of living. When he wed Mary White in 1769, he already had achieved considerable financial success. Under her direction their Philadelphia home grew into one of the city's social centers. The distinguished guests who visited the Morrises sat at polished tables of mahogany and sipped tea from the finest porcelain cups. The Marquis de Chastellux wrote that the residence was "handsome, resembling perfectly the houses in London. [Morris] lives without ostentation, but not without expense, for he spares nothing which can contribute to his happiness and that of Mrs. Morris, to whom he is much attached." In addition, the couple hosted gatherings at "The Hills," their luxurious country estate, which John Jay described as a "temple . . . erected to hospitality." There the Morrises installed an ice house and a hot house, planted imported fruit trees, and superintended lavish gatherings where good conversation and fine claret flowed abundantly.

In early 1779 Morris became the central figure in a controversy in the Congress, of which he was no longer a member. Several delegates denounced Morris and Silas Deane for their failure to separate private business transactions from their public responsibilities. Henry Laurens of South Carolina charged the company of Willing and Morris with fraud. A number of exceedingly complex events led to the charges against Morris and his partner, and in the investigation that followed neither Morris nor his accusers adhered scrupulously to the facts in presenting their cases. The Congress ultimately cleared Morris of any misconduct, including the charge of appropriating public funds for his own use, but that did not mean he was entirely blameless. Undoubtedly an element of inefficiency characterized his conduct of trade, and on at least one occasion he clearly demonstrated more concern for his own interest than that of the public. There is no doubt he should have followed the advice he often gave to associates in private business: "Short accounts are best, they keep things clear, and good Friends will then remain so." Even though Congress absolved Morris of all wrongdoing, a popular outcry against him nevertheless arose. He was defeated in his bid for reelection to the Pennsylvania Assembly, and a year passed before the power of those opposed to him diminished sufficiently for him to regain his seat.

The financial condition of the United States looked especially bleak during the winter and spring of 1781. The nation's fiscal difficulties were mainly a result of the methods previously adopted to finance the war. Congress had taken the first revenue-raising steps even before the Declaration of Independence by issuing paper money in the form of bills of credit. Congress meant for the notes to be temporary, to be retired as soon as specie was available, but the plan went awry. The first-series notes could not be redeemed, and the war emergency forced the government repeatedly to authorize new note issues.

Congress, alarmed at the amount of paper money in circulation by 1780, began exploring other sources of revenue. Despite considerable opposition, it found no alternative to borrowing if the war was to continue. Loan-office certificates and certificates of indebtedness, the equivalents of modern government bonds, were soon issued in large quantities. Congress intended to use most of those to obtain supplies by army quartermasters, purchasing agents, and commissary officers. Considerable corruption was involved in the use of the certificates, and often an exchange for supplies amounted to little more than a forced loan. Still, the certificates comprised a vital part of the war-financing effort, and later they represented an important part of the nation's domestic indebtedness. Even so, borrowing from individuals failed to cover all expenditures. Congress also obtained funds from the several states and negotiated foreign loans.

What made the financial situation of the United States more critical than ever in January 1781 was that none of these sources could be tapped for additional revenue. The paper currency had depreciated rapidly over the previous years despite attempts by Congress to buttress its value through payment of interest. It was nearly worthless by late 1780. Requisitioning had also bogged down, and the French government made clear its intention to refuse further loans. The financial position of the individual states was as dire as that of the national government in most cases, and they could not be counted on to provide additional funds. The pinching want of military supplies made the country's condition even more precarious. Washington's army, accustomed to dealing with critical logistical problems, had faced severe shortages and near bankruptcy throughout the course of the war. In previous times of difficulty, however, Congress at least provided a portion of the needed funds. This time the government verged on collapse.

Several leading figures urged the appointment of a single individual to direct the nation's finances in place of the numerous Congressional committees that had failed to secure adequate revenue. Alexander Hamilton and others suggested Robert Morris as the man for the position. Although the Congress

resigned itself to appointing a director capable of leading the nation out of its fiscal predicament, at first it disregarded Hamilton's advice on the nominee. After a time, however, the members realized that only Morris had sufficient qualifications. His business success over the preceding three years and the reputation he had earned as a consummate administrator when a member of Congress persuaded them of his indispensability. In February 1781 Congress chose him as superintendent of finance, with the appointment made without a dissenting vote.

The office was a position of tremendous responsibility, and Morris knew the burden it entailed. Before he accepted the offer he presented a series of demands to Congress. He insisted on the right to select all employees in his department, and he refused to relinquish any of his personal enterprises. Despite considerable reluctance to grant the requests Congress had no alternative. The plight of the country had grown more desperate with each passing month, and Robert Morris seemed to be the only man able to save the situation.

Morris wisely perceived that the state of the government did not accurately reflect the state of the nation's economy. The Revolution had not exhausted the country's resources, and, in fact, observers predicted a favorable economic outlook for 1781. Agriculture had suffered, but in many regions it flourished despite the difficulties created by the war. Maritime commerce was also reduced from previous levels, but it remained a bustling enterprise even though beset by difficulties. Coastal towns and cities continued to trade with the nations of Europe and with the West Indies. In some locations the losses from diminished trade were more than made up by the phenomenal successes of American privateers.

Morris went to work with his customary zeal to secure the country's finances. He centralized procedures for procuring supplies for the army, eliminating the inefficient commissary system then in use. He reduced waste in America's European financial operations and in the medical department's hospitals. He urged the states to provide the government with specie rather than with supplies. Those measures resulted in the availability of money and materiel for the victorious Yorktown campaign in the waning months of 1781, and they induced the French to lend their American ally $200,000. The superintendent next moved to establish the nation's credit. He authorized an issue of paper money se-

*Letter of instruction prepared for agents seeking investment in the Bank of North America
(Emmet Collection, New York Public Library)*

cured by his own reputation. The bills became known popularly as "Morris notes." They were drawn on the Office of Finance for $20, $50, and $80 and were payable on sight. A second type of issue was also authorized. It differed from the first in that the notes were payable after a specified period of time rather than upon presentation. The issues helped support the nation's credit, as Morris hoped they would, and they also served as a circulating medium to replace the valueless continental currency. As the government collected tax revenues it gradually retired those notes. Morris had hit on a revolutionary theory of money, even if by accident. Contrary to prevalent thought, the value of money depended on the willingness of state or national governments to accept it for taxes, not on its convertibility to specie, provided, of course, that the

citizens had confidence in the ability of the government to survive. That generated a confidence "feedback loop" in which the citizens received the assurance of the government that its money had value.

The notes mitigated the nation's financial plight, but Morris knew the country had to do more. It needed a mint to establish credit and to expand the circulating medium, he reasoned. He engaged in the preliminary planning for the project in summer 1781, and he placed a proposal before Congress in January of the following year. Morris argued that a national coinage would simplify the monetary confusion that prevailed with the use of foreign coin everywhere in the country, and that it would relieve the United States from dependence on the will or whim of foreign princes. The idea of a mint kindled little interest, but a Committee of the States and later a congressional committee approved it nonetheless. Congress granted the superintendent of finance authority to implement the project.

Another of the measures required to restore faith and credit in the United States, Morris maintained, was the establishment of a privately owned bank capitalized sufficiently to cover many of the government's needs. He discovered that raising funds for the sort of "national bank" he proposed constituted an arduous task. Throughout the summer of 1781 he urged his mercantile friends and associates to participate. He met with success in and around Philadelphia, and investors included many of the city's most prominent commercial leaders. Elsewhere his pleas for capital fell on deaf ears. The South struggled under the weight of British military operations, and in New England Morris's name and reputation were not as well known as they were in Pennsylvania. His bank obtained only $70,000 of the necessary $400,000 by summer's end, and the plan seemed doomed. At that time Morris received word that France had granted another loan of 2.5 million livres ($450,000). With funding secured, he announced that the Bank of North America would stop receiving capital subscriptions on October 1 and that an election for a board of directors would be held on November 1.

The use of funds from a French loan to purchase shares in a private venture in no way troubled Morris. He reasoned that the bank was essential to the survival of the Revolution, and employing public funds as he did benefited all the nation's citizens directly or indirectly.

Control of the Bank of North America was vested in a board composed of a dozen men, most of whom were acquaintances of Morris's. They selected his onetime business partner, Thomas Willing, as president. The bank completed arrangements for engraving bank notes by the end of November and rented a building from Tench Francis, Willing's brother-in-law. They drafted a charter for the Bank of North America and submitted it to Congress in December.

There was considerable opposition to the charter in Congress. Most objected on the ground that the Articles of Confederation did not authorize or allow the establishment of a national banking institution. Not only did the Articles contain no specific provision for such action, but there existed no

phrase or section that even implied Congress could make such authorization. Supporters of the bank claimed the country's survival depended on it, and that if the Articles did not authorize it, neither did they prohibit it. They countered the suggestion that the state of Pennsylvania charter it by pointing out that the Pennsylvania Assembly was not in session and that speed was essential if financial disaster was to be forestalled. Morris personally fought for approval. He begged, cajoled, and intimidated to obtain congressional votes. His department saw the bank as crucial, he explained, and he also required it for the great effort he made to supply the army. In the end necessity prevailed over theory. Congress voted on the last day of 1781 to approve the charter and establish the Bank of North America.

Morris promulgated the news of the bank's January 7 opening in letters that conveyed his own sense of exuberance. The bank, he explained, would "facilitate the management of the finances of the United States. The several States may, when their respective necessities require and the abilities of the bank will permit, derive occasional advantages and accommodations from it. It will afford to the individuals of all States a medium for their intercourse with each other and for the payment of taxes more convenient than the precious metals and equally safe. It will have a tendency to increase both the internal and external commerce of North America, and undoubtedly will be infinitely useful to all the traders of every State in the Union."

The "Morris notes," the mint, and the Bank of North America all contributed in important ways to the nation's fiscal recovery as the superintendent of finance envisioned it, but he knew of still another ingredient necessary for restoring public credit, the payment of the country's debt. (In many of those projects he shared the priorities of Alexander Hamilton.) Like other of Morris's measures, he designed the debt-funding scheme to link the sound private credit of American merchants to the credit of the United States. He hoped to induce wealthy men to furnish money in exchange for securities backed by the government's promise to redeem them. The key to the success of Morris's proposals was to collect adequate revenue to operate the government and simultaneously retire the public debt. Obtaining any substantial amount of money, unfortunately, proved a difficult matter. The Articles of Confederation severely limited the taxing powers of the government. The contributions of the states and a tariff provided the only funds. In February 1781 Congress introduced a proposed tariff that provided a 5 percent ad valorem duty on all "goods, wares, and merchandises of foreign growth and manufactures." Morris expended his every effort to have it enacted. Again and again he explained that a failure to provide adequate revenue for the nation would ultimately lead to disunion and defeat at the hands of the British. Restoration of public credit, he insisted, could only come after securing public faith in the government. To revive confidence in the United States, Congress needed to pass pending tariff legislation. He also pressed for a system to enable the nation to collect taxes levied for support of the national government by the states, but little enthusiasm existed in Congress for either method of raising revenue.

Specific objections to the tariff were made on several grounds. Morris did his best to support the proposed impost and to counter complaints. He cavalierly dismissed the claims of those who maintained a 5 percent impost would hinder commerce. To those who suggested crediting tariffs to the states that collected them, he explained the unfairness of such a practice to states with little foreign commerce. Unity and justice demanded impost revenues be turned over to the confederation. He included an appeal to patriotism in his rhetoric. Those who truly favored preserving the Union would support a tariff to establish the nation's credit. Opponents of the measure, he implied grimly, were those who would let the United States collapse.

Despite the hostility Morris's program encountered he refused to let it die. The tactic he adopted to build support for the tariff revealed his political sophistication. He first explained to the holders of the public debt that their certainty of receiving their due came only through adequate revenues. Then, to accentuate the truth of his words, he stopped issuing the new loan-office certificates that he customarily provided in place of interest payments on previous issues. The results of the move gave Morris considerable encouragement. His refusal to compensate public creditors enraged the classes who held most of the securities. His assurance to Benjamin Franklin that "there is a well grounded expectation that the clamors of our creditors will induce the several legislatures to [favor the impost]" was an accurate assessment of the political situation. By

January 1782 only three states had failed to support the tariff.

Once Congress approved a revenue measure for paying the public debt, Morris next had to meet the current expenditures. He issued a call to the states in the autumn of 1781 asking them to provide $8 million to prosecute the war in the next year. An elaborate but ineffective system for the collection of taxes levied by state legislatures was adopted. Despite the superintendent's pleas for funds and the administrative structure he developed to collect them, the results fell far below the amount requested, and even far below the $4 million he expected. By any method used to calculate the returns, the amount taken in scarcely exceeded the $422,000 reported by the treasurer.

That money fell far below what the government needed to operate. Even coupled with the credit supplied by the Bank of North America and the "Morris notes," the United States still fell $1 million short of its needs for 1782. Again, Morris tried to borrow money abroad. The superintendent of finance prodded Benjamin Franklin in Paris to obtain more funds, and in due course the French responded favorably. France provided a loan of 6 million livres ($1,080,000), payable in quarterly installments, to the United States for 1782. At the same time Franklin negotiated the loan in Paris, John Adams worked to obtain money from the Dutch. Dutch capitalists thwarted his initial efforts when they solicited subscriptions for the East India Company at the same time he tried to borrow funds. Investors preferred to offer their guilders to the company rather than risk them with the fledgling government of the United States. Not until early autumn did Adams secure $600,000 at 5 percent from a combination of private firms.

The two loans eased the difficulties faced by the superintendent of finance, but they did not end them. Although Morris could now draw on European funds to meet current requirements, he faced another crisis because he could not find individuals to purchase bills of exchange. The British directed their offensive of 1782 toward American commercial operations rather than against the Continental armies, and it forced a slowing of commerce everywhere in the nation and throughout the entire Atlantic trading system. The decline in activity closed most of the channels through which bills of exchange traded, and even the wealthiest merchants discovered their latitude for conducting business transactions was more constricted than in previous years.

Commercial prospects were further complicated, and Morris's task made correspondingly difficult in 1782, by the anticipated peace between Britain and the United States. Despite the heavier-than-usual pressure exerted by the Royal Navy against merchant shipping, men on both sides of the Atlantic assumed that peace was not far away. The settlement of the war and the shape of treaty arrangements to follow would have profound effects on trade, but few had any firm idea about the exact nature of those effects. In periods of severe uncertainty men of commerce tend toward caution.

To solve his immediate problems Morris tried several expedients. Like many of his countrymen he attempted unsuccessfully to operate through Havana, Cuba, as a means of circumventing the danger posed by the Royal Navy. He managed to sell some bills in Boston but never a sufficient number for his purposes. Other schemes involving bills, specie, and Caribbean exchanges were tried, but again they had only limited success. Matters were further complicated because those whose customary trade with the French was disrupted by British depredations had little need for bills of exchange drawn on France. Minor measures conceived by Morris failed to dispel the mood of trepidation over the future of American commerce, and indeed it only finally lifted when the war ended and Congress ratified the Treaty of Paris in 1783.

As superintendent of finance, Morris was charged with more than raising revenue for the nation. He also directed expenditures, and even in peacetime the chief continuing obligation of the government remained servicing the army. Incompetence, ineptitude, and occasionally fraud had characterized the military supply system during the early years of the Revolution, and Morris prided himself on the fact that he introduced considerable economy and efficiency into procurement practices. He expressed justified pride in the reforms, but even his changes and improvements in the system did not end all of the difficulties. Frequent disputes continued between the government and military contractors over payment, the quality of goods, and the meaning of contractual language. Morris never entirely succeeded in his attempts to induce harmony between officers and suppliers. Still, the fact that the army received more logistical support in 1783

than in any previous winter testified to the substantial improvements made under the new system.

In July 1782 Morris made a formal report to Congress on the state of the nation's credit. When he presented it, it attracted little interest, but by the following year, when peace seemed near, it created a political controversy that involved the Continental Army, the individual states, and the Office of Finance. As rumors of peace spread, the army grew increasingly restless. With pay in arrears and substantial amounts owed, many officers and men feared a rejection of their claims. Some observers thought the Republic stood on the brink of a coup. Early in January a delegation of officers complained to Congress over the lack of pay, their unsettled food and clothing accounts, and the failure of the government to make provision for the lifetime pensions at half-pay promised them in 1780. Congress ignored the complaints, which led to the circulation of an address to the officers of Washington's army camped near Newburgh, New York. Written by Maj. John Armstrong, although he kept his identity concealed at the time, the manifesto attacked the "coldness and severity" of Congress and warned the army to beware of men "who would advise to more moderation and longer forbearance." It called upon them to defy Congress if the members refused to meet their demands.

The summons to direct action had the backing of Gen. Horatio Gates and numerous political leaders. Even Gouverneur Morris, the close friend and chief deputy of the superintendent of finance, supported it. They hoped to use the threat of military rebellion to coerce the states into providing more funds for the confederation government. No evidence directly linked Robert Morris to the movement within the army, but he apparently supported the Newburgh movement as part of his attempt to unite all public and private creditors in an effort to create more pressure for the adoption of his fiscal program.

Many in the army agreed with Armstrong, but any effect his words might have had was turned aside by George Washington. On March 11, 1783, Washington issued an order prohibiting an unauthorized meeting called by the address. He summoned his own assembly of officers and assured them Congress would treat their claims with justice. He urged patience and cautioned them against marring the glory they had gained over the course of the war by turning against the nation and its govern-

Charles Wilson Peale's portrait of Morris

ment. In the end the victorious general prevailed over the disaffected major. The assembled officers unanimously affirmed their patriotism, expressed confidence in Congress, and denounced the "infamous propositions . . . in [the] late anonymous address."

In early 1783, when pressure from the army increased, Morris took an important step to reduce its intensity. He offered his resignation as superintendent of finance. He carefully explained the reasons for his impending departure. The danger of war had passed, he said, and his task of seeing the nation through the conflict had ended. Unfortunately, he prepared to leave before establishing the public finances on a more secure and permanent basis. Morris complained of his failure to achieve one of his most cherished goals. He chose resignation, he explained, since success proved so elusive in the political climate of the time. He planned to vacate the office on May 31 if "effectual measures are not taken by that period to make permanent provision for the public debts of every kind, . . . I will never be the minister of injustice."

The resignation statement had at least some effect on Congress. The day after its submission the members entered a full-scale debate on how to secure funding for the national debt. Arguments on ways to obtain revenues continued for several months without reaching consensus, and, unfortunately, Congress adopted no measures that satisfied the superintendent of finance. Morris complained bitterly over the rejection of his program and over the widespread criticism he received. Many in the country felt he overstepped the limits of legitimate political activity by the intensity of his efforts to stabilize the nation's finances. "There is such a disposition to traduce and vilify," he wrote, "that no prudent man will risk a fair reputation by holding an Office so important as mine."

Congress found it easier to reject Morris's fiscal plan than to ignore the demands of the army for back pay. There was no longer a threat of direct rebellion, but the presence of an unpaid and disgruntled corps of officers and men remained an implicit threat to the government. With an empty treasury and no new revenues anticipated, issuing notes payable in six months offered at least a temporary solution. The government paid out a new round of "Morris notes" for more than $500,000 by the summer of 1783. Morris again bore the brunt of criticism. This time his enemies attacked him for paying loyal soldiers in notes sure to depreciate. Stung by the charges, he denounced speculation in the notes as a "nefarious practice," but he could do little else but complain about the unfairness of the criticism. The exact rate of depreciation for the notes furnished to soldiers, while considerable, probably never exceeded that of the 1782 notes.

Issuing warrants–actually notes–to the troops only delayed the reckoning. Another temporary solution had to be found when the notes matured in six months. Morris again solved the problem for the short term, obtaining money to pay the warrants by issuing bills of exchange on funds in Holland. The lack of adequate funds in Europe to meet the new obligations created potential difficulties, but he had a plan to mitigate any catastrophe that developed. In early 1784 he realized his worst fears when he received word that creditors protested more than $300,000 of his bills. He then put his plan in action. He set out to strengthen the credit of the United States by extolling the economic potential of the nation in a flood of letters and memorials sent across the Atlantic. He also sent a few shiploads of tobacco and rice to Holland. Tax revenues provided partial payment for the commodities, and Morris supplied the remainder of the funds to load the ships from his own account.

Morris garnered his understanding of merchants and bankers from years of experience, and he knew the compensation for a shortage of $300,000 required more than a torrent of eloquence and a few shiploads of American products. He engaged Benjamin Franklin in a bill-kiting scheme that gave him more time to cover the shortfall with commodity remittances. Fortunately for the credit of the United States, John Adams ultimately negotiated a short-term, high-interest loan to cover the bills of exchange.

Through a combination of daring, luck, and measures born of sheer desperation, Morris managed to pay the warrants issued to disband the army. But he was badly mistaken if he assumed the complications with the military had ended. Peace brought a change in the nature of the difficulties, but finding solutions to the new problems continued to consume his time and energies. Only a small and inexpensive military force remained after the disbandment of the wartime army, and they had only minimal requirements. The supply system Morris previously developed remained in place after the Treaty of Paris, and it served the reduced American forces adequately. The contracts with Daniel Parker and Company, the firm which supplied the army successfully in 1783, were continued for the following year, and all seemed to be going well. Unfortunately, Parker fled the country only a hair's breadth ahead of his creditors, just after the negotiation of new contracts and after his firm received $200,000 for rations from the U.S. government. Morris took preliminary steps to recover the funds by filing suit but discovered the uncertainty of securing repayment from a fleeing debtor. The nation again failed to supply its soldiers without tapping funds slated for other expenditures, and Morris saw his plans confounded by circumstances over which he had no control.

Although Congress rejected the program devised by the superintendent of finance for funding the national debt, it enacted a measure that emphasized the need for organizing accounts as a prerequisite to paying them. Congress mandated collection of all outstanding claims. After validation, payment was to follow as soon as was practical. Mountainous problems of collection and validation existed. They involved questions of depreciation, the legality of certain charges, the reliability of evidence submitted, methods of detecting forgeries, compensation for documents destroyed during the war, and cases of officials who refused to cooperate.

The overburdened commissioners, responsible for collecting, validating, and settling claims against the government, had complicated and exacting tasks, but the superintendent of finance asked them to do even more. Morris deputized them as census takers to ascertain the condition of the new nation. Beyond matters relating strictly to the payment of the government's debts, their assignment included collecting information that fell under four general headings: geographical, moral, political, and commercial. The geographical information contained data on rivers, soils, topography, and possible locations for manufacturing and commercial enterprises. The moral inventory had little to do with the behavior of Americans. Morris wanted demographic information, and data on trades, occupations, farming, economic improvements, and the arts, "by which is not so much intended the fine as the useful arts." He hoped to learn the constitution of the various state and local governments and how they operated in practice. He also wanted names of the men who held public office at every level throughout the nation. Data on products, imports, and exports of every region, evaluations of road conditions, judgments on the value of lands, catalogs of navigation facilities, and estimates of the ease of obtaining credit followed. In addition, Morris wanted information necessary in the event of another war. He wanted to know the numbers of men available in the various states and the quality of forage in each region.

As the Revolution ended and the country struggled to place its economy on a stable peacetime footing, the nation's shippers and traders discovered many previously profitable trading patterns were closed to U.S. merchants who, having gained independence, could no longer participate in British imperial commerce. The China trade seemed the most promising new area in the first years after the war, and Morris, with his typical prescience, was a partner in the first American venture. When the *Empress of China* set sail for Canton in January 1784, a portion of her cargo belonged to him. The amount of his investment, $60,000, indicated he regarded the new trade as a major undertaking. In addition, he invested heavily in the voyages of the *Columbia* and the *Comte de Artois*, two trading vessels sailing from Europe for China.

Morris not only risked his money on untested trade routes during his reemergence as a major mercantile figure; he also acquired a new set of commercial associates. One of his postwar partners was Tench Tilghman, a former aide to George Washington. Morris supplied $12,000 in capital as his share of their joint mercantile venture. Their firm's major assets included the network of correspondents Morris established during his prerevolutionary business activities. As soon as word spread of the new partnership, letters arrived from Spain, France, England, Germany, Italy, and Portugal offering and requesting commercial services. A dispute with a European business connection led Morris to found another partnership with a longtime business associate, Benjamin Harrison, Jr., of Virginia. He also invested $20,000 in Constable, Rucker and Company, a firm organized in May 1784 with the expressed purpose of exploiting the opportunities offered by New York, the city Morris thought had potential to emerge as the most important port on the Atlantic coast.

By the time Morris actually retired from the position as superintendent of finance, he had an entire network in place to enable him to resume business operations on the grand scale that characterized his mercantile career before and during the American Revolution. No one familiar with his public and private careers imagined that within a dozen years he would be bankrupt, shielded only temporarily from his creditors behind the barricaded doors of the mansion at his country estate.

There was no indication of impending disaster when Morris left government service in May 1784. He resumed his political career and in 1785 was returned to the Pennsylvania Assembly. He had been elected to defend the Bank of North America from its enemies, and he did so effectively. Previous experience made him well aware of the role public opinion played in the formulation of fiscal policy, and he knew, too, how to manipulate it. He and other supporters of the bank hired Thomas Paine, the revolutionary war propagandist and author of *Common Sense* (1776), to write in its favor, and Morris was rumored to have contracted with publisher Matthew Carey to print and distribute the assembly's debates, which reflected favorably on the bank. In that same period he was profoundly concerned over the economic future of the nation, and attended a convention called to discuss problems bedeviling trade and commerce in the Chesapeake region. The

1786 meeting at Annapolis accomplished little. In its most noteworthy achievement, the delegates called for another convention to meet in Philadelphia the following spring to examine defects in the Articles of Confederation and to recommend modifications.

Morris went as a delegate to the Philadelphia meeting. Like Virginians Edmund Randolph and James Madison he understood the need for a national government not subservient to the whims and crochets of 13 separate states. He did not take a leading part in the debates nor did he serve actively on the committees of the meeting that became the Constitutional Convention. It is safe to assume he shared many opinions with Gouverneur Morris, his longtime friend and business associate, who spoke frequently in favor of a strong centralized government. The former superintendent of finance and seven other Pennsylvanians placed their signatures on the completed document.

After ratification of the Constitution written at the 1787 convention, Morris declined an offer to be secretary of the treasury under the new government. He chose instead to accept election to the U.S. Senate, where he served until 1795.

Unfortunately for Morris, his business affairs during these years did not go as well as his political career. In 1785 he contracted with the French Farmers-General, securing for himself a monopoly of the tobacco trade with France. This aroused the hostility of many American tobacco dealers, and the arrangement proved unsuccessful. Morris's ventures in land speculation were far more disastrous than his attempt to dominate the tobacco trade. Many Americans in the ebullience of the early national era assumed they could make vast profits by purchasing extensive tracts of land in the West and waiting for the migrations certain to follow. Farmers moving into the fertile valleys beyond the Appalachians would induce dramatic price increases, and staggering profits awaited those who had foresight enough to buy before the wave of migration.

Already a rich man by any measure of wealth used in the Republic's early years, Morris sought gain sufficient to make him rich even by European standards. He actually began his western speculations in 1780 during the Revolution and before most investors thought land purchases on the frontier could one day lift them high on a tide of profit. At that early date he formed a partnership with two other men and advanced $120,000 for procuring land in Virginia. This first investment, considered substantial when made, appeared insignificant compared to those a decade later. For Morris the era of wild and unrestricted land speculation started in 1790, when he undertook the series of purchases designed to make him the largest private landholder in America. At one point he gained a controlling interest in more than 6 million acres of Virginia, North Carolina, South Carolina, Georgia, and Kentucky. In addition, he bought several huge private estates and large areas of the land on which the new national capital was scheduled to be built. Morris channeled his investments through the North American Land Company, a $3 million partnership he organized with John Nicholson, once the comptroller general for Pennsylvania, and James Greenleaf, a former U.S. consul in Amsterdam. The company's 30,000 shares originally sold for $100 each, and Morris assured prospective purchasers of the wisdom of the investment. He advised stockholders not to expect ordinary 6 percent returns. Their investments might double or even triple in two or three years, he claimed. After 15 years they would be worth 10 or 15 times their original purchase price.

Morris did not feign enthusiasm for the potential profits in land speculation for the purpose of selling stock. He not only promoted his own company, he continually purchased more land. His transactions in New York alone involved millions of vacant acres, trust agreements that spanned the Atlantic, and hundreds of thousands of dollars.

Neither did Morris invest blindly. He traveled extensively through areas he thought might be worth acquiring and carefully analyzed their potential for profit. After a visit to the capital city, which was being laid out on the banks of the Potomac in 1796, he purchased the first of what would be holdings of more than 7,000 building sites. While there he learned of the sale of two lots for more than $4,000, and he confidently predicted a continuous rise in the city's property values for the next century.

Morris met Maj. Pierre L'Enfant on the sojourn to the future capital, and the Frenchman's talent and vision impressed him greatly. He commissioned Major L'Enfant to build him a mansion on the city block in Philadelphia he had purchased for that purpose the previous year. Although the plan called for marble walls, bas reliefs, opulent rooms, and elaborate gardens, the architect esti-

mated the cost at only $60,000. With the fervor he brought to all his undertakings, Morris ordered chairs and divans from Europe, classic statuary to grace the mansion's interior and grounds, and $25,000 worth of mirrors. He rented a residence across the street for $1,000 per year to watch construction of the house.

Morris never completed his dream palace. The first signs of impending financial collapse began to appear while it was under construction. He expected to finance the project with £75,000 from London, but a bank failure in England involved him in debts of twice that amount. Shortly afterward, the land speculation boom crumbled, and Morris ran out of cash at a time when many of his own notes came due. He reorganized his holdings, but that helped only slightly. He could not sell the vast acreage he held, he could pay neither notes nor land taxes, and work on his grand Philadelphia mansion came to a halt. Snow, rain, and sun eroded the three-story, unroofed structure, as the hapless owner struggled to resist a veritable army of men demanding payment of notes bearing his signature.

Even though his empire of paper and credit had collapsed, Morris continued at least for a time to hold property in the capital and retain ownership of his city block in Philadelphia. Still, he could not borrow money or pay the taxes coming due on his western tracts. A 200,000-acre parcel of land purchased in North Carolina for $27,000 was sold for taxes. "I believe I shall go mad," he wrote during those difficult times. "Every day brings forward scenes and troubles almost insupportable." In February 1798 he was arrested and taken to the Prune Street debtors' prison.

Morris lived in comfortable conditions while incarcerated, comfortable at least in comparison with usual prison standards in the eighteenth century. The quarters he occupied during the latter portion of his confinement were large enough to contain three writing desks, a table with a drawer, a breakfast table, a borrowed mahogany dining table, a Windsor settee, eight chairs, four trunks, three pine chests, and a letter case. The prison contained many like him, prosperous men fallen on bad times, with whom he could commiserate. Alexander Hamilton, George Washington, and Gouverneur Morris visited from time to time, and members of his family dined with him and kept him company every day. Morris remained in custody until after the passage of the Federal Bankruptcy Law in

1801. By the time of his release, he had served over three and one-half years in prison.

Morris never regained his health or fortune. He lived the remainder of his life in obscurity on a small annuity held by his wife, Mary. He died on May 8, 1806.

The life of Robert Morris cannot easily be analyzed. He was deeply involved in business, finance, and politics throughout his long career and was monumentally successful in all endeavors, at least until his last 15 years. Already one of the leading merchants in British North America on the eve of the Revolution, the knowledge and experience he acquired from his mercantile activities enabled him to serve the American cause well once the war began. He expanded his wealth during the course of the conflict with Britain through a series of partnerships that involved trading, privateering, and various types of financial transactions. As the leading merchant in the country, his experience and obvious talent for commerce led to his selection as superintendent of finance in 1781.

Morris understood the difficulties plaguing the United States as the war drew to an end. The decline of public credit, he knew, failed to reflect the condition of the nation's economy. Commerce flourished in postrevolutionary America, supported everywhere by private credit. Morris attempted to utilize the private sector to sustain the nation's finances until a permanent and stable fiscal foundation could be constructed for the government. Despite the many agonies and frustrations he endured during his term of office, Morris could congratulate himself on his achievements. He kept the country solvent under exceedingly difficult circumstances, and though the pay warrants issued to the army had been covered only by a propitious Dutch loan, a tiny surplus of $20,000 remained in the U.S. Treasury when he departed.

Had Congress adopted Morris's original plan for national fiscal recovery it is unlikely there would have been any movement for a revision of the Articles of Confederation. If, indeed, the holders of public securities induced the convening of the Constitutional Convention, their needs would have been met much earlier by the financial system he devised, and the pressure eliminated for restructuring the government. It is also likely, according to Clarence L. Ver Steeg, that if Congress enacted his program in its entirety, it would have foundered during the general commercial decline that followed the American Revolution.

Those who knew Morris well were extravagant in their praise, at least when he was successful. His expansive personality and lavish hospitality earned him the admiration of many who excoriated his politics and his habit of combining private and public interest. Although not known as a great orator, Morris's obvious command of financial details and processes enabled him to carry others with him when he spoke before the Congress, the Pennsylvania Assembly, committees, or in discussions with friends and colleagues.

Each phase of Robert Morris's career, his rise to wealth and prominence, his political successes, and his cataclysmic fall, was spectacular. Few if any possessed his speculative genius or skill at fiscal machination. His decline resulted neither from political enemies nor from those who envied his great wealth. In the end the combination of unfettered confidence in his own judgment and insatiable greed reduced him to near beggary.

Publication:

The Papers of Robert Morris, edited by E. James Ferguson and John Catanzariti, 6 volumes to date (Pittsburgh: University of Pittsburgh Press, 1973-   ).

References:

Ellis Paxson Oberholzer, *Robert Morris: Patriot and Financier* (New York: Macmillan, 1903);

Clarence L. Ver Steeg, *Robert Morris, Revolutionary Financier, With an Analysis of His Career* (Philadelphia: University of Pennsylvania Press, 1954);

Eleanor Young, *Forgotten Patriot: Robert Morris* (New York: Macmillan, 1950).

Archives:

Major collections of Robert Morris's papers are at the Historical Society of Pennsylvania, the Pennsylvania Archives, and the Library of Congress.

Levi P. Morton

(May 16, 1824-May 16, 1920)

by Dolores Greenberg

Hunter College and the Graduate
School and University Center, CUNY

CAREER: Partner, James M. Beebe & Company (1849-1855); senior partner, Morton, Grinnell & Company (1855-1861); senior partner, L. P. Morton & Company, Merchants (1861-1863); senior partner, L. P. Morton & Company, Bankers, New York; Morton, Burns & Company, London (1863-1869); senior partner, Morton, Bliss & Company, New York; Morton, Rose & Company, London (1869-1897); U.S. representative, state of New York (1879-1881); U.S. minister to France (1881-1883); vice-president of the United States (1889-1893); governor, state of New York (1895-1896); chairman of the board, Morton Trust Company (1899).

Levi Parsons Morton, vice-president from 1889 to 1893 under Benjamin Harrison, then a one-term governor of New York in 1895 and 1896, was also a prominent member of the late-nineteenth-century banking elite. Founder of the New York firm of Morton, Bliss & Company after the Civil War, he immediately extended his operations to the center of the world money market, and in 1869 established the London-based transatlantic partnership of Morton, Rose & Company. Morton's banking house quickly became one of the most important in the postbellum era. Besides being the acknowledged leader in the federal government's refunding operations and a foremost dealer in foreign exchange, it played a critical role in directing extensive railroad building during the 1870s and 1880s.

Morton's business career spanned half a century when sharp swings in the business cycle punctuated the pattern of national economic growth. Hardly a rags-to-riches story, Morton's success as an international financier reveals instead the possibilities available to a middle-class young man. Born on May 16, 1824, in Shoreham, Vermont, Morton came from a well-known family of New England

Levi P. Morton

Congregational ministers. His parents' admonishment that he work diligently, loving and serving God, did not prevent him from following the practical advice of his older brother, a lawyer, to educate himself in business rather than attend college. Consequently, at the age of eighteen Morton became a clerk in a dry goods commission store in Concord, New Hampshire. He planned to save from his salary of $200 a year and take advantage of the social connections that, as his brother had observed, were so important to a young man.

In keeping with the informality of retail operations in that era, when Morton opened a branch of the dry goods concern in Hanover, New Hampshire, he bartered local produce and dairy for such goods as cloth and tea and then received a commission from their resale in Concord. When his employer failed after the extended depression of the 1830s, the well-known Boston merchant-capitalist James Beebe, a principal creditor, continued the operation with Morton in charge. Morton prospered, soon bought Beebe out, and in 1849, at the age of twenty-five, was invited to become a junior partner in the wholesale firm of James M. Beebe & Company. He entered the wholesale trade by investing $12,000, the assets of his Hanover store.

In making the move from rural retailing to the wholesale import-export trade, Morton was following what proved to be a conventional path in the late-nineteenth-century banking community, one traveled by such German-Jewish bankers as the Seligmans, as well as by Morton's new partner, Junius S. Morgan. In 1851 Morgan joined the firm and it reorganized as Beebe, Morgan & Company. That import jobbing house, the largest in New England and second largest in the United States, facilitated the transatlantic distribution of raw materials and finished goods. Primarily it bought cotton in the American South, shipped it to England for resale, and purchased manufactured goods there for American consumption.

As a partner in Beebe's, Morton acquired specific know-how on financing foreign trade with credits advanced by English bankers, and, as important, he developed a network of valuable business contacts. His especially close tie to Morgan shaped his subsequent career. In addition, he became friends with George Boutwell, later secretary of the treasury under President Ulysses Grant, who in 1870 would offer Morton's banking house the government's first refunding contract. Cornelius Bliss, later chairman of the Republican State Committee, was also a member of Beebe's firm. Moreover, in 1852 Beebe sent Morton to London to initiate him in foreign affairs and to meet with his special financial agent, George Peabody, a New Englander who had established himself as a specialist in foreign-exchange operations in London.

When he was thirty-one, and soon after Morgan left for the House of Peabody, Morton decided to leave for New York, the nation's foremost commercial center. He achieved the goal of Horatio

Alger dreams when in 1855 he opened his own wholesale dry goods commission firm. Morton, Grinnell & Company was located on Broad Street just a few blocks away from the dry goods importer Seligman and Stettheimer and the soft goods store of Solomon Kuhn. The following year Morton, described as "a prosperous young merchant," married Lucy Kimball. He also cast his vote for the Republican presidential candidate, as he was to do ever after. His business prospered in the boom years from 1855 to 1857, selling cotton to New England mills and delivering their products south where domestically produced white sheeting was in great demand.

Scarcely had the Civil War begun when the repudiation of southern mercantile paper threatened to bring failure. Faced with the embargo on cotton and the suspension of southern trade, Morton declared bankruptcy. In 1861, having made the rounds of creditors with promissory notes, he reorganized as L. P. Morton & Company, Merchants, and took as his new junior partner Walter Burns, a Harvard graduate from a well-established mercantile family. In 1863 the two merchants turned to a more promising business, banking.

For the second time in a decade business failure served as the prelude to Morton's success. His new house, L. P. Morton & Company, Bankers, advertised its specialty as dealers in commercial paper and as drawers of foreign bills. As they were merchants adept at international credits, that business in remittances held special attraction, especially since the profits of exchange had risen continuously during the war. War supplies ordered abroad, as well as imported luxuries and goods of all sorts, meant larger foreign outlays when the gold premium was rising. The demand for foreign-exchange bills for use in actual payments effectively pushed prices up, while at the same time purchases by speculators who were investing in exchange at unprecedented rates further inflated the market. Besides remittances, Morton's firm also bought and sold government securities, took orders for stocks and bonds at home and abroad, and offered to take collection of dividends, drafts, and other moneys. To round out those general banking services and hoping to attract country bankers' balances, the bankers promised to pay interest on demand deposits.

In addition to setting up in New York, Morton correctly gauged the opening of opportunities abroad. By the winter of 1863 the mania for credit and banking operations in the world's most important money market, London, exceeded the speculative fever on Wall Street. Amidst the burgeoning of finance companies, discount houses, and new private banking partnerships, Burns opened an office in the city as the resident partner of Morton, Burns & Company.

Such were the attractions of London as a financial center that from the mid 1860s most of the outstanding banking houses in the city were of American or European origin. Morton, like the Browns, the Drexels, and the Seligmans, initially concentrated on the growth of exchange transactions. With the great cotton shipments to be covered after the war, handsome profits awaited from those transactions were handsome. But his ambitious new international banking house soon emerged as challenger in a field dominated by the Barings and the Rothschilds: government loans. During the Civil War, at the urgings of Robert Walker, Treasury Secretary Salmon P. Chase's special agent, Morton, Burns & Company floated a loan for the North. The negotiation boosted the firm's reputation and was well remembered in Washington, especially as Morton had supported the Union cause when other financiers expressed reluctance to do so. In the postwar period the foreign demand for U.S. government securities further contributed to the firm's business as speculation pushed the amount of government bonds held abroad to $1 billion by 1869.

Of all the new American transatlantic partnerships, Morton's house emerged as the acknowledged leader in the trading of U.S. government issues. As the magnitude of exchange and securities operations enlarged in the late 1860s, Morton decided to drop the firms' general banking services to concentrate on those specializations. Then in 1867 Morton took his first step in what would become another major aspect of his firms' business, investment in transportation. That year Morton became a director of the Dubuque & Sioux City, a railroad headed by New York banker Morris Ketchum Jesup.

Not only expanding opportunities but frequent reorganization characterized the growing private banking community of the late 1860s. In Morton's case, he had again to initiate the search for new partners in 1867 after Burns married Mary Morgan, the daughter of Morton's mentor and friend, Junius Morgan. As a consequence, what had started as a simple partnership developed into overlapping transatlantic copartnerships, joining two separate organizations, each with increased financial resources and connections.

The formation of Morton, Bliss & Company in New York in 1869 and Morton, Rose & Company in London allowed for two separate legal entities, each with its own members and capital. Although the senior partners in both firms insisted on close scrutiny of all investments by the other, the separate structure allowed special advantages. The individual firm was directly responsible to its clients. Management made decisions regarding foreign exchange more quickly. Each firm remained responsible for its own capital, but at the same time the companies transferred, profits and losses from the books of one firm to the other when they thought it opportune.

Morton's new senior partner in New York, George Bliss, a former Connecticut dry goods merchant, contributed experience in international credits, an interest in railroads, and substantial capital. Like Morton, he began his career as a clerk in a retail store and quickly became a partner. Bliss married the boss's daughter and in 1844 moved to New York as a partner in the newly opened import jobbing house of Simeon B. Chittenden and John Jay Phelps. He started his own wholesale dry goods business in 1853, but during the Panic of 1857 offered Phelps a partnership. The merchants prospered from the price rise during the Civil War, buying cheap in anticipation and selling on the high side before the war ended. Bliss also turned to the possibilities of railroad investment, becoming a subscriber to the New York Metropolitan Railroad Company, proposing to build the city's first underground. By 1869 his considerable real estate holdings had also contributed to his wealth, and when he entered the final phase of his career, becoming a private banker, it was estimated that he brought from $900,000 to $2.5 million to the Morton firm, while Morton's own share only came to an estimated $100,000.

The London replacement when Burns left, the former Canadian minister of finance, Sir John Rose, especially distinguished the new house. Rose's reputation as a statesman of wide experience, with government connections in Ottawa, London, and Washington, strengthened the standing and business opportunities for Morton's firm. As minister of finance for the Dominion, Rose had had close ties to Washington. When he joined the partnership he also acted as chief negotiator of the *Alabama Claims* case. He continued the special services that led to the signing of the *Alabama* Treaty and, as a consequence, in the summer of 1872 the Queen made him a baronet. As a private banker Rose remained a member of the London Committee of the Bank of Montreal and also served as the unofficial high commissioner for Canada, a post specially created by his good friend, the prime minister, Sir John Macdonald.

By the early 1870s the powerful foreign connections of the reorganized firm gave it a great advantage in the competition for business. In January 1871 not only did the Prince of Wales dine with Morton before a gala in the Prince's honor at Delmonico's, but he then arrived in Morton's carriage. The "Street," which put a value on everything, computed the honor to the new firm at a minimum of $50,000 to more than $100,000. Not surprisingly, the English government selected Morton, Bliss & Company as one of the three American firms to handle the transmission of the $15.5 million awarded to the United States by the Court of Arbitration in the *Alabama* case.

By the early 1870s Morton had also forged important political ties at home. He was known in Washington as a good friend of Secretary of the Treasury George Boutwell and of President Grant. Indeed, the partners in Jay Cooke were furious at what they charged was undue preference when Boutwell offered Morton's firm the government's first refunding contract. Morton in fact declined the business because of possible conflict-of-interest charges owing to Rose's role in the *Alabama* negotiations. However, in 1873 the four-year-old firm was offered and accepted management of the government's second refunding contract. By then Morton's banking house had the business, the political influence, and the international connections to be ranked among the foremost financial firms of the period. Morton had been dubbed "the representative of Wall Street in the Republican Party." Rumors circulated widely, much to the pleasure of his new wife, Anna Livingston Street (whom he had married two years after Lucy's death), that the president would name him secretary of the treasury. Again because of possible conflict-of-interest charges he was bypassed. Instead, in 1874 the U.S. government named Morton, Rose & Company the fiscal agent in London for the Navy and State depart-

ments, agencies they retained until the Democrats captured the presidency in 1884.

In the immediate postwar years of 1865 and 1866, trading in government securities had dominated the investment market. However, over the next two years public enthusiasm for rail building spread to the Pacific, making railroads the "big plum" for investment bankers. While the completion of the first transcontinental buoyed investor confidence, heavy purchases of government issues by national banks in 1869 sent their prices up and their yields down so that rail issues became especially attractive. By 1870 investors even subscribed to foreign issues with surprising success. The prevailing enthusiasm masked potential risk as investors willingly bought unsecured bonds, for unbuilt track, of new companies that had never paid a dividend. And up to the Panic of 1873 it was said that high interest rates made rail securities the "most popular form of investment of a personal nature open to the people of the United States."

Immediately after the formation of Morton, Bliss & Company in 1869 the partners turned to opportunities in railroad enterprise. As the crucial problem for investment bankers was what to do with money, they followed opportunities in the investment market. Morton worked behind the scenes in alliance with the era's most publicly censured rail speculators—Oakes Ames, Jay Gould, Collis Huntington, Russell Sage. But for financiers reputation counted as a valued asset. To guard the credit rating of his firm, as a matter of policy Morton refused to be identified with all of the roads with which he and his firm had affiliated, since such business would destroy his carefully fostered conservative image. For example, although Morton agreed to serve as a director on the board of the Union Pacific and his firm had become transfer agent for the transcontinental in 1871, he refused reelection when Gould entered the management in 1873. The *Commercial and Financial Chronicle* described the resignation as a "great blow" to the railroad. No publicity surfaced when an unknown junior partner replaced Morton or when Morton rejoined the board the following year. Instead, his firm continued as the financial and transfer agent for Gould's road until 1876.

Those railroad affiliations reveal a pattern of banker alliances for the direct financing of interregional routes in the South and West that date from the first postwar boom. Morton, his partners, and other prominent bankers became investors in high-risk, long-range, extensive projects. They formulated and implemented system-building strategies, provided for the financial needs of the rapidly expanding industry, and tracked the many-faceted opportunities for profit. Morton's operations during the 1870s and 1880s belie the argument that private bankers acted as protectors of their creditor clientele to check growth and competition in favor of stability. Despite the constraint of his more cautious partner, Bliss, Morton's firm encouraged new construction, acquisitions, and mergers.

The direct financing of the Milwaukee & St. Paul Railroad illustrates Morton's willingness to back an aggressive young company with grandiose plans for competitive, developmental, western expansion. He and Isaac Sherman of Duncan, Sherman & Company were named directors in 1871 to bring in new capital. Morton worked closely with Russell Sage, the president, and a board that included Oakes Ames, soon to be a central figure in the Credit Mobilier scandal. Moreover, he supported construction company methods that historians typically associate with "buccaneer promoters." Morton favored the technique as a way to finance new mileage, since it allowed the partners to increase their stocks and bonds at insider prices, to wield control in interlocking corporate structures, and to further the firm's business as a financial intermediary dealing in long-term credits. The road grew from 835 miles in 1868 to 1,399 miles by 1874; it boasted nine divisions and had purchased a controlling interest in Western Union. But according to railroad analyst Henry Varnum Poor, the expansion was unnecessary and unwise, reflecting the management's pursuit of "wild and visionary schemes."

In 1873, after the panic of that year, Morton prepared a circular urging Milwaukee & St. Paul shareholders to approve a $35 million consolidated mortgage for the road, by then renamed the Chicago, Milwaukee & St. Paul. Morton, Rose & Company successfully floated the issue in London. However, in 1875 Morton and Sage were forced out in a struggle with Alex Mitchell and Jay Gould. Nevertheless, Morton retained his security holdings and was called on to finance directly new construction by the end of the decade. In addition, during the market upsurge of 1879 Morton's firm purchased and placed millions more Chicago, Milwaukee & St. Paul bonds.

The profits of interregional construction beckoned Morton south as well as west. In 1870 he had also joined with Oakes Ames to finance, build, and operate the first all-rail route from New Orleans to Texas. Besides Morton, the banking group behind that project included Bliss, Joseph Seligman, and Louis Von Hoffman. Former New York governor and senator Edwin D. Morgan, together with Tammany boss William Tweed, and John Stewart, subtreasurer of the United States during the Civil War, completed the syndicate that intended to build west of the Mississippi as far as Houston. Construction, financed by the directors, and also subsidized by $3 million in state government donations, capital subscriptions, and guarantees, started immediately on the reorganized road, renamed the New Orleans, Mobile & Texas.

Morton had also joined the board of directors of the Missouri, Kansas & Texas by 1870. Known as the Katy, that company planned to reach the southern boundary of Kansas as part of a larger strategy to build and buy roads connecting the cattle-raising regions of Texas with northern and eastern markets. Morton supported construction from Kansas City south to New Orleans at the same time that his partner, Bliss, a director of the Illinois Central, similarly encouraged a projected north-south line to New Orleans for that company. And not surprisingly, Morton's London firm handled the sale of a $5 million sterling bond issue to finance Illinois Central construction.

During the frenzied rail-building of the early 1870s Morton looked forward to integrated systems extending east and west from Chicago and reaching south to points along the Gulf coast. He shared the naive optimism of these years and encouraged competitive overbuilding to create overlapping triangular trade routes. At the same time, as a member of the New York Chamber of Commerce, as early as 1870 Morton had supported connections to urban rail systems. He joined the board of the New York Viaduct Railroad in 1871 with high hopes for linking interstate through systems to city terminals as well as for improving local passenger service.

When money-market tightness culminated in the Panic of 1873, almost all the roads Morton had affiliated with suffered. His banking house was challenged by railroad default, insolvency, receivership, foreclosure, and reorganization before either legal or institutional precedents had been established to guide decision-making in the pioneer industry. Although the full effects of the most severe depression on record were not felt until 1875, the economic consequences quickly intensified dependence on banker services. Moreover, contrary to accepted interpretations of banker behavior, the inevitable complications did not drive Morton away from the railroad industry or signal the demise of his influence. Morton and his partners coped with constant problems and fixed policy in order to recover their direct investments by refinancing and reorganization. Also bondholder clients in New York and London, like those of the Illinois Central, turned to Morton's firms to resolve railroad tie-ups, compelling the New York partners to take an active role in the operation, leasing, and sale arrangements of defaulted property. Then, too, railroad executives such as Russell Sage and Joseph Kennedy called on Morton's firm for operating funds as well as long-term credits to complete construction projects. The depression actually enlarged the banker's sphere of influence. It schooled him and his partners in the techniques of corporate financial management in a vulnerable new industry.

Morton's New York house survived the downswing fairly well. In 1877 Bliss reported to the London partners, "On the whole I think the firm here are in a better position than at any former time." For the time being, at least until recovery occurred, he looked expectantly to new deals in government refunding transactions as the least risky and best business available. Certainly his firm was "stronger . . . than at any former period" in terms of political influence. Having won the federal refunding loan of 1873, and then that of 1876, the partners felt fairly confident of again winning syndicate management of the upcoming refunding operation despite intense competition from the other major contenders—Drexel, Morgan & Company; August Belmont, agent for the Rothschilds; and the Seligmans. Without doubt Morton's election to Congress in 1878 from New York's silk-stocking district added to his influence in Washington.

As anticipated, Morton, Bliss & Company became the acclaimed leader in the federal refunding operations of January 1879. Moreover, Morton became chairman of the National Republican Finance committee in 1879, setting up the crucial "Morton Fund" that made victory possible in the midwestern swing states of Indiana and Ohio. He fully expected to be named James Garfield's secretary of the trea-

sury and so turned down an offer of the vice-presidency at the Chicago convention. Much to his chagrin, the president proved more independent on this issue than expected. Instead of the secretaryship, he offered Morton an appointment, which he rejected, as secretary of the navy. And that rebuff of the New York financier proved a key factor in the dramatic resignations of both New York senators, Roscoe Conkling and Tom Platt. In part to save party unity and in part because the foreign appointment benefited his banking firms, Morton instead accepted the post of minister to France.

After the successful resumption of specie payments in 1879, business confidence gradually revived. By the second quarter rail stocks, even of companies previously in default, and bonds of all sorts spiraled so rapidly that it surprised Wall Street. From 1879 to 1882 speculation was the order of the day. Market manipulation puffed prices to create an irresistible demand for bonds and shares that offered quick returns in an active market. Not only did Morton, Bliss & Company increase its transactions on the New York Exchange, Morton, Rose & Company also looked to the lively market there and in London for fast returns. Reflecting the intertwining political and economic ties to the Anglo-American business elite, buying and selling was done for the accounts of both firms, for the partners' personal accounts, and for joint accounts with the partners' political friends such as Roscoe Conkling, James Blaine, William Washburn, and Sir George Stephen.

In those years Morton figured as an important participant in stock syndicates. Historians have presented the most famous of such operations, the sale of 250,000 New York Central & Hudson River shares, as a one-man operation, particularly as "J. P. Morgan's first major venture in corporate investment banking." Contemporaries more correctly identified the sale as a syndicate transaction, consisting not only of Drexel, Morgan but also of Morton's firm. The negotiation went so smoothly that Morton, Bliss & Company secretly agreed to take an interest with Sage and Gould in another ring working the market to buy the balance of the syndicate holdings. Returns from those New York Central sales were immediately slated for a syndicate of Collis P. Huntington's Central Pacific stock.

While profits came easily with only minor risks in the bull market, Morton skeptically appraised more demanding propositions for proportional returns. Yet increasingly, as rails replaced governments, he endorsed once again the "young America" credo of the early 1870s. And as losses were recouped from the profits of reorganization, compounded by stock operations, his earlier hesitancy vanished. Despite the burdens of direct investment, so onerous during the depression, Morton again became an advocate of interterritorial expansion. Before he left for Paris in 1881, his office on Nassau Street filled with a steady stream of visitors outlining new schemes. So rapidly did his firm expand its rail commitments that the possibility of inadequate cash reserves soon replaced concerns over inadequate business or the low profit margins of governments.

Just as Morton's banking house continued to play a critical role in directly shaping extensive building at home, during the 1880s Morton actively supported construction of a Canadian transcontinental. The road's early history is particularly interesting for it so well illustrates the factors that worked to obscure American involvement until the end of the decade. In fact, Stephen only agreed to assume the presidency of the company, the Canadian Pacific, if he could count on Morton's and Sir John's participation. At the same time, the prime minister, Sir John Macdonald, deliberately covered this connection with his rhetoric of economic nationalism, even though Macdonald depended from the start on this Anglo-American house to make his "Impossible Dream" a reality.

Ironically, the Americans even more than the prime minister guarded against disclosure of their support of developmental enterprise across the divide. What had long been Morton's preference to conceal his railroad affiliations was sharpened by his burgeoning political career. As a result, Morton and Bliss were secret, unlisted signatories to the original contract with the government for construction of the railway. Despite its covert character, their objections brought the reworking of the Canadian Pacific charter. And despite Morton and Bliss's refusal to take a seat on the board, in 1882 they arranged for traffic interchanges with Vanderbilt's Michigan Central and for a fresh infusion of funds for ongoing construction from a New York-based syndicate. By 1884 Morton's firms had become the road's major source of emergency funds, and they continued to provide crucially needed aid into 1885.

Although they shaped key policies and routed venture and loan capital across the border from 1881, Morton and his partners repeatedly rejected invitations to become directors. As Bliss wrote to Stephen in 1885 when again pressed to join the board, "The considerations which governed us hitherto still exist in regard to a member of our firm here assuming the responsibility of being a director in your Coy.... We are prosecuting a business of such a kind that it is desirable to avoid identifying ourselves before the public in any large outside enterprise."

In 1888, just a year after Morton finally acquiesced and became a Canadian Pacific director, Senator Arthur Gorman called for an investigation of Canadian control of U.S. rails. Gorman charged Canadian influence on American political figures, and the press pointed to L. P. Morton, Republican vice-presidential candidate, who resigned a seat on the Canadian Pacific board immediately after his nomination. According to Morton's public disclaimers, he had never attended a meeting or exercised any of his functions as a director. He had been chosen merely to fill the place temporarily until an election was held and a Canadian director chosen. Nothing could have been further from the truth. Moreover, Morton and his partners in New York and London continued to be intimately involved in Canadian Pacific affairs until the death of Bliss in 1896 and the dissolution of Morton, Bliss & Company in 1897.

Morton's firm's involvement in the reorganization of the Chesapeake & Ohio and its 1888 consolidation with the Big Four represents another instance of the long-term involvement of bankers in railroad affairs. It also places in perspective what has come to be known as "Morganization" and sheds new light on the restructuring regarded as a landmark in J. P. Morgan's career as a consolidator, and a symbol of the rescue of the industry from buccaneer promoters. Yet, seen against the events of two decades, the new system, joining the southern and western roads, represented not the beginning of banker-induced combination, but the culmination of plans that date back to the early 1870s. Bliss, John S. Kennedy, and Boston banker Thomas Perkins had taken control of the road as early as 1870 to implement interregional alliances. They continually improvised new techniques to overcome legal restraints or to mitigate financial burdens. Of the original group only Bliss remained when the company was reorganized in 1880 as the

Big Four (the Cincinnati, Indianapolis, St. Louis & Chicago), and he subsequently took a seat in every board election. Bliss, the president Melville Ingalls, and Collis Huntington of the Chesapeake & Ohio became controlling stockholders. The trio dominated policy until the mid 1880s, when the roads' financial problems and the capital straits of Morton's firm necessitated new capital alliances. It was then, after almost two decades of banker direction, that J. P. Morgan & Company reluctantly agreed to become involved in restructuring and financing this system.

In the mid 1890s, the period when banker control was publicly acknowledged, Morton's New York firm was in the process of dissolution. By 1893, at the onset of the depression, Morton had just completed his term as vice-president under Benjamin Harrison. Bypassed for renomination, he directed his energies to reordering his political career. A year after the death of Bliss in 1896 Morton entered into negotiations for the New York firm's reorganization as the Morton Trust Company. As of October 1, 1899, Morton, then seventy-five and near retirement, became chairman of the board of directors for a financial corporation that included James Alexander, president of the Equitable Life Insurance Society; George F. Baker, president of the First National Bank; Frederick Cromwell, treasurer of the Mutual Life Insurance Company; Henry Flagler, vice-president of Standard Oil; William C. Whitney of Kuhn, Loeb & Company; and W. G. Oakman, president of Guaranty Trust Company. And the subsequent merger with J. P. Morgan's Guaranty Trust Company reflected the consolidation movement that continued to mark the financial and industrial sectors into the twentieth century.

Levi P. Morton's career, revealing the very active role of reputable financiers in fostering competitive rail expansion in the 1870s and 1880s, alters the usual account of investment bankers who, it is said, took control in the 1890s to rationalize an overexpanded industry. His move from barter to banking and then his eagerness to track all opportunities for profits in the emerging rail industry, taking advantage of the ups and downs of the business cycle, sharpens historical understanding of the broader postwar patterns of economic growth. Morton and his partners were considerably more than financial intermediaries, mobilizers of other people's money, and the conservative spokesmen for a creditor clientele. The problems of the 1870s had served as a catalyst to banker-induced consolidation, and the recovery of the late 1870s also marked the displacement of individual promoters in reorganizations and related stock operations. Indeed, until the development stage drew to an end in the late 1880s, Morton and other important bankers such as the Seligmans continued to supply venture, equity, and bonded capital for projects designed to create interregional links to far-flung urban markets and overseas outlets.

Publication:
Personal Memorandum of Levi P. Morton (New York: Morton Trust Company, 1904).

References:
Dolores Greenberg, *Financiers and Railroads, 1869-1889: A Study of Morton, Bliss & Company* (Newark: University of Delaware Press, 1980);

Greenberg, "A Study of Capital Alliances: The St. Paul & Pacific," *Canadian Historical Review*, 57 (March 1976): 25-36;

Greenberg, "Yankee Financiers and the Establishment of Trans-Atlantic Partnerships: A Re-examination," *Business History*, 16 (January 1974): 17-35;

Robert McElroy, *Levi Parsons Morton: Banker, Diplomat, and Statesman* (New York: Putnam's, 1930).

Archives:
The Levi P. Morton Papers are in the New York Public Library. The George Bliss Papers, with their rich letter collection, are in the New-York Historical Society.

Mutual Savings Banks

by John Majewski

University of California, Los Angeles

In contrast to other types of banks, mutual savings banks were nonprofit organizations. There were no stockholders: all assets were owned by depositors, and all profits were deposited into their accounts. Mutual banks closely resemble trust funds, as bank managers invested the deposits, but they were not permitted to receive any profits. The purpose of a mutual was to encourage small savers. Mutuals were a close relative of nineteenth-century British trustee banks, which actually offered a government-subsidized interest rate to attract small depositors.

Community-oriented businessmen organized most mutuals in the United States. The main goal of the businessmen was to encourage thrift among the working class. Founders of mutual banks perceived thriftiness as an important social goal, an indicator of moral progress. Many mutual founders were, not surprisingly, Quakers, who deeply believed in the virtues of thrift. Mutual founders also thought that working-class savings softened the consequences of unemployment; in that sense mutuals became a form of self-help charity. Mutuals also provided economic benefits for the community by tapping into an unexploited source of capital. Many commercial banks, for example, encouraged the formation of mutuals as a source of funds.

Mutuals filled an important niche in nineteenth-century American banking. The small saver had few safe places to deposit money. Early-nineteenth-century commercial banks principally concerned themselves with note issue and usually did not accept small deposits. In some states, such as Massachusetts, laws prohibited commercial banks from paying interest on deposits. The general public also resented commercial banks as a source of economic instability. Savings and loan associations, meanwhile, usually accepted deposits only for those seeking mortgage loans.

The first mutual savings bank was the Philadelphia Savings Fund Society, which opened in 1816. By 1860 some 278 mutual savings banks with total assets of almost $1.5 million conducted business. The mutuals gained popularity in the Northeast, where a growing working class and numerous small tradesmen provided a large group of potential savers. By 1860, for example, $36.60 per capita was deposited in Massachusetts mutual savings banks; in New York $17.38 was deposited per capita. Mutuals mobilized the funds of the small saver who normally eschewed investments and thereby helped finance the rapidly growing American economy.

Mutuals stayed in the Northeast. Economic conditions initially accounted for this concentration, as the agricultural West and South did not have a large body of small savers. Later, state regulation increasingly restricted mutuals, and only 18 states allow mutual banking as of 1988. However, mutuals have remained a powerful force in America's capital markets in the twentieth century. The number of mutuals has decreased, but total deposits have continued to grow, accounting in 1964 for approximately 20 percent of all savings deposits in the United States.

References:

Emerson W. Keyes, *A History of Savings Banks in the United States,* 2 volumes (New York: Bradford Rhodes, 1876);

Hugh T. Rockoff, "Varieties of Banking and Regional Economic Development in the United States, 1840-1860," *Journal of Economic History,* 35 (March 1975): 160-181;

Alan Teck, *Mutual Savings Banks and Savings and Loan Associations: Aspects of Growth* (New York: Columbia University Press, 1968).

National Banking and Currency Acts

by Richard H. Timberlake

University of Georgia

The National Banking Act was passed as a war measure by Congress and approved by President Abraham Lincoln on February 25, 1863. Its immediate function was to create an institutional demand for the burgeoning volume of government securities that the federal government issued to finance the Civil War. The act had its roots, however, in the banking policy of the Whig party back through the decades of the nineteenth century to Henry Clay, and before him to Alexander Hamilton.

"National bank" in Whig literature meant a federally chartered supercommercial bank that would carry on a banking business with both the government and the private economy. The First and Second Banks of the United States were such institutions. They had, however, become politically unacceptable in the Jacksonian Era, especially to Andrew Jackson and the hard-money Democrats. Nonetheless, the Whigs had continued to support the national bank concept, and their Republican successors continued the tradition.

The secession of Southern states from the Union in 1860-1861 also included the secession of Southern congressmen from the federal Congress. Since those men were all Democrats, their absence left the Whig-Republicans as a congressional majority for the first time since 1840. Their new status enabled the Republicans to bring out of mothballs some of their more treasured projects, one of which was a national bank, and feel fairly certain of favorable legislative action.

The institution that finally emerged in 1863 was a multibank system and not the monolithic bank of the United States with branches that some of the earlier Whigs had envisioned. It included, however, the concept of a reserve-holding core of banks in the central-reserve cities, or redemption centers, as well as a satellite system of country banks in smaller communities.

All banks in the national system had to be chartered by the federal government–specifically by the office of the comptroller of the currency in the Treasury Department. Membership in the system was permissive and to some degree exclusive. Banks were not forced to join, and some banks could not meet the requirements. Nonetheless, the system-wide regulation to which all would be subject promised a degree of assurance to reasonably sound banks that other national banks would also be sound.

Reserve requirements of greenbacks and specie to national bank notes and deposits were specified for all banks in the system: 25 percent for banks in reserve cities, 15 percent for all others. Note issues were to be uniform in design, and all national banks had to accept each other's notes at par. The act limited total note issues to $300 million. The secretary of the treasury made allocations of notes to the participating banks, one-half of the $300 million on the basis of "representative population, and the remainder . . . [on the basis of] existing banking capital, resources, and business." National banks had to hold approved government securities as collateral for the notes, and each national bank had also to hold government securities equal to at least one-third of its capital.

Many state banks found they had little to gain by joining the new system, and, of course, until the war ended, Southern banks were not eligible.

Joining the national banking system offered several advantages, including the possibility of being chosen as a depository bank for the Treasury's tax revenues. Another advantage was the promotional advertising value of the national bank's name on the notes it circulated. To make participation even more attractive, Congress in 1865 amended the original act so that nonnational banks had to pay a 10 percent prohibitory tax on their issues of bank notes. That provision had two major effects. Many more banks became national banks, and banks that still did not want to join the system avoided the tax by using demand deposits exclusively to finance their loans and investments. Thus, the use of demand deposits greatly increased, and state bank note issues became a thing of the past. Like the treasury notes that the U.S. Treasury had issued as fiscal expedients on several occasions before 1860, the national bank notes were legal tender for all payments due to and from the federal government except for customs payments to the Treasury and payments of interest on the national debt from the Treasury.

The fixed amount of national bank notes permitted by the act proved a sticky political issue. Although most of the note apportionment came between the end of the war and early 1868, national banks in southern states comprised only 4 percent of all national banks and received allotments of only 3 percent of total national bank notes.

The reason for that misallocation, in apparent disregard of the apportionment provision in the act, resulted from a section in the Internal Revenue Act of 1864 that gave preference to all existing state banks over newly organizing banks in converting to a national status. The National Banking Act itself implied that priority. The comptroller of the currency and the secretary of the treasury also acted on the presumption that Congress, in framing the act, intended to nationalize the existing system. In practice this principle conflicted with the principle of apportionment. In July 1870 Congress supplemented the original $300 million of allowable national bank notes with an additional $54 million; but the banking fraternity still did not generally accept national banking.

The so-called inelasticity of note issue presented another perceived problem of both the greenbacks and national bank notes. Inelasticity meant the inability of the monetary system to adjust the nominal supply of money to the demands generated by long-term economic growth and to short-term seasonal agricultural requirements. The quantity of greenbacks, which the government froze in 1868, and the quantity of national bank notes, which required collateral deposits of approved U.S. government securities, both contributed to the inelasticity problem. Furthermore, the law stated that the value of the collateral securities for the issue of national bank notes was the lower of their par or market values. In addition, their production and disposition required more than six weeks after a national bank

applied for them. Since market values of the securities hovered well above par all the time after 1868, national banks that would issue notes faced a formidable cost in doing so.

The government divorced itself from all of the note issue problems of the national banks when Congress passed the Resumption Act in 1875. That act called for reductions of greenbacks on the basis of hoped-for increases in national bank notes until the planned convertibility of greenbacks into gold coin could occur in 1879 at pre-Civil War parity. The act also abolished all constraints on national bank organization and on the issue of national bank notes. From that time on only the "needs of trade" were supposed to ration the quantity of national bank note issues.

National banks never achieved the dominant position in the banking system that their supporters had expected. By 1900 deposits in national banks stood at $2,356 million while deposits in nonnational banks totaled $3,005 million. Neither did the larger national banks become the anticipated lenders of last resort for the smaller banks, both national and nonnational, that sponsors of the system had envisioned.

The passage of the Federal Reserve Act in 1913 made the national banking system largely obsolete, since all national banks had to join the new Federal Reserve System. Federal Reserve notes also supplanted national bank notes as conventional hand-to-hand currency. The government's "profits" from the gold-dollar devaluation in 1934 were used to retire the last of those notes. Nonetheless, all the trappings of the national banking system remain to this day; and the form if not the substance of national banking remains prominent in the banking industry.

References:

Philip Cagan, *Determinants and Effects of Changes in the Money Stock, 1875-1960* (New York: National Bureau of Economic Research, 1965);

Charles A. Conant, *A History of Modern Banks of Issue,* sixth edition (New York: Putnam's, 1927; reprinted, New York: Kelley, 1969);

Milton Friedman and Anna J. Schwartz, *A Monetary History of the United States, 1867-1960* (Princeton: Princeton University Press, 1963);

A. Barton Hepburn, *A History of Currency in the United States,* revised edition (New York: Macmillan, 1924);

O. M. W. Sprague, *History of Crises under the National Banking System* (Washington, D.C.: National Monetary Commission, 61st Congress, 2nd Session; Senate Document No. 538, 1910);

Richard H. Timberlake, *Origins of Central Banking in the United States* (Cambridge, Mass.: Harvard University Press, 1978);

Eugene Nelson White, *The Regulation and Reform of the American Banking System, 1900-1929* (Princeton: Princeton University Press, 1983);

Horace White, *Money and Banking*, sixth edition (New York: Ginn, 1935).

National Banks and State Banks

The term "national bank" in American financial history referred to the type of charter under which a commercial bank originated. Until 1863, when Congress passed the National Banking Act, the only national banks to exist were the First and Second Banks of the United States (BUS). Those two institutions differed greatly from the national banks chartered after 1863. First, each BUS had some "central" bank powers, meaning that to a degree they could affect the money supply through loans and note issue based on their large gold and silver (specie) reserves. Second, each had a huge capital relative to other commercial banks of the day. Third, despite the fact that 80 percent of the stock remained in private hands, each was a public institution that had certain monopoly privileges in its charter. For example, the charters stated that the government would charter no other national banks as competitors during the length of either BUS charter. Perhaps their most important advantage over other commercial banks, and the most important difference separating them from the national banks created after 1863, was their ability to establish branches in any of the several states. Thus, the two banks of the United States could engage in interstate branching more than 100 years before the question of branching across state lines emerged as a controversial issue. States did not have the authority to regulate the BUS or its branches because the banks operated under federal law. Nor could they tax the BUS or its branches, as the Supreme Court ruled in the famous *McCulloch* v. *Maryland* case (1819).

The Second BUS failed to win recharter in 1832 when President Andrew Jackson vetoed the recharter bill and Congress could not override the veto. It limped along but no longer even had any effective banking power after 1833, when Jackson removed the government's deposits, taking much of the bank's deposit base. When its charter officially expired in 1836, the nation carried on without the services of a central bank until 1913, when Congress created the Federal Reserve System. From 1836 to 1913 the U.S. Treasury handled some of the tasks that the BUS had performed, including holding government specie deposits and making the government's international payments.

Under the National Banking Act the federal government granted charters to groups of five individuals or more, provided they met the relatively high capitalization requirements of $200,000 for banks in large cities or $50,000 for banks in cities with populations of 5,000 or less. The act also required that the bank hold U.S. government bonds as collateral. In return the bank used the term "national" in its title and on its notes. National banks also received the authority to issue national bank notes, which they obtained in exchange for ownership of U.S. treasury securities. National bank notes soon circulated as the nation's only currency (with the exception of greenbacks, which existed for 20 years during and after the Civil War). National bank notes achieved their monopoly status because Congress had placed a 10 percent tax on all nonnational bank notes, effectively driving them out of existence.

Several differences existed between the earlier BUS variants and the post-1863 national banks. National banks were strictly commercial banks, and the only obligation they had to lend money to the government was an indirect one in that they held government bonds. The charters of national banks prohibited them from branching, although Congress later modified that restriction. However, they never received the privilege of interstate branching that the two banks of the United States enjoyed. Nor could national banks lend on real estate. Finally, their charters required a capitalization that many bankers considered excessively high, and states quickly discovered that they could undercut the national banks by lowering their state charter requirements.

States had chartered their own banks since the early days of the Republic, and usually the term "state bank" referred to a bank given a permit to operate by the state legislature. State charters set capitalization requirements, the length of the charter's life, and established conditions of operation. Almost all charters included a penalty, usually revoking the charter, if the bank "suspended" specie payments—that is, if the bank refused to convert the notes it issued into gold or silver coin on demand. Frequently during crises, however, when banks suspended, legislatures rattled their charter-revoking sabers a great deal but then passed laws exempting the banks from those provisions after the crisis passed. State banks, depending on their charters, could have branching privileges. After 1863, when the several states thought that the national banking system's high capitalization requirements were starving them of credit and money, many states lowered their state capitalization requirements. That liberalization process started a stampede toward state charters and away from national charters that continued into the twentieth century.

One special type of state bank lent confusion to the term: many states chartered a bank that they intended to serve as an agent of the state, and in some cases as a monopoly bank (the State Bank of Alabama, for example). While all other state-chartered banks were privately owned and operated for private profit, the legislators intended this variant of the state bank to operate for the benefit of the state. Tennessee, for example, required the profits of the Bank of Tennessee to pay for the state's educational system. Most state-controlled banks operated in competition with the numerous privately owned state-chartered banks, and despite the intentions of the legislatures, few state-controlled banks designed as monopoly banks ever really succeeded in achieving that status. When they did, they met with disaster. State monopoly banks in Arkansas, Alabama, and Missouri collapsed, usually because their lending practices were driven by political needs, not profit. A few state banks achieved some degree of success, especially the Bank of the State of Indiana, largely due to the efforts of its president, Hugh McCulloch.

The simultaneous presence of state banks and national banks led to the term "dual banking system." With the passage of the Federal Reserve Act in 1913, the government required all national banks to join the Federal Reserve System, thus placing a percentage of their deposits with the regional Reserve banks. The dual banking system continued and remains in place as of this writing.

See also:

The Bank War and the Specie Circular, Nicholas Biddle, Salmon P. Chase, Federal Reserve Act, First Bank of the United States, Alexander Hamilton, Hugh McCulloch, National Bank and Currency Acts, Second Bank of the United States.

—Editor

National City Bank

by Thomas F. Huertas

Citibank NA

National City Bank was founded in 1812 as the City Bank of New York. It became a national bank and changed its name in 1865. The bank came close to failure during the Panic of 1837 but emerged in the 1890s as the largest bank in the United States. Two factors contributed to that success: close association with the country's leading merchants and industrialists and a policy of "ready money."

The bank was established amidst political controversy. In 1811 Congress voted not to renew the charter of the Bank of the United States. In New York the Federalists who had managed the local branch of that bank applied to the state legislature for a new charter. The Republicans split into two factions, each of which wished to charter its own bank. However, the legislature would only charter one bank for each party, and not until Samuel Osgood (who had served as the nation's first postmaster general from 1789 to 1791) united the two factions did the City Bank received its state charter in June 1812.

During the first 25 years of its existence the bank functioned much like a credit union for its owners. The theory was that each owner would be able to borrow for 60 to 90 days each year a multiple of the deposits that he normally kept in the bank. During the rest of the year the merchant would be out of debt to the bank, leaving his deposits free to finance loans to other merchants. Thus, deposits constituted a revolving loan fund supplemented by the bank's note issue and capital.

In practice things did not work out so smoothly. The directors needed political connections to obtain the bank's charter, but those had only limited use in running the bank. When some of the initial borrowers failed to repay their loans, the bank's capital and lending capacity became impaired, limiting its ability to extend credit to capable merchants. That in turn reduced the bank's ability to attract deposits, and the bank responded by increasing its reliance on bank notes and interbank balances as a source of funding. During the Panic of 1837 those funding sources dried up, and the bank probably would have failed had not all New York City banks suspended payments.

The appointment of Moses Taylor as a director in 1837 brought about a marked change in the bank's policies and fortunes. Taylor was closely associated with fur merchant and financier John Jacob Astor and was a wealthy merchant in his own right. Over time Taylor acquired a controlling interest in the bank, and he served as its president from 1856 until his death in 1882, when his son-in-law, Percy Pyne, succeeded him. Taylor and Pyne used the bank as a treasury unit for the family's broad business empire, which included controlling interests in railroads, utilities, and commercial enterprises. The treasury function dictated that the bank pursue a policy of "ready money": strong liquidity, including a high cash reserve, and an aversion to volatile sources of funding such as bank notes or interbank deposits. The policy enabled the bank to gain deposits during the Panics of 1857, 1873, and 1884. Nonetheless, the bank remained relatively small. In 1890 it ranked twelfth among New York City banks.

James Stillman, president of the bank from 1891 to 1909 and chairman from 1909 to 1918, retained National City Bank's tradition of ready money but transformed the bank into a big-business firm. The bank established relationships with the nation's leading industrial and transportation enterprises, with commercial banks across the country and around the world, with the brokers of Wall Street, and with the federal government. In addition to deposits and short-term credit, the bank began to add investment banking services. At first Stillman underwrote issues for his own account, but gradually the bank took on that function, starting with gold bonds for the federal government and with the reorganization of the Union Pacific Railroad in 1895. The bank's strength lay primarily in distribution and in financing the underwriting syndicate; in originating an issue the bank worked with others, usually Kuhn, Loeb, but also J. P. Morgan and Company. By 1908 National City Bank had become one of the leading underwriters of debt securities, and it was the largest commercial bank in the country. It was also the strongest. It demonstrated that during the panics of 1893 and 1907, when the bank gained deposits and increased its loans.

But by 1908 the bank had reached a limit to its growth. It still remained largely a one-man organization. Stillman owned a controlling interest and directed its day-to-day operation. Much of the bank's underwriting and lending business depended on Stillman's personal relationships with William Rockefeller, E. H. Harriman, Henry Havemeyer, and other industrialists. As they retired from active business their enterprises became modern corporations. The bank had to respond in kind, and to seek an even broader customer base to continue to grow.

References:

Harold Van B. Cleveland and Thomas F. Huertas, *Citibank, 1812-1970* (Cambridge, Mass.: Harvard University Press, 1985);

John Moody and George Kibbe Turner, "City Bank: The Federation of the Great Merchants," *McClure's Magazine* (May 1911): 78.

New York Clearing House Association

by Richard H. Timberlake

University of Georgia

The New York Clearing House Association was the first organization of its kind and the prototype for all subsequent clearinghouse organizations in the United States. Its historical development, therefore, serves as a model for the behavior and characteristics of clearinghouses in general.

Albert Gallatin, a former secretary of the treasury, made public the first concrete suggestion for a systematic bank clearing system in 1831. His plan used the London and Scottish systems as guides. Gallatin originally wanted to see a prompt daily settlement among banks of their demand obligations. Rather than every bank sending porters to all the other banks in order to collect and pay credit and debit balances, the banks would organize a "general cash office . . . , in which each bank would place a sum in specie, proportionate to its capital, which would be carried to its credit in the books of the office. Each bank would be daily debited or credited in those books for the balance of its account with all the other banks. Each bank might at any time draw for specie on the office for the excess of its credit beyond its quota; and each bank should be obliged to replenish its quota, whenever [the quota] was diminished one-half or any other proportion agreed on."

Gallatin's proposal reflects the fact that a clearinghouse arrangement is a closed system, like a card game. What one participant loses another one gets: the sum of the exchanged items must add up to zero in the accounted units.

In 1853, more than 20 years after Gallatin proposed his plan, officers of 52 banks in New York City formally organized the New York Clearing House Association (NYCHA), with an exclusive membership. Banks that wished to become members had to qualify, then be approved by a three-fourths majority of the existing members. Member banks also had to pay admission fees. Nonmember banks could clear through member banks; but in time the association insisted that nonmembers pay fees and adhere to much the same rules that governed members.

The innovative procedure of clearing demand obligations of banks–currency and demand deposits–in a central location added greatly to the efficiency of the payments system. The NYCHA at its maturity in 1908 featured two representatives from each member bank, a "delivery clerk" and a "settling clerk." The former delivered the claims against other banks, and the latter received the packages of checks or currency from the other banks' delivery

Operations at the New York Clearing House in 1875 (Noble Foster Hoggon, Epochs in American Banking, *1929)*

clerks. If 50 banks cleared, and each bank had a payment relationship with all the other banks, then the clerks had to service 2,500 accounts.

The whole operation took place at ten o'clock in the morning each day. The delivery clerks formed a militarylike procession as they circled the stationary settling clerks and presented them with accounts due. The proof clerks in the employ of the clearinghouse recorded the sums and struck balances for the amounts due from or to each bank. This whole procedure customarily took 35 to 40 minutes.

Most member banks kept some amount of deposit at the NYCHA. If a member's balance was insufficient, the member would write a check on itself payable to the clearinghouse. The clearinghouse manager would distribute the proceeds appropriately to the creditor banks. Debtor banks could also pay daily balances due by means of legal-tender notes issued by the U.S. Treasury, gold and silver certificates, and gold coin.

The usual medium for clearing was clearinghouse certificates (CHC). This currency was issued

dollar-for-dollar by the NYCHA in denominations of $5,000, $10,000, $20,000, and even $100,000, upon deposit of the various legal-tender moneys mentioned above. Only member banks of the NYCHA could use those certificates to clear debts with each other. Banks that exchanged the CHC outside the association were fined. That strict confinement of CHC use existed to prevent any suggestion to government officials that the notes violated the laws prohibiting the private production of currency in the United States. Any time a bank wished, it could draw down its deposit by cashing in its CHC for the moneys the NYCHA held as 100 percent reserves against the outstanding certificates.

The NYCHA had virtually all the characteristics of what was known as a "bank of issue" or "central bank." The clearinghouse banks were "members"; the association issued high-denomination currency (CHC), which the members used legitimately as reserves; it required weekly statements on the condition of its member banks; it monitored members' soundness and liquidity as strategic information for all the other members. It also had a hand in specifying minimum reserve ratios. Since legal reserve requirements at the time varied—15 percent for all New York state banks and 25 percent for national banks in New York City—the association in 1908 passed a measure requiring all member banks to keep a 25 percent reserve in order to provide a uniform basis for all members' credit operations.

The extension of the NYCHA's routine clearing function to that of a lender of last resort for the associated banks when they were in the throes of a liquidity crisis is not at all surprising. Indeed, given the technical structure of the association, it was a natural development. It was also a momentous transformation. While clearing operations were commonplace to the point of boredom, the crisis conditions that saw the clearinghouse become a lender of last resort were dramatic episodes affecting the real wealth of households and business firms throughout the country.

The NYCHA undertook its first lender-of-last-resort operation in the Panic of 1857. It repeated that role several times during the early 1860s, again in the Panics of 1873, 1884, 1893, and most notably in 1907.

The distress that appeared in the New York financial sector usually took the form of high short-term interest rates, security liquidations, and bank closings. When those symptoms appeared, the NYCHA extended its certificate-issuing function to include clearinghouse loan certificates (CHLC) on a fractional reserve basis. The CHLC greatly resembled the CHC and had the same high denominations, but they were not issued upon deposit of lawful money at the clearinghouse. Rather, the association issued them as loan proceeds to member banks on the basis of interest-bearing collateral securities that member banks pledged for the loans. A loan committee of the NYCHA, usually consisting of five officers, passed judgment on the soundness of the securities. If the securities passed muster, the committee made the loan and issued the CHLC. The certificates were then used in the settlement of daily balances at the clearinghouse in the same fashion as conventional CHC.

The loans made to the member banks usually bore an annual rate of 6 percent interest plus .5 percent for administrative costs. The borrower banks paid that interest, while the creditor banks that received the loan certificates as a part of daily clearing operations realized the interest income from

them as a reward for not cashing them. The accounting department at the clearinghouse recorded the amount of interest due each bank holding the certificates by means of the daily statement of condition from each member bank.

The clearinghouse had the incentive to extend loans to sound, if illiquid, banks because the members of the clearinghouse loan committees also served as officers and stockholders of the associated member banks. The loan committees, as Theodore Gilman observed, had a "pecuniary interest as stockholders in the [member] banks, which they would endeavor to protect from loss on their contingent liability as guarantors." In short, the officers of the clearinghouse loan committees wore two hats that were inseparable. They would not jeopardize their own banks' interest by extending clearinghouse loans to banks of questionable solvency. Neither would they refuse loans to sound banks when possible failures due to a lack of reserves might have triggered a general liquidity drain and thereby threatened the viability of their own banks.

Each financial episode saw an extension of the loan certificate issues and a refinement of their uses. By 1893 clearinghouse associations in several other cities were issuing them. In addition, the denominations of the notes, which were $500 to (ultimately) $100,000 as issued by the NYCHA, breached the lower barrier (say, $100) at which borrowers would let the notes get out to the public as hand-to-hand currency. Once the lower denominations appeared, no one could stop their decline to fractional dollar denominations because their use as hand-to-hand currency required "change."

The issue of clearinghouse loan certificates extended the supply of usable money by accommodating the increased demand for liquidity. It checked the hemorrhaging of bank reserves and thereby prevented sound but illiquid banks from failing. As James Graham Cannon, an officer of the NYCHA, observed in his comprehensive treatment of the subject: the issue of CHLC "affords one of the finest examples the country has ever seen of the ability of the people when left to themselves to devise impromptu measures for their own relief." The hundreds of millions of dollars of CHLC issued over a 50-year period resulted in virtually no losses to banks or bank depositors.

The advent of the Federal Reserve System marked the end of the clearinghouse associations as lenders of last resort. Indeed, the structural organization of the Fed simply copied most of the details that the NYCHA had pioneered. The Federal Reserve Act formally legalized the issue of Federal Reserve notes, which were intended to simulate the questionably legal CHLC. Since member banks of the Federal Reserve System had to keep reserve accounts with their regional banks, the Fed banks and their branches automatically became "clearinghouse associations" for their members as well as lenders of last resort. They effectively mirrored the NYCHA and the private system of clearinghouses that they replaced.

References:

James Graham Cannon, *Clearing Houses, Senate Document 491* (Washington, D.C.: Government Printing Office, 1910);

Theodore Gilman, *A Graded Banking System* (Boston & New York: Houghton, Mifflin, 1898);

Richard H. Timberlake, Jr., "The Central Banking Role of Clearinghouse Associations," *Journal of Money, Credit and Banking*, 16 (February 1984): 1-15.

New York Safety Fund

by John Majewski

University of California, Los Angeles

Bank failures in the antebellum period usually left both noteholders and depositors with little or no compensation. In order to minimize the harmful effects of bank failures, several states adopted various insurance schemes. The most important of these was the 1829 New York Safety Fund.

Devised by a public-spirited lawyer named Joshua Forman and backed by state governor Martin Van Buren, the program forced banks to pay one-half of 1 percent of their capital into a fund for six years. Both noteholders and depositors of failed banks would be compensated from the fund. After compensation, solvent banks would replenish the fund, the size of the payments depending on the bank's capital stock. The Safety Fund comprised part of a wider package of legislation designed to prevent bank failure. Other regulations limited banks to issuing notes equal to twice their paid-up capital and permitted banks to open only after stockholders had paid in all capital stock. New York formed a state commission to enforce the regulations.

Large New York City banks strongly opposed the Safety Fund. The city banks argued that they had to pay a larger absolute amount into the fund than the smaller country banks. The city banks were also safer than the country banks, as they issued notes amounting to only one-third of their capital stock. Country banks, on the other hand, frequently issued notes well in excess of their capital stock. In the end, city bankers argued, safe banks ended up subsidizing the business of risky banks: the public, finding itself insured against loss,

Joshua Forman, who devised the system of deposit insurance known as the New York Safety Fund (engraving by Samuel Sartain)

would be more likely to take its chances with the potentially unsound country banks.

Other opponents of the system thought that the fund would be inadequate to cover both the notes and deposits of failed banks. They argued that either the fund should be enlarged or that only noteholders should be protected. Events proved that the opponents of the Safety Fund were essentially correct. Country banks failed much more often than city banks, and the fund proved inadequate to compensate both depositors and noteholders. Despite the prophetic objections, in 1829 the fund passed both houses of the legislature by large majorities.

The first eight years of the Safety Fund proved relatively uneventful, but disaster struck in the aftermath of the Panic of 1837. Two banks failed in 1837 and 11 more within the next five years. The Safety Fund, forced to pay for both deposits and note issues, did not have enough funds. The Safety Fund ended up covering the losses by issuing state stock at 6 percent interest. All banks were forced to contribute one-half of 1 percent of their capital per year until their charters expired. In 1842 the legislature moved to reduce the burden of the fund by allowing only the reimbursement of noteholders. The law also gave noteholders the first claim to the assets of a failed bank. These actions did not have a large impact, since the Safety Fund covered the notes of only two banks after 1843.

In 1838, meanwhile, the legislature guaranteed the end of the Safety Fund. Before 1838 all New York banks had to possess a state charter. The chartering process created inefficiency and corruption: existing banks tried to prevent the creation of competitors, leading to bribes and counterbribes of state legislators. An antimonopoly political faction, the Locofocos, helped pass an open-banking law that ended the chartering system. Under the open-banking law, banks did not have to belong to the Safety Fund. Hence, chartered banks belonging to the Safety Fund and "free" banks competed side by side until the last charter expired in 1866.

Although ultimately a failure, the New York Safety Fund offered an important first attempt to legislate an insurance scheme to protect bank customers. In 1831 Vermont implemented a safety fund, and in 1836 Michigan copied the system. The New York laws also provided the inspiration for more complicated schemes in states such as Ohio. Nevertheless, although originally viewed by most historians as a sophisticated measure that protected the depositor, subsequent research has shown the Safety Fund, like free banking and state banking, to have lacked the flexibility of branch banking. By concentrating on such halfway legislation, New York lawmakers avoided enacting branch-banking laws that promised greater stability.

References:

Robert E. Chaddock, *The Safety Fund Banking System in New York, 1829-1860* (Washington, D.C.: Government Printing Office, 1910);

William J. Shultz and M. R. Caine, *Financial Development of the United States* (New York: Prentice-Hall, 1937).

New York Stock Exchange

by Steven Wheeler

New York Stock Exchange Archives

The New York Stock Exchange (NYSE), America's largest securities exchange, provided a ready market for the stocks and bonds that channeled investment capital into commercial enterprise and industrial development during the nineteenth century, most notably the construction of railroads.

The NYSE's origins date back to a 1792 agreement among 24 New York City merchants and brokers to charge a standard commission on their sales of the new federal government bonds issued to repay revolutionary war debts. The Exchange was formally organized in 1817, as the New York Stock & Exchange Board, when its 27 members adopted a constitution that spelled out rules for its administration and trading. To be a member of the Exchange and enjoy the privileges of buying and selling securities at its trading sessions, one had to have a year's experience in the stock brokerage business, win election by a vote of the entire membership, and pay an admission fee of $25.

The members met twice daily to buy and sell in a "call market." From the rostrum the president read the name of each stock in turn. As he called each, the brokers shouted their bids to buy and offers to sell. When two brokers agreed on a price, the president called out the sale and the secretary recorded it. Once all sales in that stock were concluded, the next would be called out and the process began all over again.

The stocks and bonds traded at the NYSE mirrored the development of American business and industry. In its earliest days the Exchange traded about 30 different securities—the bonds of federal, state, and municipal governments and the stocks of local banks and insurance companies. By 1835 a handful of railroads, mining concerns, and gas utilities joined the list. Just after the Civil War the list grew to more than 300, swelled by a multitude of new railroad stocks and bonds that dominated trading activity through the end of the century.

The growth of the stock market ushered in many new developments at the NYSE. The Exchange opened its first building in 1865; the stock ticker began reporting stock sales to the nation in 1867; and the NYSE merged with a rival stock exchange–the Open Board of Stock Brokers–in 1869, boosting the number of members to 1,060. The increasing number of members and daily trading volume demanded a change in the manner of trading. In 1871 the Exchange abandoned the "call market" in favor of continuous trading in all stocks throughout the day. The building was redesigned to provide a large, open trading floor, and stocks were traded at specific locations marked by an iron post topped with a sign. The brokers circulated about the floor from post to post to make their sales.

The NYSE also worked to make the stock market rational and honest by regulating the conduct of its members and listed companies. As early as 1817 the Exchange expelled members making "fictitious sales." In 1868 listed companies were required to register their shares with a bank, to avoid secret issues of additional shares–watered stock. Later in the century the Exchange required listed companies to disclose financial information in annual reports to stockholders.

By the close of the nineteenth century the 1,300 securities traded at the New York Stock Exchange represented railroads, manufacturing corporations, banks, coal and iron companies, telegraph networks, and gas and electric utilities all across the United States and throughout the world. In April 1901 the Exchange set a new daily volume record of 3 million shares and began work on a new building with larger, better trading facilities that would serve the stock market of the new century.

References:

Deborah S. Gardner, *Marketplace: A Brief History of the New York Stock Exchange* (New York: New York Stock Exchange, 1982);

Robert Sobel, *The Big Board: A History of the New York Stock Market* (New York: Macmillan, 1965); Edmund Clarence Stedman, *The New York Stock Ex-* *change* (New York: Stock Exchange Historical Company, 1905).

Notes, Currency, and Legal Tender

Banks have traditionally performed the task of facilitating business by making exchanges easier and more reliable. Money traditionally provided the medium of exchange. The essence of banking involved receiving deposits from one set of customers and lending them to another and at the same time using the gold and silver (specie) reserve as a basis from which to issue the bank's own paper money. The money issued by banks was called "bank notes," or simply "notes," because the earliest bank money was literally dated and notarized. Any chartered bank could issue its own bank notes before the National Banking Act of 1863; after that time only banks with charters from the federal government, called national banks, could issue notes. People frequently called notes "currency," a term that denoted the passage of a note through several sets of hands.

Regardless of the name, neither notes nor currency necessarily carried legal-tender status, which referred to the government's commitment to accept money for all debts due the government. Making money legal tender did not guarantee it would retain value, but it did give the money value for certain purposes (such as paying taxes), which supported the value to some extent. Nevertheless, legal-tender status was only as good as the government that stood behind the commitment. During the Civil War the Confederacy made its notes legal tender for all public debts, but when the Southern armies started to lose on the battlefield, the value of the money fell along with public expectations. A government could also choose to make money legal tender for all debts "public and private" if it wished to have a monopoly on the money supply. If one money is acceptable for all debts but another is only acceptable for some debts, the first will drive out the second because it is more convenient. The National Banking Act of 1863 and its successor act in 1864 established national bank notes as the primary currency in the United States. Congress then endowed that currency with monopoly status by placing a 10 percent tax on all other notes, driving them out of existence. A series of Supreme Court cases in the 1860s and 1870s called the Legal Tender Cases ruled that U.S. government money—greenbacks—was legal tender and had to be accepted for all debts public or private. But national bank notes did not have such status, and only when the Federal Reserve System was created in 1913 did the nation's money uniformly have legal tender status.

See also:

Salmon P. Chase, Confederate Finance, Federal Reserve Act, Alexander Hamilton, Legal Tender Cases, Christopher G. Memminger.

—Editor

Ohio Life Insurance and Trust Company

by Hans Eicholz

University of California, Los Angeles

The Ohio Life Insurance and Trust Company (Ohio Life) is best known for its role in the precipitation of the Panic of 1857. The firm is blamed for transmitting to the western states a recessionary downturn originating in the Northeast, exacerbating what otherwise would have been a localized economic downturn into a full-blown national panic.

Economic trends in the 1850s had long concerned observers, who feared a recessionary course, but most thought that the bulk of the impending contraction would be felt in New York City, the country's financial center. As the largest western bank, with what were perceived to be the strongest asset holdings, Ohio Life was expected to weather the storm. A combination of mismanagement, changing market conditions, and an oppressive system of state corporate taxation, however, brought the firm down within a span of only two months.

Incorporated by an act of the General Assembly of Ohio on February 12, 1834, the result of the efforts of the prominent Bronson family of Connecticut, the purpose behind the firm's creation was to bring outside capital into the developing state, both through the sale of insurance and the acceptance of bank deposits. From the beginning the business emphasized its banking activities. Only a small percentage of its earnings came from insurance sales. In 1838 the company received $4,921.75 from insurance premiums, and by 1850 that had increased to only $5,021.01. Bank deposits increased during the same time from $600,000 to nearly $2 million. Shortly after its establishment in Cincinnati the bank opened a department in New York, "to receive and take charge of any bills of exchange, or notes in that city or vicinity." The officer in charge, the principal cashier, had the authority to invest any funds not immediately needed. Supervision was provided in the form of semi-monthly reports required to be sent to the Cincinnati office.

Initially, the business community held Ohio Life in high esteem. No doubt some of the firm's reputation stemmed from the fact that it withstood the Panic of 1837, which depressed the economy well into 1843. The late 1840s and early 1850s, however, marked a period of considerable financial growth for the nation. Due to revolution in Europe, demand for American exports surged. Moreover, emigration from Ireland brought in cheap labor, and railroad construction increased. In addition, Great Britain adopted a free-trade policy, increasing its American imports, and the Mexican War conquests opened much new territory. As the 1850s wore on, however, the European situation stabilized, and production slackened. The periodic seasonal financial downturn, which began in mid August every year, worsened. In 1857 the downturn, combined with a series of internal problems, posed a mortal threat to Ohio Life.

During the period of financial growth the firm found itself saddled with a rising tax burden that cut deep into profits. In need of funds due to liberal subsidies of improvement projects, the state government had passed a law on April 13, 1852, requiring banks to pay taxes on both their property and liabilities. The state continued to collect the established 5 percent tax on dividends. While taxes increased in Ohio, the New York cashier undertook a series of unauthorized investments and loans of a dubious nature, which amounted to nearly $3 million. Railroad issues were clearly involved: whether the cashier advanced money to a railroad on his own authority or speculated on the railroad's securities with the bank's money remains a mystery. At any rate, when the bank needed funds to meet demand at home during the 1857 downturn, the New York office was unable to call in the loans. The firm's president realized the urgency of the situation and issued the order to suspend payments. By September

26 the firm's board of trustees knew its condition was hopeless and closed down operations.

Historians have argued that Ohio Life failed because of the 1857 depreciation in railroad stock, which reduced the bank's assets. Most of the depreciation, however, seems to have taken place during the ensuing litigation against the bank by its creditors. That points toward mismanagement in New York as the greatest cause of the failure. Recession and excessive taxation no doubt helped to push the institution over the brink. The bankruptcy shocked the New York financial community. As one contemporary commentator put it, "if its [the bank's] means could be employed in desperate stock-gambling in the public market, with all the usual hypothecation of securities, and transfers, and extensive bank loans, of which the bank records must have given *some* evidence—why might not similar transactions be concealed in other institutions of which the trustees are equally well accomplished and esteemed?"

The failure of Ohio Life proved to be only one of several factors that pushed the New York banks under in 1857. Another significant problem, for example, was a New York City law that allowed country-bank arbitrageurs to bring notes into the city for conversion to gold at well above the market price of the notes. Still, Ohio Life has justifiably received much of the blame for the panic.

References:

J. S. Gibbons, *Banks of New York* (New York: Appleton, 1858), pp. 348-353;

James L. Huston, *The Panic of 1857 and the Coming of the Civil War* (Baton Rouge: Louisiana State University Press, 1987), pp. 14-15;

Mortimer Spiegelman, "The Failure of the Ohio Life Insurance and Trust Company, 1857," *Ohio State Archeological and Historical Quarterly*, 57 (July 1948): 247-265.

Oklahoma Deposit Guaranty Law

by James Smallwood

University of Texas at Tyler

The Oklahoma Deposit Guaranty Law of 1908, which was designed to protect bank depositors, resulted from various factors, the most important of which was the historic instability of banks in the prestatehood era of Oklahoma history. Although the Panic of 1907 prompted the new state's first legislature to pass a guaranty law, the most prominent advocate of such reform was William Jennings Bryan of Nebraska.

Bryan, titular leader of the national Democratic party, addressed the predominantly Democratic Oklahoma legislature in 1908 on the subject of banking reform. An orator of national prominence and three-time candidate for president, Bryan stressed the need to protect the little man—the yeoman farmer and the urban laborer—as well as the landowner and businessman. Furthermore, he asserted that a guarantee would benefit bankers. If potential depositors knew beyond all doubt that their funds would be safe, they would be more inclined to allow banks to manage them. Deposits would soar. Swayed by Bryan's arguments, the legislature passed the law.

A forerunner of the bill establishing the Federal Deposit Insurance Corporation during the New Deal years (and later the Federal Savings and Loan Insurance Corporation), the state's governor, C. N. Haskell, supported the Oklahoma law. He had earlier tried to write a bank guaranty clause into the state constitution but failed by one vote to secure its adoption. Later, he appeared before a Democratic party convention in Denver and lobbied for a guaranty plank in the national platform. Although he failed to gather the support of the national Democrats, he finally succeeded (after the push by Bryan) in Oklahoma.

Under the law any Oklahoma bank under state charter was required to contribute 1 percent of its average daily balance to a guaranty fund. Although some critics argued that the law was socialistic, most financiers and the public received it warmly. Indeed, many national banks in Oklahoma

Charles N. Haskell, governor of Oklahoma when the state inaugurated its deposit insurance system in 1909

dropped their federal charters and applied for state charters because deposits had risen so rapidly in state-chartered institutions after the law became effective. Depositors had great confidence in the new law. On February 14, 1909, the day that the guaranty took effect, state banks had deposits of $26,544,281; by September 1, 1909, deposits had risen to $65,821,048, while deposits in Oklahoma national banks had shown a corresponding decline. Of course, opponents immediately tested the constitutionality of the guaranty law, but in 1911 the U.S. Supreme Court upheld the law as a valid exercise of state police power.

Two Plains states followed Oklahoma's lead and established guaranty funds. Developments in Nebraska closely paralleled those in Oklahoma. Just as in Oklahoma, Bryan helped persuade the solons of his home state to reform the state system. The Nebraska Banking Act of 1909 established a fund that worked just like the one in Oklahoma. After the establishment of the fund, state banks in Nebraska enjoyed unbounded success for a time—success similar to that enjoyed by state banks in Oklahoma. Kansas also passed a law allowing voluntary participation in an insurance fund in 1909.

Because of bank failures in 1910 and 1911, the Oklahoma legislature in 1911 amended the guaranty law to require that state banks contribute 5 percent of their average daily balance to the fund, with 1 percent due immediately and the balance payable in installments. Though depositors felt secure in putting their money into banks covered by the law, many bankers found the new levy too costly. Several dropped their state charters and applied for national charters. In 1913 the legislature reduced the levy, but the guaranty program still did not recover the popularity among bankers it had enjoyed in 1909 and 1910.

The program continued after World War I, but the temporary recession the United States experienced after the war proved too great a burden. Oklahoma experienced many bank failures between 1918 and 1921. By the latter year the guaranty fund was virtually exhausted. Then, in the three-year period from 1921 to 1923, 70 new failures struck the state system. As a result the fund had no money to pay the claims of depositors. In January 1923 the legislature launched an investigation to examine the condition of the fund and the state banks. The reports that came back to the legislature were so bleak that the lawmakers repealed the guaranty law later in 1923.

In administering its guaranty program, Nebraska struggled through crises similar to those in Oklahoma—an economic downturn following World War I and a wave of bank failures from 1919 to 1923. But the Nebraska program recovered after the legislature created a Guaranty Fund Commission and authorized the sale of receivers' certificates. The commission operated insolvent banks that would have closed under ordinary circumstances. It operated on the expectation that liabilities to depositors could, in time, be reduced without draining the guaranty fund.

Yet by 1928 the total number and rapid pace of bank failures in Nebraska made it impossible for the commission to cover all liabilities. It called for the collection of a special assessment to be placed on the sound banks in the system. However, a majority of the state banks joined a suit to enjoin collection. A district court granted the injunction. Although both the Nebraska Supreme Court and the U. S. Supreme Court reversed the district court decision, the delay in collecting the assessment proved fatal to the fund. By the time the highest court ruled in 1931, the Nebraska legislature had already repealed the law. Just prior to its repeal the law had been the subject of an exhaustive investigation by a commission headed by ex-governor A. C. Shallenberger, who had been in office when it had taken effect in 1909. An old friend of the program, Shallenberger nevertheless concluded that as of 1930 the fund was a failure—in part because "faithless" bankers who had given "inefficient supervision" allowed their banks to place untenable strains on the fund. Shortly after Shallenberger released the commission's report, the Nebraska legislature voted for repeal. Kansas also experienced a tremendous drain on its guaranty fund, brought on by farm bankruptcies that impacted farm-area Kansas banks. By 1926 the fund had only $1.1 million to cover $6.7 million in debt.

Necessitated by wide swings in the economy, by frequent bank failures, and by mismanagement on the part of some bank officers, Plains-state guaranty programs sought to provide financial security both to depositors and bankers. The programs ultimately failed. Worse, perhaps, legislators often sought to substitute deposit insurance schemes for branch banking, which proved a far healthier and more stable organizational and regulatory device.

Deposit laws thus delayed—critically, in some cases—more desirable branch legislation. Yet even in failure they established the precedent for national action. The national systems in place today employ far more resources than the state systems did. The Federal Deposit Insurance Corporation has been successful, although the Federal Savings and Loan Insurance Corporation has recently fallen on hard times with the collapse of the savings and loan industry and may itself need a bailout.

References:

Timothy W. Hubbard and Lewis E. Davids, *Banking in Mid-America: A History of Missouri's Banks* (Washington, D.C.: Public Affairs Press, 1969);

W. E. Kuhn, *History of Nebraska Banking: A Centennial Retrospect* (Lincoln: University of Nebraska, 1968);

Edwin C. McReynolds, *Oklahoma: A History of the Sooner State* (Norman: University of Oklahoma Press, 1954);

Mary Scott Rowland, "Kansas Farming and Banking in the 1920s," *Kansas Historical Quarterly* (August 1985): 186-189;

James M. Smallwood, *An Oklahoma Adventure: Of Banks and Bankers* (Norman: University of Oklahoma Press, 1979);

Eugene N. White, *Regulation and Reform of the American Banking System, 1900-1929* (Princeton: Princeton University Press, 1983).

Rufus James Palen

(January 13, 1843-March 14, 1916)

by James Smallwood

University of Texas at Tyler

CAREER: Officer, U.S. Army (1862-1866); agent, Mutual Life Insurance Company (1866-1878); clerk, 1st Judicial District Court and Superior Court, New Mexico Territory (1873-1878); assistant cashier (1878-1883), cashier (1883-1891), president, First National Bank of Santa Fe (1895-1916); treasurer, New Mexico Territory (1891-1895).

Born in Hudson, New York, on January 13, 1843, Rufus James Palen was the son of Joseph Gilbert Palen and Caroline Anne Little Palen. He grew up in Hudson and its environs and gained his early schooling in his hometown. Following the example of his mother and father, he became a lifelong Episcopalian. Also like his father, he came to support the Republican party, endorsing the party's position on slavery and its program for economic growth.

In 1861, even though the Civil War had just begun, Palen journeyed to Ann Arbor and enrolled as a freshman in the University of Michigan. However, constant talk about and news of the Civil War stirred his nationalism and patriotism. He withdrew from school in 1862 and joined the Union Army. He became a second lieutenant in the 128th New York Volunteers and saw much action, participating in numerous campaigns in the eastern theater. He fought at Fredericksburg and Chancellorsville in Virginia. He rose through the ranks via promotions, several won during the heat of battle; by the summer of 1863 he had gained the rank of major, a position he held until he mustered out in January 1866.

After the Civil War Palen returned to Hudson and for a time clerked for a local merchant. Shortly thereafter, however, he joined the Mutual Life Insurance Company as an agent. The 20 percent commission on sales the company offered allowed Palen to save a sizable "grub-stake." In 1873 the "Major," as he was known, established a branch office of Mutual Life in Santa Fe, New Mexico Territory, realiz-

Rufus James Palen (University of New Mexico General Library, Special Collections Department, Neg. No. 989-027-001)

ing a lifelong ambition to "go west" in search of greater fortune. Beginning in 1873 he also clerked for both the 1st Judicial District Court and the Superior Court of the territory, positions that he held until 1878.

The autumn of 1878 proved noteworthy in Palen's life. First, he became a family man; on September 17, 1878, he married Ellen Seager Webbe of Santa Fe. Second, he gained the position of assistant cashier for the First National Bank of Santa Fe and joined the bank's board of directors. Earlier, both Palen and his mother had purchased stock in the bank, and when his mother transferred her stock to his name, the Major had enough leverage to win the positions. Further, he had become a close friend of Stephen Elkins, the majority shareholder and president of First National from 1871 to 1884 and later U.S. senator from West Virginia.

Palen entered the banking field at a critical time in the economic history of New Mexico. Many banks would not survive the turn of the century; others would continue to grow well into the modern era. When Palen joined the First National of Santa Fe, he quickly learned that the bank suffered from a host of lending problems. The bank always had a full discount and lending line, often accompanied by overdue paper, a problem that finally caused an inquiry by the state comptroller of the currency.

Replying to the comptroller, bank officials placed the blame for overdue loans on disruptions in the New Mexico economy–specifically on the fact that many customers of the bank were cattlemen and sheepmen who were often with their herds, hundreds of miles away from Santa Fe, when their bank notes came due. But economic disruption could only partly explain First National's lending problems. Actually, "insider" loans, especially to Elkins's friend and a bank director, Thomas Catron (who would later serve as U.S. senator from New Mexico), threatened the bank more than the herdsmen's loans. Even before Palen joined the bank, directors tried to grapple with the insider problem but for the most part had little success. In February 1879 cashier William Griffin explained to the board of directors that most of the bank's deficit of $4,200 was owed by Catron and two other directors who had secured insider loans with little collateral.

Palen determined to tighten the bank's lending policies, especially in relation to the insider loans. His course of action led him into several serious confrontations with fellow directors, including Catron, a powerful figure. Catron controlled the second largest amount of bank stock, after Elkins. Further, it had earlier been Catron, working closely with Elkins (at the time the bank's legal counsel), who had wrested control of the bank from its founders. For more than a decade Palen tried to limit the borrowing of Catron, who was forever reorganizing his own financing–borrowing from one source to pay another. In October 1883, after Palen had become cashier, he protested to Elkins that Catron's debts totaled a staggering $150,000. Outstanding loans in such large amounts, along with stiff competition from Santa Fe's Second National Bank, led to a decline in business by 1884. That year Palen reported that bank deposits had fallen by $100,000 and that the bank could lose its national depository designation.

Palen received a career blow when his friend Elkins resigned as president of First National in 1884. Griffin took over and served until his death in 1890. Pedro Perea then served until 1894. Meanwhile, Palen served as the treasurer of New Mexico Territory from 1891 to 1895, but he resigned to become president at First National upon Perea's retirement. At that time Palen forced a reorganization of the board. New directors came aboard, and as Palen said, they were "not all indebted to the bank." Nevertheless, for several more years Catron remained the bane of Palen's life; Catron continued to owe the bank large amounts of money, continued to serve on the new board, and continued to serve as the bank's vice-president.

Nevertheless, Palen managed an expanding, successful bank that withstood varied changes and crises in the coming years. First National survived the Panic of 1893, and, as the state entered into an economic expansion after 1900, the bank prospered. The reasons for Palen's success were varied. He was more conservative than his predecessors. In the 1890s he established a 6 percent limit on semiannual dividend payments and built a larger surplus fund. He continued to monitor insider loans and to limit them. In addition, he sought new investments, such as railroad bonds and the notes of national manufacturers. Palen's conservative management enabled First National to survive the Panic of 1907 just as it had the earlier panic. The bank joined the Federal Reserve System when it was organized in 1914. When Palen retired in 1916, he left behind a stable organization.

Although First National Bank of Santa Fe was the focus of Palen's attention, he nevertheless devoted much time to civic affairs. He was a trustee of the New Mexico Asylum for the Deaf and Dumb and a member of the Capitol Rebuilding Board and the Capitol Extension Board in Santa Fe. He continued to live in Santa Fe until his death on March 14, 1916.

Palen provided sound leadership for the First National Bank of Santa Fe. His work ensured that the bank thrived in the twentieth century.

References:

Ralph L. Edgel, *A Brief History of Banking in New Mexico, 1870-1959* (Albuquerque: University of New Mexico Press, 1962);

Wayne L. Mauzy, *A Century in Santa Fe: The Story of the First National Bank of Santa Fe* (Santa Fe: Vergara, 1970);

Larry Schweikart, "Early Banking in New Mexico from the Civil War to the Roaring Twenties," *New Mexico Historical Review*, 63 (January 1988): 1-24;

Paul A. F. Walter, "New Mexico's Pioneer Bank and Bankers," *New Mexico Historical Review*, 21 (July 1946): 209-225.

Archives:

Material on Rufus James Palen's business career is found in the collection on the First National Bank of Santa Fe in the Zimmerman Library at the University of New Mexico.

George Peabody

(February 18, 1795-November 4, 1869)

by Peter De Trolio III

University of Dayton

CAREER: Partner (1813-1829), senior partner, Riggs and Peabody (1830-1837); president, Eastern Railroad (1836-1869); founder and president, George Peabody and Company (1837-1864).

George Peabody was a dry goods merchant in the United States in the early part of the nineteenth century. He settled in London in 1837 and established an investment banking house, George Peabody and Company. That banking house later became J. S. Morgan and Company. Peabody was a great philanthropist, donating large sums of money to Yale and Harvard, establishing libraries in Baltimore and various New England towns, and setting up workingmen's tenements in the city of London. He never married, but rumors circulated that he had a mistress in England and fathered at least one child.

Born on February 18, 1795, in the town of South Danvers (now Peabody), Massachusetts, George Peabody was the son of Thomas and Judith Dodge Peabody. Although his family was poor, Peabody had an illustrious background. His first American ancestor, Francis Peabody, from whom all the Massachusetts Peabodys descended, came to America and settled in Topsfield, Massachusetts, in 1635. Among his ancestors numbered veterans of the French and Indian War and the American Revolution.

Peabody received a limited education, and at the age of eleven he was apprenticed to Sylvester

George Peabody

Proctor, a dry goods merchant in Danvers. He remained with Proctor for four years learning the dry goods business. Between 1810 and 1811 Peabody spent a year living with his grandfather in Vermont, helping him work his farm. He returned to Massachusetts in 1811 to work for his brother in the dry goods business in Newburyport, Massachusetts. Not long after he arrived a fire destroyed his brother's business along with a good portion of the town. At the instigation of his uncle, John Peabody, he traveled to Georgetown, D.C., to work as a financial assistant in the elder Peabody's dry goods store.

While Peabody worked for his uncle in 1812, hostilities broke out between the United States and England. Peabody joined a volunteer artillery squad and saw limited action at Fort Warburton on the Potomac River.

Peabody remained with his uncle for two years. In 1813 he entered into a partnership with Elisha Riggs to form the dry goods company of Riggs and Peabody in Georgetown. In 1815 the company moved to Baltimore, Maryland, where it grew and prospered. After only seven years of operation Riggs and Peabody had two branches, one in Philadelphia and one in New York City. In 1829 Elisha Riggs retired, and in 1830 Peabody took over as the senior partner.

Even though merchants such as George Peabody experienced considerable success on the American continent by 1835, troubled times lay ahead. Several states had defaulted on their loans abroad, and the state of Maryland verged on bankruptcy. To secure a loan for the state in England, in 1835 three commissioners were appointed, one of whom was Peabody. He had made several earlier trips to England on business for Riggs and Peabody and was familiar to British financiers. Because of his honest reputation, Peabody sold $8 million in Maryland bonds, saving the state from bankruptcy. Although at the time rumors circulated that Peabody had participated in illegal activity, they proved unfounded. He remitted his entire commission of $200,000, an early example of his philanthropy. For his service to the state he received a vote of thanks from the legislature.

In 1836 Peabody incorporated his business and became president of the Eastern Railroad. A year later he moved to London and established himself as an investment banker, founding the firm George Peabody and Company. By the 1850s the firm emerged as the financial equal of the houses of the Barings and the Rothschilds. Unlike most banks of the day where customers could get cash, Peabody's firm held deposits, discounted bills, negoti-

ated loans, and brokered in stocks. In 1854 Peabody took on Junius S. Morgan, father of J. P. Morgan, as a junior partner.

Peabody gained a reputation as a great philanthropist in his day. In 1851, when the U.S. Congress failed to provide funds for an exhibit of American products being set up by Prince Albert as part of London's Crystal Palace exhibition of 1851, Peabody gave $15,000 to finance the display. In 1852 Peabody donated $10,000 to equip the ship *Advance* for an expedition directed by Dr. Elisha Kane to find the lost Arctic explorer Sir John Franklin. To honor his generosity the searchers gave the name "Peabodyland" to the shores they visited.

Peabody became famous for the Fourth of July parties he threw for American dignitaries in London. At first many thought that the English would take offense at such gaiety, but the guest of honor at the first of the galas was Lord Nelson, the hero of Trafalgar. Inviting Lord Nelson to the first party turned out to be an act of diplomatic cunning, which secured a place for Peabody's extravaganza on the English social calendar until Peabody's death. The parties, which demonstrated to the British elite that America had come of age and hardly resembled the uncivilized wilderness of popular lore, did almost as much to secure British confidence in American prospects as Peabody's successful business dealings.

Peabody also came to the aid of many a weary American traveler in London and is memorialized to that effect in Herman Melville's *Journal of a Visit to London and the Continent* (1948). After the American Civil War broke out he helped soothe strained relations between the United States and Great Britain. He even ventured into international intrigue when he aided in the escape of Hungarian revolutionary Lajos Kossuth from an Austrian prison in 1850.

In 1852 Peabody donated $250,000 to found the Peabody Institute in Danvers on the occasion of the town's 100th anniversary. In a letter read at the celebration Peabody called education "a debt due from present to future generations." The institute contained a library and an endowment for lectures. In 1866 Peabody established the Peabody Library in Thetford, Vermont. Also in 1866 the Peabody Institute in Baltimore was founded. It received a total of $1.5 million. Peabody gave $150,000 to Yale College to establish the Peabody Museum of Natural History. Harvard University received $150,000 to endow a chair in Peabody's name and to fund the Museum of American Archaeology and Ethnology. Essex Institute in Salem, Massachusetts, received $140,000 to establish the Peabody Institute of Science. Peabody gave $3.5 million for the promotion of education in the southern states. Congress acknowledged the gift by authorizing a gold medal inscribed, "From the People of the United States to George Peabody in acknowledgment of his beneficent promotion of universal education." He also left sizable gifts to the Massachusetts Historical Society; Phillips (Andover) Academy in Andover, Massachusetts; and Kenyon College in Gambier, Ohio.

Peabody's greatest act of philanthropy occurred from 1862 to 1868, when he donated a total of $2.5 million for the erection of tenements for the laboring poor in the city of London. By 1868 the tenements had a capacity of 20,000. That same year Oxford University awarded Peabody an honorary D.C.L. In 1869 Queen Victoria asked him to accept either a baronetcy or the Grand Cross of the Order of Bath. He declined both and asked simply for an autographed letter from Victo-

ria and a miniature of the Queen. Also in 1869 the people of London erected a statue to Peabody.

After a brief visit to America, Peabody died in London on November 4, 1869. His passing was publicly mourned, and obituaries appeared in many of the world's leading newspapers. British prime minister William Gladstone attended the funeral at Westminster Abbey. Peabody's body was then transported to America and buried in Danvers.

George Peabody was instrumental in developing the British market for American bonds before the Civil War. Beyond that, his philanthropy endeared him to the hearts of many. He stands as an example of American financial willpower and as a national goodwill ambassador.

References:

Vincent P. Carosso, *Investment Banking in America* (Cambridge, Mass.: Harvard University Press, 1970);

Carosso, *The Morgans* (Cambridge, Mass.: Harvard University Press, 1987);

Franklin Parker, *George Peabody: A Biography* (Nashville: Vanderbilt University Press, 1971).

Populism and Greenbacks

by James E. Fell, Jr.

United Banks of Colorado

Populism was a late-nineteenth-century agrarian reform movement based largely in the South and West. Its origins reflected the excesses created by the industrial revolution in the post-Civil War years as well as the economic problems spawned by the overproduction and underconsumption of—and thus low prices for—wheat, tobacco, and other commodities. Ironically, the agricultural problems that produced Populism and its political expression, the Populist or People's party, reflected the success of the industrial revolution and the spectacular agricultural expansion it made possible.

American industrialization dramatically altered agricultural production. Mechanization, developments in transportation, and the rapid settlement of the arid trans-Mississippi West all had profound effects on farmers. Many of the changes were positive, but not all. Farmers resented what they consid-

ered to be exploitation by transportation and industrial interests, particularly the high freight rates and protective tariffs that farmers thought favored those industries. They also resented the debt they incurred in developing their land. As debtors, they were hurt by the general deflation of the post-Civil War years—they had to pay back loans in dollars worth more than those they borrowed.

Populism owed much to the Greenback party, which coalesced in the 1870s. Its purpose was to fight the tight money policy created by a law that called for the gradual retirement of more than $430 million in so-called "greenbacks"—paper money issued by the Union during the conflict to support the war effort. That action hurt debtors, particularly farmers. The Greenback party ran candidates for president in 1876, 1880, and 1884. Although it enjoyed little success, it developed concepts that

*James B. Weaver, presidential candidate of the Green-
back party in 1880 and the Populist party
in 1892*

power by seeking control of the Democratic party
in the Southeast and the Republican party in the Midwest. In Kansas, however, alliance members organized a third party. Party organization spread after
the success of the Kansas Populists in the 1890 election.

At conventions in Ocala, Florida, in December 1890, and Omaha, Nebraska, in 1892 the Populists advocated reforms that seemed radical in that
day. They called for a graduated income tax to
help farmers and urban workers, a postal savings
bank and a flexible currency to replace the rigid
gold standard, and a subtreasury plan for storing surplus grain. Their plans for a flexible currency included having the Treasury put into circulation a
new issue of greenbacks, the paper money issued during the Civil War. The government had not made
greenbacks convertible into gold or silver on demand (but had promised to do so at a later date).
Thus, greenbacks caused inflation, which the Populists hoped to recapture with the new issue. For the
industrial worker, they called for immigration restrictions, legislation to restrict the "money power,"
and the nationalization of the railroads, telegraph,
and telephone. To attract western miners they
called for the free and unlimited coinage of silver at
a ratio of 16 to 1 with gold, which in effect would
boost the price of silver (then coming out of the
ground at a 17 to 1 ratio) and create a measure of inflation; that plank was popular in silver-mining
areas hurt by the steady fall in the price of the
metal. Through these and other measures, the party
sought to expand its base beyond agriculture, although helping farmers remained the prime issue.
Yet the Populists remained split over the need for
and the desirability of an independent party, and
the question of race—meaning white supremacy in
the Southeast—remained a divisive problem.

In 1892 the Populists nominated for the presidency Gen. James B. Weaver, who had run for
president on the Greenback-Labor ticket in 1880.
Weaver garnered more than 1 million popular votes
and 22 electoral votes; that was hardly enough to
win, but the party elected 14 congressmen and won
several governorships. Then, as the Panic of 1893
launched the worst economic downturn the nation
had ever experienced, the Populists continued their
efforts to expand their base beyond agriculture.
They increased their popular vote in the off-year elections of 1894, but their lack of good candidates,
money, and organization suggested that ultimately

would be incorporated into Populist thinking a few
years later, notably the idea that inflation would
ease the farmers' debt burden.

Though Populism did not reach its apogee
until the economic dislocations of the 1890s, its origins came in the 1870s and 1880s, if not earlier.
Populism took root in areas where the Granger movement, through which midwestern farmers established cooperative enterprises and won legislative
reforms, was strong. Out of that ferment evolved several agricultural protest organizations, the most important being the National Farmers' Alliance (or
Northern Alliance), the National Farmers' Alliance
and Industrial Union (or Southern Alliance), and
the Colored Farmers' Alliance. By the early 1890s
those organizations collectively had several million
members.

The Populist or People's party was the political outgrowth of the rapidly growing alliance movement. The party emerged as a result of meetings
held in St. Louis, Missouri, in 1889. The next year
the movement sought to garner its first political

they had to fuse their interests with either the Republicans or the Democrats.

As the national elections of 1896 approached, the Democratic party found itself divided between the southern and western agricultural interests and more conservative eastern business interests. The southern and western wing advocated populistlike reforms, including free and unlimited coinage of silver, and successfully nominated the thirty-six-year-old congressman from Nebraska, Williams Jennings Bryan, as their candidate for president. At the convention Bryan's "cross of gold" speech stampeded the party. Equally important, it stole the Populists' thunder; when they held their convention several weeks later, they could, in the ultimate show of "me-too-ism," do little else but nominate Bryan themselves.

That sealed the party's fate. Even though Bryan lost to the Republican candidate, William McKinley, the Populists soon disappeared from the political scene. Not only had the Democrats attracted much Populist support in 1896, a period of rising farm prices further undermined the movement.

At the basis of Populism lay the belief that all wealth came from tilling the soil. Most Populists held the view that farmers had built America and laid the base for industrialization. Populism also reflected evangelical Protestantism–Populist meetings tended to manifest a revivalist impulse. The legacy of Populism has been as controversial as the party itself. Economic historians, while seeing some merit in the Populists' discontent over debt, have pointed out that other prices fell faster than farm prices in the late nineteenth century and have questioned the Populists' inability to understand the deflationary trend, which was fairly predictable for a long period of time. Still, Populist ideology contributed to the character of the Progressive Movement of the early twentieth century, and much of the Populist program for agricultural reform was enacted during the New Deal.

References:

John D. Hicks, *The Populist Revolt: A History of the Farmers' Alliance and the People's Party* (Minneapolis: University of Minnesota Press, 1931);

Norman Pollack, *The Populist Response to Industrial America: Midwestern Populist Thought* (Cambridge, Mass.: Harvard University Press, 1962).

Arsène P. Pujo

(December 16, 1861-December 31, 1939)

by Henry C. Dethloff

Texas A&M University

CAREER: Lawyer, Lake Charles, Louisiana (1886-1903, 1913-1939); U.S. representative, state of Louisiana (1903-1913).

Arsène Paulin Pujo achieved prominence in banking and financial circles when the Pujo Committee, more accurately called the Committee to Investigate the Concentration of Control of Money and Credit, was authorized by Congress in 1912 to investigate the "money trust," the alleged monopoly of the New York banking elite over American finance. Congress established the committee in response to public concerns originating in the Alliance and Populist movements of the late nineteenth century and brought into focus during the Progressive movement. Before entering the 1912 campaign for the presidency, Woodrow Wilson expressed the Progressive attitude toward banks when he declared in 1911, "The great monopoly in this country is the money monopoly. So long as it exists, our old variety and freedom and individual energy of development are out of the question."

Pujo's career aptly illustrates the association between twentieth-century progressivism and the agrarian movements of the previous generation. Born near Lake Charles, Louisiana, on December 16, 1861, Pujo attended local schools and read law before being admitted to the Louisiana bar in 1886. He began a law practice in Lake Charles, an area that experienced rapid development after completion of the Southern Pacific Railroad to New Orleans and the introduction of rice culture.

Pujo became president of the First National Bank of Welsh, Louisiana, and a director of the First National Bank of Lake Charles. At the same time he became involved in local political issues. He joined the Louisiana Farmer's Union, which merged with the Texas Farmer's Alliance in 1888 to form the Southern Farmer's Alliance. Although he was never a member of the Populist party, he supported currency reformer William Jennings Bryan for president in 1896 and 1900. In 1903 he began service in the U.S. House of Representatives as a Democrat. From 1908 to 1912 he served on the National Monetary Commission chaired by Senator Nelson B. Aldrich of Rhode Island. In 1911 he became chairman of the House Banking and Currency Committee. In that position Pujo obtained authorization to form a select committee for investigation of the money trust.

The Pujo Committee gathered information by issuing questionnaires to some 30,000 national banks, state banks, and trust companies. It was also authorized to compel the attendance of witnesses and to acquire papers. George F. Baker, chairman of the First National Bank of New York, and J. P. Morgan testified before the committee in highly publicized sessions. Some committee members believed that the investigation, which was suspended during the election of 1912 and resumed from December 1912 to February 1913, was not fully complete when the committee issued on February 28. Nevertheless, the report contributed significantly to the passage of the Federal Reserve Act later in 1913.

The committee reported that 21 percent of the total banking resources in the United States were concentrated in New York City (excluding private banking operations), and that the New Yorkers controlled national finances out of all proportion to their actual holdings. Through consolidations, stock investments, interlocking directorates, and partnerships and joint account arrangements, the 20 largest banks and trust companies in New York actually controlled 43 percent of the nation's money. The Morgan interests alone represented an estimated $22 billion in resources, 10 percent of the nation's wealth.

The power of the bankers, the committee found, radiated largely through their control over the issue and distribution of corporate securities: "Under our system of issuing and distributing corporate securities the investing public does not buy directly from the corporation. The securities travel from the issuing house through middlemen to the investor. It is only the great banks or bankers with access to the mainsprings of the concentrated resources made up of other people's money in the banks ... who have had the power to underwrite or guarantee the sale of large-scale security issues. [They] are the ones who are in position to tap those reservoirs for the venture in which they are interested and to prevent their being tapped for purposes of which they do *not* approve." Those conclusions helped convince the authors of the Federal Reserve Act to establish regional branches.

Ironically, Pujo lost his congressional seat in the year of the passage of the Federal Reserve Act. He returned to his law practice in Lake Charles, where he died on December 31, 1939.

References:

Herbert E. Dougall and Jack E. Gaumnitz, *Capital Markets and Institutions* (Englewood Cliffs, N.J.: Prentice-Hall, 1975);

Herman E. Kross and Martin R. Blyn, *A History of Financial Intermediaries* (New York: Random, 1971);

Arthur S. Link, *Woodrow Wilson and the Progressive Era, 1910-1917* (New York: Harper & Row, 1954);

Richard H. Timberlake, Jr., *The Origins of Central Banking in the United States* (Cambridge, Mass.: Harvard University Press, 1978);

Robert H. Wiebe, *The Search for Order, 1877-1920* (New York: Hill & Wang, 1967).

William Chapman Ralston

(January 12, 1826-August 27, 1875)

by Lynne Pierson Doti

Chapman College

CAREER: General merchant and travel agent, Garrison & Fretz, Panama (1849-1854), San Francisco (1854-1856); partner, Garrison, Morgan, Fretz & Ralston (1856-1857), Fretz & Ralston (1857-1861); partner, Donohoe, Ralston & Company (1861-1864); cashier (1864-1873), president, Bank of California (1873-1975).

William Chapman Ralston's career closely paralleled the exuberant history of the pioneer days of early California. He came to California with the forty-niners, and his first job was to assist others on their journeys westward. As a banker he helped finance much of the mid nineteenth-century industrial development of California, Oregon, Washington, and Nevada. He directed his banks to lend aggressively, and if customers for the loans were not available, he began his own ventures. When gold faded as the basis of the Pacific Coast economy and Nevada silver took its place, he stood in the forefront, investing heavily in the mines with his own money and that of the newly founded Bank of California, California's first incorporated bank and one of the Far West's largest enterprises. Ralston was one of San Francisco's most prominent

citizens, and the city mourned his premature death.

William Chapman Ralston was born in Plymouth, Ohio, on January 12, 1826, the eldest of four sons born to Robert Ralston III and Mary Chapman Ralston. His parents were both descended from pioneer Americans. As a young boy Ralston, called "Chapman" by his family, enjoyed horses and helped in his father's sawmills. He enjoyed being a big brother to Samuel, born in 1832, Andrew Jackson, born in 1833, and James Alpheus, born in 1835. Tragically, his mother died shortly after the birth of James. Ralston remembered the pain of the loss long into his adult years. Following frontier custom, however, the widower remarried quickly, and the boys gained a loving maternal influence in the person of Harriet Herford, daughter of a local judge. Three more children, Mary Jane, Elizabeth, and Thomas Herford, were added to the family.

At the age of fourteen Ralston left the sawmill job to become a clerk in the local general store. He continued to help in his father's shipyard business and later started delivering newly constructed boats and handling sales. He was anxious for independence, however, and he soon took a job clerking

William Chapman Ralston

for the firm of Lawson & Cavode, traveling between ports on the Ohio and the Mississippi Rivers. In a few years he went to work as chief clerk on the sidewheeler *Convoy*. The captain of that ship, Cornelius Kingsland Garrison, who played a major role in Ralston's life, was an engineer who had arrived in St. Louis in 1833 to begin a company with his brother specializing in the construction, manufacture, and wholesaling of riverboat supplies. Other brothers arrived later, and the firm Garrison & Brothers entered into the manufacture of steam engines and steel products. Ralston worked with Garrison on the *Convoy* for three years. During that time Ralston also met and was influenced by another steamboat captain, Ralph Stover Fretz. Fretz's boat, the *Memphis*, plied the southern Mississippi, and Ralston dealt with his mercantile firm in New Orleans.

New Orleans in the mid nineteenth century was no less gay than it is today. The genteel lifestyle contrasted sharply with the society on the Ohio frontier, and many of Ralston's later exuberant excesses would have seemed quite normal in New Orleans. The excitement of the city only whet-

ted Ralston's appetite, however. Captains Garrison and Fretz had joined the many Mississippi River men with gold fever. Garrison left February 15, 1849, to maintain a steamer service on the Sacramento River. Ralston also left New Orleans, on July 3, 1849.

The trip to California proved long and dangerous for the gold seekers. At first the usual route involved taking a tall-masted clipper ship such as the *Flying Cloud*, which once made the trip from New York around Cape Horn to San Francisco in a record-setting 89 days. The volume of passengers quickly exceeded clipper ship capacity, however, and many took the newer steamship lines to New Orleans, then to Aspinwall, on the east coast of Panama. From there they traveled 50 miles overland to Panama City, usually six or seven days away. Travel across the isthmus was uncertain. As one experienced traveler recommended, "a good waterproof trunk is very desirable . . . because . . . it will be likely to experience several dunkings before reaching its destination." Frequent malaria epidemics swept through the waves of migrants.

When Ralston reached Panama he encountered his old friends and mentors Garrison and Fretz. Garrison had established himself in Oregon and Washington as well as in San Francisco and Sacramento. He had built a steamer for bringing lumber down the Willamette River, had another steamer plying the Sacramento River, and built a sawmill and a larger steamer for Sacramento. He had also become an agent for Cornelius Vanderbilt's steamship line. Garrison became one of the West's leading citizens with the help of his $60,000 salary from Vanderbilt and his other business interests. He was elected mayor of San Francisco and established himself by enforcing the Sabbath laws and closing gambling establishments.

Fretz and his brother, with Garrison as a partner, had established an exchange business on the isthmus to supply travelers to California and make travel arrangements. When Ralston arrived, Fretz and Garrison convinced him to help manage this business. He once captained an ailing steamboat from Panama to San Francisco himself to accommodate the passengers. Garrison and Fretz added Ralston's name to the company stationery following that adventure. After several years of sending travelers to the land of gold, Ralston wanted to conquer new territory himself, and on September 1,

1854, he arrived in San Francisco to enter another phase of his adventurous life.

Exactly a month after his arrival, the business suffered the worst possible reversal when one of the ships of the Independent Line, for which Fretz and Ralston were agents, wrecked with the loss of about 200 passengers and a large gold shipment. Garrison brought the survivors back to San Francisco, where they complained bitterly about the fact that they were stranded there "without means to buy a meal of victuals or night's lodging." The following year brought more difficulties: gold output declined, real estate prices dropped, a series of financial panics occurred, and Garrison lost the mayor's office.

In spite of those problems, fellow banker William T. Sherman, writing in May 1856, described Ralston as a rich man. Earlier that year Ralston helped found a new bank, Garrison, Morgan, Fretz & Ralston, with money from shipping magnate Charles Morgan and from the Manhattan Bank of New York. The new bank, capitalized at $700,000, had connections in New York, New Orleans, St. Louis, Louisville, Cincinnati, and Pittsburgh. Like most early California banks, its primary activity involved the purchase and shipment of gold.

Garrison and Morgan withdrew from the partnership in 1857 to concentrate on their shipping business, which thrived in Texas, Louisiana, the Atlantic seaboard, and, especially, the Gulf region. They also invested in railroads, and Garrison soon left San Francisco to reside in New York, leaving Fretz and Ralston to announce a newly formed partnership, "Fretz & Ralston, Bankers, corner Washington and Battery Streets," on July 14, 1857. That bank served the San Francisco community in a modest way until the two joined with dry goods merchants Eugene Kelly and Joseph Donohoe to enlarge the bank. Fretz took the reorganization as an opportunity to relocate to Calaveras County. The new partnership, Donohoe, Ralston & Company, opened in 1861, reflected his lessened role. Eugene Kelly returned to New York to handle eastern sales and review the firm's actions in frequent letters and telegrams to Ralston and Donohoe. With the expanded capital base Ralston encouraged the development of local industry. He invested in the Donohoe, Booth & Company foundry and its subsidiary companies, which produced pans, steam engines, and a railroad that ran to San Jose by 1864. Ralston also contributed to the city's improvements

by underwriting bond issues and loans to building societies. Civil War inflation made gold more valuable, and California thrived.

Settled into a stable business, Ralston found time to take a wife. He had been married once before, to the granddaughter of Cornelius Vanderbilt, but she died in 1853. Ralston kept a miniature of her throughout his life. Ralston's second wife, Lizzie Fry, was probably better suited to San Francisco, having been raised in frontier Illinois. She was the adopted daughter of J. D. Fry, who had come to California in 1849 to form a partnership with William Sharon in Sacramento. Lizzie Fry and Ralston married on May 21, 1858. Although little is known of their courtship, she and Ralston had a distinctive wedding. After the ceremony at Calvary Church and a short reception, the wedding party and several of the older generation boarded the steamer *New World* and set off for a camping trip at Yosemite Valley. The venture amazed San Franciscans, not only because of the difficulty of the journey, but because the bride's going-away costume consisted of a made-for-sports bloomer dress rather than the voluminous skirts more usual for such occasions in those days, and because she wore her hair unconventionally in two braids hanging down her back. Upon returning to San Francisco the couple took hotel rooms for a short time, then spent seven years at 324 Fremont Street. The first three of their five children were born there: Samuel Fry (named after Ralston's late brother), Etna Louise, and William Chapman, Jr. The last two children, Emelita and Bertha, were born in 1865 and 1872.

While lending opportunities in California appeared everywhere and interest rates hovered at 2 to 5 percent per month, Eugene Kelly saw fruitful and safer opportunities in the East. When the Civil War ended, a battle for capital began between the Donohoe, Ralston & Company's two locations. Tension mounted, and the outcome became inevitable when Ralston, without Kelly, joined Ladd & Tilton Bank of Portland to finance new business in Oregon. "If you are going to invest outside California that way, we had better dissolve our partnership," Kelly wrote from New York. Whether because of Kelly's grip on the bank's funds or because of the increasingly critical attitude he assumed toward Ralston's activities, Ralston set about opening a new bank.

Ralston had emerged as San Francisco's most prominent citizen, perhaps the richest man in a place where incredible wealth was commonplace. His home became a social center: he once built a temporary ballroom for a theme party. He placed his faith in California's potential for renewed expansion and envisioned a bank capable of supporting it. That renewed expansion, like California's first spurt of growth, was based largely on the mineral deposits of the state. Miners searching ever farther from the original goldfields had found huge amounts of silver, the blackish substance they had once discarded. As the Comstock Lode gradually revealed its riches, miners made new fortunes, ventures revived, and silver flowed through San Francisco on its circuitous way east.

Ralston had a new goal: to capture that silver and keep it in San Francisco. A new bank, a Bank of California, would be the key. Ralston enlisted the assistance of California's most prominent citizens, including a banker who complemented his fiery nature: Darius Ogden Mills. "D. O.," as he was called, was a cautious and dignified man, always dressed in black frock coats and sporting prominent side whiskers. Mills was Sacramento's richest man and the state's most prominent banker. He had followed his brothers west in 1849 to mine gold but, like Ralston, found that commerce produced the bigger nuggets. For a year and a half he occupied himself bringing shovels, flour, and other necessities to Sacramento to sell to the miners. By 1852 a large iron safe and a reputation for honesty allowed him to declare himself a banker. The Bank of D. O. Mills stood as the oldest in the state in 1864. Ralston asked Mills to become president of the new bank, a position Ralston intended to be mostly ceremonial. Ralston took for himself the job of cashier. He decided the investments the bank made and oversaw the daily activities of shipping silver, writing drafts that the bank sent to eastern banks to pay for goods ordered there, and passing out gold or silver coin in return for gold or silver nuggets or dust. Unlike easterners, Californians demanded coin in all daily transactions. That restricted the use of bank notes to dealings among bankers and businessmen.

Ralston's new bank opened in July 1864. The bank's first customers for loans and deposits came from the ranks of successful Comstock miners. Silver mining, although lucrative, required capital. The riches of Virginia City lay ever deeper under the mountains and could only be reached by shafts and tunnels, which required the investment of huge

expenditures long before a return arrived. One way of obtaining capital involved selling shares in a successful claim to others. A lively market developed in those shares, and people from all walks of life visited the exchange to speculate in the shares. That market was volatile: a line of dark material in a dirt wall sent prices for all mining stock sailing, and the sound of water made them crash.

That latter sound shook the newly formed Bank of California in its first year. The stock market failed after a miner's pick hit subterranean water, which rendered all the mine shafts inaccessible. Ralston's correspondent bank in Virginia City failed, taking with it the money loaned by Ralston's bank for mining companies' payrolls and equipment. Ralston realized the need for a branch bank and a trusted associate to stay in Virginia City to watch the bank's considerable investment there. He planned to send his head teller but changed his mind after a momentous visit from his wife's uncle, Colonel Fry. Fry came to Ralston asking for help for an old friend of his, a friend from the days in Illinois who had seen little luck in his investments and was penniless. The always generous Ralston promptly offered $500, but Fry demurred. The gentleman required a job, and the position of Virginia City agent would be perfect. Ralston trusted his relative's judgment and agreed to the proposition, and the friend, William Sharon, departed for Virginia City. Ralston sent his brother James to assist.

Worthless investments Sharon made in the market were the key to his bad fortune, but his luck changed for the better. When he arrived in Virginia City he first sought to discover which of the failed correspondent bank's assets he could liquidate to satisfy the indebtedness. Wells Fargo had also loaned money to the failed bank and had already claimed some of its assets as its own to repay the debt. Sharon still managed to find values significant enough to satisfy the loan.

After resolving the problem, Sharon tackled another issue vital to the bank: the long-term profitability of the Comstock Lode. Flooded shafts were becoming too common. A tunnel below 500 feet was as likely as not to bring forth a stream. Dynamiting was as likely to yield a lake as a silver-filled vault. Miners brought in pumps that strained to clear the way for more mining. Bigger pumps were ordered, but none sufficed. The word on the street circulated that water had ended the Comstock bonanza, and stock prices suffered. After Sharon observed those occurences firsthand, studied mining reports, and even sent his nephew to learn assaying, he told Ralston that the real Comstock bonanza had not been seen: it lay deeper than man had yet traveled, and water barred the way. Ralston responded in a characteristic way, supplying funds to Vulcan Foundry for the construction of bigger pump engines. He proudly attended the installation of a 50-horsepower pump, considered a giant. Only eight months later that pump proved so feeble against the water that an expanding lake engulfed the machine and tore it from its foundation. Ralston ordered the foundry to construct a 120-horsepower motor, but a year passed before its installation.

Meanwhile, another man worked on a new approach to the miners' water problems. Adolph Sutro came to California with the other gold seekers, in his case, however, traveling all the way from Prussia. In 1860, as owner of a successful Comstock crushing mill of his own design, he wrote a letter to the *San Francisco Alta* describing his ideas for mechanical improvements in Comstock mines. Among his ideas was one for a tunnel to drain and ventilate the mines and provide easy downhill transportation to the crushing mill. By 1865 Sutro had a corporation well supported by Nevada dignitaries and had received exclusive rights to build a tunnel under 7,400-foot Mt. Davidson to the Comstock Lode. Thus prepared, Sutro then set out to raise money to build the tunnel. He naturally visited William Ralston at the Bank of California. Ralston listened to his plan, tearing pieces of paper into tiny bits as he frequently did when he forced his powerful and increasingly substantial body into repose.

More cautious men had laughed at the idea. But no one had ever accused Ralston of caution. He encouraged Sutro, supplying him with letters of support to help him raise the $3 million needed to complete the project. With Ralston's assistance, the owners of all the major mines reached an agreement to pay $2 per ton to Sutro forever if he completed the tunnel. Sutro proceeded to the East Coast and later to Europe to raise the money, while Ralston continued to worry, realizing his new bank sat on as unstable a foundation as Virginia City's. The bank had grown, but not in the traditional way. Ralston cut interest rates on his loans to well below his competitors' monthly 2 to 5 percent and was not overcritical of a borrower's prospects. Sharon in Virginia City loaned liberally on the mines and mills, taking stock in the companies as collateral. Ralston did the same in San Francisco. In that way Ralston and the bank came to own several mills and mines. His biographer, George D. Lyman, in only a slight bit of hyperbole, calls the Ralston of 1865 the "Atlas of the Pacific," for "upon his shoulders rested the financial structure of the Pacific Coast."

Sharon's aggressive lending policies and frequent foreclosures brought the failing Comstock under his control, but his schemes failed to produce cash. He called upon Ralston for $750,000 of that rare commodity. Long since critical of Virginia City operations, the bank's directors demanded the abandonment of the branch. Ralston and Mills went to the mines to see what they could save.

Once they arrived, however, Sharon convinced the two that the Comstock, too, rested on Atlas's shoulders. Pulling back would mean the loss of everything. Instead of retreating, Sharon argued, the bank must push ahead. The mines the bank owned could be reworked to yield more silver, and one or two of the more promising digs would surely proceed deeper into the mountain. The silver existed there in abundance, Sharon assured them. Mills demurred. Banks loaned money; they did not mine silver. Ralston saw the lack of options. Unwilling to give up his dreams and operate conventionally, he agreed to take personal responsibility if Sharon's plan failed. With that guarantee the board allowed Sharon to continue explorations. Ralston and Sharon signed a partnership agreement that applied to all their business ventures.

In 1865 the gamble paid off. The Kentuck mine yielded a promising black vein. Sharon wired the information to Ralston, who proceeded to buy stock in the Kentuck and neighboring mines. As the miners followed the vein, it grew, but not as quickly as stories of the new find. The San Francisco market became a flurry of activity, and the new partnership formed by Ralston and Sharon prospered on the speculation. The Kentuck yielded $2 million worth of silver that year. That discovery saved not only the Bank of California and Ralston, but cast a silver glow over the city.

Ralston continued to build. On land reclaimed from the bay and purchased for $67,500, Ralston built an Italianate bank building of local stone, described as "the most elegant and costly structure on the Pacific Coast." In the $275,000 building everything was as luxurious as it could be.

Memorial to Ralston published in the San Francisco Newsletter *(courtesy of the Bancroft Library, University of California, Berkeley)*

Wide mahogany counters, which served the receiving tellers and the exchange desk, extended along half of one wall. At right angles to those counters stood paying-teller counters, without the usual grilled doors above the counter to guard the piles of coin placed there. Tellers operated confidently beside stacks of gold pieces. Glass enclosed the inner office where the president and cashier sat. Other offices on the first floor housed the secretary and a land agent (realtor). At the rear of the banking room was the vault "of solid iron and elegant in its design" surmounted by a handsome clock. Over the heavy vault doors perched the head of a watchdog in a raised design. Upstairs the clerks and lawyers worked. Since one early picture shows women in the lobby, perhaps the usual "ladies banking room" was omitted. The Chinese already constituted an important part of the population of San Francisco, and Ralston had one Oriental clerk exempted from the strict employee dress code so he could wear the dark silk robes and queue deemed appropriate by the Oriental customers.

The Comstock money built far more than a bank building. Ralston reinvested the wealth as fast as he made it. He invested in every business a person was brave enough to start. Nearly $1 million went into the Pacific Woolen Mills, and nearly $2 million went to land development. More than $500,000 went to build railcars. A furniture company tried to compete with imports, although finding suitable wood was a problem. A quarter of a million dollars provided the capital for a silk company, which turned out $6,000 worth of ribbons a week. An island in the Sacramento River was reclaimed for growing wheat and fruit. Entrepreneurs built a giant dry dock, and that project provided fill for adjacent beach that other sharp-eyed businessmen then converted to land for housing. A million dollars went to a tobacco company that tried to grow, cure, and turn the tobacco into cigars. A watch factory moved from Illinois. Large loans started California's Big Four—Leland Stanford, Mark Hopkins, Charles Crocker, and Collis P. Huntington—on their railroads.

While Ralston built a city, he also created a mansion worthy of the wealthiest man in San Francisco. He bought a villa south of a town called Belmont, recently vacated by an Italian count. Despite its ample size and lovely gardens, Ralston made improvements. The building crept farther up the side of the hill, spreading sideways as it rose. Ballrooms, bedrooms, conservatories, and libraries were added. Ralston built an apartment just for Vice-President Andrew Johnson's visit, which was not slept in again. Most of the house featured the Italianate style of many of the era's buildings. Classical touches, abundant marble, and fashionable clutter added accepted touches of elegance, but distinctive elements of Ralston's personal style also showed in the decor. He loved grillwork and gadgetry. Ventilation ducts ran through the house with openings in each room covered with elaborately carved grills, producing an effect reminiscent of New Orleans. Disappearing walls were Ralston's favorite surprise. He had his guests gather in the library or the music room before dinner. Suddenly a wall glided silently upward into the ceiling, revealing the dinner table lavishly set with Sevres china, Venetian glasses, and silver for perhaps twenty courses. Chandeliers sparkled above. Ralston's waiters, always immaculately dressed Chinese in white with their pigtails glossily intact, served the meals. Sometimes 100 were needed, and they lined up behind the chairs. After dinner other walls rose to rearrange the room for dancing.

While the house grew, the grounds also received attention. The hillside was terraced and planted with azaleas, camellias, and fruit trees. Pines and cedars filtered the wind. Marble benches marked the best spots for a view of the bay. Ralston also needed numerous outbuildings. He built stables to house his beloved horses, although it proved difficult to complete them as quickly as he obtained new horses. By the middle of 1871 Ralston had spent $8,000 to $10,000 prospecting and sinking well shafts to supply the house with water. One result was a lake under the house, which Ralston enjoyed showing more adventurous guests. The entire operation needed a gas plant to keep the crystal lights of the house glowing. Later that gas plant, which cost $50,000 to build, supplied the "village" of Belmont. In the ballroom of Belmont danced the famous visitors to the city. The more sedentary could view the scene below from the mezzanine.

By that time Ralston had joined the latter group. A certain balcony projecting over the dance floor was reserved for him. Once he had taken great pride in his daily ride and swim in the cold waters of the San Francisco Bay. Rich living, however, had gradually broadened his girth, and, after he

moved to Belmont, his afternoon exercise more often consisted of driving his coach and four, usually crowded with dinner guests, as fast as possible the 22 miles home. He delighted in beating the train, although the task required two changes of horses along the way to maintain the pace. Ralston brought guests to Belmont nearly every day. The city's main booster, he insisted that every visitor see the glory of California.

Ralston's private thoughts could not always have been gay. Although he arranged for everyone else's enjoyment and exuded confidence in the city's future, one described his face in repose as "sad." Private troubles contributed to that: two of his brothers had come to work with him and met death instead of riches, and a baby daughter died after sucking sulphur matches. Danger signs appeared in the businesses as well. The mines had brought great wealth, but the flow could stop at any time.

In Virginia City, Sharon had gained control of the mills, which extracted the silver and gold from the ore, as he had gained control of the mines. He had gained control also of the best forest near the mines, so the timber for the tunnels also fell under his control. To tie the system together he created a railroad, the Virginia & Truckee. Known as the "crookedest road in the world" both for the hairpin turns in its bed and for the financing scheme that supported it, the railroad took timber to the mines and ore from the mines to the bank-controlled mills. Sharon assured Ralston that the mines were under their control, but Ralston knew well the strength of his rivals. These rivals attacked him from two directions. East of the mines Sutro gathered support for his tunnel. West of the mines, in San Francisco, a new partnership threatened Ralston's control of the city.

The Sutro tunnel had turned from hope to a threat for Ralston. The tunnel would make it less expensive to transport ore to the Sutro mill than to Ralston's mills. The Virginia & Truckee would be useless, too, and the promise still remained to pay Sutro $2 per ton of ore mined. This had seemed trivial when the ore was so rich and prices so high that ore assayed at upwards of $2,000 a ton. But mine production and prices had dropped. At the same time, laborers demanded higher wages and had succeeded in driving out the industrious Chinese.

The mines showed less profit: again only a bonanza–a rich vein–could save Ralston's plans. But on April 7, 1869, instead of a bonanza, disaster visited the mines. Fire broke out in the Yellow Jacket, Ralston's most promising mine. At 900 feet below the surface 45 men died. The mine had to be sealed for months to stop the flames. Without timber to support them, tunnels collapsed. The disaster increased worker discontent. Some believed the rumor that Sharon had set the fire so stock prices would drop and he could buy more stock in the mine. The fire did depress stock prices but caused the Bank of California to lose thousands of dollars. The fire also let Sutro gain the support of the miners for his tunnel. With $50,000 they contributed he broke ground for the tunnel on October 19, 1869.

Ralston's other income was threatened too. In 1869 the transcontinental railroad was completed. Ralston's silk and woolen mills, furniture and clock factories all suffered from the increased competition. From the West there came another threat. In 1868 James MacKay, a miner who learned to earn ownership rights rather than wages for his work in the mines, combined his cash with that of another miner, James Fair, to try speculating in mine stocks. Their combined knowledge allowed them to sort out the valid rumors and target the most promising mines. At first they made modest investments, but when the Bank of California-controlled Hale & Norcross mine appeared to be substantially undervalued, these two recruited the saloon-keeping team of James Flood and William O'Brien, and the four corporate raiders succeeded in buying sufficient stock to turn out the officers. These four men continued as rivals to Ralston, gaining ownership of several mines and mills and, later, starting a rival bank, the Nevada Bank of San Francisco (which later became part of Wells Fargo).

Whatever Ralston's private worries, he continued to act as if his wealth and that of San Francisco would grow forever. No project seemed too risky: designing a theater worthy of the most famous talent, constructing a grand hotel that spanned Stephenson Street, cutting down Rincon Hill to improve Market Street. Little wonder that Ralston was taken in by a wild hoax. Asbury Harpending, a real estate partner of Ralston, was in London when he received a $1,100 cable from him. "When I read it," Harpending said, "I felt assured that my old friend had gone mad." Diamonds had been found. Harpending hurried home. When he arrived in San Francisco in May 1872 the scheme had progressed. Two prospectors had

brought rough diamonds to the Bank of California for safe deposit. One of the miners met with Ralston and disclosed ownership of 20 acres of desert land rich with gems. Two investigators dispatched to the location returned with glowing reports. Still cautious, Ralston sent Harpending to Tiffany and Company in New York with a sample of gems found on the parcel. Their report offered more encouragement. A company was formed and went to the site. Immediately its shovels revealed not only diamonds but emeralds, rubies, and sapphires. Quickly the founders incorporated the company. Ralston was made the San Francisco and New York Mining and Commercial Company's treasurer, and among the 25 subscribers was a representative of Baron Rothschild. Of the $2 million initial subscription, the two miners accepted $300,000 for their title and then discreetly disappeared. In May a team of U.S. Geological Survey officials who worked nearby revealed the hoax. After considerable searching revealed nothing promising, one of the team found a diamond. Impressed, he proclaimed the spot "the bulliest diamond field as ever was. It not only produces diamonds, but cuts them moreover also." A wire to the company explained the details of the hoax. Overcome by guilt over his foolishness, Ralston dispersed the remaining funds and covered the losses for two friends he had encouraged to join. Harpending's embarrassment caused him to slink off eastward after selling his real estate holdings to Ralston and Sharon.

Ralston may have suffered embarrassment, but he reacted quite differently. San Francisco remained the land of milk and honey. Genuine bonanzas had grown rarer, but San Francisco grew faster than ever. The population, 150,000 in 1870, increased 25,000 the next year and reached 195,000 by 1874. Ralston's own wealth as listed on the tax rolls of 1873 came to $581,500. Only a few citizens on the list were wealthier (among the latter was Joseph Donohoe, with $1,178,000). No barriers seemed to exist to Ralston's last, greatest undertaking, the Palace hotel.

The hotel seemed to be an ideal project. Ralston's reputation as a sumptuous host would draw the guests. Income from the showcase building would spill over to support Ralston's other businesses. In 1875, when the hotel was finished according to Ralston's plan, it was everything he had hoped for. Covering 100,000 square feet, the seven-story hotel distinguished itself as the largest in the country. Not only did local companies benefit from the project, new industries appeared during the building process. The hotel featured California laurel furniture from the West Coast Furniture Company, horsehair mattresses, goose-down pillows, custom wool blankets, silk bed hangings and upholstery, bureau and door locks, elevators that held 40 guests, clocks in every room, and 27 million bricks, all from local companies. Ralston's partner, Sharon, expostulated, "If you are going to buy a foundry for a nail, a ranch for a plank and manufacture and build furniture, where is this going to end?"

Ralston spent almost $2 million on the foundation of the Palace, and $1 million more for each story that rose. The funds to finance that undertaking came more and more from purely financial sources. Although mining stocks retained their value, the gold and silver now came from other mines than those owned by Ralston and Sharon. The pair had extensive real estate holdings, speculated in stocks, and borrowed from the bank, but the rate at which Ralston spent money exceeded the income. Occasionally he did not pay bills on time. In 1873 a financial panic spread westward, the San Francisco stock market took a dip, and Ralston told the bank directors that he could not make interest payments on his loans on time. Ralston's assurances calmed most of the directors, but D. O. Mills probably sensed the depth of the problem. Although he told many people that the bank was sound, he asked to be relieved of his responsibilities as president and shareholder and departed on a world tour. Ralston paid for his shares but left the distinguished name on the list of shareholders.

Other problems followed. Germany demonetized silver in 1871, and the United States followed in 1873, causing a decline in prices. The Bank of California no longer controlled the Virginia City mines: the Bonanza Kings–Flood, Fair, O'Brien, and MacKay–were emerging as formidable rivals. Until 1873, although those four fought Ralston and Sharon for control of the mines, they had entrusted their millions to the Bank of California's vault. By 1875 they had their own large bank, the Nevada Bank of San Francisco, financed with $5 million paid up in gold. Under the ground, even deeper than the shafts, Sutro and his crew furiously dug their tunnel.

In June 1875 the financial crisis reached the West Coast. A bank in Riverside failed. The crisis spread to Los Angeles. Banks ran short of coin: some closed temporarily, and some never reopened. The panic made its way north, hitting San Francisco on August 26. The stock market turned a month-long decline into a crash. The pressure on the banks began early. Steadily customers arrived to withdraw their funds. It was not the first run the Bank of California had endured, and Ralston fought it with his usual tactics. Confidence was the key: if customers thought their money was safe, they would leave it and the run would end. Ralston had averted many a run with a display of gold coins on the counters. He sent his cashier to find the coin. Once in the past, a run had been averted by coin from the U.S. Treasury, and other times banks had supported each other in these situations. This time, however, Ralston found an unusual scarcity. Coin was the only money used in California– bank notes still did not circulate. The wheat crop had been unusually large that summer, and the farmers had just paid more than $18 million to ship their wheat crop east. Those funds would only return to California when others bought the crop and paid for it, which created a severe, though temporary, shortage.

To raise money to pay for the needed coin, Ralston sold assets. On August 23 he had sold a large amount of bills receivable to Oriental Banking Corporation. Unfortunately payment could only be made in British currency, not gold. Other bankers had too many concerns with their own solvency to lend coin to Ralston. He sold his share of the Virginia & Truckee Railroad for half its estimated value to D. O. Mills, now back from his tour. J. L. Fry also assisted Ralston as much as he could, giving him $90,000 for 16,000 acres of land in Kern County. Ralston acquired a large amount of coin by borrowing gold and silver from a company that functioned as a "depository and refinery for gold and silver" and taking it to the mint to be made into coin. Even James Flood, surprisingly, provided a loan, but Ralston's efforts proved inadequate. The lines at the bank grew longer, finally reaching outside the building. The tellers paid slowly, but the clock moved more slowly. Survival until three o'clock would have given Ralston another night to find coin. As officers measured the dwindling supply, the clock ticked steadily, and the clock outlasted the coin. At 2:35 P.M. the tellers quit paying.

Policemen urged the lobby cleared. A suspension notice was posted on the bank's iron doors.

When the Bank of California closed, runs began on other banks. One remained open late, paying out coin until after four o'clock, another demanded advance notification for withdrawals, and a third suspended operations. Several of the established banks experienced little disturbance.

The Bank of California did not open on August 27, 1875. Instead, the directors met to review the books. As a result of the meeting, they accepted Ralston's resignation. Several circumstances may have led to that result. Mills participated in the group, although he had supposedly severed his connection two years before. He must have known by that day of Ralston's failure to record the corporation's repurchase of his stock. He may also have known that Ralston had oversubscribed stock (sold it without using the funds to increase the bank's capital) and that Mills's own signature appeared on the stock certificates. It is also probable that Ralston's well-publicized reputation for high living contributed to the bank's instability; Mills's staid reputation gave the bank a chance for survival–if he accepted the presidency. At any rate, Ralston resigned and left the bank.

He visited his lawyer and signed his assets over to Sharon for the benefit of his creditors, not realizing his partner would destroy their partnership agreement to avoid liability for Ralston's debts. On the street again, Ralston passed his physician, who remarked that he appeared to be "overheated." Ralston thought he would go for a swim, and the physician remarked that he might join him. Ralston continued to the bathhouse alone. The bathhouse attendant also later remarked on Ralston's flushed appearance. The former banker assured him that a brisk rub with a turkish towel and a shower would cool him before he attempted the cold bay waters. He chatted with another bather as he entered the water, but his strong strokes soon carried him away from the young man. An engineer in the steamer *Bullion*, not far offshore, observed the bather enjoying the water; when he next looked in his direction, however, what he saw caused him quickly to lower a small boat and begin a rescue attempt. He found Ralston floating face down and tried to pull the limp body into the small boat, but it was a difficult job. A small crowd had gathered by the time he recovered the body and got his boat to shore. Several people applied the current remedies for drowning, but when a doctor arrived, he declared Ralston dead.

The news spread quickly. Ralston's physician had not yet abandoned the idea of joining his patient and friend at the beach when the news reached him. The city nearly stopped: the Bank of California had failed and the great Ralston had died. Given the timing some naturally suspected suicide. Although the exact cause of death will always be unknown, suicide seems unlikely. A complete autopsy was performed, with particular attention paid to the possibility of poison in the stomach. None was found. The doctors ruled the cause of death as "asphyxia with cerebral congestion." Little opportunity had existed for Ralston to acquire any poison that day, and before his resignation he had been unquestionably optimistic. He knew he was ruined–he owed $9.5 million and owned assets worth only $4.5 million–but hoped to rebuild, even to remain as president of his bank. Given his physique (he weighed about 200 pounds) and the normal excesses of a wealthy man of his era, a heart attack or a stroke seems most likely to have caused his death. He did not drown–no water was found in his lungs–and his body showed no signs of injury.

The city mourned. Not only was his funeral a public event, in spite of the family's wishes, but on September 8 a memorial tribute attracted 12,000 people. Prominent citizens gave eulogies, and the crowd shouted "aye" to Thomas Fitch's resolution "that the citizens of San Francisco without distinction of party, caste, or class, in public council now assembled, tender to the widow and family of our belated benefactor and friend, our tenderest sympathies for their and our great loss."

Ralston's family sued William Sharon for mismanaging the estate. Sharon settled out of court for $250,000. The Bank of California reopened on October 2 after raising $4 million in new capital. On the first day $4,430,000 in deposits came in and only $254,000 was withdrawn. The bank continued to prosper and remains a strong California bank as of 1989.

References:

James J. Hunter, *Partners in Progress, 1864-1950: A Brief History of the Bank of California, N.A., and of the Region It Has Served for 85 Years* (New York: Newcomen Society, 1950);

George D. Lyman, *Ralston's Ring: California Plunders the Comstock Lode* (New York: Scribners, 1937);

Cecil G. Tilton, *William Chapman Ralston: Courageous Builder* (Boston: Christopher, 1935).

Archives:
William Ralston's papers are at the Bancroft Library, University of California, Berkeley.

Reserves *(see* **Deposits, Reserves, and Fractional Reserve Banking***)*

Real Bills Doctrine

Early mercantilist views of wealth held that only gold, silver, and precious gems constituted true wealth (although the Physiocrats later added land to the list). By the early 1800s few people still believed in the mercantilist theory in its strict sense, but they still tended to see money as only representative of tangible wealth. The Jacksonians left their imprint on American views of money by asserting that only "hard money"—bills backed 100 percent by specie—had value. All the rest they snubbed as "worthless paper."

Attitudes had changed somewhat by the late 1800s, but only slightly: the accepted banking theory, called the "real bills" doctrine, held that all bank notes issued must represent only those assets comprised of real, tangible commodities. The real bills school allowed goods in the process of verifiable transactions to be counted as assets but not goods that had not yet been produced or grown (represented in modern "futures markets") or services.

Advocates of the real bills doctrine dominated the banking reform movement of the late nineteenth century. But many who favored a more "elastic" currency (a money supply that could be expanded or contracted more easily according to the demands of the economy) mounted a powerful challenge to the real bills school.

See also:

Nelson W. Aldrich, George F. Baker, Christopher C. Homer, John Jay Knox, Jacob Schiff, Frank Arthur Vanderlip, Amasa Walker.

—Editor

Savings and Loan Associations

Savings and Loan Associations (S&Ls) borrowed on the mutual savings bank concept, taking the savings of small depositors and making mortgage loans. Under the provisions of the Federal Home Loan Bank Act (1932), S&Ls were prohibited from making commercial loans, but as a reward they received the authority to pay slightly higher interest than banks.

Building and Loan Associations (B&Ls) were identical to S&Ls but the term was not used as frequently. Like S&Ls they provided funds specifically for financing home construction from members' deposits. Because national banks faced tight restrictions on the conditions under which they could hold real estate as collateral, B&Ls and S&Ls prospered as a means to finance home construction.

See also:

August Belmont, DeWitt Clinton, Mutual Savings Banks.

—Editor

Jacob Henry Schiff

(January 10, 1847-September 25, 1920)

by Carol M. Martel

Arizona State University

CAREER: Partner, Budge, Schiff & Company (1866-1872); manager, London and Hanseatic Bank (1873); partner (1875-1885), senior partner, Kuhn, Loeb and Company (1885-1920).

Jacob Henry Schiff, American financier and philanthropist, stood second only to J. P. Morgan among private investment bankers in the late nineteenth and early twentieth centuries. Schiff was born on January 10, 1847, in Frankfurt am Main, Germany, into a substantial German-Jewish family replete with scholars, rabbis, and businessmen. Schiff's parents, Moses and Clara Niederhofheim Schiff, provided him with a thorough secular and religious education. He had a good knowledge of Hebrew, could quote freely from the Bible, and kept abreast of developments in biblical study.

At the age of fourteen Schiff was apprenticed to a German business firm, but he wanted to immigrate to America. His father very reluctantly permitted him to go to England, where the Schiffs had relatives, and from there he left for New York City, arriving on August 6, 1865. He joined a New York brokerage firm and obtained a broker's license on November 21, 1866. He then began his own investment firm, Budge, Schiff & Company, with partners Henry Budge and Leo Lehmann. Schiff spent most of his time in Germany and Holland marketing American railroad bonds. In 1870 he was naturalized a U.S. citizen. Budge returned to his German homeland, and the firm dissolved in 1872. Schiff also returned to Germany and early the next year took a position as manager of the Hamburg branch of the London and Hanseatic Bank. Schiff's European connections proved vital to his future career, and in the Hamburg position he operated comfortably with London, Parisian, and German bankers.

Schiff's father died later in 1873, and Schiff resigned his position with the London and Hanseatic Bank to return to Frankfurt. While on a visit to Frankfurt, Abraham Kuhn invited him to return to New York to join the investment banking house of Kuhn, Loeb and Company. When Solomon Loeb re-

Jacob Henry Schiff

tired in 1885, the thirty-eight-year-old Schiff became head of the company. Schiff brought energy, foresight, and valuable European connections to the firm. Among the latter were financiers Ernest Cassel and Robert Fleming of London and Edouard Noetzlin, president of the Banque de Paris et des Pays Bas. Through those connections Schiff placed large quantities of American securities on the European market. Cassel was also his closest friend outside his family, and the two carried on a warm correspondence for 40 years.

On May 6, 1875, Schiff married Theresa Loeb, daughter of Solomon Loeb. Their son, Mortimer Leo, received training in railroad enterprise. He followed in his father's footsteps, becoming a partner and then head of Kuhn, Loeb after his father's death. The Schiffs' daughter, Frieda, married Felix Warburg, later a partner in Kuhn, Loeb.

Under Schiff's leadership Kuhn, Loeb and Company enjoyed a spectacular rise in the last two decades of the nineteenth century. The firm acquired able partners, including Felix Warburg and his brother Paul (the latter became associated with the establishment of the Federal Reserve System), Otto H. Kahn, and Abraham Wolff (whose daughter mar-

ried Kahn). Wolff had joined the company the same year as Schiff and cooperated closely with him. The Warburgs came from a Hamburg banking family, which further strengthened ties between Kuhn, Loeb and financial circles in Germany. The firm thus had a distinctly German-Jewish character prior to World War I.

After 1880 tremendous power accrued to leading investment bankers such as Schiff and J. P. Morgan. The national dominance of railroads, industrial corporations, and public-service corporations would not have been possible if investment bankers had not readily financed their legitimate needs. The bankers had to determine whether they should offer an issue of securities to the public and the price the public should have to pay. Success depended upon public confidence in a banker's judgment. Schiff felt strongly about his firm's obligation to provide funds when other investors could not, especially in times of stress. Consequently, he sometimes rejected promising opportunities because he had to consider keeping his reserves liquid more than making immediate profit. Schiff's financial achievements stemmed from his unusual grasp of problems and his unusual courage; while essentially conservative, he still, as biographer Cyrus Adler claimed, "went in where others feared to tread." Schiff rarely made a mistake in business judgment.

Kuhn, Loeb became one of the nation's leading railroad underwriters. The firm turned to the financing of railway enterprises because the prosperity of the United States depended on the extent and efficiency of its transportation. It helped finance nearly all the important railroads in the East that were not family-owned, including the Baltimore & Ohio, the Chesapeake & Ohio, the Delaware & Hudson, the Illinois Central, the Southern Pacific, the Erie, the Denver & Rio Grande, the Norfolk & Western, and others. Schiff served on the boards of directors for many of those lines. In 1915, when the Pennsylvania Railroad wanted to build a tunnel under the Hudson River and a railway station in New York City, Kuhn, Loeb floated loans of $49 million and $62 million for the road.

The great railroad boom of the late 1800s collapsed early in 1893. Schiff, Morgan, and others were called upon to reorganize companies in default. The Interstate Commerce Commission (ICC) reported in June 1894 that 192 railroads were in receivership. To rehabilitate so many large enterprises required experienced bankers able to command large resources. They provided new working capital, paid debts, and consolidated or separated unprofitable parts of the systems. By the end of the 1890s, when most of the reorganizations were completed, the bankers had earned unprecedented influence and power as well as considerable profits and prestige. Schiff helped reorganize the Baltimore & Ohio Railroad from 1896 to 1899.

Probably the most sensational episode in Schiff's career involved the struggle between the Union Pacific Railroad and the Great Northern Company for control of the Northern Pacific. That episode established Schiff's firm as one of the leading financial forces in the world. The Union Pacific had gone into receivership in 1895, at which time J. P. Morgan unsuccessfully attempted to reorganize the road. Schiff wanted the railroad for his company, but in the style of old-world banking protocol to which Schiff and Morgan adhered, Schiff demurred taking over the reorganization until Morgan assured him that he had no interest in the road except to see it rehabilitated and its creditors protected. When Schiff tried reorganizing the road, however, he encountered opposition from Edward H. Harriman, then vice-president of the Illinois Central, who informed Schiff that he intended to reorganize the Union Pacific himself. In 1896-1897, in a compromise proposed by Schiff, a syndicate took over the Union Pacific. Harriman became a member of the executive committee and cooperated with the syndicate. Morgan also cooperated with Schiff and participated in the syndicate to place the Union Pacific's main bonds. Later the Rockefeller forces and Frick steel interests joined the syndicate. Within three years under this powerful and aggressive combination, the Union Pacific showed a profit. The collaboration paid handsome dividends for Harriman and Schiff. The former advanced to the chairmanship and virtual control of the company, and the latter's firm emerged as the primary banker for the reorganized railroad.

The Harriman-Hill war of 1901 involved a clash between two rival houses of investment, J. P. Morgan and Company and Kuhn, Loeb. In May 1901 Harriman collided with James J. Hill, founder of the Great Northern Railroad and a vast empire in the Northwest. Hill had just won leading control of the Northern Pacific and the Chicago, Burlington & Quincy. Harriman sought to buy the Burlington himself. Abetted by Kuhn, Loeb, Harriman then tried to snatch the Northern Pacific from Hill.

The move brought on the panic of May 1901. In two days of frantic trading, Northern Pacific stock rose from $68 to $300 and then to $1,000. Many stockholders of other roads were caught and ruined because their securities dropped abruptly while the Northern Pacific quotations soared. A compromise ended the fight. Hill kept his pet road, Harriman edged into the Burlington directorate, and the Union Pacific received a director's seat on the Northern Pacific board. That deal was embodied in the Northern Securities Corporation, a holding company designed to protect the interests of both sides, in which Kuhn, Loeb and Company, Hill, Harriman, and Morgan placed their stock holdings in the Union Pacific, Burlington, Great Northern, and Northern Pacific railroads. President Theodore Roosevelt challenged the legality of this organization under federal antitrust laws in his first foray against the trusts. The U.S. Supreme Court ruled it an illegal corporation and ordered it dissolved. Harriman made a profit of nearly $40 million when he sold his Northern Pacific stock.

Schiff also invested heavily in mining interests, particularly the Anaconda Company in Montana. He had a close relationship with Daniel Guggenheim and his brothers. The Guggenheims' accomplishments in Alaska much impressed Schiff when he visited there in 1910.

Although Schiff did not consider the finances of the Westinghouse Electric Company to be conservatively managed, he did finance the company and give advice during its reorganization. While insisting on equitable treatment of stockholders and other creditors, Schiff helped that company reestablish itself financially. He similarly aided the Guggenheims' American Smelting and Refining Company, U.S. Rubber, Armour & Company, and American Telephone & Telegraph.

Schiff was a director of the Central Trust Company, Western Union Telegraph Company, and Wells Fargo & Company. He also had large concerns in the great insurance companies, especially the Equitable Life Assurance Society, of which he was a director. The insurance connection brought Schiff under investigation by a joint committee of the New York legislature in 1905, but it acquitted him of all knowledge of the alleged unscrupulous practices of some of his associates. Leading investment bankers such as Schiff and Morgan commonly attempted to gain influence over the large insurance companies. With the passage of the Federal Reserve Act in 1913, Schiff resigned his connection with the National City Bank, Central Trust Company, American Railway Express Company, Fifth Avenue Trust Company, and other banks.

For both personal and business reasons Schiff desired to own stock in various banks and trust companies throughout the United States and Europe. In accordance with his management policy of centralized responsibility, Kuhn, Loeb did not have branches or agencies in other centers, but preferred instead a correspondent relationship with many other institutions. Investment bankers took an interest in building up large trust companies, which had freedom to act in the field of syndicate securities, stocks not yet listed on the stock exchange but still held by syndicates. In 1912 the Pujo Committee, chaired by Congressman Arsène P. Pujo of Louisiana, investigated the "money trusts" before the House of Representatives. The committee inquired into the methods used to finance large railroad and industrial properties, the influence firms exercised over their corporate clients, and the relationships between issuing houses, their syndicate associates, and the banks and trust companies with which they affiliated. Schiff testified before the committee although his firm was not included among the institutions investigated. Schiff claimed that it was not good form to create unreasonable interference or competition, particularly after the start of negotiations. That virtually amounted to an understanding not to compete, which Schiff defended as a principle of banking ethics.

Kuhn, Loeb exported American capital throughout the world, which gave it even more of an international character than Morgan's firm. Schiff traveled to many of the locales of investment. In 1911 Schiff supported a Chinese loan, partly as a result of the influence of a young diplomat, Willard Straight, who thought that American capital invested in the Manchurian railways might serve to prevent future wars in the Far East. Along with investors such as Morgan and Harriman and two New York banks, Schiff formed the American Group with the intention of advancing the national and business interests of the United States in China. Schiff also invested in the development of railroads and other enterprises in Mexico, Canada, Sweden, Argentina, and Cuba.

Many of Kuhn, Loeb's financial interests directly related to Schiff's concerns for the conditions of worldwide Jewry. The deplorable living conditions of Jewish immigrants on the Lower East Side of New York always elicited Schiff's concern. When hostility erupted between Slavic-Jewish garment workers and German-Jewish manufacturers in New York, Schiff intervened, opposing strikers while secretly supporting their families. The persecution of Jews in czarist Russia particularly moved Schiff to action. In 1890 another Russian pogrom forced the migration of thousands of Jews from Russia to the United States. Schiff believed that the treatment of Jews in eastern Europe required formal protest by the U.S. government. He also thought the United States should encourage immigration. Occasionally his zeal outran his discretion. On one occasion he proposed to President Theodore Roosevelt that the United States intervene militarily in Russia, as it had in Cuba in 1898.

In 1904-1905 almost one-quarter of the foreign loans raised by Japan for its war against Russia came from the United States. At a dinner-party conversation in London, Schiff expressed his opinion to Korekiyo Takahashi, later president of Yokohama Specie Bank, minister of finance, and premier of Japan, that Japan could go to war against Russia even if it lacked gold. The cost of war could be met by the people who would readily take government paper. Schiff agreed to Takahashi's request that he underwrite Japanese bonds in the United States. Schiff took a leading part in those successful efforts, securing for Japan some $200 million in American bonds and encouraging his European counterparts also to help the Japanese. He made no secret of his motive for aiding Japan: the desire to undermine Russian autocracy in hope that the establishment of a constitutional government would provide some relief for Russian Jewry. Russian finances were strained by the difficulty of finding foreign financing, and within a year the country began peace negotiations with Japan. Both Japanese success and Russian failure in obtaining financing were largely attributable to the influence of Schiff and the Jewish banking community in the United States and Europe.

The American sympathy for the Japanese cause greatly facilitated the sale of Japanese bonds. The first bond issue, the first major American investment in foreign war finance, was oversubscribed by 500 percent in a day. In recognition of his service, Japan awarded Schiff the Order of the Sacred Treasure and later the more distinguished Order of the Rising Sun. Schiff took an interest in Japanese cul-

Schiff with fellow bankers Walter Frew, George F. Baker, and J. P. Morgan marching in a Liberty Loan parade, 1918

ture and its economic growth and came to consider Takahashi a close friend. The Schiffs visited Japan, where the emperor received them personally, an unprecedented gesture of gratitude to a businessman.

After the Russo-Japanese War, Japanese friends suggested to Schiff that captured Russian officers, if properly indoctrinated, would make good revolutionaries. He thereafter, in circuitous fashion, contributed money to revolutionary and other anticzarist activities in Russia.

Because of his feeling about the treatment of Jews in Russia, Schiff refused to participate in the Anglo-French loan to Russia during World War I, although it would have entailed great profit for his firm. He opposed the flotation of any Allied loans in which Russia participated and used his influence with other bankers to prevent entry of Russia into American money markets. The 1917 February Revolution in Russia brought instant support from Schiff, and he moved quickly to make his firm's resources available to the new Russian government. But after the Bolshevik Revolution in November his interest in Russian liberty bonds quickly vanished.

Schiff sponsored organizations that dispersed Russian-Jewish immigrants throughout the United States in order to relieve the concentration of Jewish immigrants in New York City. He also facilitated Russian-Jewish immigration to Latin America. In 1906 the American Jewish Committee was organized at the instigation of prominent New York Jews such as Schiff, Cyrus Adler, Judge Mayer Sulzberger, Oscar Straus, and Louis Marshall. The founders meant for the committee to represent American Jewry and to meet emergencies arising among Jews in other countries. Schiff actively supported this group, although he also emphasized that Jewish separatism in America was wrong and unpatriotic.

In 1907 Schiff founded and financed the Galveston Movement, a project to route Jewish emigrants from eastern Europe through Galveston, Texas, and settle them in midwestern and western cities. He was convinced that directing Jewish emigrants away from overcrowded New York slums was essential to their well-being. He also thought resettlement might help minimize mounting agitation for restrictive immigration legislation against eastern Europeans.

In 1905 Israel Zangwill formed the Jewish Territorial Organization in London to secure territory where Jews could settle and create an autonomous state. Schiff thought those plans impractical and not likely to alleviate the immediate problem of aiding the Jews of Russia. The organization eventually agreed to help select and direct emigrants from Russia and eastern Europe and assist them to Bremen, Germany, where they would embark for Galveston. From 1907 to 1914 about 10,000 immigrants passed through Galveston. The Galveston Movement operated as the only organized program of Jewish immigration to the United States in those years.

Schiff originally hoped that 4 million Russian Jews would immigrate to the interior of the United States and Canada, which would practically solve the Jewish problem in Russia. His greatest frustration with regard to the immigration campaign came from the unwillingness or inability of Jewish societies in Europe to close ranks and work with him without rivalry. He also expressed frustration at the unwillingness of European financial sources, such as the Rothschilds, to support the European end of the operation. Nor did the Galveston movement successfully defuse agitation for restrictive immigration laws as Schiff had hoped.

Schiff conferred and corresponded with presidents Roosevelt, Taft, and Wilson about Jewish immigration in hopes that the U.S. government would speak out concerning the treatment of Jews in eastern Europe. He wrote to the Russian government, including the premier, Count Witte, requesting action to end the pogroms and passport restrictions on American Jews traveling in Russia. During the Paris Peace Conference in 1919-1920 Schiff and other Jewish leaders played an important role in pressuring the conference to include treaty provisions to outlaw religious and racial persecution in the constitutions of the new countries.

A prestigious and powerful man in the American Jewish community, Schiff could have greatly advanced the early Zionist cause had he lent his name to it. He warmed to the idea of a cultural and religious Jewish presence in Palestine and gave large sums of money to support it. However, he firmly opposed Zionism, the campaign for a Jewish political entity. He did favor Jewish colonization in Palestine, under the direction of one of the Great Powers, but not an independent Jewish nation. He mainly objected to the political focus of Zionism, which he felt overshadowed religious and cultural motives.

Schiff admired his German homeland and despised Russia, so he wanted to help finance the Central Powers at the onset of World War I. The House of Morgan and other banks allied to financial houses in Paris and London opposed lending money to Germany. But Schiff went ahead anyway. By 1917 the Morgan group had invested some $3 billion in Britain and France while Schiff and others had invested less than $60 million in Germany.

During the war Schiff devoted most of his efforts to organizing relief for Jewish war refugees, whom the American government and the International Red Cross failed to help. He also actively worked for the American-Jewish Joint Distribution Committee to relieve suffering in Europe, and for the Jewish Welfare Board, which assisted Jewish soldiers and sailors. The Jewish War Relief Committee under the direction of son-in-law Felix Warburg distributed almost $40 million. When the United States entered the war, Schiff marched in parades, spoke at rallies, wrote generous checks, and filled executive positions to aid Liberty Loan Committees in raising money for the war effort.

In 1919, foreseeing that chaos would result from the political and economic vacuum in central Europe, Schiff proposed to noted philanthropist and chairman of the board of Sears, Roebuck, Julius Rosenwald, that they organize what amounted to a privately financed program for aid. But the men were too old and too tired to carry out their plan. Moreover, the Russian Revolution had brought in its wake an anticommunist suspicion of "international Jewry."

Schiff died at his New York home on September 25, 1920. For blocks and blocks, mourners lined the street to attend his funeral at Temple Emanu-El.

References:

Cyrus Adler, *Jacob Schiff: His Life and Letters*, 2 volumes (Garden City, N.Y.: Doubleday, Doran, 1928);

Gary Dean Best, *To Free a People: American Jewish Leaders and the Jewish Problem in Eastern Europe, 1890-1914* (Westport, Conn.: Greenwood, 1982);

Bernard Marinbach, *Galveston, Ellis Island of the West* (Albany: State University of New York Press, 1983);

Fritz Redlich, *The Molding of American Banking: Men and Ideas*, 2 volumes (New York: Johnson Reprint Co., 1968).

Archives:

The papers of Jacob Henry Schiff are at the American Jewish Archives, Hebrew Union College, Cincinnati, Ohio. Material concerning the Galveston Movement is at the American Jewish Historical Society, Brandeis University, Waltham, Massachusetts.

Second Bank of the United States and the Independent Treasury

by Jeffrey Rogers Hummel

Independent Institute

The Second Bank of the United States (BUS, 1816-1836) was a nationally chartered bank established five years after the termination of the First BUS. It arose from the financial chaos of the War of 1812. The war dealt a devastating blow to the fiscal policies of the dominant Republican party. Disrupting strict government economy and systematic debt retirement, national debt skyrocketed from $45 million at the war's outset to $127 million at its end, despite the imposition of new or expanded taxes. The Treasury borrowed more than one-third of that amount with short-term notes, acceptable for tax payments, that were little different from government-issued paper money.

The imminent prospect of war had failed to goad the Republican Congress into rechartering the First BUS in 1811. The Treasury therefore relied upon state-chartered banks to support its wartime borrowing. The number of state banks had steadily expanded, both under the First BUS and after its demise, to a total of 88 in 1811. But with the new war-engendered fiscal demands, the number exploded to 246 by 1816. The circulation of those banks grew from $45 to $68 million in bank notes, and prices in America rose to their highest point for the first half of the nineteenth century. Mounting pressure on the state banks' reserves forced them in August 1814 to suspend the redemption of their notes in specie (gold and silver), except for the New England banks, which had refused to assist the war effort. The confusing array of bank notes immediately depreciated at varying rates, compounding the national government's difficulties, since it continued to accept and spend those notes.

Republican president James Madison had supported renewal of the First BUS charter, and shortly after the suspension of specie payments he appointed Alexander Dallas as secretary of the treasury. Dallas, a wealthy Philadelphia lawyer, was known to support ardently a new national bank because of his intimate professional ties with Stephen Girard of Philadelphia and other major investors in government securities. An altered version of Dallas's proposed bank charter received Congress's reluctant assent in January 1815, while the war was still in progress, but Madison vetoed that charter because it was insufficiently attuned to the government's fiscal requirements.

Once the war ended, Congress passed a bank bill that met with Madison's and Dallas's approval, and the president signed it on April 10, 1816. The 20-year charter of the Second BUS differed only in details from that of the First. It provided for a larger establishment, with a capital stock of $35 million instead of $10 million. The national government again owned one-fifth. At least $7 million of the total stock had to be purchased with specie; the remainder, with government securities. The bank would pay the government a bonus of $1.5 million for its charter, and the president with the approval of the Senate would appoint five of its twenty-five directors.

The charter explicitly designated the Second BUS as the national government's depository. The bank did not pay the government any interest on those deposits but had to transfer government funds free of charge. It could issue as much as $35 million worth of notes, which the United States government promised to receive for all payments. The denomination of a note, however, could be no smaller than $5. Any failure to redeem a note for specie on demand made the bank liable to the note holder for a 12 percent annual penalty.

When the bank's stock went on sale, it did not prove as popular among investors as the First Bank's had been. Stephen Girard ultimately picked up $3 million worth that remained unsubscribed. The directors chose as the bank's first president Wil-

Second Bank of the United States, Philadelphia, 1816-1836 (Nicholas B. Wainwright, History of the Philadelphia National Bank, *1953)*

liam Jones, a loyal Republican politician from Pennsylvania with an undistinguished wartime record as secretary of the navy and acting secretary of the treasury. The bank's head office opened in Philadelphia on January 7, 1817, and in time 25 additional branches dotted the country.

The Madison administration convinced Congress to approve the bank's charter partially as a means of restoring specie payments among the state banks. Just to ensure that would come about, Congress passed a measure requiring that all payments to the government after February 20, 1817, be made in specie, treasury notes, notes of the BUS, or other bank notes redeemable in specie on demand. But the new national bank's willingness to lend to the state banks and to hold their notes made the scheduled specie resumption possible without any significant currency contraction.

That cooperation represented just one manifestation of the bank's early expansionary policies under Jones. He also permitted stockholders to evade the requisite specie payments for their shares, while the bank's branches became virtually autonomous. Those in the South and West had less incentive to restrain their credit because their notes

tended to be redeemed at eastern branches. The Baltimore branch suffered from outright embezzlement that cost the bank $1.5 million before being discovered.

By early 1818, after one year of operation, BUS assets had reached $41.2 million in loans and discounts, $9.5 million in government securities, $200,000 in bank premises, $1 million due from foreign banks, $1.2 million due from state banks, $1.8 million in state bank notes, and $2.5 million in specie. Among its liabilities were $8.3 million in circulating notes, $7.4 million in government deposits, and $4.9 million in other deposits. Its reserve ratio for all its notes and deposits came to 12 percent.

The Second BUS in essence propped up the monetary expansion resulting from the War of 1812. As the country enjoyed a postwar economic boom, budget surpluses rapidly reduced the Treasury's outstanding debt. The bank's circulation took up the slack, with the state banks pyramiding their own issues on top of the national bank's. But the entire currency structure hinged upon the bank's continuing ability to pay specie on demand.

Unfortunately, international drains of specie in the summer of 1818 made the bank's liquidity precarious. After the bank began calling in loans, Congress initiated an inquiry into its operations, and Jones, widely accused of mismanagement, resigned as president at the beginning of 1819. Reluctantly taking his place was Langdon Cheves, a South Carolina lawyer and former Speaker of the House. Cheves orchestrated a ruthless credit contraction.

The bank's outstanding notes and deposits dropped by more than 50 percent to $10.2 million in January of 1820; its specie holdings simultaneously rose to $3.4 million. The United States plunged into its first modern financial panic. The state banks were forced to contract, many of them again suspended specie payments or permanently closed their doors, and a wave of bankruptcies engulfed other businesses. Owing to foreclosures, the Second BUS obtained title to vast real estate holdings, including, for example, the major downtown parts of Cincinnati, Ohio. Cheves had saved the bank but only at the cost of arousing intense resentment. Memories of the Panic of 1819 eventually made the BUS known as "The Monster," an epithet popularized by Sen. Thomas Hart Benton of Missouri.

The state governments meanwhile tried to tax the national bank's branches. The Supreme Court had declined to strike down similar taxes just before the expiration of the First Bank's charter, but in 1819 a new case involving Maryland's $15,000 annual levy against all banks not chartered by the state made its way to the Court. Chief Justice John Marshall—who sold off his shares in the Second BUS beforehand to avoid a conflict of interest—delivered the Court's unanimous opinion in *McCulloch* v. *Maryland.* Using the same loose interpretation of the Constitution's "necessary and proper" clause with which Alexander Hamilton had justified the First BUS, Marshall ruled that a nationally chartered bank was constitutional and therefore immune from state taxation.

Cheves's continuing tight administration of the national bank, even after specie began to return to the country, cut into the stockholders' profits. They consequently replaced him in 1823 with thirty-seven-year-old Nicholas Biddle, a writer from a prominent Philadelphia family and one of the government-appointed bank directors. Biddle's more liberal policies increased annual dividends to 7 percent in 1828, where they remained for as long as the bank held its national charter. Biddle, however, did not overturn one of Cheves's restrictive in-

novations: honoring notes worth more than $5 only at the branch that issued them. That decentralized method of branch discipline caused the bank's notes to circulate at a slight discount when sufficiently distant from their point of issue. It thus made the bank vulnerable to charges of not providing a uniform currency.

The traditional interpretation of the Second BUS, first enunciated by its supporters and later repeated by such historians as Bray Hammond, credits Biddle's management with putting a brake upon state-chartered banks. Because the bank was a financial colossus, accounting for one-fifth of the economy's loans, one-fourth of its currency, and one-third of its specie, it acquired large quantities of state bank notes and deposits through its normal operations. The Hammond interpretation contended that, by redeeming those notes and deposits, the national bank could force the state banks to hold more specie than otherwise. The bank thereby imposed a primitive substitute for a legal reserve requirement.

More recent quantitative scholarship, notably of Peter Temin, has revealed that the Second BUS had little impact on the reserve ratios of state-chartered banks. On the contrary, the public's use of bank money increased during the Second BUS period. The bank stimulated rather than restrained state-bank credit, which probably explains the well-documented political support of the state banks for the national bank during Biddle's tenure. Hammond's oft-repeated claim that the state institutions jealously opposed the BUS appears to be nothing more than a priori assertion.

What Biddle did accomplish was to execute astute adjustments to international specie flows, much in the manner of a central bank. By 1830 the bank's outstanding notes and deposits had climbed to $29 million. Yet it held $7.6 million worth of specie, making its reserve ratio a respectable 26 percent. Its other assets included $40.7 million in loans and discounts, $11.6 million in government securities, $2.9 million in real estate, $1.4 million in bank premises, and $4.2 million in assorted liabilities of state and foreign banks.

Although Biddle's adroit expansion mollified many enemies of the bank, it did not overcome the agrarian suspicions of Andrew Jackson, who was elected to the nation's highest office in 1828. The new president questioned the bank's constitutionality in his first annual message. The Second BUS charter was not due to expire until 1836, but Biddle and Jackson's political opponents, led by Sen. Henry Clay of Kentucky, decided to press for a renewal during the next presidential race. The bank had gained such wide appeal that resistance might cost Jackson votes and possibly the election.

Congress passed a recharter bill in the summer of 1832, but Jackson did not evade the challenge. On July 10 he issued one of the most resounding presidential vetoes in American history. Not only was the BUS unconstitutional, he emphatically declared, despite what the Supreme Court said, but the bank was also a monopoly. Jackson used the term "monopoly" not in its modern sense, but with its traditional meaning of an institution granted exclusive privilege from government. Because the Second BUS was the only bank with a national charter and with the legal right to engage in interstate branching, the charge was technically correct. The bank therefore violated, the president concluded, the basic maxim that government should "confine itself to equal protection, and, as Heaven does its rain, shower its favors alike on the high and the low, the rich and the poor."

The bank veto became the primary issue in the presidential campaign. Jackson, after a decisive reelection, determined to kill what he privately called a "hydra-headed monster." Biddle arrogantly attempted to bring the administration to terms by contracting credit. BUS notes and deposits fell from a high of $44 million at the beginning of 1832 to $30 million at the end of 1833. The ensuing economic distress, however, only confirmed Jacksonian charges about Biddle's ability to abuse the bank's enormous power.

The president had already embarked upon the removal of government deposits as a way of reining in the bank. He first reorganized his cabinet and transferred Louis McLane, who opposed any removal of government deposits, from the Treasury to the State Department. When McLane's replacement, William J. Duane, also refused to carry out the removal, Jackson forced Duane's ouster and substituted the attorney general, Roger B. Taney. By October of 1833, Taney deposited all newly collected government funds within 20-odd state banks, dubbed "pet" banks by Jackson's foes.

The national bank's supporters were still numerous enough in the Senate to censure the removal policy and to reject Taney's nomination as treasury secretary but not to override a presidential veto, and the House came around to endorsing Jackson's policy. Biddle finally relented on his contraction in 1834. The BUS finished off the last years under its national charter and then in 1836 secured a state charter from Pennsylvania so it could stay in business. Within another four years, however, a new economic downturn would force Biddle's bank into liquidation.

The Independent Treasury (1840-1841, 1846-1921) eventually took the place of the Second BUS as the national government's primary fiscal agency. The war against the bank gave ideological definition to the Democratic party, which had been initially forged around Jackson's personality. Increasingly committed to a metallic monetary system, the Democrats viewed with displeasure the continuing growth of state banks—whose number had swelled to more than 700 by 1835—and the ongoing expansion of paper money—which totaled $140 million in circulation. The Jackson administration considered various proposals for regulating "pet" banks or increasing coinage, and it implemented a few of them. But Jackson's most significant move toward hard money was the Specie Circular, issued in July of 1836, less than a year before he left office.

The Specie Circular was an executive order requiring that all purchases of federal land be made only in gold or silver. It was Jackson's response to what he believed to be the inflationary potential of the recent Distribution Act. The national debt had been fully paid in January 1835, for the first and only time in U.S. history. The Whig party, organized in opposition to the Democrats, had successfully engineered Congressional approval for distributing the national government's growing surplus to the state governments.

A new financial panic in 1837, however, abruptly ended budget surpluses. The economy briefly recovered, but another panic in October 1839 ushered in four years of sustained deflation. The money stock in America dropped by more than one-third, while prices dropped by 42 percent. Despite expenditure cuts, the national government fell back into debt and even issued short-term treasury notes again. Although the bank war, the distribution of the surplus, and the Specie Circular have often received blame for these cycles of boom and bust in the late 1830s, most economic historians now concede that the paramount factor was, as in prior panics, the erratic swings in international specie flows.

Martin Van Buren, Jackson's vice-president and chosen political heir, assumed the presidency just as the Panic of 1837 struck. The accompanying suspension of specie payments discredited the state banks as government depositories, so Van Buren proposed to carry the Democratic crusade for hard money one step further. William F. Gordon of Virginia had originally suggested to Congress a complete and permanent divorce of government from the banks in 1834, and William M. Gouge, a clerk in Jackson's Treasury Department, had published details for such an Independent Treasury. Van Buren now heartily embraced the idea in his first message to Congress.

There were two aspects to this proposed divorce. The depository aspect involved holding government funds within Treasury vaults rather than depositing them in any banks, something the law already required the Treasury to do temporarily whenever the banks stopped redeeming their notes in specie. Still more controversial was the Independent Treasury's funds-receivable aspect, which in its most radical form extended the principle behind Jackson's Specie Circular to all Treasury transactions. Congress rejected Van Buren's proposal three times and, indeed, revoked the Specie Circular. But the resilient economic stringency and renewed bank suspensions brought Congressional approval for the Independent Treasury in the summer of 1840.

The triumph was short-lived, because Van Buren was defeated in his bid for reelection the same year. The victorious Whigs repealed what they preferred to call the Sub-Treasury Act before its requirement that the government be confined to receiving and paying hard money took effect. Clay, the party's congressional leader, was hoping to reinstitute a national bank. But President John Tyler vetoed the resulting Fiscal Bank Bill and the Fiscal Corporation Bill, both approved by Congress in 1842. Because Congress refused to consider the president's watered-down proposal for an Exchequer Bank, the Treasury returned to using state bank depositories.

When James Knox Polk recaptured the presidency for the Democratic party in the next election, he put the Independent Treasury, or in his terms, a "Constitutional Treasury," near the top of his agenda. Congress reenacted the measure in August of 1846, and it received its first true test during the Mexican War, which had started three months earlier. The United States financed that relatively inexpensive conflict partially with short-term treasury notes, as it had the War of 1812, but that time it did not borrow or pay out bank notes. Under the new financial regime government collections could be only in gold, silver, or treasury notes, and disbursements could be in gold, silver, or drafts on any of the subtreasury vaults scattered among several American cities. Although the national debt increased to a modest $63 million (only half the size of the debt left behind by the War of 1812, when the country was smaller and poorer), no major wartime inflation followed, and neither the banks nor the government suspended payments in specie.

The Independent Treasury System survived not only that trial but also the subsequent decade and a half. The banks as usual suspended specie payments during the next financial panic in 1857, but the Treasury did not. The system, nevertheless, was not robust enough to cope with the astronomical fiscal demands of the Civil War. Secretary of the Treasury Salmon P. Chase, although a Jacksonian by conviction, found himself compelled to negotiate a $150 million loan from northern banks in 1861. After he insisted upon adhering to the principles of the Independent Treasury by receiving that huge loan in specie, the banks suspended, followed a day later by the Union government.

The Union soon issued its own paper money, known as Greenbacks, which was not redeemable in specie but still made legal tender. Congress later established a system of nationally chartered banks whose notes carried a government guarantee. The Treasury, moreover, could use the national banks as depositories under specified conditions. Subtreasury vaults for holding government funds formally lingered on until 1921, when the Federal Reserve System entirely superseded them, but none of the motivating hard-money features remained. In all but name, the Civil War had eviscerated the Independent Treasury.

References:

Ralph C. H. Catterall, *The Second Bank of the United States* (Chicago: University of Chicago Press, 1903);

Thomas Payne Govan, *Nicholas Biddle: Nationalist and Public Banker, 1786-1844* (Chicago: University of Chicago Press, 1959);

Bray Hammond, *Banks and Politics in America: From the Revolution to the Civil War* (Princeton: Princeton University Press, 1957);

David Kinley, *The History, Organization, and Influence of the Independent Treasury of the United States* (New York: Crowell, 1893);

David A. Martin, "Metallism, Small Notes, and Jackson's War with the B.U.S.," *Explorations in Economic History,* 11 (Spring 1974): 227-247;

John M. McFaul, *The Politics of Jacksonian Finance* (Ithaca: Cornell University Press, 1972);

John Burton Phillips, "Methods of Keeping the Public Money of the United States," in *Publications of the Michigan Political Science Association,* volume 4, no. 3 (Ann Arbor: Inland, 1909);

Robert V. Remini, *Andrew Jackson and the Bank War: A Study in the Growth of Presidential Power* (New York: Norton, 1967);

Hugh Rockoff, "Money, Prices, and Banks in the Jacksonian Era," in *The Reinterpretation of American Economic History,* edited by Robert Fogel and Stanley Engerman (New York: Harper & Row, 1971);

Murray N. Rothbard, *The Panic of 1819: Reactions and Policies* (New York: Columbia University Press, 1962);

Arthur M. Schlesinger, Jr., *The Age of Jackson* (Boston: Little, Brown, 1945);

Larry Schweikart, "Jacksonian Ideology, Currency Control, and Central Banking: A Reappraisal," *Historian,* 51 (November 1988): 78-102;

Walter Buckingham Smith, *Economic Aspects of the Second Bank of the United States* (Cambridge, Mass.: Harvard University Press, 1953);

George Rogers Taylor, *The Transportation Revolution, 1815-1860* (New York: Holt, Rinehart & Winston, 1951);

Peter Temin, *The Jacksonian Economy* (New York: Norton, 1969);

Richard H. Timberlake, Jr., *The Origins of Central Banking in the United States* (Cambridge, Mass.: Harvard University Press, 1978);

Jean Alexander Wilburn, *Biddle's Bank: The Crucial Years* (New York: Columbia University Press, 1970);

Major L. Wilson, *The Presidency of Martin Van Buren* (Lawrence: University Press of Kansas, 1984).

Securities and Brokers

Securities consisted of bonds and stocks issued to finance the growth of governments (bonds only) or corporations (bonds or stocks). They were backed by the assets of the government or corporation. A bond was a loan that paid a stipulated dividend and was payable in full at the end of a designated time. In the event of a liquidation of the business's assets, bondholders received first claim on the assets. The national government and state and local governments relied on bond sales extensively for financing their enterprises.

Stocks represented shares of ownership in companies. Although their claim to assets was lower in the event of liquidation, the stockholders could elect members to the board of directors and thus partially or completely control the company.

To buy and sell bonds, customers relied on the services of "brokers," who charged a fee for negotiating the purchase or sale. (Brokers also engaged in such activities for bank notes, but after individual private notes were forced out of existence by the National Banking and Currency Acts of 1863-1864, brokers moved almost exclusively into securities operations.)

When issued, a security (or a note, for that matter) had a face value—a "par" value. But the market soon determined the real value (the market value), and the security traded at that price rather than the par price.

See also:
New York Stock Exchange.

—Editor

Joseph Seligman

(November 22, 1819-April 25, 1880)

by Charles Barber, Jr.

University of Georgia

CAREER: Peddler, merchant, Pennsylvania (1838-1841); merchant, Selma, Alabama (1841-1848); partner, J. Seligman & Brothers, Merchants, New York City (1846-1848); partner, J. Seligman & Brothers, Importers, New York City (1848-1864); managing partner, J. & W. Seligman & Company (1864-1880).

Joseph Seligman, Jewish immigrant, peddler, merchant, and international investment banker, was born on November 22, 1819, in Baiersdorf, Bavaria, and died on April 25, 1880, in New Orleans. He was the eldest son in the family of David and Fanny Seligman, a family that eventually grew to include eight sons and three daughters. David Seligman worked as a weaver and wool merchant, and Fanny ran a small dry goods shop. At the dry goods shop Joseph Seligman gained his first experience in business, serving as a money changer for travelers passing through Baiersdorf. As his mother's favorite, he had an atypical education for someone from his background. He matriculated at the University of Erlangen, where he studied liberal arts and learned Greek, French, and English.

Jewish people had a difficult life in Bavaria during the time of Seligman's youth. Due to legislation specifically designed to restrict Jews to certain fields of endeavor, ambitious young men did not face optimistic futures. As a result, many viewed immigration to the Americas as the way to success. However, due to the general poverty of German Jews and the relatively high costs of such an endeavor, immigration was difficult. Families tended to combine resources and dispatch one member with the hope he would be successful enough to send for the rest of the family.

After Seligman finished at the University of Erlangen, he realized that nothing remained for him in the repressive environment of Bavaria but a continued miserable existence. He could continue as heir

Joseph Seligman (courtesy of the New-York Historical Society)

to the town wool merchant or immigrate to America and seek his own fortune.

Though immigration was not uncommon, a stigma was attached to it. Jewish families saw immigration as a route for the very poor and felt that such a move was tantamount to admitting the family could not tend to its own. Joseph Seligman's immigration to America therefore branded his father a failure. Understandably, David Seligman did not wish to admit such a thing. For a year he held out against the entreaties of his wife and son. Finally, in July 1837, Joseph Seligman, aged seventeen, with $100 sewn into his pants, climbed into a wagon along with more than a dozen other young men from the area of Baiersdorf and journeyed to America.

The trip aboard ship proved long and arduous. Joseph had promised his father he would observe the Sabbath and the dietary laws, but the latter proved impossible. The ships provided steerage passengers of the time with only one meal a day, which invariably consisted of pork and beans.

Seligman arrived, somewhat slimmer, in New York in September and immediately set out to walk the nearly 100 miles to Mauch Chunk, Pennsylvania, where Lewis Seligman, a cousin, lived. In Mauch Chunk, Seligman found employment with Asa Packer, the town's leading businessman. For a year Seligman worked as clerk and cashier and then as private secretary to Packer. In one year he managed to save half of his annual salary of $400. He decided to strike out on his own even though Packer offered to raise Seligman's salary to $500.

For most farmers a trip into town usually constituted a miserable ordeal. Realizing that, Seligman divined that farm families might pay slightly more to have products delivered to their doors. Using the $200 he saved, Seligman purchased merchandise he noticed was popular with the farmers. He achieved instant success as a peddler. Within six months–by spring 1839–he had saved $500. With that money he sent for his next two oldest brothers, William and James.

William started peddling immediately while James worked as an apprentice carpenter. After ten months as a carpenter and the failure of two employers, James too became a peddler. With the combined profits the three brothers opened a small store in Lancaster, Pennsylvania.

Though an unsuccessful and unenthusiastic carpenter James proved his worth as a peddler. Realizing this, Joseph allowed James, late in 1840, to go south with a wagonload of merchandise. As James toured the South, a fourth brother, Jesse, arrived in America and made his way to Lancaster.

In the summer of 1841 James returned to Pennsylvania with a profit of around $1,000. His success proved so astounding that the other brothers decided to relocate their business in the South. Combining their merchandise, the brothers started with $5,000 worth of paid-up goods. In the late fall of 1841 they sailed from New York City to Mobile, Alabama. Moving into the interior of the state, the Seligmans settled on Selma as the town in which to set up shop.

At about the same time the Seligmans moved to Alabama, their father wrote informing them that their mother had died. The letter also included the news that the wool business had failed, and the old man no longer could take care of so many children by himself. The brothers scraped together the $2,000 needed for passage and sent it to Baiersdorf. In early 1842 James traveled to New York City to meet the six of his seven brothers and sisters who had made the voyage: Leopold, Abraham, Isaac, Babette, Rosalie, and Sarah. In 1843, after the wool business had collapsed completely, the last of the brothers, Henry, along with Mr. Seligman, sailed to America. Those newcomers remained in New York.

The Seligmans prospered in Alabama. Not only did the Selma store succeed but they opened additional stores in Greensboro, Eutaw, and Clinton, Alabama. Had no Seligmans lived in New York, the brothers would possibly have contented themselves to remain in the South. The South did not always welcome Jews, and though anti-Semites occasionally harassed them, the Seligmans knew that life would never be perfect. At least in Alabama they made money. However, with the arrival of the younger Seligmans their thoughts turned more and more toward New York City. In 1846 Babette married Max Stettheimer. Of the brothers in the South only Joseph attended the wedding. His trip provided an opportunity for more than a social visit. While there he founded J. Seligman & Brothers, Merchants. To anyone with the slightest business acumen it remained obvious that New York City offered more opportunities for business success than Selma. By 1848 the brothers decided to relocate north.

The marriage gave Joseph more than just an opportunity to open a store in New York–it also gave him a brother-in-law. He quickly put Max to work. In 1848 William Seligman and Stettheimer opened Stettheimer & Brothers in St. Louis, Missouri. By 1850 Stettheimer had returned to New York and joined Seligman & Stettheimer, Dry Goods Importers–the new name of J. Seligman & Brothers after the admittance of Jacob Stettheimer, Max's father.

At that same time brothers Jesse and Henry opened a store in Watertown, New York. There they made the acquaintance–soon to be strong friendship–of a young army officer, Lieut. Ulysses S. Grant. That friendship stood the Seligmans in

Birthplace of the Seligman brothers in Baiersdorf, Germany

good stead when some years later Grant became president.

Joseph Seligman kept busy the next few years. The far-flung enterprises he controlled continued to prosper and grow. He made numerous trips to Watertown and St. Louis. While those businesses might nominally have fallen under the direction of one of the other brothers, Joseph maintained ultimate authority. His relationship with his brothers at times bordered on paternal.

At that same time Joseph made his first trip back to Europe. There he paid off his father's remaining debts plus interest and married his cousin, Babet Steinhardt, in Munich.

In 1850 California gold fever hit Jesse. He seriously contemplated trying his luck in the gold fields. Joseph managed to convince Jesse that while he knew little about mining for gold he did have experience running a business. Later that year Jesse and Leopold transported $20,000 worth of dry goods via the Isthmus of Panama to San Francisco and opened J. Seligman & Company. There they marked up the merchandise to a remarkable degree. When San Francisco burned in 1851, J. Seligman & Company located in one of the few brick buildings in town that remained. Jesse had the only dry goods store in town. Though he did not mark up prices after the fire, that unfortunate incident added greatly to the Seligman brothers' coffers. As more

and more gold flowed from California to New York, Joseph closed the Watertown store and Henry went out to San Francisco to help Jesse.

In slightly more than a decade in business Joseph Seligman gained valuable financial experience. That experience taught Joseph that merchandise only made money when the store was open, but "money earns money even while you sleep." That understanding served as the guiding wisdom of the Seligmans.

The economy in the 1850s boomed. The stock market rose ever higher. Commercial bankers eased credit once and then again. Unsound business practices were not only tolerated but encouraged. But when the crash of 1857 came, the Seligmans were ready.

In 1857 Joseph Seligman overheard an employee of a New York commercial bank say that because of tight money the bank had to call in its loans. Realizing that this portended no good, Joseph had his brothers liquidate all but prime securities. When the crash came, Joseph was literally sitting on their money. He had the Seligman gold and silver in boxes under his bed. Although recovery from the crash followed quickly—due largely to the gold flowing from California and the localized nature of the recession—the Seligmans had quite an advantage under that bed.

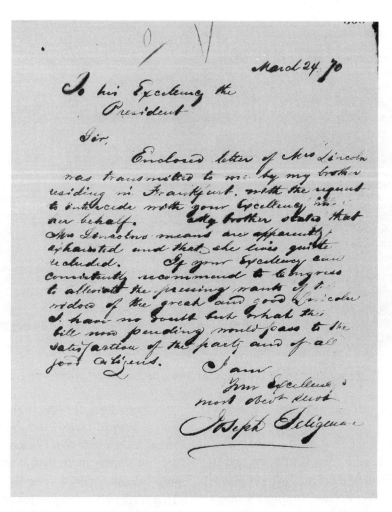

1870 letter from Joseph Seligman to President Ulysses S. Grant requesting Grant's intercession in support of a bill to give assistance to Mary Todd Lincoln (J. & W. Seligman & Company Archives, Bass Business History Collection, University of Oklahoma)

In 1860 William Seligman purchased a clothing factory. He realized that since the Seligman stores sold clothes it would be wise to own such a facility. That was indeed a wise purchase, because after the secession of the Southern states the Seligmans suddenly owned the fourteenth largest clothing factory in the Union. Though Joseph Seligman viewed the outbreak of the Civil War with regret, he did not let personal feelings distract his attention from business. In fact, soon after the firing on Fort Sumter, he and William managed to devise a method to gain army uniform contracts for the clothing factory.

Their plan, both devious and simple, involved the brothers making several personal contributions to the Union effort. The government of course appreciated those gifts. Next Joseph wrote a letter to one of the few men he knew in the government, a fellow German immigrant, Henry Gitterman. Though Gitterman was not highly placed, he was strategically placed; he held the position of provisions agent. In his letter Joseph offered to send one of the Seligman brothers, Isaac, to Washington to help Gitterman with his job. Gitterman thankfully accepted the aid, and Isaac moved to Washington to help Gitterman purchase uniforms.

Isaac soon discovered contracts were there for the asking. Given the virtually empty government treasury, many businessmen wanted nothing to do with the government. Those men viewed Union contracts as tantamount to economic suicide. Initially the Seligmans had to agree: after their first uniforms contract had been in effect for eight months and they had received no money, Joseph wrote Gitterman a somewhat panicky letter stating, "Your note just received, informing me that the appropriation for the clothing of the army is exhausted, is startling and an alarming announcement to me, for the

United States are indebted to my firm a million of dollars!" He went on to state that failure to receive the payment would lead to "suspension of our house which will drag down 20 other houses."

In the end the government paid, but Joseph had to take a large part of it in three-year Treasury 7.3 percent bonds. Unfortunately for the Seligmans, due to Union losses in the field, those bonds proved virtually unsalable. Joseph, needing cash, decided to try his luck abroad. Europeans viewed the high rate of interest–7.3 percent–as a sign of desperation. As a result Joseph also had difficulty selling the bonds there. To make matters worse, while he toured Europe, the American government gave him still more bonds. He ended up in the position of having to sell the bonds to supply money to the Union so the government could pay the Seligmans with even more bonds. Out of the gloom an idea came to Joseph. He decided to open an international banking house modeled on the influential Rothschild firm. But first he needed an end to the war.

Even though Joseph spent several years in the South, he never viewed anything but a Union victory as likely or acceptable. When it became fashionable in some circles to wish for peace, even if such a peace meant accepting the permanent separation of the nation, Joseph spoke out strongly in opposition. In one letter he wrote, "It strikes me that the country would be unfit to live in after (the disruption of the Union), in fact I do not see the least chance of peace unless thro' a reconstruction of the Union."

Once the fortunes of war turned against the South, it became much easier to place Union bonds. When William Fessenden, secretary of the treasury, announced that the issue of bonds totaled $400 million, a group of German bankers, led by Joseph, formed a syndicate to underwrite $50 million worth of those bonds. When the secretary declined to accept the group's terms, the Seligman brothers undertook to sell the bonds and sold notes in excess of $60 million.

Because of his unstinting support for the Union cause, Joseph Seligman had by the end of the war made many important friends in Washington. Though the Civil War in many ways inconvenienced the brothers, its importance to the future of the Seligman partnership cannot be overstated. Prior to the war the Seligmans were prosperous businessmen, but they differed little from many other merchants. After the war, however, they stood out–

as businessmen, as friends of the Union, and as international bankers.

For the Seligmans business in Europe hardly constituted a novel enterprise. Joseph had extensive experience selling government bonds there. In 1864 he had already organized Seligman Brothers, in London, the first overseas branch of the firm. Later in the same year Joseph also organized Seligman & Stettheimer in Frankfurt am Main, to expedite, among other things, the selling of government bonds in Europe. As a result of those already established businesses the Seligmans had not moved into wholly unfamiliar territory. As the war wound down, Joseph, then forty-five, determined that conditions were right for the move into international banking. Gathering his brothers together, he laid out his plan.

Joseph used the Rothschilds' powerful firm as a model. The House of Seligman, J. & W. Seligman & Company, created in 1864, covered the United States and Europe. The bank had offices in London, Paris, Frankfurt, New York, San Francisco, and, later, New Orleans. The Seligman brothers took assignments in the cities that seemed best to suit their skills.

In most of the cities all went well. In San Francisco, however, things took shape much more slowly. While the other brothers quickly adapted to banking, the two men running the San Francisco branch–Abraham and Leopold–did not seem to grasp the basic fundamentals of the enterprise. As the business evolved into a bank Joseph tried to correct their ineptitude by mail. By June 1867 it was obvious Joseph was losing patience, as a letter he wrote demonstrates: "I am afraid, dear Abe, you are not smart enough for the California bankers and brokers, for whenever gold goes up you appear to get stuck with currency and whenever it goes down you cannot get much."

In the summer of 1867 Joseph made the decision to close down the merchandise side of the business, J. Seligman & Company in San Francisco– even though it had comprised the "family's most prosperous enterprise"–and on October 1, 1867, J. Seligman & Company also became a bank. Not long after, the firm dispatched Abraham to Frankfurt and sent Leopold to London.

As the various enterprises of the Seligman family expanded, so did the family itself. By the end of the war Joseph and Babet Seligman had nine children–five sons and four daughters. The others were equally prolific. From the original 11 Seligman immigrants, the extended family, including husbands, wives, and children, had grown to 104. It was, as Joseph put it, "a profit in people of 845 percent." For Joseph the family presented a major difficulty. He had long believed a family member should have a position in the family business if he wished. At first that presented no obstacle. But as the family grew he discovered heredity, and more particularly marriage, did not make guarantees. His sons, nephews, and in-laws varied in their capabilities, and finding suitable positions for them constituted a chore. However, given the ever-increasing size of J. & W. Seligman & Company a place always existed for even the most maladroit.

As the Seligman brothers moved into banking and away from merchandising, Joseph's innate sense of caution grew increasingly apparent. He dealt with such large sums of money that a small mistake could mean a loss of many thousands of dollars. As he once wrote, "I may be mistaken but I prefer to err on the safe side."

That reticence took on special importance given the position the Seligmans held in the New York banking community. As newcomers, and especially as Jewish newcomers, the only issues available to them were those on which the older, more established banks had passed. Given that he chose from admittedly risky ventures, Joseph's caution was doubly important. Though the Seligmans suffered losses, they never approached the catastrophic levels that afflicted other banks. Joseph accepted such setbacks philosophically, writing to a brother, "Do not worry, as we are still getting our feet wet."

The Seligmans ventured into more than international banking in the last days of the Civil War. Following Joseph's leadership the firm also moved into the railroad business. A few years earlier Seligman had rejected the idea of investing in railroads so his about-face and newfound interest in trains surprised much of his family. Investing in railroads meant competing with Cornelius Vanderbilt, and August Belmont, who was the American representative of the House of Rothschild. Through railroads Joseph also came to know some who populated the seamier side of American business, namely, Daniel Drew, James Fisk, Jr., and Jay Gould.

The first association the Seligmans had with Drew, Fisk, and Gould came in January 1868 during a struggle between those three men and Cornel-ius Vanderbilt over control of the Erie Railroad. J. & W. Seligman & Company acted as a broker for Gould and, "regardless of their opinion of Gould's tactics," served him loyally, even guaranteeing his bail when his activities saw him temporarily jailed.

Not long after the battle over the Erie, Gould and Fisk attempted to corner the gold market by buying up all the available gold in the entire country. They succeeded and soon "owned all the gold then circulating in the United States and held contracts . . . for twice as much again." Gould thought his political contacts in Washington, including Abel Rathbone Corbin, President Grant's brother-in-law, could keep the vast governmental supply of gold off the market. Grant knew nothing about the scheme for some time. When he finally developed suspicions, on September 19, 1869, he asked Joseph Seligman to explain Gould's intentions. Joseph told him what he knew and gleaned from Grant's response that he should sell any gold he held. Grant also told Corbin to get out of the market, and Corbin in turn told Gould. On September 24, 1869, Grant ordered the Treasury to sell $5 million in gold. The price of gold plummeted, but thanks to the warning Gould made a profit of $11 million. Unfortunately, thousands of innocent investors went bankrupt. J. & W. Seligman & Company emerged from the collapse unscathed.

In 1872 an investigation was launched into the management of the Erie Railroad. Joseph Seligman testified at the hearing that J. & W. Seligman & Company "had been merely brokers for, not manipulators of, the Erie." Though his statements satisfied the committee, the mere link to Gould hurt the Seligman reputation.

After the investigation Joseph declared he would "stay out of the d----d railroads altogether." Soon, however, he jumped back in, but it was not the wisest decision. Basically Seligman did not understand railroads. While he understood the financing of railroads, the rest of the railroad business escaped him. As a result he never really knew which lines represented good buys.

Joseph agreed to help provide financing for the South Pacific Railroad of Missouri on the condition that someone from the firm serve on the board of directors. He took a place on the board himself. The South Pacific ran from St. Louis to Kansas City, with plans eventually to reach the West Coast. Joseph also helped arrange financing for the Atlan-

J. & W. SELIGMAN & CO.,

BANKERS,

59 Exchange Place, Corner of Broad Street,

NEW YORK,

Fiscal Agents

OF THE

UNITED STATES STATE DEPARTMENT.

Bills of Exchange, Commercial Credits, and Telegraphic Transfers on Great Britain and the Continent of Europe.

TRAVELLERS' CREDITS

PAYABLE IN

Any part of Europe, Asia, Africa, and America.

BRANCH HOUSES.

Messrs. SELIGMAN BROTHERS, London.
   "   SELIGMAN, FRÈRES & CO., Paris.
   "   SELIGMAN & STETTHEIMER, Frankfort.
   "   J. SELIGMAN & CO., San Francisco.
   "   SELIGMAN, HELLMAN & CO., N. Orleans.

Advances made on Consignments.

Advertisement for J. & W. Seligman & Company in a travel book (J. & W. Seligman & Company Archives, Bass Business History Collection, University of Oklahoma)

tic & Pacific Railroad, another proposed transcontinental line, that due to geographical limitations went almost nowhere. He then took an interest in the Union Pacific Railway Company, Southern Branch, later to become the Missouri, Kansas & Texas Railway Company—known as the "Katy." That line headed south on a collision course with the Atlantic & Pacific, heading west. Whichever line crossed the other's path first would effectively block the way.

Seligman, then, had financial interests in two lines—the Southern Pacific and the Atlantic & Pacific—which, in Missouri at least, ran parallel and were thus competitors, and the "Katy" attempted to block the Atlantic & Pacific. Joseph soon learned railroads were no place for the inexperienced. He told clients to stay out of railroad stocks. Unfortunately, he never followed his own advice.

Joseph also had problems in the mining industry. Of all the enterprises in which the Seligmans delved, mining proved the least profitable. Their first losing venture involved an attempt to dig a tunnel under the Comstock Lode to expedite the mining. Adolph Sutro, the man behind the scheme, finished the tunnel in 1879, but it came too late to be profitable.

Another embarrassment occurred when, against his better judgment, Joseph entered into a partnership with S. H. Bohm. Bohm operated a bank in Montana and shipped gold directly to New York. At first all went well. Then Bohm started to lend the Seligmans' money without their knowledge and to overdraw funds. The Seligmans eventually got rid of Bohm, but not before he made off with more than $250,000.

The company also expected to keep its government contacts. In 1869 the Seligmans' old friend Ulysses S. Grant became president. The Seligmans had enjoyed a comfortable working relationship under the two previous presidents—Abraham Lincoln and Andrew Johnson—and expected this relationship to continue. When Grant appointed a client of theirs, Rep. Elihu B. Washburne, secretary of state, the Seligmans wrote a letter reminding him of their past relationship and promising their "full services" to the Grant administration. Unfortunately for the Seligmans, his appointment came as a courtesy only. After 12 days in office Grant named Washburne minister to France and Hamilton Fish as the new secretary of state. Fish, who traced his lineage to Peter Stuyvesant, a man who once jailed every Jew in New York, was less a friend. As Joseph pondered this turn of events, Grant contacted him and offered him the position of secretary of the treasury.

The offer left Joseph speechless. For several days he did not reply. Obviously flattered and just as obviously capable of handling the position, he nevertheless turned it down. He "belonged to a race" that for centuries had been proscribed from entering politics. Somehow for Joseph the idea of his serving as treasury secretary seemed impossible to imagine. Though a fifty-year-old millionaire, he still saw himself as a Jewish immigrant.

Though no Seligman ever joined the Grant administration officially, the government named J. & W. Seligman & Company as financial agents of the government for the transmission of funds to foreign governments. That opened many years of similar government service.

After Joseph refused the Treasury post, Grant turned to George S. Boutwell. At Grant's request Seligman undertook to help Boutwell formulate "a policy for stabilizing United States currency and refunding the public debt." Seligman and Boutwell agreed that the government could not resume specie payments until the restoration of confidence and the lowering of interest rates paid on government bonds. Though the higher interest rates benefited the purchaser, rates so much above normal caused potential buyers to be suspicious. That reflected poorly on the nation's credit.

Just as overly high rates hurt sales of the bonds, so too interest rates below a certain point rendered the bonds unsalable. The original plan, which Seligman supported, pegged the interest rate at 5 percent, which he thought was as low as the rates could sensibly go. However, when Boutwell presented his report on the issuing of bonds to Congress in December 1869, the report stated the government issued bonds at 4.5 percent. Seligman thought such low-yield bonds would make sales next to impossible. To prove his point he wired his brothers in Europe asking them to inquire among leading bankers there as to the probability of selling the bonds. The European bankers generally agreed that 5 percent constituted the lowest reasonable figure. Even with the report from Europe in hand Boutwell refused to change his mind. Seligman then took the information to Washington and presented it in person to several congressmen. Boutwell did not appreciate this "unwarranted interference," and their relationship grew rancorous.

When Congress passed the acts of July 14, 1870, and January 20, 1871, authorizing the sale of issues of bonds to total $1.5 billion, they achieved a compromise between the two positions. The rates varied from 5 percent, at the top, down to 3.5 percent. The Seligmans expressed confidence that they would play a large share in underwriting the $200 million in bonds paying the top rate.

Boutwell, however, had other ideas. The representatives named to sell the bonds in Europe did not include the Seligmans. Initially the bonds sold so poorly that a syndicate had to be formed to sell off those remaining. The syndicate, which included the Seligmans, enjoyed much greater success. That led President Grant to announce it "had established American credit abroad."

In the early 1870s the various Seligman branches functioned as issuing houses. The New York office issued railroad and municipal bonds, while the Frankfurt branch participated in an Hungarian loan, and the Paris office issued securities to the city of Baltimore. The New York office also involved itself in corporate securities and had perhaps its greatest success with the New York Mutual Gas Light Company. Shares that earlier had literally traded for drinks at saloons grew to be worth $100 apiece. Joseph Seligman made a million dollars on that enterprise.

Though the Seligman empire grew larger and more complex, the method of remuneration for the brothers remained the same. As Isaac Seligman later noted, "the eight brothers acted as members of one firm, and what rarely occurs, no account of private income or expenditure was kept, and the profits were equally divided." That method of operation remained in place until expenses caused by their large families increased, and the company debited the brothers' share of the profits in the amount of those expenses.

By the 1870s the Seligmans were extremely prosperous. Their prosperity, however, did not blind them to their past, and as a result they involved themselves in a number of issues of interest to citizens of more modest means. Joseph Seligman served as first president of what would later be the Hebrew Orphan Asylum of the city of New York. He also helped to found the Society for Ethical Culture. He served as a member of the New York City Board of Education and as a member of the Committee of Seventy, formed to combat the Tweed Ring that was stealing millions from the city treasury. He also served as chairman of the Rapid Transit Commission and president of the American Geographical Society. In 1876, though influential friends urged Seligman to run for mayor, he refused.

By 1872, when Grant came up for reelection, most citizens recognized that his administration housed no small number of crooks and grafters. The spectacle of Grant's corrupt administration, along with his handling of Reconstruction policy, alienated some Republicans. Those dissident Republicans nominated Horace Greeley for president. Joseph Seligman, however, never abandoned his friend. At a rally at the Cooper Institute Seligman said, "That General Grant has made mistakes we do not deny; that among 60,000 office holders, some unworthy and objectionable parties had been appointed he sees himself, and is continually correcting. But that Grant tries to do his duty toward his country honestly and conscientiously, everyone who knows him must concede."

In 1872 the voters reelected Grant, and Seligman returned his full attention to banking. The next major project to occupy him, the opening of the Anglo-California Bank, involved a publicly owned commercial bank in San Francisco designed to take the place of J. Seligman & Company. Though some confusion arose concerning who would be chosen to manage the bank, by the time it opened for business on July 2, 1873, the managerial team of Richard G. Sneath and Ignatz Steinhart satisfied everyone.

Soon after the Anglo-California Bank opened, a panic developed on Wall Street. So many bankers and brokers failed that on September 22, 1873, several of the survivors implored Grant and the secretary of the treasury to travel to New York, where together they could effect a solution. Grant's solution, authorizing the Treasury to buy up to $44 million worth of government bonds, had a momentary impact. However, by September 23, Joseph Seligman told Isaac, "Things look decidedly blue this evening, most of the Banks decline to pay out Greenbacks or currency today and the Chicago Banks are reported suspended."

While Joseph struggled with the stock market crisis, William Seligman, upset at the "large amount of investments" which the New York branch held, "threatened to quit the partnership." Joseph, angered at "that selfish Bro. William," called his bluff and managed to put an end to William's rebellion. As if Joseph did not have enough to keep him busy, he also had to deal with a rancorous struggle between the comanagers of the Anglo-California Bank.

Through all the vicissitudes of 1873 Joseph Seligman managed to keep the bank solvent. Though it was not as profitable a year as he might have hoped, neither was it as disastrous as it might have been. Early in 1874, with the Panic of 1873 behind him, Joseph wrote to William, "We have all of us made mistakes, and the result has been one year's labor without pay. I am quite satisfied, provided we profit by the lessons." He continued with pride, "Think of having gone through the various crises since 1857, and especially the recent without borrowing a dollar from any bank and always having fair balances in cash, both here and in Europe." Indeed, he could take pride in his accomplishment:

how many businessmen in America could make a similar claim?

In the mid 1870s the firm accepted the position of "temporary Fiscal agents for the Navy department at London," an arrangement the navy made permanent later. That position was important more for the prestige than for the potential profits. The Seligmans, however, found it useful when they started to sell government bonds in Europe again.

Rutherford B. Hayes's accession to the office of president of the United States in 1877 might have meant an end to the Seligmans' influence in Washington had that influence rested solely on privilege and friendship. However, soon after taking office, Hayes's secretary of the treasury, John Sherman, called together several leading financial minds of the time, including Joseph Seligman. They sought to formulate "a plan for refunding the balance of the Government war debt and resuming specie payments." Sherman selected Seligman's plan, and, on December 17, 1878, "paper currency was quoted at par for the first time since 1861."

In the summer of 1877 Joseph Seligman took his family to the Grand Union Hotel in Saratoga, New York, for a holiday. He had stayed there often in the past but this time the management refused to allow him to register because he was a Jew. That touched off the first major, publicized anti-Semitic scandal in U.S. history. Speculation abounded that Seligman knew that when he went to Saratoga the hotel would refuse him admittance. If he indeed intended that, he could not have known how large the matter would grow. Lawsuits were threatened, sermons were preached, rallies and meetings were held, the boycott of a store owned by the estate of the late hotel owner contributed to its demise and sale. Seligman tried to ignore the incident, but to no avail.

That eruption polarized whole groups of people. Rather than make individuals confront their prejudices and overcome them, it simply reinforced the prejudices. Anti-Semitism became the rule in the Adirondack region rather than the exception. Whatever Seligman's intent, he could have envisioned or countenanced none of the results.

Though not admitting it, the Saratoga incident devastated Seligman. His business judgment was not as acute, and he seemed an old man at sixty. In the winter of 1880 Seligman, his wife and son, George Washington, traveled first to Florida, then New Orleans, where they visited their daughter Frances and her husband, Theodore Hellman. There, on April 25, 1880, after eating dinner in an upstairs bedroom, Seligman "called out to the maid for brandy, drank it and died."

Joseph Seligman left an estate of just more than $1 million, with $25,000 designated for charity. More important, he left behind a legacy of hard work, integrity, and decency that served as an inspiration to others.

References:
Stephen Birmingham, *"Our Crowd": The Great Jewish*

Families of New York (New York: Harper & Row, 1967);

Ross L. Muir, and Carl J. White, *Over the Long Haul: The Story of J. & W. Seligman & Company* (New York: J. & W. Seligman & Company, 1964).

Archives:
The Seligman family genealogy and letters from Joseph Seligman are contained in nine volumes at the New-York Historical Society.

John Sherman

(May 10, 1823-October 22, 1900)

by Carol Noland

Arizona State University

CAREER: Lawyer, Mansfield, Ohio (1844-1855); U.S. representative, state of Ohio (1855-1861); U.S. senator, state of Ohio (1861-1877, 1881-1897); U.S. secretary of the treasury (1877-1881); U.S. secretary of state (1897-1898).

John Sherman, long active in national financial matters, served in the U.S. House as a representative from Ohio, served two separate terms in the Senate, was appointed secretary of the treasury by President Rutherford Hayes, and served President William McKinley as secretary of state. Born on May 10, 1823, in Lancaster, Ohio, Sherman was the son of Charles Robert and Mary Hoyt Sherman. His older brother, William Tecumseh Sherman, achieved fame as a Union general during the Civil War. His father, a lawyer, rose to the bench of the state supreme court in Ohio. When Sherman's father died suddenly in 1829, Mrs. Sherman sent her 11 children to live with friends and relatives. In 1831 a cousin of his father took Sherman to live in Mount Vernon, Ohio, where he stayed for four years.

At the age of twelve Sherman returned to Lancaster and attended Homer's Academy. There he developed an interest in mathematics and surveying, and at the age of fourteen he was hired to work as a junior rodman on the Muskingum Improvement, constructing Ohio canals. By the age of sixteen he was in charge of the construction of a dam in Beverly, Ohio. He lost that job in 1838 when the Whig

party was defeated in the state election and the Democrats discontinued the project.

With his dismissal came a change in interest. Sherman gave up surveying and decided to follow in his father's footsteps and practice law. In 1840 he went to Mansfield, Ohio, to study law with his eldest brother, Charles. He proved so adept that even before his formal admission to the bar in Springfield, Ohio, on May 10, 1844, he did much of his brother's legal work. He was employed by the Pittsburgh, Fort Wayne & Chicago Railroad as a legal counselor and later became a director of that railroad, a position he held until his death.

At the same time he entered the business world as a partner in a lumber company and also began buying real estate. His reputation in the community received a boost when, on August 31, 1848, he married Cecilia Stewart, the only child of Judge James Stewart, an influential lawyer in Mansfield. The Shermans had one child, a daughter named Mary, whom they adopted.

After gaining prominence at the local level, Sherman decided to enter state politics. A staunch supporter of the Whig party, he attended many party functions. He attended both the 1848 national Whig convention in Philadelphia and the 1852 convention in Baltimore as a delegate. Sherman also proved instrumental in the organization of the Republican party and presided over the first Ohio Republican state convention in 1855.

John Sherman

That same year Sherman launched into national politics when he won election to the House of Representatives. He held moderate views on the question of slavery and was one of the few candidates upon whom both factions of the slavery issue in the state could agree. In 1856 Sherman was appointed to a three-man committee that went to Kansas to investigate the campaign for statehood there. Kansas had become a battleground between advocates of slavery from the South and opponents of slavery from the free states. The committee collected evidence of alleged fraud and coercion during the elections there and reported back to Congress. Local residents looked unfavorably on the committee's inquiries. While the committee was in Leavenworth, Kansas, a band of men threatened to burn down the town unless the committee left. Only the presence of U.S. troops at Fort Leavenworth saved the members' lives. The committee did

find instances of wrongdoing, and those findings became the basis of the 1856 Republican presidential campaign of John C. Fremont. But, despite the report of the Kansas committee, the Democratic candidate, James Buchanan, was elected president.

At the beginning of his third term in the House, Sherman emerged as a candidate for Speaker. When he could not get the three votes he needed to win the speakership, he withdrew from the candidacy and gave his vote to William Pennington, whom the House elected. Pennington immediately appointed Sherman chairman of the Ways and Means Committee. In that capacity Sherman oversaw public appropriations bills and tried to provide for the future support of the government. He secured the passage of a bill authorizing the issue of U.S. treasury notes in 1860. He also gave a boost to hopes for a transcontinental railroad when he introduced a resolution that provided for a 15-member committee to investigate the issue.

When Ohio senator Salmon P. Chase resigned in 1861 to become President Lincoln's secretary of the treasury, Sherman succeeded to that seat. Once in the Senate he became a member of the Finance Committee and spent most of his time hearing proposed amendments to tax bills. He also tried to push through a bill to issue U.S. treasury notes as legal tender, but he soon found that he was practically the only advocate of the policy. In 1862, at the request of Secretary Chase, Sherman took charge of the national banking bill in the Senate, advocating the severe taxation of banks that did not acquire national charters. He maintained that the bill would furnish a uniform currency, create a market for bonds, furnish depositories for public funds, and supply a means for payment of public dues. He argued that it was a "fitting time to inaugurate a new system, and by so simple and popular a measure as that of a National Currency teach the people that we are a Nation." Congress passed the National Banking Act in 1863.

In 1867 Sherman became chairman of the Senate Finance Committee. As chairman he brought several financial bills before Congress. The first, a currency bill, authorized an issue of $45 million in new national bank notes to replace 3 percent "temporary loan certificates," interest-bearing notes that circulated as currency. The bill was neither inflationary nor deflationary in that it did not expand or contract the currency. The notes simply replaced other issues. After six days of debate the bill passed the Senate much as Sherman had presented it.

Another bill Sherman presented proposed to refund the national debt. According to Sherman, "We give to every holder of a greenback . . . the right to present to the Treasury of the United States [that greenback] and convert it into a bond bearing four percent interest in gold." The new bonds would tie the greenbacks to gold and ensure that the public would have an interest in holding greenbacks. (No one mentioned that greenbacks already converted interchangeably with national bank notes, which in turn were convertible into gold.) Again, Sherman's bill passed the Senate virtually intact, after much discussion and debate.

Sherman won election to the Senate for the third time in 1874. That same year he initiated the move for the resumption of specie payments, which resulted in the passage of the Specie Resumption Act of 1875. The bill contained three sections, the first of which redeemed fractional paper currency in silver, and the second of which repealed the .2 percent charge for coining gold. The third section removed all limits, sectional as well as aggregate, on bank-note issues, which appealed to free-banking supporters. The bill appeased greenback supporters because it set the absolute lower limit on greenbacks at $300 million regardless of how many new bank notes were issued. The right wing was also satisfied because the bill pledged that specie payments would be resumed on January 1, 1879.

In 1877 President Hayes appointed Sherman secretary of the treasury. Sherman immediately took measures to hasten the sale of 4.5 percent bonds for refunding purposes. Within six months he secured at least $20 million for resumption, and by July 1878, six months before the date that Congress fixed by law for resumption, he had accumulated $140 million in gold in the U.S. Treasury. Once he accomplished resumption, Sherman turned his attention to refunding the remainder of the government's debt. His efforts succeeded so well that at the end of two years he had refunded nearly $850 million, saving $15 million in annual interest.

In 1880 Sherman ran as a candidate for the Republican presidential nomination. He lost the nomination to James Garfield, who had presented Sherman's name at the national convention. Although he did not receive the presidential nomination, Sherman won reelection to the Senate in 1881. He was made president pro tempore of the

Senate in 1885. Contemporaries thought highly of Sherman on matters of finance, and he spoke frequently on currency and tariff subjects.

In 1884 and again in 1888 Sherman failed to win the Republican presidential nomination. He was the leading candidate in 1888, with 249 votes on the second ballot, but he was still defeated by Benjamin Harrison. According to one source, Sherman lost the nomination because he lacked "unscrupulousness in the use of patronage, color in personality and appeal, cordial unity in the Ohio delegation, and skill in manipulating politicians, and because he had an abundance of inflationist opposition."

After the Panic of 1873 the unlimited coinage of silver became a popular issue. Because of the hard times following the panic, farmers and workingmen wanted a source of cheap money. Due to the American and European demonetization of silver and the increase in mine production, the market price of silver fell below that of gold, and many thought that silver should be used as the primary source of currency. The demand for unlimited coinage of silver caused Congress to pass the Bland-Allison Act of 1878, which required the Treasury to purchase between $2 million and $4 million dollars worth of silver bullion each month at market prices. The government coined the bullion into silver dollars, which the Congress declared legal tender. The act represented a compromise measure, and many advocates of free silver reacted negatively to its limitation on silver purchases.

By 1890 the political strength of the free silver advocates had grown so great that Congress passed the Sherman Silver Purchase Act. That act, intended to replace the Bland-Allison Act, required the government to purchase nearly twice as much silver as before and added greatly to the amount of silver already in circulation. Senator Sherman lent his name and support to the act only as an effort to placate the free-silver advocates and to save his party's strength.

In 1897 President McKinley appointed Sherman secretary of state. Sherman was mostly a figurehead in the State Department, as Assistant Secretary William Day performed most of the department's day-to-day duties. In 1898 Sherman resigned in protest to the cabinet's decision to go to war with Spain, and Day succeeded to the position.

John Sherman spent more than 40 years in government service and had great influence on the financial decisions of his day. In his memoir, *Recollections of Forty Years in the House, Senate and Cabinet* (1895), Sherman related his experiences and thoughts of the events of his time. He spent the last two years of his life in Washington, D.C., where he died on October 22, 1900.

Publication:

Recollections of Forty Years in the House, Senate and Cabinet (Chicago: Werner, 1895).

References:

Don Barrett, *The Greenbacks and Resumption of Specie Payments 1862-1879* (Glouchester, Mass.: Harvard University Press, 1965);

S. A. Bronson, *The Life of John Sherman* (Columbus, Ohio: Derby, 1880);

Walter Nugent, *Money and American Society 1865-1880* (New York: Free Press, 1968);

William Shade, *Banks or No Banks* (Detroit: Wayne State University Press, 1972).

William Tecumseh Sherman

(February 8, 1820-February 14, 1891)

by Lynne Pierson Doti

Chapman College

CAREER: Second lieutenant (1840-1841), first lieutenant (1841-1850), captain (1850-1853), U.S. Army; manager, Lucas, Turner & Company (1853-1857); business manager and law partner with Thomas Ewing (1857-1859); superintendent, Louisiana Military Academy (1859-1861); president, 5th Street Railway (1861); colonel (1861), brigadier general (1861-1862), major general (1862-1866), lieutenant general (1866-1869), commanding general (1869-1884), U.S. Army.

William Tecumseh Sherman, best known for leading the march of Union troops through the South near the end of the Civil War, spent several earlier years as a banker in California. He was born in Lancaster, Ohio, on February 8, 1820, the sixth child of Charles Robert and Mary Hoyt Sherman. Charles Sherman was a lawyer who came to Lancaster in 1811 and became a state supreme court judge in 1823. He remained in that position until his sudden death in 1829. The youngest son of the Shermans was taken in by his father's former law partner, Thomas Ewing, and his wife. The boy had been named Tecumseh at birth, after the Shawnee Indian chief, but Ewing's Catholic wife had him baptized William.

The Ewings provided Sherman a sound education at a local academy, which prepared him for the appointment to West Point that Ewing secured for the boy in 1836. He did well there, graduating sixth in his class in 1840. His first military assignment was as second lieutenant in an artillery unit in

William Tecumseh Sherman (courtesy of the New-York Historical Society)

Florida. After a year he moved to Fort Moultrie, South Carolina, as first lieutenant. His duties allowed him to take up the study of law. On his first leave he became engaged to Eleanor (Ellen) Boyle

Ewing, the daughter of his guardians. Sherman's next military assignment was at the Augusta arsenal.

When the Mexican War erupted in 1846, he was assigned to adjutant duties but desired an active post and threatened to resign his commission. His assignment to California in the new Pacific Division prevented that action. Sherman traveled to California by sea to serve with Col. Steven Kearny, whose troops had marched overland from New Mexico. Capt. Henry S. Turner brought those troops to the mountain above San Diego, where they engaged in a battle with the Californians, losing one-third of their forces and their provisions. A request for rescue was sent to San Diego, which eventually resulted in support for the army, but the bedraggled group was then sent into battle for Los Angeles, about 100 miles north of San Diego. Captain Turner had little military polish left about him when Sherman met him and, in fact, lacked even underwear. Sherman supplied those garments from his own stock. Thus originated a long friendship.

Sherman remained in California until January 1850. He saw San Francisco when it still went by the name of Yerba Buena, handled the first nuggets of the gold rush, and attended the California constitutional convention. His heart obviously lay elsewhere, however. In May 1850 he and Ellen were married in Washington, D.C., in a ceremony suitable to Thomas Ewing's prominent position. As both foster father and father-in-law, Ewing remained exceedingly generous and helpful to Sherman as long as he lived.

Sherman stayed in the army a year and a half after his marriage, residing in Washington and New Orleans. Then he requested a six-month leave of absence and sent his wife and new child to the Ewing home so he could investigate a new career. That new career took him back to California as a banker.

Many eastern and even foreign banks rushed to open branches in California to take advantage of the high interest rates and the profits possible on gold exchange. One St. Louis bank, Page & Bacon, did so well the venture attracted the attention of its neighbor and rival James Lucas of Lucas & Simonds Bank. When one of the California-branch cashiers of Page & Bacon, Benjamin Nisbet, proposed opening a branch for Lucas, Lucas decided to delay no further. Feeling Nisbet too young to manage a branch alone, he approached Sherman's former Pacific Division colleague, Henry S. Turner, with the suggestion that he return to California to oversee the operation. Turner agreed with the possibility of profit in the venture and became Lucas's partner. He did not, however, want to relocate his family to the remote and inaccessible coast. On his way to begin the branch, he visited New Orleans with the object of making Sherman the permanent manager. Sherman hesitated, probably for the same reasons. Turner continued west without a commitment. Lucas then traveled to New Orleans, also with the object of persuading Sherman to undertake the venture, and offered a one-eighth interest in the new business. Sherman agreed to give it a try. He embarked for California in March 1853, shortly after Turner arrived in San Francisco.

Sherman's journey to California proved more exciting than his military service. While he probably was relieved that the journey across Central America could be made by rail, rather than by muletrain or boat, his passage northward along the coast, never pleasant since it was made against the prevailing seas, was particularly bad. Heavy seas slowed the SS *Lewis* to a crawl. After more than two weeks at sea the ship ran aground in heavy fog. Fortunately, morning light soon revealed that the ship rested only a mile from shore, and the 385 passengers disembarked in small boats. Sherman walked along the shore to a lumber camp, and he discovered the *Lewis* actually had passed San Francisco and was wrecked 18 miles north of the Golden Gate. He bought passage on a small schooner loaded with lumber, and in a few hours the boat sailed into the bay. Fate had not finished with Sherman, however; the schooner capsized. No one drowned, and the occupants rode the hull of the wood-filled boat toward the ocean until a passing vessel rescued them. Sherman ended his adventure by being rowed to the presidio, near the entrance to the bay, and from there he journeyed by horse into town. By that evening he had comfortably settled in a boardinghouse but thought "two shipwrecks in one day is not a good beginning for a new peaceful career."

Sherman joined Lucas and Nisbet in a rented facility across the street from the famed Parrott building, where Page & Bacon was located. Turner reported the business had "taken a wonderful start." In addition to loans made at 3 percent a month, the bank bought gold at $16 per ounce and sold it on the east coast at the official government price of $18. Turner also thought real estate a safe and profitable investment. The operation required only capital. Sherman decided his future would be assured if the partners could provide this. In July 1853 Sherman sailed for Nicaragua and New York, then proceeded to St. Louis to meet Lucas, who quickly agreed to provide the needed capital to fund the bank and construct a new building. Sherman resigned his military commission and booked passage for himself, his wife, their youngest daughter, and her nurse on September 20. They arrived in San Francisco on October 16, and, after a short stay at the Claredon Hotel, rented a furnished frame house on Stockton Street.

After Turner returned to St. Louis, Sherman took over the management of the bank, Lucas, Turner & Company, communicating the events of the week to Turner in fat letters sent by steamer. One of Sherman's earliest tasks involved planning the bank building. At the northeast corner of Montgomery and Jackson streets Sherman found the best available parcel and planned a 3-story building for the bank to use and for commercial rentals. The land cost $31,000 for the 33- by 27-foot lot. The lowest estimate for erecting the building was $53,000. Sherman decided to build a large building, since business was moving toward that part of town, but to keep it plain and serviceable. The only extravagances consisted of granite facing on the first floor of the building and a vault that was "unnecessarily strong." The latter was incited by Sherman, the former by Nisbet, who, Sherman complained, thought "pearls and diamonds could not be fine enough."

The bank moved into its new building and opened for business on July 8, 1854. Many of the rooms above the banking floor rented at $270 per month, and applicants for the remaining rooms were numerous. The block south of the bank, consisting of filled tidelands, was prepared for construction, and a fire, which had destroyed the buildings built on wharves, cleared the way for more permanent buildings. Montgomery and Jackson had developed into a most desirable location. Still in use in 1989, the building has constituted the most lasting part of Sherman's career as a banker.

The year 1854 brought a fair degree of prosperity to the city of San Francisco. The gold rush had ended, and hydraulic mining companies replaced the bearded men with pans. The city on the bay grew more slowly than before but enjoyed more so-

phistication. Coal-gas lights were installed on the plank-covered streets. Clipper ships continued to arrive regularly along with coastal steamers. Sherman noted, "we have plenty of calls for money, more than we can accommodate." Interest rates still hovered at 2 to 3 percent per month. In addition to loans of the bank's funds, Sherman handled numerous trust accounts for St. Louis friends and for old army buddies whose tours in California had ended. He found those a great nuisance and tried to avoid taking more of those obligations. He also contended that the gold exchange business lacked sufficient profit, in spite of the 12.5 percent return, because of the rising costs of shipping and insurance. Redeeming East Coast bank drafts also seemed unprofitable to Sherman. He financed as many of the loans as he could with deposits rather than borrowed capital from the East, on which he had to pay about 10 percent per annum. His was the favorite bank for the military in the state, and profits totaled about $10,000 per month.

While the bank did reasonably well, indications of trouble developed. Mrs. Sherman was not fond of San Francisco. Although the Shermans added a baby boy to the household in June, she missed her oldest daughter. A city about which Sherman bragged "you do not now see troops of girls displaying themselves on horseback" could not have offered many comforts to a woman of Mrs. Sherman's upbringing. So few women lived in the city that calico and ladies' hats were considered useless, and merchants simply dumped them on the wharves. The Shermans' house was small and the yard inadequate for the needs of their active, "dirt-loving" daughter.

Signs of discontent appeared in the business world also. The correspondence of Page & Bacon for August notes a decrease in the number of drafts on San Francisco. Gold shipments dropped off because the spring run-off reflected the previous winter's low snowfall, and hydraulic mining needed large quantities of water. Prices fell, a blessing in most cases, but the real estate prices dropped, too, just as Sherman finished the bank building (although he did not notice that fact until near the end of the year). In October a prominent lumber merchant disappeared, defaulting on his numerous and dubiously acquired debts. Sherman found himself consumed with untangling the complications resulting from that defalcation.

Discontent turned into disaster in February 1855. Sherman maintained that the bank was doing well and even hired new assistants at the beginning of the month. Then one of the New York banks with whom it did business failed, tenants vacated the bank building, leaving past due rent unpaid, and several of the bank's customers experienced business failures. The closure of Burgoyne, a private banker in San Francisco, brought new customers, and, again, Sherman expanded. The bank's cash balance stood at nearly $2 million on February 15, when a bank run suddenly consumed the city.

The run began when the steamer *Oregon* arrived with news that Page & Bacon of St. Louis was bankrupt. The manager of the San Francisco branch, Henry Haight, worked to convince the public of his solvency, and the run seemed to abate after a few days. No runs on other banks occurred, but deposits slowly fell. A general panic commenced on February 23. Several banks were afraid to open, but Sherman showed no hesitation. His bank withstood the run, although the cash balance dropped from $1,145,391 to $792,307. Page & Bacon met final doom; other banks closed temporarily or permanently. The towns of Stockton, Marysville, and Sacramento also experienced runs.

For a few months business remained quiet. Sherman resumed his melancholy complaints about his asthma, moved to a nicer house with a larger yard, and planned to economize while his wife was in Ohio visiting her parents. But business steadily worsened. Credit got tighter. Sherman refused to continue to honor the overdrafts of some of his prominent customers, insisting that cash must be in the account the day before customers presented their checks for payment. The firm of Castle Brothers was so outraged by that policy that they emptied their $25,000 account and put a notice in the newspaper complaining of the practice. Several other customers also left for banks that accommodated them better. Sherman professed his joy at their departure and counseled other bankers to follow his course.

In November Sherman's bank and three others loaned $30,000 to the firm of Sather & Church to prevent its failure, but when that seemed insufficient, Sherman refused to loan more and demanded the return of the initial advance. Sather & Church repaid the loan and closed their doors. Sherman, who had prepared for a general run, expressed relief when none occurred. Palmer, Cook & Company asked Sherman for $25,000 in cash for checks writ-

ten on a New York bank, in return for a similar favor they had granted Lucas, Turner & Company in February. Sherman gave them only $15,000, assuring his partners he would get more security if the situation worsened. The year ended with the failure of a jobber who owed the bank $4,500. Sherman took possession of the merchandise.

Palmer, Cook & Company closed its doors in early 1856. Sherman discharged an employee and soon discovered his accounts were not as often over as short, indicating the employee's dishonesty. He continued to contract the bank's lending. In the summer San Francisco was disrupted by murder and the actions of a vigilante group, and Sherman made proposals to his partners that indicate he foresaw the closing of Lucas, Turner & Company in San Francisco. Business continued to decline in the city, and Sherman found his fine new building a burden. As business contracted, so did the business district—toward the wharves again; and Sherman knew the bank stood too far from the town's center. When the bank repossessed a building on Battery Street across from the custom house and post office, Sherman resolved to move. Rent on the old building had declined to $800 a month, of which the bank paid $300. Sherman at first rented the bank's old space at $200, but, as tenants continued to leave, he considered filling the building with repossessed merchandise. When businesses started to fail at a rate that made this a real prospect, it was only a matter of time before closing the bank remained the only choice. By fall 1856 Sherman complained about receiving liquor, butter, and dried apples instead of money owed. In addition to the business woes, he continued to note his own poor health and Mrs. Sherman's aversion to California. Early in January 1857 the directors decided to dissolve Lucas, Turner & Company. Sherman spent the spring planning for his withdrawal from business. He traveled to some of the mining sites in which the bank had an interest and also visited Sacramento. Suddenly the beauty of the state tugged at Sherman, who also realized he would be lost in the larger world of New York. In April announcements of the bank's impending closing appeared in the local newspapers. Sherman and his family left San Francisco on May 20.

They went to the Ewings' home in Ohio, then visited St. Louis before proceeding to New York to set up a new bank there. Sherman began cautiously, hiring no one and making few loans. San

Francisco still weighed very much on his mind, particularly as he heard that Nisbet had continued difficulty collecting loans. Nisbet had become engaged and apparently hoped the St. Louis firm would reconsider its long-standing opinion of his weaknesses and allow the bank to reopen under his management. Sherman's caution proved well founded, as a bank panic developed in October that ended the venture and nearly closed the parent company.

Nisbet abandoned the San Francisco scene at that point to take his bride east, and the board asked Sherman to complete the liquidation. He sailed to San Francisco on January 5, 1858, reaching the city on January 28. He found business conditions had worsened. In the bank rent was past due on the few rooms still occupied. Sherman proclaimed his willingness to take $6,000 for his furnished house, for which he spent $10,000. "The whole town is for sale and there are no buyers," he reported to Lucas. In May Sherman returned to St. Louis. With the exception of some further letter writing about the San Francisco accounts, his career as a banker had ended.

Ewing took Sherman into partnership for a short time, as manager for coal mines and as a law partner. Those brief careers proved as unsatisfying as banking, however, and in October 1859 Sherman accepted the post of superintendent of a new military college in Louisiana. The secession of that state forced Sherman to choose loyalty or a Confederate commission. Sherman went north. In May 1861 he was appointed colonel in the 13th infantry. He fought at Bull Run, served under Brig. Gen. Robert Anderson, then succeeded him. He earned the reputation of having a nervous temperament and was reassigned first to Henry Halleck, then Ulysses Grant. He was made major-general in 1862. In July 1864 Sherman successfully laid siege to Atlanta. He and his troops then commenced the infamous march through the South. His purpose was to break the resistance of the region by destroying the sources of supplies. His army lived off the land and often destroyed what they did not use.

After the war Sherman continued his successful military career. As commander of the Division of the Mississippi he assisted in the construction of the transcontinental railroad. Later he undertook a diplomatic mission to Mexico. He became commanding general of the army when Grant became president in 1869. He retired in 1884 and in 1886 moved to New York where he remained prominent in society until his death on February 14, 1891. Eight children survived him. His wife, Ellen, had died three years before.

References:

Dwight E. Clarke, *William Tecumseh Sherman: Gold Rush Banker* (San Francisco: California Historical Society, 1969);

Ira Cross, *Financing an Empire: History of Banking in California* (Chicago: Clarke, 1927).

Archives:

The papers of William T. Sherman and Thomas Ewing are in the Manuscript Division of the Library of Congress.

Sight Drafts (*see* Bills of Exchange, Sight Drafts, and Bills of Credit*)*

The Silver Issue and the Gold Standard

by James E. Fell, Jr.

United Banks of Colorado

The silver issue was one of the most complex and controversial monetary questions of the late nineteenth century. A major issue in the politics of the era, it reflected the economic problems afflicting the silver-producing states of the West and the agricultural states of the West and South and raised questions involving the nature of currency and the regulatory role of government.

Until 1873 the United States operated on the basis of a bimetallic currency. The mints coined silver and gold bullion into dollars at the ratio of 16 ounces of silver to 1 ounce of gold: "16 to 1" in the parlance of the day. Because the price of gold was fixed at $20 per ounce, an ounce of silver was meant to be worth $1.25. But as a practical matter, the 16 to 1 ratio undervalued silver in reference to international markets and made the overseas sale of silver more profitable than sale to the mints. As a result, in 1873 Congress decided to abandon the coinage of silver dollars–an action soon denounced as the "crime of 1873."

No sooner had Congress turned away from silver coinage than the economic status of the metal changed. Because of new silver discoveries in Nevada, western silver mines dramatically increased production at the same time many European nations made the decision to eliminate silver coinage. Overproduction and underconsumption drove down the price of silver to the point where it became profitable to sell the metal to the federal government, but that was no longer possible. Silver coinage became a political issue not only in the silver-producing states of the West but also in hard-pressed agricultural areas where debt-ridden farmers saw the remonetization of silver as a way out of their problems. What exacerbated the debt problem was that the late nineteenth century was a time of deflation; the farmers and small businessmen of the West and South envisioned silver coinage as a way to create inflation, which would make

William Jennings Bryan, presidential candidate of the Democratic and Populist parties in 1896 and the Democratic Party in 1900 and 1908. The primary issue of Bryan's first campaign was the resumption of U.S. Treasury silver purchases; he lost to Republican nominee William McKinley (Gale International Portrait Gallery).

it easier for them to pay off their creditors. The cause of bimetallism–remonetization of silver–became an important political goal in those parts of the country.

The silverites enjoyed some success in their quest. Among their champions was Congressman Richard P. "Silver Dick" Bland of Missouri. Bland expressed concern about the plight of small farmers, particularly the requirement of bankers that the farmers pay their debts in ever-scarcer specie. Having spent some of his formative years in western mining regions, he also had an interest in the travail of western miners. Through the work of Bland and others, in 1878 Congress passed the Bland-Allison Act for the remonetization of silver over the veto of President Rutherford B. Hayes. The law authorized the secretary of the treasury to purchase $2 million to $4 million in silver each month at the market price and to issue legal-tender silver dollars. While farmers and miners derived some help from that measure, they did not obtain the free and unlimited coinage of silver at 16 to 1. The Treasury tended to purchase only the minimum amount of silver required.

During the 1880s the price of silver continued to fall, hurting miners, and the problem of debt continued to plague farmers. In 1890 Congress passed the Sherman Silver Purchase Act, which required the Treasury to purchase 4.5 million ounces of silver each month at the market price and to issue legal-tender notes redeemable in silver or gold at the option of the Treasury. The Sherman Act, in effect, provided for the free and unlimited coinage of silver (since 4.5 million ounces per month was the estimated national output), but not at the ratio of 16 to 1 with gold. As a result, the circulation of redeemable paper money increased, and the nation's gold reserve declined. The price of silver also continued to fall. The situation played into the hands of the newly formed Populist party, which sought to expand its influence outside the West and South. When the Panic of 1893 set off the most severe economic downturn in American history up to that time, the drain on the nation's gold reserve intensified, and Democratic president Grover Cleveland

called Congress into special session to repeal the Sherman Act on the grounds that silver purchase constituted a major cause of the downturn. The call for repeal divided the Democratic party along sectional lines of West and South versus North and East and exacerbated urban-rural cleavages and class divisions in American society. At the Democratic convention of 1896 the party repudiated Cleveland and nominated for president the free-silver congressman from Nebraska, William Jennings Bryan. The Populist party, a third-party advocate of agricultural reform, also nominated Bryan. But farmers, who enjoyed a period of rising prices and increasing exports as the election approached, did not fully back the Democrats and Populists, and Bryan lost to the Republican candidate, William McKinley, who campaigned for "hard money," meaning the gold standard.

The severe contraction of the 1890s gradually ran its course. Easing the problem somewhat, the discovery of major gold deposits put more hard money into circulation. An act placing the United States on a gold standard passed Congress in 1900. Sentiment for free silver died away, to be replaced by calls for greater flexibility in the currency system.

References:
Milton Friedman and Anna J. Schwartz, *A Monetary History of the United States 1867-1960* (Princeton: Princeton University Press, 1963);

Robert P. Sharkey, *Money, Class, and Party: An Economic Study of the Civil War and Reconstruction* (Baltimore: Johns Hopkins University Press, 1959);

Irwin Unger, *The Greenback Era: A Social and Political History of American Finance, 1865-1879* (Princeton: Princeton University Press, 1964).

George Smith

(February 10, 1808-October 7, 1899)

by Larry Schweikart

University of Dayton

CAREER: Land speculator (1834-1863); partner, Illinois Investment Company (1837-1852); president, Wisconsin Marine and Fire Insurance Company (1839-1854); president, George Smith and Company (1839-1860); controlling stockholder, Bank of America, Washington, D.C. (1852-1853); controlling stockholder, Bank of America, Chicago (1852-1862); controlling stockholder, Bank of Atlanta (1853-1857); controlling stockholder, Interior Bank of the State of Georgia (1854-circa 1857).

Few bankers in the early 1800s have figured more prominently than George Smith in the debate over the structure of the antebellum banking system. This Scotsman demonstrated the virtues of a gold-backed currency yet at the same time showed that paper money performed indispensable economic functions.

Born on February 10, 1808, in Aberdeenshire, Scotland, Smith grew up the well-educated son of farm parents. He attended several schools, including Marischal College, in Aberdeen from 1823 to 1825, before a relative briefly tutored him as a medical student. Smith enjoyed agriculture, but even as he engaged in rental farming the distant sounds of American commerce beckoned. In the summer of 1883, after placing his Scottish businesses in the hands of his cousin Alexander Anderson, he left for New York.

Smith had hoped to work for Prime, Ward and King but found no openings. So he continued to push west, reaching Chicago in 1834. There a booming land business had turned into speculative hysteria, and Smith joined in, using the capital he brought from Scotland. Within a short time he wrote to Anderson requesting more funds. He invested in choice Chicago lots, which he sold in 1839 for $40,000. He then set his sights on lakeshore lands in Wisconsin, purchasing tracts in Green Bay and Milwaukee.

George Smith (courtesy of Saint Luke's Hospital, Chicago)

In the course of selling those lands, Smith allowed payment on time, usually a period of two or three years. He charged 10 percent interest, not excessive for the period. Even so, many buyers could not meet their obligations, and they forfeited their lands to Smith. He acquired other lands, in Sheboygan and Chicago, and sometimes worked so fast that he turned over property in a single day.

Hoping to use the results of his two-year American investment project as a base to raise still more capital, Smith returned to Aberdeenshire in 1836 to raise additional money from investors. Scottish money flowed into the banking, brokerage, and real estate firm Smith and Anderson created, the Illinois Investment Company. In March 1837 Smith and Anderson returned to Chicago, where they started their business of discounting notes, negotiating loans, and buying property. Smith also opened an office independent of the Illinois Investment Company in Chicago.

Smith's ventures did well. By 1838 the Illinois Investment Company had purchased 2,500 acres in Cook and Will counties at $1.25 per acre and had taken part interest in a $12,000 canal lot in downtown Chicago. Manager Patrick Strachan proposed to shift the company's headquarters to New York City, a move that was completed in 1839. Because the shareholders continued to receive dividends at the rate of 15 percent, few had any complaints. A fundamental change had taken place in the company, however. Strachan favored the banking and commission business to real estate speculation, and Smith, who did not want to move to New York, agreed to Strachan's plan, provided Smith could remain in the West.

In 1839 Smith established a second banking and brokerage house, that one in Milwaukee in the territory of Wisconsin. He felt that troubles lay ahead for the Illinois Investment Company and also understood that the American economy had undergone significant changes since his first visit to the country. He had observed the lack of banking facilities in Illinois and Wisconsin. As of 1851 Minnesota, Iowa, Illinois, and Wisconsin still prohibited banks, while Missouri and Indiana allowed only state banks to operate. The Illinois constitution of 1818 had permitted existing banks to continue and allowed for the creation of a state bank, which closed after ten years. A second state bank, created in 1835, like all Illinois banks suspended specie payments during the Panic of 1837 and, after a few sputtering attempts to reopen, collapsed in 1843. To Smith the Lake Michigan region desperately needed a circulating medium and a bank, but he well understood the legislative hostility to financial institutions and felt the heat of Jacksonian antibank fervor. Thus, he carefully planned his banking operation. He intended to borrow on the experience of Scottish banks, which made personal loans only

with the borrower's signature and the signatures of two sureties. Further, the Scottish banks featured branch systems to service small communities.

Smith would have preferred to operate out of Chicago, but antibank conditions there in 1838–especially acts directed against the issue of notes by nonbank entities–compelled him to originate his business farther north. Cloaking his intent to do banking under the auspices of a fire insurance company, Smith received a charter from the territory of Wisconsin on February 28, 1839, for the Wisconsin Marine and Fire Insurance Company. Within three weeks Smith turned the management of the company over to another young Scot, Alexander Mitchell, who had received his training at the North of Scotland Bank and who had served on the staff of the Illinois Investment Company. Smith remained president and a director and major stockholder. He obtained most of his stock through the sale of lands he had owned in Chicago and Milwaukee, whose values he set himself.

The Wisconsin company dealt extensively in real estate, acquiring large acreages of land in Racine and Kenosha counties. When Smith sold property, he occasionally extracted stiff rates–12 percent annually–and stretched out payments to increase the loan return. On other lands, however, he lent at more typical 8 percent rates. As soon as the company could afford it, he sold it large blocks of his own land. The business advertised its land operations widely, and its insurance sales grew along with real estate sales. Most of Smith's insurance writing was done in Chicago, where there was more need for insurance than in rural Wisconsin. By June 1843 the company had insured $770,000 worth of property, taking only $4,000 in losses.

The real goal of Smith's operations, lending, remained a concealed but profitable activity. The "bank" even loaned money to meet legislative expenses to the territory of Wisconsin, at 10 percent. The company extended other loans, on crops and on commodities such as lead and flour. With its connections to Strachan in New York, the Wisconsin business developed a growing trade in draft exchanges, for which it collected commissions. In 1839, for example, Mitchell charged 3 percent on the exchange of a New York draft, and by 1842 the company exchanged 16 drafts per month, with the business growing at a rate of 400 percent every six months.

Wisconsin Marine and Fire also received deposits, which allowed Smith to engage in his most controversial and successful venture, note issue. At first the company issued certificates of deposit in $3 denominations and in $5 "checks." Smith and Mitchell signed all certificates and issued them to depositors from Milwaukee. Initially, the only depositors to receive that money were other company officials. Later, however, the Chicago office also emitted those notes. By 1841 Wisconsin Marine and Fire had more than $34,000 in circulation. Although those certificates of deposit supposedly represented actual deposits, few actually carried gold backing. The bankers' signatures attested to a deposit having been made, but the phrase "will be paid on demand to bearer" adorning the notes identified them merely as currency. Accordingly, midwestern residents came to know them simply as "George Smith's Money."

Smith relied on the hope that some notes would be destroyed, lost, or never presented for redemption. He also knew that travel and communications difficulties permitted a considerable amount of lag time, or "float," a circumstance that had benefited many a wildcat banker. The company's most important source of profit, however, remained that on which virtually all banks operated, the fractional reserve system. Smith knew that after customers satisfied themselves that the notes were "as good as gold," they would treat them as such and not demand redemption. For each dollar deposited, the company issued five in notes. Smith even began to pay out loans in the currency. The company remained obligated to redemption in those relatively few cases when it was required.

When the Wisconsin legislature revoked the charters of its three defunct banks in 1842 and Illinois banks liquidated a year later, Smith's money became the sole circulating medium in many midwestern areas. In January 1842 Smith certificates brought a 1 to 2 percent premium in Chicago at a time when suspended banks' notes went at a discount of 10 percent. By 1842, even at a premium, circulation reached $44,161.

In 1839 Smith founded George Smith and Company in Chicago. That private bank lacked a charter, meaning it could not issue notes. It did, however, circulate the Wisconsin notes in Chicago. Indeed, local newspapers praised the stabilizing influence of the money. The Chicago business engaged primarily in lending to farmers and merchants, although Smith occasionally speculated on wheat. He played an important role in financing the wheat trade, with his account in 1846 showing $180,000 in advances. The company also engaged in the traditional banking practice of discounting drafts, often at a lower discount than other Chicago private bankers. Smith's rates and money valuations had such widespread influence that Chicago newspapers published lists and tables to make the information public. He always cashed drafts or accepted notes at discount, ranging from 12.5 to 80 percent.

In addition to those banking businesses, Smith toyed with the idea of a Great Lakes freight and passenger service, through which he met eastern dealers and merchants. He soon abandoned that business. Likewise, he also gave up on an investment in Michigan City, Indiana, a place many saw as a potential rival to Chicago. By 1844 Smith saw the light and disposed of his shares. He continued, however, to buy and sell real estate throughout Illinois. Each venture gave him further opportunity to introduce Wisconsin Marine and Fire Insurance Company certificates into circulation.

Smith's money empire had grown to the point that it required exchange centers—branches—and the first of those opened in Detroit in 1838, with another Scot, Thomas Webster, as manager. In 1841 Smith joined with a St. Louis merchant to open a branch there, quickly reorganized as Smith, Webster and Company. Another branch, in Galena, Illinois, opened in 1843. Smith also kept accounts with two Aberdeen-based competitors, Murray and Brand, in Chicago, and George Milne and Company, in Cincinnati. Both competitors closely copied Smith's methods, and they extended Smith's reach into the southern Ohio area and to Buffalo, where Murray and Brand had connections.

Throughout the creation and expansion of his banking network, Smith retained the loyalty of his employees and the trust of the customers who held his notes. A single-minded businessman, according to an employee, he "loved no woman, cared little for literature . . . had no taste for politics, no desire for public office. His work was that of a money-maker."

When the western depression pushed profits down, the Scottish investors grew uneasy. The Illinois company had divided, moved to New York and Milwaukee, created a network of agencies, and gave little evidence that its success rested on Smith's money as much as it actually did. Thus, after Wisconsin Marine and Fire cut dividends by 50 percent in 1842, and then lowered dividend payments again, the shareholders thought about either ending the business or changing the management. One of the shareholders, Alexander Johnston, deputized to investigate the companies' officers, found serious losses due to bankruptcies of Detroit and Chicago debtors. At Johnston's recommendation, Smith streamlined the organization by assuming a greater ownership in Wisconsin Marine and Fire and by selling the Galena agency (which had grown considerably under James Carter to include a booming lead trade). Johnston also discovered that the initial stockholders had made little profit, and newer investors had actually lost money. Strachan had speculated on his own with company funds and entered the losses on company books. After further battles between the New York office and the Aberdeen investors, the Illinois Investment Company was liquidated by the stockholders in 1852. Johnston discovered dozens of irregularities, and Smith could not be held blameless. Agents had operated outside anyone's control for extended periods, and losses attributable to the agents had soared. On other occasions officers—with Smith's knowledge—purchased stock at prices below those offered to other investors. Smith never questioned the practices of the New York operations. He profited handsomely from the sale of the Smith and Carter "branch" at Galena, which Wisconsin Marine and Fire purchased just at a time when the sale of mineral lands drastically drove up the value of holdings in the lead region. Smith benefited from other internal transactions as well, but the Aberdeen investors never singled him out for reprimand.

As a part of the liquidation agreement, Strachan and colleague William Scott forfeited the New York company to the shareholders. Smith continued as president in the reorganized company. Thus, with the New York firm still serving as a base for eastern exchange and Wisconsin Marine and Fire and its chain of affiliates working in the West, Smith stood poised for the recovery that followed the Panic of 1837. By the 1850s the booming midwestern wheat industry stimulated growth in Rock, Racine, Walworth, and Milwaukee counties, just where Wisconsin Marine and Fire held lands for sale. Not only did the growth stimulate the land business but the company's notes circulated more strongly than ever. Merchants specified that debtors had to pay in gold or Smith money.

Smith accomplished all this despite repeated attacks by the Wisconsin legislature. An 1843 investigating committee noted that the insurance company acted in reality as a bank and observed that the management consisted of men of exceptional shrewdness and good character, but the stockholders resided in other states or even other countries. This foreign ownership, the legislators thought, posed a problem. The committee resolved to either dissolve the company or to convert its charter into a genuine banking charter, but Smith forestalled any action through a series of delaying maneuvers. He offered amendments to the charter, proposing to include the public more often, furnish statements of condition to the stockholders, and make other concessions.

Smith and Mitchell successfully delayed committee action for a year. Mitchell then proposed to revive the charter of the Bank of Milwaukee, which had been annulled in 1839. Wisconsin Marine and Fire would then take over the charter of the defunct bank. That suggestion precipitated a kind of bank war in Wisconsin. Despite strong opposition in some quarters, the soundness of Smith's operation brought out many vocal supporters. The Milwaukee business community especially liked the proposal. But the legislature rejected the proposal and repealed the charter of the Wisconsin Marine and Fire Insurance Company on January 29, 1846.

Presented with that seemingly fatal action, Smith and Mitchell simply chose to ignore it. They slightly altered some of their practices. Real estate deals, for example, were made in Mitchell's name, not the company's. Smith also pledged his personal fortune to redeem all certificates of the company if necessary. He had purchased almost complete control and could make good the promise. The other investors were so overcommitted at the time that they could not resist successful takeover. At no time did the business suffer. In 1849 competitors, knowing that Smith's Chicago bank planned to close on Thanksgiving day, circulated announcements that the bank had suspended and closed, leading to a brief run. But even before Smith rushed additional specie to the bank, depositors had learned of the trick and had redeposited their silver.

Smith's failure to obtain a bank charter for his own business was made ironic when Illinois in 1851 and Wisconsin in 1852 both adopted free-banking laws. Chicago bankers had managed to drive out Smith's money in 1853 when they secured passage of a law imposing penalties on any notes issued in Illinois by unauthorized banks. Smith applied for permission to organize a free bank under the Wisconsin law under the old insurance company name, and the notes of this new bank replaced the old, with every dollar of the original "Smith money" redeemed at par. He also had read the handwriting on the wall in Chicago, and even before his notes were driven out of circulation there, he found a route around the law. In April 1852 he acquired control of a Washington, D.C., bank that had its headquarters in New York City, and within a few months he opened the Bank of America in Chicago with a $50,000 paid-in capitalization. Then the ingenious Smith designed notes to look like the Washington bank's, and the notes circulated in tandem, circumventing the $50,000 limit on note circulation mandated by Illinois law. When the Washington bank closed, Smith merely moved his operations to Georgia and issued notes from the Bank of Atlanta, which he also controlled. A year later, in 1854, he acquired control of yet another Georgia bank, the Interior Bank of the State of Georgia, located in Griffin. Other Chicago bankers soon copied the tactic. Smith blatantly printed the Georgia notes in Chicago, and many never circulated in Georgia.

By 1854 the Atlanta bank had $500,000 worth of notes in circulation, and by year's end $2.75 million worth of Smith's Georgia money circulated in Chicago, roughly 75 percent of the city's currency. Chicago competitors, seeking to restrain him, actually traveled to Georgia with bundles of Atlanta notes for collection. Smith retaliated with his own piratical raids. The Panic of 1857 shocked Chicago's banking circles, however, and Smith decided to retire from banking. He had already decided to shut down his banks before the panic, closing or reducing his operations to such a degree that he had departed for England before the depression. By 1862 Smith had closed his Chicago and Georgia banks (the latter had closed in the late 1850s). He had, eight years earlier, eased himself out of the Wisconsin Marine and Fire Insurance Company by selling it to Mitchell.

Out of banking, Smith became a wealthy investor in the growing American railroad network. He undertook financing of the Galena and Chicago Union Railroad, and he was a director for three railroads in the Illinois-Wisconsin region. He also invested heavily in other roads, especially the Chicago, Milwaukee & St. Paul. Later he invested in the extensions of that road. Those investments, often managed by Mitchell or Smith's agent Peter Geddes, Smith watched from Scotland, where he had returned upon his departure from Chicago. He owned two estates in the north of Scotland but resided for long stretches in London. A prominent member of the London Reform Club, Smith probably settled in London shortly after 1866. He died on October 7, 1899.

Smith's legacies were few and largely intangible: he left no bank buildings or huge companies to testify to his talents. Bray Hammond saw the Wisconsin bank as "one of the most important banks" in the United States. But even that legacy, passed to Alexander Mitchell, came to an end during the crisis of 1893, when it failed.

Smith left a fortune to scattered cousins, nephews, and other beneficiaries, including the state of New York, which collected almost $2 million on Smith's $42 million in New York holdings. In America some $52 million was divided between James Henry Smith, a cousin, and George A. Cooper, his ward's husband. Lacking a wife, son, daughter, or institutional monuments, Smith left something more than money to those who knew him. His reputation was such that in the years after he left America, the rumor that "George Smith was coming" could calm panicky markets. The common postpanic lament that "if only George Smith were here" testified to the Scotsman's influence. Most important, Smith's money provided a test case for conflicting claims about competitive money and the gold standard, the different positions of which are still debated in 1989.

References:

Don Marcus Daily, "The Development of Banking in Chicago Before 1890," Ph.D. dissertation, Northwestern University, 1934;

Bray Hammond, *Banks and Politics in America from the Revolution to the Civil War* (Princeton: Princeton University Press, 1957);

F. Cyril James, *The Growth of Chicago Banks*, 2 volumes (New York & London: Harper, 1938);

Alice E. Smith, *George Smith's Money: A Scottish Investor in America* (Madison: State Historical Society of Wisconsin, 1964).

Specie Circular (*see* **The Bank War and the
    Specie Circular**)

Specie, Hard Money, and "Suspension"

In mercantilist political economy the wealth of the world consisted of gold, silver, and precious gems. Mercantilist traditions still dominated much of early American finance, and merchants always relied on gold or silver as a final means of settling trade accounts. When banks appeared, they also adopted a healthy appreciation for gold and silver coin, called "specie." Most of the specie in the colonial and early national period consisted of British gold sovereigns, divisible into shillings and pence, and Spanish coins, called "pieces of eight" or "dollars," that were divisible into two bits, four bits, and six bits.

A bank opening for business had to have capital (assets) in the form of specie supplied by the investors and stockholders of the bank. Not all capital was "paid in" (actually physically present) when the bank opened for business, but the capital that a bank did physically hold in its vaults was made up solely of specie. No other capital assets were recognized as sufficient. Banks used specie as a basis–a "reserve"–upon which to issue paper money called "notes." Banks never maintained specie reserves equal to 100 percent of their paper money in circulation; they would go out of business if they had. Instead, they engaged in "fractional reserve banking," a time-honored practice that is successful because only a small fraction of noteholders ever present their notes for redemption (for conversion back to specie) at a given time. Even if too many noteholders presented their notes for redemption at one time, other depositors were likely to appear to deposit money at the same time. Therefore, banks only needed to maintain a small "reserve ratio";

that is, a small ratio of specie in their vaults to the total number of notes in circulation.

Paper money had several advantages over specie: people could carry it more easily, and, more important, because it was not as scarce as specie, merchants could use it in large, routine transactions. When banks made loans, they made the loans in the form of drafts (in modern parlance, a check or demand deposit) or notes. So every time a bank made a loan, the number of notes the bank had in circulation increased. Paper money proved extremely convenient, with the only problems involving the divisibility of amounts of less than $5 (due to the shortage of small change and to state laws that prohibited printing "small change notes" in amounts of 50 cents or less) and the tendencies of banks to overissue notes against their specie reserves.

In normal times healthy banks could function well with low reserve ratios, but when something in the local or even the international economy made noteholders uneasy, they rushed to convert their notes to specie. (Again, the prevailing attitude was that only gold and silver had permanent value.) During those "panics," as contemporaries termed them, banks could not possibly redeem all their notes in specie. In such cases banks either individually or collectively "suspended" specie payments, meaning that noteholders could not redeem their notes immediately. For large commercial customers during a suspension, banks occasionally "discounted," meaning that they offered to redeem their notes for a percentage of the face (par) value of the notes.

Based on mercantilist principles, many economists, politicians, and ordinary citizens espoused a doctrine called the "hard-money" position. Hard-money men intensely disliked banks and, as a rule, despised paper money. They advocated either an all-metal circulating medium (a virtual impossibility, given the limited supply of gold and silver in the world), or a 100 percent specie reserve for bank notes (again, an unrealistic position in that banks would not make a profit and would not exist). Only a few hard-money proponents held that position all their lives. Most vacillated. Salmon P. Chase, Abraham Lincoln's secretary of the treasury, advocated hard-money views in his early political career but moved to the point that as secretary of the treasury he financed the Union effort in the Civil War partly by inflating the money supply through the issue of greenbacks, which were not redeemable in specie until a future date. (Chase not only became a believer in paper money, he also got his picture on the $100 bill.) Other hard-money men adopted or abandoned their views (which inevitably went hand-in-hand with antibank views) as the political climate dictated. A good example is Andrew Jackson, who, upon becoming president in 1828, had no particular hostility toward the Second Bank of the United States (BUS). In fact, he even explored the concept of another national bank beholden to the Democratic party in 1829. But as the BUS and its president Nicholas Biddle emerged as a political threat, Jackson suddenly espoused antibank and hard-money views. Another Jacksonian, Sen. Thomas Hart Benton of Missouri, won such fame for his hard-money views that his contemporaries nicknamed him "Old Bullion."

By and large, however, as the public's understanding of banking operations grew more sophisticated, the hard-money position almost disappeared. In fact, many Jacksonians moved into Populist circles and advocated inflation through the government's new issue of greenbacks that were not redeemable in specie. After the passage of the National Banking Act in 1863, Congress placed a 10 percent tax on private bank note issue, reducing the variety of notes redeemable in specie. But that did not end suspensions or panics, which struck the nation in 1873, 1893, and 1907. In those panics, with the only money in circulation being national bank notes backed by the specie reserves of the national banks, the government started to feel more pressure to prevent runs or to rescue banks once panics started. Thus, the monetary policy of the country from 1866 to 1913, when the Federal Reserve System was created, focused on the central issue of expanding the currency during crisis situations and providing a reserve when noteholders (and later, depositors) demanded specie.

See also:

Thomas Hart Benton, Nicholas Biddle, Isaac Bronson, Henry Carey, Salmon P. Chase, Henry Clay, Davis Rich Dewey, Federal Reserve Act, Financial Panics during the Nineteenth Century, First Bank of the United States, William Gouge, Richard Hildreth, Amos Kendall, National Banking and Currency Acts, Populism and Greenbacks, Second Bank of the United States, The Silver Issue and the Gold Standard, George Tucker.

—Editor

James Speyer

(July 22, 1861-October 31, 1941)

by Hans Eicholz

University of California, Los Angeles

CAREER: Partner (1885-1899), senior partner, Speyer and Company (1899-1939).

James Speyer, a leading New York financier in the late-nineteenth and early-twentieth centuries, was the second generation of the Speyer family to do business in the United States. His father, Gustavus Speyer, left the family banking business in Frankfurt am Main, Germany, to enter into partnership with his brother, Philip Speyer, in New York. Philip Speyer had arrived in New York in 1837 to begin a branch of the business specialising in merchandizing and foreign exchange. When Gustavus Speyer arrived in 1845, they incorporated the business as Philip Speyer and Company. Economic expansion created excellent opportunities for European capital investment in the United States, and the brothers were among the first to market American securities in Europe. In 1862 Philip Speyer and Company abandoned the mercantile wing of the business to concentrate on investment banking. Because of the Speyer family connections in Europe the brothers attracted large sums of European capital, especially for investment in railroads. The firm also arranged loans to European governments and marketed federal government bonds during the Civil War. Philip Speyer and Company became a member of the New York Stock Exchange in 1868.

Meanwhile, James Speyer was born in New York on July 22, 1861, to Gustavus Speyer and his wife, Sophie. When the boy was three years old his parents decided to return to Germany, and he spent the next 20 years in Europe, where he received a public-school education. When he was twenty-one he entered the family banking business in Frankfurt am Main. When his father died in 1885, he returned to New York to work at the branch of the firm his uncle had founded.

Philip Speyer had died in 1876, leaving the firm in the hands of associates, who shortened its

James Speyer

name to Speyer and Company. By the time of the arrival of James Speyer the business was heavily involved in the burgeoning railroad bond market.

The young Speyer immediately impressed his business associates with his skill at handling sensitive business deals, especially where the railroads were concerned. He particularly impressed Jay Gould. Initially discouraged by Speyer's youthful appearance, Gould quickly gained a lasting respect for the young financier. Sent to represent the first mortgage bonds held in Germany on the troubled St. Louis & Southwestern Railroad, Speyer met with Gould, who controlled the junior securities, to arrange for the railroad's reorganization. Speyer so carefully laid out his plan that it was adopted to the satisfaction of the clients.

In 1896 Speyer introduced a new practice to American banking. That year the Baltimore & Ohio Railroad defaulted, threatening many clients of Speyer and Company. Rushing to their assistance, Speyer offered to buy back the coupons on an issue Speyer and Company had marketed for the railroad. In effect the company guaranteed the investments of its clients through a policy of self-insurance. Other prominent investment houses soon followed this practice.

Railroad builder Collis P. Huntington also recognized Speyer's business acumen. The two soon became close friends, and the Speyer family enterprises invested large sums in Huntington properties. As a consequence the Huntington roads paid their indebtedness to the U.S. government in full. At the time observers regarded that as a remarkable feat.

Speyer demonstrated his abilities in a series of other ventures, including the financing of an electric underground railway in London and railways in developing countries such as Mexico, Bolivia, and the Philippines. In Mexico City Speyer and Company contributed to the establishment of the Bank of Commerce and Industry. In Paris the firm helped set up the first organization to deal in American securities in France. Speyer and Company was also among the first to sell German securities in the United States following World War I.

In 1899 Speyer became senior partner in the firm. His marriage on November 11, 1897, to Ellen Prince, who earned a reputation in her own right for her various philanthropic activities, had produced no heirs to the Speyer fortune. Speyer came to dominate the firm and ran it as a one-man show in its later years. When he retired the business was liquidated. Speyer died in New York City on October 31, 1941.

References:

B. C. Forbes, *Men Who Are Making America* (New York: Forbes, 1917);

Fritz Redlich, *The Molding of American Banking: Men and Ideas*, 2 volumes (New York: Johnson Reprint Co., 1968).

State Banks (*see* **National Banks and State Banks**)

James Stillman

(June 9, 1850-March 15, 1918)

by Larry Schweikart

University of Dayton

CAREER: Partner, Smith, Woodward & Stillman (1871-1873), Woodward & Stillman (1873-1916); president (1891-1909), chairman of the board, National City Bank (1909-1918).

James Stillman supervised a period of great growth in National City Bank, the premier bank in the United States in the late-nineteenth century. The son of Charles and Elizabeth Pamila Goodrich Stillman, he was born in Brownsville, Texas, on June 9, 1850. His father had traveled from Wethersfield, Connecticut, where his family had settled in the seventeenth century, to the Rio Grande Valley in Texas in 1828. From 1830 he referred to himself by the Mexican name Don Carlos. He was a merchant and invested in shipping and trade, real estate, and railroads, which proved profitable enough so that he amassed a small fortune. In 1855 the family decided to find a home less subject to bandits and border raids, and they moved to New York. Stillman attended school at Cornwall-on-the-Hudson, where he established an excellent record, then continued at Churchill School in Sing Sing (now called Ossining), New York.

In 1866, using his father's connections as a cotton dealer, Stillman obtained a job at Smith and Dunning, a New York mercantile house specializing in cotton. An able worker, he started to take over the activities of his father when the older Stillman's health failed, and the firm admitted him as a junior partner in 1871, reorganizing the company as Smith, Woodward & Stillman. His father must have had high regard for his abilities, for in 1874, he filed a power of attorney that made his son the head of the family's business operations. Charles Stillman died in 1875. Through his experience at Smith, Woodward & Stillman, James Stillman developed many of the traits he later exhibited at National City Bank–those of a demanding, quiet (some said cold) taskmaster. Keeping the family busi-

James Stillman (courtesy of Citibank)

ness gave James valuable experience that he later used in his own enterprises.

Smith retired from Smith, Woodward & Stillman in 1872, and the business reorganized as Woodward & Stillman, with James holding a 45 percent share in the firm. Stillman used his profits to start a farm at Briarcliff and also purchased land at Cornwall, where he raised cattle. In the firm he handled the job of cashier and met daily with some of New York's most important businessmen. Woodward & Stillman gave James his first entry into the world of banking, both through William Woodward's brother, James T. Woodward, president of

Hanover National Bank, and millionaire financier Moses Taylor, president of National City Bank.

During his years at Smith, Woodward & Stillman, Stillman met Sarah Elizabeth Rumrill, and they were married on June 14, 1871. They had five children: Elsie, Isabel, James, Charles, and Ernest. The couple separated in 1894 and apparently had little contact after that date.

Stillman greatly impressed Moses Taylor, who sought Stillman's aid during the organization of the Houston & Texas Central Railroad. Taylor introduced Stillman to all aspects of his enterprises. Stillman, through his acquaintance with the president of the Chicago, Milwaukee & St. Paul Railroad, was elected to that company's board in 1884, and in 1885 he received a directorship on the Hanover Bank Board. Through the Chicago, Milwaukee & St. Paul board of directors, Stillman met petroleum magnate William Rockefeller. The two formed a lifelong friendship, and Stillman's daughters married sons of Rockefeller. The connection with Taylor, however, proved most rewarding. In 1882 Taylor died, leaving his son-in-law, Percy R. Pyne, as president of National City Bank. Pyne became ill after a few years and designated Stillman as his successor, and in 1891 the board of directors elected Stillman president. Early biographers of the bank, John Moody and George Turner, explain that the directors chose Stillman because "there was no one else in sight" and he "was a man of ability, sure to represent . . . the traditions of the institution."

Stillman was hardly the head of a giant firm when he assumed the presidency—the only other officer was the cashier—but he dreamed of building the bank into a major financial power. He did not have the wealth that Taylor possessed, but he had underwritten numerous railroad issues on his own account before he became president. He saw the underwriting of securities, commonly known as investment banking, as a lucrative field for the bank to pursue. National City Bank lacked the European connections of such investment firms as J. P. Morgan and Company and Kuhn, Loeb, but Stillman felt investment banking was a profitable pursuit, and he worked through his friendship with Rockefeller to achieve that end. Stillman's presidency sealed the bond between National City Bank and Standard Oil Company, not only giving the bank a market for new securities but also providing an outlet for the Standard Oil partners to enter into new investments. He also maintained his alliance with

Woodward and Hanover National Bank. The competitors engaged in a stock swap and tended to operate on a friendly basis.

During the early years of his presidency Stillman had to weather the Panic of 1893—the solid National City Bank even gained deposits during the crisis—and he developed a reputation for calmness under fire, confidence, and quiet poise. He never diverted his attention to the more exciting events on Wall Street or to nonbanking enterprises. His intensity, however, wore on his employees, but among the New York financiers few used their contacts with other businessmen as well as Stillman.

The reorganization of the Union Pacific Railroad, undertaken in 1895 in a partnership with Jacob Schiff of Kuhn, Loeb, brought National City Bank into the ranks of the major investment houses. The two houses actually complimented each other well: Kuhn, Loeb had no relationship with a commercial bank in the manner of most investment houses, and National City Bank had the funds to back large issues. Together they handled securities issues in greater amounts than they could have handled singly. When Schiff agreed to recapitalize Union Pacific in 1893, he looked to Stillman to supply the cash. Schiff organized a committee that represented the shareholders and bondholders in reorganizing the road, while National City's resources kept it operating. The bank participated on its own account in the $3.5 million syndicate to meet the payments on the mortgage bonds. In 1897 three more syndicates were organized, and in the process the National City-Kuhn, Loeb, alliance grew stronger. Stillman also brought in railroader Edward H. Harriman as a member of the road's executive committee and participated with him in the Northern Securities holding company that the Supreme Court ruled illegal in 1904. With the money from the Northern Securities stock that Harriman's companies received after selling the stock, due to the court ruling, Union Pacific purchased shares of several smaller roads to form a rail network financed by Stillman's bank.

By cementing ties with the large corporations, Stillman found that he could also win their accounts and those of the individuals who ran them, and by 1905 corporate assets at National City reached $142 million. According to Harold Cleveland and Thomas Huertas, "fourteen firms, ten of them railroads, accounted for 56 percent of the bank's total corporate deposits." The bank's assets had risen 22 percent annually since 1895, and by 1905 total National City assets reached $308 million.

To obtain those kinds of numbers Stillman had to abandon some of the old Taylor conservatism, and he ventured forth in areas other banks had previously avoided. In 1899 the bank supported Standard Oil's formation of a syndicate to control the Anaconda Copper Company in Butte, Montana. The formation created public outcry, both on grounds that it overnourished the "Money Power" and also because national banks, especially eastern banks, generally had not participated in mining enterprises.

Stillman also directed National City Bank into foreign trade, opening a foreign exchange department in 1897. Not only did the department allow the bank to pay out or receive funds abroad at virtually any time but it allowed it to finance projects in other countries. The bank also worked through European connections–correspondents–to finance the cotton trade. National City financed more than one-third of American cotton exports after the Panic of 1907. Because of the bank's size it had no trouble attracting foreign relationships. In 1912 the bank's foreign correspondent balances exceeded $6 million.

National City also profited from robust correspondent relationships with rural American banks, which deposited funds with the bank to handle exchanges in New York or for the interest. The relationships also provided a ready market for the securities that the bank financed. Stillman contributed much to building the correspondent system, as Moses Taylor saw no value in the business. When a bank with excellent correspondent networks, Third National, failed in 1897, Stillman seized the opportunity and arranged a merger. Third National's former president and the U.S. comptroller of the currency, Alonzo B. Hepburn, resigned his government job to oversee the details of the merger and to take a position as vice-president of National City Bank. That merger only whetted Stillman's appetite to acquire or have his bank acquire stock in other banks: the portfolio came to include Fidelity Bank, Bowery Savings Bank, Hanover National, Riggs National, National Citizens, National Butchers & Drovers, Lincoln National, Bank of the Metropolis, Citizens Central National, Columbia, and Second National.

Hepburn resigned in 1899 to take the presidency of Chase National Bank (National City

Bank's chief competitor), and Stillman replaced him with a man whose own talents became legendary, Frank A. Vanderlip. Vanderlip handled correspondent relationships at first, then gradually supervised other aspects of the bank's business. With Vanderlip's help, Stillman found that the bank had tremendous power in the securities market. But to sell such securities, a bank typically had to carry the securities from the date of issue until final sale. Financing these securities often involved call loans, in which the participant pledged older securities as collateral for new ones. National City's resources in call loans grew steadily. In the 1890s they accounted for one-third of the bank's total loans, and after 1900, two-thirds.

Both Stillman and Vanderlip wanted to secure a special relationship with the national government. The bank in the past had supported the government in various crises. In 1897 National City became the nation's largest depository, and after 1899 Secretary of the Treasury Lyman Gage (for whom Vanderlip had worked before he came to the bank) used deposits at National City to smooth out fluctuations in the money market. The treasury secretaries began to deposit surplus federal revenues at National City, which then distributed them to other depositories. Leslie Shaw, Gage's successor as treasury secretary, attempted to use such deposits to stabilize interest rates.

The policies Stillman encouraged exposed the bank to significant risk, and to compensate Stillman increased stockholders' equity from $3.4 million in 1891 to $49.3 million in 1907, through two stock issues. The equity increases gave National City the largest capital of any American bank. Stillman set the pace, owning 22 percent of the stock by 1904. Assets continued to rise, reaching $334 million in 1908, and profits totaled $5.2 million in 1907.

Stillman had built the bank and wanted to see it prosper when he could no longer run it. He supported the election of Vanderlip to the bank presidency in 1909. Vanderlip appreciated Stillman's contributions but had a slightly different vision of banking. National City continued to grow–in many ways it accelerated under Vanderlip. But a fundamental problem existed between the two men. Vanderlip wanted to increase his power in the bank and his wealth to go along with it. Stillman intended to hang onto his substantial interest. But the personal style on which Stillman thrived had ebbed, replaced by tiers of managerial hierarchies. Harriman died in 1909, and Rockefeller retired in 1911, negating some of Stillman's most important contacts. Both Stillman and Vanderlip thus sought to institutionalize the bank's arrangements so that they were no longer based on individual relationships.

Increasingly, however, Vanderlip made the most important decisions. Vanderlip had become a crucial figure in the reform of American banking, developing the bank's foreign department and bond department and even looking for mergers to expand the bank's securities business. To that end he had created National City Company, a holding company for National City Bank stock and the stock of 16 other banks, trust companies, and savings banks, including a Cuban bank, Banco de Habana. Stillman was a charter member of the board of directors, and he brought in Riggs National Bank of Washington D.C. But while Stillman had made National City an important national bank, Vanderlip could rightly claim, as he did in 1915, "We are really becoming a world bank in a very broad sense, and I am perfectly confident that the way is open to us to become the most powerful, most serviceable, the most far reaching world financial institution that there has ever been. The one limitation that I can see, lies in the quality of management."

Few words could have been as prophetic. In 1915 Stillman became ill in Paris, where he had recently moved. Vanderlip wrote him in July requesting an option to purchase a major portion of Stillman's stock, plus some offered him by J. P. Morgan, Jr., enough to give him effective control of the bank. Stillman refused. At the time the affair caused some bitterness, but in his autobiography, written in 1934, Vanderlip had a different view: "I quite understand him [Stillman], I think, in the attitude he took toward my request for an option on some of his City Bank stock. Of course he did not want to surrender any of it! It was a piece of himself that I was asking for."

The breach grew deeper, and Vanderlip created a new company, American International Corporation, to compliment the National City's trade finance activities. Stillman feared that Vanderlip's divided attention would cause the bank's management to suffer. Vanderlip offered to retire as president and assume the position of vice-chairman. Stillman did not like the idea, concerned that the bank could not attract a top man to the presidency with Vanderlip watching over his shoulder. Ironi-

cally, that was exactly his relationship with Vanderlip. He put Vanderlip off until his health returned, then suggested that an executive board be created. It did not work. Vanderlip could not relinquish power, and Stillman returned to New York to help direct matters.

When the United States entered World War I, Vanderlip received an invitation to head the Liberty Loan campaign of May 1917, and he threw himself into the project with zeal. William Simonson, the general executive manager, ran the bank while Vanderlip took on yet another job, chairing the War Savings Committee.

A disaster occurred while Vanderlip was in Washington. National City Bank had long coveted offices in Russia. In 1916 Vanderlip sent two vice-presidents to negotiate a $50 million bond issue with the czar as a way to examine the Russian market. A positive report came back from one of the vice-presidents, and the bank prepared to open a branch in St. Petersburg. (Indeed, Vanderlip applied to the Federal Reserve for permission to open 11 branches in Russia.) In January 1917 National City Bank opened its first branch in Russia, and even after the March revolution Vanderlip saw no reason to withdraw from the market. On November 6, 1917, the Bolsheviks seized power, and a month later they nationalized the banks. No one knew exactly to what degree National City was obligated: if it was liable for the $26 million worth of deposits in its vaults, the episode threatened to cost the bank $40 million. Although he never said as much, Stillman blamed Vanderlip for the Russian debacle, or, at least, thought his inattention to bank activities contributed to it. In February 1918 Stillman and Vanderlip discussed the matter, and Vanderlip's tenure as president ended, although he remained on the job until the end of the year.

Stillman died on March 15, 1918, shortly after the showdown with Vanderlip. He had turned National City Bank into the most powerful financial institution in the nation.

References:

Anna Robeson Burr, *The Portrait of a Banker: James Stillman, 1850-1918* (New York: Duffield, 1927);

Harold Van B. Cleveland and Thomas F. Huertas, *Citibank, 1812-1970* (Cambridge, Mass.: Harvard University Press, 1985);

Edwin Lefevre, "James Stillman," *Cosmopolitan*, 35 (July 1903);

John Moody and George Kibbe Turner, "City Bank: The Federation of the Great Merchants," *McClure's Magazine* (May 1911): 77-78;

Fritz Redlich, *The Molding of American Banking: Men and Ideas,* 2 volumes (New York: Johnson Reprint Co., 1968);

Frank Vanderlip and Boyden Sparkes, *From Farm Boy to Financier* (New York: Appleton, 1935);

John K. Winkler, *The First Billion: The Stillmans and the National Bank* (New York: Vanguard, 1934).

Suffolk System

by Hugh Rockoff

Rutgers University

From the adoption of the Constitution until the Civil War, most of the paper currency of the United States was issued by individual banks, generally private banks but sometimes public. That currency promised redemption in gold or silver on demand, but on occasion banks delayed or refused to redeem their issues. As a result merchants accepted notes from distant banks at a discount. Only the notes of sound local banks circulated at par. In most regions a system of brokers developed who exchanged "foreign" for local money. Their efforts reduced and regularized the structure of discounts, but did not produce a par currency.

In New England, however, an alternative, the Suffolk System, emerged. That system produced a par currency and has generally been given high marks by historians. The Suffolk Bank was organized in Boston in 1818 and soon decided to enter the "foreign" exchange market. Because of additional competition provided by the Suffolk, the typical discount on New England's country-bank notes in Boston soon fell from 1 to .5 percent. But the Suffolk did not find the business highly profitable, so it proposed to the other Boston banks that they sell their country notes to the Suffolk and make it the major conduit through which the country-bank notes flowing into Boston would return home. That proposal, to which several Boston banks agreed in 1824, held out the prospect of substantial gains, both for the Suffolk and for the other banks. The Suffolk hoped that the scheme would help it obtain a dominating position in the exchange market. Other banks in Boston hoped that with the Suffolk's aid they could increase the volume of their own notes in circulation at the expense of the country banks. Although there is some debate, it appears that the Bos-

ton banks failed in that objective. Five years after the agreement the ratio of currency issued by Boston banks to the total level of currency in Massachusetts had actually decreased slightly. It may even be that the Suffolk System aided the country banks in expanding their circulation by eliminating the discount on country notes.

One of the key features of the Suffolk system was the requirement that each country bank maintain a permanent deposit of $2,000 with the Suffolk plus an amount in excess sufficient to redeem any notes that reached Boston. Those balances paid no interest. A country bank that failed to maintain its redemption fund, and which did not have an agent in Boston to redeem its notes at par, then had to face a demand by the Suffolk (made, no doubt, at the worst possible moment) that it redeem its notes as promised.

By 1850 the Suffolk regularly cleared the notes, either directly or indirectly, for virtually all of the country banks in New England. The system was widely respected in other regions of the country. But New England's country banks, which had long chafed under the restrictive hand of the Suffolk, eventually found a way to undermine it. In 1858 several country banks helped form and became stockholders in the Bank of Mutual Redemption. That bank gave better terms to the country banks than did the Suffolk, and it soon acquired a substantial share of the note redemption business. Whether it could have driven the Suffolk completely from the field became a moot question with the suspension of specie payments during the Civil War and the subsequent establishment of the national banking system.

The major achievement of the Suffolk System was the establishment of a par currency in New England, an achievement that was not matched over as wide an area in other regions of the country. Par exchange facilitated the everyday process of buying and selling goods in antebellum New England. Merchants no longer had to concern themselves with the particular kind of money a customer intended to use. It is easy, however, to exaggerate the benefits of the achievement. The state of affairs previous to the rise of the Suffolk System was not one characterized by Gresham's Law: "bad money drives out good." That law only applies when moneys with different intrinsic values are forced by law or custom to exchange at equivalent values. Instead, in New England before the Suffolk, different currencies exchanged at varying prices. Rather than drive out good money, bad money tended to depreciate relative to good money. Even after the advent of the Suffolk System merchants had to exercise discrimination in accepting checks, and checks represented a growing component of the money supply.

It also appears that the major charge leveled by the country banks, that the Suffolk earned substantial monopoly profits from its domination of the note exchange business, was true. Year after year the Suffolk earned dividends at the highest rate of any bank in Boston, and its stock sold at the highest price. The excess profits did not come from the ordinary banking business of the Suffolk but rather from the large volume of permanent interest-free deposits maintained by the country banks.

But if the Suffolk went to the expense of redeeming country notes and still earned monopoly profits, who ultimately paid? Historians impressed with the elimination of the discount on New England notes seem to have neglected that question. It seems unlikely that the stockholders of the country banks paid. They may have suffered in the short run when the system was established, but in the long run capital in country banking probably earned a normal return. Of the other factors, it seems likely that depositors shouldered much of the burden in the form of lower interest and reduced services since depositors had few alternatives to reliance on the country banks. They may well have anonymously subsidized the Suffolk System.

Historians and economists have sometimes likened the Suffolk to a private central bank. The Suffolk did perform some of the functions performed by modern central banks. It prevented individual banks from issuing excessive amounts of notes and lectured them on sound banking practices. The directors of the Suffolk included members of some of the best families in Boston, even the Lawrences and Lowells, so the advice was predictably conservative: high reserve ratios and short-term commercial loans. Except to a very limited extent, the Suffolk could not alter the stock of money or the rate of interest in New England. Fundamentally the stock of specie in New England, the base of the money supply, was determined by the ebb and flow of New England's trade with other regions of the country and the rest of the world.

The Suffolk has become a symbol. To some it represents an example of how a laissez-faire banking system can generate its own regulatory system. To others it is one more example of why private banking systems need to be regulated, whether by the state or as in this case through the cooperation of public-spirited individuals. However, in pursuing such symbolism, it is important not to exaggerate the practical effects of the system.

References:

Walter W. Chadbourne, "A History of Banking in Maine, 1799-1930," *Maine Bulletin,* second series, 39 (August 1936);

N. S. B. Gras, *The Massachusetts First National Bank of Boston, 1784-1934* (Cambridge, Mass.: Harvard University Press, 1937), pp. 101-106;

Bray Hammond, *Banks and Politics in America from the Revolution to the Civil War* (Princeton: Princeton University Press, 1957), pp. 549-556;

J. Clayburn la Force, "Gresham's Law and the Suffolk System: A Misapplied Epigram," *Business History Review,* 40 (Summer 1966): 149-166;

S. Wilfred Lake, "The End of the Suffolk System," *Journal of Economic History,* 7 (November 1947): 183-207;

Fritz Redlich, *The Molding of American Banking: Men and Ideas,* 2 volumes (New York: Johnson Reprint Co., 1968);

George Trivoli, *The Suffolk Bank: A Study of a Free-Enterprise Clearing System* (London: Adam Smith Institute, 1979);

D. R. Whitney, *The Suffolk Bank* (Cambridge, Mass.: Riverside, 1878).

William Graham Sumner

(October 30, 1840-April 12, 1910)

by Robert C. Arne

University of Chicago

CAREER: Tutor (1866-1869), professor, Yale University (1872-1909); editor, *The Living Church* (1869-1870); rector, Church of the Redeemer (1870-1872); alderman, city of New Haven (1873-1876); member, Connecticut Board of Education (1882-1910); president, American Sociological Association (1909-1910).

William Graham Sumner, stigmatized by Richard Hofstadter as a "Social Darwinist," was the Gilded Age's most renowned teacher of social science and an indefatigable defender of liberalism and republicanism. Balancing justice, sympathy, and self-interest, this follower of Adam Smith made public causes the unforsaken duty of his life: academic freedom, practical education, voluntarism, hard money, honest government, peaceful foreign relations, and free trade. Sumner's political economy applied his science of society to complex problems of money, banking, tariffs, democracy, and social welfare.

Sumner was born in Paterson, New Jersey, on October 30, 1840. His father, Thomas Sumner, was a sturdy, self-educated, Lancashire yeoman who embodied the austere virtues William Sumner later defended: honesty, integrity, industry, frugality, and independence. Thomas Sumner, a railway engine repairman, and his English wife raised their son in Hartford, Connecticut. The serious, self-righteous youth relished critical thinking. He never abandoned the "conceptions of capital, labor, money, and trade" he had learned as a boy from Harriet Martineau, the famous English popularizer of laissez-faire economics. As an exceptionally bright working-class boy with an adequate education and money saved diligently by his father, Sumner enrolled at Yale. He expected to rise to the ministry. Yale educated him in the classics. Described as "reserved and repellent in manner," he graduated Phi Beta Kappa. His concern for social re-

William Graham Sumner

sponsibility and self-actualization was already apparent: "Life . . . implies the recognition of all those high purposes and vast capabilities to which our existence is but a subordinate circumstance. The man of purpose alone truly lives."

Sumner did not think he could serve society best by fighting the Civil War. Hiring a draft substitute, he went to Europe in 1863 to advance his theological studies. He was deeply affected by the dedication of his underpaid Göttingen theological tutors. From their biblical criticism he learned "rigorous and pitiless methods of investigation and deduction." Because he preferred an intellectual theology, Sumner was less impressed by the Oxford theology he studied in 1865-1866 and by the emotionalism of American religion. He returned to Yale in 1866 to tutor subjects as diverse as mathematics, Greek, and philosophy. Biographer Harris E. Starr wrote that the vigorous practicality of Sumner's teachings fascinated hundreds of students in his widely attended classes and affected their characters years later. Neatly groomed, with a gruff voice and reserved manner, Sumner "walked with great strides and the air of self-confidence and power."

Sumner left Yale in 1869 to accept a position as rector of the Morristown, New Jersey, Church of the Redeemer. Hoping to reconcile science and theology, he published a short-lived Episcopalian paper defending rational theology (*The Living Church*). Distaste for ministerial social duties, however, underscored the fact that he had chosen the wrong calling. As he struggled to become a completely rational scientist, as he put nature in God's place as the force governing man, Sumner lost his faith. But Robert Green McCloskey has concluded that Sumner's entire scholarly career was affected by his religious conception of "human virtue": "The good man was chaste, frugal, industrious, and devoted to duty; he walked alone, secure in the certainty of rectitude, and mended his own fences." Living without scandal, Sumner always upheld those ethical standards. To perfect his life, for instance, he abandoned cigars when he realized what they cost his family, and he read few novels because they detracted from his work schedule. Late in life he bicycled resolutely when his doctor ordered him to keep in shape.

Between 1872 and 1909 Sumner served Yale as a professor of political and social science. Connecticut clergymen and legislators then governed Yale and defended its classical curriculum. "Let Yale condescend to become worldly wise," responded Sumner, who soon seemed radical to his colleagues. The "Young Yale" movement of the 1870s, led by alumni such as Sumner, slowly forced the college to teach more practical subjects: natural and social science, history, modern languages, and political philosophy. The movement initiated a palace revolution that forced Yale to elect its Corporation from the alumni. Yale students loved to watch a "fearless fighter" like Sumner, a strong-willed iconoclast who shared their modern educational philosophy and, often, their love of free trade.

Putting everything "butt end foremost," Sumner refused to conceal any truth. Though he disliked the metaphysics of Herbert Spencer's *First Principles* (1863), he admired Spencer's conceptions of sociology, social forces, evolution, militancy, the industrial, and the survival of the fittest. In 1879 Yale president Noah Porter condemned Sumner's teaching of Spencer's *Study of Sociology* (1874) because it "attacks every Theistic philosophy of society" and would "bring intellectual and moral harm to the students." Breaking promises to Sumner, who threatened to resign if he could not choose his own texts, Porter attacked Sumner's use of Spencer behind his back before Yale's Board of Trustees. The press magnified the conflict: the *New York Observer* called for the resignation of professors sympathetic to Spencer. Sumner, advocating academic freedom, maintained that he was "not defending agnosticism, he was resisting obscurantism." When he explained his beliefs to colleagues, most urged him to remain at Yale. He stayed.

In spite of his teaching commitment, Sumner was elected to the New Haven City Council in 1873. Soon Republicans forced him from office for favoring the Democratic opponent of Republican machines, Samuel Tilden, in the 1876 presidential election. Sumner's subsequent renunciation of politicking did not preclude his membership on the Connecticut Board of Education from 1882 until his death. While inspecting schools around the state, he "enjoyed talking to the pupils, speaking to them about their 'sums' and what school signified. Those who heard him say that he was always simple, clear, and sympathetic." Contemporaries thought him still more humane when they witnessed the tenderness of his affection for his two sons and his semi-invalid wife, Jeannie.

William Graham Sumner's essays won him fame and infamy: he published political, economic, and sociological articles in dozens of American journals. He wrote whenever the folly of American policy upset him enough to leave the academy and engage lustily in public debate. The essays made few original contributions to theoretical economics. They were well-written polemics that applied classical economic argument against protectionism to American conditions. Thinking that his economics was completely empirical, Sumner opposed radical social innovation based on a priori theory. He intended his theory merely to assess causal relationships between facts.

Favoring the "organic" social order created by individuals acting without central direction or purpose, he rejected the protectionist's "artificial or mechanical" conception of society as a product of social engineering. Sumner feared the "social quackery" of "amateur social physicians" who preferred "remedies" like bimetallism or alcohol prohibition to scientific observations of man's evolutionary progress. He concluded, "whenever we try to get paternalized we only get policed." To Sumner, laissez-faire meant "Let us manage for ourselves." He wanted a diverse, integrated society to prosper in accordance with the infinitely complex ramifications of thousands of human decisions and actions. Rejecting the dogma that laissez-faire was a "rule of science," he willingly deviated from this "maxim of policy" in education, the maintenance of a gold standard, and other matters.

When Sumner criticized Attorney General William M. Evart's protectionist stance in 1883, the *New York Tribune* declared that Sumner was "unworthy of Yale" and fabricated a story that Sumner's students had rebelled against him. Tariffs were the federal government's largest source of income in the late nineteenth century and its greatest departure from laissez-faire principles. Republican representatives of northern manufacturers supported the tariffs while agriculturalists–who were exporting grain to the world–generally opposed them. Sumner became vice-president of the American Free Trade League. He wrote many pamphlets and a widely read 1885 booklet, *Protectionism: The -Ism Which Teaches That Waste Makes Wealth*. The booklet illustrates Sumner's general point that regulation must "*follow* custom" if it is to do anything positive; government may legitimately maintain the gold standard that custom and market experience had proven sound.

Sumner argued that the evolution of free trade paralleled the antislavery struggle, legal reformism, and the separation of church and state. He accused protectionists of creating an antievolutionary, unethical, and science-negating theory that "*national wealth can be produced by taxes and cannot be produced without them.*" Industry and intelligence create wealth, wrote Sumner, not protectionist laws that create businesses in one place by harming consumers elsewhere. Sumnerian free-trade policy called for tariffs large enough to divert capital from uses consumers most desired. What would happen if, without tariffs, America ceased to be a manufac-

turing nation? Sumner answered that "Prosperity is no more connected with one form of industry than another." What would happen if Americans imported everything and sold nothing abroad? "If so," Sumner explained, "foreigners would make us presents and support us."

Sumner always concerned himself with the neglected victims of regulatory policy. He reasoned that the consumer was actually hurt by the discovery of iron in America, since tariffs then raised prices on iron from Europe. He expressed concern for the effect of tariffs on workers. He calculated that independent sewing women had to work 15 additional minutes a day to support the Willimatic Linen Company because that company obtained a tariff that raised the price of cheap foreign thread. Tariffs hurt the working class because wage earners in one industry in effect paid taxes to support workers elsewhere. If foreign wages were lower than American wages, Sumner's opponents asked, could Americans compete? Sumner answered that farm laborers in Iowa earned three times the wages of English farm laborers, yet American farm products were competitive in England. He thought that was possible because the price of a product depended on many factors, not just the price of labor.

Sumner's criticism of tariffs illustrates his general view that the possibility of market failure must be compared with the likelihood that government might betray the common good in the name of "the selected and favored producer." He feared that "under protectionism *the government gives a license to certain interests to go out and encroach on others.*" That favoritism, he argued, caused undesirable governmental growth: "Tax A to favor B. If A complains, tax C to make it up to A. If C complains, tax B to favor C. . . . Tax them as long as anybody complains, or anybody wants anything. This is the statesmanship of the nineteenth century." He argued that Congress lacked both the will and the knowledge to regulate properly: "If now, it were possible to devise a scheme of legislation which should, according to protectionist ideas, be just the right jacket of taxation to fit this country to-day, *how long would it fit?* Not a week. . . . Every day new lines of communication are opened, new discoveries made, new inventions produced . . . and the consequence is that the industrialist system is in constant flux and change."

Sumner thought capital made civilization possible. He defined capital as "any *product* of labor

Sumner in 1907

which is used to assist production." It is labor "multiplied unto itself—raised to a higher power." He considered the savings bank depositor to be a "hero of civilization" because "every social gain, educational, ecclesiastical, political, aesthetic or other," depends upon saved capital. Sumner argued, for instance, that his reforms at Yale depended upon capital contributions. He justified the concentration of capital in few hands on grounds that few could invest capital as well as Rockefeller, Carnegie, and Morgan had. Sumner defended their riches against the "cupidity" of the "legal plunderer" because defending the institution of property was the only way Sumner could defend his family's property.

The socialism of Upton Sinclair, Sumner suggested, would waste capital by divorcing property from private interests. Laws that protected capital limited population while preserving its means of subsistence. Using Malthusian logic, he thought that welfare programs increased population and lowered wages. If laborers did not too rapidly propagate, if they did not make too many demands upon capital for wages, wage rates would rise. High profits would augment the capital that paid laborers. Sumner thought capital growth was gradually abolishing poverty and increasing the "dignity of labor": "the power of capital . . . has set women free from

the drudgery of the grain-mill and the spinning-room."

Sumner worried that capital would be squandered if America abandoned the post-1873 gold standard: "the best system of coinage yet devised." Many American farmers believed that cheaper money would reduce their debt payments and give them more dollars for their crops. When Congress abandoned greenbacks (Civil War paper currency), debtors and speculators favoring inflation turned to the palliative of bimetallism. Congress responded by passing silver purchase acts in 1878 and 1890. Indignantly aroused, Sumner thought that this fiscal irresponsibility caused the Panic of 1893. In the 1890s Sumner made himself the most conspicuous opponent of bimetallism; he spoke frequently before large and sympathetic eastern audiences in famous clubs and before smaller audiences of midwestern hecklers. Sumner and the Republicans successfully defended gold against William Jennings Bryan, the Democrats, and the Populists.

Sumner hoped that history would teach prudence. His books *A History of American Currency* (1874) and *A History of Banking in the United States* (1896) provide detailed investigations of capital flows and bank failures that simultaneously illustrated the folly of contemporaneous American money and banking policies. The books, which contain less economic theory and fewer statistics than do today's economic histories, were well received by contemporaries. Sumner thought banks should merely transfer capital to producers at market interest rates. He tried "to expose the errors involved in mistaking credit currency for money, and money for capital." Americans had repeatedly sought capital from banks and gained only speculation and unsound notes. Exemplifying those bad experiences with the story of the Second Bank of the United States, Sumner argued that banks must back notes and loans with a 100 percent specie reserve. Disguising "false credit" as real credit made banking a "high class confidence operation." He considered the Bank of the United States to be nothing less than a "swindle" by which government obtained "other people's capital": "They print notes which have no security and make the public use them as money."

Sumner's *History of Banking* argued that the law against usury had kept banks from making their profits purely from high interest rates; banks could stay in business only by issuing high volumes of "false credit" at low interest rates: "Nine-tenths of the evil practices of banks were due to attempts to evade that law in obtaining rates which were legitimately theirs by the operation of the market." Sumner conceded that "false credit" could temporarily stimulate investment and exports, but that process consumed unprofitable capital investments in "successive periods of production." Overextending credit to risky businesses exposed the entire economy, normally a healthy organism, to commercial crises. Variations in the gold stock or foreign exchange could be magnified into a depression. The liquidation of debts, banks, and enterprises and the lowering of nominal wages was then necessary as a "severe remedy" for past folly.

The greatest loser was not the politician or the "Money Shark" who profited from fluctuating monetary values; it was the "Forgotten Man" who minded his business and lost his savings. Bimetallism could not work, Sumner argued, because the metals had different and fluctuating prices on the world market. People would pay debts with the undervalued metal and trade it in for the overvalued metal if both were legally exchangeable for paper dollars. Sumner distrusted banks and government too much to favor paper currency. Irredeemable paper could lead to national disaster. Meddling with the indicators of a complex financial system—"prices, the rate of discount, and the foreign exchanges"—was tantamount to "tampering with the . . . steam gauge of a locomotive."

Sumner hesitated to endorse the Interstate Commerce Commission's regulation of railroad monopolies after 1887. He advised against hasty regulation lest responses to present difficulties create laws "unwisely adopted in the first place, but now regarded as a 'bulwark of society.' " The lack of "internal cohesion" in trusts made them less threatening than was often thought. Reserving final judgment on the ICC, he feared that attacking capital would "arrest the industrial forces in their development on which our social well-being depends." Among Sumner's papers, Bruce Curtis found an unpublished 1909 manuscript, "On the Concentration of Wealth." The manuscript suggests that Sumner favored regulating monopolies. Apparently his long-standing concern that big business might corrupt republican government finally overrode his misgivings about economic regulation.

Sumner thought most big companies earned legitimate profits because they used productive means

to acquire wealth. However, other firms in the late nineteenth century had sought tariffs, land grants, and concessions for public works. Tammany boss William Tweed and other machine politicians controlled city governments and politicized public works. Sumner denounced governance by wealth, calling it "Plutocracy." The plutocrat used his capital to get legislative privileges such as artificial monopolies: "he practices upon the industrial vices, makes an engine of venality, expends his ingenuity, not on processes of production, but on 'knowledge of men,' and on the tactics of the lobby."

In a monumental war of "numbers versus capital," Sumner saw democracy arrayed against plutocracy: "An organized interest forms a compact body, with strong wishes and motives, ready to spend money, time, and labor; it has to deal with a large mass, but it is a mass of people who are ill-informed, unorganized, and more or less indifferent." The supreme test of government was whether it could stop those distributional "cliques." Democracies, fraught with financial scandals, had failed to do so. Sumner thought that only "institutions and guarantees" that separated state and market would "cut the ground from under plutocracy."

Those constitutional guarantees might also protect property from democracy. Sumner dreaded the tendency of democracy to promote "equality" at the expense of the "Forgotten Man." Protectionists ignored consumers; trade unionists ignored workers outside their trade when they regulated apprenticeship; welfare enthusiasts forgot the taxpayer. "Their schemes," Sumner wrote, "may always be reduced to this type—that A and B decide what C shall do for D. . . . I call C the Forgotten Man, because I have never seen that any notice was taken of him in any of the discussions." Drunkenness, silliness, inefficiency, shiftlessness, and imprudence all inflicted penalties. Sumner refused to deflect those penalties to "the industrious and prudent as a responsibility and a duty." With the amoral logic of a natural scientist, he concluded: "Let it be understood that we cannot get outside this alternative: liberty, inequality, survival of the fittest; non-liberty, equality, survival of the unfittest."

Did those precepts, damned even by Sumner's contemporaries, mean that he wanted poor men to starve? In *What Social Classes Owe To Each Other* (1883), he argued that, as a matter of "patriotism and civic duty," Americans owed each other the mutual redress of grievances, the "chance" for self-help. Sumner's "law of sympathy" suggested the need for *voluntary*, direct assistance to others: "It is the common frailty in the midst of a common peril which gives us a kind of solidarity of interest to rescue the one for whom the chances of life have turned out badly just now." "Idiots, insane persons, cripples, etc., are weak and society has to support them," wrote Sumner. Aware of the progress of modern culture, he mitigated the mercilessness of natural selection in unpublished manuscripts, which claimed that "the struggle for comfort has taken the place of the struggle for existence." After 1884 Sumner refused even to use the term "survival of the fittest."

Evidence of Sumner's humanitarianism suggests that Sumner was not the "Social Darwinist" Richard Hofstadter portrayed in *Social Darwinism in American Thought* (1955). Social Darwinism means the application to social theory of Darwinian concepts of the struggle for existence, individual variation, and the survival of the fittest. It seems more likely that Sumner acquired the harshest of his worldviews from David Ricardo and Thomas Malthus, whose economic ideas were well represented in the Martineau tales he had read as a boy. Malthus's "man-land" ratio pervades his social thought. Donald Pickens argues that Sumner's use of Adam Smith and the Scottish moral philosophers, who emphasized the unintended results of individual action, was mistaken for "Social Darwinism." Because the Spencerian evolutionism Sumner admired was Lamarckian and because it also justified altruistic behavior, Spencer could not have led Sumner to strict Social Darwinism. Sumner admired Darwin greatly for his empirical method but did not accept his evolutionism until 1875. Sumner's emphasis upon voluntary cooperation proved strong enough and his references to Darwinian biology weak enough that portrayal of him as a Social Darwinist is misleading unless that term is defined broadly enough to include all forms of social evolutionism.

Sumner, like Spencer, certainly did not call for military struggle. His preference for peaceful industrial development and classical republican self-government drew the damnation of jingoists favoring the Spanish-American War of 1898. Sumner's 1899 article, "The Conquest of America by Spain," argued that America had adopted the militarist, imperialist, and absolutist policies of its vanquished opponent. "National vanity and national cupidity" made America degrade itself with the "dominion and regulation" of foreign territories while it taxed domestic citizens extra for naval protection of these colonies. When a society was relatively unfit for international struggle, as primitive societies were, Sumner believed that it deserved protection from developers.

Sumner thought men had no more natural rights "than a rattlesnake" because no man should demand anything from anyone else as a matter of right. Yet he favored a "civil liberty" that guaranteed every man *the use of all his own powers exclusively for his own welfare.* Man's civil rights include a right not to be murdered and a right to the pursuit of happiness, which meant "the right to live one's life out in one's own way." Civil liberty lets each man realize the energy within himself as society "profits by the expansion and evolution of all the power there is in it." Sumner's ideal government was a "republic" which guaranteed civil rights: a governing body with "temporary and defeasible" tenure. He thought every ruling class should seek a "Golden mean" between the preservation of its rights and the practice of its duties–particularly its duty not to exploit other classes. His ideal citizen rises to the concept of liberty by submitting to no servitude. Viewing workers as free men, Sumner admonished them to realize their own powers by accepting the duty of standing up for their own rights– perhaps with union help.

Sumner surprised his colleagues, who thought of him as an economist, when the American Sociological Association elected him president in 1909. In 1907 Sumner had published *Folkways,* a scholarly anthropological study written as a prelude to *The Science of Society.* This four-volume work, a work that Sumner initiated and for which he had always lived, was completed in 1927 by Albert Galloway Keller. Sumner held that men were fundamentally similar beings whose struggle for the earth's resources determined their actions. Men could compete or cooperate to better their chances against nature. Rejecting metaphysical teleology and theology, Sumner thought that "The end of life is to live." Rationalistic as Sumner was, his sociology highlighted man's emotions: "The four great motives which move men to social activity are hunger, love, vanity, and fear of superior powers."

Sumner described folkways as "habits of the individual and customs of the society which arise from efforts to satisfy needs." Habitual behaviors emerged from an unplanned, competitive struggle. Folkways "are like products of natural forces which men unconsciously set in operation." "Mores" were folkways enforced by moral sanctions. "Mystery" sometimes reshaped folkways into "mores" as man's supernatural beliefs affected his actions. Tradition made the "mores" relatively fixed and coercive: they determined man's ideas and his morality. Only the ruling cliques of a society could alter the mores of the custom-bound "masses" to achieve certain ends, and they could do it only gradually (usually through ritual). That conservative doctrine suggests that social engineering is virtually impossible. Nevertheless, the "dissent and free judgement of the best reason and conscience" deserves protection lest men conform forever to irrational mores.

Sumner stood as an effective advocate of intellectual freedom and economic liberty. His educational reforms seemed as radical to "the Puritan theological crowd" at Yale as his defense of free trade did to tariff-hungry capitalists. As he praised the unsung class of industrious middle-class workers and entrepreneurs, professional managerial expertise was coming to dominate increasingly large businesses. Sumner realized that the "path of greatest success" was becoming that of "distinguished service to the organization." "Progressive" reformers, "Democrats," and "Plutocrats" all exploited the "Forgotten Man" by using political organization. Sumner's science of society challenged them all by arguing that the social order was too complex to be managed by "amateur social physicians."

Sumner died of a stroke on April 12, 1910; his intellectual legacy was not great. Yale's "Sumner Club" fought the New Deal. Social scientists such as Alfred Marshall, F. Y. Edgeworth, Yves Guyot, and Franklin Giddings acknowledged respect for aspects of Sumner's work. Twentieth-century economists, however, with their specialized, quantified methods and their concern for macroeconomic issues, soon lost interest in Sumner's qualitative, microeconomic essays. Only Sumner's *Folkways* has maintained its reputation as a classic of American social science. Sumner's admonitions to wait and see how social institutions resolved problems seem incomprehensible to modern social scientists and historians. Biographer Bruce Curtis, for example, has concluded that Sumner had "few or no specific and practical prescriptions that could be used to cure social ills a century or more later." Yet

the "remedies" of professional politicians and social scientists–deficits, paper money inflation, tariffs, armies, and massive social spending–are themselves some of the problems Sumner discussed. His solutions–civil liberty, industrial cooperation, non-interventionism, and voluntarism–deserve a better hearing.

Selected Publications:

The Books of Kings, translated by Sumner (New York: Scribner, Armstrong, 1872);

A History of American Currency (New York: Holt, 1874);

Andrew Jackson as a Public Man: What He Was, What Chances He Had, and What He Did with Them (Boston: Houghton, Mifflin, 1883);

What Social Classes Owe To Each Other (New York: Harper, 1883);

Protectionism: The -Ism Which Teaches That Waste Makes Wealth (New York: Holt, 1885);

Alexander Hamilton (New York: Dodd, Mead, 1892);

A History of Banking in the United States (New York: Journal of Commerce and Commercial Bulletin, 1896);

Folkways: A Study of the Sociological Importance of Usages, Manners, Customs, Mores, and Morals (Boston: Ginn, 1907);

War and Other Essays (New Haven: Yale University Press, 1911);

Earth-Hunger and Other Essays, edited by Albert Galloway Keller (New Haven: Yale University Press, 1913);

The Challenge of Facts and Other Essays, edited by Keller (New Haven: Yale University Press, 1914);

The Forgotten Man and Other Essays (New Haven: Yale University Press, 1918);

The Science of Society, 4 volumes, by Sumner and Keller (New Haven: Yale University Press, 1927; London: Milford/Oxford University Press, 1927);

The Essays of William Graham Sumner, edited by Keller and Maurice R. Davie (New Haven: Yale University Press, 1934; London: Milford/Oxford University Press, 1934).

References:

Dominic T. Armentano, "The Political Economy of William Graham Sumner," Ph.D. dissertation, University of Connecticut, 1967;

Robert C. Bannister, *Social Darwinism: Science and Myth in Anglo-American Social Thought* (Philadelphia: Temple University Press, 1979);

Bruce Curtis, *William Graham Sumner* (Boston: Twayne, 1981);

Sidney Fine, *Laissez-Faire and the General Welfare State: A Study of Conflict in American Thought, 1861-1901* (Ann Arbor: University of Michigan Press, 1956);

Richard Hofstadter, *Social Darwinism in American Thought* (Boston: Beacon, 1955);

Albert G. Keller, *Reminiscences of William Graham Sumner* (New Haven: Yale University Press, 1933);

Robert Green McCloskey, *American Conservatism in the Age of Enterprise* (Cambridge: Harvard University Press, 1951);

Donald Pickens, "William Graham Sumner As a Critic of the Spanish American War," *Continuity*, 11 (1987);

Merwin A. Sheketoff, "William Graham Sumner: Social Christian," Ph.D. dissertation, Harvard University, 1961;

Norman Erik Smith, "William Graham Sumner as an Anti-Social Darwinist," *Pacific Sociological Review* (July 1979);

Harris E. Starr, *William Graham Sumner* (New York: Holt, 1925).

Archives:

William Graham Sumner's papers are at the Yale University Library.

Suspension *(see* Specie, Hard Money, and "Suspension"*)*

Moses Taylor

(January 11, 1806-May 23, 1882)

by Sandra L. Fraley

MARKETS

CAREER: Merchant apprentice, J. D. Brown (1821); clerk, G. G. and S. S. Howland (1821-1832); owner, Moses Taylor & Company (1832-1882); director, Manhattan Gas Light Company (1841-1882); president, Scranton Coal Company (1854-?); president, City Bank of New York (1855-1882 [reorganized as National City Bank, 1865]); president, Delaware, Lackawanna & Western Railroad (1865-1882).

Moses Taylor spent his life building the permanent industries of the United States. Operating from the president's office in the National City Bank, he seldom left his native New York City. Yet the influence of this nineteenth-century entrepreneur shaped the development of American commerce, the iron and coal industries, transportation, public utilities, and communication.

Taylor was born in New York on January 11, 1806, the son of Jacob B. Taylor, a cabinetmaker-turned-real estate broker and city politician. Jacob Taylor was elected alderman in New York at a time when the position was reserved for only the most respected men in the community. He also became famed fur trader and financier John Jacob Astor's agent for New York real estate. Home life, with its flurry of business and political activity, must have greatly influenced Moses Taylor. Even though he ap-

proached his schoolwork with the same diligence and punctuality that later characterized his business activity, scholarship or the professions held no attraction for him. With the decisiveness that later facilitated his business career, he left school at fifteen.

Taylor began his business apprenticeship in 1821 with the mercantile firm of J. D. Brown. He quickly moved to the more successful house of G. G. and S. S. Howland, where he stayed for nearly 11 years. Taylor's duties stretched from early morning labor on the docks to late evening, when he recorded the day's business activities. The Howland brothers had established themselves as the leading merchant house in the Latin American trade. With Howland's approval Taylor began to make his own investments. He tested his judgment and ability and gained valuable experience dealing with ship captains, supercargoes, and agents in foreign countries.

At the end of what the *New York Times* in 1882 called a clerkship worth "fifty years of clerks' time today," Taylor had saved $15,000 from his own enterprise. He also had earned respect and contacts in the business community that he used to his advantage throughout his life.

In 1832 Taylor made two important and enduring decisions. He opened his own merchant house (after refusing the offer of a partnership in the Howland firm), and married Catherine Wilson, the daughter of a Scotsman in business as a ship's baker and grocer. The couple had six children, two boys and four girls. A warm and loving home served as a complement to Taylor's business life. His merchant house, Moses Taylor & Company, provided the basis for his extraordinary success in commerce. A handwritten circular announced Taylor's entry into independent enterprise. He listed the Howlands and Astor as references and guaranteed that "any business in my charge . . . shall receive the best attention that industry and dispatch can give it."

One factor that seemed to secure Taylor's success was a contract from Drake Brothers of Havana, a firm that formerly dealt with the Howlands. Apparently the two firms had fallen out, and Howlands approved of Taylor serving the account. Drake Brothers shipped two-thirds of the sugar from Cuba to the United States. At that time only the United Kingdom and France surpassed Cuba in the value of goods exported to America.

Taylor became the largest sugar merchant in the United States. His net worth at the end of 1836 was $86,000. By 1840 his net worth had surpassed $200,000. In 1855 his firm paid more customs tax than any other firm in the United States except A. T. Stewart & Company, the famed dry goods merchant.

Taylor's closest and most valuable business association originated in 1836. He hired Percy Rivington Pyne, a sixteen-year-old English immigrant, as his junior clerk. In 1849 Taylor reorganized his merchant house and offered Pyne a one-quarter partnership. The relationship was cemented in 1855 when Pyne married Taylor's oldest daughter. That same year Pyne assumed major responsibilities in the merchant house, and Taylor became president of the City Bank of New York (reorganized as National City Bank in 1865). Throughout his life Pyne served as Taylor's right-hand man. After Taylor's death he perpetuated Taylor's policies.

Taylor's capacity to weather disaster was a trademark of his career and ensured his success as a merchant and entrepreneur. In 1835 a fire destroyed Wall Street and much of the surrounding business district. Taylor's South Street establishment, like many others, burned to the ground. But Taylor salvaged his account books and resumed operation the next morning from the basement of his home.

Moses Taylor (courtesy of the New-York Historical Society)

While other businesses collapsed in the financial panic of 1837, large cash reserves protected Taylor. That year he earned equal amounts from sugar commissions and investments. The firm continued to earn profits through the dull business years from 1837 to 1842.

After the slowdown ended, Taylor separated his commercial activities from his merchant house. In 1842 he removed $202,000 from Moses Taylor & Company and initiated separate commercial activities.

The board of the City Bank of New York appointed Taylor a director in 1836. In 1855 the board elected him bank president. At that time Moses Taylor & Company was the second largest importer in the United States. Taylor used National City Bank as headquarters for his financial enterprises. At the time he took control, the bank was organized as a merchants' bank. Taylor continued that tradition but consolidated the association of merchants. The bank also operated as a financial service center for his friends and associates.

Taylor's capacity for survival served the bank well. Three major panics swept the United States banking system during the Taylor and Pyne administrations—in 1857, 1873, and 1884, after Pyne assumed the president's chair following Taylor's death. City Bank's reputation for safety grew with each panic.

City Bank received a national charter and changed its name in 1865. The national charter offered a cost-free way of demonstrating high standards to the financial community. When Taylor joined the bank's board in 1836, its cash-reserve ratio was lower than any other New York bank. After 1838 it remained consistently higher. At times the cash ratio exceeded 50 percent. Taylor had no interest in growth or in using National City Bank to generate income. Instead, he maintained the bank's conservative policies of providing cash to shield customers (chiefly Taylor's companies and associates) from insolvency.

Taylor joined the board of Manhattan Gas Light Company in 1841. At the time it was the second largest utility in the city. Within a decade Taylor had helped make Manhattan Gas Light the largest gas light company in the city. Under Taylor's leadership Manhattan Gas Light Company exploited its franchise, which included providing gas lighting to streets and homes in Manhattan above Canal Street, one of the most rapidly growing urban areas in the world.

Taylor initiated policies that brought Manhattan Gas Light and New York Gas Light cooperative ventures that proved mutually beneficial. His style of hands-on management created the opportunity for gas light corporations to band together for research and other activities of mutual benefit. By the 1860s Taylor had almost total control over Manhattan Gas Light and a decade later New York Gas Light. That brought the entire industry under Taylor's influence, reduced competition, and increased profits.

Eventually Taylor gained interests in the Brooklyn Gas Company, the Buffalo Gas Company, the Chicago Gas Light Company, Metropolitan Gas Company of New York, Nassau Gas Light Company, Scranton Water and Gas Company, various Baltimore gas companies, and the New York City Gas Light Company.

The year Taylor died, the Equitable Gas Company began to compete head-on with Taylor's interests in New York City. Equitable had a more efficient manufacturing process and the financial backing of William Rockefeller and John Archibald of the Standard Oil Group.

Two years after Taylor's death, his business heir Pyne combined New York City gas interests into a single firm capable of withstanding the competition from Equitable and the coming threat of electricity. The Taylor family controlled what became New York City's premier utility.

As early as 1843 Taylor loaned money to the Forest Improvement Company, a band of New Yorkers who developed coal mining in the Schuylkill region of Pennsylvania. Taylor allowed his respected friend Charles Hecksher to guide his investments in mineral development. They expanded their investments throughout the region for the next 22 years.

Taylor's early Latin American trading activity led him to own ships even as late as 1863. In the same fashion investments in coal and subsequently iron ore development logically led to investments in railroads. While his peers invested in the exciting and speculative transcontinental railroad, Taylor worked regionally. His first investments were in the coalfields and then the railroad lines that brought the coal into New York City.

By 1852 Taylor and others had invested in the Lackawanna Iron and Coal Company. In 1854 the same group established Scranton Coal Company and elected Taylor president and his partner Pyne as treasurer. That same year he was elected to the Board of Directors of the Delaware, Lackawanna & Western Railroad.

There, too, a financial panic proved profitable for Taylor. In the depressed market of 1857, the stock price for the Delaware, Lackawanna & Western Railroad fell to $5 a share. Taylor bought controlling interest. Seven years later the stock sold for $240 a share. Taylor held his stock in the railroad for the rest of his life. Part of the stock financed the endowment for the Scranton Hospital.

When Taylor became president of the line for Delaware, Lackawanna & Western in 1865, he took what had been a locally oriented coal road and connected it with the New Jersey Central Railroad, the Morris & Essex Railroad, and the Jersey Shore Improvement Company. He later gained control of the Lackawanna & Bloomsburg Railroad, which he consolidated with the Delaware, Lackawanna & Western.

Taylor also expanded his interests to the Midwest. He became the chief financial backer for James F. Joy. Joy's Farmer's Loan and Trust Company held $900,000 in Michigan's state bonds for the Michigan Central Railroad. The institution was eager to exchange the bonds for stock. Taylor financed the development of the Michigan Central as an important regional system and developed the Chicago, Burlington & Quincy Railroad and the Joy system of roads converging on Kansas City and extending southward through public and Indian lands. In 1868 Taylor won election to the Board of Directors of the Michigan Central. He supported Joy's plan to make Michigan Central System into a new trunk line from New York City to Chicago. When a dispute arose and Joy left the presidency in 1876, Taylor's close associate Samuel Sloan replaced him.

Cornelius Vanderbilt and Jay Gould fought for control of Michigan Central against Taylor's more conservative policies. The speculators won. In 1878 Vanderbilt gained control of the road through a proxy fight. Taylor sold his stock at a handsome profit and continued his long-term association with Vanderbilt. They remained respectful of each other, but distant.

Vanderbilt had been an early associate and investor in City Bank. While he and Taylor often ran parallel business interests—in railroads, iron, and coal—they were never partners. A contemporary said, "Each of the two men was too big to be yoked. Each wanted to drive." The ostentatious Vanderbilt would have made an odd partner for the conservative Taylor, who shielded himself and his family from the public eye. Even his charities were private and related to business. Most of his charitable acts consisted of private loans to weaker friends and young men struggling for success.

Taylor's one magnificent act of public charity was the farsighted endowment of a free hospital for his workers. Four months before his death he endowed a hospital for the town of Scranton, Pennsylvania. He gave bonds from the Delaware, Lackawanna & Western Railroad and the Lackawanna Coal and Iron Company, valued at $275,000. The hospital's mandate was to provide free medical care to workers in Taylor's enterprises. While other philanthropists of that time were concerned with the spiritual redemption of the less fortunate, Taylor ministered to the physical needs of workers. "I am indebted to them for the success of my enterprises there. I want to recognize my obligation to their labor, which made my capital productive," Taylor said when he made the gift.

During the Civil War, Taylor had an active role as a Union advocate and financial adviser for the federal government. He organized the Union Defense Committee in 1860 and helped float large government bond issues in the early part of the war. Although he was a lifelong Democrat and continued to support the Democrats on the local level, he became a mainstay of the National Republican party during the war.

By 1870 Taylor had invested in the Houston & Great Northern Railroad. He joined in support of the International Railroad. In 1872 he added Central Railroad of Georgia, the last major piece of his railroad enterprise. The war had devastated the Central. With good professional management the railroad became the leading line in the postbellum period, carrying goods from the central cotton region to the sea.

Taylor also became involved in a dispute between the Franklinite Iron Company and the New Jersey Zinc Company. After litigation a new company formed, combining the two companies and giving 50 percent ownership to each side. New Jersey Zinc had also been the main producer of spiegeleisen, an important ingredient in Bessemer-steel production. As soon as his influence was secure, Taylor's Lackawanna Iron and Coal bought the contract for spiegeleisen production. Within 12 years Taylor converted a $40,000 leasehold into one-half ownership—valued at $1.5 million—of the most important zinc producer in the country.

In a conservative career that led to significant financial returns, Taylor's investment in the First Atlantic Cable Company proved an exception. Other investors saw First Atlantic as a more speculative endeavor. Typically, Taylor remained loyal through the difficult period. He responded when Cyrus W. Field asked him to help form a company that would link the United States with Great Britain via telegraph. First, Field formed a company to connect a telegraph line from Saint John's, Newfoundland, to Nova Scotia, where it would connect with existing telegraph lines in the United States. That cut 48 hours from transmission time to and from Europe. Taylor served as treasurer and director of the new company. By 1858 the company had laid one cable across the Atlantic. However, it was defective, and work halted when the Civil War erupted. It took four attempts before the operation achieved success. The Atlantic cable began operation in August 1866, bringing New York into instantaneous communication with London.

While First Atlantic worked on the transatlantic cable, Field and his associates built the American Telegraph Company. They lost in competition during the Civil War and merged with Western Union in June 1866. Taylor became a director of Western Union.

By the time of his death from pneumonia on May 23, 1882, Moses Taylor's enterprises had enabled him to participate in shaping the business structure of society. As an ancestral figure in American big business, he exhibited characteristics that Americans continue to admire in an executive. He had the capacity to establish business objectives and adapt them to changing conditions. He developed and maintained organizations and pursued efficient relations with subordinates and employees. He secured adequate financial resources, retained them, and nurtured good relations with investors. He took advantage of new technology to develop a market for his products. He was an innovator, a risk-taker, an organizer, and a decision-maker.

References:

Harold Van B. Cleveland and Thomas F. Huertas, *Citibank 1812-1970* (Cambridge, Mass.: Harvard University Press, 1985);
Daniel Hodas, *The Business Career of Moses Taylor* (New York: New York University Press, 1976).

Archives:

Material on Moses Taylor is held at Columbia University Library, the New-York Historical Society, and the New York Public Library.

Trust Companies and Trust Departments

Nineteenth-century trust companies managed property and the estates of wealthy individuals, holding them for final sale or, in the case of a trust beneficiary who still lived, for regular disbursement. The companies charged a fee for such services, but more important, they had access to the extensive funds in their care as a source of investment and lending. Thus they soon came to assume banking duties as well, although some states, such as New York, passed laws prohibiting trust companies from engaging in banking activities.

A New York company, Farmers' Loan and Trust Company (incorporated as Farmers' Insurance and Loan Company in 1922), was the nation's first company to engage in trust activities, but the first company chartered exclusively as a trust company was another New York City company, the United States Trust Company, which received a charter in 1853. That charter provided a model for New York's subsequent trust charters.

By mid century trust companies had already wedged themselves into banking businesses, and by the 1870s they emerged as important competitors to banks. In 1913 more than 1,800 trust companies conducted operations, and by that time they differed little from banks. In 1929 trust companies reached their all-time high of 18 percent of the total assets of American financial intermediaries.

See also:

Arsène P. Pujo, James Stillman, Frank Arthur Vanderlip.

—Editor

George Tucker

(August 20, 1775-April 10, 1861)

by Tiarr Martin

University of Dayton

CAREER: Lawyer, Virginia (1801-1819); state representative, Virginia (1815); U.S. representative, state of Virginia (1819-1825); professor of moral philosophy, University of Virginia (1825-1845).

George Tucker, an economist, philosopher, attorney, author, professor, and statesman, became an outspoken critic of President Andrew Jackson and a defender of Nicholas Biddle and the Second Bank of the United States during the Jacksonian Era.

Born on St. George's Island in Bermuda on August 20, 1775, Tucker was the second child and first son of Daniel and Elizabeth Tucker, who were distant cousins and descendants of a large British family that had lived in the colony for more than 150 years. His formal education on the island lasted six years and included instruction under Josiah Meigs, an attorney who later became professor of natural philosophy at Yale College and founder and president of the University of Georgia.

In July 1795 Tucker sailed for Philadelphia, intending to seek his career in America. Many members of the Tucker clan had immigrated to America, including St. George Tucker, a judge and professor of law at William and Mary College in 1795, and Thomas Tudor Tucker, a congressman from South Carolina who later served as treasurer of the United States under Thomas Jefferson. George Tucker had wanted to study law in Britain, but after seeking advice from his uncle, St. George Tucker, he enrolled at William and Mary College in Williamsburg, Virginia. He graduated in 1797.

In October of the same year Tucker married the very wealthy Mary Byrd Farley, great-granddaughter of William Byrd II, and promptly took a seven-month honeymoon in Bermuda partly because his new bride experienced poor health. Returning to Williamsburg in May 1798, Tucker intended to study for the bar examinations but instead took

George Tucker (courtesy of the New-York Historical Society)

a year-long vacation, visiting his wife's many relatives and property holdings. His life of ease came to an abrupt halt in May 1799 when Mary died, leaving him a large but bitterly contested estate. Tucker spent the next 12 months doing nothing but traveling around trying to settle the estate. After 20 years he salvaged only part of it, even though he believed himself the sole heir.

Tucker moved to Richmond during the summer of 1800 with the intent of setting up a law practice and making himself an important social and political figure. A letter of introduction from his ever-helpful uncle, St. George, to his friend Governor

James Monroe enabled Tucker to establish the elevated social standing he desired. Within a year Tucker numbered among his acquaintances several influentials, including Judge Pendleton, George Hay, George Wyth, and, of course, Governor Monroe, who introduced him to the town.

In 1801 Tucker finally received his license to practice law, and in that same year he gained his nickname, "a man of letters," when he published a piece entitled "Letter to a Member of the General Assembly of Virginia on the Subject of the Late Conspiracy of the Slaves with a Proposal for Their Colonization." In it Tucker expressed his opposition to slavery on grounds that a massive revolt was inevitable sometime in the not-too-distant future and on grounds that the ratio of blacks to whites was becoming increasingly unfavorable for whites due to the higher birth rate among blacks, caused by their guaranteed subsistence, and due to the exodus of many whites from Virginia to the West. Claiming that repatriation of blacks to Africa would be too expensive, he proposed that the federal government purchase a tract of land west of the Mississippi River for the purpose of Negro resettlement.

Tucker married Maria Ball Carter in February 1802. She was the niece of his first wife's sister and the great-niece of George Washington. Although not as wealthy as Tucker's first wife, she nevertheless proved a great asset to him in his drive for an elevated social standing.

As a lawyer, Tucker utterly failed as a result of his awkward speaking manner and insufficient knowledge of common law and courtroom procedure. Of all the legal positions offered him through family or political friendships, he found only one that he could handle—commissioner of bankruptcy—a lucrative position that he held for one year.

In politics Tucker called himself a Jeffersonian Republican, but his position had changed from near-Jacobinism to conservative, probank Republicanism. He defended the First Bank of the United States as well as the Bank of Virginia and accepted a position on the Bank of Virginia's board of directors. Tucker's social intimacy with many Federalists aroused the suspicion and anger of Republicans, including Lewis Harvey, whom Tucker eventually challenged to a duel. Tucker drew up his will (with his wife carrying their second child at the time), but, fortunately, mutual friends of the men intervened before the duel took place.

A moderately wealthy man before moving to Richmond, Tucker's financial situation steadily deteriorated. He made very little money from his law practice and constantly consumed capital from his inherited estate because of his lavish life-style and gambling habits. He also bore the expenses associated with his two children, Daniel George, born on November 23, 1802, and Eleanor Rosalie, born on May 4, 1804. In addition Tucker speculated heavily in bank stocks and real estate, which tied up most of his remaining cash.

In the fall of 1806 Tucker, realizing that he needed to start life afresh, left Richmond and moved to his wife's parents' home in Frederick County in the Shenandoah Valley. He did not sever all connections with Richmond, however, and in 1807, while he visited the capital, a loan company to which he owed $6,000 had him arrested. Tucker was released without bail and used the endorsements of Thomas Tudor and St. George Tucker to secure a loan from a Richmond bank to pay the debt. That embarrassing experience reminded Tucker that he had made a good decision in leaving Richmond in an attempt to free himself of debt and rebuild his reputation.

Tucker moved his family to Woodbridge in rural Pittsylvania County in May 1808. By December his fourth child, Eliza, was born. Maria, the third child, was born in 1806. Lelia came in 1810 and Harriet in 1813. Even though Tucker found life extremely boring in rural Virginia, he remained satisfied that he had done the right thing when he left Richmond. Slowly he developed into a competent lawyer and built up a practice.

In 1813 he wrote a series of essays as part of a self-imposed disciplinary program, and they were published in the *Philadelphia Port Folio* under the title "Thoughts of a Hermit" in 1814 and 1815. Tucker also actively participated in politics and, after two unsuccessful attempts in 1813 and 1814, was elected to the Virginia House of Delegates in 1815. Tucker sold his Woodbridge home in March 1818 and moved to Lynchburg. His financial situation had improved by that time, and his estimated property holdings exceeded $80,000. Tucker was elected to the U.S. House of Representatives and served three terms from 1819 to 1825. During that time Tucker's old habits of stylish living, indolence, and gambling returned. Also while a congressman, Tucker became very concerned about his only son, who showed signs of mental illness. In 1823 Tucker's second wife, Maria, died while she was pregnant with her seventh child. Not surprisingly, Tucker made no notable achievements while in Congress, voting the Jeffersonian Republican line most of the time and supporting the admission of Missouri without the slavery restriction in 1820. In 1824 Tucker participated in a closed Republican caucus to select William Crawford as the party's presidential candidate over his rival, Andrew Jackson. Since much of Tucker's constituency supported Jackson, Tucker had slim reelection chances.

In 1825, with his finances again in turmoil and his political career in doubt, Tucker accepted a lifetime position at Thomas Jefferson's newly established University of Virginia in Charlottesville as professor of moral philosophy. He later added political economy, belles lettres, and rhetoric to his teaching subjects. The oldest of the new faculty at age fifty, Tucker was elected faculty chairman and became responsible for student behavior. Jefferson wanted a lenient policy and assumed southern gentlemen would behave in an exemplary manner. Tucker harbored doubts concerning the wisdom of that policy, and the serious rioting that broke out in October 1825 confirmed those doubts. Students chanted slogans against European teachers and destroyed school property. They even hurled a bottle of urine through a window of the residence of professor George Long, an English-born and educated man, who was serving tea at the time. The students also intimidated and insulted local citizens. The situation whirled totally out of control, and not until Jefferson and two other ex-presidents–Madison and Monroe–personally visited the campus and addressed the students did things calm down.

Finding solitude unbearable after the death of Maria, Tucker married Louisa A. Thompson, a widow from Baltimore, in December of 1828. The following year Daniel George, Tucker's only son, was judged insane and was committed to an institution in Philadelphia, where he died in 1838.

Andrew Jackson's election to the presidency in 1828 caused much concern for Tucker, who by that time had evolved into an ultraconservative Whig, convinced that "only men of property with a tangible, taxable interest in government should be allowed to run the nation." He thought Jackson a power-hungry demagogue who had no respect for private property, and Tucker insisted that class warfare could break out. Tucker worked hard to counteract Jackson's influence, especially in the controversy

over the Second Bank of the United States. In 1831 Tucker anonymously published an article entitled "The Bank of the United States," which appeared in the *American Quarterly Review*, and in October 1833 he pseudonymously published three more articles entitled "The President's Late Act," "The President's Bank Manifesto," and "The President's Late Manifesto," which appeared in the probank *Washington National Intelligencer*. The articles defended the national bank and Nicholas Biddle's "right" to use the bank's money and influence against Jackson. After the administration discovered Tucker's authorship it accused him of being one of Biddle's hirelings, a charge Tucker always denied.

In 1839 Tucker published *The Theory of Money and Banks Investigated*, and the work remains in print today. In it Tucker defended "banks of circulation" (fractional reserve banks) against criticisms that such banks unfairly benefited a "moneyed aristocracy" at the expense of the working people. Tucker did, however, favor tighter restrictions on banks, including a requirement that start-up capital be adequate ($100,000 to $200,000 minimum) and in specie (gold and silver), not nominal, fictitious, or borrowed capital. Tucker deplored the fact that states chartered banks with inadequate capital and unscrupulous directors, thereby implying that the public could have full confidence or at least a high degree of confidence in those banks. Tucker, establishing a concept later adopted by Charles Francis Adams in his efforts for "sunshine legislation," also favored requiring all banks to give a full and public accounting of their financial condition on a regular basis and the periodic inspection of banks by examiners. Tucker suggested a four-to-one maximum ratio of outstanding notes to specie and recommended that banks forfeit to the government all profits accrued during periods of overissue and periods of suspension of specie payment.

In the book Tucker also discussed the extreme public policy positions that circulated, which ranged from government ownership of all banks to a policy of absolute laissez-faire in the banking industry. He concluded that the public welfare would be best served if the industry were left in private hands but with proper and effectively enforced government restrictions.

As another way of providing healthy checks and balances, Tucker proposed the establishment of two or three national banks. He argued, "With two national banks, placed in New York and Philadelphia, and perhaps a third in New Orleans, with charters framed according to the varied experience of more than half a century, there is every reason to believe that the United States would possess a currency, which, for cheapness, convenience, and security, would be without a parallel in any other country." His proposal for multiple national banks comprised Tucker's most significant public policy suggestion in the area of banking and foreshadowed the current Federal Reserve System.

The last few years of Tucker's professorship held much discontent for him. A wave of religious enthusiasm had engulfed the Virginia campus, which made Tucker as uncomfortable as during the riots of 1825. Tucker, himself an Episcopalian, refused to stop drinking wine or to support a temperance society that had the backing of the majority of professors and administration as well as many of the students. In 1842 the school cut his salary from $1,500 a year to $1,000, and by 1845, with investments returning him between $3,000 and $4,000 a year, Tucker retired from academia and moved to Philadelphia.

In Philadelphia Tucker actively participated in the American Philosophical Society (he had joined in 1837), presenting essays on economics and philosophy. Philadelphia's leading citizens wined and dined him, but he judged Philadelphia society to be not as "elevated" or "intelligent" as it could have been.

In 1857 Tucker's four-volume *History of the United States, from Their Colonization to the End of the Twenty-sixth Congress in 1841*, became the first important work on U.S. history written from the southern viewpoint. The following year Tucker published "Banks or No Banks" in *Merchant's Magazine* for February 1858, in which he complained of the cost of the "palaces built for our money changers." He also chastised stockholders for neglecting their duties and being partly responsible for some of the abuses during the free-banking era. He argued that stockholders should become familiar with and actively participate in the selection of the bank's directors instead of giving blind support to management's choice of directors.

After his third wife's death in 1858, Tucker, then in his eighties, continued his active social life, and he vacationed frequently with his daughters. He continued to visit the South to escape the harsh winters in Philadelphia. During one such trip in 1861 he was struck in the head by a bale of cotton while in Mobile, Alabama. He was transported to the home of his daughter, Mrs. George Rives, in Virginia. Tucker never recovered from the accident and died on April 10, 1861. He was buried in the University of Virginia cemetery located in Albemarle County, Virginia.

Selected Publications:

Essays on Various Subjects of Taste, Morals, and National Policy, by a citizen of Virginia (Georgetown: Milligan, 1822);

The Valley of the Shenandoah; or, Memoirs of the Graysons, 2 volumes (New York: Wiley, 1824);

A Voyage to the Moon: With Some Account of the Manners and Customs, Science and Philosophy, of the People of Morosofia, and Other Lunarians, as Joseph Atterley (New York: Bliss, 1827);

The Laws of Wages, Profits, and Rent, Investigated (Philadelphia: Carey & Hart, 1837);

The Life of Thomas Jefferson, 2 volumes (Philadelphia: Carey, Lea & Blanchard, 1837);

The Theory of Money and Banks Investigated (Boston: Little, Brown, 1839);

Progress of the United States in Population and Wealth in Fifty Years (New York: Hunt's Merchants' Magazine/ Boston: Little, Brown, 1843);

The History of the United States, from Their Colonization to the End of the Twenty-sixth Congress in 1841, 4 volumes (Philadelphia: Lippincott, 1856-1857);

Political Economy for the People (Philadelphia: Sherman, 1859).

References:

Joseph Dorfman, *The Economic Mind in American Civilization* (New York: Viking, 1946), pp. 539-551;

Robert Colin McLean, *George Tucker* (Chapel Hill: University of North Carolina Press, 1961).

Archives:

Material on George Tucker can be found at the University of Virginia Library and at Colonial Williamsburg.

Frank Arthur Vanderlip

(November 17, 1864-June 29, 1937)

by Larry Schweikart

University of Dayton

CAREER: Reporter (1889-1890), financial editor, *Chicago Tribune* (1890-1894); associate editor, *Economist* (1895-1897); private secretary to the U.S. secretary of the treasury (March-June 1897); assistant secretary of the treasury (June 1897-1901); vice-president (1901-1909), president, National City Bank (1909-1919); chairman, American International Corporation (1916-1919).

Powerful New York financier and banking reformer Frank Arthur Vanderlip, president of National City Bank (now Citibank), was born in Aurora, Illinois, on November 17, 1864. His relatives came to America from Holland in 1756 and settled in Pennsylvania. His father, Charles Vanderlip, who traveled west from Ohio and found work first as a blacksmith and then as a farmer, died when his son was young. His mother, Charlotte Woodworth Vanderlip, had no means of running the farm or otherwise supporting the family. His younger brother died of tuberculosis about that time, and his mother decided to sell the farm. She took Vanderlip and his younger sister to live with her mother in 1880, and Vanderlip assumed the role of head of the family, taking a job as a machine shop apprentice at $4 an hour. Young Vanderlip had obtained a public education in Aurora and demonstrated a facility with numbers. He went on to study at the University of Illinois and at the University of Chicago.

Vanderlip's early interests included stenography, and he worked in insurance for Moses Scudder at the Investors' Agency and at W. T. Baker & Company in Chicago before he got a job as a reporter for the *Chicago Tribune*. Scudder, Vanderlip recounted in his autobiography, gave him his first look at success, and the young stenographer admired his employer. In the course of his work he studied mortgages and learned about property values. He also had to make reports for the in-

Frank Arthur Vanderlip (courtesy of Citibank)

surance companies, which gave him an elementary background as a reporter. He met Joseph French Johnson, who became financial editor of the *Tribune* in 1889. Vanderlip's interest in financial affairs led Johnson to name him his successor in 1890. Word of Vanderlip's abilities spread, and soon the paper had a reputation for publishing one of the finest financial pages in the region. As a reporter Vanderlip demonstrated an ability to ferret out information, in one case purchasing stock in order to attend stockholders' meetings where, with his stenographer's memory, he mentally recorded the facts and figures presented. Impressed with Vanderlip's analysis of economic affairs, another Chicago paper, the financial weekly the *Economist*, offered him the position of associate editor, and Vanderlip resigned from the *Tribune* in 1894. By that time the young Chicagoan had made a name for himself in financial circles, and he was in demand not only as a writer but as a lecturer at colleges and universities.

In 1897 Vanderlip resigned his job at the *Economist* to serve as private secretary to Secretary of the Treasury Lyman Gage. That position lasted only from March to June, for on June 1 President William McKinley appointed Vanderlip assistant secretary of the treasury. He inherited considerable authority in his new position, especially in matters of personnel, then later in the financial bureaus, which imbued him with valuable experience in money matters. He met "thousands of bankers," contacts that stood him in good stead when he later solicited correspondent accounts for National City Bank. As assistant secretary he directed the first loan in the Spanish-American War of $200,000, a feat he later called "the most intensive clerical undertaking in which the government had ever engaged over a similar length of time." He also made several reforms in the Bureau of Printing and Engraving and improved operations at the mints in Philadelphia and New Orleans. He made key appointments both at the Bureau of Standards and the Secret Service.

Vanderlip left government service in 1901, when National City Bank, on Gage's recommendation, named him to replace another influential banking figure, A. Barton Hepburn, as vice-president. Gage had important ties to National City. Since 1899 Gage had used Treasury deposits at the bank to regulate partially the money market, purchasing government securities on the open market, prepaying the interest on the government debt, and permitting internal revenue funds to accumulate outside the Treasury as deposits in national banks. He also had designated National City to receive tax revenues and distribute them to other depositories, because, in Gage's view, it was the only bank that had a volume of securities adequate to cover daily transactions pledged for deposits. The bank's president, James Stillman, noted with approval Vanderlip's handling of the Spanish-American War bond issue, and he even arranged for Vanderlip to take an extended trip on the company's behalf before he came to the bank, to visit overseas financial centers and solidify contacts with finance ministers and important foreign borrowers. That trip gave Vanderlip valuable foreign contacts. He observed bank-

ing practices in Europe firsthand and attended the international conference of commerce and industry at Ostend, Belgium. Upon his return he produced a 1902 paper entitled the "American Commercial Invasion of Europe," which contended that Europe offered great possibilities for American investment and credit and that the U.S. empire could penetrate European markets.

Stillman singled out the young vice-president for still other special treatment by extending Vanderlip invitations to attend meetings of the board of directors. At first he had not much else to do. On his first day in the new position he took a desk "in a very good location in the parlors of the bank and possessing a pleasant outlook on Wall Street." But the bank assigned him no duties. "Here he was," one journalist wrote, "a high-salaried officer, a part of one of the smoothest-running machines in existence, but with no apparent obligation to make this machine go." All Vanderlip had to do was be Stillman's idea man.

Vanderlip soon found ways to expand the bank's business. His position at the Treasury had generated contacts with independent bankers across the country, and now he sought their accounts. He instituted an advertising campaign emphasizing bond trading. The bank created a special wire network to receive correspondents' orders and published, beginning in 1904, a monthly newsletter which furnished "detailed information regarding any issue of bonds in which a correspondent bank may be interested."

The bank dealt primarily in U.S. government securities, and, because the National Bank Act required all national banks to hold those bonds as collateral, National City found a steady market, both in buying and selling. The bank assured its correspondents that it could handle all the securities they wanted to purchase or sell. More likely at Stillman's suggestion than Vanderlip's, the bank also acquired controlling interest in a Washington, D.C., bank, Riggs National (the descendant of the firm of Riggs and Corcoran, which financed the Mexican War). National City utilized that Washington bank as a subsidiary—almost a "branch"—to facilitate the issue and retirement of national bank notes by correspondent banks, a task easily performed by Riggs National due to its location across the street from the U.S. Treasury building. The bank also offered foreign-currency exchange to correspondents, who previously had to pay commission merchants. The system allowed domestic correspondents to draw directly on National City's foreign correspondents.

Although Vanderlip was hardly a pioneer, those innovations took root in the American banking system largely due to his energy and careful cultivation. National City's U.S. correspondents more than doubled in three years, to 1,230 in 1905. More important than correspondents (competitors such as Chase and Hanover had more) were deposits, and by 1905 National City's interbank deposits constituted almost 20 percent of the bank's total deposit base.

On January 12, 1909, the National City board of directors elected Vanderlip president to replace Stillman, who took the newly created position of chairman of the board. Stillman had engineered the entire process from his home in Paris and did not even attend the election meeting. He had groomed Vanderlip as his protégé for several years and, once he handed over the reins of power, delegated most of the operational authority of the bank to the new president. The chairman, however, was still the bank's major stockholder and had a veto over policy decisions; as Harold Van B. Cleveland and Thomas F. Huertas put it, "Vanderlip proposed and Stillman disposed."

Stillman perceived that the days of individual deal making had begun to wane. Even the great J. P. Morgan had seen his resources extended in the Panic of 1907, and few bankers thought that a single financial house would have the ability to support the nation's economy in the future. Correspondent relationships had grown more important than ever, and both Stillman and Vanderlip knew they needed to restructure the bank's relationships for it to remain competitive in the modern business climate.

National City had rescued many of the customers of the investment firm of Kuhn, Loeb in the Panic of 1907, giving that house enough short-term credit to allow it to market its bonds at a reasonable price. Kuhn, Loeb remembered National City's generosity. In 1909 Vanderlip faced his first significant management test when J. Ogden Armour, the famous meat baron and a regular customer of the bank since 1897, requested that the bank underwrite a $50 million bond issue to finance the Armour meat-packing plants in the United States and foreign countries. The request exceeded the bank's resources, so Vanderlip turned to Kuhn, Loeb to mar-

ket the bond deal jointly. He expressed to Stillman a concern that he would be "eaten alive" at Kuhn, Loeb. Instead, he could cheerily report to Stillman after the deal was consummated that "I have succeeded in getting absolutely everything that I thought the bank was entitled to . . . and have gotten it with absolute good nature and friendliness throughout all discussions." While negotiating the Armour deal Vanderlip also persuaded Kuhn, Loeb to accept a joint venture on the "Farmers Loan [and Trust Co.]," although that was one of the particularly difficult things to do." Vanderlip took exceptional pleasure in working out the new arrangement, which he thought put National City "on all fours" with Kuhn, Loeb. The new working arrangement served as the standard by which the two banks assessed future profits and fees in their joint underwriting ventures.

Vanderlip, however, did not content himself with an exclusive relationship to Kuhn, Loeb. That had characterized the old arrangement–Stillman's arrangement–and did not serve the bank's changing needs. He cultivated a link to the syndicate of J. P. Morgan, still the nation's leading bank. Stillman had joined the Morgan-led syndicate in financing the reorganization of the Northern Pacific Railroad in the 1890s, and in 1896 one of Morgan's partners, Robert Bacon, joined the bank's board of directors, holding a seat until 1903. George W. Perkins, another Morgan partner, also held a seat in the first decade of the new century. The relationship grew after National City regularly participated in the originating group of the Morgan companies after the Panic of 1907. That meant that the bank obtained securities on the same terms as Morgan, earned a larger spread than sellers, and received some of the sales as deposits until the borrower decided to use them. Morgan, First National Bank, and National City formed an alliance under which the house originating the underwriting received 50 percent of the issue, and the other two banks received 25 percent. But working with companies as different and as occasionally antagonistic as Morgan and Kuhn, Loeb required Vanderlip to display "some acrobatic ability." Nevertheless, in 1914 Vanderlip reported the bank was "at peace with everybody, we do business with everybody."

In addition to the alliances it had cemented with Kuhn, Loeb and Morgan, National City began to participate with smaller banks in investment syndicates involving electric and gas utilities (areas Morgan and other large houses thought too risky). The bank gave particularly extensive support to Pacific Gas and Electric, a company Stillman had helped organize in 1906.

Vanderlip had achieved such success in the investment field that William Rockefeller suggested that he develop a retail distribution network for securities. National City's correspondents had started to buy securities as secondary reserves and resell them to their own customers. The bond sales campaigns were successful, and the bank developed a full-time securities sales force. The bank's ability to place bond issues increased commensurately. The bank also had to locate new customers to issue the securities. Vanderlip saw a natural outlet in the newly developing large corporations of the time, and he won their business by offering them credit lines and favorable deposit facilities. He established programs across the country to develop the new corporate customer base. By 1914 the bank had added such important corporations to its customer list as Morris & Company (meat packing), American Sugar Refining, the Joseph Schlitz Brewing Company, the American Tobacco Company, the American Cigar Company, the U.S. Rubber Company, Firestone Rubber Company, American Brass, General Electric, Western Electric, U.S. Cast Iron Pipe & Foundry, International Harvester, W. R. Grace, American Telephone & Telegraph, Pullman Company, Westinghouse Air Brake, Lackawanna Steel, Central Leather, Endicott-Johnson, New York Edison, Consolidated Gas, Ford Motor, Detroit Cadillac Motor, Packard Motor, and Peerless Motor, not to mention Standard Oil and 11 of the top 26 railroad firms, including the top four.

Those accounts gave National City important advantages over its competitors. It was already the nation's largest bank (a position it would retain until the 1980s, when Bank of America edged ahead for a short time) and had emerged as a powerful investment bank. Thanks to the bank's unique joint alliance with both Morgan and Kuhn, Loeb, it had access to issues that only one of the other houses independently enjoyed, and as a result participated in more issues than either Morgan or Kuhn, Loeb. National City took advantage of the Panic of 1907 to lend to other banks, and in the process made itself the largest lender to business among all New York institutions. The bank's earnings reached $7 million in 1911, with bond underwriting and trad-

ing accounting for almost half of the bank's gross income.

Vanderlip expressed concern, though, about the bank's ability to maintain the commercial side of the business and its tendency to rely too heavily on bond activity. State banks, which faced fewer restrictions, had made inroads into the business of all the national banks. State-chartered banks could, if laws permitted, open branch offices; National City could not. State banks also had lower reserve requirements, which allowed them to offer more services at a higher rate of interest than National City. Trust companies, which frequently merged with state banks, had trust powers and services, and Vanderlip's institution lacked those powers. Vanderlip saw a need for an expansion of the powers of national banks. When he told Stillman that "something radical is going to be necessary in order to meet the banking competition that we are facing," he made it clear that his support for banking reform came not from concern for the public or the financial community as a whole, but from his anxiety over threats to National City's market position.

By that time Vanderlip was in his prime. A large-featured man with sad eyes, white hair, a prominent cleft chin, and a robust mustache, he had a dignified yet sympathetic look. With his glasses on he slightly resembled Theodore Roosevelt. On May 19, 1903, he had married Narcissa Cox, and they had five children, Narcissa, Charlotte, Frank, Virginia, and Kelvin. They made their home in Scarborough, New York. Although frequently honored in his life (Vanderlip received honorary degrees from Illinois, Colgate, Princeton, and Brown; was decorated with the Chevalier Legion of Honor by the French, the Order of Danilo I by the Montenegrans, and the Order of George I by the Greeks; and was made a commander in the Belgian Order of Leopold), Vanderlip saw himself as coming from simple roots.

Few individuals combined so many necessary qualities for promoting banking reform as Frank Vanderlip. He knew Washington from his Treasury days, had read widely on economics, and headed the largest bank in the nation. Even before he became president of National City he had displayed reformist concerns. While still vice-president he developed the positions for strong central banking he later championed.

Petrograd, Russia, branch of National City Bank, 1917 (courtesy of Citibank)

Only a handful of bankers appreciated the depth and breadth of the change that had occurred in banking during the great period of American industrialization and consolidation. In 1905 Vanderlip wrote that "the banking tendency of recent years has resulted in increasing rapidly the number of banks that do not find in their own community a sufficient borrowing demand at all seasons," a condition resulting from the nation's increased wealth, the emergence of large corporations that no longer turned to local banks for financing, and the rise in bank deposits. He also understood that the extension of bank credit against the collateral of securities marked another point in the evolution of banking services. George F. Baker, president of New York's First National Bank, complained to Vanderlip that the city's banks had gotten away from "old time banking" and that "the method of doing business had changed." Vanderlip already knew that and welcomed the change. Finally, he saw that the numbers of banks in the system had declined relative to the total number of financial institutions and especially took note of the expansion of trust companies. In a 1902 speech to the Northeastern Bankers Association, reprinted in *Bankers Magazine* as "The Expansion of Credit in the United States," he noted that in the three previous years "the movement to aggregate industrial establishments into single great corporate units, and to con-

vert the evidence of ownership into corporate securities" had inaugurated a new epoch in American banking. Deposits in national banks had grown from $3.26 billion in 1899 to $4.5 billion in 1902, while legal reserves had declined due to the conversion of fixed property into corporate securities. Those in turn had provided the basis for the expansion of bank deposits. The corporations then turned the bank credit into "improvement, betterment, and extension" of plant capacity–"a fixed form of investment." But, he warned, in that form it could not be returned to a "liquid fund of capital," except through increased earnings, until it had been completely depreciated. The assets, then, were not "self-liquidating" and did not conform to the "real bills" doctrine. Negotiable securities representing claims on fixed capital represented "a loaning of bank credit for conversion into a fixed form of property."

Vanderlip's wish to reshape the banking system by establishing a central bank was a reaction to the tremendous responsibility National City had assumed in previous panics by providing money, a responsibility from which he wanted to free his bank. Vanderlip saw reform as a way to unshackle the national banks from unnecessary limits on their powers, which restrained their ability to compete. His position was not altruistic; it embodied defensive concerns similar to those that had encouraged the railroaders to form pools. But he did see gold in "them thar hills": if a central bank was formed "at which we can rediscount commercial paper, making commercial paper a liquid asset, then we will have no necessity for devoting a large amount of our funds to call loans on stock exchange collateral, and can divert the funds now used for that purpose to commercial loans."

In 1901 Rep. Charles N. Fowler of New Jersey, chairman of the House Banking and Currency Committee, drafted a reform bill that proposed to allow national banks to increase currency elasticity by issuing notes without first investing in government bonds and depositing them with the comptroller. The bill also permitted excess U.S. moneys to be placed in national banks that deposited bonds with the government for security. Finally, Fowler's bill sought to centralize control over bank reserves and make interest rates uniform by including branch banking and branch clearinghouse associations.

When the Fowler bill failed, Sen. Nelson W. Aldrich "assumed the leadership of the search party" for an elastic currency. By that time bankers were regularly meeting with the comptroller of the currency, William B. Ridgely, and with each other to seek "quasi-legal methods of stabilization." In 1903 Morgan, Baker, Stillman, and Vanderlip held a meeting with the comptroller to reduce the volume of "long-distance loaning" by country banks in the New York market. Within a short time the secretary of the treasury started to stretch the definition of acceptable securities to allow greater elasticity.

So, even before that old demon "inelasticity" raised its head again in the Panic of 1907, the banking community had set itself on the road to reform. According to James Livingston, the event that spurred decisive action was Jacob Schiff's 1906 speech denouncing the existing system to the New York Chamber of Commerce. Schiff recommended that the Finance Committee of the Chamber investigate the problem of currency elasticity, and from then on the issue lay at the center of the reformers' efforts. Interestingly, the Finance Committee's report was judged to be totally unsatisfactory: Stillman remarked that it showed Wall Street was far denser about money and finance than anyone had suspected. Stillman suggested the Chamber appoint a five-man commission to study the system and suggest reforms. The committee, made up of Vanderlip, Isador Straus, Dumont Clarke, Charles A. Co-

nant, and John Claflin, began its deliberations in March 1906, and it quickly dispatched Conant to Europe to examine European central banks. He returned in June, and the committee drafted its report, which it presented to the Chamber on October 4. In the report the committee emphasized the danger of inflation as much as inelasticity and observed that the lack of coordination of the capital market made it difficult to check expansion of the money supply. The committee concluded that only a central bank could solve those problems.

Selling the concept of a central bank to other businessmen, let alone the rest of the nation, required considerable skill, and Vanderlip was the natural committee member to fulfill the task. He undertook a writing campaign to the currency committees of the New York Produce Exchange and the Manufacturer's Association of New York, "centering public attention," as he put it, on the money and currency issue. The American Bankers Association (ABA) also debated the concept of a central bank but rejected it. However, the ABA decided to continue to study the matter with a commission of its own, and that group met in November with the Chamber's representatives, Vanderlip and Conant. Vanderlip said the meetings resulted in "complete and harmonious" agreement, and their joint proposals contributed to the ABA's plan for currency reform, which scarcely differed from the Chamber's. Both plans proposed ways to create emergency currency for purposes of "elasticity," and both accepted an "assets" currency. Vanderlip, Conant, and James Forgan, of Chicago's First National Bank, all agreed that the critical plank in both plans called for prompt redemption in lawful money. Redemption required adequate reserves against both bank notes and deposits as well as adequate facilities. As long as national bank notes were not considered reserves, the system would prevent inflation. Vanderlip saw a problem with the increasing number of state banks, and in 1907 admitted that the possibility that those banks "might count [national bank] notes in their reserves" left doubt about the creation of enough redemption points to drive in the "redundant circulation."

Those fears led Paul Warburg of Kuhn, Loeb to hammer on the solution proposed earlier as a safeguard against such problems: a national bank. His 1907 arguments impressed Vanderlip enough that he sent copies to bank reformers in the Midwest. By December 1907, thanks to the panic crisis, which had begun in October, Vanderlip could report growing sentiment in favor of a national bank. Indeed, even a month before the panic he had observed that "the subject is [only] technical" and needed no more debate—his polite way of saying that the politicians should leave it to the bankers.

Continuing to support reform publicly in whatever way he could, Vanderlip participated in a January 1908 symposium sponsored by the American Association for the Advancement of Science. He called the Panic of 1907 "one of the great calamities of history" and contended that the trouble lay in the decentralized system, in which each bank "stands alone, concerned first with its own safety." The banking systems of other countries had solved the problems facing the United States with elastic currency that could be quickly mobilized, and centralized reserves. Vanderlip went on to criticize the tendency of Americans to "look alike upon banking panics and crop failures as dispensations of an inscrutable Providence." In Progressive fashion he appealed to science as a guide to reform.

From late 1907 to 1908 a congressional committee on banking chaired by Senator Aldrich held private conferences with several bankers, including Vanderlip. The reform bill introduced by the committee in February 1908 provided for an emergency currency: national banks would be permitted to issue such currency if it was secured by bond deposits. The bill also required 15 percent reserve in lawful money as a method of controlling the volume of money loaned on call in New York by those banks. Aldrich also added a section proposing the appointment of a National Monetary Commission, to "keep the financial issue out of politics" just as Vanderlip had urged. Eventually, congressional debate centered on which securities should constitute the backing for the emergency currency, and Edward Vreeland of New York offered a compromise designating commercial paper. The Aldrich-Vreeland Act passed both houses in 1908. But it was a stopgap measure, and everyone awaited the proposals of the National Monetary Commission.

The National Monetary Commission, again chaired by Aldrich, called upon financial leaders such as Vanderlip, Warburg, Henry P. Davison of J. P. Morgan and Company, Benjamin Strong of Bankers' Trust Company (who was destined to head the New York Federal Reserve Board), A. Barton Hepburn of Chase, and Charles C. Homer to testify on the state of American finance. The group advocated reform in the direction of central banking along the model of the Bank of England and the German Reichsbank, and the commission spent four months in Europe learning about those and other systems. Vanderlip continued as one of the inner circle of banking experts regularly consulted by Aldrich and the commission.

Aldrich needed details, and he needed bankers to fill them in for him. In November 1910, at the suggestion of Davison, a secret meeting took place on Jekyll Island, Georgia. The secrecy was so complete that particulars of the meeting remained undisclosed until Aldrich's autobiography appeared in 1935. Along with Vanderlip, Warburg, and Aldrich, two of the National Monetary Commission's European inquiry group, Davison and Abram Piatt Andrew, a Harvard professor, attended. They met for weeks and emerged with a plan that fully outlined the bank proposal. Aldrich presented the document to Congress on January 16, 1911. It called for the creation of a national reserve association to hold the reserves of commercial banks, issue bank notes, and rediscount bank paper. More important (from Vanderlip's point of view), it expanded and liberalized the powers of national banks. The big New York banks supported the plan and even launched a publicity campaign on its behalf, which may have doomed it from the outset. The advertising blitz, combined with renewed economic growth, dampened enthusiasm for centralization. The public came to believe that supporting the commission proposal would put more power in the hands of New York bankers than they already possessed. The suspicion against the New York "money power" remained especially strong in rural areas. In 1909 *Banking Law Journal* had mailed out a letter to all national and state banks and trust companies with the question, "Do you favor a central bank if not controlled by 'Wall Street' or any Monopolistic Interest?" Nearly 60 percent of the replies favored a central bank of some type. But among western or country bankers a common sentiment reverberated: "There is no way," wrote a Minnesota banker, "to keep a central bank free from Wall St. . . . a central bank means concentrating wealth at the expense of the small banks."

Apparently defeated in his quest for revision of the national bank system, Vanderlip, like other big bankers, determined to create a subsidiary not subject to the existing regulations. He had good reason to think that the federal government would approve an application for a corporate affiliate to institutionalize the investments that National City's owners had made in smaller banks and trust companies over the years. Vanderlip announced his intention to the stockholders in June 1911. Using as a model George F. Baker's First National Bank's affiliate, First Security Company, Vanderlip proposed an institution in which the shareholders of the affiliate vested their ownership in trustees who served concurrently as officers of the bank. The trustees would elect the affiliate's board of directors. In July 1911 National City Company was incorporated under New York laws, with Vanderlip, Stillman, and Stephen Palmer, a bank director, as the trustees. The new company had a capital of $10 million, making it the largest bank affiliate in the country. It also became a huge holding company, acquiring the stock holdings of Stillman and others. National City Company also held shares in seven New York banks, which the bank operated as if they were branches, granting them overdraft allowances, collecting their out-of-town checks, and giving them access to the loan packages the bank administered. The bank's venture into a quasi-interstate branch-bank arrangement marked a departure from traditional practice and anticipated the development of large-scale branch banking.

National City's move into holding companies further inflamed suspicions of the public. Rep. Charles A. Lindbergh, Sr., father of the aviator, suspected that the Aldrich Plan, as the commission's reform program came to be known, merely constituted a means to institutionalize the "money trust." Many Americans thought that Wall Street banks conspired to manipulate interest rates or the supply of money. As Vincent P. Carosso has noted, "suspicion and fear of the moneyed interests had been a constant since the earliest days of the republic." At the time, Harvard University economist Charles Bullock contended that Morgan and John D. Rockefeller in effect controlled the nation's economy, and muckraker Lincoln Steffens called Morgan "the boss of the United States." In that atmosphere, and with the Aldrich Plan seemingly stalled, the House Banking and Currency Committee established an investigatory subcommittee in February 1912.

Even before the House investigation began, National City had received notice that the attorney general (apparently on his own authority) planned to investigate the bank. The investigation concluded that National City's acquisition of the other national banks constituted a violation of the National Banking Act. The secretary of the treasury, however, disagreed. Facing a public battle between his treasury secretary and his attorney general, President William Howard Taft chose to decide the case himself. The president feared that a decision in favor of National City might imply a lack of executive department support for congressional action on the National Monetary Commission plan. Luckily, Taft in the end did not have to decide. Vanderlip wisely unloaded the domestic-bank stock by November 1911.

The House subcommittee, chaired by Rep. Arsène P. Pujo of Louisiana, began its investigation in an atmosphere of hostility to the national banks. Although J. P. Morgan delivered a powerful defense of investment banking and an emphatic rebuttal of the "money trust" notion during the hearings, the committee succeeded in exposing the concentration of banking power in New York, Boston, and Chicago. Stillman's name came up several times, but Vanderlip remained in the shadows, preparing for the inevitable reform. The change from Republican to Democratic control of the executive branch in 1912 temporarily stalled developments, as partisanship demanded at least a cosmetic change in the character of the reform. The bill introduced by Rep. Carter Glass of Virginia and presented to President Woodrow Wilson in December 1912 was much like the Aldrich plan. The proposal still featured a centralized system, but the centralization would be accomplished through the establishment of several independent reserve banks. Wilson clearly favored a central bank but admitted it would not pass political muster. To mollify country bankers the independent reserve banks were to be scattered across the country. To maintain federal control over the system—something the government had sought since the times of Andrew Jackson—several political appointees were to stock the organization's policy board.

Vanderlip disliked the notion of decentralizing the reserve banks. He saw decentralization as one of the shortcomings of the system as it existed and argued that the "most important thing that legislation can accomplish is to relate all these reserves to one another by placing [them] in a common reservoir." He also deplored the political control of the Glass bill: any board "subject to the vicissitudes of political pressure and party trading in its make-up, will fail to assume successfully [central bank responsibilities]." Vanderlip wanted experienced financial men, not political cronies, to handle the complex issues of central banking. The Glass bill threatened to remove control of the credit system "from the active responsibility of bank management." Vanderlip should have known that the history of American banking recorded many instances in which the centralization of financial power, even in state hands, led to abuse and, ultimately, destabilization of the money supply. Despite an energetic campaign for a banker-merged system, Vanderlip's bank, which in the public mind seemed to be "the very fangs and claws of the 'Money Trust,'" could not overcome the forces that sought to put the banking system under the control of the federal government. The Glass bill passed as the Federal Reserve Act in September 1913.

Vanderlip had continued to try to convince the politicians of the need for financial-community management of the central bank. In July 1913 he argued, "the fundamental objection to the [Glass] plan is the character of the control which is provided." He objected "not to the powers granted but to the hands in which they are placed." An administrator based in Washington with the Cabinet members looking over his shoulder promised to "very rapidly lose the power to direct wisely." But while Vanderlip wanted the governing body "in close, active, working touch with the everyday problems, conditions and atmosphere of the financial world," he certainly never intended it to get too close to the country banks. Wall Street should decide, he thought, and Main Street should accept, because local bankers lacked the sophistication to deal with complex financial arrangements. In July Glass had promised to recast the system so that the Cabinet would have less influence on its operations, and they also added an advisory council made up of delegates from the reserve banks.

Vanderlip took further encouragement when members of the Senate Banking and Currency Committee requested that he draw up a compromise plan. He suggested that the president appoint seven Federal Reserve Board members, who then would appoint the other officials of the Federal Reserve. Vanderlip also envisioned public ownership of the common stock of the Reserve Bank. The plan met with significant public and legislative support. Glass, however, saw it as an attempt to circumvent his own bill and persuaded Wilson to reject Vanderlip's proposal. The president refused even to meet with the banker. Wilson's reply to Vanderlip's

request for a meeting was curt: "It would be quite useless for me to discuss it [your plan] with you." Vanderlip responded in a heated debate with Glass at the Economic Club of New York in November 1913. He tried to portray himself as a man of the people, pointing out that he had risen from poverty and had worn "the blue overalls of a farm hand and a machine shop apprentice." He touched a raw nerve when he criticized those who "started in the most humble surroundings and remained there."

What had given Glass much of the ammunition to defeat Vanderlip was the fact that many bankers, including Hepburn and Warburg, had parted company with Vanderlip on the issue of political control. Warburg even helped guide the Glass bill through Congress. Glass enjoyed pointing out that the bankers had displayed disunity.

The Federal Reserve Act changed the way National City did business in two ways. Country-bank deposits held by New York banks, which previously counted toward their reserves, were no longer counted as such. Country banks now had an incentive to withdraw their deposits from New York banks. Also, the system's clearing and collecting services offered at no cost what National City and other banks had up to that time earned fees for providing. As Vanderlip saw it, those changes only encouraged the larger city banks to compete with the country banks, which previously had provided their correspondent and customer base. He predicted that the large banks "will become competitors for business in a much wider circle." The system offered some compensation: it permitted the national banks to open overseas branches; lowered the reserve requirements on demand deposits by 7 percent; and allowed member banks to discount commercial paper with the Federal Reserve, thus enhancing the banks' ability to make commercial loans. Congress also avoided legislating against investment banking, which had formed the crux of the Pujo committee's criticisms.

Still, Vanderlip, once in the vanguard of investment banking for the major corporations, began to see the value of cultivating the accounts of smaller firms. "I welcome the growth in number of accounts. I know it means more work, more officers," he noted, but "in the end it is safer for a bank to have this foundation of a great number of medium-sized growing accounts." He dispatched officers to drum up new business and encouraged them to sign up all healthy firms. Between September 1912 and July 1916 National City added 2,050 corporate accounts. To go along with the aggressive marketing campaigns, the bank also experienced an increase in loan demand when war broke out in Europe. During the first three years of war National City tripled its commercial loans to $213 million, or 29 percent of its total assets. Vanderlip took some satisfaction in the fact that the Federal Reserve Act "has made the City Bank far more a national bank than ever before." While the framers had meant the act "to curb the great New York banks in their growth . . . it has given them the broadest opportunities for development."

Other avenues for expanding the bank's customer base presented themselves in the new system. Opportunities existed for overseas branches, most notably in those countries where the bank's corporate customers had manufacturing plants or distribution facilities. James A. Farrell, president of U.S. Steel, not only approved of the idea of overseas branches for National City but he encouraged it by promising to give the bank access to its credit files on foreign customers if it established foreign branches. Several companies with Latin American connections wanted branches in that part of the world: Du Pont, W. R. Grace and Company, International Harvester, Armour and Company, and Standard Oil. But Stillman discouraged Vanderlip from foreign branching, even though Stillman had invested in the Cuban Banco de Habana in 1905. Some of Stillman's criticisms of overseas trade had merit. Language, custom, and government all stood as barriers to easy entry and reliable trade. Vanderlip thought the growth potential of the foreign markets outweighed those concerns, and a year after the Federal Reserve Act permitted it, he insisted on a "modest trial of South American banking." He persuaded Stillman with the argument that National City needed to be "first in the field" or "some other bank will." The bank's first foreign branch (and the first American foreign bank) opened in Buenos Aires on November 10, 1914.

Historians have tended to view Vanderlip's foray into South America with a certain cynicism. But, as historians Cleveland and Huertas note, Vanderlip looked at the venture strictly as a way to satisfy American corporate customers and to attract new domestic business. He was under no false illusions about the ability of poverty-level developing republics to repay loans. The Argentine branch performed well at the time. It "virtually eliminated

competition from German and British banks" and by 1917 had become Argentina's ninth largest bank, with 1.8 percent of total Argentinean deposits, a ratio approximately equal to National City's share of deposits in the United States. Of course, much of the competition had folded when the war erupted. Other National City branches, in Rio de Janeiro, Santos, São Paulo, Montevideo, Havana, Bahia, Santiago, and Valparaiso, soon followed. Under Vanderlip's tenure the bank set up college training courses to prepare employees for overseas work.

With Latin America firmly added to the bank's service area, Vanderlip turned his attention to the Far East. There an American corporation operating under a special charter from the Connecticut legislature, the International Banking Corporation, had branches in Manila, Singapore, and Shanghai, as well as in London. Vanderlip had wanted to acquire that company as early as 1909, and in 1915 he succeeded. He noted, "We have got it at a time when it has really gotten pretty well on its feet."

By 1916 National City had become a truly international bank, integrating overseas branch banking, trade finance for domestic corporations, banking for foreign correspondents, and foreign exchange trading. At the same time Vanderlip moved the focus of the bank toward corporate business. Between 1914 and 1917 the bank's assets increased by more than $600 million, at an annual rate of 34 percent. Profits grew at an astounding rate, by 65 percent, shooting upward from $5.1 million in 1914 to $8.4 million in 1917.

Vanderlip had also engineered the bank's foray into investment banking, and the bond department consistently remitted large profits. The growing bond market included investors of average means from across the nation. N. W. Halsey, among other firms, retained securities among those new buyers and also developed relationships with cities and utilities that traditional bond brokers ignored. By tapping into that large sector, houses such as Halsey presented tremendous opportunities for growth. Vanderlip had expressed interest in acquiring Halsey as early as 1913, but National City failed to complete the acquisition. So Stillman and Vanderlip increased National City's own underwriting business. Lending to foreigners was difficult because of America's neutral status in the war, but the French succeeded in convincing Vanderlip to lend them $10 million in 1914. Although Secretary of State William Jennings Bryan had stated that such loans were "inconsistent" with neutrality, Vanderlip pushed ahead, granting the loan at about double the call rate, subject to approval of the State Department. Only then did he notify Bryan, but the proposal was worded so as to make the loan appear as bank "credit." Bryan, and later Wilson, approved the loan, satisfied that it was not actually a loan.

A flood of war borrowing ensued. By 1917 foreign governments had received $2.5 billion from American investors. Vanderlip continued his drive to expand the bank's distribution and underwriting capabilities, and when the Halsey company came on the market in 1916, National City snapped it up.

The acquisition of Halsey marked the culmination of Vanderlip's strategy for reshaping the bank. By searching out customers in niches Morgan and Kuhn, Loeb would not explore, National City emerged as a stronger institution. Its contacts with correspondent banks and its underwriting potential gave it important advantages over Chase and First National. Vanderlip remained the driving force. As Cleveland and Huertas observe, even though each new activity developed out of existing functions, "Vanderlip's strategic thinking was critical." Stillman "in his declining years was the balance wheel . . . [but] Vanderlip supplied the drive, the imagination, the vision of what National City could be: an all-purpose, worldwide financial intermediary."

Vanderlip noted in his autobiography, "it was high time I took some steps to secure my own fortune." He tried to obtain a major stock issue in the bank. That proved difficult, as the six largest stockholders held a majority of the stock. He requested from Stillman an option on his stock as well as a huge loan with which to acquire other stock, which would give him a substantial stake in the bank. Stillman refused to sell and declined Vanderlip's loan request as well. He made Vanderlip a counter offer of substantially fewer shares. Morgan provided the loan to acquire another block of stock, but Vanderlip still came far short of what he desired.

Vanderlip's disappointment over the stock maneuvers coincided with the war bonanza, and he created a new business, American International Corporation, to purchase European holdings in the buyer's market. Stillman did not want the bank involved in the new company. He saw that Vanderlip was seeking to gain outside the bank what was denied him inside: control and recognition. Vanderlip proceeded to set up the new company, without Stillman's blessing, in 1916. He offered the bank's stockholders the right to subscribe to the new firm's common stock. American International's board of directors contained many of the bank's board members. Vanderlip retained a large class of managerial securities and served as chairman. The company had a deliberately vague charter, which gave it wide financial berth, and it soon expanded worldwide.

American International required much of Vanderlip's attention and energy, forcing him to divide time between it and the bank. He offered to step up to the position of vice-chairman of the bank, relinquishing the presidency. Stillman, who had been insulted by Vanderlip's request for more control in National City, grew increasingly concerned about the bank's management. A new president would still have to report to Vanderlip, making him more an administrative assistant to Vanderlip than a company leader. And Stillman worried about the surge of competition from the Europeans destined to follow the war's end. He put Vanderlip off for a time, then in 1916 met with the president to work out the details. Vanderlip quickly learned that finding a capable replacement would be difficult, so he and Stillman agreed to set up an executive board to handle administrative duties. The system, borrowed from British banks, never worked as planned. Vanderlip held on to the actual operating authority, and the board had no real decision-making powers. Vanderlip remained divided in his loyalties between the bank and the American International Corporation.

Vanderlip also began to decentralize the bank along regional lines. That increased the necessity for a firmer hand at the top. And his attention continued to wander. In 1917 he jumped at the opportunity to head the Liberty Loan campaign for the Federal Reserve Bank of New York. The job put Vanderlip back in the spotlight—something he had missed since his days as reformer of the banking system. As head of the Liberty Loan campaign, he brought lower-income individuals into the war finance effort through a thrift-stamp savings program. It worked so well that Vanderlip contemplated other thrift programs based on "loose change in the pockets of people," including lotteries. He enjoyed the new task so much and performed it so well that the secretary of the treasury asked him to chair the War Savings Committee, and he accepted, taking a leave of absence from the bank.

Just before Vanderlip assumed his new duties in Washington, he had set in motion at National City a program designed to penetrate the Russian market. His timing could not have been worse. Vanderlip had long sought a Russian opening. The bank had important customers who desired banking services in Russia to support their field operations. National City had underwritten some bonds for the Russian government and had served as a depository for funds so the czarist regime could purchase war materiel. Vanderlip, in rather mercenary fashion, saw the war as a chance to dot the country with National City branches, ahead of the bank's German competitors. He sent two vice-presidents to negotiate a bond issue with the Russian government in 1916, and at first all seemed well. The vice-presidents made preparations for a branch in Petrograd (Leningrad), and Vanderlip exuded such confidence that he requested permission from the Federal Reserve Board to open 11 branches in Russia or its dominions.

The National City branch opened in January 1917 despite the winds of revolution swirling about it. Vanderlip thought the heavy wartime debts assumed by the Russian government gave it a certain stability: after all, he reasoned, no government could safely repudiate. But Vanderlip had not read Lenin. The Bolsheviks nationalized Russian banks soon after taking power, and within months National City held more than $5 million in worthless government bonds. In addition, the bank had advanced $2 million to the Russian branches and owed $26 million to depositors from the Russian branches. No one knew what the bank's liabilities were. National City ultimately lost $10 million, and it could have been worse had more depositors filed suits to recover their money.

Vanderlip and Stillman parted ways after the Russian debacle. Stillman came out of retirement intent on taking complete control of the bank, but he died shortly after meeting with Vanderlip to arrange the switch. For a short time after Stillman's death Vanderlip remained president, but the board elected Stillman's son Joseph A. Stillman to serve as chairman. On June 3, 1919, Vanderlip resigned.

After his departure from National City, Vanderlip continued to buy and sell stocks successfully. He continued to write as well and in 1935 published his autobiography, written with the aid of Boyden Sparkes. He also actively participated in the Metropolitan, Century, and Union League Clubs in New York and the Cosmos Club in Washington. He died on June 29, 1937.

Frank Vanderlip was one of the most influential bankers in American history. Had J. P. Morgan not been a contemporary, he would have dominated his age. Reformer, centralizer, and visionary in the area of bank branching and overseas expansion, Vanderlip helped bring about marked changes on the American banking landscape.

Publications:

Business and Education (New York: Duffield, 1907);

What Happened to Europe (New York: Macmillan, 1919);

What Next in Europe? (New York: Harcourt, Brace, 1922);

Tomorrow's Money: A Financial Program for America (New York: Reynal & Hitchcock, 1934);

From Farm Boy to Financier, with Boyden Sparkes (New York & London: Appleton, 1935).

References:

Vincent P. Carosso, *Investment Banking in America: A History* (Cambridge, Mass.: Harvard University Press, 1970);

Harold Van B. Cleveland and Thomas F. Huertas, *Citibank, 1812-1970* (Cambridge, Mass.: Harvard University Press, 1985);

Milton Friedman and Anna J. Schwartz, *A Monetary History of the United States, 1867-1960* (Princeton: Princeton University Press, 1963);

James Livingston, *Origins of the Federal Reserve System: Money, Class, and Corporate Capitalism* (Ithaca, N.Y.: Cornell University Press, 1986);

Robert Mayer, "The Origins of the American Banking Empire in Latin America: Frank A. Vanderlip and the National City Bank," *Journal of Interamerican Studies and World Affairs,* 15 (1973);

W. Nelson Peach, *The Security Affiliates of National Banks* (Baltimore: Johns Hopkins University Press, 1941);

Clyde William Phelps, *The Foreign Expansion of American Banks: American Branch Banking Abroad* (New York: Ronald Press, 1927);

Fritz Redlich, *The Molding of American Banking: Men and Ideas,* 2 volumes (New York: Johnson Reprint Co., 1968);

Richard Timberlake, Jr., *The Origins of Central Banking in the United States* (Cambridge, Mass.: Harvard University Press, 1978);

Robert Craig West, *Banking Reform and the Federal Reserve, 1863-1923* (Ithaca, N.Y.: Cornell University Press, 1974);

Eugene Nelson White, *Regulation and Reform of the American Banking System, 1900-1929* (Princeton: Princeton University Press, 1983).

Amasa Walker

(May 4, 1799-October 29, 1875)

Archives:

The papers of Frank Vanderlip are at Columbia University.

by Michael F. Konig

Westfield State College

CAREER: Teacher, Brookfield, Massachusetts (1818-1820); mercantile partnership (1820-1823); sales agent, Methuen Manufacturing Company (1823-1825); merchant, Boston (1825-18??); director, Franklin Bank (1832-1840); director, Western Railroad (1832-1840); lecturer, Oberlin College (1842-1848); state representative, Massachusetts (1849-1851, 1859-1861); secretary of state, Massachusetts (1851-1853); secretary, Massachusetts Board of Agriculture (1852-1853); examiner in political economy, Harvard University (1853-1860); lecturer, Amherst College (1859-1869); U.S. representative, state of Massachusetts (1862).

Born May 4, 1799, in Woodstock, Connecticut, Amasa Walker descended from an early New England family. His lineage can be traced to Samuel Walker, who lived in Lynn, Reading, and Woburn, Massachusetts, between 1630 and 1684. Samuel and Priscilla Carpenter Walker, Amasa Walker's parents, moved from Woodstock to Brookfield, Massachusetts, in 1800. There Walker attended the local district school, worked on the family farm, and labored in the card manufacturing centers of nearby Leicester.

At the age of fifteen Walker found employment as a clerk in a local country store. For the next six years he worked alternately at that and at his family's farm in order to support himself while preparing for entrance into Amherst College. Unfortunately his unrelenting work schedule broke his rather fragile health and forced Walker to abandon his Amherst aspirations. From 1818 to 1820 he taught school while continuing to work on the farm.

In October 1820 Walker formed a partnership with a local businessman, Allen Newell, in order to purchase a store in West Brookfield. Walker continued in this business successfully but disposed of his

Amasa Walker (engraving by F. T. Stuart)

interest in 1823. During the next two years he served as the agent for Methuen Manufacturing Company, and in 1825 he moved to Boston where he established a boot-and-shoe outlet with a local retailer, Charles G. Carleton. Walker married Carleton's sister, Emeline, in July 1826. Unfortunately, Emeline died two years later. Walker remarried shortly thereafter. He and his second wife, Hannah Ambrose of Concord, New Hampshire, had three children.

By 1829 Walker had founded an additional independent business and had also demonstrated a substantial interest in community affairs. He assisted in the organization of the Boston Lyceum, the earliest such institution in Massachusetts, and was elected the Lyceum's first secretary. Walker became president of that institution in 1832 and also participated in a movement against Masonry. He maintained that the Masons' secretive orientation worked against a "free and virtuous society." Walker continued to exhibit concern for public affairs throughout his life.

In 1832 officials of the Franklin Bank in Boston elected Walker a director. He also served as a director of the Western Railroad. Walker continued in those positions through 1837 but incurred heavy financial losses during the panic of that same year. The reversal had a profound effect upon Walker. He retired completely from commercial affairs in 1840 and took up residence at his father's estate in North Brookfield.

Yet Walker's interest in community affairs did not waver. He became increasingly committed to the cause of temperance, serving as the Boston Temperance Society's president during the 1840s. Other public issues gained his attention. Between 1842 and 1848 Walker delivered an annual course of lectures on political economy at Oberlin College, an institution he had financially supported. At the same time he became involved in the cause for world peace. In 1843 Walker served as a delegate and vice-president for the First International Peace Congress, in London. A few years later, in 1849, he attended a similar congress in Paris.

Walker's support for temperance and peace coincided with his strident abolitionist position. He participated in some of the earliest Free Soil party activities and in 1848 attended the national Free Soil convention in Buffalo, New York, which nominated Martin Van Buren for the presidency. Walker's public service continued when he was elected a representative to the Massachusetts State House in 1849. In that position he helped to carry through a secret ballot law and a bill stipulating that *Webster's Dictionary* be used in the public schools.

In 1851 Massachusetts Free Soilers and Democrats helped to elect Walker secretary of state, and in 1852 he became ex officio secretary of the Massachusetts Board of Agriculture. He also served as a member of the convention for revising the constitution of Massachusetts and chaired the commonwealth's legislative committee on suffrage.

Despite impressive commitment and participation in public affairs, Walker never lost his interest in commercial and economic matters. Between 1853 and 1860 he served as one of the examiners in political economy at Harvard and during the years 1859 through 1869 annually lectured on that subject at Amherst College.

Walker's reputation as an expert in the area of political economy increased dramatically when in 1857 he published a series of articles in *Hunt's Merchant's Magazine and Commercial Review*. Those articles also appeared in pamphlet form as *The Nature and Uses of Money and Mixed Currency* (1857).

Those works appeared at a time when a financial panic shook much of the nation. Thus Walker put his opinions and theories to a practical test. Boston merchants and bankers invited Walker to attend an important meeting at which they hoped to formulate a united response to the rapidly spreading economic dilemma. At that meeting the merchants and bankers agreed to maintain specie payment throughout Boston's financial and banking community. Walker argued that such an act could not be sustained for more than two weeks and that the tightened credit necessitated by that effort would ruin many of the city's other merchants and businessmen. He alternately proposed that specie payment be suspended immediately.

The majority of the attending business and banking leaders expressed shock and disapproval at Walker's position. Twelve days later every bank in Boston failed, as well as many large mercantile houses. Those failures, which fulfilled Walker's prediction, made him an authority on finance and currency matters. In 1859, after gaining election a second time to the state legislature, Walker played a prominent role in the revision of laws pertaining to banking and the issuing of paper money. He reached the culmination of his political career with his election to the U.S. House of Representatives in 1862.

In 1866 Walker's most considerable publication in the fields of economy and finance, *The Science of Wealth: A Manual of Political Economy*, appeared. The work received widespread attention, passed through eight editions, and was even translated into Italian. The work served as an essential source for the even better-known work, *The Wages Question*, which Walker's son, Francis Amasa Walker, published in 1876. Amasa Walker's self-professed qualifications for his presentation of his treatise described "a practical knowledge of business and banking affairs generally, and a most earnest and persistent search for the truth in all matters pertaining to [his] favorite science."

As in his other publications Walker's primary focus in *The Science of Wealth* was currency and banking. Contemporaries and scholars of economic history have regarded Walker as a devotee of the famous "currency school," which favored 100 percent specie reserves behind bank note currency. In *The Science of Wealth* Walker also developed the conception of the entrepreneur as a separate productive factor distinguished from the capitalist.

While *The Science of Wealth* marked the culmination of Walker's contributions to the field of political economy, his theories and positions continued

to appear in noteworthy periodicals and newspapers. Amherst College recognized Walker's achievements by conferring upon him an honorary LL.D. degree in 1867. Continually in poor health, Walker died on October 29, 1875.

Publications:

The Nature and Uses of Money and Mixed Currency, with a History of the Wickaboag Bank (Boston: Crosby, Nichols, 1857);

The Science of Wealth: A Manual of Political Economy (Boston: Little, Brown, 1866; revised and enlarged, 1867);

Our National Currency (New York: Barnes, 1874);

The National Currency and the Money Problem (New York & Chicago: Barnes, 1878).

Francis Amasa Walker

(July 2, 1840-January 5, 1897)

by Michael F. Konig

Westfield State College

CAREER: Deputy special commissioner of the revenue, U.S. Department of the Treasury (1869-1870); superintendent, Ninth U.S. Census (1870); commissioner, U.S. Office of Indian Affairs (1870-1873); professor of political economy and history, Sheffield Scientific School, Yale University (1873-1881); president, Massachusetts Institute of Technology (1881-1897); president, American Statistical Association (1881-1897); president, American Economic Association (1885-1892).

Francis Amasa Walker, son of political economist and statesman Amasa Walker and an important economist, educator, and statistician in his own right, was born on July 2, 1840, in Boston, Massachusetts. He profited from a positive home life stimulated by his father's economic, political, and social-advocacy activities. Following his graduation from Amherst College in 1860, Walker spent nine years studying law, fighting in the Civil War, teaching Latin and Greek at Williston Seminary in Easthampton, Massachusetts, and writing editorials for the prominent Samuel Bowles's *Springfield Daily Republican*. On August 16, 1865, he married Exene Stoughton, of Gill, Massachusetts. The couple had seven children.

In January 1869 Walker relocated to Washington, D.C., and began his work as statistician in the capacity as deputy special commissioner of the revenue in charge of the Bureau of Statistics in the U.S. Treasury Department. He continued as a statistician in various capacities throughout his life.

Walker reorganized the Bureau of Statistics and restored its reputation and prestige. As a result he secured an appointment in 1870 as superintendent of the Ninth U.S. Census. In that position he acquired an international reputation as a statistician. He also strongly urged that the census bureau be given a permanent organization to allow uninterrupted service and more accurate enumeration.

The federal government failed to act on Walker's suggestions. In fact, funds for Walker's retention as superintendent of the 1870 census failed to materialize. Yet the administration of President Ulysses S. Grant still valued Walker's services and appointed him commissioner of the Office of Indian Affairs. The Indian Affairs Office had suffered from numerous scandals, and the opening for Walker's position became a reality during subsequent reform efforts. Since the Department of the Interior encompassed both the Census Bureau and the In-

Francis Amasa Walker (courtesy of the Massachusetts Institute of Technology)

dian Affairs Office, Walker continued to supervise the census while he drew his commissioner's salary.

Walker exposed fraud and abuses associated with Indian affairs and produced a forthright book on the problems facing the native Americans entitled *The Indian Question* (1874). At the same time he continued his labor on the census, substantially contributing to the *1874 Statistical Atlas of the United States*. Those accomplishments earned a strong reputation for Walker among the nation's most prominent reformers, including Henry Adams, James A. Garfield, Edwin L. Godkin, Horace White, and Charles Francis Adams, Jr.

By 1873 Walker had resigned from the Indian Affairs Office to pursue a career in his brother-in-law's shoe factory. An appointment as professor of political economy and history at the Sheffield Scientific School of Yale University became available, however, and Walker quickly accepted the position.

At the Yale graduate school Walker taught with the famous economist William Graham Sumner. The pair instituted one of the nation's first courses in statistics, entitled "Statistics of Indus-

try." Walker's past governmental service afforded him a tremendous amount of information on the social and economic conditions of the United States. He also understood quite clearly the realities of the American political situation because of his numerous and necessary contacts with elected and bureaucratic officials. Thus Walker emerged as a dynamic educator and public administrator. He dared to be a pioneer and thus markedly stimulated the development of economics as a field of study in America.

Walker emerged as an important figure in a new inductive and historical approach to economics. He stipulated that wages did not depend entirely on the amount of preexisting capital but more on the productivity of labor. He articulated this and other important economic theories in his internationally famous book, *The Wages Question*, published in 1876. That treatise weakened support for the wage-fund theory in the United States and Great Britain and further developed his father's concept of the entrepreneur as an agent of production distinct from the capitalist. *The Wages Question* firmly established Walker's reputation as an economist of international stature.

In his continual battle for the independence of economic thought, Walker directly confronted the controversial post-Civil War issue of money. That issue encompassed several facets, including the resumption of specie payments on greenbacks, the use of silver as a monetary metal, and the worldwide concern caused by the demonetization of silver. Walker addressed those difficult questions through a series of lectures he presented at Johns Hopkins University in 1877 and 1878 and through a general monetary treatise entitled *Money* (1878). That book served as the forerunner of a more extensive work, *Money and Its Relations to Trade and Industry* (1879). In the latter Walker defined money to include not only bank notes but everything serving as a medium of exchange. He maintained that the federal government had the right to declare paper legal tender but also stated that governments were not well versed enough in economic matters to avoid currency overissue. In conjunction with W. Stanley Jevon's *Money and the Mechanism of Exchange*, the work became the standard treatise on money in the English-speaking world for the next 25 years.

Money and Its Relations to Trade and Industry demonstrated Walker's increasingly adamant position in favor of international bimetallism. In 1878

Walker served as a delegate to the International Monetary Conference, where his adherence to that view began to develop. Walker did not attend an abortive Brussels Conference in 1892 on international bimetallism, but he became increasingly convinced that a lack of consensus among the world's industrializing nations in regard to bimetallism led to the disastrous panic of 1893. Walker maintained that the demonetization of silver by Germany in 1873 and the subsequent abandonment of bimetallism by France and other western nations precipitated the economic cataclysm. His support of an international bimetallic system led to the publication of his final major treatise, *International Bimetallism* (1896).

Walker's writings on bimetallism served as an important focal point of the debate over the issue during the American presidential election of 1896. William Jennings Bryan, the Democratic candidate, argued that the United States could accomplish its conversion to a bimetallic monetary system, devoid of cooperation from other western nations. Walker disagreed, pointing to Great Britain's seeming shift toward a bimetallic standard. He also sensed the sectional animosity surrounding the issue and took a position favoring tolerance and understanding between creditors and debtors. Walker also attempted to undercut the free-coinage movement by organizing businessmen behind international bimetallism. While those efforts were important from a long-term theoretical perspective, they did not immediately succeed. William McKinley won the presidency, due in large measure to the support he received from conservative, gold-standard bankers and industrialists.

As a theorist, Walker also took a position against the blind acceptance of laissez-faire as it applied to the government's regulation of the American economic process. He advocated a limited reduction of the workday from 14 to 10 hours in the interests of increased efficiency. But he did not believe that the nation's industrial community could maintain an eight-hour law.

Immigration also concerned Walker. He argued that immigrant labor participated in boycotts, strikes, and sabotage more readily than did native Americans. In fact, he attributed decreasing native birthrate to what he termed the "competitive shock" of immigration.

Contemporaries described Walker as "unquestionably the most prominent and best known of American [economic] writers." His influence extended to both Great Britain and France. As a theoristic economist he may even have enjoyed a greater reputation abroad than at home. In America government officials and other economists often maintained that Walker's excellent work as statistician and administrator eclipsed his theoretical accomplishments. They may have made that claim because Walker often took positions unpopular with the majority of economists and businessmen of his day. For example, Walker espoused a free-trade position, partly because protectionism undermined international bimetallism. Yet free traders attacked him because he maintained that, in all fairness, protectionists deserved a hearing.

Walker's reputation and ability as a statistician and as an economist enabled him to assist in the professionalization of those fields in the United States. He contributed articles to newly established professional academic journals and precipitated a debate in the *Quarterly Journal of Economics* over the desirability of private land ownership.

Walker left Yale in 1881 to become president of the Massachusetts Institute of Technology. He also served as the president of the American Economic Association (AEA) from 1885 through 1892, when a "new school" of young German-trained economists comprised the majority of that organization's membership. The AEA adopted a statement of principle that "affirmed the State as a positive agency for human progress and asserted the importance of historical and statistical study as against deductive analysis." Walker also served as president of the American Statistical Association between 1883 and 1897, when that organization evolved from a local to a national institution.

Walker was a college professor, a college administrator, a government administrator, a statistician, an army officer, and an author, but he still found time for civic activities. He served on the New Haven School Committee from 1878 through 1881, as member of the Massachusetts Board of Education intermittently from 1879 through 1890, and as a trustee for the Boston Public Library in 1896. Upon his death in January 1897 the *Springfield Daily Republican* stated that "in him a sense of life abounded." In light of Walker's numerous accomplishments that seems almost an understatement.

Publications:

The Indian Question (Boston: Osgood, 1874);

The Wages Question: A Treatise on Wages and the Wages Class (New York: Holt, 1876);

Money (New York: Holt, 1878);

Money and Its Relations to Trade and Industry (New York: Holt, 1879);

Political Economy (New York: Holt, 1883; revised and enlarged, 1887; revised and enlarged again, 1888);

History of the Second Army Corps in the Army of the Potomac (New York: Scribners, 1886);

Land and Its Rent (Boston: Little, Brown, 1888);

First Lessons in Political Economy (New York: Holt, 1889);

Hancock in the War of the Rebellion (New York: Little, 1891);

General Hancock (New York: Appleton, 1894);

The Making of the Nation (New York: Scribners, 1895);

International Bimetallism (New York: Holt, 1896);

Discussions in Economics and Statistics, edited by Davis Rich Dewey, 2 volumes (New York: Holt, 1899);

Discussions in Education, edited by James Munroe Phinney (New York: Holt, 1899).

References:

Bernard Newton, *The Economics of Francis Amasa Walker: American Economics in Transition* (New York: Kelly, 1968).

James Munroe Phinney, *A Life of Francis Amasa Walker* (New York: Holt, 1923).

Thomas Wren Ward

(November 20, 1786-March 4, 1858)

by Michael F. Konig

Westfield State College

CAREER: Agent, Baring Brothers and Company, London (1828-1853); partner, Ropes and Ward (1828-1853); partner, Prime, Ward and King (1828-1853).

Thomas Wren Ward was born in Salem, Massachusetts, on November 20, 1786, the son of William and Martha Proctor Ward, themselves descended from a longtime colonial Bay State family. Between roughly 1830 and 1853 Ward played an important if not particularly obtrusive role in the development of American financial and commercial affairs.

Ward's commercial activities began with his association with the Boston importing and exporting house of Ropes and Ward. In 1828, while serving as full partner in this firm, he traveled to England, ostensibly to visit an intimate friend, Joshua Bates. The friendship culminated in a profitable business relationship. Bates had recently been admitted to a partnership in the leading English firm at that time, Baring Brothers and Company, which financed the foreign trade of the United States. Through his association with Bates, Ward became the primary American agent of this formidable London financial house.

In this position Ward exercised considerable responsibility. He facilitated almost all of the Barings' American business, which annually involved several

Thomas Wren Ward (S. G. Ward, Ward Family Papers, 1900)

million pounds sterling. During Ward's first three years as the Barings' agent, he granted credits and exclusive bond operations to American merchants totaling nearly $50 million. He also arranged for the transfer of shipping documents, negotiated loans, collected debts, contacted correspondents, and reported on economic conditions. British merchant bankers regarded the relationship as highly significant. As one of his most difficult tasks Ward attempted to prevent the repudiation of bonded indebtedness by the states of Pennsylvania, Maryland, and Louisiana. The Baring Brothers had previously sold the securities of those states to English investors. In Louisiana he partly succeeded in preventing full repudiation and thus maintained the state's credit rating.

Ward served in other capacities for the Barings. Upon his initiative the firm retained Daniel Webster as counsel. Diplomatic considerations guided this decision, as many considered the appointment of Webster an important factor in maintaining peaceful relations between Great Britain and the United States. Ward described the American statesman as "able . . . in defending the true principles of the Constitution and upholding the rights of property" but also as "reckless in pecuniary matters." Webster tended to "pass the hat among wealthy men" and rarely repaid them. Ward advised the Barings that if they lent money to Webster they would probably have to write it off to profit and loss. This insight into Webster's financial affairs Ward provided more than likely prevented them from becoming disillusioned with their American counsel. Ward further counseled U.S. president James K. Polk in 1845 as to British financial considerations when the two nations incurred strained relations over the division of the Oregon Territory.

The Barings appreciated Ward's blunt honesty and considered him one of the "soundest" men of finance in the United States. Many within the firm regarded Ward's judicious advice as the chief factor enabling the firm to weather the financial downturn of 1837-1842. Bray Hammond provides a similar appraisal of Ward's personal character and financial abilities, describing Ward as "a businessman of foremost ability and character."

Ward was also involved in the affairs of the Second Bank of the United States (BUS). The success and ultimate failure of that institution reflected the changing attitudes of Americans toward the banking and financial community during the antebellum period. The rechartering of the BUS had become a major issue in the 1832 presidential contest. Politi-

cal opponents of Andrew Jackson, notably Henry Clay and BUS president, Nicholas Biddle, had thrust the issue into the forefront of national affairs as a means to weaken Andrew Jackson's support in the election. They miscalculated, however, the lack of support for the bank by both the president and the American people. Jackson defeated Clay in the election and at the same time effectively destroyed any possibility of recharter. The controversy distracted the attention of Biddle from the institution's internal affairs and policies. According to Hammond, the BUS management never recovered its poise and judgment after the 1832 contest.

Through their agent, Ward, the Barings had become involved with the BUS. In 1833 Ward reported to the London firm that the condition of the bank was less than secure. During that year the federal government paid off $6 million in bonds for which insufficient reserves existed at the BUS. The situation was embarrassing to Biddle, and he turned to Ward and the Barings for assistance. The Barings held a large portion of those bonds and through Ward attempted to consummate an agreement beneficial to both themselves and the BUS. But the agreement controverted the bank's charter and had to be disavowed, and the Barings had to borrow in order to assist. The BUS only tardily responded by facilitating a $7 million loan Ward and the Barings had undertaken for the Union Bank of Louisiana. Ward stated he "never had confidence" in Biddle's ability to manage the bank and described him as a "man of talent and resource" but "an intriguer." For Jackson's second term in office he would have preferred that "a plain and straightforward man of good judgement and prudence" manage the bank's affairs.

Jackson substantially reduced the power of the BUS after 1832 by depositing federal revenues in state "pet" banks. The president arrived at that course through the advice of financial figures who had opposed what they thought was Biddle's highhanded dominance of the nation's fiscal affairs. Ward appears to have been one of those advisers. He also recognized that an increasingly powerful New York City banking community, which had continually taken an antagonistic position against the BUS, hoped to increase its influence and prestige through the receipt of federal revenues. In response Biddle created an artificial financial panic by calling in the short-term loans of the BUS. Ward opposed that action in a dispatch to the Barings.

Biddle's defense of the BUS was futile, and, as the institution's deposits dwindled along with its prestige and power, state banks initiated a frenzy of land-mortgage speculation. Many state institutions issued notes without adequate specie reserves and loaned the currency to western farmers purchasing federal land. Jackson expressed concern that this speculation had reached unsafe proportions, and Congress passed the Specie Circular, requiring that payments to the federal government for land purchases be made only in specie, gold or silver coin. That abrupt change in federal monetary policy coincided with the sudden halt of silver that once flowed steadily out of Mexican mines—silver the United States sent to China in payment for Chinese silks and porcelain. This in turn shut off the specie flow to Britain, and the British responded by raising interest rates, precipitating the Panic of 1837.

Other factors contributed to the deteriorating economic situation. Britain had become the paramount industrial and financial power in the world, and the United States constituted its major market. Years of speculation and hasty expansion had overheated the British and American transatlantic economy. Great Britain had become almost overly dependent upon the United States as a market for its goods, its capital, and as a source of cotton for its mills. The British felt the negative effects of the decline of the BUS and the Panic of 1837.

As the reserves of the BUS continued to dwindle the Bank of England attempted to provide some support through the proscription of American credit, temporarily invigorating BUS stocks. The measure, however, proved to be of only temporary value to the rapidly declining institution, and in his dispatches to the Barings, Ward expressed concern over the position taken by the Bank of England. Ward foresaw danger in the increasingly polarized nature of the transatlantic economy. He feared that Great Britain had become overly speculative in its lending policies and that American financial business and commercial interests had become too dependent upon British credit.

Ward predicted disaster and was correct. A contraction in the British demand for American cotton and the higher interest rates occurring in conjunction with the negative effects of the Specie Circular sent the U.S. economy reeling. American business and financial institutions could not sell, buy, borrow, or pay. Ward's financial firm, Prime, Ward

and King, felt the negative effects as did the faltering BUS.

Because the federal government would accept only specie in exchange for land and because many business and financial transactions had been suspended by March and April of 1837, the government and private citizens began to hoard gold. This only compounded the problems faced by the British and American transatlantic economy. To alleviate the situation, Ward, through his financial firm and through his position as agent for the Baring Brothers, arranged a program in which prominent American institutions such as the BUS, the Bank of America, and the Girard and Morris Canal and Banking Company sold their obligations in the form of bonds in London, Paris, and Amsterdam. The sales totaled nearly $12 million. A $1 million shipment of specie from the United States Bank of New York to the Bank of England supported the arrangement.

Ward's actions contributed to a stabilization of the transatlantic economy, but the BUS could not put its house in order. Following the advice of Ward, the Baring Brothers closed their credit with the BUS, a damaging blow.

As the BUS came to play an increasingly smaller regulatory role, major Wall Street banks became indifferent to governmental presence in national or international monetary affairs. Ward was convinced that some measure of governmental regulation of banking was necessary. His view, however, constituted a minority in the American financial community. As historian Hammond contends, "The Jacksonian ideal of diminishing the responsibilities of Washington accorded with Wall Street's fully."

By 1840 an era of "free banking," with private banks filling the vacuum left by the BUS, had established the New York institutions as the most dominant in the field. These included the powerful Bank of Commerce, in which Ward advised his Baring Brothers associates to invest, and they did by purchasing $100,000 of the stock of this new bank. Ward privately purchased between $30,000 to $40,000 of the Bank of Commerce stock as well. He also helped to facilitate a merger between the Bank of Commerce and the Manhattan Bank. That arrangement produced a type of regulatory effect not only upon the Wall Street banking community but also upon the banking communities of Philadelphia and Boston. The merger reflected Ward's conservative approach to monetary affairs and served the financial community well in this post-BUS era. In addition, the combined Bank of Commerce and Manhattan Bank, known simply as the Bank of Commerce, continued on a prominent course for nearly a century. In 1929 it was amalgamated with the Guaranty Trust Company.

Ward's fiscal endeavors, while having an important effect on American and international finance, also made him a wealthy man. But those endeavors did not consume all of Ward's public life. From 1828 to 1836 he served as the treasurer of the Boston Athenaeum, and between 1830 and 1842 he held a similar position at Harvard University. Ward retired from active business in 1853 and died on March 4, 1858. His will bequeathed portions of his $650,000 estate to the Boston Athenaeum and Harvard, as well as to the American Peace Society and the Boston Missionary Society.

Reference:
Bray Hammond, *Banks and Politics in America from the Revolution to the Civil War* (Princeton: Princeton University Press, 1957).

Archives:
Material relating to Thomas Wren Ward's dealings with Baring Brothers and Company is in the Baring Papers at the Public Archives, Ottawa, Ontario.

Henry Wells

(December 12, 1805-December 10, 1878)

by Robert J. Chandler

Wells Fargo Bank

CAREER: Apprentice, Jessup & Palmer (1821-1826); tanner and shoemaker, Port Byron, New York (1826-1829); educational therapist (1820s-1840s); steamboat business (1830s-1841); agent, Harnden's Express (1841); partner, Pomeroy & Company (1841-1843); partner, Livingston, Wells & Pomeroy (1843-1844); partner, Wells & Company (1845-1846, 1847-1850); partner, Livingston, Wells & Company (1844-1846); partner, Livingston & Wells (1846-1847); president (1850-1868), director, American Express Company (1850-1875); director, Wells, Fargo & Company (1852-1866).

Henry Wells was a pioneer in the express and communications businesses and an early advocate of women's education. In the 1840s he battled for cheap postage, financed and built several of the earliest telegraph lines, and pushed the express business westward. He founded two well-known financial institutions, American Express Company and Wells, Fargo & Company, and also founded Wells College for women in Aurora, New York.

Wells was born on December 12, 1805, in Thetford, Vermont, the third son and fourth child of Shipley Wells, an itinerant Presbyterian minister, and Dolly Randall Wells. The Reverend Wells soon headed west, briefly settling in Crown Point, New York, on the Vermont border. The family moved shortly thereafter, arriving at Seneca Falls near Cayuga Lake in Upstate New York in 1814. Shipley Wells farmed and made bricks when he was not preaching.

Henry Wells attended school in nearby Fayette, living with Deacon James Huff. A friend recalled Wells as a "lively rollicking boy who liked to have his own way, and could generally command the respect of his fellows by superior muscular power when all other arguments failed." Wells stammered, and perhaps that encouraged his use of physical strength in argument; he grew to be more than six feet tall and was broad shouldered.

In 1821, at the age of sixteen, Wells became an apprentice to Deacon Jessup, of Jessup & Palmer, tanners and shoemakers of Palmyra. Completing his apprenticeship in 1826, Wells married Sarah Daggett; the couple had four children, Charles, Mary, Oscar, and Edward. Following Sarah's death in 1859, Wells wed Mary Prentice of Boston in 1861.

Wells began work in Port Byron, New York, but he was not content to be a shoemaker, and his stuttering offered opportunity. About 1824 he had visited a therapist in Rochester and found means to control his speech defect. He opened several ther-

Henry Wells (courtesy of Wells Fargo Bank)

apy schools of his own. During the next fifteen years schools appeared in Rochester, Buffalo, Lockport, Utica, New York City, Pittsburgh, Cincinnati, and Cleveland. Wells had moderate success. Describing his educational career, he once humorously quoted New York Republican boss Thurlow Weed: "I cured everybody but myself." Throughout his life Wells avoided public speaking and usually had others give his addresses. However, he sometimes used stammering to emphasize his statements.

In the 1830s Wells became interested in transportation. By 1836 he was a passenger and freight forwarder on the Erie Canal, traveling 363 miles from Albany to Buffalo, New York, and forwarding freight overland through Pennsylvania to the Ohio River. The gregarious Wells made friends with men such as Daniel Drew, who controlled the Hudson River steamers; Erastus Corning, a New York railroader; and Ezra Cornell, a telegraph pioneer.

In 1841, at thirty-six, Wells entered his best-known career: expressing. The industry had begun only two years earlier. James W. Hale, proprietor of the Tontine Reading Room in New York City, was also a steamboat agent and forwarder of mail, news, and parcels to Boston. In the winter of

1838-1839 he persuaded young William F. Harnden to inaugurate the first scheduled express between the two cities. Banks and bankers particularly needed the service since the 1839 demise of the Bank of the United States destroyed the area's central clearing system, resulting in a high discount when banks sent drafts for collection. In 1841 Harnden expanded his express up the Hudson River, and, working through Wells's friendship with Daniel Drew, he obtained a steamboat contract to Albany. Appropriately, Wells served as Harnden's agent in that city.

Within a few months, Harnden and Wells's interests diverged. Harnden looked east to Europe, which had sent hordes of immigrants to the United States. Wells looked west to the land of his youth and the territory of his forwarding business. Wells proposed to Harnden that he extend his express to Buffalo, and "as the facilities of transportation would permit," to Chicago and the Far West. Harnden declined. "If *you* choose to run an Express to the Rocky mountains," snapped Harnden to Wells, "you had better do it on your own account; *I* choose to run an Express where there is business." Wells accepted the challenge.

For the next ten years Wells was a partner in various firms offering expressing, at first weekly, then daily, from New York to Buffalo and west to St. Louis, Missouri. Three like-minded men were his associates: George E. Pomeroy, Crawford Livingston, and William George Fargo. For Wells, profit and public service were intertwined.

Beginning in 1841 and continuing for 18 months, proprietor Wells worked as a messenger on the Albany to Buffalo run, and during the first year he never missed a trip. It took four nights and three days to reach Buffalo using railroads, stagecoaches, and virtually anything else that moved. Twenty years later Wells remembered the journey as "ugly," "horrible," and, at best, "endurable." Bankers, businessmen, and the public supported the infant enterprise. Early in 1842 James Leidley of the Seneca Street House in Buffalo wished to feature oysters on his menu, telling Wells, "If I pay for them— charge what you will" to move them. That motive, declared Wells, was "the keystone to all success in enterprise." His fee was $3 per 100 oysters, and as the fame of the Seneca House spread, so did that of the express. In 1842 workers completed the last of the seven railroads between Albany and Buffalo, cutting the journey to 24 rugged hours. Wells paid for his seat and an extra one for his trunk, with the less valuable material in the baggage car. One railroad official noted of the expanding express business: "Of all the wonderful growths which he had seen in the West, none equalled Wells' trunk!"

In 1843 the firm of Livingston, Wells & Pomeroy started running the Buffalo express daily, and on April 1, 1845, Wells, Fargo, and Daniel Dunning formed Wells & Company to head westward to Cleveland, Detroit, Cincinnati, Chicago, and St. Louis. As usual, Wells stressed public service and efficiency and did much of the work himself. He recalled being on the steamer *St. Louis* on Lake Erie on October 18 and 19, 1844, during one of the worst storms on record. "It was the duty of the Express to go," he asserted. In contrast to Harnden's voluminous written rules, Wells once told a messenger, "Young man, my instructions will be very short: You are bound for Cleveland, and you are expected to get there. That is all." Wells stuttered when he became excited, and he made "get" into a word of three syllables. Each was "pronounced with such decided emphasis," declared the teller of the tale, that the messenger knew he must not fail. "The much tried yet never failing integrity" of the expressmen, wrote Wells, brought public confidence, but mere success was not enough. "There was one very powerful business rule," he added. "It was concentrated in the word–courtesy."

"Government should do little as possible of that which the People can do," philosophized Wells, and one area where the people could do better was the delivery of mail. During the 1840s U.S. postage depended on distance traveled. It ranged from 6 cents for a letter going under 30 miles to 25 cents for one sent more than 400 miles. Mail from New York City to Buffalo went at the highest rate.

In 1842 Wells fought the government postal monopoly. He charged 6 cents a letter or sold 20 adhesive stamps for $1. By 1844 several carriers had joined the battle, offering postal delivery at the same rates. James W. Hale and Lysander Spooner served the seaboard commercial centers of Philadelphia, Boston, and New York, while the Letter Expresses of George Pomeroy and Wells brought mail to Buffalo and on to Detroit and Chicago. The government appeared to concentrate its efforts at suppression in upper New York State, but the public supported Henry Wells. At Utica the government arrested express messengers daily, but citizens immediately posted bail, allowing them to continue their journeys. Between Buffalo and Rochester, reported A. L. Stimson, the "entire letter mail" went by express.

Henry Wells counterattacked. Representing several expressmen, he proposed to First Assistant Postmaster General Selah Hobbie that they would deliver all letters for 5 cents each. "Zounds, Sir," exclaimed that official, having a knowledge of the political patronage system. "It would throw 16,000 Postmasters out of office!" Congress responded slowly, passing a law on March 3, 1845, fixing postage after July 1 at 5 cents for letters sent less than 300 miles, and 10 cents for letters sent farther. The government still charged double the price for which Wells carried a letter to Buffalo until June 30, 1851, when the cost of mail traveling under 3,000 miles fell to 3 cents.

Wells took pride in his crusade to bring cheap postage and recalled 20 years later, "I was then known as the People's Postmaster General." He praised the express business for its gift of "this important and peaceful revolution." However, a business must make a profit to survive, and as with the oysters to Buffalo, Wells did not ignore the task of making money. Stimson observed that the Letter Express "was the most profitable part of the Express business," while James Hale remarked that the government would have kept the 25 cent rate indefinitely, "if Wells and myself had not seen a business opening in it."

The telegraph constituted the last of the "public acts" Wells pioneered in the 1840s. Surprisingly, capitalists in New York and Boston, the commercial centers of the nation, did not recognize the telegraph as a means "to extinguish distance and annihilate time," as telegrapher James D. Reid aptly expressed its advantages. They left it to central New Yorkers with a more far-seeing view. On July 16, 1845, former stagecoach drivers John Butterfield, Theodore S. Faxton, and Hiram Greenman, and expressmen Wells and Crawford Livingston united to build a telegraph from New York City to Albany to Buffalo. Faxton became president of the new company, while Ezra Cornell of Ithaca, an early associate of Samuel F. B. Morse, was a large stockholder. Wells claimed credit for building the line from Buffalo to Lockport, which, on November 7, 1845, became the first telegraph line opened for commercial business in the United States. Before the entire line was ready on September 9, 1846, Wells, Livingston, Pomeroy, Cornell,

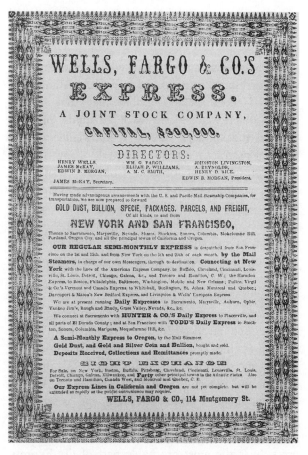

Business directory page advertising the express service of Wells, Fargo & Company

and others had opened a line from New York City to Boston on June 27. Wells finished his last telegraph venture in 1847. He and Livingston strung the wires of the Montreal Telegraph Company, under the presidency of Cornell's brother-in-law, from Buffalo to Toronto, Montreal, and Quebec.

In late 1846 Wells turned over the express business west of Buffalo to William A. Livingston, Crawford's brother, and William G. Fargo in order to devote his energy to the eastern business from New York City to Buffalo. However, his years as an express messenger and telegraph builder had sapped his health, while death claimed his partner Crawford Livingston in 1847 and Livingston's successor, Edward C. Winslow, in 1849. Until 1849, when Johnston Livingston joined him, Wells virtually singlehandedly ran Wells & Company.

John Butterfield, Wells's telegraph partner, saw opportunity in Wells's misfortune. Joining with James D. Wasson, he formed a joint-stock company capitalized at $50,000, secured an exclusive contract over the seven upstate railroads that Erastus Corning consolidated into the New York Central in

1853, and gave battle to Wells. The fierce war brought heavy financial losses. The two resolved to establish the traditional express monopoly over a certain territory and fix rates with neighboring express companies. Livingston & Fargo, the western ally of Wells & Company, was invited to join, and on March 18, 1850, the American Express Company came into being.

Capitalized at $150,000, American Express was a joint-stock association and an umbrella over two autonomous companies. Wells, Butterfield & Company, under line superintendent Butterfield, controlled eastern expressing, while Fargo ran western business through Livingston, Fargo & Company. On the board of directors, Fargo and William Livingston fought Butterfield and Wasson, while Wells, Johnston Livingston, and James McKay formed a third group dedicated to the preservation of American Express. As an indication of his role as mediator, the directors elected Wells president while he was in Europe. Fargo became secretary, and Alexander Holland, Butterfield's son-in-law, was treasurer.

Within a few months, the forty-four-year-old Wells withdrew further from active involvement. In late summer 1850 he moved to Aurora, across Cayuga Lake from his boyhood home, a tiring 24-hour journey from the American Express New York headquarters. He complained of being "completely exhausted" after meetings that dragged on, even for days, with little accomplished, all laced with Butterfield's profanity. Since directors viewed most proposals as benefiting one faction or the other, American Express did not innovate, but thanks to Wells, neither did it fly apart. Wells paid less attention to express business in the 1860s, when record wartime profits stilled board dissension, and his health declined. A carriage accident in 1859 badly injured a leg, leaving him with a limp for life, and in the 1860s he wintered in warmer climates. He retired in 1868, after a bruising battle with the Merchants Union Express. Surprisingly, Wells wanted to assess stockholders for funds and fight on, while Fargo argued for compromise and merger, and became president.

Wells is better remembered for founding a company that contained his name and is today a respected California financial institution. On February 11, 1852, Fargo suggested that American Express "extend this line to California." On March 6, in the midst of an acrimonious monthlong debate initiated by Butterfield, Wells asked the board to "immediately put into operation a California Express." Two days later, to keep peace and avoid strengthening Fargo's faction, Johnston Livingston and McKay voted with Butterfield and Wasson against Wells and Fargo.

On March 18, 1852, Wells, Fargo, and others organized Wells, Fargo & Company as a joint-stock association capitalized at $300,000 to conduct an "Express and Exchange business" on the Pacific Coast. Others among the nine directors included Elijah P. Williams, Fargo's brother-in-law, and the American Express swing voters, Livingston and McKay. Edwin D. Morgan, an Aurora merchant whom Wells had known since 1832, was president. In June 1852 Samuel P. Carter, an express and telegraph agent in Albany for Wells since the 1840s, arrived in San Francisco and set up operations. Reuben W. Washburn, formerly of the Bank of Syracuse, arrived in early July, and Wells Fargo opened for business on July 13, 1852, at 424 Montgomery Street, virtually on the site of its current headquarters.

Very quickly Carter and Washburn complained that the eastern directors did not understand expensive, tumultuous California gold-rush business conditions or Wells Fargo's activities. On the expressing side, the directors concentrated on San Francisco to New York shipping, while the two San Francisco agents felt the internal California express was the most profitable. In addition, recalling Wells's campaign in 1844 for reliable mail delivery, the Letter Express became of supreme importance, as few trusted the government mails.

Wells Fargo's banking proved the most difficult feature for the directors to comprehend. California banking revolved around purchasing gold dust from miners and selling them drafts—bills of exchange—to transfer money home. Eastern express companies often had relatively little paid-in capital; they often used the amount of capital stock to allot shares to claim dividends. However, Wells Fargo required money to purchase dust, and Carter and Washburn complained continually that the $50,000 on hand was not enough. "This is the best Country that I know to make money with money," they wrote. They felt it "urgent" that directors Wells, Fargo, or Morgan come to California.

In February 1853 Wells arrived in San Francisco, exhilarated over the trip. "Give me credit for being the first man across the Isthmus in a race of six hundred," he exclaimed. "I passed every thing

on the road." He quickly agreed with Carter and Washburn. "This is a great Country & a greater people," he rejoiced, but after observing the fast pace of commerce, concluded, "I am an old Fogey here." He also demanded an increased capital, remarking that Wells Fargo was "now but a one horse bank compared with those around us." In January 1854 the directors tripled the capital available in California to $150,000.

At fifty-nine, expressing ceased to interest Wells. In 1865 he began planning what he called "the dream of my life," a college for women. In the mid 1830s he had seen banker Stephen Girard's unfinished college in Philadelphia. "Standing there alone," he recalled, "I thought I would rather be Girard, as he was thus represented, than the President of the United States." Though Wells only stood on the threshold of fame and fortune, he resolved "that if I ever had the ability I would go and do likewise." Wells met the critics of women's education as he had met other great challenges in life. "Give her the opportunity!" he bluntly replied. Instruction at Wells College in Aurora, New York, began on September 16, 1868, making it the nation's second college, after Vassar (founded in 1861), devoted exclusively to the education of women. "The practical education of our daughters," explained Wells in an 1871 circular addressed to Wells Fargo employees, was the college's goal. His college "would make wives and mothers who would be companions for sensible men, and properly to train their children for the higher walks of life." Wells donated $200,000 worth of land, buildings, and equipment and provided other services. He was president of the First National Bank of Aurora and of the Cayuga Lake Railroad that connected Aurora with Auburn and Ithaca.

In 1871, 1875, and 1876 Wells visited the Golden State to escape harsh New York winters. While in San Diego in 1875, he was an incorporator and the moving spirit behind the Arizona & New Mexico Express Company, which his son Charles supervised. Unfortunately, Charles Wells lacked the abilities of his father, and the company failed the next year. Wells continued to maintain an elegant life-style while his fortune declined. His friend Edwin Morgan became the second founder of Wells College, giving more than $300,000 for buildings and operating expenses. Wells died on December 10, 1878, in Glasgow, Scotland, two days short of his seventy-third birthday, on his way to sunny Italy. He left an estate of only $40,000.

"Our lives are not measured by the number of years and days we exist," wrote Wells in 1875, "but by what we accomplish while we live, and the good we may render to our fellow men." Henry Wells was a risk taker and a self-made man with a vision of public service. He claimed four major accomplishments: "I claim to be the Father of the present Express system," Wells wrote in 1871. Though he was not the first, Wells led the express into new lands and built strong companies serving large territories. His moderating influence kept American Express from dissolving due to the Fargo-Butterfield feud. To his express company, opined Wells in 1864, "are the people indebted for the *de*creased cost and *in*creased accommodation of postal arrangements." His battle in the 1840s for cheap government postage brought great public benefit. His vision of the potential of the telegraph surpassed that of urban capitalists, and he used his money, time, and health to promote rapid electronic communications. His final achievement, continuing his pioneering spirit, was the creation of Wells College for women. With the news of his death at hand, the *New York Times* concluded that Henry Wells had "used his great wealth in a truly philanthropic spirit."

Publications:

The American Express in its Relations to Buffalo (Albany, N.Y.: Van Benthuysen's, 1863; Buffalo, N.Y.: Buffalo Historical Society, 1938);

Sketch of the Rise, Progress, and Present Condition of the Express System (Albany, N.Y.: Van Benthuysen's, 1864);

Truly yours HENRY WELLS: A Group of Letters by Henry Wells to Edwin B. Morgan (Aurora, N.Y.: Wells College Press, 1945).

References:

American Express Company, *Promises to Pay* (New York: American Express, 1977);

Morris Bishop, "Henry, How Could You Do It?" *Wells College Alumnae News/Express* (March 1968);

Peter Z. Grossman, *American Express: An Unauthorized History* (New York: Crown, 1987);

Noel Loomis, *Wells Fargo* (New York, 1968);

James D. Reid, *The Telegraph in America* (New York: Derby, 1879);

A. L. Stimson, *History of the Express Business* (New York, 1858; revised, 1860; revised again, 1881).

Archives:

Material on Henry Wells can be found at the corporate archives of the American Express Company in New York City, at Wells Fargo Bank in San Francisco, and at Wells College, Aurora, New York.

Wells Fargo & Company

by Robert J. Chandler

Wells Fargo Bank

Wells, Fargo & Company is the holding company for the San Francisco-based Wells Fargo Bank founded in 1852, now the oldest bank in the West. Its logo, a Concord stagecoach pulled by six running horses, recalls the company's dedicated employees and its diversified services that aided western development and symbolizes its continuing commitment to the region.

In New York City, on March 18, 1852, Henry Wells, William G. Fargo, and others formed Wells, Fargo & Company as a joint-stock association capitalized at $300,000 to operate on the Pacific Coast. The company developed four main lines of business: banking (1852 to the present), expressing (1852-1918), mail delivery (1852-1895), and overland stagecoaching (1857-1870).

On July 13, 1852, Wells Fargo opened for business in San Francisco under expressman Samuel P. Carter and banker Reuben W. Washburn. Transitory miners and merchants needed two basic services. Wells Fargo's Banking Department bought their placer gold, paying for it with standard-value gold coins, and sold them bills of exchange payable in the East so they could send their newfound fortunes home. Wells Fargo quickly established offices in Sacramento and Placer County to express gold, and it contracted with small banking and express firms to serve other areas. Its main rival was Adams & Company, a branch of an eastern express company that had arrived in 1849 and opened a network of agencies throughout gold-rush California.

A test came in February 1855, when Page, Bacon & Company and Adams & Company, California's two largest banking houses, failed, precipitating a financial panic. Wells Fargo's San Francisco office closed for three days to gather money, as the company held its assets in the mining regions to purchase gold dust. The company's gold-country agents withstood runs and sent surplus funds to the head office. Wells Fargo emerged from the panic as

Wells Fargo expressmen, circa 1870 (courtesy of Wells Fargo Bank)

a leading bank and the dominant express company in the region. At the end of 1855 it had more than 60 West Coast agencies, including large branch banking offices in Marysville, Sacramento, Stockton, and Portland, Oregon. In 1867, adding 13 correspondent bankers who were also express agents, Wells Fargo served 17 of the 35 California towns and cities that had banks. Wells, Fargo & Company express transported most of the gold and silver mined in the West and between 1858 and 1900 published statistics on precious metals production.

The joint-stock association proved to be a good investment. Henry Wells wrote on February 18, 1854, that Wells Fargo was "at last in a position to make money," and it paid a 15 percent dividend that year. Following a year of losses after the California panic of 1855, Wells Fargo regularly paid 10 to 12 percent. By 1859 its capital stock had tripled to $1 million (10,000 shares), and in 1863, because of Civil War prosperity, that figure doubled. Most of the new shares went to old stockholders.

Wells Fargo seized opportunities to enter the transportation business as it followed miners eastward from California. At first four, and then five, of its directors, including president Danford N. Barney, aided the formation, building, and operation of the Overland Mail Company that in 1858 began running stagecoaches to California along a southern route through Texas. With the outbreak of the Civil War, Wells Fargo served the central route through Salt Lake City. For six months in 1861 it ran the famed Pony Express, the best-known segment of its highly regarded Letter Express business, to the Mormon capital. General Agent Louis McLane, son of the president of the Baltimore & Ohio Railroad, had a great interest in the iron horse. Since 1856 Wells Fargo had ridden the rails of the Sacramento Valley Railroad from the state capital to Folsom. In the 1860s Wells Fargo worked with the railroad's affiliates to lay the iron rails over the Sierra Mountains. However, the rival Central Pacific Railroad won the race.

On November 1, 1866, Wells Fargo assembled the greatest American stagecoach empire. It united its Pioneer line to Virginia City, the Overland Mail Company's route to Salt Lake City, and Ben Holladay's stage lines east and north of the Mormon city. In contrast to the major eastern express companies, which remained secretive joint-stock associations, Wells Fargo assumed Holladay's 1866 Colorado incorporation and its $10 million capital stock. Wells Fargo's stagecoaches ran between railheads at Cisco, California, and North Platte, Nebraska; north from Salt Lake City to Fort Benton, Montana, and Boise, Idaho; around the mining towns near Denver; and south to the White Pine mining district of Nevada. A visiting eastern editor characterized Wells Fargo as "the omnipresent, universal business agent" of the West and concluded, "It is the Ready Companion of civilization."

In 1869 the new transcontinental railroad ended Wells Fargo's stagecoaching and brought a change in ownership. The shrewd Lloyd Tevis, with the cooperation of the Central Pacific Railroad, staged a raid that brought the road one-third of the Wells Fargo stock (increased to $15 million for that purpose) in return for an exclusive express contract. In 1870 Wells Fargo reduced its capital stock to $5 million and in 1871 resumed its dividend, which had been suspended since 1867. The Company regularly paid 8 percent thereafter.

In the 1860s the California economy expanded from placer mining to hardrock mining, agriculture, and manufacturing. All demanded long-term investment, and Wells Fargo's banking survived the transition from the era of gold-rush banking. In 1866 Wells Fargo joined other bankers to form the San Francisco Assay and Refining Works to coin bullion at a loss so that California would have sufficient circulating money. In 1876 Wells, Fargo & Company's bank was one of 15 that formed the San Francisco Clearing House, and later that year it moved into an elegant building separate from express operations. The bank also had branches in Virginia City and Carson City, Nevada; Salt Lake City, Utah; and New York City. In the 1890s the bank closed its offices in the Silver State, but reopened in Portland, Oregon. Normally, the bank contributed one-third of the company's profits, but during the Panic of 1893 its share surpassed the express.

Wells, Fargo & Company's express expanded through railroad contracts. In 1875 it lost the territory east of Ogden, Utah, when it refused to give capital stock to the Union Pacific. But Wells Fargo worked with the Santa Fe and the Southern Pacific through the Southwest to reach Chicago in 1887 and New York City in 1888. Wells Fargo became the first express to offer ocean-to-ocean service, and from 1890 to 1892 its national rail network boosted company earnings above $1 million annually. Wells Fargo's agents were respected men and women, often merchants, postmasters, telegraphers, and railroad agents who offered their communities a variety of financial, collection, commission, and package services. Taking advantage of Wells Fargo's fleet of railroad refrigerator cars, they actively marketed agricultural products.

In 1899, as Wells Fargo recovered from the Panic of 1893, company earnings again exceeded $1 million, and in 1909 they reached almost $5 million. Profitability increased in the new century. In 1898 the company's surplus exceeded $1 million and grew rapidly to $27 million in 1909. In 1910 shareholders received a special $24 million dividend. However, the express business declined due to regulation by the Interstate Commerce Commission, competition from the Post Office's parcel post service, and railroad disruptions caused by World War I. On July 1, 1918, Wells Fargo's 35,000 employees, working in 10,000 domestic offices on 80,000 miles of railroad and stagecoach lines, joined the American Railway Express as part of a wartime consolidation of the express business.

In 1905 Wells, Fargo & Company's bank merged with the Nevada National Bank. "Our ambition is not to be the largest bank in San Francisco," declared President Isaias W. Hellman of the new Wells Fargo Nevada National Bank, "but to be the soundest and the best." From the 1920s through the 1940s Wells Fargo remained a strong unit bank, easily weathering the Great Depression. Under bank president Frederick L. Lipman it preferred to do business with professional bankers through correspondent relationships. California's population expanded after World War II, and Wells Fargo entered retail branch banking on a large scale following a merger in 1960 with the American Trust Company. In 1986 it doubled in size through the acquisition of The Crocker Bank, and today Wells Fargo is a well-managed regional bank.

References:

Lucius Beebe and Charles Clegg, *U.S. West: The Saga of Wells Fargo* (New York: Dutton, 1949);

Anson S. Blake, ed., "Working for Wells Fargo— 1860-1863: Letters of Charles T. Blake," *California Historical Society Quarterly*, 16 (March-June 1937): 30-42, 172-181;

Robert J. Chandler, "Wells Fargo: 'We Never Forget,'" *Quarterly of the National Association and Center for Outlaw and Lawman History*, 11 (Winter-Spring 1987): 5-11;

Richard Dillon, *Wells Fargo Detective: A Biography of James B. Hume* (New York: Coward-McCann, 1969);

Edward Hungerford, *Wells Fargo: Advancing the American Frontier* (New York: Random House, 1949);

W. Turrentine Jackson, *Wells Fargo & Co. in Idaho Territory* (Boise: Idaho State Historical Society, 1984);

Jackson, *Wells Fargo in Colorado Territory* (Denver: Colorado Historical Society, 1982);

Jackson, *Wells Fargo Stagecoaching in Montana* (Helena: Montana Historical Society, 1979);

Noel Loomis, *Wells Fargo* (New York, 1968);

Wells Fargo Bank, *Wells Fargo: Since 1852* (San Francisco: Wells Fargo, 1988).

Archives

The archives of Wells, Fargo & Company are at the History Department of Wells Fargo Bank, San Francisco.

Horace White

(August 10, 1834-September 16, 1916)

by Joseph Logsdon

University of New Orleans

CAREER: Editor in chief, *Chicago Tribune* (1865-1874); treasurer, Oregon Railway and Navigation Company (1879-1883); coeditor, (1881-1899), editor in chief, *New York Evening Post* and the *Nation* (1899-1902); chairman, Governor's Committee on Speculation in Securities and Commodities, state of New York (1909).

Horace White was a consummate journalist of the late-nineteenth century. As the editor of such leading publications as the *Chicago Tribune*, the *Nation*, and the *New York Evening Post*, he wrote daily columns for almost half a century. Throughout his journalistic career he was always more than a reporter or an editor: he also shaped national affairs as a social activist, scholar, businessman, and intimate adviser to prominent leaders in both business and government. He focused his most lasting influence on the field of economics by debating the key issues of political economy during the Gilded Age. His classical-liberal ideology found its way into popular treatises on money and banking that helped mold the nation's dominant financial and fiscal concepts until the 1930s.

White liked to think of himself as a midwesterner, but he was really a product of New England. Born in Colebrook, New Hampshire, on August 10, 1834, he learned little about his place of birth because in 1838 his father, Horace White, Sr., led his young family together with an organized group from New Hampshire to a site in the Wisconsin Territory that became the town of Beloit. There White's father also laid the groundwork for a Congregational church and an academy now known as Beloit College. White knew little of his father, a Dartmouth-trained physician who died in 1843. Instead, he was raised by a stepfather, Samuel Hinman, who was a much sterner Calvinist in his role as church deacon and trustee of Beloit College.

Horace White

The Yale University graduates who had set up Beloit College furthered White's Yankee tutelage and encouraged his attachment to the Whig party and the interests of the "best people," as White's family and early associates often referred to themselves. One of his teachers left a special imprint on White–Aaron L. Chapin, an early American economist who had studied under a Yale pioneer in the field, Francis Wayland. Under normal circumstances White would probably have utilized his very privileged college education to become either a small-town banker or a doctor like his father, but his life took on new direction as he came of age during the nation's most explosive political era.

According to White's own recollections, the Free Soil campaign of 1848 made him feel a "new birth" and convinced him to become a journalist so that he could enter the political fray against slavery.

In 1853, when he was just nineteen, he set out for Chicago immediately after his graduation from Beloit College in order to start his long newspaper career. While a reporter for the *Chicago Journal*, a Whig newspaper, White began covering local politics just as the Kansas-Nebraska Act of 1854 not only set the stage for the legendary senate-campaign encounters between Stephen A. Douglas and Abraham Lincoln but also shifted the storm center of national politics out to the prairies of the Midwest.

White threw himself into the excitement of the political maelstrom. He abandoned a promising career in the bituminous coal mines of southern Illinois and eschewed a settled family life after 1856, when he married Martha Root, a childhood sweetheart and the daughter of a prominent Congregational minister and abolitionist. Instead, White seized upon an opportunity to become the secretary and field agent of the National Kansas Committee, which enabled him to supply and arm John Brown and other militant Free Soilers in Kansas. In taking such actions White became part of a unique generation of independent-minded, middle-class Americans who stood ready to use force even against the federal government if it remained opposed to their particular causes.

White almost moved to Kansas himself in 1857, but the panic of that year depressed his financial investments and forced him to return to full-time journalism with a new Republican newspaper, the *Chicago Tribune*. By then thoroughly captivated by Abraham Lincoln, White developed a close relationship with the future president after his new editors assigned him to cover the Lincoln-Douglas contest for the U.S. Senate in 1858. The two men often traveled together by rail through Illinois, and White repaid the friendship with unabashedly partisan coverage for the *Tribune*. Their relationship led to White's authorship of a portion of Lincoln's campaign biography in 1860 and a postelection vow to the new president that he and other young Republicans stood ready to "plunge into blood to the horses' bridles" to defend Lincoln's "newly acquired prerogatives."

Although White joined a volunteer military unit in 1861, he resigned in response to his wife's pleas and accepted an assignment as Washington correspondent for the *Chicago Tribune*. In that capacity the twenty-six-year-old reporter not only urged abolition and radical prosecution of the war but also cultivated close contacts with such important Republican leaders as William Pitt Fessenden, senator from Maine; and Edwin Stanton, secretary of war. Both leaders helped him augment his income as a correspondent by helping him secure federal clerkships that gave him access not only to news scoops but also to inside information about an increase of excise taxes that allowed him to speculate heavily in pretax whiskey. In addition, the enterprising reporter also started a newspaper wire service, the Independent News Room, in competition with the Associated Press. By the spring of 1865 White's personal contacts, new wealth, and skill as a journalist won him the post as editor in chief of the *Chicago Tribune*.

White assumed his new position on the eve of Lincoln's assassination and thereafter remained at the center of the terrible feud in the Republican party that followed the accession of Andrew Johnson and his unpopular Reconstruction program. After White led the *Tribune* into open opposition to the president's policies, he quickly became a leading voice in the Radical wing of the Republican party. His editorial policy, which threatened to make a "frog pond" of the recalcitrant state of Mississippi, reached its radical apex in 1866 when the *Chicago Tribune* became one of the first major Republican dailies to demand universal male suffrage and direct congressional control in the former Confederate states.

The Reconstruction imbroglio carried White well beyond his own philosophic and social moorings. As early as 1868 he began a retreat toward an increasingly conservative outlook that eventually made him renounce his earlier opposition to Andrew Johnson and repudiate equal citizenship for black southerners. Indeed, in less than a decade he espoused the tenets of a classical liberalism that denounced almost all governmental interference in society except the protection of private property. The seeds of such views had been sown by his early education and social standing, but the issue of slavery had pushed him into bolder thought and action after he and his friends gained control of the federal government.

White had, for example, always questioned the wisdom of the protective tariff but had subordinated those convictions during the battle over slavery and presidential Reconstruction. True, the demands of Republican farmers and mercantile interests in the Midwest had also caused him to steer the *Tribune* in support of state governmental regulations of railroads and warehouses that culminated in the Granger laws of the early 1870s, but White's renewed study of classical economics, particularly the writings of the French free trader Frédéric Bastiat, drew him inexorably toward conservatism. In 1869 White edited an English translation of Bastiat's work *Sophisms of Protectionism*, and through the auspices of the American Free Trade Society he engaged in a dialogue with such English liberals as John Bright and John Stuart Mill. In 1869 White's founding membership in the American Social Science Association also brought him into regular contact with like-minded laissez-faire intellectuals, and eventually he also joined the Cobden Club of London and gave addresses before it in England. By mid-life he confessed open admiration for the political and social institutions that prevailed under the British Liberal party and saw himself as part of a transatlantic, Anglo-American class of liberal reformers.

Such thinking moved White away from the Republican party Stalwarts who supported President Ulysses S. Grant. After trying to alter national policies over the tariff, the national debt, and federal intervention in the South, White and other newspaper editors sponsored the Liberal Republican rebellion of 1872. Their laissez-faire platform, however, was quickly embarrassed when the Ku Klux Klan went on a rampage in 1872 and the Liberal Republican convention nominated the nation's leading protectionist, Horace Greeley, as their presidential candidate. Grant's overwhelming reelection not only undermined White's national stature but also jeopardized his control of the *Chicago Tribune*, as the newspaper's circulation and advertising declined. Adding to those difficulties, losses in the Chicago fire of 1872 and the sudden death of his wife in 1873 convinced White to resign as editor and to transfer the financial and editorial control of the *Chicago Tribune* to Joseph Medill in November 1874.

Early retirement as a moderately wealthy but still young man of forty brought major changes in White's life. First, he married a much younger woman, Amelia McDougall, with whom he had his first children, three daughters. He also moved to New York City and began to work in the railroad and financial empire of Henry Villard, his closest friend since the 1860s, when they both had worked as reporters in Washington, D.C.

From 1876 to 1891 White helped to manage Villard's interests in such western railroads as the Kansas-Pacific, the Oregon & California, and the Northern Pacific. He proved a successful lobbyist before Congress and also won favors from his former Liberal Republican compatriot, Carl Schurz, then secretary of the interior in the Rutherford B. Hayes administration. In corporate boardrooms White proved equally adept in bargaining with Villard's rival tycoons and fashioning gentlemen's agreements and profit pools. Officially listed as treasurer of a Villard holding company, the Oregon Railway and Navigation Company, White kept trusted watch over Villard's entire financial front in New York while Villard raced across the Atlantic to negotiate with European investors or out to the Pacific Northwest to supervise the construction of his transportation network.

Flushed with capital by the opening of the 1880s, Villard helped White reenter journalism in 1881 by providing most of the cash to buy both the *New York Evening Post* and the *Nation* and also to hire Carl Schurz and Edwin L. Godkin to work with White in an editorial triumvirate. Under that arrangement Schurz became editor in chief, and the *Nation* served as the weekly edition of the *Evening Post*.

The impressive newspaper combine never lived up to its financial expectations. As an afternoon paper, the *Evening Post* could not compete successfully with the morning papers for the commercial advertising that increasingly dominated the operations of large dailies. Moreover, feuds between Schurz, Villard, and Godkin over editorial policy defied White's constant efforts as a peacemaker and led by 1883 to the resignation of Schurz and to Godkin's promotion as editor in chief.

In 1883 White, who had become moderately wealthy while managing Villard's interests, returned to full-time journalism as coeditor with Godkin, after Villard was forced to resign from the presidency of the Northern Pacific following a brief financial panic. White found working with Godkin less difficult than it had been for Schurz, because White fully shared Godkin's laissez-faire, conservative outlook. Together they turned the *Evening Post* and the *Nation* into major journals of opinion for the literary and intellectual elites of the day. Their brand of independent, nonpartisan reporting also set new standards for American journalism.

Since the depression of the 1870s White not only abandoned almost all traces of his youthful radicalism, but he also turned from the optimistic, liberal views of Adam Smith and Frédéric Bastiat to the more pessimistic outlook of Thomas Malthus and David Ricardo. The outbreak of violent strikes in the late 1870s as well as a more assertive agrarianism among western and southern farmers caused him to discard his earlier expectation that the United States would escape the class strife and violence of Europe. During the last quarter of the nineteenth century he consistently condemned labor strikes, farmers' movements for governmental regulation, and, particularly, all fiscal nostrums such as greenbacks, bimetallism, and the free coinage of silver.

In turn, White looked upon free trade as a rather simple solution for social ills and for what he recognized as the apparent dangers of corporate monopoly. He resisted all new strains of reform economics, not merely socialism but also the ideas of his fellow journalists Henry George and Henry Demerest Lloyd, as well as the concepts of "New School" professional economists such as Henry C. Adams, Richard T. Ely, and Benjamin Andrews. Indeed, he personally led campaigns to get Ely and Andrews fired from their university positions for their support of American labor unions.

In pronouncing such views in the *Evening Post* and the *Nation* during the last two decades of the nineteenth century, White and Godkin helped to set the ideological and political agenda of the Republican independents known as the Mugwumps, who showed their national influence in bolstering the Democratic candidacy of Grover Cleveland for president in 1884, 1888, and 1892. After contributing to Cleveland's first victory in 1884 by publishing a new batch of Mulligan letters that thwarted the Republican candidacy of James G. Blaine, White turned increasingly to economic commentary in his editorials and columns.

White's influence with top Cabinet officers in the Cleveland administrations of 1885 and 1893 gave his columns an air of official news. Indeed, White proved to be more than just an inside pundit; together with Henry Villard he also dabbled directly in Democratic party circles in several states

to gain support for Cleveland's repeal of silver coinage in 1893. Later, in 1896, he also cooperated closely with the Republican campaign in his role as a leader of the Gold Democrats in order to defeat his bête noire, William Jennings Bryan. His chief contribution that year was a popular booklet, *Coin's Financial Fool* (1895), distributed in a 300,000-copy edition to counter the famous Populist pamphlets of William "Coin" Harvey, who promoted the free coinage of silver at an inflated price. White relished the 1896 campaign because "the cheap-money men, repudiators, Populists, anarchists, and Coxeyites" had gathered "under one banner" where they could "all be raked by one fire."

It was during that period of heated political debate over the nation's monetary and financial policies that White published his major work, *Money and Banking Illustrated by American History*. The book went through ten editions after its first publication in 1895 and became a standard text for American college classes until the Great Depression. After passage of the Currency Act of 1900, which legalized the gold standard for the United States, leaders of the financial and banking community in New York City honored White as a chief proponent of that victory.

Despite such plaudits from leading conservative businessmen and politicians, White demonstrated that he was an independent advocate of classical economics rather than a mere propagandist for the William McKinley administration. Indeed, by 1898 he was already engaged in renewed rebellion against the national Republican leadership for their seizure of Puerto Rico and the Philippines after the Spanish-American War. Just as he had earlier branded his erstwhile hero, Grover Cleveland, as an international anarchist for his jingoism in the crisis with Great Britain over Venezuela in 1895, he condemned McKinley's seizure of colonies as a foolish return to the discredited policies of mercantilism. By 1900, after Godkin's retirement made him editor in chief, White wanted to oppose McKinley's reelection but pulled back as soon as the Democrats renominated Bryan as their candidate. At that point White resolved to wait for McKinley's reelection and organize Republican anti-imperialists such as his friend Andrew Carnegie to pressure the administration through a Supreme Court case either to abandon colonies or give them constitutional rights of self-government and statehood. With an outlook that mixed racism and democratic idealism, White opposed autonomous self-government or colonial rule for the nonwhite population of the Philippines. He favored total independence.

When Theodore Roosevelt became president after McKinley's assassination in 1901, White feared even greater colonial adventure by the former vice-president, who had led the administration's earlier attacks on the anti-imperialists. But Roosevelt held several quiet meetings with his former opponents to convince them that he would not extend colonial possessions and would turn the Philippines into a self-governing American protectorate along the lines of Cuba. Unlike Carnegie and most of the anti-imperialists, White refused to end his criticism until the Republicans clearly spelled out such an arrangement. He maintained his opposition to U.S. policy in the Philippines, longer than most of the anti-imperialists. Even after his retirement from the *Evening Post* in 1902, he served as president of the Filipino Progress Association until 1906, when the Roosevelt administration drafted a declaration of principles agreeable to White's organization.

The Progressive Era encouraged White to reconsider his resolute, laissez-faire liberalism. He gave support to the labor unions in the 1902 coal strike and recognized the need for banking reform after the financial panic of 1907. In his last major public service, in 1909, he went further and chaired a New York State blue-ribbon commission, the Governor's Committee on Speculation in Securities and Commodities, which recommended some forms of state regulation for those markets. The relative social calm of the Progressive Era seemed to have given him an opportunity to view issues in a less frightening atmosphere.

After 1902, during his retirement from active journalism, White also helped to write the history of his era by encouraging the work of James Ford Rhodes and William Dunning as well as by writing memoirs of Abraham Lincoln and a biography of Lyman Trumbull, a former senator of Illinois, whose career dovetailed with White's until Trumbull diverged dramatically in support of the Populists during the 1890s. White's biography is, as a result, often autobiographical. When he died in 1916 at the age of eighty-two, he was part of a comfortable and wealthy gentry in the United States. One of his daughters married a son of William Dean Howells, and another became a patron of the arts in Santa Fe, New Mexico.

Publications:

Coin's Financial Fool: A Reply to Coin's Financial School (New York: Ogilvie, 1895);

Money and Banking Illustrated by American History (Boston: Ginn, 1895);

Abraham Lincoln in 1854 (Springfield: Illinois State Historical Society, 1908);

The Life of Lyman Trumbull (Boston: Houghton Mifflin, 1913);

The Lincoln and Douglas Debates (Chicago: University of Chicago Press, 1914).

References:

Joseph Logsdon, *Horace White, Nineteenth Century Liberal* (Westport, Conn.: Greenwood, 1971);

John G. Sproat, *"The Best Men": Liberal Reformers in the Gilded Age* (New York: Oxford University Press, 1968).

Archives:

The bulk of Horace White's papers is in the White Collection at the Illinois State Historical Society. The papers related to the 1909 New York State investigation of the stock market that White chaired are in the Horace White Committee Papers at the New-York Historical Society.

Hugh Lawson White

(October 30, 1773-April 10, 1840)

by Kurt Schuler

George Mason University

CAREER: Lawyer (1796-1825); judge, Tennessee Superior Court for Law and Equity (1801-1807); state senator, Tennessee (1807-1809, 1817-1819); U.S. district attorney for East Tennessee (1808-1809); judge, Tennessee Supreme Court of Errors and Appeals (1809-1815); president, Bank of the State of Tennessee (1812-1827); Florida land claims commissioner (1821-1824); Virginia-Kentucky military land claims commissioner (1822); U.S. senator, state of Tennessee (1825-1840).

Hugh Lawson White, jurist, banker, and U. S. senator, was born in Iredell County, North Carolina, on October 30, 1773. He was the second of seven children and the eldest son of James White and Mary Lawson White. His father was of Irish descent. For James White's services in the American Revolution, the North Carolina government gave him a tract on the site that later became Knoxville, Tennessee. In 1785 the family moved there from Fort Chiswell, Virginia.

White's mother was responsible for much of his early education. Starting at age fifteen he studied classics for three years with the Reverend Samuel Carrick (a Presbyterian minister) and with a lawyer. In 1793, when war broke out with the Creek and Cherokee Indians, Hugh White volunteered for militia duty. Both he and his father distinguished themselves in the conflict. James White led the defense of Knoxville against a much larger Indian force. Hugh White, serving under Gen. James Sevier, killed the Indian chief King Fisher at the Battle of Etowah. His modesty and his dislike for bloodshed led him never to publicize the deed.

Shortly after his militia duty, Hugh White accepted a job as private secretary to the territorial governor, William Blount, who was a friend of his father. He learned much about government, especially Indian relations, and made many political acquaintances. However, he wished to continue his

Hugh Lawson White (engraving by Thomas B. Welch from a portrait by Emanuel Leutze)

formal education. White went to Philadelphia in 1794 and studied mathematics for a year, then studied under a lawyer in Lancaster, Pennsylvania. He returned to Knoxville in 1796, at the end of his twenty-second year, and entered the practice of law. On December 13, 1798, he married Elizabeth Moore Carrick, the Reverend Carrick's daughter, who was ten years younger than he. They had twelve children. All but two died before their father, most from tuberculosis, a disease from which White also suffered.

Among White's noteworthy successes as a lawyer was an action to get the federal government to pay the veterans of the Battle of Etowah, which it had previously refused to acknowledge. Andrew Jackson, a recently elected Tennessee congressman, proved instrumental in securing pay for the veterans. The episode inaugurated White's lifelong involvement with Jackson. When in 1801 the state legislature appointed White a judge on the Superior Court for Law and Equity, Jackson was a supporter and colleague.

A desire to improve the court system induced White to resign his judgeship in 1807 to run successfully for state senator. He pressed the legislature to create a state supreme court to correct inconsistencies in the decisions of the superior courts and worked for other reforms. The reforms having passed, he declined reelection in 1809. He served briefly as the U. S. district attorney for East Tennessee before resigning to sit on the state supreme court, where he served until 1815.

When in good health White had great capacity for work. Besides keeping up his farm, his legal practice, and his judgeship, he founded the Bank of the State of Tennessee in November 1811. It was the second bank founded in the state—the Bank of Nashville had been chartered in 1807—and the first to have branches. Its maximum authorized capital was $400,000, which later doubled. The state government reserved the right to own up to $20,000 of its stock.

White was the bank's president from 1812 to 1827, for which he refused salary. His formal knowledge of banking seems to have been limited to what he observed on a trip to the East Coast to have the bank's notes engraved. However, he managed the bank with rare skill. It stood out as one of the few in the West to maintain specie payments continuously, even in the financial panics of 1814 and 1819.

White vehemently opposed the federally chartered Second Bank of the United States (BUS). When the U.S. House of Representatives considered the bill to establish it, his former employer, William Blount, who had become the congressman for Knoxville, sought White's opinion. White urged Blount to vote against the bill, and Blount became the only Tennessee congressman to do so. Andrew Jackson, Felix Grundy, and others had urged the BUS to establish a Nashville branch in competition with a branch of White's bank. (Later, of course, Jackson opposed the BUS; White may have influenced his change of opinion.) BUS supporters expected that it

would increase bank credit availability for merchants.

To protect his bank White ran successfully for state senator again in 1817. He pushed through a bill taxing any bank not chartered by the state at $50,000 per year, which kept the BUS out of Tennessee until 1827. White had strong support in rural areas, which saw the BUS as a threat to the business of ten small-town unit banks that the legislature chartered in the same session. Merchants in the commercial centers, on the other hand, were afraid that the unit banks would circulate a mass of untrustworthy, hard-to-redeem notes. Their animosity subsided when the bill allowed the newly created unit banks to join the Bank of the State of Tennessee or the Bank of Nashville as branches. The bill also permitted the Bank of Nashville to merge with the Bank of the State of Tennessee. Evidently White intended to meld the unit banks into a statewide empire. But the Panic of 1819, which broke most of the unit banks, and White's involvement in national politics prevented him from realizing his plan. The Bank of the State of Tennessee so depended on White's leadership that when he resigned as its president in 1827, it closed shortly afterward. White's other main accomplishment in his second term as state senator was a law prohibiting duelling. He apparently did not run for reelection.

In November 1812 White persuaded first his father, and then a brother-in-law, Col. John Williams, to reinforce Andrew Jackson's militia in the war against Tecumseh and the Creek Indians. The aid proved invaluable to Jackson. By 1820 Williams had become a U.S. senator and Jackson was governor of Florida. They probably influenced President James Monroe to appoint White to a three-man federal commission to resolve property claims against the former Spanish government of Florida. The Florida commission met intermittently for three years in Washington, where White made acquaintance with important politicians. In 1822 White also served on a commission to resolve land grants that Virginia had made to revolutionary war veterans in what had become Kentucky.

In 1823 White supported Jackson over Williams for one of the Tennessee seats in the U. S. Senate, creating a family split that never healed. White worked in Jackson's unsuccessful campaign for the presidency the following year, and, in 1825, when Jackson resigned from the Senate to prepare for his next presidential campaign, Jackson urged the legislature to choose White for the vacant seat. White won unanimously.

White was fifty-two years old when he entered his Senate career. Five feet eleven inches tall, very thin and pale, with flowing gray hair, his almost ghostly appearance belied his great endurance. His clear blue, but small and very deep-set eyes sparkled when he was engaged in thought. Stern and earnest, White seldom expressed great emotion, though at times he enjoyed humor. He had no intellectual interests outside of the law, and certainly banking theory never absorbed his time or attention. His punctuality and sense of duty were so strict as to be almost eccentric. White's fellow senators grew to appreciate these qualities, and his influence spread.

White, though a stalwart Democrat, remained independent-minded. He refused to follow Jackson in denouncing Henry Clay as corrupt for having thrown electoral votes to John Quincy Adams. (Adams had defeated Jackson, then had appointed Clay secretary of state.) However, White's first notable action in Congress was to oppose Clay's proposal to send a delegation to a Pan-American Congress that Simon Bolivar was organizing in Panama. White led the attack in the foreign relations committee and on the Senate floor, where he made his maiden speech. Among the problems he saw with the Panama Congress was that it planned to consider abolishing the slave trade. White, who owned two dozen slaves, argued that slavery remained a state matter, not a federal one. On that, as on other subjects, he upheld states' rights and a strict construction of the Constitution. The Senate approved a delegation to the convention but it never took place.

White also took a leading part in court reform. He supported a bill to create badly needed circuit court judgeships in the west. Many western Democrats opposed the bill because they wanted to wait until a Democratic president could appoint new judges. However, since the Jacksonians split on the issue, White never really "defected" to the administration side. The bill finally passed in April 1828. On other topics White voted the Democratic position, but he seldom made speeches. He opposed Clay's program of protective tariffs and federally financed internal improvements. He held that tariffs should only raise revenue, not protect manufacturers, and that only states should finance internal improvements. White opposed the BUS as unconsti-

tutional and unnecessary, just as he had done in the Tennessee senate.

White worked hard for Jackson's victory in the election of 1828. Shortly after the Tennessee legislature elected White to another Senate term, Jackson offered him the post of secretary of war, but admonished that if he did not want it, he should convince John Eaton, another Tennesseean, to take it. Eaton wanted the job so badly that he employed the ruse of writing White that Jackson had made the offer to both of them, and that Jackson wanted them to decide between themselves who would take it. Eaton professed a desire for the job, and a sense of propriety compelled White to bow out.

White disliked Jackson's cabinet, which he considered narrowminded and selfish. He disapproved of its political cronyism. Yet in a test of loyalty to Jackson, his capacity for cordiality toward John Eaton's wife, Peggy, he passed easily. Much of Washington society ostracized Peggy Eaton because her morals were supposedly impure. This treatment angered Jackson, who remembered similar rumors that had circulated about his own wife, who had since died. White could more easily be gallant towards Peggy Eaton than many other members of Congress could because his own wife was ill and not involved in Washington social life. Mrs. White died on March 25, 1831. In the preceding six years, ten of their children had also died. Though grief-stricken, White did not remain a widower long. On November 30, 1832, he married Mrs. Ann E. Peyton, a divorcee who ran the boardinghouse where he usually stayed when in Washington.

The brouhaha over Peggy Eaton brought conflicts within the Democratic party to a head. Vice-President John C. Calhoun, whose wife shunned Peggy Eaton, broke with Jackson. Jackson then chose Martin Van Buren as his political heir in the spring of 1831, purging Calhoun supporters from the cabinet. John Eaton also resigned, and Jackson again offered the secretary of war job to White, but White declined, citing bad health and the sorrows his family had suffered. It also seems likely that he did not wish to appear to support Van Buren, though he worked for the Jackson-Van Buren ticket in 1832. White's refusal dashed Eaton's hopes of taking over White's Senate seat. White also on several occasions declined a Supreme Court appointment.

As chairman of the Senate Indian affairs committee, White generally attempted to ensure that the federal government and the states kept their treaty obligations to the Indians. However, he supported Jackson's forced removal of Indians from Georgia, which the Supreme Court had declared illegal, because he argued that settlers would accomplish such a result eventually, only with more bloodshed. He proposed in an 1830 report that the federal government permanently reserve western lands for Indians.

White at first opposed Henry Clay's bill to give the proceeds from federal land sales to the states, because the budget was in deficit, but later, when it moved into surplus, he favored the measure. He made outstanding speeches in June and July 1832 and March 1834 against rechartering the BUS. In his first speech he contended that the praise the bank's supporters had lavished on it had no justification. The federal government, not the bank, had been responsible for compelling state-chartered banks to resume specie payments, which they had suspended long after the War of 1812 had ended. The bank had not been especially well-managed. In 1819 it had been on the brink of collapse when Langdon Cheves stepped in as its president and rescued it. At present it did a large business, but, White said, nothing guaranteed its soundness. Merchants every ten or fifteen years wound up their affairs to discover whether the debts owed them were good, and the BUS should also do so. Furthermore, White asserted that the bank's custody of federal deposits gave it an unhealthy monopoly power over foreign and domestic exchange and over the state banks. However, he did not favor undoing the monopoly by granting federal charters to competitors, as a present-day economist might advocate. Rather, he argued that the framers of the Constitution never intended for Congress to charter a bank. They reserved that power for the states; the framers intended to limit the congressional purview to gold and silver coinage.

White's second speech against the bank, supporting Jackson's veto of the recharter bill, deprecated Daniel Webster's claim that forcing the bank to close would bring distress to the country. The charter still had four years to run, White pointed out; that provided ample time for a calm liquidation. He reiterated his attack on the bank's monopoly. And, taking up his constitutional argument from a different angle, he attacked the bank's ability to exercise certain powers that the Constitution denied to the federal government itself, such as the power to purchase land within a state without its consent.

White backed the administration policy of letting federal funds in the BUS run down and depositing all new revenue with state banks. When Jackson asked his advice on such a step, White cautioned that public opinion opposed it. Yet when Jackson removed the deposits anyway, by an executive order of September 1833, White held that the president had acted lawfully. The following March, Daniel Webster introduced a bill to extend the bank's charter six years from its expiration in 1836. White's final speech against recharter presented an elaborate restatement of his positions. He denied that the commercial distress that many parts of the country suffered could be cured by a recharter; on the contrary, he held that the bank's control of exchange was responsible for it and that the proper remedy was to deprive the bank of that control. That incorrect argument typified the level of reasoning in much congressional debate both for and against the bank. White inveighed against the bank's involvement in politics. Apparently he saw no contradiction in his own past political activity as state senator to protect the bank he headed, though his activity had differed only in scale from that of the BUS.

Most of White's colleagues were angry that Jackson had not sought congressional approval for removing the deposits from the BUS, and the Senate passed a resolution censuring Jackson. For the next three years the Jacksonians fought to have the censure removed from the Senate journal. White found that attempt to rewrite history as repugnant as the censure itself, enraging Jackson. White had earlier aroused Jackson's animosity by supporting Henry Clay's compromise in the tariff nullification controversy of 1832 and 1833. As president pro tempore of the Senate (a position he held from December 1832 to 1833) he appointed an opponent of Jackson's tariff proposals to head a committee on tariffs. However, he supported Jackson's "force bill" to intimidate South Carolina nullificationists.

In 1833 the Tennessee legislature almost nominated White for president to succeed Jackson in 1836, but White blocked the move. Jackson threatened to make White "odious" throughout Tennessee if White stood in Van Buren's way. Anti-Van Buren sentiment among Democrats grew so strong that on December 20, 1834, the Tennessee congressional delegation nominated White for president without his permission. White accepted, saying that he felt it a citizen's duty to accept a nomination thrust upon him by the people. The Van Buren forces, alarmed at the support for White, maneuvered to hold the Democratic convention early, in May 1835. They successfully isolated White's supporters; the Tennessee delegation never attended the convention.

White stood for reelection to the Senate in October 1835. The Jacksonians' effort to defeat him emerged as the major issue within the Tennessee Democratic party. The legislature vindicated White by returning him to the Senate unanimously for a third term and nominating him for president.

The Whig party seized on White's popularity as a vote-getting strategem. Though his principles had little in common with theirs, they ran him as a regional candidate for president. They hoped an electoral-vote deadlock would throw the election into the House of Representatives, where the most popular Whig (probably William Henry Harrison) could defeat Van Buren. White appeared on the ballot in ten states—Illinois and all states from Virginia south and west except Kentucky and South Carolina. Daniel Webster headed the Whig ticket in New England, and Harrison in the rest of the country. John Tyler, a Virginia Whig senator, was White's running mate.

White carried Tennessee, where he defeated Van Buren even in Jackson's Hermitage district; and Georgia, where a States Rights party supported him; but he lost elsewhere. Van Buren received 764,176 popular votes, to 146,107 for White and 593,251 for others, and 170 electoral votes, to 26 for White and 98 for others.

White returned to the Senate soured. His influence noticeably diminished, he often found himself on the losing side. The Senate expunged the censure of Jackson from its journal. It also passed the Independent Treasury Act, which White opposed. He objected not to separating government deposits from the banking system, but to allowing the Treasury to issue interest-bearing notes receivable for payment of taxes. That emergency measure, which was intended to enable the government to carry on while its deposits in the state banks remained largely useless because of the Panic of 1837, would, White feared, produce permanent inflation. To him, the Independent Treasury potentially posed as much danger as the BUS had. "Pass this bill, and we put it in the *power of the President, through his Secretary of*

the Treasury, to control the whole *pecuniary active capital* of the country," he exclaimed. The state banks, on the other hand, were too numerous and too independent of federal control to be tools for executive branch abuse, he said. Like many other legislators, White saw nothing wrong with federal laws to encourage state banks not to issue low-denomination notes. Reflecting his experience as a banker, though, he claimed that bank notes constituted credit, and not money in the sense that specie constituted money, hence bank notes were not inflationary. He favored state bank note issues so long as they were convertible into specie; White was not a pure "hard money" man.

The Democrats' split into pro- and anti-White factions enabled the Whigs to dominate Tennessee politics from 1836 to 1839. In 1839 the Democrats swept to power. During a severe illness in the fall of 1838, White had submitted a letter of resignation to the Whig governor, Newton Cannon, which Cannon had refused to accept. The Democrats now attempted to procure the letter from the lame-duck governor and declare White's resignation accepted. Cannon would not cooperate, so they fixed on another scheme. They knew that White believed senators had a moral obligation to follow the instructions of the state legislatures that had elected them, if the instructions seemed to represent popular opinion and were constitutional. White had never received instructions that he opposed, but other senators occasionally had, and some had resigned in response. The Democrats hoped that White would follow that custom, so the legislature instructed him to vote for the Independent Treasury Bill. Rather than do so, White resigned on January 13, 1840.

Many considered White a political martyr, and a backlash of support for him developed in Tennessee. The Whigs regained power in the state elections of 1840. Though he never officially changed parties, White backed Henry Clay and later William Henry Harrison for the Whig presidential nomination. The Whigs chose him as an electoral college representative. White never intended to take an active part in the presidential campaign, in part because of his health, which deteriorated on the month-long journey on horseback from Washington to Knoxville. He died of tuberculosis at his farm outside of Knoxville on April 10, 1840, at the age of sixty-six. He was buried in the family plot in the graveyard of the First Presbyterian Church of Knoxville. His constituents remembered him fondly, but, as one biographer remarked, "when his own generation died his fame very nearly died with it."

White embodied a rare combination of banking and political talent. His overriding concerns were practical, and he never developed a deep intellectual position on banks and money. His consistent opposition to federally chartered banks and to federal note issue sprang from a firm conviction that the Constitution reserved banking as a matter for the states alone.

References:

Claude A. Campbell, "Branch Banking in Tennessee Prior

to the Civil War," *East Tennessee Historical Society Publications* (1939): 34-46;

Lunia Paul Gresham, "Hugh Lawson White," *Tennessee Historical Quarterly* (1944): 291-318;

Gresham, *The Public Career of Hugh Lawson White* (Nashville: Privately printed, 1945);

Nancy N. Scott, ed., *A Memoir of Hugh Lawson White* (Philadelphia: Lippincott, 1856);

Leslie H. Southwick, *Presidential Also-Rans and Running Mates, 1788-1982* (Jefferson, N.C.: McFarland).

Archives:

The Calvin Morgan McClung collection of the Lawson McGhee Library in Knoxville has letters by White.

Levi Woodbury

(December 22, 1789-September 4, 1851)

by Carol M. Martel

Arizona State University

CAREER: Lawyer and public official, Francestown, New Hampshire (1812-1822); governor of New Hampshire (1822-1823); U.S. senator, state of New Hampshire (1825-1831, 1841-1845); U.S. secretary of the navy (1831-1834); U.S. secretary of the treasury (1834-1841); associate justice, U.S. Supreme Court (1845-1851).

Levi Woodbury served as secretary of the navy and secretary of the treasury in President Andrew Jackson's cabinet and as an associate justice of the U.S. Supreme Court. Earlier, in his home state, New Hampshire, he attained prominence as governor, senator, and Superior Court justice. Born on December 22, 1789, in Francestown, New Hampshire, the second of twelve children and first son of Peter and Mary Woodbury, Woodbury came from a family that was among the earliest settlers of New England. His father owned a farm near Francestown and also developed a small retail trade. The free Francestown village school provided Woodbury with his basic education. Then the family sacrificed to send him to Atkinson Academy to prepare for Dartmouth College. He graduated Phi Beta Kappa from Dartmouth in 1809. During his college years he kept a journal in which he wrote about his drive to excel and his egotism about his intellectual ability. He also recorded what he viewed as his character faults and how he planned to correct them. The

journal entries reveal an idealistic, ambitious, and ethical young man.

After graduating from Dartmouth, Woodbury studied law at Judge Tapping Reeve's law school in Litchfield, Connecticut, the first formal law school in the United States. He was the first Supreme Court justice to study at a law school. He continued his studies at the law offices of well-known jurists Samuel Dana of Boston and Jeremiah Smith of Exeter. After the New Hampshire bar admitted him in 1812, he opened a law practice in Francestown.

During the War of 1812 Woodbury defended the policy of President James Madison. As one of the few in New England who approved of Madison's conduct of the war, he soon became identified with local Republican party leadership. He helped draft the Hillsborough County Resolves, which defended Republicans against the criticism of briefly resurgent Federalists. He became well known for his efforts to develop a strong local Republican organization and was a popular speaker at county conventions. He became secretary of the Francestown School Inspecting Committee, a justice of the peace, and a Francestown selectman. By 1815 he had established his law practice, which consisted primarily of civil suits and debt collection, and he stood ready to take a more active role in public service.

Levi Woodbury (engraving by F. B. Longacre)

A vacancy existed on the state Superior Court when William Plumer became governor of New Hampshire, but he had difficulty finding acceptable candidates. Plumer wanted a nonpartisan judiciary of able men. Too many Federalist judges had already been named, and other potential candidates were either obnoxious personally or declined the job. In 1816 Plumer appointed the twenty-seven-year-old Woodbury an associate justice. The governor praised his appointee as a "gentleman of talents, science, & legal requirements, & of an irreproachable character. No other man in the State of half his merit would have accepted the office." Despite earning the sobriquet "baby judge," Woodbury was determined to succeed. Plumer quipped that time would cure his fault of youthfulness. The legislature quickly approved the appointment.

Although accepting the judgeship entailed considerable financial sacrifice and sidetracked his political ambitions, Woodbury believed that refusing the challenge would have offended the Republican party leaders he had been trying so hard to cultivate. On the bench he played a respectable but subordinate role to the state's chief justice, William M. Richardson. Not surprisingly, he endorsed Richardson's opinion upholding the state's right to reorganize Dartmouth College as a public university. In 1819 the Supreme Court overturned the state court decision, ruling that the colonial-era charter establishing the college could not be altered by the state legislature.

In 1819, Woodbury married Elizabeth Williams Clapp, the daughter of prominent Maine politician and wealthy businessman Asa Clapp, who played an important role among leading New England Republicans who later became Jacksonians. He aided Woodbury by use of his financial and political power. The couple settled in Portsmouth, which put them in direct contact with the merchant aristocracy and Republican leadership of the state. Their home soon became a center for Woodbury's political friends. The couple's first child, Charles Levi, was born in 1820 and was followed by four sisters, Mary Elizabeth, Frances, Virginia, and Ellen.

The Superior Court position became less and less attractive to Woodbury. His circuit duties kept him in touch with the judges, lawyers, and political leaders in the state and New England, but his wife disliked the long absences. She would return to Maine while he was on circuit. Moreover, judges did not receive a generous salary. Woodbury made it clear that he preferred political life and would leave the bench in a relatively short time.

By that time factionalism and personality politics marked the New Hampshire Republican party. Woodbury became a cause in part of the growing factionalism within the Republican ranks. In 1822 Republican editor and political boss Isaac Hill attempted to force the election of a weak and unappealing man, General Samuel Dinsmoor, to the governorship. An independent group of Republicans met in convention to nominate Woodbury as their candidate, which he did nothing to discourage. The two Republican groups fought over the election, and Woodbury emerged the victor. In town meetings during March, voters went against the regular party nominee to support Woodbury.

The diversity of Woodbury's support surprised everyone. Ex-governor Plumer wholeheartedly endorsed his protégé. Federalists led by Daniel Webster's brother Ezekiel worked actively for Woodbury. Many Republican leaders also threw their support behind Woodbury because Dinsmoor was an unsatisfactory candidate. The latter group included Benjamin Pierce, father of future president Franklin Pierce. Biographer Vincent J. Capowski contends that the broadness of Woodbury's support caused him to lose in 1823, because "the gap between Ezekiel Webster and Benjamin Pierce was a chasm that defied Woodbury's best attempts at bridging." Those who resented the margin of victory provided by the Federalists in 1822 blocked Woodbury's efforts to reunify his party in 1823.

In his inaugural message to the legislature, Governor Woodbury commented on the need for judicial reform, especially the need for a limit on the discretion of the courts in awarding fines and prison terms for contempt and breaches of common law. Then he espoused the tenets that guided him throughout his public career: "My education and political faith have always led me to rank the general diffusion of knowledge, equality of rights, liberty of conscience, and a strict accountability of all public servants."

Woodbury saw education as the key to social progress. In his inaugural speech he argued that free education could eliminate poverty and would increase national prosperity and therefore should be expanded. As for higher education, Woodbury proposed that the state create a public, but not a free, university in the future. Although politically conservative, he advocated the establishment of lyceums, institutes, and museums for adult education. He looked forward to free lecture halls, Sunday libraries, cheaper newspapers, prison reform and poor relief, and, above all, enlightened democracy.

The new governor made an honest if somewhat naive attempt to unify the Republican party. He not only failed to bring the various factions together, he alienated all but his closest allies. He failed to bring about a reconciliation with Isaac Hill, although he made many of his appointments with that purpose in mind. Hill never respected Woodbury and spoke disparagingly about "these pretended days of good feelings." Woodbury's limited legislative program got lost in the partisan clamor. When it came time for the next annual election, Woodbury had fewer votes than David L. Morril. Since neither candidate had a clear majority, the legislature chose Morril, who went on to serve three terms as governor. Woodbury's year as governor had been a disaster, but he had learned some hard political lessons. He reflected to his father-in-law that "every public man in this country, who has any kind of talent, or independence, or opinions of his own, must expect abuse and ingratitude." Nevertheless, a self-respecting politician would do his duty

and "leave some memorial to his children and friends, that his life was not that of a mere vegetable or an oyster."

Woodbury went back to his private life and his law practice in Portsmouth, but he soon returned to his chosen profession, politics. In 1825 he entered the state legislature as a representative from Portsmouth and immediately won the position of speaker. Then the legislature appointed him to a vacant seat in the U.S. Senate.

The unsuccessful governor had become a senator, and the Woodburys left New Hampshire for the world of national politics. Elizabeth reluctantly left the society of Portsmouth and Portland, but soon gained a reputation as a leading Washington hostess. The Woodburys organized an informal eating group that consisted of southern statesmen such as John C. Calhoun of South Carolina and John Randolph of Virginia, New England men of commerce, and Martin Van Buren's Regency New Yorkers. Woodbury formed a natural bridge for these sectional interests, which greatly benefited his entire political career. The term "Republican" had come to encompass such a diversity of opinion that men such as Woodbury began to use the word "Democrat" to describe their politics.

Woodbury went to Washington to represent New England commerce. During an 1829 Senate debate on a bill that would have slowed down government participation in western expansion, Thomas Hart Benton nicknamed Woodbury the "Rock of New England Democracy." Woodbury's strict-constructionist remarks had so pleased the Missouri senator that he declaimed, "This is Peter, and Peter is the rock on which the church of New England democracy shall be built."

During a Senate debate about a conference in Panama, Woodbury first became identified with the Jacksonians. President John Quincy Adams made a major effort in his administration to cooperate with Latin American governments. Adams appointed two delegates to attend an international conference in Panama in 1826. This issue became a catalyst for the formation of an opposition party centered around Andrew Jackson to which Woodbury committed himself. In their efforts to discredit the administration, the Jacksonians charged that participating in the Panama Congress would sacrifice American interests and involve the nation in an entangling alliance. The antiadministration coalition filibustered and delayed the Panama mission so long that by the time it finally won approval it was too late.

Woodbury developed into an integral part of the Jacksonian machine in the Senate. In the late 1820s sectional disputes on tariff questions constituted a prominent feature of American political life. Woodbury identified with the Jacksonians in voting to defeat amendments to the Tariff Bill of 1828 that would have lowered the duties, even though the bill penalized New Hampshire's powerful commercial interests in favor of establishing high duties on items produced in the American West. This distressed New England manufacturers, who now would have to pay more for raw materials. For example, Woodbury voted for a higher duty on woolens even though New Hampshire produced finished goods. Many New Englanders, however, supported the tariff of 1828 because they supported the principle of protection. On the other hand, Southerners, heavy consumers of manufactured goods, were so shocked by what they regarded as outrageous rates that they labeled the bill the "tariff of abominations." Woodbury's vote indicated his close cooperation with the Jacksonians. Possibly he had already set his mind on a cabinet post. Although the bill passed and President Adams signed it, the surrounding conflict completed the schism within the Republican party.

Woodbury opposed a judiciary bill that proposed to expand the Supreme Court from seven to ten members. He considered it an "unprecedented increase" that would have provided Congress with an opportunity to pack the court. He did not oppose expansion of the federal court system in the Southwest, however. He also advocated the annexation of Texas, even if it led to war, and supported the occupation of Oregon.

In the presidential campaign of 1828 the National Republicans supported the reelection of John Quincy Adams, but he lost to Jackson and the group then identified as Democratic Republicans. Woodbury campaigned for Jackson on the national, regional, and local levels. He flooded New Hampshire with campaign literature, gave frequent speeches, and organized party caucuses. The Democrats dominated New Hampshire for the next 30 years.

After his Senate term expired in 1831, Woodbury returned to Portsmouth and won an appointment to the state senate. He had refused a ministerial post in Spain, because his wife and children

Silhouette of Woodbury (photograph by Bill Finney; courtesy of the New Hampshire Historical Society)

did not want to go there. Almost immediately after assuming his seat in the state senate, Jackson offered him the post of secretary of the navy. Although some historians claim he accomplished nothing noteworthy as navy secretary, others have commended him. Woodbury reformed the rules of Navy conduct and procedure, for example, by restraining the power of subordinate officers to inflict punishment on sailors and reorganizing the method of allotting service among the officers. His experience on the Senate naval committee served him in good stead, and he personally visited the country's naval yards. He also sent a fleet to Charleston, South Carolina, to back up customs authorities against the nullifying threats of South Carolina politicians.

Woodbury's cabinet colleagues described him as a "truly noncommittal man." Although of strong and shrewd mind, he seemed wary and never committed himself to a position upon which he was not immediately obliged to act. In heated Cabinet discussions about rechartering the Second Bank of the United States (BUS), Woodbury usually mediated between Secretary of the Treasury Louis McLane and Attorney General Roger Taney without indicating his own views. Taney once remarked that Woodbury was honest and a good lawyer, but that if he expressed an opinion, he "most commonly added to it many qualifications and hesitations and doubts that sometimes appeared to take it back again." Churchill Cambreleng added that "Woodbury keeps snug and plays out of all the corners of his eyes."

That equivocation evolved as an essential part of Woodbury's political tactics. As governor he had been rebuffed in his attempt to align himself with the regular Republicans. As senator, cabinet member, and, later, Supreme Court justice, he never took an open position until the situation demanded it. He did try to define a position on the basis of principle, so political necessity, not opportunism, guided his actions. It is well to point out that Woodbury was one of the few men who was simultaneously trusted by such a diverse group as Calhoun, Van Buren, and Jackson.

While Woodbury served as navy secretary, the war over the Second BUS raged. President Jackson did not dislike all banks or all businesses, but he distrusted monopolistic bankers and large business concerns. He disliked paper money generally and, moreover, believed the BUS served the interests of the wealthy classes at the expense of the average citizen. He concluded that the bank, as a privileged, centralized, and powerful monied institution, threatened republican government and liberty.

The Second BUS was imposing when Jackson became president. The main branch was in Philadelphia, with 29 branches located in other cities. The bank had been chartered by the federal government in 1816. Public money deposited in the bank amounted to between $6 million and $7 million, with personal deposits totaling another $6 million. It held about 50 percent of U.S. specie reserves. The bank had stockholders in every state and in many foreign countries. The federal government owned only one-fifth of its stock, but the bank provided important services to the national economy because of the credit it provided for profit-making enterprises. Its bank notes circulated on a par with gold in every part of the country. The BUS also received and disbursed the revenue of the nation. Public funds were deposited in the bank, which also served as an agent in the collection and transmittal of taxes. It did not charge the government for that service. But even though the government placed all its deposits in the bank, the interest earned was not shared by the taxpayers but went to the stockholders.

President Jackson suggested he would have tolerated a charter renewal with the introduction of safeguards. However, pro-BUS forces antagonized him by sponsoring an early move to recharter the bank in 1832, four years before its charter expired. Nicholas Biddle, president of the bank since 1823, concluded that Jackson would not interfere with the recharter fight in an election year.

The recharter bill passed both the Senate and the House in the summer of 1832, but a scorching veto from Jackson killed it. In his veto message Jackson denied that Congress had the right to delegate its power in carrying out governmental functions. He went on to condemn the BUS as anti-American, since a substantial minority of its stockholders were foreigners. The president's sweeping accusations may have seemed demagogic to the moneyed interests of the country, but they made good sense to common men. The Bank War reaffirmed the Democratic party's institutional cohesiveness and commitment to the principles of limited government and individual initiative.

Woodbury did not automatically oppose the bank. He had used it for his own accounts and had occasionally dined with Biddle. As early as 1829, though, he charged the bank's officers with political favoritism and opposed the policies of the bank. As a member of Jackson's cabinet, he cautiously sided with the president in opposition to rechartering the bank.

In the 1832 election Jackson easily defeated Henry Clay. Jackson interpreted his reelection as a mandate to continue the war on the bank. He could not abolish the institution, but he could lessen its power. He resolved to slay the "hydra-headed monster" by removing the government's deposits. The secretary of the treasury had to give the actual order to remove the deposits. The incumbent secretary, Louis McLane, believed such an action would destabilize the financial system and refused to give the order. McLane was "promoted" to the State Department, and Jackson appointed Pennsylvania politician William Duane to the Treasury post in June 1833. Duane opposed the BUS but also refused to take any action against it. Jackson fired him and named Attorney General Roger B. Taney the new secretary of the treasury.

Although the Senate struggled to prevent Jackson from removing the BUS deposits, he went ahead with his campaign to destroy the bank. New funds were placed in selected state banks, called "pets." Jackson claimed that the state banks would provide equivalent services and security to the public without the dangerous concentration of power inherent in the national bank. As money was withdrawn from the bank to pay government expenses, its resources decreased.

The BUS responded by calling in loans, raising interest rates, and instituting other policies aimed at forcing the country by means of an economic squeeze to demand recharter. The squeeze pitched the country into recession in 1833-1834 and frightened many people into believing that Jackson's BUS policy had produced catastrophe. The Senate registered its disapproval when it refused to confirm Taney as secretary of the treasury. Taney continued to advise Jackson on money matters, and from 1836 until his death in 1864 he served as one of the greatest chief justices of the Supreme Court. On June 27, 1834, Woodbury was named to the Treasury post, and the Senate quickly confirmed him.

Woodbury loyally continued the war on the BUS. He insisted that Congress had no authority to charter a national bank. He also had moderate hard-money views and opposed the issue of paper money to inflate the currency. Jacksonian hard-money policy made Woodbury's job more difficult, especially in an expanding, credit-hungry country. But he emerged as an efficient administrator of the state banking system. He developed rules and procedures for regulating the banks and implemented Jackson's hard-money theories. He eventually came to favor an independent treasury, maintaining that the government did not need banks to care for its funds.

Beginning in January 1835 Woodbury refused to receive BUS drafts in payment of debts owed to the United States. His policy in managing pet banking operations made it necessary to favor some banks. He decided to concentrate funds in three Wall Street banks (the Bank of America, the Manhattan Company, and the Mechanics Bank). That was a sound decision because New York City was the financial and economic capital of the United States. An element of favoritism also factored in the decision, since the vice-president, Martin Van Buren, led the New York Democrats.

Through his official dealings with the pets Woodbury managed to install order and control over the banking system. The Treasury instituted regulation of small notes by forbidding deposit banks to accept notes of less than $5, which was raised to $10 a year later by Congress. Woodbury insisted that the security of the public money was of primary importance, so the pet banks were required to pledge security in specie for the funds they held whenever the amount exceeded one-half of the bank's capital. Also, the order for banks to increase their specie holdings reduced the money available for loans. The Treasury thus imposed restraint on credit.

Woodbury continually encouraged the banks to increase vault specie. He claimed that the ratio of specie to paper money deteriorated between 1834 and late 1835. Paper money issues had increased, and bank credit had expanded more rapidly than specie reserves. Political opposition to his conservative specie policies undermined his efforts, which even Democratic faithfuls failed to appreciate.

Woodbury concentrated an increased federal surplus in the pet banks. However, that policy had an economic impact that affected the entire state of New York and, indirectly, the whole nation. New York banks were limited by the Safety Fund Act to loaning 2 1/3 times each bank's capital. So loans based on the funds Woodbury concentrated on Wall Street were limited, and the public money lay idle. He opposed using surplus public money for "reloaning and for private gain," although many bankers insisted that more public money be made available for loans. Woodbury claimed that loaning public money had never been part of the original intention of the public banking system. Woodbury minimized the surplus in his annual report to Congress, arguing that the funds came available only for a short time, prior to expenditure or disposition by Congress, and stated that the administration did have a plan for investing the surplus in state stocks. Along with some Jacksonians, he hoped that the surplus would vanish. Other Democrats demanded a more flexible money market.

Resentment against the financial dominance of Wall Street made Woodbury's task more difficult. He strived to develop a Treasury policy that would satisfy the banking community and still maintain the support of antibank Democrats. Antibank forces, however, considered a satisfied banking community evidence of financial conspiracy. Their evaluation of Treasury proposals rested on the amount of opposition they generated within financial circles.

Congress had been asked to pass laws regulating deposit banks but did not do so until the political attack on pet banking resulted in the passage of the Distribution-Deposit Act of 1836. The new law reflected the financial and political resentment against Woodbury's management of the public funds, especially his non-expansionist policy. In the opinion of his critics, the secretary was "too regulatory, too deflationary, and too selective." The provisions of the Deposit Act increased the number of pet banks. The act also restricted government deposits in any one bank to an amount not exceeding three-fourths of the bank's capital, which resulted in an extensive transferal of funds between banks and required that interest be paid on the deposits. Consequently, the bankers required freer use of the public money for loans in order to recoup the interest. The Deposit Bank system provided many of the same important functions that the Second Bank of the United States had, in regulating and facilitating the flow of currency and exchange throughout the banks.

Woodbury generally opposed the 1836 Deposit Act. He refused to select other pet banks in New York State on the grounds that not enough money was collected and disbursed by those banks that applied for pet-bank status. He continued the policy of urging the pets to increase specie holdings, which made transfer of money more difficult. An interbank scramble for specie endangered an already precarious banking structure. The state banks began issuing millions of dollars in paper money, which Jackson hated.

In order to curb paper money issues and break the cycle of western land speculation that bank credit fed, Jackson issued the Specie Circular in 1836. Only gold and silver would be accepted for the purchase of land from the government. Technically, the order came from the secretary of the treasury, and Woodbury signed it, but he took no initiative in drafting it. The resistance of conservative Democrats hampered Jackson's attempts to pass more regulatory measures. In 1837 Congress passed a bill repealing the Specie Circular, but Jackson employed a pocket veto to defeat it. In the end, Jackson's deposit system failed to promote a specie

currency. However, the flood of silver that flowed into the country from Mexico allowed the banks to issue notes that in turn helped to sustain and augment the industrial growth and expansion of the period.

Woodbury had not intended to transform the Treasury into the focal point of central banking operations. Jacksonian banking policy had evolved from a simple emphasis on specie to a specific control over credit. The interests of the Wall Street pets coincided with Woodbury's growing concern over the unregulated credit structure. But the Deposit-Distribution Act of 1836 intervened in the process of giving the Treasury even greater command of banking and credit.

Less than two weeks after Martin Van Buren became president in 1837, the country suffered a major financial collapse. The bankruptcy of one of the largest New York dealers in domestic bills set off a chain reaction of bankruptcies and suspensions. During the panic Woodbury failed to maintain the credit of the federal government. When the pet banks suspended specie payments, Woodbury protected public holders of drafts drawn on federal deposits so that they would not lose because of depreciated paper money.

How much effect Woodbury's policies had on the Panic of 1837 is arguable. Richard H. Timberlake, for example, contends that Woodbury's failure to impose defensive reserve requirements on the pet banks when deposits were building up in late 1836 was a mistake. Woodbury played it safe by following the letter of the distribution law, which absolved him of any responsibility for the collapse that followed. It would have been within his power to have increased reserve requirements on depository banks, which would have restricted the expansion of bank credit. Most recently, Peter Temin has shown that the 1837 panic stemmed from the rise in British interest rates and had little to do with the Specie Circular or even the destruction of the BUS.

Van Buren spent most of his presidency trying to cope with the depression. He finally won passage of an Independent Treasury Act, which required public money to be managed by the government without the assistance of banks. Deposits would be stored in subtreasury buildings around the country and withdrawn as needed by the government. The principle that the collection, transfer, and disbursement of public money should be managed by public officers became a vital feature of American financial life. In this way, no private agency could profit from the use of public funds. (Although soon after the National Banking Act was passed in 1863 the advantages of holding public deposits were clear: not only did public depositories have huge sums available to lend, but national bank notes provided free advertising.)

It was well known that Woodbury was not a strong figure in the administration. Attempts were made to ease him out of office. In 1838 Isaac Hill, then governor of New Hampshire, nominated Woodbury chief justice of the state court. Everyone assumed that Woodbury would accept in order to "escape to the quiet scenes and calm enjoyments of his native State," as Horace Greeley said. Woodbury decided to stay on in Washington.

Woodbury retired from the Treasury post in 1841, when William Henry Harrison became president. He returned to the Senate, where he continued to emphasize states' rights, always one of his staunchest principles. He could not be classified as prosouthern and certainly had no proslavery instincts, but he did act as a conservative in regard to federal-state relations. He was mentioned as a vice-presidential candidate in 1844 because of his acceptability to all sections of the country. Despite the fact that Southerners and New Englanders alike trusted him, Woodbury did not win the nomination. He might have been too politically timid to fight for it.

On September 20, 1845, after Woodbury declined the ambassadorship to the Court of St. James, President James Polk appointed him an associate justice of the Supreme Court. His former cabinet colleague, Taney, was chief justice. Woodbury wrote most notable opinions in dissent. He enunciated his political philosophy, based on the concept of limited government and strict construction of the United States Constitution.

In *Jones* v. *Van Zandt* (1846-1847), involving the constitutionality of the Federal Fugitive Slave Act of 1793, Woodbury earned respect from Southerners and northern constitutional conservatives. Van Zandt, an abolitionist, was being sued for harboring a fugitive slave. His defense argued that the act of 1793 was unconstitutional because moral law took precedence over statutory law. Woodbury rejected all technical objections and the claim of unconstitutionality when he reminded the Court and the nation that the compromises of the Constitu-

tion required the honest enforcement of laws such as that of 1793. The Court had no choice but the "straight and narrow path." Although strongly opposed to slavery, Woodbury insisted that it was a political question to be settled by each state and not a federal one.

In *Waring* v. *Clarke* (1847) Woodbury held that the application of admiralty law stopped at the shoreline of a nation. He noted that "a great principle at the foundation of our political system applies strongly to the present case and is, that while supporting all the power clearly granted to the general government, we ought to forbear interfering with what has been preserved to the states, and in cases of doubt to follow where that principle leads."

In *Luther* v. *Borden* (1849) he broke with the Court's finding that it had no power to restrict the decision of Congress or the president to recognize either party in a state conflict over lawful government. Taney had declared that the federal courts could not interfere with the domestic concerns of the states. Woodbury agreed that the Court should avoid political issues, but he believed that the use of martial law in Rhode Island, the state in question, had gone too far. He believed the Court had "evinced a manifest and sleepless opposition in all cases of a political bearing, to the strict constitution of the Constitution," which threw "chains over States-Rights, chains never dreamed of at the formation of the General Government."

In the *Passenger Cases* (1849) Woodbury declared for regulation when he held as constitutional laws in New York and Massachusetts that levied a head tax on entering aliens. He argued that if Congress had full power over the admission or exclusion of aliens, that power might be used to force the admission of slaves or other persons into unwilling states. Only state sovereignty could properly exercise a police function, not the federal government.

In writing his well-researched, logical decisions, Woodbury showed no gift for clarity and tight reasoning. But he sought a middle ground between private rights and the public interest. Democratic writers praised his work on the Court. According to one editor, Woodbury retained the common touch and an affection for the people.

With a presidential election coming up in 1848, Woodbury's previous political prominence, combined with his opinions on cases such as *Jones* v. *Van Zandt*, made him a contender for the Democratic nomination. Southerners expressed special interest in finding someone who would uphold states' rights. Woodbury and Lewis Cass of Michigan were the front-runners a few months before the convention. Cass obtained the nomination but lost the election to Zachary Taylor.

During the campaign, the more conservative of the southern states' rights advocates regretted that Woodbury had not been the nominee. Woodbury continued to favor constitutionalism at every opportunity. He strongly supported the Compromise of 1850, including the Fugitive Slave Law of that year, at a time when it was not popular for a New Englander to do so. For the sake of the preservation of the Union, Woodbury argued that the legal rights of slaveholders ought to be upheld. Northern authorities had the duty to uphold southern rights, "boldly, faithfully, with true loyalty to the Union, and not with evasion and procrastination." The highest law was the Constitution, and to try to overturn any part of it would not only be ruinous to the nation but treasonable.

Woodbury served on the Supreme Court until his death in Portsmouth on September 4, 1851. If he had lived he might have been the Democratic presidential candidate in 1852. One newspaper lauded him as a "sagacious, sound, and always republican expounder of the Constitution . . . possessing also every personal quality, urbanity, courtesy, dignity, and every moral requisite of firmness, fidelity, and discretion." The *Washington Union* said of Woodbury, "No man is more thoroughly known in the country as the firm and unwavering supporter of the Union, the Constitution, and the laws."

Woodbury's judicial career paralleled his previous political experience. It was "temperate, sound, progressively conservative, but not overly successful. He had too much talent to be a mediocrity, but not enough verve to use his talents dynamically." But from the earliest days of his political career in New Hampshire a consistent philosophy underlaid his politics. He began his career as a Jeffersonian Republican in 1812, at a time when the Republican party in New Hampshire was well organized and constructionist in ideology. Gradually the lack of an opposition party during the Era of Good Feelings brought out factionalism among Republicans and resulted in Woodbury's election as governor. Because of his strong Republican bias he ignored the factional leaders in favor of the regular Republican organization, but satisfied neither group. When his reelection bid failed, Woodbury became much more

cautious and pragmatic about political alliances. In the Senate the vote against the Panama mission marked Woodbury's break with John Quincy Adams. His Jacksonianism evolved from a series of political alliances based on mutual self-interest and compatible political ideologies. In recognition of Woodbury's major contributions to the construction of the Jacksonian party, he was appointed to Jackson's cabinet. Despite much Congressional opposition to Jacksonian banking policies, Woodbury held his job as secretary of the treasury through two administrations.

Woodbury achieved a broad cross section of support from diverse political leaders even though he was also criticized for being too noncommital, too reluctant to take action, and too pragmatic. No suggestion of malfeasance in office or scandal in personal life surfaced about Woodbury. Indeed, John M. McFaul describes him as a "rather colorless, unimaginative administrator concerned mainly with his own reputation and political future." But he consistently followed his conservative principles of strict adherence to the Constitution, respect for states' rights, limited federal government, and the progressive ideals of education and the rights of individual citizens.

Publications:

Writings of Levi Woodbury, LL. D., 3 volumes (Boston: Little, Brown, 1852).

References:

Vincent J. Capowski, "The Making of a Jacksonian Democrat: Levi Woodbury 1789-1831," Ph.D. dissertation, Fordham University, 1966;

Richard B. Latner, *The Presidency of Andrew Jackson* (Athens, Ga.: University of Georgia Press, 1979);

John M. McFaul, *The Politics of Jacksonian Finance* (Ithaca, N.Y.: Cornell University Press, 1972);

James Roger Sharp, *The Jacksonians versus the Banks* (New York: Columbia University Press, 1970);

Peter Temin, *The Jacksonian Economy* (New York: Norton, 1969);

Richard H. Timberlake, *The Origins of Central Banking in the United States* (Cambridge, Mass.: Harvard University Press, 1978);

Charles Warren, *The Supreme Court in United States History*, 2 volumes (Boston: Little, Brown, 1926).

Archives:

The papers of Levi Woodbury are housed in the Library of Congress, the Dartmouth College Library, and the New Hampshire Historical Society.

Contributors

Roberta Sue Alexander–*University of Dayton*
Robert C. Arne–*University of Chicago*
Charles Barber, Jr.–*University of Georgia*
David T. Beito–*University of Nevada at Las Vegas*
B. R. Burg–*Arizona State University*
Charles W. Calomiris–*Northwestern University*
Robert J. Chandler–*Wells Fargo Bank*
Janet L. Coryell–*Auburn University*
Jennifer Davis–*University of Dayton*
Henry C. Dethloff–*Texas A&M University*
Peter De Trolio III–*University of Dayton*
Lynne Pierson Doti–*Chapman College*
Hans Eicholz–*University of California, Los Angeles*
Saul Englebourg–*Boston University*
James E. Fell, Jr.–*United Banks of Colorado*
Sandra L. Fraley–*MARKETS*
Dolores Greenberg–*Hunter College and the Graduate School and University Center, CUNY*
Thomas F. Huertas–*Citibank NA*
Jeffrey Rogers Hummel–*Independent Institute*
Gregory S. Hunter–*ITT Corporation*
Benjamin J. Klebaner–*City College, CUNY*
Michael F. Konig–*Westfield State College*
John Landry–*Brown University*
Joseph Logsdon–*University of New Orleans*
John Majewski–*University of California, Los Angeles*
John W. Malsberger–*Muhlenberg College*
Carol M. Martel–*Arizona State University*
Albro Martin–*Bradley University, Emeritus*
Tiarr Martin–*University of Dayton*
Irene D. Neu–*Indiana University*
Carol Noland–*Arizona State University*
Gary M. Pecquet–*Southwest Texas State University*
Edwin J. Perkins–*University of Southern California*
Joseph F. Rishel–*Duquesne University*
Hugh Rockoff–*Rutgers University*
Kurt Schuler–*George Mason University*
Larry Schweikart–*University of Dayton*
James Smallwood–*University of Texas at Tyler*
Richard H. Timberlake–*University of Georgia*
Kirby Turner–*Montgomery County Historical Society*
Steven Wheeler–*New York Stock Exchange Archives*

Index